Practical
Business
Math
Procedures

The McGraw-Hill/Irwin Series in Operations and Decision Sciences

Supply Chain Management

Benton
Purchasing and Supply Chain Management
Second Edition

Burt, Petcavage, and Pinkerton
Supply Management
Eighth Edition

Bowersox, Closs, and Cooper
Supply Chain Logistics Management
Fourth Edition

Johnson, Leenders, and Flynn
Purchasing and Supply Management
Fourteenth Edition

Simchi-Levi, Kaminsky, and Simchi-Levi
**Designing and Managing the Supply Chain:
Concepts, Strategies, Case Studies**
Third Edition

Project Management

Brown and Hyer
Managing Projects: A Team-Based Approach
Second Edition

Larson and Gray
**Project Management:
The Managerial Process**
Fifth Edition

Service Operations Management

Fitzsimmons and Fitzsimmons
**Service Management: Operations,
Strategy, Information Technology**
Seventh Edition

Management Science

Hillier and Hillier
**Introduction to Management Science:
A Modeling and Case Studies
Approach with Spreadsheets**
Fourth Edition

Stevenson and Ozgur
**Introduction to Management Science
with Spreadsheets**
First Edition

Manufacturing Control Systems

Jacobs, Berry, Whybark, and Vollmann
**Manufacturing Planning & Control
for Supply Chain Management**
Sixth Edition

Business Research Methods

Cooper-Schindler
Business Research Methods
Eleventh Edition

Business Forecasting

Wilson, Keating, and John Galt
Solutions, Inc.
Business Forecasting
Sixth Edition

Linear Statistics and Regression

Kutner, Nachtsheim, and Neter
Applied Linear Regression Models
Fourth Edition

Business Systems Dynamics

Sterman
**Business Dynamics: Systems Thinking
and Modeling for a Complex World**
First Edition

Operations Management

Cachon and Terwiesch
**Matching Supply with Demand:
An Introduction to Operations
Management**
Third Edition

Finch
**Interactive Models for Operations
and Supply Chain Management**
First Edition

Jacobs and Chase
**Operations and Supply Chain
Management: The Core**
Third Edition

Jacobs and Chase
**Operations and Supply Chain
Management**
Fourteenth Edition

Jacobs and Whybark
**Why ERP? A Primer on SAP
Implementation**
First Edition

Schroeder, Goldstein, and
Rungtusanatham
**Operations Management in the
Supply Chain: Decisions and Cases**
Sixth Edition

Stevenson
Operations Management
Eleventh Edition

Swink, Melnyk, Cooper, and Hartley
**Managing Operations across the
Supply Chain**
First Edition

Product Design

Ulrich and Eppinger
Product Design and Development
Fifth Edition

Business Math

Slater/Wittry
Practical Business Math Procedures
Eleventh Edition

Slater/Wittry
**Practical Business Math Procedures,
Brief Edition**
Eleventh Edition

Slater/Wittry
**Math for Business and Finance:
An Algebraic Approach**
First Edition

Business Statistics

Bowerman, O'Connell, Murphree,
and Orris
Essentials of Business Statistics
Fourth Edition

Bowerman, O'Connell, and Murphree
Business Statistics in Practice
Sixth Edition

Doane and Seward
**Applied Statistics in Business and
Economics**
Fourth Edition

Jaggia and Kelly
**Business Statistics: Communicating
with Numbers**
First Edition

Lind, Marchal, and Wathen
**Basic Statistics for Business and
Economics**
Eighth Edition

Lind, Marchal, and Wathen
**Statistical Techniques in Business
and Economics**
Fifteenth Edition

Practical Business Math Procedures

Eleventh Edition

JEFFREY SLATER
North Shore Community College
Danvers, Massachusetts

SHARON M. WITTRY
Pikes Peak Community College
Colorado Springs, Colorado

McGraw-Hill
Irwin

McGraw-Hill
Irwin

PRACTICAL BUSINESS MATH PROCEDURES, ELEVENTH EDITION
Published by McGraw-Hill/Irwin, a business unit of The McGraw-Hill Companies, Inc., 1221 Avenue of the Americas, New York, NY, 10020. Copyright © 2014 by The McGraw-Hill Companies, Inc. All rights reserved. Printed in the United States of America. Previous editions © 2011, 2008, and 2006. No part of this publication may be reproduced or distributed in any form or by any means, or stored in a database or retrieval system, without the prior written consent of The McGraw-Hill Companies, Inc., including, but not limited to, in any network or other electronic storage or transmission, or broadcast for distance learning.

Some ancillaries, including electronic and print components, may not be available to customers outside the United States.

This book is printed on acid-free paper.

6 7 8 9 0 DOW/DOW 1 0 9 8 7 6 5

ISBN   978-0-07-337754-4 (student edition)
MHID   0-07-337754-6 (student edition)
ISBN   978-0-07-753391-5 (teacher's edition)
MHID   0-07-753391-7 (teacher's edition)

Senior Vice President, Products & Markets: *Kurt L. Strand*
Vice President, Content Production & Technology Services: *Kimberly Meriwether David*
Managing Director: *Douglas Reiner*
Senior Brand Manager: *Thomas Hayward*
Executive Director of Development: *Ann Torbert*
Development Editor: *Kaylee Putbrese*
Director of Digital Content: *Doug Ruby*
Digital Development Editor: *Meg B. Maloney*
Marketing Manager: *Heather Kazakoff*
Lead Project Manager: *Lori Koetters*
Senior Buyer: *Michael R. McCormick*
Senior Designer: *Matt Diamond*
Cover Image: *Mark Dierker*
Senior Content Licensing Specialist: *Jeremy Cheshareck*
Photo Researcher: *Ira C. Roberts*
Lead Media Project Manager: *Daryl Horrocks*
Typeface: *10/12 Times Roman*
Compositor: *Aptara®, Inc.*
Printer: *R. R. Donnelley*

All credits appearing on page or at the end of the book are considered to be an extension of the copyright page.

Library of Congress Cataloging-in-Publication Data

Slater, Jeffrey, 1947-
    Practical business math procedures / Jeffrey Slater, Sharon M. Wittry.—11th ed.
        p. cm.—(The McGraw-Hill/Irwin series in operations and decision sciences)
    Includes index.
    ISBN-13: 978-0-07-337754-4 (student edition : alk. paper)
    ISBN-10: 0-07-337754-6 (student edition : alk. paper)
    ISBN-13: 978-0-07-753391-5 (teacher's edition : alk. paper)
    ISBN-10: 0-07-753391-7 (teacher's edition : alk. paper)
    1. Business mathematics—Problems, exercises, etc. I. Wittry, Sharon M. II. Title.
HF5694.S57 2014
650.01'513—dc23
                                                                2012038963

The Internet addresses listed in the text were accurate at the time of publication. The inclusion of a website does not indicate an endorsement by the authors or McGraw-Hill, and McGraw-Hill does not guarantee the accuracy of the information presented at these sites.

www.mhhe.com

Dedication

To Mia, Matt, Sam, and Hope.
How lucky I am to have such wonderful grandkids!
—Love, PaPa Jeff

To my loving husband. You make every day shine.
—Love, Sharon

Note to Students

ROADMAP TO SUCCESS

How to use this book and the Total Slater/Wittry Learning System.

Step 1: **Each chapter is broken down into Learning Units. Read and master one Learning Unit at a time.**

How do I know whether I understand it?

- Try the practice quiz. All the worked-out solutions are provided. If you still have questions, watch the authors on your DVD (comes with your text) or on YouTube or Connect and work each problem out.

- For more practice, try the extra practice quiz. Worked-out solutions are in Appendix B.

Once you feel confident with the subject matter, go on to the next Learning Unit in the chapter.

Step 2: **Review the Interactive Chapter Organizer at the end of the chapter.**

How do I know if I understand it?

- The third column, "You try it," gives you the chance to do additional practice.

Step 3: **Do assigned problems at the end of the chapter (or Appendix A). These may include discussion questions, drill, word problems, challenge problems, video cases, as well as projects from Surf to Save and Kiplinger's magazine.**

Can I check my homework?

- Appendix C has check figures for all the odd-numbered problems.

Step 4: **Take the Summary Practice Test.**

Can I check my progress?

- Appendix C has check figures for all problems.

What do I do if I do not match check figures?

- Review the video tutorial on the student DVD—the authors work out each problem. You can also see the videos on YouTube and Connect.

To aid you in studying the book, we have developed the following color code:

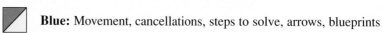 **Blue:** Movement, cancellations, steps to solve, arrows, blueprints

 **Purple and yellow:** Formulas and steps

 **Green:** Tables and forms

Red: Key items we are solving for

If you have difficulty with any text examples, pay special attention to the red and the blue. These will help remind you of what you are looking for as well as what the procedures are.

FEATURES   The following are the features students have told us have helped them the most.

Blueprint Aid Boxes   For the first eight chapters (not in Chapter 4), blueprint aid boxes are available to help you map out a plan to solve a word problem. We know the harder thing to do in solving word problems is often figuring out where to start. Use the blueprint as a model to get started.

Business Math Handbook   This reference guide contains all the tables found in the text. It makes homework, exams, etc., easier to deal with than flipping back and forth through the text.

Interactive Chapter Organizer   At the end of each chapter is a quick reference guide called the Interactive Chapter Organizer, in which key points, formulas, and examples are provided. A list of vocabulary terms is also included, as well as Check Figures for Extra Practice Quizzes. All have page references. A new column called "You Try It" gives you a chance to do additional practice. And solutions are provided in Appendix B. (A complete glossary is found at the end of the text.) Think of the Interactive Chapter Organizer as your set of notes and use it as a reference when doing homework problems and reviewing before exams.

DVD-ROM   The DVD packaged with the text includes tutorial videos that cover all of the Learning Unit Practice Quizzes and Summary Practice Tests.

For **extra help** from your authors–Sharon and Jeff–see the student DVD

The Business Math Website   Visit the site at www.mhhe.com/slater11e and find the Internet Resource Guide with hot links, tutorials, practice quizzes, Excel® workbook and templates, and other study materials useful for the course.

Video Cases   There are six video cases applying business math concepts to real companies such as Six Flags, Subaru of Indiana Automotive, Noodles & Company, Buycostume.com, and DHL. You can watch these videos at **www.mhhe.com/slater11e**. Some background case information and assignment problems incorporating information on the companies are included at the end of Chapters 6, 7, 8, 13, 16, and 19.

Compounding/Present Value Overlays   A set of color overlays are inserted in Chapter 13. These color graphics are intended to demonstrate the concepts of present value and future value and, even more important, the basic relationship between the two.

Surf to Save   At the end of each chapter you will find word problems with links to sites and publications. These problems give you a chance to apply the theory provided in the chapter to the real world. Put your math skills to work.

Group Activity: Personal Finance, a Kiplinger Approach   In each chapter you can debate a business math issue based on a *Kiplinger's Personal Finance* magazine article. This is great for critical thinking, as well as improving your writing skills.

Spreadsheet Templates   Excel® templates are available for selected end-of-chapter problems. You can run these templates as-is or enter your own data. The templates also include an interest table feature that enables you to input any percentage rate and any terms. The program then generates table values for you.

Cumulative Reviews   At the end of Chapters 3, 8, and 13 are word problems that test your retention of business math concepts and procedures. Check figures for *all* cumulative review problems are in Appendix C.

Vocabulary   Each chapter opener includes a Vocabulary Preview covering the key terms in the chapter. The Interactive Chapter Organizer includes page references to the terms. There's also a glossary at the end of the text.

Acknowledgments

Academic Experts, Contributors

Dawn P. Addington
Tom Bilyeu
James P. DeMeuse
Joe Hanson
Deborah Layton
Lynda L. Mattes

Joseph M. Nicassio
Jo Ann Rawley
Karen Ruedinger
Kelly Russell
Marge Sunderland
Mary Frey

Jason Tanner
Patrick Cunningham
Paul Tomko
Peter VanderWeyst

Company/*Applications*

Chapter 1

Subway—*Chapter introduction*
Starbucks—*Problem solving*
Whole Foods—*Reading and writing numbers*
Disney—*Rounding numbers*
Tootsie Roll Industries—*Dissecting word problems and rounding*
Walmart—*Subtraction of whole numbers*
Hershey—*Subtraction of whole numbers*
Facebook—*Multiplying and dividing whole numbers*

Chapter 2

McDonald's—*Fractions*
M&M'S/Mars—*Fractions and multiplication*
Albertsons—*Dissecting word problems with fractions*

Chapter 3

Honda, Toyota, BMW, GM, Chrysler, Mercedes-Benz—*Decimals*
Google—*Adding, subtracting, multiplying, and dividing decimals*
Apple—*International currency*

Chapter 4

Charles Schwab, Fidelity Investments, JPMorgan Chase & Co., T. Rowe Price—*New deposits with use of technology*
TD Bank Financial Group—*ATM fees*
JPMorgan Chase Bank—*Mobile banking*

Chapter 5

Stop & Shop—*Word problems*

Chapter 6

Google, Facebook—*Introduction to percents*
Family Dollar Stores, J.M. Smucker Co.—*Understanding percents*
Walt Disney Co.—*Converting decimals to percents*
Ford, Toyota, Honda, Chrysler, Nissan—*Percent increase and decrease*
M&M'S/Mars—*Rate, portion, and base*

Chapter 7

Groupon, Facebook—*Introduction to decimals*
Procter & Gamble, Samsung Venture Investment Corp.—*Trade discounts*
Amazon.com Inc., Toys "R" Us, Newegg.com—*Shipping terms*

Chapter 8

Macy's Inc., Microsoft, Mozilla Corp.—*Introduction to retailing*
Gap—*Markup on cost and selling price*

Chapter 9

McDonald's—*Health plans*
Google Inc., Apple Inc., Walt Disney Co., Facebook—*Employee satisfaction*
IRS—*Circular E tables*

Chapter 10

Research Services Inc.—*Credit unions versus banks for borrowing*

Chapter 11

Prosper Marketplace Inc., Lending Club Corp., eBay—*Introduction to promissory notes*
U.S. Treasury—*Buying treasuries*
General Motors Co.—*Lines of credit*

Chapter 12

U.S. Department of Labor—*Magic of compounding*

Chapter 13

T. Rowe Price Group—*Retirement payoff*
Dunkin' Donuts—*Power of compounding*

Chapter 14

Edmunds.com—*FICO scores*
U.S. government—*Credit Card Act of 2009*
Citibank Mastercard—*Calculation of finance charge*

Chapter 15

Bank of America, JPMorgan Chase & Co., Freddie Mac—*Lowering mortgage payment*
FICO—*Credit score*
HSH Associates—*Refinancing a mortgage*

Chapter 16

SEC—*Sarbanes-Oxley Act*
Greystone Bakery—*Benefit corporation*

Campbell Soup Co.—*Income statement*

Zyngz Corp.—*Elements of the income statement*

General Mills Inc.—*Gross margin*

Sara Lee, ConAgra, Kraft, Hershey, Kellogg, Heinz—*Cost of goods sold*

Chapter 17

Intellichoice.com—*Depreciation reductions over the years for cars*

Joint Committee on Taxation—*Corporate tax breaks*

Chapter 18

Walmart—*Electronic inventory tags*

American Eagle Outfitters, Abercrombie & Fitch, Aeropostale—*Inventory competition*

Certified Public Accountants—*GAAP and IFRS*

McGraw-Hill Co.—*Textbook pricing*

Gap—*Distribution of overhead*

Chapter 19

Target, Walmart, Amazon—*Collecting taxes online*

Chapter 20

TIAA-CREF, USAA—*Introduction to insurance*

Chapter 21

Morningstar—*Mix of investments*

Putnam Investments Inc., Schwab Funds—*Mutual funds*

Chapter 22

Ford Motor Inc., Facebook, Yahoo!, AOL, Microsoft, Google—*Internet advertising breakdown*

Pike Research—*Bar chart of electric vehicles*

Contents

Note to Students   vi

Kiplinger's Personal Finance Magazine Subscription Form   xiii

CHAPTER 1   Whole Numbers: How to Dissect and Solve Word Problems   2

LU 1–1   Reading, Writing, and Rounding Whole Numbers   4
LU 1–2   Adding and Subtracting Whole Numbers   10
LU 1–3   Multiplying and Dividing Whole Numbers   14

CHAPTER 2   Fractions   34

LU 2–1   Types of Fractions and Conversion Procedures   36
LU 2–2   Adding and Subtracting Fractions   41
LU 2–3   Multiplying and Dividing Fractions   47

CHAPTER 3   Decimals   64

LU 3–1   Rounding Decimals; Fraction and Decimal Conversions   66
LU 3–2   Adding, Subtracting, Multiplying, and Dividing Decimals   71
Cumulative Review: A Word Problem Approach—Chapters 1–3   89

CHAPTER 4   Banking   90

LU 4–1   The Checking Account   92
LU 4–2   Bank Statement and Reconciliation Process; Latest Trends in Mobile Banking   96

CHAPTER 5   Solving for the Unknown: A How-To Approach for Solving Equations   116

LU 5–1   Solving Equations for the Unknown   118
LU 5–2   Solving Word Problems for the Unknown   123

CHAPTER 6   Percents and Their Applications   142

LU 6–1   Conversions   143
LU 6–2   Application of Percents—Portion Formula   149
Video Case: Project Management at Six Flags, New Jersey   173

CHAPTER 7   Discounts: Trade and Cash   176

LU 7–1   Trade Discounts—Single and Chain (Includes Discussion of Freight)   178
LU 7–2   Cash Discounts, Credit Terms, and Partial Payments   185
Video Case: Recycling at Subaru of Indiana Automotive   204

CHAPTER 8   Markups and Markdowns: Perishables and Breakeven Analysis   208

LU 8–1   Markups Based on Cost (100%)   210
LU 8–2   Markups Based on Selling Price (100%)   215
LU 8–3   Markdowns and Perishables   221
LU 8–4   Breakeven Analysis   224
Video Case: Noodles & Company   237
Cumulative Review: A Word Problem Approach—Chapters 6–8   241

CHAPTER 9   Payroll   242

LU 9–1   Calculating Various Types of Employees' Gross Pay   244
LU 9–2   Computing Payroll Deductions for Employees' Pay; Employers' Responsibilities   248

CHAPTER 10   Simple Interest   264

LU 10–1   Calculation of Simple Interest and Maturity Value   265

LU 10–2   Finding Unknown in Simple Interest Formula   268

LU 10–3   U.S. Rule—Making Partial Note Payments before Due Date   270

CHAPTER 11   Promissory Notes, Simple Discount Notes, and the Discount Process   284

LU 11–1   Structure of Promissory Notes; the Simple Discount Note   286

LU 11–2   Discounting an Interest-Bearing Note before Maturity   289

CHAPTER 12   Compound Interest and Present Value   300

LU 12–1   Compound Interest (Future Value)—The Big Picture   301

LU 12–2   Present Value—The Big Picture   309

CHAPTER 13   Annuities and Sinking Funds   322

LU 13–1   Annuities: Ordinary Annuity and Annuity Due (Find Future Value)   324

LU 13–2   Present Value of an Ordinary Annuity (Find Present Value)   330

LU 13–3   Sinking Funds (Find Periodic Payments)   333

Video Case: DHL Global Delivery   342

Cumulative Review: A Word Problem Approach—Chapters 10–13   346

CHAPTER 14   Installment Buying   348

LU 14–1   Cost of Installment Buying   350

LU 14–2   Revolving Charge Credit Cards   355

CHAPTER 15   The Cost of Home Ownership   372

LU 15–1   Types of Mortgages and the Monthly Mortgage Payment   374

LU 15–2   Amortization Schedule—Breaking Down the Monthly Payment   378

CHAPTER 16   How to Read, Analyze, and Interpret Financial Reports   390

LU 16–1   Balance Sheet—Report as of a Particular Date   392

LU 16–2   Income Statement—Report for a Specific Period of Time   398

LU 16–3   Trend and Ratio Analysis   405

Video Case: Buycostumes.com   420

CHAPTER 17   Depreciation   424

LU 17–1   Concept of Depreciation and the Straight-Line Method   425

LU 17–2   Units-of-Production Method   428

LU 17–3   Declining-Balance Method   429

LU 17–4   Modified Accelerated Cost Recovery System (MACRS) with Introduction to ACRS (1986, 1989, 2010)   431

CHAPTER 18   Inventory and Overhead   442

LU 18–1   Assigning Costs to Ending Inventory—Specific Identification; Weighted Average; FIFO; LIFO   444

LU 18–2   Retail Method; Gross Profit Method; Inventory Turnover; Distribution of Overhead   450

CHAPTER 19   Sales, Excise, and Property Taxes   468

LU 19–1   Sales and Excise Taxes   469

LU 19–2   Property Tax   471

Video Case: EDP Renewables   480

CHAPTER 20   Life, Fire, and Auto Insurance   484

LU 20–1   Life Insurance   485

LU 20–2   Fire Insurance   490

LU 20–3   Auto Insurance   493

CHAPTER 21   Stocks, Bonds, and Mutual Funds   508

LU 21–1   Stocks   509

LU 21–2   Bonds   514

LU 21–3   Mutual Funds   516

CHAPTER 22   Business Statistics   528

LU 22–1   Mean, Median, and Mode   530

LU 22–2   Frequency Distributions and Graphs   533

LU 22–3   Measures of Dispersion (Optional)   538

APPENDIX A: Additional Homework by Learning Unit   A

APPENDIX B: Worked-Out Solutions to Extra Practice Quizzes and You Try It Problems   B-1

APPENDIX C: Check Figures   C

APPENDIX D: Metric System   D-1

Glossary/Index   G-1

Because Money Matters...

Get *Kiplinger's Personal Finance* at a Special Low Student Rate, Just $1 a Month!

Practical Business Math Procedures

CHAPTER 1

Whole Numbers: How to Dissect and Solve Word Problems

A Foot Long but a Dollar Short

New numbers released this week prove it: There are more Subway stores on the planet then McDonald's. Has McDonald's lost its grip? Not overseas, where it has nearly twice as many stores as the sandwich chain, and not in terms of world-wide sales. Still, it's a coup for Subway. The chain has been promoting the healthful aspects of its food since 1996, well before Jared went on TV with his Subway diet in 2000, and this without even 'reformulating the meat,' according to Subway spokesman Les Winograd.

—Sarah Slobin

TOTAL STORES IN 2010

		U.S.	International
33,749	Subway	23,722	10,027
32,737	McDonald's	14,027	18,710
17,009	Starbucks	11,158	5,851
16,756	KFC	4,986	11,770
13,356	Pizza Hut	7,528	5,828

Are You What You Eat?
Some of the most popular sandwiches world-wide and their vital statistics.

	6" turkey breast sub	Big Mac
Serving size (g)	219	214
Calories	280	540
Calories from fat	30	260
Total fat (g)	3.5	29
Saturated fat	1.0	10
Trans fat	0.0	1.5
Cholesterol (mg)	20	75
Sodium (mg)	920	1,040
Carbohydrates	47	45
Dietary fiber (g)	5	3
Sugars (g)	6	9
Protein (g)	18	25

Sources: Technomic Top 500 Report; the companies

LU 1–1: Reading, Writing, and Rounding Whole Numbers

1. Use place values to read and write numeric and verbal whole numbers *(pp. 4–6)*.
2. Round whole numbers to the indicated position *(pp. 6–7)*.
3. Use blueprint aid for dissecting and solving a word problem *(pp. 7–8)*.

LU 1–2: Adding and Subtracting Whole Numbers

1. Add whole numbers; check and estimate addition computations *(pp. 10–11)*.
2. Subtract whole numbers; check and estimate subtraction computations *(pp. 11–12)*.

LU 1–3: Multiplying and Dividing Whole Numbers

1. Multiply whole numbers; check and estimate multiplication computations *(pp. 14–16)*.
2. Divide whole numbers; check and estimate division computations *(pp. 16–17)*.

VOCABULARY PREVIEW

Here are key terms in this chapter. After completing the chapter, if you know the term, place a checkmark in the parentheses. If you don't know the term, look it up and put the page number where it can be found.

**Addends ( )   Decimal point ( )   Decimal system ( )   Difference ( )   Dividend ( )   Divisor ( )   Minuend ( )
Multiplicand ( )   Multiplier ( )   Partial products ( )   Partial quotient ( )   Product ( )   Quotient ( )
Remainder ( )   Rounding all the way ( )   Subtrahend ( )   Sum ( )   Whole number ( )**

In the chapter opener we see that Subway has more total stores in the United States (23,722) than does McDonald's (14,027). Keeping track of store count is just one way numbers tell us something about a business.

GLOBAL

People of all ages make personal business decisions based on the answers to number questions. Numbers also determine most of the business decisions of companies. For example, go to the website of a company such as Starbucks and note the importance of numbers in the company's business decision-making process.

The following *Wall Street Journal* clipping "Starbucks Menu Expands in China" announces plans to reach a greater number of people in China:

© Yan daming–Imaginechina via AP Images

Starbucks Menu Expands in China

BY LAURIE BURKITT

BEIJING—**Starbucks** Corp. is introducing its instant-coffee packets in China, expanding beyond coffee stores to also sell consumer packaged goods.

The Seattle-based coffee company's Via single-serving coffee packets will be available in at least 800 Starbucks stores across China, Hong Kong and Taiwan beginning on April 6, John Culver, president of Starbucks International, said Tuesday at a news conference here.

The packets also will be distributed in grocery and convenience stores and later in hotels and entertainment venues, Mr. Culver said. He added that a schedule hasn't been set. "We see a big opportunity in packaged goods in China," he said.

The move signals Starbucks's intention to expand not only its coffee business in China but beyond the beverage as well.

Starbucks has been exploring new tactics in the U.S. and internationally to boost its offerings into a broader array of consumer goods. Starbucks dropped the company's name and the word "coffee" from its logo in January. The company rolled out the new logo Tuesday in China.

Companies often follow a general problem-solving procedure to arrive at a change in company policy. Using Starbucks as an example, the following steps illustrate this procedure:

Step 1. State the problem(s).   Globally increase market share and profitability.

Step 2. Decide on the best methods to solve the problem(s).   Expand operations in China beyond coffee sales.

Step 3. Does the solution make sense?   Adapt to Chinese eating habits—more tea products and consumer packaged goods.

Step 4. Evaluate the results.   Starbucks will evaluate new plan.

Your study of numbers begins with a review of basic computation skills that focuses on speed and accuracy. You may think, "But I can use my calculator." Even if your instructor allows you to use a calculator, you still must know the basic computation skills. You need these skills to know what to calculate, how to interpret your calculations, how to make estimates to recognize errors you made in using your calculator, and how to make calculations when you do not have a calculator.

The United States' numbering system is the **decimal system** or *base 10 system*. Your calculator gives the 10 single-digit numbers of the decimal system—0, 1, 2, 3, 4, 5, 6, 7, 8, and 9. The center of the decimal system is the **decimal point.** When you have a number with a decimal point, the numbers to the left of the decimal point are **whole numbers** and the numbers to the right of the decimal point are decimal numbers (discussed in Chapter 3). When you have a number *without* a decimal, the number is a whole number and the decimal is assumed to be after the number.

This chapter discusses reading, writing, and rounding whole numbers; adding and subtracting whole numbers; and multiplying and dividing whole numbers.

Learning Unit 1–1: Reading, Writing, and Rounding Whole Numbers

LO 1

Whole Foods Market has more than 2,100,000 followers on Twitter. Tweets involve recipes, food tips, and answers to customer questions. Are you one of those two million, one hundred thousand followers?

Now let's begin our study of whole numbers.

GLOBAL

Reading and Writing Numeric and Verbal Whole Numbers

The decimal system is a *place-value system* based on the powers of 10. Any whole number can be written with the 10 digits of the decimal system because the position, or placement, of the digits in a number gives the value of the digits.

To determine the value of each digit in a number, we use a place-value chart (Figure 1.1) that divides numbers into named groups of three digits, with each group separated by a comma. To separate a number into groups, you begin with the last digit in the number and insert commas every three digits, moving from right to left. This divides the number into the named groups (units, thousands, millions, billions, trillions) shown in the place-value chart. Within each group, you have a ones, tens, and hundreds place. Keep in mind that the leftmost group may have fewer than three digits.

In Figure 1.1 (p. 5), the numeric number 1,605,743,891,412 illustrates place values. When you study the place-value chart, you can see that the value of each place in the chart is 10 times the value of the place to the right. We can illustrate this by analyzing the last four digits in the number 1,605,743,891,412 :

$$1{,}412 = (1 \times 1{,}000) + (4 \times 100) + (1 \times 10) + (2 \times 1)$$

So we can also say, for example, that in the number 745, the "7" means seven hundred (700); in the number 75, the "7" means 7 tens (70).

To read and write a numeric number in verbal form, you begin at the left and read each group of three digits as if it were alone, adding the group name at the end (except the last units group and groups of all zeros). Using the place-value chart in Figure 1.1, the number 1,605,743,891,412 is read as one trillion, six hundred five billion, seven hundred forty-three million, eight hundred ninety-one thousand, four hundred twelve. You do not read zeros. They fill vacant spaces as placeholders so that you can correctly state the number values. Also, the numbers twenty-one to ninety-nine must have a hyphen. And most important, when you read or write whole numbers in

Whole number place-value chart

Whole Number Groups

Trillions				Billions				Millions				Thousands				Units			
Hundred trillions	Ten trillions	Trillions	Comma	Hundred billions	Ten billions	Billions	Comma	Hundred millions	Ten millions	Millions	Comma	Hundred thousands	Ten thousands	Thousands	Comma	Hundreds	Tens	Ones (units)	Decimal Point
		1	,	6	0	5	,	7	4	3	,	8	9	1	,	4	1	2	.

verbal form, do not use the word *and*. In the decimal system, *and* indicates the decimal, which we discuss in Chapter 3.

By reversing this process of changing a numeric number to a verbal number, you can use the place-value chart to change a verbal number to a numeric number. Remember that you must keep track of the place value of each digit. The place values of the digits in a number determine its total value.

Before we look at how to round whole numbers, we should look at how to convert a number indicating parts of a whole number to a whole number. We will use the following *Wall Street Journal* clip about Whole Foods as an example.

@WholeFoods

FOLLOWERS:
2.1 MILLION
Recipes, food tips and answers to customers' questions

WRITTEN BY:
One person who tweets from the main account; individual accounts are created for, and handled by, each store

Whole Foods' 2,100,000 followers on Twitter could be written as 2.1 million. This amount is two million plus one hundred thousand of an additional million. The following steps explain how to convert these decimal numbers into a regular whole number:

CONVERTING PARTS OF A MILLION, BILLION, TRILLION, ETC., TO A REGULAR WHOLE NUMBER
Step 1. Drop the decimal point and insert a comma.
Step 2. Add zeros so the leftmost digit ends in the word name of the amount you want to convert. Be sure to add commas as needed.

EXAMPLE   Convert 2.1 million to a regular whole number.

Step 1. 2.1 million

2,1   Change the decimal point to a comma.

Step 2. 2,100,000   Add zeros and commas so the whole number indicates million.

Rounding Whole Numbers

Many of the whole numbers you read and hear are rounded numbers. Government statistics are usually rounded numbers. The financial reports of companies also use rounded numbers. All rounded numbers are *approximate* numbers. The more rounding you do, the more you approximate the number.

Rounded whole numbers are used for many reasons. With rounded whole numbers you can quickly estimate arithmetic results, check actual computations, report numbers that change quickly such as population numbers, and make numbers easier to read and remember.

Numbers can be rounded to any identified digit place value, including the first digit of a number (rounding all the way). To round whole numbers, use the following three steps:

ROUNDING WHOLE NUMBERS
Step 1. Identify the place value of the digit you want to round.
Step 2. If the digit to the right of the identified digit in Step 1 is 5 or more, increase the identified digit by 1 (round up). If the digit to the right is less than 5, do not change the identified digit.
Step 3. Change all digits to the right of the rounded identified digit to zeros.

EXAMPLE 1   Round 9,362 to the nearest hundred.

Step 1. 9,362   The digit 3 is in the hundreds place value.

Step 2.   The digit to the right of 3 is 5 or more (6). Thus, 3, the identified digit in Step 1, is now rounded to 4. You change the identified digit only if the digit to the right is 5 or more.

9,462

Step 3. 9,400   Change digits 6 and 2 to zeros, since these digits are to the right of 4, the rounded number.

By rounding 9,362 to the nearest hundred, you can see that 9,362 is closer to 9,400 than to 9,300.

Next, we show you how to round to the nearest thousand.

EXAMPLE 2   Round 67,951 to the nearest thousand.

Step 1. 67,951   The digit 7 is in the thousands place value.

Step 2.   The digit to the right of 7 is 5 or more (9). Thus, 7, the identified digit in Step 1, is now rounded to 8.

68,951

Step 3. 68,000   Change digits 9, 5, and 1 to zeros, since these digits are to the right of 8, the rounded number.

By rounding 67,951 to the nearest thousand, you can see that 67,951 is closer to 68,000 than to 67,000.

Now let's look at **rounding all the way.** To round a number all the way, you round to the first digit of the number (the leftmost digit) and have only one nonzero digit remaining in the number.

EXAMPLE 3   Round 7,843 all the way.

Step 1. 7,843   Identified leftmost digit is 7.

Step 2. └─────► Digit to the right of 7 is greater than 5, so 7 becomes 8.

      8,843
      ↓↓↓
      ▼▼▼

Step 3. 8,000   Change all other digits to zeros.

Rounding 7,843 all the way gives 8,000.

    Remember that rounding a digit to a specific place value depends on the degree of accuracy you want in your estimate. For example, in the *Wall Street Journal* clip "Phineas and Ferb," 628,000 rounds all the way to 600,000 because the digit to the right of 6 (leftmost digit) is less than 5. The 600,000 is 28,000 less than the original 628,000. You would be more accurate if you rounded 628,000 to the ten thousand place value of 1 identified digit, which is 630,000.

    Before concluding this unit, let's look at how to dissect and solve a word problem.

How to Dissect and Solve a Word Problem

As a student, your author found solving word problems difficult. Not knowing where to begin after reading the word problem caused the difficulty. Today, students still struggle with word problems as they try to decide where to begin.

    Solving word problems involves *organization* and *persistence.* Recall how persistent you were when you learned to ride a two-wheel bike. Do you remember the feeling of success you experienced when you rode the bike without help? Apply this persistence to word problems. Do not be discouraged. Each person learns at a different speed. Your goal must be to FINISH THE RACE and experience the success of solving word problems with ease.

    To be organized in solving word problems, you need a plan of action that tells you where to begin—a blueprint aid. Like a builder, you will refer to this blueprint aid constantly until you know the procedure. The blueprint aid for dissecting and solving a word problem appears below. Note that the blueprint aid serves an important function—**it decreases your math anxiety.**

Blueprint Aid for Dissecting and Solving a Word Problem

LO 3

	The facts	Solving for?	Steps to take	Key points
BLUEPRINT				

© Roberts Publishing Services

Now let's study this blueprint aid. The first two columns require that you *read* the word problem slowly. Think of the third column as the basic information you must know or calculate before solving the word problem. Often this column contains formulas that provide the foundation for the step-by-step problem solution. The last column reinforces the key points you should remember.

It's time now to try your skill at using the blueprint aid for dissecting and solving a word problem.

The Word Problem On the 100th anniversary of Tootsie Roll Industries, the company reported sharply increased sales and profits. Sales reached one hundred ninety-four million dollars and a record profit of twenty-two million, five hundred fifty-six thousand dollars. The company president requested that you round the sales and profit figures all the way.

Study the following blueprint aid and note how we filled in the columns with the information in the word problem. You will find the organization of the blueprint aid most helpful. Be persistent! You *can* dissect and solve word problems! When you are finished with the word problem, make sure the answer seems reasonable.

	The facts	Solving for?	Steps to take	Key points
BLUEPRINT	*Sales:* One hundred ninety-four million dollars. *Profit:* Twenty-two million, five hundred fifty-six thousand dollars.	Sales and profit rounded all the way.	Express each verbal form in numeric form. Identify leftmost digit in each number.	Rounding all the way means only the left-most digit will remain. All other digits become zeros.

Steps to solving problem

1. Convert verbal to numeric.
   One hundred ninety-four million dollars ⟶ $194,000,000
   Twenty-two million, five hundred fifty-six thousand dollars ⟶ $ 22,556,000

2. Identify leftmost digit of each number.
   $194,000,000 $22,556,000

3. Round.
   $200,000,000 $20,000,000

Note that in the final answer, $200,000,000 and $20,000,000 have only one nonzero digit.

Remember that you cannot round numbers expressed in verbal form. You must convert these numbers to numeric form.

Now you should see the importance of the information in the third column of the blueprint aid. When you complete your blueprint aids for word problems, do not be concerned if the order of the information in your boxes does not follow the order given in the text boxes. Often you can dissect a word problem in more than one way.

Your first Practice Quiz follows. Be sure to study the paragraph that introduces the Practice Quiz.

MONEY tips

Do not carry your Social Security card in your wallet. Keep it and other important documents in a safe deposit box or fireproof container. Shred any document that contains personal information, such as anything with your Social Security number on it, old bank statements, applications for loans, and so on.

LU 1–1 PRACTICE QUIZ

Complete this **Practice Quiz** to see how you are doing.

At the end of each learning unit, you can check your progress with a Practice Quiz. If you had difficulty understanding the unit, the Practice Quiz will help identify your area of weakness. Work the problems on scrap paper. Check your answers with the worked-out solutions that follow the quiz. Ask your instructor about specific assignments and the videos available on your DVD for each unit Practice Quiz.

1. Write in verbal form:
   a. 7,948   **b.** 48,775   **c.** 814,410,335,414

2. Round the following numbers as indicated:

Nearest ten	Nearest hundred	Nearest thousand	Rounded all the way
a. 92	**b.** 745	**c.** 8,341	**d.** 4,752

3. Kellogg's reported its sales as five million, one hundred eighty-one thousand dollars. The company earned a profit of five hundred two thousand dollars. What would the sales and profit be if each number were rounded all the way? (*Hint:* You might want to draw the blueprint aid since we show it in the solution.)

*For **extra help** from your authors—Sharon and Jeff–see the student DVD*

✓ Solutions

1. **a.** Seven thousand, nine hundred forty-eight
   b. Forty-eight thousand, seven hundred seventy-five
   c. Eight hundred fourteen billion, four hundred ten million, three hundred thirty-five thousand, four hundred fourteen

2. **a.** 90   **b.** 700   **c.** 8,000   **d.** 5,000

3. Kellogg's sales and profit:

	The facts	Solving for?	Steps to take	Key points
BLUEPRINT	*Sales:* Five million, one hundred eighty-one thousand dollars. *Profit:* Five hundred two thousand dollars.	Sales and profit rounded all the way.	Express each verbal form in numeric form. Identify leftmost digit in each number.	Rounding all the way means only the left-most digit will remain. All other digits become zeros.

Steps to solving problem

1. Convert verbal to numeric.
   Five million, one hundred eighty-one thousand ⟶ $5,181,000
   Five hundred two thousand ⟶ $ 502,000

2. Identify leftmost digit of each number.
   $5,181,000 $502,000

3. Round.
   $5,000,000 $500,000

LU 1–1a EXTRA PRACTICE QUIZ WITH WORKED-OUT SOLUTIONS

Need more practice? Try this **Extra Practice Quiz** (check figures in the Interactive Chapter Organizer, p. 21). Worked-out Solutions can be found in Appendix B at end of text.

1. Write in verbal form:
   a. 8,682   **b.** 56,295   **c.** 732,310,444,888

2. Round the following numbers as indicated:

Nearest ten	Nearest hundred	Nearest thousand	Rounded all the way
a. 43	**b.** 654	**c.** 7,328	**d.** 5,980

3. Kellogg's reported its sales as three million, two hundred ninety-one thousand dollars. The company earned a profit of four hundred five thousand dollars. What would the sales and profit be if each number were rounded all the way?

Learning Unit 1–2: Adding and Subtracting Whole Numbers

LO 1

We all know the cost of car rentals and hotel rates vary around the world. The following *Wall Street Journal* clip identifies some of the most and least expensive car rental and hotel rates in the world. For example, note the difference in daily costs between the hotel rates in Brisbane, Australia, and Albuquerque, New Mexico.

Brisbane	$259
Albuquerque	− 65
	$194

CAR RENTAL		$187	HOTEL RATE		$103

MOST EXPENSIVE		LEAST EXPENSIVE		MOST EXPENSIVE		LEAST EXPENSIVE	
Rome	$440	Hong Kong	$62	Perth, Australia	$284	Tulsa, Okla.	$64
Barcelona, Spain	$428	Bangalore, India	$69	Brisbane, Australia	$259	Albuquerque, N.M.	$65
Seoul, South Korea	$417	Mumbai, India	$75	Sydney, Australia	$255	Jacksonville, Fla.	$69

Reprinted with permission of *The Wall Street Journal*, Copyright © 2011 Dow Jones & Company, Inc. All Rights Reserved Worldwide.

This unit teaches you how to manually add and subtract whole numbers. When you least expect it, you will catch yourself automatically using this skill.

Addition of Whole Numbers

To add whole numbers, you unite two or more numbers called **addends** to make one number called a **sum,** *total,* or *amount.* The numbers are arranged in a column according to their place values—units above units, tens above tens, and so on. Then, you add the columns of numbers from top to bottom. To check the result, you re-add the columns from bottom to top. This procedure is illustrated in the steps that follow.

"*Mistakes were made.*"

From The Wall Street Journal, copyright © 2010, permission of Cartoon Features Syndicate.

ADDING WHOLE NUMBERS
Step 1. Align the numbers to be added in columns according to their place values, beginning with the units place at the right and moving to the left.
Step 2. Add the units column. Write the sum below the column. If the sum is more than 9, write the units digit and carry the tens digit.
Step 3. Moving to the left, repeat Step 2 until all place values are added.

EXAMPLE

Adding	2 11		Checking	**Alternate check**
top	1,362	↑	bottom to	Add each column as a
bottom	5,913		to top	separate total and then
	8,924			combine. The end
	+6,594			result is the same.
	22,793			

$$
\begin{array}{r}
1,362 \\
5,913 \\
8,924 \\
+\ 6,594 \\
\hline
13 \\
18 \\
2\,6 \\
20 \\
\hline
22,793
\end{array}
$$

How to Quickly Estimate Addition by Rounding All the Way   In Learning Unit 1–1, you learned that rounding whole numbers all the way gives quick arithmetic estimates. Using the following *Wall Street Journal* clipping "International Ambitions" note how you can round each number all the way and the total will not be rounded all the way. Remember that rounding all the way does not replace actual computations, but it is helpful in making quick commonsense decisions.

GLOBAL

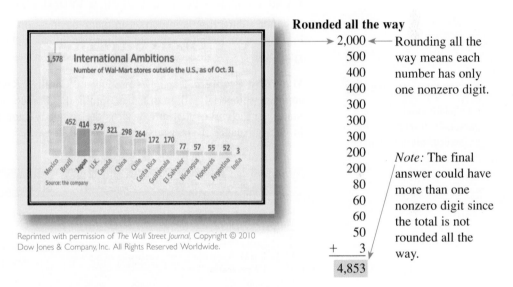

Reprinted with permission of *The Wall Street Journal,* Copyright © 2010 Dow Jones & Company, Inc. All Rights Reserved Worldwide.

Rounded all the way

2,000	← Rounding all the
500	way means each
400	number has only
400	one nonzero digit.
300	
300	
300	
200	*Note:* The final
200	answer could have
80	more than one
60	nonzero digit since
60	the total is not
50	rounded all the
+ 3	way.
4,853	

LO 2

Subtraction of Whole Numbers

Subtraction is the opposite of addition. Addition unites numbers; subtraction takes one number away from another number. In subtraction, the top (largest) number is the **minuend.** The number you subtract from the minuend is the **subtrahend,** which gives you the **difference** between the minuend and the subtrahend. The steps for subtracting whole numbers follow.

SUBTRACTING WHOLE NUMBERS
Step 1. Align the minuend and subtrahend according to their place values.
Step 2. Begin the subtraction with the units digits. Write the difference below the column. If the units digit in the minuend is smaller than the units digit in the subtrahend, borrow 1 from the tens digit in the minuend. One tens digit is 10 units.
Step 3. Moving to the left, repeat Step 2 until all place values in the subtrahend are subtracted.

MONEY tips

Be vigilant about sharing personal information. Change passwords often and do not share them.

EXAMPLE   The *Wall Street Journal* clipping "International Ambitions" illustrates the subtraction of whole numbers:

What is the difference in the number of Walmart stores in Japan and the UK? As shown below you can use subtraction to arrive at the 35 difference.

$$
\begin{array}{r}
{\scriptstyle 3\,10\,14} \\
\cancel{4}\,\cancel{1}\,\cancel{4} \leftarrow \text{Minuend (larger number)} \\
-379 \leftarrow \text{Subtrahend} \\
\hline
35 \leftarrow \text{Difference}
\end{array}
$$

Check
$$
\begin{array}{r}
35 \\
+379 \\
\hline
414
\end{array}
$$

In subtraction, borrowing from the column at the left is often necessary. Remember that 1 ten = 10 units, 1 hundred = 10 tens, and 1 thousand = 10 hundreds.

In the units column in the example above, 9 cannot be subtracted from 4 so we borrow from the tens column, resulting in 14 less 9 equals 5. In the tens column, we cannot subtract 7 from 0 so we borrow 10 tens from the hundreds column, leaving 3 hundreds. Ten less 7 equals 3.

Checking subtraction requires adding the difference (35) to the subtrahend (379) to arrive at the minuend (414).

How to Dissect and Solve a Word Problem

Accurate subtraction is important in many business operations. In Chapter 4 we discuss the importance of keeping accurate subtraction in your checkbook balance. Now let's check your progress by dissecting and solving a word problem.

The Word Problem   Hershey's produced 25 million Kisses in one day. The same day, the company shipped 4 million to Japan, 3 million to France, and 6 million throughout the United States. At the end of that day, what is the company's total inventory of Kisses? What is the inventory balance if you round the number all the way?

	The facts	Solving for?	Steps to take	Key points
BLUEPRINT	*Produced:* 25 million. *Shipped:* Japan, 4 million; France, 3 million; United States, 6 million.	Total Kisses left in inventory. Inventory balance rounded all the way.	Total Kisses produced − Total Kisses shipped = Total Kisses left in inventory.	Minuend − Subtrahend = Difference. Rounding all the way means rounding to last digit on the left.

Steps to solving problem

1. Calculate the total Kisses shipped.

2. Calculate the total Kisses left in inventory.

3. Rounding all the way.

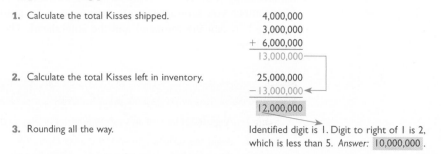

Identified digit is 1. Digit to right of 1 is 2, which is less than 5. *Answer:* 10,000,000 .

The Practice Quiz that follows will tell you how you are progressing in your study of Chapter 1.

Complete this **Practice Quiz** to see how you are doing.

1. Add by totaling each separate column:
   8,974
   6,439
   + 6,941

2. Estimate by rounding all the way (do not round the total of estimate) and then do the actual computation:
   4,241
   8,794
   + 3,872

3. Subtract and check your answer:
   9,876
   − 4,967

4. Jackson Manufacturing Company projected its year 2013 furniture sales at $900,000. During 2013, Jackson earned $510,000 in sales from major clients and $369,100 in sales from the remainder of its clients. What is the amount by which Jackson over- or underestimated its sales? Use the blueprint aid, since the answer will show the completed blueprint aid.

For **extra help** from your authors–Sharon and Jeff–see the student DVD

YouTube

✓ **Solutions**

1.   14
      14
      2 2
      20
      22,354

2. **Estimate**   **Actual**
      4,000   4,241
      9,000   8,794
    + 4,000   + 3,872
    17,000   **16,907**

3.   8 18 6 16
     9,876
     − 4,967
     4,909

   Check
     4,909
   + 4,967
     9,876

4. Jackson Manufacturing Company over- or underestimated sales:

	The facts	Solving for?	Steps to take	Key points
BLUEPRINT	Projected 2013 sales: $900,000. Major clients: $510,000. Other clients: $369,100.	How much were sales over- or underestimated?	Total projected sales − Total actual sales = Over- or underestimated sales.	Projected sales (minuend) − Actual sales (subtrahend) = Difference.

Steps to solving problem

1. Calculate total actual sales.
   $510,000
   + 369,100
   $879,100

2. Calculate overestimated or underestimated sales.
   $900,000
   − 879,100
   $ 20,900 (overestimated)

Need more practice? Try this **Extra Practice Quiz** (check figures in the Interactive Chapter Organizer, p. 21). Worked-out Solutions can be found in Appendix B at end of text.

1. Add by totaling each separate column:
   9,853
   7,394
   + 8,843

2. Estimate by rounding all the way (do not round the total of estimate) and then do the actual computation:
   3,482
   6,981
   + 5,490

3. Subtract and check your answer:

$$
\begin{array}{r}
9{,}787 \\
-5{,}968 \\
\hline
\end{array}
$$

4. Jackson Manufacturing Company projected its year 2013 furniture sales at $878,000. During 2013, Jackson earned $492,900 in sales from major clients and $342,000 in sales from the remainder of its clients. What is the amount by which Jackson over- or under-estimated its sales?

Learning Unit 1–3: Multiplying and Dividing Whole Numbers

The *Wall Street Journal* clip in the margin shows that Facebook agreed to a 20-year privacy settlement with the government. If Facebook violates the settlement, it can be fined $16,000 per day. What would it cost if Facebook violated the settlement for 4 days?

$$4 \text{ days} \times \$16{,}000 = \$64{,}000$$

If you divide $64,000 by $16,000 per day you get 4 days.

This unit will sharpen your skills in two important arithmetic operations—multiplication and division. These two operations frequently result in knowledgeable business decisions.

Multiplication of Whole Numbers—Shortcut to Addition

From calculating the cost of Facebook's settlement you know that multiplication is a *shortcut to addition:*

$$\$16{,}000 \times 4 = \$64{,}000 \qquad \text{or} \qquad \$16{,}000 + \$16{,}000 + \$16{,}000 + \$16{,}000 = \$64{,}000$$

Before learning the steps used to multiply whole numbers with two or more digits, you must learn some multiplication terminology.

Note in the following example that the top number (number we want to multiply) is the **multiplicand.** The bottom number (number doing the multiplying) is the **multiplier.** The final number (answer) is the **product.** The numbers between the multiplier and the product are **partial products.** Also note how we positioned the partial product 2090. This number is the result of multiplying 418 by 50 (the 5 is in the tens position). On each line in the partial products, we placed the first digit directly below the digit we used in the multiplication process.

EXAMPLE

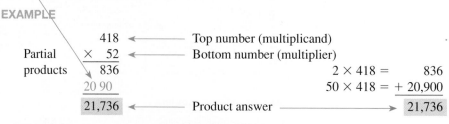

"I'm not late. Everyone learns at their own speed."

We can now give the following steps for multiplying whole numbers with two or more digits:

MULTIPLYING WHOLE NUMBERS WITH TWO OR MORE DIGITS
Step 1. Align the multiplicand (top number) and multiplier (bottom number) at the right. Usually, you should make the smaller number the multiplier.
Step 2. Begin by multiplying the right digit of the multiplier with the right digit of the multiplicand. Keep multiplying as you move left through the multiplicand. Your first partial product aligns at the right with the multiplicand and multiplier.
Step 3. Move left through the multiplier and continue multiplying the multiplicand. Your partial product right digit or first digit is placed directly below the digit in the multiplier that you used to multiply.
Step 4. Continue Steps 2 and 3 until you have completed your multiplication process. Then add the partial products to get the final product.

Checking and Estimating Multiplication   We can check the multiplication process by reversing the multiplicand and multiplier and then multiplying. Let's first estimate 52×418 by rounding all the way.

EXAMPLE
$$
\begin{array}{r}
50 \;\leftarrow\; 52 \\
\times\; 400 \;\leftarrow\; \times\, 418 \\
\hline
20{,}000 \qquad 416 \\
52 \\
20\,8 \\
\hline
\boxed{21{,}736}
\end{array}
$$

By estimating before actually working the problem, we know our answer should be about 20,000. When we multiply 52 by 418, we get the same answer as when we multiply 418×52—and the answer is about 20,000. Remember, if we had not rounded all the way, our estimate would have been closer. If we had used a calculator, the rounded estimate would have helped us check the calculator's answer. Our commonsense estimate tells us our answer is near 20,000—not 200,000.

Before you study the division of whole numbers, you should know (1) the multiplication shortcut with numbers ending in zeros and (2) how to multiply a whole number by a power of 10.

MULTIPLICATION SHORTCUT WITH NUMBERS ENDING IN ZEROS
Step 1. When zeros are at the end of the multiplicand or the multiplier, or both, disregard the zeros and multiply.
Step 2. Count the number of zeros in the multiplicand and multiplier.
Step 3. Attach the number of zeros counted in Step 2 to your answer.

EXAMPLE

$$
\begin{array}{r}
65{,}000 \\
\times\; 420 \\
\hline
\end{array}
\qquad
\begin{array}{r}
65 \\
\times\; 42 \\
\hline
1\,30 \\
26\;0 \\
\hline
27{,}300{,}000
\end{array}
\qquad
\begin{array}{r}
3 \text{ zeros} \\
+\,1 \text{ zero} \\
\hline
4 \text{ zeros}
\end{array}
$$

No need to multiply rows of zeros

$$
\begin{array}{r}
65{,}000 \\
\times\; 420 \\
\hline
00\,000 \\
1\,300\,00 \\
26\,000\,0 \\
\hline
\boxed{27{,}300{,}000}
\end{array}
$$

MULTIPLYING A WHOLE NUMBER BY A POWER OF 10
Step 1. Count the number of zeros in the power of 10 (a whole number that begins with 1 and ends in one or more zeros such as 10, 100, 1,000, and so on).
Step 2. Attach that number of zeros to the right side of the other whole number to obtain the answer. Insert comma(s) as needed every three digits, moving from right to left.

EXAMPLE 99×10 $= 99\underline{0}$ $= \boxed{990}$ ← Add 1 zero

99×100 $= 9,9\underline{00}$ $= \boxed{9,900}$ ← Add 2 zeros

$99 \times 1,000 = 99,\underline{000} = \boxed{99,000}$ ← Add 3 zeros

When a zero is in the center of the multiplier, you can do the following:

EXAMPLE

$$\begin{array}{r} 658 \\ \times\ 403 \\ \hline 1\ 974 \\ 263\ 2\square \\ \hline \boxed{265,174} \end{array}$$

$$\begin{array}{r} 3 \times 658 = 1,974 \\ 400 \times 658 = +\ 263,200 \\ \hline \boxed{265,174} \end{array}$$

Division of Whole Numbers

Division is the reverse of multiplication and a time-saving shortcut related to subtraction. For example, in the introduction of this learning unit you determined that Facebook would pay $64,000 for a 4-day settlement penalty. You multiplied $16,000 $\times$ 4 to get $64,000. Since division is the reverse of multiplication you can also say that $64,000 $\div$ 4 = $16,000.

Division can be indicated by the common symbols $\div$ and $)$, or by the bar — in a fraction and the forward slant / between two numbers, which means the first number is divided by the second number. Division asks how many times one number (**divisor**) is contained in another number (**dividend**). The answer, or result, is the **quotient.** When the divisor (number used to divide) doesn't divide evenly into the dividend (number we are dividing), the result is a **partial quotient,** with the leftover amount the **remainder** (expressed as fractions in later chapters). The following example illustrates *even division* (this is also an example of *long division* because the divisor has more than one digit).

EXAMPLE

$$\begin{array}{r} 18 \leftarrow \text{Quotient} \\ \text{Divisor} \longrightarrow 15\overline{)270} \leftarrow \text{Dividend} \\ \underline{15} \\ 120 \\ \underline{120} \end{array}$$

This example divides 15 into 27 once with 12 remaining. The 0 in the dividend is brought down to 12. Dividing 120 by 15 equals 8 with no remainder; that is, even division. The following example illustrates *uneven division with a remainder* (this is also an example of *short division* because the divisor has only one digit).

EXAMPLE

$$\begin{array}{r} 24\ \text{R1} \leftarrow \text{Remainder} \\ 7\overline{)169} \\ \underline{14} \\ 29 \\ \underline{28} \\ 1 \end{array}$$

Check

$(7 \times 24) + 1 = 169$

Divisor $\times$ Quotient + Remainder = Dividend

Note how doing the check gives you assurance that your calculation is correct. When the divisor has one digit (short division) as in this example, you can often calculate the division mentally as illustrated in the following examples:

EXAMPLES

$$\begin{array}{r} 108 \\ 8\overline{)864} \end{array}$$

$$\begin{array}{r} 16\ \text{R6} \\ 7\overline{)118} \end{array}$$

Next, let's look at the value of estimating division.

Estimating Division Before actually working a division problem, estimate the quotient by rounding. This estimate helps you check the answer. The example that follows is rounded all the way. After you make an estimate, work the problem and check your answer by multiplication.

EXAMPLE

	36 R111	**Estimate**	**Check**
	138)5,079	50	138
	4 14	100)5,000	× 36
	939		828
	828		4 14
	111		4,968
			+ 111 ←— Add remainder
			5,079

Now let's turn our attention to division shortcuts with zeros.

Division Shortcuts with Zeros The steps that follow show a shortcut that you can use when you divide numbers with zeros.

DIVISION SHORTCUT WITH NUMBERS ENDING IN ZEROS

Step 1. When the dividend and divisor have ending zeros, count the number of ending zeros in the divisor.

Step 2. Drop the same number of zeros in the dividend as in the divisor, counting from right to left.

Note the following examples of division shortcuts with numbers ending in zeros. Since two of the symbols used for division are ÷ and)‾ , our first examples show the zero shortcut method with the ÷ symbol.

EXAMPLES

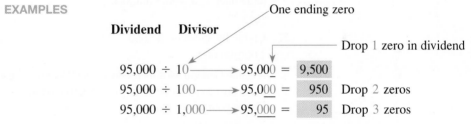

In a long division problem with the)‾ symbol, you again count the number of ending zeros in the divisor. Then drop the same number of ending zeros in the dividend and divide as usual.

EXAMPLE   6,5̲0̲0̲)88,0̲0̲0̲ ←— Drop 2 zeros

	13 R35
	65)880
	65
	230
	195
	35

65)880 ←——

You are now ready to practice what you learned by dissecting and solving a word problem.

How to Dissect and Solve a Word Problem

The blueprint aid on page 18 will be your guide to dissecting and solving the following word problem.

The Word Problem Dunkin' Donuts sells to four different companies a total of $3,500 worth of doughnuts per week. What is the total annual sales to these companies? What is the yearly sales per company? (Assume each company buys the same amount.) Check your answer to show how multiplication and division are related.

MONEY tips

College *is* worth it! College graduates earn substantially more money each year than high school graduates *and that* wage premium is increasing steadily—almost twice as much. Stay in school.

	The facts	Solving for?	Steps to take	Key points
BLUEPRINT	*Sales per week:* $3,500. *Companies:* 4.	Total annual sales to all four companies. Yearly sales per company.	Sales per week × Weeks in year (52) = Total annual sales. Total annual sales ÷ Total companies = Yearly sales per company.	Division is the reverse of multiplication.

Steps to solving problem

1. Calculate total annual sales. $3,500 × 52 weeks = $182,000

2. Calculate yearly sales per company, $182,000 ÷ 4 = $45,500

Check

$45,500 × 4 = $182,000

It's time again to check your progress with a Practice Quiz.

LU 1–3 | **PRACTICE QUIZ**

Complete this **Practice Quiz** to see how you are doing.

1. Estimate the actual problem by rounding all the way, work the actual problem, and check:
   Actual   **Estimate**   **Check**
   3,894
   × 18

2. Multiply by shortcut method:
   77,000
   × 1,800

3. Multiply by shortcut method:
   95 × 10,000

4. Divide by rounding all the way, complete the actual calculation, and check, showing remainder as a whole number.
   $26)\overline{5,325}$

5. Divide by shortcut method:
   $4,000)\overline{96,000}$

6. Assume General Motors produces 960 Chevrolets each workday (Monday through Friday). If the cost to produce each car is $6,500, what is General Motors' total cost for the year? Check your answer.

*For **extra help** from your authors—Sharon and Jeff—see the student DVD*

✓ Solutions

1. **Estimate**   **Actual**   **Check**
   4,000   3,894   8 × 3,894 =   31,152
   ×   20   ×   18   10 × 3,894 = + 38,940
   80,000   31 152   70,092
                         38 94
                         70,092

2. 77 × 18 = 1,386 + 5 zeros = 138,600,000

3. 95 + 4 zeros = 950,000

4. **Rounding**   **Actual**   **Check**
       166 R20   204 R21   26 × 204 = 5,304
   30)5,000   26)5,325   +   21
      3 0   5 2   5,325
      2 00   125
      1 80   104
       200   21
       180
        20

5. Drop 3 zeros = $\dfrac{24}{4)\overline{96}}$

6. General Motors' total cost per year:

	The facts	Solving for?	Steps to take	Key points
BLUEPRINT	*Cars produced each workday:* 960. *Workweek:* 5 days. *Cost per car:* $6,500.	Total cost per year.	Cars produced per week × 52 = Total cars produced per year. Total cars produced per year × Total cost per car = Total cost per year.	Whenever possible, use multiplication and division shortcuts with zeros. Multiplication can be checked by division.

Steps to solving problem

1. Calculate total cars produced per week.

    5 × 960 = 4,800 cars produced per week

2. Calculate total cars produced per year.

    4,800 cars × 52 weeks = 249,600 total cars produced per year

3. Calculate total cost per year.

    249,600 cars × $6,500 = $1,622,400,000
    (multiply 2,496 × 65 and add zeros)

    Check

    $1,622,400,000 ÷ 249,600 = $6,500 (drop 2 zeros before dividing)

LU 1–3a   EXTRA PRACTICE QUIZ WITH WORKED-OUT SOLUTIONS

Need more practice? Try this **Extra Practice Quiz** (check figures in the Interactive Chapter Organizer, p. 21). Worked-out Solutions can be found in Appendix B at end of text.

1. Estimate the actual problem by rounding all the way, work the actual problem, and check:

    Actual　　　**Estimate**　　　**Check**

    4,938
    × 　19

2. Multiply by shortcut method:

    86,000
    × 1,900

3. Multiply by shortcut method:

    86 × 10,000

4. Divide by rounding all the way, complete the actual calculation, and check, showing remainder as a whole number.

    26)6,394

5. Divide by the shortcut method:

    3,000)99,000

6. Assume General Motors produces 850 Chevrolets each workday (Monday through Friday). If the cost to produce each car is $7,000, what is General Motors' total cost for the year? Check your answer.

INTERACTIVE CHAPTER ORGANIZER

Topic/procedure/formula	Examples	You try it*
Reading and writing numeric and verbal whole numbers, p. 4 Placement of digits in a number gives the value of the digits (Figure 1.1). Commas separate every three digits, moving from right to left. Begin at left to read and write number in verbal form. Do not read zeros or use *and*. Hyphenate numbers twenty-one to ninety-nine. Reverse procedure to change verbal number to numeric.	462 → Four hundred sixty-two 6,741 → Six thousand, seven hundred forty-one	**Write in verbal form** 571 → 7,943 →
Rounding whole numbers, p. 6 1. Identify place value of the digit to be rounded. 2. If digit to the right is 5 or more, round up; if less than 5, do not change. 3. Change all digits to the right of rounded identified digit to zeros.	643 to nearest ten 4 in tens place value 3 is not 5 or more Thus, 643 rounds to 640.	**Round to nearest ten** 691
Rounding all the way, p. 6 Round to first digit of number. One nonzero digit remains. In estimating, you round each number of the problem to one nonzero digit. The final answer is not rounded.	468,451 → 500,000 The 5 is the only nonzero digit remaining.	**Round all the way** 429,685 →
Adding whole numbers, p. 10 1. Align numbers at the right. 2. Add units column. If sum is more than 9, carry tens digit. 3. Moving left, repeat Step 2 until all place values are added. Add from top to bottom. Check by adding bottom to top or adding each column separately and combining.	$\begin{array}{r} 65 \\ +\ 47 \\ \hline 112 \end{array}$ $\begin{array}{r} 12 \\ +10 \\ \hline 112 \end{array}$ Checking sum of each digit	**Add** 76 +38
Subtracting whole numbers, p. 11 1. Align minuend and subtrahend at the right. 2. Subtract units digits. If necessary, borrow 1 from tens digit in minuend. 3. Moving left, repeat Step 2 until all place values are subtracted. Minuend less subtrahend equals difference.	**Check** $\begin{array}{r} {}^{5\,18} \\ 6\not85 \\ -492 \\ \hline 193 \end{array}$ $\begin{array}{r} 193 \\ +492 \\ \hline 685 \end{array}$	**Subtract** 629 −134
Multiplying whole numbers, p. 14 1. Align multiplicand and multiplier at the right. 2. Begin at the right and keep multiplying as you move to the left. First partial product aligns at the right with multiplicand and multiplier. 3. Move left through multiplier and continue multiplying multiplicand. Partial product right digit or first digit is placed directly below digit in multiplier. 4. Continue Steps 2 and 3 until multiplication is complete. Add partial products to get final product.	$\begin{array}{r} 223 \\ \times\ 32 \\ \hline 446 \\ 6\ 69 \\ \hline 7,136 \end{array}$	**Multiply** 491 × 28

Shortcuts: (a) When multiplicand or multiplier, or both, end in zeros, disregard zeros and multiply; attach same number of zeros to answer. If zero is in center of multiplier, no need to show row of zeros. (b) If multiplying by power of 10, attach same number of zeros to whole number multiplied.	a. $\begin{array}{r}48,000 \\ \times\ \ \ 40\end{array}$ $\begin{array}{r}48 \\ \times\ 4\end{array}$ 3 zeros
	    +1 zero
	1,920,000 ← 4 zeros
	
	$\begin{array}{r} 524 \\ \times\ 206 \\ \hline 3\ 144 \\ 104\ 8 \\ \hline 107,944 \end{array}$
	
	b. 14 × 10 = 140 (attach 1 zero)
	  14 × 1,000 = 14,000 (attach 3 zeros)
		Multiply by shortcut
		13 × 10 =
		13 × 1,000 =

INTERACTIVE CHAPTER ORGANIZER

Topic/procedure/formula	Examples	You try it*
Dividing whole numbers, p. 16 1. When divisor is divided into the dividend, the remainder is less than divisor. 2. Drop zeros from dividend right to left by number of zeros found in the divisor. Even division has no remainder; uneven division has a remainder; divisor with one digit is short division; and divisor with more than one digit is long division.	1. $\begin{array}{r} 5\ R6 \\ 14\overline{)76} \\ 70 \\ \hline 6 \end{array}$ 2. $5{,}000 \div 100 = 50 \div 1 = \boxed{50}$ $\quad 5{,}000 \div 1{,}000 = 5 \div 1 = \boxed{5}$	**Divide** 1. $16\overline{)95}$ **Divide by shortcut** 2. $4{,}000 \div 100$ $\quad 4{,}000 \div 1{,}000$

KEY TERMS			
	Addends, *p. 10* Decimal point, *p. 4* Decimal system, *p. 4* Difference, *p. 11* Dividend, *p. 16* Divisor, *p. 16*	Minuend, *p. 11* Multiplicand, *p. 14* Multiplier, *p. 14* Partial products, *p. 14* Partial quotient, *p. 16* Product, *p. 14*	Quotient, *p. 16* Remainder, *p. 16* Rounding all the way, *p. 6* Subtrahend, *p. 11* Sum, *p. 10* Whole number, *p. 4*

| **Check Figures for Extra Practice Quizzes with Page References. (Worked-out Solutions in Appendix B.)** | LU 1–1a (p. 9)
1. A. Eight thousand, six hundred eighty-two; B. Fifty-six thousand, two hundred ninety-five; C. Seven hundred thirty-two billion, three hundred ten million, four hundred forty-four thousand, eight hundred eighty-eight
2. A. 40; B. 700; C. 7,000; D. 6,000
3. $3,000,000; $400,000 | LU 1–2a (p. 13)
1. 26,090
2. 15,000; 15,953
3. 3,819
4. $43,100 (over) | LU 1–3a (p. 19)
1. 100,000; 93,822
2. 163,400,000
3. 860,000
4. 245 R24
5. 33
6. $1,547,000,000 |

*Worked-out solutions are in Appendix B.

Critical Thinking Discussion Questions with Chapter Concept Check

1. List the four steps of the decision-making process. Do you think all companies should be required to follow these steps? Give an example.

2. Explain the three steps used to round whole numbers. Pick a whole number and explain why it should not be rounded.

3. How do you check subtraction? If you were to attend a movie, explain how you might use the subtraction check method.

4. Explain how you can check multiplication. If you visit a local supermarket, how could you show multiplication as a shortcut to addition?

5. Explain how division is the reverse of multiplication. Using the supermarket example, explain how division is a time-saving shortcut related to subtraction.

6. **Chapter Concept Check.** Using all the math you learned in Chapter 1, go to the chapter opener and plan out a dinner for a family of four. You need to calculate the difference in cost and calories from dining at Subway versus McDonald's. Go online or visit these stores in your area to find current food prices.

Classroom Notes

END-OF-CHAPTER PROBLEMS

 www.mhhe.com/slater11e

Check figures for odd-numbered problems in Appendix C.   Name _____   Date _____

DRILL PROBLEMS

Add the following: *LU 1-2(1)*

1–1.   75
  + 19

1–2.   850
  + 670

1–3.   88
  + 88

1–4.   88
  + 75

1–5.   6,251
  + 7,329

1–6.   59,481
  51,411
  + 70,821

1–7.   78,159
  15,850
  + 19,681

Subtract the following: *LU 1-2(2)*

1–8.   68
  −19

1–9.   80
  −42

1–10.   287
   −199

1–11.   9,000
   −5,400

1–12.   9,800
   −8,900

1–13.   1,622
   − 548

Multiply the following: *LU 1-3(1)*

1–14.   60
  × 7

1–15.   510
  × 61

1–16.   800
  × 200

1–17.   677
  × 503

1–18.   309
  × 850

1–19.   450
  × 280

Divide the following by short division: *LU 1-3(2)*

1–20. 4)1,600

1–21. 9)810

1–22. 4)164

Divide the following by long division. Show work and remainder. *LU 1-3(2)*

1–23. 6)520

1–24. 62)8,915

Add the following without rearranging: *LU 1-2(1)*

1–25. 95 + 310

1–26. 1,055 + 88

1–27. 666 + 950

1–28. 1,011 + 17

1–29. Add the following and check by totaling each column individually without carrying numbers: *LU 1-2(1)*

Check

  8,539
  6,842
+ 9,495

Estimate the following by rounding all the way and then do actual addition: *LU 1-1(2), LU 1-2(1)*

	Actual	**Estimate**		**Actual**	**Estimate**
1–30.	7,700		**1–31.**	6,980	
	9,286			3,190	
	+ 3,900			+ 7,819	

Subtract the following without rearranging: *LU 1-2(2)*

1–32. $190 - 66$

1–33. $950 - 870$

1–34. Subtract the following and check answer: *LU 1-2(2)*

  591,001
− 375,956

Multiply the following horizontally: *LU 1-3(1)*

1–35. 19×7 **1–36.** 84×8 **1–37.** 27×8 **1–38.** 19×5

Divide the following and check by multiplication: *LU 1-2(2)*

1–39. $45\overline{)876}$ **Check**   **1–40.** $46\overline{)1,950}$ **Check**

Complete the following: *LU 1-2(2)*

1–41.	9,200	**1–42.**	3,000,000
	− 1,510		− 769,459
	− 700		− 68,541

1–43. Estimate the following problem by rounding all the way and then do the actual multiplication: *LU 1-1(2), LU 1-3(1)*

Actual   **Estimate**

 870
$\times$ 81

Divide the following by the shortcut method: *LU 1-3(2)*

1–44. $1,000\overline{)950,000}$ **1–45.** $100\overline{)70,000}$

1–46. Estimate actual problem by rounding all the way and do actual division: *LU 1-1(2), LU 1-3(2)*

Actual   **Estimate**

$695\overline{)8,950}$

WORD PROBLEMS

1–47. The *Wall Street Journal* reported that the cost for lightbulbs over a 10-year period at a local Walmart parking lot in Kansas would be $248,134 if standard lightbulbs were used. If LED lightbulbs were used over the same period, the total cost would be $220,396. What would Walmart save by using LED bulbs? *LU 1-2(2)*

1–48. An education can be the key to higher earnings. In a U.S. Census Bureau study, high school graduates earned $30,400 per year. Associate's degree graduates averaged $38,200 per year. Bachelor's degree graduates averaged $52,200 per year. Assuming a 50-year work-life, calculate the lifetime earnings for a high school graduate, associate's degree graduate, and bachelor's degree graduate. What's the lifetime income difference between a high school and associate's degree? What about the lifetime difference between a high school and bachelor's degree? *LU 1-3(1), LU 1-2(2)*

1–49. Assume season-ticket prices in the lower bowl for the Buffalo Bills will rise from $480 for a 10-game package to $600. Fans sitting in the best seats in the upper deck will pay an increase from $440 to $540. Don Manning plans to purchase two season tickets for either lower bowl or upper deck. **(a)** How much more will two tickets cost for lower bowl? **(b)** How much more will two tickets cost for upper deck? **(c)** What will be his total cost for a 10-game package for lower bowl? **(d)** What will be his total cost for a 10-game package for upper deck? *LU 1-2(2), LU 1-3(1)*

1–50. Some ticket prices for *Lion King* on Broadway were $70, $95, $200, and $250. For a family of four, estimate the cost of the $95 tickets by rounding all the way and then do the actual multiplication: *LU 1-1(2), LU 1-3(1)*

1–51. Walt Disney World Resort and United Vacations got together to create a special deal. The air-inclusive package features accommodations for three nights at Disney's All-Star Resort, hotel taxes, and a four-day unlimited Magic Pass. Prices are $609 per person traveling from Washington, DC, and $764 per person traveling from Los Angeles. **(a)** What would be the cost for a family of four leaving from Washington, DC? **(b)** What would be the cost for a family of four leaving from Los Angeles? **(c)** How much more will it cost the family from Los Angeles? *LU 1-3(1)*

1–52. NTB Tires bought 910 tires from its manufacturer for $36 per tire. What is the total cost of NTB's purchase? If the store can sell all the tires at $65 each, what will be the store's gross profit, or the difference between its sales and costs (Sales − Costs = Gross profit)? *LU 1-3(1), LU 1-2(2)*

1–53. What was the total average number of visits for these websites? *LU 1-2(1), LU 1-3(2)*

Website	Average daily unique visitors
1. Orbitz.com	1,527,000
2. Mypoints.com	1,356,000
3. Americangreetings.com	745,000
4. Bizrate.com	503,000
5. Half.com	397,000

1–54. As the Boston MarketWatch for January 2012 states, "The Approved Card" from Suze Orman provides a pretty fair deal. This prepaid debit card costs $3 to purchase and there is a $3 monthly account maintenance fee (the first month's charge is waived). Withdrawals at ATMs cost $2. If Hanna Lind used this card for 8 months and had nine ATM withdrawals, what would her charge be? *LU 1-3(1)*

1–55. A report from the Center for Science in the Public Interest—a consumer group based in Washington, DC—released a study listing calories of various ice cream treats sold by six of the largest ice cream companies. The worst treat tested by the group was 1,270 total calories. People need roughly 2,200 to 2,500 calories per day. Using a daily average, how many additional calories should a person consume after eating ice cream? *LU 1-2(1), LU 1-3(2)*

1–56. At Rose State College, Alison Wells received the following grades in her online accounting class: 90, 65, 85, 80, 75, and 90. Alison's instructor, Professor Clark, said he would drop the lowest grade. What is Alison's average? *LU 1-2(1)*

1–57. The Bureau of Transportation's list of the 10 most expensive U.S. airports and their average fares is given below. Please use this list to answer the questions that follow. *LU 1-2(1, 2)*

1. Houston, TX	$477
2. Huntsville, AL	473
3. Newark, NJ	470
4. Cincinnati, OH	466
5. Washington, DC	465
6. Charleston, SC	460
7. Memphis, TN	449
8. Knoxville, TN	449
9. Dallas–Fort Worth, TX	431
10. Madison, WI	429

a. What is the total of all the fares?
b. What would the total be if all the fares were rounded all the way?
c. How much does the actual number differ from the rounded estimate?

1–58. Ron Alf, owner of Alf's Moving Company, bought a new truck. On Ron's first trip, he drove 1,200 miles and used 80 gallons of gas. How many miles per gallon did Ron get from his new truck? On Ron's second trip, he drove 840 miles and used 60 gallons. What is the difference in miles per gallon between Ron's first trip and his second trip? *LU 1-3(2)*

1–59. In Bankrate.com's Smart Spending column for early 2012, Jan Fandrich of Billings, Montana, explains how she saves money, stays healthy, and helps the environment by using baking soda and vinegar instead of toxic commercial cleaners. She puts a little bit of vinegar in the rinse cycle instead of fabric softener, and mops the floors and cleans the showers with a mix of baking soda and vinegar in water. If a box of baking soda costs $1 and a bottle of vinegar is $2, how much will her cleaning supplies cost if she uses five boxes of baking soda and 10 bottles of vinegar in 1 year? *LU 1-3(1)*

1–60. Assume BarnesandNoble.com has 289 business math texts in inventory. During one month, the online bookstore ordered and received 1,855 texts; it also sold 1,222 on the web. What is the bookstore's inventory at the end of the month? If each text costs $59, what is the end-of-month inventory cost? *LU 1-2(1), LU 1-2(2)*

1–61. Assume Cabot Company produced 2,115,000 cans of paint in August. Cabot sold 2,011,000 of these cans. If each can cost $18, what were Cabot's ending inventory of paint cans and its total ending inventory cost? *LU 1-2(2), LU 1-3(1)*

1–62. A local community college has 20 faculty members in the business department, 40 in psychology, 26 in English, and 140 in all other departments. What is the total number of faculty at this college? If each faculty member advises 25 students, how many students attend the local college? *LU 1-2(1), LU 1-3(1)*

1–63. Hometown Buffet had 90 customers on Sunday, 70 on Monday, 65 on Tuesday, and a total of 310 on Wednesday to Saturday. How many customers did Hometown Buffet serve during the week? If each customer spends $9, what were the total sales for the week? *LU 1-2(1), LU 1-3(1)*

If Hometown Buffet had the same sales each week, what were the sales for the year?

1–64. A local travel agency projected its year 2013 sales at $880,000. During 2013, the agency earned $482,900 sales from its major clients and $116,500 sales from the remainder of its clients. How much did the agency overestimate its sales? *LU 1-2(2)*

1–65. Ryan Seary works at US Airways and earned $71,000 last year before tax deductions. From Ryan's total earnings, his company subtracted $1,388 for federal income taxes, $4,402 for Social Security, and $1,030 for Medicare taxes. What was Ryan's actual, or net, pay for the year? *LU 1-2(1, 2)*

1–66. An article in *The New York Times* on January 5, 2012, discussed how individuals with little or no prior credit sources may benefit from a new tracking procedure. Experian, one of the three leading credit reporting companies, is now tracking on-time rent payments, thereby raising the credit scores of many people. Experian uses FICO scores, a three-digit rating system ranging generally from 300–850, to rate how risky a borrower is. If you currently have a FICO score of 550 and on-time rent payments increase your FICO score by 80, what is your new FICO score? *LU 1-2(1)*

1–67. Roger Company produces beach balls and operates three shifts. Roger produces 5,000 balls per shift on shifts 1 and 2. On shift 3, the company can produce 6 times as many balls as on shift 1. Assume a 5-day workweek. How many beach balls does Roger produce per week and per year? *LU 1-2(1), LU 1-3(1)*

1–68. Assume 6,000 children go to Disneyland today. How much additional revenue will Disneyland receive if it raises the cost of admission from $31 to $41 and lowers the age limit for adults from 12 years old to 10 years old? *LU 1-2(1), LU 1-3(1)*

1–69. Moe Brink has a $900 balance in his checkbook. During the week, Moe wrote the following checks: rent, $350; telephone, $44; food, $160; and entertaining, $60. Moe also made a $1,200 deposit. What is Moe's new checkbook balance? *LU 1-2(1, 2)*

1–70. A local Sports Authority store, an athletic sports shop, bought and sold the following merchandise: *LU 1-2(1, 2)*

	Cost	Selling price
Tennis rackets	$ 2,900	$ 3,999
Tennis balls	70	210
Bowling balls	1,050	2,950
Sneakers	+ 8,105	+ 14,888

What was the total cost of the merchandise bought by Sports Authority? If the shop sold all its merchandise, what were the sales and the resulting gross profit (Sales − Costs = Gross profit)?

1–71. Rich Engel, the bookkeeper for Engel's Real Estate, and his manager are concerned about the company's telephone bills. eXcel Last year the company's average monthly phone bill was $32. Rich's manager asked him for an average of this year's phone bills. Rich's records show the following: *LU 1-2(1), LU 1-3(2)*

January	$ 34	July	$ 28
February	60	August	23
March	20	September	29
April	25	October	25
May	30	November	22
June	59	December	41

What is the average of this year's phone bills? Did Rich and his manager have a justifiable concern?

1–72. On Monday, a local True Value Hardware sold 15 paint brushes at $3 each, six wrenches at $5 each, seven bags of grass *eXcel* seed at $3 each, four lawn mowers at $119 each, and 28 cans of paint at $8 each. What were True Value's total dollar sales on Monday? *LU 1-2(1), LU 1-3(1)*

1–73. While redecorating, Lee Owens went to Carpet World and bought 150 square yards of commercial carpet. The total cost of the carpet was $6,000. How much did Lee pay per square yard? *LU 1-3(2)*

1–74. Washington Construction built 12 ranch houses for $115,000 each. From the sale of these houses, Washington received *eXcel* $1,980,000. How much gross profit (Sales − Costs = Gross profit) did Washington make on the houses? *LU 1-2(2), LU 1-3(1, 2)*

The four partners of Washington Construction split all profits equally. How much will each partner receive?

CHALLENGE PROBLEMS

1–75. A mall in Lexington has 18 stores. The following is a breakdown of what each store pays for rent per month. The rent is based on square footage.

5 department/computer stores	$1,250	2 bakeries	$ 500
5 restaurants	860	2 drugstores	820
3 bookstores	750	1 supermarket	1,450

Calculate the total rent that these stores pay annually. What would the answer be if it were rounded all the way? How much more each year do the drugstores pay in rent compared to the bakeries? *LU 1-2(2), LU 1-3(1)*

1–76. Paula Sanchez is trying to determine her 2014 finances. Paula's actual 2013 finances were as follows: *LU 1-1, LU 1-2, LU 1-3*

Income:		Assets:	
Gross income	$69,000	Checking account	$ 1,950
Interest income	450	Savings account	8,950
Total	$69,450	Automobile	1,800
Expenses:		Personal property	14,000
Living	$24,500	Total	$26,700
Insurance premium	350	Liabilities:	
Taxes	14,800	Note to bank	4,500
Medical	585	Net worth	$22,200 ($26,700 − $4,500)
Investment	4,000		
Total	$44,235		

Net worth = Assets − Liabilities
(own)   (owe)

Paula believes her gross income will double in 2014 but her interest income will decrease $150. She plans to reduce her 2014 living expenses by one-half. Paula's insurance company wrote a letter announcing that her insurance premiums would triple in 2014. Her accountant estimates her taxes will decrease $250 and her medical costs will increase $410. Paula also hopes to cut her investments expenses by one-fourth. Paula's accountant projects that her savings and checking accounts will each double in value. On January 2, 2014, Paula sold her automobile and began to use public transportation. Paula forecasts that her personal property will decrease by one-seventh. She has sent her bank a $375 check to reduce her bank note. Could you give Paula an updated list of her 2014 finances? If you round all the way each 2013 and 2014 asset and liability, what will be the difference in Paula's net worth?

 SUMMARY PRACTICE TEST YouTube™

Do you need help? The DVD has step-by-step worked-out solutions.

1. Translate the following verbal forms to numbers and add. *(p. 4)   LU 1-1(1), LU 1-2(1)*

   a. Four thousand, eight hundred thirty-nine

   b. Seven million, twelve

   c. Twelve thousand, three hundred ninety-two

2. Express the following number in verbal form. *(p. 4)   LU 1-1(1)*
   9,622,364

3. Round the following numbers. *(p. 6)   LU 1-1(2)*

Nearest ten	Nearest hundred	Nearest thousand	Round all the way
a. 68	**b.** 888	**c.** 8,325	**d.** 14,821

4. Estimate the following actual problem by rounding all the way, work the actual problem, and check by adding each column of digits separately. *(pp. 6, 10)   LU 1-1(2), LU 1-2(1)*

Actual	**Estimate**	**Check**
1,886		
9,411		
+ 6,395		

5. Estimate the following actual problem by rounding all the way and then do the actual multiplication. *(pp. 6, 14)   LU 1-1(2), LU 1-3(1)*

Actual	**Estimate**
8,843	
✕ 906	

6. Multiply the following by the shortcut method. *(p. 14)   LU 1-3(1)*

829,412 ✕ 1,000

7. Divide the following and check the answer by multiplication. *(pp. 14, 16)   LU 1-3(1, 2)*

Check

39)‾14,800

8. Divide the following by the shortcut method. *(p. 16)   LU 1-3(2)*

6,000 ÷ 60

9. Ling Wong bought a $299 iPod that was reduced to $205. Ling gave the clerk three $100 bills. What change will Ling receive? *(p. 11)   LU 1-2(2)*

10. Sam Song plans to buy a $16,000 Ford Focus with an interest charge of $4,000. Sam figures he can afford a monthly payment of $400. If Sam must pay 40 equal monthly payments, can he afford the Ford Focus? *(pp. 10, 16)   LU 1-2(1), LU 1-3(2)*

11. Lester Hal has the oil tank at his business filled 20 times per year. The tank has a capacity of 200 gallons. Assume **(a)** the price of oil fuel is $3 per gallon and **(b)** the tank is completely empty each time Lester has it filled. What is Lester's average monthly oil bill? Complete the following blueprint aid for dissecting and solving the word problem. *(pp. 14, 16)   LU 1-3(1, 2)*

	The facts	**Solving for?**	**Steps to take**	**Key points**
BLUEPRINT				

Steps to solving problem

SURF TO SAVE

Earning and spending money 🔍

PROBLEM 1
Budget your laptop purchase

Imagine you have a budget of $2,500 to purchase 5 identical laptops for your family. Go to http://www.officemax.com, select a laptop to meet your needs, and then calculate how much 5 of those laptops would cost. Round prices to the nearest dollar and ignore sales tax and delivery charges. Is $2,500 enough? If so, how much money do you have left? If not, how much more money do you need?

Discussion Questions

1. What is the importance of having a budget?

2. Should college students, who are traditionally low wage earners, still utilize a budget? Why?

PROBLEM 2
Budget expenses for a trip

Imagine you are planning a 4-night stay, Monday through Thursday, in New York City. Go to http://www.hertz.com to find the daily rate for the car you'd like. Then, go to http://www2.choicehotels.com to choose a hotel and determine the nightly room rate. Calculate your total cost for the car and lodging, ignoring taxes and rounding rates to the nearest dollar.

Discussion Questions

1. Using your existing salary, how would you budget for this trip to ensure you have the appropriate funds? Be specific.

2. What types of expenses might you incur once you are on this trip?

PROBLEM 3
Determine wage breakdowns

Go to http://www.nascar.com. Choose the Standings, Spring Cup Series link. Look at the Top 5 money earners for any 3-year period. Based on total winnings, how much money did each earn per month, per week, per day, and per hour, assuming a 40-hour workweek? What is the difference in each of these earning amounts across the 3 years you selected?

Discussion Questions

1. How much do you expect to earn after graduating from college?

2. What is your expected salary breakdown by month, week, day, and hour?

PROBLEM 4
How much reading can you afford?

Go to http://www.amazon.com. Search for the list of "Top 100 books." If you have $100 to spend, how many of the Top 100 books could you buy if you started with the number one book and worked your way down the list? Ignore shipping and handling and taxes.

Discussion Questions

1. If you owned an e-reader, how many more e-books could you purchase with the same $100?

2. Based on your current salary, how many hours must you work to afford spending this $100 on books?

MOBILE APPS ✕

MathPad 4 (Clay Cat Designs) Focuses on solving word problems through addition, subtraction, division, and multiplication.

Basic Math (Explorer Technologies) Uses repetition of problems to build up basic math skills.

INTERNET PROJECTS ✕

See text website
www.mhhe.com/slater11e_sse_ch01

PAID FOR
COLLEGE
ON HIS OWN

David Leestma, 21, is a junior at Ferris State University, in Big Rapids, Mich. He will graduate in 2012 with a bachelor's degree in heating, ventilating and air conditioning, and with zero debt.

YOU TOOK A YEAR OFF BETWEEN HIGH SCHOOL AND COLLEGE. HOW COME? I wasn't sure what I wanted to do for a career, and I didn't want to go to school unless I knew. So I got a job at Sam's Club working at the café for $9 an hour. Over the year, it became clear what I *didn't* want to do—I didn't want to work in retail the rest of my life. I went on a couple of job shadows with friends of my family. On one, I spent time with a mechanical engineer. He designed HVAC systems and got me interested in that.

WHY DID YOU START AT A COMMUNITY COLLEGE RATHER THAN A FOUR-YEAR COLLEGE? Grand Rapids Community College was cheaper, and it gave me the option to live at home. The plan when I started was to transfer to Ferris. As far as I know, it is one of only a few colleges in the country that offer a bachelor's degree in HVAC. The community college had a program with Ferris, so I had a guarantee that I wouldn't have a problem transferring my credits.

YOU HAVE FOUR YOUNGER SIBLINGS. WERE YOUR PARENTS ABLE TO HELP WITH THE COLLEGE COSTS? They said that I could live at home free and eat all I wanted. But I haven't gotten any money from them for college.

WHAT WERE SOME OF THE WAYS IN WHICH YOU PAID FOR COLLEGE? I had a paper route from ages 12 to 18, and I saved all my money from that—about $6,000. I saved most of my money while I worked at Sam's Club. At the community college, I had a Pell grant [a need-based federal grant, up to $5,550 this year] that covered most of my college costs. I still get a Pell grant, and I also have a scholarship—$4,000 a year, which covers over half of my tuition. I pay a couple of thousand dollars a year more for tuition and fees, plus $3,000 a year for room and board. I have enough money to cover this year's costs, and I should have enough to cover my last year.

WHAT HAS BEEN YOUR BIGGEST CHALLENGE SO FAR? At Grand Rapids, I did two summer, two fall and two winter semesters in one year, and I worked part-time at Sam's Club. I went to school and worked pretty much round the clock, except for Sundays. I did homework on lunch breaks. It was crazy.

DO YOU HAVE ADVICE FOR OTHER STUDENTS? From the start, I've always looked at what job I'm going to get when I finish. That's the whole goal of going to college for me. So take your time to choose what you want to do. You can change your mind after you start college, but taking more classes costs money and extra time.

ANY REGRETS ABOUT THE WAY YOU'VE DONE IT? No. A lot of the other students I talk to are $10,000 or more in debt. I like where I'm sitting financially right now. It's a blessing. ■

Interview by
JANE
BENNETT
CLARK

BUSINESS MATH ISSUE

Going into debt in order to attend college will always pay off.

1. List the key points of the article and information to support your position.
2. Write a group defense of your position using math calculations to support your view.

Fractions

Rhymes with Orange © 2012 Hilary B. Price. King Features Syndicate.

About half of the
vehicles sold in th
U.S. are now mad
foreign-owned fi

LU 2–1: Types of Fractions and Conversion Procedures

1. Recognize the three types of fractions *(pp. 36–37)*.
2. Convert improper fractions to whole or mixed numbers and mixed numbers to improper fractions *(pp. 37–38)*.
3. Convert fractions to lowest and highest terms *(pp. 38–39)*.

LU 2–2: Adding and Subtracting Fractions

1. Add like and unlike fractions *(pp. 41–42)*.
2. Find the least common denominator by inspection and prime numbers *(pp. 42–43)*.
3. Subtract like and unlike fractions *(p. 44)*.
4. Add and subtract mixed numbers with the same or different denominators *(pp. 44–46)*.

LU 2–3: Multiplying and Dividing Fractions

1. Multiply and divide proper fractions and mixed numbers *(pp. 47–48)*.
2. Use the cancellation method in the multiplication and division of fractions *(pp. 48–49)*.

VOCABULARY PREVIEW

Here are key terms in this chapter. After completing the chapter, if you know the term, place a checkmark in the parentheses. If you don't know the term, look it up and put the page number where it can be found.

Cancellation ( ) Common denominator ( ) Denominator ( ) Equivalent ( ) Fraction ( ) Greatest common divisor ( ) Higher terms ( ) Improper fraction ( ) Least common denominator (LCD) ( ) Like fractions ( ) Lowest terms ( ) Mixed numbers ( ) Numerator ( ) Prime numbers ( ) Proper fraction ( ) Reciprocal ( ) Unlike fractions ( )

The *Wall Street Journal* clipping "Asia Delivers for McDonald's" illustrates the use of a fraction. From the clipping you learn that one-third ($\frac{1}{3}$) of sales at a McDonald's in Cairo, Egypt, is from delivery.

Now let's look at Milk Chocolate M&M'S® candies as another example of using fractions.

As you know, M&M'S® candies come in different colors. Do you know how many of each color are in a bag of M&M'S®? If you go to the M&M'S website, you learn that a typical bag of M&M'S® contains approximately 17 brown, 11 yellow, 11 red, and 5 each of orange, blue, and green M&M'S®.[1]

Asia Delivers For McDonald's

BY JULIE JARGON

When Americans are too busy or lazy to cook, they often place an order with their favorite Chinese restaurant. So who do people in China call when they want food delivered? Increasingly, McDonald's and KFC.

Delivery is becoming an important part of the growth strategy at **McDonald's** Corp. and **Yum Brands Inc.**'s KFC chain in parts of the world where cities are too crowded and real estate costs too high to justify building drive-throughs.

A McDonald's moped in Cairo, Egypt, where delivery is a third of sales.

© Peter Macdiarmid/Getty Images

GLOBAL

The 1.69-ounce bag of M&M'S® shown on page 36 contains 55 M&M'S®. In this bag, you will find the following colors:

18 yellow	9 blue	6 brown
10 red	7 orange	5 green

[1]Off 1 due to rounding.

55 pieces in the bag

The number of yellow candies in a bag might suggest that yellow is the favorite color of many people. Since this is a business math text, however, let's look at the 55 M&M'S® in terms of fractional arithmetic.

Of the 55 M&M'S® in the 1.69-ounce bag, 5 of these M&M'S® are green, so we can say that 5 parts of 55 represent green candies. We could also say that 1 out of 11 M&M'S® is green. Are you confused?

For many people, fractions are difficult. If you are one of these people, this chapter is for you. First you will review the types of fractions and the fraction conversion procedures. Then you will gain a clear understanding of the addition, subtraction, multiplication, and division of fractions.

Learning Unit 2–1: Types of Fractions and Conversion Procedures

LO 1

This chapter explains the parts of whole numbers called **fractions.** With fractions you can divide any object or unit—a whole—into a definite number of equal parts. For example, the bag of 55 M&M'S® described above contains 6 brown candies. If you eat only the brown M&M'S®, you have eaten 6 parts of 55, or 6 parts of the whole bag of M&M'S®. We can express this in the following fraction:

$$\frac{6}{55}$$

6 is the **numerator,** or top of the fraction. The numerator describes the number of equal parts of the whole bag that you ate.

55 is the **denominator,** or bottom of the fraction. The denominator gives the total number of equal parts in the bag of M&M'S®.

Before reviewing the arithmetic operations of fractions, you must recognize the three types of fractions described in this unit. You must also know how to convert fractions to a workable form.

Types of Fractions

In *The Wall Street Journal* it was reported that in the United States two-thirds ($\frac{2}{3}$) of all sales in fast-food restaurants is from drive-through orders. The fraction $\frac{2}{3}$ is a proper fraction.

© Photodisc/Getty Images

PROPER FRACTIONS

A **proper fraction** has a value less than 1; its numerator is smaller than its denominator.

EXAMPLES $\dfrac{1}{4}, \dfrac{1}{2}, \dfrac{1}{10}, \dfrac{1}{12}, \dfrac{1}{3}, \dfrac{4}{7}, \dfrac{2}{3}, \dfrac{9}{10}, \dfrac{12}{13}, \dfrac{18}{55}$

IMPROPER FRACTIONS

An **improper fraction** has a value equal to or greater than 1; its numerator is equal to or greater than its denominator.

EXAMPLES $\dfrac{14}{14}, \dfrac{7}{6}, \dfrac{15}{14}, \dfrac{22}{19}$

MIXED NUMBERS

A **mixed number** is the sum of a whole number greater than zero and a proper fraction.

EXAMPLES $5\dfrac{1}{6}, 5\dfrac{9}{10}, 8\dfrac{7}{8}, 33\dfrac{5}{6}, 139\dfrac{9}{11}$

Conversion Procedures

In Chapter 1 we worked with two of the division symbols ($\div$ and $\overline{)}$). The horizontal line (or the diagonal) that separates the numerator and the denominator of a fraction also indicates division. The numerator, like the dividend, is the number we are dividing into. The denominator, like the divisor, is the number we use to divide. Then, referring to the 6 brown M&M'S® in the bag of 55 M&M'S® ($\frac{6}{55}$) shown at the beginning of this unit, we can say that we are dividing 55 into 6, or 6 is divided by 55. Also, in the fraction $\frac{3}{4}$, we can say that we are dividing 4 into 3, or 3 is divided by 4.

Working with the smaller numbers of simple fractions such as $\frac{3}{4}$ is easier, so we often convert fractions to their simplest terms. In this unit we show how to convert improper fractions to whole or mixed numbers, mixed numbers to improper fractions, and fractions to lowest and highest terms.

Converting Improper Fractions to Whole or Mixed Numbers   Business situations often make it necessary to change an improper fraction to a whole number or mixed number. You can use the following steps to make this conversion:

CONVERTING IMPROPER FRACTIONS TO WHOLE OR MIXED NUMBERS

LO 2

Step 1. Divide the numerator of the improper fraction by the denominator.

Step 2. **a.** If you have no remainder, the quotient is a whole number.

   b. If you have a remainder, the whole number part of the mixed number is the quotient. The remainder is placed over the old denominator as the proper fraction of the mixed number.

EXAMPLES

$$\frac{15}{15} = 1 \qquad \frac{16}{5} = 3\frac{1}{5} \qquad 5\overline{)16} \;\; 3\,R1$$
$$\frac{15}{1}$$

Converting Mixed Numbers to Improper Fractions   By reversing the procedure of converting improper fractions to mixed numbers, we can change mixed numbers to improper fractions.

CONVERTING MIXED NUMBERS TO IMPROPER FRACTIONS
Step 1. Multiply the denominator of the fraction by the whole number.
Step 2. Add the product from Step 1 to the numerator of the old fraction.
Step 3. Place the total from Step 2 over the denominator of the old fraction to get the improper fraction.

EXAMPLE $6\frac{1}{8} = \frac{(8 \times 6) + 1}{8} = \frac{49}{8}$ Note that the denominator stays the same.

Converting (Reducing) Fractions to Lowest Terms   When solving fraction problems, you always reduce the fractions to their lowest terms. This reduction does not change the value of the fraction. For example, in the bag of M&M'S®, 5 out of 55 were green. The fraction for this is $\frac{5}{55}$. If you divide the top and bottom of the fraction by 5, you have reduced the fraction to $\frac{1}{11}$ without changing its value. Remember, we said in the chapter introduction that 1 out of 11 M&M'S® in the bag of 55 M&M'S® represents green candies. Now you know why this is true.

To reduce a fraction to its lowest terms, begin by inspecting the fraction, looking for the largest whole number that will divide into both the numerator and the denominator without leaving a remainder. This whole number is the **greatest common divisor,** which cannot be zero. When you find this largest whole number, you have reached the point where the fraction is reduced to its **lowest terms.** At this point, no number (except 1) can divide evenly into both parts of the fraction.

LO 3

REDUCING FRACTIONS TO LOWEST TERMS BY INSPECTION
Step 1. By inspection, find the largest whole number (greatest common divisor) that will divide evenly into the numerator and denominator (does not change the fraction value).
Step 2. Divide the numerator and denominator by the greatest common divisor. Now you have reduced the fraction to its lowest terms, since no number (except 1) can divide evenly into the numerator and denominator.

EXAMPLE $\frac{24}{30} = \frac{24 \div 6}{30 \div 6} = \frac{4}{5}$

Using inspection, you can see that the number 6 in the above example is the greatest common divisor. When you have large numbers, the greatest common divisor is not so obvious. For large numbers, you can use the following step approach to find the greatest common divisor:

STEP APPROACH FOR FINDING GREATEST COMMON DIVISOR
Step 1. Divide the smaller number (numerator) of the fraction into the larger number (denominator).
Step 2. Divide the remainder of Step 1 into the divisor of Step 1.
Step 3. Divide the remainder of Step 2 into the divisor of Step 2. Continue this division process until the remainder is a 0, which means the last divisor is the greatest common divisor.

EXAMPLE

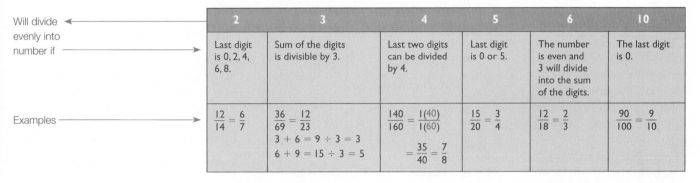

	Step 1	Step 2	
$\dfrac{24}{30}$	$\begin{array}{r} 1 \\ 24\overline{)30} \\ \underline{24} \\ 6 \end{array}$	$\begin{array}{r} 4 \\ 6\overline{)24} \\ \underline{24} \\ 0 \end{array}$	$\dfrac{24 \div 6}{30 \div 6} = \dfrac{4}{5}$

Reducing a fraction by inspection is to some extent a trial-and-error method. Sometimes you are not sure what number you should divide into the top (numerator) and bottom (denominator) of the fraction. The following reference table on divisibility tests will be helpful. Note that to reduce a fraction to lowest terms might result in more than one division.

2	3	4	5	6	10
Last digit is 0, 2, 4, 6, 8.	Sum of the digits is divisible by 3.	Last two digits can be divided by 4.	Last digit is 0 or 5.	The number is even and 3 will divide into the sum of the digits.	The last digit is 0.
$\dfrac{12}{14} = \dfrac{6}{7}$	$\dfrac{36}{69} = \dfrac{12}{23}$ $3 + 6 = 9 \div 3 = 3$ $6 + 9 = 15 \div 3 = 5$	$\dfrac{140}{160} = \dfrac{1(40)}{1(60)}$ $= \dfrac{35}{40} = \dfrac{7}{8}$	$\dfrac{15}{20} = \dfrac{3}{4}$	$\dfrac{12}{18} = \dfrac{2}{3}$	$\dfrac{90}{100} = \dfrac{9}{10}$

Will divide evenly into number if →

Examples →

Converting (Raising) Fractions to Higher Terms Later, when you add and subtract fractions, you will see that sometimes fractions must be raised to **higher terms.** Recall that when you reduced fractions to their lowest terms, you looked for the largest whole number (greatest common divisor) that would divide evenly into both the numerator and the denominator. When you raise fractions to higher terms, you do the opposite and multiply the numerator and the denominator by the same whole number. For example, if you want to raise the fraction $\frac{1}{4}$, you can multiply the numerator and denominator by 2.

EXAMPLE $\quad \dfrac{1}{4} \times \dfrac{2}{2} = \dfrac{2}{8}$

The fractions $\frac{1}{4}$ and $\frac{2}{8}$ are **equivalent** in value. By converting $\frac{1}{4}$ to $\frac{2}{8}$, you only divided it into more parts.

Let's suppose that you have eaten $\frac{4}{7}$ of a pizza. You decide that instead of expressing the amount you have eaten in 7ths, you want to express it in 28ths. How would you do this?

To find the new numerator when you know the new denominator (28), use the steps that follow.

RAISING FRACTIONS TO HIGHER TERMS WHEN DENOMINATOR IS KNOWN
Step 1. Divide the *new* denominator by the *old* denominator to get the common number that raises the fraction to higher terms.
Step 2. Multiply the common number from Step 1 by the old numerator and place it as the new numerator over the new denominator.

EXAMPLE $\quad \dfrac{4}{7} = \dfrac{?}{28}$

Step 1. Divide 28 by 7 = 4.

Step 2. Multiply 4 by the numerator 4 = 16.

Result:

$$\dfrac{4}{7} = \dfrac{16}{28} \qquad \left(\textit{Note: This is the same as multiplying } \dfrac{4}{7} \times \dfrac{4}{4}. \right)$$

Note that the $\frac{4}{7}$ and $\frac{16}{28}$ are equivalent in value, yet they are different fractions.

Now try the following Practice Quiz to check your understanding of this unit.

LU 2–1 **PRACTICE QUIZ**

Complete this **Practice Quiz** to see how you are doing.

1. Identify the type of fraction—proper, improper, or mixed:

   a. $\dfrac{4}{5}$ **b.** $\dfrac{6}{5}$ **c.** $19\dfrac{1}{5}$ **d.** $\dfrac{20}{20}$

2. Convert to a mixed number:

   $\dfrac{160}{9}$

3. Convert the mixed number to an improper fraction:

   $9\dfrac{5}{8}$

4. Find the greatest common divisor by the step approach and reduce to lowest terms:

   a. $\dfrac{24}{40}$ **b.** $\dfrac{91}{156}$

5. Convert to higher terms:

   a. $\dfrac{14}{20} = \dfrac{}{200}$ **b.** $\dfrac{8}{10} = \dfrac{}{60}$

*For **extra help** from your authors–Sharon and Jeff–see the student DVD*

You Tube™

✓ **Solutions**

1. **a.** Proper
   b. Improper
   c. Mixed
   d. Improper

2.
   $$\begin{array}{r} 17\frac{7}{9} \\ 9\overline{)160} \\ \underline{9} \\ 70 \\ \underline{63} \\ 7 \end{array}$$

3. $\dfrac{(9 \times 8) + 5}{8} = \dfrac{77}{8}$

4. **a.**
   $$\begin{array}{r} 1 \\ 24\overline{)40} \\ \underline{24} \\ 16 \end{array} \quad \begin{array}{r} 1 \\ 16\overline{)24} \\ \underline{16} \\ 8 \end{array} \quad \begin{array}{r} 2 \\ 8\overline{)16} \\ \underline{16} \\ 0 \end{array}$$ 8 is greatest common divisor.

   $\dfrac{24 \div 8}{40 \div 8} = \dfrac{3}{5}$

   b.
   $$\begin{array}{r} 1 \\ 91\overline{)156} \\ \underline{91} \\ 65 \end{array} \quad \begin{array}{r} 1 \\ 65\overline{)91} \\ \underline{65} \\ 26 \end{array} \quad \begin{array}{r} 2 \\ 26\overline{)65} \\ \underline{52} \\ 13 \end{array} \quad \begin{array}{r} 2 \\ 13\overline{)26} \\ \underline{26} \\ 0 \end{array}$$ 13 is greatest common divisor.

   $\dfrac{91 \div 13}{156 \div 13} = \dfrac{7}{12}$

5. **a.**
   $\begin{array}{r} 10 \\ 20\overline{)200} \end{array}$ $10 \times 14 = 140$ $\dfrac{14}{20} = \dfrac{140}{200}$

   b.
   $\begin{array}{r} 6 \\ 10\overline{)60} \end{array}$ $6 \times 8 = 48$ $\dfrac{8}{10} = \dfrac{48}{60}$

LU 2–1a **EXTRA PRACTICE QUIZ WITH WORKED-OUT SOLUTIONS**

Need more practice? Try this **Extra Practice Quiz** (check figures in the Interactive Chapter Organizer, p. 53). Worked-out Solutions can be found in Appendix B at end of text.

1. Identify the type of fraction—proper, improper, or mixed:

   a. $\dfrac{2}{5}$ **b.** $\dfrac{7}{6}$ **c.** $18\dfrac{1}{3}$ **d.** $\dfrac{40}{40}$

2. Convert to a mixed number (do not reduce):

   $\dfrac{155}{7}$

3. Convert the mixed number to an improper fraction:

   $8\dfrac{7}{9}$

4. Find the greatest common divisor by the step approach and reduce to lowest terms:

    a. $\dfrac{42}{70}$ **b.** $\dfrac{96}{182}$

5. Convert to higher terms:

    a. $\dfrac{16}{30} = \dfrac{}{300}$ **b.** $\dfrac{9}{20} = \dfrac{}{60}$

Learning Unit 2–2: Adding and Subtracting Fractions

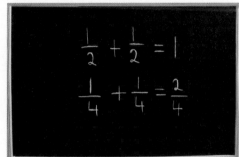

© Roberts Publishing Services

LO 1

More teachers are using online video-sharing sites that are modeled after Google Inc.'s YouTube. As you can see in the video screenshot provided, these fractions can be added because the fractions have the same denominator. These are called *like fractions*.

    In this unit you learn how to add and subtract fractions with the same denominators (**like fractions**) and fractions with different denominators (**unlike fractions**). We have also included how to add and subtract mixed numbers.

Addition of Fractions

When you add two or more quantities, they must have the same name or be of the same denomination. You cannot add 6 quarts and 3 pints unless you change the denomination of one or both quantities. You must either make the quarts into pints or the pints into quarts. The same principle also applies to fractions. That is, to add two or more fractions, they must have a **common denominator.**

Adding Like Fractions   In our video-sharing clipping at the beginning of this unit we stated that because the fractions had the same denominator, or a common denominator, they were *like fractions*. Adding like fractions is similar to adding whole numbers.

ADDING LIKE FRACTIONS
Step 1. Add the numerators and place the total over the original denominator.
Step 2. If the total of your numerators is the same as your original denominator, convert your answer to a whole number; if the total is larger than your original denominator, convert your answer to a mixed number.

EXAMPLE $\dfrac{1}{7} + \dfrac{4}{7} = \boxed{\dfrac{5}{7}}$

The denominator, 7, shows the number of pieces into which some whole was divided. The two numerators, 1 and 4, tell how many of the pieces you have. So if you add 1 and 4, you get 5, or $\frac{5}{7}$.

Adding Unlike Fractions   Since you cannot add *unlike fractions* because their denominators are not the same, you must change the unlike fractions to *like fractions*—fractions with the same denominators. To do this, find a denominator that is common to all the fractions you want to add. Then look for the **least common denominator (LCD).**[2] The LCD is the smallest nonzero whole number into which all denominators will divide evenly. You can find the LCD by inspection or with prime numbers.

Finding the Least Common Denominator (LCD) by Inspection The example that follows shows you how to use inspection to find an LCD (this will make all the denominators the same).

EXAMPLE $\dfrac{3}{7} + \dfrac{5}{21}$

Inspection of these two fractions shows that the smallest number into which denominators 7 and 21 divide evenly is 21. Thus, $\boxed{21}$ is the LCD.

---

[2]Often referred to as the *lowest common denominator.*

You may know that 21 is the LCD of $\frac{3}{7} + \frac{5}{21}$, but you cannot add these two fractions until you change the denominator of $\frac{3}{7}$ to 21. You do this by building (raising) the equivalent of $\frac{3}{7}$, as explained in Learning Unit 2–1. You can use the following steps to find the LCD by inspection:

Step 1. Divide the new denominator (21) by the old denominator (7): $21 \div 7 = 3$.

Step 2. Multiply the 3 in Step 1 by the old numerator (3): $3 \times 3 = 9$. The new numerator is 9.

Result:

$$\frac{3}{7} = \frac{9}{21}$$

Now that the denominators are the same, you add the numerators.

$$\frac{9}{21} + \frac{5}{21} = \frac{14}{21} = \frac{2}{3}$$

Note that $\frac{14}{21}$ is reduced to its lowest terms $\frac{2}{3}$. Always reduce your answer to its lowest terms.

You are now ready for the following general steps for adding proper fractions with different denominators. These steps also apply to the following discussion on finding LCD by prime numbers.

LO 2

ADDING UNLIKE FRACTIONS
Step 1. Find the LCD.
Step 2. Change each fraction to a like fraction with the LCD.
Step 3. Add the numerators and place the total over the LCD.
Step 4. If necessary, reduce the answer to lowest terms.

Finding the Least Common Denominator (LCD) by Prime Numbers When you cannot determine the LCD by inspection, you can use the prime number method. First you must understand prime numbers.

PRIME NUMBERS
A **prime number** is a whole number greater than 1 that is only divisible by itself and 1. The number 1 is not a prime number.

EXAMPLES   2, 3, 5, 7, 11, 13, 17, 19, 23, 29, 31, 37, 41, 43

Note that the number 4 is not a prime number. Not only can you divide 4 by 1 and by 4, but you can also divide 4 by 2. A whole number that is greater than 1 and is only divisible by itself and 1 has become a source of interest to some people.

EXAMPLE $\dfrac{1}{3} + \dfrac{1}{8} + \dfrac{1}{9} + \dfrac{1}{12}$

Step 1. Copy the denominators and arrange them in a separate row.

   3 8 9 12

Step 2. Divide the denominators in Step 1 by prime numbers. Start with the smallest number that will divide into at least two of the denominators. Bring down any number that is not divisible. Keep in mind that the lowest prime number is 2.

$$2\,\big/\,\underline{3 \quad 8 \quad 9 \quad 12}$$
$$3 \quad 4 \quad 9 \quad 6$$

Note: The 3 and 9 were brought down, since they were not divisible by 2.

Step 3. Continue Step 2 until no prime number will divide evenly into at least two numbers.

Note: The 3 is used, $2\,\big/\,\underline{3 \quad 8 \quad 9 \quad 12}$
since 2 can no longer $2\,\big/\,\underline{3 \quad 4 \quad 9 \quad 6}$
divide evenly into at $3\,\big/\,\underline{3 \quad 2 \quad 9 \quad 3}$
least two numbers. $1 \quad 2 \quad 3 \quad 1$

Step 4. To find the LCD, multiply all the numbers in the divisors (2, 2, 3) and in the last row (1, 2, 3, 1).

$$\boxed{2 \times 2 \times 3} \times \boxed{1 \times 2 \times 3 \times 1} = \boxed{72} \ (\text{LCD})$$

   Divisors $\times$ Last row

Step 5. Raise each fraction so that each denominator will be 72 and then add fractions.

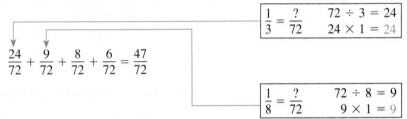

$$\dfrac{24}{72} + \dfrac{9}{72} + \dfrac{8}{72} + \dfrac{6}{72} = \dfrac{47}{72}$$

  The above five steps used for finding LCD with prime numbers are summarized as follows:

FINDING LCD FOR TWO OR MORE FRACTIONS
Step 1. Copy the denominators and arrange them in a separate row.
Step 2. Divide the denominators by the smallest prime number that will divide evenly into at least two numbers.
Step 3. Continue until no prime number divides evenly into at least two numbers.
Step 4. Multiply all the numbers in divisors and last row to find the LCD.
Step 5. Raise all fractions so each has a common denominator and then complete the computation.

Adding Mixed Numbers The following steps will show you how to add mixed numbers:

ADDING MIXED NUMBERS
Step 1. Add the fractions (remember that fractions need common denominators, as in the previous section).
Step 2. Add the whole numbers.
Step 3. Combine the totals of Steps 1 and 2. Be sure you do not have an improper fraction in your final answer. Convert the improper fraction to a whole or mixed number. Add the whole numbers resulting from the improper fraction conversion to the total whole numbers of Step 2. If necessary, reduce the answer to lowest terms.

EXAMPLE

$$4\frac{7}{20} \qquad 4\frac{7}{20} \qquad \frac{3}{5}=\frac{?}{20}$$

$$6\frac{3}{5} \qquad 6\frac{12}{20} \qquad 20 \div 5 = 4$$

$$+\;7\frac{1}{4} \qquad +\;7\frac{5}{20} \qquad \times\;3$$

$$\qquad\qquad\qquad\qquad 12$$

Step 1 → $\frac{24}{20} = 1\frac{4}{20}$

Step 2 → $+\;17$

Step 3 → $= 18\frac{4}{20} = 18\frac{1}{5}$

Subtraction of Fractions

The subtraction of fractions is similar to the addition of fractions. This section explains how to subtract like and unlike fractions and how to subtract mixed numbers.

Subtracting Like Fractions   To subtract like fractions, use the steps that follow.

LO 3

SUBTRACTING LIKE FRACTIONS

Step 1. Subtract the numerators and place the answer over the common denominator.

Step 2. If necessary, reduce the answer to lowest terms.

EXAMPLE $\frac{9}{10} - \frac{1}{10} = \frac{8 \div 2}{10 \div 2} = \frac{4}{5}$

Step 1   Step 2

Subtracting Unlike Fractions   Now let's learn the steps for subtracting unlike fractions.

SUBTRACTING UNLIKE FRACTIONS

Step 1. Find the LCD.

Step 2. Raise the fraction to its equivalent value.

Step 3. Subtract the numerators and place the answer over the LCD.

Step 4. If necessary, reduce the answer to lowest terms.

EXAMPLE

$$\frac{5}{8} \qquad \frac{40}{64}$$
$$-\frac{2}{64} \qquad -\frac{2}{64}$$
$$\frac{38}{64} = \frac{19}{32}$$

By inspection, we see that LCD is 64.
Thus $64 \div 8 = 8 \times 5 = 40$.

Subtracting Mixed Numbers   When you subtract whole numbers, sometimes borrowing is not necessary. At other times, you must borrow. The same is true of subtracting mixed numbers.

LO 4

SUBTRACTING MIXED NUMBERS

When Borrowing Is Not Necessary	*When Borrowing Is Necessary*
Step 1. Subtract fractions, making sure to find the LCD.	**Step 1.** Make sure the fractions have the LCD.
Step 2. Subtract whole numbers.	**Step 2.** Borrow from the whole number of the minuend (top number).
Step 3. Reduce the fraction(s) to lowest terms.	**Step 3.** Subtract the whole numbers and fractions.
	Step 4. Reduce the fraction(s) to lowest terms.

EXAMPLE   Where borrowing is not necessary: Find LCD of 2 and 8. LCD is 8.

$$6\frac{1}{2} \qquad\qquad 6\frac{4}{8}$$
$$-\ \frac{3}{8} \qquad\qquad -\ \frac{3}{8}$$
$$\qquad\qquad\qquad\quad 6\frac{1}{8}$$

EXAMPLE   Where borrowing is necessary:

$$3\frac{1}{2} = \qquad 3\frac{2}{4} = \qquad 2\frac{6}{4}\ \left(\frac{4}{4} + \frac{2}{4}\right)$$
$$-\ 1\frac{3}{4} = \quad -\ 1\frac{3}{4} = \quad -\ 1\frac{3}{4}$$
$$\text{LCD is } 4. \qquad\qquad\qquad 1\frac{3}{4}$$

© Stockbroker/Purestock/Superstock

Since $\frac{3}{4}$ is larger than $\frac{2}{4}$, we must borrow 1 from the 3. This is the same as borrowing $\frac{4}{4}$. A fraction with the same numerator and denominator represents a whole. When we add $\frac{4}{4} + \frac{2}{4}$, we get $\frac{6}{4}$. Note how we subtracted the whole number and fractions, being sure to reduce the final answer if necessary.

How to Dissect and Solve a Word Problem

Let's now look at how to dissect and solve a word problem involving fractions.

The Word Problem The Albertsons grocery store has $550\frac{1}{4}$ total square feet of floor space. Albertsons' meat department occupies $115\frac{1}{2}$ square feet, and its deli department occupies $145\frac{7}{8}$ square feet. If the remainder of the floor space is for groceries, what square footage remains for groceries?

	The facts	Solving for?	Steps to take	Key points
BLUEPRINT	Total square footage: $550\frac{1}{4}$ sq. ft. Meat department: $115\frac{1}{2}$ sq. ft. Deli department: $145\frac{7}{8}$ sq. ft.	Total square footage for groceries.	Total floor space − Total meat and deli floor space = Total grocery floor space.	Denominators must be the same before adding or subtracting fractions. $\frac{8}{8} = 1$ Never leave improper fraction as final answer.

Steps to solving problem

1. Calculate total square footage of the meat and deli departments.

Meat: $\qquad 115\frac{1}{2} = \qquad 115\frac{4}{8}$

Deli: $\quad +\ 145\frac{7}{8} = +\ 145\frac{7}{8}$

$$\qquad\qquad\qquad 260\frac{11}{8} = 261\frac{3}{8} \text{ sq. ft.}$$

2. Calculate total grocery square footage.

$$\qquad\qquad\qquad\qquad\qquad\qquad\qquad\qquad\quad \textbf{Check}$$

$$550\frac{1}{4} = \quad 550\frac{2}{8} = \quad 549\frac{10}{8} \qquad\qquad 261\frac{3}{8}$$
$$-\ 261\frac{3}{8} = -\ 261\frac{3}{8} = -\ 261\frac{3}{8} \quad \left(\frac{2}{8} + \frac{8}{8}\right) \qquad +\ 288\frac{7}{8}$$
$$\qquad\qquad\qquad\qquad\qquad 288\frac{7}{8} \text{ sq. ft.} \qquad\qquad 549\frac{10}{8} = 550\frac{2}{8} = 550\frac{1}{4} \text{ sq. ft.}$$

Note how the above blueprint aid helped to gather the facts and identify what we were looking for. To find the total square footage for groceries, we first had to sum the areas for meat and deli. Then we could subtract these areas from the total square footage. Also note that in Step 1 above, we didn't leave the answer as an improper fraction. In Step 2, we borrowed from the 550 so that we could complete the subtraction.

It's your turn to check your progress with a Practice Quiz.

LU 2–2 **PRACTICE QUIZ**

Complete this **Practice Quiz** to see how you are doing.

1. Find LCD by the division of prime numbers:

   12, 9, 6, 4

2. Add and reduce to lowest terms if needed:

   a. $\dfrac{3}{40} + \dfrac{2}{5}$ b. $2\dfrac{3}{4} + 6\dfrac{1}{20}$

3. Subtract and reduce to lowest terms if needed:

   a. $\dfrac{6}{7} - \dfrac{1}{4}$ b. $8\dfrac{1}{4} - 3\dfrac{9}{28}$ c. $4 - 1\dfrac{3}{4}$

4. Computerland has $660\dfrac{1}{4}$ total square feet of floor space. Three departments occupy this floor space: hardware, $201\dfrac{1}{8}$ square feet; software, $242\dfrac{1}{4}$ square feet; and customer service, _____ square feet. What is the total square footage of the customer service area? You might want to try a blueprint aid, since the solution will show a completed blueprint aid.

*For **extra help** from your authors–Sharon and Jeff–see the student DVD*

✓ **Solutions**

1. $\begin{array}{r} 2\;\big/\;\overline{12\quad 9\quad 6\quad 4} \\ 2\;\big/\;\overline{6\quad 9\quad 3\quad 2} \\ 3\;\big/\;\overline{3\quad 9\quad 3\quad 1} \\ \overline{1\quad 3\quad 1\quad 1} \end{array}$ $\text{LCD} = 2 \times 2 \times 3 \times 1 \times 3 \times 1 \times 1 = \boxed{36}$

2. a. $\dfrac{3}{40} + \dfrac{2}{5} = \dfrac{3}{40} + \dfrac{16}{40} = \boxed{\dfrac{19}{40}}$ $\left(\begin{array}{c} \dfrac{2}{5} = \dfrac{?}{40} \\ 40 \div 5 = 8 \times 2 = 16 \end{array} \right)$

   b. $\begin{array}{r} 2\dfrac{3}{4} \\ +\,6\dfrac{1}{20} \\ \hline \end{array}$ $\begin{array}{r} 2\dfrac{15}{20} \\ +\,6\dfrac{1}{20} \\ \hline 8\dfrac{16}{20} = 8\dfrac{4}{5} \end{array}$ $\dfrac{3}{4} = \dfrac{?}{20}$

   $20 \div 4 = 5 \times 3 = 15$

3. a. $\begin{array}{r} \dfrac{6}{7} = \dfrac{24}{28} \\ -\dfrac{1}{4} = -\dfrac{7}{28} \\ \hline \dfrac{17}{28} \end{array}$ b. $\begin{array}{r} 8\dfrac{1}{4} = \quad 8\dfrac{7}{28} = \quad 7\dfrac{35}{28} \\ -3\dfrac{9}{28} = -3\dfrac{9}{28} = -3\dfrac{9}{28} \\ \hline 4\dfrac{26}{28} = 4\dfrac{13}{14} \end{array}$ $\left(\dfrac{28}{28} + \dfrac{7}{28} \right)$

   c. $\begin{array}{r} 3\dfrac{4}{4} \\ -\,1\dfrac{3}{4} \\ \hline 2\dfrac{1}{4} \end{array}$ Note how we showed the 4 as $3\dfrac{4}{4}$.

4. Computerland's total square footage for customer service:

	The facts	Solving for?	Steps to take	Key points
B L U E P R I N T	*Total square footage:* $660\frac{1}{4}$ *sq. ft.* *Hardware:* $201\frac{1}{8}$ *sq. ft.* *Software:* $242\frac{1}{4}$ *sq. ft.*	Total square footage for customer service.	Total floor space − Total hardware and software floor space = Total customer service floor space.	Denominators must be the same before adding or subtracting fractions.

Steps to solving problem

1. Calculate the total square footage of hardware and software.

$$20 1\frac{1}{8} = \quad 201\frac{1}{8} \text{ (hardware)}$$
$$+ \, 242\frac{1}{4} = + \, 242\frac{2}{8} \text{ (software)}$$
$$\overline{\qquad\qquad\qquad\quad 443\frac{3}{8}}$$

2. Calculate the total square footage for customer service.

$$660\frac{1}{4} = \quad 660\frac{2}{8} = \quad 659\frac{10}{8} \text{ (total square footage)}$$
$$- 443\frac{3}{8} = - \, 443\frac{3}{8} = - \, 443\frac{3}{8} \text{ (hardware plus software)}$$
$$\overline{\qquad\qquad\qquad\qquad 216\frac{7}{8} \text{ sq. ft. (customer service)}}$$

LU 2–2a	EXTRA PRACTICE QUIZ WITH WORKED-OUT SOLUTIONS

Need more practice? Try this **Extra Practice Quiz** (check figures in the Interactive Chapter Organizer, p. 53). Worked-out Solutions can be found in Appendix B at end of text.

1. Find the LCD by the division of prime numbers:
   10, 15, 9, 4

2. Add and reduce to lowest terms if needed:
   a. $\dfrac{2}{25} + \dfrac{3}{5}$ **b.** $3\dfrac{3}{8} + 6\dfrac{1}{32}$

3. Subtract and reduce to lowest terms if needed:
   a. $\dfrac{5}{6} - \dfrac{1}{3}$ **b.** $9\dfrac{1}{8} - 3\dfrac{7}{32}$ **c.** $6 - 1\dfrac{2}{5}$

4. Computerland has $985\frac{1}{4}$ total square feet of floor space. Three departments occupy this floor space: hardware, $209\frac{1}{8}$ square feet; software, $382\frac{1}{4}$ square feet; and customer service, _____ square feet. What is the total square footage of the customer service area?

Learning Unit 2–3: Multiplying and Dividing Fractions

LO	1

The following recipe for Coconutty "M&M'S"® Brand Brownies makes 16 brownies. What would you need if you wanted to triple the recipe and make 48 brownies?

Coconutty "M&M'S"® Brand Brownies

6 squares (1 ounce each) semi-sweet chocolate
½ cup (1 stick) butter
¾ cup granulated sugar
2 large eggs
1 tablespoon vegetable oil
1 teaspoon vanilla extract
1¼ cups all-purpose flour
3 tablespoons unsweetened cocoa powder
1 teaspoon baking powder
½ teaspoon salt
1½ cups "M&M'S"® Brand MINIS Chocolate
   Candies, divided

Preheat oven to 350°F. Grease 8 × 8 × 2-inch pan; set aside. In small saucepan combine chocolate, butter, and sugar over low heat; stir constantly until smooth. Remove from heat; let cool. In bowl beat eggs, oil, and vanilla; stir in chocolate mixture until blended. Stir in flour, cocoa powder, baking powder, and salt. Stir in 1 cup "M&M'S"® Brand MINIS

Chocolate Candies. Spread batter in prepared pan. Bake 35 to 40 minutes or until toothpick inserted in center comes out clean. Cool. Prepare a coconut topping. Spread over brownies; sprinkle with $\frac{1}{2}$ cup "M&M'S"® Brand MINIS Chocolate Candies.

In this unit you learn how to multiply and divide fractions.

Multiplication of Fractions

Multiplying fractions is easier than adding and subtracting fractions because you do not have to find a common denominator. This section explains the multiplication of proper fractions and the multiplication of mixed numbers.

MULTIPLYING PROPER FRACTIONS[3]
Step 1. Multiply the numerators and the denominators.
Step 2. Reduce the answer to lowest terms or use the cancellation method.

First let's look at an example that results in an answer that we do not have to reduce.

EXAMPLE $\dfrac{1}{7} \times \dfrac{5}{8} = \boxed{\dfrac{5}{56}}$

In the next example, note how we reduce the answer to lowest terms.

EXAMPLE $\dfrac{5}{1} \times \dfrac{1}{6} \times \dfrac{4}{7} = \dfrac{20}{42} = \boxed{\dfrac{10}{21}}$ Keep in mind $\dfrac{5}{1}$ is equal to 5.

We can reduce $\frac{20}{42}$ by the step approach as follows:

$$
\begin{array}{r}
2 \\
20\overline{)42} \\
40 \\
\hline
2
\end{array}
\qquad
\begin{array}{r}
10 \\
2\overline{)20} \\
20 \\
\hline
0
\end{array}
$$

We could also have found
the greatest common divisor
by inspection.

$$\dfrac{20 \div 2}{42 \div 2} = \boxed{\dfrac{10}{21}}$$

As an alternative to reducing fractions to lowest terms, we can use the **cancellation** technique. Let's work the previous example using this technique.

LO 2

EXAMPLE $\dfrac{5}{1} \times \dfrac{1}{\cancel{6}} \times \dfrac{\overset{2}{\cancel{4}}}{7} = \boxed{\dfrac{10}{21}}$ 2 divides evenly into 4 twice
and into 6 three times.

Note that when we cancel numbers, we are reducing the answer before multiplying. We know that multiplying or dividing both numerator and denominator by the same number gives an equivalent fraction. So we can divide both numerator and denominator by any number that divides them both evenly. It doesn't matter which we divide first. Note that this division reduces $\frac{10}{21}$ to its lowest terms.

Multiplying Mixed Numbers   The following steps explain how to multiply mixed numbers:

MULTIPLYING MIXED NUMBERS
Step 1. Convert the mixed numbers to improper fractions.
Step 2. Multiply the numerators and denominators.
Step 3. Reduce the answer to lowest terms or use the cancellation method.

EXAMPLE

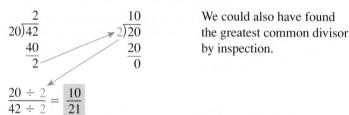

$$2\frac{1}{3} \times 1\frac{1}{2} = \frac{7}{\cancel{3}} \times \frac{\cancel{3}}{2} = \frac{7}{2} = \boxed{3\frac{1}{2}}$$

Step 1   Step 2   Step 3

[3]You would follow the same procedure to multiply improper fractions.

Division of Fractions

When you studied whole numbers in Chapter 1, you saw how multiplication can be checked by division. The multiplication of fractions can also be checked by division, as you will see in this section on dividing proper fractions and mixed numbers.

Dividing Proper Fractions   The division of proper fractions introduces a new term—the **reciprocal.** To use reciprocals, we must first recognize which fraction in the problem is the divisor—the fraction that we divide by. Let's assume the problem we are to solve is $\frac{1}{8} \div \frac{2}{3}$. We read this problem as "$\frac{1}{8}$ divided by $\frac{2}{3}$." The divisor is the fraction after the division sign (or the second fraction). The steps that follow show how the divisor becomes a reciprocal.

DIVIDING PROPER FRACTIONS
Step 1. Invert (turn upside down) the divisor (the second fraction). The inverted number is the *reciprocal.*
Step 2. Multiply the fractions.
Step 3. Reduce the answer to lowest terms or use the cancellation method.

Do you know why the inverted fraction number is a reciprocal? Reciprocals are two numbers that when multiplied give a product of 1. For example, 2 (which is the same as $\frac{2}{1}$) and $\frac{1}{2}$ are reciprocals because multiplying them gives 1.

EXAMPLE $\frac{1}{8} \div \frac{2}{3}$ $\frac{1}{8} \times \frac{3}{2} = \boxed{\frac{3}{16}}$

Dividing Mixed Numbers   Now you are ready to divide mixed numbers by using improper fractions.

DIVIDING MIXED NUMBERS
Step 1. Convert all mixed numbers to improper fractions.
Step 2. Invert the divisor (take its reciprocal) and multiply. If your final answer is an improper fraction, reduce it to lowest terms. You can do this by finding the greatest common divisor or by using the cancellation technique.

EXAMPLE $8\frac{3}{4} \div 2\frac{5}{6}$

Step 1. $\frac{35}{4} \div \frac{17}{6}$

Step 2. $\frac{35}{\cancel{4}_{2}} \times \frac{\cancel{6}^{3}}{17} = \frac{105}{34} = \boxed{3\frac{3}{34}}$ Here we used the cancellation technique.

How to Dissect and Solve a Word Problem

The Word Problem   Jamie Slater ordered $5\frac{1}{2}$ cords of oak. The cost of each cord is $150. He also ordered $2\frac{1}{4}$ cords of maple at $120 per cord. Jamie's neighbor, Al, said that he would share the wood and pay him $\frac{1}{5}$ of the total cost. How much did Jamie receive from Al?

Note how we filled in the blueprint aid columns. We first had to find the total cost of all the wood before we could find Al's share—$\frac{1}{5}$ of the total cost.

MONEY tips

Make good buying decisions. Do not spend more money than you make. In fact, remember to pay yourself first by putting away money each paycheck for your retirement—even $10 each paycheck adds up.

	The facts	Solving for?	Steps to take	Key points
BLUEPRINT	Cords ordered: $5\frac{1}{2}$ at $150 per cord; $2\frac{1}{4}$ at $120 per cord. Al's cost share: $\frac{1}{5}$ the total cost.	What will Al pay Jamie?	Total cost of wood × $\frac{1}{5}$ = Al's cost.	Convert mixed numbers to improper fractions when multiplying. Cancellation is an alternative to reducing fractions.

Steps to solving problem

1. Calculate the cost of oak.

$$5\frac{1}{2} \times \$150 = \frac{11}{2} \times \$\overset{\$75}{\cancel{150}} = \$825$$

2. Calculate the cost of maple.

$$2\frac{1}{4} \times \$120 = \frac{9}{\cancel{4}} \times \$\overset{\$30}{\cancel{120}} = +270$$

$$\overline{\$1,095} \text{ (total cost of wood)}$$

3. What Al pays.

$$\frac{1}{\cancel{5}} \times \$\overset{\$219}{\cancel{1,095}} = \boxed{\$219}$$

You should now be ready to test your knowledge of the final unit in the chapter.

LU 2–3 PRACTICE QUIZ

Complete this **Practice Quiz** to see how you are doing.

1. Multiply (use cancellation technique):

   a. $\frac{4}{8} \times \frac{4}{6}$ **b.** $35 \times \frac{4}{7}$

2. Multiply (do not use canceling; reduce by finding the greatest common divisor):

   $$\frac{14}{15} \times \frac{7}{10}$$

3. Complete the following. Reduce to lowest terms as needed.

   a. $\frac{1}{9} \div \frac{5}{6}$ **b.** $\frac{51}{5} \div \frac{5}{9}$

4. Jill Estes bought a mobile home that was $8\frac{1}{8}$ times as expensive as the home her brother bought. Jill's brother paid $16,000 for his mobile home. What is the cost of Jill's new home?

For **extra help** from your authors—Sharon and Jeff—see the student DVD

You Tube™

✓ Solutions

1. **a.** $\dfrac{\overset{1}{\cancel{\underset{2}{\cancel{4}}}}}{\underset{1}{\cancel{\underset{2}{8}}}} \times \dfrac{\overset{1}{\cancel{4}}}{\underset{3}{\cancel{6}}} = \boxed{\dfrac{1}{3}}$ **b.** $\overset{5}{\cancel{35}} \times \dfrac{4}{\cancel{7}} = \boxed{20}$

2. $\dfrac{14}{15} \times \dfrac{7}{10} = \dfrac{98 \div 2}{150 \div 2} = \boxed{\dfrac{49}{75}}$

   $$
   \begin{array}{cccccc}
   \overset{1}{98\overline{)150}} & \overset{1}{52\overline{)98}} & \overset{1}{46\overline{)52}} & \overset{7}{6\overline{)46}} & \overset{1}{4\overline{)6}} & \overset{2}{2\overline{)4}} \\
   \underline{98} & \underline{52} & \underline{46} & \underline{42} & \underline{4} & \underline{4} \\
   52 & 46 & 6 & 4 & 2 & 0
   \end{array}
   $$

3. **a.** $\dfrac{1}{9} \times \dfrac{6}{5} = \dfrac{6 \div 3}{45 \div 3} = \boxed{\dfrac{2}{15}}$ **b.** $\dfrac{51}{5} \times \dfrac{9}{5} = \dfrac{459}{25} = \boxed{18\dfrac{9}{25}}$

4. Total cost of Jill's new home:

	The facts	Solving for?	Steps to take	Key points
BLUEPRINT	Jill's mobile home: $8\frac{1}{8}$ as expensive as her brother's. Brother paid: $16,000.	Total cost of Jill's new home.	$8\frac{1}{8}$ × Total cost of Jill's brother's mobile home = Total cost of Jill's new home.	Canceling is an alternative to reducing.

Steps to solving problem

1. Convert $8\frac{1}{8}$ to a mixed number. $\frac{65}{8}$

2. Calculate the total cost of Jill's home. $\frac{65}{8} \times \$\overset{\$2,000}{\cancel{16,000}} = \$130,000$

| LU 2–3a | **EXTRA PRACTICE QUIZ WITH WORKED-OUT SOLUTIONS** |

Need more practice? Try this **Extra Practice Quiz** (check figures in the Interactive Chapter Organizer, p. 53). Worked-out Solutions can be found in Appendix B at end of text.

1. Multiply (use cancellation technique):

   a. $\frac{6}{8} \times \frac{3}{6}$ b. $42 \times \frac{1}{7}$

2. Multiply (do not use canceling; reduce by finding the greatest common divisor):

   $\frac{13}{117} \times \frac{9}{5}$

3. Complete the following. Reduce to lowest terms as needed.

   a. $\frac{1}{8} \div \frac{4}{5}$ b. $\frac{61}{6} \div \frac{6}{7}$

4. Jill Estes bought a mobile home that was $10\frac{1}{8}$ times as expensive as the home her brother bought. Jill's brother paid $10,000 for his mobile home. What is the cost of Jill's new home?

INTERACTIVE CHAPTER ORGANIZER

Topic/procedure/formula	Examples	You try it*
Types of fractions, p. 36 *Proper:* Value less than 1; numerator smaller than denominator. *Improper:* Value equal to or greater than 1; numerator equal to or greater than denominator. *Mixed:* Sum of whole number greater than zero and a proper fraction.	$\frac{3}{5}, \frac{7}{9}, \frac{8}{15}$ $\frac{14}{14}, \frac{19}{18}$ $6\frac{3}{8}, 9\frac{8}{9}$	**Identify type of fraction** $\frac{3}{10}, \frac{9}{8}, 1\frac{4}{5}$
Fraction conversions, p. 37 *Improper to whole or mixed:* Divide numerator by denominator; place remainder over *old* denominator. *Mixed to improper:* $\frac{\text{Whole number} \times \text{Denominator} + \text{Numerator}}{\text{Old denominator}}$	$\frac{17}{4} = 4\frac{1}{4}$ $4\frac{1}{8} = \frac{32+1}{8} = \frac{33}{8}$	**Convert to mixed number** $\frac{18}{7}$ **Convert to improper fraction** $5\frac{1}{7}$
Reducing fractions to lowest terms, p. 38 1. Divide numerator and denominator by largest possible divisor (does not change fraction value). 2. When reduced to lowest terms, no number (except 1) will divide evenly into both numerator and denominator.	$\frac{18 \div 2}{46 \div 2} = \frac{9}{23}$	**Reduce to lowest terms** $\frac{16}{24}$
Step approach for finding greatest common denominator, p. 38 1. Divide smaller number of fraction into larger number. 2. Divide remainder into divisor of Step 1. Continue this process until no remainder results. 3. The last divisor used is the greatest common divisor.	$15 \longrightarrow \overset{4}{15\overline{)65}} \quad \overset{3}{5\overline{)15}}$ $\quad\;\; \underline{60} \qquad\;\; \underline{15}$ $\quad\;\;\; 5 \qquad\quad 0$ $\boxed{5}$ is greatest common divisor.	**Find greatest common denominator** $\frac{20}{50}$
Raising fractions to higher terms, p. 39 Multiply numerator and denominator by same number. Does not change fraction value.	$\frac{15}{41} = \frac{?}{410}$ $410 \div 41 = 10 \times 15 = \boxed{150}$	**Raise to higher terms** $\frac{16}{31} = \frac{?}{310}$

(continues)

INTERACTIVE CHAPTER ORGANIZER

Topic/procedure/formula	Examples	You try it*
Adding and subtracting like and unlike fractions, p. 41 When denominators are the same (like fractions), add (or subtract) numerators, place total over original denominator, and reduce to lowest terms. When denominators are different (unlike fractions), change them to like fractions by finding LCD using inspection or prime numbers. Then add (or subtract) the numerators, place total over LCD, and reduce to lowest terms.	$\frac{4}{9} + \frac{1}{9} = \boxed{\frac{5}{9}}$ $\frac{4}{9} - \frac{1}{9} = \frac{3}{9} = \boxed{\frac{1}{3}}$ $\frac{4}{5} + \frac{2}{7} = \frac{28}{35} + \frac{10}{35} = \frac{38}{35} = \boxed{1\frac{3}{35}}$	**Add** $\frac{3}{7} + \frac{2}{7}$ **Subtract** $\frac{5}{7} - \frac{2}{7}$ **Add** $\frac{5}{8} + \frac{3}{40}$
Prime numbers, p. 42 Whole numbers larger than 1 that are only divisible by itself and 1.	$2, 3, 5, 7, 11$	**List the next two prime numbers after 11**
LCD by prime numbers, p. 42 1. Copy denominators and arrange them in a separate row. 2. Divide denominators by smallest prime number that will divide evenly into at least two numbers. 3. Continue until no prime number divides evenly into at least two numbers. 4. Multiply all the numbers in the divisors and last row to find LCD. 5. Raise fractions so each has a common denominator and complete computation.	$\frac{1}{3} + \frac{1}{6} + \frac{1}{8} + \frac{1}{12} + \frac{1}{9}$ $\begin{array}{r|ccccc} 2 & 3 & 6 & 8 & 12 & 9 \\ 2 & 3 & 3 & 4 & 6 & 9 \\ 3 & 3 & 3 & 2 & 3 & 9 \\ \hline & 1 & 1 & 2 & 1 & 3 \end{array}$ $2 \times 2 \times 3 \times 1 \times 1 \times 2 \times 1 \times 3 = \boxed{72}$	**Find LCD** $\frac{1}{2} + \frac{1}{4} + \frac{1}{5}$
Adding mixed numbers, p. 43 1. Add fractions. 2. Add whole numbers. 3. Combine totals of Steps 1 and 2. If denominators are different, a common denominator must be found. Answer cannot be left as improper fraction.	$1\frac{4}{7} + 1\frac{3}{7}$ Step 1: $\frac{4}{7} + \frac{3}{7} = \frac{7}{7}$ Step 2: $1 + 1 = 2$ Step 3: $2\frac{7}{7} = \boxed{3}$	**Add mixed numbers** $2\frac{1}{4} + 3\frac{3}{4}$
Subtracting mixed numbers, p. 44 1. Subtract fractions. 2. If necessary, borrow from whole numbers. 3. Subtract whole numbers and fractions if borrowing was necessary. 4. Reduce fractions to lowest terms. If denominators are different, a common denominator must be found.	$12\frac{2}{5} - 7\frac{3}{5}$ $11\frac{7}{5} - 7\frac{3}{5}$ $= \boxed{4\frac{4}{5}}$ Due to borrowing $\frac{5}{5}$ from number 12 $\frac{5}{5} + \frac{2}{5} = \frac{7}{5}$ The whole number is now 11.	**Subtract mixed numbers** $11\frac{1}{3}$ $-2\frac{2}{3}$
Multiplying proper fractions, p. 48 1. Multiply numerators and denominators. 2. Reduce answer to lowest terms or use cancellation method.	$\frac{4}{7} \times \frac{\overset{1}{\cancel{7}}}{9} = \boxed{\frac{4}{9}}$	**Multiply and reduce** $\frac{4}{5} \times \frac{25}{26}$
Multiplying mixed numbers, p. 48 1. Convert mixed numbers to improper fractions. 2. Multiply numerators and denominators. 3. Reduce answer to lowest terms or use cancellation method.	$1\frac{1}{8} \times 2\frac{5}{8}$ $\frac{9}{8} \times \frac{21}{8} = \frac{189}{64} = \boxed{2\frac{61}{64}}$	**Multiply and reduce** $2\frac{1}{4} \times 3\frac{1}{4}$

(continues)

INTERACTIVE CHAPTER ORGANIZER

Topic/procedure/formula	Examples	You try it*
Dividing proper fractions, p. 49 1. Invert divisor. 2. Multiply. 3. Reduce answer to lowest terms or use cancellation method.	$\dfrac{1}{4} \div \dfrac{1}{8} = \dfrac{1}{4} \times \dfrac{\overset{2}{8}}{\underset{1}{1}} = 2$	**Divide** $\dfrac{1}{8} \div \dfrac{1}{4}$
Dividing mixed numbers, p. 49 1. Convert mixed numbers to improper fractions. 2. Invert divisor and multiply. If final answer is an improper fraction, reduce to lowest terms by finding greatest common divisor or using the cancellation method.	$1\dfrac{1}{2} \div 1\dfrac{5}{8} = \dfrac{3}{2} \div \dfrac{13}{8}$ $= \dfrac{3}{2} \times \dfrac{\overset{4}{8}}{\underset{1}{13}}$ $= \dfrac{12}{13}$	**Divide mixed numbers** $3\dfrac{1}{4} \div 1\dfrac{4}{5}$

KEY TERMS	Cancellation, *p. 48* Common denominator, *p. 41* Denominator, *p. 36* Equivalent, *p. 39* Fraction, *p. 36* Greatest common divisor, *p. 38*	Higher terms, *p. 39* Improper fraction, *p. 37* Least common denominator (LCD), *p. 41* Like fractions, *p. 41* Lowest terms, *p. 38*	Mixed numbers, *p. 37* Numerator, *p. 36* Prime numbers, *p. 42* Proper fraction, *p. 37* Reciprocal, *p. 49* Unlike fractions, *p. 41*

Check Figures for Extra Practice Quizzes with Page References. (Worked-out Solutions in Appendix B.)	LU 2–1a (p. 40) 1. a. P b. I c. M d. I 2. $22\dfrac{1}{7}$ 3. $\dfrac{79}{9}$ 4. a. 14; $\dfrac{3}{5}$ b. 2; $\dfrac{48}{91}$ 5. a. 160; b. 27	LU 2–2a (p. 47) 1. 180 2. a. $\dfrac{17}{25}$ b. $9\dfrac{13}{32}$ 3. a. $\dfrac{1}{2}$ b. $5\dfrac{29}{32}$ c. $4\dfrac{3}{5}$ 4. $393\dfrac{7}{8}$ sq. ft.	LU 2–3a (p. 51) 1. a. $\dfrac{3}{8}$ b. 6 2. $117; \dfrac{1}{5}$ 3. a. $\dfrac{5}{32}$ b. $11\dfrac{31}{36}$ 4. $101,250

*Worked-out solutions are in Appendix B.

Critical Thinking Discussion Questions with Chapter Concept Check

1. What are the steps to convert improper fractions to whole or mixed numbers? Give an example of how you could use this conversion procedure when you eat at Pizza Hut.

2. What are the steps to convert mixed numbers to improper fractions? Show how you could use this conversion procedure when you order doughnuts at Dunkin' Donuts.

3. What is the greatest common divisor? How could you use the greatest common divisor to write an advertisement showing that 35 out of 60 people prefer MCI to AT&T?

4. Explain the step approach for finding the greatest common divisor. How could you use the MCI–AT&T example in question 3 to illustrate the step approach?

5. Explain the steps of adding or subtracting unlike fractions. Using a ruler, measure the heights of two different-size cans of food and show how to calculate the difference in height.

6. What is a prime number? Using the two cans in question 5, show how you could use prime numbers to calculate the LCD.

7. Explain the steps for multiplying proper fractions and mixed numbers. Assume you went to Staples (a stationery superstore). Give an example showing the multiplying of proper fractions and mixed numbers.

8. **Chapter Concept Check.** In the chapter opener it was stated that half of the vehicles sold in the United States are made by foreign firms. Using all the information you have learned about fractions, search the web to find out how many cars are produced in the United States in a year and what fractional part represents cars produced by foreign-owned firms. Finally, present calculations using fractions to agree or disagree with the chapter opener statement.

Classroom Notes

Check figures for odd-numbered problems in Appendix C.   Name _____   Date _____

DRILL PROBLEMS

Identify the following types of fractions: *LU 2-1(1)*

2–1. $\dfrac{6}{7}$

2–2. $\dfrac{12}{11}$

2–3. $\dfrac{14}{11}$

Convert the following to mixed numbers: *LU 2-1(2)*

2–4. $\dfrac{91}{10} =$

2–5. $\dfrac{921}{15} =$

Convert the following to improper fractions: *LU 2-1(2)*

2–6. $8\dfrac{7}{8}$

2–7. $19\dfrac{2}{3}$

Reduce the following to the lowest terms. Show how to calculate the greatest common divisor by the step approach.   *LU 2-1(3)*

2–8. $\dfrac{16}{38}$

2–9. $\dfrac{44}{52}$

Convert the following to higher terms: *LU 2-1(3)*

2–10. $\dfrac{9}{10} = \dfrac{}{70}$

Determine the LCD of the following (a) by inspection and (b) by division of prime numbers: *LU 2-2(2)*

2–11. $\dfrac{3}{4}, \dfrac{7}{12}, \dfrac{5}{6}, \dfrac{1}{5}$ **Check**

   Inspection

2–12. $\dfrac{5}{6}, \dfrac{7}{18}, \dfrac{5}{9}, \dfrac{2}{72}$ **Check**

   Inspection

2–13. $\dfrac{1}{4}, \dfrac{3}{32}, \dfrac{5}{48}, \dfrac{1}{8}$ **Check**

   Inspection

Add the following and reduce to lowest terms: *LU 2-2(1), LU 2-1(3)*

2–14. $\dfrac{3}{9} + \dfrac{3}{9}$

2–15. $\dfrac{3}{7} + \dfrac{4}{21}$

2–16. $6\dfrac{1}{8} + 4\dfrac{3}{8}$

2–17. $6\dfrac{3}{8} + 9\dfrac{1}{24}$

2–18. $9\dfrac{9}{10} + 6\dfrac{7}{10}$

Subtract the following and reduce to lowest terms: *LU 2-2(3), LU 2-1(3)*

2–19. $\dfrac{11}{12} - \dfrac{1}{12}$

2–20. $14\dfrac{3}{8} - 10\dfrac{5}{8}$

2–21. $12\dfrac{1}{9} - 4\dfrac{2}{3}$

Multiply the following and reduce to lowest terms. Do not use the cancellation technique for these problems.   *LU 2-3(1), LU 2-1(3)*

2–22. $17 \times \dfrac{4}{2}$

2–23. $\dfrac{5}{6} \times \dfrac{3}{8}$

2–24. $8\dfrac{7}{8} \times 64$

Multiply the following. Use the cancellation technique.   *LU 2-3(1), LU 2-1(2)*

2–25. $\dfrac{4}{10} \times \dfrac{30}{60} \times \dfrac{6}{10}$

2–26. $3\dfrac{3}{4} \times \dfrac{8}{9} \times 4\dfrac{9}{12}$

Divide the following and reduce to lowest terms. Use the cancellation technique as needed.   *LU 2-3(2), LU 2-1(2)*

2–27. $\dfrac{12}{9} \div 4$

2–28. $18 \div \dfrac{1}{5}$

2–29. $4\dfrac{2}{3} \div 12$

2–30. $3\dfrac{5}{6} \div 3\dfrac{1}{2}$

WORD PROBLEMS

2–31. Michael Wittry has been investing in his Roth IRA retirement account for 20 years. Two years ago, his account was worth $215,658. After losing $\frac{1}{3}$ of its original value, it then gained $\frac{1}{2}$ of its new value back. What is the current value of his Roth IRA?   *LU 2-3(1)*

2–32. Delta pays Pete Rose $180 per day to work in the maintenance department at the airport. Pete became ill on Monday and went home after $\frac{1}{6}$ of a day. What did he earn on Monday? Assume no work, no pay.   *LU 2-3(1)*

2–33 As reported by *The New York Times* in January 2012, about $\frac{3}{4}$ of the top 1% of North America's wealthiest people reported they spent less than they earned in 2011—compared to almost $\frac{1}{2}$ for all others. If the top 1% equals 312,935 people, how many spent less than they earned (round to the nearest person)?   *LU 2-3(3)*

2–34. Joy Wigens, who works at Putnam Investments, received a check for $1,600. She deposited $\frac{1}{4}$ of the check in her Citibank account. How much money does Joy have left after the deposit?   *LU 2-3(1)*

2–35. Lee Jenkins worked the following hours as a manager for a local Pizza Hut: $14\frac{1}{4}$, $5\frac{1}{4}$, $8\frac{1}{2}$, and $7\frac{1}{4}$. How many total hours did Lee work?   *LU 2-2(1)*

2–36. Lester bought a piece of property in Vail, Colorado. The sides of the land measure $115\frac{1}{2}$ feet, $66\frac{1}{4}$ feet, $106\frac{1}{8}$ feet, and $110\frac{1}{4}$ feet. Lester wants to know the perimeter (sum of all sides) of his property. Can you calculate the perimeter for Lester?   *LU 2-2(1)*

2–37. Tiffani Lind got her new weekly course schedule from Roxbury Community College in Boston. Following are her classes and their length: Business Math, $2\frac{1}{2}$ hours; Introduction to Business, $1\frac{1}{2}$ hours; Microeconomics, $1\frac{1}{2}$ hours; Spanish, $2\frac{1}{4}$ hours; Marketing, $1\frac{1}{4}$ hours; and Business Statistics, $1\frac{3}{4}$ hours. How long will she be in class each week?   *LU 2-2(1)*

2–38. Seventy-seven million people were born between 1946 and 1964. The U.S. Census classifies this group of individuals as baby boomers. It is said that today and every day for the next 18 years, 10,000 baby boomers will reach 65. If $\frac{1}{4}$ of the 65 and older age group uses e-mail, $\frac{1}{5}$ obtains the news from the Internet, and $\frac{1}{6}$ searches the Internet, find the LCD and determine total technology usage for this age group as a fraction.   *LU 2-2(1, 2)*

2–39. At a local Walmart store, a Coke dispenser held $19\frac{1}{4}$ gallons of soda. During working hours, $12\frac{3}{4}$ gallons were dispensed. How many gallons of Coke remain?   *LU 2-2(2, 3)*

2–40. Bernie Falls bought a home from Century 21 in Houston, Texas, that is $9\frac{1}{2}$ times as expensive as the home his parents bought. Bernie's parents paid $30,000 for their home. What is the cost of Bernie's new home?   *LU 2-1(2), LU 2-3(1)*

2–41. A local garden center charges $250 per cord of wood. If Logan Grace orders $3\frac{1}{2}$ cords, what will the total cost be?   *LU 2-3(1)*

2–42. A local Target store bought 90 pizzas at Pizza Hut for its holiday party. Each guest ate $\frac{1}{6}$ of a pizza and there was no pizza left over. How many guests did Target have for the party?   *LU 2-3(1)*

2–43. Marc, Steven, and Daniel entered into a Subway sandwich shop partnership. Marc owns $\frac{1}{9}$ of the shop and Steven owns $\frac{1}{4}$. What part does Daniel own?   *LU 2-2(1, 2)*

2–44. Lionel Sullivan works for Burger King. He is paid time and one-half for Sundays. If Lionel works on Sunday for 6 hours at a regular pay of $8 per hour, what does he earn on Sunday?   *LU 2-3(1)*

2–45. InternetWorldStats.com shows $\frac{1}{2}$ of North America's population is on Facebook. If there are 312,934,968 people in the United States, how many are on Facebook?   *LU 2-2(3)*

2–46. A trip to the White Mountains of New Hampshire from Boston will take you $2\frac{3}{4}$ hours. Assume you have traveled $\frac{1}{11}$ of the **eXcel** way. How much longer will the trip take? *LU 2-3(1, 2)*

2–47. Andy, who loves to cook, makes apple cobbler for his family. The recipe (serves 6) calls for $1\frac{1}{2}$ pounds of apples, $3\frac{1}{4}$ cups **eXcel** of flour, $\frac{1}{4}$ cup of margarine, $2\frac{3}{8}$ cups of sugar, and 2 teaspoons of cinnamon. Since guests are coming, Andy wants to make a cobbler that will serve 15 (or increase the recipe $2\frac{1}{2}$ times). How much of each ingredient should Andy use? *LU 2-3(1, 2)*

2–48. Mobil allocates $1,692\frac{3}{4}$ gallons of gas per month to Jerry's Service Station. The first week, Jerry sold $275\frac{1}{2}$ gallons; second week, $280\frac{1}{4}$ gallons; and third week, $189\frac{1}{8}$ gallons. If Jerry sells $582\frac{1}{2}$ gallons in the fourth week, how close is Jerry to selling his allocation? *LU 2-2(4)*

2–49. A marketing class at North Shore Community College conducted a viewer preference survey. The survey showed that $\frac{5}{6}$ of the people surveyed preferred Apple's iPhone over the Blackberry. Assume 2,400 responded to the survey. How many favored using a Blackberry? *LU 2-3(1, 2)*

2–50. The price of a used Toyota LandCruiser has increased to $1\frac{1}{4}$ times its earlier price. If the original price of the LandCruiser was $30,000, what is the new price? *LU 2-3(1, 2)*

2–51. Tempco Corporation has a machine that produces $12\frac{1}{2}$ baseball gloves each hour. In the last 2 days, the machine has run for a total of 22 hours. How many baseball gloves has Tempco produced? *LU 2-3(2)*

2–52. Alicia, an employee of Dunkin' Donuts, receives $23\frac{1}{4}$ days per year of vacation time. So far this year she has taken $3\frac{1}{8}$ days in January, $5\frac{1}{2}$ days in May, $6\frac{1}{4}$ days in July, and $4\frac{1}{4}$ days in September. How many more days of vacation does Alicia have left? *LU 2-2(1, 2, 3)*

2–53. A Hamilton multitouch watch was originally priced at $600. At a closing of the Alpha Omega Jewelry Shop, the watch is **eXcel** being reduced by $\frac{1}{4}$. What is the new selling price? *LU 2-3(1)*

2–54. Shelly Van Doren hired a contractor to refinish her kitchen. The contractor said the job would take $49\frac{1}{2}$ hours. To date, the contractor has worked the following hours:

Monday	$4\frac{1}{4}$
Tuesday	$9\frac{1}{8}$
Wednesday	$4\frac{1}{4}$
Thursday	$3\frac{1}{2}$
Friday	$10\frac{5}{8}$

How much longer should the job take to be completed? *LU 2-2(4)*

ADDITIONAL SET OF WORD PROBLEMS

2–55. An issue of *Taunton's Fine Woodworking* included plans for a hall stand. The total height of the stand is $81\frac{1}{2}$ inches. If the base is $36\frac{5}{16}$ inches, how tall is the upper portion of the stand? *LU 2-2(4)*

2–56. Albertsons grocery planned a big sale on apples and received 750 crates from the wholesale market. Albertsons will bag these apples in plastic. Each plastic bag holds $\frac{1}{9}$ of a crate. If Albertsons has no loss to perishables, how many bags of apples can be prepared? *LU 2-3(1)*

2–57. Frank Puleo bought 6,625 acres of land in ski country. He plans to subdivide the land into parcels of $13\frac{1}{4}$ acres each. Each parcel will sell for \$125,000. How many parcels of land will Frank develop? If Frank sells all the parcels, what will be his total sales? *LU 2-3(1)*

If Frank sells $\frac{3}{5}$ of the parcels in the first year, what will be his total sales for the year?

2–58. A local Papa Gino's conducted a food survey. The survey showed that $\frac{1}{9}$ of the people surveyed preferred eating pasta to hamburger. If 5,400 responded to the survey, how many actually favored hamburger? *LU 2-3(1)*

2–59. Tamara, Jose, and Milton entered into a partnership that sells men's clothing on the web. Tamara owns $\frac{3}{8}$ of the company and Jose owns $\frac{1}{4}$. What part does Milton own? *LU 2-2(1, 3)*

2–60. *Quilters Newsletter Magazine* gave instructions on making a quilt. The quilt required $4\frac{1}{2}$ yards of white-on-white print, 2 yards blue check, $\frac{1}{2}$ yard blue-and-white stripe, $2\frac{3}{4}$ yards blue scraps, $\frac{3}{4}$ yard yellow scraps, and $4\frac{7}{8}$ yards lining. How many total yards are needed? *LU 2-2(1, 2)*

2–61. A trailer carrying supplies for a Krispy Kreme from Virginia to New York will take $3\frac{1}{4}$ hours. If the truck traveled $\frac{1}{5}$ of the way, how much longer will the trip take? *LU 2-3(1, 2)*

2–62. Land Rover has increased the price of a FreeLander by $\frac{1}{5}$ from the original price. The original price of the FreeLander was $30,000. What is the new price? *LU 2-3(1, 2)*

CHALLENGE PROBLEMS

2–63. *Woodsmith* magazine gave instructions on how to build a pine cupboard. Lumber will be needed for two shelves $10\frac{1}{4}$ inches long, two base sides $12\frac{1}{2}$ inches long, and two door stiles $29\frac{1}{8}$ inches long. Your lumber comes in 6 foot lengths. **(a)** How many feet of lumber will you need? **(b)** If you want $\frac{1}{2}$ a board left over, is this possible with two boards? *LU 2-2(1, 2, 3, 4)*

2–64. Jack MacLean has entered into a real estate development partnership with Bill Lyons and June Reese. Bill owns $\frac{1}{4}$ of the partnership, while June has a $\frac{1}{5}$ interest. The partners will divide all profits on the basis of their fractional ownership.

The partnership bought 900 acres of land and plans to subdivide each lot into $2\frac{1}{4}$ acres. Homes in the area have been selling for $240,000. By time of completion, Jack estimates the price of each home will increase by $\frac{1}{3}$ of the current value. The partners sent a survey to 12,000 potential customers to see whether they should heat the homes with oil or gas. One-fourth of the customers responded by indicating a 5-to-1 preference for oil. From the results of the survey, Jack now plans to install a 270-gallon oil tank at each home. He estimates that each home will need five fills per year. The current price of home heating fuel is $1 per gallon. The partnership estimates its profit per home will be $\frac{1}{8}$ the selling price of each home.

From the above, please calculate the following: *LU 2-1(1, 2, 3), LU 2-2(1, 2, 3, 4), LU 2-3(1, 2)*

a. Number of homes to be built.　　　　　　　　**b.** Selling price of each home.

c. Number of people responding to survey.　　　**d.** Number of people desiring oil.

e. Average monthly cost per house to heat using oil.

f. Amount of profit Jack will receive from the sale of homes.

SUMMARY PRACTICE TEST You Tube™

Do you need help? The DVD has step-by-step worked-out solutions.

Identify the following types of fractions. *(p. 36)   LU 2-1(1)*

1. $5\frac{1}{8}$

2. $\frac{2}{7}$

3. $\frac{20}{19}$

4. Convert the following to a mixed number. *(p. 37)   LU 2-1(2)*

$\frac{163}{9}$

5. Convert the following to an improper fraction. *(p. 37)   LU 2-1(2)*

$8\frac{1}{8}$

6. Calculate the greatest common divisor of the following by the step approach and reduce to lowest terms. *(p. 39)   LU 2-2(1, 2)*

$\frac{63}{90}$

7. Convert the following to higher terms. *(p. 39)   LU 2-1(3)*

$\frac{16}{94} = \frac{?}{376}$

8. Find the LCD of the following by using prime numbers. Show your work. *(p. 42)   LU 2-2(2)*

$\frac{1}{8} + \frac{1}{3} + \frac{1}{2} + \frac{1}{12}$

9. Subtract the following. *(p. 44)   LU 2-2(4)*

$15\frac{4}{5}$
$-8\frac{19}{20}$

Complete the following using the cancellation technique. *(p. 49)   LU 2-3(1, 2)*

10. $\frac{3}{4} \times \frac{2}{4} \times \frac{6}{9}$

11. $7\frac{1}{9} \times \frac{6}{7}$

12. $\frac{3}{7} \div 6$

13. A trip to Washington from Boston will take you $5\frac{3}{4}$ hours. If you have traveled $\frac{1}{3}$ of the way, how much longer will the trip take? *(p. 48)   LU 2-3(1)*

14. Quiznos produces 640 rolls per hour. If the oven runs $12\frac{1}{4}$ hours, how many rolls will the machine produce? *(p. 49)   LU 2-3(1, 2)*

15. A taste-testing survey of Zing Farms showed that $\frac{2}{3}$ of the people surveyed preferred the taste of veggie burgers to regular burgers. If 90,000 people were in the survey, how many favored veggie burgers? How many chose regular burgers? *(p. 48)   LU 2-3(1)*

16. Jim Janes, an employee of Enterprise Co., worked $9\frac{1}{4}$ hours on Monday, $4\frac{1}{2}$ hours on Tuesday, $9\frac{1}{4}$ hours on Wednesday, $7\frac{1}{2}$ hours on Thursday, and 9 hours on Friday. How many total hours did Jim work during the week? *(p. 41)   LU 2-2(1, 2)*

17. JCPenney offered a $\frac{1}{3}$ rebate on its \$39 hair dryer. Joan bought a JCPenney hair dryer. What did Joan pay after the rebate? *(p. 48)   LU 2-3(1)*

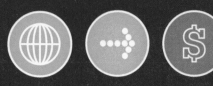

Can you afford to eat? 🔍

PROBLEM 1
Avoid fees

Go to http://money.cnn.com/2001/12/12/debt/q_costcutting/index.htm. Read "The hunt for extra cash," by Annelena Lobb, to learn strategies for reducing banking fees and other personal living expenses. Based on the article, determine how many of the 8,300 traditional banks offer free checking. How many of the 10,599 credit unions offer free checking?

Discussion Questions

1. Why do banks charge fees?
2. What types of fees does your bank charge?

PROBLEM 2
Cook up a winner!

Go to http://www.campbellsoup.com. Search for the recipe called "Festive Chicken."

1 tsp. onion powder; 1/2 tsp. paprika; 1/4 tsp. garlic powder; 1/4 tsp. pepper; 2 lb. chicken parts, skin removed; 1 can (10 3/4 oz.) Campbell's Cream of Mushroom soup OR 98% Fat Free Cream of Mushroom soup; 1/3 cup buttermilk; 1 small red pepper, chopped; 4 green onions, sliced; chopped fresh parsley

The recipe makes 4 servings. If you needed 20 servings for a company outing, how much of each ingredient would you need?

Discussion Questions

1. How much would it cost you to make 20 servings?
2. Would it be less expensive for you to purchase five pizzas to share?

PROBLEM 3
What is your grocery budget?

Visit http://www.walmart.com/cp/Grocery/976759 to find the prices for 20 grocery items that you normally buy within a 1-week time frame. What is the total cost for these items? Determine the fraction of your weekly income needed to cover this expenditure. Now expand this expenditure for the entire month and year. Based on the monthly and yearly expense, determine the fraction of your earnings that would be needed to make these purchases.

Discussion Questions

1. Do you prefer to buy name brand or store brand items? Why?
2. Assume your salary will increase by 1/3 of your current earnings. Would it affect which groceries you would purchase?

PROBLEM 4
Saving for a rainy day

Go to http://www.bankrate.com/finance/financial-literacy/family-learns-to-spend-less-live-more-1.aspx. Read "Family learns to spend less, live more." According to the article, what fraction of disposable income are U.S. households now saving? According to Ellie Kay, is this enough? What fraction does she suggest?

Discussion Questions

1. If you saved 1/10 of your current income for 1 year, how much would you have?
2. If you continued, how much would you have after 10 years of saving? What are some ways you would like to spend this money?

MOBILE APPS ✕

Everyday Mathematics Equivalent Fractions (McGraw-Hill School Education Group) Offers a quick and easy approach to understand concepts related to fractions.

Fractions Calculator (PCB Enterprises) Assists in the addition, subtraction, multiplication, and division of fractions.

INTERNET PROJECTS ✕

See text website
www.mhhe.com/slater11e_sse_ch02

A KIPLINGER APPROACH

MONEY & ETHICS
KNIGHT KIPLINGER

IS IT ETHICAL TO OPT OUT OF HEALTH INSURANCE?

Q. I have a 32-year-old friend—single, healthy, earning a good salary—who doesn't have employer health insurance and declines to buy his own. He thinks it's unlikely he'll need expensive care, and he calls the new individual insurance mandate an infringement on his liberty. Is his position ethical?

The Supreme Court will rule on the *constitutionality* of the health care law's mandate, but to me, the key principle of ethical living is taking responsibility for oneself and not putting a burden on others.

The vast majority of people—including your friend—would never be able to pay out-of-pocket for a very expensive medical need. So the cost would fall on someone else—family members, friends, unreimbursed doctors and hospitals, or taxpayers and fellow citizens who have been paying for insurance long before a need arose.

Only the rich—those able to pay personally for an organ transplant, very premature baby or $100,000-a-year miracle drug—can ethically choose to go naked on health insurance.

Hospitals have long been required by law (and motivated by medical ethics) to provide emergency care to everyone who comes through their doors, regardless of insurance. I don't hear *that* mandate being challenged.

Similarly, polls show that some people who oppose an individual mandate also approve of the government's plan to force insurers to accept new customers with a preexisting health problem. That seems ethically inconsistent.

In the absence of an individual mandate, many people would simply wait until they get really sick to start paying into an insurance pool that has to take them. With some restrictions, their near-term medical costs would be covered by the premiums of more-responsible citizens who had been contributing to the system for a long time.

There is ethical symmetry—as well as economic sense—to a health care system into which everyone must be accepted and to which everyone who is financially able to contribute is required to do so.

HAVE A MONEY-AND-ETHICS QUESTION YOU'D LIKE ANSWERED IN THIS COLUMN? WRITE TO EDITOR IN CHIEF KNIGHT KIPLINGER AT ETHICS@KIPLINGER.COM.

■ SUZANNE BERNIER IS BACK AT MOM AND DAD'S.

■ STARTING OUT

GROUND RULES FOR BOOMERANG KIDS
IT'S OKAY TO HELP, BUT DON'T CODDLE.

SUZANNE BERNIER IS ONE OF the lucky ones. Just before graduating from Brandeis University in 2010, she landed a job at a medical software company. Yet after graduation, the frugal 24-year-old moved back in with her parents. "I wanted to save as much money as possible," she says.

More than one-fifth of people ages 25 to 34 live in multi-generational homes, the highest level since the 1950s, reports Pew Research. The hospitality helps boomerangers stay positive in tough times. More than three-fourths of people ages 25 to 34 who have lived at home are upbeat about their future finances, according to Pew.

Laying ground rules can help prevent a clash of the generations. "Put a game plan together with expectations," says Linda Leitz, a certified financial planner in Colorado. Parents who open their homes should establish a time limit for the stay and get regular progress reports. The child should pay rent, save money or pay off debt. Don't subsidize a lavish lifestyle. If kids can't contribute money, consider requiring household chores instead.

Parents should gradually turn up the heat, Leitz says. Raise the cost of rent by a certain date, for example, even if your plan is to make a gift of the money when your child departs. The comfort of home shouldn't be cushy enough to erode financial independence.
JOHN MILEY

BUSINESS MATH ISSUE

In the long run, living at home after college results in losing one's independence.

1. List the key points of the article and information to support your position.
2. Write a group defense of your position using math calculations to support your view.

Decimals

What retailers and publishers might get from an e-book vs. a traditional print book, using a hypothetical hardcover:

E-Book

$12.99
retail price
per e-book

−$3.90
to the retailer

−$2.27
royalty payment
to the author

−$0.90
for digital rights
management, digital
warehousing,
production, and
distribution

$5.92
per unit
to the publisher

Print book

$26.00
retail price per
hardcover book

−$13.00
to the retailer

−$3.90
royalty payment
to the author

−$3.25
for shipping,
warehousing
and production

$5.85
per unit
to the publisher**

... and for total U.S.
publishing industry
**$27.9
billion**

LU 3–1: Rounding Decimals; Fraction and Decimal Conversions

1. Explain the place values of whole numbers and decimals; round decimals *(pp. 66–68)*.

2. Convert decimal fractions to decimals, proper fractions to decimals, mixed numbers to decimals, and pure and mixed decimals to decimal fractions *(pp. 68–70)*.

LU 3–2: Adding, Subtracting, Multiplying, and Dividing Decimals

1. Add, subtract, multiply, and divide decimals *(pp. 71–73)*.

2. Complete decimal applications in foreign currency *(p. 74)*.

3. Multiply and divide decimals by shortcut methods *(pp. 74–75)*.

VOCABULARY PREVIEW

Here are key terms in this chapter. After completing the chapter, if you know the term, place a checkmark in the parentheses. If you don't know the term, look it up and put the page number where it can be found.

Decimal ( ) Decimal fraction ( ) Decimal point ( ) Mixed decimal ( ) Pure decimal ( ) Repeating decimal ( ) Rounding decimals ( )

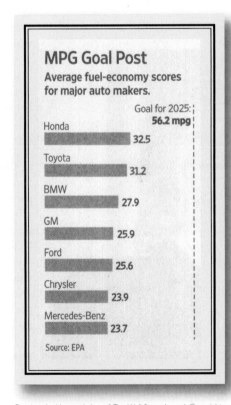

MPG Goal Post
Average fuel-economy scores for major auto makers.

Goal for 2025: **56.2 mpg**

Make	mpg
Honda	32.5
Toyota	31.2
BMW	27.9
GM	25.9
Ford	25.6
Chrysler	23.9
Mercedes-Benz	23.7

Source: EPA

The way gas prices are rising, fuel economy may be a big consideration in your next car purchase. As you can see from the *Wall Street Journal* clip, "MPG Goal Post," automakers' goal for 2025 is to produce vehicles that get 56.2 miles per gallon. To reach this goal, Honda will have to increase its mpg by 23.7.

$$
\begin{array}{ll}
\text{Honda:} & 56.2 \text{ mpg} \\
& \underline{-32.5} \\
& 23.7 \text{ mpg}
\end{array}
$$

TABLE   **3.1**

Analyzing a bag of M&M'S®

LO **1**

© Sharon Hoogstraten

Color*	Fraction	Decimal
Yellow	$\frac{18}{55}$	.33
Red	$\frac{10}{55}$	.18
Blue	$\frac{9}{55}$	.16
Orange	$\frac{7}{55}$	.13
Brown	$\frac{6}{55}$	.11
Green	$\frac{5}{55}$	.09
Total	$\frac{55}{55} = 1$	1.00

*The color ratios currently given are a sample used for educational purposes. They do not represent the manufacturer's color ratios.

Chapter 2 introduced the 1.69-ounce bag of M&M'S® shown in Table 3.1. In Table 3.1, the six colors in the 1.69-ounce bag of M&M'S® are given in fractions and their values expressed in decimal equivalents that are rounded to the nearest hundredths.

This chapter is divided into two learning units. The first unit discusses rounding decimals, converting fractions to decimals, and converting decimals to fractions. The second unit shows you how to add, subtract, multiply, and divide decimals, along with some shortcuts for multiplying and dividing decimals. Added to this unit is a global application of decimals dealing with foreign exchange rates. One of the most common uses of decimals occurs when we spend dollars and cents, which is a *decimal number.*

A **decimal** is a decimal number with digits to the right of a *decimal point,* indicating that decimals, like fractions, are parts of a whole that are less than one. Thus, we can interchange the terms *decimals* and *decimal numbers.* Remembering this will avoid confusion between the terms *decimal, decimal number,* and *decimal point.*

Learning Unit 3–1: Rounding Decimals; Fraction and Decimal Conversions

Remember to read the decimal point as *and*.

In Chapter 1 we stated that the **decimal point** is the center of the decimal numbering system. So far we have studied the whole numbers to the left of the decimal point and the parts of whole numbers called fractions. We also learned that the position of the digits in a whole number gives the place values of the digits (Figure 1.1, p. 5). Now we will study the position (place values) of the digits to the right of the decimal point (Figure 3.1, p. 67). Note that the words to the right of the decimal point end in *ths*.

You should understand why the decimal point is the center of the decimal system. If you move a digit to the left of the decimal point by place (ones, tens, and so on), *you increase its value 10 times for each place (power of 10).* If you move a digit to the right of the decimal point by place (tenths, hundredths, and so on), *you decrease its value 10 times for each place.*

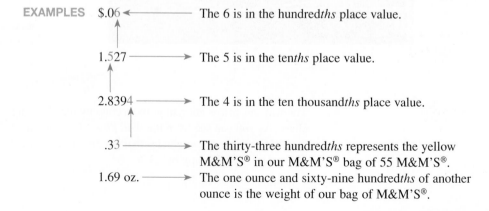

EXAMPLES $.06 \longleftarrow$ The 6 is in the hundred*ths* place value.

1.527 $\longrightarrow$ The 5 is in the ten*ths* place value.

2.8394 $\longrightarrow$ The 4 is in the ten thousand*ths* place value.

.33 $\longrightarrow$ The thirty-three hundred*ths* represents the yellow M&M'S® in our M&M'S® bag of 55 M&M'S®.

1.69 oz. $\longrightarrow$ The one ounce and sixty-nine hundred*ths* of another ounce is the weight of our bag of M&M'S®.

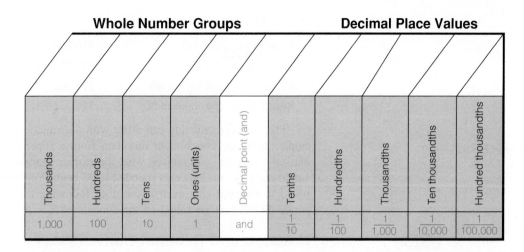

FIGURE 3.1

Decimal place-value chart

Do you recall from Chapter 1 how you used a place-value chart to read or write whole numbers in verbal form? To read or write decimal numbers, you read or write the decimal number as if it were a whole number. Then you use the name of the decimal place of the last digit as given in Figure 3.1. For example, you would read or write the decimal .0796 as seven hundred ninety-six ten thousandths (the last digit, 6, is in the ten thousandths place).

To read a decimal with four or fewer whole numbers, you can also refer to Figure 3.1. For larger whole numbers, refer to the whole-number place-value chart in Chapter 1 (Figure 1.1, p. 5). For example, from Figure 3.1 you would read the number 126.2864 as one hundred twenty-six and two thousand eight hundred sixty-four ten thousandths. Remember that the *and* is the decimal point.

Now let's round decimals. Rounding decimals is similar to the rounding of whole numbers that you learned in Chapter 1.

Rounding Decimals

From Table 3.1, you know that the 1.69-ounce bag of M&M'S® introduced in Chapter 2 contained $\frac{18}{55}$, or .33, yellow M&M'S®. The .33 was rounded to the nearest hundredth. **Rounding decimals** involves the following steps:

ROUNDING DECIMALS TO A SPECIFIED PLACE VALUE

Step 1. Identify the place value of the digit you want to round.

Step 2. If the digit to the right of the identified digit in Step 1 is 5 or more, increase the identified digit by 1. If the digit to the right is less than 5, do not change the identified digit.

Step 3. Drop all digits to the right of the identified digit.

Let's practice rounding by using the $\frac{18}{55}$ yellow M&M'S® that we rounded to .33 in Table 3.1. Before we rounded $\frac{18}{55}$ to .33, the number we rounded was .32727. This is an example of a **repeating decimal** since the 27 repeats itself.

EXAMPLE   Round .3272727 to the nearest hundredth.

Step 1.   .3272727   The identified digit is 2, which is in the hundredths place (two places to the right of the decimal point).

Step 2.   → The digit to the right of 2 is more than 5 (7). Thus, 2, the identified digit in Step 1, is changed to 3.

.3372727

Step 3.   .33   Drop all other digits to the right of the identified digit 3.

We could also round the .3272727 M&M'S® to the nearest tenth or thousandth as follows:

OTHER EXAMPLES

Round to nearest dollar:	$166.39 ⟶	$166
Round to nearest cent:	$1,196.885 ⟶	$1,196.89
Round to nearest hundredth:	$38.563 ⟶	$38.56
Round to nearest thousandth:	$1,432.9981 ⟶	$1,432.998

The rules for rounding can differ with the situation in which rounding is used. For example, have you ever bought one item from a supermarket produce department that was marked "3 for $1" and noticed what the cashier charged you? One item marked "3 for $1" would not cost you $33\frac{1}{3}$ cents rounded to 33 cents. You will pay 34 cents. Many retail stores round to the next cent even if the digit following the identified digit is less than $\frac{1}{2}$ of a penny. In this text we round on the concept of 5 or more.

LO 2

Fraction and Decimal Conversions

In business operations we must frequently convert fractions to decimal numbers and decimal numbers to fractions. This section begins by discussing three types of fraction-to-decimal conversions. Then we discuss converting pure and mixed decimals to decimal fractions.

Converting Decimal Fractions to Decimals   From Figure 3.1 you can see that a **decimal fraction** (expressed in the digits to the right of the decimal point) is a fraction with a denominator that has a power of 10, such as $\frac{1}{10}$, $\frac{17}{100}$, and $\frac{23}{1,000}$. To convert a decimal fraction to a decimal, follow these steps:

CONVERTING DECIMAL FRACTIONS TO DECIMALS

Step 1. Count the number of zeros in the denominator.

Step 2. Place the numerator of the decimal fraction to the right of the decimal point the same number of places as you have zeros in the denominator. (The number of zeros in the denominator gives the number of digits your decimal has to the right of the decimal point.) Do not go over the total number of denominator zeros.

Now let's change $\frac{3}{10}$ and its higher multiples of 10 to decimals.

EXAMPLES

Verbal form	Decimal fraction	Decimal[1]	Number of decimal places to right of decimal point
a. Three tenths	$\frac{3}{10}$	.3	1
b. Three hundredths	$\frac{3}{100}$	.03	2
c. Three thousandths	$\frac{3}{1,000}$	.003	3
d. Three ten thousandths	$\frac{3}{10,000}$	.0003	4

Note how we show the different values of the decimal fractions above in decimals. The zeros after the decimal point and before the number 3 indicate these values. If you add zeros after the number 3, you do not change the value. Thus, the numbers .3 , .30 , and .300 have the same value. So 3 tenths of a pizza, 30 hundredths of a pizza, and 300 thousandths of a pizza are the same total amount of pizza. The first pizza is sliced into 10 pieces. The second pizza is sliced into 100 pieces. The third pizza is sliced into 1,000 pieces. Also, we don't need to place a zero to the left of the decimal point.

---

[1]From .3 to .0003, the values get smaller and smaller, but if you go from .3 to .3000, the values remain the same.

Converting Proper Fractions to Decimals   Recall from Chapter 2 that proper fractions are fractions with a value less than 1. That is, the numerator of the fraction is smaller than its denominator. How can we convert these proper fractions to decimals? Since proper fractions are a form of division, it is possible to convert proper fractions to decimals by carrying out the division.

CONVERTING PROPER FRACTIONS TO DECIMALS
Step 1. Divide the numerator of the fraction by its denominator. (If necessary, add a decimal point and zeros to the number in the numerator.)
Step 2. Round as necessary.

EXAMPLES

$$\frac{3}{4} = 4\overline{)3.00} = .75 \qquad \frac{3}{8} = 8\overline{)3.000} = .375 \qquad \frac{1}{3} = 3\overline{)1.000} = .33\overline{3}$$

$$\frac{3}{4} = 4\overline{)3.00}$$
$$\underline{2\,8}$$
$$20$$
$$\underline{20}$$

$$\frac{3}{8} = 8\overline{)3.000}$$
$$\underline{2\,4}$$
$$60$$
$$\underline{56}$$
$$40$$
$$\underline{40}$$

$$\frac{1}{3} = 3\overline{)1.000}$$
$$\underline{9}$$
$$10$$
$$\underline{9}$$
$$10$$
$$\underline{9}$$
$$1$$

Note that in the last example $\frac{1}{3}$, the 3 in the quotient keeps repeating itself (never ends). The short bar over the last 3 means that the number endlessly repeats.

Converting Mixed Numbers to Decimals

A mixed number, you will recall from Chapter 2, is the sum of a whole number greater than zero and a proper fraction. To convert mixed numbers to decimals, use the following steps:

CONVERTING MIXED NUMBERS TO DECIMALS
Step 1. Convert the fractional part of the mixed number to a decimal (as illustrated in the previous section).
Step 2. Add the converted fractional part to the whole number.

EXAMPLE

$$8\frac{2}{5} = \textbf{(Step 1)} \quad 5\overline{)2.0} = .4 \qquad \textbf{(Step 2)} = \begin{array}{r} 8.00 \\ +\ .40 \\ \hline 8.40 \end{array}$$

$$\underline{2\,0}$$

Now that we have converted fractions to decimals, let's convert decimals to fractions.

Converting Pure and Mixed Decimals to Decimal Fractions   A **pure decimal** has no whole number(s) to the left of the decimal point (.43, .458, and so on). A **mixed decimal** is a combination of a whole number and a decimal. An example of a mixed decimal follows.

EXAMPLE   737.592 = Seven hundred thirty-seven and five hundred ninety-two thousandths

Note the following conversion steps for converting pure and mixed decimals to decimal fractions:

CONVERTING PURE AND MIXED DECIMALS TO DECIMAL FRACTIONS

Step 1. Place the digits to the right of the decimal point in the numerator of the fraction. Omit the decimal point. (For a decimal fraction with a fractional part, see examples **c** and **d** below.)

Step 2. Put a 1 in the denominator of the fraction.

Step 3. Count the number of digits to the right of the decimal point. Add the same number of zeros to the denominator of the fraction. For mixed decimals, add the fraction to the whole number.

If desired, you can reduce the fractions in Step 3.

EXAMPLES		Step 1	Step 2	Places	Step 3
a.	.3	$\underline{3}$	$\dfrac{3}{1}$	1	$\dfrac{3}{10}$
b.	.24	$\underline{24}$	$\dfrac{24}{1}$	2	$\dfrac{24}{100}$
c.	$.24\frac{1}{2}$	$\underline{245}$	$\dfrac{245}{1}$	3	$\dfrac{245}{1,000}$

Before completing Step 1 in example **c,** we must remove the fractional part, convert it to a decimal ($\frac{1}{2} = .5$), and multiply it by .01 ($.5 \times .01 = .005$). We use .01 because the 4 of .24 is in the hundredths place. Then we add $.005 + .24 = .245$ (three places to right of the decimal) and complete Steps 1, 2, and 3.

d.	$.07\frac{1}{4}$	$\underline{725}$	$\dfrac{725}{1}$	4	$\dfrac{725}{10,000}$

In example **d,** be sure to convert $\frac{1}{4}$ to .25 and multiply by .01. This gives .0025. Then add .0025 to .07, which is .0725 (four places), and complete Steps 1, 2, and 3.

e.	17.45	$\underline{45}$	$\dfrac{45}{1}$	2	$\dfrac{45}{100} = 17\dfrac{45}{100}$

Example **e** is a mixed decimal. Since we substitute *and* for the decimal point, we read this mixed decimal as seventeen and forty-five hundredths. Note that after we converted the .45 of the mixed decimal to a fraction, we added it to the whole number 17.

The Practice Quiz that follows will help you check your understanding of this unit.

MONEY tips

Set up automatic payments for the minimum payment due on your debt and eliminate late fees. Create an alert with your smartphone or computer for each bill. Pay more than the minimum whenever possible.

LU 3–1 PRACTICE QUIZ

*Complete this **Practice Quiz** to see how you are doing.*

Write the following as a decimal number.

1. Four hundred eight thousandths

Name the place position of the identified digit:

2. 6.8241   **3.** 9.3942

Round each decimal to place indicated:

		Tenth	Thousandth
4.	.62768	**a.**	**b.**
5.	.68341	**a.**	**b.**

Convert the following to decimals:

6. $\dfrac{9}{10,000}$ **7.** $\dfrac{14}{100,000}$

Convert the following to decimal fractions (do not reduce):

8. .819   **9.** 16.93   **10.** $.05\frac{1}{4}$

Convert the following fractions to decimals and round answer to nearest hundredth:

11. $\dfrac{1}{6}$ **12.** $\dfrac{3}{8}$ **13.** $12\frac{1}{8}$

✓ Solutions

1. .408 (3 places to right of decimal)
2. Hundredths
3. Thousandths
4. a. .6 (identified digit 6—digit to right less than 5)
    b. .628 (identified digit 7—digit to right greater than 5)
5. a. .7 (identified digit 6—digit to right greater than 5)
    b. .683 (identified digit 3—digit to right less than 5)
6. .0009 (4 places)
7. .00014 (5 places)
8. $\dfrac{819}{1,000}$ $\left(\dfrac{819}{1 + 3 \text{ zeros}}\right)$
9. $16\dfrac{93}{100}$
10. $\dfrac{525}{10,000}$ $\left(\dfrac{525}{1 + 4 \text{ zeros}}\ \dfrac{1}{4} \times .01 = .0025 + .05 = .0525\right)$
11. .16666 = .17
12. .375 = .38
13. 12.125 = 12.13

| **LU 3–1a** | **EXTRA PRACTICE QUIZ WITH WORKED-OUT SOLUTIONS** |

Need more practice? Try this **Extra Practice Quiz** (check figures in the Interactive Chapter Organizer, p. 79). Worked-out Solutions can be found in Appendix B at end of text.

Write the following as a decimal number:

1. Three hundred nine thousandths

Name the place position of the identified digit:

2. 7.9324
3. 8.3682

Round each decimal to place indicated:

	Tenth	**Thousandth**
4. .84361	a.	b.
5. .87938	a.	b.

Convert the following to decimals:

6. $\dfrac{8}{10,000}$
7. $\dfrac{16}{100,000}$

Convert the following to decimal fractions (do not reduce):

8. .938
9. 17.95
10. $.03\frac{1}{4}$

Convert the following fractions to decimals and round answer to nearest hundredth:

11. $\dfrac{1}{8}$
12. $\dfrac{4}{7}$
13. $13\dfrac{1}{9}$

Learning Unit 3–2: Adding, Subtracting, Multiplying, and Dividing Decimals

GLOBAL

The *Wall Street Journal* clip "Google+ Pulls in 20 Million in 3 Weeks" (p. 72) reveals that Google reported 19.93 million visitors since the launch of its social networking service, Google+. The following calculations show how many visitors were from outside the United States.

Total visitors:	19.93 million
U.S. visitors:	−5.31
International visitors:	14.62 million

This learning unit shows you how to add, subtract, multiply, and divide decimals. You also make calculations involving decimals, including decimals used in foreign currency.

LO 1

Addition and Subtraction of Decimals

Since you know how to add and subtract whole numbers, to add and subtract decimal numbers you have only to learn about the placement of the decimals. The following steps on page 72 will help you:

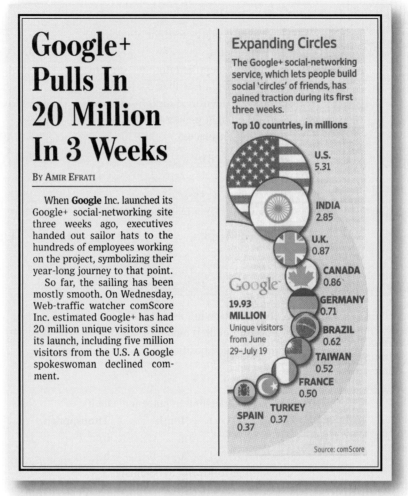

ADDING AND SUBTRACTING DECIMALS

Step 1. Vertically write the numbers so that the decimal points align. You can place additional zeros to the right of the decimal point if needed without changing the value of the number.

Step 2. Add or subtract the digits starting with the right column and moving to the left.

Step 3. Align the decimal point in the answer with the above decimal points.

EXAMPLES   Add 4 + 7.3 + 36.139 + .0007 + 8.22.

Whole number to the right of the last digit is assumed to have a decimal.

$$
\begin{array}{r}
4.0000 \\
7.3000 \\
36.1390 \\
.0007 \\
8.2200 \\
\hline
55.6597
\end{array}
$$

Extra zeros have been added to make calculation easier.

Subtract 45.3 − 15.273.

$$
\begin{array}{r}
45.\overset{2\ 9\ 10}{300} \\
-\ 15.273 \\
\hline
30.027
\end{array}
$$

Subtract 7 − 6.9.

$$
\begin{array}{r}
\overset{6\ 10}{7.0} \\
-\ 6.9 \\
\hline
.1
\end{array}
$$

Multiplication of Decimals

The multiplication of decimal numbers is similar to the multiplication of whole numbers except for the additional step of placing the decimal in the answer (product). The steps that follow simplify this procedure.

MULTIPLYING DECIMALS

Step 1. Multiply the numbers as whole numbers, ignoring the decimal points.

Step 2. Count and total the number of decimal places in the multiplier and multiplicand.

Step 3. Starting at the right in the product, count to the left the number of decimal places totaled in Step 2. Place the decimal point so that the product has the same number of decimal places as totaled in Step 2. If the total number of places is greater than the places in the product, insert zeros in front of the product.

EXAMPLES

	8.52	(2 decimal places)
Step 1	× 6.7	(1 decimal place) **Step 2**
	5 964	
	51 12	
	57.084	
Step 3		

	2.36	(2 places)
	× .016	(3 places)
	1416	
	236	
	.03776	Need to add zero

Division of Decimals

If the divisor in your decimal division problem is a whole number, first place the decimal point in the quotient directly above the decimal point in the dividend. Then divide as usual. If the divisor has a decimal point, complete the steps that follow.

DIVIDING DECIMALS

Step 1. Make the divisor a whole number by moving the decimal point to the right.

Step 2. Move the decimal point in the dividend to the right the same number of places that you moved the decimal point in the divisor (Step 1). If there are not enough places, add zeros to the right of the dividend.

Step 3. Place the decimal point in the quotient above the new decimal point in the dividend. Divide as usual.

EXAMPLE

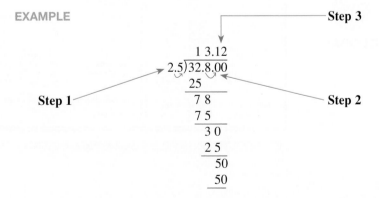

Stop a moment and study the above example. Note that the quotient does not change when we multiply the divisor and the dividend by the same number. This is why we can move the decimal point in division problems and always divide by a whole number.

Decimal Applications in Foreign Currency

GLOBAL

Sharon Wittry, who lives in Canada, wanted to buy a new Apple iPad 2. She went on eBay and found that the cost would be $600 U.S. dollars. Wanting to know how much this would cost in Canadian dollars, Sharon consulted the *Wall Street Journal*'s currency table and found that a Canadian dollar was worth $0.9794 in U.S. dollars. Therefore, for each Canadian dollar it would cost $1.0210 to buy a U.S. good.

Using this information, Sharon completed the following calculation to determine what an iPad would cost her:

$$\$600 \qquad \times \quad \$1.0210 \quad = \quad \$612.60$$
| (cost of the iPad in | | (cost of the iPad in |
| U.S. dollars) | | Canadian dollars) |

To check her findings, Sharon did the following calculation:

$$\$612.60 \qquad \times \quad \$0.9794 \qquad = \quad \$599.98 \text{ (off due to rounding)}$$
(cost of the iPad in	(what the Canadian dollar	(U.S. selling price)
Canadian dollars)	is worth against the	
	U.S. dollar)	

"The dollar held its value today against the yen, the euro, the peso, the comic book and the baseball card."

GLOBAL

Currencies

U.S.-dollar foreign-exchange rates in late New York trading on Friday

Country/currency	Fri in US$	Fri per US$	US$ vs, YTD chg (%)	Country/currency	Fri in US$	Fri per US$	US$ vs, YTD chg (%)
Americas				**Europe**			
Argentina peso*	.2321	4.3089	8.6	**Czech Rep.** koruna	.05063	19.751	5.8
Brazil real	.5360	1.8657	12.3	**Denmark** krone	.1743	5.7373	3.1
Canada dollar	.9794	1.0210	2.6	**Euro area** euro	1.2960	.7716	3.3
Chile peso	.001924	519.86	11.1	**Hungary** forint	.004113	243.14	17.7
Colombia peso	.0005153	1940.50	1.1	**Norway** krone	.1673	5.9766	2.6
Ecuador US dollar	1	1	unch	**Poland** zloty	.2901	3.4470	16.9
Mexico peso*	.0717	13.9461	13.1	**Russia** ruble‡	.03110	32.150	5.2
Peru new sol	.3709	2.696	-3.9	**Sweden** krona	.1453	6.8800	2.6
Uruguay peso†	.05047	19.8130	1.9	**Switzerland** franc	1.0670	.9372	0.2
Venezuela b. fuerte	.229885	4.3500	unch	1-mos forward	1.0675	.9368	0.2
Asia-Pacific				3-mos forward	1.0691	.9354	0.2
Australian dollar	1.0208	.9796	0.3	6-mos forward	1.0718	.9330	0.1
1-mos forward	1.0170	.9832	0.2	**Turkey** lira**	.5217	1.9170	23.5
3-mos forward	1.0107	.9894	0.1	**UK pound**	1.5542	.6434	0.4
6-mos forward	1.0024	.9976	-0.2	1-mos forward	1.5537	.6436	0.4
China yuan	.1583	6.3190	-4.3	3-mos forward	1.5528	.6440	0.4
Hong Kong dollar	.1288	7.7669	-0.1	6-mos forward	1.5513	.6446	0.4
India rupee	.01886	53.025	18.3				
Indonesia rupiah	.0001107	9033	1.6	**Middle East/Africa**			
Japan yen	.013001	76.92	-5.2	**Bahrain** dinar	2.6520	.3771	unch
1-mos forward	.013008	76.88	-5.5	**Egypt** pound*	.1653	6.0498	6.3
3-mos forward	.013025	76.78	-5.6	**Israel** shekel	.2624	3.8110	7.8
6-mos forward	.013054	76.60	-5.6	**Jordan** dinar	1.4095	.7095	0.1
Malaysia ringgit	.3147	3.1775	5.1	**Kuwait** dinar	3.5945	.2782	-1.3
New Zealand dollar	.7776	1.2860	0.3	**Lebanon** pound	.0006645	1504.95	0.4
Pakistan rupee	.01113	89.845	4.9	**Saudi Arabia** riyal	.2666	3.7504	unch
Philippines peso	.0228	43.850	0.3	**South Africa** rand	.1237	8.0873	22.2
Singapore dollar	.7713	1.2965	1.1	**UAE** dirham	.2722	3.6731	unch
South Korea won	.0008616	1160.60	5.6				
Taiwan dollar	.03304	30.265	4.2	*Floating rate †Financial §Government rate			
Thailand baht	.03165	31.600	7.3	‡Russian Central Bank rate **Commercial rate			
Vietnam dong	.00004753	21038	8.2	Source: ICAP plc.			

Multiplication and Division Shortcuts for Decimals

The shortcut steps that follow show how to solve multiplication and division problems quickly involving multiples of 10 (10, 100, 1,000, 10,000, etc.).

SHORTCUTS FOR MULTIPLES OF 10

Multiplication

Step 1. Count the zeros in the multiplier.

Step 2. Move the decimal point in the multiplicand the same number of places to the right as you have zeros in the multiplier.

Division

Step 1. Count the zeros in the divisor.

Step 2. Move the decimal point in the dividend the same number of places to the left as you have zeros in the divisor.

LO 3

© Zumawirewestphotostwo/Newscom

In multiplication, the answers are *larger* than the original number.

EXAMPLE   If Toyota spends $60,000 for magazine advertising, what is the total value if it spends this same amount for 10 years? What would be the total cost?

$$\$60,000 \times 10 = \boxed{\$600,000}$$ (1 place to the right)

OTHER EXAMPLES $6.89 \times 10 = \boxed{68.9}$ (1 place to the right)

$6.89 \times 100 = \boxed{689.}$ (2 places to the right)

$6.89 \times 1,000 = \boxed{6,890.}$ (3 places to the right)

In division, the answers are *smaller* than the original number.

EXAMPLES $6.89 \div 10 = \boxed{.689}$ (1 place to the left)

$6.89 \div 100 = \boxed{.0689}$ (2 places to the left)

$6.89 \div 1,000 = \boxed{.00689}$ (3 places to the left)

$6.89 \div 10,000 = \boxed{.000689}$ (4 places to the left)

Next, let's dissect and solve a word problem.

How to Dissect and Solve a Word Problem

The Word Problem May O'Mally went to Sears to buy wall-to-wall carpet. She needs 101.3 square yards for downstairs, 16.3 square yards for the upstairs bedrooms, and 6.2 square yards for the halls. The carpet cost $14.55 per square yard. The padding cost $3.25 per square yard. Sears quoted an installation charge of $6.25 per square yard. What was May O'Mally's total cost?

By completing the following blueprint aid, we will slowly dissect this word problem. Note that before solving the problem, we gather the facts, identify what we are solving for, and list the steps that must be completed before finding the final answer, along with any key points we should remember. Let's go to it!

MONEY tips

Formula for Financial Success: Reduce Spending + Decrease Debt + Increase Savings (Investing) = Healthy Net Worth

	The facts	Solving for?	Steps to take	Key points
BLUEPRINT	*Carpet needed:* 101.3 sq. yd.; 16.3 sq. yd.; 6.2 sq. yd. *Costs:* Carpet, $14.55 per sq. yd.; padding, $3.25 per sq. yd.; installation, $6.25 per sq. yd.	Total cost of carpet, padding, and installation.	Total square yards × Cost per square yard = Total cost.	Align decimals. Round answer to nearest cent.

Steps to solving problem

1. Calculate the total number of square yards.

$$
\begin{array}{r}
101.3 \\
16.3 \\
6.2 \\
\hline
123.8 \text{ square yards}
\end{array}
$$

2. Calculate the total cost per square yard.

$$
\begin{array}{r}
\$14.55 \\
3.25 \\
6.25 \\
\hline
\$24.05
\end{array}
$$

3. Calculate the total cost of carpet, padding, and installation.

123.8 × $24.05 = $2,977.39

It's time to check your progress.

LU 3–2 PRACTICE QUIZ

Complete this **Practice Quiz** to see how you are doing.

1. Rearrange vertically and add:
14, .642, 9.34, 15.87321

2. Rearrange and subtract:
28.1549 − .885

3. Multiply and round the answer to the nearest tenth:
28.53 × 17.4

4. Divide and round to the nearest hundredth:
2,182 ÷ 2.83

Complete by the shortcut method:

5. 14.28 × 100   **6.** 9,680 ÷ 1,000   **7.** 9,812 ÷ 10,000

8. Could you help Mel decide which product is the "better buy"?

   Dog food A: $9.01 for 64 ounces   **Dog food B:** $7.95 for 50 ounces
Round to the nearest cent as needed.

9. At Avis Rent-A-Car, the cost per day to rent a medium-size car is $39.99 plus 29 cents per mile. What will it cost to rent this car for 2 days if you drive 602.3 miles? Since the solution shows a completed blueprint, you might use a blueprint also.

10. A trip to Mexico cost 6,000 pesos. What would this be in U.S. dollars? Check your answer.

✓ **Solutions**

1.
$$
\begin{array}{r}
14.00000 \\
.64200 \\
9.34000 \\
15.87321 \\
\hline
39.85521
\end{array}
$$

2.
$$
\begin{array}{r}
^{7\ 101414} \\
28.\cancel{1}\cancel{5}\cancel{4}9 \\
-\ .8850 \\
\hline
27.2699
\end{array}
$$

3.
$$
\begin{array}{r}
28.53 \\
\times\ 17.4 \\
\hline
11\ 412 \\
199\ 71 \\
285\ 3 \\
\hline
496.422
\end{array} = \boxed{496.4}
$$

4.
$$
\begin{array}{r}
771.024 = 771.02 \\
2.83\overline{)218200.000} \\
1981 \\
\hline
2010 \\
1981 \\
\hline
290 \\
283 \\
\hline
7\ 00 \\
5\ 66 \\
\hline
1\ 340 \\
1\ 132
\end{array}
$$

5. 14.28 = 1,428   **6.** 9.680 = 9.680   **7.** .9812 = .9812

8. **A:** $9.01 ÷ 64 = $.14   **B:** $7.95 ÷ 50 = $.16   Buy A.

9. Avis Rent-A-Car total rental charge:

	The facts	Solving for?	Steps to take	Key points
BLUEPRINT	Cost per day, $39.99. 29 cents per mile. Drove 602.3 miles. 2-day rental.	Total rental charge.	Total cost for 2 days' rental + Total cost of driving = Total rental charge.	In multiplication, count the number of decimal places. Starting from right to left in the product, insert decimal in appropriate place. Round to nearest cent.

Steps to solving problem

1. Calculate total costs for 2 days' rental. $39.99 $\times$ 2 = $79.98

2. Calculate the total cost of driving. $.29 $\times$ 602.3 = $174.667 = $174.67

3. Calculate the total rental charge.
$$\begin{array}{r} \$\,79.98 \\ +\,174.67 \\ \hline \$254.65 \end{array}$$

10. 6,000 $\times$ $.0717 = $430.20

   Check $430.20 $\times$ 13.9461 = 5,999.61 pesos due to rounding

---

LU 3–2a   EXTRA PRACTICE QUIZ WITH WORKED-OUT SOLUTIONS

Need more practice? Try this **Extra Practice Quiz** (check figures in the Interactive Chapter Organizer, p. 79). Worked-out Solutions can be found in Appendix B at end of text.

1. Rearrange vertically and add:
   16, .831, 9.85, 17.8321

2. Rearrange and subtract:
   29.5832 − .998

3. Multiply and round the answer to the nearest tenth:
   29.64 $\times$ 18.2

4. Divide and round to the nearest hundredth:
   3,824 ÷ 4.94

Complete by the shortcut method:

5. 17.48 $\times$ 100   6. 8,432 ÷ 1,000   7. 9,643 ÷ 10,000

8. Could you help Mel decide which product is the "better buy"?
   Dog food A: $8.88 for 64 ounces   **Dog food B:** $7.25 for 50 ounces

Round to the nearest cent as needed:

9. At Avis Rent-A-Car, the cost per day to rent a medium-size car is $29.99 plus 22 cents per mile. What will it cost to rent this car for 2 days if you drive 709.8 miles?

10. A trip to Mexico costs 7,000 pesos. What would this be in U.S. dollars? Check your answer.

INTERACTIVE CHAPTER ORGANIZER

Topic/procedure/formula	Examples	You try it*
Identifying place value, p. 67 $10, 1, \dfrac{1}{10}, \dfrac{1}{100}, \dfrac{1}{1,000},$ etc.	.439 in thousandths place value	**Identify place value** .8256
Rounding decimals, p. 67 1. Identify place value of digit you want to round. 2. If digit to right of identified digit in Step 1 is 5 or more, increase identified digit by 1; if less than 5, do not change identified digit. 3. Drop all digits to right of identified digit.	.875 rounded to nearest tenth = .9 Identified digit	**Round to nearest tenth** .841
Converting decimal fractions to decimals, p. 68 1. Decimal fraction has a denominator with multiples of 10. Count number of zeros in denominator. 2. Zeros show how many places are in the decimal.	$\dfrac{8}{1,000} = .008$ $\dfrac{6}{10,000} = .0006$	**Convert to decimal** $\dfrac{9}{1,000}$ $\dfrac{3}{10,000}$
Converting proper fractions to decimals, p. 69 1. Divide numerator of fraction by its denominator. 2. Round as necessary.	$\dfrac{1}{3}$ (to nearest tenth) = .3	**Convert to decimal (to nearest tenth)** $\dfrac{1}{7}$
Converting mixed numbers to decimals, p. 69 1. Convert fractional part of the mixed number to a decimal. 2. Add converted fractional part to whole number.	$6\dfrac{1}{4}$ $\dfrac{1}{4} = .25 + 6 = 6.25$	**Convert to decimal** $5\dfrac{4}{5}$
Converting pure and mixed decimals to decimal fractions, p. 69 1. Place digits to right of decimal point in numerator of fraction. 2. Put 1 in denominator. 3. Add zeros to denominator, depending on decimal places of original number. For mixed decimals, add fraction to whole number.	.984 (3 places) 1. $\dfrac{984}{}$ 2. $\dfrac{984}{1}$ 3. $\dfrac{984}{1,000}$	**Convert to fraction** .865

Adding and subtracting decimals, p. 71
1. Vertically write and align numbers on decimal points.
2. Add or subtract digits, starting with right column and moving to the left.
3. Align decimal point in answer with above decimal points.
	Add 1.3 + 2 + .4
	1.3
	2.0
	.4
	——
	3.7
	Subtract 5 − 3.9 $\overset{4\ 10}{\cancel{5}.\cancel{0}}$
	           −3.9
	          ——
	          1.1
		Add
		1.7 + 3 + .8
		
		Subtract
		6 − 4.1

Multiplying decimals, p. 73 1. Multiply numbers, ignoring decimal points. 2. Count and total number of decimal places in multiplier and multiplicand. 3. Starting at right in the product, count to the left the number of decimal places totaled in Step 2. Insert decimal point. If number of places greater than space in answer, add zeros.	2.48 (2 places) × .018 (3 places) ——— 1 984 2 48 ——— .04464	**Multiply** 3.49 × .015

(continues)

INTERACTIVE CHAPTER ORGANIZER

Topic/procedure/formula	Examples	You try it*
Dividing a decimal by a whole number, p. 73 1. Place decimal point in quotient directly above the decimal point in dividend. 2. Divide as usual.	$$\begin{array}{r} 1.1 \\ 42\overline{)46.2} \\ \underline{42} \\ 42 \\ \underline{42} \end{array}$$	**Divide (to nearest tenth)** $33\overline{)49.5}$
Dividing if the divisor is a decimal, p. 73 1. Make divisor a whole number by moving decimal point to the right. 2. Move decimal point in dividend to the right the same number of places as in Step 1. 3. Place decimal point in quotient above decimal point in dividend. Divide as usual.	$$\begin{array}{r} 14.2 \\ 2.9\overline{)41.39} \\ \underline{29} \\ 123 \\ \underline{116} \\ 79 \\ \underline{58} \\ 21 \end{array}$$	**Divide (to nearest tenth)** $3.2\overline{)1.48}$
Shortcuts on multiplication and division of decimals, p. 74 When multiplying by 10, 100, 1,000, and so on, move decimal point in multiplicand the same number of places to the right as you have zeros in multiplier. For division, move decimal point to the left.	$4.85 \times 100 =$ 485 $4.85 \div 100 =$ .0485	**Multiply by shortcut** 6.92×100 **Divide by shortcut** $6.92 \div 100$

KEY TERMS	Decimal, *p. 66* Decimal fraction, *p. 68* Decimal point, *p. 66*	Mixed decimal, *p. 69* Pure decimal, *p. 69* Repeating decimal, *p. 67*	Rounding decimals, *p. 67*

Check Figures for Extra Practice Quizzes with Page References. (Worked-out Solutions in Appendix B.)	LU 3–1a (p. 71)		LU 3–2a (p. 77)	

	1. .309
	2. Hundredths
	3. Ten-thousandths
	4. A. .8
	   B. .844
	5. A. .9
	   B. .879
	6. .0008
	7. .00016
		8. $\frac{938}{1,000}$
		9. $17\frac{95}{100}$
		10. $\frac{325}{10,000}$
		11. .13
		12. .57
		13. 13.11
			1. 44.5131
			2. 28.5852
			3. 539.4
			4. 774.09
			5. 1,748
				6. 8.432
				7. .9643
				8. Buy A $.14
				9. $216.14
				10. $501.90

Note: For how to dissect and solve a word problem, see page 75.

*Worked-out solutions are in Appendix B.

Critical Thinking Discussion Questions with Chapter Concept Check

1. What are the steps for rounding decimals? Federal income tax forms allow the taxpayer to round each amount to the nearest dollar. Do you agree with this?

2. Explain how to convert fractions to decimals. If 1 out of 20 people buys a Land Rover, how could you write an advertisement in decimals?

3. Explain why .07, .70, and .700 are not equal. Assume you take a family trip to Disney World that covers 500 miles. Show that $\frac{8}{10}$ of the trip, or .8 of the trip, represents 400 miles.

4. Explain the steps in the addition or subtraction of decimals. Visit a car dealership and find the difference between two sticker prices. Be sure to check each sticker price for accuracy. Should you always pay the sticker price?

5. **Chapter Concept Check.** In the chapter opener, the e-book was compared to a print book through the use of whole numbers and decimals. Visit a publisher's website and calculate the difference between the prices for a printed text and an e-book. Estimate what you think the profit is to the publisher based on what you read in the chapter opener.

Classroom Notes

END-OF-CHAPTER PROBLEMS

Check figures for odd-numbered problems in Appendix C.   Name _____ Date _____

DRILL PROBLEMS

Identify the place value for the following: *LU 3-1(1)*

3–1. 7.9382 ↑

3–2. 462.8391 ↑

Round the following as indicated: *LU 3-1(1)*

	Tenth	**Hundredth**	**Thousandth**
3–3. .7391			
3–4. 6.8629			
3–5. 5.8312			
3–6. 6.8415			
3–7. 6.5555			
3–8. 75.9913			

Round the following to the nearest cent: *LU 3-1(1)*

3–9. $4,822.775

3–10. $4,892.046

Convert the following types of decimal fractions to decimals (round to nearest hundredth as needed): *LU 3-1(2)*

3–11. $\dfrac{8}{100}$

3–12. $\dfrac{3}{10}$

3–13. $\dfrac{61}{1,000}$

3–14. $\dfrac{610}{1,000}$

3–15. $\dfrac{91}{100}$

3–16. $\dfrac{979}{1,000}$

3–17. $16\dfrac{61}{100}$

Convert the following decimals to fractions. Do not reduce to lowest terms. *LU 3-1(2)*

3–18. .9

3–19. .71

3–20. .009

3–21. .0125

3–22. .609

3–23. .825

3–24. .9999

3–25. .7065

Convert the following to mixed numbers. Do not reduce to the lowest terms. *LU 3-1(2)*

3–26. 7.1

3–27. 28.48

3–28. 6.025

Write the decimal equivalent of the following: *LU 3-1(2)*

3–29. Five thousandths

3–30. Three hundred three and two hundredths

3–31. Eighty-five ten thousandths

3–32. Seven hundred seventy-five thousandths

Rearrange the following and add: *LU 3-2(1)*

3–33. .115, 10.8318, 4.7, 802.4811

3–34. .005, 2,002.181, 795.41, 14.0, .184

Rearrange the following and subtract: *LU 3-2(1)*

3–35. 9.2 − 5.8

3–36. 7 − 2.0815

3–37. 3.4 − 1.08

Estimate by rounding all the way and multiply the following (do not round final answer): *LU 3-2(1)*

3–38. 6.24 × 3.9

Estimate

3–39. .413 × 3.07

Estimate

3–40. 675 × 1.92

Estimate

3–41. 4.9 × .825

Estimate

Divide the following and round to the nearest hundredth: *LU 3-2(1)*

3–42. .8931 ÷ 3

3–43. 29.432 ÷ .0012

3–44. .0065 ÷ .07

3–45. 7,742.1 ÷ 48

3–46. 8.95 ÷ 1.18

3–47. 2,600 ÷ .381

Convert the following to decimals and round to the nearest hundredth: *LU 3-1(2)*

3–48. $\frac{1}{8}$

3–49. $\frac{1}{25}$

3–50. $\frac{5}{6}$

3–51. $\frac{5}{8}$

Complete these multiplications and divisions by the shortcut method (do not do any written calculations):   *LU 3-2(3)*

3–52. 96.7 ÷ 10

3–53. 258.5 ÷ 100

3–54. 8.51 × 1,000

3–55. .86 ÷ 100

3–56. 9.015 × 100

3–57. 48.6 × 10

3–58. 750 × 10

3–59. 3,950 ÷ 1,000

3–60. 8.45 ÷ 10

3–61. 7.9132 × 1,000

WORD PROBLEMS

As needed, round answers to the nearest cent.

3–62. A Chevy Volt costs $29,000 in the United States. Using the exchange rate given on page 74, what would it cost in Canada? Check your answer.   *LU 3-2(2)*

3–63. Dustin Pedroia got 7 hits out of 12 at bats. What was his batting average to the nearest thousandths place?   *LU 3-1(2)*

3–64. Pete Ross read in a *Wall Street Journal* article that the cost of parts and labor to make an Apple iPhone 4S were as follows: *LU 3-2(1)*

Display	$37.00	Wireless	$23.54
Memory	$28.30	Camera	$17.60
Labor	$ 8.00	Additional items	$81.56

Assuming Pete pays $649 for an iPhone 4S, how much profit does the iPhone generate?

3–65. At the Party Store, Joan Lee purchased 21.50 yards of ribbon. Each yard costs 91 cents. What was the total cost of the ribbon? Round to the nearest cent.   *LU 3-2(1)*

3–66. Douglas Noel went to Home Depot and bought four doors at $42.99 each and six bags of fertilizer at $8.99 per bag. What was the total cost to Douglas? If Douglas had $300 in his pocket, what does he have left to spend?   *LU 3-2(1)*

3–67. The stock of Intel has a high of $30.25 today. It closed at $28.85. How much did the stock drop from its high?   *LU 3-2(1)*

3–68. Pete is traveling by car to a computer convention in San Diego. His company will reimburse him $.48 per mile. If Pete travels 210.5 miles, how much will Pete receive from his company?   *LU 3-2(1)*

3–69. Mark Ogara rented a truck from Avis Rent-A-Car for the weekend (2 days). The base rental price was $29.95 per day plus $14\frac{1}{2}$ cents per mile. Mark drove 410.85 miles. How much does Mark owe?   *LU 3-2(1)*

3–70. Nursing home costs are on the rise as consumeraffairs.com reports in its quarterly newsletter. The average cost is around $192 a day with an average length of stay of 2.5 years. Calculate the cost of the average nursing home stay. *LU 3-2(1)*

3–71. Bob Ross bought a Blackberry on the web for $89.99. He saw the same Blackberry in the mall for $118.99. How much did Bob save by buying on the web? *LU 3-2(1)*

3–72. Russell is preparing the daily bank deposit for his coffee shop. Before the deposit, the coffee shop had a checking account balance of $3,185.66. The deposit contains the following checks:

No. 1	$ 99.50	No. 3	$8.75
No. 2	110.35	No. 4	6.83

Russell included $820.55 in currency with the deposit. What is the coffee shop's new balance, assuming Russell writes no new checks? *LU 3-2(1)*

3–73. Facebook announced it is going public in 2012. As a result, billionaires and millionaires will be created in a scenario similar to what happened when Microsoft and Google went public. Facebook's founder, Mark Zuckerberg, 27 years old, has 533.8 million shares in Facebook worth $28.4 billion. Peter Thiel, Facebook's first outside investor, has 44.7 million shares. Accel Partners has 201.4 million shares. Marc Andreessen, Netscape's founder, has 3.6 million shares. Sheryl Sandberg, the COO of Facebook, has 1.9 million shares. What is the total number of shares owned by these individuals? *LU 3-2(1)*

3–74. Randi went to Lowe's to buy wall-to-wall carpeting. She needs 110.8 square yards for downstairs, 31.8 square yards for the halls, and 161.9 square yards for the bedrooms upstairs. Randi chose a shag carpet that costs $14.99 per square yard. She ordered foam padding at $3.10 per square yard. The carpet installers quoted Randi a labor charge of $3.75 per square yard. What will the total job cost Randi? *LU 3-2(1)*

3–75. Paul Rey bought four new Dunlop tires at Goodyear for $95.99 per tire. Goodyear charged $3.05 per tire for mounting, $2.95 per tire for valve stems, and $3.80 per tire for balancing. If Paul paid no sales tax, what was his total cost for the four tires? *LU 3-2(1)*

3–76. Shelly is shopping for laundry detergent, mustard, and canned tuna. She is trying to decide which of two products is the better buy. Using the following information, can you help Shelly? *LU 3-2(1)*

Laundry detergent A	Mustard A	Canned tuna A
$2.00 for 37 ounces	$.88 for 6 ounces	$1.09 for 6 ounces

Laundry detergent B	Mustard B	Canned tuna B
$2.37 for 38 ounces	$1.61 for $12\frac{1}{2}$ ounces	$1.29 for $8\frac{3}{4}$ ounces

3–77. Roger bought season tickets for weekend games to professional basketball games. The cost was $945.60. The season pack-
eXcel age included 36 home games. What is the average price of the tickets per game? Round to the nearest cent. Marcelo, Roger's
friend, offered to buy four of the tickets from Roger. What is the total amount Roger should receive? *LU 3-2(1)*

3–78. A nurse was to give each of her patients a 1.32-unit dosage of a prescribed drug. The total remaining units of the drug at
the hospital pharmacy were 53.12. The nurse has 38 patients. Will there be enough dosages for all her patients? *LU 3-2(1)*

3–79. Jill Horn went to Japan and bought an animation cel of Spongebob. The price was 25,000 yen. Using the *Wall Street Journal*
currency table on page 74, what is the price in U.S. dollars? Check your answer. *LU 3-2(2)*

ADDITIONAL SET OF WORD PROBLEMS

3–80. As *USA TODAY* reported early in 2012, the U.S. debt is now larger than the U.S. economy. The debt is $15.23 trillion while
the value of all goods and services the U.S. economy produces in 1 year is $15.17 trillion. How much more debt in trillions
does the United States have than it produces each year? *LU 3-2(1)*

3–81. Eastman Kodak announced in a January 19, 2012, press release that it has filed for bankruptcy protection. The 131-year-
old company has struggled to adapt to the digital world and has incurred far more debt than assets. The company reported
it has $5.1 billion in assets and nearly $6.8 billion in debt. How much more does it have in debt than assets? *LU 3-2(1)*

3–82. Morris Katz bought four new tires at Goodyear for $95.49 per tire. Goodyear also charged Morris $2.50 per tire for mounting,
$2.40 per tire for valve stems, and $3.95 per tire for balancing. Assume no tax. What was Morris's total cost for the four
tires? *LU 3-2(1)*

3–83. The *Denver Post* reported that Xcel Energy is revising customer charges for monthly residential electric bills and gas bills.
Electric bills will increase $3.32. Gas bills will decrease $1.74 a month. **(a)** What is the resulting new monthly increase for
the entire bill? **(b)** If Xcel serves 2,350 homes, how much additional revenue would Xcel receive each month? *LU 3-2(1)*

3–84. Steven is traveling to an auto show by car. His company will reimburse him $.29 per mile. If Steven travels 890.5 miles,
how much will he receive from his company? *LU 3-2(1)*

3–85. Gracie went to Home Depot to buy wall-to-wall carpeting for her house. She needs 104.8 square yards for downstairs,
17.4 square yards for halls, and 165.8 square yards for the upstairs bedrooms. Gracie chose a shag carpet that costs
$13.95 per square yard. She ordered foam padding at $2.75 per square yard. The installers quoted Gracie a labor cost of
$5.75 per square yard in installation. What will the total job cost Gracie? *LU 3-2(1)*

CHALLENGE PROBLEMS

3–86. Fred and Winnie O'Callahan have put themselves on a very strict budget. Their goal at the end of the year is to buy a car
eXcel for $14,000 in cash. Their budget includes the following per dollar:

        $.40 food and lodging
         .20 entertainment
         .10 educational

Fred earns $2,000 per month and Winnie earns $2,500 per month. After 1 year will Fred and Winnie have enough cash to buy the car?   *LU 3-2(1)*

3–87. Jill and Frank decided to take a long weekend in New York. City Hotel has a special getaway weekend for $79.95. The price is per person per night, based on double occupancy. The hotel has a minimum two-night stay. For this price, Jill and Frank will receive $50 credit toward their dinners at City's Skylight Restaurant. Also included in the package is a $3.99 credit per person toward breakfast for two each morning.

Since Jill and Frank do not own a car, they plan to rent a car. The car rental agency charges $19.95 a day with an additional charge of $.22 a mile and $1.19 per gallon of gas used. The gas tank holds 24 gallons.

From the following facts, calculate the total expenses of Jill and Frank (round all answers to nearest hundredth or cent as appropriate). Assume no taxes.   *LU 3-2(1)*

Car rental (2 days):		Dinner cost at Skylight	$182.12
Beginning odometer reading	4,820	Breakfast for two:	
Ending odometer reading	4,940	Morning No. 1	24.17
Beginning gas tank: $\frac{3}{4}$ full		Morning No. 2	26.88
Gas tank on return: $\frac{1}{2}$ full		Hotel room	79.95
Tank holds 24 gallons			

 SUMMARY PRACTICE TEST

Do you need help? The DVD has step-by-step worked-out solutions. You Tube™

1. Add the following by translating the verbal form to the decimal equivalent. *(pp. 67, 71)*   *LU 3-1(1), LU 3-2(1)*

   Three hundred thirty-eight and seven hundred five thousandths
   Nineteen and fifty-nine hundredths
   Five and four thousandths
   Seventy-five hundredths
   Four hundred three and eight tenths

Convert the following decimal fractions to decimals. *(p. 68)*   *LU 3-1(2)*

2. $\dfrac{7}{10}$

3. $\dfrac{7}{100}$

4. $\dfrac{7}{1,000}$

Convert the following to proper fractions or mixed numbers. Do not reduce to the lowest terms. *(p. 69)* *LU 3-1(2)*

5. .9

6. 6.97

7. .685

Convert the following fractions to decimals (or mixed decimals) and round to the nearest hundredth as needed. *(p. 69)* *LU 3-1(2)*

8. $\frac{2}{7}$

9. $\frac{1}{8}$

10. $4\frac{4}{7}$

11. $\frac{1}{13}$

12. Rearrange the following decimals and add. *(p. 71)* *LU 3-2(1)*

5.93,   11.862,   284.0382,   88.44

13. Subtract the following and round to the nearest tenth. *(p. 72)* *LU 3-2(1)*

13.111 − 3.872

14. Multiply the following and round to the nearest hundredth. *(p. 73)* *LU 3-2(1)*

7.4821 × 15.861

15. Divide the following and round to the nearest hundredth. *(p. 73)* *LU 3-2(1)*

203,942 ÷ 5.88

Complete the following by the shortcut method. *(p. 74)* *LU 3-2(3)*

16. 62.94 × 1,000

17. 8,322,249.821 × 100

18. The average pay of employees is $795.88 per week. Lee earns $820.44 per week. How much is Lee's pay over the average? *(p. 72)* *LU 3-2(1)*

19. Lowes reimburses Ron $.49 per mile. Ron submitted a travel log for a total of 1,910.81 miles. How much will Lowes reimburse Ron? Round to the nearest cent. *(p. 73)* *LU 3-2(1)*

20. Lee Chin bought two new car tires from Michelin for $182.11 per tire. Michelin also charged Lee $3.99 per tire for mounting, $2.50 per tire for valve stems, and $4.10 per tire for balancing. What is Lee's final bill? *(pp. 71, 73)* *LU 3-2(1)*

21. Could you help Judy decide which of the following products is cheaper per ounce? *(p. 73)* *LU 3-2(1)*

Canned fruit A

$.37 for 3 ounces

Canned fruit B

$.58 for $3\frac{3}{4}$ ounces

22. Paula Smith bought a computer tablet for 350 euros. Using the *Wall Street Journal* currency table on page 74, what is this price in U.S. dollars? *(p. 74)* *LU 3-2(2)*

23. Google stock traded at a high of $438.22 and closed at $410.12. How much did the stock fall from its high? *(p. 72)* *LU 3-2(1)*

SURF TO SAVE

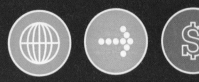

How far does your money go? 🔍

PROBLEM 1
Get ready for your new job

Go to http://www.officemax.com. Choose an expensive pen, briefcase, and portfolio. If you were to order all three of these items for your new job, how much would they cost before taxes? (Assume shipping on your order is free.) Assuming your sales tax is 6%, how much would you pay in sales tax on this purchase? Note: Expensive pens are found under "Fine & Better" pens in the pen section. Searching for "Briefcase" is the easiest way to find briefcases at the site.

Discussion Questions

1. What other expenses will you most likely incur as you start your new career?

2. How will these expenses impact the starting salary you will need to earn?

PROBLEM 2
Dollars and yen

Go to http://www.oanda.com/converter/classic. Suppose you converted $10,000 to Japanese yen on July 24, 2004. If you convert those yen back to dollars at today's exchange rate, how much money would you have?

Discussion Questions

1. What did you notice in the conversion of these monetary amounts based on the date of the conversion?

2. What does this tell you about the state of the economy in the U.S. versus Japan?

PROBLEM 3
Affordable trades

Go to http://www.kiplinger.com/columns/ask/archive/2004/q0105.htm. Read the "Ask Kim" question and answer by Kimberly Lankford. At the price quoted in the article for BuyandHold's lower-priced ($6.99) service, how much would it cost to make three trades per month for 1 year?

Discussion Questions

1. Assume you made three trades per month for an entire year. How much would you need to earn in profit on each trade to cover your yearly expense for these trades?

2. How comfortable are you in making such stock trades? By how much would the individual investments have to change in value to encourage you to make these trades? Why?

PROBLEM 4
Mind over matter

Airlines charge almost $200 if a suitcase weighs more than 50 pounds. The skycap tells you your suitcase weighs 22 kilograms. You think that each kilogram is equal to 2.2 pounds. Do you owe additional fees for an overweight suitcase? Use the converter at http://www.metric-conversions.org/weight/kilograms-to-pounds.htm to verify your answer.

Discussion Questions

1. Why do you think airlines charge for overweight baggage and additional baggage?

2. Do these fees impact which airline you fly?

MOBILE APPS ✕

Equations with Decimals (YourTeacher.com) Provides a tutorial on decimals.

Fractions to Decimal and vice versa (Essence Computing) Assists in the conversion of fractions to their decimal equivalents and vice versa.

INTERNET PROJECTS ✕

See text website
www.mhhe.com/slater11e_sse_ch03

Cash In Your Old Electronics

You may be surprised at how much some online retailers will pay. BY JEFF BERTOLUCCI

YOU PROBABLY HAVE PLENTY of old electronic gizmos and gadgets tucked away in drawers. It's easy to convert those cell phones, computers, iPods and movie DVDs into quick cash.

A number of big-name shopping sites, including Amazon, Best Buy, eBay and Gazelle, will offer cash or store credit for your gear. The process is quick and painless, and you won't have to pay shipping costs—even if the buyer rejects your stuff and returns it. Although you may earn more by auctioning gear on eBay, it's hard to top the simplicity of the cash-for-electronics marketplaces.

You'll often get top dollar for trading in high-demand items (such as anything from Apple). That's the case with Gazelle. Gazelle chief gadget officer Anthony Scarsella says you can estimate what you'd get for your used item by seeing what it's selling for at the Gazelle stores on Amazon and eBay. Figure you'll get 10% to 20% less because the merchants add a markup.

Easy sell. As you might expect from the world's top e-tailer, Amazon has an extremely user-friendly interface with its Trade-In Store. The site accepts trade-ins for store credit in four categories: Books, Video Games, Movies & TV (on DVD), and Electronics. To submit an item, you enter the product's name in a search window, then answer a few questions about its condition. If Amazon is interested, you'll get an offer on the spot. If Amazon decides, upon receiving your device, that the product is worth less than its original offer, you can accept a reduced price or have it returned at no charge.

I gave the service a try. Amazon offered $63.25 for my Apple iPod nano, which was a few years old but in excellent condition. I accepted the offer and printed Amazon's free UPS mailing label, which popped up in a browser window. Next, I boxed up the iPod and dropped it off at the nearest UPS store. Painless. Within two weeks, Amazon e-mailed that it had accepted my iPod and credited my gift-card balance.

Could I have made more by auctioning the device on eBay? Probably. I checked eBay and discovered that bidders were offering up to $100 for iPod models similar to mine. Lesson learned: If you want top dollar, trade-ins aren't necessarily the way to go—though getting a good price at auction is always a gamble.

The eBay difference. EBay's Instant Sale works pretty much the same way as Amazon's Trade-In Store, albeit with a notable difference. Unlike Amazon, eBay gives you cash, not store credit. The fastest way to get paid is to open an account with eBay's PayPal service (if you haven't already), then transfer the funds to your checking account.

EBay offered $36.35 for my Apple TV video-streaming device, sight unseen. After examining it, however, eBay lowered the offer to $30.90; "visible scratches" were to blame, they said. (What scratches? I wondered. Am I blind?)

Nevertheless, I accepted the lower offer, mostly because it was higher than competing trade-in sites were willing to pay. Gazelle, for instance, offered just $27, and Amazon wasn't interested in my Apple device at all.

In addition to eBay, other sites offer cash, including Gazelle (www.gazelle.com). Gazelle also operates online trade-in services for big-name retailers, such as Costco and Walmart. If you'd rather not pack up your gear, take it to a participating Best Buy or Radio Shack store, where someone will appraise and buy your products on the spot. Many trade-in services offer to recycle your device free if they don't want to buy it.

Always compare prices at several sites before you accept an offer. While you're at it, surf over to eBay to see how much sellers and auctioneers are asking for your product. ∎

HOW MUCH YOU'LL POCKET

Here's a list of in-demand electronics at two major buyers, and an idea of how much they'll pay.

Trade-in service	Most popular electronic trade-ins	Trade-in price*
Amazon	Apple iPod touch 8GB (Black, 4th generation)	$109
	Amazon Kindle 3G	$30
	Garmin nuvi 2555LMT GPS Navigator	$87
	Garmin nuvi 1450LMT GPS Navigator	$74
Gazelle	Apple iPhone 3GS	$132
	Apple iPhone 3G	$62
	Apple iPhone 4	$187
	Apple iPad 2	$380
	BlackBerry Torch 9800	$79

*Amazon's prices are maximum offered for the product; Gazelle's are average selling prices for February 2012.

A Word Problem Approach—Chapters 1, 2, 3

1. The top rate at the Waldorf Towers Hotel in New York is $390. The top rate at the Ritz Carlton in Boston is $345. If John spends 9 days at the hotel, how much can he save if he stays at the Ritz? *(pp. 10, 14)* *LU 1-2(2), LU 1-3(1)*

2. Robert Half Placement Agency was rated best by 4 to 1 in an independent national survey. If 250,000 responded to the survey, how many rated Robert Half the best? *(p. 47)* *LU 2-3(1)*

3. Of the 63.2 million people who watch professional football, only $\frac{1}{5}$ watch the commercials. How many viewers do not watch the commercials? *(p. 47)* *LU 2-3(1)*

4. AT&T advertised a 10-minute call for $2.27. MCI WorldCom's rate was $2.02. Assuming Bill Splat makes forty 10-minute calls, how much could he save by using MCI WorldCom? *(pp. 72–73)* *LU 3-2(1)*

5. A square foot of rental space in New York City, Boston, and Providence costs as follows: New York City, $6.25; Boston, $5.75; and Providence, $3.75. If Compaq Computer wants to rent 112,500 square feet of space, what will Compaq save by renting in Providence rather than Boston? *(pp. 72–73)* *LU 3-2(1)*

6. American Airlines has a frequent-flier program. Coupon brokers who buy and sell these awards pay between 1 and $1\frac{1}{2}$ cents for each mile earned. Fred Dietrich earned a 50,000-mile award (worth two free tickets to any city). If Fred decided to sell his award to a coupon broker, approximately how much would he receive? *(p. 71)* *LU 3-2(1)*

7. Lillie Wong bought four new Firestone tires at $82.99 each. Firestone also charged $2.80 per tire for mounting, $1.95 per tire for valves, and $3.15 per tire for balancing. Lillie turned her four old tires in to Firestone, which charged $1.50 per tire to dispose of them. What was Lillie's final bill? *(p. 72)* *LU 3-2(1)*

8. Tootsie Roll Industries bought Charms Company for $65 million. Some analysts believe that in 4 years the purchase price could rise to three times as much. If the analysts are right, how much did Tootsie Roll save by purchasing Charms immediately? *(p. 14)* *LU 1-3(1)*

9. Today the average business traveler will spend $47.73 a day on food. The breakdown is dinner, $22.26; lunch, $10.73; breakfast, $6.53; tips, $6.23; and tax, $1.98. If Clarence Donato, an executive for Honeywell, spends only .33 of the average, what is Clarence's total cost for food for the day? If Clarence wanted to spend $\frac{1}{3}$ more than the average on the next day, what would be his total cost on the second day? Round to the nearest cent. *(pp. 48, 71)* *LU 2-3(1), LU 3-2(1)*

Be sure you use the fractional equivalent in calculating $.3\overline{3}$.

Banking

Use a Phone for Deposits on the Go

By Emily Glazer

Depositing checks into investment accounts is getting easier—for some.

Both **Charles Schwab** Corp. and **Fidelity Investments** rolled out new software applications at the end of May allowing customers to deposit checks into brokerage accounts with their smartphones. After signing up for the service, customers photograph the front and back of a check with their iPhone or Android, then follow a few steps to send the deposit on its way in minutes.

"We don't have the pervasive locations that traditional banks and [their] ATMs have," says Richard Blunck, Fidelity's executive vice president for Web distribution. A smartphone, he adds, "is a lot better than stamps and mailing."

After registering for mobile deposits, you select which account the deposits will go to. With Schwab, you'll receive an email acknowledging receipt of a check within four hours if it's sent before 4 p.m., or the next business day if it's sent after 4, says Diane Russell, Schwab's senior vice president of platform services.

Deposits by smartphone may arrive faster than checks sent in the mail, but the money won't become available in your account any faster. As with most check deposits, the funds become available within a few days of the deposit, based on regulations and financial institution policies.

After the check clears, Ms. Russell recommends shredding or tearing up the paper. If a check is deposited twice, "by accident or abuse," an error message will appear, she says.

Though neither Schwab nor Fidelity enables direct mobile deposit into retirement accounts, Fidelity allows you to transfer money into retirement accounts using the mobile app, Mr. Blunck says. Schwab does not allow that because of "the complexity of IRS rules governing contributions," according to a Schwab spokeswoman.

A recent Schwab survey found nearly seven in 10 Americans between the ages of 18 and 44 were interested in using their mobile phones to deposit checks, largely based on convenience.

Schwab and Fidelity join a batch of banks—including **J.P. Morgan Chase** & Co., **PNC Financial Services Group** Inc. and **U.S. Bancorp**—that have launched similar applications allowing mobile deposits.

Other investment companies say they are exploring the option, including **Vanguard Group** and **T. Rowe Price Group** Inc. "We're on a journey toward that end," says Chip Weldon, T. Rowe Price's vice president of interactive strategies. But he adds he doesn't anticipate rolling out the service in the next year.

"If you fill out this little card, sir, we can switch over to direct deposit."

w you car
bank anytim
anywh...

Visit www.oc...m/m...
for more det...ay!

LU 4–1: The Checking Account

1. Define and state the purpose of signature cards, checks, deposit slips, check stubs, check registers, and endorsements *(pp. 92–94)*.

2. Correctly prepare deposit slips and write checks *(pp. 92–94)*.

LU 4–2: Bank Statement and Reconciliation Process; Latest Trends in Mobile Banking

1. Explain trends in the banking industry *(p. 96)*.

2. Define and state the purpose of the bank statement *(pp. 96–98)*.

3. Complete a check register and a bank reconciliation *(pp. 98–101)*.

4. Explain the trends in mobile banking *(p. 101)*.

VOCABULARY PREVIEW

Here are key terms in this chapter. After completing the chapter, if you know the term, place a checkmark in the parentheses. If you don't know the term, look it up and put the page number where it can be found.

Automatic teller machine (ATM) ( ) Bank reconciliation ( ) Bank statement ( ) Banking apps ( ) Blank endorsement ( ) Check ( ) Check register ( ) Check stub ( ) Credit memo (CM) ( ) Debit card ( ) Debit memo (DM) ( ) Deposit slip ( ) Deposits in transit ( ) Draft ( ) Drawee ( ) Drawer ( ) Electronic funds transfer (EFT) ( ) Endorse ( ) Full endorsement ( ) Mobile banking ( ) Nonsufficient funds (NSF) ( ) Outstanding checks ( ) Overdrafts ( ) Payee ( ) Restrictive endorsement ( ) Signature card ( )

The *Wall Street Journal* clip "Use a Phone for Deposits on the Go" in the chapter opener shows how technology is affecting your bank transactions. In this chapter we will look at how to do banking transactions manually, followed by a look at the latest trends in banking.

An important fixture in today's banking is the **automatic teller machine (ATM).** The ability to get instant cash is a convenience many bank customers enjoy.

The effect of using an ATM card is the same as using a **debit card**—both transactions result in money being immediately deducted from your checking account balance. As a result, debit cards have been called enhanced ATM cards or *check cards*. Often banks charge fees for these card transactions. The frequent complaints of bank customers have made many banks offer their ATMs as a free service, especially if customers use an ATM in the same network as their bank. Some banks charge fees for using another bank's ATM. The following *Wall Street Journal* clip "ATM Fees Heading Higher" (p. 92) shows how ATM fees are on the rise again.

Remember that the use of debit cards involves planning. As *check cards,* you must be aware of your bank balance every time you use a debit card. Also, if you use a credit card instead of a debit card, you can only be held responsible for $50 of illegal charges; and during the time the credit card company

ATM Fees Heading Higher

BY ROBIN SIDEL

Some of the nation's biggest banks are imposing a variety of new fees on people who withdraw money from automated-teller machines.

The move is the latest example of the burgeoning new fees that banks are imposing on customers accustomed to years of free services. Banks are scrambling to replace billions of dollars in revenue expected to be lost from new federal regulations on overdraft charges and debit cards.

J.P. Morgan Chase & Co., **TD Bank Financial Group**, and **PNC Financial Services Group** already are changing their ATM policies to collect more fees.

J.P. Morgan's Chase retail division, for example, is going after noncustomers who withdraw money from the bank's ATMs, according to people familiar with the matter. Chase executives have grumbled about customers of rival banks using the company's machines even though it charges them $3, which is standard in the banking industry. Chase is now testing fees of $5

and $4 in Illinois and Texas, respectively, for noncustomer withdrawals.

More ATM fee rises are expected in the coming months. As regulations limit certain profitable practices in the industry, the banks are replacing lost funds with new fees. Some financial institutions recently introduced new charges on checking accounts as a way to make up some of the revenue that will be choked from rules imposed by the Dodd-Frank financial-overhaul law.

investigates the illegal charges, they are removed from your account. However, with a debit card, this legal limit only applies if you report your card lost or stolen within two business days.

This chapter begins with a discussion of the checking account. You will follow Molly Kate as she opens a checking account for Gracie's Natural Superstore and performs her banking transactions. Pay special attention to the procedure used by Gracie's to reconcile its checking account and bank statement. This information will help you reconcile your checkbook records with the bank's record of your account. The chapter concludes by discussing the latest technology trends in banking.

Learning Unit 4–1: The Checking Account

LO 1

A **check** or **draft** is a written order instructing a bank, credit union, or savings and loan institution to pay a designated amount of your money on deposit to a person or an organization. Checking accounts are offered to individuals and businesses. Note that the business checking account usually receives more services than the personal checking account but may come with additional fees.

Most small businesses depend on a checking account for efficient record keeping. In this learning unit you will follow the checking account procedures of a newly organized small business. You can use many of these procedures in your personal check writing. You will also learn about e-checks—a new trend.

Opening the Checking Account

Molly Kate, treasurer of Gracie's Natural Superstore, went to Ipswich Bank to open a business checking account. The bank manager gave Molly a **signature card.** The signature card contained space for the company's name and address, references, type of account, and the signature(s) of the person(s) authorized to sign checks. If necessary, the bank will use the signature card to verify that Molly signed the checks. Some companies authorize more than one person to sign checks or require more than one signature on a check.

Molly then lists on a **deposit slip** (or deposit ticket) the checks and/or cash she is depositing in her company's business account. The bank gave Molly a temporary checkbook to use until the company's printed checks arrived. Molly also will receive *preprinted* checking account deposit slips like the one shown in Figure 4.1 (p. 93). Since the deposit slips are in duplicate, Molly can keep a record of her deposit. Note that the increased use of making deposits at ATM machines has made it more convenient for people to make their deposits.

LO 2

Writing business checks is similar to writing personal checks. Before writing any checks, however, you must understand the structure of a check and know how to write a check. Carefully study Figure 4.2 (p. 93). Note that the verbal amount written in the check should match the figure amount. If these two amounts are different, by law the bank uses

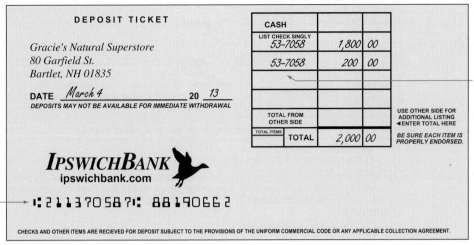

FIGURE 4.1   Deposit slip

Preprinted numbers in magnetic ink identify bank number, routing and sorting of the check, and Gracie's Natural Superstore account number

The 53-7058 is taken from the upper right corner of the check from the top part of the fraction. This number is known as the American Bankers Association transit number. The 53 identifies the city or state where the bank is located and the 7058 identifies the bank.

Check Stub

It should be completed before the check is written.

the verbal amount. Also, note the bank imprint on the bottom right section of the check. When processing the check, the bank imprints the check's amount. This makes it easy to detect bank errors.

Using the Checking Account

Once the check is written, the writer must keep a record of the check. Knowing the amount of your written checks and the amount in the bank should help you avoid writing a bad check. Business checkbooks usually include attached **check stubs** to keep track of written checks. The sample check stub in the margin shows the information that the check writer will want to record. Some companies use a **check register** to keep their check records instead of check stubs. Figure 4.6 (p. 99) shows a check register with a ✓ column that is often used in balancing the checkbook with the bank statement (Learning Unit 4–2).

FIGURE 4.2   The structure of a check

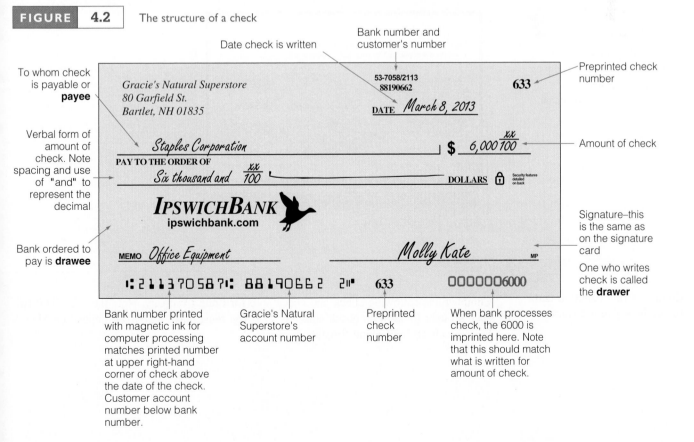

Date check is written

Bank number and customer's number

To whom check is payable or **payee**

Preprinted check number

Verbal form of amount of check. Note spacing and use of "and" to represent the decimal

Amount of check

Bank ordered to pay is **drawee**

Signature–this is the same as on the signature card

One who writes check is called the **drawer**

Bank number printed with magnetic ink for computer processing matches printed number at upper right-hand corner of check above the date of the check. Customer account number below bank number.

Gracie's Natural Superstore's account number

Preprinted check number

When bank processes check, the 6000 is imprinted here. Note that this should match what is written for amount of check.

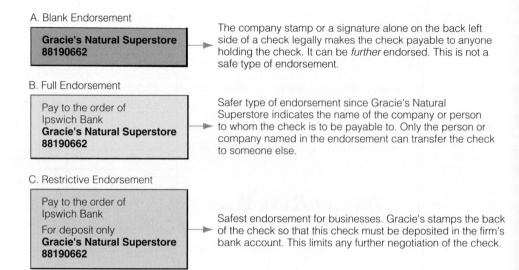

Types of common endorsements

Gracie's Natural Superstore has had a busy week, and Molly must deposit its checks in the company's checking account. However, before she can do this, Molly must **endorse,** or sign, the back left side of the checks. Figure 4.3 above explains the three types of check endorsements: **blank endorsement, full endorsement,** and **restrictive endorsement.** These endorsements transfer Gracie's ownership to the bank, which collects the money from the person or company issuing the check. Federal Reserve regulation limits all endorsements to the top $1\frac{1}{2}$ inches of the trailing edge on the back left side of the check.

After the bank receives Molly's deposit slip, shown in Figure 4.1 (p. 93), it increases (or credits) Gracie's account by $2,000. Often Molly leaves the deposit in a locked bag in a night depository. Then the bank credits (increases) Gracie's account when it processes the deposit on the next working day.

In the following *Wall Street Journal* clip "Fee, Not Free," see how the cost of regular checking has increased. Banks are looking for new ways to increase their profit. Later in the chapter we will look at online banking and the decrease in check writing.

MONEY tips

Conduct an annual check of your bank's interest rates and fees. You may find higher rates and lower fees at a credit union.

LU 4–1   **PRACTICE QUIZ**

Complete this **Practice Quiz** to see how you are doing.

Complete the following check and check stub for Long Company. Note the $9,500.60 balance brought forward on check stub No. 113. You must make a $690.60 deposit on May 3. Sign the check for Roland Small.

Date	Check no.	Amount	Payable to	For
June 5, 2013	113	$83.76	Angel Corporation	Rent

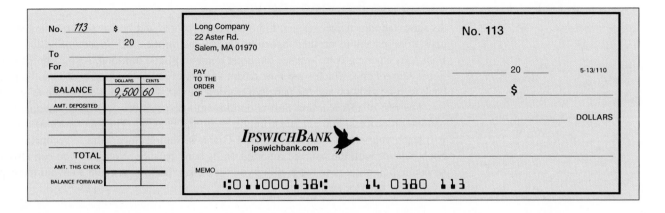

For **extra help** from your authors—Sharon and Jeff—see the student DVD

✓ **Solution**

You Tube™

| LU 4–1a | EXTRA PRACTICE QUIZ WITH WORKED-OUT SOLUTIONS |

Need more practice? Try this **Extra Practice Quiz** (check figures in the Interactive Chapter Organizer, p. 103). Worked-out Solutions can be found in Appendix B at end of text.

Complete the following check and stub for Long Company. Note the $10,800.80 balance brought forward on check stub No. 113. You must make an $812.88 deposit on May 3. Sign the check for Roland Small.

Date	Check no.	Amount	Payable to	For
July 8, 2013	113	$79.88	Lowe Corp.	Advertising

Learning Unit 4–2: Bank Statement and Reconciliation Process; Latest Trends in Mobile Banking

LO 1

Trends in Banking Industry

As shown in the chapter opener, more and more people and businesses are using smartphone apps from lenders to do their banking transactions. In the *Wall Street Journal* clip "Need to Bank? Try Phoning It In," we see the latest trend in **mobile banking.** Also, note the other *Wall Street Journal* clip, which shows the recent amount of online banking accounts, the number of bank website visitors, and the penalty for using a teller if a person is signed up as an e-banker.

The rest of this learning unit is divided into two sections: (1) bank statement and reconciliation process, and (2) latest trends in mobile banking. The bank statement discussion will teach you why it was important for Gracie's Natural Superstore to reconcile its checkbook balance with the balance reported on its bank balance. Note that you can also use this reconciliation process in reconciling your personal checking account to avoid the expensive error of an overdrawn account.

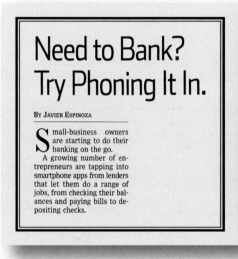

Need to Bank? Try Phoning It In.

BY JAVIER ESPINOZA

Small-business owners are starting to do their banking on the go.
A growing number of entrepreneurs are tapping into smartphone apps from lenders that let them do a range of jobs, from checking their balances and paying bills to depositing checks.

29.7 Million	24.3 Million	$8.95
Active online banking accounts, more than half of which use bill-paying services.	Unique visitors to the bank's site during August, most among U.S. banks.	Monthly charge to users of Bank of America's eBanking service who visit a teller.

LO 2

Bank Statement and Reconciliation Process

Each month, Ipswich Bank sends Gracie's Natural Superstore a **bank statement** (Figure 4.4, p. 97). We are interested in the following:

1. Beginning bank balance.

2. Total of all the account increases. Each time the bank increases the account amount, it *credits* the account.

3. Total of all account decreases. Each time the bank decreases the account amount, it *debits* the account.

4. Final ending balance.

Due to differences in timing, the bank balance on the bank statement frequently does not match the customer's checkbook balance. Also, the bank statement can show transactions that have not been entered in the customer's checkbook. Figure 4.5, page 97, tells you what to look for when comparing a checkbook balance with a bank balance.

FIGURE   4.4

Bank statement

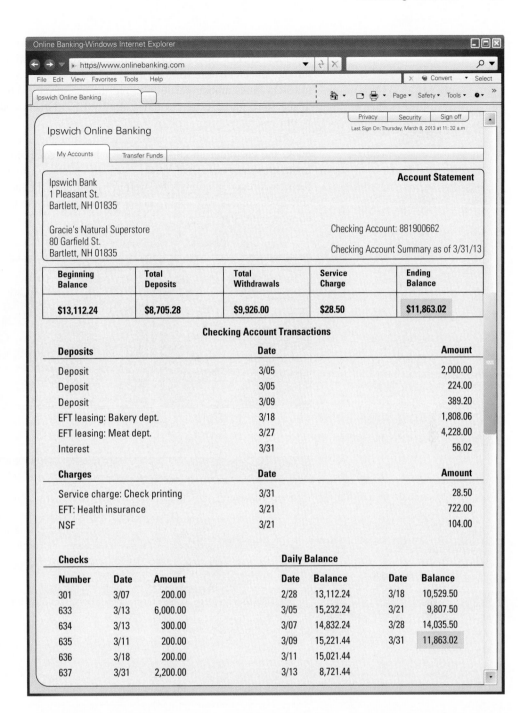

FIGURE   4.5

Reconciling checkbook with
bank statement

Checkbook balance		Bank balance
+ EFT (electronic funds transfer)	− NSF check	+ Deposits in transit
+ Interest earned	− Online fees	− Outstanding checks
+ Notes collected	− Automatic payments*	± Bank errors
+ Direct deposits	− Overdrafts†	
− ATM withdrawals	− Service charges	
− Automatic withdrawals	− Stop payments‡	
	± Book errors§	

*Preauthorized payments for utility bills, mortgage payments, insurance, etc.

†**Overdrafts** occur when the customer has no overdraft protection and a check bounces back to the company or person who received the check because the customer has written a check without enough money in the bank to pay for it.

‡A stop payment is issued when the writer of the check does not want the receiver to cash the check.

§If a $60 check is recorded at $50, the checkbook balance must be decreased by $10.

Gracie's Natural Superstore is planning to offer to its employees the option of depositing their checks directly into each employee's checking account. This is accomplished through the **electronic funds transfer (EFT)**—a computerized operation that electronically transfers funds among parties without the use of paper checks. Gracie's, who sublets space in the store, receives rental payments by EFT. Gracie's also has the bank pay the store's health insurance premiums by EFT.

LO 3

To reconcile the difference between the amount on the bank statement and in the checkbook, the customer should complete a **bank reconciliation.** Today, many companies and home computer owners are using software such as Quicken and QuickBooks to complete their bank reconciliation. Also, we have mentioned the increased use of **banking apps** available to customers. However, you should understand the following steps for manually reconciling a bank statement.

RECONCILING A BANK STATEMENT

Step 1. Identify the outstanding checks (checks written but not yet processed by the bank). You can use the ✓ column in the check register (Figure 4.6) to check the canceled checks listed in the bank statement against the checks you wrote in the check register. The unchecked checks are the outstanding checks.

Step 2. Identify the deposits in transit (deposits made but not yet processed by the bank), using the same method in Step 1.

Step 3. Analyze the bank statement for transactions not recorded in the check stubs or check registers (like EFT).

Step 4. Check for recording errors in checks written, in deposits made, or in subtraction and addition.

Step 5. Compare the adjusted balances of the checkbook and the bank statement. If the balances are not the same, repeat Steps 1–4.

Molly uses a check register (Figure 4.6, p. 99) to keep a record of Gracie's checks and deposits. By looking at Gracie's check register, you can see how to complete Steps 1 and 2 above. The explanation that follows for the first four bank statement reconciliation steps will help you understand the procedure.

Step 1. Identify Outstanding Checks   **Outstanding checks** are checks that Gracie's Natural Superstore has written but Ipswich Bank has not yet recorded for payment when it sends out the bank statement. Gracie's treasurer identifies the following checks written on 3/31 as outstanding:

No. 638	$572.00
No. 639	638.94
No. 640	166.00
No. 641	406.28
No. 642	917.06

FIGURE   **4.6**

Gracie's Natural Superstore check register

NUMBER	DATE 2013	DESCRIPTION OF TRANSACTION	PAYMENT/DEBIT (−)	√	FEE (IF ANY) (−)	DEPOSIT/CREDIT (+)	BALANCE $ 12,912	24
	3/04	Deposit	$		$	$ 2,000 00	+ 2,000	00
							14,912	24
	3/04	Deposit				224 00	+ 224	00
							15,136	24
633	3/08	Staples Company	6,000 00	✓			− 6,000	00
							9,136	24
634	3/09	Health Foods Inc.	1,020 00	✓			− 1,020	00
							8,116	24
	3/09	Deposit				389 20	+ 389	20
							8,505	44
635	3/10	Liberty Insurance	200 00	✓			− 200	00
							8,305	44
636	3/18	Ryan Press	200 00	✓			− 200	00
							8,105	44
637	3/29	Logan Advertising	2,200 00	✓			− 2,200	00
							5,905	44
	3/30	Deposit				3,383 26	+ 3,383	26
							9,288	70
638	3/31	Sears Roebuck	572 00				− 572	00
							8,716	70
639	3/31	Flynn Company	638 94				− 638	94
							8,077	76
640	3/31	Lynn's Farm	166 00				− 166	00
							7,911	76
641	3/31	Ron's Wholesale	406 28				− 406	28
							7,505	48
642	3/31	Grocery Natural, Inc.	917 06				− 917	06
							$6,588	42

RECORD ALL CHARGES OR CREDITS THAT AFFECT YOUR ACCOUNT

REMEMBER TO RECORD AUTOMATIC PAYMENTS/DEPOSITS ON DATE AUTHORIZED.

Step 2. Identify Deposits in Transit   **Deposits in transit** are deposits that did not reach Ipswich Bank by the time the bank prepared the bank statement. The March 30 deposit of $3,383.26 did not reach Ipswich Bank by the bank statement date. You can see this by comparing the company's bank statement with its check register.

Step 3. Analyze Bank Statement for Transactions Not Recorded in Check Stubs or Check Register   The bank statement of Gracie's Natural Superstore (Figure 4.4, p. 97) begins with the deposits, or increases, made to Gracie's bank account. Increases to accounts are known as credits. These are the result of a **credit memo (CM).** Gracie's received the following increases or credits in March:

1. *EFT leasing:* $1,808.06 and $4,228.00.   Each month the bakery and meat departments pay for space they lease in the store.

2. *Interest credited:* $56.02.   Gracie's has a checking account that pays interest; the account has earned $56.02.

When Gracie's has charges against its bank account, the bank decreases, or debits, Gracie's account for these charges. Banks usually inform customers of a debit transaction by a **debit memo (DM).** The following items will result in debits to Gracie's account:

1. *Service charge:* $28.50.   The bank charged $28.50 for printing Gracie's checks.

2. *EFT payment:* $722.   The bank made a health insurance payment for Gracie's.

3. *NSF check:* $104.   One of Gracie's customers wrote Gracie's a check for $104. Gracie's deposited the check, but the check bounced for **nonsufficient funds (NSF).** Thus, Gracie's has $104 less than it figured.

Step 4. Check for Recording Errors The treasurer of Gracie's Natural Superstore, Molly Kate, recorded check No. 634 for the wrong amount—$1,020 (see the check register). The bank statement showed that check No. 634 cleared for $300. To reconcile Gracie's checkbook balance with the bank balance, Gracie's must add $720 to its checkbook balance. Neglecting to record a deposit also results in an error in the company's checkbook balance. As you can see, reconciling the bank's balance with a checkbook balance is a necessary part of business and personal finance.

Step 5. Completing the Bank Reconciliation Now we can complete the bank reconciliation on the back side of the bank statement as shown in Figure 4.7. This form is usually on the back of a bank statement. If necessary, however, the person reconciling the bank statement can construct a bank reconciliation form similar to Figure 4.8 (p. 101).

FIGURE **4.7**

Reconciliation process

CHECKS OUTSTANDING (NOT YET CHARGED TO ACCOUNT)		
NUMBER OR DATE	**DOLLARS**	**CENTS**
638	8572	00
639	638	94
640	166	00
641	406	28
642	911	06
TOTAL	**$2,700**	**28**

CHECKING ACCOUNT RECONCILEMENT

Enter the new balance shown on the other side of this statement. $ 11,863.02

ADD
Deposits not shown 3,383.26

ADD
Advances and Transfers to Checking not shown.

SUBTOTAL 15,246.28

DEDUCT
Checks outstanding 2,700.28

SUBTOTAL 12,546.00

DEDUCT
Transfers from Checking not shown
This amount should agree with the balance in your checkbook register. $ 12,546.00

Checkbook balance	$6,588.42
+ EFT leasing	$6,036.06
+ Interest	56.02
+ Checkbook error	720.00 6,812.08
– Service charge	$ 28.50
– EFT: health insurance	722.00
– NSF	104.00 854.50
Ending checkbook balance	$12,546.00

GRACIE'S NATURAL SUPERSTORE
Bank Reconciliation as of March 31, 2013

Checkbook balance			Bank balance		
Gracie's checkbook balance		$6,588.42	Bank balance		$11,863.02
Add:			Add:		
EFT leasing: Bakery dept.	$1,808.06		Deposit in transit, 3/30		3,383.26
EFT leasing: Meat dept.	4,228.00				$15,246.28
Interest	56.02				
Error: Overstated check No. 634	720.00	$ 6,812.08			
		$13,400.50			
Deduct:			Deduct:		
Service charge	$ 28.50		Outstanding checks:		
NSF check	104.00		No. 638	$572.00	
EFT health insurance payment	722.00	854.50	No. 639	638.94	
			No. 640	166.00	
			No. 641	406.28	
			No. 642	917.06	2,700.28
Reconciled balance		$12,546.00	Reconciled balance		$12,546.00

Trends in Mobile Banking

The hottest trend in banking is the use of bank apps. For example, JPMorgan Chase & Co. offers customers a free app to use with an iPad, iPhone, Android, Blackberry, or Kindle.

MONEY tips

Always review your monthly bank statement to ensure there are no errors. The earlier you catch an error, the easier it is to remedy.

www.chase.com

LU 4–2 PRACTICE QUIZ

Complete this **Practice Quiz** to see how you are doing.

Rosa Garcia received her February 3, 2013, bank statement showing a balance of $212.80. Rosa's checkbook has a balance of $929.15. The bank statement showed that Rosa had an ATM fee of $12.00 and a deposited check returned fee of $20.00. Rosa earned interest of $1.05. She had three outstanding checks: No. 300, $18.20; No. 302, $38.40; and No. 303, $68.12. A deposit for $810.12 was not on her bank statement. Prepare Rosa Garcia's bank reconciliation.

*For **extra help** from your authors—Sharon and Jeff—see the student DVD*

✓ Solution

ROSA GARCIA					
Bank Reconciliation as of February 3, 2013					
Checkbook balance			**Bank balance**		
Rosa's checkbook balance		$929.15	Bank balance		$ 212.80
Add:			Add:		
Interest		1.05	Deposit in transit		810.12
		$930.20			$1,022.92
Deduct:			Deduct:		
Deposited check returned fee	$20.00		Outstanding checks:		
ATM	12.00	32.00	No. 300	$18.20	
			No. 302	38.40	
			No. 303	68.12	124.72
Reconciled balance		$898.20	Reconciled balance		$ 898.20

LU 4–2a EXTRA PRACTICE QUIZ WITH WORKED-OUT SOLUTIONS

Need more practice? Try this **Extra Practice Quiz** (check figures in the Interactive Chapter Organizer, p. 103). Worked-out Solutions can be found in Appendix B at end of text.

Earl Miller received his March 8, 2013, bank statement, which had a $300.10 balance. Earl's checkbook has a $1,200.10 balance. The bank statement showed a $15.00 ATM fee and a $30.00 deposited check returned fee. Earl earned $24.06 interest. He had three outstanding checks: No. 300, $22.88; No. 302, $15.90; and No. 303, $282.66. A deposit for $1,200.50 was not on his bank statement. Prepare Earl's bank reconciliation.

INTERACTIVE CHAPTER ORGANIZER

Topic/procedure/formula	Examples	You try it*
Types of endorsements, p. 94 *Blank:* Not safe; can be further endorsed.	Jones Co. 21-333-9	**Write a sample of a blank, full, and restrictive endorsement.**
Full: Only person or company named in endorsement can transfer check to someone else.	Pay to the order of Regan Bank Jones Co. 21-333-9	Use Pete Co. Acct. # 24-111-9
Restrictive: Check must be deposited. Limits any further negotiation of the check.	Pay to the order of Regan Bank. For deposit only. Jones Co. 21-333-9	

(continues)

INTERACTIVE CHAPTER ORGANIZER

Topic/procedure/formula	Examples	You try it*
Bank reconciliation, p. 98	**Checkbook balance**	**Calculate ending checkbook balance**
Checkbook balance	Balance $800	
+ EFT (electronic funds transfer)	− NSF 40	1. Beg. checkbook bal.: $300
+ Interest earned	$760	2. NSF: $50
+ Notes collected	− Service charge 4	3. Deposit in transit: $100
+ Direct deposits	$756	4. Outstanding check: $60
− ATM withdrawals		5. ATM service charge: $20
− NSF check	**Bank balance**	
− Online fees	Balance $ 632	
− Automatic withdrawals	+ Deposits in transit 416	
− Overdrafts	$1,048	
− Service charges	− Outstanding checks 292	
− Stop payments	$ 756	
± Book errors (see note, below)		
CM—adds to balance		
DM—deducts from balance		
Bank balance		
+ Deposits in transit		
− Outstanding checks		
± Bank errors		

KEY TERMS	Automatic teller machine (ATM), *p. 91*	Debit card, *p. 91*	Full endorsement, *p. 94*
	Bank reconciliation, *p. 98*	Debit memo (DM), *p. 99*	Mobile banking, *p. 96*
	Bank statement, *p. 96*	Deposit slip, *p. 92*	Nonsufficient funds (NSF), *p. 99*
	Banking apps, *p. 98*	Deposits in transit, *p. 99*	Outstanding checks, *p. 98*
	Blank endorsement, *p. 94*	Draft, *p. 92*	Overdrafts, *p. 97*
	Check, *p. 92*	Drawee, *p. 93*	Payee, *p. 93*
	Check register, *p. 93*	Drawer, *p. 93*	Restrictive endorsement, *p. 94*
	Check stub, *p. 93*	Electronic funds transfer (EFT), *p. 98*	Signature card, *p. 92*
	Credit memo (CM), *p. 99*	Endorse, *p. 94*	

Check Figures for Extra Practice Quizzes with Page References. (Worked-out Solutions in Appendix B.)	LU 4–1a (p. 95) Ending Balance Forward $11,533.80	LU 4–2a (p. 102) Reconciled Balance $1,179.16

Note: If a $60 check is recorded as $50, we must decrease checkbook balance by $10.

*Worked-out solutions are in Appendix B.

Critical Thinking Discussion Questions with Chapter Concept Check

1. Explain the structure of a check. The trend in bank statements is not to return the canceled checks. Do you think this is fair?

2. List the three types of endorsements. Endorsements are limited to the top $1\frac{1}{2}$ inches of the trailing edge on the back left side of your check. Why do you think the Federal Reserve made this regulation?

3. List the steps in reconciling a bank statement. Today, many banks charge a monthly fee for certain types of checking accounts. Do you think all checking accounts should be free? Please explain.

4. What are some of the trends in mobile banking? Will we become a cashless society in which all transactions are made with some type of credit card?

5. What do you think of the government's intervention in trying to bail out banks? Should banks be allowed to fail?

6. **Chapter Concept Check.** Create your own company and provide needed data to prepare a bank reconciliation. Then go to a bank website and explain how you would use the bank's app versus the manual system of banking.

Classroom Notes

END-OF-CHAPTER PROBLEMS  connect (plus+) www.mhhe.com/slater11e

Check figures for odd-numbered problems in Appendix C.   Name _____   Date _____

DRILL PROBLEMS

4–1. Fill out the check register that follows with this information: *LU 4-1(1)*

2013

July 7	Check No. 482	AOL	$143.50
15	Check No. 483	Staples	66.10
19	Deposit		800.00
20	Check No. 484	Sprint	451.88
24	Check No. 485	Krispy Kreme	319.24
29	Deposit		400.30

		RECORD ALL CHARGES OR CREDITS THAT AFFECT YOUR ACCOUNT					BALANCE	
NUMBER	DATE 2013	DESCRIPTION OF TRANSACTION	PAYMENT/DEBIT (−)	√	FEE (IF ANY) (−)	DEPOSIT/CREDIT (+)	$ 4,500	75
			$		$	$		

4–2. November 1, 2013, Payroll.com, an Internet company, has a $10,481.88 checkbook balance. Record the following transactions for Payroll.com by completing the two checks and check stubs provided. Sign the checks Garth Scholten, controller.   *LU 4-1(2)*

a. November 8, 2013, deposited $688.10

b. November 8, check No. 190 payable to Staples for office supplies—$766.88

c. November 15, check No. 191 payable to Best Buy for computer equipment—$3,815.99.

No. _____ $ _____
_____ 20 ____
To _____
For _____

	DOLLARS	CENTS
BALANCE		
AMT. DEPOSITED		
TOTAL		
AMT. THIS CHECK		
BALANCE FORWARD		

PAYROLL.COM
1 LEDGER RD.
ST. PAUL, MN 55113

No. 190

PAY TO THE ORDER OF _____   _____ 20 ____   5-13/110

$ _____

_____ DOLLARS

IPSWICHBANK
ipswichbank.com

MEMO _____

⑈0⑈⑈000⑈38⑈: 25 ⑈⑈⑈03 ⑈90

No. _____ $ _____
_____ 20 ____
To _____
For _____

	DOLLARS	CENTS
BALANCE		
AMT. DEPOSITED		
TOTAL		
AMT. THIS CHECK		
BALANCE FORWARD		

PAYROLL.COM
1 LEDGER RD.
ST. PAUL, MN 55113

No. 191

PAY TO THE ORDER OF _____   _____ 20 ____   5-13/110

$ _____

_____ DOLLARS

IPSWICHBANK
ipswichbank.com

MEMO _____

⑈0⑈⑈000⑈38⑈: 25 ⑈⑈⑈03 ⑈9⑈

4–3. Using the check register in Problem 4–1 and the following bank statement, prepare a bank reconciliation for Lee.com. *LU 4-2(3)*

BANK STATEMENT			
Date	Checks	Deposits	Balance
7/1 balance			$4,500.75
7/18	$143.50		4,357.25
7/19		$ 800.00	5,157.25
7/26	319.24		4,838.01
7/30	15.00 SC		4,823.01

WORD PROBLEMS

4–4. The World Bank forecasts growth of world trade to be 4.7% in 2012, down from 12.4% in 2010. This change has caused *eXcel* Peru's Apple Blossom Florist to analyze its current financial situation, beginning with reconciling its accounts. Apple Blossom received its bank statement showing a balance of $8,788. Its checkbook balance is $15,252. Deposits in transit are $3,450 and $6,521. There is a service charge of $45 and interest earned of $3. Notes collected total $1,575. Outstanding checks are No. 1021 for $1,260 and No. 1022 for $714. All numbers are in U.S. dollars. Help Apple Blossom Florist reconcile its balances. *LU 4-2(3)*

4–5. The U.S. Chamber of Commerce provides a free monthly bank reconciliation template at business.uschamber.com/tools/ bankre_m.asp. Annie Moats just received her bank statement notice online. She wants to reconcile her checking account with her bank statement and has chosen to reconcile her accounts manually. Her checkbook shows a balance of $698. Her bank statement reflects a balance of $1,348. Checks outstanding are No. 2146, $25; No. 2148, $58; No. 2152, $198; and No. 2153, $464. Deposits in transit are $100 and $50. There is a $15 service charge and $5 ATM charge in addition to notes collected of $50 and $25. Reconcile Annie's balances. *LU 4-2(3)*

4–6. A local bank began charging $2.50 each month for returning canceled checks. The bank also has an $8.00 "maintenance" fee if a checking account slips below $750. Donna Sands likes to have copies of her canceled checks for preparing her income tax returns. She has received her bank statement with a balance of $535.85. Donna received $2.68 in interest and has been charged for the canceled checks and the maintenance fee. The following checks were outstanding: No. 94, $121.16; No. 96, $106.30; No. 98, $210.12; and No. 99, $64.84. A deposit of $765.69 was not recorded on Donna's bank statement. Her checkbook shows a balance of $806.94. Prepare Donna's bank reconciliation. *LU 4-2(3)*

4–7. Ben Luna received his bank statement with a $27.04 fee for a bounced check (NSF). He has an $815.75 monthly mortgage payment paid through his bank. There was also a $3.00 teller fee and a check printing fee of $3.50. His ATM card fee was $6.40. There was also a $530.50 deposit in transit. The bank shows a balance of $119.17. The bank paid Ben $1.23 in interest. Ben's checkbook shows a balance of $1,395.28. Check No. 234 for $80.30 and check No. 235 for $28.55 were outstanding. Prepare Ben's bank reconciliation. *LU 4-2(3)*

4–8. Kameron Gibson's bank statement showed a balance of $717.72. Kameron's checkbook had a balance of $209.50. Check No. 104 for $110.07 and check No. 105 for $15.55 were outstanding. A $620.50 deposit was not on the statement. He has his payroll check electronically deposited to his checking account—the payroll check was for $1,025.10. There was also a $4 teller fee and an $18 service charge. Prepare Kameron Gibson's bank reconciliation. *LU 4-2(3)*

4–9. Banks are finding more ways to charge fees, such as a $25 overdraft fee. Sue McVickers has an account in Fayetteville; she has received her bank statement with this $25 charge. Also, she was charged a $6.50 service fee; however, the good news is she earned $5.15 interest. Her bank statement's balance was $315.65, but it did not show the $1,215.15 deposit she had made. Sue's checkbook balance shows $604.30. The following checks have not cleared: No. 250, $603.15; No. 253, $218.90; and No. 254, $130.80. Prepare Sue's bank reconciliation. *LU 4-2(3)*

4–10. Carol Stokke receives her April 6 bank statement showing a balance of $859.75; her checkbook balance is $954.25. The bank statement shows an ATM charge of $25.00, NSF fee of $27.00, earned interest of $2.75, and Carol's $630.15 refund check, which was processed by the IRS and deposited to her account. Carol has two checks that have not cleared—No. 115 for $521.15 and No. 116 for $205.50. There is also a deposit in transit for $1,402.05. Prepare Carol's bank reconciliation.   *LU 4-2(3)*

4–11. Lowell Bank reported the following checking account fees: $2 to see a real-live teller, $20 to process a bounced check, and $1 to $3 if you need an original check to prove you paid a bill or made a charitable contribution. This past month you had to transact business through a teller six times—a total $12 cost to you. Your bank statement shows a $305.33 balance; your checkbook shows a $1,009.76 balance. You received $1.10 in interest. An $801.15 deposit was not recorded on your statement. The following checks were outstanding: No. 413, $28.30; No. 414, $18.60; and No. 418, $60.72. Prepare your bank reconciliation.   *LU 4-2(3)*

4–12. According to New York City's public records, a single-family town house at 247 Central Park West with a 60-foot lap pool, e**X**cel fitness/massage area, and media room sold for $22.375 million on January 13, 2012. If you were the owner, reconcile your checkbook and bank balance according to the following: bank statement balance, $18,769; checkbook balance, $22,385,015; interest earned, $3,948; deposits in transit, $100,656 and $22,375,000; ATM card fees, $150; outstanding checks— No. 10189, $55,678; No. 10192, $15,287; No. 10193, $22,350; and No. 10194, $12,297.   *LU 4-2(3)*

4–13. Labeled as one of the top 20 best countries to open a small business in, Thailand offers many business strengths as noted by "Doing Business in Thailand: 2011 Country Commercial Guide for U.S. Companies." A restaurant on Koh Phi Phi, Ton Sai Seafood, wants to conduct a bank reconciliation with the following information in U.S. dollars: bank statement balance, $12,568; checkbook balance, $6,485; earned interest, $4; deposits in transit, $2,000; outstanding checks—No. 255, $5,500; No. 261, $2,500; No. 262, $79. Prepare the bank reconciliation.   *LU 4-2(3)*

CHALLENGE PROBLEMS

4–14. Carolyn Crosswell, who banks in New Jersey, wants to balance her checkbook, which shows a balance of $985.20. The bank shows a balance of $1,430.33. The following transactions occurred: $135.20 automatic withdrawal to the gas company, $6.50 ATM fee, $8.00 service fee, and $1,030.05 direct deposit from the IRS. Carolyn used her debit card five times and was charged 45 cents for each transaction; she was also charged $3.50 for check printing. A $931.08 deposit was not shown on her bank statement. The following checks were outstanding: No. 235, $158.20; No. 237, $184.13; No. 238, $118.12; and No. 239, $38.83. Carolyn received $2.33 interest. Prepare Carolyn's bank reconciliation.   *LU 4-2(3)*

4–15. Melissa Jackson, bookkeeper for Kinko Company, cannot prepare a bank reconciliation. From the following facts, can you eXcel help her complete the June 30, 2013, reconciliation? The bank statement showed a $2,955.82 balance. Melissa's checkbook showed a $3,301.82 balance.

Melissa placed a $510.19 deposit in the bank's night depository on June 30. The deposit did not appear on the bank statement. The bank included two DMs and one CM with the returned checks: $690.65 DM for NSF check, $8.50 DM for service charges, and $400.00 CM (less $10 collection fee) for collecting a $400.00 non-interest-bearing note. Check No. 811 for $110.94 and check No. 912 for $82.50, both written and recorded on June 28, were not with the returned checks. The bookkeeper had correctly written check No. 884, $1,000, for a new cash register, but she recorded the check as $1,069. The May bank reconciliation showed check No. 748 for $210.90 and check No. 710 for $195.80 outstanding on April 30. The June bank statement included check No. 710 but not check No. 748.   *LU 4-2(3)*

SUMMARY PRACTICE TEST You Tube

Do you need help? The DVD has step-by-step worked-out solutions.

1. Walgreens has a $12,925.55 beginning checkbook balance. Record the following transactions in the check stubs provided. (*p. 92*)   *LU 4-1(2)*
    a. November 4, 2013, check No. 180 payable to Ace Medical Corporation, $1,700.88 for drugs.
    b. $5,250 deposit—November 24.
    c. November 24, 2013, check No. 181 payable to John's Wholesale, $825.55 merchandise.

No. _____ $ _____		
_____ 20 ____		
To _____		
For _____		
	DOLLARS	CENTS
BALANCE		
AMT. DEPOSITED		
TOTAL		
AMT. THIS CHECK		
BALANCE FORWARD		

No. _____ $ _____		
_____ 20 ____		
To _____		
For _____		
	DOLLARS	CENTS
BALANCE		
AMT. DEPOSITED		
TOTAL		
AMT. THIS CHECK		
BALANCE FORWARD		

2. On April 1, 2013, Lester Company received a bank statement that showed a $8,950 balance. Lester showed an $8,000 checking account balance. The bank did not return check No. 115 for $750 or check No. 118 for $370. A $900 deposit made on March 31 was in transit. The bank charged Lester $20 for check printing and $250 for NSF checks. The bank also collected a $1,400 note for Lester. Lester forgot to record a $400 withdrawal at the ATM. Prepare a bank reconciliation. *(p. 98) LU 4-2(3)*

3. Felix Babic banks at Role Federal Bank. Today he received his March 31, 2013, bank statement showing a $762.80 balance. Felix's checkbook shows a balance of $799.80. The following checks have not cleared the bank: No. 140, $130.55; No. 149, $66.80; and No. 161, $102.90. Felix made a $820.15 deposit that is not shown on the bank statement. He has his $617.30 monthly mortgage payment paid through the bank. His $1,100.20 IRS refund check was mailed to his bank. Prepare Felix Babic's bank reconciliation. *(p. 98) LU 4-2(3)*

4. On June 30, 2013, Wally Company's bank statement showed a $7,500.10 bank balance. Wally has a beginning checkbook balance of $9,800.00. The bank statement also showed that it collected a $1,200.50 note for the company. A $4,500.10 June 30 deposit was in transit. Check No. 119 for $650.20 and check No. 130 for $381.50 are outstanding. Wally's bank charges $.40 cents per check. This month, 80 checks were processed. Prepare a reconciled statement. *(p. 98)* *LU 4-2(3)*

PROBLEM 1
Bank costs

Go to http://www.bankrate.com/brm/rate/bank_home.asp. Select the Checking/Savings tab. Search for a "Local, Interest Checking Account in a State and City near where you live." Select an interest-bearing account. Which account requires the highest average minimum balance to avoid monthly service fees? Which account requires the lowest average minimum balance to avoid monthly service fees? Which account would you select for your personal checking account from this list?

Discussion Questions

1. What are the most important criteria for you in selecting a checking account? Why?

2. Discuss the pros and cons of using a local versus an Internet-based checking account.

PROBLEM 2
Checkbook vs. bank statement balance

Go to http://googolplex.cuna.org/12433/cnote/article.php?doc_id=2502. Use the Checking/Debit Account Calculator and "Go Figure" based on the following: your register balance, $525.89; interest earnings, $1.23; bank fees, $8.99; statement balance, $698.00; deposits in transit, $150.00; withdrawals in transit, $250.00.

Discussion Questions

1. Based on the difference you found in the adjusted balances, where would you begin to look to determine what is causing this discrepancy?

2. How could this tool be useful for your own checking account?

PROBLEM 3
Online vs. on-site

Go to http://www.bankrate.com/finance/checking/online-banking-still-favorable.aspx. Read the article about online banking. List the pros and cons of online banking compared to a traditional checking account. Which account type do you feel would be the best fit for a typical banking customer? Which type of account would be the best for you, and why?

Discussion Questions

1. In the future, will we see more or less online banking? Why?

2. Why do you feel these differences exist between online and traditional checking accounts?

PROBLEM 4
What's in your checkbook?

Go to http://www.cpasitesolutions.com/content/calcs/CheckBook.html. Calculate your checkbook balance for the month if you started out with $561.00 and wrote four checks for $112.45, $100.00, $45.00, and $245.00, and made three deposits of $100.00, $55.00, and $200.00.

Discussion Questions

1. How often do you update your checkbook balance? Why?

2. Discuss some potential problems that could arise if your checkbook balance is not kept up to date.

MOBILE APPS

Easy Checkbook (Poetry Outdoors) Helps track purchases and balance a check register.

PocketMoney (Catamount Software) Tracks finances on multiple devices and analyzes spending with a variety of reporting functions.

INTERNET PROJECTS

See text website
www.mhhe.com/slater11e_sse_ch04

Credit Unions Anyone Can Join

Become a member and get a better deal on checking accounts, mortgages and car loans.

BY JOAN GOLDWASSER

CREDIT UNIONS OFFER THE same services that banks provide. But they tend to charge lower loan rates, pay higher yields on savings and "treat borrowers who are struggling more sympathetically," says Stephen Brobeck, executive director of the Consumer Federation of America. The rate on new-car loans at credit unions recently averaged 3.4%, or 1.5 percentage points less than at banks; the rate on gold and platinum credit cards was 9.8%, or about 1.4 percentage points lower.

A big reason for the friendlier terms is that credit unions are member-owned, not-for-profit institutions, so they are exempt from federal income taxes. You qualify for membership if you have a "common bond"—because of where you work, live, attend school or worship; because you belong to an affiliated association; or because a family member belongs.

To find a credit union near you, go to www .culookup.com or www .asmarterchoice.org. Or you can bank online at the credit unions below, which are open to anyone if you join the affiliated association (for more choices, go to kiplinger.com/links/ creditunions). Deposits are federally insured by the National Credit Union Administration up to $250,000 per account.

ALLIANT CREDIT UNION
www.alliantcreditunion.org
HOW TO JOIN: Contribute $10 to nonprofit Foster Care to Success and open a $5 savings account.

CHECKING: No monthly service fee or minimum balance. High Rate Checking option pays 0.90%. You have free access to more than 80,000 ATMs.

LOAN RATES: Fixed-rate 30-year mortgages at 4.25%. Loans for new and used cars are 1.99% for up to 72 months.

CONNEXUS CREDIT UNION
www.connexuscu.org
HOW TO JOIN: Make a one-time, $5 donation to the nonprofit Connexus Association and open a $5 savings account.

CHECKING: All three individual accounts have no minimum balance or monthly fees and entitle you to a 1% reduction on consumer loans. With Xtraordinary Checking, you earn 2% on balances up to $25,000 and are eligible for up to $25 a month in ATM rebates.

LOAN RATES: Fixed-rate 30-year mortgages at 4.25%. Auto loans range from 2.49% (36 months) to 5.99% (84 months).

LAKE MICHIGAN CREDIT UNION
www.lmcu.org
HOW TO JOIN: Donate $5 to the West Michigan Chapter of the ALS Association and open a $5 savings account.

CHECKING: Free Checking has no monthly fees but pays no interest. Max Checking pays 3% on balances up to $15,000 and refunds of up to $15 per month in ATM surcharges. Members have free access to 92 proprietary ATMs in Michigan.

LOAN RATES: Fixed-rate 30-year mortgages are as low as 3.9%. Auto loans for new and used cars run 2.99% for up to 63 months. ∎

BUSINESS MATH ISSUE

A credit union is always a better choice than a large bank.

1. List the key points of the article and information to support your position.
2. Write a group defense of your position using math calculations to support your view.

CHAPTER 5

Solving for the Unknown: A How-to Approach for Solving Equations

From *The Wall Street Journal*, Copyright © 2010, permissio
Features Syndicate.

Study Challenges Old Weight-Loss Equation

By Katherine Hobson

There's new math out on how to calculate weight loss that may be disappointing to those relying on the old math.

Many people may remember an old—and apparently incorrect—piece of dietary advice: eat 500 fewer calories per day, and in a week you'll have a deficit of 3,500 calories and will thus lose a pound.

BEST OF THE HEALTH BLOG

That calculation, however, assumes that if "I cut 500 calories from my diet ... the number of calories I'm burning will stay the same," says Kevin Hall, a physiologist at the National Institute of Diabetes and Digestive and Kidney Diseases. That's not so, however, because metabolism "slows down right away, and continues to slow as body weight is lost," Dr. Hall says.

So if people use that math, they are not going to lose as much weight as they think they should.

Dr. Hall and colleagues just published a paper in the Lancet—part of the journal's obesity series—that provides an alternative model. It is based on data from controlled feeding studies and captures that metabolic slowdown as well as other effects, such as the fact that the same amount and intensity of exercise will burn off fewer calories as a person loses weight.

It predicts that for a typical overweight adult, every reduction of 10 calories per day will lead to a weight loss not of about a pound a year, but only about half a pound. The next half-pound will take about two more years to lose.

The authors note this casts doubt on public-health messages about making small changes (like scrapping a soda a day) in order to reap big weight-loss gains over time. Using their model to predict, say, the effects of a soda tax produces a much more modest impact on obesity.

Eric Ravussin, a professor at Pennington Biomedical Research Center and director of the institution's Nutrition and Obesity Research Center, says this paper is important because many physicians are still advising their patients to rely on the cut-500-calories-per-day-lose-a-pound-a-week model. (He was a reviewer on this paper and has collaborated with Dr. Hall.)

The website for the NIDDK features a Web-based tool that allows you to tailor the rate at which you want to lose weight based on how much you're willing to change your physical activity in the short and long term.

© JGI/Blend Images

LU 5–1: Solving Equations for the Unknown

1. Explain the basic procedures used to solve equations for the unknown *(pp. 118–119)*.

2. List the five rules and the mechanical steps used to solve for the unknown in seven situations; know how to check the answers *(pp. 119–122)*.

LU 5–2: Solving Word Problems for the Unknown

1. List the steps for solving word problems *(p. 123)*.

2. Complete blueprint aids to solve word problems; check the solutions *(pp. 124–126)*.

VOCABULARY PREVIEW

Here are key terms in this chapter. After completing the chapter, if you know the term, place a checkmark in the parentheses. If you don't know the term, look it up and put the page number where it can be found.

Constants ( ) Equation ( ) Expression ( ) Formula ( ) Knowns ( ) Unknown ( ) Variables ( )

Did you know that Google handles nearly two-thirds of the world's web searches? The following *Wall Street Journal* clip, "Google Revamps To Fight Cheaters," shows how Google uses math formulas to weed out "low-quality" sites.

Learning Unit 5–1 explains how you can solve for unknowns in equations. In Learning Unit 5–2 you learn how to solve for unknowns in word problems. When you complete these learning units, you will not have to memorize as many formulas to solve business and personal math applications. With the increasing use of computer software, a basic working knowledge of solving for the unknown has become necessary.

GLOBAL

© AP Photo/Paul Sakuma

Google Revamps To Fight Cheaters

BY AMIR EFRATI

Google Inc., long considered the gold standard of Internet search, is changing the secret formula it uses to rank Web pages as it struggles to combat websites that have been able to game its system.

The Internet giant, which handles nearly two-thirds of the world's Web searches, has been under fire recently over the quality of its results. Google said it changed its mathematical formula late Thursday in order to better weed out "low-quality" sites that offer users little value. Some such sites offer just enough content to appear in search results and lure users to pages loaded with advertisements.

Google generates billions of dollars from advertising linked to its search engine, whose influence as a front door to the world's online content and commerce continues to grow by the year. Google's power over the fortunes of so many other companies has made it a target of competitor complaints. It has also faced government investigations, including scrutiny by regulators in the U.S. and Europe.

The Silicon Valley company built its business on the strength of algorithms that yield speedy results. The company constantly refines those formulas, and sometimes takes manual action to penalize companies that it believes use tricks to artificially rise in search rankings. In recent weeks, it has cracked down on retailers **J.C. Penney** Co. and **Overstock.com** Inc.

Learning Unit 5–1: Solving Equations for the Unknown

LO 1

The Rose Smith letter below is based on a true story. Note how Rose states that the blueprint aids, the lesson on repetition, and the chapter organizers were important factors in the successful completion of her business math course.

Rose Smith
15 Locust Street
Lynn, MA 01915

Dear Professor Slater,

   Thank you for helping me get through your Business Math class. When I first started, my math anxiety level was real high. I felt I had no head for numbers. When you told us we would be covering the chapter on solving equations, I'll never forget how I started to shake. I started to panic. I felt I could never solve a word problem. I thought I was having an algebra attack.

   Now that it's over (90 on the chapter on unknowns), I'd like to tell you what worked for me so you might pass this on to other students. It was your blueprint aids. Drawing boxes helped me to think things out. They were a <u>tool</u> that helped me more clearly understand how to dissect each word problem. They didn't solve the problem for me, but gave me the direction I needed. <u>Repetition</u> was the key to my success. At first I got them all wrong but after the third time, things started to click. I felt more confident. Your chapter organizers at the end of the chapter were great. Thanks for your patience – your repetition breeds success – now students are asking me to help them solve a word problem. Can you believe it!

Best,

Rose

Rose Smith

Many of you are familiar with the terms *variables* and *constants*. If you are planning to prepare for your retirement by saving only what you can afford each year, your saving is a *variable;* if you plan to save the same amount each year, your saving is a *constant.* Now you can also say that you cannot buy clothes by size because of the many variables involved. This unit explains the importance of mathematical variables and constants when solving equations.

Basic Equation-Solving Procedures

In the chapter opener, the old weight-loss equation was challenged with a new equation based on metabolism. The definition of "equation" that follows may suggest to you what the new equation means.

   Do you know the difference between a mathematical expression, equation, and formula? A mathematical **expression** is a meaningful combination of numbers and letters called *terms.* Operational signs (such as $+$ or $-$) within the expression connect the terms to show a relationship between them. For example, $6 + 2$ and $6A - 4A$ are mathematical expressions. An **equation** is a mathematical statement with an equals sign showing that a mathematical expression on the left equals the mathematical expression on the right. An equation has an equals sign; an expression does not have an equals sign. A **formula** is an equation that expresses in symbols a general fact, rule, or principle. Formulas are shortcuts for expressing a word concept. For example, in Chapter 10 you will learn that the formula for simple interest is Interest (I) = Principal (P) $\times$ Rate (R) $\times$ Time (T). This means that when you see $I = P \times R \times T$, you recognize the simple interest formula. Now let's study basic equations.

   As a mathematical statement of equality, equations show that two numbers or groups of numbers are equal. For example, $6 + 4 = 10$ shows the equality of an equation. Equations also use letters as symbols that represent one or more numbers. These symbols, usually a letter of the alphabet, are **variables** that stand for a number. We can use a variable even though we may not know what it represents. For example, $A + 2 = 6$. The variable A

represents the number or **unknown** (4 in this example) for which we are solving. We distinguish variables from numbers, which have a fixed value. Numbers such as 3 or −7 are **constants** or **knowns,** whereas *A* and 3*A* (this means 3 times the variable *A*) are variables. So we can now say that variables and constants are *terms of mathematical expressions.*

Usually in solving for the unknown, we place variable(s) on the left side of the equation and constants on the right. The following rules for variables and constants are important.

VARIABLES AND CONSTANTS RULES

1. If no number is in front of a letter, it is a 1: $B = 1B$; $C = 1C$.

2. If no sign is in front of a letter or number, it is a +: $C = +C$; $4 = +4$.

You should be aware that in solving equations, the meaning of the symbols $+$, $-$, $\times$, and $\div$ has not changed. However, some variations occur. For example, you can also write $A \times B$ (*A* times *B*) as $A \cdot B$, $A(B)$, or AB. Also, *A* divided by *B* is the same as A/B. Remember that to solve an equation, you must find a number that can replace the unknown in the equation and make it a true statement. Now let's take a moment to look at how we can change verbal statements into variables.

Assume Dick Hersh, an employee of Nike, is 50 years old. Let's assign Dick Hersh's changing age to the symbol *A*. The symbol *A* is a variable.

Verbal statement	Variable A (age)
Dick's age 8 years ago	$A - 8$
Dick's age 8 years from today	$A + 8$
Four times Dick's age	$4A$
One-fifth Dick's age	$A/5$

To visualize how equations work, think of the old-fashioned balancing scale shown in Figure 5.1. The pole of the scale is the equals sign. The two sides of the equation are the two pans of the scale. In the left pan or left side of the equation, we have $A + 8$; in the right pan or right side of the equation, we have 58. To solve for the unknown (Dick's present age), we isolate or place the unknown (variable) on the left side and the numbers on the right. We will do this soon. For now, remember that to keep an equation (or scale) in balance, we must perform mathematical operations (addition, subtraction, multiplication, and division) to *both* sides of the equation.

FIGURE 5.1

Equality in equations

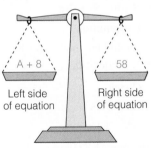

Left side of equation   Right side of equation

Dick's age in 8 years will equal 58.

LO 2

SOLVING FOR THE UNKNOWN RULE

Whatever you do to one side of an equation, you must do to the other side.

How to Solve for Unknowns in Equations

This section presents seven drill situations and the rules that will guide you in solving for unknowns in these situations. We begin with two basic rules—the opposite process rule and the equation equality rule.

OPPOSITE PROCESS RULE

If an equation indicates a process such as addition, subtraction, multiplication, or division, solve for the unknown or variable by using the opposite process. For example, if the equation process is addition, solve for the unknown by using subtraction.

EQUATION EQUALITY RULE

You can add the same quantity or number to both sides of the equation and subtract the same quantity or number from both sides of the equation without affecting the equality of the equation. You can also divide or multiply both sides of the equation by the same quantity or number *(except zero)* without affecting the equality of the equation.

To check your answer(s), substitute your answer(s) for the letter(s) in the equation. The sum of the left side should equal the sum of the right side.

Drill Situation 1: Subtracting Same Number from Both Sides of Equation

Example	Mechanical steps	Explanation
$A + 8 = 58$	$A + 8 = 58$	8 is subtracted from *both* sides of equation to isolate variable A on the left.
Dick's age A plus 8 equals 58.	$\underline{\quad -8 \quad -8 \quad}$	
	$A \quad = \quad 50$	

Check

$$50 + 8 = 58$$
$$58 = 58$$

Note: Since the equation process used *addition*, we use the opposite process rule and solve for variable A with *subtraction*. We also use the equation equality rule when we subtract the same quantity from both sides of the equation.

Drill Situation 2: Adding Same Number to Both Sides of Equation

Example	Mechanical steps	Explanation
$B - 50 = 80$	$B - 50 = 80$	50 is added to *both* sides to isolate variable B on the left.
Some number B less 50 equals 80.	$\underline{\quad +50 \quad +50 \quad}$	
	$B \quad = \quad 130$	**Check**

$$130 - 50 = 80$$
$$80 = 80$$

Note: Since the equation process used *subtraction*, we use the opposite process rule and solve for variable B with *addition*. We also use the equation equality rule when we add the same quantity to both sides of the equation.

Drill Situation 3: Dividing Both Sides of Equation by Same Number

Example	Mechanical steps	Explanation
$7G = 35$	$7G = 35$	By dividing both sides by 7, G equals 5.
Some number G times 7 equals 35.	$\dfrac{7G}{7} = \dfrac{35}{7}$	
	$G = 5$	**Check**

$$7(5) = 35$$
$$35 = 35$$

Note: Since the equation process used *multiplication*, we use the opposite process rule and solve for variable G with *division*. We also use the equation equality rule when we divide both sides of the equation by the same quantity.

Drill Situation 4: Multiplying Both Sides of Equation by Same Number

Example	Mechanical steps	Explanation
$\dfrac{V}{5} = 70$	$\dfrac{V}{5} = 70$	By multiplying both sides by 5, V is equal to 350.
Some number V divided by 5 equals 70.	$5\left(\dfrac{V}{5}\right) = 70(5)$	**Check**
	$V = 350$	$\dfrac{350}{5} = 70$

$$70 = 70$$

Note: Since the equation process used *division*, we use the opposite process rule and solve for variable V with *multiplication*. We also use the equation equality rule when we multiply both sides of the equation by the same quantity.

Drill Situation 5: Equation That Uses Subtraction and Multiplication to Solve for Unknown

MULTIPLE PROCESSES RULE

When solving for an unknown that involves more than one process, do the addition and subtraction before the multiplication and division.

Example

$$\frac{H}{4} + 2 = 5$$

When we divide unknown H by 4 and add the result to 2, the answer is 5.

Mechanical steps

$$\frac{H}{4} + 2 = 5$$

$$\frac{H}{4} + 2 = 5$$

$$\underline{\quad -2 \quad\quad -2 \quad}$$

$$\frac{H}{4} = 3$$

$$\cancel{4}\left(\frac{H}{\cancel{4}}\right) = \cancel{4}(3)$$

$$H = \boxed{12}$$

Explanation

1. Move constant to right side by subtracting 2 from both sides.

2. To isolate H, which is divided by 4, we do the opposite process and multiply 4 times *both* sides of the equation.

Check

$$\frac{12}{4} + 2 = 5$$
$$3 + 2 = 5$$
$$5 = 5$$

Drill Situation 6: Using Parentheses in Solving for Unknown

PARENTHESES RULE

When equations contain parentheses (which indicate grouping together), you solve for the unknown by first multiplying each item inside the parentheses by the number or letter just outside the parentheses. Then you continue to solve for the unknown with the opposite process used in the equation. Do the additions and subtractions first; then the multiplications and divisions.

Example

$5(P - 4) = 20$

The unknown P less 4, multiplied by 5 equals 20.

Mechanical steps

$$5(P - 4) = 20$$

$$5P - 20 = 20$$

$$\underline{\quad +20 \quad\quad +20 \quad}$$

$$\frac{\cancel{5}P}{\cancel{5}} = \frac{40}{5}$$

$$P = \boxed{8}$$

Explanation

1. Parentheses tell us that everything inside parentheses is multiplied by 5. Multiply 5 by P and 5 by -4.

2. Add 20 to both sides to isolate $5P$ on left.

3. To remove 5 in front of P, divide both sides by 5 to result in P equals 8.

Check

$$5(8 - 4) = 20$$
$$5(4) = 20$$
$$20 = 20$$

MONEY tips

Negotiate. Over 90% of customers who ask for a discount on items such as electronics, appliances, furniture, and medical bills receive one. Just ask. You could be saving money.

Drill Situation 7: Combining Like Unknowns

LIKE UNKNOWNS RULE
To solve equations with like unkowns, you first combine the unknowns and then solve with the opposite process used in the equation.

Example

$4A + A = 20$

Mechanical steps

$4A + A = 20$

$\dfrac{\cancel{5}A}{\cancel{5}} = \dfrac{20}{5}$

$\boxed{A = 4}$

Explanation

To solve this equation: $4A + 1A = 5A$. Thus, $5A = 20$. To solve for A, divide both sides by 5, leaving A equals 4.

Check

$4(4) + 4 = 20$

$20 = 20$

Before you go to Learning Unit 5–2, let's check your understanding of this unit.

LU 5–1   PRACTICE QUIZ

Complete this **Practice Quiz** to see how you are doing.

For **extra help** from your authors–Sharon and Jeff–see the student DVD

1. Write equations for the following (use the letter Q as the variable). Do not solve for the unknown.
    a. Nine less than one-half a number is fourteen.
    b. Eight times the sum of a number and thirty-one is fifty.
    c. Ten decreased by twice a number is two.
    d. Eight times a number less two equals twenty-one.
    e. The sum of four times a number and two is fifteen.
    f. If twice a number is decreased by eight, the difference is four.

2. Solve the following:
    a. $B + 24 = 60$ b. $D + 3D = 240$ c. $12B = 144$
    d. $\dfrac{B}{6} = 50$ e. $\dfrac{B}{4} + 4 = 16$ f. $3(B - 8) = 18$

✓ Solutions

1. a. $\dfrac{1}{2}Q - 9 = 14$ b. $8(Q + 31) = 50$ c. $10 - 2Q = 2$
    d. $8Q - 2 = 21$ e. $4Q + 2 = 15$ f. $2Q - 8 = 4$

2. a. $B + 24 = 60$
        $\underline{-24 -24}$
        $B \boxed{36}$

    b. $\dfrac{\cancel{4}D}{\cancel{4}} = \dfrac{240}{4}$
        $D = \boxed{60}$

    c. $\dfrac{\cancel{12}B}{\cancel{12}} = \dfrac{144}{12}$
        $B = \boxed{12}$

    d. $\cancel{6}\left(\dfrac{B}{\cancel{6}}\right) = 50(6)$
        $B = \boxed{300}$

    e. $\dfrac{B}{4} + 4 = 16$
        $\phantom{\dfrac{B}{4}}\underline{- 4 - 4}$
        $\dfrac{B}{4} = 12$
        $\cancel{4}\left(\dfrac{B}{\cancel{4}}\right) = 12(4)$
        $B = \boxed{48}$

    f. $3(B - 8) = 18$
        $3B - 24 = 18$
        $\underline{+ 24 +24}$
        $\dfrac{\cancel{3}B}{\cancel{3}} = \dfrac{42}{3}$
        $B = \boxed{14}$

LU 5–1a   **EXTRA PRACTICE QUIZ WITH WORKED-OUT SOLUTIONS**

Need more practice? Try this **Extra Practice Quiz** (check figures in the Interactive Chapter Organizer, p. 130). Worked-out Solutions can be found in Appendix B at end of text.

1. Write equations for the following (use the letter Q as the variable). Do not solve for the unknown.
   a. Eight less than one-half a number is sixteen.
   b. Twelve times the sum of a number and forty-one is 1,200.
   c. Seven decreased by twice a number is one.
   d. Four times a number less two equals twenty-four.
   e. The sum of three times a number and three is nineteen.
   f. If twice a number is decreased by six, the difference is five.

2. Solve the following:
   a. $B + 14 = 70$ b. $D + 4D = 250$ c. $11B = 121$
   d. $\dfrac{B}{8} = 90$ e. $\dfrac{B}{2} + 2 = 250$ f. $3(B - 6) = 18$

Learning Unit 5–2: Solving Word Problems for the Unknown

LO 1

When you buy a candy bar such as a Snickers, you should turn the candy bar over and carefully read the ingredients and calories contained on the back of the candy bar wrapper.

For example, on the back of the Snickers wrapper you will read that there are "170 calories per piece." You could misread this to mean that the entire Snickers bar has 170 calories. However, look closer and you will see that the Snickers bar is divided into three pieces, so if you eat the entire bar, instead of consuming 170 calories, you will consume 510 calories. Making errors like this could result in a weight gain that you cannot explain.

$$\frac{1}{3}S = 170 \text{ calories}$$

$$3\left(\frac{1}{3}S\right) = 170 \times 3$$

$$S = \boxed{510} \text{ calories per bar}$$

In this unit, we use blueprint aids in six different situations to help you solve for unknowns. Be patient and *persistent*. Remember that the more problems you work, the easier the process becomes. Do not panic! Repetition is the key. Study the five steps that follow. They will help you solve for unknowns in word problems.

SOLVING WORD PROBLEMS FOR UNKNOWNS
Step 1. Carefully read the entire problem. You may have to read it several times.
Step 2. Ask yourself: What is the problem looking for?
Step 3. When you are sure what the problem is asking, let a variable represent the unknown. If the problem has more than one unknown, represent the second unknown in terms of the same variable. For example, if the problem has two unknowns, Y is one unknown. The second unknown is $4Y$—4 times the first unknown.
Step 4. Visualize the relationship between unknowns and variables. Then set up an equation to solve for unknown(s).
Step 5. Check your result to see if it is accurate.

This clip from the *Wall Street Journal,* "How to Ace That Test," may also help you in the process of solving word problems.

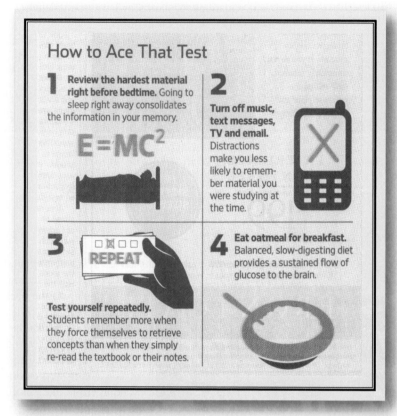

How to Ace That Test

1 **Review the hardest material right before bedtime.** Going to sleep right away consolidates the information in your memory.

$E = MC^2$

2 **Turn off music, text messages, TV and email.** Distractions make you less likely to remember material you were studying at the time.

3 REPEAT

Test yourself repeatedly. Students remember more when they force themselves to retrieve concepts than when they simply re-read the textbook or their notes.

4 **Eat oatmeal for breakfast.** Balanced, slow-digesting diet provides a sustained flow of glucose to the brain.

Word Problem Situation 1: Number Problems Today on sale at a local Stop and Shop supermarket, the price of a 1-pound can of Chock full o'Nuts coffee is $9.99. This is a $2 savings. What was the original price of the can of coffee?

LO 2

	Unknown(s)	Variable(s)	Relationship*
BLUEPRINT	Original price of Chock full o'Nuts	P	$P - \$2 = $ New price

Mechanical steps

$$P - 2 = \$\ 9.99$$
$$+ 2 \quad + 2$$
$$P \quad = \ \$11.99$$

*This column will help you visualize the equation before setting up the actual equation.

Explanation

The original price less $2 = $9.99. Note that we added $2 to both sides to isolate P on the left. Remember, $1P = P$.

Check

$11.99 − 2 = $9.99
$9.99 = $9.99

Word Problem Situation 2: Finding the Whole When Part Is Known A local Burger King budgets $\frac{1}{8}$ of its monthly profits on salaries. Salaries for the month were $12,000. What were Burger King's monthly profits?

	Unknown(s)	Variable(s)	Relationship
BLUEPRINT	Monthly profits	P	$\frac{1}{8}P$ Salaries = $12,000

Mechanical steps

$$\frac{1}{8}P = \$12,000$$
$$8\left(\frac{P}{8}\right) = \$12,000(8)$$
$$P = \boxed{\$96,000}$$

Explanation

$\frac{1}{8}P$ represents Burger King's monthly salaries. Since the equation used division, we solve for P by multiplying both sides by 8.

Check

$\frac{1}{8}(\$96,000) = \$12,000$
$12,000 = $12,000

Word Problem Situation 3: Difference Problems ICM Company sold 4 times as many computers as Ring Company. The difference in their sales is 27. How many computers of each company were sold?

	Unknown(s)	Variable(s)	Relationship
BLUEPRINT	ICM Ring	$4C$ C	$4C$ $-C$ 27

Note: If problem has two unknowns, assign the variable to smaller item or one who sells less. Then assign the other unknown using the same variable. *Use the same letter.*

Mechanical steps

$$4C − C = 27$$
$$\frac{3C}{3} = \frac{27}{3}$$
$$C = \boxed{9}$$

Ring = $\boxed{9}$ computers

ICM = 4(9)

$= \boxed{36}$ computers

Explanation

The variables replace the names ICM and Ring. We assigned Ring the variable C, since it sold fewer computers. We assigned ICM $4C$, since it sold 4 times as many computers.

Check

36 computers
$\underline{-9}$
27 computers

Word Problem Situation 4: Calculating Unit Sales Together Barry Sullivan and Mitch Ryan sold a total of 300 homes for Regis Realty. Barry sold 9 times as many homes as Mitch. How many did each sell?

	Unknown(s)	Variable(s)	Relationship
BLUEPRINT	Homes sold: B. Sullivan M. Ryan	 $9H$ H*	 $9H$ $+ H$ 300 homes

*Assign H to Ryan since he sold less.

Mechanical steps

$$9H + H = 300$$
$$\frac{10H}{10} = \frac{300}{10}$$
$$H = \boxed{30}$$

Ryan: $\boxed{30}$ homes

Sullivan: 9(30) = $\boxed{270}$ homes

Explanation

We assigned Mitch H, since he sold fewer homes. We assigned Barry $9H$, since he sold 9 times as many homes. Together Barry and Mitch sold 300 homes.

Check

30 + 270 = 300

Word Problem Situation 5: Calculating Unit and Dollar Sales (Cost per Unit) When Total Units Are Not Given Andy sold watches ($9) and alarm clocks ($5) at a flea market. Total sales were $287. People bought 4 times as many watches as alarm clocks. How many of each did Andy sell? What were the total dollar sales of each?

	Unknown(s)	Variable(s)	Price	Relationship
BLUEPRINT	*Unit sales:*			
	Watches	4C	$9	36C
	Clocks	C	5	+ 5C
				$287 total sales

Mechanical steps

$$36C + 5C = 287$$
$$\frac{41C}{41} = \frac{287}{41}$$
$$C = \boxed{7}$$

$\boxed{7}$ clocks

$4(7) = \boxed{28}$ watches

Explanation

Number of watches times $9 sales price plus number of alarm clocks times $5 sales price equals $287 total sales.

Check

$7(\$5) + 28(\$9) = \$287$
$\$35 + \$252 = \$287$
$\$287 = \$287$

Word Problem Situation 6: Calculating Unit and Dollar Sales (Cost per Unit) When Total Units Are Given Andy sold watches ($9) and alarm clocks ($5) at a flea market. Total sales for 35 watches and alarm clocks were $287. How many of each did Andy sell? What were the total dollar sales of each?

	Unknown(s)	Variable(s)	Price	Relationship
BLUEPRINT	*Unit sales:*			
	Watches	W*	$9	9W
	Clocks	35 − W	5	+ 5(35 − W)
				$287 total sales

*The more expensive item is assigned to the variable first only for this situation to make the mechanical steps easier to complete.

Mechanical steps

$$9W + 5(35 - W) = 287$$
$$9W + 175 - 5W = 287$$
$$4W + 175 = 287$$
$$\underline{\quad - 175 \quad} \quad \underline{- 175}$$
$$\frac{4W}{4} = \frac{112}{4}$$
$$W = \boxed{28}$$

Watches = $\boxed{28}$

Clocks = 35 − 28 = $\boxed{7}$

Explanation

Number of watches (W) times price per watch plus number of alarm clocks times price per alarm clock equals $287. Total units given was 35.

Check

$28(\$9) + 7(\$5) = \$287$
$\$252 + \$35 = \$287$
$\$287 = \$287$

Why did we use 35 − W? Assume we had 35 pizzas (some cheese, others meatball). If I said that I ate all the meatball pizzas (5), how many cheese pizzas are left? Thirty? Right, you subtract 5 from 35. Think of 35 − W as meaning one number.

Note in Word Problem Situations 5 and 6 that the situation is the same. In Word Problem Situation 5, we were not given total units sold (but we were told which sold better). In Word Problem Situation 6, we were given total units sold, but we did not know which sold better.

Now try these six types of word problems in the Practice Quiz. Be sure to complete blueprint aids and the mechanical steps for solving the unknown(s).

LU 5–2 PRACTICE QUIZ

Complete this **Practice Quiz** to see how you are doing.

Situations

1. An L. L. Bean sweater was reduced $30. The sale price was $90. What was the original price?

2. Kelly Doyle budgets $\frac{1}{8}$ of her yearly salary for entertainment. Kelly's total entertainment bill for the year is $6,500. What is Kelly's yearly salary?

3. Micro Knowledge sells 5 times as many computers as Morse Electronics. The difference in sales between the two stores is 20 computers. How many computers did each store sell?

4. Susie and Cara sell stoves at Elliott's Appliances. Together they sold 180 stoves in January. Susie sold 5 times as many stoves as Cara. How many stoves did each sell?

5. Pasquale's Pizza sells meatball pizzas ($6) and cheese pizzas ($5). In March, Pasquale's total sales were $1,600. People bought 2 times as many cheese pizzas as meatball pizzas. How many of each did Pasquale's sell? What were the total dollar sales of each?

6. Pasquale's Pizza sells meatball pizzas ($6) and cheese pizzas ($5). In March, Pasquale's sold 300 pizzas for $1,600. How many of each did Pasquale's sell? What was the dollar sales price of each?

✓ **Solutions**

1.

	Unknown(s)	Variable(s)	Relationship
BLUEPRINT	Original price	P^*	$P - \$30$ = Sale price Sale price = $90

*P = Original price.

Mechanical steps

$$P - \$30 = \$90$$
$$\underline{+\ 30 \qquad +\ 30}$$
$$P \qquad = \boxed{\$120}$$

2.

	Unknown(s)	Variable(s)	Relationship
BLUEPRINT	Yearly salary	S^*	$\frac{1}{8}S$ Entertainment = $6,500

*S = Salary.

Mechanical steps

$$\frac{1}{8}S = \$6,500$$
$$8\left(\frac{S}{8}\right) = \$6,500(8)$$
$$S = \boxed{\$52,000}$$

3.

	Unknown(s)	Variable(s)	Relationship
BLUEPRINT	Micro Morse	$5C^*$ C	$5C$ $-C$ 20 computers

*C = Computers.

Mechanical steps

$$5C - C = 20$$
$$\frac{4C}{4} = \frac{20}{4}$$
$$C = \boxed{5} \text{ (Morse)}$$
$$5C = \boxed{25} \text{ (Micro)}$$

4.

	Unknown(s)	Variable(s)	Relationship
BLUEPRINT	*Stoves sold:* Susie Cara	$5S^*$ S	$5S$ $-S$ 180 stoves

*S = Stoves.

Mechanical steps

$$5S + S = 180$$
$$\frac{6S}{6} = \frac{180}{6}$$
$$S = \boxed{30} \text{ (Cara)}$$
$$5S = \boxed{150} \text{ (Susie)}$$

5.

	Unknown(s)	Variable(s)	Price	Relationship
BLUEPRINT	Meatball Cheese	M $2M$	$6 5	$6M$ $+ 10M$ $1,600 total sales

Mechanical steps

$$6M + 10M = 1,600$$
$$\frac{16M}{16} = \frac{1,600}{16}$$
$$M = \boxed{100} \text{ (meatball)}$$
$$2M = \boxed{200} \text{ (cheese)}$$

Check

$$(100 \times \$6) + (200 \times \$5) = \$1,600$$
$$\$600 + \$1,000 = \$1,600$$
$$\$1,600 = \$1,600$$

6.

	Unknown(s)	Variable(s)	Price	Relationship
BLUEPRINT	*Unit sales:*			
	Meatball	M*	$6	$6M$
	Cheese	$300 - M$	5	$+ 5(300 - M)$
				$1,600 total sales

Mechanical steps

$$6M + 5(300 - M) = 1,600$$
$$6M + 1,500 - 5M = 1,600$$
$$M + 1,500 = 1,600$$
$$\underline{- 1,500 \qquad - 1,500}$$
$$M = \boxed{100}$$

Meatball = $\boxed{100}$

Cheese = $300 - 100 = \boxed{200}$

*We assign the variable to the most expensive item to make the mechanical steps easier to complete.

Check

$$100(\$6) + 200(\$5) = \$600 + \$1,000$$
$$= \$1,600$$

LU 5–2a EXTRA PRACTICE QUIZ WITH WORKED-OUT SOLUTIONS

Need more practice? Try this **Extra Practice Quiz** (check figures in the Interactive Chapter Organizer, p. 130). Worked-out Solutions can be found in Appendix B at end of text.

Situations

1. An L. L. Bean sweater was reduced $50. The sale price was $140. What was the original price?
2. Kelly Doyle budgets $\frac{1}{7}$ of her yearly salary for entertainment. Kelly's total entertainment bill for the year is $7,000. What is Kelly's yearly salary?
3. Micro Knowledge sells 8 times as many computers as Morse Electronics. The difference in sales between the two stores is 49 computers. How many computers did each store sell?
4. Susie and Cara sell stoves at Elliott's Appliances. Together they sold 360 stoves in January. Susie sold 2 times as many stoves as Cara. How many stoves did each sell?
5. Pasquale's Pizza sells meatball pizzas ($7) and cheese pizzas ($6). In March, Pasquale's total sales were $1,800. People bought 3 times as many cheese pizzas as meatball pizzas. How many of each did Pasquale's sell? What were the total dollar sales of each?
6. Pasquale's Pizza sells meatball pizzas ($7) and cheese pizzas ($6). In March, Pasquale's sold 288 pizzas for $1,800. What was the dollar sales price of each?

INTERACTIVE CHAPTER ORGANIZER

Solving for unknowns from basic equations	Mechanical steps to solve unknowns	Key point(s)	You try it*
Situation 1: Subtracting same number from both sides of equation, p. 120	$D + 10 = 12$ $\underline{- 10 \quad - 10}$ $D = 2$	Subtract 10 from both sides of equation to isolate variable D on the left. Since equation used addition, we solve by using opposite process—subtraction.	**Solve** $E + 15 = 14$
Situation 2: Adding same number to both sides of equation, p. 120	$L - 24 = 40$ $\underline{+ 24 \quad + 24}$ $L = 64$	Add 24 to both sides to isolate unknown L on left. We solve by using opposite process of subtraction—addition.	**Solve** $B - 40 = 80$
Situation 3: Dividing both sides of equation by same number, p. 120	$6B = 24$ $\dfrac{6B}{6} = \dfrac{24}{6}$ $B = 4$	To isolate B on the left, divide both sides of the equation by 6. Thus, the 6 on the left cancels—leaving B equal to 4. Since equation used multiplication, we solve unknown by using opposite process—division.	**Solve** $5C = 75$

(continues)

INTERACTIVE CHAPTER ORGANIZER

Solving for unknowns from basic equations	Mechanical steps to solve unknowns	Key point(s)	You try it*
Situation 4: Multiplying both sides of equation by same number, p. 120	$$\frac{R}{3} = 15$$ $$3\left(\frac{R}{3}\right) = 15(3)$$ $$R = \boxed{45}$$	To remove denominator, multiply both sides of the equation by 3—the 3 on the left side cancels, leaving R equal to 45. Since equation used division, we solve unknown by using opposite process—multiplication.	**Solve** $$\frac{A}{6} = 60$$
Situation 5: Equation that uses subtraction and multiplication to solve for unknown, p. 121	$$\frac{B}{3} + 6 = 13$$ $$\underline{-6 \quad -6}$$ $$\frac{B}{3} = 7$$ $$3\left(\frac{B}{3}\right) = 7(3)$$ $$B = \boxed{21}$$	1. Move constant 6 to right side by subtracting 6 from both sides. 2. Isolate B on left by multiplying both sides by 3.	**Solve** $$\frac{C}{4} + 10 = 17$$
Situation 6: Using parentheses in solving for unknown, p. 121	$$6(A - 5) = 12$$ $$6A - 30 = 12$$ $$\underline{+30 \quad +30}$$ $$\frac{6A}{6} = \frac{42}{6}$$ $$A = \boxed{7}$$	Parentheses indicate multiplication. Multiply 6 times A and 6 times -5. Result is $6A - 30$ on left side of the equation. Now add 30 to both sides to isolate $6A$ on left. To remove 6 in front of A, divide both sides by 6, to result in A equal to 7. Note that when deleting parentheses, we did not have to multiply the right side.	**Solve** $$7(B - 10) = 35$$
Situation 7: Combining like unknowns, p. 122	$$6A + 2A = 64$$ $$\frac{8A}{8} = \frac{64}{8}$$ $$A = \boxed{8}$$	$6A + 2A$ combine to $8A$. To solve for A, we divide both sides by 8.	**Solve** $$5B + 3B = 17$$

Solving for unknowns from word problems	Blueprint aid	Mechanical steps to solve unknown with check	You try it*
Situation 1: Number problems, p. 124 **U.S. Air reduced its airfare to California by $60. The sale price was $95. What was the original price?**	BLUEPRINT <table><tr><td>Unknown(s)</td><td>Variable(s)</td><td>Relationship</td></tr><tr><td>Original price</td><td>P</td><td>P − $60 = Sale price Sale price = $95</td></tr></table>	$$P - \$60 = \$95$$ $$\underline{+60 \quad +60}$$ $$P = \boxed{\$155}$$ **Check** $$\$155 - \$60 = \$95$$ $$\$95 = \$95$$	**Solve** U.S. Air reduced its airfare to California by $53. The sale price was $110. What was the original price?
Situation 2: Finding the whole when part is known, p. 125 **K. McCarthy spends $^1/_8$ of her budget for school. What is the total budget if school costs $5,000?**	BLUEPRINT <table><tr><td>Unknown(s)</td><td>Variable(s)</td><td>Relationship</td></tr><tr><td>Total budget</td><td>B</td><td>$^1/_8 B$ School = $5,000</td></tr></table>	$$\frac{1}{8}B = \$5,000$$ $$8\left(\frac{B}{8}\right) = \$5,000(8)$$ $$B = \boxed{\$40,000}$$ **Check** $$\frac{1}{8}(\$40,000) = \$5,000$$ $$\$5,000 = \$5,000$$	**Solve** K. McCarthy spends $^1/_7$ of her budget for school. What is the total budget if school costs $6,000?

(continues)

INTERACTIVE CHAPTER ORGANIZER

Solving for unknowns from word problems	Blueprint aid	Mechanical steps to solve unknown with check	You try it*
Situation 3: Difference problems, p. 125 Moe sold 8 times as many suitcases as Bill. The difference in their sales is 280 suitcases. How many suitcases did each sell?	**BLUEPRINT** | Unknown(s)	Variable(s)	Relationship
---	---	---
Suitcases sold:		
Moe	8S	8S
Bill	S	$\underline{- S}$
		280 suitcases		$8S - S = 280$ $\dfrac{7S}{7} = \dfrac{280}{7}$ $S = \boxed{40}$ (Bill) $8(40) = \boxed{320}$ (Moe) **Check** $320 - 40 = 280$ $280 = 280$	**Solve** Moe sold 9 times as many suitcases as Bill. The difference in their sales is 640 suitcases. How many suitcases did each sell?
Situation 4: Calculating unit sales, p. 125 Moe sold 8 times as many suitcases as Bill. Together they sold a total of 360. How many did each sell?	**BLUEPRINT** | Unknown(s)	Variable(s)	Relationship
---	---	---
Suitcases sold:		
Moe	8S	8S
Bill	S	$\underline{+ S}$
		360 suitcases		$8S + S = 360$ $\dfrac{9S}{9} = \dfrac{360}{9}$ $S = \boxed{40}$ (Bill) $8(40) = \boxed{320}$ (Moe) **Check** $320 + 40 = 360$ $360 = 360$	**Solve** Moe sold 9 times as many suitcases as Bill. Together they sold a total of 640. How many did each sell?
Situation 5: Calculating unit and dollar sales (cost per unit) when *total units not given*, p. 126 Blue Furniture Company ordered sleepers ($300) and nonsleepers ($200) that cost $8,000. Blue expects sleepers to out-sell nonsleepers 2 to 1. How many units of each were ordered? What were dollar costs of each?	**BLUEPRINT** 	Unknown(s)	Variable(s)	Price	Relationship
Sleepers	2N	$300	600N
Nonsleepers	N	200	+200N
			$8,000 total cost		$600N + 200N = 8,000$ $\dfrac{800N}{800} = \dfrac{8,000}{800}$ $N = \boxed{10}$ (nonsleepers) $2N = \boxed{20}$ (sleepers) **Check** $10 \times \$200 = \$2,000$ $20 \times \$300 = \underline{\ 6,000}$ $= \$8,000$	**Solve** Blue Furniture Company ordered sleepers ($400) and nonsleepers ($300) that cost $15,000. Blue expects sleepers to outsell nonsleepers 3 to 1. How many units of each were ordered? What were dollar costs of each?
Situation 6: Calculating unit and dollar sales (cost per unit) when *total units given*, p. 126 Blue Furniture Company ordered 30 sofas (sleepers and nonsleepers) that cost $8,000. The whole-sale unit cost was $300 for the sleepers and $200 for the nonsleepers. How many units of each were ordered? What were dollar costs of each?	**BLUEPRINT** 	Unknown(s)	Variable(s)	Price	Relationship
Unit costs			
Sleepers	S	$300	300S
Nonsleepers	30 − S	200	+200(30 − S)
			$8,000 total cost	 *Note:* When the total units are given, the higher-priced item (sleepers) is assigned to the variable first. This makes the mechanical steps easier to complete.	$300S + 200(30 - S) = 8,000$ $300S + 6,000 - 200S = 8,000$ $100S + 6,000 = 8,000$ $\underline{\ \ \ \ \ - 6,000 \ \ \ \ \ \ \ \ - 6,000}$ $\dfrac{100S}{100} = \dfrac{2,000}{100}$ $S = \boxed{20}$ Nonsleepers $= 30 - 20$ $= \boxed{10}$ **Check** $20(\$300) + 10(\$200) = \$8,000$ $\$6,000 + \ \$2,000 = \$8,000$ $\$8,000 = \$8,000$	**Solve** Blue Furniture Company ordered 40 sofas (sleepers and nonsleepers) that cost $15,000. The wholesale unit cost was $400 for the sleepers and $300 for the non-sleepers. How many units of each were ordered? What were dollar costs of each?

KEY TERMS	Constants, p. 119	Formula, p. 118	Variables, p. 118
	Equation, p. 118	Knowns, p. 119	
	Expression, p. 118	Unknown, p. 119	

| **Check Figures for Extra Practice Quizzes with Page References. (Worked-out Solutions in Appendix B.)** | LU 5–1a (p. 123)
1. a. $Q/2 - 8 = 16$ b. $12(Q + 41) = 1,200$
   c. $7 - 2Q = 1$ d. $4Q - 2 = 24$
   e. $3Q + 3 = 19$ f. $2Q - 6 = 5$
2. a. 56   b. 50   c. 11
   d. 720   e. 496   f. 12 | LU 5–2a (p. 128)
1. $P = \$190$
2. $S = \$49,000$
3. Morse 7; Micro 56
4. Cara 120; Susie 240
5. Meatball 72; cheese 216; Meatball = $504; cheese = $1,296
6. Meatball $504; cheese $1,296 |

*Worked-out solutions are in Appendix B.

Critical Thinking Discussion Questions with Chapter Concept Check

1. Explain the difference between a variable and a constant. What would you consider your monthly car payment—a variable or a constant?

2. How does the opposite process rule help solve for the variable in an equation? If a Mercedes costs 3 times as much as a Saab, how could the opposite process rule be used? The selling price of the Mercedes is $60,000.

3. What is the difference between Word Problem Situations 5 and 6 in Learning Unit 5–2? Show why the more expensive item in Word Problem Situation 6 is assigned to the variable first.

4. **Chapter Concept Check.** Based on the article in the chapter opener and all of the information you have learned about equations in this chapter, go to a weight-loss website and create several equations on how to lose weight. Be sure to create a word problem and specify the steps you need to take to solve this weight-loss problem.

Classroom Notes

Check figures for odd-numbered problems in Appendix C.   Name _____ Date _____

DRILL PROBLEMS (First of Three Sets)

Solve the unknown from the following equations: *LU 5-1(2)*

5–1. $C - 40 = 315$ **5–2.** $B + 110 = 400$ **5–3.** $Q + 100 = 400$ **5–4.** $Q - 60 = 850$

5–5. $5Y = 75$ **5–6.** $\dfrac{P}{6} = 92$ **5–7.** $8Y = 96$ **5–8.** $\dfrac{N}{16} = 5$

5–9. $4(P - 9) = 64$ **5–10.** $3(P - 3) = 27$

WORD PROBLEMS (First of Three Sets)

5–11. Lee and Fred are elementary school teachers. Fred works for a charter school in Pacific Palisades, California, where class size reduction is a goal for 2013. Lee works for a noncharter school where funds do not allow for class size reduction policies. Lee's fifth-grade class has 1.4 times as many students as Fred's. If there are a total of 60 students, how many students does Fred's class have? How many students does Lee's class have? *LU 5-2(2)*

5–12. In 1955 an antique car that originally cost \$3,668 is valued today at \$62,125 if in excellent condition, which is $1\frac{3}{4}$ times as **eXcel** much as a car in very nice condition—if you can find an owner willing to part with one for any price. What would be the value of the car in very nice condition? *LU 5-2(2)*

5–13. Joe Sullivan and Hugh Kee sell cars for a Ford dealer. Over the past year, they sold 300 cars. Joe sells 5 times as many cars as Hugh. How many cars did each sell? *LU 5-2(2)*

5–14. Nanda Yueh and Lane Zuriff sell homes for ERA Realty. Over the past 6 months they sold 120 homes. Nanda sold 3 times **eXcel** as many homes as Lane. How many homes did each sell? *LU 5-2(2)*

5–15. Dots sells T-shirts ($2) and shorts ($4). In April, total sales were $600. People bought 4 times as many T-shirts as shorts. How many T-shirts and shorts did Dots sell? Check your answer. *LU 5-2(2)*

5–16. Dots sells a total of 250 T-shirts ($2) and shorts ($4). In April, total sales were $600. How many T-shirts and shorts did Dots sell? Check your answer. *Hint:* Let S = Shorts. *LU 5-2(2)*

DRILL PROBLEMS (Second of Three Sets)

Solve the unknown from the following equations: *LU 5-1(2)*

5–17. $7B = 490$

5–18. $7(A - 5) = 63$

5–19. $\dfrac{N}{9} = 7$

5–20. $18(C - 3) = 162$

5–21. $9Y - 10 = 53$

5–22. $7B + 5 = 26$

WORD PROBLEMS (Second of Three Sets)

5–23. On a flight from Boston to San Diego, American reduced its Internet price by $190.00. The new sale price was $420.99. What was the original price? *LU 5-2(2)*

5–24. Jill, an employee at Old Navy, budgets $\frac{1}{5}$ of her yearly salary for clothing. Jill's total clothing bill for the year is $8,000. What is her yearly salary? *LU 5-2(2)*

5–25. Bill's Roast Beef sells 5 times as many sandwiches as Pete's Deli. The difference between their sales is 360 sandwiches. **eXcel** How many sandwiches did each sell? *LU 5-2(2)*

5–26. The count of discouraged unemployed workers rose to 503,000, $2\frac{1}{2}$ times as many as in the previous year. How many discouraged unemployed workers were there in the previous year?   *LU 5-2(2)*

5–27. A local Computer City sells batteries ($3) and small boxes of pens ($5). In August, total sales were $960. Customers bought 5 times as many batteries as boxes of pens. How many of each did Computer City sell? Check your answer.   *LU 5-2(2)*

5–28. Staples sells boxes of pens ($10) and rubber bands ($4). Leona ordered a total of 24 cartons for $210. How many boxes of each did Leona order? Check your answer. *Hint:* Let P = Pens.   *LU 5-2(2)*

DRILL PROBLEMS (Third of Three Sets)

Solve the unknown from the following equations: *LU 5-1(2)*

5–29. $A + 90 - 15 = 210$ **5–30.** $5Y + 15(Y + 1) = 35$

5–31. $3M + 20 = 2M + 80$ **5–32.** $20(C - 50) = 19,000$

WORD PROBLEMS (Third of Three Sets)

5–33. If Colorado Springs, Colorado, has 1.2 times as many days of sunshine than Boston, Massachusetts, how many days of sunshine does each city have if there are a total of 464 days of sunshine between the two in a year? (Round to the nearest day.)   *LU 5-2(2)*

5–34. At General Electric, shift 1 produced 4 times as much as shift 2. General Electric's total production for July was 5,500 jet engines. What was the output for each shift? *LU 5-2(2)*

5–35. Ivy Corporation gave 84 people a bonus. If Ivy had given 2 more people bonuses, Ivy would have rewarded $\frac{2}{3}$ of the workforce. How large is Ivy's workforce? *LU 5-2(2)*

5–36. Jim Murray and Phyllis Lowe received a total of $50,000 from a deceased relative's estate. They decided to put $10,000 in a trust for their nephew and divide the remainder. Phyllis received $\frac{3}{4}$ of the remainder; Jim received $\frac{1}{4}$. How much did Jim and Phyllis receive? *LU 5-2(2)*

5–37. The first shift of GME Corporation produced $1\frac{1}{2}$ times as many lanterns as the second shift. GME produced 5,600 lanterns in November. How many lanterns did GME produce on each shift? *LU 5-2(2)*

5–38. Walmart sells thermometers ($2) and hot-water bottles ($6). In December, Walmart's total sales were $1,200. Customers bought 7 times as many thermometers as hot-water bottles. How many of each did Walmart sell? Check your answer. *LU 5-2(2)*

5–39. Ace Hardware sells boxes of wrenches ($100) and hammers ($300). Howard ordered 40 boxes of wrenches and hammers for $8,400. How many boxes of each are in the order? Check your answer. *LU 5-2(2)*

5–40. The Susan Hansen Group in St. George, Utah, sells $16,000,000 of single-family homes and townhomes a year. If single-family homes, with an average selling price of $250,000, sell 3.5 times more often than townhomes, with an average selling price of $190,000, how many of each are sold? (Round to nearest whole.) *LU 5-2(2)*

5–41. Want to donate to a better cause? Consider micro-lending. Micro-lending is a process where you lend directly to entrepreneurs in developing countries. You can lend starting at $25. Kiva.org boasts a 99% repayment rate. The average loan to an entrepreneur is $388.44 and the average loan amount is $261.14. With a total amount loaned of $283,697,150, how many people are lending money if the average number of loans per lender is 8? *LU 5-2(2)*

CHALLENGE PROBLEMS

5–42. Myron Corporation is sponsoring a walking race at its company outing. Leona Jackson and Sam Peterson love to walk. Leona walks at the rate of 5 miles per hour. Sam walks at the rate of 6 miles per hour. Assume they start walking from the same place and walk in a straight line. Sam starts $\frac{1}{2}$ hour after Leona. Answer the questions that follow. *Hint:* Distance = Rate $\times$ Time. *LU 5-2(2)*

  a. How long will it take Sam to meet Leona?

  b. How many miles would each have walked?

  c. Assume Leona and Sam meet in Lonetown Station where two buses leave along parallel routes in opposite directions. The bus travelling east has a 60 mph speed. The bus traveling west has a 40 mph speed. In how many hours will the buses be 600 miles apart?

5–43. Bessy has 6 times as much money as Bob, but when each earns $6, Bessy will have 3 times as much money as Bob. How much does each have before and after earning the $6? *LU 5-2(2)*

SUMMARY PRACTICE TEST You Tube™

Do you need help? The DVD has step-by-step worked-out solutions.

1. Delta reduced its round-trip ticket price from Portland to Boston by $140. The sale price was $401.90. What was the original price? *(p. 124)   LU 5-2(2)*

2. David Role is an employee of Google. He budgets $\frac{1}{7}$ of his salary for clothing. If David's total clothing for the year is $12,000, what is his yearly salary? *(p. 125)   LU 5-2(2)*

3. A local Best Buy sells 8 times as many iPods as Sears. The difference between their sales is 490 iPods. How many iPods did each sell? *(p. 125)   LU 5-2(2)*

4. Working at Staples, Jill Reese and Abby Lee sold a total of 1,200 calculators. Jill sold 5 times as many calculators as Abby. How many did each sell? *(p. 125)   LU 5-2(2)*

5. Target sells sets of pots ($30) and dishes ($20) at the local store. On the July 4 weekend, Target's total sales were $2,600. People bought 6 times as many pots as dishes. How many of each did Target sell? Check your answer. *(p. 126)* *LU 5-2(2)*

6. A local Dominos sold a total of 1,600 small pizzas ($9) and pasta dinners ($13) during the Super Bowl. How many of each did Dominos sell if total sales were $15,600? Check your answer. *(p. 126)* *LU 5-2(2)*

How can you solve the world's problems?

PROBLEM 1
Ticket to ride

Your student business club has U.S. $1,000 to spend on a day trip to Toronto. You estimate U.S. $200 for gas and tolls for the bus, and C$10 for parking at the science center. Go to the Ontario Science Center, website (http://www.ontariosciencecentre.ca), to find the cost of admission, including the two OMNIMAX films. Based on these costs, how many students can the business club afford to send on this trip? (*Hint:* Go to http://www.oanda.com/converter/classic for exchange rates.)

Discussion Questions

1. How much money would you budget for meals and other expenses on this trip?

2. What would be some fundraiser ideas to earn more money for your club to take this trip? How much additional revenue could you gain from these fundraisers?

PROBLEM 2
More People, More Debt

Go to http://www.census.gov/main/www/popclock.html to find the U.S. population. Then, go to http://www.brillig.com/debt_clock to find the U.S. national debt. Use these data to determine the U.S. government's debt per person. Compare this with the number quoted on the debt clock site.

Discussion Questions

1. What do you feel is fueling the growth in the U.S. population?
2. Do you think the national debt will continue to rise? Why?

PROBLEM 3
Fueling Your Travels

Go to http://www.fuelcostcalculator.com. Find the average cost of fuel for your state. If the vehicle you drive averages 25 miles per gallon, what would it cost for you to travel 1,500 miles for your summer vacation?

Discussion Questions

1. Based on rising fuel prices, should you consider an electric or hybrid car for your next purchase? Why?

2. How would the price of driving to your destination compare to other forms of travel (i.e., air, train, bus, etc.)? Which would be your preferred method of travel for your vacation?

PROBLEM 4
Stocking up on Gap

Go to http://finance.yahoo.com/lookup and find the current stock price for Gap, Inc. How many shares of this stock could be purchased at the current price for $1,500.00?

Discussion Questions

1. Is Gap's stock price a value for the money? Why?
2. What are some factors that would cause Gap's stock price to increase? What factors may cause its stock price to decrease?

Tax-Smart Ways to Help Your Kids

Uncle Sam (and some states) give a little back when you help pay college bills or save for their future. BY KIMBERLY LANKFORD

GENEROSITY MAY BE ITS OWN reward, but it's even better when your gift garners a tax break. There are several tax-smart ways to help your kids or grandkids:

Feed a 529 plan. Money in a 529 plan may be used tax-free for college costs, and you may get a state income-tax break for your contributions. To qualify for a state tax break, you usually need to contribute to your own state's 529 plan (although five states—Arizona, Kansas, Maine, Missouri and Pennsylvania—allow a deduction for contributions made to any state's plan). Some states let anyone take a tax deduction for their contributions; others give the tax break only to the owner of the account. But there's no limit to the number of 529 accounts that may be opened for one child, so parents and grandparents, for example, can open separate accounts and deduct contributions (see www .savingforcollege.com for details about each state's plan and tax rules).

Get a big gift-tax break. In 2011, you may generally give up to $13,000 per person without being subject to gift-tax rules. Or you may make five years' worth of 529 contributions in one year—up to $65,000 per child, or up to $130,000 per child per married couple—without triggering the gift tax. Caveat: If you give money to that person again within the next five years, you'll eat into your lifetime maximum of $5 million in tax-free gifts.

Take credit for tuition payments. The American Opportunity credit can cut your tax bill by up to $2,500 per student if you're paying tuition for the first four years of college. To qualify for the full credit, the student must be considered your dependent and you must spend at least $4,000 in tuition and qualified expenses (including fees, books and other course materials). Plus, your modified adjusted gross income must be below $160,000 if married filing jointly or $80,000 if single or head of household (couples earning up to $180,000 or singles earning up to $90,000 can get a partial credit).

Pay college tuition directly. Direct payments of tuition (but not room and board) to educational institutions are excluded from the $13,000 annual gift-tax limit. This rule applies to anyone making the tuition payment and is particularly popular with grandparents who want to give some extra money to their grandkids without running up against the gift-tax limits.

Help contribute to a Roth IRA. Kids of any age can open a Roth IRA as long as they have earned income from a job—even if it's just baby-sitting or lawn mowing. They may contribute up to the amount of their earned income for the year—with a $5,000 maximum in 2011—and you can give them the money to make the contributions. You won't get a tax break for your gift, but the kids will reap the benefits in the future—by withdrawing all of the money (including the earnings) tax-free after age 59½. And they can access the contributions at any time without taxes or penalties.

Open a custodial account. Open an account for your children or grandchildren at a brokerage firm or mutual fund company and make it a learning experience by making the investing decisions together. You can use the money for anything that benefits the child until he or she reaches the age of majority (21 in most states; 18 in a few) and takes over control of the account. Custodial accounts for children younger than 19 and full-time students younger than 24 are generally subject to the kiddie-tax rules: The first $950 of the child's investment income is tax-free; the next $950 is taxed at the child's own, low rate. Any investment income that tops $1,900 in 2011 is taxed at the parents' higher rate. ∎

BUSINESS MATH ISSUE

Saving for your kids at an early age is not the best use of your cash.

1. List the key points of the article and information to support your position.
2. Write a group defense of your position using math calculations to support your view.

Percents and Their Applications

Google to Give Staff 10% Raise

BY AMIR EFRATI
AND SCOTT MORRISON

Moving to staunch the defection of staff to competitors, **Google** Inc. is giving a 10% raise to all of its 23,000 employees, according to people familiar with the matter.

The raise, which will be given to executives and staff across the globe, is effective in January.

The pay hike comes as Google ramps up its battle with competitors, especially neighboring **Facebook** Inc., in a fight to secure talented staff. Roughly 10% of Facebook's employees are Google veterans, and other Silicon Valley companies have aggressively poached employees from the Internet giant.

Chief Executive Eric Schmidt disclosed the raise in an email to employees, saying the company wants to lift morale. "We want to make sure that you feel rewarded for your hard work," Mr. Schmidt wrote. "We want to continue to attract the best people to Google."

IF WE BUILD OUR SOFTWARE WITH NO BUGS, WE CAN MAKE A 10% RETURN ON OUR INVESTMENT.

10%

BUT IF WE DO A POOR JOB, WE CAN MAKE A 40% RETURN BY SELLING UPGRADES AND SERVICE.

BUT DON'T WORRY, WE ONLY HAVE THE BUDGET FOR A POOR JOB.

I CAN REMEMB IF WE CHEAP SMAR

PHEW!

DILBERT: © Scott Adams/Dist. by United Feature Syndicate, Inc.

LU 6–1: Conversions

1. Convert decimals to percents (including rounding percents), percents to decimals, and fractions to percents *(pp. 143–147)*.

2. Convert percents to fractions *(p. 147)*.

LU 6–2: Application of Percents—Portion Formula

1. List and define the key elements of the portion formula *(p. 149)*.

2. Solve for one unknown of the portion formula when the other two key elements are given *(pp. 149–153)*.

3. Calculate the rate of percent increases and decreases *(pp. 153–156)*.

VOCABULARY PREVIEW

Here are key terms in this chapter. After completing the chapter, if you know the term, place a checkmark in the parentheses. If you don't know the term, look it up and put the page number where it can be found.

Base ( ) Percent decrease ( ) Percent increase ( ) Percents ( ) Portion ( ) Rate ( )

The following *Wall Street Journal* clips illustrate the use of percents to show relationships between numbers. For example, profit at the Family Dollar is up by 23% from an earlier period of time. On the other hand, J.M. Smucker is reporting that it will cut its workforce by 15% and close four plants. Additionally, in the chapter opener, we read that Google is giving a 10% raise to its employees.

To understand percents, you should first understand the conversion relationship between decimals, percents, and fractions as explained in Learning Unit 6–1. Then, in Learning Unit 6–2, you will be ready to apply percents to personal and business events.

Family Dollar's Profit Rises 23%

BY MELISSA KORN

Family Dollar Stores Inc., which posted a 23% rise in fiscal-fourth-quarter profit Wednesday, said low-income shoppers are being joined by middle-class consumers in the discount chain's aisles.

The company said customers are still struggling financially and continue to seek bargains in apparel, pantry staples and other items. Family Dollar also said it plans to accelerate new-store growth and begin a store-renovation program.

Smucker to Cut Workers, Shut Plants

J.M. Smucker Co. said it will cut 15% of its work force, or about 700 jobs, over the next three years, closing four plants and building a new one.

The company said once the measures are fully in place, it expects to save $60 million annually.

The maker of fruit spreads, Folgers coffee and other foods also will close two fruit-spreads plants in 2013 and consolidate all coffee production into facilities in New Orleans, shuttering two other plants over the next two years.

Meanwhile, the company plans to spend $220 million over the next three years in its coffee and namesake businesses, building a new plant and expenditures for new equipment and technology.

Learning Unit 6–1: Conversions

LO 1

When we described parts of a whole in previous chapters, we used fractions and decimals. Percents also describe parts of a whole. The word *percent* means per 100. The percent symbol (%) indicates hundredths (division by 100). **Percents** are the result of expressing numbers as part of 100.

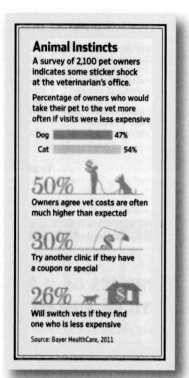

GLOBAL

Disney To Launch Channel In Russia

By Ethan Smith
And Greg White

Walt Disney Co. said it reached a deal to start a Disney Channel in Russia, after more than three years of effort.

The new channel is to be a joint venture between Disney and UTH Russia, a media holding company. UTH's Seven TV is to become Disney Channel. Disney will own 49% of the channel with UTH holding the other 51%.

Russia's Interfax news agency said Disney was spending $300 million for its stake. Disney declined to discuss financial terms.

© Design Pics/Ben Welsh

Percents can provide some revealing information. The *Wall Street Journal* clipping "Animal Instincts" in the margin shows that 30% of pet owners would try another clinic if they had a coupon or special. This 30% represents 30 pet owners out of 100.

Let's return to the M&M'S® example from earlier chapters. In Table 6.1, we use our bag of 55 M&M'S® to show how fractions, decimals, and percents can refer to the same parts of a whole. For example, the bag of 55 M&M'S® contains 18 yellow M&M'S®. As you can see in Table 6.1, the 18 candies in the bag of 55 can be expressed as a fraction ($\frac{18}{55}$), decimal (.33), and percent (32.73%). If you visit the M&M'S® website, you will see that the standard is 11 yellow M&M'S®. The clipping (below) "What Colors Come in Your Bag?" shows an M&M'S® Milk Chocolate Candies Color Chart.

In this unit we discuss converting decimals to percents (including rounding percents), percents to decimals, fractions to percents, and percents to fractions. You will see when you study converting fractions to percents why you should first learn how to convert decimals to percents.

What Colors Come In Your Bag?

Information adapted from http://us.mms.com/us/about/products/milkchocolate/

| TABLE | 6.1 | Analyzing a bag of M&M'S® |

Color	Fraction	Decimal (hundredth)	Percent (hundredth)
Yellow	$\frac{18}{55}$	.33	32.73%
Red	$\frac{10}{55}$	.18	18.18
Blue	$\frac{9}{55}$	.16	16.36
Orange	$\frac{7}{55}$	.13	12.73
Brown	$\frac{6}{55}$	.11	10.91
Green	$\frac{5}{55}$	.09	9.09
Total	$\frac{55}{55}=1$	1.00	100.00%

Converting Decimals to Percents

The *Wall Street Journal* clip "Disney To Launch Channel In Russia" shows that Disney is starting a new Disney channel in Russia with 49% Disney ownership. If the clipping had stated the 49% as a decimal (.49), could you give its equivalent in percent? The decimal .49 in decimal fraction is $\frac{49}{100}$. As you know, percents are the result of expressing numbers as part of 100, so 49% = $\frac{49}{100}$. You can now conclude that .49 = $\frac{49}{100}$ = 49%.

The steps for converting decimals to percents are as follows:

CONVERTING DECIMALS TO PERCENTS

Step 1. Move the decimal point two places to the right. You are multiplying by 100. If necessary, add zeros. This rule is also used for whole numbers and mixed decimals.

Step 2. Add a percent symbol at the end of the number.

EXAMPLES

$$.49 = .49. = \boxed{49\%}$$ $$.8 = .80. = \boxed{80\%}$$ $$8 = 8.00. = \boxed{800\%}$$

Add 1 zero to make two places.   Add 2 zeros to make two places.

$$.425 = .42.5 = \boxed{42.5\%}$$ $$.007 = .00.7 = \boxed{.7\%}$$ $$2.51 = 2.51. = \boxed{251\%}$$

Caution: One percent means 1 out of every 100. Since .7% is less than 1%, it means $\frac{7}{10}$ of 1%—a very small amount. Less than 1% is less than .01. To show a number less than 1%, you must use more than two decimal places and add 2 zeros. Example: .7% = .007.

Rounding Percents

When necessary, percents should be rounded. Rounding percents is similar to rounding whole numbers. Use the following steps to round percents:

ROUNDING PERCENTS
Step 1. When you convert from a fraction or decimal, be sure your answer is in percent before rounding.
Step 2. Identify the specific digit. If the digit to the right of the identified digit is 5 or greater, round up the identified digit.
Step 3. Delete digits to the right of the identified digit.

For example, Table 6.1 (p. 144) shows that the 18 yellow M&M'S® rounded to the nearest hundredth percent is 32.73% of the bag of 55 M&M'S®. Let's look at how we arrived at this figure.

When using a calculator, you press 18 ÷ 55 %. This allows you to go right to percent, avoiding the decimal step.

Step 1. $\frac{18}{55} = .3272727 = 32.72727\%$ Note that the number is in percent! Identify the hundredth percent digit.

Step 2.   32.73727%   Digit to the right of the identified digit is greater than 5, so the identified digit is increased by 1.

Step 3. $\boxed{32.73\%}$ Delete digits to the right of the identified digit.

Converting Percents to Decimals

Note in the following *Wall Street Journal* clip "The New Ice Age" that ice cream sales are down by .4%.

In the paragraph and steps that follow, you will learn how to convert percents to decimals. The example using .4% comes from the clipping "The New Ice Age."

To convert percents to decimals, you reverse the process used to convert decimals to percents. In our earlier discussion on converting decimals to percents (p. 144), we asked if the 49% in the "Disney" clipping had been in decimals and not percent, could you convert the decimals to the 49%? Once again, the definition of percent states that $49\% = \frac{49}{100}$. The fraction $\frac{49}{100}$ can be written in decimal form as .49. You can conclude that $49\% = \frac{49}{100} = .49$. Now you can see this procedure in the following conversion steps:

CONVERTING PERCENTS TO DECIMALS
Step 1. Drop the percent symbol.
Step 2. Move the decimal point two places to the left. You are dividing by 100. If necessary, add zeros.

EXAMPLES

Note that when a percent is less than 1%, the decimal conversion has at least two leading zeros before the number .004.

$.4\% = .00.4 = \boxed{.004}$ $2\% = .02. = \boxed{.02}$ $49\% = .49. = \boxed{.49}$

Add 2 zeros to make two places.   Add 1 zero to make two places.

$54.5\% = .54.5 = \boxed{.545}$ $824.4\% = 8.24.4 = \boxed{8.244}$

Now we must explain how to change fractional percents such as $\frac{1}{5}\%$ to a decimal. Remember that fractional percents are values less than 1%. For example, $\frac{1}{5}\%$ is $\frac{1}{5}$ of 1%. Fractional percents can appear singly or in combination with whole numbers. To convert them to decimals, use the following steps:

CONVERTING FRACTIONAL PERCENTS TO DECIMALS
Step 1. Convert a single fractional percent to its decimal equivalent by dividing the numerator by the denominator. If necessary, round the answer.
Step 2. If a fractional percent is combined with a whole number (mixed fractional percent), convert the fractional percent first. Then combine the whole number and the fractional percent.
Step 3. Drop the percent symbol; move the decimal point two places to the left (this divides the number by 100).

EXAMPLES

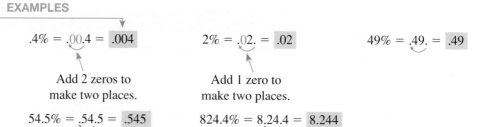

$\frac{1}{5}\% = .20\% = .00.20 = \boxed{.0020}$ Think of $7\frac{3}{4}\%$ as

$\frac{1}{4}\% = .25\% = .00.25 = \boxed{.0025}$ $7\% = \quad .07$

$7\frac{3}{4}\% = 7.75\% = .07.75 = \boxed{.0775}$ $+ \frac{3}{4}\% = \ + .0075$

$6\frac{1}{2}\% = 6.5\% = .06.5 = \boxed{.065}$ $7\frac{3}{4}\% = \quad .0775$

Converting Fractions to Percents

When fractions have denominators of 100, the numerator becomes the percent. Other fractions must be first converted to decimals; then the decimals are converted to percents.

CONVERTING FRACTIONS TO PERCENTS
Step I. Divide the numerator by the denominator to convert the fraction to a decimal.
Step 2. Move the decimal point two places to the right; add the percent symbol.

EXAMPLES

$$\frac{3}{4} = .75 = .75. = \boxed{75\%} \qquad \frac{1}{5} = .20 = .20. = \boxed{20\%} \qquad \frac{1}{20} = .05 = .05. = \boxed{5\%}$$

LO 2

Converting Percents to Fractions

Using the definition of percent, you can write any percent as a fraction whose denominator is 100. Thus, when we convert a percent to a fraction, we drop the percent symbol and write the number over 100, which is the same as multiplying the number by $\frac{1}{100}$. This method of multiplying by $\frac{1}{100}$ is also used for fractional percents.

CONVERTING A WHOLE PERCENT (OR A FRACTIONAL PERCENT) TO A FRACTION
Step I. Drop the percent symbol.
Step 2. Multiply the number by $\frac{1}{100}$.
Step 3. Reduce to lowest terms.

EXAMPLES

$$76\% = 76 \times \frac{1}{100} = \frac{76}{100} = \boxed{\frac{19}{25}} \qquad\qquad \frac{1}{8}\% = \frac{1}{8} \times \frac{1}{100} = \boxed{\frac{1}{800}}$$

$$156\% = 156 \times \frac{1}{100} = \frac{156}{100} = 1\frac{56}{100} = \boxed{1\frac{14}{25}}$$

Sometimes a percent contains a whole number and a fraction such as $12\frac{1}{2}\%$ or 22.5%. Extra steps are needed to write a mixed or decimal percent as a simplified fraction.

MONEY tips

Nearly half, 47%, of adult Americans have no life insurance coverage. Consider the impact on survivors. At a minimum, carry burial insurance and a letter of last instruction stating your burial wishes.

CONVERTING A MIXED OR DECIMAL PERCENT TO A FRACTION
Step I. Drop the percent symbol.
Step 2. Change the mixed percent to an improper fraction.
Step 3. Multiply the number by $\frac{1}{100}$.
Step 4. Reduce to lowest terms.
Note: If you have a mixed or decimal percent, change the decimal portion to its fractional equivalent and continue with Steps I to 4.

EXAMPLES
$$12\frac{1}{2}\% = \frac{25}{2} \times \frac{1}{100} = \frac{25}{200} = \boxed{\frac{1}{8}}$$

$$12.5\% = 12\frac{1}{2}\% = \frac{25}{2} \times \frac{1}{100} = \frac{25}{200} = \boxed{\frac{1}{8}}$$

$$22.5\% = 22\frac{1}{2}\% = \frac{45}{2} \times \frac{1}{100} = \frac{45}{200} = \boxed{\frac{9}{40}}$$

It's time to check your understanding of Learning Unit 6–1.

Complete this **Practice Quiz** to see how you are doing.

Convert to percents (round to the nearest tenth percent as needed):

1. .6666 _____   **2.** .832 _____

3. .004 _____   **4.** 8.94444 _____

Convert to decimals (remember, decimals representing less than 1% will have at least 2 leading zeros before the number):

5. $\frac{1}{4}$% _____   **6.** $6\frac{3}{4}$% _____

7. 87% _____   **8.** 810.9% _____

Convert to percents (round to the nearest hundredth percent):

9. $\frac{1}{7}$ _____   **10.** $\frac{2}{9}$ _____

Convert to fractions (remember, if it is a mixed number, first convert to an improper fraction):

11. 19% _____   **12.** $71\frac{1}{2}$% _____   **13.** 130% _____

14. $\frac{1}{2}$% _____   **15.** 19.9% _____

*For **extra help** from your authors—Sharon and Jeff—see the student DVD*

✓ **Solutions**

1. $.\underset{\smile}{66}.66 =$ 66.7%

3. $.\underset{\smile}{00}.4 =$ .4%

5. $\frac{1}{4}$% = .25% = .0025

7. 87% = $.\underset{\smile}{87}.$ = .87

9. $\frac{1}{7}$ = $.\underset{\smile}{14}.285$ = 14.29%

11. 19% = $19 \times \frac{1}{100}$ = $\boxed{\frac{19}{100}}$

13. 130% = $130 \times \frac{1}{100} = \frac{130}{100} = 1\frac{30}{100} = 1\frac{3}{10}$

15. $19\frac{9}{10}$% = $\frac{199}{10} \times \frac{1}{100}$ = $\boxed{\frac{199}{1,000}}$

2. $.\underset{\smile}{83}.2 =$ 83.2%

4. $8.94.444 =$ 894.4%

6. $6\frac{3}{4}$% = 6.75% = .0675

8. 810.9% = $8.\underset{\smile}{10}.9$ = 8.109

10. $\frac{2}{9}$ = $.22.2\overline{2}$ = 22.22%

12. $71\frac{1}{2}$% = $\frac{143}{2} \times \frac{1}{100}$ = $\boxed{\frac{143}{200}}$

14. $\frac{1}{2}$% = $\frac{1}{2} \times \frac{1}{100}$ = $\boxed{\frac{1}{200}}$

Need more practice? Try this **Extra Practice Quiz** (check figures in the Interactive Chapter Organizer, p. 161). Worked-out Solutions can be found in Appendix B at end of text.

Convert to percents (round to the nearest tenth percent as needed):

1. .4444   **2.** .782

3. .006   **4.** 7.93333

Convert to decimals (remember, decimals representing less than 1% will have at least 2 leading zeros before the number):

5. $\frac{1}{5}$%   **6.** $7\frac{4}{5}$%

7. 92%   **8.** 765.8%

Convert to percents (round to the nearest hundredth percent):

9. $\frac{1}{3}$ **10.** $\frac{3}{7}$

Convert to fractions (remember, if it is a mixed number, first convert to an improper fraction):

11. 17%   **12.** $82\frac{1}{4}$%   **13.** 150%

14. $\frac{1}{4}$%   **15.** 17.8%

Learning Unit 6–2: Application of Percents—Portion Formula

LO 1

The bag of M&M'S® we have been studying contains Milk Chocolate M&M'S®. M&M/Mars also makes Peanut M&M'S® and some other types of M&M'S®. To study the application of percents to problems involving M&M'S®, we make two key assumptions:

1. Total sales of Milk Chocolate M&M'S®, Peanut M&M'S®, and other M&M'S® chocolate candies are $400,000.

2. Eighty percent of M&M'S® sales are Milk Chocolate M&M'S®. This leaves the Peanut and other M&M'S® chocolate candies with 20% of sales (100% − 80%).

80% M&M'S®		20% M&M'S®		100%
Milk Chocolate M&M'S®	+	Peanut and other chocolate candies	=	Total sales ($400,000)

Before we begin, you must understand the meaning of three terms—*base, rate,* and *portion.* These terms are the key elements in solving percent problems.

- **Base (*B*).** The **base** is the beginning whole quantity or value (100%) with which you will compare some other quantity or value. Often the problems give the base after the word *of.* For example, the whole (total) sales of M&M'S®—Milk Chocolate M&M'S, Peanut, and other M&M'S® chocolate candies—are $400,000.

- **Rate (*R*).** The **rate** is a percent, decimal, or fraction that indicates the part of the base that you must calculate. The percent symbol often helps you identify the rate. For example, Milk Chocolate M&M'S® currently account for 80% of sales. So the rate is 80%. Remember that 80% is also $\frac{4}{5}$, or .80.

- **Portion (*P*).** The **portion** is the amount or part that results from the base multiplied by the rate. For example, total sales of M&M'S® are $400,000 (base); $400,000 times .80 (rate) equals $320,000 (portion), or the sales of Milk Chocolate M&M'S®. *A key point to remember is that portion is a number and not a percent. In fact, the portion can be larger than the base if the rate is greater than 100%.*

Solving Percents with the Portion Formula

LO 2

In problems involving portion, base, and rate, we give two of these elements. You must find the third element. Remember the following key formula:

> Portion (*P*) = Base (*B*) × Rate (*R*)

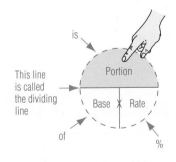

To help you solve for the portion, base, and rate, this unit shows pie charts. The shaded area in each pie chart indicates the element that you must solve for. For example, since we shaded *portion* in the pie chart at the left, you must solve for portion. To use the pie charts, put your finger on the shaded area (in this case portion). The formula that remains tells you what to do. So in the pie chart at the left, you solve the problem by multiplying base by the rate. Note the circle around the pie chart is broken since we want to emphasize that portion can be larger than base if rate is greater than 100%. The horizontal line in the pie chart is called the dividing line, and we will use it when we solve for base or rate.

The following example summarizes the concept of base, rate, and portion. Assume that you received a small bonus check of $100. This is a gross amount—your company did not withhold any taxes. You will have to pay 20% in taxes.

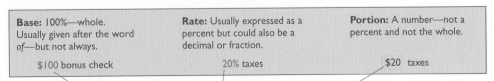

Base: 100%—whole. Usually given after the word *of*—but not always.	**Rate:** Usually expressed as a percent but could also be a decimal or fraction.	**Portion:** A number—not a percent and not the whole.
$100 bonus check	20% taxes	$20 taxes

First decide what you are looking for. You want to know how much you must pay in taxes—the portion. How do you get the portion? From the portion formula Portion (*P*) = Base (*B*) × Rate (*R*), you know that you must multiply the base ($100) by the rate (20%). When you do this, you get $100 × .20 = $20. So you must pay $20 in taxes.

Let's try our first word problem by taking a closer look at the M&M'S® example to see how we arrived at the $320,000 sales of Milk Chocolate M&M'S® given earlier. We will be using blueprint aids to help dissect and solve each word problem.

Solving for Portion

The Word Problem Sales of Milk Chocolate M&M'S® are 80% of the total M&M'S® sales. Total M&M'S® sales are $400,000. What are the sales of Milk Chocolate M&M'S®?

	The facts	Solving for?	Steps to take	Key points
BLUEPRINT	*Milk Chocolate M&M'S® sales: 80%.* *Total M&M'S® sales: $400,000.*	Sales of Milk Chocolate M&M'S®.	Identify key elements. *Base:* $400,000. *Rate:* .80. *Portion:* ? Portion = Base × Rate.	Amount or part of beginning Portion (?) Base × Rate ($400,000) (.80) Beginning whole quantity (often after "of") Percent symbol or word (here we put into decimal) Portion and rate must relate to same piece of base.

Steps to solving problem

1. Set up the formula.

   Portion = Base × Rate

2. Calculate portion (sales of Milk Chocolate M&M'S®).

   $P = \$400,000 \times .80$

   $P = \$320,000$

In the first column of the blueprint aid, we gather the facts. In the second column, we state that we are looking for sales of Milk Chocolate M&M'S®. In the third column, we identify each key element and the formula needed to solve the problem. Review the pie chart in the fourth column. Note that the portion and rate must relate to the same piece of the base. In this word problem, we can see from the solution below the blueprint aid that sales of Milk Chocolate M&M'S® are $320,000. The $320,000 does indeed represent 80% of the base. Note here that the portion ($320,000) is less than the base of $400,000 since the rate is less than 100%.

Now let's work another word problem that solves for the portion.

The Word Problem Sales of Milk Chocolate M&M'S® are 80% of the total M&M'S® sales. Total M&M'S® sales are $400,000. What are the sales of Peanut and other M&M'S® chocolate candies?

	The facts	Solving for?	Steps to take	Key points
BLUEPRINT	*Milk Chocolate M&M'S® sales: 80%.* *Total M&M'S® sales: $400,000.*	Sales of Peanut and other M&M'S® chocolate candies.	Identify key elements. *Base:* $400,000. *Rate:* .20 (100% − 80%). *Portion:* ? Portion = Base × Rate.	If 80% of sales are Milk Chocolate M&M'S, then 20% are Peanut and other M&M'S® chocolate candies. Portion (?) Base × Rate ($400,000) (.20) Portion and rate must relate to same piece of base.

Steps to solving problem

1. Set up the formula.

Portion = Base × Rate

2. Calculate portion (sale of Peanut and other M&M'S® chocolate candies).

$P = \$400,000 \times .20$

$P = \$80,000$

In the previous blueprint aid, note that we must use a rate that agrees with the portion so the portion and rate refer to the same piece of the base. Thus, if 80% of sales are Milk Chocolate M&M'S®, 20% must be Peanut and other M&M'S® chocolate candies (100% − 80% = 20%). So we use a rate of .20.

In Step 2, we multiplied $\$400,000 \times .20$ to get a portion of $80,000. This portion represents the part of the sales that were *not* Milk Chocolate M&M'S®. Note that the rate of .20 and the portion of $80,000 relate to the same piece of the base—$80,000 is 20% of $400,000. Also note that the portion ($80,000) is less than the base ($400,000) since the rate is less than 100%.

Take a moment to review the two blueprint aids in this section. Be sure you understand why the rate in the first blueprint aid was 80% and the rate in the second blueprint aid was 20%.

Solving for Rate

The Word Problem Sales of Milk Chocolate M&M'S® are $320,000. Total M&M'S® sales are $400,000. What is the percent of Milk Chocolate M&M'S® sales compared to total M&M'S® sales?

	The facts	Solving for?	Steps to take	Key points
BLUEPRINT	*Milk Chocolate M&M'S® sales:* $320,000. *Total M&M'S® sales:* $400,000.	Percent of Milk Chocolate M&M'S® sales to total M&M'S® sales.	Identify key elements. *Base:* $400,000. *Rate:* ? *Portion:* $320,000 Rate = $\dfrac{\text{Portion}}{\text{Base}}$	Since portion is less than base, the rate must be less than 100% Portion ($320,000) Base ($400,000) × Rate (?) Portion and rate must relate to the same piece of base.

Steps to solving problem

1. Set up the formula.

Rate = $\dfrac{\text{Portion}}{\text{Base}}$

2. Calculate rate (percent of Milk Chocolate M&M'S® sales).

$R = \dfrac{\$320,000}{\$400,000}$

$R = 80\%$

Note that in this word problem, the rate of 80% and the portion of $320,000 refer to the same piece of the base.

The Word Problem Sales of Milk Chocolate M&M'S® are $320,000. Total sales of Milk Chocolate M&M'S, Peanut, and other M&M'S® chocolate candies are $400,000. What percent of Peanut and other M&M'S® chocolate candies are sold compared to total M&M'S® sales?

(continued on p. 152)

	The facts	Solving for?	Steps to take	Key points
BLUEPRINT	Milk Chocolate M&M'S® sales: $320,000. Total M&M'S® sales: $400,000.	Percent of Peanut and other M&M'S® chocolate candies sales compared to total M&M'S® sales.	Identify key elements. Base: $400,000. Rate: ? Portion: $80,000 ($400,000 − $320,000). Rate = $\frac{\text{Portion}}{\text{Base}}$	Represents sales of Peanut and other M&M'S® chocolate candies Portion ($80,000) Base × Rate ($400,000) (?) When portion becomes $80,000, the portion and rate now relate to same piece of base.

Steps to solving problem

1. Set up the formula. $\text{Rate} = \frac{\text{Portion}}{\text{Base}}$

2. Calculate rate. $R = \frac{\$80,000}{\$400,000}$ ($400,000 − $320,000)

$R = \boxed{20\%}$

The word problem asks for the rate of candy sales that are *not* Milk Chocolate M&M'S. Thus, $400,000 of total candy sales less sales of Milk Chocolate M&M'S® ($320,000) allows us to arrive at sales of Peanut and other M&M'S® chocolate candies ($80,000). The $80,000 portion represents 20% of total candy sales. The $80,000 portion and 20% rate refer to the same piece of the $400,000 base. Compare this blueprint aid with the blueprint aid for the previous word problem. Ask yourself why in the previous word problem the rate was 80% and in this word problem the rate is 20%. In both word problems, the portion was less than the base since the rate was less than 100%.

Now we go on to calculate the base. Remember to read the word problem carefully so that you match the rate and portion to the same piece of the base.

Solving for Base

The Word Problem Sales of Peanut and other M&M'S® chocolate candies are 20% of total M&M'S® sales. Sales of Milk Chocolate M&M'S® are $320,000. What are the total sales of all M&M'S®?

	The facts	Solving for?	Steps to take	Key points
BLUEPRINT	Peanut and other M&M'S® chocolate candies sales: 20%. Milk Chocolate M&M'S® sales: $320,000.	Total M&M'S® sales.	Identify key elements. Base: ? Rate: .80 (100% − 20%) Portion: $320,000 Base = $\frac{\text{Portion}}{\text{Rate}}$	Portion ($320,000) Base × Rate (?) (.80) (100% − 20%) Portion ($320,000) and rate (.80) do relate to the same piece of base.

Steps to solving problem

1. Set up the formula. $\text{Base} = \frac{\text{Portion}}{\text{Rate}}$

2. Calculate the base. $B = \frac{\$320,000}{.80}$ ← $320,000 is 80% of base

$B = \boxed{\$400,000}$

Note that we could not use 20% for the rate. The $320,000 of Milk Chocolate M&M'S® represents 80% (100% − 20%) of the total sales of M&M'S®. We use 80% so that the portion and rate refer to same piece of the base. Remember that the portion ($320,000) is less than the base ($400,000) since the rate is less than 100%.

LO 3

Calculating Percent Increases and Decreases

The following *Wall Street Journal* clipping shows that sales for Ford are up 19%, while Toyota showed a 4.4% decrease in sales. Using this clipping, let's look at how to calculate percent increases and decreases.

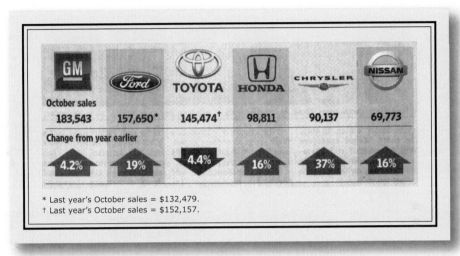

Reprinted with permission of The Wall Street Journal, Copyright © 2010 Dow Jones & Company, Inc. All Rights Reserved Worldwide.

The Ford Example: Rate of Percent Increase

Assume: Sales increase from $132,479 to $157,650.

$$\text{Rate} = \frac{\text{Portion}}{\text{Base}} \quad \longleftarrow \text{Difference between old and new sales}$$
$$\longleftarrow \text{Old sales}$$

$$R = \frac{\$25,171\,(\$157,650 - \$132,479)}{\$132,479}$$

$$R = \boxed{18.99\%} \quad (\text{Rounded to 19\% in clip.})$$

Let's prove the 19% with a pie chart.

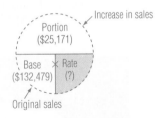

The formula for calculating sales **percent increase** is as follows:

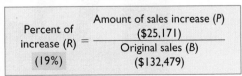

Now let's look at how to calculate the math for a decrease in sales for Toyota.

The Toyota Example: Rate of Percent Decrease

Assume: Sales drop from $152,157 to $145,474.

$$\text{Rate} = \frac{\text{Portion}}{\text{Base}} \quad\begin{array}{l}\longleftarrow\text{Difference between old and new sales}\\ \longleftarrow\text{Old sales}\end{array}$$

$$R = \frac{\$6,683\,(\$152,157 - \$145,474)}{\$152,157}$$

$$R = \boxed{4.39\%} = 4.4\%$$

Let's prove the 4.4% with a pie chart.

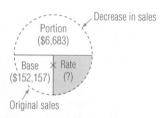

The formula for calculating sales **percent decrease** is as follows:

Percent decrease

Percent of decrease (R) (4.4%)	=	Amount of sales decrease (P) ($6,683)
		Original sales (B) ($152,157)

In conclusion, the following steps can be used to calculate percent increases and decreases:

CALCULATING PERCENT INCREASES AND DECREASES

Step 1. Find the difference between amounts (such as sales).

Step 2. Divide Step 1 by the original amount (the base): $R = P \div B$. Be sure to express your answer in percent.

Before concluding this chapter, we will show how to calculate a percent increase and decrease using M&M'S® (Figure 6.1).

FIGURE **6.1**

Bag of 18.40-ounce M&M'S®

Additional Examples Using M&M'S

The Word Problem Sheila Leary went to her local supermarket and bought the bag of M&M'S® shown in Figure 6.1 (p. 154). The bag gave its weight as 18.40 ounces, which was 15% more than a regular 1-pound bag of M&M'S®. Sheila, who is a careful shopper, wanted to check and see if she was actually getting a 15% increase. Let's help Sheila dissect and solve this problem.

	The facts	Solving for?	Steps to take	Key points
BLUEPRINT	New bag of M&M'S®: 18.40 oz. 15% increase in weight. *Original bag of M&M'S®:* 16 oz. (1 lb.)	Checking percent increase of 15%.	Identify key elements. *Base:* 16 oz. *Rate:* ? *Portion:* 2.40 oz. $\left(\begin{array}{r} 18.40 \text{ oz.} \\ -\ 16.00 \\ \hline 2.40 \text{ oz.} \end{array}\right)$ Rate = $\dfrac{\text{Portion}}{\text{Base}}$	Difference between base and new weight. Portion (2.40 oz.) Base × Rate (16 oz.) (?) Original amount sold

Steps to solving problem

1. Set up the formula.   Rate = $\dfrac{\text{Portion}}{\text{Base}}$

2. Calculate the rate. $R = \dfrac{2.40 \text{ oz.}}{16.00 \text{ oz.}}$ ← Difference between base and new weight. ← Old weight equals 100%.

R = 15% increase

The new weight of the bag of M&M'S® is really 115% of the old weight:

$$\begin{array}{rclcl} 16.00 \text{ oz.} & = & 100\% & & \\ +\ 2.40 & = & +\ 15 & & \\ \hline 18.40 \text{ oz.} & = & 115\% & = & 1.15 \end{array}$$

We can check this by looking at the following pie chart:

Portion = Base × Rate

18.40 oz. = 16 oz. × 1.15

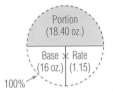

Why is the portion greater than the base? Remember that the portion can be larger than the base only if the rate is greater than 100%. Note how the portion and rate relate to the same piece of the base—18.40 oz. is 115% of the base (16 oz.).

Let's see what could happen if M&M/Mars has an increase in its price of sugar. This is an additional example to reinforce the concept of percent decrease.

The Word Problem The increase in the price of sugar caused the M&M/Mars company to decrease the weight of each 1-pound bag of M&M'S® to 12 ounces. What is the rate of percent decrease?

	The facts	Solving for?	Steps to take	Key points
BLUEPRINT	16-oz. bag of M&M'S®: reduced to 12 oz.	Rate of percent decrease.	Identify key elements. *Base:* 16 oz. *Rate:* ? *Portion:* 4 oz. (16 oz. − 12 oz.) Rate = $\dfrac{\text{Portion}}{\text{Base}}$	Amount of decrease. Portion (4 oz.) Base × Rate (16 oz.) (?) Old base 100%

MONEY tips

When planning for retirement, a rule of thumb is that you will need 70% of your preretirement pay to live comfortably. This number assumes your house is paid off and you are in good health. Automating your savings can be a huge factor in helping you reach your goals. So, begin planning early in life and start saving for a financially sound retirement.

Steps to solving problem

1. Set up the formula.

$$\text{Rate} = \frac{\text{Portion}}{\text{Base}}$$

2. Calculate the rate.

$$R = \frac{4 \text{ oz.}}{16.00 \text{ oz.}}$$

$$R = 25\% \text{ decrease}$$

The new weight of the bag of M&M'S® is 75% of the old weight:

$$
\begin{array}{rcr}
16 \text{ oz.} & = & 100\% \\
- \;\; 4 & & - \;\; 25 \\
\hline
12 \text{ oz.} & = & 75\% \\
\end{array}
$$

We can check this by looking at the following pie chart:

Portion = Base × Rate

12 oz. = 16 oz. × .75

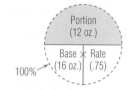

100%

Portion (12 oz.)

Base (16 oz.) × Rate (.75)

Note that the portion is smaller than the base because the rate is less than 100%. Also note how the portion and rate relate to the same piece of the base—12 ounces is 75% of the base (16 oz.).

After your study of Learning Unit 6–2, you should be ready for the Practice Quiz.

LU 6–2   PRACTICE QUIZ

Complete this **Practice Quiz** to see how you are doing.

Solve for portion:

1. 38% of 900.

2. 60% of $9,000.

Solve for rate (round to the nearest tenth percent as needed):

3. 430 is _____% of 5,000.

4. 200 is _____% of 700.

Solve for base (round to the nearest tenth as needed):

5. 55 is 40% of _____.

6. 900 is $4\frac{1}{2}$% of _____.

Solve the following (blueprint aids are shown in the solution; you might want to try some on scrap paper):

7. Five out of 25 students in Professor Ford's class received an A grade. What percent of the class *did not* receive the A grade?

8. Abby Biernet has yet to receive 60% of her lobster order. Abby received 80 lobsters to date. What was her original order?

9. Assume in 2013, Dunkin' Donuts Company had $300,000 in doughnut sales. In 2014, sales were up 40%. What are Dunkin' Donuts sales for 2014?

10. The price of an Apple computer dropped from $1,600 to $1,200. What was the percent decrease?

11. In 1982, a ticket to the Boston Celtics cost $14. In 2013, a ticket cost $50. What is the percent increase to the nearest hundredth percent?

For extra help from your authors—Sharon and Jeff—see the student DVD

✓ Solutions

1. $\boxed{342} = 900 \times .38$
$(P) = (B) \times (R)$

2. $\boxed{\$5,400} = \$9,000 \times .60$
$(P) \;\;=\;\; (B) \;\; \times (R)$

3. $\dfrac{(P)430}{(B)5,000} = .086 = \boxed{8.6\% \; (R)}$

4. $\dfrac{(P)200}{(B)700} = .2857 = \boxed{28.6\% \; (R)}$

5. $\dfrac{(P)55}{(R).40} = \boxed{137.5 \; (B)}$

6. $\dfrac{(P)900}{(R).045} = \boxed{20,000 \; (B)}$

7. Percent of Professor Ford's class that did not receive an A grade:

	The facts	Solving for?	Steps to take	Key points
BLUEPRINT	5 As. 25 in class.	Percent that did not receive A.	Identify key elements. *Base:* 25 *Rate:* ? *Portion:* 20 (25 − 5). $Rate = \dfrac{Portion}{Base}$	Portion (20) Base (25) × Rate (?) The whole Portion and rate must relate to same piece of base.

Steps to solving problem

1. Set up the formula. $Rate = \dfrac{Portion}{Base}$

2. Calculate the base rate. $R = \dfrac{20}{25}$

$R = 80\%$

8. Abby Biernet's original order:

	The facts	Solving for?	Steps to take	Key points
BLUEPRINT	60% of the order not in. 80 lobsters received.	Total order of lobsters.	Identify key elements. *Base:* ? *Rate:* .40 (100% − 60%) *Portion:* 80. $Base = \dfrac{Portion}{Rate}$	Portion (80) Base (?) × Rate (.40) 80 lobsters represent 40% of the order Portion and rate must relate to same piece of base.

Steps to solving problem

1. Set up the formula. $Base = \dfrac{Portion}{Rate}$

2. Calculate the base rate. $B = \dfrac{80}{.40}$ ← 80 lobsters is 40% of base.

$B = 200\ lobsters$

9. Dunkin' Donuts Company sales for 2014:

	The facts	Solving for?	Steps to take	Key points
BLUEPRINT	*2013:* $300,000 sales. *2014:* Sales up 40% from 2013.	Sales for 2014.	Identify key elements. *Base:* $300,000. *Rate:* 1.40. Old year 100% New year +40 140% *Portion:* ? Portion = Base × Rate.	2014 sales Portion (?) Base ($300,000) × Rate (1.40) 2013 sales When rate is greater than 100%, portion will be larger than base.

Steps to solving problem

1. Set up the formula.   Portion = Base × Rate

2. Calculate the portion. P = \$300,000 × 1.40

                                           P = \$420,000

10. Percent decrease in Apple computer price:

	The facts	Solving for?	Steps to take	Key points
BLUEPRINT	Apple computer was \$1,600; now, \$1,200.	Percent decrease in price.	Identify key elements. *Base:* \$1,600. *Rate:* ? *Portion:* \$400 (\$1,600 − \$1,200). Rate = $\dfrac{\text{Portion}}{\text{Base}}$	Difference in price Portion (\$400) Base ($1,600) × Rate (?) Original price

Steps to solving problem

1. Set up the formula.   Rate = $\dfrac{\text{Portion}}{\text{Base}}$

2. Calculate the rate. R = $\dfrac{\$400}{\$1,600}$

                                           R = 25%

11. Percent increase in Boston Celtics ticket:

© AP Photo/Charles Krupa

	The facts	Solving for?	Steps to take	Key points
BLUEPRINT	\$14 ticket (old). \$50 ticket (new).	Percent increase in price.	Identify key elements. *Base:* \$14 *Rate:* ? *Portion:* \$36 (\$50 − \$14) Rate = $\dfrac{\text{Portion}}{\text{Base}}$	Difference in price Portion (\$36) Base ($14) × Rate (?) Original price When portion is greater than base, rate will be greater than 100%.

Steps to solving problem

1. Set up the formula.   Rate = $\dfrac{\text{Portion}}{\text{Base}}$

2. Calculate the rate. R = $\dfrac{\$36}{\$14}$

                                           R = 2.5714 = 257.14%

Need more practice? Try this **Extra Practice Quiz** (check figures in the Interactive Chapter Organizer, p. 161). Worked-out Solutions can be found in Appendix B at end of text.

Solve for portion:

1. 42% of 1,200

2. 7% of $8,000

Solve for rate (round to nearest tenth percent as needed):

3. 510 is _____ % of 6,000.

4. 400 is _____% of 900.

Solve for base (round to the nearest tenth as needed):

5. 30 is 60% of _____.

6. 1,200 is $3\frac{1}{2}$% of _____.

7. Ten out of 25 students in Professor Ford's class received an A grade. What percent of the class did not receive the A grade?

8. Abby Biernet has yet to receive 70% of her lobster order. Abby received 90 lobsters to date. What was her original order?

9. A local Dunkin' Donuts Company had $400,000 in doughnut sales in 2013. In 2014, sales were up 35%. What are Dunkin' Donuts sales for 2014?

10. The price of an Apple computer dropped from $1,800 to $1,000. What was the percent decrease? (Round to the nearest hundredth percent.)

11. In 1982, a ticket to the Boston Celtics cost $14. In 2013, a ticket cost $75. What is the percent increase to the nearest hundredth percent?

INTERACTIVE CHAPTER ORGANIZER

Topic/procedure/formula	Examples	You try it*
Converting decimals to percents, p. 144 1. Move decimal point two places to right. If necessary, add zeros. This rule is also used for whole numbers and mixed decimals. 2. Add a percent symbol at end of number.	.81 = .81. = 81% .008 = .00.8 = .8% 4.15 = 4.15. = 415%	**Convert to percent** .92 .009 5.46
Rounding percents, p. 145 1. Answer must be in percent before rounding. 2. Identify specific digit. If digit to right is 5 or greater, round up. 3. Delete digits to right of identified digit.	Round to the nearest hundredth percent. $\frac{3}{7}$ = .4285714 = 42.85714% = 42.86%	**Round to the nearest hundredth percent** $\frac{2}{9}$
Converting percents to decimals, pp. 145–146 1. Drop percent symbol. 2. Move decimal point two places to left. If necessary, add zeros. For fractional percents: 1. Convert to decimal by dividing numerator by denominator. If necessary, round answer. 2. If a mixed fractional percent, convert fractional percent first. Then combine whole number and fractional percent. 3. Drop percent symbol, move decimal point two places to left.	.89% = .0089 95% = .95 195% = 1.95 $8\frac{3}{4}$% = 8.75% = .0875 $\frac{1}{4}$% = .25% = .0025 $\frac{1}{5}$% = .20% = .0020	**Convert to decimal** .78% 96% 246% $7\frac{3}{4}$% $\frac{3}{4}$% $\frac{1}{2}$%

(continues)

INTERACTIVE CHAPTER ORGANIZER

Topic/procedure/formula	Examples	You try it*
Converting fractions to percents, p. 147 1. Divide numerator by denominator. 2. Move decimal point two places to right; add percent symbol.	$\frac{4}{5} = .80 = 80\%$	**Convert to percent** $\frac{3}{5}$
Converting percents to fractions, p. 147 Whole percent (or fractional percent) to a fraction: 1. Drop percent symbol. 2. Multiply number by $\frac{1}{100}$. 3. Reduce to lowest terms. Mixed or decimal percent to a fraction: 1. Drop percent symbol. 2. Change mixed percent to an improper fraction. 3. Multiply number by $\frac{1}{100}$. 4. Reduce to lowest terms. If you have a mixed or decimal percent, change decimal portion to fractional equivalent and continue with Steps 1 to 4.	$64\% \longrightarrow 64 \times \frac{1}{100} = \frac{64}{100} = \frac{16}{25}$ $\frac{1}{4}\% \longrightarrow \frac{1}{4} \times \frac{1}{100} = \frac{1}{400}$ $119\% \longrightarrow 119 \times \frac{1}{100} = \frac{119}{100} = 1\frac{19}{100}$ $16\frac{1}{4}\% \longrightarrow \frac{65}{4} \times \frac{1}{100} = \frac{65}{400} = \frac{13}{80}$ $16.25\% \longrightarrow 16\frac{1}{4}\% = \frac{65}{4} \times \frac{1}{100}$ $= \frac{65}{400} = \frac{13}{80}$	**Convert to fractions** 74% $\frac{1}{5}\%$ 121% $17\frac{1}{5}\%$ 17.75%
Solving for portion, p. 150 "is" Portion (?) Base ($1,000) × Rate (.10) "of" "%"	10% of Mel's paycheck of $1,000 goes for food. What portion is deducted for food? $\$100 = \$1,000 \times .10$ *Note:* If question was what amount does not go for food, the portion would have been: $\$900 = \$1,000 \times .90$ $(100\% - 10\% = 90\%)$	**Find portion** Base $2,000 Rate 80%
Solving for rate, p. 151 Portion ($100) Base ($1,000) × Rate (?)	Assume Mel spends $100 for food from his $1,000 paycheck. What percent of his paycheck is spent on food? $\frac{\$100}{\$1,000} = .10 = 10\%$ *Note:* Portion is less than base since rate is less than 100%.	**Find rate** Base $2,000 Portion $500
Solving for base, p. 152 Portion ($100) Base (?) × Rate (.10)	Assume Mel spends $100 for food, which is 10% of his paycheck. What is Mel's total paycheck? $\frac{\$100}{.10} = \$1,000$	**Find base** Rate 20% Portion $200

(continues)

INTERACTIVE CHAPTER ORGANIZER

Topic/procedure/formula	Examples	You try it*
Calculating percent increases and decreases, pp. 153–156 Amount of decrease or increase Portion Base × Rate (?) Original price	Stereo, $2,000 original price. Stereo, $2,500 new price. $\dfrac{\$500}{\$2,000} = .25 = \boxed{25\%}$ increase **Check** $\$2,000 \times 1.25 = \$2,500$ *Note:* Portion is greater than base since rate is greater than 100%. Portion ($2,500) Base × Rate ($2,000) (1.25)	**Find percent increase** Old price $500 New price $600

KEY TERMS	Base, *p. 149* Percent decrease, *p. 154*	Percent increase, *p. 153* Percents, *p. 143*	Portion, *p. 149* Rate, *p. 149*

Check Figures for Extra Practice Quizzes with Page References. (Worked-out Solutions in Appendix B.)	LU 6–1a (p. 148)		LU 6–2a (p. 159)	
	1. 44.4%	8. 7.658	1. 504	7. 60%
	2. 78.2%	9. 33.33%	2. 560	8. 300
	3. .6%	10. 42.86%	3. 8.5%	9. $540,000
	4. 793.3%	11. $\dfrac{17}{100}$	4. 44.4%	10. 44.44%
	5. .0020	12. $\dfrac{329}{400}$	5. 50	11. 435.71%
	6. .0780	13. $1\dfrac{1}{2}$	6. 34,285.7	
	7. .92	14. $\dfrac{1}{400}$		
		15. $\dfrac{89}{500}$		

Note: For how to dissect and solve a word problem, see page 150.

*Worked-out solutions are in Appendix B.

Critical Thinking Discussion Questions with Chapter Concept Check

1. In converting from a percent to a decimal, when will you have at least 2 leading zeros before the whole number? Explain this concept, assuming you have 100 bills of $1.

2. Explain the steps in rounding percents. Count the number of students who are sitting in the back half of the room as a percent of the total class. Round your answer to the nearest hundredth percent. Could you have rounded to the nearest whole percent without changing the accuracy of the answer?

3. Define portion, rate, and base. Create an example using Walt Disney World to show when the portion could be larger than the base. Why must the rate be greater than 100% for this to happen?

4. How do we solve for portion, rate, and base? Create an example using IBM computer sales to show that the portion and rate do relate to the same piece of the base.

5. Explain how to calculate percent decreases or increases. Many years ago, comic books cost 10 cents a copy. Visit a bookshop or newsstand. Select a new comic book and explain the price increase in percent compared to the 10-cent comic. How important is the rounding process in your final answer?

6. **Chapter Concept Check.** Go to the Google or Facebook site and find out how many people the company employs. Assuming a 10% increase in employment this year, calculate the total number of new employees by the end of the year, and identify the base rate and portion. If, in the following year, the 10% increase in employment fell by 5%, what would the total number of current employees be?

Classroom Notes

END-OF-CHAPTER PROBLEMS

Check figures for odd-numbered problems in Appendix C.   Name _____   Date _____

DRILL PROBLEMS

Convert the following decimals to percents: *LU 6-1(1)*

6–1. .78   **6–2.** .943   **6–3.** .7

6–4. 8.00   **6–5.** 3.561   **6–6.** 6.006

Convert the following percents to decimals: *LU 6-1(1)*

6–7. 8%   **6–8.** 14%   **6–9.** $64\frac{3}{10}\%$

6–10. 75.9%   **6–11.** 119%   **6–12.** 89%

Convert the following fractions to percents (round to the nearest tenth percent as needed):   *LU 6-1(1)*

6–13. $\frac{1}{12}$ **6–14.** $\frac{1}{400}$

6–15. $\frac{7}{8}$ **6–16.** $\frac{11}{12}$

Convert the following percents to fractions and reduce to the lowest terms: *LU 6-1(2)*

6–17. 4%   **6–18.** $18\frac{1}{2}\%$

6–19. $31\frac{2}{3}\%$ **6–20.** $61\frac{1}{2}\%$

6–21. 6.75%   **6–22.** 182%

Solve for the portion (round to the nearest hundredth as needed):   *LU 6-2(2)*

6–23. 7% of 150   **6–24.** 125% of 4,320   **6–25.** 25% of 410
eXcel   eXcel   eXcel

6–26. 119% of 128.9   **6–27.** 17.4% of 900   **6–28.** 11.2% of 85
eXcel   eXcel   eXcel

6–29. $12\frac{1}{2}\%$ of 919   **6–30.** 45% of 300

6–31. 18% of 90   **6–32.** 30% of 2,000

Solve for the base (round to the nearest hundredth as needed):   *LU 6-2(2)*

6–33. 170 is 120% of _____   **6–34.** 36 is .75% of _____

6–35. 50 is .5% of _____   **6–36.** 10,800 is 90% of _____

6–37. 800 is $4\frac{1}{2}\%$ of _____

Solve for rate (round to the nearest tenth percent as needed):   *LU 6-2(2)*

6–38. _____ of 80 is 50   **6–39.** _____ of 85 is 92

6–40. _____ of 250 is 65   **6–41.** 110 is _____ of 100

6–42. .09 is _____ of 2.25   **6–43.** 16 is _____ of 4

Solve the following problems. Be sure to show your work. Round to the nearest hundredth or hundredth percent as needed: *LU 6-2(2)*

6–44. What is 180% of 310?

6–45. 66% of 90 is what?

6–46. 40% of what number is 20?

6–47. 770 is 70% of what number?

6–48. 4 is what percent of 90?

6–49. What percent of 150 is 60?

Complete the following table: *LU 6-2(3)*

	Selling price		Amount of decrease	Percent change (to nearest
Product	**2013**	**2014**	**or increase**	**hundredth percent as needed)**
6–50. Apple iPad	$650	$500		
6–51. Smartphone	$100	$120		

WORD PROBLEMS (First of Four Sets)

6–52. At a local Dunkin' Donuts, a survey showed that out of 1,200 customers eating lunch, 240 ordered coffee with their meal. e**X**cel What percent of customers ordered coffee? *LU 6-2(2)*

6–53. What percent of customers in Problem 6–52 did not order coffee? *LU 6-2(2)*
e**X**cel

6–54. In January 2012, gas was selling for $3.60 a gallon. The price of a gallon of regular unleaded dropped to $3.50 on February 11, 2012. What was the percent decrease? Round to the nearest hundredth percent. *LU 6-2(3)*

6–55. Wally Chin, the owner of an ExxonMobil station, bought a used Ford pickup truck, paying $2,000 as a down payment. He still owes 80% of the selling price. What was the selling price of the truck? *LU 6-2(2)*

6–56. Maria Fay bought four Dunlop tires at a local Goodyear store. The salesperson told her that her mileage would increase by 8%. Before this purchase, Maria was getting 24 mpg. What should her mileage be with the new tires to the nearest hundredth? *LU 6-2(2)*

6–57. The Social Security Administration announced the following rates to explain what percent of your Social Security benefits *eXcel* you will receive based on how old you are when you start receiving Social Security benefits.

Age	Percent of benefit
62	75
63	80
64	86.7
65	93.3
66	100

Assume Shelley Kate decides to take her Social Security at age 63. What amount of Social Security money will she receive each month, assuming she is entitled to $800 per month? *LU 6-2(2)*

6–58. Assume that in the year 2013, 800,000 people attended the Christmas Eve celebration at Walt Disney World. In 2014, atten- *eXcel* dance for the Christmas Eve celebration is expected to increase by 35%. What is the total number of people expected at Walt Disney World for this event? *LU 6-2(2)*

6–59. Pete Smith found in his attic a Woody Woodpecker watch in its original box. It had a price tag on it for $4.50. The watch was made in 1949. Pete brought the watch to an antiques dealer and sold it for $35. What was the percent of increase in price? Round to the nearest hundredth percent. *LU 6-2(3)*

6–60. Christie's Auction sold a painting for $24,500. It charges all buyers a 15% premium of the final bid price. How much did the bidder pay Christie's? *LU 6-2(2)*

WORD PROBLEMS (Second of Four Sets)

6–61. Out of 9,000 college students surveyed, 540 responded that they do not eat breakfast. What percent of the students do not eat breakfast? *LU 6-2(2)*

6–62. What percent of college students in Problem 6–61 eat breakfast? *LU 6-2(2)*

6–63. The January/February 2012 *Discover* magazine article "Could Random Airplane Boarding Speed Your Trip?" demonstrates that random boarding saved 3.5 minutes off of a typical 22.5-minute boarding process. What percent savings is this to the nearest whole percent? *LU 6-2(2)*

6–64. Rainfall for January in Fiji averages 12″ according to *World Travel Guide*. This year it rained 5% less. How many inches (to the nearest tenth) did it rain this year? *LU 6-2(2)*

6–65. Jim and Alice Lange, employees at Walmart, have put themselves on a strict budget. Their goal at year's end is to buy a boat for $15,000 in cash. Their budget includes the following:

    40% food and lodging   20% entertainment   10% educational

Jim earns $1,900 per month and Alice earns $2,400 per month. After 1 year, will Alice and Jim have enough cash to buy the boat? *LU 6-2(2)*

6–66. Epiq Systems reported bankruptcy filings of 2 million in 2011. Seventy percent of the filings are Chapter 7 bankruptcies allowing individuals to avoid repaying their debts if they meet certain requirements. Thirty percent of the filings are Chapter 13 filings, where a portion of the debt will need to be repaid over 3 to 5 years. How many bankruptcies in 2011 were Chapter 7 and how many bankruptcies were Chapter 13? *LU 6-2(2)*

6–67. The Museum of Science in Boston estimated that 64% of all visitors came from within the state. On Saturday, 2,500 people attended the museum. How many attended the museum from out of state? *LU 6-2(2)*

6–68. Staples pays George Nagovsky an annual salary of $36,000. Today, George's boss informs him that he will receive a $4,600 raise. What percent of George's old salary is the $4,600 raise? Round to the nearest tenth percent. *LU 6-2(2)*

6–69. In 2013, a local Dairy Queen had $550,000 in sales. In 2014, Dairy Queen's sales were up 35%. What were Dairy Queen's sales in 2014?   *LU 6-2(2)*

6–70. Blue Valley College has 600 female students. This is 60% of the total student body. How many students attend Blue Valley College?   *LU 6-2(2)*

6–71. Dr. Grossman was reviewing his total accounts receivable. This month, credit customers paid $44,000, which represented 20% of all receivables (what customers owe) due. What was Dr. Grossman's total accounts receivable?   *LU 6-2(2)*

6–72. Massachusetts has a 5% sales tax. Timothy bought a Toro lawn mower and paid $20 sales tax. What was the cost of the lawn mower before the tax?   *LU 6-2(2)*

6–73. The price of an antique doll increased from $600 to $800. What was the percent of increase? Round to the nearest tenth percent.   *LU 6-2(3)*

6–74. A local Barnes and Noble bookstore ordered 80 marketing books but received 60 books. What percent of the order was missing?   *LU 6-2(2)*

WORD PROBLEMS (Third of Four Sets)

6–75. RealtyTrac reported that the amount of foreclosures filed fell from 2.9 million properties in 2010 to 2 million properties in 2011. This equated to 1 in every 69 U.S. homes. What percent of U.S. homes were foreclosed against (to the nearest tenth percent)?   *LU 6-2(2)*

6–76. Due to increased mailing costs, the new rate will cost publishers $50 million; this is 12.5% more than they paid the previous year. How much did it cost publishers last year? Round to the nearest hundreds.   *LU 6-2(2)*

6–77. In 2013, Jim Goodman, an employee at Walgreens, earned $45,900, an increase of 17.5% over the previous year. What were Jim's earnings in 2012? Round to the nearest cent.   *LU 6-2(2)*

6–78. If the number of mortgage applications declined by 7% to 1,625,415, what had been the previous year's number of applications?   *LU 6-2(2)*

6–79. In 2013, the price of a business math text rose to $150. This is 8% more than the 2012 price. What was the old selling price? Round to the nearest cent.   *LU 6-2(2)*

6–80. Web Consultants, Inc., pays Alice Rose an annual salary of $48,000. Today, Alice's boss informs her that she will receive a $6,400 raise. What percent of Alice's old salary is the $6,400 raise? Round to the nearest tenth percent.   *LU 6-2(2)*

6–81. Earl Miller, a lawyer, charges Lee's Plumbing, his client, 25% of what he can collect for Lee from customers whose accounts are past due. The attorney also charges, in addition to the 25%, a flat fee of $50 per customer. This month, Earl collected $7,000 from three of Lee's past-due customers. What is the total fee due to Earl?   *LU 6-2(2)*

6–82. A local Petco ordered 100 dog calendars but received 60. What percent of the order was missing?   *LU 6-2(2)*

6–83. Ray's Video uses MasterCard. MasterCard charges $2\frac{1}{2}\%$ on net deposits (credit slips less returns). Ray's made a net deposit of $4,100 for charge sales. How much did MasterCard charge Ray's?   *LU 6-2(2)*

6–84. In 2013, Internet Access had $800,000 in sales. In 2014, Internet Access's sales were up 45%. What are the sales for 2014? *LU 6-2(2)*

WORD PROBLEMS (Fourth of Four Sets)

6–85. Chevrolet raised the base price of its Volt by $1,200 to $33,500. What was the percent increase? Round to the nearest tenth percent.   *LU 6-2(2)*

6–86. The sales tax rate is 8%. If Jim bought a new Buick and paid a sales tax of $1,920, what was the cost of the Buick before the tax?   *LU 6-2(2)*

6–87. Puthina Unge bought a new Compaq computer system on sale for $1,800. It was advertised as 30% off the regular price. What was the original price of the computer? Round to the nearest dollar.   *LU 6-2(2)*

6–88. John O'Sullivan has just completed his first year in business. His records show that he spent the following in advertising:

Internet $600   Radio $650   Yellow Pages $700   Local flyers $400

What percent of John's advertising was spent on the Yellow Pages? Round to the nearest hundredth percent.   *LU 6-2(2)*

6–89. Jay Miller sold his ski house at Attitash Mountain in New Hampshire for $35,000. This sale represented a loss of 15% off the original price. What was the original price Jay paid for the ski house? Round your answer to the nearest dollar. *LU 6-2(2)*

6–90. Out of 4,000 colleges surveyed, 60% reported that SAT scores were not used as a high consideration in viewing their applications. How many schools view the SAT as important in screening applicants? *LU 6-2(2)*

6–91. If refinishing your basement at a cost of $45,404 would add $18,270 to the resale value of your home, what percent of your cost is recouped? Round to the nearest percent. *LU 6-2(2)*

6–92. A major airline laid off 4,000 pilots and flight attendants. If this was a 12.5% reduction in the workforce, what was the size of the workforce after the layoffs? *LU 6-2(2)*

6–93. Assume 450,000 people line up on the streets to see the Macy's Thanksgiving Parade in 2012. If attendance is expected to increase 30%, what will be the number of people lined up on the street to see the 2013 parade? *LU 6-2(2)*

CHALLENGE PROBLEMS

6–94. Each Tuesday, Ryan Airlines reduces its one-way ticket from Fort Wayne to Chicago from $125 to $40. To receive this special $40 price, the customer must buy a round-trip ticket. Ryan has a nonrefundable 25% penalty fare for cancellation; it estimates that about nine-tenths of 1% will cancel their reservations. The airline also estimates this special price will cause a passenger traffic increase from 400 to 900. Ryan expects revenue for the year to be 55.4% higher than the previous year. Last year, Ryan's sales were $482,000. To receive the special rate, Janice Miller bought two round-trip tickets. On other airlines, Janice has paid $100 round trip (with no cancellation penalty). Calculate the following: *LU 6-2(2)*
a. Percent discount Ryan is offering.

b. Percent passenger travel will increase.

c. Sales for new year.
d. Janice's loss if she cancels one round-trip flight.
e. Approximately how many more cancellations can Ryan Airlines expect (after Janice's cancellation)?

6–95. A local Dunkin' Donuts shop reported that its sales have increased exactly 22% per year for the last 2 years. This year's sales were $82,500. What were Dunkin' Donuts' sales 2 years ago? Round each year's sales to the nearest dollar. *LU 6-2(2)*

 SUMMARY PRACTICE TEST You Tube™

Do you need help? The DVD has step-by-step worked-out solutions.

Convert the following decimals to percents. *(p. 144) LU 6-1(1)*

1. .921   **2.** .4   **3.** 15.88   **4.** 8.00

Convert the following percents to decimals. *(p. 145) LU 6-1(1)*

5. 42%   **6.** 7.98%   **7.** 400%   **8.** $\frac{1}{4}$%

Convert the following fractions to percents. Round to the nearest tenth percent. *(p. 147) LU 6-1(1)*

9. $\frac{1}{6}$ **10.** $\frac{1}{3}$

Convert the following percents to fractions and reduce to the lowest terms as needed. *(p. 147) LU 6-1(2)*

11. $19\frac{3}{8}$%   **12.** 6.2%

Solve the following problems for portion, base, or rate:

13. An Arby's franchise has a net income before taxes of $900,000. The company's treasurer estimates that 40% of the company's net income will go to federal and state taxes. How much will the Arby's franchise have left? *(p. 149) LU 6-2(2)*

14. Domino's projects a year-end net income of $699,000. The net income represents 30% of its annual sales. What are Domino's projected annual sales? *(p. 152) LU 6-2(2)*

15. Target ordered 400 iPods. When Target received the order, 100 iPods were missing. What percent of the order did Target receive? *(p. 151) LU 6-2(2)*

16. Matthew Song, an employee at Putnam Investments, receives an annual salary of $120,000. Today his boss informed him that he would receive a $3,200 raise. What percent of his old salary is the $3,200 raise? Round to the nearest hundredth percent. *(p. 151) LU 6-2(2)*

17. The price of a Delta airline ticket from Los Angeles to Boston increased to $440. This is a 15% increase. What was the old fare? Round to the nearest cent. *(p. 152)   LU 6-2(2)*

18. Scupper Grace earns a gross pay of $900 per week at Office Depot. Scupper's payroll deductions are 29%. What is Scupper's take-home pay? *(p. 149)   LU 6-2(2)*

19. Mia Wong is reviewing the total accounts receivable of Wong's department store. Credit customers paid $90,000 this month. This represents 60% of all receivables due. What is Mia's total accounts receivable? *(p. 152)   LU 6-2(2)*

www.mhhe.com/
slater11e_vc

In a constantly changing business environment, new product and service development can invigorate a company, improve market share, and ensure desired financial performance. Six Flags, with its "Go Big! Go Six Flags" motto, knows it must regularly add new rides and upgrade existing ones in its theme parks to remain on top.

Located in Grand Prairie, Texas, Six Flags first opened in 1961 and grew to become the largest regional theme park system in the world. Central to this growth was the constant development of new and record-setting theme park rides, following a well-defined process of product development. Consider the Kingda Ka roller coaster that opened in May 2005 at the Six Flags Great Adventure & Wild Safari in Jackson, New Jersey. This is the largest of the Six Flags parks, and Kingda Ka is the tallest and fastest coaster in North America.

Getting to the May 2005 ride opening required significant planning and a coordinated effort. Six Flags' new product development process ensures both. It guides and choreographs the hundreds of tasks involved in building a roller coaster, from preparing the foundation to erecting the steel frame to installing the hydraulic system that allows for speeds of 128 mph to fitting out the cars.

Six Flags relies on several key documents to control and monitor all resources, including raw materials, equipment, and the people involved in the construction of the ride. The Statement of Work (SOW) is a written statement that describes the work to be done and includes a preliminary project schedule and completion dates. The SOW details project milestones, key completion events, and budget parameters. The Work Breakdown Structure (WBS) defines the hierarchy of tasks, subtasks, and work packages and is key to managing the logistics of the project. The project Gantt chart illustrates the project schedule and helps identify the critical path within the project. The critical path represents the longest chain of tasks in terms of time to complete. If there is a delay in any step in the critical path, the whole project can be delayed.

The Kingda Ka ride had a 15-month project schedule of which 9 to 10 months were actual construction time. The coaster took 16 months to complete and came in 10% over budget. Success in new product development requires careful planning, well-defined milestones, teamwork, and flexibility to respond to unforeseen changes. The successful Kingda Ka ride was no exception.

PROBLEM 1

As stated in the case, the original project schedule for the Kingda Ka coaster was 15 months but the project actually took 16 months to complete. What was the percent increase over the original scheduled completion time? Round your answer to the nearest percent.

PROBLEM 2

Review the video case to identify the timing of key steps in the construction of the Kingda Ka, including start of conceptual planning, start of foundation construction, start of steel erection, and completion of the project. What percent of the actual total project time had elapsed by the time foundation construction began? By the time steel erection began? Round answers to the nearest percent.

PROBLEM 3

The project Gantt chart shown in the video indicated that 145 days were planned for site preparation, 119 days for foundations, and 133 for steel erection. What was the percentage of time needed for each of these three steps assuming 397 days were needed in total? Round answers to the nearest percent.

PROBLEM 4

The Kindga Ka is currently the tallest steel roller coaster, at 456 feet high. The second tallest is the Top Thrill Dragster at Cedar Point in Sandusky, Ohio, at 420 feet. How much taller is the Kingda Ka in both feet and percentage (to the nearest tenth percent)?

PROBLEM 5

If Six Flags wanted to build a roller coaster that was 5% taller than the Kingda Ka, how tall would the coaster need to be? Round answer to the nearest foot.

PROBLEM 6

Six Flags rates its rides as mild, moderate, or max. The Six Flags Great Adventure park where the Kingda Ka ride is located has a total of 49 rides. Of these, 12 have a max rating, 8 have a moderate rating, and the remainder are rated mild. Express each of the ride types as a fraction and then determine the percentage each comprises of the total. Reduce fractions to the lowest possible terms and round percentages to the nearest percent.

PROBLEM 7

The Kingda Ka ride covers 3,118 feet of track. The Green Lantern, a new ride at the same park, has ¾ mile of track. Which ride is longer and by what percent? Round answer to the nearest percent.

PROBLEM 8

As the case states, the Kingda Ka ride reaches speeds of 128 mph due to its hydraulic system. The Green Lantern ride is designed to reach speeds of 63 mph. What percent increase would be needed for the Green Lantern ride to match the speed attained on the Kingda Ka? Round answer to the nearest tenth percent.

Class Discussion In any project, project managers must balance three key variables—time, cost, and quality. Typically one variable is most critical in a project and should problems arise, the other two may be sacrificed to achieve the one that is key to the project's success. Discuss how these three variables were managed in the Kingda Ka project.

PROBLEM 1
All-in-one and one for all

Assume you want to buy an all-in-one printer/scanner/copier/fax machine. Go to www.staples.com and choose an all-in-one machine to meet your needs. How much does it cost? If your state charged 7% sales tax; what would be the amount of the tax on this purchase?

Discussion Questions

1. Is the all-in-one machine less expensive than purchasing separate machines for all of these tasks?

2. When might it be a better option to buy individual machines versus an all-in-one? Why?

PROBLEM 3
Investment know-how

Go to http://biz.yahoo.com/r. From Research Tools go to the Historical Quotes page. Enter a ticker symbol (search by company name if you do not know the symbol) to find the price of a particular stock last Wednesday and on the same date 1 year ago. (Use the closing price.) What was the percent change in the stock you chose?

Discussion Questions

1. What may have caused this change in stock price?

2. How is the current stock price a reflection of the products the company sells?

PROBLEM 2
What do your neighbors earn?

Go to http://www.census.gov/hhes/www/income/data/statemedian/index.html. Find the Median Household Income by State—Single-Year Estimates for a four-person family in your state (use the U.S. average if you are taking this course outside the United States) for the last 3 consecutive years. Find the percent increase (or decrease) in income each year for a family of four.

Discussion Questions

1. How does the median income for your state compare to a neighboring state?

2. What accounts for the differences in median income between your state and neighboring states?

PROBLEM 4
On the move, will my money follow?

Assume your employer is relocating to another state. You can keep your current job and salary if you move. Go to http://cgi.money.cnn.com/tools/costofliving/costofliving.html, enter your current state and city, a new destination state and city, and your current yearly salary. Click on Get result. Based on the calculation, what is the percent increase or decrease of your salary? Is this move worth your while financially?

Discussion Questions

1. Other than income, what factors would influence your decision to move to another state?

2. What factors help explain the change in income between the two locations you selected?

A KIPLINGER APPROACH

New Jobs, New Skills

The best route to a rewarding career is to pick a growing field and stay flexible.

WHAT IT'S ALL ABOUT. Jobs will trickle into the labor market over the next several months, but don't expect significant improvement until late next year. We'll recoup the eight million jobs lost in the recession by late 2013 or early 2014. But new workers will be entering the labor force, so achieving a full-employment economy—an unemployment rate of about 5% to 5.5%—could take much longer.

HOW IT'S DIFFERENT THIS TIME. Even profitable companies with plenty of cash aren't hiring until confidence in the economy improves. Nevertheless, job openings have risen 26% since July 2009. Why not a bigger dent in unemployment? Partly it's a mismatch between what employers are looking for and what workers have to offer. Success now depends less on years of experience in a particular industry or finely honed expertise, and more on flexibility and a knack for adapting a set of transferable skills.

HOW YOU CAN PROFIT. New grads will find the highest demand for degrees in accounting, business administration, computer science, engineering and math. An occupational certificate or associate's degree might help snag a lucrative job. But consider the number of job openings in the field. Employment in biomedical engineering is projected to grow 72% from 2008 through 2018— but that works out to just 1,400 openings per year.

The fastest-growing occupations with a lot of openings have a familiar ring, says occupational expert Laurence Shatkin. Over ten years (beginning in 2008), the number of computer network systems and database administrator openings could grow by 46,000 a year on average. Registered nurses could see 104,000 job openings per year. There will be a huge need for accountants and auditors, with about 50,000 openings per year.

Have a job already? Look for a raise of 3% or less, on average, but superstars might see 4.5%. Cover four bases to show you've added value: quantity (more output); quality (reduced errors); cost (on budget or below); and timeliness (deadlines beaten). Ask for a raise immediately after a big success. **ANNE KATES SMITH**

The More You Learn, the More You Earn

What a Degree WILL PAY
You can make a decent wage at the lower end of the educational spectrum. Figures are for median salaries.

BUSINESS

OFFICE MANAGEMENT
CERTIFICATE: $26,952
ASSOCIATE'S DEGREE: $34,296
BUSINESS MANAGEMENT
BACHELOR'S: $57,000
MASTER'S: $75,204

ENGINEERING

DRAFTING
CERTIFICATE: $36,000
ASSOCIATE'S DEGREE: $47,004
CHEMICAL, ELECTRICAL, CIVIL, OTHER
BACHELOR'S: $66,000
MASTER'S: $88,503

HEALTH

HEALTH CARE (LPN)
CERTIFICATE: $23,328
PHYSIOTHERAPIST, X-RAY TECH, OTHER
ASSOCIATE'S DEGREE: $40,524
BACHELOR'S: $45,549
MASTER'S: $60,276

COMPUTERS

INFORMATION MANAGEMENT
CERTIFICATE: $33,504
ASSOCIATE'S DEGREE: $42,000
INFORMATION SCIENCES
BACHELOR'S: $74,406
MASTER'S: $80,004

Where the JOB OPENINGS are
There will be 32.4 million replacement job openings between 2008 and 2018, as baby-boomers exit the workforce.

Financial services	1.9 MILLION
Government and public education services	2.3 MILLION
Manufacturing	2.6 MILLION
Private education services	2.8 MILLION
Health care	3.3 MILLION
Professional and business services	4.5 MILLION

SOURCE: Georgetown University Center on Education and the Workforce

BUSINESS MATH ISSUE

The impact of technology today will result in fewer job openings in the future.

1. List the key points of the article and information to support your position.
2. Write a group defense of your position using math calculations to support your view.

Discounts: Trade and Cash

Facebook Takes Aim at Groupon

BY SCOTT MORRISON

Facebook Inc. will soon start testing a service to provide discounts and other offers to its more than 500 million members, a move that will thrust the social network into direct competition with daily deals provider **Groupon** Inc.

The new service will be tested in Dallas, Austin, Atlanta, San Francisco and San Diego, and will expand upon Facebook's existing service that offers deals to members when they use Facebook Places to check into a specific location, the company said.

Users will be able locate deals on a special page listing all local promotions running at any given time. Users will be able to find a link to the deals page on the left side of their home page.

Facebook said the new service will let people buy deals on Facebook and share them with their friends.

"Local businesses will be able to sign up to use this feature soon and people will be able to find deals in the coming weeks," according to a company statement.

The push into social deals could step up pressure on Groupon and rival LivingSocial, which lead the rapidly growing market but only have a small percentage of Facebook's users.

Facebook declined to say whether it will require members to use the company's virtual currency, Facebook Credits, to purchase deals. The Palo Alto, Calif., company has been pushing the use of Credits for the purchase of digital goods in games, for which Facebook takes a 30% cut of revenue.

Requiring users to buy daily deals with Credits would push the virtual currency beyond the digital realm and could drive adoption among a broader base of users.

Facebook spokeswoman Annie Ta declined to rule out the possibility that deal buyers would be required to use Facebook Credits, saying the company was exploring different ways to purchase deals.

© AP Photo/L.G. Patterson

LU 7–1: Trade Discounts—Single and Chain (Includes Discussion of Freight)

1. Calculate single trade discounts with formulas and complements *(pp. 178–179)*.
2. Explain the freight terms *FOB shipping point* and *FOB destination (pp. 179–180)*.
3. Find list price when net price and trade discount rate are known *(pp. 181–182)*.
4. Calculate chain discounts with the net price equivalent rate and single equivalent discount rate *(pp. 182–184)*.

LU 7–2: Cash Discounts, Credit Terms, and Partial Payments

1. List and explain typical discount periods and credit periods that a business may offer *(pp. 185–192)*.
2. Calculate outstanding balance for partial payments *(p. 192)*.

Here are key terms in this chapter. After completing the chapter, if you know the term, place a checkmark in the parentheses. If you don't know the term, look it up and put the page number where it can be found.

Cash discount ( ) Chain discounts ( ) Complement ( ) Credit period ( ) Discount period ( )

Due dates ( ) End of credit period ( ) End of month (EOM) ( ) FOB destination ( ) FOB shipping

point ( ) Freight terms ( ) Invoice ( ) List price ( ) Net price ( ) Net price equivalent rate ( )

Ordinary dating ( ) Receipt of goods (ROG) ( ) Series discounts ( ) Single equivalent discount rate ( )

Single trade discount ( ) Terms of the sale ( ) Trade discount ( ) Trade discount amount ( ) Trade

discount rate ( )

Have you ever tried to find discounts online when buying fashion products? The *Wall Street Journal* clipping below, "How to Find Discount Fashion Online," shows how searching the web can provide some impressive discounts that you may miss by shopping at your local mall.

This chapter discusses two types of discounts taken by retailers—trade and cash. A **trade discount** is a reduction off the original selling price (list price) of an item and is not related to early payment. A **cash discount** is the result of an early payment based on the terms of the sale.

How to Find Discount Fashion Online

Stephanie Phair, director at discount online retailer **theOutnet.com**, says there are "two different people in the discount world." Some people buy discount but don't tell anyone. Others, like her, tell the world. "There's an element of pride," she says.

But searching site upon site for discounts takes time—just like going from store to store in the mall. A better bet is to try a search engine called an aggregator, which can pull up items from multiple sites. If Ms. Phair has something specific in mind, say, a pair of gold strappy sandals, she starts with ShopStyle or another aggregator. "It's a good way to cover a lot of ground," she says.

Since discount clothes are more likely to be sold out in some sizes, she sorts results by size. Another way to start, if you

have loyalties to specific brands, is to sign up for sales alerts on sites like shopittome.com.

Ms. Phair generally prefers discount sites, which are always open, to flash-sale sites, which offer sales between prescribed hours, because she likes the freedom to shop when her schedule permits. If you try shopping flash sales, also known as "pop-up" sales, being decisive is key: "You can't wait because it will likely be gone," Ms. Phair says. "You have to know what you want and know what your [price] threshold is."

It's helpful to know whether 30% or 60% is a decent discount, though that depends on what's being sold. Shoes and handbags are popular items at full price, so their discounts may hover around the 40% or 50% range. Denim might go for as much as 60% off, while expensive evening

dresses can be found for 70% off.

High-end designer labels, which have limited runs and cult followings, are harder to find at a discount. "Marni is not a brand readily available at discount. If I find [Marni] at 30% or 40% off, that's awesome," Ms. Phair says. Beyond labels, she looks for high-quality pieces that she can expect to last for several seasons and go with items she already owns.

Rather than push bathing suits in September, some discount retailers, including theOutnet, now highlight season-appropriate clothing. But the collections may include a lot from past seasons—and it often isn't clear what's new and what's from, say, fall 2007. Ms. Phair doesn't scorn older clothes, noting that trends usually run for a few seasons. For example, animal prints, camel and minimalist

dressing, which came into fashion a few years ago, will be in again for fall 2010.

Many online retailers have made the return process as easy as it is at their offline counterparts by including return shipping labels with each purchase. But read the fine print: Very deeply discounted items may be on final sale. Some sites accept returns for store credit only.

There are a few things that Ms. Phair normally won't buy online. Expensive jewelry is one, because she prefers to handle the jewelry in person. Also, Ms. Phair, who plans to get married in February, is debating whether to buy her wedding dress off the web, as new ones are very hard to find at a discount online.

Still, she'll start her search online. "If it's full price, so be it. But if it's discount, even better."

—*Elva Ramirez*

Learning Unit 7–1: Trade Discounts—Single and Chain (Includes Discussion of Freight)

© Inti St. Clair/Getty Images

The merchandise sold by retailers is bought from manufacturers and wholesalers who sell only to retailers and not to customers. These manufacturers and wholesalers offer retailer discounts so retailers can resell the merchandise at a profit. The discounts are off the manufacturers' and wholesalers' **list price** (suggested retail price), and the amount of discount that retailers receive off the list price is the **trade discount amount.** The *Wall Street Journal* clip "P&G Clears Plan for Mobile Coupons" shows how consumers use technology, such as smartphones and digital coupons, to obtain discounts. But consumers are not the only ones to benefit; the article also discusses how retailers can track customer preferences based on where and when digital coupons are redeemed.

When you make a purchase, the retailer (seller) gives you a purchase **invoice.** Invoices are important business documents that help sellers keep track of sales transactions and buyers keep track of purchase transactions. North Shore Community College Bookstore is a retail seller of textbooks to students. The bookstore

LO 1

P&G Clears Plan for Mobile Coupons

BY HANNAH KARP

Digital coupons are catching on with consumers, but the market's growth has been hampered by a pesky problem: Many retailers still aren't equipped with laser scanners that can detect bar codes off of the reflective, shiny, backlit screen of a smartphone. **Procter & Gamble** Co. is working on a potential solution. The consumer-goods giant said Monday it is working with start-up **mobeam** Inc. on a pilot program that will allow consumers to redeem coupons for P&G products straight from their phones. San Francisco-based mobeam has patented a way to beam out a bar code from the screen of a phone that is legible to normal laser scanners.

U.S. consumers saved more than $1.2 billion from redeeming digital coupons in 2010, according to a research report by digital-coupon provider Coupons.com, up 41% from a year earlier.

The challenge for mobeam now will be to get its technology integrated into smartphones so consumers can use it.

The technology must be installed in the guts of a phone, which requires the cooperation of device makers.

Mobeam says it is working with handset makers so that tens of millions of phones hitting the market in 2012 will include its technology, though it declined to say what device makers it is in discussions with. **Samsung Venture Investment** Corp., the venture-capital arm of **Samsung Group**, a large maker of mobile devices, recently invested money in mobeam.

Scanning technology is improving slowly. Airlines and some retailers like Target and Walgreens have developed tech-

nology to scan bar codes off of the mobile coupons they issue themselves, but consumer companies cannot guarantee exactly where customers will be able to use their coupons since they don't control the checkout lines.

For P&G, another potential payoff could come from the data it could gather from consumers who use the digital coupons. Mobeam says it will provide its partners with a trove of information about their mobile coupon users with consumer permission, allowing companies to track where and when they redeem them and what they buy.

Reprinted with permission of *The Wall Street Journal*, Copyright © 2011 Dow Jones & Company, Inc. All Rights Reserved Worldwide.

usually purchases its textbooks directly from publishers. Figure 7.1 (p. 179) shows a sample of what a textbook invoice from McGraw-Hill/Irwin Publishing Company to the North Shore Community College Bookstore would look like. Note that the trade discount amount is given in percent. This is the **trade discount rate,** which is a percent off the list price that retailers can deduct. The following formula for calculating a trade discount amount gives the numbers from the Figure 7.1 invoice in parentheses:

TRADE DISCOUNT AMOUNT FORMULA		
Trade discount amount = List price × Trade discount rate		
($1,943.88)	($7,775.50)	(25%)

The price that the retailer (bookstore) pays the manufacturer (publisher) or wholesaler is the **net price.** The following formula for calculating the net price gives the numbers from the Figure 7.1 invoice in parentheses:

NET PRICE FORMULA				
Net price	=	List price	−	Trade discount amount
($5,831.62)		($7,775.50)		($1,943.88)

Bookstore invoice showing a
trade discount

Invoice No.: 5582

McGraw-Hill/Irwin Publishing Co.
1333 Burr Ridge Parkway
Burr Ridge, Illinois 60527

Date: July 8, 2013
Ship: Two-day UPS
Terms: 2/10, n/30

Sold to: North Shore Community College Bookstore
1 Ferncroft Road
Danvers, MA 01923

Description	Unit list price	Total amount
50 Financial Management—Block/Hirt	$135.10	$6,755.00
10 Introduction to Business—Nichols	102.05	1,020.50
	Total List Price	$7,775.50
	Less: Trade Discount 25%	−1,943.88
	Net Price	$5,831.62
	Plus: Prepaid Shipping Charge	+125.00
	Total Invoice Amount	$5,956.62

© Frances Roberts/Alamy

Frequently, manufacturers and wholesalers issue catalogs to retailers containing list prices of the seller's merchandise and the available trade discounts. To reduce printing costs when prices change, these sellers usually update the catalogs with new *discount sheets*. The discount sheet also gives the seller the flexibility of offering different trade discounts to different classes of retailers. For example, some retailers buy in quantity and service the products. They may receive a larger discount than the retailer who wants the manufacturer to service the products. Sellers may also give discounts to meet a competitor's price, to attract new retailers, and to reward the retailers who buy product-line products. Sometimes the ability of the retailer to negotiate with the seller determines the trade discount amount.

Retailers cannot take trade discounts on freight, returned goods, sales tax, and so on. Trade discounts may be single discounts or a chain of discounts. Before we discuss single trade discounts, let's study freight terms.

LO 2

Freight Terms

The most common **freight terms** are *FOB shipping point* and *FOB destination*. These terms determine how the freight will be paid. The key words in the terms are *shipping point* and *destination*.

FOB shipping point means free on board at shipping point; that is, the buyer pays the freight cost of getting the goods to the place of business.

For example, assume that IBM in San Diego bought goods from Argo Suppliers in Boston. Argo ships the goods FOB Boston by plane. IBM takes title to the goods when the aircraft in Boston receives the goods, so IBM pays the freight from Boston to San Diego. Frequently, the seller (Argo) prepays the freight and adds the amount to the buyer's (IBM) invoice. When paying the invoice, the buyer takes the cash discount off the net price and adds the freight cost. FOB shipping point can be illustrated as follows:

FOB shipping point (Boston)

Boston   San Diego

Argo Suppliers
(IBM takes title here)

Buyer pays the freight

IBM
(Buyer pays the freight costs)

FOB destination means the seller pays the freight cost until it reaches the buyer's place of business. If Argo ships its goods to IBM FOB destination or FOB San Diego, the title to the goods remains with Argo. Then it is Argo's responsibility to pay the freight from Boston to IBM's place of business in San Diego. FOB destination can be illustrated as follows:

FOB destination (San Diego)

Boston

Argo Suppliers (Has title)	→ Seller pays the freight →	**IBM** (Gets title on arrival of goods)

The following *Wall Street Journal* clipping, "Ship Free or Lose Out," reveals that more and more online and retail stores are offering free shipping.

GLOBAL

Ship Free or Lose Out

More Retailers Absorb Cost of Sending Packages to Vie With Web-Only Rivals

By Ann Zimmerman and Dana Mattioli

Traditional retailers are taking the expensive step of offering more free-shipping deals this holiday season, as they seek to lure the growing number of Internet shoppers to their websites and away from online-only rivals, particularly **Amazon.com** Inc.

Amazon offers free shipping on most orders over $25, as well as cheap, low-hassle delivery options such as its Prime membership program, which other retailers have found hard to match. The online retail giant also offers low prices, since it doesn't have to pay for spar-

kly stores or cheery salespeople and— as rivals like to point out—because it doesn't collect sales taxes for the most part.

To fight back, **Toys "R" Us,** which last year had only select items available for free shipping, has made its entire online inventory eligible as long as customers spend $49. Similarly, **Wal-Mart Stores** Inc. has made every consumer-electronics item—rather than just select gadgets—on its website available for free shipping through Dec. 19 with a minimum $45 purchase. And **Best Buy** Co. is offering free shipping for every product it offers online, including giant TV sets.

For consumers, free shipping

can make a big difference in the ultimate price they pay. Amazon and Wal-Mart on Tuesday both were selling a hot holiday toy, Let's Rock Elmo, for $49.66 and offered free standard shipping—about a $6 savings. To keep up, the Toys "R" Us website is waiving its $10 shipping fee for the holidays. (It is charging $10 more for the toy itself, though.)

"Free shipping used to be a way to entice customers to your store over another site, but now it's just the price of entry," said Kevin Mansell, chief executive of **Kohl's** Corp., the discount department store.

Newegg.com, which specializes in electronics and is the

second-biggest online-only retailer, also offers free shipping on many products.

High shipping costs can turn off customers altogether. Amanda Lordy, a 29-year-old from Hoboken, N.J., does about half of her holiday shopping online. She recently canceled an order for $30 of gourmet cheese because the site was charging $14 for shipping.

Now you are ready for the discussion on single trade discounts.

Single Trade Discount

In the introduction to this unit, we showed how to use the trade discount amount formula and the net price formula to calculate the McGraw-Hill/Irwin Publishing Company textbook sale to the North Shore Community College Bookstore. Since McGraw-Hill/Irwin gave the bookstore only one trade discount, it is a **single trade discount.** In the following word problem, we use the formulas to solve another example of a single trade discount. Again, we will use a blueprint aid to help dissect and solve the word problem.

The Word Problem The list price of a Macintosh computer is $2,700. The manufacturer offers dealers a 40% trade discount. What are the trade discount amount and the net price?

	The facts	Solving for?	Steps to take	Key points
BLUEPRINT	*List price:* $2,700. *Trade discount rate:* 40%.	Trade discount amount. Net price.	Trade discount amount = List price × Trade discount rate. Net price = List price − Trade discount amount.	Trade discount amount — Portion (?) — Base ($2,700) × Rate (.40) — List price — Trade discount rate

Steps to solving problem

1. Calculate the trade discount amount. $2,700 × .40 = $1,080

2. Calculate the net price. $2,700 − $1,080 = $1,620

Now let's learn how to check the dealers' net price of $1,620 with an alternate procedure using a complement.

How to Calculate the Net Price Using Complement of Trade Discount Rate
The **complement** of a trade discount rate is the difference between the discount rate and 100%. The following steps show you how to use the complement of a trade discount rate:

CALCULATING NET PRICE USING COMPLEMENT OF TRADE DISCOUNT RATE

Step 1. To find the complement, subtract the single discount rate from 100%.

Step 2. Multiply the list price times the complement (from Step 1).

Think of a complement of any given percent (decimal) as the result of subtracting the percent from 100%.

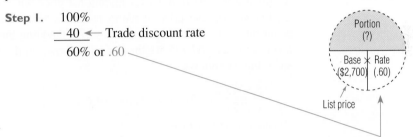

Step 1.   100%
        − 40 ← Trade discount rate
        60% or .60

Portion
(?)

Base × Rate
($2,700) (.60)

List price

The complement means that we are spending 60 cents per dollar because we save 40 cents per dollar. Since we planned to spend $2,700, we multiply .60 by $2,700 to get a net price of $1,620.

Step 2. $1,620 = $2,700 × .60

Note how the portion ($1,620) and rate (.60) relate to the same piece of the base ($2,700). The portion ($1,620) is smaller than the base, since the rate is less than 100%.

Be aware that some people prefer to use the trade discount amount formula and the net price formula to find the net price. Other people prefer to use the complement of the trade discount rate to find the net price. The result is always the same.

LO 3

Finding List Price When You Know Net Price and Trade Discount Rate   The following formula has many useful applications:

CALCULATING LIST PRICE WHEN NET PRICE AND TRADE DISCOUNT RATE ARE KNOWN

$$\text{List price} = \frac{\text{Net price}}{\text{Complement of trade discount rate}}$$

Next, let's see how to dissect and solve a word problem calculating list price.

The Word Problem   A Macintosh computer has a $1,620 net price and a 40% trade discount. What is its list price?

(continued on p. 182)

	The facts	Solving for?	Steps to take	Key points
BLUEPRINT	*Net price:* $1,620. *Trade discount rate:* 40%.	List price.	List price = $\dfrac{\text{Net price}}{\text{Complement of trade discount rate}}$	Net price Portion ($1,620) Base (?) × Rate (.60) List price 100% −40%

Steps to solving problem

1. Calculate the complement of the trade discount.

$$\begin{array}{r} 100\% \\ -\ 40 \\ \hline 60\% = .60 \end{array}$$

2. Calculate the list price.

$$\dfrac{\$1,620}{.60} = \boxed{\$2,700}$$

Note that the portion ($1,620) and rate (.60) relate to the same piece of the base.

Let's return to the McGraw-Hill/Irwin invoice in Figure 7.1 (p. 179) and calculate the list price using the formula for finding list price when the net price and trade discount rate are known. The net price of the textbooks is $5,831.62. The complement of the trade discount rate is 100% − 25% = 75% = .75. Dividing the net price $5,831.62 by the complement .75 equals $7,775.50, the list price shown in the McGraw-Hill/Irwin invoice. We can show this as follows:

$$\dfrac{\$5,831.62}{.75} = \$7,775.50^*, \text{ the list price}$$

*Off one cent due to rounding.

Chain Discounts

LO 4

Frequently, manufacturers want greater flexibility in setting trade discounts for different classes of customers, seasonal trends, promotional activities, and so on. To gain this flexibility, some sellers give **chain** or **series discounts**—trade discounts in a series of two or more successive discounts.

Sellers list chain discounts as a group, for example, 20/15/10. Let's look at how Mick Company arrives at the net price of office equipment with a 20/15/10 chain discount.

EXAMPLE   The list price of the office equipment is $15,000. The chain discount is 20/15/10. The long way to calculate the net price is as follows:

Step 1	**Step 2**	**Step 3**	**Step 4**
$15,000	$15,000	$12,000	$10,200
× .20	− 3,000	− 1,800	− 1,020
$ 3,000	$12,000	$10,200	$ 9,180 net price
	× .15	× .10	
	$ 1,800	$ 1,020	

Never add the 20/15/10 together

Note how we multiply the percent (in decimal) times the new balance after we subtract the previous trade discount amount. For example, in Step 3, we change the last discount, 10%, to decimal form and multiply times $10,200. Remember that each percent is multiplied by a successively *smaller* base. You could write the 20/15/10 discount rate in any order and still arrive at the same net price. Thus, you would get the $9,180 net price if the discount were 10/15/20 or 15/20/10. However, sellers usually give the larger discounts first. *Never try to shorten this step process by adding the discounts.* Your net price will be incorrect because, when done properly, each percent is calculated on a different base.

Net Price Equivalent Rate   In the example above, you could also find the $9,180 net price with the **net price equivalent rate**—a shortcut method. Let's see how to use this rate to calculate net price.

CALCULATING NET PRICE USING NET PRICE EQUIVALENT RATE
Step 1. Subtract each chain discount rate from 100% (find the complement) and convert each percent to a decimal.
Step 2. Multiply the decimals. Do not round off decimals, since this number is the net price equivalent rate.
Step 3. Multiply the list price times the net price equivalent rate (Step 2).

The following word problem with its blueprint aid illustrates how to use the net price equivalent rate method.

The Word Problem   The list price of office equipment is $15,000. The chain discount is 20/15/10. What is the net price?

	The facts	Solving for?	Steps to take	Key points
BLUEPRINT	List price: $15,000. Chain discount: 20/15/10	Net price.	Net price equivalent rate. Net price = List price $\times$ Net price equivalent rate.	Do not round net price equivalent rate.

Steps to solving problem

1. Calculate the complement of each rate and convert each percent to a decimal.

$$
\begin{array}{ccc}
100\% & 100\% & 100\% \\
-\ 20 & -\ 15 & -\ 10 \\
\hline
80\% & 85\% & 90\% \\
\downarrow & \downarrow & \downarrow \\
.8 & .85 & .9
\end{array}
$$

2. Calculate the net price equivalent rate. (Do not round.)

$.8 \times .85 \times .9 = .612$ Net price equivalent rate. For each $1, you are spending about 61 cents.

3. Calculate the net price (actual cost to buyer).

$15,000 \times .612 = \boxed{\$9,180}$

Next we see how to calculate the trade discount amount with a simpler method. In the previous word problem, we could calculate the trade discount amount as follows:

$15,000 ← List price
$\underline{-\ 9,180}$ ← Net price
$\boxed{\$\ 5,820}$ ← Trade discount amount

Single Equivalent Discount Rate   You can use another method to find the trade discount by using the **single equivalent discount rate.**

MONEY tips

Double-check invoices. On average 9 out of 10 invoices contain an error.

CALCULATING TRADE DISCOUNT AMOUNT USING SINGLE EQUIVALENT DISCOUNT RATE
Step 1. Subtract the net price equivalent rate from 1. This is the single equivalent discount rate.
Step 2. Multiply the list price times the single equivalent discount rate. This is the trade discount amount.

Let's now do the calculations.

Step 1.   1.000 ← If you are using a calculator, just press 1.
$\underline{-\ .612}$
.388 ← This is the single equivalent discount rate.

Step 2. $15,000 $\times$ .388 = $\boxed{\$5,820}$ → This is the trade discount amount.

Remember that when we use the net price equivalent rate, the buyer of the office equipment pays \$.612 on each \$1 of list price. Now with the single equivalent discount rate, we can say that the buyer saves \$.388 on each \$1 of list price. The .388 is the single equivalent discount rate for the 20/15/10 chain discount. Note how we use the .388 single equivalent discount rate as if it were the only discount.

It's time to try the Practice Quiz.

LU 7–1 PRACTICE QUIZ

Complete this **Practice Quiz** to see how you are doing.[1]

1. The list price of a dining room set with a 40% trade discount is \$12,000. What are the trade discount amount and net price? (Use the complement method for net price.)
2. The net price of a video system with a 30% trade discount is \$1,400. What is the list price?
3. Lamps Outlet bought a shipment of lamps from a wholesaler. The total list price was \$12,000 with a 5/10/25 chain discount. Calculate the net price and trade discount amount. (Use the net price equivalent rate and single equivalent discount rate in your calculation.)

*For **extra help** from your authors–Sharon and Jeff–see the student DVD*

YouTube

✓ Solutions

1. Dining room set trade discount amount and net price:

BLUEPRINT	The facts	Solving for?	Steps to take	Key points
	List price: \$12,000. *Trade discount rate:* 40%.	Trade discount amount. Net price.	Trade discount amount = List price × Trade discount rate. Net price = List price × Complement of trade discount rate.	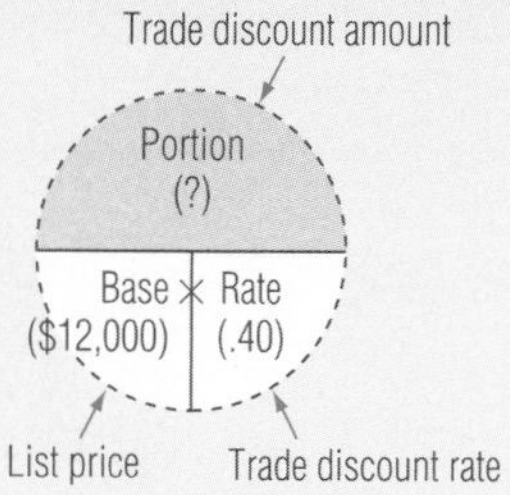

Steps to solving problem

1. Calculate the trade discount. $\$12,000 \times .40 =$ **\$4,800** Trade discount amount
2. Calculate the net price. $\$12,000 \times .60 =$ **\$7,200** (100% − 40% = 60%)

2. Video system list price:

BLUEPRINT	The facts	Solving for?	Steps to take	Key points
	Net price: \$1,400. *Trade discount rate:* 30%.	List price.	List price = $\dfrac{\text{Net price}}{\text{Complement of trade discount}}$	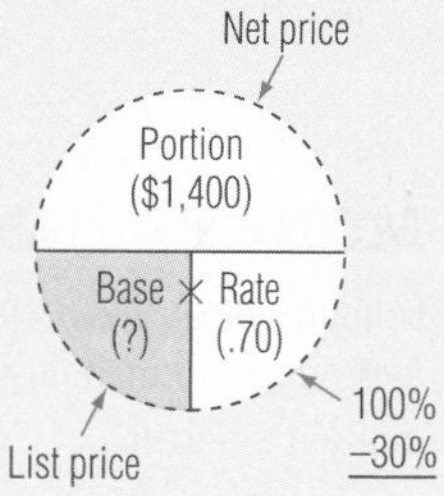

Steps to solving problem

1. Calculate the complement of trade discount.

$$\begin{array}{r} 100\% \\ -\ 30 \\ \hline 70\% \end{array} = .70$$

2. Calculate the list price.

$$\frac{\$1,400}{.70} = \$2,000$$

[1]For all three problems we will show blueprint aids. You might want to draw them on scrap paper.

3. Lamps Outlet's net price and trade discount amount:

	The facts	Solving for?	Steps to take	Key points
BLUEPRINT	List price: $12,000. Chain discount: 5/10/25.	Net price. Trade discount amount.	Net price = List price × Net price equivalent rate. Trade discount amount = List price × Single equivalent discount rate.	Do not round off net price equivalent rate or single equivalent discount rate.

Steps to solving problem

1. Calculate the complement of each chain discount.	$$\begin{array}{ccc} 100\% & 100\% & 100\% \\ -\ 5 & -\ 10 & -\ 25 \\ \hline 95\% & 90\% & 75\% \end{array}$$
2. Calculate the net price equivalent rate.	$.95 \times .90 \times .75 = .64125$
3. Calculate the net price.	$\$12{,}000 \times .64125 = \boxed{\$7{,}695}$
4. Calculate the single equivalent discount rate.	$$\begin{array}{r} 1.00000 \\ -\ .64125 \\ \hline .35875 \end{array}$$
5. Calculate the trade discount amount.	$\$12{,}000 \times .35875 = \boxed{\$4{,}305}$

LU 7–1a   EXTRA PRACTICE QUIZ WITH WORKED-OUT SOLUTIONS

Need more practice? Try this **Extra Practice Quiz** (check figures in the Interactive Chapter Organizer, p. 196). Worked-out Solutions can be found in Appendix B at end of text.

1. The list price of a dining room set with a 30% trade discount is $16,000. What are the trade discount amount and net price? (Use the complement method for net price.)

2. The net price of a video system with a 20% trade discount is $400. What is the list price?

3. Lamps Outlet bought a shipment of lamps from a wholesaler. The total list price was $14,000 with a 4/8/20 chain discount. Calculate the net price and trade discount amount. (Use the net price equivalent rate and single equivalent discount rate in your calculation.)

Learning Unit 7–2: Cash Discounts, Credit Terms, and Partial Payments

LO 1

To introduce this learning unit, we will use the New Hampshire Propane Company invoice that follows. The invoice shows that if you pay your bill early, you will receive a 19-cent discount. Every penny counts.

New Hampshire Propane Company				
Date	Description	Qty.	Price	Total
	Previous Balance			**$0.00**
06/24/14	PROPANE	3.60	$3.40	$12.24

Invoice No. 004433L	Totals this invoice: $12.24 **AMOUNT DUE:** $12.24
Invoice Date 6/26/14	Prompt Pay Discount: $0.19 **Net Amount Due if RECEIVED by 07/10/14:** $12.05
	Due Date 7/26/14

Now let's study cash discounts.

Cash Discounts

In the New Hampshire Propane Company invoice, we receive a cash discount of 19 cents. This amount is determined by the **terms of the sale,** which can include the credit period, cash discount, discount period, and freight terms.

Buyers can often benefit from buying on credit. The time period that sellers give buyers to pay their invoices is the **credit period.** Frequently, buyers can sell the goods bought during this credit period. Then, at the end of the credit period, buyers can pay sellers with the funds from the sales of the goods. When buyers can do this, they can use the consumer's money to pay the invoice instead of their money.

Sellers can also offer a cash discount, or reduction from the invoice price, if buyers pay the invoice within a specified time. This time period is the **discount period,** which is part of the total credit period. Sellers offer this cash discount because they can use the dollars to better advantage sooner than later. Buyers who are not short of cash like cash discounts because the goods will cost them less and, as a result, provide an opportunity for larger profits.

Remember that buyers do not take cash discounts on freight, returned goods, sales tax, and trade discounts. Buyers take cash discounts on the *net price* of the invoice. Before we discuss how to calculate cash discounts, let's look at some aids that will help you calculate credit **due dates** and **end of credit periods.**

Aids in Calculating Credit Due Dates   Sellers usually give credit for 30, 60, or 90 days. Not all months of the year have 30 days. So you must count the credit days from the date of the invoice. The trick is to remember the number of days in each month. You can choose one of the following three options to help you do this.

Option 1: Days-in-a-Month Rule   You may already know this rule. Remember that every 4 years is a leap year.

> Thirty days has September, April, June, and November; all the rest have 31 except February has 28, and 29 in leap years.

Option 2: Knuckle Months   Some people like to use the knuckles on their hands to remember which months have 30 or 31 days. Note in the following diagram that each knuckle represents a month with 31 days. The short months are in between the knuckles.

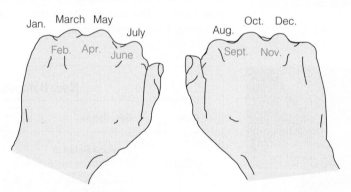

31 days: Jan., March, May, July, Aug., Oct., Dec.

Option 3: Days-in-a-Year Calendar   The days-in-a-year calendar (excluding leap year) is another tool to help you calculate dates for discount and credit periods (Table 7.1, p. 187). For example, let's use Table 7.1 to calculate 90 days from August 12.

EXAMPLE   By Table 7.1: August 12 = $\begin{array}{r} 224 \text{ days} \\ +\ 90 \\ \hline 314 \text{ days} \end{array}$

Search for day 314 in Table 7.1. You will find that day 314 is November 10. In this example, we stayed within the same year. Now let's try an example in which we overlap from year to year.

A cash discount is for prompt payment. A trade discount is not.

Trade discounts should be taken before cash discounts.

Years divisible by 4 are leap years. Leap years occur in 2012 and 2016.

| TABLE | 7.1 | Exact days-in-a-year calendar (excluding leap year)* |

Day of month	31 Jan.	28 Feb.	31 Mar.	30 Apr.	31 May	30 June	31 July	31 Aug.	30 Sept.	31 Oct.	30 Nov.	31 Dec.
1	1	32	60	91	121	152	182	213	244	274	305	335
2	2	33	61	92	122	153	183	214	245	275	306	336
3	3	34	62	93	123	154	184	215	246	276	307	337
4	4	35	63	94	124	155	185	216	247	277	308	338
5	5	36	64	95	125	156	186	217	248	278	309	339
6	6	37	65	96	126	157	187	218	249	279	310	340
7	7	38	66	97	127	158	188	219	250	280	311	341
8	8	39	67	98	128	159	189	220	251	281	312	342
9	9	40	68	99	129	160	190	221	252	282	313	343
10	10	41	69	100	130	161	191	222	253	283	314	344
11	11	42	70	101	131	162	192	223	254	284	315	345
12	12	43	71	102	132	163	193	224	255	285	316	346
13	13	44	72	103	133	164	194	225	256	286	317	347
14	14	45	73	104	134	165	195	226	257	287	318	348
15	15	46	74	105	135	166	196	227	258	288	319	349
16	16	47	75	106	136	167	197	228	259	289	320	350
17	17	48	76	107	137	168	198	229	260	290	321	351
18	18	49	77	108	138	169	199	230	261	291	322	352
19	19	50	78	109	139	170	200	231	262	292	323	353
20	20	51	79	110	140	171	201	232	263	293	324	354
21	21	52	80	111	141	172	202	233	264	294	325	355
22	22	53	81	112	142	173	203	234	265	295	326	356
23	23	54	82	113	143	174	204	235	266	296	327	357
24	24	55	83	114	144	175	205	236	267	297	328	358
25	25	56	84	115	145	176	206	237	268	298	329	359
26	26	57	85	116	146	177	207	238	269	299	330	360
27	27	58	86	117	147	178	208	239	270	300	331	361
28	28	59	87	118	148	179	209	240	271	301	332	362
29	29	—	88	119	149	180	210	241	272	302	333	363
30	30	—	89	120	150	181	211	242	273	303	334	364
31	31	—	90	—	151	—	212	243	—	304	—	365

*Often referred to as a Julian calendar.

EXAMPLE   What date is 80 days after December 5?

Table 7.1 shows that December 5 is 339 days from the beginning of the year. Subtracting 339 from 365 (the end of the year) tells us that we have used up 26 days by the end of the year. This leaves 54 days in the new year. Go back in the table and start with the beginning of the year and search for 54 (80 − 26) days. The 54th day is February 23.

By table	Without use of table

By table

   365 days in year
− 339 days until December 5
    26 days used in year

          80 days from December 5
       − 26 days used in year
        54 days in new year or
          February 23

Without use of table

  December 31
− December   5
          26
+ 31 days in January
       57
+ 23 due date (February 23)
  80 total days

When you know how to calculate credit due dates, you can understand the common business terms sellers offer buyers involving discounts and credit periods. Remember that discount and credit terms vary from one seller to another.

Common Credit Terms Offered by Sellers

The common credit terms sellers offer buyers include *ordinary dating, receipt of goods (ROG),* and *end of month (EOM).* In this section we examine these credit terms. To determine the due dates, we used the exact days-in-a-year calendar (Table 7.1, p. 187).

Ordinary Dating   Today, businesses frequently use the **ordinary dating** method. It gives the buyer a cash discount period that begins with the invoice date. The credit terms of two common ordinary dating methods are 2/10, n/30 and 2/10, 1/15, n/30.

2/10, n/30 Ordinary Dating Method   The 2/10, n/30 is read as "two ten, net thirty." Buyers can take a 2% cash discount off the gross amount of the invoice if they pay the bill within 10 days from the invoice date. If buyers miss the discount period, the net amount—without a discount—is due between day 11 and day 30. *Freight, returned goods, sales tax, and trade discounts must be subtracted from the gross before calculating a cash discount.*

EXAMPLE $400 invoice dated July 5: terms 2/10, n/30; no freight; paid on July 11.

Step 1. Calculate end of 2% discount period:

> July   5 date of invoice
> $\underline{+\ 10}$ days
> July 15 end of 2% discount period

Step 2. Calculate end of credit period:

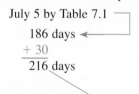

> July 5 by Table 7.1
> 186 days
> $\underline{+\ 30}$
> 216 days

Search in Table 7.1 for 216 → August 4 → end of credit period

Step 3. Calculate payment on July 11:

> .02 × $400 = $8 cash discount
> $400 − $8 = $392 paid

> *Note:* A 2% cash discount means that you save 2 cents on the dollar and pay 98 cents on the dollar. Thus, $.98 × $400 = $392.

The following time line illustrates the 2/10, n/30 ordinary dating method beginning and ending dates of the above example:

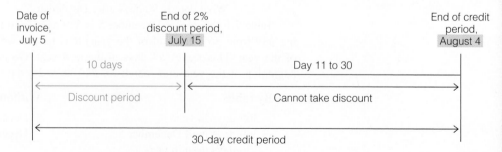

2/10, 1/15, n/30 Ordinary Dating Method   The 2/10, 1/15, n/30 is read "two ten, one fifteen, net thirty." The seller will give buyers a 2% (2 cents on the dollar) cash discount if they pay within 10 days of the invoice date. If buyers pay between day 11 and day 15 from the date of the invoice, they can save 1 cent on the dollar. If buyers do not pay on day 15, the net or full amount is due 30 days from the invoice date.

EXAMPLE $600 invoice dated May 8; $100 of freight included in invoice price; paid on May 22. Terms 2/10, 1/15, n/30.

Step 1. Calculate the end of the 2% discount period:

May 8 date of invoice
+ 10 days
May 18 end of 2% discount period

Step 2. Calculate end of 1% discount period:

May 18 end of 2% discount period
+ 5 days
May 23 end of 1% discount period

Step 3. Calculate end of credit period:

May 8 by Table 7.1
128 days
+ 30
158 days

Search in Table 7.1 for 158 → June 7 → end of credit period

Step 4. Calculate payment on May 22 (14 days after date of invoice):

$600 invoice
− 100 freight
$500
× .01
$5.00

$500 − $5.00 + $100 freight = $595

A 1% discount means we pay $.99 on the dollar or
$500 × $.99 = $495 + $100 freight = $595.

Note: Freight is added back since no cash discount is taken on freight.

The following time line illustrates the 2/10, 1/15, n/30 ordinary dating method beginning and ending dates of the above example:

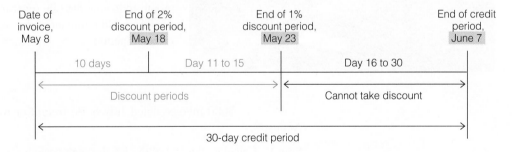

Receipt of Goods (ROG)

3/10, n/30 ROG With the **receipt of goods (ROG),** the cash discount period begins when buyer receives goods, *not* the invoice date. Industry often uses the ROG terms when buyers cannot expect delivery until a long time after they place the order. Buyers can take a 3% discount within 10 days *after* receipt of goods. The full amount is due between day 11 and day 30 if the cash discount period is missed.

EXAMPLE $900 invoice dated May 9; no freight or returned goods; the goods were received on July 8; terms 3/10, n/30 ROG; payment made on July 20.

Step 1. Calculate the end of the 3% discount period:

July 8 date goods arrive
+ 10 days
July 18 end of 3% discount period

(continued on p. 190)

Step 2. Calculate the end of the credit period:

July 8 by Table 7.1 ⎯⎤
    189 days ⟵⎯⎯⎯⎯⎯⎯⎯⎯⎯⎤
    + 30
     219 days

Search in Table 7.1 for 219 → August 7 → end of credit period

Step 3. Calculate payment on July 20:

Missed discount period and paid net or full amount of $900.

The following time line illustrates 3/10, n/30 ROG beginning and ending dates of the above example:

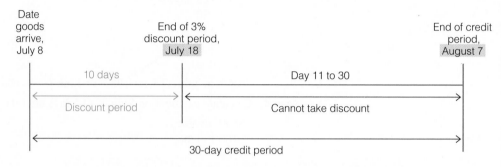

Date goods arrive, July 8	End of 3% discount period, July 18	End of credit period, August 7
10 days	Day 11 to 30	
Discount period	Cannot take discount	
30-day credit period		

© The McGraw-Hill Companies, Inc./Christopher Kerrigan, photographer

End of Month (EOM)[2]   In this section we look at invoices involving **end of month (EOM)** terms. If an invoice is dated the *25th or earlier* of a month, we follow one set of rules. If an invoice is dated after the 25th of the month, a new set of rules is followed. Let's look at each situation.

Invoice Dated 25th or Earlier in Month, 1/10 EOM If sellers date an invoice on the 25th or earlier in the month, buyers can take the cash discount if they pay the invoice by the first 10 days of the month following the sale (next month). If buyers miss the discount period, the full amount is due within 20 days after the end of the discount period.

EXAMPLE $600 invoice dated July 6; no freight or returns; terms 1/10 EOM; paid on August 8.

Step 1. Calculate the end of the 1% discount period: ⎯⎤

August 10 ⟵⎯⎯⎯⎯⎯⎯⎯⎯⎯⎯⎤   First 10 days of month following sale.

Step 2. Calculate the end of the credit period: ⎯⎯→

August 10
   + 20 days
August 30 → Credit period is 20 days after discount period.

Step 3. Calculate payment on August 8:

.99 × $600 = $594

---

[2]Sometimes the Latin term *proximo* is used. Other variations of EOM exist, but the key point is that the seller guarantees the buyer 15 days' credit. We assume a 30-day month.

The following time line illustrates the beginning and ending dates of the EOM invoice of the previous example:

| Date of invoice, July 6 | Next month following sale, August* | End of 1% discount period, August 10 | End of credit period, August 30 |

*Even though the discount period begins with the next month following the sale, if buyers wish, they can pay before the discount period (date of invoice until the discount period).

Invoice Dated after 25th of Month, 2/10 EOM When sellers sell goods *after* the 25th of the month, buyers gain an additional month. The cash discount period ends on the 10th day of the second month that follows the sale. Why? This occurs because the seller guarantees the 15 days' credit of the buyer. If a buyer bought goods on August 29, September 10 would be only 12 days. So the buyer gets the extra month.

EXAMPLE $800 invoice dated April 29; no freight or returned goods; terms 2/10 EOM; payment made on June 18.

Step 1. Calculate the end of the 2% discount period:

June 10 ←

First 10 days of second month following sale

Step 2. Calculate the end of the credit period:

June 10
+ 20 days
June 30 ←

Credit period is 20 days after discount period.

Step 3. Calculate the payment on June 18:

No discount; $800 paid.

The following time line illustrates the beginning and ending dates of the EOM invoice of the above example:

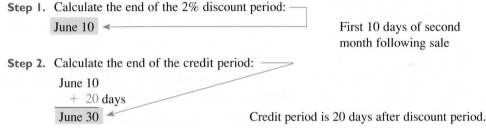

| Date of invoice, April 29 | 2nd month following sale, June* | End of 2% discount period, June 10 | End of credit period, June 30 |

*Even though the discount period begins with the second month following the sale, if buyers wish, they can pay before the discount date (date of invoice until the discount period)

Solving a Word Problem with Trade and Cash Discount

Now that we have studied trade and cash discounts, let's look at a combination that involves both a trade and a cash discount.

The Word Problem Hardy Company sent Regan Corporation an invoice for office equipment with a $10,000 list price. Hardy dated the invoice July 29 with terms of 2/10 EOM (end of month). Regan receives a 30% trade discount and paid the invoice on September 6. Since terms were FOB destination, Regan paid no freight charge. What was the cost of office equipment for Regan?

	The facts	Solving for?	Steps to take	Key points
BLUEPRINT	List price: $10,000. Trade discount rate: 30%. Terms: 2/10 EOM. Invoice date: 7/29. Date paid: 9/6.	Cost of office equipment.	Net price = List price × Complement of trade discount rate. After 25th of month for EOM. Discount period is 1st 10 days of second month that follows sale.	Trade discounts are deducted before cash discounts are taken. Cash discounts are not taken on freight or returns.

(continued on p. 192)

Steps to solving problem

1. Calculate the net price.

$$\$10,000 \times .70 = \$7,000 \qquad \begin{bmatrix} 100\% \\ - 30\% \text{ (trade discount)} \end{bmatrix}$$

2. Calculate the discount period.

Sale: 7/29 Month 1: Aug. Month 2: Sept 10 → Paid on Sept. 6—is entitled to 2% off.

3. Calculate the cost of office equipment.

$$\$7,000 \times .98 = \boxed{\$6,860}$$ If you save 2 cents on a dollar, you are spending 98 cents.

$$\begin{matrix} 100\% \\ - 2\% \end{matrix}$$

LO 2

Partial Payments

Often buyers cannot pay the entire invoice before the end of the discount period. To calculate partial payments and outstanding balance, use the following steps:

CALCULATING PARTIAL PAYMENTS AND OUTSTANDING BALANCE
Step 1. Calculate the complement of a discount rate.
Step 2. Divide partial payments by the complement of a discount rate (Step 1). This gives the amount credited.
Step 3. Subtract Step 2 from the total owed. This is the outstanding balance.

EXAMPLE Molly McGrady owed $400. Molly's terms were 2/10, n/30. Within 10 days, Molly sent a check for $80. The actual credit the buyer gave Molly is as follows:

Step 1. $100\% - 2\% = 98\% \to .98$

Step 2. $\dfrac{\$80}{.98} = \$81.63$ $\qquad \dfrac{\$80}{1 - .02}$ ← Discount rate

Step 3. $\$400.00$
$\quad - \underline{81.63}$ partial payment—although sent in $80
$\quad \boxed{\$318.37}$ outstanding balance

Note: We do not multiply $.02 \times \$80$ because the seller did not base the original discount on $80. When Molly makes a payment within the 10-day discount period, 98 cents pays each $1 she owes. Before buyers take discounts on partial payments, they must have permission from the seller. Not all states allow partial payments.

You have completed another unit. Let's check your progress.

MONEY tips

The formula for determining your credit score is roughly: 35% from your payment history (may include library fines and parking tickets); 30% determined by your debt to available credit ratio; 15% on the length of your credit history—the fewer and older the accounts, the better; 10% based on how many recent accounts were opened along with the number of inquiries made by lenders on your credit report; and, finally, 10% for the types of credit used.

LU 7–2 PRACTICE QUIZ

Complete this **Practice Quiz** to see how you are doing.

Complete the following table:

	Date of invoice	Date goods received	Terms	Last day* of discount period	End of credit period
1.	July 6		2/10, n/30		
2.	February 19	June 9	3/10, n/30 ROG		
3.	May 9		4/10, 1/30, n/60		
4.	May 12		2/10 EOM		
5.	May 29		2/10 EOM		

*If more than one discount, assume date of last discount.

6. Metro Corporation sent Vasko Corporation an invoice for equipment with an $8,000 list price. Metro dated the invoice May 26. Terms were 2/10 EOM. Vasko receives a 20% trade discount and paid the invoice on July 3. What was the cost of equipment for Vasko? (A blueprint aid will be in the solution to help dissect this problem.)

7. Complete amount to be credited and balance outstanding:

Amount of invoice: $600
Terms: 2/10, 1/15, n/30
Date of invoice: September 30
Paid October 3: $400

✓ Solutions

1. End of discount period: July 6 + 10 days = July 16
   End of credit period: By Table 7.1, July 6 =
   $$\begin{array}{r} 187 \text{ days} \\ + 30 \text{ days} \\ \hline 217 \end{array} \rightarrow \text{search} \longrightarrow \text{Aug. 5}$$

2. End of discount period: June 9 + 10 days = June 19
   End of credit period: By Table 7.1, June 9 =
   $$\begin{array}{r} 160 \text{ days} \\ + 30 \text{ days} \\ \hline 190 \end{array} \rightarrow \text{search} \longrightarrow \text{July 9}$$

3. End of discount period: By Table 7.1, May 9 =
   $$\begin{array}{r} 129 \text{ days} \\ + 30 \text{ days} \\ \hline 159 \end{array} \rightarrow \text{search} \longrightarrow \text{June 8}$$
   End of credit period: By Table 7.1, May 9 =
   $$\begin{array}{r} 129 \text{ days} \\ + 60 \text{ days} \\ \hline 189 \end{array} \rightarrow \text{search} \longrightarrow \text{July 8}$$

4. End of discount period: June 10
   End of credit period: June 10 + 20 = June 30

5. End of discount period: July 10
   End of credit period: July 10 + 20 = July 30

6. Vasko Corporation's cost of equipment:

	The facts	Solving for?	Steps to take	Key points
BLUEPRINT	List price: $8,000. Trade discount rate: 20%. Terms: 2/10 EOM. Invoice date: 5/26. Date paid: 7/3.	Cost of equipment.	Net price = List price × Complement of trade discount rate. EOM before 25th: Discount period is 1st 10 days of month that follows sale.	Trade discounts are deducted before cash discounts are taken. Cash discounts are not taken on freight or returns.

Steps to solving problem

1. Calculate the net price. $8,000 × .80 = $6,400   ⎡ 100% ⎣ − 20%
2. Calculate the discount period. Until July 10
3. Calculate the cost of office equipment. $6,400 × .98 = $6,272 (100% − 2%)

7. $\dfrac{\$400}{.98} = \$408.16$, amount credited.

$600 − $408.16 = **$191.84**, balance outstanding.

LU 7–2a EXTRA PRACTICE QUIZ WITH WORKED-OUT SOLUTIONS

Need more practice? Try this **Extra Practice Quiz** (check figures in the Interactive Chapter Organizer, p. 196). Worked-out Solutions can be found in Appendix B at end of text.

Complete the following table:

	Date of invoice	Date goods received	Terms	Last day of discount period*	End of credit period
1.	July 8		2/10, n/30		
2.	February 24	June 12	3/10, n/30 ROG		
3.	May 12		4/10, 1/30, n/60		
4.	April 14		2/10 EOM		
5.	April 27		2/10 EOM		

*If more than one discount, assume date of last discount.

6. Metro Corporation sent Vasko Corporation an invoice for equipment with a $9,000 list price. Metro dated the invoice June 29. Terms were 2/10 EOM. Vasko receives a 30% trade discount and paid the discount on August 9. What was the cost of equipment for Vasko?

7. Complete amount to be credited and balance outstanding:

Amount of invoice: $700
Terms: 2/10, 1/15, n/30
Date of invoice: September 28
Paid October 3: $600

INTERACTIVE CHAPTER ORGANIZER

Topic/procedure/formula	Examples	You try it*
Trade discount amount, p. 178 Trade discount amount = List price × Trade discount rate	$600 list price 30% trade discount rate Trade discount amount = $600 × .30 = $180	**Calculate trade discount amount** $700 list price 20% trade discount
Calculating net price, p. 178 Net price = List price − Trade discount amount or List price × Complement of trade discount price	$600 list price 30% trade discount rate Net price = $600 × .70 = $420 1.00 − .30 .70	**Calculate net price** $700 list price 20% trade discount
Freight, p. 179 FOB shipping point—buyer pays freight. FOB destination—seller pays freight.	Moose Company of New York sells equipment to Agee Company of Oregon. Terms of shipping are FOB New York. Agee pays cost of freight since terms are FOB shipping point.	**Calculate freight** If a buyer in Boston buys equipment with shipping terms of FOB destination, who will pay cost of freight?
Calculating list price when net price and trade discount rate are known, p. 181 List price = Net price / Complement of trade discount rate	40% trade discount rate Net price, $120 $120 / .60 = $200 list price (1.00 − .40)	**Calculate list price** 60% trade discount rate Net price, $240
Chain discounts, p. 182 Successively lower base.	5/10 on a $100 list item $ 100 $ 95 × .05 × .10 $ 5.00 $9.50 (running balance) $95.00 − 9.50 $85.50 net price	**Calculate net price** 6/8 on $200 list item

(continues)

INTERACTIVE CHAPTER ORGANIZER

Topic/procedure/formula	Examples	You try it*
Net price equivalent rate, pp. 182–183 $\dfrac{\text{Actual cost}}{\text{to buyer}} = \dfrac{\text{List}}{\text{price}} \times \dfrac{\text{Net price}}{\text{equivalent rate}}$ Take complement of each chain discount and multiply—do not round. $\dfrac{\text{Trade discount}}{\text{amount}} = \dfrac{\text{List}}{\text{price}} - \dfrac{\text{Actual cost}}{\text{to buyer}}$	Given: 5/10 on $1,000 list price Take complement: .95 × .90 = .855 　　　　　　　　　(net price equivalent) $1,000 × .855 = $855 　　　　　　　(actual cost or net price) 　　　$1,000 　　－　855 　　　$ 145　trade discount amount	**Calculate net price equivalent rate, net price, and trade discount amount** 6/8 on $2,000 list
Single equivalent discount rate, p. 183 $\dfrac{\text{Trade discount}}{\text{amount}} = \dfrac{\text{List}}{\text{price}} \times \dfrac{1 - \text{Net price}}{\text{equivalent rate}}$	See preceding example for facts: 1 − .855 = .145 .145 × $1,000 = $145	**From the above You Try It, calculate single equivalent discount**
Cash discounts, p. 186 Cash discounts, due to prompt payment, are not taken on freight, returns, etc.	Gross 　 $1,000 (includes freight) Freight 　$25　　　Terms 2/10, n/30 Returns 　$25　　　Purchased: Sept. 9; 　　　　　　　　　　　paid Sept. 15 　Cash discount = $950 × .02 = $19	**Calculate cash discount** Gross 　 $2,000 (includes freight) Freight 　$40　　　Terms 2/10, n/30 Returns 　$40　　　Purchased: Sept. 2; 　　　　　　　　　　　paid Sept. 8
Calculating due dates, pp. 186–187 *Option 1:* Thirty days has September, April, June, and November; all the rest have 31 except February has 28, and 29 in leap years. *Option 2:* Knuckles—31-day month; in between knuckles are short months. *Option 3:* Days-in-a-year table.	Invoice $500 on March 5; terms 2/10, n/30　　　　March 5 *End of discount*　　　　　　+ 10 *period:* ─────────→ March 15 *End of credit*　　March 5 = 64 days *period by*　　　　　　+ 30 *Table 7.1:* ──────→ 94 days 　　　　　　　　　　　↓ 　　Search in Table 7.1　April 4	**Calculate end of discount and end of credit periods** Invoice $600 on April 2; terms 2/10, n/30
Common terms of sale **a. Ordinary dating, p. 188** Discount period begins from date of invoice. Credit period ends 20 days from the end of the discount period unless otherwise stipulated; example, 2/10, n/60—the credit period ends 50 days from end of discount period.	Invoice $600 (freight of $100 included in price) dated March 8; payment on March 16; 3/10, n/30.　　March 8 *End of discount*　　　　　　+ 10 *period:* ─────────→ March 18 *End of credit*　　March 8 = 67 days *period by*　　　　　　+ 30 *Table 7.1:* ──────→ 97 days 　　　　　　　　　　　↓ 　　Search in Table 7.1　April 7 *If paid on March 16:* .97 × $500 = $485 　　　　　　+ 100 freight 　　　　　　$585	**Calculate amount paid** Invoice $700 (freight of $100 included in price) dated May 7; payment May 15; 2/10, n/30
b. Receipt of goods (ROG), p. 189 Discount period begins when goods are received. Credit period ends 20 days from end of discount period.	4/10, n/30, ROG. $600 invoice; no freight; dated August 5; goods received October 2, payment made October 20.　October 2 *End of discount*　　　　　　+ 10 *period:* ─────────→ October 12 *End of*　　　　October 2 = 275 *credit period*　　　　　+ 30 *by Table 7.1:* ──────→ 305 　　　　　　　　　　　↓ Search in Table 7.1　November 1 *Payment on October 20:* No discount, pay $600	**Calculate amount paid** 3/10, n/30, ROG. $700 invoice; no freight; dated September 6; goods received September 20; payment made October 15.

(continues)

INTERACTIVE CHAPTER ORGANIZER

Topic/procedure/formula	Examples	You try it*
c. End of month (EOM), p. 190 On or before 25th of the month, discount period is 10 days after month following sale. After 25th of the month, an additional month is gained.	$1,000 invoice dated May 12; no freight or returns; terms 2/10 EOM. *End of discount period* → June 10 *End of credit period* → June 30	**Calculate end of discount and end of credit periods** $2,000 invoice dated October 11; terms 2/10 EOM
Partial payments, p. 192 Amount credited = $\dfrac{\text{Partial payment}}{1 - \text{Discount rate}}$	$200 invoice; terms 2/10, n/30; dated March 2; paid $100 on March 5. $\dfrac{\$100}{1-.02} = \dfrac{\$100}{.98} = \$102.04$	**Calculate amount credited** $400 invoice; terms 2/10, n/30; dated May 4; paid $300 on May 7.

KEY TERMS			
	Cash discount, *p. 177*	FOB shipping point, *p. 179*	Single equivalent discount
	Chain discounts, *p. 182*	Freight terms, *p. 179*	rate, *p. 183*
	Complement, *p. 181*	Invoice, *p. 178*	Single trade discount, *p. 180*
	Credit period, *p. 186*	List price, *p. 178*	Terms of the sale, *p. 186*
	Discount period, *p. 186*	Net price, *p. 178*	Trade discount, *p. 177*
	Due dates, *p. 186*	Net price equivalent rate, *p. 182*	Trade discount amount, *p. 178*
	End of credit period, *p. 186*	Ordinary dating, *p. 188*	Trade discount rate, *p. 178*
	End of month (EOM), *p. 190*	Receipt of goods (ROG), *p. 189*	
	FOB destination, *p. 180*	Series discounts, *p. 182*	

Check Figures for Extra Practice Quizzes with Page References. (Worked-out Solutions in Appendix B.)	LU 7–1a (p. 185) 1. $4,800 TD; $11,200 NP 2. $500 3. $9,891.84 NP; TD $4,108.16	LU 7–2a (p. 194) 1. July 18; Aug. 7 2. June 22; July 12 3. June 11; July 11 4. May 10; May 30 5. June 10; June 30 6. $6,174 7. a) $612.24 b) $87.76

*Worked-out solutions are in Appendix B.

Critical Thinking Discussion Questions with Chapter Concept Check

1. What is the net price? June Long bought a jacket from a catalog company. She took her trade discount off the original price plus freight. What is wrong with June's approach? Who would benefit from June's approach—the buyer or the seller?

2. How do you calculate the list price when the net price and trade discount rate are known? A publisher tells the bookstore its net price of a book along with a suggested trade discount of 20%. The bookstore uses a 25% discount rate. Is this ethical when textbook prices are rising?

3. If Jordan Furniture ships furniture FOB shipping point, what does that mean? Does this mean you get a cash discount?

4. What are the steps to calculate the net price equivalent rate? Why is the net price equivalent rate *not* rounded?

5. What are the steps to calculate the single equivalent discount rate? Is this rate off the list or net price? Explain why this calculation of a single equivalent discount rate may not always be needed.

6. What is the difference between a discount and credit period? Are all cash discounts taken before trade discounts? Do you agree or disagree? Why?

7. Explain the following credit terms of sale:
   a. 2/10, n/30.
   b. 3/10, n/30 ROG.
   c. 1/10 EOM (on or before 25th of month).
   d. 1/10 EOM (after 25th of month).

8. Explain how to calculate a partial payment. Whom does a partial payment favor—the buyer or the seller?

9. **Chapter Concept Check.** Search Facebook to find out what customer discounts companies offer to Facebook users (see chapter opener for specifics). Be sure to talk about shipping charges and trade and cash discounts. What kind of savings can you find?

END-OF-CHAPTER PROBLEMS

 **McGraw Hill** connect™ (plus+) www.mhhe.com/slater11e

Check figures for odd-numbered problems in Appendix C.   Name _____   Date _____

DRILL PROBLEMS

For all problems, round your final answer to the nearest cent. Do not round net price equivalent rates or single equivalent discount rates.

Complete the following: *LU 7-1(4)*

Item	List price	Chain discount	Net price equivalent rate (in decimals)	Single equivalent discount rate (in decimals)	Trade discount	Net price
7-1. Apple iPad	$599	3/1				
7-2. Panasonic DVD player	$199	8/4/3				
7-3. IBM scanner	$269	7/3/1				

Complete the following: *LU 7-1(4)*

Item	List price	Chain discount	Net price	Trade discount
7-4. Trotter treadmill	$3,000	9/4		
7-5. Maytag dishwasher	$450	8/5/6		
7-6. Hewlett-Packard scanner	$320	3/5/9		
7-7. Land Rover roofrack	$1,850	12/9/6		

7-8. Which of the following companies, A or B, gives a higher discount? Use the single equivalent discount rate to make your
eXcel choice (convert your equivalent rate to the nearest hundredth percent).

Company A	Company B
8/10/15/3	10/6/16/5

Complete the following: *LU 7-2(1)*

	Invoice	Date goods are received	Terms	Last day* of discount period	Final day bill is due (end of credit period)
7–9.	June 18		1/10, n/30		
7–10.	Nov. 27		2/10 EOM		
7–11.	May 15	June 5	3/10, n/30, ROG		
7–12.	April 10		2/10, 1/30, n/60		
7–13.	June 12		3/10 EOM		
7–14.	Jan. 10	Feb. 3 (no leap year)	4/10, n/30, ROG		

*If more than one discount, assume date of last discount.

Complete the following by calculating the cash discount and net amount paid: *LU 7-2(1)*

	Gross amount of invoice (freight charge already included)	Freight charge	Date of invoice	Terms of invoice	Date of payment	Cash discount	Net amount paid
7–15.	$7,000	$100	4/8	2/10, n/60	4/15		
7–16.	$600	None	8/1	3/10, 2/15, n/30	8/13		
7–17.	$200	None	11/13	1/10 EOM	12/3		
7–18.	$500	$100	11/29	1/10 EOM	1/4		

Complete the following: *LU 7-2(2)*

	Amount of invoice	Terms	Invoice date	Actual partial payment made	Date of partial payment	Amount of payment to be credited	Balance outstanding
7–19.	$700	2/10, n/60	5/6	$400	5/15		
7–20.	$600	4/10, n/60	7/5	$400	7/14		

WORD PROBLEMS (Round to Nearest Cent as Needed)

7–21. The list price of a smartphone is $299. A local Verizon dealer receives a trade discount of 20%. Find the trade discount amount and the net price. *LU 7-1(1)*

7–22. A model NASCAR race car lists for $79.99 with a trade discount of 40%. What is the net price of the car? *LU 7-1(1)*

eXcel

7–23. Lucky you! You went to couponcabin.com and found a 20% off coupon to your significant other's favorite store. Armed with that coupon, you went to the store only to find a storewide sale offering 10% off everything in the store. In addition, your credit card has a special offer that allows you to save 10% if you use your credit card for all purchases that day. Using your credit card, what will you pay before tax for the $155 gift you found? Use the single equivalent discount to calculate how much you save and then calculate your final price. *LU 7-1(4)*

7–24. Levin Furniture buys a living room set with a $4,000 list price and a 55% trade discount. Freight (FOB shipping point) of $50 is not part of the list price. What is the delivered price (including freight) of the living room set, assuming a cash discount of 2/10, n/30, ROG? The invoice had an April 8 date. Levin received the goods on April 19 and paid the invoice on April 25. *LU 7-1(1, 2)*

7–25. A manufacturer of skateboards offered a 5/2/1 chain discount to many customers. Bob's Sporting Goods ordered 20 skateboards for a total $625 list price. What was the net price of the skateboards? What was the trade discount amount? *LU 7-1(4)*

7–26. Home Depot wants to buy a new line of fertilizers. Manufacturer A offers a 21/13 chain discount. Manufacturer B offers a 26/8 **eXcel** chain discount. Both manufacturers have the same list price. What manufacturer should Home Depot buy from? *LU 7-1(4)*

7–27. Maplewood Supply received a $5,250 invoice dated 4/15/06. The $5,250 included $250 freight. Terms were 4/10, 3/30, n/60. **(a)** If Maplewood pays the invoice on April 27, what will it pay? **(b)** If Maplewood pays the invoice on May 21, what will it pay? *LU 7-2(1)*

7–28. A local Sports Authority ordered 50 pairs of tennis shoes from Nike Corporation. The shoes were priced at $85 for each **eXcel** pair with the following terms: 4/10, 2/30, n/60. The invoice was dated October 15. Sports Authority sent in a payment on October 28. What should have been the amount of the check? *LU 7-2(1)*

7–29. Macy of New York sold LeeCo. of Chicago office equipment with a $6,000 list price. Sale terms were 3/10, n/30 FOB New **eXcel** York. Macy agreed to prepay the $30 freight. LeeCo. pays the invoice within the discount period. What does LeeCo. pay Macy? *LU 7-2(2)*

7–30. Royal Furniture bought a sofa for $800. The sofa had a $1,400 list price. What was the trade discount rate Royal received? Round to the nearest hundredth percent. *LU 7-2(1)*

7–31. The Consumer Electronics Show (CES) reports that the HP Spectre laptop computer starts at $999.99 for a base configuration. The model displayed at its recent show costs $1,399, $100 more than the comparable 13-inch Apple MacBook Air. If Computers-R-Us buys the HP Spectre at the show with 3/15, net 30 terms on August 22, how much does it need to pay on September 5? *LU 7-2(1)*

7–32. Bally Manufacturing sent Intel Corporation an invoice for machinery with a $14,000 list price. Bally dated the invoice July 23 with 2/10 EOM terms. Intel receives a 40% trade discount. Intel pays the invoice on August 5. What does Intel pay Bally? *LU 7-2(1)*

7–33. On August 1, Intel Corporation (Problem 7–32) returns $100 of the machinery due to defects. What does Intel pay Bally on August 5? Round to nearest cent. *LU 7-2(1)*

7–34. Stacy's Dress Shop received a $1,050 invoice dated July 8 with 2/10, 1/15, n/60 terms. On July 22, Stacy's sent a $242 partial payment. What credit should Stacy's receive? What is Stacy's outstanding balance? *LU 7-2(2)*

7–35. On March 11, Jangles Corporation received a $20,000 invoice dated March 8. Cash discount terms were 4/10, n/30. On March 15, Jangles sent an $8,000 partial payment. What credit should Jangles receive? What is Jangles' outstanding balance? *LU 7-2(2)*

ADDITIONAL SET OF WORD PROBLEMS

7–36. The 2012 Mini Cooper S retails starting at $23,800. If the dealership can purchase five with a 20/10/5 chain discount, what is its net price? *LU 7-1(4)*

7–37. A local Barnes and Noble paid a $79.99 net price for each calculus textbook. The publisher offered a 20% trade discount. What was the publisher's list price? *LU 7-2(3)*

7–38. HomeOffice.com buys a computer from Compaq Corporation. The computer has a $1,200 list price with a 30% trade discount. What is the trade discount amount? What is the net price of the computer? Freight charges are FOB destination. *LU 7-1(1)*

7–39. Vail Ski Shop received a $1,201 invoice dated July 8 with 2/10, 1/15, n/60 terms. On July 22, Vail sent a $485 partial payment. What credit should Vail receive? What is Vail's outstanding balance? *LU 7-2(2)*

7–40. True Value received an invoice dated 4/15/02. The invoice had a $5,500 balance that included $300 freight. Terms were 4/10, 3/30, n/60. True Value pays the invoice on April 29. What amount does True Value pay? *LU 7-1(1, 2)*

7–41. Baker's Financial Planners purchased seven new computers for $850 each. It received a 15% discount because it purchased more than five and an additional 6% discount because it took immediate delivery. Terms of payment were 2/10, n/30. Baker's pays the bill within the cash discount period. How much should the check be? Round to the nearest cent. *LU 7-1(4)*

7–42. On May 14, Talbots of Boston sold Forrest of Los Angeles $7,000 of fine clothes. Terms were 2/10 EOM FOB Boston. Talbots agreed to prepay the $80 freight. If Forrest pays the invoice on June 8, what will Forrest pay? If Forrest pays on June 20, what will Forrest pay? *LU 7-1(2), LU 7-2(1)*

7–43. Sam's Ski Boards.com offers 5/4/1 chain discounts to many of its customers. The Ski Hut ordered 20 ski boards with a total list price of $1,200. What is the net price of the ski boards? What was the trade discount amount? Round to the nearest cent. *LU 7-1(4)*

7–44. Majestic Manufacturing sold Jordans Furniture a living room set for an $8,500 list price with 35% trade discount. The $100 freight (FOB shipping point) was not part of the list price. Terms were 3/10, n/30 ROG. The invoice date was May 30. Jordans received the goods on July 18 and paid the invoice on July 20. What was the final price (include cost of freight) of the living room set? *LU 7-1(1, 2), LU 7-2(1)*

7–45. Boeing Truck Company received an invoice showing 8 tires at $110 each, 12 tires at $160 each, and 15 tires at $180 each. Shipping terms are FOB shipping point. Freight is $400; trade discount is 10/5; and a cash discount of 2/10, n/30 is offered. Assuming Boeing paid within the discount period, what did Boeing pay? *LU 7-1(4)*

7–46. Verizon offers to sell cellular phones listing for $99.99 with a chain discount of 15/10/5. Cellular Company offers to sell its cellular phones that list at $102.99 with a chain discount of 25/5. If Irene is to buy six phones, how much could she save if she buys from the lower-priced company? *LU 7-1(4)*

7–47. The 2012 iPhone 4S launch in China did not go as planned. Because of an overwhelming number of scalpers, Apple halted sales. After implementing a lottery system, Apple resumed selling the device online with shipments promised by March 2. If phones sell for U.S.$199 2/10, n/30 ROG, and 15 were purchased for resale on February 10 and received March 11, how much is owed if the invoice is paid on March 20? *LU 7-2(1)*

7–48. The original price of a 2012 Honda Insight to the dealer is $17,995, but the dealer will pay only $16,495. If the dealer pays Honda within 15 days, there is a 1% cash discount. **(a)** How much is the rebate? **(b)** What percent is the rebate? Round to nearest hundredth percent. **(c)** What is the amount of the cash discount if the dealer pays within 15 days? **(d)** What is the dealer's final price? **(e)** What is the dealer's total savings? Round answer to the nearest hundredth. *LU 7-1(1), LU 7-2(1)*

7–49. On March 30, Century Television received an invoice dated March 28 from ACME Manufacturing for 50 televisions at a cost of $125 each. Century received a 10/4/2 chain discount. Shipping terms were FOB shipping point. ACME prepaid the $70 freight. Terms were 2/10 EOM. When Century received the goods, 3 sets were defective. Century returned these sets to ACME. On April 8, Century sent a $150 partial payment. Century will pay the balance on May 6. What is Century's final payment on May 6? Assume no taxes. *LU 7-1(1, 2, 4), LU 7-2(1)*

SUMMARY PRACTICE TEST (Round to the Nearest Cent as Needed)   You Tube™

Do you need help? The DVD has step-by-step worked-out solutions.

Complete the following: *(pp. 178–179)   LU 7-1(1)*

	Item	List price	Single trade discount	Net price
1.	Apple iPod	$350	5%	
2.	Palm Pilot		10%	$190

Calculate the net price and trade discount (use net price equivalent rate and single equivalent discount rate) for the following: *(pp. 182–184)   LU 7-1(4)*

	Item	List price	Chain discount	Net price	Trade discount
3.	Sony HD flat-screen TV	$899	5/4		

4. From the following, what is the last date for each discount period and credit period? *(pp. 178–179)   LU 7-1(1)*

Date of invoice	Terms	End of discount period	End of credit period
a. Nov. 4	2/10, n/30		
b. Oct. 3, 2009	3/10, n/30 ROG (Goods received March 10, 2010)		
c. May 2	2/10 EOM		
d. Nov. 28	2/10 EOM		

5. Best Buy buys an iPod from a wholesaler with a $300 list price and a 5% trade discount. What is the trade discount amount? e**X**cel What is the net price of the iPod? *(pp. 178–179)   LU 7-1(1)*

6. Jordan's of Boston sold Lee Company of New York computer equipment with a $7,000 list price. Sale terms were 4/10, n/30 FOB Boston. Jordan's agreed to prepay the $400 freight. Lee pays the invoice within the discount period. What does Lee pay Jordan's? *(pp. 179–180; 185–192)   LU 7-1(2), LU 7-2(1)*

7. Julie Ring wants to buy a new line of Tonka trucks for her shop. Manufacturer A offers a 14/8 chain discount. Manufacturer B e**X**cel offers a 15/7 chain discount. Both manufacturers have the same list price. Which manufacturer should Julie buy from? *(pp. 182–184)   LU 7-1(4)*

8. Office.com received a $8,000 invoice dated April 10. Terms were 2/10, 1/15, n/60. On April 14, Office.com sent a $1,900 partial payment. What credit should Office.com receive? What is Office.com's outstanding balance? Round to the nearest cent. *(p. 192)   LU 7-2(2)*

9. Logan Company received from Furniture.com an invoice dated September 29. Terms were 1/10 EOM. List price on the invoice was $8,000 (freight not included). Logan receives a 8/7 chain discount. Freight charges are Logan's responsibility, but Furniture.com agreed to prepay the $300 freight. Logan pays the invoice on November 7. What does Logan Company pay Furniture.com? *(pp. 182–184)   LU 7-1(4)*

www.mhhe.com/
slater11e_vc

In 2002, Fuju Heavy Industries Ltd., parent company of Subaru of Indiana Automotive (SIA), challenged SIA with a goal no domestic manufacturing facility had achieved—zero landfill within 4 years. What seemed like a daunting goal was achieved in half the time by combining a comprehensive approach to identifying and eliminating waste with a powerful motivator.

Located in Lafayette, Indiana, SIA builds the Subaru Outback, Legacy, and Tribeca vehicle lines as well as the Toyota Camry in partnership with Toyota. SIA is currently the only Subaru auto assembly plant in the United States. Getting started on the zero landfill goal, SIA went about systematically identifying, weighing, and inventorying all waste in its 2.3 million-square-foot manufacturing facility, which performs integrated operations from stamping to final assembly.*

Once waste was identified, SIA made section managers responsible for the waste in their section and even went so far as to tie their bonus to waste elimination. Section managers along with their teams eagerly set out to find alternatives to the landfill.

For SIA, a key aspect of the solution included a rigorous approach to sorting waste and finding recyclers who were specifically interested in each type of waste and then only giving them that waste and nothing more. As an example, SIA sorts up to 17 different kinds of plastic. A second key component was SIA's partnership with Allegiant Global Services, which located recyclers, picked up waste line-side, and paid for all shipping charges.

For SIA's part, it invested in equipment that significantly reduced the volume and therefore cost of shipping waste. SIA compacts its cardboard, typically reducing 50–60 cubic yards of material to 2 cubic yards. Smaller bales weigh 350–400 lbs and large ones upwards of 1,000 lbs. SIA also has a bulb crusher on hand to crush fluorescent bulbs, separating the glass from the hazardous chemicals. This saves $2 per bulb to ship them to a recycler.

For its efforts, SIA was the first domestic auto plant to achieve Zero Landfill status in May 2004, the first to receive ISO 14001 certification, and the first to be officially designated a wildlife habitat. Clearly Subaru Indiana Automotive has found responsible environmental stewardship to be the right thing to do for the planet as well as for the bottom line.

Note: The following problems contain data that have been created by the author.

*Subaru of Indiana Automotive Inc. website: http://www.subaru-sia.com/Company/history/index.html.

PROBLEM 1

As the case states, Allegiant Global Services covers the cost of all shipping charges. If the terms included FOB for scraps Allegiant purchased from SIA, what would the terms specify? *Hint:* Research Allegiant's location to detail the terms fully.

PROBLEM 2

Suppose SIA sells each 350–400 lb bale of cardboard to Allegiant for $150. Further assume that SIA has 400 such bales to sell and offers a trade discount of 20% to Allegiant. What would the total trade discount be? What would the net price be? Round answers to the nearest dollar.

PROBLEM 3

If SIA offered a chain discount of 20/15/10 instead of the single discount, what would the net price equivalent rate be? Express your answer as a decimal and do not round.

PROBLEM 4

Suppose an invoice to Allegiant in the amount of $2,500 dated May 11 had the terms 2/10, 1/30, n/60. If the invoice were paid on June 1, how much would Allegiant owe SIA? Round your answer to the nearest dollar.

PROBLEM 5

If Allegiant were to pay $25,000 for recycled steel and SIA offered a 15% trade discount, what would the list price be? Round your answer to the nearest cent.

PROBLEM 6

Imagine an invoice to Allegiant in the amount of $15,250, dated September 8, that had the terms 2/10 EOM. If the invoice were paid on October 11, how much would Allegiant owe SIA? Round your answer to the nearest dollar.

PROBLEM 7

Suppose Allegiant had an invoice from SIA in the amount of $42,000, dated November 16. If the invoice had the terms 2/10, n/30 and Allegiant made a partial payment in the amount of $14,000 on November 23, what would the outstanding balance due be for the invoice? Round your answer to the nearest cent.

Class Discussion The case does not indicate whether Subaru Indiana Automotive has generated a net savings from its recycling efforts. Discuss the economics of the recycling program as you would anticipate them to be and determine whether you feel such a commitment would be warranted even if it cost SIA money to sustain the program.

PROBLEM 1
Free shipping!

Visit www.staples.com and search for DVD+RW media. Select enough of the DVD+RWs to equal an amount over $45 in order to qualify for free shipping. How much did you save on shipping? What is your discount percent when you receive free shipping on your order?

Discussion Questions

1. Why do online merchants require a certain minimum dollar purchase before giving free shipping?
2. What other incentives could the online merchant use to achieve the same goal?

PROBLEM 2
Pay early, or not?

Go to http://www.fms.treas.gov/prompt/discount.html. If there are 30 days left in the discount period and 60 days left in the payment period, find out what the discount must be for it not to be worthwhile to pay early.

Discussion Questions

1. Would there ever be a situation in which it would still not be advantageous to pay early, even if a discount were available?
2. Why do companies offer a discount for paying early?

PROBLEM 3
Buying software at deep discounts

Go to http://www.academicsuperstore.com. Choose one product listed on the Students tab. What discount off the suggested retail price is the manufacturer offering through Academic Superstore?

Discussion Questions

1. Why do retailers show inflated suggested retail prices?
2. How can consumers be sure they are getting a good deal?

PROBLEM 4
Money in bloom!

Go to http://ww11.1800flowers.com. Click on Deal of the Week. Select any of the flower deals and calculate the discount percentage.

Discussion Questions

1. Why would 1-800-Flowers run promotions such as the Deal of the Week?
2. If there is a deal every week that allows you to save money on flowers, would you ever purchase from its standard flower arrangements? Why?

MOBILE APPS ✕

Calculate Discounts & Sales Tax (Blue Sodium Corp) Helps calculate discounts in percentages or as dollar values.

Discount Calculator (ChuChu Train Productions) Calculates the prices of items after applying discounts to determine item cost and amount saved.

INTERNET PROJECTS ✕

See text website
www.mhhe.com/slater11e_sse_ch07

The App of Haggling

IN THE ARENA OF HAGGLING, knowledge is power. And the right application can put that power at your fingertips. Specifically, free price-matching apps are available for the Apple iPhone and dozens of mobile phones that run Google's Android software.

How do they work? Rather than combing through ads, you check the phone to see which nearby store has the best offer. If you're already at a store and find a better price elsewhere, simply ask the retailer if it will match or beat the competitor's price.

To try phone haggling, I used a T-Mobile G2 ($200 with a two-year contract) and two free apps available in Google's Android Market, an online store with more than 100,000 software programs accessible via the G2's main screen. Because of their power, simplicity and ease of use, my favorite shopping tools are Google Shopper and ShopSavvy, although there are many more.

All price-matching apps work pretty much the same way. The easiest is to use your phone's camera as a bar-code scanner. For instance, using Google Shopper, select "Image Search" on the app's home screen, and then aim the camera at the bar code. Once it recognizes the code, the app beeps. Within seconds, Google Shopper displays all local and online stores that sell the product, the price they're asking, the stores' addresses, and their distance in miles from your current location.

But what if you can't find the bar code? Try a voice-recognition search—say, for example, "Samsung 50-inch 3D plasma HDTV"— or go old school and type in the product's name. A voice search may seem inherently unreliable, but it worked well in my tests of Google Shopper in Best Buy's noisy electronics department. Shop-Savvy has a bar-code scanner and text search, but no voice option.

Putting the apps to the test. At Best Buy I spotted a 32-inch Sony LCD TV for $400. Google Shopper found the same model at a Sears 27 miles away for $356. Too far. But at Staples, ShopSavvy discovered that a $210 APC Backup Battery, handy for surge protection and power outages, was $150 at Office Depot and $180 at Best Buy. And both stores were less than a mile away.

Cha-ching. The app showed me that a short drive would save me 60 bucks. But would I have to make the schlep? I asked clerks at both stores whether they'd match the price I'd found with my phone. In both instances, they said they'd need to see a print ad to give me the better deal. (So last century.)

Undaunted, I went to another Best Buy and scanned a Panasonic cordless phone kit with four handsets. Best Buy wanted $100, but a Wal-Mart nine miles away had it for $89. Would Best Buy match Wal-Mart's price? Yes. All I had to do was bring the Panasonic box to customer service, which would call Wal-Mart to verify the lower price.

Next I ventured into Fry's Electronics, a big-box retailer with stores in nine states, where Shop-Savvy informed me that a $499 Toshiba 32-inch LCD TV was $30 cheaper at a Best Buy a half-mile away. Fry's agreed to match the lower price after making the requisite confirmation call. I couldn't, however, get them to *beat* the competitor's price.

I called retailers to see whether they had a policy on shopping apps, and Best Buy said it does honor prices from them. Given my experiences, it's safe to say some clerks aren't aware of their store's policy, and it's incumbent on shoppers to seek out store managers and push the issue.

Sometimes, shopping apps show that the price you see is the best in town. A Best Buy in my area, for instance, had a Currie Ezip 400 electric scooter on sale for $200; the next best price Google Shopper could find was $300. And Costco's $100 price for the iHome IP45BZ rechargeable stereo speaker (with FM radio and alarm, iPod and iPhone dock) was $3 less than I found elsewhere. No buyer's remorse here.

If you suspect a certain item will go on sale soon—after the holidays, say—use ShopSavvy to create a price alert. Simply enter your target price and e-mail address, and the app will notify you when the price hits your target. Both ShopSavvy and Google Shopper keep a history of the products you've researched— a handy feature for checking prices over time without having to reenter the same information again and again. **JEFF BERTOLUCCI**

BUSINESS MATH ISSUE

Retailers should not allow customers to use the haggling app in their store.

1. List the key points of the article and information to support your position.
2. Write a group defense of your position using math calculations to support your view.

CHAPTER 8

Markups and Markdowns: Perishables and Breakeven Analysis

Macy's Catalog Shoppers' Habi

During the past few thousands of **Macy's** In ers received spring cata surprise there. The diffe however, was how they lored and targeted to th tomers, obviously aware ous purchases.

Indeed, there were te thousands of different ve out of the millions mailed geted to the customers a customized with names. A female in her 30s, for exa might receive a catalog off up clothing, shoes and han based on preferences glean from her prior purchases, a posed to one filled with pa baby clothing.

A spokesman says that mining the data in the recor purchases on Macy's credit the store can sharpen its dir mail. "Customers who shop f quently for men's apparel, fo ample, will see more menswe in their catalog, along with a smaller or no presence of oth categories," he says.

The catalogs help Macy's tomers browse products they' far more likely to buy, says Bri Sozzi, a retail analyst at Wall Street Strategies. Other stores are likely to follow suit, he says using records like bridal or baby registries or loyalty cards to col lect customer information.

He adds, however, "They know what you're buying, and boy is it creepy."

LU 8–1: Markups[1] Based on Cost (100%)

1. Calculate dollar markup and percent markup on cost *(pp. 211–212)*.
2. Calculate selling price when you know the cost and percent markup on cost *(p. 212)*.
3. Calculate cost when you know the selling price and percent markup on cost *(p. 212)*.
4. Calculate cost when dollar markup and percent markup on cost are known *(p. 213)*.

LU 8–2: Markups Based on Selling Price (100%)

1. Calculate dollar markup and percent markup on selling price *(pp. 215–216)*.
2. Calculate selling price when dollar markup and percent markup on selling price are known *(p. 216)*.
3. Calculate selling price when cost and percent markup on selling price are known *(p. 216)*.
4. Calculate cost when selling price and percent markup on selling price are known *(p. 217)*.
5. Convert from percent markup on cost to percent markup on selling price and vice versa *(pp. 217–218)*.

LU 8–3: Markdowns

1. Calculate markdowns; compare markdowns and markups *(pp. 221–222)*.

Here are key terms in this chapter. After completing the chapter, if you know the term, place a checkmark in the parentheses. If you don't know the term, look it up and put the page number where it can be found.

**Cost ( )   Dollar markdown ( )   Dollar markup ( )   Gross profit ( )   Margin ( )   Markdowns ( )
Markup ( )   Net profit (net income) ( )   Operating expenses (overhead) ( )   Percent markup on cost ( )
Percent markup on selling price ( )   Selling price ( )**

The chapter opening clip shows how Macy's can track the buying patterns of its customers. Macy's targets customers by sending specific catalogues based on consumer buying habits. Now let's turn our attention to another store you may be familiar with—Gap.

We will look at some of Gap's pricing options for its fleece hoody jackets. Note the clip in the margin that shows that during the holiday season, Gap used Facebook to announce 30% off everything in the store.

Before we study the two pricing methods available to Gap (percent markup on cost and percent markup on selling price), we must know the following terms:

- **Selling price.** The price retailers charge consumers. The total selling price of all the goods sold by a retailer (like Gap) represents the retailer's total sales.

- **Cost.** The price retailers pay to a manufacturer or supplier to bring the goods into the store.

- **Markup, margin,** or **gross profit.** These three terms refer to the difference between the cost of bringing the goods into the store and the selling price of the goods.

DUSTIN © 2011 Steve Kelley & Jeff Parker. King Features Syndicate.

[1]Some texts use the term *markon* (selling price minus cost).

© AP Photo/Eric Risberg

DUSTIN © 2011 Steve Kelley & Jeff Parker. King Features Syndicate.

- **Operating expenses** or **overhead.** The regular expenses of doing business such as wages, rent, utilities, insurance, and advertising.
- **Net profit** or **net income.** The profit remaining after subtracting the cost of bringing the goods into the store and the operating expenses from the sale of the goods (including any returns or adjustments). In Learning Unit 8–4 we will take a closer look at the point at which costs and expenses are covered. This is called the *breakeven* point.

From these definitions, we can conclude that *markup* represents the amount that retailers must add to the cost of the goods to cover their operating expenses and make a profit.[2]

Let's assume Gap plans to sell hooded fleece jackets for $23 that cost $18.[3]

Basic selling price formula

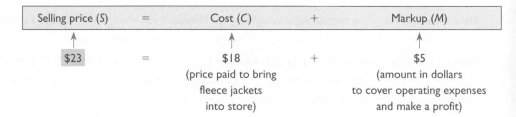

Selling price (S)	=	Cost (C)	+	Markup (M)
$23	=	$18	+	$5
		(price paid to bring fleece jackets into store)		(amount in dollars to cover operating expenses and make a profit)

In the Gap example, the markup is a dollar amount, or a **dollar markup.** Markup is also expressed in percent. When expressing markup in percent, retailers can choose a percent based on *cost* (Learning Unit 8–1) or a percent based on *selling price* (Learning Unit 8–2).

When you go out to dinner at a salad bar, you might be amazed to discover how much certain foods are marked up. For example, at one restaurant, potatoes are marked up 62.5% and shrimp are marked up 75%. Now let's look at how to calculate markup percents.

Learning Unit 8–1: Markups Based on Cost (100%)

In Chapter 6 you were introduced to the portion formula, which we used to solve percent problems. We also used the portion formula in Chapter 7 to solve problems involving trade and cash discounts. In this unit you will see how we use the basic selling price formula and the portion formula to solve percent markup situations based on cost. We will be using blueprint aids to show how to dissect and solve all word problems in this chapter.

Many manufacturers mark up goods on cost because manufacturers can get cost information more easily than sales information. Since retailers have the choice of using percent markup on cost or selling price, in this unit we assume Gap has chosen percent markup on cost. In Learning Unit 8–2 we show how Gap would determine markup if it decided to use percent markup on selling price.

Businesses that use **percent markup on cost** recognize that cost is 100%. This 100% represents the base of the portion formula. All situations in this unit use cost as 100%.

To calculate percent markup on cost, we will use the hooded fleece jacket sold by Gap and begin with the basic selling price formula given in the chapter introduction.

[2]In this chapter, we concentrate on the markup of retailers. Manufacturers and suppliers also use markup to determine selling price.

[3]These may not be actual store prices but we assume these prices in our examples.

When we know the dollar markup, we can use the portion formula to find the percent markup on cost.

Markup expressed in dollars:

Selling price ($23) = Cost ($18) + Markup ($5)

Markup expressed as a percent markup on cost:

Cost	100.00%
+ Markup	+ 27.78
= Selling price	127.78%

> Cost is 100%—the base. Dollar markup is the portion, and percent markup on cost is the rate.

In Situation 1 (below) we show why Gap has a 27.78% markup (dollar markup [$5] divided by cost [$18]) based on cost by presenting the hooded fleece jacket as a word problem. We solve the problem with the blueprint aid used in earlier chapters. In the second column, however, you will see footnotes after two numbers. These refer to the steps we use below the blueprint aid to solve the problem. Throughout the chapter, the numbers that we are solving for are in red. Remember that cost is the base for this unit.

LO 1

Situation 1: Calculating Dollar Markup and Percent Markup on Cost

Dollar markup is calculated with the basic selling price formula $S = C + M$. When you know the cost and selling price of goods, reverse the formula to $M = S - C$. Subtract the cost from the selling price, and you have the dollar markup.

The percent markup on cost is calculated with the portion formula. For Situation 1 the *portion* (P) is the dollar markup, which you know from the selling price formula. In this unit the *rate* (R) is always the percent markup on cost and the *base* (B) is always the cost (100%). To find the percent markup on cost (R), use the portion formula $R = \frac{P}{B}$ and divide the dollar markup (P) by the cost (B). Convert your answer to a percent and round if necessary.

Now we will look at the Gap example to see how to calculate the 27.78% markup on cost.

The Word Problem   The Gap pays $18 for a hooded fleece jacket, which the store plans to sell for $23. What is Gap's dollar markup? What is the percent markup on cost (rounded to the nearest hundredth percent)?

	The facts	Solving for?	Steps to take	Key points
BLUEPRINT	Hooded fleece jacket cost: $18. Hooded fleece jacket selling price: $23.	% $ C 100.00% $18 + M 27.78[2] 5[1] = S 127.78% $23	Dollar markup = Selling price − Cost. Percent markup on cost = Dollar markup / Cost	Dollar markup Portion ($5) Base × Rate ($18) (?) Cost

[1]Dollar markup. See Step 1, below.
[2]Percent markup on cost. See Step 2, below.

Steps to solving problem

1. Calculate the dollar markup.

   Dollar markup = Selling price − Cost

   $5 = $23 − $18

2. Calculate the percent markup on cost.

   Percent markup on cost = $\dfrac{\text{Dollar markup}}{\text{Cost}}$

   $= \dfrac{\$5}{\$18} = 27.78\%$

To check the percent markup on cost, you can use the basic selling price formula $S = C + M$. Convert the percent markup on cost found with the portion formula to a decimal and multiply it by the cost. This gives the dollar markup. Then add the cost and the dollar markup to get the selling price of the goods.

You could also check the cost (B) by dividing the dollar markup (P) by the percent markup on cost (R).

Check

Selling price = Cost + Markup	or	Cost (B) = $\dfrac{\text{Dollar markup } (P)}{\text{Percent markup on cost } (R)}$

$$\$23 = \$18 + .2778(\$18) \longleftarrow$$
$$\$23 = \$18 + \$5$$
$$\$23 = \$23$$

$$= \dfrac{\$5}{.2778} = \$18$$

Parentheses mean that you multiply the percent markup on cost in decimal by the cost.

LO 2

Situation 2: Calculating Selling Price When You Know Cost and Percent Markup on Cost

When you know the cost and the percent markup on cost, you calculate the selling price with the basic selling formula $S = C + M$. Remember that when goods are marked up on cost, the cost is the base (100%). So you can say that the selling price is the cost plus the markup in dollars (percent markup on cost times cost).

Now let's look at Mel's Furniture where we calculate Mel's dollar markup and selling price.

The Word Problem   Mel's Furniture bought a lamp that cost $100. To make Mel's desired profit, he needs a 65% markup on cost. What is Mel's dollar markup? What is his selling price?

	The facts	Solving for?	Steps to take	Key points
BLUEPRINT	Lamp cost: $100. Markup on cost: 65%.	$\begin{array}{lcc} & \% & \$ \\ C & 100\% & \$100 \\ + M & 65 & 65^1 \\ = S & 165\% & \$165^2 \end{array}$	Dollar markup: $S = C + M$. or $S = \text{Cost} \times \left(1 + \begin{matrix}\text{Percent}\\\text{markup}\\\text{on cost}\end{matrix}\right)$	Selling price / Portion (?) / Base × Rate ($100) (1.65) / Cost 100% +65%

¹Dollar markup. See Step 1, below.
²Selling price. See Step 2, below.

Steps to solving problem

1. Calculate the dollar markup. $S = C + M$

   $S = \$100 + .65(\$100) \longleftarrow$ Parentheses mean you multiply the percent markup in decimal by the cost.

   $S = \$100 + \boxed{\$65} \longleftarrow$ Dollar markup

2. Calculate the selling price. $S = \boxed{\$165}$

You can check the selling price with the formula $P = B \times R$. You are solving for the portion (P)—the selling price. Rate (R) represents the 100% cost plus the 65% markup on cost. Since in this unit the markup is on cost, the base is the cost. Convert 165% to a decimal and multiply the cost by 1.65 to get the selling price of $165.

Check

Selling price = Cost × (1 + Percent markup on cost)	$= \$100 \times 1.65 = \boxed{\$165}$
(P) (B) (R)	

LO 3

Situation 3: Calculating Cost When You Know Selling Price and Percent Markup on Cost

When you know the selling price and the percent markup on cost, you calculate the cost with the basic selling formula $S = C + M$. Since goods are marked up on cost, the percent markup on cost is added to the cost.

Let's see how this is done in the following Jill Sport example.

The Word Problem Jill Sport, owner of Sports, Inc., sells tennis rackets for $50. To make her desired profit, Jill needs a 40% markup on cost. What do the tennis rackets cost Jill? What is the dollar markup?

	The facts	Solving for?	Steps to take	Key points
BLUEPRINT	Selling price: $50. Markup on cost: 40%.		%	$
		C	100%	$35.71[1]
		+ M	40	14.29[2]
		= S	140%	$50.00

Steps to take: $S = C + M$. or $Cost = \dfrac{Selling\ price}{1 + \left[\begin{array}{c}Percent\\ markup\\ on\ cost\end{array}\right]}$ $M = S - C$.

Key points: Selling price / Portion ($50) / Base (?) × Rate (1.40) / Cost / 100% +40%

[1]Cost. See Step 1, below.
[2]Dollar markup. See Step 2, below.

LO 4

MONEY tips

Automate your savings. Save more money from each paycheck starting now. If you have 1% automatically taken out of your check, you will never miss it. Over time, it can add up to six figures and will help you start building a financially healthy retirement today.

Steps to solving problem

1. Calculate the cost.

$S = C + M$

$50.00 = C + .40C$ ← This means 40% times cost. C is the same as 1C. Adding .40C to 1C gives the percent markup on cost of 1.40C in decimal.

$\dfrac{\$50.00}{1.40} = \dfrac{1.40C}{1.40}$

$\$35.71 = C$

2. Calculate the dollar markup.

$M = S - C$
$M = \$50.00 - \$35.71$
$M = \$14.29$

You can check your cost answer with the portion formula $B = \frac{P}{R}$. Portion (P) is the selling price. Rate (R) represents the 100% cost plus the 40% markup on cost. Convert the percents to decimals and divide the portion by the rate to find the base, or cost.

Check

$$Cost\ (B) = \dfrac{Selling\ price\ (P)}{1 + Percent\ markup\ on\ cost\ (R)} = \dfrac{\$50.00}{1.40} = \$35.71$$

Now try the following Practice Quiz to check your understanding of this unit.

LU 8–1 PRACTICE QUIZ

Complete this **Practice Quiz** to see how you are doing.

Solve the following situations (markups based on cost):

1. Irene Westing bought a desk for $400 from an office supply house. She plans to sell the desk for $600. What is Irene's dollar markup? What is her percent markup on cost? Check your answer.
2. Suki Komar bought dolls for her toy store that cost $12 each. To make her desired profit, Suki must mark up each doll 35% on cost. What is the dollar markup? What is the selling price of each doll? Check your answer.
3. Jay Lyman sells calculators. His competitor sells a new calculator line for $14 each. Jay needs a 40% markup on cost to make his desired profit, and he must meet price competition. At what cost can Jay afford to bring these calculators into the store? What is the dollar markup? Check your answer.

*For **extra help** from your authors–Sharon and Jeff–see the student DVD*

✓ Solutions

1. Irene's dollar markup and percent markup on cost:

	The facts	Solving for?			Steps to take	Key points
BLUEPRINT	Desk cost: $400. Desk selling price: $600.		%	$	Dollar markup $=$ Selling price $-$ Cost.	Dollar markup
		C	100%	$400		Portion ($200)
		+ M	50²	200¹	Percent markup on cost $= \dfrac{\text{Dollar markup}}{\text{Cost}}$	Base × Rate ($400) (?)
		= S	150%	$600		Cost

¹Dollar markup. See Step 1, below.
²Percent markup on cost. See Step 2, below.

Steps to solving problem

1. Calculate the dollar markup.

$$\text{Dollar markup} = \text{Selling price} - \text{Cost}$$
$$\boxed{\$200} \quad = \quad \$600 \quad - \$400$$

2. Calculate the percent markup on cost.

$$\text{Percent markup on cost} = \frac{\text{Dollar markup}}{\text{Cost}}$$
$$= \frac{\$200}{\$400} = \boxed{50\%}$$

Check

$$\text{Selling price} = \text{Cost} + \text{Markup} \qquad \textbf{or} \qquad \text{Cost }(B) = \frac{\text{Dollar markup }(P)}{\text{Percent markup on cost }(R)}$$
$$\$600 = \$400 + .50(\$400)$$
$$\$600 = \$400 + \$200$$
$$\$600 = \$600 \qquad\qquad\qquad\qquad\qquad = \frac{\$200}{.50} = \$400$$

2. Dollar markup and selling price of doll:

	The facts	Solving for?			Steps to take	Key points
BLUEPRINT	Doll cost: $12 each. Markup on cost: 35%.		%	$	Dollar markup: $S = C + M.$	Selling price
		C	100%	$12.00	or	Portion (?)
		+ M	35	4.20¹	$S = \text{Cost} \times \left(1 + \begin{array}{c}\text{Percent} \\ \text{markup} \\ \text{on cost}\end{array}\right)$	Base × Rate ($12) (1.35)
		= S	135%	$16.20²		Cost $\quad$ 100% $+35\%$

¹Dollar markup. See Step 1, below.
²Selling price. See Step 2, below.

Steps to solving problem

1. Calculate the dollar markup.
$$S = C + M$$
$$S = \$12.00 + .35(\$12.00)$$
$$S = \$12.00 + \boxed{\$4.20} \leftarrow \text{Dollar markup}$$

2. Calculate the selling price.
$$S = \boxed{\$16.20}$$

Check

$$\underset{(P)}{\text{Selling price}} = \underset{(B)}{\text{Cost}} \times (1 + \underset{(R)}{\text{Percent markup on cost}}) = \$12.00 \times 1.35 = \boxed{\$16.20}$$

3. Cost and dollar markup:

	The facts	Solving for?	Steps to take	Key points
BLUEPRINT	Selling price: $14. Markup on cost: 40%.	$\begin{array}{ccc} & \% & \$ \\ C & 100\% & \$10^1 \\ +M & 40 & 4^2 \\ =S & 140\% & \$14 \end{array}$	$S = C + M.$ or $Cost = \dfrac{Selling\ price}{1 + \begin{bmatrix} Percent \\ markup \\ on\ cost \end{bmatrix}}$ $M = S - C.$	Selling price Portion ($14) Base × Rate (?) (1.40) Cost 100% +40%

¹Cost. See Step 1, below.
²Dollar markup. See Step 2, below.

Steps to solving problem

1. Calculate the cost.

$$S = C + M$$
$$\$14 = C + .40C$$
$$\frac{\$14}{1.40} = \frac{1.40C}{1.40}$$
$$\$10 = C$$

2. Calculate the dollar markup.

$$M = S - C$$
$$M = \$14 - \$10$$
$$M = \boxed{\$4}$$

Check

$$Cost\ (B) = \frac{Selling\ price\ (P)}{1 + Percent\ markup\ on\ cost\ (R)} = \frac{\$14}{1.40} = \$10$$

LU 8–1a **EXTRA PRACTICE QUIZ WITH WORKED-OUT SOLUTIONS**

Need more practice? Try this **Extra Practice Quiz** (check figures in the Interactive Chapter Organizer, p. 228). Worked-out Solutions can be found in Appendix B at end of text.

Solve the following situations (markups based on cost):

1. Irene Westing bought a desk for $800 from an office supply house. She plans to sell the desk for $1,200. What is Irene's dollar markup? What is her percent markup on cost? Check your answer.

2. Suki Komar bought dolls for her toy store that cost $14 each. To make her desired profit, Suki must mark up each doll 38% on cost. What is the dollar markup? What is the selling price of each doll? Check your answer.

3. Jay Lyman sells calculators. His competitor sells a new calculator line for $16 each. Jay needs a 42% markup on cost to make his desired profit, and he must meet price competition. At what cost can Jay afford to bring these calculators into the store? What is the dollar markup? Check your answer.

Learning Unit 8-2: Markups Based on Selling Price (100%)

© Bloomberg via Getty Images

Many retailers mark up their goods on the selling price since sales information is easier to get than cost information. These retailers use retail prices in their inventory and report their expenses as a percent of sales.

Businesses that mark up their goods on selling price recognize that selling price is 100%. We begin this unit by assuming Gap has decided to use percent markup based on selling price. We repeat Gap's selling price formula expressed in dollars.

Markup expressed in dollars:

Selling price ($23) = Cost ($18) + Markup ($5)

Markup expressed as **percent markup on selling price:**

Cost	78.26%
+ Markup	+21.74
= Selling price	100.00%

Selling price is 100%—the base. Dollar markup is the portion, and percent markup on selling price is the rate.

In Situation 1 (below) we show why Gap has a 21.74% markup based on selling price. In the last unit, markups were based on *cost*. In this unit, markups are based on *selling price*.

LO 1

Situation 1: Calculating Dollar Markup and Percent Markup on Selling Price

The dollar markup is calculated with the selling price formula used in Situation 1, Learning Unit 8–1: $M = S - C$. To find the percent markup on selling price, use the portion formula $R = \frac{P}{B}$, where rate (the percent markup on selling price) is found by dividing the portion (dollar markup) by the base (selling price). Note that when solving for percent markup on cost in Situation 1, Learning Unit 8–1, you divided the dollar markup by the cost.

The Word Problem The cost to Gap for a hooded fleece jacket is $18; the store then plans to sell them for $23. What is Gap's dollar markup? What is its percent markup on selling price? (Round to the nearest hundredth percent.)

	The facts	Solving for?		Steps to take	Key points
BLUEPRINT	Hooded fleece jacket *cost:* $18. Hooded fleece jacket *price:* $23.	C 78.26% $+ M$ 21.74%[2] $= S$ 100.00%	$18 5[1] $23	Dollar markup = Selling price − Cost. Percent markup on selling price = Dollar markup / Selling price	Dollar markup / Portion ($5) / Base ($23) × Rate (?) / Selling price

[1]Dollar markup. See Step 1, below.
[2]Percent markup on selling price. See Step 2, below.

Steps to solving problem

1. Calculate the dollar markup.

$$\text{Dollar markup} = \text{Selling price} - \text{Cost}$$
$$\$5 = \$23 - \$18$$

2. Calculate the percent markup on selling price.

$$\frac{\text{Percent markup}}{\text{on selling price}} = \frac{\text{Dollar markup}}{\text{Selling price}}$$
$$= \frac{\$5}{\$23} = 21.74\%$$

You can check the percent markup on selling price with the basic selling price formula $S = C + M$. You can also use the portion formula by dividing the dollar markup (P) by the percent markup on selling price (R).

Check

Selling price = Cost + Markup	or	Selling price $(B) = \dfrac{\text{Dollar markup } (P)}{\text{Percent markup on selling price } (R)}$

$$\$23 = \$18 + .2174(\$23)$$

$$\$23 = \$18 + \$5$$

$$\$23 = \$23$$

$$= \frac{\$5}{.2174} = \$23$$

Parentheses mean you multiply the percent markup on selling price in decimal by the selling price.

LO 3

Situation 2: Calculating Selling Price When You Know Cost and Percent Markup on Selling Price

When you know the cost and percent markup on selling price, you calculate the selling price with the basic selling formula $S = C + M$. Remember that when goods are marked up on selling price, the selling price is the base (100%). Since you do not know the selling price, the percent markup is based on the unknown selling price. To find the dollar markup after you find the selling price, use the selling price formula $M = S - C$.

The Word Problem Mel's Furniture bought a lamp that cost $100. To make Mel's desired profit, he needs a 65% markup on selling price. What are Mel's selling price and his dollar markup?

LO 2

	The facts	Solving for?	Steps to take	Key points
BLUEPRINT	Lamp cost: $100. Markup on selling price: 65%.	%　　$ C　35%　$100.00 + M　65　185.71[2] = S　100%　$285.71[1]	$S = C + M.$ or $S = \dfrac{\text{Cost}}{1 - \begin{array}{c}\text{Percent markup}\\\text{on selling price}\end{array}}$	Cost Portion ($100) Base (?) × Rate (.35) Selling price 100% −65%

[1]Selling price. See Step 1, below.
[2]Dollar markup. See Step 2, below.

Steps to solving problem

1. Calculate the selling price.

$$S = C + M$$
$$S = \$100.00 + .65S$$
$$\underline{-.65S \qquad\qquad -.65S}$$
$$\dfrac{.35S}{.35} = \dfrac{\$100.00}{.35}$$
$$S = \boxed{\$285.71}$$

$$\begin{array}{r}1.00S\\-.65S\\\hline=.35S\end{array}$$

Do not multiply the .65 times $100.00. The 65% is based on selling price not cost.

2. Calculate the dollar markup.

$$M = S - C$$
$$\boxed{\$185.71} = \$285.71 - \$100.00$$

You can check your selling price with the portion formula $B = \frac{P}{R}$. To find the selling price (B), divide the cost (P) by the rate (100% − Percent markup on selling price).

Check

$$\text{Selling price } (B) = \dfrac{\text{Cost } (P)}{1 - \text{Percent markup on selling price } (R)}$$

$$= \dfrac{\$100.00}{1 - .65} = \dfrac{\$100.00}{.35} = \boxed{\$285.71}$$

LO 4

Situation 3: Calculating Cost When You Know Selling Price and Percent Markup on Selling Price

When you know the selling price and the percent markup on selling price, you calculate the cost with the basic formula $S = C + M$. To find the dollar markup, multiply the markup percent by the selling price. When you have the dollar markup, subtract it from the selling price to get the cost.

The Word Problem Jill Sport, owner of Sports, Inc., sells tennis rackets for $50. To make her desired profit, Jill needs a 40% markup on the selling price. What is the dollar markup? What do the tennis rackets cost Jill?

	The facts	Solving for?	Steps to take	Key points
BLUEPRINT	Selling price: $50. Markup on selling price: 40%.	%　　$ C　60%　$30[2] + M　40　20[1] = S　100%　$50	$S = C + M.$ or $\text{Cost} = \text{Selling price} \times \left(1 - \begin{array}{c}\text{Percent markup}\\\text{on selling price}\end{array}\right)$	Cost Portion (?) Base ($50) × Rate (.60) Selling price 100% −40%

[1]Dollar markup. See Step 1, below.
[2]Cost. See Step 2, below.

Steps to solving problem

1. Calculate the dollar markup.

$$S = C + \quad M$$
$$\$50 = C + .40(\$50)$$

2. Calculate the cost.

$$\$50 = C + \boxed{\$20} \leftarrow \text{Dollar markup}$$
$$\underline{-20 \qquad -20}$$
$$\boxed{\$30} = C$$

To check your cost, use the portion formula Cost (P) = Selling price (B) × (100% selling price − Percent markup on selling price) (R).

Check

$$\underset{(P)}{\text{Cost}} = \underset{(B)}{\underset{\text{price}}{\text{Selling}}} \times \left(1 - \underset{(R)}{\underset{\text{on selling price}}{\text{Percent markup}}}\right) = \$50 \times .60 = \boxed{\$30}$$

$$(1.00 - .40)$$

In Table 8.1, we compare percent markup on cost with percent markup on retail (selling price). This table is a summary of the answers we calculated from the word problems in Learning Units 8–1 and 8–2. The word problems in the units were the same except in Learning Unit 8–1, we assumed markups were on cost, while in Learning Unit 8–2, markups were on selling price. Note that in Situation 1, the dollar markup is the same $5, but the percent markup is different.

Let's now look at how to convert from percent markup on cost to percent markup on selling price and vice versa. We will use Situation 1 from Table 8.1.

LO 5

Formula for Converting Percent Markup on Cost to Percent Markup on Selling Price

To convert percent markup on cost to percent markup on selling price:

$$\frac{\text{Percent markup on cost}}{1 + \text{Percent markup on cost}}$$

$$\frac{.2778}{1 + .2778} = \boxed{21.74\%}$$

TABLE 8.1

Comparison of markup on cost versus markup on selling price

Markup based on cost—Learning Unit 8–1	Markup based on selling price—Learning Unit 8–2
Situation 1: Calculating dollar amount of markup and percent markup on cost.	*Situation 1: Calculating dollar amount of markup and percent markup on selling price.*
Hooded fleece jacket cost, $18.	Hooded fleece jacket cost, $18.
Hooded fleece jacket selling price, $23.	Hooded fleece jacket selling price, $23.
$M = S - C$	$M = S - C$
$M = \$23 - \$18 = \$5$ markup (p. 211)	$M = \$23 - \$18 = \$5$ markup (p. 216)
$M \div C = \$5 \div \$18 = 27.78\%$	$M \div S = \$5 \div \$23 = 21.74\%$
Situation 2: Calculating selling price on cost.	*Situation 2: Calculating selling price on selling price.*
Lamp cost, $100. 65% markup on cost	Lamp cost, $100. 65% markup on selling price
$S = C \times (1 + \text{Percent markup on cost})$	$S = C \div (1 - \text{Percent markup on selling price})$
$S = \$100 \times 1.65 = \$165$ (p. 212)	$S = \$100.00 \div .35$
	$(100\% - 65\% = 35\% = .35)$
$(100\% + 65\% = 165\% = 1.65)$	$S = \$285.71$ (p. 217)
Situation 3: Calculating cost on cost.	*Situation 3: Calculating cost on selling price.*
Tennis racket selling price, $50. 40% markup on cost	Tennis racket selling price, $50. 40% markup on selling price
$C = S \div (1 + \text{Percent markup on cost})$	$C = S \times (1 - \text{Percent markup on selling price})$
$C = \$50.00 \div 1.40$	$C = \$50 \times .60 = \$30$ (p. 217)
$(100\% + 40\% = 140\% = 1.40)$	
$C = \$35.71$ (p. 213)	$(100\% - 40\% = 60\% = .60)$

MONEY tips

When analyzing a job offer, make sure you include the value of the benefits. Salary alone will not let you know the value of the offer.

Formula for Converting Percent Markup on Selling Price to Percent Markup on Cost

To convert percent markup on selling price to percent markup on cost:

Percent markup on selling price
1 − Percent markup on selling price

$$\frac{.2174}{1-.2174} = 27.78\%$$

Key point: A 21.74% markup on selling price or a 27.78% markup on cost results in the same dollar markup of $5.

Now let's test your knowledge of Learning Unit 8–2.

LU 8–2   PRACTICE QUIZ

Complete this **Practice Quiz** to see how you are doing.

Solve the following situations (markups based on selling price). Note numbers 1, 2, and 3 are parallel problems to those in Practice Quiz 8–1.

1. Irene Westing bought a desk for $400 from an office supply house. She plans to sell the desk for $600. What is Irene's dollar markup? What is her percent markup on selling price (rounded to the nearest tenth percent)? Check your answer. Selling price will be slightly off due to rounding.

2. Suki Komar bought dolls for her toy store that cost $12 each. To make her desired profit, Suki must mark up each doll 35% on the selling price. What is the selling price of each doll? What is the dollar markup? Check your answer.

3. Jay Lyman sells calculators. His competitor sells a new calculator line for $14 each. Jay needs a 40% markup on the selling price to make his desired profit, and he must meet price competition. What is Jay's dollar markup? At what cost can Jay afford to bring these calculators into the store? Check your answer.

4. Dan Flow sells wrenches for $10 that cost $6. What is Dan's percent markup on cost? Round to the nearest tenth percent. What is Dan's percent markup on selling price? Check your answer.

*For **extra help** from your authors–Sharon and Jeff–see the student DVD*

✓ Solutions

1. Irene's dollar markup and percent markup on selling price:

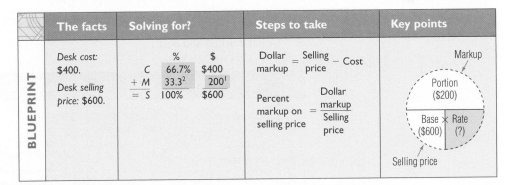

	The facts	Solving for?			Steps to take	Key points
BLUEPRINT	Desk cost: $400. Desk selling price: $600.	C + M = S	% 66.7% 33.3² 100%	$ $400 200¹ $600	$\text{Dollar markup} = \text{Selling price} - \text{Cost}$ $\text{Percent markup on selling price} = \dfrac{\text{Dollar markup}}{\text{Selling price}}$	Markup / Portion ($200) / Base ($600) × Rate (?) / Selling price

¹Dollar markup. See Step 1, below.
²Percent markup on selling price. See Step 2, below.

Steps to solving problem

1. Calculate the dollar markup.

   Dollar markup = Selling price − Cost

   $200 = $600 − $400

2. Calculate the percent markup on selling price.

   $$\text{Percent markup on selling price} = \frac{\text{Dollar markup}}{\text{Selling price}}$$

   $$= \frac{\$200}{\$600} = 33.3\%$$

Check

$$\text{Selling price} = \text{Cost} + \text{Markup} \quad \textbf{or} \quad \text{Selling price } (B) = \frac{\text{Dollar markup } (P)}{\text{Percent markup on selling price } (R)}$$

$$\$600 = \$400 + .333(\$600)$$

$$\$600 = \$400 + \$199.80$$

$$\$600 = \$599.80 \text{ (off due to rounding)}$$

$$= \frac{\$200}{.333} = \$600.60$$

(not exactly $600 due to rounding)

2. Selling price of doll and dollar markup:

	The facts	Solving for?			Steps to take	Key points
BLUEPRINT	*Doll cost:* $12 each. *Markup on selling price:* 35%.	C $+M$ $=S$	**%** 65% 35 100%	**$** $12.00 6.46² $18.46¹	$S = C + M$ or $S = \dfrac{\text{Cost}}{1 - \text{Percent markup on selling price}}$	Cost — Portion ($12) — Base × Rate (?) (.65) — Selling price — 100% −35%

¹Selling price. See Step 1, below.
²Dollar markup. See Step 2, below.

Steps to solving problem

1. Calculate the selling price.

$$S = C + M$$
$$S = \$12.00 + .35S$$
$$-.35S \qquad\qquad -.35S$$
$$\frac{.65S}{.65} = \frac{\$12.00}{.65}$$
$$S = \$18.46$$

2. Calculate the dollar markup.

$$M = S - C$$
$$\$6.46 = \$18.46 - \$12.00$$

Check

$$\text{Selling price } (B) = \frac{\text{Cost } (P)}{1 - \text{Percent markup on selling price } (R)} = \frac{\$12.00}{.65} = \$18.46$$

3. Dollar markup and cost:

	The facts	Solving for?			Steps to take	Key points
BLUEPRINT	*Selling price:* $14. *Markup on selling price:* 40%.	C $+M$ $=S$	**%** 60% 40 100%	**$** $8.40² 5.60¹ $14.00	$S = C + M$ or $\text{Cost} = \text{Selling price} \times \left(1 - \dfrac{\text{Percent markup}}{\text{on selling price}}\right)$	Cost — Portion (?) — Base × Rate ($14) (.60) — Selling price — 100% −40%

¹Dollar markup. See Step 1, below.
²Cost. See Step 2, below.

Steps to solving problem

1. Calculate the dollar markup.

$$S = C + M$$
$$\$14.00 = C + .40(\$14.00)$$

2. Calculate the cost.

$$\$14.00 = C + \$5.60 \leftarrow \text{Dollar markup}$$
$$-5.60 \qquad -5.60$$
$$\$8.40 = C$$

Check

$$\text{Cost} = \text{Selling price} \times (1 - \text{Percent markup on selling price}) = \$14.00 \times .60 = \boxed{\$8.40}$$
$$\quad (P) \qquad\qquad (B) \qquad\qquad\qquad\qquad (R)$$

$$(1.00 - .40)$$

4. $\text{Cost} = \dfrac{\$4}{\$6} = \boxed{66.7\%}$ $\dfrac{.40}{1 - .40} = \dfrac{.40}{.60} = \dfrac{2}{3} = 66.7\%$

   $\text{Selling price} = \dfrac{\$4}{\$10} = \boxed{40\%}$ $\dfrac{.667}{1 + .667} = \dfrac{.667}{1.667} = 40\%$ (due to rounding)

LU 8–2a   EXTRA PRACTICE QUIZ WITH WORKED-OUT SOLUTIONS

Need more practice? Try this **Extra Practice Quiz** (check figures in the Interactive Chapter Organizer, p. 228). Worked-out Solutions can be found in Appendix B at end of text.

Solve the following situations (markups based on selling price).

1. Irene Westing bought a desk for $800 from an office supply house. She plans to sell the desk for $1,200. What is Irene's dollar markup? What is her percent markup on selling price (rounded to the nearest tenth percent)? Check your answer. Selling price will be slightly off due to rounding.

2. Suki Komar bought dolls for her toy store that cost $14 each. To make her desired profit, Suki must mark up each doll 38% on selling price. What is the selling price of each doll? What is the dollar markup? Check your answer.

3. Jay Lyman sells calculators. His competitor sells a new calculator line for $16 each. Jay needs a 42% markup on the selling price to make his desired profit, and he must meet price competition. What is Jay's dollar markup? At what cost can Jay afford to bring these calculators into the store? Check your answer.

4. Dan Flow sells wrenches for $12 that cost $7. What is Dan's percent markup on cost? Round to the nearest tenth percent. What is Dan's percent markup on selling price? Check your answer.

Learning Unit 8–3: Markdowns and Perishables

The following *Wall Street Journal* clip, "Do the Holiday-Shopping Math," provides some insights that may make you a better shopper. Check it out.

Do the Holiday-Shopping Math

1. Which represents the biggest savings, in total dollars?
A) A markdown from $85.27 to $70.66
B) A markdown from $83.99 to $69.99
C) A markdown from $80 to $70

2. Which represents the biggest percentage discount?
A) $300 off a $1,299.99 refrigerator
B) Buy one sweater for the regular price of $40, get another for 50% off.
C) A bottle of perfume marked down from $15 to $10

3. Which represents the biggest percentage off a $2,000 item?
A) 50% off
B) 25% off, then another 25% off the reduced price
C) 20% off, then another 20% off the reduced price, then 20% off the twice-reduced price.

4. On a $40 pair of pants, which offer will yield the best discount?
A) Buy one, get 50% off the second.
B) $20 off all purchases of $50 or more.
C) A markdown of $10 on the pants.

ANSWERS
Question from D1. Answer C: All three offers could theoretically yield a 20% discount, but in most cases, the first two will yield less. To get that much savings from the gift card, you'd have to spend exactly $100, then exactly $25 with the gift card. More likely—since it can be hard to find items totalling exactly that much—you'd spend more than $125 to get $25 off. Both A and B may push you to spend more than you'd planned; the straight percentage discount doesn't create that incentive.

1. Answer A: Answering this requires three simple subtractions, yet pricing researchers say shoppers skip the math by taking cognitive shortcuts, such as associating precise prices with low prices. Answer A ($14.61) may seem small, but it's greater than B and C ($14 and $10, respectively). Also, those 9s at the end of the prices in Choice B may help make the decline in the left-most digit (from 8 to 6) seem larger than the decline in Choice A (from 8 to 7).

2. Answer C: Retailers often use absolute discounts on expensive items. A $300 reduction sounds good, but it's just 23% off the full price. As for those sweaters, you're getting two for $60, compared with $80 without a discount—a savings of 25%. The perfume discount may seem most modest, but $5 off $15 is a 33.3% savings.

3. Answer A: Discounts layered on top of discounts sound more impressive than they really are, because each successive discount is taken off a lower price base. Option A yields a sale price of $1,000, compared with a sale price of $1,125 in option B. In Option C, the first reduction brings the price down to $1,600, the second to $1,280, and the third to $1,024. Those three discounts might appear to add up to 60%, but they save less than one 50% discount.

4. Answer C: The discounts only look identical. When you buy two pairs of pants, you spend $60 to get the discount. If you want just one pair, options A and B don't represent any savings. Option C saves only $10, but you don't end up with pants you don't need.

This learning unit focuses your attention on how to calculate markdowns. Then you will learn how a business prices perishable items that may spoil before customers buy them.

LO 1

Markdowns

Markdowns are reductions from the original selling price caused by seasonal changes, special promotions, style changes, and so on. We calculate the markdown percent as follows:

$$\text{Markdown percent} = \frac{\text{Dollar markdown}}{\text{Selling price (original)}}$$

Let's look at the following Kmart example:

EXAMPLE Kmart marked down an $18 video to $10.80. Calculate the **dollar markdown** and the markdown percent.

Dollar markdown
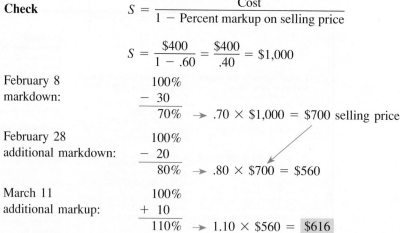

Portion
($7.20)

Base × Rate
($18)   (?)

Original selling price

$18.00 Original selling price
− 10.80 Sale price
$ 7.20 Markdown

$$\frac{\text{Dollar markdown, }\$7.20}{\text{Selling price (original), }\$18.00} = 40\%$$

Calculating a Series of Markdowns and Markups   Often the final selling price is the result of a series of markdowns (and possibly a markup in between markdowns). We calculate additional markdowns on the previous selling price. Note in the following example how we calculate markdown on selling price after we add a markup.

EXAMPLE Jones Department Store paid its supplier $400 for a TV. On January 10, Jones marked the TV up 60% on selling price. As a special promotion, Jones marked the TV down 30% on February 8 and another 20% on February 28. No one purchased the TV, so Jones marked it up 10% on March 11. What was the selling price of the TV on March 11?

January 10: Selling price = Cost   + Markup

S = $400 + .60S$

$- .60S$ $- .60S$

$$\frac{.40S}{.40} = \frac{\$400}{.40}$$

S = $1,000

Check $$S = \frac{\text{Cost}}{1 - \text{Percent markup on selling price}}$$

$$S = \frac{\$400}{1 - .60} = \frac{\$400}{.40} = \$1,000$$

February 8
markdown:

100%
− 30
70% → .70 × $1,000 = $700 selling price

February 28
additional markdown:

100%
− 20
80% → .80 × $700 = $560

March 11
additional markup:

100%
+ 10
110% → 1.10 × $560 = $616

"To hit our goal, we need to sell these last muffins for a hundred dollars each."

LO 2

Pricing Perishable Items

The following formula can be used to determine the price of goods that have a short shelf life such as fruit, flowers, and pastry. (We limit this discussion to obviously **perishable** items.)

$$\text{Selling price of perishables} = \frac{\text{Total dollar sales}}{\text{Number of units produced} - \text{Spoilage}}$$

The Word Problem Audrey's Bake Shop baked 20 dozen bagels. Audrey expects 10% of the bagels to become stale and not salable. The bagels cost Audrey $1.20 per dozen. Audrey wants a 60% markup on cost. What should Audrey charge for each dozen bagels so she will make her profit? Round to the nearest cent.

	The facts	Solving for?	Steps to take	Key points
BLUEPRINT	Bagels cost: $1.20 per dozen. Not salable: 10%. Baked: 20 dozen. Markup on cost: 60%.	Price of a dozen bagels.	Total cost. Total dollar markup. Total selling price. Bagel loss. $TS = TC + TM$.	Markup is based on cost.

Steps to solving problem

1. Calculate the total cost.

$$TC = 20 \text{ dozen} \times \$1.20 = \$24.00$$

2. Calculate the total dollar markup.

$$\boxed{TS = TC + TM}$$

$$TS = \$24.00 + .60(\$24.00)$$

$$TS = \$24.00 + \$14.40 \;\longleftarrow\; \text{Total dollar markup}$$

3. Calculate the total selling price.

$$TS = \$38.40 \;\longleftarrow\; \text{Total selling price}$$

4. Calculate the bagel loss.

$$20 \text{ dozen} \times .10 = 2 \text{ dozen}$$

5. Calculate the selling price for a dozen bagels.

$$\frac{\$38.40}{18} = \boxed{\$2.13} \text{ per dozen} \qquad \begin{array}{r} 20 \\ -\ 2 \\ \hline 18 \end{array}$$

It's time to try the Practice Quiz.

LU 8–3 PRACTICE QUIZ

Complete this **Practice Quiz** to see how you are doing.

1. Sunshine Music Shop bought a stereo for $600 and marked it up 40% on selling price. To promote customer interest, Sunshine marked the stereo down 10% for 1 week. Since business was slow, Sunshine marked the stereo down an additional 5%. After a week, Sunshine marked the stereo up 2%. What is the new selling price of the stereo to the nearest cent? What is the markdown percent based on the original selling price to the nearest hundredth percent?

2. Alvin Rose owns a fruit and vegetable stand. He knows that he cannot sell all his produce at full price. Some of his produce will be markdowns, and he will throw out some produce. Alvin must put a high enough price on the produce to cover markdowns and rotted produce and still make his desired profit. Alvin bought 300 pounds of tomatoes at 14 cents per pound. He expects a 5% spoilage and marks up tomatoes 60% on cost. What price per pound should Alvin charge for the tomatoes?

For **extra help** from your authors–Sharon and Jeff–see the student DVD

✓ Solutions

1.
$$S = C + M$$

$$S = \$600 + .40S$$

$$\underline{-.40S \qquad\qquad -.40S}$$

$$\frac{.60S}{.60} = \frac{\$600}{.60}$$

$$S = \$1{,}000$$

Check

$$S = \frac{\text{Cost}}{1 - \text{Percent markup on selling price}}$$

$$S = \frac{\$600}{1 - .40} = \frac{\$600}{.60} = \$1{,}000$$

First markdown: $.90 \times \$1{,}000 = \$900$ selling price

Second markdown: $.95 \times \$900 = \$855$ selling price

Markup: $1.02 \times \$855 = \boxed{\$872.10}$ final selling price

$$\$1{,}000 - \$872.10 = \frac{\$127.90}{\$1{,}000} = \boxed{12.79\%}$$

2. Price of tomatoes per pound:

	The facts	Solving for?	Steps to take	Key points
BLUEPRINT	300 lb. tomatoes at $.14 per pound. *Spoilage: 5%.* *Markup on cost: 60%.*	Price of tomatoes per pound.	Total cost. Total dollar markup. Total selling price. Spoilage amount. TS = TC + TM.	Markup is based on cost.

Steps to solving problem

1. Calculate the total cost.

$TC = 300 \text{ lb.} \times \$.14 = \$42.00$

2. Calculate the total dollar markup.

$TS = TC + TM$

$TS = \$42.00 + .60(\$42.00)$

$TS = \$42.00 + \$25.20 \leftarrow$ Total dollar markup

3. Calculate the total selling price.

$TS = \$67.20 \leftarrow$ Total selling price

4. Calculate the tomato loss.

300 pounds $\times$ .05 = 15 pounds spoilage

5. Calculate the selling price per pound of tomatoes.

$\dfrac{\$67.20}{285} = \boxed{\$.24}$ per pound (rounded to nearest hundredth)

$(300 - 15)$

LU 8–3a EXTRA PRACTICE QUIZ WITH WORKED-OUT SOLUTIONS

Need more practice? Try this **Extra Practice Quiz** (check figures in the Interactive Chapter Organizer, p. 228). Worked-out Solutions can be found in Appendix B at end of text.

1. Sunshine Music Shop bought a stereo for $800 and marked it up 30% on selling price. To promote customer interest, Sunshine marked the stereo down 10% for 1 week. Since business was slow, Sunshine marked the stereo down an additional 5%. After a week, Sunshine marked the stereo up 2%. What is the new selling price of the stereo to the nearest cent? What is the markdown percent based on the original selling price to the nearest hundredth percent?

2. Alvin Rose owns a fruit and vegetable stand. He knows that he cannot sell all his produce at full price. Some of his produce will be markdowns, and he will throw out some produce. Alvin must put a high enough price on the produce to cover markdowns and rotted produce and still make his desired profit. Alvin bought 500 pounds of tomatoes at 16 cents per pound. He expects a 10% spoilage and marks up tomatoes 55% on cost. What price per pound should Alvin charge for the tomatoes?

Learning Unit 8–4: Breakeven Analysis

One Shirt's Cost

Fabric	$6.80
Fabric for placket & vent	$0.99
4 buttons (including 1 extra)	$0.12
Thread	$0.09
Labels	$1.10
Hang tag	$0.40
Waste fabric	$0.85
Labor	$11.05
Packing materials	$0.17
Ship materials to N.Y. factory, then shirts to Atlanta	$5.00
Hand-embroidered linen bag	$3.00
Total	**$29.57**
Wholesale price	**$65.00**
Retail price	**$155.00**

Source: KP MacLane

Bryan Derballa for The Wall Street Journal (9)

So far in this chapter, cost is the price retailers pay to a manufacturer or supplier to bring the goods into the store. In this unit, we view costs from the perspective of manufacturers or suppliers who produce goods to sell in units, such as polo shirts, pens, calculators, lamps, and so on. These manufacturers or suppliers deal with two costs—fixed costs (*FC*) and variable costs (*VC*).

The *Wall Street Journal* clip in the margin shows the cost associated with producing one $155 retail MacLane polo shirt.

To understand how the owners of manufacturers or suppliers that produce goods per unit operate their businesses, we must understand fixed costs (*FC*), variable costs (*VC*), contribution margin (*CM*), and breakeven point (*BE*). Carefully study the following definitions of these terms:

- **Fixed costs (*FC*).** Costs that *do not change* with increases or decreases in sales; they include payments for insurance, a business license, rent, a lease, utilities, labor, and so on.

- **Variable costs (*VC*).** Costs that *do change* in response to changes in the volume of sales; they include payments for material, some labor, and so on.

- **Selling price (*S*).** In this unit we focus on manufacturers and suppliers who produce goods to sell in units.

- **Contribution margin (*CM*).** The difference between selling price (*S*) and variable costs (*VC*). This difference goes *first* to pay off total fixed costs (*FC*); when they are covered, *profits* (*or losses*) start to accumulate.

- **Breakeven point (*BE*).** The point at which the seller has covered all expenses and costs of a unit and has not made any profit or suffered any loss. Every unit sold after the breakeven point (*BE*) will bring some profit or cause a loss.

Learning Unit 8–4 is divided into two sections: calculating a contribution margin (*CM*) and calculating a breakeven point (*BE*). You will learn the importance of these two concepts and the formulas that you can use to calculate them. Study the example given for each concept to help you understand why the success of business owners depends on knowing how to use these two concepts.

LO 1

Calculating a Contribution Margin (*CM*)

Before we calculate the breakeven point, we must first calculate the contribution margin. The formula is as follows:

> Contribution margin (*CM*) = Selling price (*S*) − Variable cost (*VC*)

EXAMPLE   Assume Jones Company produces pens that have a selling price (*S*) of $2.00 and a variable cost (*VC*) of $.80. We calculate the contribution margin (*CM*) as follows:

Contribution margin (*CM*) = $2.00 (*S*) − $.80 (*VC*)
$$CM = \boxed{\$1.20}$$

This means that for each pen sold, $1.20 goes to cover fixed costs (*FC*) and results in a profit. It makes sense to cover fixed costs (*FC*) first because the nature of a *FC* is that it does not change with increases or decreases in sales.

Now we are ready to see how Jones Company will reach a breakeven point (*BE*).

LO 2

Calculating a Breakeven Point (*BE*)

Sellers like Jones Company can calculate their profit or loss by using a concept called the **breakeven point (*BE*)**. This important point results after sellers have paid all their expenses and costs. Study the following formula and the example:

> $$\text{Breakeven point } (BE) = \frac{\text{Fixed costs } (FC)}{\text{Contribution margin } (CM)}$$

EXAMPLE   Jones Company produces pens. The company has a fixed cost (*FC*) of $60,000. Each pen sells for $2.00 with a variable cost (*VC*) of $.80 per pen.

Fixed cost (*FC*)	$60,000
Selling price (*S*) per pen	$2.00
Variable cost (*VC*) per pen	$.80

$$\text{Breakeven point } (BE) = \frac{\$60,000\ (FC)}{\$2.00\ (S) - \$.80\ (VC)} = \frac{\$60,000\ (FC)}{\$1.20\ (CM)} = \boxed{50,000 \text{ units (pens)}}$$

At 50,000 units (pens), Jones Company is just covering its costs. Each unit after 50,000 brings in a profit of $1.20 (*CM*).

It is time to try the Practice Quiz.

LU 8–4 PRACTICE QUIZ

Complete this **Practice Quiz** to see how you are doing.

Blue Company produces holiday gift boxes. Given the following, calculate (1) the contribution margin (*CM*) and (2) the breakeven point (*BE*) for Blue Company.

Fixed cost (*FC*)	$45,000
Selling price (*S*) per gift box	$20
Variable cost (*VC*) per gift box	$8

For **extra help** from your authors–Sharon and Jeff–see the student DVD

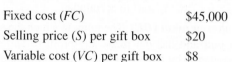

✓ Solutions

1. Contribution margin (*CM*) = $20 (*S*) − $8 (*VC*) = $12

2. Breakeven point (*BE*) = $\dfrac{\$45{,}000\ (FC)}{\$20\ (S) - \$8\ (VC)} = \dfrac{\$45{,}000\ (FC)}{\$12\ (CM)} = $ 3,750 units (gift boxes)

LU 8–4a EXTRA PRACTICE QUIZ WITH WORKED-OUT SOLUTIONS

Need more practice? Try this **Extra Practice Quiz** (check figures in the Interactive Chapter Organizer, p. 228). Worked-out Solutions can be found in Appendix B at end of text.

Angel Company produces car radios. Given the following, calculate (1) the contribution margin (*CM*) and (2) the breakeven point (*BE*) for Angel Company.

Fixed cost (*FC*)	$96,000
Selling price (*S*) per radio	$240
Variable cost (*VC*) per radio	$80

INTERACTIVE CHAPTER ORGANIZER

Topic/procedure/formula	Examples	You try it*
Markups based on cost: **Cost is 100% (base), p. 211** Selling price (*S*) = Cost (*C*) + Markup (*M*)	$400 = $300 + $100 $S\ \ =\ \ C\ +\ M$	**Calculate selling price** Cost, $400; Markup, $200
Percent markup on cost, p. 211 $\dfrac{\text{Dollar markup (portion)}}{\text{Cost (base)}} = \dfrac{\text{Percent markup}}{\text{on cost (rate)}}$	$\dfrac{\$100}{\$300} = \dfrac{1}{3} = 33\dfrac{1}{3}\%$	**Calculate percent markup on cost** Dollar markup, $50; Cost, $200
Cost, p. 212 $C = \dfrac{\text{Dollar markup}}{\text{Percent markup on cost}}$	$\dfrac{\$100}{.33} = \$303$ Off slightly due to rounding	**Calculate cost** Dollar markup, $50; Percent markup on cost, 25%
Calculating selling price, p. 212 $S = C + M$ **Check** S = Cost × (1 + Percent markup on cost)	Cost, $6; percent markup on cost, 20% S = $6 + .20($6) **Check** S = $6 + $1.20 ↓ S = $7.20 $6 × 1.20 = $7.20	**Calculate selling price** Cost, $8; Percent markup on cost, 10%
Calculating cost, p. 213 $S = C + M$ **Check** $\text{Cost} = \dfrac{\text{Selling price}}{1 + \text{Percent markup on cost}}$	S = $100; M = 70% of cost $\qquad$ S = C + M $\qquad \left(\begin{smallmatrix}\text{Remember,}\\ C = 1.00C\end{smallmatrix}\right)$ $\qquad$ $100 = C + .70C $\qquad$ $100 = 1.7C $\qquad \dfrac{\$100}{1.7} = C$ **Check** $\qquad$ ↓ $\$58.82 = C$ $\dfrac{\$100}{1 + .70} = \$58.82$	**Calculate cost** Selling price, $200; Markup on cost, 60%

(continues)

INTERACTIVE CHAPTER ORGANIZER

Topic/procedure/formula	Examples	You try it*
Markups based on selling price: selling price is 100% (Base), p. 216 Dollar markup = Selling price − Cost	$M = S - C$ $\boxed{\$600} = \$1,000 - \$400$	**Calculate dollar markup** Cost, $2,000; Selling price, $4,500
Percent markup on selling price, p. 216 $\dfrac{\text{Dollar markup (portion)}}{\text{Selling price (base)}} = \dfrac{\text{Percent markup on}}{\text{selling price (rate)}}$	$\dfrac{\$600}{\$1,000} = \boxed{60\%}$	**Calculate percent markup on selling price** Dollar markup, $700; Selling price, $2,800
Selling price, p. 216 $S = \dfrac{\text{Dollar markup}}{\text{Percent markup on selling price}}$	$\dfrac{\$600}{.60} = \boxed{\$1,000}$	**Calculate selling price** Dollar markup, $700; Percent markup on selling price, 50%
Calculating selling price, p. 216 $S = C + M$ **Check** $\text{Selling price} = \dfrac{\text{Cost}}{1 - \begin{array}{c}\text{Percent markup}\\\text{on selling price}\end{array}}$	Cost, $400; percent markup on S, 60% $S = C + M$ $S = \$400 + .60S$ $S - .60S = \$400 + .60S - .60S$ $\dfrac{.40S}{.40} = \dfrac{\$400}{.40} \quad \boxed{S = \$1,000}$ Check $\rightarrow$ $\boxed{\dfrac{\$400}{1 - .60} = \dfrac{\$400}{.40} = \$1,000}$	**Calculate selling price** Cost, $800; Markup on selling price, 40%
Calculating cost, p. 217 $S = C + M$ **Check** $\text{Cost} = \dfrac{\text{Selling}}{\text{price}} \times \left(1 - \begin{array}{c}\text{Percent markup}\\\text{on selling price}\end{array}\right)$	$\$1,000 = C + 60\%(\$1,000)$ $\$1,000 = C + \$600$ $\boxed{\$400} = C$ Check $\longrightarrow$ $\boxed{\begin{array}{l}\$1,000 \times (1 - .60)\\\$1,000 \times .40 = \$400\end{array}}$	**Calculate cost** Selling price, $2,000; 70% markup on selling price
Conversion of markup percent, p. 218 $\begin{array}{ccc}\text{Percent markup} & & \text{Percent markup}\\\text{on cost} & \text{to} & \text{on selling price}\end{array}$ $\boxed{\dfrac{\text{Percent markup on cost}}{1 + \text{Percent markup on cost}}}$ $\begin{array}{ccc}\text{Percent markup} & & \text{Percent markup}\\\text{on selling price} & \text{to} & \text{on cost}\end{array}$ $\boxed{\dfrac{\text{Percent markup on selling price}}{1 - \text{Percent markup on selling price}}}$	*Round to nearest percent:* 54% markup on cost $\rightarrow$ $\boxed{35\%}$ markup on selling price $\boxed{\dfrac{.54}{1 + .54} = \dfrac{.54}{1.54} = 35\%}$ 35% markup on $\longrightarrow$ $\boxed{54\%}$ markup selling price $\qquad$ on cost $\boxed{\dfrac{.35}{1 - .35} = \dfrac{.35}{.65} = 54\%}$	**Calculate percent markup on selling price** Convert 47% markup on cost to markup on selling price. Round to nearest percent.
Markdowns, p. 222 $\text{Markdown percent} = \dfrac{\text{Dollar markdown}}{\text{Selling price (original)}}$	$40 selling price 10% markdown $\$40 \times .10 = \$4$ markdown $\dfrac{\$4}{\$40} = \boxed{10\%}$	**Calculate markdown percent** Selling price, $50; Markdown, 20%
Pricing perishables, p. 222 1. Calculate total cost and total selling price. 2. Calculate selling price per unit by dividing total sales in Step 1 by units expected to be sold after taking perishables into account.	50 pastries cost 20 cents each; 10 will spoil before being sold. Markup is 60% on cost. 1. $TC = 50 \times \$.20 = \$10$ $\quad TS = TC + TM$ $\quad TS = \$10 + .60(\$10)$ $\quad TS = \$10 + \$6$ $\quad TS = \$16$ 2. $\dfrac{\$16}{40 \text{ pastries}} = \boxed{\$.40}$ per pastry	**Calculate cost of each pastry** 30 pastries cost 30 cents each; 15 will spoil; Markup is 30% on cost

(continues)

INTERACTIVE CHAPTER ORGANIZER

Topic/procedure/formula	Examples	You try it*
Breakeven point (BE), p. 225 $BE = \dfrac{\text{Fixed cost } (FC)}{\text{Contribution margin } (CM)}$ (Selling price, S − Variable cost, VC)	Fixed cost (FC) \qquad\qquad $60,000 Selling price ($S$) \qquad\qquad $90 Variable cost ($VC$) \qquad\qquad $30 $BE = \dfrac{\$60,000}{\$90 - \$30} = \dfrac{\$60,000}{\$60} = 1,000$ units	**Calculate BE** Fixed cost (FC) $70,000 Selling price ($S$) $80 Variable cost ($VC$) $60

KEY TERMS	Breakeven point, *p. 225* Contribution margin, *p. 225* Cost, *p. 209* Dollar markdown, *p. 222* Dollar markup, *p. 210* Fixed cost, *p. 224* Gross profit, *p. 209*	Margin, *p. 209* Markdowns, *p. 222* Markup, *p. 209* Net profit (net income), *p. 210* Operating expenses (overhead), *p. 210* Percent markup on cost, *p. 210*	Percent markup on selling price, *p. 215* Perishables, *p. 222* Selling price, *pp. 209, 225* Variable cost, *p. 224*

Check Figures for Extra Practice Quizzes with Page References. (Worked-out Solutions in Appendix B.)	LU 8–1a (p. 215) **1.** $400; 50% **2.** $5.32; $19.32 **3.** $11.27; $4.73	LU 8–2a (p. 221) **1.** $400; 33.3% **2.** $22.58; $8.58 **3.** $6.72; $9.28 **4.** 71.4%; 41.7%	LU 8–3a (p. 224) **1.** $996.69; 12.79% **2.** .28	LU 8–4a (p. 226) **1.** $160; 600

*Worked-out solutions are in Appendix B.

Critical Thinking Discussion Questions with Chapter Concept Check

1. Assuming markups are based on cost, explain how the portion formula could be used to calculate cost, selling price, dollar markup, and percent markup on cost. Pick a company and explain why it would mark goods up on cost rather than on selling price.

2. Assuming markups are based on selling price, explain how the portion formula could be used to calculate cost, selling price, dollar markup, and percent markup on selling price. Pick a company and explain why it would mark up goods on selling price rather than on cost.

3. What is the formula to convert percent markup on selling price to percent markup on cost? How could you explain that a 40% markup on selling price, which is a 66.7% markup on cost, would result in the same dollar markup?

4. Explain how to calculate markdowns. Do you think stores should run 1-day-only markdown sales? Would it be better to offer the best price "all the time"?

5. Explain the five steps in calculating a selling price for perishable items. Recall a situation where you saw a store that did *not* follow the five steps. How did it sell its items?

6. Explain how Walmart uses breakeven analysis. Give an example.

7. **Chapter Concept Check.** Consider the *Wall Street Journal* clip in the chapter opener that discusses how Macy's (like many other retailers) can track what customers buy (and what they will want). Visit a retailer's website and find out how that retailer marks up goods and marks down specials. Present calculations based on this chapter to support your findings.

END-OF-CHAPTER PROBLEMS

Check figures for odd-numbered problems in Appendix C.

Name _____ Date _____

DRILL PROBLEMS

Assume markups in Problems 8–1 to 8–6 are based on cost. Find the dollar markup and selling price for the following problems. Round answers to the nearest cent. *LU 8-1(1, 2)*

	Item	Cost	Markup percent	Dollar markup	Selling price
8–1.	Blackberry iPad	$500	20%		
8–2.	Hamilton khaki multi-touch watch	$400	40%		

Solve for cost (round to the nearest cent): *LU 8-1(3)*

8–3. Selling price of office furniture at Staples, $6,000

Percent markup on cost, 40%

Actual cost?

8–4. Selling price of lumber at Home Depot, $4,000

Percent markup on cost, 30%

Actual cost?

Complete the following: *LU 8-1(1)*

	Cost	Selling price	Dollar markup	Percent markup on cost*
8–5.	$15.10	$22.00	?	?
8–6.	?	?	$4.70	102.17%

*Round to the nearest hundredth percent.

Assume markups in Problems 8–7 to 8–12 are based on selling price. Find the dollar markup and cost (round answers to the nearest cent): *LU 8-2(1, 2)*

	Item	Selling price	Markup percent	Dollar markup	Cost
8–7.	Sony LCD TV	$1,000	45%		
8–8.	IBM scanner	$80	30%		

Solve for the selling price (round to the nearest cent):   *LU 8-2(3)*

8–9. Selling price of a complete set of pots and pans at Walmart?

40% markup on selling price

Cost, actual, $66.50

8–10. Selling price of a dining room set at Macy's?

55% markup on selling price

Cost, actual, $800

Complete the following: *LU 8-2(1)*

	Cost	Selling price	Dollar markup	Percent markup on selling price (round to nearest tenth percent)
8–11.	$14.80	$49.00	?	?
8–12.	?	?	$4	20%

By conversion of the markup formula, solve the following (round to the nearest whole percent as needed):   *LU 8-2(5)*

	Percent markup on cost	Percent markup on selling price
8–13.	12.4%	?
8–14.	?	13%

Complete the following: *LU 8-3(1, 2)*

8–15. Calculate the final selling price to the nearest cent and markdown percent to the nearest hundredth percent:

eXcel

Original selling price	First markdown	Second markdown	Markup	Final markdown
$5,000	20%	10%	12%	5%

Item	Total quantity bought	Unit cost	Total cost	Percent markup on cost	Total selling price	Percent that will spoil	Selling price per brownie
8–16. Brownies	20	$.79	?	60%	?	10%	?

Complete the following: *LU 8-4(1, 2)*

	Breakeven point	Fixed cost	Contribution margin	Selling price per unit	Variable cost per unit
8–17.		$65,000		$5.00	$1.00
8–18.		$90,000		$9.00	$4.00

WORD PROBLEMS

8–19. Bari Jay, a gown manufacturer, received an order for 600 prom dresses from China. Her cost is $35 a gown. If her markup based on selling price is 79%, what is the selling price of each gown? Round to the nearest cent. *LU 8-2(2)*

8–20. Chin Yov, store manager for Best Buy, does not know how to price a GE freezer that cost the store $600. Chin knows his boss wants a 45% markup on cost. Help Chin price the freezer. *LU 8-1(2)*

8–21. Cecil Green sells golf hats. He knows that most people will not pay more than $20 for a golf hat. Cecil needs a 40% markup on cost. What should Cecil pay for his golf hats? Round to the nearest cent. *LU 8-1(4)*

8–22. Macy's was selling Calvin Klein jean shirts that were originally priced at $58.00 for $8.70. **(a)** What was the amount of the markdown? **(b)** Based on the selling price, what is the percent markdown? *LU 8-3(1)*

8–23. Brownsville, Texas, boasts being the southernmost international seaport and the largest city in the lower Rio Grande Valley. Ben Supple, an importer in Brownsville, has just received a shipment of Peruvian opals that he is pricing for sale. He paid $150 for the shipment. If he wants a 75% markup, calculate the selling price based on selling price. Then calculate the selling price based on cost. *LU 8-1(2), LU 8-2(2)*

8–24. Front Range Cabinet Distributors in Colorado Springs, Colorado, sells to its contractors with a 42% markup on cost. If the selling price for cabinets is $9,655, what is the cost to contractors based on cost? Round to the nearest tenth. Check your answer. *LU 8-1(3)*

8–25. Misu Sheet, owner of the Bedspread Shop, knows his customers will pay no more than $120 for a comforter. Misu wants *eXcel* a 30% markup on selling price. What is the most that Misu can pay for a comforter?   *LU 8-2(4)*

8–26. Assume Misu Sheet (Problem 8–25) wants a 30% markup on cost instead of on selling price. What is Misu's cost? Round *eXcel* to the nearest cent.   *LU 8-1(4)*

8–27. Misu Sheet (Problem 8–25) wants to advertise the comforter as "percent markup on cost." What is the equivalent rate of percent markup on cost compared to the 30% markup on selling price? Check your answer. Is this a wise marketing decision? Round to the nearest hundredth percent.   *LU 8-2(5)*

8–28. DeWitt Company sells a kitchen set for $475. To promote July 4, DeWitt ran the following advertisement:

eXcel Beginning each hour up to 4 hours we will mark down the kitchen set 10%. At the end of each hour, we will mark up the set 1%.

Assume Ingrid Swenson buys the set 1 hour 50 minutes into the sale. What will Ingrid pay? Round each calculation to the nearest cent. What is the markdown percent? Round to the nearest hundredth percent.   *LU 8-3(1)*

8–29. Angie's Bake Shop makes birthday chocolate chip cookies that cost $2 each. Angie expects that 10% of the cookies will *eXcel* crack and be discarded. Angie wants a 60% markup on cost and produces 100 cookies. What should Angie price each cookie? Round to the nearest cent.   *LU 8-3(2)*

8–30. Assume that Angie (Problem 8–29) can sell the cracked cookies for $1.10 each. What should Angie price each cookie?   *LU 8-3(2)*

8–31. Jane Corporation produces model toy cars. Each sells for $29.99. Its variable cost per unit is $14.25. What is the breakeven point for Jane Corporation assuming it has a fixed cost of $314,800?   *LU 8-4(2)*

ADDITIONAL SET OF WORD PROBLEMS

8–32. Aunt Sally's "New Orleans Most Famous Pralines" sells pralines costing $1.10 each to make. If Aunt Sally's wants a 35% markup based on selling price and produces 45 pralines with an anticipated 15% spoilage (rounded to the nearest whole number), what should each praline be sold for? *LU 8-3(2)*

8–33. Sachi Wong, store manager for Hawk Appliance, does not know how to price a GE dishwasher that cost the store $399. Sachi knows her boss wants a 40% markup on cost. Can you help Sachi price the dishwasher? *LU 8-1(2)*

8–34. Working off an 18% margin, with markups based on cost, the Food Co-op Club boasts that it has 5,000 members and a 200% increase in sales. The markup is 36% based on cost. What would be its percent markup if selling price were the base? Round to the nearest hundredth percent. *LU 8-2(5)*

8–35. At a local Bed and Bath Superstore, the manager, Jill Roe, knows her customers will pay no more than $300 for a bedspread. Jill wants a 35% markup on selling price. What is the most that Jill can pay for a bedspread? *LU 8-2(4)*

8–36. Jim Abbott purchased a $60,000 RV with a 40 percent markup on selling price. **(a)** What was the amount of the dealer's markup? **(b)** What was the dealer's original cost? *LU 8-2(4)*

8–37. Best Buy sells a handheld personal planner for $199.99. Best Buy marked up the personal planner 35% on the selling price. What is the cost of the handheld personal planner? *LU 8-2(4)*

8–38. Arley's Bakery makes fat-free cookies that cost $1.50 each. Arley expects 15% of the cookies to fall apart and be eXcel discarded. Arley wants a 45% markup on cost and produces 200 cookies. What should Arley price each cookie? Round to the nearest cent. *LU 8-3(2)*

8–39. Assume that Arley (Problem 8–38) can sell the broken cookies for $1.40 each. What should Arley price each cookie? *LU 8-3(2)*

8–40. An Apple Computer Center sells computers for $1,258.60. Assuming the computers cost $10,788 per dozen, find for each computer the **(a)** dollar markup, **(b)** percent markup on cost, and **(c)** percent markup on selling price, to the nearest hundredth percent. *LU 8-1(1), LU 8-2(1)*

Prove **(b)** and **(c)** of the above problem using the equivalent formulas.

8–41. Pete Corporation produces bags of peanuts. Its fixed cost is $17,280. Each bag sells for $2.99 with a unit cost of $1.55. What is Pete's breakeven point? *LU 8-4(2)*

CHALLENGE PROBLEMS

8–42. Nissan Appliances bought two dozen camcorders at a cost of $4,788. The markup on the camcorders is 25% of the selling price. What was the original selling price of each camcorder? *LU 8-2(3)*

8–43. On July 8, 2013, Leon's Kitchen Hut bought a set of pots with a $120 list price from Lambert Manufacturing. Leon's receives a 25% trade discount. Terms of the sale were 2/10, n/30. On July 14, Leon's sent a check to Lambert for the pots. Leon's expenses are 20% of the selling price. Leon's must also make a profit of 15% of the selling price. A competitor marked down the same set of pots 30%. Assume Leon's reduces its selling price by 30%. *LU 8-2(3)*

   a. What is the sale price at Kitchen Hut?

   b. What was the operating profit or loss?

Do you need help? The DVD has step-by-step worked-out solutions.

1. Sunset Co. marks up merchandise 40% on cost. A DVD player costs Sunset $90. What is Sunset's selling price? Round to the nearest cent. *(p. 212)* *LU 8-1(2)*

2. JCPenney sells jeans for $49.50 that cost $38.00. What is the percent markup on cost? Round to the nearest hundredth percent. Check the cost. *(p. 211)* *LU 8-1(1)*

3. Best Buy sells a flat-screen high-definition TV for $700. Best Buy marks up the TV 45% on cost. What is the cost and dollar markup of the TV? *(pp. 211, 213)* *LU 8-1(1, 3)*

4. Sports Authority marks up New Balance sneakers $30 and sells them for $109. Markup is on cost. What are the cost and percent markup to the nearest hundredth percent? *(pp. 211, 213)* *LU 8-1(1, 3)*

5. The Shoe Outlet bought boots for $60 and marks up the boots 55% on the selling price. What is the selling price of the boots? Round to the nearest cent. *(p. 216)* *LU 8-2(2)*

6. Office Max sells a desk for $450 and marks up the desk 35% on the selling price. What did the desk cost Office Max? Round to the nearest cent. *(p. 217)* *LU 8-2(4)*

7. Zales sells diamonds for $1,100 that cost $800. What is Zales's percent markup on selling price? Round to the nearest hundredth percent. Check the selling price. *(p. 216)* *LU 8-2(1)*

8. Earl Miller, a customer of J. Crew, will pay $400 for a new jacket. J. Crew has a 60% markup on selling price. What is the most that J. Crew can pay for this jacket? *(p. 217)* *LU 8-2(4)*

9.   Home Liquidators marks up its merchandise 35% on cost. What is the company's equivalent markup on selling price? Round to the nearest tenth percent. *(p. 218)   LU 8-2(5)*

10.   The Muffin Shop makes no-fat blueberry muffins that cost $.70 each. The Muffin Shop knows that 15% of the muffins will spoil. If The Muffin Shop wants 40% markup on cost and produces 800 muffins, what should The Muffin Shop price each muffin? Round to the nearest cent. *(p. 222)   LU 8-3(2)*

11.   Angel Corporation produces calculators selling for $25.99. Its unit cost is $18.95. Assuming a fixed cost of $80,960, what is the breakeven point in units? *(p. 225)   LU 8-4(2)*

Noodles & Company is a rapidly expanding restaurant in the "quick-casual" dining world. Close attention to detail through effective and efficient operations management is the core attribute that enables Noodles & Company to provide hot, fresh food in a timely manner. With time a scarce resource for many, Noodles & Company has found a way to satisfy the time-hungry niche market by providing high-quality food quickly.

Management spends much time analyzing business processes and functions to ensure customers receive a premium food experience. Noodles & Company plans the customers' experience from the moment they enter the restaurant to the moment they leave. Operations goals require each customer to have his or her meal within five minutes of placing an order.

Once the order is taken through the guest interaction point of purchase (30 seconds), the order is sent to the kitchen technologically. Through the division of tasks, every function of the kitchen is made as efficient as possible. The line is set up with previously portioned meats and vegetables that flow in the same flow process each dish requires. Stations have a "job aid" providing the appropriate weight and ingredients for each dish. The preheated pan is critical to throughput and operational efficiency. With the help of 30,000 BTU burners, each dish gets through the sauté line in 3.5 minutes. An additional 30 seconds is used at the garnish station and the meal is served to the customer within 5 minutes.

Just-in-time inventory maintains that only what is needed is prepared. First-in first-out (FIFO) inventory method ensures the freshest ingredients. Food preparation is conducted throughout the day to ensure freshness. Focusing on every element from entry to exit allows Noodles & Company to deliver on the company's promise of quick, fresh, customized food served in a no-tip welcoming setting.

Note: The following problems contain some data that has been created by the author.

PROBLEM 1

The video discusses the extensive planning required to meet the operational goals for serving high-quality foods quickly. The goal of 5 minutes from order-taking to serving each meal is critical to maintaining Noodles & Company's promise to the customer of high-quality food served quickly. If a meal needs to be remade due to a processing error, what percent increase is this additional 3.5 minutes?

PROBLEM 2

Noodles & Company has won numerous accolades for its unique menu offerings. In 2011 *Parents* magazine ranked the chain number 6 in its top 10 list of Best Family Restaurants. The company also earned recognition as one of America's healthiest fast-food restaurants by *Health* magazine in 2008/2009. Its CEO, Kevin Reddy, was named a Top 10 Who to Watch Executive in 2010 and 2011 by *Nation's Restaurant News*. All of this success translates to revenue growth for the chain. According to *Inc.* magazine, the company's revenues grew from $136.7 million in 2007 to $220.8 million in 2010. What was its 3-year growth? Round your answer to the nearest percent.

PROBLEM 3

Currently Noodles & Company has approximately 300 locations in 22 states. If it planned to grow by 12% in 2012, how many new restaurants would it open and how many locations would it then have by the end of the year if it met its target? Round answers to the nearest whole number.

PROBLEM 4

The Noodles & Company location in Ann Arbor, Michigan, sells its Japanese Pan Noodle dish for $4.49 for a small bowl and $5.59 for a regular bowl. Protein (chicken, beef, shrimp, or tofu) is available for an additional $2.35 for either size. Imagine Noodles & Company is making a 250% markup based on cost. What is the cost for a regular Japanese Pan Noodle dish with chicken? What is the dollar markup? Round answers to the nearest cent.

PROBLEM 5

In Problem 4 above, the hypothetical markup based on cost was 250%. What is the corresponding markup based on selling price? Round your answer to the nearest percent.

PROBLEM 6

Noodles & Company offers shrimp as one of its protein options. Assume that each restaurant purchases frozen shrimp in large quantities and defrosts only as much as it expects to use each day. The restaurant would likely use past daily sales to estimate how much to take out for each day's business. But even then, some amount of loss could occur because shrimp should not be refrozen. Assume further that once defrosted, shrimp can be used for up to 2 days, each portion of shrimp costs $1.80, and the company wants an 80% markup on cost. If a given location takes out enough shrimp to sell 240 portions over a 2-day period and expects that as much as 10% could go bad before selling it, how should it price each portion of shrimp to account for the possible 10% loss?

Class Discussion   Given the explosive growth of the "quick-casual" dining segment with franchises such as Noodles & Company, Chipotle Mexican Grill, and Qdoba, discuss how Noodles & Company might position itself to stand out in this increasingly crowded field of options.

PROBLEM 1
What can I afford to drive?

Go to http://www.kbb.com and find the dealer's invoice price of a new car of your choice. Then go to http://www.edmunds.com/car-buying/dealer-holdback to find the dealer holdback for that manufacturer. (Choose another car if that manufacturer does not have a holdback.) If the dealer sells you the car for invoice price, how much profit does the dealer make? If the dealer's cost is the invoice price minus the holdback, then what is the dealer's percent markup based on cost?

Discussion Questions

1. Why do dealers utilize holdbacks?

2. Based on your findings, would you purchase new or used when you graduate from college? Why?

PROBLEM 2
Do you really save at Amazon?

Go to http://www.amazon.com and choose five books you would like to read. Use the List Price and the Our Price to confirm the percentage on the You Save line.

Discussion Questions

1. Why does Amazon list pricing in this manner?

2. Do you expect deep discounts on all your purchases at Amazon? Why?

PROBLEM 3
Save big—instantly

Go to http://www.bestbuy.com. Find a product with a rebate or instant savings. Calculate the percent markdown after rebate.

Discussion Questions

1. What are the pros and cons of rebates from the seller's perspective?

2. What are the pros and cons of rebates from the consumer's perspective?

PROBLEM 4
A picture is worth how much?

Go to www.staples.com and search for a photo printer for your home. Select one that has Total Savings details attached to it and click on See Details to get the original and sale price. What is the percent markdown on the original price?

Discussion Questions

1. How do the photo printers that advertise these special savings compare to those without the savings?

2. What is the seller's advantage in promoting particular photo printers using the Total Savings approach?

MOBILE APPS ✕

iMarkup (SUI Solutions) Assists in calculating markup given a particular sale price, cost, or markup percentage.

MarkUp Markdown (Dynamic Circle, Inc.) Margin calculator and sale price tool that helps determine sale price based on a given percentage off the original price.

INTERNET PROJECTS ✕

 See text website
www.mhhe.com/slater11e_sse_ch08

A Fresh Look at Extended Warranties

Your tech toys are pricey and precious. What can you do to protect them? BY JEFF BERTOLUCCI

THESE DAYS WE TAKE OUR tablets, e-readers and smart phones with us everywhere. That means our gadgets are more liable to be damaged, lost or stolen. Is it time to rethink buying extended warranties, long thought to benefit retailers at the expense of consumers? We recently surveyed protection packages peddled at the point of purchase to see what they offer.

Pricey plans. Retailers' extended warranties and service contracts are often expensive. Take Staples' tablet-protection plan. When you buy the iPad-like Samsung Galaxy Tab 10.1 for $500 and add Staples' optional two-year service plan, which covers accidental damage from spills and drops, you'll pay an extra $240—nearly half the cost of the tablet itself.

Similarly, Sprint offers the Assurant Advanced Protection Pack, which covers repair or replacement of a tablet, laptop, or netbook that has a mechanical or electrical breakdown, is accidentally damaged, or is lost or stolen. It costs $13 a month, or $156 a year. Pricey, yes, and its gets uglier: There's a $100 deductible on claims for loss, theft and accidental damage.

Overlapping coverage. Be wary of warranties that don't cover your equipment for as long as advertised. For example, the Dell Inspiron 15R 2nd Gen laptop ($600) comes with one year of service. For an extra $119, Dell's Three-Year Good Service Package extends the plan for an additional *two* years—you're really buying two, not three, years of coverage because the first year is free.

Many retailers offer service plans that pick up where the manufacturer's warranty ends. For example, the Wal-Mart Product Protection Plan, which costs $65 for TVs priced from $500 to $1,000, adds two years of coverage, including in-home repair. The retailer also offers a $99, two-year "Drop, Spill, and Broken Screen Protection Plan" with no deductible for iPads, tablet computers and e-readers.

Those are actually decent deals, as these plans go. But before you sign up, see whether you can get coverage free. Some retailers and credit card companies provide extended coverage at no extra charge. Costco, for instance, adds a second year to the manufacturer's one-year warranty on TVs, computers and projectors. Gold and platinum MasterCards, Visa Signature cards and American Express cards all extend the manufacturer's warranty by up to one year when you buy items with the cards. American Express cards and Citi's new ThankYou Premier card will pay to repair broken items or replace lost purchases within 90 days—up to $1,000 per claim (the $450-per-year Platinum card has a limit of $10,000).

Devil in the details. Read the fine print carefully. The AppleCare Protection Plan for the iPad ($79) and the iPhone ($69) extends Apple's standard one year of repair or replacement coverage, plus 90 days of phone support, to two years. However, the plan doesn't cover damage caused by accidents. Nor will it replace a lost or stolen device.

Some service contracts that seem affordable and comprehensive provide coverage you may not need. The Costco SquareTrade plan, which costs just $30 for TVs under $500, extends coverage for mechanical and electrical failures for the third through the fifth years of ownership.

But a TV lemon generally turns sour right away. Says Jack Gillis, director of public affairs for the Consumer Federation of America: "Stick the cost of extended service contracts under your mattress, and save it for the next version of that product you want to buy." ∎

BUSINESS MATH ISSUE

Extended warranties are a waste of money.

1. List the key points of the article and information to support your position.
2. Write a group defense of your position using math calculations to support your view.

A Word Problem Approach—Chapters 6, 7, 8

1. Assume Kellogg's produced 715,000 boxes of Corn Flakes this year. This was 110% of the annual production last year. What was last year's annual production? *(p. 152)   LU 6-2(2)*

2. A new Sony camcorder has a list price of $420. The trade discount is 10/20 with terms of 2/10, n/30. If a retailer pays the invoice within the discount period, what is the amount the retailer must pay? *(pp. 182, 185)   LU 7-1(4), LU 7-2(1)*

3. JCPenney sells loafers with a markup of $40. If the markup is 30% on cost, what did the loafers cost JCPenney? Round to the nearest dollar. *(p. 213)   LU 8-1(3)*

4. Aster Computers received from Ring Manufacturers an invoice dated August 28 with terms 2/10 EOM. The list price of the invoice is $3,000 (freight not included). Ring offers Aster a 9/8/2 trade chain discount. Terms of freight are FOB shipping point, but Ring prepays the $150 freight. Assume Aster pays the invoice on October 9. How much will Ring receive? *(pp. 182, 185)   LU 7-1(4), LU 7-2(1)*

5. Runners World marks up its Nike jogging shoes 25% on selling price. The Nike shoe sells for $65. How much did the store pay for them? *(p. 217)   LU 8-2(4)*

6. Ivan Rone sells antique sleds. He knows that the most he can get for a sled is $350. Ivan needs a 35% markup on cost. Since Ivan is going to an antiques show, he wants to know the maximum he can offer a dealer for an antique sled. *(p. 213)   LU 8-1(3)*

7. Bonnie's Bakery bakes 60 loaves of bread for $1.10 each. Bonnie's estimates that 10% of the bread will spoil. Assume a 60% markup on cost. What is the selling price of each loaf? If Bonnie's can sell the old bread for one-half the cost, what is the selling price of each loaf? *(p. 222)   LU 8-3(2)*

Payroll

McDonald's Says It

Plan With Limits

McDonald's offers hourly workers a set of health-insurance plans that have low weekly premiums and low annual benefit caps. Details of the plans for individual policies for crew members:

	Premiums	Maximum annual benefit
BASIC PLAN	$13.99 (weekly) $727.48 (yearly)	$2,000
MEDIUM BENEFITS	$24.30 $1,263.60	$5,000 (outpatient; $1,500)
HIGHER BENEFITS	$32.30 $1,679.60	$10,000 (outpatient; $2,000)

What all of the plans pay for, up to annual maximum:

- 100% of visit to primary-care or specialist doctor, after $20 co-pay
- 100% of prescription drug costs, after $5 co-pay for generic and $50 co-pay for brand
- 70% of inpatient hospital services

Source: McDonald's benefit handout

LU 9–1: Calculating Various Types of Employees' Gross Pay

1. Define, compare, and contrast weekly, biweekly, semimonthly, and monthly pay periods *(p. 244).*

2. Calculate gross pay with overtime on the basis of time *(pp. 244–245).*

3. Calculate gross pay for piecework, differential pay schedule, straight commission with draw, variable commission scale, and salary plus commission *(pp. 245–247).*

LU 9–2: Computing Payroll Deductions for Employees' Pay; Employers' Responsibilities

1. Prepare and explain the parts of a payroll register *(pp. 248–251).*

2. Explain and calculate federal and state unemployment taxes *(pp. 251–252).*

VOCABULARY PREVIEW

Here are key terms in this chapter. After completing the chapter, if you know the term, place a checkmark in the parentheses. If you don't know the term, look it up and put the page number where it can be found.

Biweekly ( )   Deductions ( )   Differential pay schedule ( )   Draw ( )   Employee's Withholding Allowance Certificate (W-4) ( )   Fair Labor Standards Act ( )   Federal income tax withholding (FIT) ( )   Federal Insurance Contribution Act (FICA) ( )   Federal Unemployment Tax Act (FUTA) ( )   Gross pay ( )   Medicare ( )   Monthly ( )   Net pay ( )   Overrides ( )   Overtime ( )   Payroll register ( )   Percentage method ( )   Semimonthly ( )   Social Security ( )   State income tax (SIT) ( )   State Unemployment Tax Act (SUTA) ( )   Straight commission ( )   Variable commission scale ( )   W-4 ( )   Weekly ( )

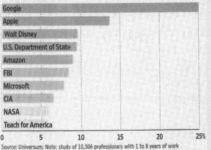

Google Is No. 1 on List Of Desired Employers

BY JOE LIGHT

One in four young professionals wants to work at **Google** Inc., according to a survey by Universum, a consulting firm that helps companies improve their attractiveness to prospective employees.

Nearly 25% of survey respondents picked Google, almost twice as many as chose **Apple** Inc., which ranked second. **Walt Disney** Co., the U.S. State Department and **Amazon.com** Inc. rounded out the top five.

To conduct the survey, Universum asked 10,306 young professionals—defined as college graduates with one to eight years of work experience—to pick as many as five ideal employers out of a list of 150.

Respondents also could write in companies not on the list. The top write-in was **Facebook** Inc., followed by the Department of Homeland Security and the United Nations.

Young professionals generally want to work at companies that the professionals like as consumers, said Kasia Do, a project manager for Universum. Such people also appear to be drawn to companies that seem financially strong and can offer

job stability, Ms. Do said.

Google, in particular, has tailored the image it projects to potential employees, said John Sullivan, a management professor at San Francisco State University.

The company regularly hosts open houses and tech-related talks in areas where it wants to recruit, said Yolanda Mangolini, director of outreach programs for Google. "It's incredibly powerful and helps them imagine themselves at Google," she said. The company also runs blogs, Twitter feeds and YouTube channels that try to show what it's like to work there, she said.

Government agencies, such as the National Aeronautics and Space Administration, the Federal Bureau of Investigation and the Central Intelligence Agency, also ranked in the top 10. That might be in part because the federal government hasn't laid off as many employees as the private sector has, Ms. Do said.

Plus, "Those government agencies can articulate a reason for being that gives employees a sense of purpose," said Jon Picoult of brand consultant Watermark Consulting. "For young people looking to make a difference in the world, they have a good story to tell."

Highly Recommended
Percentage of respondents who named the company as an ideal employer

Google, Apple, Walt Disney, U.S. Department of State, Amazon, FBI, Microsoft, CIA, NASA, Teach for America

Source: Universum; Note: study of 10,306 professionals with 1 to 8 years of work experience between November 2010 and January 2011; List only includes top 10 companies

Which company would you like to work for? The *Wall Street Journal* clip "Google Is No. 1 on List of Desired Employers" shows the results of a survey of young professionals. Note that the top write-in was Facebook.

This chapter discusses (1) the type of pay people work for, (2) how employers calculate paychecks and deductions, and (3) what employers must report and pay in taxes.

Learning Unit 9–1: Calculating Various Types of Employees' Gross Pay

LO 1

Logan Company manufactures dolls of all shapes and sizes. These dolls are sold world-wide. We study Logan Company in this unit because of the variety of methods Logan uses to pay its employees.

Companies usually pay employees **weekly, biweekly, semimonthly,** or **monthly.** How often employers pay employees can affect how employees manage their money. Some employees prefer a weekly paycheck that spreads the inflow of money. Employees who have monthly bills may find the twice-a-month or monthly paycheck more convenient. All employees would like more money to manage.

Let's assume you earn $50,000 per year. The following table shows what you would earn each pay period. Remember that 13 weeks equals one quarter. Four quarters or 52 weeks equals a year.

Salary paid	Period (based on a year)	Earnings for period (dollars)
Weekly	52 times (once a week)	$ 961.54 ($50,000 ÷ 52)
Biweekly	26 times (every two weeks)	$1,923.08 ($50,000 ÷ 26)
Semimonthly	24 times (twice a month)	$2,083.33 ($50,000 ÷ 24)
Monthly	12 times (once a month)	$4,166.67 ($50,000 ÷ 12)

Now let's look at some pay schedule situations and examples of how Logan Company calculates its payroll for employees of different pay status.

LO 2

Situation 1: Hourly Rate of Pay; Calculation of Overtime

The **Fair Labor Standards Act** sets minimum wage standards and overtime regulations for employees of companies covered by this federal law. The law provides that employees working for an hourly rate receive time-and-a-half pay for hours worked in excess of their regular 40-hour week. Many managerial people, however, are exempt from the time-and-a-half pay for all hours in excess of a 40-hour week. Other workers may also be exempt.

The current federal hourly minimum wage is $7.25. Various states have passed their own minimum wages. For example, in Illinois it is $8.25; Massachusetts, $8.00; Nevada, $8.25; Ohio, $7.70; Oregon, $8.80; and Washington, $9.04. Note in the *Wall Street Journal* clipping "Stacking Up" how the average hourly wage even varies by different occupations in New York City.

"Don't think of it as overtime. Think of it as an encore."

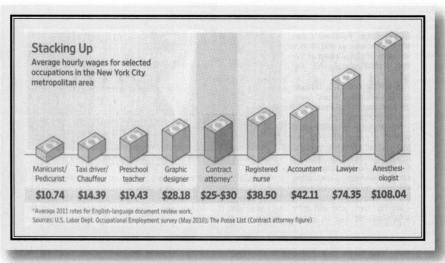

Stacking Up
Average hourly wages for selected occupations in the New York City metropolitan area

Manicurist/Pedicurist	Taxi driver/Chauffeur	Preschool teacher	Graphic designer	Contract attorney*	Registered nurse	Accountant	Lawyer	Anesthesiologist
$10.74	$14.39	$19.43	$28.18	$25–$30	$38.50	$42.11	$74.35	$108.04

*Average 2011 rates for English-language document review work.
Sources: U.S. Labor Dept. Occupational Employment survey (May 2010); The Posse List (Contract attorney figure)

Now we return to our Logan Company example. Logan Company is calculating the weekly pay of Ramon Valdez who works in its manufacturing division. For the first 40 hours Ramon works, Logan calculates his **gross pay** (earnings before **deductions**) as follows:

> Gross pay = Hours employee worked × Rate per hour

Ramon works more than 40 hours in a week. For every hour over his 40 hours, Ramon must be paid an **overtime** pay of at least 1.5 times his regular pay rate. The following formula is used to determine Ramon's overtime:

> Hourly overtime pay rate = Regular hourly pay rate × 1.5

Logan Company must include Ramon's overtime pay with his regular pay. To determine Ramon's gross pay, Logan uses the following formula:

> Gross pay = Earnings for 40 hours + Earnings at time-and-a-half rate (1.5)

We are now ready to calculate Ramon's gross pay from the following data:

EXAMPLE

Employee	M	T	W	Th	F	S	Total hours	Rate per hour
Ramon Valdez	13	$8\frac{1}{2}$	10	8	$11\frac{1}{4}$	$10\frac{3}{4}$	$61\frac{1}{2}$	$9

$$
\begin{array}{l}
61\frac{1}{2} \text{ total hours} \\
\underline{-40 \ \text{ regular hours}} \\
21\frac{1}{2} \text{ hours overtime}^1
\end{array}
\qquad \text{Time-and-a-half pay: } \$9 \times 1.5 = \$13.50
$$

$$
\begin{aligned}
\text{Gross pay} &= (40 \text{ hours} \times \$9) + (21\tfrac{1}{2} \text{ hours} \times \$13.50) \\
&= \quad \$360 \quad + \quad \$290.25 \\
&= \boxed{\$650.25}
\end{aligned}
$$

Note that the $13.50 overtime rate came out even. However, throughout the text, *if an overtime rate is greater than two decimal places, do not round it. Round only the final answer. This gives greater accuracy.*

Situation 2: Straight Piece Rate Pay

LO 3

Some companies, especially manufacturers, pay workers according to how much they produce. Logan Company pays Ryan Foss for the number of dolls he produces in a week. This gives Ryan an incentive to make more money by producing more dolls. Ryan receives $.96 per doll, less any defective units. The following formula determines Ryan's gross pay:

> Gross pay = Number of units produced × Rate per unit

Companies may also pay a guaranteed hourly wage and use a piece rate as a bonus. However, Logan uses straight piece rate as wages for some of its employees.

EXAMPLE During the last week of April, Ryan Foss produced 900 dolls. Using the above formula, Logan Company paid Ryan $864.

$$
\begin{aligned}
\text{Gross pay} &= 900 \text{ dolls} \times \$.96 \\
&= \boxed{\$864}
\end{aligned}
$$

---

[1]Some companies pay overtime for time over 8 hours in one day; Logan Company pays overtime for time over 40 hours per week.

Situation 3: Differential Pay Schedule

Some of Logan's employees can earn more than the $.96 straight piece rate for every doll they produce. Logan Company has set up a **differential pay schedule** for these employees. The company determines the rate these employees make by the amount of units the employees produce at different levels of production.

EXAMPLE   Logan Company pays Abby Rogers on the basis of the following schedule:

	Units produced	Amount per unit
First 50 →	1–50	$ .50
Next 100 →	51–150	.62
Next 50 →	151–200	.75
	Over 200	1.25

Last week Abby produced 300 dolls. What is Abby's gross pay?
    Logan calculated Abby's gross pay as follows:

$$(50 \times \$.50) + (100 \times \$.62) + (50 \times \$.75) + (100 \times \$1.25)$$

$$\$25 \quad + \quad \$62 \quad + \quad \$37.50 \quad + \quad \$125 \quad = \boxed{\$249.50}$$

Now we will study some of the other types of employee commission payment plans.

Situation 4: Straight Commission with Draw

Companies frequently use **straight commission** to determine the pay of salespersons. This commission is usually a certain percentage of the amount the salesperson sells. An example of one group of companies ceasing to pay commissions is the rental-car companies.

Companies such as Logan Company allow some of its salespersons to draw against their commission at the beginning of each month. A **draw** is an advance on the salesperson's commission. Logan subtracts this advance later from the employee's commission earned based on sales. When the commission does not equal the draw, the salesperson owes Logan the difference between the draw and the commission.

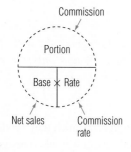

EXAMPLE   Logan Company pays Jackie Okamoto a straight commission of 15% on her net sales (net sales are total sales less sales returns). In May, Jackie had net sales of $56,000. Logan gave Jackie a $600 draw in May. What is Jackie's gross pay?
    Logan calculated Jackie's commission minus her draw as follows:

$$\$56,000 \times .15 = \$8,400$$
$$\underline{- \quad 600}$$
$$\boxed{\$7,800}$$

Logan Company pays some people in the sales department on a variable commission scale. Let's look at this, assuming the employee had no draw.

Situation 5: Variable Commission Scale

A company with a **variable commission scale** uses different commission rates for different levels of net sales.

EXAMPLE   Last month, Jane Ring's net sales were $160,000. What is Jane's gross pay based on the following schedule?

Up to $35,000	4%
Excess of $35,000 to $45,000	6%
Over $45,000	8%

$$\text{Gross pay} = (\$35,000 \times .04) + (\$10,000 \times .06) + (\$115,000 \times .08)$$

$$= \quad \$1,400 \quad + \quad \$600 \quad + \quad \$9,200$$

$$= \boxed{\$11,200}$$

MONEY tips

Understand the costs of credit. Do not spend money you do not currently have–especially if it is for entertainment. Avoid reaching or coming close to the maximum on your credit cards. Be careful to fully understand the terms of any credit card you use.

Situation 6: Salary Plus Commission

Logan Company pays Joe Roy a $3,000 monthly salary plus a 4% commission for sales over $20,000. Last month Joe's net sales were $50,000. Logan calculated Joe's gross monthly pay as follows:

Gross pay = Salary + (Commission × Sales over $20,000)

= $3,000 +   (.04 × $30,000)

= $3,000 + $1,200

= $4,200

Before you take the Practice Quiz, you should know that many managers today receive **overrides.** These managers receive a commission based on the net sales of the people they supervise.

LU 9–1 PRACTICE QUIZ

Complete this **Practice Quiz** to see how you are doing.

*For **extra help** from your authors–Sharon and Jeff–see the student DVD*

1. Jill Foster worked 52 hours in one week for Delta Airlines. Jill earns $10 per hour. What is Jill's gross pay, assuming overtime is at time-and-a-half?

2. Matt Long had $180,000 in sales for the month. Matt's commission rate is 9%, and he had a $3,500 draw. What was Matt's end-of-month commission?

3. Bob Meyers receives a $1,000 monthly salary. He also receives a variable commission on net sales based on the following schedule (commission doesn't begin until Bob earns $8,000 in net sales):

$8,000–$12,000	1%	Excess of $20,000 to $40,000	5%
Excess of $12,000 to $20,000	3%	More than $40,000	8%

   Assume Bob earns $40,000 net sales for the month. What is his gross pay?

✓ Solutions

1. 40 hours × $10.00 = $400.00
    12 hours × $15.00 =   180.00 ($10.00 × 1.5 = $15.00)
                         $580.00

2. $180,000 × .09 = $16,200
                      −   3,500
                        $12,700

3. Gross pay = $1,000 + ($4,000 × .01) + ($8,000 × .03) + ($20,000 × .05)
              = $1,000 + $40   + $240   + $1,000
              = $2,280

LU 9–1a EXTRA PRACTICE QUIZ WITH WORKED-OUT SOLUTIONS

Need more practice? Try this **Extra Practice Quiz** (check figures in the Interactive Chapter Organizer, p. 254). Worked-out Solutions can be found in Appendix B at end of text.

1. Jill Foster worked 54 hours in one week for Delta Airlines. Jill earns $12 per hour. What is Jill's gross pay, assuming overtime is at time-and-a-half?

2. Matt Long had $210,000 in sales for the month. Matt's commission rate is 8%, and he had a $4,000 draw. What was Matt's end-of-month commission?

3. Bob Myers receives a $1,200 monthly salary. He also receives a variable commission on net sales based on the following schedule (commission doesn't begin until Bob earns $9,000 in net sales).

$9,000 to $12,000	1%	Excess of $20,000 to $40,000	5%
Excess of $12,000 to $20,000	3%	More than $40,000	8%

   Assume Bob earns $60,000 net sales for the month. What is his gross pay?

Learning Unit 9–2: Computing Payroll Deductions for Employees' Pay; Employers' Responsibilities

The following *Wall Street Journal* clip, "Pay Check," shows the average income of the most and least stressful jobs.

This unit begins by dissecting a paycheck. Then we give you an insight into the tax responsibilities of employers.

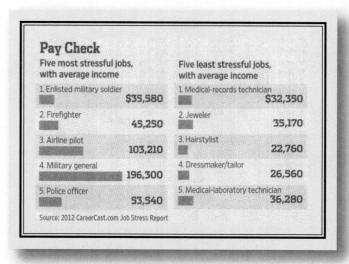

Pay Check

Five most stressful jobs, with average income		Five least stressful jobs, with average income	
1. Enlisted military soldier	$35,580	1. Medical-records technician	$32,350
2. Firefighter	45,250	2. Jeweler	35,170
3. Airline pilot	103,210	3. Hairstylist	22,760
4. Military general	196,300	4. Dressmaker/tailor	26,560
5. Police officer	53,540	5. Medical-laboratory technician	36,280

Source: 2012 CareerCast.com Job Stress Report

Reprinted with permission of *The Wall Street Journal*, Copyright © 2012 Dow Jones & Company, Inc. All Rights Reserved Worldwide.

LO 1

Computing Payroll Deductions for Employees

Companies often record employee payroll information in a multicolumn form called a **payroll register.** The increased use of computers in business has made computerized registers a time-saver for many companies.

Glo Company uses a multicolumn payroll register. Below is Glo's partial payroll register showing the payroll information for Alice Rey during week 49. Let's check each column to see if Alice's take-home pay of $1,517.81 is correct. Note how the circled letters in the register correspond to the explanations that follow.

GLO COMPANY
Payroll Register
Week #49

Employee name	Allow. & marital status	Cum. earn.	Sal. per week	Earnings			Cum. earn.	FICA Taxable Earnings		FICA				Health ins.	Net pay
				Reg.	Ovt.	Gross		S.S.	Med.	S.S.	Med.	FIT	SIT		
Rey, Alice	M-2	108,000	2,250	2,250	—	2,250	110,250	2,100	2,250	130.20	32.63	334.36	135	100	1,517.81
	(A)	(B)	(C)		(D)		(E)	(F)	(G)	(H)	(I)	(J)	(K)	(L)	(M)

Payroll Register Explanations
(A)—Allowance and marital status
(B), (C), (D)—Cumulative earnings before payroll, salaries, earnings
(E)—Cumulative earnings after payroll

When Alice was hired, she completed the **W-4 (Employee's Withholding Allowance Certificate)** form shown in Figure 9.1 stating that she is married and claims an allowance (exemption) of 2. Glo Company will need this information to calculate the federal income tax (J).

Before this pay period, Alice has earned $108,000 (48 weeks × $2,250 salary per week). Since Alice receives no overtime, her $2,250 salary per week represents her gross pay (pay before any deductions).

After this pay period, Alice has earned $110,250 ($108,000 + $2,250).

FIGURE 9.1

Employee's W-4 form

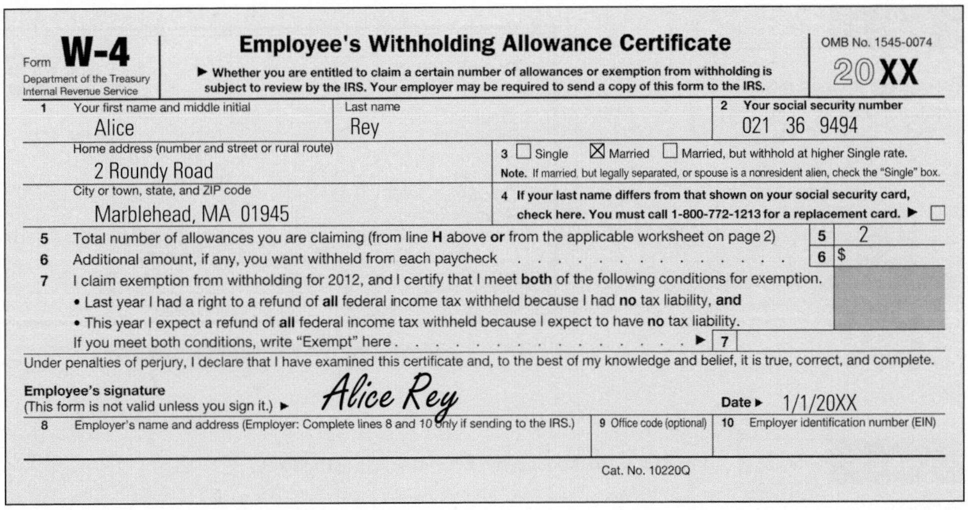

Form **W-4** Department of the Treasury Internal Revenue Service

Employee's Withholding Allowance Certificate

▶ Whether you are entitled to claim a certain number of allowances or exemption from withholding is subject to review by the IRS. Your employer may be required to send a copy of this form to the IRS.

OMB No. 1545-0074 **20XX**

1 Your first name and middle initial: Alice | Last name: Rey | 2 Your social security number: 021 36 9494

Home address (number and street or rural route): 2 Roundy Road | 3 ☐ Single ☒ Married ☐ Married, but withhold at higher Single rate. Note. If married, but legally separated, or spouse is a nonresident alien, check the "Single" box.

City or town, state, and ZIP code: Marblehead, MA 01945 | 4 If your last name differs from that shown on your social security card, check here. You must call 1-800-772-1213 for a replacement card. ▶ ☐

5 Total number of allowances you are claiming (from line **H** above **or** from the applicable worksheet on page 2) 5 2

6 Additional amount, if any, you want withheld from each paycheck . . . 6 $

7 I claim exemption from withholding for 2012, and I certify that I meet **both** of the following conditions for exemption.
- Last year I had a right to a refund of **all** federal income tax withheld because I had **no** tax liability, **and**
- This year I expect a refund of **all** federal income tax withheld because I expect to have **no** tax liability.

If you meet both conditions, write "Exempt" here . . . ▶ 7

Under penalties of perjury, I declare that I have examined this certificate and, to the best of my knowledge and belief, it is true, correct, and complete.

Employee's signature (This form is not valid unless you sign it.) ▶ Alice Rey   **Date ▶** 1/1/20XX

8 Employer's name and address (Employer: Complete lines 8 and 10 only if sending to the IRS.) | 9 Office code (optional) | 10 Employer identification number (EIN)

Cat. No. 10220Q

The **Federal Insurance Contribution Act (FICA)** funds the **Social Security** program. The program includes Old Age and Disability, Medicare, Survivor Benefits, and so on. The FICA tax requires separate reporting for Social Security and **Medicare.** We will use the following rates for Glo Company:

	Rate	Base
Social Security	6.20%	$110,100
Medicare	1.45	No base

These rates mean that Alice Rey will pay Social Security taxes on the first $110,100 she earns this year. After earning $110,100, Alice's wages will be exempt from Social Security. Note that Alice will be paying Medicare taxes on all wages since Medicare has no base cutoff.

Ⓕ,Ⓖ—Taxable earnings for Social Security and Medicare

To help keep Glo's record straight, the *taxable earnings column only shows what wages will be taxed. This amount is not the tax.* For example, in week 49, only $2,100 of Alice's salary will be taxable for Social Security.

$110,100 Social Security base
− 108,000 Ⓑ
$ 2,100

Ⓗ—Social Security

To calculate Alice's Social Security tax, we multiply $2,100 Ⓕ by 6.2%:

$2,100 × .062 = **$130.20**

Ⓘ—Medicare

Since Medicare has no base, Alice's entire weekly salary is taxed 1.45%, which is multiplied by $2,250.

$2,250 × .0145 = **$32.63**

Ⓙ—FIT

Using the W-4 form Alice completed, Glo deducts **federal income tax withholding (FIT).** The more allowances an employee claims, the less money Glo deducts from the employee's paycheck. Glo uses the percentage method to calculate FIT.[2]

The Percentage Method[3] Today, since many companies do not want to store the tax tables, they use computers for their payroll. These companies use the **percentage method.** For this method we use Table 9.1 and Table 9.2 on page 250 from Circular E to calculate Alice's FIT.

Step 1. In Table 9.1, locate the weekly withholding for one allowance. Multiply this number by 2.

$73.08 × 2 = $146.16

[2]The *Business Math Handbook* has a sample of the wage bracket method.

[3]An alternative method is the wage bracket method shown in the *Business Math Handbook.*

TABLE 9.1

Percentage method income tax withholding allowances

Payroll Period	One Withholding Allowance
Weekly	$ 73.08
Biweekly	146.15
Semimonthly	158.33
Monthly	316.67
Quarterly	950.00
Semiannually	1,900.00
Annually	3,800.00
Daily or miscellaneous (each day of the payroll period)	14.62

TABLE 9.2   Percentage method income tax withholding schedules

TABLE 1—WEEKLY Payroll Period

(a) SINGLE person (including head of household)—

If the amount of wages (after subtracting withholding allowances) is: The amount of income tax to withhold is:

Not over $41 . . . . $0

Over—	But not over—		of excess over—
$41	—$209	. . . . $0.00 plus 10%	—$41
$209	—$721	. . . . $16.80 plus 15%	—$209
$721	—$1,688	. . . . $93.60 plus 25%	—$721
$1,688	—$3,477	. . . . $335.35 plus 28%	—$1,688
$3,477	—$7,510	. . . . $836.27 plus 33%	—$3,477
$7,510	. . . .	$2,167.16 plus 35%	—$7,510

(b) MARRIED person—

If the amount of wages (after subtracting withholding allowances) is: The amount of income tax to withhold is:

Not over $156 . . . . $0

Over—	But not over—		of excess over—
$156	—$490	. . . . $0.00 plus 10%	—$156
$490	—$1,515	. . . . $33.40 plus 15%	—$490
$1,515	—$2,900	. . . . $187.15 plus 25%	—$1,515
$2,900	—$4,338	. . . . $533.40 plus 28%	—$2,900
$4,338	—$7,624	. . . . $936.04 plus 33%	—$4,338
$7,624	. . . .	$2,020.42 plus 35%	—$7,624

TABLE 2—BIWEEKLY Payroll Period

(a) SINGLE person (including head of household)—

If the amount of wages (after subtracting withholding allowances) is: The amount of income tax to withhold is:

Not over $83 . . . . $0

Over—	But not over—		of excess over—
$83	—$417	. . . . $0.00 plus 10%	—$83
$417	—$1,442	. . . . $33.40 plus 15%	—$417
$1,442	—$3,377	. . . . $187.15 plus 25%	—$1,442
$3,377	—$6,954	. . . . $670.90 plus 28%	—$3,377
$6,954	—$15,019	. . . . $1,672.46 plus 33%	—$6,954
$15,019	. . . .	$4,333.91 plus 35%	—$15,019

(b) MARRIED person—

If the amount of wages (after subtracting withholding allowances) is: The amount of income tax to withhold is:

Not over $312 . . . . $0

Over—	But not over—		of excess over—
$312	—$981	. . . . $0.00 plus 10%	—$312
$981	—$3,031	. . . . $66.90 plus 15%	—$981
$3,031	—$5,800	. . . . $374.40 plus 25%	—$3,031
$5,800	—$8,675	. . . . $1,066.65 plus 28%	—$5,800
$8,675	—$15,248	. . . . $1,871.65 plus 33%	—$8,675
$15,248	. . . .	$4,040.74 plus 35%	—$15,248

TABLE 3—SEMIMONTHLY Payroll Period

(a) SINGLE person (including head of household)—

If the amount of wages (after subtracting withholding allowances) is: The amount of income tax to withhold is:

Not over $90 . . . . $0

Over—	But not over—		of excess over—
$90	—$452	. . . . $0.00 plus 10%	—$90
$452	—$1,563	. . . . $36.20 plus 15%	—$452
$1,563	—$3,658	. . . . $202.85 plus 25%	—$1,563
$3,658	—$7,533	. . . . $726.60 plus 28%	—$3,658
$7,533	—$16,271	. . . . $1,811.60 plus 33%	—$7,533
$16,271	. . . .	$4,695.14 plus 35%	—$16,271

(b) MARRIED person—

If the amount of wages (after subtracting withholding allowances) is: The amount of income tax to withhold is:

Not over $338 . . . . $0

Over—	But not over—		of excess over—
$338	—$1,063	. . . . $0.00 plus 10%	—$338
$1,063	—$3,283	. . . . $72.50 plus 15%	—$1,063
$3,283	—$6,283	. . . . $405.50 plus 25%	—$3,283
$6,283	—$9,398	. . . . $1,155.50 plus 28%	—$6,283
$9,398	—$16,519	. . . . $2,027.70 plus 33%	—$9,398
$16,519	. . . .	$4,377.63 plus 35%	—$16,519

TABLE 4—MONTHLY Payroll Period

(a) SINGLE person (including head of household)—

If the amount of wages (after subtracting withholding allowances) is: The amount of income tax to withhold is:

Not over $179 . . . . $0

Over—	But not over—		of excess over—
$179	—$904	. . . . $0.00 plus 10%	—$179
$904	—$3,125	. . . . $72.50 plus 15%	—$904
$3,125	—$7,317	. . . . $405.65 plus 25%	—$3,125
$7,317	—$15,067	. . . . $1,453.65 plus 28%	—$7,317
$15,067	—$32,542	. . . . $3,623.65 plus 33%	—$15,067
$32,542	. . . .	$9,390.40 plus 35%	—$32,542

(b) MARRIED person—

If the amount of wages (after subtracting withholding allowances) is: The amount of income tax to withhold is:

Not over $675 . . . . $0

Over—	But not over—		of excess over—
$675	—$2,125	. . . . $0.00 plus 10%	—$675
$2,125	—$6,567	. . . . $145.00 plus 15%	—$2,125
$6,567	—$12,567	. . . . $811.30 plus 25%	—$6,567
$12,567	—$18,796	. . . . $2,311.30 plus 28%	—$12,567
$18,796	—$33,038	. . . . $4,055.42 plus 33%	—$18,796
$33,038	. . . .	$8,755.28 plus 35%	—$33,038

Step 2. Subtract $146.16 in Step 1 from Alice's total pay.

$$\begin{array}{r} \$2,250.00 \\ -\ \ \ 146.16 \\ \hline \$2,103.84 \end{array}$$

Step 3. In Table 9.2, locate the married person's weekly pay table. The $2,103.84 falls between $1,515 and $2,900. The tax is $187.15 plus 25% of the excess over $1,515.

$$\begin{array}{r} \$2,103.84 \\ -\ 1,515.00 \\ \hline \$\ \ \ 588.84 \end{array}$$

Tax $187.15 + .25\ (\$588.84)$

$187.15 + \$147.21 = \boxed{\$334.36}$

We assume a 6% **state income tax (SIT).**

$2,250 \times .06 = \boxed{\$135.00}$

Alice contributes $100 per week for health insurance.
Alice's **net pay** is her gross pay less all deductions.

$$\begin{array}{rl} \$2,250.00 & \text{gross} \\ -\ \ \ 130.20 & \text{Social Security} \\ -\ \ \ \ \ 32.63 & \text{Medicare} \\ -\ \ \ 334.36 & \text{FIT} \\ -\ \ \ 135.00 & \text{SIT} \\ -\ \ \ 100.00 & \text{health insurance} \\ \hline =\ \$1,517.81 & \text{net pay} \end{array}$$

Employers' Responsibilities

The chapter opener shows the benefits plan McDonald's is offering its hourly workers. In the first section of this unit, we saw that Alice contributed to Social Security and Medicare. Glo Company has the legal responsibility to match her contributions. Besides matching Social Security and Medicare, Glo must pay two important taxes that employees do not have to pay—federal and state unemployment taxes.

Federal Unemployment Tax Act (FUTA)   The federal government participates in a joint federal-state unemployment program to help unemployed workers. At this writing, employers pay the government a 6.2% **FUTA** tax on the first $7,000 paid to employees as wages during the calendar year. Any wages in excess of $7,000 per worker are exempt wages and are not taxed for FUTA. If the total cumulative amount the employer owes the government is less than $100, the employer can pay the liability yearly (end of January in the following calendar year). If the tax is greater than $100, the employer must pay it within a month after the quarter ends.

Companies involved in a state unemployment tax fund can usually take a 5.4% credit against their FUTA tax. *In reality, then, companies are paying .8% (.008) to the federal unemployment program.* In all our calculations, FUTA is .008.

EXAMPLE   Assume a company had total wages of $19,000 in a calendar year. No employee earned more than $7,000 during the calendar year. The FUTA tax is .8% (6.2% minus the company's 5.4% credit for state unemployment tax). How much does the company pay in FUTA tax?

The company calculates its FUTA tax as follows:

$$\begin{array}{rl} 6.2\% & \text{FUTA tax} \\ -\ 5.4\% & \text{credit for SUTA tax} \\ \hline =\ .8\% & \text{tax for FUTA} \end{array}$$

$.008 \times \$19,000 = \boxed{\$152}$ FUTA tax due to federal government

© Corbis/RF

LO 2

MONEY tips

The IRS has twelve items it looks for on a return that raise the chances of an audit from the average rate of 1.1%: making too much money; failing to report all taxable income; taking large charitable deductions; claiming the home office deduction; claiming rental losses; deducting business meals, travel, and entertainment; claiming 100% business use of a vehicle; writing off a loss for a hobby; running a cash business; failing to report a foreign bank account; engaging in currency transactions; and taking higher-than-average deductions.

Ⓚ—SIT

Ⓛ—Health insurance
Ⓜ—Net pay

State Unemployment Tax Act (SUTA)   The current **SUTA** tax in many states is 5.4% on the first $7,000 the employer pays an employee. Some states offer a merit rating system that results in a lower SUTA rate for companies with a stable employment period. The federal government still allows 5.4% credit on FUTA tax to companies entitled to the lower SUTA rate. Usually states also charge companies with a poor employment record a higher SUTA rate. However, these companies cannot take any more than the 5.4% credit against the 6.2% federal unemployment rate.

EXAMPLE   Assume a company has total wages of $20,000 and $4,000 of the wages are exempt from SUTA. What are the company's SUTA and FUTA taxes if the company's SUTA rate is 5.8% due to a poor employment record?

The exempt wages (over $7,000 earnings per worker) are not taxed for SUTA or FUTA. So the company owes the following SUTA and FUTA taxes:

$20,000
$-\underline{4,000}$ (exempt wages)
$\overline{\$16,000} \times .058 = \boxed{\$928}$ SUTA

Federal FUTA tax would then be:
$\$16,000 \times .008 = \boxed{\$128}$

You can check your progress with the following Practice Quiz.

LU 9–2   PRACTICE QUIZ

Complete this **Practice Quiz** to see how you are doing.

*For **extra help** from your authors–Sharon and Jeff–see the student DVD*

You Tube

1. Calculate Social Security taxes, Medicare taxes, and FIT for Joy Royce. Joy's company pays her a monthly salary of $9,500. She is single and claims 1 deduction. Before this payroll, Joy's cumulative earnings were $106,600. (Social Security maximum is 6.2% on $110,100, and Medicare is 1.45%.) Calculate FIT by the percentage method.

2. Jim Brewer, owner of Arrow Company, has three employees who earn $300, $700, and $900 a week. Assume a state SUTA rate of 5.1%. What will Jim pay for state and federal unemployment taxes for the first quarter?

✓ Solutions

1. **Social Security**

$110,100
$-\underline{106,600}$
$\overline{\$3,500} \times .062 = \boxed{\$217.00}$

Medicare

$\$9,500 \times .0145 = \$137.75$

FIT

Percentage method: $9,500.00
$\$316.67 \times 1 =$ $\underline{-316.67}$ (Table 9.1)
$\$9,183.33$

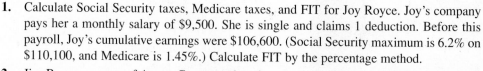

$7,317 to $15,067 ➞ $1,453.65 plus 28% of excess over $7,317
(Table 9.2)

$9,183.33
$-\underline{7,317.00}$
$\overline{\$1,866.33} \times .28 =$ $\$522.57$
$+\underline{1,453.65}$
$\boxed{\$1,976.22}$

2. 13 weeks × $300 = $ 3,900
    13 weeks × $700 =   9,100 ($9,100 − $7,000) ➞ $2,100 ⎫ Exempt wages
    13 weeks × $900 = $\underline{11,700}$ ($11,700 − $7,000) ➞ $\underline{4,700}$ ⎬ (not taxed for
    $\$24,700$ $\$6,800$ ⎭ FUTA or SUTA)

    $24,700 − $6,800 = $17,900 taxable wages
    SUTA = .051 × $17,900 = $\boxed{\$912.90}$
    FUTA = .008 × $17,900 = $\boxed{\$143.20}$

    Note: FUTA remains at .008 whether SUTA rate is higher or lower than standard.

LU 9–2a **EXTRA PRACTICE QUIZ WITH WORKED-OUT SOLUTIONS**

Need more practice? Try this **Extra Practice Quiz** (check figures in the Interactive Chapter Organizer, p. 254). Worked-out Solutions can be found in Appendix B at end of text.

1. Calculate Social Security taxes, Medicare taxes, and FIT for Joy Royce. Joy's company pays her a monthly salary of $10,000. She is single and claims 1 deduction. Before this payroll, Joy's cumulative earnings were $109,600. (Social Security maximum is 6.2% on $110,100, and Medicare is 1.45%.) Calculate FIT by the percentage method.

2. Jim Brewer, owner of Arrow Company, has three employees who earn $200, $800, and $950 a week. Assume a state SUTA rate of 5.1%. What will Jim pay for state and federal unemployment taxes for the first quarter?

INTERACTIVE CHAPTER ORGANIZER

Topic/procedure/formula	Examples	You try it*
Gross pay, p. 245 Hours employee worked × Rate per hour	$6.50 per hour at 36 hours Gross pay = 36 × $6.50 = $234	**Calculate gross pay** $9.25 per hour; 38 hours
Overtime, p. 245 Gross earnings (pay) = Regular pay + Earnings at overtime rate $(1\frac{1}{2})$	$6 per hour; 42 hours Gross pay = (40 × $6) + (2 × $9) = $240 + $18 = $258	**Calculate gross pay** $7 per hour; 43 hours
Straight piece rate, p. 245 Gross pay = Number of units produced × Rate per unit	1,185 units; rate per unit, $.89 Gross pay = 1,185 × $.89 = $1,054.65	**Calculate gross pay** 2,250 units; $.79 per unit
Differential pay schedule, p. 246 Rate on each item is related to the number of items produced.	1–500 at $.84; 501–1,000 at $.96; 900 units produced. Gross pay = (500 × $.84) + (400 × $.96) = $420 + $384 = $804	**Calculate gross pay** 1–600 at $.79; 601–1,000 at $.88; 900 produced
Straight commission, p. 246 Total sales × Commission rate Any draw would be subtracted from earnings.	$155,000 sales; 6% commission $155,000 × .06 = $9,300	**Calculate straight commission** $175,000 sales; 7% commission
Variable commission scale, p. 246 Sales at different levels pay different rates of commission.	Up to $5,000, 5%; $5,001 to $10,000, 8%; over $10,000, 10% Sold: $6,500 Solution: ($5,000 × .05) + ($1,500 × .08) = $250 + $120 = $370	**Calculate commission** Up to $6,000, 5%; $6,001 to $8,000, 9%; Over $8,000, 12% Sold: $12,000
Salary plus commission, p. 247 Regular wages (fixed) + Commissions earned	Base $400 per week + 2% on sales over $14,000 Actual sales: $16,000 $400 (base) + (.02 × $2,000) = $440	**Calculate gross pay** Base $600 per week plus 4% on sales over $16,000. Actual sales $22,000.
Payroll register, p. 248 Multicolumn form to record payroll. Married and paid weekly. (Table 9.2) Claims 1 allowance. FICA rates from chapter.	<table><tr><td rowspan="2">Earnings Gross</td><td colspan="3">Deductions</td><td rowspan="2">Net pay</td></tr><tr><td colspan="3">FICA</td></tr><tr><td></td><td>S.S.</td><td>Med.</td><td>FIT</td><td></td></tr><tr><td>1,515</td><td>93.93</td><td>21.97</td><td>176.19</td><td>1,222.91</td></tr></table>	**Calculate net pay** Gross pay, $490; Married, paid weekly. Claims, one allowance. Use rates in text for Social Security, Medicare, and FIT.
FICA, p. 249 **Social Security Medicare** 6.2% on $110,100 (S.S.) 1.45% (Med.)	If John earns $120,000, what did he contribute for the year to Social Security and Medicare? S.S.: $110,100 × .062 = $6,826.20 Med.: $120,000 × .0145 = $1,740.00	**Calculate FICA** If John earns $150,000, what did he contribute to Social Security and Medicare?

(continues)

INTERACTIVE CHAPTER ORGANIZER

Topic/procedure/formula	Examples	You try it*

FIT calculation (percentage method), pp. 249–251
Facts:
  Al Doe: Married
  Claims: 2
  Paid weekly: $1,600
	$1,600.00
	− 146.16 ($73.08 × 2) Table 9.1
	$1,453.84
	By Table 9.2
	  $1,453.84
	− 490.00
	$ 963.84
	$33.40 + .15($963.84)
	$33.40 + $144.58 = $177.98
		Calculate FIT
		Jim Smith, married, claims 3;
		Paid weekly, $1,400

State and federal unemployment, pp. 251–252 Employer pays these taxes. Rates are 6.2% on $7,000 for federal and 5.4% for state on $7,000. 6.2% − 5.4% = .8% federal rate after credit. If state unemployment rate is higher than 5.4%, no additional credit is taken. If state unemployment rate is less than 5.4%, the full 5.4% credit can be taken for federal unemployment.	Cumulative pay before payroll, $6,400; this week's pay, $800. What are state and federal unemployment taxes for employer, assuming a 5.2% state unemployment rate? State → .052 × $600 = $31.20 Federal → .008 × $600 = $4.80 ($6,400 + $600 = $7,000 maximum)	**Calculate SUTA and FUTA** Cumulative pay before payroll, $6,800. This week's payroll, $9,000. State rate is 5.4%.

| **KEY TERMS** | Biweekly, p. 244
Deductions, p. 245
Differential pay schedule, p. 246
Draw, p. 246
Employee's Withholding Allowance
  Certificate (W-4), p. 248
Fair Labor Standards Act, p. 244
Federal income tax withholding
  (FIT), p. 249
Federal Insurance Contribution
  Act (FICA), p. 249 | Federal Unemployment Tax Act
  (FUTA), p. 251
Gross pay, p. 245
Medicare, p. 249
Monthly, p. 244
Net pay, p. 251
Overrides, p. 247
Overtime, p. 245
Payroll register, p. 248
Percentage method, p. 249
Semimonthly, p. 244 | Social Security, p. 249
State income tax (SIT), p. 251
State Unemployment Tax Act
  (SUTA), p. 252
Straight commission, p. 246
Variable commission
  scale, p. 246
W-4, p. 248
Weekly, p. 244 |
| **Check Figures for Extra Practice Quizzes with Page References. (Worked-out Solutions in Appendix B.)** | LU 9–1a (p. 247)
1. $732
2. $12,800
3. $4,070 | LU 9–2a (p. 253)
1. $31; 145; $2,116.22
2. $846.60; $132.80 |

*Worked-out solutions are in Appendix B.

Critical Thinking Discussion Questions with Chapter Concept Check

1. Explain the difference between biweekly and semimonthly. Explain what problems may develop if a retail store hires someone on straight commission to sell cosmetics.

2. Explain what each column of a payroll register records (p. 248) and how each number is calculated. Social Security tax is based on a specific rate and base; Medicare tax is based on a rate but has no base. Do you think this is fair to all taxpayers?

3. What taxes are the responsibility of the employer? How can an employer benefit from a merit-rating system for state unemployment?

4. **Chapter Concept Check.** Visit the Starbucks website to see how its benefits plan compares to McDonald's health insurance plan discussed in the chapter opener. Be sure to discuss the responsibilities of the employee and the employer.

END-OF-CHAPTER PROBLEMS

Check figures for odd-numbered problems in Appendix C.

Name _____ Date _____

DRILL PROBLEMS

Complete the following table: *LU 9-1(2)*

Employee	M	T	W	Th	F	Hours	Rate per hour	Gross pay
9–1. Roger Rial	11	6	9	7	6		$7.95	
9–2. Kristina Shaw	5	9	10	8	8		$8.10	

Complete the following table (assume the overtime for each employee is a time-and-a-half rate after 40 hours): *LU 9-1(2)*

Employee	M	T	W	Th	F	Sa	Total regular hours	Total overtime hours	Regular rate	Overtime rate	Gross earnings
9–3. Blue	12	9	9	9	9	3			$8.00		
9–4. Tagney	14	8	9	9	5	1			$7.60		

Calculate gross earnings: *LU 9-1(3)*

Worker	Number of units produced	Rate per unit	Gross earnings
9–5. Lang	480	$3.50	
9–6. Swan	846	$ .58	

Calculate the gross earnings for each apple picker based on the following differential pay scale: *LU 9-1(3)*

1–1,000: $.03 each	1,001–1,600: $.05 each	Over 1,600: $.07 each

Apple picker	Number of apples picked	Gross earnings
9–7. Ryan	1,600	
9–8. Rice	1,925	

Calculate the end-of-month commission. *LU 9-1(3)*

Employee	Total sales	Commission rate	Draw	End-of-month commission received
9–9. Reese	$300,000	7%	$8,000	

Ron Company has the following commission schedule:

Commission rate	Sales
2%	Up to $80,000
3.5%	Excess of $80,000 to $100,000
4%	More than $100,000

Calculate the gross earnings of Ron Company's two employees: *LU 9-1(3)*

Employee	Total sales	Gross earnings
9–10. Bill Moore	$ 70,000	
9–11. Ron Ear	$155,000	

Complete the following table, given that A Publishing Company pays its salespeople a weekly salary plus a 2% commission on all net sales over $5,000 (no commission on returned goods): *LU 9-1(3)*

	Employee	Gross sales	Return	Net sales	Given quota	Commission sales	Commission rates	Total commission	Regular wage	Total wage
9–12. eXcel	Ring	$ 8,000	$ 25		$5,000		2%		$250	
9–13. eXcel	Porter	$12,000	$100		$5,000		2%		$250	

Calculate the Social Security and Medicare deductions for the following employees (assume a tax rate of 6.2% on $110,100 for Social Security and 1.45% for Medicare): *LU 9-2(1)*

	Employee	Cumulative earnings before this pay period	Pay amount this period	Social Security	Medicare
9–14.	Logan	$110,000	$3,000		
9–15.	Rouche	$104,000	$7,000		
9–16.	Cleaves	$400,000	$6,000		

Complete the following payroll register. Calculate FIT by the percentage method for this weekly period; Social Security and Medicare are the same rates as in the previous problems. No one will reach the maximum for FICA. *LU 9-2(1)*

	Employee	Marital status	Allowances claimed	Gross pay	FIT	FICA S.S.	Med.	Net pay
9–17.	Mike Rice	M	2	$1,600				
9–18.	Pat Brown	M	4	$2,100				

9–19. Given the following, calculate the state (assume 5.3%) and federal unemployment taxes that the employer must pay for each of the first two quarters. The federal unemployment tax is .8% on the first $7,000.   *LU 9-2(2)*

PAYROLL SUMMARY		
	Quarter 1	Quarter 2
Bill Adams	$4,000	$ 8,000
Rich Haines	8,000	14,000
Alice Smooth	3,200	3,800

WORD PROBLEMS

9–20. Lai Xiaodong, a 22-year-old college-educated man, accepted a job at Foxconn Technology (where the iPad was being produced for Apple) in Chengdu, China, for $22 a day at 12 hours a day, 6 days a week. A company perk included company housing in dorms for the 70,000 employees. It was common for 20 people to be assigned to the same three-bedroom apartment. What were Lai's hourly (rounded to the nearest cent), weekly, and annual gross pay?   *LU 9-1(1)*

9–21. Rhonda Brennan found her first job after graduating from college through the classifieds of the *Miami Herald*. She was delighted when the offer came through at $18.50 per hour. She completed her W-4 stating that she is married with a child and claims an allowance of 3. Her company will pay her biweekly for 80 hours. Calculate her take-home pay for her first check. *LU 9-2(1)*

9–22. The Social Security Administration increased the taxable wage base from $106,800 to $110,100. The 6.2% tax rate is unchanged. Joe Burns earned over $120,000 each of the past two years. **(a)** What is the percent increase in the base? Round to the nearest hundredth percent. **(b)** What is Joe's increase in Social Security tax for the new year?   *LU 9-2(1)*

9–23. In an effort to stimulate economic growth, President Obama proposed "The American Jobs Act," which reduced both employer and employee payroll taxes from 6.2% to 3.1%. If the act passed as originated, how much would Juan Carlos Soto, Jr., have saved in his net pay if he earned $6,548 in March 2012 with earnings to date of $24,356? (Round to the nearest cent.)   *LU 9-2(1)*

9–24. Maggie Vitteta, single, works 38 hours per week at $9.00 an hour. How much is taken out for federal income tax with one withholding exemption? *LU 9-2(1)*

9–25. Robin Hartman earns $600 per week plus 3% of sales over $6,500. Robin's sales are $14,000. How much does Robin earn? *LU 9-1(3)*

9–26. Pat Maninen earns a gross salary of $3,000 each week. What are Pat's first week's deductions for Social Security and Medicare? Will any of Pat's wages be exempt from Social Security and Medicare for the calendar year? Assume a rate of 6.2% on $110,100 for Social Security and 1.45% for Medicare. *LU 9-2(1)*

9–27. Richard Gaziano is a manager for Health Care, Inc. Health Care deducts Social Security, Medicare, and FIT (by percentage method) from his earnings. Assume the same Social Security and Medicare rates as in Problem 9–26. Before this payroll, Richard is $1,000 below the maximum level for Social Security earnings. Richard is married, is paid weekly, and claims 2 exemptions. What is Richard's net pay for the week if he earns $1,300? *LU 9-2(1)*

9–28. Len Mast earned $2,200 for the last 2 weeks. He is married, is paid biweekly, and claims 3 exemptions. What is Len's income tax? Use the percentage method. *LU 9-2(1)*

9–29. Westway Company pays Suzie Chan $2,200 per week. By the end of week 51, how much did Westway deduct for Suzie's *eXcel* Social Security and Medicare for the year? Assume Social Security is 6.2% on $110,100 and 1.45% for Medicare. What state and federal unemployment taxes does Westway pay on Suzie's yearly salary? The state unemployment rate is 5.1%. FUTA is .8%. *LU 9-2(1, 2)*

9–30. Morris Leste, owner of Carlson Company, has three employees who earn $400, $500, and $700 per week. What are the total state and federal unemployment taxes that Morris owes for the first 11 weeks of the year and for week 30? Assume a state rate of 5.6% and a federal rate of .8%. *LU 9-2(2)*

9–31. Tiffani Lind earned $1,200 during her biweekly pay period. She is married and claims 4 deductions. Her annual earnings *eXcel* to date are $52,521. Calculate her net pay.   *LU 9-2(1)*

CHALLENGE PROBLEMS

9–32. The San Bernardino County Fair hires about 150 people during fair time. Their wages range from $6.75 to $8.00. California has a state income tax of 9%. Sandy Denny earns $8.00 per hour; George Barney earns $6.75 per hour. They both worked 35 hours this week. Both are married; however, Sandy claims 2 exemptions and George claims 1 exemption. Assume a rate of 6.2% on $110,100 for Social Security and 1.45% for Medicare. **(a)** What is Sandy's net pay after FIT (use the tables in the text), Social Security tax, state income tax, and Medicare have been taken out? **(b)** What is George's net pay after the same deductions? **(c)** How much more is Sandy's net pay versus George's net pay? Round to the nearest cent.   *LU 9-2(1)*

9–33. Bill Rose is a salesperson for Boxes, Inc. He believes his $1,460.47 monthly paycheck is in error. Bill earns a $1,400 salary per month plus a 9.5% commission on sales over $1,500. Last month, Bill had $8,250 in sales. Bill believes his traveling expenses are 16% of his weekly gross earnings before commissions. Monthly deductions include Social Security, $126.56; Medicare, $29.60; FIT, $189.50; union dues, $25.00; and health insurance, $16.99. Calculate the following: **(a)** Bill's monthly take-home pay, and indicate the amount his check was under- or overstated, and **(b)** Bill's weekly traveling expenses. Round your final answer to the nearest dollar.   *LU 9-2(1)*

SUMMARY PRACTICE TEST YouTube™

Do you need help? The DVD has step-by-step worked-out solutions.

1. Calculate Sam's gross pay (he is entitled to time-and-a-half). *(p. 245) LU 9-1(2)*

M	T	W	Th	F	Total hours	Rate per hour	Gross pay
$9\frac{1}{4}$	$9\frac{1}{4}$	$10\frac{1}{2}$	$8\frac{1}{2}$	$11\frac{1}{2}$		$8.00	

2. Mia Kaminsky sells shoes for Macy's. Macy's pays Mia $12 per hour plus a 5% commission on all sales. Assume Mia works 37 hours for the week and has $7,000 in sales. What is Mia's gross pay? *(p. 246) LU 9-1(3)*

3. Lee Company pays its employees on a graduated commission scale: 6% on the first $40,000 sales, 7% on sales from $40,001 to $80,000, and 13% on sales of more than $80,000. May West, an employee of Lee, has $230,000 in sales. What commission did May earn? *(p. 246) LU 9-1(3)*

4. Matty Kim, an accountant for Vernitron, earned $102,600 from January to June. In July, Matty earned $20,000. Assume a tax rate of 6.2% for Social Security on $110,100 and 1.45% on Medicare. How much are the July taxes for Social Security and Medicare? *(p. 249) LU 9-2(1)*

5. Grace Kelley earns $2,000 per week. She is married and claims 2 exemptions. What is Grace's income tax? Use the percentage method. *(p. 249) LU 9-2(1)*

6. Jean Michaud pays his two employees $900 and $1,200 per week. Assume a state unemployment tax rate of 5.7% and a federal unemployment tax rate of .8%. What state and federal unemployment taxes will Jean pay at the end of quarter 1 and quarter 2? *(pp. 251–252) LU 9-2(2)*

SURF TO SAVE

Looking for ways to make money?

PROBLEM 1
Sell it on Amazon.com?

Go to http://www.amazon.com. At the bottom of the page, under Make Money with Us, click on sell on Amazon. Suppose you sold 10 PCs for $500 each and the buyers paid the cost of shipping. After deducting the per-item and referral fees Amazon charges and the $400 you paid for each PC, what was your total profit on these transactions?

Discussion Questions

1. Is it worth the money for you to sell products through this site? Why?
2. Why does Amazon.com charge sellers fees?

PROBLEM 2
Single vs. married taxpayers

Go to http://www.paycheckcity.com/coapa/netpaycalculator.asp. Suppose you are single and earn $2,000 semimonthly. Assume it is July 1 and you have already earned $24,000. How much more federal income tax is withheld from your paycheck compared to a married person, earning the same salary, with four dependents?

Discussion Questions

1. Why do you feel the tax rates differ based on marital status?
2. Will your federal tax withholding likely increase, decrease, or stay the same over the next 10 years? Why?

PROBLEM 3
Can you afford to retire?

Go to http://www.ssa.gov/OACT/quickcalc/index.html. Assume that you plan to retire at the age of 70 and that you will make an average of $55,000 per year. Calculate your benefit using both today's dollars and inflated (future) dollars. How do the two values differ? Click to see the earnings that were used. Which number is more realistic?

Discussion Questions

1. How does this tool help you prepare for your future retirement?
2. Will the amounts you have seen for your eventual retirement cover all of your expected expenses during your retirement? Why or why not?

PROBLEM 4
Worthy commission?

Go to http://www.nytimes.com/2011/01/30/realestate/30cov.html?pagewanted=all and read "You Don't Have to Pay It." According to the article, real estate agents' average commission rate is 6%. If a real estate agent sold five homes with an average price of $250,000 last year, what would be his/her total commission earned for the year?

Discussion Questions

1. Based on the article, what causes drops in agents' commissions?
2. Would you take on more of the tasks involved in selling your house to pay a smaller commission? Why?

MOBILE APPS ✕

Withholding Calc (3 Dogs and a Cat Software) Helps you estimate your paychecks and the impact changes to your withholdings will have on take-home pay.

Payrollguru (Payrollguru, Inc.) Assists in the calculation of paychecks, including the net pay as well as applicable taxes taken out of gross pay amounts.

INTERNET PROJECTS ✕

See text website
www.mhhe.com/slater11e_sse_ch09

Health Coverage on Your Own

New resources and rules help you find an affordable policy. BY KIMBERLY LANKFORD

■ YOU'LL SAVE WITH A HIGH-DEDUCTIBLE POLICY, AND YOU COULD BE ELIGIBLE FOR WELL-CHILD VISITS AT NO COST.

UNLESS A SUPREME COURT decision derails the 2010 health-care-reform law, the marketplace for individual health insurance is scheduled to change drastically in 2014—when policies will be sold on state-run exchanges and insurers will no longer be able to deny you coverage or charge higher rates because of your health. Until then, take advantage of new rules and resources to help you find coverage.

Resources. A new tool at the government's HealthCare .gov site provides extensive information about the policies available in your area and makes it easy to narrow your search based on the size of the deductible, out-of-pocket expenses and the type of plan (such as HMO or PPO). You'll see details about benefits, co-payment rates, exclusions and base premiums.

For premium information based on your medical condition, go to eHealthInsurance.com, which queries you about your health and lists prices and policy details from many companies. You can also get help from a health insurance agent through www.nahu.org.

If you have the option of continuing coverage through COBRA—the federal law that requires employers to offer coverage for up to 18 months after you leave your job—shop around before you take it. If you're healthy, you may find a better deal on your own.

Adult children can now remain on their parents' policies until age 26 if they don't have coverage through their own jobs. That can be a great deal if you have family coverage for younger siblings and wouldn't need to pay extra to add a grown kid. But if you'd have to switch from coverage for a single or a couple to family coverage, compare the extra cost with the price of buying a separate individual policy—healthy people in their early twenties can generally get a high-deductible policy for $100 per month or less.

High-deductible plans. The money you save in premiums may more than make up for a higher deductible. And new laws now require most insurers to provide preventive-care screenings without charging deductibles or co-payments, even if you have a high-deductible policy. Depending on your age, you could be eligible for blood-pressure, diabetes and cholesterol tests, mammograms and colonoscopies, flu shots, routine vaccines, well-baby and well-child visits, and other preventive services without any out-of-pocket costs (see www.healthcare.gov/prevention for a list of eligible services).

If your health insurance policy has a deductible of at least $1,200 for individual coverage (or $2,400 for family coverage), you can make tax-deductible contributions up to $3,100 ($6,250 for family coverage) to a health savings account for 2012, plus $1,000 if you're 55 or older. That gives you a stash of tax-free money to use for medical expenses in any year.

If you have a preexisting health condition. You'll usually be able to keep coverage from a former employer for up to 18 months under COBRA, no matter how poor your health is. Most states must provide a continuation policy after you've used up your coverage (see www .coverageforall.org for your state's rules).

If you aren't eligible for COBRA, you may be able to find coverage through the new Pre-Existing Condition Insurance Plan, which was introduced as part of the health-care-reform law. The federal government runs the plans in 23 states and the District of Columbia; 27 states run their own plans, which must also follow the federal rules. However, there's a big catch: You can qualify for this coverage only if you've been uninsured for at least six months.

Even if you haven't gone that long without insurance, you may still qualify for a policy through your state's high-risk insurance pool, which may not require a six-month waiting period. For a list of options and rules, see www.healthcare.gov or www.coverageforall.org. ■

BUSINESS MATH ISSUE

Higher deductibles are a great way to save money on health premiums.

1. List the key points of the article and information to support your position.
2. Write a group defense of your position using math calculations to support your view.

Classroom Notes

Simple Interest

LOAN OFFICER — Gottschalk

"Just why do you think you deserve a better standard of living?"

What's the Difference?

Credit unions typically charge lower fees—and pay out higher rates—than commercial banks. A sampling of current averages:

DEPOSIT ACCOUNTS	Credit Unions	Banks	Differer
12-Month CD ($10,000)	0.72%	0.56%	0.16 pt
Personal Savings ($1,000)	0.29%	0.20%	0.09 p
Personal Interest Checking ($2,500)	0.39%	0.23%	0.16 p
Insufficient Funds Fee	$26.29	$29.11	$2.
CONSUMER LOANS			
Unsecured Personal Loan ($5,000; 4 Years)	10.62%	11.05%	0.43
New Auto Loan (5 Years)	3.93%	5.40%	1.47
Used Auto Loan (2-Year-Old Vehicle; 4 Years)	4.06%	5.66%	1.6
CREDIT CARDS			
Platinum	10.22%	12.09%	1.
Annual Fee	$26.60	$34.63	
Maximum Late Fee	$24.98	$34.13	
Reward	10.91%	12.91%	
Annual Fee	$27.93	$88.44	
Maximum Late Fee	$23.58	$33.56	

Source: Informa Research Services Inc.

Note: Data as of Ju

citiban

Sarah Vargas

LU 10–1: Calculation of Simple Interest and Maturity Value

1. Calculate simple interest and maturity value for months and years *(pp. 265–266)*.

2. Calculate simple interest and maturity value by **(a)** exact interest and **(b)** ordinary interest *(pp. 266–267)*.

LU 10–2: Finding Unknown in Simple Interest Formula

1. Using the interest formula, calculate the unknown when the other two (principal, rate, or time) are given *(pp. 268–269)*.

LU 10–3: U.S. Rule—Making Partial Note Payments before Due Date

1. List the steps to complete the U.S. Rule as well as calculate proper interest credits *(pp. 270–271)*.

Here are key terms in this chapter. After completing the chapter, if you know the term, place a checkmark in the parentheses. If you don't know the term, look it up and put the page number where it can be found.

Adjusted balance ( ) Banker's Rule ( ) Exact interest ( ) Interest ( ) Maturity value ( ) Ordinary interest ( ) Principal ( ) Simple interest ( ) Simple interest formula ( ) Time ( ) U.S. Rule ( )

Do you shop around for the best bank rates? In the chapter opener, the *Wall Street Journal* clip "What's the Difference?" shows that credit unions may be a good choice when it comes to rates for deposits, consumer loans, or credit cards. Note that in the *Wall Street Journal* article "Peer-to-Peer Loans Grow" (in the margin below) borrowers are using the Internet to get loans.

In this chapter, you will study simple interest. The principles discussed apply whether you are paying interest or receiving interest. Let's begin by learning how to calculate simple interest.

Learning Unit 10–1: Calculation of Simple Interest and Maturity Value

LO 1

Peer-to-Peer Loans Grow

Fed Up With Banks, Entrepreneurs Turn to Internet Sites

BY ANGUS LOTEN

Some small-business owners, rejected by banks or fed up with bad lending terms, are turning to Internet sites that match borrowers with giant pools of lenders when they need funds. That has driven growth and increased the public profile of a sector that was briefly shut down by regulators during the financial crisis.

In the past year, **Prosper Marketplace** Inc. and **Lending Club** Corp., which run the nation's two biggest peer-to-peer lending sites, have reported a sharp upturn in personal loans used to fund small businesses. The sites work like **eBay**-style marketplaces, matching prequalified borrowers to lenders.

Hope Slater, a young attorney, rented an office in a professional building. Since Hope recently graduated from law school, she was short of cash. To purchase office furniture for her new office, Hope went to her bank and borrowed $40,000 for 6 months at a 4% annual interest rate. **Interest** expense is the cost of borrowing money.

The original amount Hope borrowed ($40,000) is the **principal** (face value) of the loan. Hope's price for using the $40,000 is the interest rate (4%) the bank charges on a yearly basis. Since Hope is borrowing the $40,000 for 6 months, Hope's loan will have a **maturity value** of $40,800—the principal plus the interest on the loan. Thus, Hope's price for using the furniture before she can pay for it is $800 interest, which is a percent of the principal for a specific time period. To make this calculation, we use the following formula:

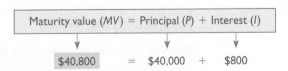

Maturity value (*MV*) = Principal (*P*) + Interest (*I*)

$40,800 = $40,000 + $800

Hope's furniture purchase introduces **simple interest**—the cost of a loan, usually for 1 year or less. Simple interest is only on the original principal or amount borrowed. Let's examine how the bank calculated Hope's $800 interest.

Simple Interest Formula

To calculate simple interest, we use the following **simple interest formula:**

> Simple interest (I) = Principal (P) $\times$ Rate (R) $\times$ Time (T)

In this formula, rate is expressed as a decimal, fraction, or percent; and time is expressed in years or a fraction of a year.

EXAMPLE Hope Slater borrowed $40,000 for office furniture. The loan was for 6 months at an annual interest rate of 4%. What are Hope's interest and maturity value?

Using the simple interest formula, the bank determined Hope's interest as follows:

In your calculator, multiply $40,000 times .04 times 6. Divide your answer by 12. You could also use the % key—multiply $40,000 times 4% times 6 and then divide your answer by 12.

Step 1. Calculate the interest.

$$I = \$40,000 \times .04 \times \frac{6}{12}$$
$$\quad\quad (P)\quad (R)\quad (T)$$
$$= \$800$$

Step 2. Calculate the maturity value.

$$MV = \$40,000 + \$800$$
$$\quad\quad\quad (P)\quad\quad (I)$$
$$= \$40,800$$

Now let's use the same example and assume Hope borrowed $40,000 for 1 year. The bank would calculate Hope's interest and maturity value as follows:

Step 1. Calculate the interest.

$$I = \$40,000 \times .04 \times 1 \text{ year}$$
$$\quad\quad (P)\quad\quad (R)\quad\quad (T)$$
$$= \$1,600$$

Step 2. Calculate the maturity value.

$$MV = \$40,000 + \$1,600$$
$$\quad\quad\quad (P)\quad\quad\quad (I)$$
$$= \$41,600$$

Let's use the same example again and assume Hope borrowed $40,000 for 18 months. Then Hope's interest and maturity value would be calculated as follows:

Step 1. Calculate the interest.

$$I = \$40,000 \times .04 \times \frac{18^1}{12}$$
$$\quad\quad (P)\quad\quad (R)\quad (T)$$
$$= \$2,400$$

Step 2. Calculate the maturity value.

$$MV = \$40,000 + \$2,400$$
$$\quad\quad\quad (P)\quad\quad\quad (I)$$
$$= \$42,400$$

Next we'll turn our attention to two common methods we can use to calculate simple interest when a loan specifies its beginning and ending dates.

LO 2

Two Methods for Calculating Simple Interest and Maturity Value

Method 1: Exact Interest (365 Days) The Federal Reserve banks and the federal government use the **exact interest** method. The *exact interest* is calculated by using a 365-day year. For **time,** we count the exact number of days in the month that the borrower has the loan. The day the loan is made is not counted, but the day the money is returned is counted

---

[1]This is the same as 1.5 years.

as a full day. This method calculates interest by using the following fraction to represent time in the formula:

$$\text{Time} = \frac{\text{Exact number of days}}{365} \longleftarrow \text{Exact interest}$$

From the *Business Math Handbook*

July 6	187th day
March 4	− 63rd day
	124 days
	(exact time of loan)
March	31
	− 4
	27
April	30
May	31
June	30
July	+ 6
	124 days

For this calculation, we use the exact days-in-a-year calendar from the *Business Math Handbook*. You learned how to use this calendar in Chapter 7, page 187.

EXAMPLE On March 4, Joe Bench borrowed $50,000 at 5% interest. Interest and principal are due on July 6. What are the interest cost and the maturity value?

Step 1. Calculate the interest.

$$I = P \times R \times T$$
$$= \$50,000 \times .05 \times \frac{124}{365}$$
$$= \$849.32 \text{ (rounded to nearest cent)}$$

Step 2. Calculate the maturity value.

$$MV = P + I$$
$$= \$50,000 + \$849.32$$
$$= \boxed{\$50,849.32}$$

Method 2: Ordinary Interest (360 Days) In the **ordinary interest** method, time in the formula $I = P \times R \times T$ is equal to the following:

$$\text{Time} = \frac{\text{Exact number of days}}{360} \longleftarrow \text{Ordinary interest}$$

Since banks commonly use the ordinary interest method, it is known as the **Banker's Rule.** Banks charge a slightly higher rate of interest because they use 360 days instead of 365 in the denominator. (Here's a hint: The word *ordinary* starts with an "O" and "360" ends with a "0.") By using 360 instead of 365, the calculation is supposedly simplified. Consumer groups, however, are questioning why banks can use 360 days, since this benefits the bank and not the customer. The use of computers and calculators no longer makes the simplified calculation necessary. For example, after a court case in Oregon, banks began calculating interest on 365 days except in mortgages.

Now let's replay the Joe Bench example we used to illustrate Method 1 to see the difference in bank interest when we use Method 2.

EXAMPLE On March 4, Joe Bench borrowed $50,000 at 5% interest. Interest and principal are due on July 6. What are the interest cost and the maturity value?

Step 1. Calculate the interest.

$$I = \$50,000 \times .05 \times \frac{124}{360}$$
$$= \$861.11$$

Step 2. Calculate the maturity value.

$$MV = P + I$$
$$= \$50,000 + \$861.11$$
$$= \boxed{\$50,861.11}$$

Note: By using Method 2, the bank increases its interest by $11.79.

$$\begin{array}{r} \$861.11 \longleftarrow \text{Method 2} \\ - \ 849.32 \\ \hline \$ \ 11.79 \longleftarrow \text{Method 1} \end{array}$$

Now you should be ready for your first Practice Quiz in this chapter.

MONEY tips

Because debit cards draw money directly from your checking account, it is critical that you protect your account. Be cautious of the ATMs you use. Any outdoor transaction is at risk if the public has access to the machine—even at gas stations. Skimming devices can easily be used to pick up your information and leave your account at risk. Never use an ATM that has been tampered with.

Complete this **Practice Quiz** to see how you are doing.

Calculate simple interest (rounded to the nearest cent):

1. $14,000 at 4% for 9 months
2. $25,000 at 7% for 5 years
3. $40,000 at $10\frac{1}{2}$% for 19 months
4. On May 4, Dawn Kristal borrowed $15,000 at 8%. Dawn must pay the principal and interest on August 10. What are Dawn's simple interest and maturity value if you use the exact interest method?
5. What are Dawn Kristal's (Problem 4) simple interest and maturity value if you use the ordinary interest method?

For **extra help** from your authors–Sharon and Jeff–see the student DVD

You**Tube**

✓ **Solutions**

1. $14,000 \times .04 \times \dfrac{9}{12} = $ $420

2. $25,000 \times .07 \times 5 = $ $8,750

3. $40,000 \times .105 \times \dfrac{19}{12} = $ $6,650

4. August 10 → 222
   May 4 → − 124
   _____
   98

   $15,000 \times .08 \times \dfrac{98}{365} = $ $322.19

   $MV = $15,000 + $322.19 = $ $15,322.19

5. $15,000 \times .08 \times \dfrac{98}{360} = $ $326.67

   $MV = $15,000 + $326.67 = $ $15,326.67

Need more practice? Try this **Extra Practice Quiz** (check figures in the Interactive Chapter Organizer, p. 273). Worked-out Solutions can be found in Appendix B at end of text.

Calculate simple interest (rounded to the nearest cent):

1. $16,000 at 3% for 8 months
2. $15,000 at 6% for 6 years
3. $50,000 at 7% for 18 months
4. On May 6, Dawn Kristal borrowed $20,000 at 7%. Dawn must pay the principal and interest on August 14. What are Dawn's simple interest and maturity value if you use the exact interest method?
5. What are Dawn Kristal's (Problem 4) simple interest and maturity value if you use the ordinary interest method?

Learning Unit 10–2: Finding Unknown in Simple Interest Formula

LO 1

This unit begins with the formula used to calculate the principal of a loan. Then it explains how to find the *principal, rate,* and *time* of a simple interest loan. In all the calculations, we use 360 days and round only final answers.

Finding the Principal

EXAMPLE Tim Jarvis paid the bank $19.48 interest at 9.5% for 90 days. How much did Tim borrow using the ordinary interest method?

The following formula is used to calculate the principal of a loan:

Interest
($19.48)

Principal × Rate × Time
? (.095) ($\frac{90}{360}$)

$$\text{Principal} = \frac{\text{Interest}}{\text{Rate} \times \text{Time}}$$

Note how we illustrated this in the margin. The shaded area is what we are solving for. When solving for principal, rate, or time, you are dividing. Interest will be in the numerator, and the denominator will be the other two elements multiplied by each other.

Step 2. When using a calculator, press

.095 × 90 ÷ 360 M+ .

Step 3. When using a calculator, press

19.48 ÷ MR = .

Step 1. Set up the formula.

$$P = \frac{\$19.48}{.095 \times \frac{90}{360}}$$

Step 2. Multiply the denominator.

.095 times 90 divided by 360 (do not round)

$$P = \frac{\$19.48}{.02375}$$

Step 3. Divide the numerator by the result of Step 2.

$P = \$820.21$

Step 4. Check your answer.

$$\$19.48 = \$820.21 \times .095 \times \frac{90}{360}$$

(I) (P) (R) (T)

Finding the Rate

EXAMPLE Tim Jarvis borrowed $820.21 from a bank. Tim's interest is $19.48 for 90 days. What rate of interest did Tim pay using the ordinary interest method?

The following formula is used to calculate the rate of interest:

$$\text{Rate} = \frac{\text{Interest}}{\text{Principal} \times \text{Time}}$$

Step 1. Set up the formula.

$$R = \frac{\$19.48}{\$820.21 \times \frac{90}{360}}$$

Step 2. Multiply the denominator. Do not round the answer.

$$R = \frac{\$19.48}{\$205.0525}$$

Step 3. Divide the numerator by the result of Step 2.

$R = 9.5\%$

Step 4. Check your answer.

$$\$19.48 = \$820.21 \times .095 \times \frac{90}{360}$$

(I) (P) (R) (T)

Finding the Time

Step 2. When using a calculator, press

820.21 × .095 M+ .

Step 3. When using a calculator, press

19.48 ÷ MR = .

EXAMPLE Tim Jarvis borrowed $820.21 from a bank. Tim's interest is $19.48 at 9.5%. How much time does Tim have to repay the loan using the ordinary interest method?

The following formula is used to calculate time:

$$\text{Time (in years)} = \frac{\text{Interest}}{\text{Principal} \times \text{Rate}}$$

MONEY tips

For each checking account you have, make certain to apply for overdraft protection to protect your account from human error and unintentional overdrafts.

Step 1. Set up the formula.

$$T = \frac{\$19.48}{\$820.21 \times .095}$$

Step 2. Multiply the denominator. Do not round the answer.

$$T = \frac{\$19.48}{\$77.91995}$$

Step 3. Divide the numerator by the result of Step 2.

$T = .25$ years

Step 4. Convert years to days (assume 360 days).

$.25 \times 360 =$ **90 days**

Step 5. Check your answer.

$$\$19.48 = \$820.21 \times .095 \times \frac{90}{360}$$

(I) (P) (R) (T)

Before we go on to Learning Unit 10–3, let's check your understanding of this unit.

LU 10–2 PRACTICE QUIZ

Complete this **Practice Quiz** to see how you are doing.

Complete the following (assume 360 days):

	Principal	Interest rate	Time (days)	Simple interest
1.	?	5%	90 days	$8,000
2.	$7,000	?	220 days	$350
3.	$1,000	8%	?	$300

For **extra help** from your authors–Sharon and Jeff–see the student DVD

You Tube

✓ Solutions

1. $\dfrac{\$8,000}{.05 \times \dfrac{90}{360}} = \dfrac{\$8,000}{.0125} = \boxed{\$640,000}$ $\qquad P = \dfrac{I}{R \times T}$

2. $\dfrac{\$350}{\$7,000 \times \dfrac{220}{360}} = \dfrac{\$350}{\$4,277.7777} = \boxed{8.18\%}$ $\qquad R = \dfrac{I}{P \times T}$

(do not round)

3. $\dfrac{\$300}{\$1,000 \times .08} = \dfrac{\$300}{\$80} = 3.75 \times 360 = \boxed{1,350 \text{ days}}$ $\qquad T = \dfrac{I}{P \times R}$

LU 10–2a EXTRA PRACTICE QUIZ WITH WORKED-OUT SOLUTIONS

Need more practice? Try this **Extra Practice Quiz** (check figures in the Interactive Chapter Organizer, p. 273). Worked-out Solutions can be found in Appendix B at end of text.

Complete the following (assume 360 days):

	Principal	Interest rate	Time (days)	Simple interest
1.	?	4%	90 days	$9,000
2.	$6,000	?	180 days	$280
3.	$900	6%	?	$190

Learning Unit 10–3: U.S. Rule—Making Partial Note Payments before Due Date

Often a person may want to pay off a debt in more than one payment before the maturity date. The **U.S. Rule** allows the borrower to receive proper interest credits. This rule states that any partial loan payment first covers any interest that has built up. The remainder of the partial payment reduces the loan principal. Courts or legal proceedings generally use the U.S. Rule. The Supreme Court originated the U.S. Rule in the case of *Story* v. *Livingston*.

LO 1

EXAMPLE Jeff Edsell owes $5,000 on a 4%, 90-day note. On day 50, Jeff pays $600 on the note. On day 80, Jeff makes an $800 additional payment. Assume a 360-day year. What is Jeff's adjusted balance after day 50 and after day 80? What is the ending balance due?

To calculate $600 payment on day 50:

Step 1. Calculate interest on principal from date of loan to date of first principal payment. Round to nearest cent.

$I = P \times R \times T$

$I = \$5,000 \times .04 \times \dfrac{50}{360}$

$I = \$27.78$

Step 2. Apply partial payment to interest due. Subtract remainder of payment from principal. This is the **adjusted balance** (principal).

600.00 payment
$-\ \ 27.78$ interest
$\overline{\$572.22}$

$\$5,000.00$ principal
$-\ \ \ 572.22$
$\overline{\$4,427.78}$ adjusted balance—principal

(continued on p. 271)

© The McGraw-Hill Companies, Inc./John Flournoy, photographer

MONEY tips

Pay off debt instead of moving it around unless you have been offered 0% interest. Be wary of companies offering to consolidate your debt into a single loan. If you do, be certain to read and understand all the terms.

To calculate $800 payment on day 80:

Step 3. Calculate interest on adjusted balance that starts from previous payment date and goes to new payment date. Then apply Step 2.

Compute interest on $4,427.78 for 30 days (80 − 50)

$$I = \$4,427.78 \times .04 \times \frac{30}{360}$$

$$I = \$14.76$$

$$\begin{array}{r} \$800.00 \text{ payment} \\ -14.76 \text{ interest} \\ \hline \$785.24 \end{array}$$

$$\begin{array}{r} \$4,427.78 \\ -785.24 \\ \hline \$3,642.54 \text{ adjusted} \\ \text{balance} \end{array}$$

Step 4. At maturity, calculate interest from last partial payment. *Add* this interest to adjusted balance.

Ten days are left on note since last payment.

$$I = \$3,642.54 \times .04 \times \frac{10}{360}$$

$$I = \$4.05$$

$$\text{Balance owed} = \boxed{\$3,646.59} \left(\begin{array}{r} \$3,642.54 \\ +4.05 \end{array} \right)$$

Note that when Jeff makes two partial payments, Jeff's total interest is $46.59 ($27.78 + $14.76 + $4.05). If Jeff had repaid the entire loan after 90 days, his interest payment would have been $50—a total savings of $3.41.

Let's check your understanding of the last unit in this chapter.

LU 10–3 | PRACTICE QUIZ

Complete this **Practice Quiz** to see how you are doing.

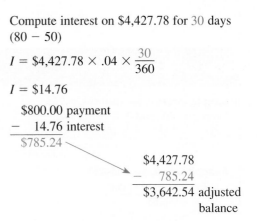

For **extra help** from your authors—Sharon and Jeff—see the student DVD

You Tube™

Polly Flin borrowed $5,000 for 60 days at 8%. On day 10, Polly made a $600 partial payment. On day 40, Polly made a $1,900 partial payment. What is Polly's ending balance due under the U.S. Rule (assuming a 360-day year)?

✓ **Solutions**

$$\$5,000 \times .08 \times \frac{10}{360} = \$11.11$$

$$\begin{array}{r} \$600.00 \\ -11.11 \\ \hline \$588.89 \end{array} \qquad \begin{array}{r} \$5,000.00 \\ -588.89 \\ \hline \$4,411.11 \end{array}$$

$$\$4,411.11 \times .08 \times \frac{30}{360} = \$29.41$$

$$\begin{array}{r} \$1,900.00 \\ -29.41 \\ \hline \$1,870.59 \end{array} \qquad \begin{array}{r} \$4,411.11 \\ -1,870.59 \\ \hline \$2,540.52 \end{array}$$

$$\$2,540.52 \times .08 \times \frac{20}{360} = \$11.29$$

$$\begin{array}{r} \$11.29 \\ +2,540.52 \\ \hline \boxed{\$2,551.81} \end{array}$$

LU 10–3a | EXTRA PRACTICE QUIZ WITH WORKED-OUT SOLUTION

Need more practice? Try this **Extra Practice Quiz** (check figure in the Interactive Chapter Organizer, p. 273). Worked-out Solution can be found in Appendix B at end of text.

Polly Flin borrowed $4,000 for 60 days at 4%. On day 15, Polly made a $700 partial payment. On day 40, Polly made a $2,000 partial payment. What is Polly's ending balance due under the U.S. Rule (assuming a 360-day year)?

INTERACTIVE CHAPTER ORGANIZER

Topic/procedure/formula	Examples	You try it*
Simple interest for months, p. 266 Interest = Principal × Rate × Time (I) (P) (R) (T)	$2,000 at 9% for 17 months $I = \$2,000 \times .09 \times \dfrac{17}{12}$ $I = \$255$	**Calculate simple interest** $4,000 at 3% for 18 months
Exact interest, pp. 266–267 $T = \dfrac{\text{Exact number of days}}{365}$ $I = P \times R \times T$	$1,000 at 10% from January 5 to February 20 $I = \$1,000 \times .10 \times \dfrac{46}{365}$ Feb. 20: 51 days Jan. 5: − 5 46 days $I = \$12.60$	**Calculate exact interest** $3,000 at 4% from January 8 to February 22
Ordinary interest (Banker's Rule), p. 267 $T = \dfrac{\text{Exact number of days}}{360}$ $I = P \times R \times T$ Higher interest costs	$I = \$1,000 \times .10 \times \dfrac{46}{360}$ (51 − 5) $I = \$12.78$	**Calculate ordinary interest** $3,000 at 4% from January 8 to February 22
Finding unknown in simple interest formula (use 360 days), p. 268 $I = P \times R \times T$	Use this example for illustrations of simple interest formula parts: $1,000 loan at 9%, 60 days $I = \$1,000 \times .09 \times \dfrac{60}{360} = \$15$	**Calculate interest (use 360 days)** $2,000 loan at 4%, 90 days
Finding the principal, pp. 268–269 $P = \dfrac{I}{R \times T}$	$P = \dfrac{\$15}{.09 \times \dfrac{60}{360}} = \dfrac{\$15}{.015} = \$1,000$	**Calculate principal** *Given:* interest, $20; rate, 4%; 90 days
Finding the rate, p. 269 $R = \dfrac{I}{P \times T}$	$R = \dfrac{\$15}{\$1,000 \times \dfrac{60}{360}} = \dfrac{\$15}{166.66666} = .09$ = 9% *Note:* We did not round the denominator.	**Calculate rate** *Given:* interest, $20; principal, $2,000; 90 days
Finding the time, p. 269 $T = \dfrac{I}{P \times R}$ (in years) Multiply answer by 360 days to convert answer to days for ordinary interest.	$T = \dfrac{\$15}{\$1,000 \times .09} = \dfrac{\$15}{\$90} = .1666666$ $.1666666 \times 360 = 59.99 = 60$ days	**Calculate number of days** *Given:* principal, $2,000; rate, 4%; interest, $20

(continues)

INTERACTIVE CHAPTER ORGANIZER

Topic/procedure/formula	Examples	You try it*
U.S. Rule (use 360 days), pp. 270–271 Calculate interest on principal from date of loan to date of first partial payment. Calculate adjusted balance by subtracting from principal the partial payment less interest cost. The process continues for future partial payments with the adjusted balance used to calculate cost of interest from last payment to present payment.	12%, 120 days, $2,000 *Partial payments:* On day 40: $250 On day 60: $200 *First payment:* $I = \$2,000 \times .12 \times \dfrac{40}{360}$ $I = \$26.67$ $\$250.00$ payment -26.67 interest $\overline{\$223.33}$ $\$2,000.00$ principal -223.33 $\overline{\$1,776.67}$ adjusted balance *Second payment:* $I = \$1,776.67 \times .12 \times \dfrac{20}{360}$ $I = \$11.84$ $\$200.00$ payment -11.84 interest $\overline{\$188.16}$ $\$1,776.67$ -188.16 $\overline{\$1,588.51}$ adjusted balance	**Calculate balance due and total interest** *Given:* $4,000; 4%; 90 days *Partial payments:* On day 30: $400 On day 70: $300
Balance owed equals last adjusted balance plus interest cost from last partial payment to final due date.	*60 days left:* $\$1,588.51 \times .12 \times \dfrac{60}{360} = \$31.77$ $\$1,588.51 + \$31.77 = \boxed{\$1,620.28}$ balance due Total interest $=\$26.67$ 11.84 $+31.77$ $\overline{\$70.28}$	

KEY TERMS	Adjusted balance, *p. 270* Banker's Rule, *p. 267* Exact interest, *p. 266* Interest, *p. 265*	Maturity value, *p. 265* Ordinary interest, *p. 267* Principal, *p. 265* Simple interest, *p. 265*	Simple interest formula, *p. 266* Time, *p. 266* U.S. Rule, *p. 270*
Check Figures for Extra Practice Quizzes with Page References. (Worked-out Solutions in Appendix B.)	LU 10–1a (p. 268) **1.** $320 **2.** $5,400 **3.** $5,250 **4.** $20,383.56; Interest = $383.56 **5.** $20,388.89; Interest = $388.89	LU 10–2a (p. 270) **1.** $900,000 **2.** 9.33% **3.** 1,267 days	LU 10–3a (p. 271) $1,318.78

*Worked-out solutions are in Appendix B.

Critical Thinking Discussion Questions with Chapter Concept Check

1. What is the difference between exact interest and ordinary interest? With the increase of computers in banking, do you think that the ordinary interest method is a dinosaur in business today?

2. Explain how to use the portion formula to solve the unknowns in the simple interest formula. Why would rounding the answer of the denominator result in an inaccurate final answer?

3. Explain the U.S. Rule. Why in the last step of the U.S. Rule is the interest added, not subtracted?

4. Do you believe the government bailout of banks is in the best interest of the country? Defend your position.

5. **Chapter Concept Check.** Referring to the chapter opener, prepare calculations based on the concepts in this chapter to prove credit unions would save you money in your personal life.

END-OF-CHAPTER PROBLEMS  www.mhhe.com/slater11e

Check figures for odd-numbered problems in Appendix C.   Name _____   Date _____

DRILL PROBLEMS

Calculate the simple interest and maturity value for the following problems. Round to the nearest cent as needed. *LU 10-1(1)*

	Principal	Interest rate	Time	Simple interest	Maturity value
10–1.	$17,000	$2\frac{1}{2}\%$	18 mo.		
10–2.	$21,000	5%	$1\frac{3}{4}$ yr.		
10–3.	$20,000	$6\frac{3}{4}\%$	9 mo.		

Complete the following, using ordinary interest: *LU 10-1(2)*

	Principal	Interest rate	Date borrowed	Date repaid	Exact time	Interest	Maturity value
10–4. eXcel	$1,000	8%	Mar. 8	June 9			
10–5. eXcel	$585	9%	June 5	Dec. 15			
10–6. eXcel	$1,200	12%	July 7	Jan. 10			

Complete the following, using exact interest: *LU 10-1(2)*

	Principal	Interest rate	Date borrowed	Date repaid	Exact time	Interest	Maturity value
10–7.	$1,000	8%	Mar. 8	June 9			
10–8.	$585	9%	June 5	Dec. 15			
10–9.	$1,200	12%	July 7	Jan. 10			

Solve for the missing item in the following (round to the nearest hundredth as needed):   *LU 10-2(1)*

	Principal	Interest rate	Time (months or years)	Simple interest
10–10.	$400	5%	?	$100
10–11.	?	7%	$1\frac{1}{2}$ years	$200
10–12.	$5,000	?	6 months	$300

10–13. Use the U.S. Rule to solve for total interest costs, balances, and final payments (use ordinary interest).   *LU 10-3(1)*

   Given   Principal: $10,000, 8%, 240 days

   Partial payments: On 100th day, $4,000

   On 180th day, $2,000

WORD PROBLEMS

10–14. Diane Van Os decided to buy a new car since her credit union was offering such low interest rates. She borrowed $32,000 at 3.5% on December 26, 2012, and paid it off February 21, 2014. How much did she pay in interest? (Assume ordinary interest.)   *LU 10-1(2)*

10–15. Leslie Hart borrowed $15,000 to pay for her child's education at Riverside Community College. Leslie must repay the loan at the end of 9 months in one payment with $5\frac{1}{2}$% interest. How much interest must Leslie pay? What is the maturity value?   *LU 10-1(1)*

10–16. On September 12, Jody Jansen went to Sunshine Bank to borrow $2,300 at 9% interest. Jody plans to repay the loan on January 27. Assume the loan is on ordinary interest. What interest will Jody owe on January 27? What is the total amount Jody must repay at maturity? *LU 10-1(2)*

10–17. Kelly O'Brien met Jody Jansen (Problem 10–16) at Sunshine Bank and suggested she consider the loan on exact interest. Recalculate the loan for Jody under this assumption. How much would she save in interest? *LU 10-1(2)*

10–18. On May 3, 2014, Leven Corp. negotiated a short-term loan of $685,000. The loan is due October 1, 2014, and carries a 6.86% interest rate. Use ordinary interest to calculate the interest. What is the total amount Leven would pay on the maturity date? *LU 10-1(2)*

10–19. Gordon Rosel went to his bank to find out how long it will take for $1,200 to amount to $1,650 at 8% simple interest. Please solve Gordon's problem. Round time in years to the nearest tenth. *LU 10-2(1)*

10–20. Bill Moore is buying a used Winnebago. His April monthly interest at 12% was $125. What was Bill's principal balance at the beginning of April? Use 360 days. *LU 10-2(1)*

10–21. On April 5, 2014, Janeen Camoct took out an $8\frac{1}{2}$% loan for $20,000. The loan is due March 9, 2015. Use ordinary interest to calculate the interest. What total amount will Janeen pay on March 9, 2015? *LU 10-1(2)*

10–22. Sabrina Bowers took out the same loan as Janeen (Problem 10–21). Sabrina's terms, however, are exact interest. What is Sabrina's difference in interest? What will she pay on March 9, 2015? *LU 10-1(2)*

10–23. Max Wholesaler borrowed $2,000 on a 10%, 120-day note. After 45 days, Max paid $700 on the note. Thirty days later, Max paid an additional $630. What is the final balance due? Use the U.S. Rule to determine the total interest and ending balance due. Use ordinary interest. *LU 10-3(1)*

ADDITIONAL SET OF WORD PROBLEMS

10–24. Lane French had a bad credit rating and went to a local cash center. He took out a $100 loan payable in two weeks at $115. What is the percent of interest paid on this loan? Do not round denominator before dividing. *LU 10-2(1)*

10–25. Joanne and Ed Greenwood built a new barn with an attached arena. To finance the loan, they paid $1,307 interest on $45,000 at 4.0%. What was the time, using exact interest (rounded up to the nearest day)? *LU 10-2(1)*

10–26. On September 14, Jennifer Rick went to Park Bank to borrow $2,500 at $11\frac{3}{4}\%$ interest. Jennifer plans to repay the loan on January 27. Assume the loan is on ordinary interest. What interest will Jennifer owe on January 27? What is the total amount Jennifer must repay at maturity? *LU 10-1(2)*

10–27. Steven Linden met Jennifer Rick (Problem 10–26) at Park Bank and suggested she consider the loan on exact interest. Recalculate the loan for Jennifer under this assumption. *LU 10-1(2)*

10–28. Lance Lopes went to his bank to find out how long it will take for $1,000 to amount to $1,700 at 12% simple interest. e*X*cel Can you solve Lance's problem? Round time in years to the nearest tenth. *LU 10-2(1)*

10–29. Andres Michael bought a new boat. He took out a loan for $24,500 at 4.5% interest for 2 years. He made a $4,500 partial payment at 2 months and another partial payment of $3,000 at 6 months. How much is due at maturity? *LU 10-3(1)*

10–30. Shawn Bixby borrowed $17,000 on a 120-day, 12% note. After 65 days, Shawn paid $2,000 on the note. On day 89, Shawn paid an additional $4,000. What is the final balance due? Determine total interest and ending balance due by the U.S. Rule. Use ordinary interest. *LU 10-3(1)*

10–31. Carol Miller went to Europe and forgot to pay her $740 mortgage payment on her New Hampshire ski house. For her 59 days overdue on her payment, the bank charged her a penalty of $15. What was the rate of interest charged by the bank? Round to the nearest hundredth percent. (Assume 360 days.) *LU 10-2(1)*

10–32. Abe Wolf bought a new kitchen set at Sears. Abe paid off the loan after 60 days with an interest charge of $9. If Sears charges 10% interest, what did Abe pay for the kitchen set? (Assume 360 days.) *LU 10-2(1)*

10–33. Joy Kirby made a $300 loan to Robinson Landscaping at 11%. Robinson paid back the loan with interest of $6.60. How long in days was the loan outstanding? (Assume 360 days.) Check your answer. *LU 10-2(1)*

10–34. Molly Ellen, bookkeeper for Keystone Company, forgot to send in the payroll taxes due on April 15. She sent the payment November 8. The IRS sent her a penalty charge of 8% simple interest on the unpaid taxes of $4,100. Calculate the penalty. (Remember that the government uses exact interest.) *LU 10-1(2)*

10–35. Oakwood Plowing Company purchased two new plows for the upcoming winter. In 200 days, Oakwood must make a single payment of $23,200 to pay for the plows. As of today, Oakwood has $22,500. If Oakwood puts the money in a bank today, what rate of interest will it need to pay off the plows in 200 days? (Assume 360 days.) *LU 10-2(1)*

10–36. Debbie McAdams paid 8% interest on a $12,500 loan balance. Jan Burke paid $5,000 interest on a $62,500 loan. Based on 1 year: **(a)** What was the amount of interest paid by Debbie? **(b)** What was the interest rate paid by Jan? **(c)** Debbie and Jan are both in the 28% tax bracket. Since the interest is deductible, how much would Debbie and Jan each save in taxes? *LU 10-2(1)*

10–37. Janet Foster bought a computer and printer at Computerland. The printer had a $600 list price with a $100 trade discount and 2/10, n/30 terms. The computer had a $1,600 list price with a 25% trade discount but no cash discount. On the computer, Computerland offered Janet the choice of (1) paying $50 per month for 17 months with the 18th payment paying the remainder of the balance or (2) paying 8% interest for 18 months in equal payments. *LU 10-1(2)*

   a. Assume Janet could borrow the money for the printer at 8% to take advantage of the cash discount. How much would Janet save? (Assume 360 days.)

   b. On the computer, what is the difference in the final payment between choices 1 and 2?

 SUMMARY PRACTICE TEST You Tube™

Do you need help? The DVD has step-by-step worked-out solutions.

1. Lorna Hall's real estate tax of $2,010.88 was due on December 14, 2009. Lorna lost her job and could not pay her tax bill until February 27, 2010. The penalty for late payment is $6\frac{1}{2}$% ordinary interest. *(pp. 265–266) LU 10-1(1)*

   a. What is the penalty Lorna must pay?

   b. What is the total amount Lorna must pay on February 27?

2. Ann Hopkins borrowed $60,000 for her child's education. She must repay the loan at the end of 8 years in one payment with $5\frac{1}{2}$% interest. What is the maturity value Ann must repay? *(p. 266) LU 10-1(1)*

3. On May 6, Jim Ryan borrowed $14,000 from Lane Bank at $7\frac{1}{2}$% interest. Jim plans to repay the loan on March 11. Assume the loan is on ordinary interest. How much will Jim repay on March 11? *(p. 267)* *LU 10-1(2)*

4. Gail Ross met Jim Ryan (Problem 3) at Lane Bank. After talking with Jim, Gail decided she would like to consider the same loan on exact interest. Can you recalculate the loan for Gail under this assumption? *(pp. 266–267)* *LU 10-1(2)*

5. Claire Russell is buying a car. Her November monthly interest was $210 at $7\frac{3}{4}$% interest. What is Claire's principal balance (to the nearest dollar) at the beginning of November? Use 360 days. Do not round the denominator in your calculation. *(pp. 268–269)* *LU 10-2(1)*

6. Comet Lee borrowed $16,000 on a 6%, 90-day note. After 20 days, Comet paid $2,000 on the note. On day 50, Comet paid $4,000 on the note. What are the total interest and ending balance due by the U.S. Rule? Use ordinary interest. *(pp. 270–271)* *LU 10-3(1)*

PROBLEM 1
"Same as cash"?

Go to http://www.consumercity.org/sameascash.html and read the article. Suppose you purchased $5,000 worth of furniture and missed the 90-day deadline to pay it off. If you are charged 18% simple annual interest for the 90 days (1/4 year) on the $5,000, how much will you owe?

Discussion Questions

1 Why do so many companies offer these "same as cash" deals?

2. Do you think most consumers pay off their "same as cash" purchases within the free financing period? Why or why not?

PROBLEM 2
Not free forever

Go to http://www.bestbuy.com/site/null/Credit-Cards/pcmcat102500050032.c?id=pcmcat161200050007 and select a couple of products that would put you over the $149 minimum to receive the 6-month financing offer. Estimate how much interest you would owe if you missed the 6-month deadline.

Discussion Questions

1. What are the pros and cons of "same as cash" offers for the consumer?

2. What are the pros and cons of "same as cash" offers for the seller?

PROBLEM 3
Costs of early out

Go to https://www.afbank.com/rates/cd.cfm. Find the rate for a 60-month certificate of deposit (CD). Now, navigate the site to find the penalty for early withdrawal on 60-month CDs. Calculate the penalty you would pay for early withdrawal if you initially invested $30,000.

Discussion Questions

1. Based on the penalties for early withdrawal, for what reasons would you consider taking money out early?

2. What is the value to the bank to have your money invested for a specific period of time in which you are not allowed to make withdrawals?

PROBLEM 4
Shopping for a new car

Go to http://www.kbb.com/new-cars and choose a new car you would like to purchase. Note the MSRP and then go to https://www.chase.com and click on Auto Loans. Under new car loans, click on check today's rates. Input your zip code, and click continue. Assume you are taking the loan out for 60 months. What would the simple interest and the maturity value be on your new car purchase?

Discussion Questions

1. What are some options for you to reduce the amount of money you would need to finance your new car purchase?

2. How does the purchase price of the car you desire impact whether you would want to finance your purchase or save money to pay for the car in full?

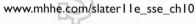

SMART WAYS TO MANAGE STUDENT DEBT

PAYING OFF LOANS EARLY MAY NOT BE THE TOP PRIORITY. BY MICHAEL STRATFORD

SINCE GRADUATING FROM pharmacy school last May, Caitlin has been attempting a balancing act familiar to many recent graduates. She is staring down $120,000 in student debt while also gearing up to buy a house and save for retirement. Fortunately, as a pharmacist for a major retail chain, she's well compensated, with a salary of more than $100,000.

Caitlin knows this income gives her options most of her contemporaries don't enjoy. But that doesn't make managing life a breeze. "I just don't know what to do with my paychecks," Caitlin says. "Should I pay off all my loans right away? Or invest some of the money that I have?" Aside from student loans, Caitlin has no debt and has $20,000 in the bank. She'd like a new car, and hopes to move to Hawaii, where her mother lives, and buy a house there in five to ten years.

Those goals require cash. Caitlin's first step should be to build up her savings and to set aside a rainy-day fund, just in case. Because she has a secure job in a growing field, a six-month reserve fund should be sufficient. Certificates of deposit are her best bet because CDs aren't easy to spend on a whim. "Having an emergency fund locked up in a CD makes it harder to nibble away at it for items that aren't really emergencies," says Andy Tilp, of Trillium Valley Financial Planning, in Sherwood, Ore.

Caitlin would also do well to buy long-term disability insurance. "Right now, her ability to earn a living is her best asset, and it's important to insure that asset," says William Stewart, of Rehmann Financial, in Troy, Mich. The cost to guarantee 60% of her salary if she were permanently disabled should be in the range of $300 a month—or less, if she can get a discount through her employer.

About those loans. Because Caitlin has other financial goals, her student loans aren't a priority. She's currently paying $1,400

a month on a ten-year repayment plan. If she temporarily extends the term of the debt to 25 years, she'll lower her monthly payment by as much as 50% and be able to put aside the difference for other purposes.

At her salary, Caitlin should aim to save as much as 25% to 30% of her take-home pay, advises Paul Baumbach, of Mallard Advisors, in Newark, Del. He also advises that she rejigger her student-debt repayment schedule while she saves for a down payment on a house in Hawaii, where real estate is expensive. In addition, Baumbach says, she should contribute the full $17,000 permitted in 2012 to her 401(k) once she is eligible for matching contributions. That will save about $6,300 in state and federal taxes.

Still, the longer the payment period on her student loans, the more interest Caitlin will pay overall. So if she can afford at some point to return to the ten-year schedule, she should try.

The principle remains the same even for young people who earn less than Caitlin: Set up a loan-repayment schedule you can live with so that you maximize your cash flow for living expenses and other purposes. Discipline works for everyone. ∎

BUSINESS MATH ISSUE

Paying a loan back early is a smart strategy.

1. List the key points of the article and information to support your position.
2. Write a group defense of your position using math calculations to support your view.

CHAPTER 11

Promissory Notes, Simple Discount Notes, and the Discount Process

Smaller Businesses Seeking Loans Still Come Up Empty

BY EMILY MALTBY

Small businesses expected 2011 to be the moment a years-long credit freeze would finally begin to thaw. But borrowing has only gotten worse.

Loans outstanding to small businesses totaled $609 billion at the end of March, an 8.6% drop from a year earlier, according to the most recent data from the Federal Deposit Insurance Corporation, which analyzes loans of less than $1 million.

John S. Dykes

LU 11–1: Structure of Promissory Notes; the Simple Discount Note

1. Differentiate between interest-bearing and non-interest-bearing notes *(p. 286)*.

2. Calculate bank discount and proceeds for simple discount notes *(pp. 286–287)*.

3. Calculate and compare the interest, maturity value, proceeds, and effective rate of a simple interest note with a simple discount note *(p. 287)*.

4. Explain and calculate the effective rate for a Treasury bill *(p. 288)*.

LU 11–2: Discounting an Interest-Bearing Note before Maturity

1. Calculate the maturity value, bank discount, and proceeds of discounting an interest-bearing note before maturity *(pp. 289–290)*.

2. Identify and complete the four steps of the discounting process *(pp. 289–290)*.

VOCABULARY PREVIEW

Here are key terms in this chapter. After completing the chapter, if you know the term, place a checkmark in the parentheses. If you don't know the term, look it up and put the page number where it can be found.

Bank discount ( ) Bank discount rate ( ) Contingent liability ( ) Discounting a note ( ) Discount period ( ) Effective rate ( ) Face value ( ) Interest-bearing note ( ) Maker ( ) Maturity date ( ) Maturity value (MV) ( ) Non-interest-bearing note ( ) Payee ( ) Proceeds ( ) Promissory note ( ) Simple discount note ( ) Treasury bill ( )

The *Wall Street Journal* clip "Smaller Businesses Seeking Loans Still Come Up Empty" in the chapter opener shows that many small businesses have a problem getting credit. The *Wall Street Journal* clip "Peer-to-Peer Loans Grow" shows that some businesses are turning to the Internet to secure funds from pools of lenders rather than being rejected by bankers.

This chapter begins with a discussion of the structure of promissory notes and simple discount notes. We also look at the application of discounting with Treasury bills. The chapter concludes with an explanation of how to calculate the discounting of promissory notes.

Peer-to-Peer Loans Grow

Fed Up With Banks, Entrepreneurs Turn to Internet Sites

BY ANGUS LOTEN

Some small-business owners, rejected by banks or fed up with bad lending terms, are turning to Internet sites that match borrowers with giant pools of lenders when they need funds. That has driven growth and increased the public profile of a sector that was briefly shut down by regulators during the financial crisis.

In the past year, **Prosper Marketplace** Inc. and **Lending Club** Corp., which run the nation's two biggest peer-to-peer lending sites, have reported a sharp upturn in personal loans used to fund small businesses. The sites work like **eBay**-style marketplaces, matching prequalified borrowers to lenders.

Together, the sites have generated more than $500 million in personal loans in the past five years. And while most of the loans are used to pay off credit cards, the proportion of the funds used to finance small businesses is rising.

Learning Unit 11–1: Structure of Promissory Notes; the Simple Discount Note

Although businesses frequently sign promissory notes, customers also sign promissory notes. For example, some student loans may require the signing of promissory notes. Appliance stores often ask customers to sign a promissory note when they buy large appliances on credit. In this unit, promissory notes usually involve interest payments.

LO 1

Structure of Promissory Notes

To borrow money, you must find a lender (a bank or a company selling goods on credit). You must also be willing to pay for the use of the money. In Chapter 10 you learned that interest is the cost of borrowing money for periods of time.

Money lenders usually require that borrowers sign a **promissory note.** This note states that the borrower will repay a certain sum at a fixed time in the future. The note often includes the charge for the use of the money, or the rate of interest. Figure 11.1 shows a sample promissory note with its terms identified and defined. Take a moment to look at each term.

In this section you will learn the difference between interest-bearing notes and non-interest-bearing notes.

Interest-Bearing versus Non-Interest-Bearing Notes   A promissory note can be interest bearing or non–interest bearing. To be interest bearing, the note must state the rate of interest. Since the promissory note in Figure 11.1 states that its interest is 9%, it is an **interest-bearing note.** When the note matures, Regal Corporation will pay back the original amount (**face value**) borrowed plus interest. The simple interest formula (also known as the interest formula) and the maturity value formula from Chapter 10 are used for this transaction.

> Interest = Face value (principal) × Rate × Time
> Maturity value = Face value (principal) + Interest

FIGURE 11.1

Interest-bearing promissory note

$10,000 a.	LAWTON, OKLAHOMA *October 2, 2014* c.
Sixty days b.	AFTER DATE we PROMISE TO PAY TO
THE ORDER OF	*G.J. Equipment Company* d.
Ten thousand and 00/100-------------------DOLLARS.	
PAYABLE AT	*Able National Bank*
VALUE RECEIVED WITH INTEREST AT _9%_ e. REGAL CORPORATION f.	
NO. _114_ DUE *December 1, 2014* g.	*J.M. Moore* TREASURER

a. **Face value:** Amount of money borrowed—$10,000. The face value is also the principal of the note.
b. **Term:** Length of time that the money is borrowed—60 days.
c. **Date:** The date that the note is issued—October 2, 2014.
d. **Payee:** The company extending the credit—G.J. Equipment Company.
e. **Rate:** The annual rate for the cost of borrowing the money—9%.
f. **Maker:** The company issuing the note and borrowing the money—Regal Corporation.
g. **Maturity date:** The date the principal and interest rate are due—December 1, 2014.

If you sign a **non-interest-bearing** promissory note for $10,000, you pay back $10,000 at maturity. The maturity value of a non-interest-bearing note is the same as its face value. Usually, non-interest-bearing notes occur for short time periods under special conditions. For example, money borrowed from a relative could be secured by a non-interest-bearing promissory note.

LO 2

Simple Discount Note

The total amount due at the end of the loan, or the **maturity value (MV),** is the sum of the face value (principal) and interest. Some banks deduct the loan interest in advance. When banks do this, the note is a **simple discount note.**

In the simple discount note, the **bank discount** is the interest that banks deduct in advance and the **bank discount rate** is the percent of interest. The amount that the borrower receives after the bank deducts its discount from the loan's maturity value is the note's **proceeds.** Sometimes we refer to simple discount notes as non-interest-bearing notes. Remember, however, that borrowers *do* pay interest on these notes.

In the example that follows, Pete Runnels has the choice of a note with a simple interest rate (Chapter 10) or a note with a simple discount rate (Chapter 11). Table 11.1 provides a summary of the calculations made in the example and gives the key points that you should remember. Now let's study the example, and then you can review Table 11.1.

EXAMPLE   Pete Runnels has a choice of two different notes that both have a face value (principal) of $14,000 for 60 days. One note has a simple interest rate of 8%, while the other note has a simple discount rate of 8%. For each type of note, calculate **(a)** interest owed, **(b)** maturity value, **(c)** proceeds, and **(d)** effective rate.

LO 3

Simple interest note—Chapter 10	Simple discount note—Chapter 11
Interest	**Interest**
a. $I = \text{Face value (principal)} \times R \times T$ $I = \$14,000 \times .08 \times \dfrac{60}{360}$ $I = \$186.67$	**a.** $I = \text{Face value (principal)} \times R \times T$ $I = \$14,000 \times .08 \times \dfrac{60}{360}$ $I = \$186.67$
Maturity value	**Maturity value**
b. $MV = \text{Face value} + \text{Interest}$ $MV = \$14,000 + \$186.67$ $MV = \$14,186.67$	**b.** $MV = \text{Face value}$ $MV = \$14,000$
Proceeds	**Proceeds**
c. $\text{Proceeds} = \text{Face value}$ $= \$14,000$	**c.** $\text{Proceeds} = MV - \text{Bank discount}$ $= \$14,000 - \$186.67$ $= \$13,813.33$
Effective rate	**Effective rate**
d. $\text{Rate} = \dfrac{\text{Interest}}{\text{Proceeds} \times \text{Time}}$ $= \dfrac{\$186.67}{\$14,000 \times \dfrac{60}{360}}$ $= 8\%$	**d.** $\text{Rate} = \dfrac{\text{Interest}}{\text{Proceeds} \times \text{Time}}$ $= \dfrac{\$186.67}{\$13,813.33 \times \dfrac{60}{360}}$ $= 8.11\%$

TABLE   11.1

Comparison of simple interest note and simple discount note (Calculations from the Pete Runnels example)

Simple interest note (Chapter 10)	Simple discount note (Chapter 11)
1. A promissory note for a loan with a term of usually less than 1 year. *Example:* 60 days.	1. A promissory note for a loan with a term of usually less than 1 year. *Example:* 60 days.
2. Paid back by one payment at maturity. Face value equals actual amount (or principal) of loan (this is not maturity value).	2. Paid back by one payment at maturity. Face value equals maturity value (what will be repaid).
3. Interest computed on face value or what is actually borrowed. *Example:* $186.67.	3. Interest computed on maturity value or what will be repaid and not on actual amount borrowed. *Example:* $186.67.
4. Maturity value = Face value + Interest. *Example:* $14,186.67.	4. Maturity value = Face value. *Example:* $14,000.
5. Borrower receives the face value. *Example:* $14,000.	5. Borrower receives proceeds = Face value − Bank discount. *Example:* $13,813.33.
6. Effective rate (true rate is same as rate stated on note). *Example:* 8%.	6. Effective rate is higher since interest was deducted in advance. *Example:* 8.11%.
7. Used frequently instead of the simple discount note. *Example:* 8%.	7. Not used as much now because in 1969 congressional legislation required that the true rate of interest be revealed. Still used where legislation does not apply, such as personal loans.

Note that the interest of $186.67 is the same for the simple interest note and the simple discount note. The maturity value of the simple discount note is the same as the face value. In the simple discount note, interest is deducted in advance, so the proceeds are less than the face value. Note that the **effective rate** for a simple discount note is higher than the stated rate, since the bank calculated the rate on the face value of the note and not on what Pete received.

Application of Discounting—Treasury Bills   When the government needs money, it sells Treasury bills. A **Treasury bill** is a loan to the federal government for 28 days (4 weeks), 91 days (13 weeks), or 1 year. Note that the *Wall Street Journal* clipping "Treasury to Auction $147 Billion in Securities" announces a new sale.

Treasury to Auction $147 Billion in Securities

BY JEFF BATER

WASHINGTON—The Treasury on Thursday announced plans to sell $147 billion in bills, notes and bonds next week.

Details of the offerings (all with minimum denominations of $100):

■ **Monday:** In the usual weekly sale, $29 billion in three-month bills and $27 billion in six-month bills will be sold. The bills will be dated Jan. 12, 2012, and mature April 12, 2012, and July 12, 2012, respectively. The Cusip number for the three-

month bills is 9127955H0 and for the six-month bills is 9127955W7.

Noncompetitive tenders for the bills must be received by 11 a.m. Eastern time Monday and competitive tenders by 11:30 a.m.

■ **Tuesday:** $25 billion in 52-week bills will be sold, dated Jan. 12, 2012, and maturing Jan. 10, 2013. Cusip number is 9127955V9. Noncompetitive tenders for the bills must be received by 11 a.m. Tuesday and competitive tenders by 11:30 a.m.

■ **Tuesday:** $32 billion in three-year notes will be sold. The dated date is Jan. 15, 2012. The issue date is Jan. 17, 2012. The notes mature Jan. 15, 2015. Cusip number is 912828RZ5. Noncompetitive tenders for the notes must be received by noon Tuesday and competitive tenders by 1 p.m. (Details on the usual four-week bill sale will be announced on Monday.)

■ **Wednesday:** $21 billion in reopened 10-year notes will be sold. The dated date is Nov. 15, 2011. The issue date is Jan. 17, 2012. The notes mature Nov. 15,

2021. Cusip number is 912828RR3.

Noncompetitive tenders for the notes must be received by noon Wednesday and competitive tenders by 1 p.m.

■ **Thursday:** $13 billion in re-opened 30-year bonds will be sold. The dated date is Nov. 15, 2011. The issue date is Jan. 17, 2012. The bonds mature Nov. 15, 2041. Cusip number is 912810QT8.

Noncompetitive tenders for the bonds must be received by noon Thursday and competitive tenders by 1 p.m.

MONEY tips

Paying your rent on time can help improve your credit rating. Leaving a lease before it is up and bouncing checks to a landlord will reduce it.

Treasury bills can be bought over the phone or on the government website. The purchase price (or proceeds) of a Treasury bill is the value of the Treasury bill less the discount. For example, if you buy a $10,000, 13-week Treasury bill at 8%, you pay $9,800 since you have not yet earned your interest ($10,000 × .08 × $\frac{13}{52}$ = $200). At maturity—13 weeks—the government pays you $10,000. You calculate your effective yield (8.16% rounded to the nearest hundredth percent) as follows:

$$\text{($10,000 - $200)} \longrightarrow \frac{\$200}{\$9,800 \times \frac{13}{52}} = \boxed{8.16\%} \text{ effective rate}$$

Now it's time to try the Practice Quiz and check your progress.

LU 11–1   PRACTICE QUIZ

Complete this **Practice Quiz** to see how you are doing.

1. Warren Ford borrowed $12,000 on a non-interest-bearing, simple discount, $9\frac{1}{2}$%, 60-day note. Assume ordinary interest. What are **(a)** the maturity value, **(b)** the bank's discount, **(c)** Warren's proceeds, and **(d)** the effective rate to the nearest hundredth percent?

2. Jane Long buys a $10,000, 13-week Treasury bill at 6%. What is her effective rate? Round to the nearest hundredth percent.

*For **extra help** from your authors—Sharon and Jeff—see the student DVD*

You Tube™

✓ **Solutions**

1. **a.** Maturity value = Face value = $12,000

   b. Bank discount = MV × Bank discount rate × Time

   $$= \$12,000 \times .095 \times \frac{60}{360}$$

   $$= \boxed{\$190}$$

   c. Proceeds = MV − Bank discount
   $$= \$12,000 - \$190$$
   $$= \boxed{\$11,810}$$

   d. Effective rate = $\dfrac{\text{Interest}}{\text{Proceeds} \times \text{Time}}$

   $$= \frac{\$190}{\$11,810 \times \frac{60}{360}}$$

   $$= \boxed{9.65\%}$$

2. $\$10,000 \times .06 \times \dfrac{13}{52} = \$150$ interest $\dfrac{\$150}{\$9,850 \times \dfrac{13}{52}} = \boxed{6.09\%}$

LU 11–1a | **EXTRA PRACTICE QUIZ WITH WORKED-OUT SOLUTIONS**

Need more practice? Try this **Extra Practice Quiz** (check figures in the Interactive Chapter Organizer, p. 292). Worked-out Solutions can be found in Appendix B at end of text.

1. Warren Ford borrowed $14,000 on a non-interest-bearing, simple discount, $4\frac{1}{2}\%$, 60-day note. Assume ordinary interest. What are (a) the maturity value, (b) the bank's discount, (c) Warren's proceeds, and (d) the effective rate to the nearest hundredth percent?

2. Jane Long buys a $10,000, 13-week Treasury bill at 4%. What is her effective rate? Round to the nearest hundredth percent.

Learning Unit 11–2: Discounting an Interest-Bearing Note before Maturity

LO 1

Manufacturers frequently deliver merchandise to retail companies and do not request payment for several months. For example, Roger Company manufactures outdoor furniture that it delivers to Sears in March. Payment for the furniture is not due until September. Roger will have its money tied up in this furniture until September. So Roger requests that Sears sign promissory notes.

If Roger Company needs cash sooner than September, what can it do? Roger Company can take one of its promissory notes to the bank, assuming the company that signed the note is reliable. The bank will buy the note from Roger. Now Roger has discounted the note and has cash instead of waiting until September when Sears would have paid Roger.

Remember that when Roger Company discounts the promissory note to the bank, the company agrees to pay the note at maturity if the maker of the promissory note fails to pay the bank. The potential liability that may or may not result from discounting a note is called a **contingent liability.**

Think of **discounting a note** as a three-party arrangement. Roger Company realizes that the bank will charge for this service. The bank's charge is a **bank discount.** The actual amount Roger receives is the **proceeds** of the note. The four steps below and the formulas in the example that follows will help you understand this discounting process.

LO 2

DISCOUNTING A NOTE
Step 1. Calculate the interest and maturity value.
Step 2. Calculate the discount period (time the bank holds note).
Step 3. Calculate the bank discount.
Step 4. Calculate the proceeds.

EXAMPLE   Roger Company sold the following promissory note to the bank:

Date of note	Face value of note	Length of note	Interest rate	Bank discount rate	Date of discount
March 8	$2,000	185 days	6%	5%	August 9

What are Roger's (1) interest and maturity value (MV)? What are the (2) discount period and (3) bank discount? (4) What are the proceeds?

1. *Calculate Roger's interest and maturity value (MV):*

MV = Face value (principal) + Interest

   Interest = $2,000 × .06 × $\frac{185}{360}$ ⟵ Exact number of days over 360

   = $61.67

   MV = $2,000 + $61.67

   = $2,061.67

Calculating days without table:

March	31
	$\underline{-\ 8}$
	23
April	30
May	31
June	30
July	31
August	$\underline{\ \ 9}$
	154

185 days—length of note
$\underline{-154}$ days Roger held note
  31 days bank waits

2. *Calculate **discount period:***

Determine the number of days that the bank will have to wait for the note to come due (discount period).

August 9	221 days
March 8	$\underline{-\ 67}$
	154 days passed before
	note is discounted
	185 days
	$\underline{-\ 154}$
	31 days bank waits for
	note to come due

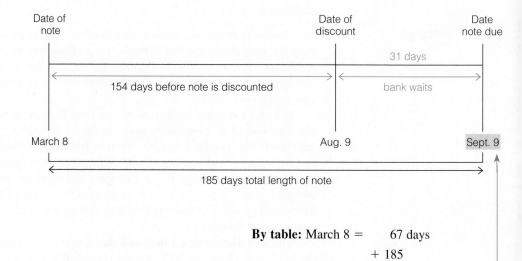

By table: March 8 =   67 days
$\underline{+\ 185}$
252 search in table

3. *Calculate bank discount (bank charge):*

$$\$2,061.67 \times .05 \times \frac{31}{360} = \$8.80$$

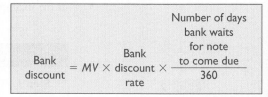

$$\text{Bank discount} = MV \times \text{Bank discount rate} \times \frac{\text{Number of days bank waits for note to come due}}{360}$$

Step 1
↓

$$\text{Proceeds} = MV - \text{Bank discount (charge)}$$

↑
Step 3

4. *Calculate proceeds:*

$2,061.67
$\underline{-\ \ \ \ \ 8.80}$
$2,052.87

If Roger had waited until September 9, it would have received $2,061.67. Now, on August 9, Roger received $2,000 plus $52.87 interest.

Now let's assume Roger Company received a non-interest-bearing note. Then we follow the four steps for discounting a note except the maturity value is the amount of the loan. No interest accumulates on a non-interest-bearing note. Today, many banks use simple interest instead of discounting. Also, instead of discounting notes, many companies set up *lines of credit* so that additional financing is immediately available.

The *Wall Street Journal* clipping "When the Home Bank Closes" on page 291 describes how a bank canceled a line of credit from a home equity loan that was used to inject cash into the home owner's company, Gamer Grub.

The Practice Quiz that follows will test your understanding of this unit.

When the Home Bank Closes

BY ROBBIE WHELAN

Keith Mullin's start-up snack-food company, Gamer Grub, needs cash to become a player.

The San Diego company, which makes bags of high-energy snack food for videogame fanatics, recently struck a promotional partnership to sell its product at stores across the U.S. as part of the launch of "Call of Duty: Modern Warfare 3," the country's top-selling videogame. While more than 3,000 stores have agreed to sell the snacks, Mr. Mullin can't get the funds he needs to hire workers and launch a marketing campaign.

In prior years, Mr. Mullin tapped his home-equity line of credit to inject cash into the business. But the credit line was canceled by his lender after the value of his home plummeted. That set off a chain of events that ended in Mr. Mullin losing his home. Now his business can't find the funds to grow.

Tighter Lending
Total debt from second mortgages and home-equity lines of credit

2Q 2011 **$828B**

$1.25 trillion
1.00
0.75
0.50
0.25
0

2000   '05   '10

Source: Inside Mortgage Finance
The Wall Street Journal

"On one side of the coin, things are great," he says. "But on the back side of the coin, it's fire and brimstone, and it's just totally brutal."

It is well known that the housing bust has taken a devastating toll on American families, nearly three million of which have lost their homes to foreclosure. Less known is the impact that the housing collapse is having on owners of small businesses, which have often relied upon home-equity borrowing to finance the early stages of growth and development.

American business history is packed with stories of company builders, from Wal-Mart Stores Inc.'s Sam Walton to Sam Adams beer brewer Jim Koch, who got key early funding from their homes. Nearly one in three small-business owners has

LU 11–2 PRACTICE QUIZ

Complete this **Practice Quiz** to see how you are doing.

Date of note	Face value (principal) of note	Length of note	Interest rate	Bank discount rate	Date of discount
April 8	$35,000	160 days	11%	9%	June 8

From the above, calculate **(a)** interest and maturity value, **(b)** discount period, **(c)** bank discount, and **(d)** proceeds. Assume ordinary interest.

For **extra help** from your authors—Sharon and Jeff—see the student DVD

✓ Solutions

a. $I = \$35,000 \times .11 \times \dfrac{160}{360} = \boxed{\$1,711.11}$

$MV = \$35,000 + \$1,711.11 = \boxed{\$36,711.11}$

b. Discount period = $160 - 61 = \boxed{99 \text{ days.}}$

April	30
	− 8
	22
May	+ 31
	53
June	+ 8
	61

Or by table:
June 8	159
April 8	− 98
	61

c. Bank discount = $\$36,711.11 \times .09 \times \dfrac{99}{360} = \boxed{\$908.60}$

d. Proceeds = $\$36,711.11 - \$908.60 = \boxed{\$35,802.51}$

LU 11–2a EXTRA PRACTICE QUIZ WITH WORKED-OUT SOLUTION

Need more practice? Try this **Extra Practice Quiz** (check figure in the Interactive Chapter Organizer, p. 292). Worked-out Solution can be found in Appendix B at end of text.

From the information below, calculate **(a)** interest and maturity value, **(b)** discount period, **(c)** bank discount, and **(d)** proceeds. Assume ordinary interest.

Date of note	Face value (principal) of note	Length of note	Interest rate	Bank discount rate	Date of discount
April 10	$40,000	170 days	5%	2%	June 10

INTERACTIVE CHAPTER ORGANIZER

Topic/procedure/formula	Examples	You try it*
Simple discount note, pp. 286–287 Bank Bank discount = MV × discount × Time (interest) rate Interest based on amount paid back and not on actual amount received.	$6,000 × .09 × $\frac{60}{360}$ = $90 Borrower receives $5,910 (the proceeds) and pays back $6,000 at maturity after 60 days. A Treasury bill is a good example of a simple discount note.	**Calculate proceeds** $4,000 note at 2% for 30 days
Effective rate, pp. 287–288 $\frac{\text{Interest}}{\text{Proceeds} \times \text{Time}}$ ↑ What borrower receives (Face value − Discount)	*Example:* $10,000 note, discount rate 12% for 60 days. I = $10,000 × .12 × $\frac{60}{360}$ = $200 Effective rate: $\frac{\$200}{\$9,800 \times \frac{60}{360}}$ = $\frac{\$200}{\$1,633.3333}$ = 12.24% ↑ Amount borrower received	**Calculate effective rate** $15,000 note at 4% for 40 days

Discounting an interest-bearing note, pp. 289–290
 1. Calculate interest and maturity value.
    I = Face value × Rate × Time
    MV = Face value + Interest
 2. Calculate number of days bank will wait for note to come due (discount period).
 3. Calculate bank discount (bank charge).
    Bank
    MV × discount × $\frac{\text{Number of days bank waits}}{360}$
    rate
 4. Calculate proceeds.
    MV − Bank discount (charge)
	Example: $1,000 note, 6%, 60-day, dated November 1 and discounted on December 1 at 8%.
	
	 1. I = $1,000 × .06 × $\frac{60}{360}$ = $10
	    MV = $1,000 + $10 = $1,010
	 2. 30 days
	 3. $1,010 × .08 × $\frac{30}{360}$ = $6.73
	 4. $1,010 − $6.73 = $1,003.27
		Calculate proceeds
		 $2,000 note, 3%, 60 days, dated November 5 and discounted on December 15 at 5%

KEY TERMS	Bank discount, pp. 286, 289 Bank discount rate, p. 286 Contingent liability, p. 289 Discounting a note, p. 289 Discount period, p. 290 Effective rate, p. 288	Face value, p. 286 Interest-bearing note, p. 286 Maker, p. 286 Maturity date, p. 286 Maturity value (MV), p. 286 Non-interest-bearing note, p. 286	Payee, p. 286 Proceeds, pp. 287, 289 Promissory note, p. 286 Simple discount note, p. 286 Treasury bill, p. 288

Check Figures for Extra Practice Quizzes with Page References. (Worked-out Solutions in Appendix B.)	LU 11–1a (p. 289)
	 1. A. $14,000
	     B. $105
	     C. $13,895
	     D. 4.53%
	 2. 4.04%
			LU 11–2a (p. 291)
			 1. A. Int. = $944.44; $40,944.44
			     B. 109 days
			     C. $247.94
			     D. $40,696.50

*Worked-out solutions are in Appendix B.

Critical Thinking Discussion Questions with Chapter Concept Check

1. What are the differences between a simple interest note and a simple discount note? Which type of note would have a higher effective rate of interest? Why?

2. What are the four steps of the discounting process? Could the proceeds of a discounted note be less than the face value of the note?

3. What is a line of credit? What could be a disadvantage of having a large credit line?

4. Discuss the impact of a slow economy on small business borrowing.

5. **Chapter Concept Check.** Based on the chapter opener, go to the Internet and determine the current status of business loans. In your answer, please include concepts you learned in this chapter.

Check figures for odd-numbered problems in Appendix C.   Name _____   Date _____

DRILL PROBLEMS

Complete the following table for these simple discount notes. Use the ordinary interest method.   *LU 11-1(2)*

	Amount due at maturity	Discount rate	Time	Bank discount	Proceeds
11–1.	$16,000	$2\frac{1}{2}\%$	190 days		
11–2.	$20,000	$6\frac{1}{4}\%$	180 days		

Calculate the discount period for the bank to wait to receive its money: *LU 11-2(1)*

	Date of note	Length of note	Date note discounted	Discount period
11–3.	April 12	45 days	May 2	
11–4.	March 7	120 days	June 8	

Solve for maturity value, discount period, bank discount, and proceeds (assume for Problems 11–5 and 11–6 a bank discount rate of 9%).   *LU 11-2(1, 2)*

	Face value (principal)	Rate of interest	Length of note	Maturity value	Date of note	Date note discounted	Discount period	Bank discount	Proceeds
11–5.	$50,000	11%	95 days		June 10	July 18			
11–6.	$25,000	9%	60 days		June 8	July 10			

11–7.   Calculate the effective rate of interest (to the nearest hundredth percent) of the following Treasury bill.
eXcel   **Given:** $10,000 Treasury bill, 4% for 13 weeks.   *LU 11-1(4)*

WORD PROBLEMS

Use ordinary interest as needed.

11–8. Carl Sonntag wanted to compare what proceeds he would receive with a simple interest note versus a simple discount note. Both had the same terms: $19,500 at 8% for 2 years. Compare the proceeds. *LU 11-1(3)*

11–9. Bill Blank signed an $8,000 note at Citizen's Bank. Citizen's charges a $6\frac{1}{2}$% discount rate. If the loan is for 300 days, find **(a)** the proceeds and **(b)** the effective rate charged by the bank (to the nearest tenth percent). *LU 11-1(3)*

11–10. You were offered the opportunity to issue either a simple interest note or a simple discount note with the following terms: $33,353 at 7% for 18 months. Based on the effective interest rate, which would you choose? *LU 11-1(3)*

11–11. On September 5, Sheffield Company discounted at Sunshine Bank a $9,000 (maturity value), 120-day note dated June 5. Sunshine's discount rate was 9%. What proceeds did Sheffield Company receive? *LU 11-2(1)*

11–12. The Treasury Department auctioned $21 billion in 3-month bills in denominations of $10,000 at a discount rate of 4.965%. What would be the effective rate of interest? Round your answer to the nearest hundredth percent. *LU 11–1(4)*

11–13. Toyota Motor Corporation has faced tough times after losing production due to natural disasters. This, coupled with the yen's appreciation against the dollar, has Toyota anticipating net profits 51% lower than last year. If Toyota had a ¥20,000 note at 2.5% interest for 340 days, what would Toyota's proceeds be if it discounted the note on day 215 at 4%? (Round to the nearest yen for each answer.) *LU 11-2(1)*

11–14. Ron Prentice bought goods from Shelly Katz. On May 8, Shelly gave Ron a time extension on his bill by accepting a $3,000, 8%, 180-day note. On August 16, Shelly discounted the note at Roseville Bank at 9%. What proceeds does Shelly Katz receive? *LU 11-2(1)*

11–15. Rex Corporation accepted a $5,000, 8%, 120-day note dated August 8 from Regis Company in settlement of a past bill. On *eXcel* October 11, Rex discounted the note at Park Bank at 9%. What are the note's maturity value, discount period, and bank discount? What proceeds does Rex receive? *LU 11-2(1)*

11–16. On May 12, Scott Rinse accepted an $8,000, 12%, 90-day note for a time extension of a bill for goods bought by Ron Prentice. On June 12, Scott discounted the note at Able Bank at 10%. What proceeds does Scott receive? *LU 11-2(1)*

11–17. Hafers, an electrical supply company, sold $4,800 of equipment to Jim Coates Wiring, Inc. Coates signed a promissory note May 12 with 4.5% interest. The due date was August 10. Short of funds, Hafers contacted Charter One Bank on July 20; the bank agreed to take over the note at a 6.2% discount. What proceeds will Hafers receive? *LU 11-2(1)*

CHALLENGE PROBLEMS

11–18. Assume that 3-month Treasury bills totaling $12 billion were sold in $10,000 denominations at a discount rate of 3.605%. In addition, the Treasury Department sold 6-month bills totaling $10 billion at a discount rate of 3.55%. **(a)** What is the discount amount for 3-month bills? **(b)** What is the discount amount for 6-month bills? **(c)** What is the effective rate for 3-month bills? **(d)** What is the effective rate for 6-month bills? Round to the nearest hundredth percent. *LU 11-1(4)*

11–19. Tina Mier must pay a $2,000 furniture bill. A finance company will loan Tina $2,000 for 8 months at a 9% discount rate. The finance company told Tina that if she wants to receive exactly $2,000, she must borrow more than $2,000. The finance company gave Tina the following formula:

$$\text{What to ask for} = \frac{\text{Amount in cash to be received}}{1 - (\text{Discount} \times \text{Time of loan})}$$

Calculate Tina's loan request and the effective rate of interest to the nearest hundredth percent. *LU 11-1(3)*

 SUMMARY PRACTICE TEST You Tube™

Do you need help? The DVD has step-by-step worked-out solutions.

1. On December 12, Lowell Corporation accepted a $160,000, 120-day, non-interest-bearing note from Able.com. What is the maturity value of the note? *(p. 286) LU 11-1(1)*

2. The face value of a simple discount note is $17,000. The discount is 4% for 160 days. Calculate the following. *(pp. 287, 288)*
e**X**cel *LU 11-1(3)*

    a. Amount of interest charged for each note.

    b. Amount borrower would receive.

    c. Amount payee would receive at maturity.

    d. Effective rate (to the nearest tenth percent).

3. On July 14, Gracie Paul accepted a $60,000, 6%, 160-day note from Mike Lang. On November 12, Gracie discounted the note at Lend Bank at 7%. What proceeds did Gracie receive? *(p. 289) LU 11-2(1)*

Credit

LOWER YOUR RATE ON ALL YOUR LOANS

THE FEDS' EFFORTS TO INJECT MORE LIFE INTO the economy have torpedoed savings yields. But the flip side is lower rates for borrowers.

CREDIT CARDS. The average rate on an outstanding balance was recently 13%, but you can probably do better. Lowering your rate can be as simple as asking the issuer to give you a better deal; but you may save more by snapping up a 0% rate (usually for an introductory period of up to 21 months) for a balance transfer. You'll likely pay a transfer fee of 3% to 4%. If you can't pay off the debt during the introductory period, see whether shifting to a card with no transfer fee and a lower rate will benefit you more. The Simmons First Visa Platinum card, available to those with excellent credit, imposes no transfer fee or annual fee, and it has a 7.25% variable rate.

Or look into an unsecured personal loan to refinance credit card debt. The average rate for a 24-month personal loan was recently about 11%, according to the Federal Reserve.

If your credit score is in the mid 700s or higher, you might get a rate in the single digits.

AUTO LOANS. Refinancing an auto loan could save you big bucks, and it's less complex than a mortgage refi. Use the tool at www.bankrate.com/funnel/auto to see competitive local rates. Recently, Pentagon Fed-

eral Credit Union was offering rates as low as 1.99% to those who applied online to refinance. Plus, check out www.rategenius.com, which matches applicants with lending institutions. One caveat: If your current loan levies a prepayment penalty, it could cancel out the savings you'd get by refinancing.

Another option for credit card debt or a car loan: a home-equity loan (recent average, 6.9%) or line of credit (5.2%). Americans overindulged in home-equity borrowing during the housing bubble, and lenders are wary of extending too much credit. Still, they're making loans again to homeowners with plenty of equity, and interest on home-equity debt is tax-deductible up to certain limits.

Or, if you are planning to refinance your mortgage, consider a cash-out refi, says Adrian Nazari, chief executive of Credit Sesame.com, and use the extra funds to pay off debt. Average rates on 30-year fixed mortgages are about 4%, and the interest is tax-deductible. **LISA GERSTNER**

BUSINESS MATH ISSUE

Lines of credit should not be used to lower debt.

1. List the key points of the article and information to support your position.
2. Write a group defense of your position using math calculations to support your view.

CHAPTER 12

Compound Interest and Present Value

"We met with our retirement financial planner. You each owe us $100,000."

From *The Wall Street Journal*, copyright © 2010, permission of Cartoon Features Syndicate.

Reprinted with permission of *The Wall Street Journal*, Copyright © 2010 Dow Jones & Company, Inc. All Rights Reserved Worldwide.

Where the Money Goes

A middle-income family will spend an estimated $222,360 to raise a baby born in 2009 to age 18. The chart on the left shows how that amount is spent by an average family. The chart on the right is a budget breakdown in the same categories by the Morgan family.

National average
- Clothing 6%
- Miscellaneous 8%
- Housing 32%
- Health care 8%
- Transportation 14%
- Food 16%
- Child care and education 16%

Morgans (2010)
- 1%
- 9%
- 57%
- 13%
- 7%
- 3%
- 10%

Note: Housing costs in the national figure represent the average cost of an additional bedroom; in the Morgan budget, the housing figure represents the family's total outlay.

Sources: Department of Agriculture; the Morgan family

© Blend Images/Ariel Skelley/Getty Images RF

Note: **A complete set of plastic overlays showing the concepts of compound interest and present value is found in Chapter 13.**

LU 12–1: Compound Interest (Future Value)—The Big Picture

1. Compare simple interest with compound interest *(pp. 303–304)*.
2. Calculate the compound amount and interest manually and by table lookup *(pp. 304–306)*.
3. Explain and compute the effective rate (APY) *(pp. 306–307)*.

LU 12–2: Present Value—The Big Picture

1. Compare present value (PV) with compound interest (FV) *(pp. 309–310)*.
2. Compute present value by table lookup *(pp. 310–312)*.
3. Check the present value answer by compounding *(pp. 310–311)*.

Here are key terms in this chapter. After completing the chapter, if you know the term, place a checkmark in the parentheses. If you don't know the term, look it up and put the page number where it can be found.

Annual percentage yield (APY) ( ) Compound amount ( ) Compounded annually ( ) Compounded daily ( ) Compounded monthly ( ) Compounded quarterly ( ) Compounded semiannually ( ) Compounding ( ) Compound interest ( ) Effective rate ( ) Future value (FV) ( ) Nominal rate ( ) Number of periods ( ) Present value (PV) ( ) Rate for each period ( )

Wow! The chapter opening *Wall Street Journal* clip "Where the Money Goes" shows that it will cost about $222,360 to raise a child to the age of 18. So how does one prepare for such a large cost? It is through the magic of compounding.

In this chapter we look at the power of compounding—interest paid on earned interest. Let's begin by studying Learning Unit 12–1, which shows you how to calculate compound interest.

The Magic of Compounding

Compounding investment earnings is what can make even small investments become large investments given enough time.

How It Works - The money you save (either in a savings account, a mutual funds or in individual stocks) earns interest. Then you earn interest on the money you originally save, plus on the interest you've accumulated. As your savings grow, you earn interest on a bigger and bigger pool of money.

For example, the value of $1000 compounded at various rates of return over time is shown in the following chart.

Years	4%	6%	8%	10%
10	$1,481	$1,791	$2,159	$2,594
20	$2,191	$3,207	$4,661	$6,728
30	$3,243	$5,743	$10,063	$17,449

Start Saving Early - For every 10 years you delay before starting to save for retirement, you will need to save three times as much each month to catch up.

www.dol.gov

Learning Unit 12–1: Compound Interest (Future Value)— The Big Picture

So far we have discussed only simple interest, which is interest on the principal alone. Simple interest is either paid at the end of the loan period or deducted in advance. From the chapter introduction, you know that interest can also be compounded.

Compounding involves the calculation of interest periodically over the life of the loan (or investment). After each calculation, the interest is added to the principal. Future calculations are on the adjusted principal (old principal plus interest). **Compound interest,** then, is the interest on the principal plus the interest of prior periods. **Future value (FV),** or the

compound amount, is the final amount of the loan or investment at the end of the last period. In the beginning of this unit, do not be concerned with how to calculate compounding but try to understand the meaning of compounding.

Figure 12.1 shows how $1 will grow if it is calculated for 4 years at 8% annually. This means that the interest is calculated on the balance once a year. In Figure 12.1, we start with $1, which is the **present value (PV).** After year 1, the dollar with interest is worth $1.08. At the end of year 2, the dollar is worth $1.17. By the end of year 4, the dollar is worth $1.36 . Note how we start with the present and look to see what the dollar will be worth in the future. *Compounding goes from present value to future value.*

Check out the plastic overlays that appear at the end of Chapter 13 to review these concepts.

FIGURE	12.1

Future value of $1 at 8% for four periods

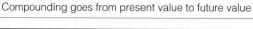

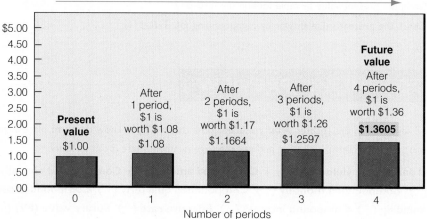

Before you learn how to calculate compound interest and compare it to simple interest, you must understand the terms that follow. These terms are also used in Chapter 13.

- **Compounded annually:** Interest calculated on the balance once a year.
- **Compounded semiannually:** Interest calculated on the balance every 6 months or every $\frac{1}{2}$ year.
- **Compounded quarterly:** Interest calculated on the balance every 3 months or every $\frac{1}{4}$ year.
- **Compounded monthly:** Interest calculated on the balance each month.
- **Compounded daily:** Interest calculated on the balance each day.
- **Number of periods:**[1] Number of years multiplied by the number of times the interest is compounded per year. For example, if you compound $1 for 4 years at 8% annually, semiannually, or quarterly, the following periods will result:

    Annually: 4 years × 1 = 4 periods
    Semiannually: 4 years × 2 = 8 periods
    Quarterly: 4 years × 4 = 16 periods

- **Rate for each period:**[2] Annual interest rate divided by the number of times the interest is compounded per year. Compounding changes the interest rate for annual, semiannual, and quarterly periods as follows:

    Annually: 8% ÷ 1 = 8%
    Semiannually: 8% ÷ 2 = 4%
    Quarterly: 8% ÷ 4 = 2%

Note that both the number of periods (4) and the rate (8%) for the annual example did not change. You will see later that rate and periods (not years) will always change unless interest is compounded yearly.

Now you are ready to learn the difference between simple interest and compound interest.

---

[1]Periods are often expressed with the letter *N* for number of periods.

[2]Rate is often expressed with the letter *i* for interest.

LO 1

Simple versus Compound Interest

Did you know that money invested at 6% will double in 12 years? The following *Wall Street Journal* clipping "Confused by Investing?" shows how to calculate the number of years it takes for your investment to double. Although this clip is from 2003, its information is as current today as it was then. It explains compounding and the rule of 72, so read it carefully.

Confused by Investing?

If there's something about your investment portfolio that doesn't seem to add up, maybe you should check your math.

Lots of folks are perplexed by the mathematics of investing, so I thought a refresher course might help. Here's a look at some key concepts:

■ **10 Plus 10 is 21**

Imagine you invest $100, which earns 10% this year and 10% next. How much have you made? If you answered 21%, go to the head of the class.

Here's how the math works. This year's 10% gain turns your $100 into $110. Next year, you also earn 10%, but you start the year with $110. Result? You earn $11, boosting your wealth to $121.

Thus, your portfolio has earned a *cumulative* 21% return over two years, but the *annualized* return is just 10%. The fact that 21% is more than double 10% can be attributed to the effect of investment compounding, the way that you earn money each year not only on your original investment, but also on earnings from prior years that you've reinvested.

■ **The Rule of 72**

To get a feel for compounding, try the rule of 72. What's that? If you divide a particular annual return into 72, you'll find out how many years it will take to double your money. Thus, at 10% a year, an investment will double in value in a tad over seven years.

Reprinted with permission of *The Wall Street Journal,* Copyright © 2003 Dow Jones & Company, Inc. All Rights Reserved Worldwide.

The following three situations of Bill Smith will clarify the difference between simple interest and compound interest.

Situation 1: Calculating Simple Interest and Maturity Value

EXAMPLE   Bill Smith deposited $80 in a savings account for 4 years at an annual interest rate of 8%. What is Bill's simple interest?

To calculate simple interest, we use the following simple interest formula:

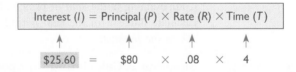

$$\text{Interest } (I) = \text{Principal } (P) \times \text{Rate } (R) \times \text{Time } (T)$$

$$\$25.60 \quad = \quad \$80 \quad \times \quad .08 \quad \times \quad 4$$

In 4 years Bill receives a total of $105.60 ($80.00 + $25.60)—principal plus simple interest.

Now let's look at the interest Bill would earn if the bank compounded Bill's interest on his savings.

Situation 2: Calculating Compound Amount and Interest without Tables[3]

You can use the following steps to calculate the compound amount and the interest manually:

CALCULATING COMPOUND AMOUNT AND INTEREST MANUALLY
Step 1. Calculate the simple interest and add it to the principal. Use this total to figure next year's interest.
Step 2. Repeat for the total number of periods.
Step 3. Compound amount − Principal = Compound interest.

---

[3]For simplicity of presentation, round each calculation to the nearest cent before continuing the compounding process. The compound amount will be off by 1 cent.

© 2011 Joe Martin. Dist. by Neatly Chiseled Features.

EXAMPLE   Bill Smith deposited $80 in a savings account for 4 years at an annual compounded rate of 8%. What are Bill's compound amount and interest?

The following shows how the compounded rate affects Bill's interest:

	Year 1	Year 2	Year 3	Year 4
	$80.00	$86.40	$ 93.31	$100.77
	× .08	× .08	× .08	× .08
Interest	$ 6.40	$ 6.91	$ 7.46	$ 8.06
Beginning balance	+ 80.00	+ 86.40	+ 93.31	+ 100.77
Amount at year-end	$86.40	$93.31	$100.77	$108.83

Note that the beginning year 2 interest is the result of the interest of year 1 added to the principal. At the end of each interest period, we add on the period's interest. This interest becomes part of the principal we use for the calculation of the next period's interest. We can determine Bill's compound interest as follows:[4]

Compound amount	$108.83
Principal	− 80.00
Compound interest	$ 28.83 *Note:* In Situation 1 the interest was $25.60.

We could have used the following simplified process to calculate the compound amount and interest:

Year 1	Year 2	Year 3	Year 4
$80.00	$86.40	$ 93.31	$100.77
× 1.08	× 1.08	× 1.08	× 1.08
$86.40	$93.31	$100.77	$108.83 ← Future value

When using this simplification, you do not have to add the new interest to the previous balance. Remember that compounding results in higher interest than simple interest. Compounding is the *sum* of principal and interest multiplied by the interest rate we use to calculate interest for the next period. So, 1.08 above is 108%, with 100% as the base and 8% as the interest.

LO 2

Situation 3: Calculating Compound Amount by Table Lookup   To calculate the compound amount with a future value table (p. 305), use the following steps:

CALCULATING COMPOUND AMOUNT BY TABLE LOOKUP

Step 1. Find the periods: Years multiplied by number of times interest is compounded in 1 year.

Step 2. Find the rate: Annual rate divided by number of times interest is compounded in 1 year.

Step 3. Go down the Period column of the table to the number of periods desired; look across the row to find the rate. At the intersection of the two columns is the table factor for the compound amount of $1.

Step 4. Multiply the table factor by the amount of the loan. This gives the compound amount.

[4]The formula for compounding is $A = P(1 + i)^N$, where A equals compound amount, P equals the principal, i equals interest per period, and N equals number of periods. The calculator sequence would be as follows for Bill Smith: 1 $+$ .08 y^x 4 × 80 $=$ 108.84. A Financial Calculator Guide booklet is available online that shows how to operate HP 10BII and TI BA II Plus.

TABLE	12.1	Future value of $1 at compound interest

Period	1%	1½%	2%	3%	4%	5%	6%	7%	8%	9%	10%
1	1.0100	1.0150	1.0200	1.0300	1.0400	1.0500	1.0600	1.0700	1.0800	1.0900	1.1000
2	1.0201	1.0302	1.0404	1.0609	1.0816	1.1025	1.1236	1.1449	1.1664	1.1881	1.2100
3	1.0303	1.0457	1.0612	1.0927	1.1249	1.1576	1.1910	1.2250	1.2597	1.2950	1.3310
4	1.0406	1.0614	1.0824	1.1255	1.1699	1.2155	1.2625	1.3108	1.3605	1.4116	1.4641
5	1.0510	1.0773	1.1041	1.1593	1.2167	1.2763	1.3382	1.4026	1.4693	1.5386	1.6105
6	1.0615	1.0934	1.1262	1.1941	1.2653	1.3401	1.4185	1.5007	1.5869	1.6771	1.7716
7	1.0721	1.1098	1.1487	1.2299	1.3159	1.4071	1.5036	1.6058	1.7138	1.8280	1.9487
8	1.0829	1.1265	1.1717	1.2668	1.3686	1.4775	1.5938	1.7182	1.8509	1.9926	2.1436
9	1.0937	1.1434	1.1951	1.3048	1.4233	1.5513	1.6895	1.8385	1.9990	2.1719	2.3579
10	1.1046	1.1605	1.2190	1.3439	1.4802	1.6289	1.7908	1.9672	2.1589	2.3674	2.5937
11	1.1157	1.1780	1.2434	1.3842	1.5395	1.7103	1.8983	2.1049	2.3316	2.5804	2.8531
12	1.1268	1.1960	1.2682	1.4258	1.6010	1.7959	2.0122	2.2522	2.5182	2.8127	3.1384
13	1.1381	1.2135	1.2936	1.4685	1.6651	1.8856	2.1329	2.4098	2.7196	3.0658	3.4523
14	1.1495	1.2318	1.3195	1.5126	1.7317	1.9799	2.2609	2.5785	2.9372	3.3417	3.7975
15	1.1610	1.2502	1.3459	1.5580	1.8009	2.0789	2.3966	2.7590	3.1722	3.6425	4.1772
16	1.1726	1.2690	1.3728	1.6047	1.8730	2.1829	2.5404	2.9522	3.4259	3.9703	4.5950
17	1.1843	1.2880	1.4002	1.6528	1.9479	2.2920	2.6928	3.1588	3.7000	4.3276	5.0545
18	1.1961	1.3073	1.4282	1.7024	2.0258	2.4066	2.8543	3.3799	3.9960	4.7171	5.5599
19	1.2081	1.3270	1.4568	1.7535	2.1068	2.5270	3.0256	3.6165	4.3157	5.1417	6.1159
20	1.2202	1.3469	1.4859	1.8061	2.1911	2.6533	3.2071	3.8697	4.6610	5.6044	6.7275
21	1.2324	1.3671	1.5157	1.8603	2.2788	2.7860	3.3996	4.1406	5.0338	6.1088	7.4002
22	1.2447	1.3876	1.5460	1.9161	2.3699	2.9253	3.6035	4.4304	5.4365	6.6586	8.1403
23	1.2572	1.4084	1.5769	1.9736	2.4647	3.0715	3.8197	4.7405	5.8715	7.2579	8.9543
24	1.2697	1.4295	1.6084	2.0328	2.5633	3.2251	4.0489	5.0724	6.3412	7.9111	9.8497
25	1.2824	1.4510	1.6406	2.0938	2.6658	3.3864	4.2919	5.4274	6.8485	8.6231	10.8347
26	1.2953	1.4727	1.6734	2.1566	2.7725	3.5557	4.5494	5.8074	7.3964	9.3992	11.9182
27	1.3082	1.4948	1.7069	2.2213	2.8834	3.7335	4.8223	6.2139	7.9881	10.2451	13.1100
28	1.3213	1.5172	1.7410	2.2879	2.9987	3.9201	5.1117	6.6488	8.6271	11.1672	14.4210
29	1.3345	1.5400	1.7758	2.3566	3.1187	4.1161	5.4184	7.1143	9.3173	12.1722	15.8631
30	1.3478	1.5631	1.8114	2.4273	3.2434	4.3219	5.7435	7.6123	10.0627	13.2677	17.4494

Note: For more detailed tables, see your reference booklet, the *Business Math Handbook.*

In Situation 2, Bill deposited $80 into a savings account for 4 years at an interest rate of 8% compounded annually. Bill heard that he could calculate the compound amount and interest by using tables. In Situation 3, Bill learns how to do this. Again, Bill wants to know the value of $80 in 4 years at 8%. He begins by using Table 12.1.

Four Periods

No. of times compounded × No. of years in 1 year

1   ×   4

Looking at Table 12.1, Bill goes down the Period column to period 4, then across the row to the 8% column. At the intersection, Bill sees the number 1.3605. The marginal notes show how Bill arrived at the periods and rate. The 1.3605 table number means that $1 compounded at this rate will increase in value in 4 years to about $1.36. Do you recognize the $1.36? Figure 12.1 showed how $1 grew to $1.36. Since Bill wants to know the value of $80, he multiplies the dollar amount by the table factor as follows:

$80.00   ×   1.3605   = $108.84 [5]

Principal × Table factor = Compound amount (future value)

[5]Off 1 cent due to rounding.

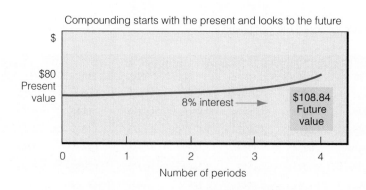

FIGURE **12.2**

Compounding (FV)

Compounding starts with the present and looks to the future

$

$80
Present
value

8% interest ⟶ $108.84
Future
value

0   1   2   3   4

Number of periods

8% Rate

$8\%\ \text{rate} = \dfrac{8\%}{1}$ → Annual rate

→ No. of times compounded in 1 year

Figure 12.2 illustrates this compounding procedure. We can say that compounding is a future value (FV) since we are looking into the future. Thus,

$108.84 − $80.00 = $28.84 interest for 4 years at 8% compounded annually on $80.00

Now let's look at two examples that illustrate compounding more than once a year.

EXAMPLE Find the interest on $6,000 at 10% compounded semiannually for 5 years. We calculate the interest as follows:

Periods = 2 × 5 years = 10

Rate = 10% ÷ 2 = 5%

10 periods, 5%, in Table 12.1 = 1.6289 (table factor)

$6,000 × 1.6289 = $9,773.40
− 6,000.00
$3,773.40
interest

EXAMPLE Pam Donahue deposits $8,000 in her savings account that pays 6% interest compounded quarterly. What will be the balance of her account at the end of 5 years?

Periods = 4 × 5 years = 20

Rate = $6\% \div 4 = 1\frac{1}{2}\%$

20 periods, $1\frac{1}{2}\%$, in Table 12.1 = 1.3469 (table factor)

$8,000 × 1.3469 = $10,775.20

Next, let's look at bank rates and how they affect interest.

LO 3

Bank Rates—Nominal versus Effective Rates (Annual Percentage Yield, or APY)

Banks often advertise their annual (nominal) interest rates and *not* their true or effective rate (annual percentage yield, or APY). This has made it difficult for investors and depositors to determine the actual rates of interest they were receiving. The Truth in Savings law forced savings institutions to reveal their actual rate of interest. The APY is defined in the Truth in Savings law as the percentage rate expressing the total amount of interest that would be received on a $100 deposit based on the annual rate and frequency of compounding for a 365-day period. As you can see from the advertisement on the left, banks now refer to the effective rate of interest as the annual percentage yield.

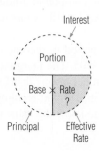

Let's study the rates of two banks to see which bank has the better return for the investor. Blue Bank pays 8% interest compounded quarterly on $8,000. Sun Bank offers 8% interest compounded semiannually on $8,000. The 8% rate is the **nominal rate,** or stated rate, on which the bank calculates the interest. To calculate the **effective rate (annual percentage yield,** or **APY),** however, we can use the following formula:

$$\text{Effective rate (APY)}^6 = \frac{\text{Interest for I year}}{\text{Principal}}$$

Now let's calculate the effective rate (APY) for Blue Bank and Sun Bank.

Note the effective rates (APY) can be seen from Table 12.1 for $1:
1.0824 ← 4 periods, 2%
1.0816 ← 2 periods, 4%

Blue, 8% compounded quarterly	Sun, 8% compounded semiannually
Periods = 4 (4 × 1)	Periods = 2 (2 × 1)
Percent = $\frac{8\%}{4}$ = 2%	Percent = $\frac{8\%}{2}$ = 4%
Principal = $8,000	Principal = $8,000
Table 12.1 lookup: 4 periods, 2%	Table 12.1 lookup: 2 periods, 4%
1.0824 × $8,000 Less $8,659.20 principal − 8,000.00 $ 659.20	1.0816 × $8,000 $8,652.80 − 8,000.00 $ 652.80
Effective rate (APY) = $\frac{\$659.20}{\$8,000}$ = .0824	$\frac{\$652.80}{\$8,000}$ = .0816
= 8.24%	= 8.16%

FIGURE 12.3

Nominal and effective rates (APY) of interest compared

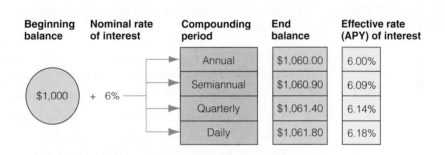

Beginning balance	Nominal rate of interest	Compounding period	End balance	Effective rate (APY) of interest
		Annual	$1,060.00	6.00%
$1,000	+ 6%	Semiannual	$1,060.90	6.09%
		Quarterly	$1,061.40	6.14%
		Daily	$1,061.80	6.18%

MONEY tips

Are you financially "on track"? Here is a simple calculation to help estimate what your net worth should be:
(Age × Pre-tax income) ÷ 10

Figure 12.3 illustrates a comparison of nominal and effective rates (APY) of interest. This comparison should make you question any advertisement of interest rates before depositing your money.

Before concluding this unit, we briefly discuss compounding interest daily.

Compounding Interest Daily

Although many banks add interest to each account quarterly, some banks pay interest that is **compounded daily,** and other banks use *continuous compounding.* Remember that continuous compounding sounds great, but in fact, it yields only a fraction of a percent more interest over a year than daily compounding. Today, computers perform these calculations.

Table 12.2 (p. 308) is a partial table showing what $1 will grow to in the future by daily compounded interest, 360-day basis. For example, we can calculate interest compounded daily on $900 at 6% per year for 25 years as follows:

$900 × 4.4811 = $4,032.99 daily compounding

---

[6]Round to the nearest hundredth percent as needed. In practice, the rate is often rounded to the nearest thousandth.

TABLE	12.2	Interest on a $1 deposit compounded daily—360-day basis

Number of years	6.00%	6.50%	7.00%	7.50%	8.00%	8.50%	9.00%	9.50%	10.00%
1	1.0618	1.0672	1.0725	1.0779	1.0833	1.0887	1.0942	1.0996	1.1052
2	1.1275	1.1388	1.1503	1.1618	1.1735	1.1853	1.1972	1.2092	1.2214
3	1.1972	1.2153	1.2337	1.2523	1.2712	1.2904	1.3099	1.3297	1.3498
4	1.2712	1.2969	1.3231	1.3498	1.3771	1.4049	1.4333	1.4622	1.4917
5	1.3498	1.3840	1.4190	1.4549	1.4917	1.5295	1.5682	1.6079	1.6486
6	1.4333	1.4769	1.5219	1.5682	1.6160	1.6652	1.7159	1.7681	1.8220
7	1.5219	1.5761	1.6322	1.6904	1.7506	1.8129	1.8775	1.9443	2.0136
8	1.6160	1.6819	1.7506	1.8220	1.8963	1.9737	2.0543	2.1381	2.2253
9	1.7159	1.7949	1.8775	1.9639	2.0543	2.1488	2.2477	2.3511	2.4593
10	1.8220	1.9154	2.0136	2.1168	2.2253	2.3394	2.4593	2.5854	2.7179
15	2.4594	2.6509	2.8574	3.0799	3.3197	3.5782	3.8568	4.1571	4.4808
20	3.3198	3.6689	4.0546	4.4810	4.9522	5.4728	6.0482	6.6842	7.3870
25	4.4811	5.0777	5.7536	6.5195	7.3874	8.3708	9.4851	10.7477	12.1782
30	6.0487	7.0275	8.1645	9.4855	11.0202	12.8032	14.8747	17.2813	20.0772

Now it's time to check your progress with the following Practice Quiz.

LU 12–1	PRACTICE QUIZ

Complete this **Practice Quiz** to see how you are doing.

1. Complete the following without a table (round each calculation to the nearest cent as needed):

Principal	Time	Rate of compound interest	Compounded	Number of periods to be compounded	Total amount	Total interest
$200	1 year	8%	Quarterly	a.	b.	c.

2. Solve the previous problem by using compound value (FV) in Table 12.1.
3. Lionel Rodgers deposits $6,000 in Victory Bank, which pays 3% interest compounded semiannually. How much will Lionel have in his account at the end of 8 years?
4. Find the effective rate (APY) for the year: principal, $7,000; interest rate, 12%; and compounded quarterly.
5. Calculate by Table 12.2 what $1,500 compounded daily for 5 years will grow to at 7%.

*For **extra help** from your authors–Sharon and Jeff–see the student DVD*

You Tube

Check out the plastic overlays that appear at the end of Chapter 13 to review these concepts.

✓ **Solutions**

1. **a.** 4 (4 × 1)   **b.** $216.48   **c.** $16.48 ($216.48 − $200)

   $200 × 1.02 = $204 × 1.02 = $208.08 × 1.02 = $212.24 × 1.02 = $216.48

2. $200 × 1.0824 = $216.48 (4 periods, 2%)

3. 16 periods, 1½%, $6,000 × 1.2690 = $7,614

4. 4 periods, 3%,

   $7,000 × 1.1255 = $\begin{array}{r} \$7,878.50 \\ -\ 7,000.00 \\ \hline \$\ 878.50 \end{array}$ $\dfrac{\$878.50}{\$7,000.00}$ = 12.55%

5. $1,500 × 1.4190 = $2,128.50

Need more practice? Try this **Extra Practice Quiz** (check figures in the Interactive Chapter Organizer, p. 314). Worked-out Solutions can be found in Appendix B at end of text.

1. Complete the following without a table (round each calculation to the nearest cent as needed):

Principal	Time	Rate of compound interest	Compounded	Number of periods to be compounded	Total amount	Total interest
$500	1 year	8%	Quarterly	a.	b.	c.

2. Solve the previous problem by using compound value (FV). See Table 12.1.

3. Lionel Rodgers deposits $7,000 in Victory Bank, which pays 4% interest compounded semiannually. How much will Lionel have in his account at the end of 8 years?

4. Find the effective rate (APY) for the year: principal, $8,000; interest rate, 6%; and compounded quarterly. Round to the nearest hundredth percent.

5. Calculate by Table 12.2 what $1,800 compounded daily for 5 years will grow to at 6%.

Learning Unit 12–2: Present Value—The Big Picture

Figure 12.1 (p. 302) in Learning Unit 12–1 showed how by compounding, the *future value* of $1 became $1.36. This learning unit discusses *present value*. Before we look at specific calculations involving present value, let's look at the concept of present value.

Figure 12.4 shows that if we invested 74 cents today, compounding would cause the 74 cents to grow to $1 in the future. For example, let's assume you ask this question: "If I need $1 in 4 years in the future, how much must I put in the bank *today* (assume an 8% annual interest)?" To answer this question, you must know the present value of that $1 today. From Figure 12.4, you can see that the present value of $1 is .7350. Remember that the $1 is only worth 74 cents if you wait 4 periods to receive it. This is one reason why so many athletes get such big contracts—much of the money is paid in later years when it is not worth as much.

FIGURE 12.4

Present value of $1 at 8% for four periods

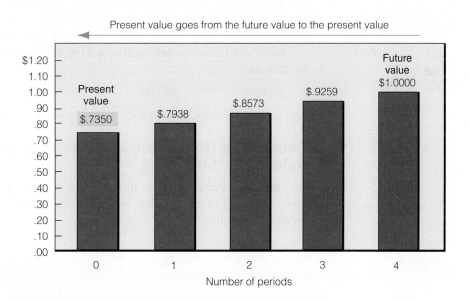

Present value goes from the future value to the present value

Number of periods

LO 1

Relationship of Compounding (FV) to Present Value (PV)— The Bill Smith Example Continued

In Learning Unit 12–1, our consideration of compounding started in the *present* ($80) and looked to find the *future* amount of $108.84. Present value (PV) starts with the *future* and tries to calculate its worth in the *present* ($80). For example, in Figure 12.5 (p. 310), we assume Bill Smith knew that in 4 years he wanted to buy a bike that cost $108.84 (future). Bill's bank pays 8% interest compounded annually. How much money must Bill put in the bank *today* (present) to have $108.84 in 4 years? To work from the future to the present, we can use a present value (PV) table. In the next section you will learn how to use this table.

<table>
<tr><td>**FIGURE** **12.5**</td></tr>
</table>

Present value

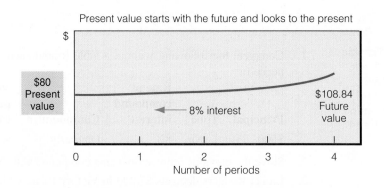

Present value starts with the future and looks to the present

How to Use a Present Value (PV) Table[7]

To calculate present value with a present value table, use the following steps:

LO 2

CALCULATING PRESENT VALUE BY TABLE LOOKUP
Step 1. Find the periods: Years multiplied by number of times interest is compounded in 1 year.
Step 2. Find the rate: Annual rate divided by number of times interest is compounded in 1 year.
Step 3. Go down the Period column of the table to the number of periods desired; look across the row to find the rate. At the intersection of the two columns is the table factor for the compound value of $1.
Step 4. Multiply the table factor times the future value. This gives the present value.

Periods

$$4 \quad \times \quad 1 \quad = \quad 4$$

No. of years   No. of times compounded in 1 year

      Table 12.3 (p. 311) is a present value (PV) table that tells you what $1 is worth today at different interest rates. To continue our Bill Smith example, go down the Period column in Table 12.3 to 4. Then go across to the 8% column. At 8% for 4 periods, we see a table factor of .7350. This means that $1 in the future is worth approximately 74 cents today. If Bill invested 74 cents today at 8% for 4 periods, Bill would have $1 in 4 years.

      Since Bill knows the bike will cost $108.84 in the future, he completes the following calculation:

$$\$108.84 \times .7350 = \boxed{\$80.00}$$

This means that $108.84 in today's dollars is worth $80.00. Now let's check this.

Comparing Compound Interest (FV) Table 12.1 with Present Value (PV) Table 12.3

We know from our calculations that Bill needs to invest $80 for 4 years at 8% compound interest annually to buy his bike. We can check this by going back to Table 12.1 and comparing it with Table 12.3. Let's do this now.

LO 3

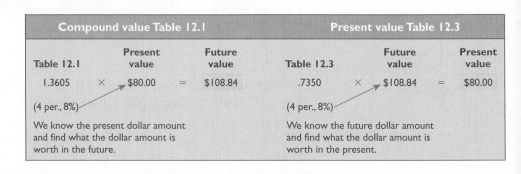

Compound value Table 12.1			Present value Table 12.3		
Table 12.1	Present value	Future value	Table 12.3	Future value	Present value
1.3605	× $80.00	= $108.84	.7350	× $108.84	= $80.00
(4 per., 8%)			(4 per., 8%)		
We know the present dollar amount and find what the dollar amount is worth in the future.			We know the future dollar amount and find what the dollar amount is worth in the present.		

[7]The formula for present value is $PV = \dfrac{A}{(1 + i)^N}$, where A equals future amount (compound amount), N equals number of compounding periods, and i equals interest rate per compounding period. The calculator sequence for Bill Smith would be as follows: 1 $\boxed{+}$ .08 $\boxed{y^x}$ 4 $\boxed{=}$ $\boxed{M+}$ 108.84 $\boxed{\div}$ $\boxed{MR}$ $\boxed{=}$ 80.03.

| TABLE | 12.3 | | Present value of $1 at end of period | | | | | | | | | |

Period	1%	1½%	2%	3%	4%	5%	6%	7%	8%	9%	10%
1	.9901	.9852	.9804	.9709	.9615	.9524	.9434	.9346	.9259	.9174	.9091
2	.9803	.9707	.9612	.9426	.9246	.9070	.8900	.8734	.8573	.8417	.8264
3	.9706	.9563	.9423	.9151	.8890	.8638	.8396	.8163	.7938	.7722	.7513
4	.9610	.9422	.9238	.8885	.8548	.8227	.7921	.7629	.7350	.7084	.6830
5	.9515	.9283	.9057	.8626	.8219	.7835	.7473	.7130	.6806	.6499	.6209
6	.9420	.9145	.8880	.8375	.7903	.7462	.7050	.6663	.6302	.5963	.5645
7	.9327	.9010	.8706	.8131	.7599	.7107	.6651	.6227	.5835	.5470	.5132
8	.9235	.8877	.8535	.7894	.7307	.6768	.6274	.5820	.5403	.5019	.4665
9	.9143	.8746	.8368	.7664	.7026	.6446	.5919	.5439	.5002	.4604	.4241
10	.9053	.8617	.8203	.7441	.6756	.6139	.5584	.5083	.4632	.4224	.3855
11	.8963	.8489	.8043	.7224	.6496	.5847	.5268	.4751	.4289	.3875	.3505
12	.8874	.8364	.7885	.7014	.6246	.5568	.4970	.4440	.3971	.3555	.3186
13	.8787	.8240	.7730	.6810	.6006	.5303	.4688	.4150	.3677	.3262	.2897
14	.8700	.8119	.7579	.6611	.5775	.5051	.4423	.3878	.3405	.2992	.2633
15	.8613	.7999	.7430	.6419	.5553	.4810	.4173	.3624	.3152	.2745	.2394
16	.8528	.7880	.7284	.6232	.5339	.4581	.3936	.3387	.2919	.2519	.2176
17	.8444	.7764	.7142	.6050	.5134	.4363	.3714	.3166	.2703	.2311	.1978
18	.8360	.7649	.7002	.5874	.4936	.4155	.3503	.2959	.2502	.2120	.1799
19	.8277	.7536	.6864	.5703	.4746	.3957	.3305	.2765	.2317	.1945	.1635
20	.8195	.7425	.6730	.5537	.4564	.3769	.3118	.2584	.2145	.1784	.1486
21	.8114	.7315	.6598	.5375	.4388	.3589	.2942	.2415	.1987	.1637	.1351
22	.8034	.7207	.6468	.5219	.4220	.3418	.2775	.2257	.1839	.1502	.1228
23	.7954	.7100	.6342	.5067	.4057	.3256	.2618	.2109	.1703	.1378	.1117
24	.7876	.6995	.6217	.4919	.3901	.3101	.2470	.1971	.1577	.1264	.1015
25	.7798	.6892	.6095	.4776	.3751	.2953	.2330	.1842	.1460	.1160	.0923
26	.7720	.6790	.5976	.4637	.3607	.2812	.2198	.1722	.1352	.1064	.0839
27	.7644	.6690	.5859	.4502	.3468	.2678	.2074	.1609	.1252	.0976	.0763
28	.7568	.6591	.5744	.4371	.3335	.2551	.1956	.1504	.1159	.0895	.0693
29	.7493	.6494	.5631	.4243	.3207	.2429	.1846	.1406	.1073	.0822	.0630
30	.7419	.6398	.5521	.4120	.3083	.2314	.1741	.1314	.0994	.0754	.0573
35	.7059	.5939	.5000	.3554	.2534	.1813	.1301	.0937	.0676	.0490	.0356
40	.6717	.5513	.4529	.3066	.2083	.1420	.0972	.0668	.0460	.0318	.0221

Note: For more detailed tables, see your booklet, the *Business Math Handbook.*

Note that the table factor for compounding is over 1 (1.3605) and the table factor for present value is less than 1 (.7350). The compound value table starts with the present and goes to the future. The present value table starts with the future and goes to the present.

Let's look at another example before trying the Practice Quiz.

EXAMPLE   Rene Weaver needs $20,000 for college in 4 years. She can earn 8% compounded quarterly at her bank. How much must Rene deposit at the beginning of the year to have $20,000 in 4 years?

Remember that in this example the bank compounds the interest *quarterly.* Let's first determine the period and rate on a quarterly basis:

$$\text{Periods} = 4 \times 4 \text{ years} = 16 \text{ periods} \qquad \text{Rate} = \frac{8\%}{4} = 2\%$$

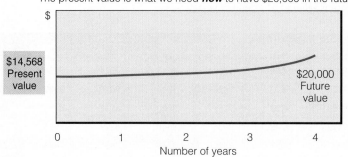

FIGURE 12.6

Present value

The present value is what we need ***now*** to have $20,000 in the future

Now we go to Table 12.3 and find 16 under the Period column. We then move across to the 2% column and find the .7284 table factor.

$20,000 × .7284 = **$14,568**

(future value)   (present value)

We illustrate this in Figure 12.6.

We can check the $14,568 present value by using the compound value Table 12.1:

16 periods, 2% column = 1.3728 × $14,568 = $19,998.95[8]

Let's test your understanding of this unit with the Practice Quiz.

LU 12–2 PRACTICE QUIZ

Complete this **Practice Quiz** to see how you are doing.

Use the present value Table 12.3 to complete:

	Future amount desired	Length of time	Rate compounded	Table period	Rate used	PV factor	PV amount
1.	$ 7,000	6 years	6% semiannually	_____	_____	_____	_____
2.	$15,000	20 years	10% annually	_____	_____	_____	_____

3. Bill Blum needs $20,000 6 years from today to attend V.P.R. Tech. How much must Bill put in the bank today (12% quarterly) to reach his goal?

4. Bob Fry wants to buy his grandson a Ford Taurus in 4 years. The cost of a car will be $24,000. Assuming a bank rate of 8% compounded quarterly, how much must Bob put in the bank today?

For ***extra help*** from your authors–Sharon and Jeff–see the student DVD

✓ Solutions

1. 12 periods (6 years × 2)   3% (6% ÷ 2)   .7014 $4,909.80 ($7,000 × .7014)

2. 20 periods (20 years × 1)   10% (10% ÷ 1)   .1486 $2,229.00 ($15,000 × .1486)

3. 6 years × 4 = 24 periods $\dfrac{12\%}{4} = 3\%$ .4919 × $20,000 = **$9,838**

4. 4 × 4 years = 16 periods $\dfrac{8\%}{4} = 2\%$ .7284 × $24,000 = **$17,481.60**

[8]Not quite $20,000 due to rounding of table factors.

LU 12–2a EXTRA PRACTICE QUIZ WITH WORKED-OUT SOLUTIONS

Need more practice? Try this **Extra Practice Quiz** (check figures in the Interactive Chapter Organizer, p. 314). Worked-out Solutions can be found in Appendix B at end of text.

Use the *Business Math Handbook* to complete:

Future amount desired	Length of time	Rate compounded	Table period	Rate used	PV factor	PV amount
1. $ 9,000	7 years	$2\frac{1}{2}\%$ semiannually	____	____	____	____
2. $20,000	20 years	4% annually	____	____	____	____

3. Bill Blum needs $40,000 6 years from today to attend V.P.R. Tech. How much must Bill put in the bank today (8% quarterly) to reach his goal?

4. Bob Fry wants to buy his grandson a Ford Taurus in 4 years. The cost of a car will be $28,000. Assuming a bank rate of 4% compounded quarterly, how much must Bob put in the bank today?

INTERACTIVE CHAPTER ORGANIZER

Topic/procedure/formula	Examples	You try it*
Calculating compound amount without tables (future value),† p. 303 Determine new amount by multiplying rate times new balance (that includes interest added on). Start in present and look to future. $\dfrac{\text{Compound}}{\text{interest}} = \dfrac{\text{Compound}}{\text{amount}} - \text{Principal}$ ⊢——Compounding——⊣ PV ⟶ FV	$100 in savings account, compounded annually for 2 years at 8%: $100 $108 × 1.08 × 1.08 $108 $116.64 (future value)	**Calculate compound amount (future value)** $200 for 2 years at 4%, compounded annually
Calculating compound amount (future value) by table lookup, p. 304 Periods = $\dfrac{\text{Number of times}}{\text{compounded}}$ × $\dfrac{\text{Years of}}{\text{loan}}$ per year Rate = $\dfrac{\text{Annual rate}}{\text{Number of times compounded per year}}$ Multiply table factor (intersection of period and rate) times amount of principal.	*Example:* $2,000 at 12% for 5 years and compounded quarterly: Periods = 4 × 5 years = 20 Rate = $\dfrac{12\%}{4}$ = 3% 20 periods, 3% = 1.8061 (table factor) $2,000 × 1.8061 = $3,612.20 (future value)	**Calculate compound amount by table lookup** $4,000 at 6% for 6 years, compounded semiannually

Calculating effective rate (APY), pp. 306–307
 	
Effective rate (APY) = $\dfrac{\text{Interest for 1 year}}{\text{Principal}}$
or
Rate can be seen in Table 12.1 factor.
	$1,000 at 10% compounded semiannually for 1 year.
	By Table 12.1: 2 periods, 5%
	1.1025 means at end of year investor has earned 110.25% of original principal. Thus the interest is 10.25%.
	$1,000 × 1.1025 = $1,102.50
	      − 1,000.00
	       $ 102.50
	
	$\dfrac{\$102.50}{\$1,000}$ = 10.25%
	    effective rate (APY)
		Calculate effective rate
		$4,000 at 6% for 1 year, compounded semiannually

(continues)

INTERACTIVE CHAPTER ORGANIZER

Topic/procedure/formula	Examples	You try it*
Calculating present value (PV) by table lookup‡, p. 310 Start with future and calculate worth in the present. Periods and rate computed like in compound interest. ⊢——Present value——⊣ PV ⟵⟶ FV Find periods and rate. Multiply table factor (intersection of period and rate) times amount of loan.	*Example:* Want \$3,612.20 after 5 years with rate of 12% compounded quarterly: Periods = 4 × 5 = 20; % = 3% By Table 12.3: 20 periods, 3% = .5537 \$3,612.20 × .5537 = \$2,000.08 ↙ Invested today will yield desired amount in future	**Calculate present value by table lookup** Want \$6,000 after 4 years with rate of 6%, compounded quarterly

KEY TERMS			
	Annual percentage yield (APY), *p. 307* Compound amount, *p. 302* Compounded annually, *p. 302* Compounded daily, *pp. 302, 308* Compounded monthly, *p. 302*	Compounded quarterly, *p. 302* Compounded semiannually, *p. 302* Compounding, *p. 301* Compound interest, *p. 301* Effective rate, *p. 307*	Future value (FV), *p. 301* Nominal rate, *p. 307* Number of periods, *p. 302* Present value (PV), *p. 302* Rate for each period, *p. 302*

| Check Figures for Extra Practice Quizzes with Page References. (Worked-out Solutions in Appendix B.) | LU 12–1a (p. 309)
1. 4 periods; Int. = \$41.22; \$541.21
2. \$541.21
3. \$9,609.60
4. 6.14%
5. \$2,429.64 | LU 12–2a (p. 313)
1. 14 periods; $2\frac{1}{2}$%; \$6,369.30
2. 20 periods; 4%; \$9,128
3. \$24,868
4. \$23,878.40 |

*Worked-out solutions are in Appendix B.

†$A = P(1 + i)^N$.

‡$\dfrac{A}{(1 + i)^N}$ if table not used.

Critical Thinking Discussion Questions with Chapter Concept Check

1. Explain how periods and rates are calculated in compounding problems. Compare simple interest to compound interest.

2. What are the steps to calculate the compound amount by table? Why is the compound table factor greater than \$1?

3. What is the effective rate (APY)? Why can the effective rate be seen directly from the table factor?

4. Explain the difference between compounding and present value. Why is the present value table factor less than \$1?

5. **Chapter Concept Check.** Using the information from the chapter opener that shows the cost of raising a child, create a problem using present value and compounding to show the amount you would need to put away today in a bank to have enough money to pay for a child's costs through the age of 18. Assume your own rates and periods and that the amount you put in the bank is one lump sum that will grow through compounding (without new investments).

Check figures for odd-numbered problems in Appendix C. Name _____ Date _____

DRILL PROBLEMS

Complete the following without using Table 12.1 (round to the nearest cent for each calculation) and then check your answer by Table 12.1 (check will be off due to rounding). *LU 12-1(2)*

	Principal	Time (years)	Rate of compound interest	Compounded	Periods	Rate	Total amount	Total interest
12–1.	$1,600	2	6%	Semiannually				

Complete the following using compound future value Table 12.1: *LU 12-1(2)*

	Time	Principal	Rate	Compounded	Amount	Interest
12–2.	12 years	$15,000	$3\frac{1}{2}\%$	Annually		
12–3.	6 months	$15,000	6%	Semiannually		
12–4.	3 years	$6,000	6%	Quarterly		

Calculate the effective rate (APY) of interest for 1 year. *LU 12-1(3)*

12–5. Principal: $15,500
Interest rate: 12%
Compounded quarterly
Effective rate (APY):

12–6. Using Table 12.2, calculate what $700 would grow to at $6\frac{1}{2}\%$ per year compounded daily for 7 years. *LU 12-1(3)*

Complete the following using present value Table 12.3 or the present value table in the *Business Math Handbook*. *LU 12-2(2)*

	Amount desired at end of period	Length of time	Rate	Compounded	On PV Table 12.3 Period used	On PV Table 12.3 Rate used	PV factor used	PV of amount desired at end of period
12–7. eXcel	$6,000	8 years	3%	Semiannually				
12–8. eXcel	$8,900	4 years	6%	Monthly				
12–9. eXcel	$17,600	7 years	12%	Quarterly				

12–10. $20,000   20 years   8%   Annually

eXcel

12–11. Check your answer in Problem 12–9 by the compound value Table 12.1. The answer will be off due to rounding. *LU 12-2(3)*

WORD PROBLEMS

12–12. Sam Long anticipates he will need approximately $225,000 in 15 years to cover his 3-year-old daughter's college bills for a 4-year degree. How much would he have to invest today at an interest rate of 8 percent compounded semiannually? *LU 12-2(2)*

12–13. Lynn Ally, owner of a local Subway shop, loaned $40,000 to Pete Hall to help him open a Subway franchise. Pete plans to repay Lynn at the end of 8 years with 6% interest compounded semiannually. How much will Lynn receive at the end of 8 years? *LU 12-1(2)*

12–14. Molly Hamilton deposited $50,000 at Bank of America at 8% interest compounded quarterly. What is the effective rate (APY) to the nearest hundredth percent? *LU 12-1(3)*

12–15. Melvin Indecision has difficulty deciding whether to put his savings in Mystic Bank or Four Rivers Bank. Mystic offers eXcel 10% interest compounded semiannually. Four Rivers offers 8% interest compounded quarterly. Melvin has $10,000 to invest. He expects to withdraw the money at the end of 4 years. Which bank gives Melvin the better deal? Check your answer. *LU 12-1(3)*

12–16. Lee Holmes deposited $15,000 in a new savings account at 9% interest compounded semiannually. At the beginning of year 4, Lee deposits an additional $40,000 at 9% interest compounded semiannually. At the end of 6 years, what is the balance in Lee's account? *LU 12-1(2)*

12–17. Lee Wills loaned Audrey Chin $16,000 to open Snip Its Hair Salon. After 6 years, Audrey will repay Lee with 8% interest eXcel compounded quarterly. How much will Lee receive at the end of 6 years? *LU 12-1(2)*

12–18. If you receive a $3,750 tax refund, bonus, or other lump sum of money, how much will it be worth in 25 years if you invest it today at 4% interest compounded annually? *LU 12-1(2)*

12–19. John Roe, an employee of the Gap, loans $3,000 to another employee at the store. He will be repaid at the end of 4 years with interest at 6% compounded quarterly. How much will John be repaid? *LU 12-1(2)*

12–20. The International Monetary Fund is trying to raise $500 billion in 5 years for new funds to lend to developing countries. At 6% interest compounded quarterly, how much must it invest today to reach $500 billion in 5 years? *LU 12-2(2)*

12–21. Security National Bank is quoting 1-year certificates of deposit with an interest rate of 5% compounded semiannually. Joe Saver purchased a $5,000 CD. What is the CD's effective rate (APY) to the nearest hundredth percent? Use tables in the *Business Math Handbook*. *LU 12-1(2, 3)*

12–22. Jim Ryan, an owner of a Burger King restaurant, assumes that his restaurant will need a new roof in 7 years. He estimates the roof will cost him $9,000 at that time. What amount should Jim invest today at 6% compounded quarterly to be able to pay for the roof? Check your answer. *LU 12-2(2)*

12–23. Tony Ring wants to attend Northeast College. He will need $60,000 4 years from today. Assume Tony's bank pays *eXcel* 12% interest compounded semiannually. What must Tony deposit today so he will have $60,000 in 4 years? *LU 12-2(2)*

12–24. Check your answer (to the nearest dollar) in Problem 12–23 by using the compound value Table 12.1. The answer will be slightly off due to rounding. *LU 12-1(3)*

12–25. Pete Air wants to buy a used Jeep in 5 years. He estimates the Jeep will cost $15,000. Assume Pete invests $10,000 now at 12% interest compounded semiannually. Will Pete have enough money to buy his Jeep at the end of 5 years? *LU 12-1(2), LU 12-2(2)*

12–26. Lance Jackson deposited $5,000 at Basil Bank at 9% interest compounded daily. What is Lance's investment at the end of 4 years? *LU 12-1(2)*

12–27. Paul Havlik promised his grandson Jamie that he would give him $6,000 8 years from today for graduating from high school. Assume money is worth 6% interest compounded semiannually. What is the present value of this $6,000? *LU 12-2(2)*

12–28. Earl Ezekiel wants to retire in San Diego when he is 65 years old. Earl is now 50. He believes he will need $300,000 to retire comfortably. To date, Earl has set aside no retirement money. Assume Earl gets 6% interest compounded semiannually. How much must Earl invest today to meet his $300,000 goal? *LU 12-2(2)*

12–29. Jackie Rich would like to buy a $19,000 Toyota hybrid car in 4 years. Jackie wants to put the money aside now. Jackie's bank offers 8% interest compounded semiannually. How much must Jackie invest today? *LU 12-2(2)*

12–30. Treasure Mountain International School in Park City, Utah, is a public middle school interested in raising money for next year's Sundance Film Festival. If the school raises $2,989 and invests it for 1 year at 3% interest compounded annually, what is the APY earned? *LU 12-1(2, 3)*

CHALLENGE PROBLEMS

12–31. Pete's Real Estate is currently valued at $65,000. Pete feels the value of his business will increase at a rate of 10% per year, compounded semiannually for the next 5 years.

At a local fundraiser, a competitor offered Pete $70,000 for the business. If he sells, Pete plans to invest the money at 6% compounded quarterly. What price should Pete ask? Verify your answer. *LU 12-1(2), LU 12-2(2)*

12–32. You are the financial planner for Johnson Controls. Assume last year's profits were $700,000. The board of directors decided to forgo dividends to stockholders and retire high-interest outstanding bonds that were issued 5 years ago at a face value of $1,250,000. You have been asked to invest the profits in a bank. The board must know how much money you will need from the profits earned to retire the bonds in 10 years. Bank A pays 6% compounded quarterly, and Bank B pays $6\frac{1}{2}$% compounded annually. Which bank would you recommend, and how much of the company's profit should be placed in the bank? If you recommended that the remaining money not be distributed to stockholders but be placed in Bank B, how much would the remaining money be worth in 10 years? Use tables in the *Business Math Handbook.** Round final answer to nearest dollar. *LU 12-1(2, 3), LU 12-2(2)*

*Check glossary for unfamiliar terms.

Do you need help? The DVD has step-by-step worked-out solutions.

1. Lorna Ray, owner of a Starbucks franchise, loaned $40,000 to Lee Reese to help him open a new flower shop online. Lee plans to repay Lorna at the end of 5 years with 4% interest compounded semiannually. How much will Lorna receive at the end of 5 years? *(p. 304)   LU 12-1(2)*

2. Joe Beary wants to attend Riverside College. Eight years from today he will need $50,000. If Joe's bank pays 6% interest compounded semiannually, what must Joe deposit today to have $50,000 in 8 years? *(p. 310)   LU 12-2(2)*

3. Shelley Katz deposited $30,000 in a savings account at 5% interest compounded semiannually. At the beginning of year 4, Shelley deposits an additional $80,000 at 5% interest compounded semiannually. At the end of 6 years, what is the balance in Shelley's account? *(p. 304)   LU 12-1(2)*

4. Earl Miller, owner of a Papa Gino's franchise, wants to buy a new delivery truck in 6 years. He estimates the truck will cost $30,000. If Earl invests $20,000 now at 5% interest compounded semiannually, will Earl have enough money to buy his delivery truck at the end of 6 years? *(pp. 304, 310)   LU 12-1(2), LU 12-2(2)*

5. Minnie Rose deposited $16,000 in Street Bank at 6% interest compounded quarterly. What was the effective rate (APY)? Round to the nearest hundredth percent. *(pp. 304, 306)   LU 12-1(2, 3)*

6. Lou Ling, owner of Lou's Lube, estimates that he will need $70,000 for new equipment in 7 years. Lou decided to put aside money today so it will be available in 7 years. Reel Bank offers Lou 6% interest compounded quarterly. How much must Lou invest to have $70,000 in 7 years? *(p. 310)   LU 12-2(2)*

7. Bernie Long wants to retire to California when she is 60 years of age. Bernie is now 40. She believes that she will need $900,000 to retire comfortably. To date, Bernie has set aside no retirement money. If Bernie gets 8% compounded semiannually, how much must Bernie invest today to meet her $900,000 goal? *(p. 310)   LU 12-2(2)*

8. Jim Jones deposited $19,000 in a savings account at 7% interest compounded daily. At the end of 6 years, what is the balance in Jim's account? *(p. 304)   LU 12-1(2)*

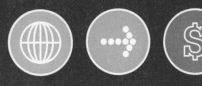

PROBLEM 1
"Plant" a money tree

Go to http://www.finaid.org/calculators/compoundinterest.phtml. If you invest $1,000 for 20 years at an 8% nominal annual interest rate, how much will you earn with monthly compounding? Daily compounding? How much difference between the monthly and the daily compounding?

Discussion Questions

1. What are the pros and cons of investing your money for an extended period of time such as 20 years?

2. What is the advantage to the financial institution paying the interest on your investment while holding your investment money?

PROBLEM 2
CD countdown

Go to http://www.bankrate.com. Get a rate for a 5-year certificate of deposit (CD). If you invest $5,000 today, what will the value be at maturity?

Discussion Questions

1. What are the advantages of investing in a CD versus in a regular savings account?

2. What are the advantages of offering CD investments from the perspective of the financial institution?

PROBLEM 3
Double your money!

Go to http://invest-faq.com/articles/analy-rule-72.html. Create another column for the table there where you divide each number of years into 70. Which gives results closer to the true result—the Rule of 72, or the Rule of 70? Can you find a number that when you divide the years into the number you get even closer to the true value? Why do you think the Rule of 72 is used?

Discussion Questions

1. Why would we want to look at our investments from the perspective of doubling our money?

2. What types of investments might be able to earn more than 10% per year?

PROBLEM 4
You can afford your dream home

Go to http://bankrate.com/brm/calc/savecalc.asp. Suppose you want to save $25,000 for a down payment on a house and you have 10 years to save this amount. How much would you need to save monthly to achieve this goal if the interest rate is 5% compounded monthly? What happens if you can increase your interest rate to 8%?

Discussion Questions

1. How would your down payment impact the type of house you purchase?

2. How does breaking up your investment into monthly contributions assist in meeting your ultimate goals?

MOBILE APPS

Compound Interest Calculator (Space Age Industries LLC) Calculates compound interest with varying amounts, duration, interest, and frequency.

InvestCalc (Fred Boratto) Figures investment values based upon present values as well as future values and what it will take to achieve these values in the future.

INTERNET PROJECTS

See text website
www.mhhe.com/slater11e_sse_ch12

Retirement Reality Check: Are You Saving Enough?

To maintain a comfortable lifestyle in retirement, you should aim to replace about 80% of your current gross income. Social Security will supply about 30% of that amount for most middle-income workers. (You can get your personalized estimate of how much to expect from Social Security at www.ssa.gov/estimator.) The rest of your retirement income may come from pension benefits, a job or personal savings. To establish a nest egg target, you need a rough idea of how much money you'll want to draw from your savings each month.

Steps	How It Works	What to Do	Your Answers
1	**Meet John.** He's 55, plans to retire in ten years and thinks he may live until 90. He assumes an average 6% return on his investments and he estimates that he'll need $2,500 per month from his savings. John looks at table 1 and finds where 25 years and 6% intersect: $205,000. That's how much he'll need to produce $1,000 per month of retirement income. But he needs more than twice that much. So he divides $2,500 by $1,000 and comes up with a factor of 2.5. Then he calculates his target nest egg amount: $205,000 x 2.5 = $512,500.	**Divide your monthly income needs by 1,000 and multiply it by the amount in table 1.**	TARGET NEEDS $
2	Table 2 will help you calculate the future value of your existing investments. With ten years to go before retiring and an assumed rate of return of 6%, John's factor from table 2 is 1.79. When he multiplies his current balance of $250,000 by 1.79, the future value of his account at retirement is $447,500.	**Multiply your current account balance by the factor in table 2.**	$
3	Table 3 shows the future value of your ongoing monthly contributions. John is also saving $500 per month and assumes his savings will earn 6% over the next ten years. The future value of his monthly contribution is $82,350 ($500 x 164.70 = $82,350).	**Multiply your monthly contributions by the factor in table 3.**	$
4	Using John's example, his projected savings are step 2 ($447,500) + step 3 ($82,350) = $529, 850.	**Add your answers in step 2 and step 3 together.**	PROJECTED SAVINGS $

TABLE 1 (dollar values needed to produce $1,000 per month; assumes 3% annual inflation)

Rate of return	Years in retirement						
	5	10	15	20	25	30	35
2%	$60,000	$123,000	$189,000	$259,000	$331,000	$408,000	$488,000
4	57,000	111,000	162,000	211,000	258,000	302,000	344,000
6	54,000	100,000	140,000	175,000	**205,000**	231,000	254,000
8	51,000	91,000	122,000	147,000	167,000	182,000	194,000
10	48,000	83,000	108,000	125,000	138,000	148,000	154,000

TABLE 2 (current balance factor)

Time to retire.	Rate of return			
	4%	6%	8%	10%
5 years	1.22	1.34	1.47	1.61
10 years	1.48	**1.79**	2.16	2.60
15 years	1.80	2.34	3.17	4.18
20 years	2.19	3.21	4.66	6.73

TABLE 3 (monthly contribution factor)

Time to retire.	Rate of return			
	4%	6%	8%	10%
5 years	66.52	70.11	73.97	78.08
10 years	147.74	**164.70**	184.17	206.55
15 years	246.91	292.27	348.35	417.92
20 years	368.00	464.35	592.95	765.70

*John's results in bold. SOURCE: Strategic Distribution Institute

WHAT DOES IT MEAN?

If step 4 is larger than step 1, congratulations, you're on track.

If step 4 is smaller than step 1, you need to make some changes to reach your nest egg goal. Consider working a few years longer, saving more each month or adjusting your investment mix to achieve a higher return. Or reconsider how much retirement income you will need.

In John's example, he is slightly ahead of his goal ($529,850 - $512,500 = $17,350). But because this is just a rough estimate, he should continue his current savings plan. Very few people have reached retirement regretting that they saved too much. But John is relieved that his savings are on track after all.

BUSINESS MATH ISSUE

Most people should start building their nest egg by the age of 40.

1. List the key points of the article and information to support your position.
2. Write a group defense of your position using math calculations to support your view.

CHAPTER 13

Annuities and Sinking Funds

Hold Off on Those Retirement Parties

Among the states requiring or urging public workers to delay retiring:

■ **Arizona:** Increased the 'retirement rule'—worker's age plus years of service before retirement—to 85 from 80.

■ **Colorado:** Increased the 'retirement rule' to 88 from 85 as of 2011, and to 90 as of 2017.

■ **Illinois:** Increased retirement age to 67 from 60.

■ **Michigan:** Minimum retirement age of 60; before, workers needed 30 years of service at any age.

■ **Minnesota:** Increased penalty for early retirement for state patrol and correctional workers.

■ **Missouri:** Increased retirement age to 67 with 10 years of service up from age 62 with 5 years of service; some very-long term workers may be able to retire earlier.

■ **Utah:** Increased total service years before retirement for fire and public safety employees to 25 from 20; for most other state workers to 35 from 30.

Source: National Conference of State Legislatures and pension systems. Retirement age refers to the age at which a worker can retire without a reduced pension. Changes don't apply to all state workers and they take effect at different times. Most affect only new hires.

How long might a $2 million portfolio last?

If withdrawals start at age 65 and rise 3% a year, here are the ages at which T. Rowe Price Group figures there's a significant chance the portfolio will run dry.

First-year withdrawal	Danger zone* (Age)
$80,000 (4%)	97
$120,000	82
$160,000	77
$200,000	74

* Based on 10,000 market scenarios, these are the ages at which there's a 1-in-10 chance of having no money left. Assumes an investment mix of 60% stocks and 40% bonds.
Source: T. Rowe Price Group

Douglas B. Jones

Note: **A complete set of plastic overlays showing the concept of annuities is found at the end of the chapter.**

LU 13–1: Annuities: Ordinary Annuity and Annuity Due (Find Future Value)

1. Differentiate between contingent annuities and annuities certain *(p. 325).*
2. Calculate the future value of an ordinary annuity and an annuity due manually and by table lookup *(pp. 325–329).*

LU 13–2: Present Value of an Ordinary Annuity (Find Present Value)

1. Calculate the present value of an ordinary annuity by table lookup and manually check the calculation *(pp. 330–331).*
2. Compare the calculation of the present value of one lump sum versus the present value of an ordinary annuity *(p. 332).*

LU 13–3: Sinking Funds (Find Periodic Payments)

1. Calculate the payment made at the end of each period by table lookup *(pp. 333–334).*
2. Check table lookup by using ordinary annuity table *(p. 334).*

Here are key terms in this chapter. After completing the chapter, if you know the term, place a checkmark in the parentheses. If you don't know the term, look it up and put the page number where it can be found.

Annuities certain ( ) Annuity ( ) Annuity due ( ) Contingent annuities ( ) Future value of an annuity ( ) Ordinary annuity ( ) Payment periods ( ) Present value of an ordinary annuity ( ) Sinking fund ( ) Term of the annuity ( )

The *Wall Street Journal* clip "How Long Might a $2 Million Portfolio Last?" in the chapter opener shows that a large amount saved for retirement could be quickly reduced in future years. Note also in the *Wall Street Journal* clip "Hold Off on Those Retirement Parties" that many states are increasing the age requirements for retiring public workers. As the following clip shows, many factors—even small ones like your daily coffee spending—could affect your retirement savings.

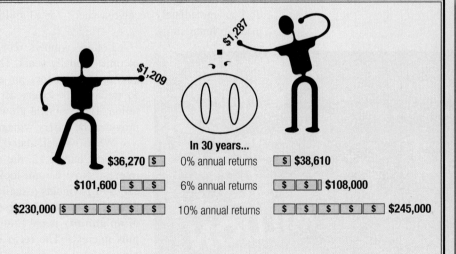

INVESTING YOUR SAVINGS
Assuming the price of coffee remains the same, we added up what you would save if you gave up coffee over 30 years and what you would save if you made coffee at home instead of buying it.

We then invested the savings. We compounded each amount weekly at annual rates: 0 percent, which means you did nothing with the money; at 6 percent, which is an average expected rate of return on a stock portfolio, and at 10 percent, an aggressive expected rate of return.

$1,209

$1,287

In 30 years...

$36,270 — 0% annual returns — $38,610

$101,600 — 6% annual returns — $108,000

$230,000 — 10% annual returns — $245,000

© Tim Boyle/Getty Images

So, would you like to save $1,287? A *Boston Globe* article entitled "Cost of Living: A Cup a Day" began by explaining that each month the *Globe* runs a feature on an everyday expense to see how much it costs an average person. Since many people are coffee drinkers, the *Globe* assumed that a person drank 3 cups a day of Dunkin' Donuts coffee at the cost of $1.65 a cup. For a 5-day week, the person would spend $1,287 annually (52 weeks). If the person brewed the coffee at home, the cost of the beans per cup would be $0.10 with an annual expense of $78, saving $1,209 over the Dunkin' Donuts coffee. If a person gave up drinking coffee, the person would save $1,287.

The article continued with the discussion on "Investing Your Savings" (page 323). Note how much you would have in 30 years if you invested your money in 0%, 6%, and 10% annual returns. Using the magic of compounding, if you saved $1,287 a year, your money could grow to a quarter of a million dollars.

This chapter shows how to compute compound interest that results from a *stream* of payments, or an annuity. Chapter 12 showed how to calculate compound interest on a lump-sum payment deposited at the beginning of a particular time. Knowing how to calculate interest compounding on a lump sum will make the calculation of interest compounding on annuities easier to understand.

We begin the chapter by explaining the difference between calculating the future value of an ordinary annuity and an annuity due. Then you learn how to find the present value of an ordinary annuity. The chapter ends with a discussion of sinking funds.

Learning Unit 13–1: Annuities: Ordinary Annuity and Annuity Due (Find Future Value)

Many parents of small children are concerned about being able to afford to pay for their children's college educations. (See Chapter 12 opener.) Some parents deposit a lump sum in a financial institution when the child is in diapers. The interest on this sum is compounded until the child is 18, when the parents withdraw the money for college expenses. Parents could also fund their children's educations with annuities by depositing a series of payments for a certain time. The concept of annuities is the first topic in this learning unit.

Concept of an Annuity—The Big Picture

All of us would probably like to win $1 million in a state lottery. What happens when you have the winning ticket? You take it to the lottery headquarters. When you turn in the ticket, do you immediately receive a check for $1 million? No. Lottery payoffs are not usually made in lump sums.

© Daniel Acker/Bloomberg via Getty Images

Lottery winners receive a series of payments over a period of time—usually years. This *stream* of payments is an **annuity.** By paying the winners an annuity, lotteries do not actually spend $1 million. The lottery deposits a sum of money in a financial institution. The continual growth of this sum through compound interest provides the lottery winner with a series of payments.

When we calculated the maturity value of a lump-sum payment in Chapter 12, the maturity value was the principal and its interest. Now we are looking not at lump-sum payments but at a series of payments (usually of equal amounts over regular **payment periods**) plus the interest that accumulates. So the **future value of an annuity** is the future *dollar amount* of a series of payments plus interest.[1] The **term of the annuity** is the time from the beginning of the first payment period to the end of the last payment period.

---

[1]The term *amount of an annuity* has the same meaning as *future value of an annuity.*

FIGURE   **13.1**

Future value of an annuity of
$1 at 8%

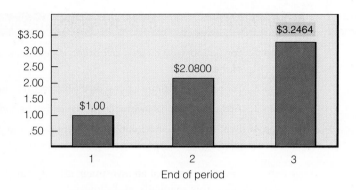

The concept of the future value of an annuity is illustrated in Figure 13.1. Do not be concerned about the calculations (we will do them soon). Let's first focus on the big picture of annuities. In Figure 13.1 we see the following:

At end of period 1:   The $1 is still worth $1 because it was invested at the *end* of the period.

At end of period 2:   An additional $1 is invested. The $2.00 is now worth $2.08. Note the $1 from period 1 earns interest but not the $1 invested at the end of period 2.

At end of period 3:   An additional $1 is invested. The $3.00 is now worth $3.25. Remember that the last dollar invested earns no interest.

Before learning how to calculate annuities, you should understand the two classifications of annuities.

LO 1

How Annuities Are Classified

Annuities have many uses in addition to lottery payoffs. Some of these uses are insurance companies' pension installments, Social Security payments, home mortgages, businesses paying off notes, bond interest, and savings for a vacation trip or college education.

Annuities are classified into two major groups: contingent annuities and annuities certain. **Contingent annuities** have no fixed number of payments but depend on an uncertain event (e.g., life insurance payments that cease when the insured dies). **Annuities certain** have a specific stated number of payments (e.g., mortgage payments on a home). Based on the time of the payment, we can divide each of these two major annuity groups into the following:

1. **Ordinary annuity**—regular deposits (payments) made at the *end* of the period. Periods could be months, quarters, years, and so on. An ordinary annuity could be salaries, stock dividends, and so on.

2. **Annuity due**—regular deposits (payments) made at the *beginning* of the period, such as rent or life insurance premiums.

The remainder of this unit shows you how to calculate and check ordinary annuities and annuities due. Remember that you are calculating the *dollar amount* of the annuity at the end of the annuity term or at the end of the last period.

Ordinary Annuities: Money Invested at End of Period (Find Future Value)

Before we explain how to use a table that simplifies calculating ordinary annuities, let's first determine how to calculate the future value of an ordinary annuity manually.

LO 2

Calculating Future Value of Ordinary Annuities Manually   Remember that an ordinary annuity invests money at the *end* of each year (period). After we calculate ordinary annuities manually, you will see that the total value of the investment comes from the *stream* of yearly investments and the buildup of interest on the current balance.

Check out the plastic overlays that appear at the end of this chapter to review these concepts.

CALCULATING FUTURE VALUE OF AN ORDINARY ANNUITY MANUALLY

Step 1. For period 1, no interest calculation is necessary, since money is invested at the end of the period.

Step 2. For period 2, calculate interest on the balance and add the interest to the previous balance.

Step 3. Add the additional investment at the end of period 2 to the new balance.

Step 4. Repeat Steps 2 and 3 until the end of the desired period is reached.

EXAMPLE Find the value of an investment after 3 years for a $3,000 ordinary annuity at 8%. We calculate this manually as follows:

Step 1. ⟶ End of year 1: $3,000.00 → No interest, since this is put in at end of year 1. (Remember, payment is made at the end of the period.)

Year 2: $3,000.00 → Value of investment before investment at end of year 2.

Step 2. ⟶ + 240.00 → Interest (.08 × $3,000) for year 2.

$3,240.00 → Value of investment at end of year 2 before second investment.

Step 3. ⟶ End of year 2: + 3,000.00 → Second investment at end of year 2.

Year 3: $6,240.00 → Investment balance going into year 3.

+ 499.20 → Interest for year 3 (.08 × $6,240).

Step 4. ⟶ $6,739.20 → Value before investment at end of year 3.

⟶ + 3,000.00 → Investment at end of year 3.

End of year 3: $9,739.20 → Total value of investment after investment at end of year 3.

Note: We invested a total of $9,000 over three different periods. It is now worth $9,739.20

Early years

```
1           2           3
+-----------+-----------+
$3,000 ----------------->
     $3,000 ------------>
              $3,000
```

When you deposit $3,000 at the end of each year at an annual rate of 8%, the total value of the annuity is $9,739.20. What we called *maturity value* in compounding is now called the *future value of the annuity*. Remember that Interest = Principal × Rate × Time, with the principal changing because of the interest payments and the additional deposits. We can make this calculation easier by using Table 13.1 (p. 327).

Calculating Future Value of Ordinary Annuities by Table Lookup Use the following steps to calculate the future value of an ordinary annuity by table lookup.[2]

CALCULATING FUTURE VALUE OF AN ORDINARY ANNUITY BY TABLE LOOKUP

Step 1. Calculate the number of periods and rate per period.

Step 2. Look up the periods and rate in an ordinary annuity table. The intersection gives the table factor for the future value of $1.

Step 3. Multiply the payment each period by the table factor. This gives the future value of the annuity.

$$\frac{\text{Future value of}}{\text{ordinary annuity}} = \frac{\text{Annuity payment}}{\text{each period}} \times \frac{\text{Ordinary annuity}}{\text{table factor}}$$

---

[2]The formula for an ordinary annuity is $FV = PMT \times \left[\frac{(1+i)^n - 1}{i}\right]$ where FV equals future value of an ordinary annuity, PMT equals annuity payment, i equals interest, and n equals number of periods. The calculator sequence for this example is: 1 $+$ .08 $=$ y^x 3 $-$ 1 $\div$ .08 $\times$ 3,000 $=$ 9,739.20. A *Financial Calculator Guide* booklet is available that shows how to operate HP 10BII and TI BA II Plus.

TABLE	13.1		Ordinary annuity table: Compound sum of an annuity of $1									
Period	**2%**	**3%**	**4%**	**5%**	**6%**	**7%**	**8%**	**9%**	**10%**	**11%**	**12%**	**13%**
1	1.0000	1.0000	1.0000	1.0000	1.0000	1.0000	1.0000	1.0000	1.0000	1.0000	1.0000	1.0000
2	2.0200	2.0300	2.0400	2.0500	2.0600	2.0700	2.0800	2.0900	2.1000	2.1100	2.1200	2.1300
3	3.0604	3.0909	3.1216	3.1525	3.1836	3.2149	3.2464	3.2781	3.3100	3.3421	3.3744	3.4069
4	4.1216	4.1836	4.2465	4.3101	4.3746	4.4399	4.5061	4.5731	4.6410	4.7097	4.7793	4.8498
5	5.2040	5.3091	5.4163	5.5256	5.6371	5.7507	5.8666	5.9847	6.1051	6.2278	6.3528	6.4803
6	6.3081	6.4684	6.6330	6.8019	6.9753	7.1533	7.3359	7.5233	7.7156	7.9129	8.1152	8.3227
7	7.4343	7.6625	7.8983	8.1420	8.3938	8.6540	8.9228	9.2004	9.4872	9.7833	10.0890	10.4047
8	8.5829	8.8923	9.2142	9.5491	9.8975	10.2598	10.6366	11.0285	11.4359	11.8594	12.2997	12.7573
9	9.7546	10.1591	10.5828	11.0265	11.4913	11.9780	12.4876	13.0210	13.5795	14.1640	14.7757	15.4157
10	10.9497	11.4639	12.0061	12.5779	13.1808	13.8164	14.4866	15.1929	15.9374	16.7220	17.5487	18.4197
11	12.1687	12.8078	13.4863	14.2068	14.9716	15.7836	16.6455	17.5603	18.5312	19.5614	20.6546	21.8143
12	13.4120	14.1920	15.0258	15.9171	16.8699	17.8884	18.9771	20.1407	21.3843	22.7132	24.1331	25.6502
13	14.6803	15.6178	16.6268	17.7129	18.8821	20.1406	21.4953	22.9534	24.5227	26.2116	28.0291	29.9847
14	15.9739	17.0863	18.2919	19.5986	21.0150	22.5505	24.2149	26.0192	27.9750	30.0949	32.3926	34.8827
15	17.2934	18.5989	20.0236	21.5785	23.2759	25.1290	27.1521	29.3609	31.7725	34.4054	37.2797	40.4174
16	18.6392	20.1569	21.8245	23.6574	25.6725	27.8880	30.3243	33.0034	35.9497	39.1899	42.7533	46.6717
17	20.0120	21.7616	23.6975	25.8403	28.2128	30.8402	33.7503	36.9737	40.5447	44.5008	48.8837	53.7390
18	21.4122	23.4144	25.6454	28.1323	30.9056	33.9990	37.4503	41.3014	45.5992	50.3959	55.7497	61.7251
19	22.8405	25.1169	27.6712	30.5389	33.7599	37.3789	41.4463	46.0185	51.1591	56.9395	63.4397	70.7494
20	24.2973	26.8704	29.7781	33.0659	36.7855	40.9954	45.7620	51.1602	57.2750	64.2028	72.0524	80.9468
25	32.0302	36.4593	41.6459	47.7270	54.8644	63.2489	73.1060	84.7010	98.3471	114.4133	133.3338	155.6194
30	40.5679	47.5754	56.0849	66.4386	79.0580	94.4606	113.2833	136.3077	164.4941	199.0209	241.3327	293.1989
40	60.4017	75.4012	95.0254	120.7993	154.7616	199.6346	259.0569	337.8831	442.5928	581.8260	767.0913	1013.7030
50	84.5790	112.7968	152.6669	209.3470	290.3351	406.5277	573.7711	815.0853	1163.9090	1668.7710	2400.0180	3459.5010

Note: This is only a sampling of tables available. The *Business Math Handbook* shows tables from $\frac{1}{2}$% to 15%.

EXAMPLE   Find the value of an investment after 3 years for a $3,000 ordinary annuity at 8%.

Step 1. Periods = 3 years × 1 = 3   Rate = $\dfrac{8\%}{\text{Annually}} = 8\%$

Step 2. Go to Table 13.1, an ordinary annuity table. Look for 3 under the Period column. Go across to 8%. At the intersection is the table factor, 3.2464. (This was the example we showed in Figure 13.1.)

Step 3. Multiply $3,000 × 3.2464 = $9,739.20 (the same figure we calculated manually).

Annuities Due: Money Invested at Beginning of Period (Find Future Value)

In this section we look at what the difference in the total investment would be for an annuity due. As in the previous section, we will first make the calculation manually and then use the table lookup.

Calculating Future Value of Annuities Due Manually   Use the steps that follow to calculate the future value of an annuity due manually.

CALCULATING FUTURE VALUE OF AN ANNUITY DUE MANUALLY
Step 1. Calculate the interest on the balance for the period and add it to the previous balance.
Step 2. Add additional investment at the *beginning* of the period to the new balance.
Step 3. Repeat Steps 1 and 2 until the end of the desired period is reached.

Remember that in an annuity due, we deposit the money at the *beginning* of the year and gain more interest. Common sense should tell us that the *annuity due* will give a higher final value. We will use the same example that we used before.

EXAMPLE Find the value of an investment after 3 years for a $3,000 annuity due at 8%. We calculate this manually as follows:

Beginning year 1: $3,000.00 → First investment (will earn interest for 3 years).

Step 1. ————————→ + 240.00 → Interest (.08 × $3,000).

$3,240.00 → Value of investment at end of year 1.

Step 2. ————————→ Year 2: + 3,000.00 → Second investment (will earn interest for 2 years).

$6,240.00

Step 3. ————————→ + 499.20 → Interest for year 2 (.08 × $6,240).

$6,739.20 → Value of investment at end of year 2.

Year 3: + 3,000.00

$9,739.20 → Third investment (will earn interest for 1 year).

+ 779.14 → Interest (.08 × $9,739.20).

End of year 3: $10,518.34 → At the end of year 3, final value.

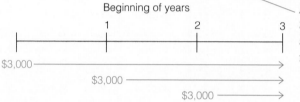

Beginning of years

1   2   3

$3,000 —————————————————→

$3,000 —————————————→

$3,000 —————→

Note: Our total investment of $9,000 is worth $10,518.34. For an ordinary annuity, our total investment was only worth $9,739.20.

Calculating Future Value of Annuities Due by Table Lookup To calculate the future value of an annuity due with a table lookup, use the steps that follow.

CALCULATING FUTURE VALUE OF AN ANNUITY DUE BY TABLE LOOKUP[3]

Step 1. Calculate the number of periods and the rate per period. Add one extra period.

Step 2. Look up in an ordinary annuity table the periods and rate. The intersection gives the table *factor* for future value of $1.

Step 3. Multiply payment each period by the table factor.

Step 4. Subtract 1 payment from Step 3.

$$\text{Future value of an annuity due} = \left(\begin{array}{c} \text{Annuity} \\ \text{payment} \\ \text{each period} \end{array} \times \begin{array}{c} \text{Ordinary*} \\ \text{annuity} \\ \text{table factor} \end{array} \right) - 1 \text{ Payment}$$

*Add 1 period.

Let's check the $10,518.34 by table lookup.

Step 1. Periods = 3 years × 1 = 3
                                    + 1 extra
                                  ———————
                                      4

Rate = $\dfrac{8\%}{\text{Annually}}$ = 8%

Step 2. Table factor, 4.5061

Step 3. $3,000 × 4.5061 = $13,518.30

Step 4.   − 3,000.00 ← Be sure to subtract 1 payment.
                             ——————————
                           = $10,518.30 (off 4 cents due to rounding)

---

[3]The formula for an annuity due is FV = PMT × $\frac{(1 + i)^n - 1}{i}$ × (1 + i), where FV equals future value of annuity due, PMT equals annuity payment, *i* equals interest, and *n* equals number of periods. This formula is the same as that in footnote 2 except we multiply the future value of annuity by 1 + *i* since payments are made at the beginning of the period. The calculator sequence for this example is: 1 $\boxed{+}$ .08 $\boxed{=}$ $\boxed{\times}$ 9,739.20 $\boxed{=}$ 10,518.34.

Note that the annuity due shows an ending value of $10,518.30, while the ending value of ordinary annuity was $9,739.20. We had a higher ending value with the annuity due because the investment took place at the beginning of each period.

Annuity payments do not have to be made yearly. They could be made semiannually, monthly, quarterly, and so on. Let's look at one more example with a different number of periods and the same rate.

Different Number of Periods and Rates   By using a different number of periods and the same rate, we will contrast an ordinary annuity with an annuity due in the following example:

EXAMPLE   Using Table 13.1 (p. 327), find the value of a $3,000 investment after 3 years made quarterly at 8%.

In the annuity due calculation, be sure to add one period and subtract one payment from the total value.

	Ordinary annuity	Annuity due	
Step 1.	Periods = 3 years × 4 = 12	Periods = 3 years × 4 = 12	Step 1
	Rate = 8% ÷ 4 = 2%	Rate = 8% ÷ 4 = 2%	
Step 2.	Table 13.1:	Table 13.1:	Step 2
	12 periods, 2% = 13.4120	13 periods, 2% = 14.6803	
Step 3.	$3,000 × 13.4120 = $40,236	$3,000 × 14.6803 = $44,040.90	Step 3
Step 4.		− 3,000.00	Step 4
		$41,040.90	

Again, note that with annuity due, the total value is greater since you invest the money at the beginning of each period.

Now check your progress with the Practice Quiz.

LU 13–1   PRACTICE QUIZ

Complete this **Practice Quiz** to see how you are doing.

1. Using Table 13.1, (a) find the value of an investment after 4 years on an ordinary annuity of $4,000 made semiannually at 10%; and (b) recalculate, assuming an annuity due.

2. Wally Beaver won a lottery and will receive a check for $4,000 at the beginning of each 6 months for the next 5 years. If Wally deposits each check into an account that pays 6%, how much will he have at the end of the 5 years?

For **extra help** from your authors—Sharon and Jeff—see the student DVD

You Tube™

✓ Solutions

1. **a.** Step 1.   Periods = 4 years × 2 = 8

    Step 2.   Factor = 9.5491

    Step 3. $4,000 × 9.5491

    = $38,196.40

    10% ÷ 2 = 5%

    b. Periods = 4 years × 2   Step 1

    = 8 + 1 = 9

    10% ÷ 2 = 5%

    Factor = 11.0265   Step 2

    $4,000 × 11.0265 = $44,106   Step 3

    − 1 payment   − 4,000   Step 4

    $40,106

2. Step 1.   5 years × 2 =   10

    + 1

    11 periods

    $\frac{6\%}{2} = 3\%$

    Step 2.   Table factor, 12.8078

    Step 3. $4,000 × 12.8078 = $51,231.20

    Step 4.   − 4,000.00

    $47,231.20

Need more practice? Try this **Extra Practice Quiz** (check figures in the Interactive Chapter Organizer, p. 335). Worked-out Solutions can be found in Appendix B at end of text.

1. Using Table 13.1, **(a)** find the value of an investment after 4 years on an ordinary annuity of $5,000 made semiannually at 4%; and **(b)** recalculate, assuming an annuity due.

2. Wally Beaver won a lottery and will receive a check for $2,500 at the beginning of each 6 months for the next 6 years. If Wally deposits each check into an account that pays 6%, how much will he have at the end of the 6 years?

Learning Unit 13–2: Present Value of an Ordinary Annuity (Find Present Value)[4]

This unit begins by presenting the concept of present value of an ordinary annuity. Then you will learn how to use a table to calculate the present value of an ordinary annuity.

LO 1

Concept of Present Value of an Ordinary Annuity— The Big Picture

Let's assume that we want to know how much money we need to invest *today* to receive a stream of payments for a given number of years in the future. This is called the **present value of an ordinary annuity.**

In Figure 13.2 you can see that if you wanted to withdraw $1 at the end of one period, you would have to invest 93 cents *today*. If at the end of each period for three periods you wanted to withdraw $1, you would have to put $2.58 in the bank *today* at 8% interest. (Note that we go from the future back to the present.)

FIGURE **13.2**

Present value of an annuity of $1 at 8%

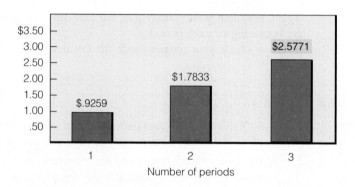

Now let's look at how we could use tables to calculate the present value of annuities and then check our answer.

Calculating Present Value of an Ordinary Annuity by Table Lookup

Use the steps below to calculate the present value of an ordinary annuity by table lookup.[5]

CALCULATING PRESENT VALUE OF AN ORDINARY ANNUITY BY TABLE LOOKUP
Step 1. Calculate the number of periods and rate per period.
Step 2. Look up the periods and rate in the present value of an annuity table. The intersection gives the table factor for the present value of $1.
Step 3. Multiply the withdrawal for each period by the table factor. This gives the present value of an ordinary annuity.

$$\text{Present value of ordinary annuity payment} = \text{Annuity payment} \times \text{Present value of ordinary annuity table factor}$$

---

[4]For simplicity we omit a discussion of present value of annuity due that would require subtracting a period and adding a 1.

[5]The formula for the present value of an ordinary annuity is PV = PMT $\times \frac{1 - 1 \div (1 + i)^n}{i}$, where PV equals present value of annuity, PMT equals annuity payment, i equals interest, and n equals number of periods. The calculator sequence would be as follows for the John Fitch example that follows on page 331: 1 $\boxed{+}$ .08 $\boxed{y^x}$ 3 $\boxed{+/-}$ $\boxed{=}$ $\boxed{M+}$ 1 $\boxed{-}$ $\boxed{MR}$ $\boxed{\div}$ .08 $\boxed{\times}$ 8,000 $\boxed{=}$ 21,000.

TABLE | **13.2** | Present value of an annuity of $1

Period	2%	3%	4%	5%	6%	7%	8%	9%	10%	11%	12%	13%
1	0.9804	0.9709	0.9615	0.9524	0.9434	0.9346	0.9259	0.9174	0.9091	0.9009	0.8929	0.8850
2	1.9416	1.9135	1.8861	1.8594	1.8334	1.8080	1.7833	1.7591	1.7355	1.7125	1.6901	1.6681
3	2.8839	2.8286	2.7751	2.7232	2.6730	2.6243	2.5771	2.5313	2.4869	2.4437	2.4018	2.3612
4	3.8077	3.7171	3.6299	3.5459	3.4651	3.3872	3.3121	3.2397	3.1699	3.1024	3.0373	2.9745
5	4.7134	4.5797	4.4518	4.3295	4.2124	4.1002	3.9927	3.8897	3.7908	3.6959	3.6048	3.5172
6	5.6014	5.4172	5.2421	5.0757	4.9173	4.7665	4.6229	4.4859	4.3553	4.2305	4.1114	3.9975
7	6.4720	6.2303	6.0021	5.7864	5.5824	5.3893	5.2064	5.0330	4.8684	4.7122	4.5638	4.4226
8	7.3255	7.0197	6.7327	6.4632	6.2098	5.9713	5.7466	5.5348	5.3349	5.1461	4.9676	4.7988
9	8.1622	7.7861	7.4353	7.1078	6.8017	6.5152	6.2469	5.9952	5.7590	5.5370	5.3282	5.1317
10	8.9826	8.5302	8.1109	7.7217	7.3601	7.0236	6.7101	6.4177	6.1446	5.8892	5.6502	5.4262
11	9.7868	9.2526	8.7605	8.3064	7.8869	7.4987	7.1390	6.8052	6.4951	6.2065	5.9377	5.6869
12	10.5753	9.9540	9.3851	8.8632	8.3838	7.9427	7.5361	7.1607	6.8137	6.4924	6.1944	5.9176
13	11.3483	10.6350	9.9856	9.3936	8.8527	8.3576	7.9038	7.4869	7.1034	6.7499	6.4235	6.1218
14	12.1062	11.2961	10.5631	9.8986	9.2950	8.7455	8.2442	7.7862	7.3667	6.9819	6.6282	6.3025
15	12.8492	11.9379	11.1184	10.3796	9.7122	9.1079	8.5595	8.0607	7.6061	7.1909	6.8109	6.4624
16	13.5777	12.5611	11.6523	10.8378	10.1059	9.4466	8.8514	8.3126	7.8237	7.3792	6.9740	6.6039
17	14.2918	13.1661	12.1657	11.2741	10.4773	9.7632	9.1216	8.5436	8.0216	7.5488	7.1196	6.7291
18	14.9920	13.7535	12.6593	11.6896	10.8276	10.0591	9.3719	8.7556	8.2014	7.7016	7.2497	6.8399
19	15.6784	14.3238	13.1339	12.0853	11.1581	10.3356	9.6036	8.9501	8.3649	7.8393	7.3658	6.9380
20	16.3514	14.8775	13.5903	12.4622	11.4699	10.5940	9.8181	9.1285	8.5136	7.9633	7.4694	7.0248
25	19.5234	17.4131	15.6221	14.0939	12.7834	11.6536	10.6748	9.8226	9.0770	8.4217	7.8431	7.3300
30	22.3964	19.6004	17.2920	15.3724	13.7648	12.4090	11.2578	10.2737	9.4269	8.6938	8.0552	7.4957
40	27.3554	23.1148	19.7928	17.1591	15.0463	13.3317	11.9246	10.7574	9.7790	8.9511	8.2438	7.6344
50	31.4236	25.7298	21.4822	18.2559	15.7619	13.8007	12.2335	10.9617	9.9148	9.0417	8.3045	7.6752

EXAMPLE   John Fitch wants to receive an $8,000 annuity in 3 years. Interest on the annuity is 8% annually. John will make withdrawals at the end of each year. How much must John invest today to receive a stream of payments for 3 years? Use Table 13.2. Remember that interest could be earned semiannually, quarterly, and so on, as shown in the previous unit.

Step 1. 3 years × 1 = 3 periods $\dfrac{8\%}{\text{Annually}} = 8\%$

Step 2. Table factor, 2.5771 (we saw this in Figure 13.2)

Step 3. $8,000 × 2.5771 = **$20,616.80**

If John wants to withdraw $8,000 at the end of each period for 3 years, he will have to deposit $20,616.80 in the bank *today*.

$20,616.80
+   1,649.34 → Interest at end of year 1 (.08 × $20,616.80)
$22,266.14
−   8,000.00 → First payment to John
$14,266.14
+   1,141.29 → Interest at end of year 2 (.08 × $14,266.14)
$15,407.43
−   8,000.00 → Second payment to John
$ 7,407.43
+   592.59 → Interest at end of year 3 (.08 × $7,407.43)
$ 8,000.02
−   8,000.00 → After end of year 3 John receives his last $8,000
        .02   (off 2 cents due to rounding)

Before we leave this unit, let's work out two examples that show the relationship of Chapter 13 to Chapter 12. Use the tables in your *Business Math Handbook.*

Lump Sum versus Annuities

EXAMPLE John Sands made deposits of $200 semiannually to Floor Bank, which pays 8% interest compounded semiannually. After 5 years, John makes no more deposits. What will be the balance in the account 6 years after the last deposit?

Step 1. Calculate amount of annuity: Table 13.1

10 periods, 4% $200 × 12.0061 = $2,401.22

Step 2. Calculate how much the final value of the annuity will grow by the compound interest table. Table 12.1

12 periods, 4% $2,401.22 × 1.6010 = $3,844.35

For John, the stream of payments grows to $2,401.22. Then this *lump sum* grows for 6 years to $3,844.35. Now let's look at a present value example.

EXAMPLE Mel Rich decided to retire in 8 years to New Mexico. What amount should Mel invest today so he will be able to withdraw $40,000 at the end of each year for 25 years *after* he retires? Assume Mel can invest money at 5% interest (compounded annually).

Step 1. Calculate the present value of the annuity: Table 13.2

25 periods, 5% $40,000 × 14.0939 = $563,756

Step 2. Find the present value of $563,756 since Mel will not retire for 8 years:

Table 12.3

8 periods, 5% (PV table) $563,756 × .6768 = $381,550.06

If Mel deposits $381,550 in year 1, it will grow to $563,756 after 8 years.

It's time to try the Practice Quiz and check your understanding of this unit.

LU 13–2 PRACTICE QUIZ

Complete this **Practice Quiz** to see how you are doing.

1. What must you invest today to receive an $18,000 annuity for 5 years semiannually at a 10% annual rate? All withdrawals will be made at the end of each period.

2. Rase High School wants to set up a scholarship fund to provide five $2,000 scholarships for the next 10 years. If money can be invested at an annual rate of 9%, how much should the scholarship committee invest today?

3. Joe Wood decided to retire in 5 years in Arizona. What amount should Joe invest today so he can withdraw $60,000 at the end of each year for 30 years after he retires? Assume Joe can invest money at 6% compounded annually.

✓ Solutions

1. **Step 1.** Periods = 5 years × 2 = 10; Rate = 10% ÷ 2 = 5%
   Step 2. Factor, 7.7217
   Step 3. $18,000 × 7.7217 = $138,990.60
2. **Step 1.** Periods = 10; Rate = 9%
   Step 2. Factor, 6.4177
   Step 3. $10,000 × 6.4177 = $64,177
3. **Step 1.** Calculate present value of annuity: 30 periods, 6%.
   $60,000 × 13.7648 = $825,888
   Step 2. Find present value of $825,888 for 5 years: 5 periods, 6%.
   $825,888 × .7473 = $617,186.10

MONEY tips

The best rates on mortgages, loans, and credit cards are offered to those with credit scores above 700. Pay your bills on time, have one long-term credit card, keep low balances, pay off balances each month, and review your credit report regularly.

Need more practice? Try this **Extra Practice Quiz** (check figures in the Interactive Chapter Organizer, p. 335). Worked-out Solutions can be found in Appendix B at end of text.

1. What must you invest today to receive a $20,000 annuity for 5 years semiannually at a 5% annual rate? All withdrawals will be made at the end of each period.

2. Rase High School wants to set up a scholarship fund to provide five $3,000 scholarships for the next 10 years. If money can be invested at an annual rate of 4%, how much should the scholarship committee invest today?

3. Joe Wood decided to retire in 5 years in Arizona. What amount should Joe invest today so he can withdraw $80,000 at the end of each year for 30 years after he retires? Assume Joe can invest money at 3% compounded annually.

Learning Unit 13–3: Sinking Funds (Find Periodic Payments)

LO 1

A **sinking fund** is a financial arrangement that sets aside regular periodic payments of a particular amount of money. Compound interest accumulates on these payments to a specific sum at a predetermined future date. Corporations use sinking funds to discharge bonded indebtedness, to replace worn-out equipment, to purchase plant expansion, and so on.

A sinking fund is a different type of an annuity. In a sinking fund, you determine the amount of periodic payments you need to achieve a given financial goal. In the annuity, you know the amount of each payment and must determine its future value. Let's work with the following formula:

> Sinking fund payment = Future value × Sinking fund table factor[6]

EXAMPLE To retire a bond issue, Moore Company needs $60,000 in 18 years from today. The interest rate is 10% compounded annually. What payment must Moore make at the end of each year? Use Table 13.3.

TABLE 13.3

Sinking fund table based on $1

Period	2%	3%	4%	5%	6%	8%	10%
1	1.0000	1.0000	1.0000	1.0000	1.0000	1.0000	1.0000
2	0.4951	0.4926	0.4902	0.4878	0.4854	0.4808	0.4762
3	0.3268	0.3235	0.3203	0.3172	0.3141	0.3080	0.3021
4	0.2426	0.2390	0.2355	0.2320	0.2286	0.2219	0.2155
5	0.1922	0.1884	0.1846	0.1810	0.1774	0.1705	0.1638
6	0.1585	0.1546	0.1508	0.1470	0.1434	0.1363	0.1296
7	0.1345	0.1305	0.1266	0.1228	0.1191	0.1121	0.1054
8	0.1165	0.1125	0.1085	0.1047	0.1010	0.0940	0.0874
9	0.1025	0.0984	0.0945	0.0907	0.0870	0.0801	0.0736
10	0.0913	0.0872	0.0833	0.0795	0.0759	0.0690	0.0627
11	0.0822	0.0781	0.0741	0.0704	0.0668	0.0601	0.0540
12	0.0746	0.0705	0.0666	0.0628	0.0593	0.0527	0.0468
13	0.0681	0.0640	0.0601	0.0565	0.0530	0.0465	0.0408
14	0.0626	0.0585	0.0547	0.0510	0.0476	0.0413	0.0357
15	0.0578	0.0538	0.0499	0.0463	0.0430	0.0368	0.0315
16	0.0537	0.0496	0.0458	0.0423	0.0390	0.0330	0.0278
17	0.0500	0.0460	0.0422	0.0387	0.0354	0.0296	0.0247
18	0.0467	0.0427	0.0390	0.0355	0.0324	0.0267	0.0219
19	0.0438	0.0398	0.0361	0.0327	0.0296	0.0241	0.0195
20	0.0412	0.0372	0.0336	0.0302	0.0272	0.0219	0.0175
24	0.0329	0.0290	0.0256	0.0225	0.0197	0.0150	0.0113
28	0.0270	0.0233	0.0200	0.0171	0.0146	0.0105	0.0075
32	0.0226	0.0190	0.0159	0.0133	0.0110	0.0075	0.0050
36	0.0192	0.0158	0.0129	0.0104	0.0084	0.0053	0.0033
40	0.0166	0.0133	0.0105	0.0083	0.0065	0.0039	0.0023

MONEY tips

If you are trying to build credit by using a credit card, each time you make a purchase using the credit card, deduct that amount from your checking account. When your credit card bill is due, add up all your credit card deductions in your checking account. You will have enough to pay the credit card off in full.

[6]Sinking fund table is the reciprocal of the ordinary annuity table.

We begin by looking down the Period column in Table 13.3 until we come to 18. Then we go across until we reach the 10% column. The table factor is .0219.

Now we multiply $60,000 by the factor as follows:

$$\$60,000 \times .0219 = \boxed{\$1,314}$$

LO 2

This states that if Moore Company pays $1,314 at the end of each period for 18 years, then $60,000 will be available to pay off the bond issue at maturity.

We can check this by using Table 13.1 on page 327 (the ordinary annuity table):

$$\$1,314 \times 45.5992 = \$59,917.35 \text{ (off due to rounding)}$$

It's time to try the following Practice Quiz.

LU 13–3 | PRACTICE QUIZ

Complete this **Practice Quiz** to see how you are doing.

*For **extra help** from your authors–Sharon and Jeff–see the student DVD*

Today, Arrow Company issued bonds that will mature to a value of $90,000 in 10 years. Arrow's controller is planning to set up a sinking fund. Interest rates are 12% compounded semiannually. What will Arrow Company have to set aside to meet its obligation in 10 years? Check your answer. Your answer will be off due to the rounding of Table 13.3.

✓ **Solution**

10 years × 2 = 20 periods $\dfrac{12\%}{2} = 6\%$ $\$90,000 \times .0272 = \boxed{\$2,448}$

Check $\$2,448 \times 36.7855 = \$90,050.90$

LU 13–3a | EXTRA PRACTICE QUIZ WITH WORKED-OUT SOLUTION

Need more practice? Try this **Extra Practice Quiz** (check figure in the Interactive Chapter Organizer, p. 335). Worked-out Solution can be found in Appendix B at end of text.

Today Arrow Company issued bonds that will mature to a value of $120,000 in 20 years. Arrow's controller is planning to set up a sinking fund. Interest rates are 6% compounded semiannually. What will Arrow Company have to set aside to meet its obligation in 10 years? Check your answer. Your answer will be off due to rounding of Table 13.3.

INTERACTIVE CHAPTER ORGANIZER

Topic/procedure/formula	Examples	You try it*
Ordinary annuities (find future value), pp. 326–327 Invest money at end of each period. Find future value at maturity. Answers question of how much money accumulates. $\dfrac{\text{Future value of ordinary annuity}}{} = \dfrac{\text{Annuity payment each period}}{} \times \dfrac{\text{Ordinary annuity table factor}}{}$ $FV = PMT \left[\dfrac{(1 + i)^n - 1}{i} \right]$	Use Table 13.1: 2 years, $4,000 ordinary annuity at 8% annually. Value = $4,000 × 2.0800 = $8,320 (2 periods, 8%) $FV = 4,000 \left[\dfrac{(1 + .08)^2 - 1}{.08} \right] = \$8,320$	**Calculate value of ordinary annuity** $6,000, 7% annually, 4 years

(continues)

INTERACTIVE CHAPTER ORGANIZER

Topic/procedure/formula	Examples	You try it*
Annuities due (find future value), pp. 327–329 Invest money at beginning of each period. Find future value at maturity. Should be higher than ordinary annuity since it is invested at beginning of each period. Use Table 13.1, but add one period and subtract one payment from answer. $$\begin{pmatrix} \text{Future} \\ \text{value} \\ \text{of an} \\ \text{annuity} \\ \text{due} \end{pmatrix} = \begin{pmatrix} \text{Annuity} \\ \text{payment} \\ \text{each} \\ \text{period} \end{pmatrix} \times \begin{pmatrix} \text{Ordinary*} \\ \text{annuity} \\ \text{table} \\ \text{factor} \end{pmatrix} - 1\ \text{Payment}$$ *Add 1 period. $$FV_{due} = PMT\left[\frac{(1+i)^n - 1}{i}\right](1+i)$$	*Example:* Same example as above but invest money at beginning of period. $$\begin{aligned} \$4,000 \times 3.2464 &= \$12,985.60 \\ &\quad -\ 4,000.00 \\ &= \boxed{\$\ 8,985.60} \\ &\quad (3\ \text{periods, }8\%) \end{aligned}$$ $$FV_{due} = 4,000\left(\frac{(1+.08)^2 - 1}{.08}\right)(1+.08)$$ $$= \$8,985.60$$	**Calculate value of annuity due** $6,000, 7% annually, 4 years
Present value of an ordinary annuity (find present value), pp. 330–331 Calculate number of periods and rate per period. Use Table 13.2 to find table factor for present value of $1. Multiply withdrawal for each period by table factor to get present value of an ordinary annuity. $$\begin{pmatrix} \text{Present} \\ \text{value of an} \\ \text{ordinary} \\ \text{annuity} \\ \text{payment} \end{pmatrix} = \begin{pmatrix} \text{Annuity} \\ \text{payment} \end{pmatrix} \times \begin{pmatrix} \text{Present} \\ \text{value of} \\ \text{ordinary} \\ \text{annuity} \\ \text{table factor} \end{pmatrix}$$ $$PV = PMT\left[\frac{1 - (1+i)^{-n}}{i}\right]$$	*Example:* Receive $10,000 for 5 years. Interest is 10% compounded annually. Table 13.2: 5 periods, 10% $$\text{What you put in today} = \begin{aligned} 3.7908 \\ \underline{\times\ \$10,000} \\ \boxed{\$37,908} \end{aligned}$$ $$PV = 10,000\left[\frac{1 - (1+.1)^{-5}}{.1}\right] = \$37,907.88$$	**Calculate present value of ordinary annuity** $20,000, 6 years, 4% interest compounded annually
Sinking funds (find periodic payment), pp. 333–334 Paying a particular amount of money for a set number of periodic payments to accumulate a specific sum. We know the future value and must calculate the periodic payments needed. Answer can be proved by ordinary annuity table. $$\begin{pmatrix} \text{Sinking} \\ \text{fund} \\ \text{payment} \end{pmatrix} = \begin{pmatrix} \text{Future} \\ \text{value} \end{pmatrix} \times \begin{pmatrix} \text{Sinking} \\ \text{fund table} \\ \text{factor} \end{pmatrix}$$	*Example:* $200,000 bond to retire 15 years from now. Interest is 6% compounded annually. By Table 13.3: $$\$200,000 \times .0430 = \boxed{\$8,600}$$ Check by Table 13.1: $$\$8,600 \times 23.2759 = \$200,172.74$$	**Calculate periodic payment** $400,000 bond to retire 20 years from now. Interest is 5% compounded annually.

KEY TERMS	Annuities certain, *p. 325* Annuity, *p. 324* Annuity due, *p. 325* Contingent annuities, *p. 325*	Future value of an annuity, *p. 324* Ordinary annuity, *p. 325* Payment periods, *p. 324*	Present value of an ordinary annuity, *p. 330* Sinking fund, *p. 333* Term of the annuity, *p. 324*
Check Figures for Extra Practice Quizzes with Page References. (Worked-out Solutions in Appendix A.)	LU 13–1a (p. 330) **1.** a. $42,914.50 b. $43,773 **2.** $36,544.50	LU 13–2a (p. 333) **1.** $175,042 **2.** $121,663.50 **3.** $1,352,584.40	LU 13–3a (p. 334) $1,596

*Worked-out solutions are in Appendix B.

Critical Thinking Discussion Questions with Chapter Concept Check

1. What is the difference between an ordinary annuity and an annuity due? If you were to save money in an annuity, which would you choose and why?

2. Explain how you would calculate ordinary annuities and annuities due by table lookup. Create an example to explain the meaning of a table factor from an ordinary annuity.

3. What is a present value of an ordinary annuity? Create an example showing how one of your relatives might plan for retirement by using the present value of an ordinary annuity. Would you ever have to use lump-sum payments in your calculation from Chapter 12?

4. What is a sinking fund? Why could an ordinary annuity table be used to check the sinking fund payment?

5. With the tight economy, more businesses are cutting back on matching the retirement contributions of their employees. Do you think this is ethical?

6. **Chapter Concept Check.** Using the information from the chapter opener clip, create your own assumptions for retirement planning. Back up your retirement planning with calculations involving ordinary annuities as well as the present value of annuities.

END-OF-CHAPTER PROBLEMS  www.mhhe.com/slater11e

Check figures for odd-numbered problems in Appendix C.

Name _____ Date _____

DRILL PROBLEMS

Complete the ordinary annuities for the following using tables in the *Business Math Handbook:*   *LU 13-1(2)*

	Amount of payment	Payment payable	Years	Interest rate	Value of annuity
13–1.	$20,000	Annually	9	3%	
13–2.	$7,000	Semiannually	8	7%	

Redo Problem 13–1 as an annuity due:

13–3.

Calculate the value of the following annuity due without a table. Check your results by Table 13.1 or the *Business Math Handbook* (they will be slightly off due to rounding):   *LU 13-1(2)*

	Amount of payment	Payment payable	Years	Interest rate
13–4.	$2,000	Annually	3	6%

Complete the following using Table 13.2 or the *Business Math Handbook* for the present value of an ordinary annuity: *LU 13-2(1)*

	Amount of annuity expected	Payment	Time	Interest rate	Present value (amount needed now to invest to receive annuity)
13–5.	$900	Annually	4 years	6%	
13–6.	$15,000	Quarterly	4 years	8%	

13–7.   Check Problem 13–5 without the use of Table 13.2.

Using the sinking fund Table 13.3 or the *Business Math Handbook*, complete the following: *LU 13-3(1)*

	Required amount	Frequency of payment	Length of time	Interest rate	Payment amount end of each period
13–8.	$25,000	Quarterly	6 years	8%	
13–9.	$15,000	Annually	8 years	8%	

13–10.   Check the answer in Problem 13–9 by Table 13.1.   *LU 13-3(2)*

13–11. John Regan, an employee at Home Depot, made deposits of $800 at the end of each year for 4 years. Interest is 4% compounded annually. What is the value of Regan's annuity at the end of 4 years? *LU 13-1(2)*

13–12. Ed Long promised to pay his son $400 semiannually for 12 years. Assume Ed can invest his money at 6% in an ordinary annuity. How much must Ed invest today to pay his son $400 semiannually for 12 years? *LU 13-2(1)*

13–13. To help you reach financial security upon retirement, you should invest 20% of your income annually. If you automatically transferred $3,000 at the end of each year to a retirement account earning 4% interest compounded annually, how much would you have after 25 years? 30 years? *LU 13-1(2)*

13–14. After paying off a car loan or credit card, don't remove this amount from your budget. Instead, invest in your future by applying some of it to your retirement account. How much would $450 invested at the end of each quarter be worth in 10 years at 4% interest? (Use the *Business Math Handbook* tables.) *LU 13-1(2)*

13–15. The average American has $99 lying about. Stick $99 in an ordinary annuity account each year for 10 years at 5% interest and watch it grow. What is the cash value of this annuity at the end of year 10? Round to the nearest dollar. *LU 13-1(2)*

13–16. Patricia and Joe Payne are divorced. The divorce settlement stipulated that Joe pay $525 a month for their daughter Suzanne until she turns 18 in 4 years. How much must Joe set aside today to meet the settlement? Interest is 6% a year. *LU 13-2(1)*

13–17. Josef Company borrowed money that must be repaid in 20 years. The company wants to make sure the loan will be repaid at the end of year 20, so it invests $12,500 at the end of each year at 12% interest compounded annually. What was the amount of the original loan? *LU 13-1(2)*

13–18. Bankrate.com reported on a shocking statistic: only 54% of workers participate in their company's retirement plan. This means that 46% do not. With such an uncertain future for Social Security, this can leave almost 1 in 2 individuals without proper income during retirement. Jill Collins, 20, decided she needs to have $250,000 in her retirement account upon retiring at 60. How much does she need to invest each year at 5% compounded annually to meet her goal? *Tip:* She is setting up a sinking fund. *LU 13-3(1)*

13–19. Toby Martin invests $2,000 at the end of each year for 10 years in an ordinary annuity at 11% interest compounded annually. What is the final value of Toby's investment at the end of year 10? *LU 13-1(2)*

13–20. Alice Longtree has decided to invest $400 quarterly for 4 years in an ordinary annuity at 8%. As her financial adviser, *eXcel* calculate for Alice the total cash value of the annuity at the end of year 4.   *LU 13-1(2)*

13–21. At the beginning of each period for 10 years, Merl Agnes invests $500 semiannually at 6%. What is the cash value of this annuity due at the end of year 10?   *LU 13-1(2)*

13–22. Jeff Associates needs to repay $30,000. The company plans to set up a sinking fund that will repay the loan at the end of 8 years. Assume a 12% interest rate compounded semiannually. What must Jeff pay into the fund each period of time? Check your answer by Table 13.1.   *LU 13-3(1, 2)*

13–23. On Joe Martin's graduation from college, Joe's uncle promised him a gift of $12,000 in cash or $900 every quarter for *eXcel* the next 4 years after graduation. If money could be invested at 8% compounded quarterly, which offer is better for Joe? *LU 13-1(2), LU 13-2(1)*

13–24. You are earning an average of $46,500 and will retire in 10 years. If you put 20% of your gross average income in an *eXcel* ordinary annuity compounded at 7% annually, what will be the value of the annuity when you retire?   *LU 13-1(2)*

13–25. A local Dunkin' Donuts franchise must buy a new piece of equipment in 5 years that will cost $88,000. The company is setting up a sinking fund to finance the purchase. What will the quarterly deposit be if the fund earns 8% interest?   *LU 13-3(1)*

13–26. Mike Macaro is selling a piece of land. Two offers are on the table. Morton Company offered a $40,000 down payment and $35,000 a year for the next 5 years. Flynn Company offered $25,000 down and $38,000 a year for the next 5 years. If money can be invested at 8% compounded annually, which offer is better for Mike?   *LU 13-1(2)*

13–27. Al Vincent has decided to retire to Arizona in 10 years. What amount should Al invest today so that he will be able to withdraw $28,000 at the end of each year for 15 years *after* he retires? Assume he can invest the money at 8% interest compounded annually.   *LU 13-2(1)*

13–28. Victor French made deposits of $5,000 at the end of each quarter to Book Bank, which pays 8% interest compounded quarterly. After 3 years, Victor made no more deposits. What will be the balance in the account 2 years after the last deposit? *LU 13-1(2)*

13–29. Janet Woo decided to retire to Florida in 6 years. What amount should Janet invest today so she can withdraw $50,000 at the end of each year for 20 years after she retires? Assume Janet can invest money at 6% compounded annually.   *LU 13-2(1)*

13–30. Assume that you can buy a $6,000 computer system in monthly installments for 3 years. The seller charges you 12% interest compounded monthly. What is your monthly payment? Assume your first payment is due at the end of the month. Use tables in the *Business Math Handbook*.   *LU 13-2(1)*

$$\text{Monthly payment} = \frac{\text{Amount owed}}{\text{Table factor}}$$
$$\text{for PV of annuity}$$

13–31. Ajax Corporation has hired Brad O'Brien as its new president. Terms included the company's agreeing to pay retirement benefits of $18,000 at the end of each semiannual period for 10 years. This will begin in 3,285 days. If the money can be invested at 8% compounded semiannually, what must the company deposit today to fulfill its obligation to Brad?   *LU 13-2(1)*

 SUMMARY PRACTICE TEST (Use Tables in the *Business Math Handbook*)

Do you need help? The DVD has step-by-step worked-out solutions.

1. Lin Lowe plans to deposit $1,800 at the end of every 6 months for the next 15 years at 8% interest compounded semiannually. What is the value of Lin's annuity at the end of 15 years? *(p. 326)   LU 13-1(2)*

2. On Abby Ellen's graduation from law school, Abby's uncle, Bull Brady, promised her a gift of $24,000 or $2,400 every quarter for the next 4 years after graduating from law school. If the money could be invested at 6% compounded quarterly, which offer should Abby choose? *(pp. 330–332)   LU 13-2(1, 2)*

3. Sanka Blunck wants to receive $8,000 each year for 20 years. How much must Sanka invest today at 4% interest compounded annually? *(p. 330)   LU 13-2(1)*

4. In 9 years, Rollo Company will have to repay a $100,000 loan. Assume a 6% interest rate compounded quarterly. How much must Rollo Company pay each period to have $100,000 at the end of 9 years? *(p. 333)   LU 13-3(1)*

5. Lance Industries borrowed $130,000. The company plans to set up a sinking fund that will repay the loan at the end of 18 years. Assume a 6% interest rate compounded semiannually. What amount must Lance Industries pay into the fund each period? Check your answer by Table 13.1. *(pp. 333–334)   LU 13-3(1, 2)*

6. Joe Jan wants to receive $22,000 each year for the next 22 years. Assume a 6% interest rate compounded annually. How much must Joe invest today? *(pp. 330–331)   LU 13-2(1)*

7. Twice a year for 15 years, Warren Ford invested $1,700 compounded semiannually at 6% interest. What is the value of this annuity due? *(pp. 327–328)   LU 13-1(2)*

8. Scupper Molly invested $1,800 semiannually for 23 years at 8% interest compounded semiannually. What is the value of this annuity due? *(pp. 327–328)   LU 13-1(2)*

9. Nelson Collins decided to retire to Canada in 10 years. What amount should Nelson deposit so that he will be able to withdraw $80,000 at the end of each year for 25 years after he retires? Assume Nelson can invest money at 7% interest compounded annually. *(pp. 330–331)   LU 13-2(1)*

10. Bob Bryan made deposits of $10,000 at the end of each quarter to Lion Bank, which pays 8% interest compounded quarterly. After 9 years, Bob made no more deposits. What will be the account's balance 4 years after the last deposit? *(pp. 325–327)   LU 13-1(2)*

Part of Deutsche Post, the world's leading mail and logistics group, DHL maintains a presence in 220 countries and territories and generates in excess of $50 billion in annual revenues. Its 275,000 employees provide services in the following areas:

- Parcel/document express delivery services
- Freight by air, ocean, road, and rail
- Warehousing and distribution
- Supply chain solutions
- International mail solutions

Moving west across the globe, DHL's global expansion strategy was fueled by key acquisitions such as Airborne Express in the United States, which provided a much needed distribution network in North America and included an expedited shipping infrastructure on the domestic level. This acquisition propelled DHL to become a respected third player in the U.S. market, behind market leaders Federal Express and UPS.

The investment in U.S. operations enabled DHL to become equally strong in Asia, Europe, and the U.S. Its strategy for differentiation includes the three cornerstones of flexibility, responsiveness, and the human touch.

Flexibility and responsiveness are supported by an efficient regional hub system. In the U.S. DHL maintains two air/ground hubs that service five gateway locations. While the hubs service the gateways, gateways serve the DHL service centers and export to foreign destinations. This structure allows DHL to move goods efficiently with the confidence of "track 'n trace," a bar coding system that since 1986 has allowed customers to track the status of a package from the point of pickup to delivery.

The human touch refers to DHL's commitment to maintaining its own staff, rather than using subcontractors who might also provide transport services for other companies. DHL has also invested in offering "Industry Sector Solutions" essentially providing expertise in select industries such as aerospace, automotive, chemical, and consumer to name a few. The DHL brand is known for "personal commitment, proactive solutions and local strength," and key to all of this is the DHL employee.

Note: The following problems contain some data that has been created by the author.

PROBLEM 1

Assume DHL will need to replace a piece of equipment in 12 years that will cost $240,000. The company will set up a sinking fund to finance this future purchase. What amount should DHL put away quarterly if it can earn 10% interest? Round to the nearest cent.

PROBLEM 2

If DHL were to sell off a used aircraft and had the following two offers to consider, which one would be a better deal? How much better is the better deal? Assume 6% interest compounded annually, and down payments are not invested. Round to the nearest cent.

Offer 1: $150,000 down payment and $30,000 a year for the next 5 years.

Offer 2: $75,000 down payment and $45,000 a year for the next 5 years.

PROBLEM 3

Suppose the retirement plan for DHL salaried personnel included a $1,000 company contribution paid quarterly at the beginning of the month. Assuming these funds could be invested at 8% interest compounded quarterly, what would be the cash value at the end of 3 years? Round to the nearest cent.

PROBLEM 4

Imagine that DHL borrowed capital that needed to be repaid in 5 years. If DHL paid $150,000 at the end of each year at 10% interest compounded annually, what was the original loan amount? Round to the nearest cent.

PROBLEM 5

Assume DHL needs access to a stream of capital for the next 10 years. If DHL needs $2.5 million per year and can earn 4% interest compounded annually, how much must the company put away today to have these funds when needed? How much of DHL's capital need will come from interest earned? Round to the nearest dollar.

Class Discussion. The mail and logistics industry is a dynamic one. Consider how electronic communication might impact DHL's business. Review the DHL website for insights on how the company is responding to new forms of communication.

Class Discussion. DHL has a clear strategy for market differentiation as discussed in the video case. Research U.S. market leaders Federal Express and UPS and compare each company's strategy for differentiation.

SURF TO SAVE

Securing money for your future 🔍

PROBLEM 1
Never too early to start saving

Go to http://www.bankrate.com/brm/news/ira/20021211a.asp and read the article "Start Your Kids on the Roth Road." Suppose you open a Roth IRA for your daughter and deposit $1,000 at the end of each year to match her earned income from age 14 to age 21 (8 years). Assuming she makes no withdrawals or additions to that account after the year that she turns 21, how much will she have in the account at the end of the year that she turns 60? Assume the money in the Roth IRA account earns 8% annually on average. (*Hint:* This is like an annuity for the first 8 years, then like a savings account.)

Discussion Questions

1. What is the value in starting investments at such an early age?

2. How might having such an investment set up impact the child's future savings?

PROBLEM 2
Retire in style

Go to http://www.homefederal.com/ResourceCenter/Calculators. Suppose you want to save $1,000,000 for retirement. If you plan to retire in 20 years what would be the monthly payment to your sinking fund? What if you plan to retire in 30 years? In 40 years? Is the 40-year annual contribution half the 20-year contribution? Explain why, or why not.

Discussion Questions

1. What does this problem tell us about the importance of starting a savings plan early in life?

2. At what age will you likely retire? How would this impact your savings plan as a college student?

PROBLEM 3
You're a winner!

Go to http://www.straightdope.com/mailbag/mlottery.html and read the information about lotteries. Then use the "What is my future value worth today?" calculator at http://www.timevalue.com/Tools.aspx?CALCULATORID=IC04&TEMPLATE_ID=www.timevalue.com_2 to answer the following. If a friend won the lottery and is guaranteed payments of $100,000 for the next 30 years (total payout of $3,000,000) and long-term interest rates are at 6%, then what immediate lump-sum payment is equivalent to the 30-year payout?

Discussion Questions

1. Which would you prefer to receive, a lump sum or yearly payments for a lottery win? Why?

2. Why would the lottery organization prefer to use the payment option versus lump sum?

PROBLEM 4
Regroup, retire, and relax

Go to http://www.timevalue.com/tcalc.aspx and click "How much do I need to fund my retirement?" If you were planning to retire and can live comfortably on $3,000.00 per month for 10 years, how much money would you need to deposit now in an account earning 5% interest to be able to afford this amount? If you cut your monthly payout in half, how much would you need to deposit now?

Discussion Questions

1. How can you estimate your monthly expenses by the time you are able to retire?

2. Calculate your current monthly expenses. How might these expenses change once you reach retirement age?

MOBILE APPS ✕

Annuity Pro (RIEU Limited) Calculates future values, present values, interest rates, time periods, and more for annuity investments.

TimeMoney (Dalasoft Limited) Calculates the time value of money in many scenarios including annuities, loans, and sinking funds.

INTERNET PROJECTS ✕

See text website
www.mhhe.com/slater11e_sse_ch13

A KIPLINGER APPROACH

IT'S NEVER TOO LATE FOR A ROTH IRA

THE PROSPECT OF TAX-FREE INCOME IN RETIREMENT MAY BE TOO GOOD TO PASS UP, REGARDLESS OF YOUR AGE. BY LAURA COHN

OUR READER

WHO: **BILL SEGUR, 60**

WHERE: **WILMINGTON, N.C.**

QUESTION: **I'VE FINALLY PAID OFF MY MORTGAGE. WHAT SHOULD I DO WITH THE EXTRA CASH?**

NOW THAT THEY'VE PAID OFF their home loan early, Bill is wondering how he and his wife, Susan, should use the extra $600 a month. Bill is a registered nurse at a hospital and hopes to retire in a few years. He wants to maximize what he and Susan (also an RN) are socking away while they're still working. So their focus is on adding to their savings kitty.

Bill and Susan, 54, figure they have three options. They can increase their contributions to their 403(b) and 401(k) retirement plans, add more to their established traditional IRAs, or start up Roth IRAs. Bill appreciates the tax advantages of a Roth. Although there is no upfront tax break, all withdrawals, including investment earnings, are tax-free once you are 59½ and the account has been open at least five years.

But Bill wonders whether it makes sense for him and Susan to open Roths at their age. "At this late date in our work experiences, do we start new Roth IRAs or add to our traditional

accounts?" he asks. The couple have an adequate emergency savings fund and little debt, so they can comfortably bulk up their retirement assets.

Carlo Panaccione, a financial planner in Redwood City, Cal., says that Bill and Susan should pat themselves on the back for paying off their mortgage and committing to put the money toward savings rather than going on a spending spree. "People always say: 'If I have money

left at the end of the year, I'll save it,'" says Panaccione. "It never happens." Instead, he says, household budgets simply tend to expand whenever a family has money to spare.

Tax advantages. So, to answer Bill's question directly: It's not too late to start a Roth IRA. Because both Bill and Susan are older than 50 and their joint income is less than $167,000, each of them can contribute the maximum $6,000 (including

$1,000 in catch-up contributions) to a Roth in 2010.

No matter how long you maintain the retirement account, the tax benefits of a Roth are simply too good to pass up. When you withdraw money from a 401(k) or a regular IRA, it's taxed at your ordinary income-tax rate. With a Roth, you can withdraw cash in retirement without paying Uncle Sam a penny.

And once Bill and Susan retire, they won't need to tap their Roth IRAs right away, given their modest living expenses, their income from workplace retirement plans and Social Security. Because Roths have no required-minimum-distribution rules, you can leave the investments in place as long as you like. "That money can just sit there and cook," says Larry Rosenthal, a financial planner in Manassas, Va. With income-tax rates likely to rise to offset growing budget deficits, the Roth stands out as an increasingly valuable tax shelter. In other words, it's a good way for the couple to diversify their future tax liability.

Roth accounts could also prove helpful to Bill and Susan's estate planning. They can leave the accounts to their two daughters, who would inherit them tax-free. ∎

BUSINESS MATH ISSUE

Roth IRAs are best to establish over the age of 60.

1. List the key points of the article and information to support your position.
2. Write a group defense of your position using math calculations to support your view.

A Word Problem Approach—Chapters 10, 11, 12, 13

1. Amy O'Mally graduated from high school. Her uncle promised her as a gift a check for $2,000 or $275 every quarter for 2 years. If money could be invested at 6% compounded quarterly, which offer is better for Amy? (Use the tables in the *Business Math Handbook*.) *(p. 330)   LU 13-2(1)*

2. Alan Angel made deposits of $400 semiannually to Sag Bank, which pays 10% interest compounded semiannually. After 4 years, Alan made no more deposits. What will be the balance in the account 3 years after the last deposit? (Use the tables in the *Business Math Handbook*.) *(p. 326)   LU 13-1(2)*

3. Roger Disney decides to retire to Florida in 12 years. What amount should Roger invest today so that he will be able to withdraw $30,000 at the end of each year for 20 years *after* he retires? Assume he can invest money at 8% interest compounded annually. (Use tables in the *Business Math Handbook*.) *(p. 330)   LU 13-2(2)*

4. On September 15, Arthur Westering borrowed $3,000 from Vermont Bank at $10\frac{1}{2}$% interest. Arthur plans to repay the loan on January 25. Assume the loan is based on exact interest. How much will Arthur totally repay? *(p. 266)   LU 10-1(2)*

5. Sue Cooper borrowed $6,000 on an $11\frac{3}{4}$%, 120-day note. Sue paid $300 toward the note on day 50. On day 90, Sue paid an additional $200. Using the U.S. Rule, Sue's adjusted balance after her first payment is the following. *(p. 270)   LU 10-3(1)*

6. On November 18, Northwest Company discounted an $18,000, 12%, 120-day note dated September 8. Assume a 10% discount rate. What will be the proceeds? Use ordinary interest. *(p. 289)   LU 11-2(1)*

7. Alice Reed deposits $16,500 into Rye Bank, which pays 10% interest compounded semiannually. Using the appropriate table, what will Alice have in her account at the end of 6 years? *(p. 304)   LU 12-1(2)*

8. Peter Regan needs $90,000 5 years from today to retire in Arizona. Peter's bank pays 10% interest compounded semiannually. What will Peter have to put in the bank today to have $90,000 in 5 years? *(p. 310)   LU 12-2(2)*

Special Supplement

Time-Value Relationship Using Plastic Overlays
Contents

One Lump Sum (Single Amount)

EXHIBIT 13.1   Compound (future value) of $.68 at 10% for 4 periods

EXHIBIT 13.2   Present value of $1.00 at 10% for 4 periods

Annuity (Stream of Payments)

EXHIBIT 13.3   Present value of a 4-year annuity of $1.00 at 10%

EXHIBIT 13.4   Future value of a 4-year annuity of $1.00 at 10%

Turn transparency over to see relationship of compounding to present value.

EXHIBIT | **13.1** | Compound (future value) of $.68 at 10% for 4 periods

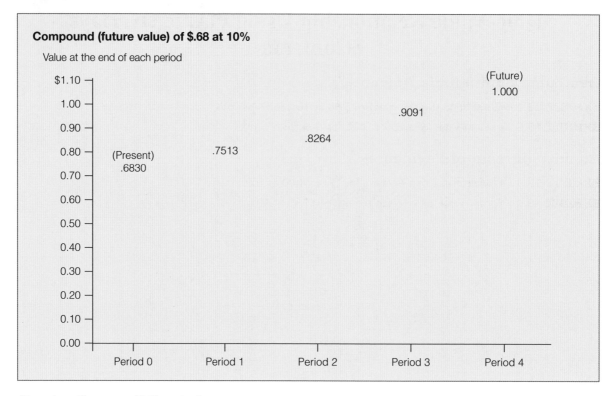

Compound (future value) of $.68 at 10%

Value at the end of each period

68¢ today will grow to $1.00 in the future.

What Exhibit 13.1 Means

If you take $.68 to a bank that pays 10% after 4 periods you will be able to get $1.00. The $.68 is the present value, and the $1.00 is the compound value or future value. Keep in mind that the $.68 is a one lump-sum investment.

EXHIBIT **13.2** Present value of $1.00 at 10% for 4 periods

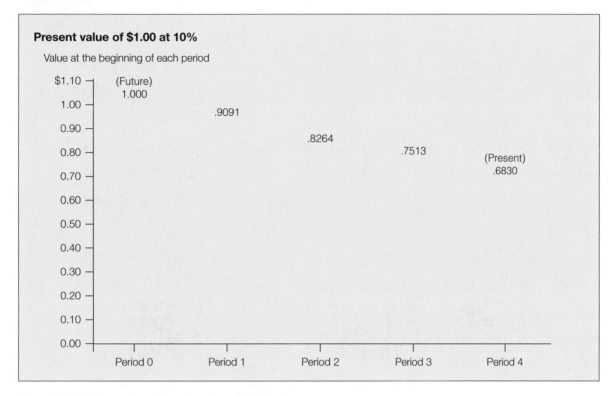

Present value of $1.00 at 10%

Value at the beginning of each period

If I need $1 in four periods, I need to invest $0.68 today.

What Exhibit 13.2 Means

If you want to receive $1.00 at the end of 4 periods at a bank paying 10%, you will have to deposit $.68 in the bank today. The longer you have to wait for your money, the less it is worth. The $1.00 is the compound or future amount, and the $.68 is the present value of a dollar that you will not receive for 4 periods.

EXHIBIT **13.3** Present value of a 4-year annuity of $1.00 at 10%

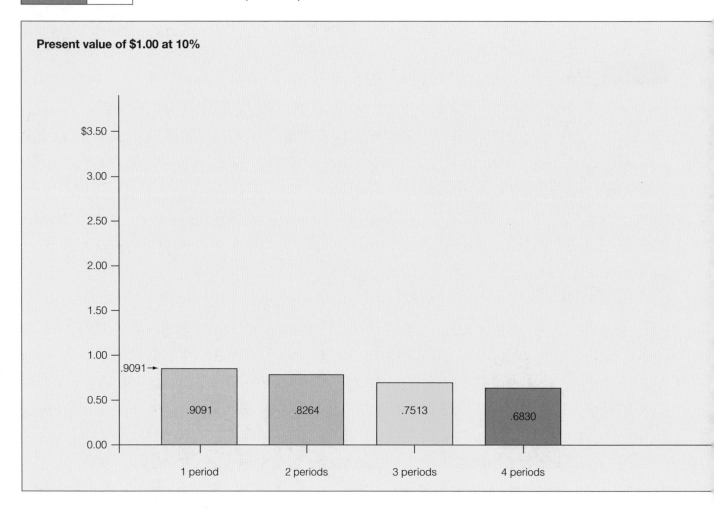

Present value of $1.00 at 10%

EXHIBIT **13.4** Future value of a 4-year annuity of $1.00 at 10%

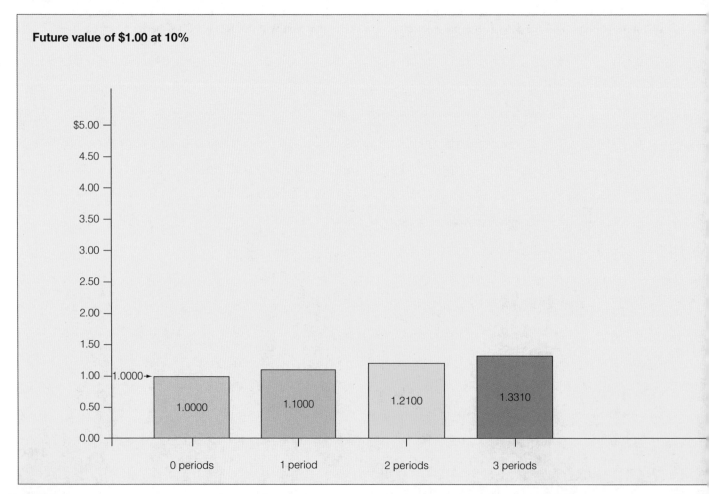

Future value of $1.00 at 10%

What Exhibit 13.3 Means*

BLUE BOX
(Top box)

Blue shows how to receive $1.00 after 1 period. You must put in $.91 today.

PURPLE BOX
(2nd box from top)

Purple shows how to receive $1.00 after 2 periods. You must put in $.83 today to get $1.00 for 2 periods. You must put in the bank today $1.74 ($.91 + $.83) to take out $1.00 for 2 periods.

YELLOW BOX
(3rd box from top)

Yellow shows how to receive $1.00 after 3 periods. You must put in $.75 today to get $1.00 for 3 periods. You also must put in the bank today $2.49 ($.91 + $.83 + $.75) to take out $1.00 for 3 periods.

GREEN BOX
(4th box from top)

Green shows how to receive $1.00 after 4 periods. You must put in $.68 today to get $1.00 for 4 periods. You also must put in the bank today $3.17 ($.91 + $.83 + $.75 + $.68) to take out $1.00 for 4 periods.

What Exhibit 13.4 Means*

BLUE BOX
(Top box)

Blue shows $1.00 invested at the end of each period. The $1.00 has no time to earn interest.

PURPLE BOX
(2nd box from top)

Purple shows the value of $1.00 after 2 periods. The $1.00 is now worth $1.10 due to compounding for 1 period.

YELLOW BOX
(3rd box from top)

Yellow shows the value of $1.00 after 3 periods. The $1.00 is now worth $1.21 due to compounding for 2 periods.

GREEN BOX
(4th box from top)

Green shows that the value of $1.00 after 4 periods is $1.33 due to compounding for 3 periods. If you put $1.00 in the bank at 10% for 4 years, the $4.00 grows to $4.64.

*From table in Handbook for 10%.

Periods	Amount of annuity	Present value of an annuity
1	1. 1.0000	.9091
2	2. 2.1000	1.7355
3	3. 3100	2.4869
4	4. 6410	3.1699

Classroom Notes

Installment Buying

Inside the Fee Machine

The Credit Card Act prohibited a number of controversial billing practices. So issuers cranked up their ordinary fees—and dreamed up new ways to squeeze customers.

Ordinary charges have risen since the card act was passed...

Foreign-transaction fees	+50%
Balance transfers	+33%
Cash-advance fees	+33%
Annual fees	+18%
Penalty interest rates	+3.4%

... And issuers are getting more creative

AMPLE TIME TO PAY

Under the Card Act, companies must allot 21 days between when a statement is mailed and when payment is due. Some cardholders say they aren't getting the full time required—and then are getting slammed with late-payment fees.

ADVICE

Watch out for shortened payment dates.

SUNDAY DUE DATES

The Card Act encourages banks not to process payments on Sundays and holidays. But some banks say they're open for business even when there's no mail delivery.

ADVICE

Even though the Card Act deals with billing dates, don't assume you are safe.

LOW-LIMIT CARDS

These cards, popular with students, now can't levy fees greater than 25% of a borrower's credit line.

ADVICE

Watch out for processing and other fees not included in the total tally.

FAUX INACTIVITY FEES

While inactivity fees will be banned under the Card Act, some issuers are charging an annual fee that's waived if cardholders reach a certain spending threshold.

ADVICE

Pay attention to conditional annual fees.

REBATE OFFERS

Some credit cards offer refunds on finance charges when customers pay on time. But such offers can be revoked suddenly and for any reason, leaving cardholders stuck with higher charges than they bargained for.

ADVICE

Don't mistake rebates for real savings in finance charges.

LU 14–1: Cost of Installment Buying

1. Calculate the amount financed, finance charge, and deferred payment *(pp. 350–351)*.
2. Calculate the estimated APR by table lookup *(pp. 351–353)*.
3. Calculate the monthly payment by formula and by table lookup *(pp. 353–355)*.

LU 14–2: Revolving Charge Credit Cards

1. Calculate the finance charges on revolving charge credit card accounts *(pp. 356–358)*.

VOCABULARY PREVIEW

Here are key terms in this chapter. After completing the chapter, if you know the term, place a checkmark in the parentheses. If you don't know the term, look it up and put the page number where it can be found.

**Amortization ( ) Amount financed ( ) Annual percentage rate (APR) ( ) Average daily balance ( )
Cash advance ( ) Credit Card Act ( ) Daily balance ( ) Deferred payment price ( ) Down payment ( )
Fair Credit and Charge Card Disclosure Act of 1988 ( ) Finance charge ( ) Installment loan ( ) Loan
amortization table ( ) Open-end credit ( ) Outstanding balance ( ) Revolving charge account ( )
Truth in Lending Act ( )**

2010 Honda CR-V

$424   **$444**

Typical monthly   Typical monthly
payment, NEW   payment, USED
model   1-year-old model

Edmunds.com looked at the monthly payments for various new vehicles and their one-year-old counterparts and found in many instances, the old models' payments were pricier than the younger models.

Reprinted with permission of *The Wall Street Journal*, Copyright © 2010 Dow Jones & Company, Inc. All Rights Reserved Worldwide.

Do you know your FICO score? In the chapter opener we see how credit card companies may try to "squeeze customers." As a good consumer you should know your *FICO score*. "FICO" stands for Fair Isaac Corporation. It is a measure of your credit score. Factors making up your score may include payment history and types of credit used. Scores range from 300 to 850. Approximately 60% of people's FICO scores fall between 650 and 799. You are entitled to a free report by the Fair and Accurate Credit Card Transaction Act when you borrow once a year. The higher your score, the better your interest rates will be when you borrow.

If you are thinking of buying a car, the *Wall Street Journal* clipping, above, may be of interest to you. Edmunds.com indicates that the monthly payment on a year-old car could be more than the monthly payment on a new car. Buyer beware!

This chapter discusses the cost of buying products via installments (closed-end credit) and revolving credit card (open-end credit). You will see in Learning Unit 14–1 that to buy a 4×4 pickup a qualified buyer must have a credit score of 720 or higher (see clip below).

Learning Unit 14–1: Cost of Installment Buying

Installment buying, a form of *closed-end credit,* can add a substantial amount to the cost of big-ticket purchases. To illustrate this, we follow the procedure of buying a pickup truck, including the amount financed, finance charge, and deferred payment price. Then we study the effect of the Truth in Lending Act.

LO 1

Amount Financed, Finance Charge, and Deferred Payment

This advertisement for the sale of a pickup truck appeared in a local paper. As you can see from this advertisement, after customers make a **down payment,** they can buy the truck with an **installment loan.** This loan is paid off with a series of equal periodic payments. These payments include both interest and principal. The payment process is called **amortization.** In the promissory notes of earlier chapters, the loan was paid off in one ending payment. Now let's look at the calculations involved in buying a pickup truck.

© AP Photo/Orlin Wagner

$194.38 MONTH

4X4 Pickup*
$9,345

With $300 down cash or trade for 60 months at Annual Percentage Rate of 10.5%. Amt. financed—$9,045.00. Finance chg.—$2,617.80. Total note—$11,662.80. Total deferred payment price—$11,962.80. Taxes, title, insurance additional.

*Financing is available to qualified buyers with credit scores of 720 or higher.

Checking Calculations in Pickup Advertisement

Calculating Amount Financed The **amount financed** is what you actually borrow. To calculate this amount, use the following formula:

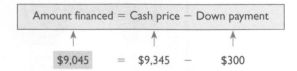

$$\text{Amount financed} = \text{Cash price} - \text{Down payment}$$

$$\$9,045 = \$9,345 - \$300$$

Calculating Finance Charge The words "**finance charge**" in the advertisement represent the *interest* charge. The interest charge resulting in the finance charge includes the cost of credit reports, mandatory bank fees, and so on. You can use the following formula to calculate the total interest on the loan:

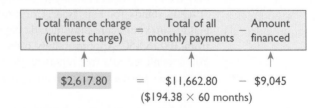

$$\begin{array}{ccc} \text{Total finance charge} & = & \text{Total of all} & - & \text{Amount} \\ \text{(interest charge)} & & \text{monthly payments} & & \text{financed} \end{array}$$

$$\$2,617.80 = \$11,662.80 - \$9,045$$
$$(\$194.38 \times 60 \text{ months})$$

Calculating Deferred Payment Price The **deferred payment price** represents the total of all monthly payments plus the down payment. The following formula is used to calculate the deferred payment price:

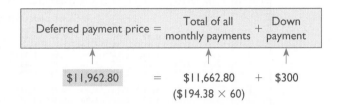

$$\text{Deferred payment price} = \frac{\text{Total of all}}{\text{monthly payments}} + \frac{\text{Down}}{\text{payment}}$$

$$\$11,962.80 \quad = \quad \$11,662.80 \quad + \quad \$300$$
$$(\$194.38 \times 60)$$

Truth in Lending: APR Defined and Calculated

In 1969, the Federal Reserve Board established the **Truth in Lending Act** (Regulation Z). The law doesn't regulate interest charges; its purpose is to make the consumer aware of the true cost of credit.

The Truth in Lending Act requires that creditors provide certain basic information about the actual cost of buying on credit. Before buyers sign a credit agreement, creditors must inform them in writing of the amount of the finance charge and the **annual percentage rate (APR).** The APR represents the true or effective annual interest creditors charge. This is helpful to buyers who repay loans over different periods of time (1 month, 48 months, and so on).

To illustrate how the APR affects the interest rate, assume you borrow $100 for 1 year and pay a finance charge of $9. Your interest rate would be 9% if you waited until the end of the year to pay back the loan. Now let's say you pay off the loan and the finance charge in 12 monthly payments. Each month that you make a payment, you are losing some of the value or use of that money. So the true or effective APR is actually greater than 9%.

The APR can be calculated by formula or by tables. We will use the table method since it is more exact.

LO 2

Calculating APR Rate by Table 14.1 (p. 352) Note the following steps for using a table to calculate APR:

CALCULATING APR BY TABLE
Step 1. Divide the finance charge by amount financed and multiply by $100 to get the table lookup factor.
Step 2. Go to APR Table 14.1. At the left side of the table are listed the number of payments that will be made.
Step 3. When you find the number of payments you are looking for, move to the right and look for the two numbers closest to the table lookup number. This will indicate the APR.

Now let's determine the APR for the pickup truck advertisement given earlier in the chapter.

As stated in Step 1, we begin by dividing the finance charge by the amount financed and multiply by $100:

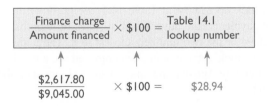

$$\frac{\text{Finance charge}}{\text{Amount financed}} \times \$100 = \frac{\text{Table 14.1}}{\text{lookup number}}$$

$$\frac{\$2,617.80}{\$9,045.00} \times \$100 = \$28.94$$

We multiply by $100, since the table is based on $100 of financing.

TABLE   14.1   Annual percentage rate table per $100

NUMBER OF PAYMENTS	ANNUAL PERCENTAGE RATE

NUMBER OF PAYMENTS	10.00%	10.25%	10.50%	10.75%	11.00%	11.25%	11.50%	11.75%	12.00%	12.25%	12.50%	12.75%	13.00%	13.25%	13.50%	13.75%
	(FINANCE CHARGE PER $100 OF AMOUNT FINANCED)															
1	0.83	0.85	0.87	0.90	0.92	0.94	0.96	0.98	1.00	1.02	1.04	1.06	1.08	1.10	1.12	1.15
2	1.25	1.28	1.31	1.35	1.38	1.41	1.44	1.47	1.50	1.53	1.57	1.60	1.63	1.66	1.69	1.72
3	1.67	1.71	1.76	1.80	1.84	1.88	1.92	1.96	2.01	2.05	2.09	2.13	2.17	2.22	2.26	2.30
4	2.09	2.14	2.20	2.25	2.30	2.35	2.41	2.46	2.51	2.57	2.62	2.67	2.72	2.78	2.83	2.88
5	2.51	2.58	2.64	2.70	2.77	2.83	2.89	2.96	3.02	3.08	3.15	3.21	3.27	3.34	3.40	3.46
6	2.94	3.01	3.08	3.16	3.23	3.31	3.38	3.45	3.53	3.60	3.68	3.75	3.83	3.90	3.97	4.05
7	3.36	3.45	3.53	3.62	3.70	3.78	3.87	3.95	4.04	4.12	4.21	4.29	4.38	4.47	4.55	4.64
8	3.79	3.88	3.98	4.07	4.17	4.26	4.36	4.46	4.55	4.65	4.74	4.84	4.94	5.03	5.13	5.22
9	4.21	4.32	4.43	4.53	4.64	4.75	4.85	4.96	5.07	5.17	5.28	5.39	5.49	5.60	5.71	5.82
10	4.64	4.76	4.88	4.99	5.11	5.23	5.35	5.46	5.58	5.70	5.82	5.94	6.05	6.17	6.29	6.41
11	5.07	5.20	5.33	5.45	5.58	5.71	5.84	5.97	6.10	6.23	6.36	6.49	6.62	6.75	6.88	7.01
12	5.50	5.64	5.78	5.92	6.06	6.20	6.34	6.48	6.62	6.76	6.90	7.04	7.18	7.32	7.46	7.60
13	5.93	6.08	6.23	6.38	6.53	6.68	6.84	6.99	7.14	7.29	7.44	7.59	7.75	7.90	8.05	8.20
14	6.36	6.52	6.69	6.85	7.01	7.17	7.34	7.50	7.66	7.82	7.99	8.15	8.31	8.48	8.64	8.81
15	6.80	6.97	7.14	7.32	7.49	7.66	7.84	8.01	8.19	8.36	8.53	8.71	8.88	9.06	9.23	9.41
16	7.23	7.41	7.60	7.78	7.97	8.15	8.34	8.53	8.71	8.90	9.08	9.27	9.46	9.64	9.83	10.02
17	7.67	7.86	8.06	8.25	8.45	8.65	8.84	9.04	9.24	9.44	9.63	9.83	10.03	10.23	10.43	10.63
18	8.10	8.31	8.52	8.73	8.93	9.14	9.35	9.56	9.77	9.98	10.19	10.40	10.61	10.82	11.03	11.24
19	8.54	8.76	8.98	9.20	9.42	9.64	9.86	10.08	10.30	10.52	10.74	10.96	11.18	11.41	11.63	11.85
20	8.98	9.21	9.44	9.67	9.90	10.13	10.37	10.60	10.83	11.06	11.30	11.53	11.76	12.00	12.23	12.46
21	9.42	9.66	9.90	10.15	10.39	10.63	10.88	11.12	11.36	11.61	11.85	12.10	12.34	12.59	12.84	13.08
22	9.86	10.12	10.37	10.62	10.88	11.13	11.39	11.64	11.90	12.16	12.41	12.67	12.93	13.19	13.44	13.70
23	10.30	10.57	10.84	11.10	11.37	11.63	11.90	12.17	12.44	12.71	12.97	13.24	13.51	13.78	14.05	14.32
24	10.75	11.02	11.30	11.58	11.86	12.14	12.42	12.70	12.98	13.26	13.54	13.82	14.10	14.38	14.66	14.95
25	11.19	11.48	11.77	12.06	12.35	12.64	12.93	13.22	13.52	13.81	14.10	14.40	14.69	14.98	15.28	15.57
26	11.64	11.94	12.24	12.54	12.85	13.15	13.45	13.75	14.06	14.36	14.67	14.97	15.28	15.59	15.89	16.20
27	12.09	12.40	12.71	13.03	13.34	13.66	13.97	14.29	14.60	14.92	15.24	15.56	15.87	16.19	16.51	16.83
28	12.53	12.86	13.18	13.51	13.84	14.16	14.49	14.82	15.15	15.48	15.81	16.14	16.47	16.80	17.13	17.46
29	12.98	13.32	13.66	14.00	14.33	14.67	15.01	15.35	15.70	16.04	16.38	16.72	17.07	17.41	17.75	18.10
30	13.43	13.78	14.13	14.48	14.83	15.19	15.54	15.89	16.24	16.60	16.95	17.31	17.66	18.02	18.38	18.74
31	13.89	14.25	14.61	14.97	15.33	15.70	16.06	16.43	16.79	17.16	17.53	17.90	18.27	18.63	19.00	19.38
32	14.34	14.71	15.09	15.46	15.84	16.21	16.59	16.97	17.35	17.73	18.11	18.49	18.87	19.25	19.63	20.02
33	14.79	15.18	15.57	15.95	16.34	16.73	17.12	17.51	17.90	18.29	18.69	19.08	19.47	19.87	20.26	20.66
34	15.25	15.65	16.05	16.44	16.85	17.25	17.65	18.05	18.46	18.86	19.27	19.67	20.08	20.49	20.90	21.31
35	15.70	16.11	16.53	16.94	17.35	17.77	18.18	18.60	19.01	19.43	19.85	20.27	20.69	21.11	21.53	21.95
36	16.16	16.58	17.01	17.43	17.86	18.29	18.71	19.14	19.57	20.00	20.43	20.87	21.30	21.73	22.17	22.60
37	16.62	17.06	17.49	17.93	18.37	18.81	19.25	19.69	20.13	20.58	21.02	21.46	21.91	22.36	22.81	23.25
38	17.08	17.53	17.98	18.43	18.88	19.33	19.78	20.24	20.69	21.15	21.61	22.07	22.52	22.99	23.45	23.91
39	17.54	18.00	18.46	18.93	19.39	19.86	20.32	20.79	21.26	21.73	22.20	22.67	23.14	23.61	24.09	24.56
40	18.00	18.48	18.95	19.43	19.90	20.38	20.86	21.34	21.82	22.30	22.79	23.27	23.76	24.25	74.73	25.22
41	18.47	18.95	19.44	19.93	20.42	20.91	21.40	21.89	22.39	22.88	23.38	23.88	24.38	24.88	25.38	25.88
42	18.93	19.43	19.93	20.43	20.93	21.44	21.94	22.45	22.96	23.47	23.98	24.49	25.00	25.51	26.03	26.55
43	19.40	19.91	20.42	20.94	21.45	21.97	22.49	23.01	23.53	24.05	24.57	25.10	25.62	26.15	26.68	27.21
44	19.86	20.39	20.91	21.44	21.97	22.50	23.03	23.57	24.10	24.64	25.17	25.71	26.25	26.79	27.33	27.88
45	20.33	20.87	21.41	21.95	22.49	23.03	23.58	24.12	24.67	25.22	25.77	26.32	26.88	27.43	27.99	28.55
46	20.80	21.35	21.90	22.46	23.01	23.57	24.13	24.69	25.25	25.81	26.37	26.94	27.51	28.08	28.65	29.22
47	21.27	21.83	22.40	22.97	23.53	24.10	24.68	25.25	25.82	26.40	26.98	27.56	28.14	28.72	29.31	29.89
48	21.74	22.32	22.90	23.48	24.06	24.64	25.23	25.81	26.40	26.99	27.58	28.18	28.77	29.37	29.97	30.57
49	22.21	22.80	23.39	23.99	24.58	25.18	25.78	26.38	26.98	27.59	28.19	28.80	29.41	30.02	30.63	31.24
50	22.69	23.29	23.89	24.50	25.11	25.72	26.33	26.95	27.56	28.18	28.80	29.42	30.04	30.67	31.29	31.92
51	23.16	23.78	24.40	25.02	25.64	26.26	26.89	27.52	28.15	28.78	29.41	30.05	30.68	31.32	31.96	32.60
52	23.64	24.27	24.90	25.53	26.17	26.81	27.45	28.09	28.73	29.38	30.02	30.67	31.32	31.98	32.63	33.29
53	24.11	24.76	25.40	26.05	26.70	27.35	28.00	28.66	29.32	29.98	30.64	31.30	31.97	32.63	33.30	33.97
54	24.59	25.25	25.91	26.57	27.23	27.90	28.56	29.23	29.91	30.58	31.25	31.93	32.61	33.29	33.98	34.66
55	25.07	25.74	26.41	27.09	27.77	28.44	29.13	29.81	30.50	31.18	31.87	32.56	33.26	33.95	34.65	35.35
56	25.55	26.23	26.92	27.61	28.30	28.99	29.69	30.39	31.09	31.79	32.49	33.20	33.91	34.62	35.33	36.04
57	26.03	26.73	27.43	28.13	28.84	29.54	30.25	30.97	31.68	32.39	33.11	33.83	34.56	35.28	36.01	36.74
58	26.51	27.23	27.94	28.66	29.37	30.10	30.82	31.55	32.27	33.00	33.74	34.47	35.21	35.95	36.69	37.43
59	27.00	27.72	28.45	29.18	29.91	30.65	31.39	32.13	32.87	33.61	34.36	35.11	35.86	36.62	37.37	38.13
60	27.48	28.22	28.96	29.71	30.45	31.20	31.96	32.71	33.47	34.23	34.99	35.75	36.52	37.29	38.06	38.83

Note: For a more detailed set of tables from 2% to 21.75%, see the reference tables in the *Business Math Handbook*.

To look up $28.94 in Table 14.1, we go down the left side of the table until we come to 60 payments (the advertisement states 60 months). Then, moving to the right, we look for $28.94 or the two numbers closest to it. The number $28.94 is between $28.22 and $28.96. So we look at the column headings and see a rate between 10.25% and 10.5%. The Truth in Lending Act requires that when creditors state the APR, it must be accurate to the nearest $\frac{1}{4}$ of 1%.[1]

[1]If we wanted an exact reading of APR when the number is not exactly in the table, we would use the process of interpolating. We do not cover this method in this course.

TABLE 14.1 (concluded)

NUMBER OF PAYMENTS	ANNUAL PERCENTAGE RATE															
	14.00%	14.25%	14.50%	14.75%	15.00%	15.25%	15.50%	15.75%	16.00%	16.25%	16.50%	16.75%	17.00%	17.25%	17.50%	17.75%
	(FINANCE CHARGE PER $100 OF AMOUNT FINANCED)															
1	1.17	1.19	1.21	1.23	1.25	1.27	1.29	1.31	1.33	1.35	1.37	1.40	1.42	1.44	1.46	1.48
2	1.75	1.78	1.82	1.85	1.88	1.91	1.94	1.97	2.00	2.04	2.07	2.10	2.13	2.16	2.19	2.22
3	2.34	2.38	2.43	2.47	2.51	2.55	2.59	2.64	2.68	2.72	2.76	2.80	2.85	2.89	2.93	2.97
4	2.93	2.99	3.04	3.09	3.14	3.20	3.25	3.30	3.36	3.41	3.46	3.51	3.57	3.62	3.67	3.73
5	3.53	3.59	3.65	3.72	3.78	3.84	3.91	3.97	4.04	4.10	4.16	4.23	4.29	4.35	4.42	4.48
6	4.12	4.20	4.27	4.35	4.42	4.49	4.57	4.64	4.72	4.79	4.87	4.94	5.02	5.09	5.17	5.24
7	4.72	4.81	4.89	4.98	5.06	5.15	5.23	5.32	5.40	5.49	5.58	5.66	5.75	5.83	5.92	6.00
8	5.32	5.42	5.51	5.61	5.71	5.80	5.90	6.00	6.09	6.19	6.29	6.38	6.48	6.58	6.67	6.77
9	5.92	6.03	6.14	6.25	6.35	6.46	6.57	6.68	6.78	6.89	7.00	7.11	7.22	7.32	7.43	7.54
10	6.53	6.65	6.77	6.88	7.00	7.12	7.24	7.36	7.48	7.60	7.72	7.84	7.96	8.08	8.19	8.31
11	7.14	7.27	7.40	7.53	7.66	7.79	7.92	8.05	8.18	8.31	8.44	8.57	8.70	8.83	8.96	9.09
12	7.74	7.89	8.03	8.17	8.31	8.45	8.59	8.74	8.88	9.02	9.16	9.30	9.45	9.59	9.73	9.87
13	8.36	8.51	8.66	8.81	8.97	9.12	9.27	9.43	9.58	9.73	9.89	10.04	10.20	10.35	10.50	10.66
14	8.97	9.13	9.30	9.46	9.63	9.79	9.96	10.12	10.29	10.45	10.67	10.78	10.95	11.11	11.28	11.45
15	9.59	9.76	9.94	10.11	10.29	10.47	10.64	10.82	11.00	11.17	11.35	11.53	11.71	11.88	12.06	12.24
16	10.20	10.39	10.58	10.77	10.95	11.14	11.33	11.52	11.71	11.90	12.09	12.28	12.46	12.65	12.84	13.03
17	10.82	11.02	11.22	11.42	11.62	11.82	12.02	12.22	12.42	12.62	12.83	13.03	13.23	13.43	13.63	13.83
18	11.45	11.66	11.87	12.08	12.29	12.50	12.72	12.93	13.14	13.35	13.57	13.78	13.99	14.21	14.42	14.64
19	12.07	12.30	12.52	12.74	12.97	13.19	13.41	13.64	13.86	14.09	14.31	14.54	14.76	14.99	15.22	15.44
20	12.70	12.93	13.17	13.41	13.64	13.88	14.11	14.35	14.59	14.82	15.06	15.30	15.54	15.77	16.01	16.25
21	13.33	13.58	13.82	14.07	14.32	14.57	14.82	15.06	15.31	15.56	15.81	16.06	16.31	16.56	16.81	17.07
22	13.96	14.22	14.48	14.74	15.00	15.26	15.52	15.78	16.04	16.30	16.57	16.83	17.09	17.36	17.62	17.88
23	14.59	14.87	15.14	15.41	15.68	15.96	16.23	16.50	16.78	17.05	17.32	17.60	17.88	18.15	18.43	18.70
24	15.23	15.51	15.80	16.08	16.37	16.65	16.94	17.22	17.51	17.80	18.09	18.37	18.66	18.95	19.24	19.53
25	15.87	16.17	16.46	16.76	17.06	17.35	17.65	17.95	18.25	18.55	18.85	19.15	19.45	19.75	20.05	20.36
26	16.51	16.82	17.13	17.44	17.75	18.06	18.37	18.68	18.99	19.30	19.62	19.93	20.24	20.56	20.87	21.19
27	17.15	17.47	17.80	18.12	18.44	18.76	19.09	19.41	19.74	20.06	20.39	20.71	21.04	21.37	21.69	22.02
28	17.80	18.13	18.47	18.80	19.14	19.47	19.81	20.15	20.48	20.82	21.16	21.50	21.84	22.18	22.52	22.86
29	18.45	18.79	19.14	19.49	19.83	20.18	20.53	20.89	21.23	21.58	21.94	22.29	22.64	22.99	23.35	23.70
30	19.10	19.45	19.81	20.17	20.54	20.90	21.26	21.62	21.99	22.35	22.72	23.08	23.45	23.81	24.18	24.55
31	19.75	20.12	20.49	20.87	21.24	21.61	21.99	22.37	22.74	23.12	23.50	23.88	24.26	24.64	25.02	25.40
32	20.40	20.79	21.17	21.56	21.95	22.33	22.72	23.11	23.50	23.89	24.28	24.68	25.07	25.46	25.86	26.25
33	21.06	21.46	21.85	22.25	22.65	23.06	23.46	23.86	24.26	24.67	25.07	25.48	25.88	26.29	26.70	27.11
34	21.72	22.13	22.54	22.95	23.37	23.78	24.19	24.61	25.03	25.44	25.86	26.28	26.70	27.12	27.54	27.97
35	22.38	22.80	23.23	23.65	24.08	24.51	24.94	25.36	25.79	26.23	26.66	27.09	27.52	27.96	28.39	28.83
36	23.04	23.48	23.92	24.35	24.80	25.24	25.68	26.12	26.57	27.01	27.46	27.90	28.35	28.80	29.25	29.70
37	23.70	24.16	24.61	25.06	25.51	25.97	26.42	26.88	27.34	27.80	28.26	28.72	29.18	29.64	30.10	30.57
38	24.37	24.84	25.30	25.77	26.24	26.70	27.17	27.64	28.11	28.59	29.06	29.53	30.01	30.49	30.96	31.44
39	25.04	25.52	26.00	26.48	26.96	27.44	27.92	28.41	28.89	29.38	29.87	30.36	30.85	31.34	31.83	32.32
40	25.71	26.20	26.70	27.19	27.69	28.18	28.68	29.18	29.68	30.18	30.69	31.19	31.69	32.19	32.69	33.20
41	26.39	26.89	27.40	27.91	28.41	28.92	29.44	29.95	30.46	30.97	31.49	32.01	32.52	33.04	33.56	34.08
42	27.06	27.58	28.10	28.62	29.15	29.67	30.19	30.72	31.25	31.78	32.31	32.84	33.37	33.90	34.44	34.97
43	27.74	28.27	28.81	29.34	29.88	30.42	30.96	31.50	32.04	32.58	33.13	33.67	34.22	34.76	35.31	35.86
44	28.42	28.97	29.52	30.07	30.62	31.17	31.72	32.28	32.83	33.39	33.95	34.51	35.07	35.63	36.19	36.76
45	29.11	29.67	30.23	30.79	31.36	31.92	32.49	33.06	33.63	34.20	34.77	35.35	35.92	36.50	37.08	37.66
46	29.79	30.36	30.94	31.52	32.10	32.68	33.26	33.84	34.43	35.01	35.60	36.19	36.78	37.37	37.96	38.56
47	30.48	31.07	31.66	32.25	32.84	33.44	34.03	34.63	35.23	35.83	36.43	37.04	37.64	38.25	38.86	39.46
48	31.17	31.77	32.37	32.98	33.59	34.20	34.81	35.42	36.03	36.65	37.27	37.88	38.50	39.13	39.75	40.37
49	31.86	32.48	33.09	33.71	34.34	34.96	35.59	36.21	36.84	37.47	38.10	38.74	39.37	40.01	40.65	41.29
50	32.55	33.18	33.82	34.45	35.09	35.73	36.37	37.01	37.65	38.30	38.94	39.59	40.24	40.89	41.55	42.20
51	33.25	33.89	34.54	35.19	35.84	36.49	37.15	37.81	38.46	39.12	39.79	40.45	41.11	41.78	42.45	43.12
52	33.95	34.61	35.27	35.93	36.60	37.27	37.94	38.61	39.28	39.96	40.63	41.31	41.99	42.67	43.36	44.04
53	34.65	35.32	36.00	36.68	37.36	38.04	38.72	39.41	40.10	40.79	41.48	42.17	42.87	43.57	44.27	44.97
54	35.35	36.04	36.73	37.42	38.12	38.82	39.52	40.22	40.92	41.63	42.33	43.04	43.75	44.47	45.18	45.90
55	36.05	36.76	37.46	38.17	38.88	39.60	40.31	41.03	41.74	42.47	43.19	43.91	44.64	45.37	46.10	46.83
56	36.76	37.48	38.20	38.92	39.65	40.38	41.11	41.84	42.57	43.31	44.05	44.79	45.53	46.27	47.02	47.77
57	37.47	38.20	38.94	39.68	40.42	41.16	41.91	42.65	43.40	44.15	44.91	45.66	46.42	47.18	47.94	48.71
58	38.18	38.93	39.68	40.43	41.19	41.95	42.71	43.47	44.23	45.00	45.77	46.54	47.32	48.09	48.87	49.65
59	38.89	39.66	40.42	41.19	41.96	42.74	43.51	44.29	45.07	45.85	46.64	47.42	48.21	49.01	49.80	50.60
60	39.61	40.39	41.17	41.95	42.74	43.53	44.32	45.11	45.91	46.71	47.51	48.31	49.12	49.92	50.73	51.55

LO 3

Calculating the Monthly Payment by Formula and Table 14.2 (p. 354)   The pickup truck advertisement showed a $194.38 monthly payment. We can check this by formula and by table lookup.

By Formula

$$\frac{\text{Finance charge} + \text{Amount financed}}{\text{Number of payments of loan}} = \frac{\$2{,}617.80 + \$9{,}045}{60} = \$194.38$$

| TABLE 14.2 | Loan amortization table (monthly payment per $1,000 to pay principal and interest on installment loan) |

Terms in months	7.50%	8%	8.50%	9%	10.00%	10.50%	11.00%	11.50%	12.00%
6	$170.34	$170.58	$170.83	$171.20	$171.56	$171.81	$172.05	$172.30	$172.55
12	86.76	86.99	87.22	87.46	87.92	88.15	88.38	88.62	88.85
18	58.92	59.15	59.37	59.60	60.06	60.29	60.52	60.75	60.98
24	45.00	45.23	45.46	45.69	46.14	46.38	46.61	46.84	47.07
30	36.66	36.89	37.12	37.35	37.81	38.04	38.28	38.51	38.75
36	31.11	31.34	31.57	31.80	32.27	32.50	32.74	32.98	33.21
42	27.15	27.38	27.62	27.85	28.32	28.55	28.79	29.03	29.28
48	24.18	24.42	24.65	24.77	25.36	25.60	25.85	26.09	26.33
54	21.88	22.12	22.36	22.59	23.07	23.32	23.56	23.81	24.06
60	20.04	20.28	20.52	20.76	21.25	21.49	21.74	21.99	22.24

By Table 14.2 The **loan amortization table** (many variations of this table are available) in Table 14.2 can be used to calculate the monthly payment for the pickup truck. To calculate a monthly payment with a table, use the following steps:

MONEY tips

Control your debt. Check for errors monthly by reviewing each line item on your bank statement and credit card bills. Record your bank transactions and save credit card receipts to cross-check each. Review your credit card's year-end summary to see where your money goes.

CALCULATING MONTHLY PAYMENT BY TABLE LOOKUP

Step 1. Divide the loan amount by $1,000 (since Table 14.2 is per $1,000):

$$\frac{\$9,045}{\$1,000} = 9.045$$

Step 2. Look up the rate (10.5%) and number of months (60). At the intersection is the table factor showing the monthly payment per $1,000.

Step 3. Multiply quotient in Step 1 by the table factor in Step 2:

9.045 × $21.49 = **$194.38.**

Remember that this $194.38 fixed payment includes interest and the reduction of the balance of the loan. As the number of payments increases, interest payments get smaller and the reduction of the principal gets larger.[2]

Now let's check your progress with the Practice Quiz.

| LU 14–1 | PRACTICE QUIZ |

Complete this **Practice Quiz** to see how you are doing.

From the partial advertisement at the right calculate the following:

1. **a.** Amount financed.
   b. Finance charge.
   c. Deferred payment price.
   d. APR by Table 14.1.
   e. Monthly payment by formula.

$288 per month	
Sale price	$14,150
Down payment	$ 1,450
Term/Number of payments	60 months

2. Jay Miller bought a New Brunswick boat for $7,500. Jay put down $1,000 and financed the balance at 10% for 60 months. What is his monthly payment? Use Table 14.2.

Courtesy of Brunswick Corporation

[2]In Chapter 15 we give an amortization schedule for home mortgages that shows how much of each fixed payment goes to interest and how much reduces the principal. This repayment schedule also gives a running balance of the loan.

TABLE 14.2   (concluded)

Terms in months	12.50%	13.00%	13.50%	14.00%	14.50%	15.00%	15.50%	16.00%
6	$172.80	$173.04	$173.29	$173.54	$173.79	$174.03	$174.28	$174.53
12	89.08	89.32	89.55	89.79	90.02	90.26	90.49	90.73
18	61.21	61.45	61.68	61.92	62.15	62.38	62.62	62.86
24	47.31	47.54	47.78	48.01	48.25	48.49	48.72	48.96
30	38.98	39.22	39.46	39.70	39.94	40.18	40.42	40.66
36	33.45	33.69	33.94	34.18	34.42	34.67	34.91	35.16
42	29.52	29.76	30.01	30.25	30.50	30.75	31.00	31.25
48	26.58	26.83	27.08	27.33	27.58	27.83	28.08	28.34
54	24.31	24.56	24.81	25.06	25.32	25.58	25.84	26.10
60	22.50	22.75	23.01	23.27	23.53	23.79	24.05	24.32

For **extra help** from your authors–Sharon and Jeff–see the student DVD

You Tube™

✓ Solutions

1. **a.** $14,150 − $1,450 = $12,700

   b. $17,280 ($288 × 60) − $12,700 = $4,580

   c. $17,280 ($288 × 60) + $1,450 = $18,730

   d. $\dfrac{\$4,580}{\$12,700} \times \$100 = \$36.06$; between 12.75% and 13%

   e. $\dfrac{\$4,580 + \$12,700}{60} = \$288$

2. $\dfrac{\$6,500}{\$1,000} = 6.5 \times \$21.25 = \$138.13$ (10%, 60 months)

LU 14–1a   EXTRA PRACTICE QUIZ WITH WORKED-OUT SOLUTIONS

Need more practice? Try this **Extra Practice Quiz** (check figures in the Interactive Chapter Organizer, p. 360). Worked-out Solutions can be found in Appendix B at end of text.

From the partial advertisement at the right calculate the following:

1. **a.** Amount financed.
   b. Finance charge.
   c. Deferred payment price.
   d. APR by Table 14.1.
   e. Monthly payment by formula.

$295 per month	
Sale price	$13,999
Down payment	$ 1,480
Term/Number of payments	60 months

2. Jay Miller bought a New Brunswick boat for $9,000. Jay put down $1,000 and financed the balance at 8% for 60 months. What is his monthly payment? Use Table 14.2.

Learning Unit 14–2: Revolving Charge Credit Cards

Do you owe a balance on your credit card? Let's look at how long it will take to pay off your credit card balance by making payments for the minimum amount. Study the clipping "Pay Just the Minimum, and Get Nowhere Fast" on page 356.

The clipping assumes that the minimum rate on the balance of a credit card is 2%. Note that if the annual interest cost is 17%, it will take 17 years, 3 months to pay off a balance of $1,000, and the total cost will be $2,590.35. If the balance on your revolving charge credit card is more than $1,000, you can see how fast the total cost rises. If you cannot afford the total cost of paying only the minimum, it is time for you to reconsider how you use your revolving credit card. This is why when you have financial difficulties, experts often advise you first to work on getting rid of your revolving credit card debt.

Do you know why revolving credit cards are so popular? Businesses encourage customers to use credit cards because consumers tend to buy more when they can use a credit card for their purchases. Consumers find credit cards convenient to use and valuable in establishing credit. The problem is that when consumers do not pay their balance in full

Pay Just the Minimum, and Get Nowhere Fast

THE COST—IN YEARS AND DOLLARS—OF PAYING THE MINIMUM 2% OF BALANCES ON CREDIT CARDS CHARGING 17% ANNUAL INTEREST

Balance	Total Cost	Total Time
$1,000	$2,590.35	17 years, 3 months
$2,500	$7,733.49	30 years, 3 months
$5,000	$16,305.34	40 years, 2 months

SOURCE: WWW.BANKRATE.COM

Reprinted with permission of *The Wall Street Journal,* Copyright © 2009 Dow Jones & Company, Inc. All Rights Reserved Worldwide.

each month, they do not realize how expensive it is to pay only the minimum of their balance. In 2011 American Express offered a new card called Serve that does not allow a customer to carry a balance. It is a *prepaid* card. It allows customers to use their smartphone to transfer money and pay for their purchases.

To protect consumers, Congress passed the **Fair Credit and Charge Card Disclosure Act of 1988.** This act requires that for direct-mail application or solicitation, credit card companies must provide specific details involving all fees, grace period, calculation of finance charges, and so on. In 2009 the **Credit Card Act** was passed to provide better consumer protection in dealing with credit card companies (see the chapter opener chip).

We begin the unit by seeing how Moe's Furniture Store calculates the finance charge on Abby Jordan's previous month's credit card balance. Then we learn how to calculate the average daily balance on the partial bill of Joan Ring.

LO 1

Calculating Finance Charge on Previous Month's Balance

Abby Jordan bought a dining room set for $8,000 on credit. She has a **revolving charge account** at Moe's Furniture Store. A revolving charge account gives a buyer **open-end credit.** Abby can make as many purchases on credit as she wants until she reaches her maximum $10,000 credit limit.

Often customers do not completely pay their revolving charge accounts at the end of a billing period. When this occurs, stores add interest charges to the customers' bills. Moe's Furniture Store calculates its interest using the *unpaid balance method.* It charges $1\frac{1}{2}\%$ on the *previous month's balance,* or 18% per year. Moe's has no minimum monthly payment (many stores require $10 or $15, or a percent of the outstanding balance).

Abby has no other charges on her revolving charge account. She plans to pay $500 per month until she completely pays off her dining room set. Abby realizes that when she makes a payment, Moe's Furniture Store first applies the money toward the interest and then reduces the **outstanding balance** due. (This is the U.S. Rule we discussed in Chapter 10.) For her own information, Abby worked out the first 3-month schedule of payments, shown in Table 14.3. Note how the interest payment is the rate times the outstanding balance.

TABLE 14.3 Schedule of payments

Monthly payment number	Outstanding balance due	$1\frac{1}{2}\%$ interest payment	Amount of monthly payment	Reduction in balance due	Outstanding balance due
1	$8,000.00	$120.00	$500.00	$380.00	$7,620.00
		(.015 × $8,000.00)		($500.00 − $120.00)	($8,000.00 − $380.00)
2	$7,620.00	$114.30	$500.00	$385.70	$7,234.30
		(.015 × $7,620.00)		($500.00 − $114.30)	($7,620.00 − $385.70)
3	$7,234.30	$108.51	$500.00	$391.49	$6,842.81
		(.015 × $7,234.30)		($500.00 − $108.51)	($7,234.30 − $391.49)

$20.00	**$957.19**

Payment Due Date:

01/16/2011   Payment must be received by 5:00 PM local time on the payment due date.

Late Payment Warning: If we do not receive your minimum payment by the date listed above, you may have to pay a late fee of up to $35 and your APRs may be increased up to the variable Penalty APR of 29.99%.

Today, most companies with credit card accounts calculate the finance charge, or interest, as a percentage of the average daily balance. Interest on credit cards can be very expensive for consumers; however, interest is a source of income for credit card companies. In the exhibit shown to the left, note the late payment warning issued by the credit card company. It states that a late payment could result in interest penalties close to 30%. The following is a letter I received from my credit card company when I questioned how my finance charge was calculated.

How Citibank Calculates My Finance Charge

Thank you for your recent inquiry regarding your Citi® / AAdvantage® MasterCard® account and how finance charges are calculated.

Finance charges for purchases, balance transfers, and cash advances will begin to accrue from the date the transaction is added to your balance. They will continue to accrue until payment in full is credited to your account. This means that when you make your final payment on these balances, you will be billed finance charges for the time between the date your last statement prints and the date your payment is received.

Paying your purchase balance in full each billing period by the payment due date saves you money because it allows you to take advantage of your grace period on purchases, which is not less than 20 days. You can avoid periodic finance charges on purchases (excluding balance transfers) that appear on your current billing statement if you paid the New Balance on the last statement by the payment due date on that statement and you pay your New Balance by the payment due date on your current statement. If you made a balance transfer, you may be unable to avoid periodic finance charges on new purchases, as described in the balance transfer offer.

Calculating Average Daily Balance   Let's look at the following steps for calculating the **average daily balance.** Remember that a **cash advance** is a cash loan from a credit card company.

CALCULATING AVERAGE DAILY BALANCE AND FINANCE CHARGE
Step 1. Calculate the daily balance or amount owed at the end of each day during the billing cycle:
$$\frac{\text{Daily}}{\text{balance}} = \frac{\text{Previous}}{\text{balance}} + \frac{\text{Cash}}{\text{advances}} + \text{Purchases} - \text{Payments}$$
Step 2. When the daily balance is the same for more than 1 day, multiply it by the number of days the daily balance remained the same, or the number of days of the current balance. This gives a cumulative daily balance.
Step 3. Add the cumulative daily balances.
Step 4. Divide the sum of the cumulative daily balances by the number of days in the billing cycle.
Step 5. Finance charge = Rate per month × Average daily balance.

Following is the partial bill of Joan Ring and an explanation of how Joan's average daily balance and finance charge were calculated. Note how we calculated each **daily balance** and then multiplied each daily balance by the number of days the balance remained the same. Take a moment to study how we arrived at 8 days. The total of the cumulative daily balances was $16,390. To get the average daily balance, we divided by the number of days in the billing cycle—30. Joan's finance charge is $1\frac{1}{2}$% per month on the average daily balance.

7 days had a balance of $450

30-day cycle − 22 (7 + 3 + 9 + 3) equals 8 days left with a balance of $620.

30-day billing cycle			
6/20	Billing date	Previous balance	$450
6/27	Payment		$ 50 cr.
6/30	Charge: JCPenney		200
7/9	Payment		40 cr.
7/12	Cash advance		60

MONEY tips
Don't fall behind. Social media is the new method many companies are choosing to interact with their customers. Mobile technologies are used by 50% of companies. Apps are available to calculate retirement needs, mortgages, interest on a loan, and so much more.

	No. of days of current balance	Current daily balance	Extension	
Step 1 →	7	$450	$ 3,150	← Step 2
	3	400 ($450 − $50)	1,200	
	9	600 ($400 + $200)	5,400	
	3	560 ($600 − $40)	1,680	
	8	620 ($560 + $60)	4,960	
	30		$16,390	← Step 3

$$\text{Average daily balance} = \frac{\$16,390}{30} = \$546.33 \quad \leftarrow \text{Step 4}$$

Step 5 → Finance charge = $546.33 × .015 = $8.19

Now try the following Practice Quiz to check your understanding of this unit.

LU 14–2 PRACTICE QUIZ

Complete this **Practice Quiz** to see how you are doing.

1. Calculate the balance outstanding at the end of month 2 (use U.S. Rule) given the following: purchased $600 desk; pay back $40 per month; and charge of $2\frac{1}{2}$% interest on unpaid balance.

2. Calculate the average daily balance and finance charge from the information that follows.

31-day billing cycle			
8/20	Billing date	Previous balance	$210
8/27	Payment		$50 cr.
8/31	Charge: Staples		30
9/5	Payment		10 cr.
9/10	Cash advance		60

Rate = 2% per month on average daily balance.

*For **extra help** from your authors–Sharon and Jeff–see the student DVD*

You Tube

✓ Solutions

1. Month	Balance due	Interest	Monthly payment	Reduction in balance	Balance outstanding
1	$600	$15.00 (.025 × $600)	$40	$25.00 ($40 − $15)	$575.00
2	$575	$14.38 (.025 × $575)	$40	$25.62	$549.38

2. Average daily balance calculated as follows:

No. of days of current balance	Current balance	Extension
7	$210	$1,470
4	160 ($210 − $50)	640
5	190 ($160 + $30)	950
5	180 ($190 − $10)	900
10	240 ($180 + $60)	2,400
31		$6,360

31 − 21 (7 + 4 + 5 + 5) ⟶ 10

$$\text{Average daily balance} = \frac{\$6,360}{31} = \boxed{\$205.16}$$

$$\text{Finance charge} = \boxed{\$4.10}\ (\$205.16 \times .02)$$

LU 14–2a EXTRA PRACTICE QUIZ WITH WORKED-OUT SOLUTIONS

Need more practice? Try this **Extra Practice Quiz** (check figures in the Interactive Chapter Organizer, p. 360). Worked-out Solutions can be found in Appendix B at end of text.

1. Calculate the balance outstanding at the end of month 2 (use U.S. Rule) given the following: purchased $300 desk; pay back $20 per month; and charge of $1\frac{1}{4}\%$ interest on unpaid balance.

2. Calculate the average daily balance and finance charge from the following information:

31-day billing cycle			
8/21	Billing date	Previous balance	$400
8/24	Payment		$100 cr.
8/31	Charge: Staples		60
9/5	Payment		20 cr.
9/10	Cash Advance		200

Finance charge is 2% on average daily balance.

INTERACTIVE CHAPTER ORGANIZER

Topic/procedure/formula	Examples	You try it*
Amount financed, p. 350 $\frac{\text{Amount}}{\text{financed}} = \frac{\text{Cash}}{\text{price}} - \frac{\text{Down}}{\text{payment}}$	60 payments of $125.67 per month; cash price $5,295 with a $95 down payment Cash price $5,295 − Down payment − 95 = Amount financed $5,200	**Calculate amount financed** 60 payments of $129.99 per month; Cash price $5,400 with a $100 down payment
Total finance charge (interest), p. 350 $\frac{\text{Total}}{\text{finance}} = \frac{\text{Total of}}{\text{all monthly}} - \frac{\text{Amount}}{\text{financed}}$ $\text{charge} \quad \text{payments}$	(continued from above) $\frac{\$125.67}{\text{per month}} \times \frac{60}{\text{months}} = \$7,540.20$ − Amount financed − 5,200.00 = Finance charge $2,340.20	**Calculate total finance charge** (continued from above)
Deferred payment price, p. 351 $\frac{\text{Deferred}}{\text{payment}} = \frac{\text{Total of}}{\text{all monthly}} + \frac{\text{Down}}{\text{payment}}$ $\text{price} \quad \text{payments}$	(continued from above) $7,540.20 + $95 = $7,635.20	**Calculate deferred payment price** (continued from above)

(continues)

INTERACTIVE CHAPTER ORGANIZER

Topic/procedure/formula	Examples	You try it*
Calculating APR by Table 14.1, p. 351 $\dfrac{\text{Finance charge}}{\text{Amount financed}} \times \$100 = \begin{matrix}\text{Table 14.1}\\ \text{lookup number}\end{matrix}$	*(continued from information provided on page 359)* $\dfrac{\$2,340.20}{\$5,200.00} \times \$100 = \$45.004$ Search in Table 14.1 between 15.50% and 15.75% for 60 payments.	**Calculate APR by table** *(continued from information provided on page 359)*
Monthly payment, pp. 353–354 *By formula:* $\dfrac{\text{Finance charge} + \text{Amount financed}}{\text{Number of payments of loan}}$ *By table:* $\dfrac{\text{Loan}}{\$1,000} \times \begin{matrix}\text{Table}\\\text{factor}\end{matrix}\text{ (rate, months)}$	*(continued from above)* $\dfrac{\$2,340.20 + \$5,200.00}{60} = \$125.67$ Given: 15.5% $\quad\quad$ 60 months $\quad\quad$ \$5,200 loan $\dfrac{\$5,200}{\$1,000} = 5.2 \times \$24.05 = \$125.06$ $\quad\quad$ (off due to rounding of rate)	**Calculate monthly payment** *(continued from information provided on page 359; use 16%)*
Open-end credit, p. 356 Monthly payment applied to interest first before reducing balance outstanding.	\$4,000 purchase \$250 a month payment $2\frac{1}{2}\%$ interest on unpaid balance \$4,000 × .025 = \$100 interest \$250 − \$100 = \$150 to lower balance \$4,000 − \$150 = \$3,850 Balance outstanding after month 1.	**Calculate balance outstanding after month 1** \$5,000 purchase; \$275 monthly payment; $3\frac{1}{2}\%$ interest on unpaid balance
Average daily balance and finance charge, p. 357 $\begin{matrix}\text{Daily}\\\text{balance}\end{matrix} = \begin{matrix}\text{Previous}\\\text{balance}\end{matrix} + \begin{matrix}\text{Cash}\\\text{advances}\end{matrix}$ $\quad + \text{Purchases} - \text{Payments}$ $\begin{matrix}\text{Average}\\\text{daily}\\\text{balance}\end{matrix} = \dfrac{\begin{matrix}\text{Sum of cumulative}\\\text{daily balances}\end{matrix}}{\begin{matrix}\text{Number of days}\\\text{in billing cycle}\end{matrix}}$ $\begin{matrix}\text{Finance}\\\text{charge}\end{matrix} = \begin{matrix}\text{Monthly}\\\text{rate}\end{matrix} \times \begin{matrix}\text{Average}\\\text{daily}\\\text{balance}\end{matrix}$	*30-day billing cycle; $1\frac{1}{2}\%$ finance charge per month* *Example:* 8/21 Balance $\quad$ \$100 $\quad\quad$ 8/29 Payment \$10 $\quad\quad$ 9/12 Charge $\quad$ 50 30-day billing cycle less the 8 and 14. *Average daily balance equals:* 8 days × \$100 = \$ 800 14 days × $\quad$ 90 = 1,260 8 days × $\quad$ 140 = 1,120 $\quad\quad\quad\quad$ \$3,180 ÷ 30 Average daily balance = \$106 Finance charge = \$106 × .015 = \$1.59	**Calculate daily balance and finance charge** 30-day billing cycle; $2\frac{1}{2}\%$ finance charge per month Given: 9/4 bal \$200 $\quad\quad$ 9/16 payment \$80 $\quad\quad$ 9/20 charge \$60

KEY TERMS	Amortization, *p. 350* Amount financed, *p. 350* Annual percentage rate $\quad$ (APR), *p. 351* Average daily balance, *p. 357* Cash advance, *p. 357* Credit Card Act, *p. 356*	Daily balance, *p. 358* Deferred payment price, *p. 351* Down payment, *p. 350* Fair Credit and Charge Card $\quad$ Disclosure Act of 1988, *p. 356* Finance charge, *p. 350* Installment loan, *p. 350*	Loan amortization table, *p. 354* Open-end credit, *p. 356* Outstanding balance, *p. 356* Revolving charge account, *p. 356* Truth in Lending Act, *p. 351*

Check Figures for Extra Practice Quizzes with Page References. (Worked-out Solutions in Appendix B.)	LU 14–1a (p. 355) 1. a. \$12,519 $\quad$ b. \$5,181 $\quad$ c. \$19,180 $\quad$ d. Bet. 14.50%–14.75% $\quad$ e. \$295 2. \$162.24	LU 14–2 (p. 359) 1. \$267.30 $\quad$ end of month 2 2. \$410.97 $\quad$ \$8.22

*Worked-out solutions are in Appendix B.

Critical Thinking Discussion Questions with Chapter Concept Check

1. Explain how to calculate the amount financed, finance charge, and APR by table lookup. Do you think the Truth in Lending Act should regulate interest charges?

2. Explain how to use the loan amortization table. Check with a person who owns a home and find out what part of each payment goes to pay interest versus the amount that reduces the loan principal.

3. What steps are used to calculate the average daily balance? Many credit card companies charge 18% annual interest. Do you think this is a justifiable rate? Defend your answer.

4. **Chapter Concept Check.** Based on the chapter opener regarding the Credit Card Act, visit the web and find information on how social networks like Facebook have had some influence on credit card companies' policies. Defend your position with the concepts learned in this chapter.

Classroom Notes

END-OF-CHAPTER PROBLEMS

McGraw Hill **connect** (plus+)   www.mhhe.com/slater11e

Check figures for odd-numbered problems in Appendix C.   Name _____   Date _____

DRILL PROBLEMS

Complete the following table: *LU 14-1(1)*

	Purchase price of product	Down payment	Amount financed	Number of monthly payments	Amount of monthly payments	Total of monthly payments	Total finance charge
14-1.	Chevy Volt $32,000	$10,000		80	$320		
14-2.	Apple iPhone $299	$100		12	$20.50		

Calculate **(a)** the amount financed, **(b)** the total finance charge, and **(c)** APR by table lookup.   *LU 14-1(1, 2)*

	Purchase price of a used car	Down payment	Number of monthly payments	Amount financed	Total of monthly payments	Total finance charge	APR
14-3.	$5,673	$1,223	48		$5,729.76		
14-4.	$4,195	$95	60		$5,944.00		

Calculate the monthly payment for Problems 14-3 and 14-4 by table lookup and formula. (Answers will not be exact due to rounding of percents in table lookup.)   *LU 14-1(3)*

14-5. **(14-3)** (Use 13% for table lookup.)

14-6. **(14-4)** (Use 15.5% for table lookup.)

14-7. Calculate the average daily balance and finance charge.   *LU 14-2(1)*

30-day billing cycle			
9/16	Billing date	Previous balance	$2,000
9/19	Payment	$ 60 cr.	
9/30	Charge: Home Depot	1,500	
10/3	Payment	60 cr.	
10/7	Cash advance	70	
Finance charge is $1\frac{1}{2}$% on average daily balance			

WORD PROBLEMS

14–8. Before purchasing a used car, Cody Lind checked www.kbb.com to learn what he should offer for the used car he wanted to buy. Then he conducted a carfax.com search on the car he found to see if the car had ever been in an accident. The Carfax was clean so he purchased the used car for $14,750. He put $2,000 down and financed the rest with a 48-month, 7.5% loan. What is his monthly car payment by table lookup?   *LU 14-1(1, 2)*

14–9. For the best terms on a loan or credit card, you need a credit score above 700. To achieve this, start establishing credit now. Pay all of your bills on time. In addition, use only one-third of your available credit limit and pay off your revolving balance(s) each month. R. J. Johnson has excellent credit. She wants to purchase a piece of equipment for her business and was offered 6% for 60 months for the $55,000 unit. What is her monthly payment by formula?   *LU 14-1(3)*

14–10. Ramon Hernandez saw the following advertisement for a used Volkswagen Bug and decided to work out the numbers to be sure the ad had no errors. Please help Ramon by calculating **(a)** the amount financed, **(b)** the finance charge, **(c)** APR by table lookup, **(d)** the monthly payment by formula, and **(e)** the monthly payment by table lookup (will be off slightly). *LU 14-1(1, 2, 3)*

a. Amount financed:

b. Finance charge:

c. APR by table lookup:

d. Monthly payment by formula:

e. Monthly payment by table lookup (use 14.50%):

14–11. From this partial advertisement calculate: *LU 14-1(1, 2, 3)*

$95.10 per month
#43892 Used car. Cash price $4,100. Down payment $50. For 60 months.

a. Amount financed.

b. Finance charge.

c. Deferred payment price.

d. APR by Table 14.1.

e. Monthly payment (by formula).

14–12. If you are trying to build credit by using a credit card, each time you make a purchase with the credit card, deduct that

eXcel amount from your checking account. That way, when your credit card bill is due, you will have enough to pay the credit card off in full. Kathy Lehner is going to start doing this. She plans on paying her credit card bill in full this month. How much does she owe with a 12% APR and the following transactions? *LU 14-2(1)*

31-day billing cycle			
10/1	Previous balance		$1,168
10/3	Credit	$75 cr.	
10/12	Charge: King Soopers	152	
10/15	Payment	350 cr.	
10/25	Charge: Delta	325	
10/30	Charge: Holiday Fun	65	

14–13. Shirley Stewart is planning to buy a Toyota hybrid for $18,999 with $2,000 down and plans to finance the car. Citizens' Financial Bank quoted a finance charge at 8% for 48 months; Charter One Bank quoted her a finance charge at 7.50% for 60 months. **(a)** What would be her monthly payment to Citizens' Financial Bank to the nearest cent? **(b)** What would be her monthly payment to Charter One Bank to the nearest cent? Use the loan amortization table. **(c)** How much more would her monthly payment be on the 48-month loan? *LU 14-1(3)*

14–14. First America Bank's monthly payment charge on a 48-month, $20,000 loan is $488.26. U.S. Bank's monthly payment fee

eXcel is $497.70 for the same loan amount. What would be the APR for an auto loan for each of these banks? (Use the *Business Math Handbook*.) *LU 14-1(1, 2)*

14–15. From the following facts, Molly Roe has requested you to calculate the average daily balance. The customer believes the average daily balance should be $877.67. Respond to the customer's concern. *LU 14-2(1)*

28-day billing cycle		
3/18	Billing date Previous balance	$800
3/24	Payment	$ 60 cr.
3/29	Charge: Sears	250
4/5	Payment	20 cr.
4/9	Charge: Macy's	200

14–16. Jill bought a $500 rocking chair. The terms of her revolving charge are $1\frac{1}{2}\%$ on the unpaid balance from the previous month. If she pays $100 per month, complete a schedule for the first 3 months like Table 14.3. Be sure to use the U.S. Rule. *LU 14-2(1)*

Monthly payment number	Outstanding balance due	$1\frac{1}{2}\%$ interest payment	Amount of monthly payment	Reduction in balance due	Outstanding balance due

---

CHALLENGE PROBLEMS

14–17. Peg Gasperoni bought a $50,000 life insurance policy for $100 per year. Ryan Life Insurance Company sent her the following billing instructions along with a premium plan example:

"Your insurance premium notice will be mailed to you in a few days. You may pay the entire premium in full without a finance charge or you may pay the premium in installments after a down payment and the balance in monthly installments of $30. The finance charge will be added to the unpaid balance. The finance charge is based on an annual percentage rate of 15%."

If the total policy premium is:	And you put down:	The balance subject to finance charge will be:	The total number of monthly installments ($30 minimum) will be:	The monthly installment before adding the finance charge will be:	The total finance charge for all installments will be:	And the total deferred payment price will be:
$100	$30.00	$ 70.00	3	$30.00	$ 1.75	$101.75
200	50.00	150.00	5	30.00	5.67	205.67
300	75.00	225.00	8	30.00	12.84	312.84

Peg feels that the finance charge of $1.75 is in error. Who is correct? Check your answer. *LU 14-2(1)*

14–18. You have a $1,100 balance on your 15% credit card. You have lost your job and been unemployed for 6 months. You have been unable to make any payments on your balance. However, you received a tax refund and want to pay off the credit card. How much will you owe on the credit card, and how much interest will have accrued? What will be the effective rate of interest after the 6 months (to the nearest hundredth percent)? *LU 14-2(1)*

SUMMARY PRACTICE TEST You Tube™

Do you need help? The DVD has step-by-step worked-out solutions.

1. Walter Lantz buys a Volvo SUV for $42,500. Walter made a down payment of $16,000 and paid $510 monthly for 60 months. What are the total amount financed and the total finance charge that Walter paid at the end of the 60 months? *(p. 350)* *LU 14-1(1)*

2. Joyce Mesnic bought an HP laptop computer at Staples for $699. Joyce made a $100 down payment and financed the balance at 10% for 12 months. What is her monthly payment? (Use the loan amortization table.) *(pp. 353–354)* *LU 14-1(3)*

3. Lee Remick read the following partial advertisement: price, $22,500; down payment, $1,000 cash or trade; and $399.99 per month for 60 months. Calculate **(a)** the total finance charge and **(b)** the APR by Table 14.1 (use the tables in *Business Math Handbook*) to the nearest hundredth percent. *(pp. 350–353)* *LU 14-1(1, 2)*

4.	Nancy Billows bought a $7,000 desk at Furniture.com. Based on her income, Nancy could only afford to pay back $700 per month. The charge on the unpaid balance is 3%. The U.S. Rule is used in the calculation. Calculate the balance outstanding at the end of month 2. *(pp. 356–358) LU 14-2(1)*

Month	Balance due	Interest	Monthly payment	Reduction in balance	Balance outstanding

5.	Calculate the average daily balance and finance charge on the statement below. *(pp. 356–358) LU 14-2(1)*

30-day billing cycle		
7/3	Balance	$400
7/18	Payment	100 cr.
7/27	Charge Walmart	250

Assume 2% finance charge on average daily balance.

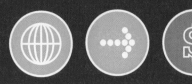

PROBLEM 1
How much car can I afford?

Go to http://www.bankrate.com. Find an auto loan rate for a 3-year loan. Then go to http://www.bankofamerica.com/vehicle_and_personal_loans/index.cfm?template=learn_calculators&context=financenter&calcid=auto05 and select your state to find the monthly payment calculator. Calculate your payments if you borrow $23,000 for 3 years at the rate you found. Suppose the auto dealer was offering a special 2.9% rate. How much could you save over the life of the loan by borrowing at the lower rate?

Discussion Questions

1. How does the interest rate you secure impact the type of car you would purchase?

2. What is the incentive to the dealer in offering such low rates on car purchases?

PROBLEM 2
Not-so-free credit

Go to http://www.bankrate.com. Follow the link to credit cards and then to "Find a Credit Card." Choose Student Cards from the drop-down menu to see your available options. Suppose you kept an average daily balance of $1,000 on the credit card for the entire introductory period. How much interest would you save versus the regular APR during the 0.0% introductory period? (You may assume the monthly rate is the annual rate divided by 12. If given an APR range, use the lower percentage in the range.) Suppose you continued to use the same card after the introductory period expired. How much interest would you pay over the same amount of time as the introductory period?

Discussion Questions

1. Why would banks want to offer such low rates as an introductory offer to new customers?

2. What are the pros and cons to carrying a balance on your credit card during these low introductory rate periods?

PROBLEM 3
Debt debunked!

Go to http://www.leadfusion.com/products/researching-solutions/calculator-showcase#iframe, select the Credit Card tab, and then the "What will it take to pay off my balance?" calculator. Suppose you carry a credit card balance of $9,000. The interest rate on the credit card is fixed at 18% and you aren't charged an annual fee. You decide to stop using the credit card until you pay off the balance. Your goal is to do so in 18 months and you plan to pay $500 per month. Will you pay off the balance in 18 months at that rate? If not, what will it take?

Discussion Questions

1. In 2002 the average family carried a balance of $9,000 in credit card debt. What are some reasons that could lead someone to carry that much debt?

2. How would such a credit card balance impact your spending ability and budgeting in other areas of your finances?

PROBLEM 4
Does my credit score matter?

Go to http://learn.bankofamerica.com/articles/managing-credit/how-to-improve-your-credit-score.html to learn about how to improve your credit score.

Discussion Questions

1. How would these suggestions help your credit score?

2. Do you feel you could follow these suggestions? Why or why not?

MOBILE APPS

Payment Calculator Pro—A Simple Loan Calculator (CS Software) Calculates payments for auto or home loans simply.

GooBiq Credit Card Rates (GooBiq.com) Locates current rates on a variety of credit cards including fees, credit limits, and more.

INTERNET PROJECTS

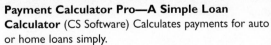

See text website
www.mhhe.com/slater11e_sse_ch14

■ LOWDOWN

What You Need to Know About Pay-As-You-Go Plastic

Slam on the brakes with a card that won't let you run up a balance. BY JOAN GOLDWASSER

1. SWITCH FROM A CREDIT CARD TO A CHARGE CARD. Charge cards, such as an American Express card (www.americanexpress .com), don't let you carry a balance; you must pay what you owe each month. The AmEx Green card costs $95 annually (the fee is waived the first year) and offers a generous travel-rewards program.

2. USE YOUR BANK DEBIT CARD. Maybe you want to impose the discipline of spending only what's in your checking account. Debit cards are free—with no interest charges and no monthly fees—and those that bear either the MasterCard or Visa logo may be used at millions of retailers. If you sign for your purchases, you get the same protections as with a credit card, and you may qualify for rewards programs. Plus, you can take out cash at an ATM or punch in your PIN to get cash at many retailers.

3. WATCH OUT FOR PREPAID DEBIT CARDS. They look like other plastic, and you may use them like credit and bank debit cards. Banks hoping to replace lost revenue because of restrictions in the CARD Act of 2009 may soon be marketing them aggressively. But prepaid debit cards are loaded with land mines. Cardholders usually pay an activation fee (which can run as high as $19.95), plus a monthly fee (as high as $9.95). There may also be fees to reload the card and check your balance, in addition to an ATM-withdrawal fee. The Kardashian sisters of reality-TV fame launched a prepaid card for teens last November that cost $99.95 for a year. The uproar about marketing such an expensive card to teenagers was so great that the Kardashians canceled the card less than a month later.

4. THIS PIGGY IS DIFFERENT. SmartyPig, the online savings Web site, offers a prepaid Cash Rewards MasterCard (www.smarty pig.com) that costs $4.95 but has no monthly or reloading fees and offers cash-back rewards up to 10% from participating retailers. If you use an ATM to withdraw cash, you'll pay $1.95; but, as with other debit cards, you may request cash at a retailer by punching in your PIN.

5. GET PIN MONEY IN PARIS. Consider the free Travelex Cash Passport card (http:// travelex.com). You can load the card in either euros or pounds, so you avoid foreign-currency transaction fees. Travelex does not charge an ATM-withdrawal fee, but you will pay the overseas bank's fee when you obtain cash. One drawback: If the card sits in your drawer for more than 12 months, you'll pay a monthly inactivity fee.

6. MAKE A COMEBACK WITH A SECURED CARD. If you don't qualify for a traditional card, you can rebuild your credit by getting a secured card. Make a deposit in the issuing bank; that amount becomes your credit limit. The bank reports your payments to the credit bureaus each month, creating a good payment history. Secured cards usually carry an annual fee and high interest rates—the BankAmericard Visa Fully Secured card (www.bankofamerica .com; click on "borrow," then "credit cards") comes with a 20.24% rate and a $39 annual fee—but credit unions generally charge less. Secure First Credit Union, in Birmingham, Ala. (www.securefirstcu.org), offers a secured Visa card with a 12.9% rate and a $35 fee. To find a credit union near you, go to www .creditunion.coop. ■

Classroom Notes

The Cost of Home Ownership

A New Way to Cut a Mortgage

'Recasting' Your Home Loan Can Lower Monthly Payments With Fewer Hassles

BY M.P. MCQUEEN

Some homeowners who already have refinanced into low-interest-rate mortgages are using a little-known strategy to make their monthly payments even smaller.

Called "recasting" or "re-amortizing," the strategy allows a borrower to lower the monthly payment on an existing fixed-rate home loan for a small fee without having to apply for a new loan and without having to pay reappraisal and other fees.

Recasting also may enable homeowners to save on interest paid over the life of the loan, merely by putting a large sum of cash against the principal, whether or not they have refinanced already.

The bad news? Banks don't advertise the strategy, perhaps because it is less lucrative than refinancing a mortgage. And not all loans are eligible. To find out more, you will have to ask your lender directly.

At **J.P. Morgan Chase** & Co.'s Chase Home Finance unit, less than 200 mortgages a month are recast out of 10 million home loans outstanding, a spokesman says. At **Bank of America** Corp., about 200 to 300 a month recasting requests are received out of about 14 million home loans serviced by the company, a spokesman says. Neither bank has seen increased demand.

Here is how it works: A homeowner asks his loan servicer if he can put a large sum of money against the outstanding principal on the mortgage. Ordinarily, doing so would enable him to pay off the loan early, but he would still have to pay the same monthly note. But if the lender agrees to recast the mortgage, he may be able to reduce the monthly payment over the remaining term of the loan.

For example, a person with a 30-year $300,000 fixed-rate mortgage and an interest rate of 4.75% who recasted one year into the loan by putting in $60,000 toward the principal would trim his balance to $235,371. Assuming there were 29 years left on the loan, that would result in a monthly payment of $1,247 instead of the original $1,565.

There are downsides to the strategy. Many financial experts advise against putting additional cash into one's residence, arguing that higher returns historically have been available in the financial markets and interest rates on bonds are likely to rise eventually.

LU 15–1: Types of Mortgages and the Monthly Mortgage Payment

1. List the types of mortgages available *(p. 374)*.

2. Utilize an amortization chart to compute monthly mortgage payments *(pp. 375–376)*.

3. Calculate the total cost of interest over the life of a mortgage *(pp. 376–377)*.

LU 15–2: Amortization Schedule—Breaking Down the Monthly Payment

1. Calculate and identify the interest and principal portion of each monthly payment *(pp. 378–379)*.

2. Prepare an amortization schedule *(p. 379)*.

VOCABULARY PREVIEW

Here are key terms in this chapter. After completing the chapter, if you know the term, place a checkmark in the parentheses. If you don't know the term, look it up and put the page number where it can be found.

Adjustable rate mortgage (ARM) ( ) Amortization schedule ( ) Amortization table ( ) Biweekly mortgage ( ) Closing costs ( ) Escrow account ( ) Fixed rate mortgage ( ) Foreclosure ( ) Graduated-payment mortgages (GPM) ( ) Home equity loan ( ) Interest-only mortgage ( ) Monthly payment ( ) Mortgages ( ) Points ( ) Reverse mortgage ( ) Short sale ( ) Subprime loans ( )

For many years the price of real estate has fallen. As a result, foreclosures and short sales are on the rise. **Foreclosure** results when property owners fail to make their mortgage payments. A **short sale** results when the lender sells a piece of property for less than the balance owed on the mortgage. The chapter opener *Wall Street Journal* clip "A New Way to Cut a Mortgage" offers tips on how to lower mortgage payments to avoid such bitter outcomes. The *Wall Street Journal* clip "Credit Crunch" shows that your credit score may also be affected by late mortgage payments, which might affect future loans and mortgages too.

This chapter explores the various costs involved in purchasing a home.

Credit Crunch
How housing missteps affect your credit score.

	ESTIMATED STARTING SCORE			APROXIMATE TIME TO RETURN TO ORIGINAL SCORE		
	680	**720**	**780**	**680**	**720**	**780**
30 days late on mortgage	600-620	630-650	670-690	9 months	2.5 years	3 years
Short sale or deed in lieu of foreclosure	610-630	605-625	655-675	3 years	7 years	7 years
Foreclosure or short sale with amount of unpaid balance disclosed	575-595	570-590	620-640	3 years	7 years	7 years

Source: FICO

Learning Unit 15–1: Types of Mortgages and the Monthly Mortgage Payment

LO 1

Figure 15.1 lists various loan types. A type of adjustable rate mortgage called a **subprime loan** was at the root of so many foreclosures in the past few years. This type of home loan allowed buyers to have a very low interest rate—sometimes even a zero rate. This helped customers qualify for expensive homes that they would not otherwise have qualified for. Lenders offering subprimes assumed prices of homes would rise and most buyers would convert to a fixed rate before the rate was substantially adjusted upward. As we now know, prices of homes have fallen.

Purchasing a home usually involves paying a large amount of interest. Note how your author was able to save $70,121.40.

Over the life of a 30-year **fixed rate mortgage** (see Figure 15.1) of $100,000, the interest would have cost $207,235. Monthly payments would have been $849.99. This would not include taxes, insurance, and so on.

Your author chose a **biweekly mortgage** (see Figure 15.1). This meant that every 2 weeks (26 times a year) the bank would receive $425. By paying every 2 weeks instead of once a month, the mortgage would be paid off in 23 years instead of 30—a $70,121.40 *savings* on interest. Why? When a payment is made every 2 weeks, the principal is reduced more quickly, which substantially reduces the interest cost.

The question facing prospective buyers concerns which type of mortgage will be best for them. Depending on how interest rates are moving when you purchase a home, you may find one type of **mortgage** to be the most advantageous for you (see Figure 15.1).

The *Wall Street Journal* clip "Downsizing" (page 375) shows that interest rates (like 3.5%) for a mortgage are at record lows. The monthly payment at 6% is $2,398.20 and it drops to $1,796.18 at a 3.5% interest rate—a savings of $602.02 per month.

Have you heard that elderly people who are house-rich and cash-poor can use their home to get cash or monthly income? The Federal Housing Administration makes it possible for older homeowners to take out a **reverse mortgage** on their homes. Under reverse mortgages, senior homeowners borrow against the equity in their property, often getting fixed monthly checks. The debt is repaid only when the homeowners or their estate sells

FIGURE 15.1 | Types of mortgages available

Loan types	Advantages	Disadvantages
30-year fixed rate mortgage	A predictable monthly payment.	If interest rates fall, you are locked in to higher rate unless you refinance. (Application and appraisal fees along with other closing costs will result.)
15-year fixed rate mortgage	Interest rate lower than 30-year fixed (usually $\frac{1}{4}$ to $\frac{1}{2}$ of a percent). Your equity builds up faster while interest costs are cut by more than one-half.	A larger down payment is needed. Monthly payment will be higher.
Graduated-payment mortgage (GPM)	Easier to qualify for than 30- or 15-year fixed rate. Monthly payments start low and increase over time.	May have higher APR than fixed or variable rates.
Biweekly mortgage	Shortens term loan; saves substantial amount of interest; 26 biweekly payments per year. Builds equity twice as fast.	Not good for those not seeking an early loan payoff. Extra payments per year.
Adjustable rate mortgage (ARM)	Lower rate than fixed. If rates fall, could be adjusted down without refinancing. Caps available that limit how high rate could go for each adjustment period over term of loan.	Monthly payment could rise if interest rates rise. Riskier than fixed rate mortgage in which monthly payment is stable.
Home equity loan	Cheap and reliable accessible lines of credit backed by equity in your home. Tax-deductible. Rates can be locked in. Reverse mortgages may be available to those 62 or older.	Could lose home if not paid. No annual or interest caps.
Interest-only mortgages	Borrowers pay interest but no principal in the early years (5 to 15) of the loan.	Early years build up no equity.

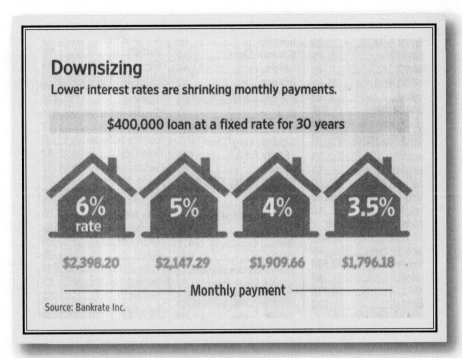

Downsizing
Lower interest rates are shrinking monthly payments.

$400,000 loan at a fixed rate for 30 years

6% rate — $2,398.20

5% — $2,147.29

4% — $1,909.66

3.5% — $1,796.18

—————— Monthly payment ——————

Source: Bankrate Inc.

the home. The *Wall Street Journal* clip "Debate on Reverse-Mortgage Risks Heats Up" raises the question whether reverse mortgages are too risky due to scams and deceptive marketing targeting the elderly.

Debate on Reverse-Mortgage Risks Heats Up

BY MAYA JACKSON RANDALL

A report by Consumers Union and other advocacy groups has ignited a debate about whether reverse mortgages are too risky for house-rich seniors in need of extra cash, just as the nation's new consumer agency is starting to examine the issue.

The groups are urging the new Consumer Financial Protection Bureau to boost oversight of the complex loans and to move to fight scams and deceptive marketing. Other groups, however, defend reverse mortgages.

The market for reverse mortgages is poised for expansion as the baby-boom generation retires. Meanwhile, lenders are aggressively marketing reverse

mortgages, tapping celebrities such as actor and former U.S. Sen. Fred Thompson as spokesmen and holding seminars at senior centers to sell the loans.

Most reverse mortgages are made under the Home Equity Conversion Mortgage program, begun in 1988. A borrower must be at least 62 years old and have paid off all or most of the mortgage. Instead of a monthly mortgage payment, the borrower receives payments as a lump sum, monthly cash advances or line of credit. When the homeowner dies, moves or sells the house, the loan must be repaid.

The consumer advocates say seniors should use reverse mortgages—which allow older Americans to tap into the equity in

their home—only as a last resort because fees can be high and the loans could affect eligibility for government-assistance programs such as Medicaid. Also, if borrowers deplete home equity, they won't have much to pass on to heirs and could have a harder time funding long-term care.

"The public, policy makers and legislators should be aware that this time, yesterday's subprime lenders are now preying on a growing elderly population who are trying to remain financially independent in their own homes during a depressed economy," says the report from Consumers Union, the California Advocates for Nursing Home Reform and the Council on Aging Silicon Valley that was released

last week.

Defending reverse mortgages, groups such as RetireSafe and the National Reverse Mortgage Lenders Association say the report fails to acknowledge recent pro-consumer changes. "I think they're rattling the cages here without having much concrete to offer or any evidence to back up their allegations that there are widespread problems," said Peter Bell, president of the association.

The advocacy groups say reverse mortgages are reasonable for some seniors in foreclosure who don't plan to move into assisted living and for low-income seniors who lack other retirement assets, don't qualify for lower-cost alternatives and can't meet their mortgage obligations.

Now let's learn how to calculate a monthly mortgage payment and the total cost of loan interest over the life of a mortgage. We will use the following example in our discussion.

EXAMPLE   Gary bought a home for $200,000. He made a 20% down payment. The 9% mortgage is for 30 years (30 × 12 = 360 payments). What are Gary's monthly payment and total cost of interest?

LO 2

Computing the Monthly Payment for Principal and Interest

You can calculate the principal and interest of Gary's **monthly payment** using the **amortization table** shown in Table 15.1 (p. 376) and the following steps. (Remember that this is the same type of amortization table used in Chapter 14 for installment loans.)

| TABLE | 15.1 | Amortization table (mortgage principal and interest per $1,000) |

Term in years	\multicolumn{15}{c}{INTEREST}
	$3\frac{1}{2}$%	5%	$5\frac{1}{2}$%	6%	$6\frac{1}{2}$%	7%	$7\frac{1}{2}$%	8%	$8\frac{1}{2}$%	9%	$9\frac{1}{2}$%	10%	$10\frac{1}{2}$%	11%
10	9.89	10.61	10.86	11.11	11.36	11.62	11.88	12.14	12.40	12.67	12.94	13.22	13.50	13.78
12	8.52	9.25	9.51	9.76	10.02	10.29	10.56	10.83	11.11	11.39	11.67	11.96	12.25	12.54
15	7.15	7.91	8.18	8.44	8.72	8.99	9.28	9.56	9.85	10.15	10.45	10.75	11.06	11.37
17	6.52	7.29	7.56	7.84	8.12	8.40	8.69	8.99	9.29	9.59	9.90	10.22	10.54	10.86
20	5.80	6.60	6.88	7.17	7.46	7.76	8.06	8.37	8.68	9.00	9.33	9.66	9.99	10.33
22	5.44	6.20	6.51	6.82	7.13	7.44	7.75	8.07	8.39	8.72	9.05	9.39	9.73	10.08
25	5.01	5.85	6.15	6.45	6.76	7.07	7.39	7.72	8.06	8.40	8.74	9.09	9.45	9.81
30	4.50	5.37	5.68	6.00	6.33	6.66	7.00	7.34	7.69	8.05	8.41	8.78	9.15	9.53
35	3.99	5.05	5.38	5.71	6.05	6.39	6.75	7.11	7.47	7.84	8.22	8.60	8.99	9.37

COMPUTING MONTHLY PAYMENT BY USING AN AMORTIZATION TABLE

Step 1. Divide the amount of the mortgage by $1,000.

Step 2. Look up the rate and term in the amortization table. At the intersection is the table factor.

Step 3. Multiply Step 1 by Step 2.

For Gary, we calculate the following:

$$\frac{\$160,000 \text{ (amount of mortgage)}}{\$1,000} = 160 \times \$8.05 \text{ (table rate)} = \boxed{\$1,288}$$

So $160,000 is the amount of the mortgage ($200,000 less 20%). The $8.05 is the table factor of 9% for 30 years per $1,000. Since Gary is mortgaging 160 units of $1,000, the factor of $8.05 is multiplied by 160. Remember that the $1,288 payment does not include taxes, insurance, and so on.

LO 3

What Is the Total Cost of Interest?

We can use the following formula to calculate Gary's total interest cost over the life of the mortgage:

$$\begin{array}{ccccc} \text{Total cost} \\ \text{of interest} \end{array} = \begin{array}{c} \text{Total of all} \\ \text{monthly payments} \end{array} - \begin{array}{c} \text{Amount of} \\ \text{mortage} \end{array}$$

$$\$303,680 = \underset{(\$1,288 \times 360)}{\$463,680} - \$160,000$$

Effects of Interest Rates on Monthly Payment and Total Interest Cost

Table 15.2 (p. 377) shows the effect that an increase in interest rates would have on Gary's monthly payment and his total cost of interest. Note that if Gary's interest rate rises to 11%, the 2% increase will result in Gary paying an additional $85,248 in total interest.

For most people, purchasing a home is a major lifetime decision. Many factors must be considered before this decision is made. Being informed about related costs and the types of available mortgages can save you thousands of dollars.

TABLE   15.1   (concluded)

Term in years	11½%	11¾%	12%	12½%	12¾%	13%	13½%	13¾%	14%	14½%	14¾%	15%	15½%
						INTEREST							
10	14.06	14.21	14.35	14.64	14.79	14.94	15.23	15.38	15.53	15.83	15.99	16.14	16.45
12	12.84	12.99	13.14	13.44	13.60	13.75	14.06	14.22	14.38	14.69	14.85	15.01	15.34
15	11.69	11.85	12.01	12.33	12.49	12.66	12.99	13.15	13.32	13.66	13.83	14.00	14.34
17	11.19	11.35	11.52	11.85	12.02	12.19	12.53	12.71	12.88	13.23	13.41	13.58	13.94
20	10.67	10.84	11.02	11.37	11.54	11.72	12.08	12.26	12.44	12.80	12.99	13.17	13.54
22	10.43	10.61	10.78	11.14	11.33	11.51	11.87	12.06	12.24	12.62	12.81	12.99	13.37
25	10.17	10.35	10.54	10.91	11.10	11.28	11.66	11.85	12.04	12.43	12.62	12.81	13.20
30	9.91	10.10	10.29	10.68	10.87	11.07	11.46	11.66	11.85	12.25	12.45	12.65	13.05
35	9.77	9.96	10.16	10.56	10.76	10.96	11.36	11.56	11.76	12.17	12.37	12.57	12.98

TABLE   15.2   Effect of interest rates on monthly payments

	9%	11%	Difference
Monthly payment	$1,288	$1,524.80	$236.80 per month
	(160 × $8.05)	(160 × $9.53)	
Total cost of interest	$303,680	$388,928	$85,248
	($1,288 × 360) − $160,000	($1,524.80 × 360) − $160,000	($236.80 × 360)

MONEY tips

Should you buy or rent your home? Buying actually saves you $1,743 more, on average, per year if you stay in your home for 6 years or longer. This savings results from the allowed deduction of property taxes and mortgage interest on your personal income taxes.

In addition to the mortgage payment, buying a home can include the following costs:

- *Closing costs:* When property passes from seller to buyer, **closing costs** may include fees for credit reports, recording costs, lawyer's fees, points, title search, and so on. A **point** is a one-time charge that is a percent of the mortgage. Two points means 2% of the mortgage.

- *Escrow amount:* Usually, the lending institution, for its protection, requires that each month 1/12 of the insurance cost and 1/12 of the real estate taxes be kept in a special account called the **escrow account.** The monthly balance in this account will change depending on the cost of the insurance and taxes. Interest is paid on escrow accounts.

- *Repairs and maintenance:* This includes paint, wallpaper, landscaping, plumbing, electrical expenses, and so on.

- *PMI insurance:* When buying a house, if you do not have 20% in cash to put as a down payment lenders will require you to purchase PMI (Private Mortgage Insurance). This can be very expensive and only benefits the lender. It is important to know that as soon as 20% equity is reached in the home (determined by an appraisal), the borrower must petition to have the PMI removed. The mortgage lender will not be tracking this and you may continue to pay PMI after it is no longer required.

As you can see, the cost of owning a home can be expensive. But remember that all interest costs of your monthly payment and your real estate taxes are deductible. For many, owning a home can have advantages over renting.

Before you study Learning Unit 15–2, let's check your understanding of Learning Unit 15–1.

LU 15–1 PRACTICE QUIZ

Complete this **Practice Quiz** to see how you are doing.

*For **extra help** from your authors–Sharon and Jeff–see the student DVD*

You Tube

Given: Price of home, $225,000; 20% down payment; 9% interest rate; 25-year mortgage. Solve for:

1. Monthly payment and total cost of interest over 25 years.
2. If rate fell to 8%, what would be the total decrease in interest cost over the life of the mortgage?

✓ **Solutions**

1. $225,000 − $45,000 = $180,000

    $$\frac{\$180,000}{\$1,000} = 180 \times \$8.40 = \boxed{\$1,512}$$

    $$\boxed{\$273,600} = \quad \$453,600 - \$180,000$$
    $$(\$1,512 \times 300) \quad 25 \text{ years} \times 12 \text{ payments per year}$$

2. 8% = $1,389.60 monthly payment
    (180 × $7.72)
    Total interest cost $236,880 = ($1,389.60 × 300) − $180,000
    Savings $\boxed{\$36,720}$ = ($273,600 − $236,880)

LU 15–1a EXTRA PRACTICE QUIZ WITH WORKED-OUT SOLUTIONS

Need more practice? Try this **Extra Practice Quiz** (check figures in the Interactive Chapter Organizer, p. 381). Worked-out Solutions can be found in Appendix B at end of text.

Given: Price of home, $180,000; 30% down payment; 7% interest rate; 30-year mortgage. Solve for:

1. Monthly payment and total cost of interest over 30 years.
2. If rate fell to 5%, what would be the total decrease in interest cost over the life of the mortgage?

Learning Unit 15–2: Amortization Schedule—Breaking Down the Monthly Payment

LO 1

In Learning Unit 15–1, we saw that over the life of Gary's $160,000 loan, he would pay $303,680 in interest. Now let's use the following steps to determine what portion of Gary's first monthly payment reduces the principal and what portion is interest.

CALCULATING INTEREST, PRINCIPAL, AND NEW BALANCE OF MONTHLY PAYMENT
Step 1. Calculate the interest for a month (use current principal): Interest = Principal × Rate × Time.
Step 2. Calculate the amount used to reduce the principal: Principal reduction = Monthly payment − Interest (Step 1).
Step 3. Calculate the new principal: Current principal − Reduction of principal (Step 2) = New principal.

Step 1. Interest (I) = Principal (P) × Rate (R) × Time (T)

$$\$1,200 = \$160,000 \times .09 \times \frac{1}{12}$$

Step 2. The reduction of the $160,000 principal each month is equal to the payment less interest. So we can calculate Gary's new principal balance at the end of month 1 as follows:

Monthly payment at 9% (from Table 15.1)	$1,288 (160 × $8.05)
− Interest for first month	− 1,200
= Principal reduction	$ 88

Step 3. As the years go by, the interest portion of the payment decreases and the principal portion increases.

Principal balance	$160,000
Principal reduction	− 88
Balance of principal	$159,912

Let's do month 2:

Step 1. Interest = Principal × Rate × Time

$$= \$159,912 \times .09 \times \frac{1}{12}$$

$$= \$1,199.34$$

Step 2. $1,288.00 monthly payment
− 1,199.34 interest for month 2
$ 88.66 principal reduction

Step 3. $159,912.00 principal balance
−   88.66 principal reduction
$159,823.34 balance of principal

Note that in month 2, interest costs drop 66 cents ($1,200.00 − $1,199.34). So in 2 months, Gary has reduced his mortgage balance by $176.66 ($88.00 + $88.66). After 2 months, Gary has paid a total interest of $2,399.34 ($1,200.00 + $1,199.34).

MONEY tips

Make one extra mortgage payment a year (lump sum or biweekly). It may save you thousands of dollars in interest.

LO 2

Example of an Amortization Schedule

The partial **amortization schedule** given in Table 15.3 shows the breakdown of Gary's monthly payment. Note the amount that goes toward reducing the principal and toward payment of actual interest. Also note how the outstanding balance of the loan is reduced. After 7 months, Gary still owes $159,369.97. Often when you take out a mortgage loan, you receive an amortization schedule from the company that holds your mortgage.

TABLE   15.3   Partial amortization schedule

Payment number	Principal (current)	MONTHLY PAYMENT, $1,288		Balance of principal
		Interest	Principal reduction	
1	$160,000.00 $\left(\$160,000 \times .09 \times \frac{1}{12}\right)$	$1,200.00 ($1,288 − $1,200)	$88.00 ($160,000 − $88)	$159,912.00
2	$159,912.00 $\left(\$159,912 \times .09 \times \frac{1}{12}\right)$	$1,199.34 ($1,288 − $1,199.34)	$88.66 ($159,912 − $88.66)	$159,823.34
3	$159,823.34	$1,198.68	$89.32	$159,734.02
4	$159,734.02	$1,198.01	$89.99	$159,644.03
5	$159,644.03	$1,197.33	$90.67	$159,553.36
6	$159,553.36	$1,196.65	$91.35	$159,462.01
7	$159,462.01	$1,195.97*	$92.04	$159,369.97

*Off 1 cent due to rounding.

Refinancing Gets Even More Attractive

BY ANNAMARIA ANDRIOTIS

Homeowners who have resisted the urge to refinance their mortgages until now could be rewarded for their will-power. Mortgage rates have fallen to new lows—and banks are rolling out in-centives to win business.

Economic uncertainty in Europe and slow growth in the U.S. are prompting investors to pile into ultrasafe U.S. Treasurys. That, in turn, is pushing down mortgage rates, which are tied to Treasurys.

The average interest rate on a 30-year mortgage fell to 4.05% for the week ended Dec. 23, the lowest in 60 years, according to HSH Associates, a mortgage-data firm. And rates on jumbo mortgages—private loans that in most parts of the country are larger than $417,000—also have hit new lows, averaging 4.61%.

"It's hard to argue rates will get much lower than they are today," says Stuart Gabriel, director of the Ziman Center for Real Estate at the University of California, Los Angeles.

That's good news for homeowners. A person who refinanced a $400,000 30-year mortgage in February would pay an interest rate of 5.04% on average, ac-cording to HSH Associates, and fork over $2,157 a month; at the current rate of 4.05%, he'd save $236 per month, or $2,830 per year.

With interest rates falling, the *Wall Street Journal* clip, "Refinancing Gets Even More Attractive," may help you decide if refinancing is in your future.

It's time to test your knowledge of Learning Unit 15–2 with a Practice Quiz.

LU 15–2 PRACTICE QUIZ

Complete this **Practice Quiz** to see how you are doing.

For **extra help** from your authors—Sharon and Jeff—see the student DVD

You Tube

$100,000 mortgage; monthly payment, $953 (100 × $9.53)

Prepare an amortization schedule for the first three periods for the following: mortgage, $100,000; 11%; 30 years.

✓ Solution

Payment number	Principal (current)	PORTION TO— Interest	PORTION TO— Principal reduction	Balance of principal
I	$100,000	$916.67 $\left(\$100{,}000 \times .11 \times \frac{1}{12}\right)$	$36.33 ($953.00 − $916.67)	$99,963.67 ($100,000 − $36.33)
2	$99,963.67	$916.33 $\left(\$99{,}963.67 \times .11 \times \frac{1}{12}\right)$	$36.67 ($953.00 − $916.33)	$99,927.00 ($99,963.67 − $36.67)
3	$99,927	$916.00 $\left(\$99{,}927 \times .11 \times \frac{1}{12}\right)$	$37.00 ($953.00 − $916.00)	$99,890.00 ($99,927.00 − $37.00)

LU 15–2a EXTRA PRACTICE QUIZ WITH WORKED-OUT SOLUTION

Need more practice? Try this **Extra Practice Quiz** (check figures in the Interactive Chapter Organizer, p. 381). Worked-out Solution can be found in Appendix B at end of text.

Prepare an amortization schedule for the first two periods for the following: mortgage, $70,000; 7%; 30 years.

INTERACTIVE CHAPTER ORGANIZER

Topic/procedure/formula	Examples	You try it*
Computing monthly mortgage payment, p. 376 Based on per $1,000 (Table 15.1): $\frac{\text{Amount of mortgage}}{\$1,000} \times$ Table rate	Use Table 15.1: 12% on $60,000 mortgage for 30 years. $\frac{\$60,000}{\$1,000} = 60 \times \$10.29$ $= \$617.40$	**Calculate monthly payment** $70,000 mortgage at 3.5% for 30 years
Calculating total interest cost, p. 376 $\frac{\text{Total of all}}{\text{monthly payments}} - \frac{\text{Amount of}}{\text{mortgage}}$	Using example above: 30 years = 360 (payments) $\times \$617.40$ $\$222,264$ $- 60,000$ $\$162,264$ (mortgage interest over life of mortgage)	**Calculate total interest cost** Use the data from the problem above.
Amortization schedule, pp. 378–379 $I = P \times R \times T$ $\left(I \text{ for month} = P \times R \times \frac{1}{12}\right)$ $\frac{\text{Principal}}{\text{reduction}} = \frac{\text{Monthly}}{\text{payment}} - \text{Interest}$ $\frac{\text{New}}{\text{principal}} = \frac{\text{Current}}{\text{principal}} - \frac{\text{Reduction of}}{\text{principal}}$	Using same example: **Payment number / Interest / Principal reduction / Balance of principal** 1 / $600 / $17.40 / $59,982.60 $\left(\$60,000 \times .12 \times \frac{1}{12}\right)$ $\left(\begin{array}{c}\$617.40\\-\$600.00\end{array}\right)$ $\left(\begin{array}{c}\$60,000.00\\-\$17.40\end{array}\right)$ 2 / $599.83 / $17.57 / $59,965.03 $\left(\$59,982.60 \times .12 \times \frac{1}{12}\right)$ $\left(\begin{array}{c}\$617.40\\-\$599.83\end{array}\right)$ $\left(\begin{array}{c}\$59,982.60\\-\$17.57\end{array}\right)$	**Prepare amortization for first two payments** Use the data from the problem above.

KEY TERMS	Adjustable rate mortgage, (ARM), p. 374 Amortization schedule, p. 379 Amortization table, p. 375 Biweekly mortgage, p. 374 Closing costs, p. 377 Escrow account, p. 377	Fixed rate mortgage, p. 374 Foreclosure, p. 373 Graduated-payment mortgages (GPM), p. 374 Home equity loan, p. 374 Interest-only mortgage, p. 374 Monthly payment, p. 375	Mortgages, p. 374 Points, p. 377 Reverse mortgage, p. 374 Short sale, p. 373 Subprime loans, p. 374

Check Figures for Extra Practice Quizzes with Page References. (Worked-out Solutions in Appendix B.)	LU 15–1a (p. 378) 1. $839.16 $176,097.60 2. $117,583.20 $58,514.40		LU 15–2a (p. 380) $408.33 $57.87 $69,942.13 $408.00 $58.20 $69,883.93

*Worked-out solutions are in Appendix B.

Critical Thinking Discussion Questions with Chapter Concept Check

1. Explain the advantages and disadvantages of the following loan types: 30-year fixed rate, 15-year fixed rate, graduated-payment mortgage, biweekly mortgage, adjustable rate mortgage, and home equity loan. Why might a bank require a home buyer to establish an escrow account?

2. How is an amortization schedule calculated? Is there a best time to refinance a mortgage?

3. What is a point? Is paying points worth the cost?

4. Explain the use of the subprime loan and when it is best used.

5. Explain a short sale.

6. Explain subprime loans and how foreclosures result.

7. **Chapter Concept Check.** Based on the chapter opener, create an example to show how recasting works. Use concepts in the chapter to support your case.

Classroom Notes

END-OF-CHAPTER PROBLEMS

Check figures for odd-numbered problems in Appendix C.   Name _____ Date _____

DRILL PROBLEMS

Complete the following amortization chart by using Table 15.1.   *LU 15-1(2)*

	Selling price of home	Down payment	Principal (loan)	Rate of interest	Years	Payment per $1,000	Monthly mortgage payment
15–1. eXcel	$140,000	$10,000		$3\frac{1}{2}\%$	25		
15–2. eXcel	$90,000	$5,000		$5\frac{1}{2}\%$	30		
15–3. eXcel	$190,000	$50,000		7%	35		

15–4. What is the total cost of interest in Problem 15–2? *LU 15-1(3)*
eXcel

15–5. If the interest rate rises to 7% in Problem 15–2, what is the total cost of interest? *LU 15-1(3)*

Complete the following: *LU 15-2(1)*

	Selling price	Down payment	Amount mortgage	Rate	Years	Monthly payment	First Payment Broken Down Into—		Balance at end of month
							Interest	Principal	
15–6.	$125,000	$5,000		7%	30				
15–7.	$199,000	$40,000		$12\frac{1}{2}\%$	35				

15–8. Bob Jones bought a new log cabin for $70,000 at 11% interest for 30 years. Prepare an amortization schedule for the first three periods. *LU 15-2(2)*

Payment number	Portion to—		Balance of loan outstanding
	Interest	Principal	

WORD PROBLEMS

15–9. FreddieMac reports that the average rate on a 30-year fixed rate mortgage is 3.92% as of January 2012. This is down from 4.76% in January 2011 and 5.03% in January 2010. If you have a $225,000, 5%, 30-year mortgage, how much interest will you save if you refinance your loan at 3.5% for 15 years?   *LU 15-1(2, 3)*

15–10. Oprah Winfrey has closed on a 42-acre estate near Santa Barbara, California, for $50,000,000. If Oprah puts 20% down and finances at 7% for 30 years, what would her monthly payment be?   *LU 15-1(2)*

15–11. Joe Levi bought a home in Arlington, Texas, for $140,000. He put down 20% and obtained a mortgage for 30 years at $5\frac{1}{2}\%$.
eXcel What is Joe's monthly payment? What is the total interest cost of the loan?   *LU 15-1(2, 3)*

15–12. If in Problem 15–11 the rate of interest is $7\frac{1}{2}\%$, what is the difference in interest cost?   *LU 15-1(3)*
eXcel

15–13. Mike Jones bought a new split-level home for $150,000 with 20% down. He decided to use Victory Bank for his mortgage. Victory was offering $13\frac{3}{4}\%$ for 25-year mortgages. Provide Mike with an amortization schedule for the first three periods. *LU 15-2(1, 2)*

Payment number	Portion to—		Balance of loan outstanding
	Interest	**Principal**	

15–14. Harriet Marcus is concerned about the financing of a home. She saw a small cottage that sells for $50,000. If she puts 20% down, what will her monthly payment be at **(a)** 25 years, $11\frac{1}{2}\%$; **(b)** 25 years, $12\frac{1}{2}\%$; **(c)** 25 years, $13\frac{1}{2}\%$; and **(d)** 25 years, 15%? What is the total cost of interest over the cost of the loan for each assumption? **(e)** What is the savings in interest cost between $11\frac{1}{2}\%$ and 15%? **(f)** If Harriet uses 30 years instead of 25 for both $11\frac{1}{2}\%$ and 15%, what is the difference in interest?   *LU 15-1(2, 3)*

15–15. Mortgage lenders base the mortgage interest rate they offer you on your credit rating. This makes it financially critical to maintain a credit score of 700 or higher. How much more interest would you pay on a $195,000 home if you put 20% down and financed the remaining with a 30-year mortgage at 6% interest compared to a 30-year mortgage at $3\frac{1}{2}\%$ interest? *LU 15-1(2, 3)*

15–16. Daniel and Jan agreed to pay $560,000 for a four-bedroom colonial home in Waltham, Massachusetts, with a $60,000 down payment. They have a 30-year mortgage at a fixed rate of 6.00%. **(a)** How much is their monthly payment? **(b)** After the first payment, what would be the balance of the principal? *LU 15-1(2), LU 15-2(1)*

15–17. You can save a significant amount of mortgage interest paid if you make one additional principal and interest payment a year. This will reduce a 30-year mortgage by around 6 years. It also increases your equity in the home faster. If you choose to pay one additional mortgage payment a year by paying 1/12 of it each month (make certain to note the extra money is to reduce principal), how much will you pay each month for a mortgage of $150,000 at $3\frac{1}{2}\%$ for 20 years? *LU 15-1(2)*

CHALLENGE PROBLEMS

15–18. Rick Rueta purchased a $90,000 home at 9% for 30 years with a down payment of $20,000. His annual real estate tax is **eXcel** $1,800 along with an annual insurance premium of $960. Rick's bank requires that his monthly payment include an escrow deposit for the tax and insurance. What is the total payment each month for Rick? *LU 15-1(2)*

15–19. Sharon Fox decided to buy a home in Marblehead, Massachusetts, for $275,000. Her bank requires a 30% down payment. Sue Willis, an attorney, has notified Sharon that besides the 30% down payment there will be the following additional costs:

Recording of the deed	$ 30.00
A credit and appraisal report	155.00
Preparation of appropriate documents	48.00

In addition, there will be a transfer tax of 1.8% of the purchase price and a loan origination fee of 2.5% of the mortgage amount.

Assume a 30-year mortgage at a rate of 10%.   *LU 15-1(2, 3)*

a. What is the initial amount of cash Sharon will need?

b. What is her monthly payment?

c. What is the total cost of interest over the life of the mortgage?

 SUMMARY PRACTICE TEST You Tube™

Do you need help? The DVD has step-by-step worked-out solutions.

1. Pat Lavoie bought a home for $180,000 with a down payment of $10,000. Her rate of interest is 6% for 30 years. Calculate **eXcel** her **(a)** monthly payment; **(b)** first payment, broken down into interest and principal; and **(c)** balance of mortgage at the end of the month. *(pp. 375–377)   LU 15-1(2, 3)*

2. Jen Logan bought a home in Iowa for $110,000. She put down 20% and obtained a mortgage for 30 years at $5\frac{1}{2}$%. What are Jen's monthly payment and total interest cost of the loan? *(pp. 375–377)   LU 15-1(2, 3)*

3. Christina Sanders is concerned about the financing of a home. She saw a small Cape Cod–style house that sells for $90,000. If she puts 10% down, what will her monthly payment be at **(a)** 30 years, 5%; **(b)** 30 years, $5\frac{1}{2}$% **(c)** 30 years, 6%; and **(d)** 30 years, $6\frac{1}{2}$%? What is the total cost of interest over the cost of the loan for each assumption? *(pp. 375–377) LU 15-1(2, 3)*

4. Loretta Scholten bought a home for $210,000 with a down payment of $30,000. Her rate of interest is 6% for 35 years. Calculate Loretta's payment per $1,000 and her monthly mortgage payment. *(pp. 375–376)   LU 15-1(2)*

5. Using Problem 4, calculate the total cost of interest for Loretta Scholten. *(pp. 376–377)   LU 15-1(3)*

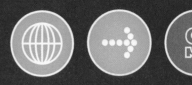
 PROBLEM 1
15- versus 30-year loan

Go to http://www.bankrate.com/calculators/mortgages/mortgage-calculator.aspx. Suppose you can get a $90,000 loan at 8% interest and that you can make a $25,000 down payment. What would your monthly payment be on a 30-year loan? What would the monthly payment be on a 15-year loan? How much interest would you pay altogether for each loan? (Ignore property taxes and insurance in the calculations.)

Discussion Questions

1. What are the pros and cons of a 30-year versus 15-year loan?
2. Which loan period would you feel more comfortable borrowing within? Why?

 PROBLEM 2
Moving on

Go to http://www.interest.com. Choose a state to which you would like to move. Follow the link to "Mortgage Rates in Your State." Choose a 30-year fixed-rate loan. Compare the total amount of interest you would pay to borrow $100,000 from three different lenders. Remember to include the points, or interest fees, you pay up front. For example, 2 points means a 2% fee at the start of the loan, or $100,000 $\times$ 2% = $2,000.

Discussion Questions

1. Why would researching your house costs in another state assist you in planning such a move?
2. What might explain the differences you found among lenders?

 PROBLEM 3
Points of interest

Go to http://www.usbank.com/cgi_w/cfm/personal/products_and_services/mortgage/interest_rates.cfm. If you need to borrow $200,000 to pay for your house, how much will the 2-point discount fee be on the mortgage? What rate will you receive after paying the fee? What rate would you receive if you did not pay the discount fee?

Discussion Questions

1. What are you actually paying for in your points expense? Do you feel this is a necessary charge? Why?
2. Why would some banks offer loans without points due from the borrower?

 PROBLEM 4
Reverse a mortgage?

Your parents or grandparents have asked for your advice on a reverse mortgage. Go to http://www.mlsreversemortgage.com/reverse-mortgage-calculator and read about reverse mortgages. Now calculate how much of a payment your parents or grandparents would receive if they were born in 1924 and their home is worth $150,000.

Discussion Questions

1. Based on your research, what would you advise your parents or grandparents to do?
2. What are the pros and cons of reverse mortgages?

MOBILE APPS

Mortgage Rates (Left Coast R&D, Inc.) Assists you in shopping for the best rates currently available.

Mortgage (MortgageSuite) Calculates fixed rate mortgages simply with the ability to run "what-if" scenarios for overpayments, loan term, loan amount, and interest rate.

INTERNET PROJECTS

See text website
www.mhhe.com/slater11e_sse_ch15

Downsize Your Mortgage?

Sometimes it makes sense to add cash or shorten the term when you refinance. BY SETH FIEGERMAN

BEFORE THE HOUSING BUST, homeowners often saw soaring real estate values as an opportunity to get cash out of their home by refinancing or taking out a home-equity loan. But now that home prices have headed in the other direction, homeowners are seeing the wisdom of the cash-in refi.

Many refinancers who want to lock in historically low rates (recently an average of 4.3% for a 30-year fixed-rate mortgage) are bringing extra funds—beyond closing costs—to the

settlement table. They may be underwater on their mortgage and need to pony up cash in order to refinance. They may want to boost the equity in their home to avoid paying for private mortgage insurance. Or they may want a smaller monthly payment and lower interest payments over the life of the loan. Freddie Mac, which buys mortgages from lenders, says that 22% of households that refinanced in the second quarter of 2010 put extra cash into their homes.

At the same time, shorter-term mortgages—of 15 or 20 years—are in vogue. They are especially popular with people nearing retirement who want to finish paying off the mortgage and trim interest costs as well. For example, if you refinance a $200,000 mortgage at 4.3% for 30 years, your monthly principal-and-interest payments will be $990, and you'll pay $156,307 in interest over the life of the loan. If you choose a 15-year loan at the going rate of 3.7%, your payments will be $1,449 a month—but you'll pay only $60,908 in interest.

Some homeowners also see accelerated mortgage payments as an investment, earning the equivalent of the rate you pay on the loan. In that sense, paying down your mortgage beats money-market funds and CDs. And unlike an investment in the stock market, the returns are guaranteed. "Realizing that your money works harder paying down the mortgage than it does in savings is a powerful incentive," says Guy Cecala, publisher of the newsletter *Inside Mortgage Finance.*

Making the decision. Of course, higher monthly payments on your mortgage would decrease your cash flow. "You need to look at whether that money could be better spent elsewhere," says Keith Gumbinger, of HSH Associates. "Maybe it could be used to pay down credit-card debt or go toward your retirement plan."

Some financial planners think younger homeowners should not pay down their

mortgage early. "Anyone under 40 should be funding a retirement plan, and anyone over 50 should be concentrating on paying off the house," says Rick Kahler, of the Kahler Financial Group, in Rapid City, S.D. However, if you're close to retirement and paying off the mortgage would mean raiding too much of your savings, it may not be a good idea.

Whenever you consider a refi, make sure it will really save you money. Although rules of thumb abound—some say that refinancing makes sense when rates are one point lower than you're currently paying, others say two points—you have to crunch the numbers to see when the lower payments will make up for your closing costs. You should also consider your tax situation—remember that mortgage interest is deductible—and how long you plan to stay in your home. (For help, use the calculator at http://zwicke.nber.org/refinance. It will estimate how far interest rates need to fall before you should refinance your fixed-rate mortgage with a new fixed-rate loan, and it takes your tax bracket into consideration.)

If committing to higher monthly payments concerns you, or you're worried about whether you will qualify for a new mortgage, you always have the option of making extra payments on your current loan. Doing so can potentially turn your existing loan into a 15-year mortgage, says Cecala, "although you must be pretty disciplined to do that." ∎

BUSINESS MATH ISSUE

Refinancing has very little risk.

1. List the key points of the article and information to support your position.
2. Write a group defense of your position using math calculations to support your view.

Classroom Notes

CHAPTER 16

How to Read, Analyze, and Interpret Financial Reports

Kellogg, Sara Lee Raise Prices, Get Mixed Results

BY PAUL ZIOBRO
AND MARSHALL ECKBLAD

Kellogg Co. and **Sara Lee** Corp. relied on higher prices to grow sales for the three months ended Dec. 31, passing on higher costs for everything from cookies to coffee.

Results from the two food makers, reported Thursday, show some willingness among consumers to pay higher prices on many products. Sara Lee's coffee and tea sales in Europe rose 12%, while Kellogg's U.S. snacks and frozen foods business saw sales rise 8.1% and 13.5%, respectively.

But Sara Lee's sliced meats business in the U.S. saw sales volume decline, resulting in flat sales. The company said its Hillshire Farms brand lunchmeat has fallen behind competitors that have introduced new products that resonate more with consumers. Sara Lee brands also include Jimmy Dean and the Senseo line of coffee products.

"We have to tip our hat to competition that out-innovated us in lunch meat," said Marcel Smits, who heads up Sara Lee's meats division.

Kellogg's U.S. cereal business posted only slight growth, with executives saying that some consumers haven't adjusted to higher prices. Sales were also challenged in Europe, where heavy discounting by competitors has pressured results.

Kellogg's fourth-quarter earnings were up 23% to $232 million, rising more than expected due to sales growth of 5.4% to $3.02 billion on higher prices. The company, whose brands include Rice Krispies, Pop Tarts and Eggo waffles, also expects sales to remain strong as it introduces new products, boosts advertising and continues to reap benefits from higher prices.

Kellogg expects the European market will continue to remain weak, and also forecast another challenging year for the U.S. cereal category.

Meanwhile, Sara Lee saw its fiscal second-quarter earnings drop 44% to $469 million, hurt by impairment charges. Net sales were up 6.3% to $2.08 billion.

Both companies say they still are facing pressure from higher costs. Kellogg sees another year of "unusually" high commodity inflation, with projections that costs will rise 7%, leading to a slight drop in gross margins.

Sara Lee will soon cleave itself in two, separating its North American meat-focused business, which includes brands like Jimmy Dean and Hillshire Farms, from its surging European coffee-and-tea unit. The company says the split will likely take place in the next six months.

Sara Lee's costs for commodities have risen nearly $1 billion over the last six quarters, with expectations the costs will rise an additional $90 million over the next two quarters. Costs for the coffee-and-tea business appear to be stabilizing, but other ingredients like raw pork continue to pose problems.

LU 16–1: Balance Sheet—Report as of a Particular Date

1. Explain the purpose and the key items on the balance sheet *(pp. 392–395)*.
2. Explain and complete vertical and horizontal analysis *(pp. 395–397)*.

LU 16–2: Income Statement—Report for a Specific Period of Time

1. Explain the purpose and the key items on the income statement *(pp. 398–403)*.
2. Explain and complete vertical and horizontal analysis *(pp. 403–404)*.

LU 16–3: Trend and Ratio Analysis

1. Explain and complete a trend analysis *(p. 405)*.
2. List, explain, and calculate key financial ratios *(pp. 405–407)*.

VOCABULARY PREVIEW

Here are key terms in this chapter. After completing the chapter, if you know the term, place a checkmark in the parentheses. If you don't know the term, look it up and put the page number where it can be found.

**Accounts payable ( ) Accounts receivable ( ) Acid test ( ) Assets ( ) Asset turnover ( )
Balance sheet ( ) Benefit corporation ( ) Capital ( ) Common stock ( ) Comparative statement ( )
Corporation ( ) Cost of merchandise (goods) sold ( ) Current assets ( ) Current liabilities ( )
Current ratio ( ) Expenses ( ) Gross profit from sales ( ) Gross sales ( ) Horizontal analysis ( )
Income statement ( ) Liabilities ( ) Long-term liabilities ( ) Merchandise inventory ( ) Mortgage
note payable ( ) Net income ( ) Net purchases ( ) Net sales ( ) Operating expenses ( ) Owner's
equity ( ) Partnership ( ) Plant and equipment ( ) Prepaid expenses ( ) Purchase discounts ( )
Purchase returns and allowances ( ) Purchases ( ) Quick assets ( ) Quick ratio ( ) Ratio analysis ( )
Retained earnings ( ) Return on equity ( ) Revenues ( ) Salaries payable ( ) Sales (not trade)
discounts ( ) Sales returns and allowances ( ) Sole proprietorship ( ) Stockholders' equity ( )
Trend analysis ( ) Vertical analysis ( )**

The Sarbanes-Oxley Act (2002) was passed to ensure public companies are accurately reporting their financial statements. The *Wall Street Journal* article, "Justices Keep Sarbanes-Oxley, Adjust Structure," (see next page) discusses how the Sarbanes-Oxley law was kept intact with technical changes. As you will see in this chapter, an understatement of expenses overstates the reported earnings or net income of a company. This overstatement presents a false picture of the company's financial position.

This chapter explains how to analyze two key financial reports: the *balance sheet* (shows a company's financial condition at a particular date) and the *income statement* (shows a company's profitability over a time period).[1] Business owners must understand their financial statements to avoid financial difficulties. This includes knowing how to read, analyze, and interpret financial reports.

---

[1]The third key financial report is the statement of cash flows. We do not discuss this statement. For more information on the statement of cash flows, check your accounting text.

Justices Keep Sarbanes-Oxley, Adjust Structure

BY KARA SCANNELL,
AND MICHAEL RAPOPORT

The nation's highest court ordered a technical change Monday to the Sarbanes-Oxley accounting rules but left the broader law intact.

A government body that oversees accounting firms is structured in a way that's unconstitutional, the Supreme Court said. Under the 5-4 ruling, the Public Company Accounting Oversight Board can continue to operate with only minor changes.

The decision hands a victory to opponents of the 2002 corporate-governance law that created the panel, but it has little practical impact. Had the court ruled more broadly, it could have invalidated the accounting panel or even Sarbanes-Oxley itself.

The case had drawn significant attention because of the continuing debates over Sarbanes-Oxley. Congress created the law in response to a wave of accounting scandals punctuated by frauds at Enron and World-Com. The law required corporate executives to sign off on financial statements, pushed for greater independence in board-

rooms and approved stiffer penalties for corporate wrongdoers.

The court mandated that the SEC be able to remove any accounting-board member 'at will.'

Learning Unit 16–1: Balance Sheet—Report as of a Particular Date

LO 1

The **balance sheet** gives a financial picture of what a company is worth as of a particular date, usually at the end of a month or year. This report lists (1) how much the company owns (assets), (2) how much the company owes (liabilities), and (3) how much the owner (**owner's equity**) is worth.

Note that assets and liabilities are divided into two groups: current (*short term*, usually less than 1 year); and *long term*, usually more than 1 year. The basic formula for a balance sheet is as follows:

$$\text{Assets} - \text{Liabilities} = \text{Owner's equity}$$

Like all formulas, the items on both sides of the equal sign must balance.

By reversing the above formula, we have the following common balance sheet layout:

$$\text{Assets} = \text{Liabilities} + \text{Owner's equity}$$

To introduce you to the balance sheet, let's assume that you collect baseball cards and decide to open a baseball card shop. As the owner of The Card Shop, your investment, or owner's equity, is called **capital.** Since your business is small, your balance sheet is short. After the first year of operation, The Card Shop balance sheet is shown as follows:

"Capital" does not mean "cash." It is the owner's investment in the company.

THE CARD SHOP Balance Sheet December 31, 2014		Report as of a particular date	
Assets		**Liabilities**	
Cash	$ 3,000	Accounts payable	$ 2,500
Merchandise inventory (baseball cards)	4,000	**Owner's Equity**	
Equipment	3,000	E. Slott, capital	7,500
Total assets	$10,000	Total liabilities and owner's equity	$10,000

The heading gives the name of the company, title of the report, and date of the report. Note how the totals of both sides of the balance sheet are the same. This is true of all balance sheets.

We can take figures from the balance sheet of The Card Shop and use our first formula to determine how much the business is worth:

© Lana Sundman/Alamy

Assets − Liabilities = Owner's equity (capital)

$10,000 − $2,500 = $7,500

Since you are the single owner of The Card Shop, your business is a **sole proprietorship.** If a business has two or more owners, it is a **partnership.** A **corporation** has many owners or stockholders, and the equity of these owners is called **stockholders' equity.** The following *Wall Street Journal* clip discusses America's newest type of corporation: the **benefit corporation.** Now let's study the balance sheet elements of a corporation.

America's Newest Company Type: The 'Benefit Corporation'

What is a 'benefit corporation'? A company whose charter allows the board to consider social or environmental objectives ahead of profits.

What is the advantage? Protection from investor allegations of not maximizing shareholder value.

Does that make it a nonprofit? No, a benefit corporation isn't a nonprofit nor is it tax exempt.

How many states allow it? Seven. With bills introduced in four additional states.

What are the downsides? 'For an investor, this is a terrible idea' due to lack of accountability, says Charles Elson, who teaches corporate governance at the University of Delaware. If management makes a bad decision, 'there's very little you can do about it as a shareholder.'

Mike Brady, right, president of Greyston Bakery, which has goals for hiring locally and child care.

Elements of the Balance Sheet

The format and contents of all corporation balance sheets are similar. Figure 16.1 shows the balance sheet of Mool Company (p. 394). As you can see, the formula Assets = Liabilities + Stockholders' equity (we have a corporation in this example) is also the framework of this balance sheet.

FIGURE 16.1   Balance sheet

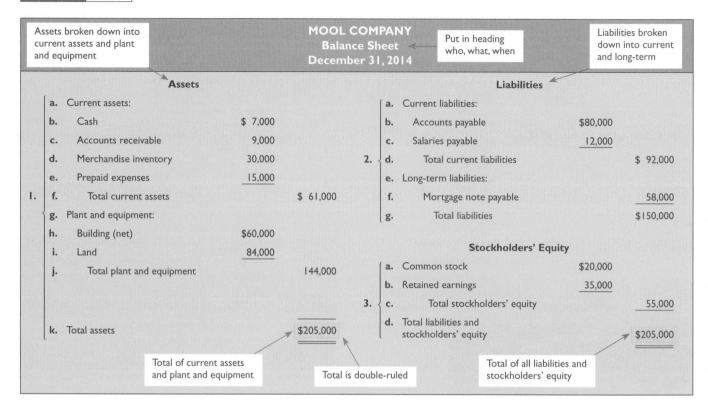

To help you understand the three main balance sheet groups (assets, liabilities, and stockholders' equity) and their elements, we have labeled them in Figure 16.1. An explanation of these groups and their elements follows this paragraph. Do not try to memorize the elements. Just try to understand their meaning. Think of Figure 16.1 (above) as a reference aid. You will find that the more you work with balance sheets, the easier it is for you to understand them.

1. **Assets:** Things of value *owned* by a company (economic resources of the company) that can be measured and expressed in monetary terms.
    a. **Current assets:** Assets that companies consume or convert to cash *within 1 year* or a normal operating cycle.
    b. **Cash:** Total cash in checking accounts, savings accounts, and on hand.
    c. **Accounts receivable:** Money *owed* to a company by customers from sales on account (buy now, pay later).
    d. **Merchandise inventory:** Cost of goods in stock for resale to customers.
    e. **Prepaid expenses:** The purchases of a company are assets until they expire (insurance or rent) or are consumed (supplies).
    f. **Total current assets:** Total of all assets that the company will consume or convert to cash within 1 year.
    g. **Plant and equipment:** Assets that will last longer than 1 year. These assets are used in the operation of the company.
    h. **Building (net):** The cost of the building minus the depreciation that has accumulated. Usually, balance sheets show this as "Building less accumulated depreciation." In Chapter 17 we discuss accumulated depreciation in greater detail.
    i. **Land:** This asset does not depreciate, but it can increase or decrease in value.
    j. **Total plant and equipment:** Total of building and land, including machinery and equipment.
    k. **Total assets:** Total of current assets and plant and equipment.
2. **Liabilities:** Debts or obligations of the company.
    a. **Current liabilities:** Debts or obligations of the company that are *due within 1 year.*
    b. **Accounts payable:** A current liability that shows the amount the company owes to creditors for services or items purchased.

Rhymes with Orange (105945) © 2012 Hilary B. Price. King Features Syndicate.

    c. **Salaries payable:** Obligations that the company must pay within 1 year for salaries earned but unpaid.

    d. **Total current liabilities:** Total obligations that the company must pay within 1 year.

    e. **Long-term liabilities:** Debts or obligations that the company does not have to pay within 1 year.

    f. **Mortgage note payable:** Debt owed on a building that is a long-term liability; often the building is the collateral.

    g. **Total liabilities:** Total of current and long-term liabilities.

3. **Stockholders' equity (owner's equity):** The rights or interest of the stockholders to assets of a corporation. If the company is not a corporation, the term *owner's equity* is used. The word *capital* follows the owner's name under the title *Owner's Equity*.

    a. **Common stock:** Amount of the initial and additional investment of corporation owners by the purchase of stock.

    b. **Retained earnings:** The amount of corporation earnings that the company retains, not necessarily in cash form.

    c. **Total stockholders' equity:** Total of stock plus retained earnings.

    d. **Total liabilities and stockholders' equity:** Total current liabilities, long-term liabilities, stock, and retained earnings. This total represents all the claims on assets—prior and present claims of creditors, owners' residual claims, and any other claims.

Now that you are familiar with the common balance sheet items, you are ready to analyze a balance sheet.

Vertical Analysis and the Balance Sheet

LO 2

Often financial statement readers want to analyze reports that contain data for two or more successive accounting periods. To make this possible, companies present a statement showing the data from these periods side by side. As you might expect, this statement is called a **comparative statement.**

Comparative reports help illustrate changes in data. Financial statement readers should compare the percents in the reports to industry percents and the percents of competitors.

Figure 16.2 (p. 396) shows the comparative balance sheet of Roger Company. Note that the statement analyzes each asset as a percent of total assets for a single period. The statement then analyzes each liability and equity as a percent of total liabilities and stockholders' equity. We call this type of analysis **vertical analysis.**

The following steps use the portion formula to prepare a vertical analysis of a balance sheet.

PREPARING A VERTICAL ANALYSIS OF A BALANCE SHEET
Step 1. Divide each asset (the portion) as a percent of total assets (the base). Round as indicated.
Step 2. Round each liability and stockholders' equity (the portions) as a percent of total liabilities and stockholders' equity (the base). Round as indicated.

We can also analyze balance sheets for two or more periods by using **horizontal analysis.** Horizontal analysis compares each item in 1 year by amount, percent, or both with the same item of the previous year. Note the Abby Ellen Company horizontal analysis shown

FIGURE **16.2**

Comparative balance sheet:
Vertical analysis

We divide each item by
the total of assets.

Portion
($8,000)

Base × Rate
($85,000) (?)

	ROGER COMPANY Comparative Balance Sheet December 31, 2013 and 2014			
	2014		**2013**	
	Amount	Percent	Amount	Percent
Assets				
Current assets:				
Cash	$22,000	25.88	$18,000	22.22
Accounts receivable	8,000	9.41	9,000	11.11
Merchandise inventory	9,000	10.59	7,000	8.64
Prepaid rent	4,000	4.71	5,000	6.17
Total current assets	$43,000	50.59	$39,000	48.15*
Plant and equipment:				
Building (net)	$18,000	21.18	$18,000	22.22
Land	24,000	28.24	24,000	29.63
Total plant and equipment	$42,000	49.41*	$42,000	51.85
Total assets	$85,000	100.00	$81,000	100.00
Liabilities				
Current liabilities:				
Accounts payable	$14,000	16.47	$ 8,000	9.88
Salaries payable	18,000	21.18	17,000	20.99
Total current liabilities	$32,000	37.65	$25,000	30.86*
Long-term liabilities:				
Mortgage note payable	12,000	14.12	20,000	24.69
Total liabilities	$44,000	51.76*	$45,000	55.56*
Stockholders' Equity				
Common stock	$20,000	23.53	$20,000	24.69
Retained earnings	21,000	24.71	16,000	19.75
Total stockholders' equity	$41,000	48.24	$36,000	44.44
Total liabilities and stockholders' equity	$85,000	100.00	$81,000	100.00

We divide each item by the total of
liabilities and stockholders' equity.

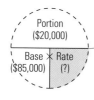
Portion
($20,000)

Base × Rate
($85,000) (?)

Note: All percents are rounded to the nearest hundredth percent.
*Due to rounding.

in Figure 16.3 (p. 397). To make a horizontal analysis, we use the portion formula and the steps that follow:

PREPARING A HORIZONTAL ANALYSIS OF A COMPARATIVE BALANCE SHEET
Step 1. Calculate the increase or decrease (portion) in each item from the base year.
Step 2. Divide the increase or decrease in Step 1 by the old or base year.
Step 3. Round as indicated.

MONEY tips

Make a video of your home
to inventory your belongings.
Keep this in a safety deposit or
fireproof box. In the event of a
loss, you will have a recording
of your belongings. It is amazing
how much can be forgotten
without it.

You can see the difference between vertical analysis and horizontal analysis by looking at the example of vertical analysis in Figure 16.2 (above). The percent calculations in Figure 16.2 are for each item of a particular year as a percent of that year's total assets or total liabilities and stockholders' equity.

Horizontal analysis needs comparative columns because we take the difference *between* periods. In Figure 16.3, for example, the accounts receivable decreased $1,000 from 2013

FIGURE 16.3

Comparative balance sheet:
Horizontal analysis

Difference between
2013 and 2014

Portion
−($1,000)

Base × Rate
($6,000)   (?)

2013

ABBY ELLEN COMPANY Comparative Balance Sheet December 31, 2013 and 2014				
			INCREASE (DECREASE)	
	2014	2013	Amount	Percent
Assets				
Current assets:				
Cash	$ 6,000	$ 4,000	$2,000	50.00*
Accounts receivable	5,000	6,000	(1,000)	− 16.67
Merchandise inventory	9,000	4,000	5,000	125.00
Prepaid rent	5,000	7,000	(2,000)	− 28.57
Total current assets	$25,000	$21,000	$4,000	19.05
Plant and equipment:				
Building (net)	$12,000	$12,000	–0–	–0–
Land	18,000	18,000	–0–	–0–
Total plant and equipment	$30,000	$30,000	–0–	–0–
Total assets	$55,000	$51,000	$4,000	7.84
Liabilities				
Current liabilities:				
Accounts payable	$ 3,200	$ 1,800	$1,400	77.78
Salaries payable	2,900	3,200	(300)	− 9.38
Total current liabilities	$ 6,100	$ 5,000	$1,100	22.00
Long-term liabilities:				
Mortgage note payable	17,000	15,000	2,000	13.33
Total liabilities	$23,100	$20,000	$3,100	15.50
Owner's Equity				
Abby Ellen, capital	$31,900	$31,000	$ 900	2.90
Total liabilities and owner's equity	$55,000	$51,000	$4,000	7.84

*The percents are not summed vertically in horizontal analysis.

to 2014. Thus, by dividing $1,000 (amount of change) by $6,000 (base year), we see that Abby's receivables decreased 16.67%.

Let's now try the following Practice Quiz.

LU 16–1 PRACTICE QUIZ

Complete this **Practice Quiz** to see how you are doing.

1. Complete this partial comparative balance sheet by vertical analysis. Round percents to the nearest hundredth.

	2014		2013	
	Amount	Percent	Amount	Percent
Assets				
Current assets:				
a. Cash	$ 42,000		$ 40,000	
b. Accounts receivable	18,000		17,000	
c. Merchandise inventory	15,000		12,000	
d. Prepaid expenses	17,000		14,000	
•	•		•	
•	•		•	
•	•		•	
Total current assets	$160,000		$150,000	

2. What is the amount of change in merchandise inventory and the percent increase?

✓ **Solutions**

			2014		**2013**	
1.	**a.**	Cash	$\dfrac{\$42,000}{\$160,000} =$	26.25%	$\dfrac{\$40,000}{\$150,000} =$	26.67%
	b.	Accounts receivable	$\dfrac{\$18,000}{\$160,000} =$	11.25%	$\dfrac{\$17,000}{\$150,000} =$	11.33%
	c.	Merchandise inventory	$\dfrac{\$15,000}{\$160,000} =$	9.38%	$\dfrac{\$12,000}{\$150,000} =$	8.00%
	d.	Prepaid expenses	$\dfrac{\$17,000}{\$160,000} =$	10.63%	$\dfrac{\$14,000}{\$150,000} =$	9.33%

2.

$$\begin{array}{r} \$15,000 \\ -\ 12,000 \\ \hline \end{array}$$
Amount = $\boxed{\$\ 3,000}$

$\text{Percent} = \dfrac{\$3,000}{\$12,000} = \boxed{25\%}$

LU 16–1a EXTRA PRACTICE QUIZ WITH WORKED-OUT SOLUTIONS

Need more practice? Try this **Extra Practice Quiz** (check figures in the Interactive Chapter Organizer, p. 409). Worked-out Solutions can be found in Appendix B at end of text.

1. Complete this partial comparative balance sheet by vertical analysis. Round percents to the nearest hundredth.

	2014		**2013**	
	Amount	**Percent**	**Amount**	**Percent**
Assets				
Current assets:				
a. Cash	$ 38,000		$ 35,000	
b. Accounts receivable	19,000		18,000	
c. Merchandise inventory	16,000		11,000	
d. Prepaid expenses	20,000		16,000	
.	.		.	
.	.		.	
.	.		.	
Total current assets	$180,000		$140,000	

2. What is the amount of change in merchandise inventory and the percent increase?

Learning Unit 16–2: Income Statement—Report for a Specific Period of Time

LO 1

One of the most important departments in a company is its accounting department. The job of the accounting department is to determine the financial results of the company's operations. Is the company making money or losing money? The following *Wall Street Journal* clip "Campbell Soup to Exit Russia" (p. 399) reveals that profits there have fallen below projected expectations. Campbell believes that China offers stronger profit potentials.

GLOBAL

Campbell Soup To Exit Russia

By Julie Jargon

Campbell Soup Co. said it is exiting Russia just four years after betting it would be a simmering new market.

On Tuesday, Campbell Chief Operating Officer and CEO-elect Denise Morrison said results in Russia fell below the company's expectations.

"We believe that opportunities currently under exploration in other emerging markets, notably China, offer stronger prospects for driving profitable growth within an acceptable time frame," Ms. Morrison said.

In this learning unit we look at the **income statement**—a financial report that tells how well a company is performing (its profitability or net profit) during a specific period of time (month, year, etc.). In general, the income statement reveals the inward flow of revenues (sales) against the outward or potential outward flow of costs and expenses.

The form of income statements varies depending on the company's type of business. However, the basic formula of the income statement is the same:

$$\text{Revenues} - \text{Operating expenses} = \text{Net income}$$

In a merchandising business like The Card Shop, we can expand on this formula:

> After any returns, allowances, or discounts
>
> Revenues (sales)
> − Cost of merchandise or goods ◄── Baseball cards
> = Gross profit from sales
> − Operating expenses
> = Net income (profit)

THE CARD SHOP Income Statement For Month Ended December 31, 2014	
Revenues (sales)	$8,000
Cost of merchandise (goods) sold	3,000
Gross profit from sales	$5,000
Operating expenses	750
Net income	$4,250

Now let's look at The Card Shop's income statement to see how much profit The Card Shop made during its first year of operation. For simplicity, we assume The Card Shop sold all the cards it bought during the year. For its first year of business, The Card Shop made a profit of $4,250.

We can now go more deeply into the income statement elements as we study the income statement of a corporation.

Elements of the Corporation Income Statement

Figure 16.4 (p. 401) gives the format and content of the Mool Company income statement—a corporation. The five main items of an income statement are revenues, cost of merchandise (goods) sold, gross profit on sales, operating expenses, and net income. We will follow the same pattern we used in explaining the balance sheet and define the main items and the letter-coded subitems.

1. **Revenues:** Total earned sales (cash or credit) less any sales returns and allowances or sales discounts. Note from the following *Wall Street Journal* clip that games from Zynga and other companies provide Facebook with 15% of its revenue.

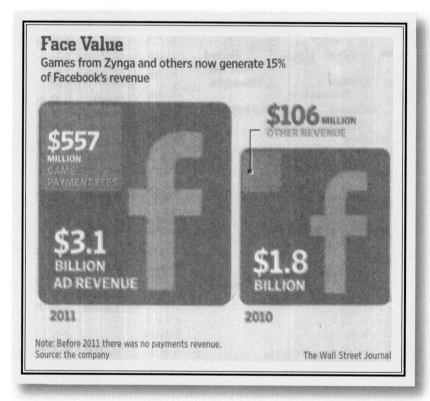

    a. Gross sales: Total earned sales before sales returns and allowances or sales discounts.

    b. Sales returns and allowances: Reductions in price or reductions in revenue due to goods returned because of product defects, errors, and so on. When the buyer keeps the damaged goods, an allowance results.

    c. Sales (not trade) discounts: Reductions in the selling price of goods due to early customer payment. For example, a store may give a 2% discount to a customer who pays a bill within 10 days.

    d. Net sales: Gross sales less sales returns and allowances less sales discounts.

2. **Cost of merchandise (goods) sold:** All the costs of getting the merchandise that the company sold. The cost of all unsold merchandise (goods) will be subtracted from this item (ending inventory).

    a. Merchandise inventory, December 1, 2014: Cost of inventory in the store that was for sale to customers at the beginning of the month.

    b. Purchases: Cost of additional merchandise brought into the store for resale to customers.

    c. Purchase returns and allowances: Cost of merchandise returned to the store due to damage, defects, errors, and so on. Damaged goods kept by the buyer result in a cost reduction called an *allowance*.

FIGURE 16.4 Income statement

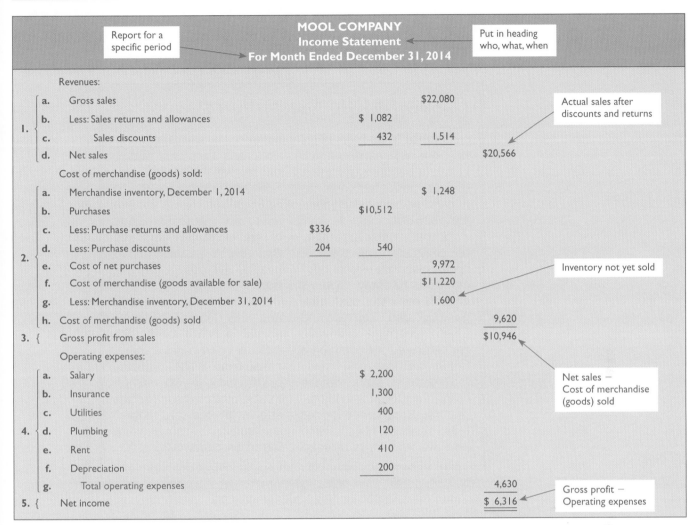

		MOOL COMPANY Income Statement For Month Ended December 31, 2014			
	Revenues:				
1. a.	Gross sales		$22,080		Actual sales after discounts and returns
b.	Less: Sales returns and allowances	$ 1,082			
c.	Sales discounts	432	1,514		
d.	Net sales			$20,566	
	Cost of merchandise (goods) sold:				
2. a.	Merchandise inventory, December 1, 2014		$ 1,248		
b.	Purchases	$10,512			
c.	Less: Purchase returns and allowances	$336			
d.	Less: Purchase discounts	204	540		
e.	Cost of net purchases		9,972		Inventory not yet sold
f.	Cost of merchandise (goods available for sale)		$11,220		
g.	Less: Merchandise inventory, December 31, 2014		1,600		
h.	Cost of merchandise (goods) sold			9,620	
3. {	Gross profit from sales			$10,946	
	Operating expenses:				
4. a.	Salary	$ 2,200			Net sales − Cost of merchandise (goods) sold
b.	Insurance	1,300			
c.	Utilities	400			
d.	Plumbing	120			
e.	Rent	410			
f.	Depreciation	200			
g.	Total operating expenses			4,630	Gross profit −
5. {	Net income			$ 6,316	Operating expenses

Note: Numbers are subtotaled from left to right.

Farm to Table

Expected inflation in the cost of goods sold over the next 12 months for food companies

Sara Lee	11.7%
ConAgra	7.4
Kraft	5.3
Hershey	4.0
Kellogg	3.6
Heinz	2.0

Source: Sanford C. Bernstein

d. **Purchase discounts:** Savings received by the buyer for paying for merchandise before a certain date. These discounts can result in a substantial savings to a company.

e. **Cost of net purchases:** Cost of purchases less purchase returns and allowances less purchase discounts.

f. **Cost of merchandise (goods available for sale):** Sum of beginning inventory plus cost of net purchases.

g. **Merchandise inventory, December 31, 2014:** Cost of inventory remaining in the store to be sold.

h. **Cost of merchandise (goods) sold:** Beginning inventory plus net purchases less ending inventory. Note in the accompanying *Wall Street Journal* clipping the amount of inflation in the cost of goods sold for companies like Hershey.

3. **Gross profit from sales:** Net sales less cost of merchandise (goods) sold.

4. **Operating expenses:** Additional costs of operating the business beyond the actual cost of inventory sold.

a.–f. **Expenses:** Individual expenses broken down.

g. **Total operating expenses:** Total of all the individual expenses.

5. **Net income:** Gross profit less operating expenses.

You can read in the following *Wall Street Journal* clipping that while General Mills' sales were up 8.9% its gross margin fell to 37.6% from 43.1%, due to rising costs.

In the next section you will learn some formulas that companies use to calculate various items on the income statement.

General Mills Net Falls 14%

General Mills Inc.'s fiscal first-quarter earnings fell 14% as a bigger advertising budget and higher costs cut into the packaged-food company's profit.

"A challenging first-quarter comparison is now behind us, and we expect General Mills to show earnings growth over the next nine months," said Chairman and Chief Executive Ken Powell, who affirmed the company's full-year guidance.

General Mills—whose brands includes Cheerios cereal and Hamburger Helper —has recently been able to improve its profits by rais-ing prices or shrinking package sizes to offset higher raw-material costs.

Sales jumped 8.9% to $3.85 billion. Gross margin fell to 37.6% from 43.1%, due to higher input costs and changing its business mix to include the Yoplait acquisition.

For the quarter ended Aug. 28, General Mills reported a profit of $405.6 million, or 61 cents a share, down from $472.1 million, or 70 cents, a year earlier. Excluding items such as the effects of mark-to-market accounting, earnings were flat at 64 cents.

Calculating Net Sales, Cost of Merchandise (Goods) Sold, Gross Profit, and Net Income of an Income Statement

It is time to look closely at Figure 16.4 (p. 401) and see how each section is built. Use the previous vocabulary as a reference. We will study Figure 16.4 step by step.

Step 1. Calculate the net sales—what Mool earned:

$$\text{Net sales} = \text{Gross sales} - \frac{\text{Sales returns}}{\text{and allowances}} - \text{Sales discounts}$$

$$\$20{,}566 = \$22{,}080 - \$1{,}082 - \$432$$

Step 2. Calculate the cost of merchandise (goods) sold:

$$\begin{matrix}\text{Cost of} \\ \text{merchandise} \\ \text{(goods) sold}\end{matrix} = \begin{matrix}\text{Beginning} \\ \text{inventory}\end{matrix} + \begin{matrix}\text{Net purchases} \\ \text{(purchases less} \\ \text{returns and discounts)}\end{matrix} - \begin{matrix}\text{Ending} \\ \text{inventory}\end{matrix}$$

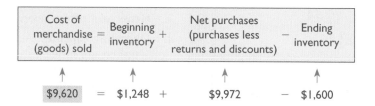

$$\$9{,}620 = \$1{,}248 + \$9{,}972 - \$1{,}600$$

Step 3. Calculate the gross profit from sales—profit before operating expenses:

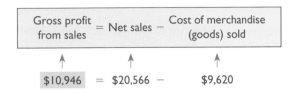

$$\begin{array}{c} \text{Gross profit} \\ \text{from sales} \end{array} = \text{Net sales} - \begin{array}{c} \text{Cost of merchandise} \\ \text{(goods) sold} \end{array}$$

$$\boxed{\$10{,}946} = \$20{,}566 - \$9{,}620$$

Step 4. Calculate the net income—profit after operating expenses:

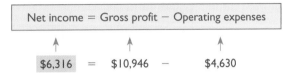

$$\text{Net income} = \text{Gross profit} - \text{Operating expenses}$$

$$\boxed{\$6{,}316} = \$10{,}946 - \$4{,}630$$

LO 2

Analyzing Comparative Income Statements

We can apply the same procedures of vertical and horizontal analysis to the income statement that we used in analyzing the balance sheet. Let's first look at the vertical analysis for Royal Company, Figure 16.5. Then we will look at the horizontal analysis of Flint Company's 2013 and 2014 income statements shown in Figure 16.6 (p. 404). Note in the margin how numbers are calculated.

FIGURE **16.5**

Vertical analysis

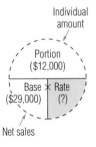

ROYAL COMPANY Comparative Income Statement For Years Ended December 31, 2013 and 2014				
	2014	**Percent of net**	**2013**	**Percent of net**
Net sales	$45,000	100.00	$29,000	100.00*
Cost of merchandise sold	19,000	42.22	12,000	41.38
Gross profit from sales	$26,000	57.78	$17,000	58.62
Operating expenses:				
Depreciation	$ 1,000	2.22	$ 500	1.72
Selling and advertising	4,200	9.33	1,600	5.52
Research	2,900	6.44	2,000	6.90
Miscellaneous	500	1.11	200	.69
Total operating expenses	$ 8,600	19.11†	$ 4,300	14.83
Income before interest and taxes	$17,400	38.67	$12,700	43.79
Interest expense	6,000	13.33	3,000	10.34
Income before taxes	$11,400	25.33†	$ 9,700	33.45
Provision for taxes	5,500	12.22	3,000	10.34
Net income	$ 5,900	13.11	$ 6,700	23.10†

*Net sales = 100%

†Off due to rounding.

Horizontal analysis

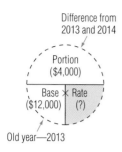

Difference from
2013 and 2014

Portion
($4,000)

Base × Rate
($12,000)   (?)

Old year—2013

MONEY tips

Keep a record of how much you
owe and to whom you owe it.
Create a plan to pay each debt off,
one by one. Pay off the highest
interest rate balance first.

FLINT COMPANY Comparative Income Statement For Years Ended December 31, 2013 and 2014				
			INCREASE (DECREASE)	
	2014	**2013**	**Amount**	**Percent**
Sales	$90,000	$80,000	$ 10,000	
Sales returns and allowances	2,000	2,000	–0–	
Net sales	$88,000	$78,000	$ 10,000	+ 12.82
Cost of merchandise (goods) sold	45,000	40,000	5,000	+ 12.50
Gross profit from sales	$43,000	$38,000	$ 5,000	+ 13.16
Operating expenses:				
Depreciation	$ 6,000	$ 5,000	$ 1,000	+ 20.00
Selling and administrative	16,000	12,000	4,000	+ 33.33
Research	600	1,000	(400)	– 40.00
Miscellaneous	1,200	500	700	+ 140.00
Total operating expenses	$23,800	$18,500	$ 5,300	+ 28.65
Income before interest and taxes	$19,200	$19,500	$ (300)	– 1.54
Interest expense	4,000	4,000	–0–	
Income before taxes	$15,200	$15,500	$ (300)	– 1.94
Provision for taxes	3,800	4,000	(200)	– 5.00
Net income	$11,400	$11,500	$ (100)	– .87

The following Practice Quiz will test your understanding of this unit.

Complete this **Practice Quiz**
to see how you are doing.

*For **extra help** from
your authors—Sharon
and Jeff—see the
student DVD*

From the following information, calculate:

a. Net sales.

b. Cost of merchandise (goods) sold.

c. Gross profit from sales.

d. Net income.

Given Gross sales, $35,000; sales returns and allowances, $3,000; beginning inventory,
$6,000; net purchases, $7,000; ending inventory, $5,500; operating expenses, $7,900.

✓ **Solutions**

a. $35,000 − $3,000 = $32,000 (Gross sales − Sales returns and allowances)

b. $6,000 + $7,000 − $5,500 = $7,500 (Beginning inventory + Net purchases − Ending inventory)

c. $32,000 − $7,500 = $24,500 (Net sales − Cost of merchandise sold)

d. $24,500 − $7,900 = $16,600 (Gross profit from sales − Operating expenses)

Need more practice? Try this
Extra Practice Quiz (check
figures in the Interactive
Chapter Organizer, p. 409).
Worked-out Solutions can
be found in Appendix B at
end of text.

From the following information, calculate:

a. Net sales

b. Cost of merchandise (goods) sold

c. Gross profit from sales

d. Net income

Given: Gross sales, $36,000; sales returns and allowances, $2,800; beginning inventory,
$5,900; net purchases, $6,800; ending inventory, $5,200; operating expenses,
$8,100.

Learning Unit 16–3: Trend and Ratio Analysis

Now that you understand the purpose of balance sheets and income statements, you are ready to study how experts look for various trends as they analyze the financial reports of companies. This learning unit discusses trend analysis and ratio analysis. The study of these trends is valuable to businesses, financial institutions, and consumers.

LO 1

Trend Analysis

Many tools are available to analyze financial reports. When data cover several years, we can analyze changes that occur by expressing each number as a percent of the base year. The base year is a past period of time that we use to compare sales, profits, and so on, with other years. We call this **trend analysis.**

Using the data below, we complete a trend analysis with the following steps:

COMPLETING A TREND ANALYSIS
Step 1. Select the base year (100%).
Step 2. Express each amount as a percent of the base year amount (rounded to the nearest whole percent).

GIVEN (BASE YEAR 2012)			
	2015	2014	2013	2012
Sales	$621,000	$460,000	$340,000	$420,000
Gross profit	182,000	141,000	112,000	124,000
Net income	48,000	41,000	22,000	38,000

TREND ANALYSIS			
	2015	2014	2013	2012
Sales	148%	110%	81%	100%
Gross profit	147	114	90	100
Net income	126	108	58	100

How to Calculate Trend Analysis

$$\frac{\text{Each item}}{\text{Base amount}} = \frac{\$340,000}{\$420,000}\overset{\text{Sales for 2013}}{\underset{\text{Sales for 2012}}{}} = 80.95\% = \boxed{81\%}$$

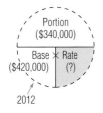

Portion
($340,000)

Base × Rate
($420,000)   (?)

2012

What Trend Analysis Means Sales of 2013 were 81% of the sales of 2012. Note that you would follow the same process no matter which of the three areas you were analyzing. All categories are compared to the base year—sales, gross profit, or net income.

We now will examine **ratio analysis**—another tool companies use to analyze performance.

Ratio Analysis

LO 2

A *ratio* is the relationship of one number to another. Many companies compare their ratios with those of previous years and with ratios of other companies in the industry. Companies can get ratios of the performance of other companies from their bankers, accountants, local small business centers, libraries, and newspaper articles. It is important to choose companies from similar industries when comparing ratios. For example, ratios at McDonald's will be different from ratios at Toys "R" Us. McDonald's sells more perishable products. Note in the following *Wall Street Journal* clip (p. 406) how Yahoo!'s revenue fell 5%. Ratios will be needed to find out why.

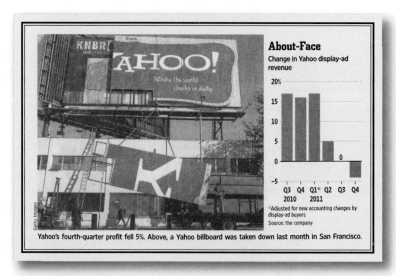

Yahoo's fourth-quarter profit fell 5%. Above, a Yahoo billboard was taken down last month in San Francisco.

Reprinted with permission of *The Wall Street Journal,* Copyright © 2012 Dow Jones & Company, Inc. All Rights Reserved Worldwide.

Percentage ratios are used by companies to determine the following:

1. How well the company manages its assets—*asset management ratios.*
2. The company's debt situation—*debt management ratios.*
3. The company's profitability picture—*profitability ratios.*

Each company must decide the true meaning of what the three types of ratios (asset management, debt management, and profitability) are saying. Table 16.1 (p. 407) gives a summary of the key ratios, their calculations (rounded to the nearest hundredth), and what they mean. All calculations are from Figures 16.1 (p. 394) and 16.4 (p. 401).

Now you can check your knowledge with the Practice Quiz that follows.

LU 16–3 **PRACTICE QUIZ**

Complete this **Practice Quiz** to see how you are doing.

1. Prepare a trend analysis from the following sales, assuming a base year of 2012. Round to the nearest whole percent.

	2015	**2014**	**2013**	**2012**
Sales	$29,000	$44,000	$48,000	$60,000

2. **Given** Total current assets (CA), $15,000; accounts receivable (AR), $6,000; total current liabilities (CL), $10,000; inventory (Inv), $4,000; net sales, $36,000; total assets, $30,000; net income (NI), $7,500.

   Calculate
   a. Current ratio.
   b. Acid test.
   c. Average day's collection.
   d. Profit margin on sales (rounded to the nearest hundredth percent).

For **extra help** from your authors–Sharon and Jeff–see the student DVD

You Tube™

✓ Solutions

		2015	**2014**	**2013**	**2012**
1.	Sales	48%	73%	80%	100%

$$\left(\frac{\$29,000}{\$60,000}\right) \quad \left(\frac{\$44,000}{\$60,000}\right) \quad \left(\frac{\$48,000}{\$60,000}\right)$$

2. a. $\dfrac{CA}{CL} = \dfrac{\$15,000}{\$10,000} = 1.5$

   b. $\dfrac{CA - Inv}{CL} = \dfrac{\$15,000 - \$4,000}{\$10,000} = 1.1$

   c. $\dfrac{AR}{\frac{Net\ sales}{360}} = \dfrac{\$6,000}{\frac{\$36,000}{360}} = 60\ days$

   d. $\dfrac{NI}{Net\ sales} = \dfrac{\$7,500}{\$36,000} = 20.83\%$

LU 16–3a EXTRA PRACTICE QUIZ WITH WORKED-OUT SOLUTIONS

Need more practice? Try this **Extra Practice Quiz** (check figures in the Interactive Chapter Organizer, p. 409). Worked-out Solutions can be found in Appendix B at end of text.

1. Prepare a trend analysis from the following sales, assuming a base year of 2012. Round to the nearest whole percent.

	2015	**2014**	**2013**	**2012**
Sales	$25,000	$60,000	$50,000	$70,000

2. **Given:** Total current assets (CA), $14,000; accounts receivable (AR), $5,500; total current liabilities (CL), $9,000; inventory (Inv), $3,900; net sales, $36,500; total assets, $32,000; net income (NI), $8,000. Calculate:

   a. Current ratio.

   b. Acid test.

   c. Average day's collection.

   d. Profit margin on sales (round to the nearest hundredth percent).

TABLE   16.1   Summary of key ratios: A reference guide*

Ratio	Formula	Actual calculations	What it says	Questions that could be raised
Current ratio[†]	Current assets / Current liabilities (Current assets include cash, accounts receivable, and marketable securities.)	$\dfrac{\$61,000}{\$92,000} = .66{:}1$ Industry average, 2 to 1	Business has 66¢ of current assets to meet each $1 of current debt.	Not enough current assets to pay off current liabilities. Industry standard is $2 for each $1 of current debt.
Acid test (quick ratio) Top of fraction often → referred to as *quick assets*	Current assets − Inventory − Prepaid expenses / Current liabilities (Inventory and prepaid expenses are excluded because it may not be easy to convert these to cash.)	$\dfrac{\$61,000 - \$30,000 - \$15,000}{\$92,000}$ $= .17{:}1$ Industry average, 1 to 1	Business has only 17¢ to cover each $1 of current debt. This calculation excludes inventory and prepaid expenses.	Same as above but more severe.
Average day's collection	Accounts receivable / $\dfrac{\text{Net sales}}{360}$	$\dfrac{\$9,000}{\frac{\$20,566}{360}} = 158 \text{ days}$ Industry average, 90–120 days	On the average, it takes 158 days to collect accounts receivable.	Could we speed up collection since industry average is 90–120 days?
Total debt to total assets	Total liabilities / Total assets	$\dfrac{\$150,000}{\$205,000} = 73.17\%$ Industry average, 50%–70%	For each $1 of assets, the company owes 73¢ in current and long-term debt.	73% is slightly higher than industry average.
Return on equity	Net income / Stockholders' equity	$\dfrac{\$6,316}{\$55,000} = 11.48\%$ Industry average, 15%–20%	For each $1 invested by the owner, a return of 11¢ results.	Could we get a higher return on money somewhere else?
Asset turnover	Net sales / Total assets	$\dfrac{\$20,566}{\$205,000} = 10¢$ Industry average, 3¢ to 8¢	For each $1 invested in assets, it returns 10¢ in sales.	Are assets being utilized efficiently?
Profit margin on net sales	Net income / Net sales	$\dfrac{\$6,316}{\$20,566} = 30.71\%$ Industry average, 25%–40%	For each $1 of sales, company produces 31¢ in profit.	Compared to competitors, are we showing enough profits versus our increased sales?

*Inventory turnover is discussed in Chapter 18.

[†]For example, Wal-Mart Stores, Inc., has a current ratio of 1.51.

INTERACTIVE CHAPTER ORGANIZER

Topic/procedure/formula	Examples	You try it*
Balance sheet		
Vertical analysis, p. 395 Process of relating each figure on a financial report (down the column) to a total figure.	Current assets $ 520 52% Plant and equipment 480 48 Total assets $1,000 100%	**Do vertical analysis** CA $ 400 ? P + E 600 ? Total assets $1,000 ?
Horizontal analysis, p. 396 Analyzing comparative financial reports shows rate and amount of change across columns item by item.	**2014** | **2013** | **Change** | **%** Cash, $5,000 | $4,000 | $1,000 | 25% ← ($1,000) ($4,000)	**Do horizontal analysis** | **2014** | **2013** | **Change** | **%** Cash | $8,000 | $2,000 | ? | ?
Income statement formulas (Horizontal and vertical analysis can also be done for income statements.)		
Net sales, p. 402 Gross _ Sales returns _ Sales sales and allowances discounts	$200 gross sales − 10 sales returns and allowances − 2 sales discounts $188 net sales	**Calculate net sales** Gross sales, $400 Sales returns and allowances, $20 Sales discount, $5
Cost of merchandise (goods) sold, p. 402 Beginning + Net − Ending inventory purchases inventory	$50 + $100 − $20 = $130 Beginning inventory + Net purchases − Ending inventory = Cost of merchandise (goods) sold	**Calculate cost of merchandise sold** Beginning inventory, $50 Net purchases, $200 Ending inventory, $20
Gross profit from sales, p. 403 Net sales − Cost of merchandise (goods) sold	$188 − $130 = $58 gross profit from sales Net sales − Cost of merchandise (goods) sold = Gross profit from sales	**Calculate gross profit** Net sales, $400 Cost of merchandise sold, $250
Net income, p. 403 Gross profit − Operating expenses	$58 − $28 = $30 Gross profit from sales − Operating expenses = Net income	**Calculate net income** Gross profit, $210 Operating expenses, $180
Trend analysis, p. 405 Each number expressed as a percent of the base year. Each item Base amount	2016 2015 2014 Sales $200 $300 $400 ←Base year 50% 75% 100% ($200/$400) ($300/$400)	**Prepare a trend analysis** 2016 2015 2014 $1,200 $800 $1,000 ←Base year
Ratios, pp. 405–407 Tools to interpret items on financial reports.	Use this example for calculating the following ratios: current assets, $30,000; accounts receivable, $12,000; total current liabilities, $20,000; inventory, $6,000; prepaid expenses, $2,000; net sales, $72,000; total assets, $60,000; net income, $15,000; total liabilities, $30,000.	**Use this example for calculating the following ratios:** Current assets, $40,000; Accounts receivable, $44,000; Total current liabilities, $160,000; Inventory, $2,000; Prepaid expenses, $3,000; Net sales, $60,000; Total assets, $70,000; Net income, $16,000; Total liabilities, $180,000.
Current ratio, p. 407 Current assets Current liabilities	$30,000/$20,000 = 1.5	Use the information from the example above.

(continues)

INTERACTIVE CHAPTER ORGANIZER

Topic/procedure/formula	Examples	You try it*
Acid test (quick ratio), p. 407 ⤴ Called quick assets $\dfrac{\text{Current assets} - \text{Inventory} - \text{Prepaid expenses}}{\text{Current liabilities}}$	$\dfrac{\$30,000 - \$6,000 - \$2,000}{\$20,000} = 1.1$	Use the information from the example on page 408.
Average day's collection, p. 407 $\dfrac{\text{Accounts receivable}}{\dfrac{\text{Net sales}}{360}}$	$\dfrac{\$12,000}{\dfrac{\$72,000}{360}} = 60 \text{ days}$	Use the information from the example on page 408.
Total debt to total assets, p. 407 $\dfrac{\text{Total liabilities}}{\text{Total assets}}$	$\dfrac{\$30,000}{\$60,000} = 50\%$	Use the information from the example on page 408.
Return on equity, p. 407 $\dfrac{\text{Net income}}{\text{Stockholders' equity (A - L)}}$	$\dfrac{\$15,000}{\$30,000} = 50\%$	Use the information from the example on page 408.
Asset turnover, p. 407 $\dfrac{\text{Net sales}}{\text{Total assets}}$	$\dfrac{\$72,000}{\$60,000} = 1.2$	Use the information from the example on page 408.
Profit margin on net sales, p. 407 $\dfrac{\text{Net income}}{\text{Net sales}}$	$\dfrac{\$15,000}{\$72,000} = .2083 = 20.83\%$	Use the information from the example on page 408.

KEY TERMS			

	Accounts payable, *p. 394*
	 Accounts receivable, *p. 394*
	 Acid test, *p. 407*
	 Assets, *p. 394*
	 Asset turnover, *p. 407*
	 Balance sheet, *p. 392*
	 Benefit corporation, *p. 393*
	 Capital, *p. 393*
	 Common stock, *p. 395*
	 Comparative statement, *p. 395*
	 Corporation, *p. 393*
	 Cost of merchandise (goods)
	   sold, *pp. 400, 401*
	 Current assets, *p. 394*
	 Current liabilities, *p. 394*
	 Current ratio, *p. 407*
	 Expenses, *p. 401*
		Gross profit from sales, *p. 401*
		 Gross sales, *p. 400*
		 Horizontal analysis, *p. 395*
		 Income statement, *p. 399*
		 Liabilities, *p. 394*
		 Long-term liabilities, *p. 395*
		 Merchandise inventory, *p. 394*
		 Mortgage note payable, *p. 395*
		 Net income, *p. 401*
		 Net purchases, *p. 401*
		 Net sales, *p. 400*
		 Operating expenses, *p. 401*
		 Owner's equity, *pp. 392, 395*
		 Partnership, *p. 393*
		 Plant and equipment, *p. 394*
		 Prepaid expenses, *p. 394*
		 Purchase discounts, *p. 401*
			Purchase returns and
			   allowances, *p. 400*
			 Purchases, *p. 400*
			 Quick assets, *p. 407*
			 Quick ratio, *p. 407*
			 Ratio analysis, *p. 405*
			 Retained earnings, *p. 395*
			 Return on equity, *p. 407*
			 Revenues, *p. 400*
			 Salaries payable, *p. 395*
			 Sales (not trade) discounts, *p. 400*
			 Sales returns and
			   allowances, *p. 400*
			 Sole proprietorship, *p. 393*
			 Stockholders' equity, *pp. 393, 395*
			 Trend analysis, *p. 405*
			 Vertical analysis, *p. 395*

| Check Figures for Extra Practice Quizzes with Page References. (Worked-out Solutions in Appendix B.) | LU 16–1a (p. 398)
 1. a. 21.11%; 25%
   b. 10.56%; 12.86%
   c. 8.89%; 7.86%
   d. 11.11%; 11.43%
 2. 45.45% | LU 16–2a (p. 404)
 1. a. $33,200
   b. $7,500
   c. $25,700
   d. $17,600 | LU 16–3a (p. 407)
 1. 36%; 86%; 71%; 100%
 2. a. 1.6
   b. 1.12
   c. 54.2
   d. 21.92% |

*Worked-out solutions are in Appendix B.

Critical Thinking Discussion Questions with Chapter Concept Check

1. What is the difference between current assets and plant and equipment? Do you think land should be allowed to depreciate?

2. What items make up stockholders' equity? Why might a person form a sole proprietorship instead of a corporation?

3. Explain the steps to complete a vertical or horizontal analysis relating to balance sheets. Why are the percents not summed vertically in horizontal analysis?

4. How do you calculate net sales, cost of merchandise (goods) sold, gross profit, and net income? Why do we need two separate figures for inventory in the cost of merchandise (goods) sold section?

5. Explain how to calculate the following: current ratios, acid test, average day's collection, total debt to assets, return on equity, asset turnover, and profit margin on net sales. How often do you think ratios should be calculated?

6. What is trend analysis? Explain how the portion formula assists in preparing a trend analysis.

7. In light of the economic crises of 2009, explain how companies such as GE are trying to gain market share and increase profit margins.

8. **Chapter Concept Check.** Consider the chapter opener and go online to look up the financial statement of Kellogg to see how it is doing. Use ratio analysis based on concepts presented in this chapter.

END-OF-CHAPTER PROBLEMS

Check figures for odd-numbered problems in Appendix C.   Name _____   Date _____

DRILL PROBLEMS

16–1. As the accountant for Ron's Donut Shop, prepare a December 31, 2015, balance sheet like that for The Card Shop (LU 16–1) from the following: cash, $40,000; accounts payable, $28,000; merchandise inventory, $14,000; Vic Sullivan, capital, $46,000; and equipment, $20,000.   *LU 16-1(1)*

16–2. From the following, prepare a classified balance sheet for Ranger Company as of December 31, 2015. Ending merchandise inventory was $4,000 for the year.   *LU 16-1(1)*

Cash	$6,000	Accounts payable	$1,800
Prepaid rent	1,600	Salaries payable	1,600
Prepaid insurance	4,000	Note payable (long term)	8,000
Office equipment (net)	5,000	J. Lowell, capital*	9,200

*What the owner supplies to the business. Replaces common stock and retained earnings section.

16–3. Complete a horizontal analysis for Brown Company, rounding percents to the nearest hundredth: *LU 16-1(2)*

eXcel

BROWN COMPANY Comparative Balance Sheet December 31, 2014 and 2015				
			INCREASE (DECREASE)	
	2015	2014	Amount	Percent
Assets				
Current assets:				
Cash	$ 15,750	$ 10,500		
Accounts receivable	18,000	13,500		
Merchandise inventory	18,750	22,500		
Prepaid advertising	54,000	45,000		
Total current assets	$106,500	$ 91,500		
Plant and equipment:				
Building (net)	$120,000	$126,000		
Land	90,000	90,000		
Total plant and equipment	$210,000	$216,000		
Total assets	$316,500	$307,500		
Liabilities				
Current liabilities:				
Accounts payable	$132,000	$120,000		
Salaries payable	22,500	18,000		
Total current liabilities	$154,500	$138,000		
Long-term liabilities:				
Mortgage note payable	99,000	87,000		
Total liabilities	$253,500	$225,000		
Owner's Equity				
J. Brown, capital	63,000	82,500		
Total liabilities and owner's equity	$316,500	$307,500		

16–4. Prepare an income statement for Munroe Sauce for the year ended December 31, 2015. Beginning inventory was $1,248. Ending inventory was $1,600. *LU 16-2(1)*

Sales	$34,900
Sales returns and allowances	1,092
Sales discount	1,152
Purchases	10,512
Purchase discounts	540
Depreciation expense	115
Salary expense	5,200
Insurance expense	2,600
Utilities expense	210
Plumbing expense	250
Rent expense	180

16–5. Assume this is a partial list of financial highlights from a Best Buy annual report:

	2013	**2012**
	(dollars in millions)	
Net sales	$37,580	$33,075
Earnings before taxes	2,231	1,283
Net earnings	1,318	891

Complete a horizontal and vertical analysis from the above information. Round to the nearest hundredth percent. *LU 16-2(2)*

16–6. From the French Instrument Corporation second-quarter report ended 2014, do a vertical analysis for the second quarter of 2014. *LU 16-2(2)*

FRENCH INSTRUMENT CORPORATION AND SUBSIDIARIES Consolidated Statements of Operation (Unaudited) (In thousands of dollars, except share data)			
	SECOND QUARTER		
	2014	**2013**	**Percent of net**
Net sales	$6,698	$6,951	
Cost of sales	4,089	4,462	
Gross margin	2,609	2,489	
Expenses:			
Selling, general and administrative	1,845	1,783	
Product development	175	165	
Interest expense	98	123	
Other (income), net	(172)	(99)	
Total expenses	1,946	1,972	
Income before income taxes	663	517	
Provision for income taxes	265	209	
Net income	$398	$308	
Net income per common share*	$.05	$.03	
Weighted average number of common shares and equivalents	6,673,673	6,624,184	

*Income per common share reflects the deduction of the preferred stock dividend from net income.
†Off due to rounding.

16–7. Complete the comparative income statement and balance sheet for Logic Company, rounding percents to the nearest hundredth: *LU 16-1(2), LU 16-2(2)*

LOGIC COMPANY Comparative Income Statement For Years Ended December 31, 2014 and 2015			INCREASE (DECREASE)	
	2015	2014	Amount	Percent
Gross sales	$19,000	$15,000		
Sales returns and allowances	1,000	100		
Net sales	$18,000	$14,900		
Cost of merchandise (goods) sold	12,000	9,000		
Gross profit	$ 6,000	$ 5,900		
Operating expenses:				
Depreciation	$ 700	$ 600		
Selling and administrative	2,200	2,000		
Research	550	500		
Miscellaneous	360	300		
Total operating expenses	$ 3,810	$ 3,400		
Income before interest and taxes	$ 2,190	$ 2,500		
Interest expense	560	500		
Income before taxes	$ 1,630	$ 2,000		
Provision for taxes	640	800		
Net income	$ 990	$ 1,200		

LOGIC COMPANY Comparative Balance Sheet December 31, 2014 and 2015	2015		2014	
	Amount	Percent	Amount	Percent
Assets				
Current assets:				
Cash	$12,000		$ 9,000	
Accounts receivable	16,500		12,500	
Merchandise inventory	8,500		14,000	
Prepaid expenses	24,000		10,000	
Total current assets	$61,000		$45,500	
Plant and equipment:				
Building (net)	$14,500		$11,000	
Land	13,500		9,000	
Total plant and equipment	$28,000		$20,000	
Total assets	$89,000		$65,500	
Liabilities				
Current liabilities:				
Accounts payable	$13,000		$ 7,000	
Salaries payable	7,000		5,000	
Total current liabilities	$20,000		$12,000	
Long-term liabilities:				
Mortgage note payable	22,000		20,500	
Total liabilities	$42,000		$32,500	
Stockholders' Equity				
Common stock	$21,000		$21,000	
Retained earnings	26,000		12,000	
Total stockholders' equity	$47,000		$33,000	
Total liabilities and stockholders' equity	$89,000		$65,500	

*Due to rounding.

From Problem 16–7, your supervisor has requested that you calculate the following ratios, rounded to the nearest hundredth: *LU 16-3(2)*

	2015	**2014**

16–8. Current ratio.

16–9. Acid test.

16–10. Average day's collection.

16–11. Asset turnover.

16–12. Total debt to total assets.

16–13. Net income (after tax) to the net sales.

16–14. Return on equity (after tax).

16–8.

16–9.

16–10.

16–11.

16–12.

16–13.

16–14.

WORD PROBLEMS

16–15. William Burris invested $100,000 in an Australian-based franchise, Rent Your Boxes, purchasing three territories in the *eXcel* Washington area. After finding out the company had gone bankrupt, he rallied 10 other franchisees to join him and created a new company, Rent Our Boxes. If Rent Our Boxes had net income of $38,902 with net sales of $286,585, what was its profit margin on net sales to the nearest hundredth percent? *LU 16-3(2)*

16–16. General Motors announced a quarterly profit of $472 million. In 2011, GM earned $7.6 billion—a 62% increase from 2010. Below is a portion of its balance sheet. Conduct a horizontal analysis of the following line items (rounding percent to nearest hundredth): *LU 16-1(2)*

	2011 (dollars in millions)	**2010 (dollars in millions)**	**Difference**	**% CHG**
Cash and cash equivalents	$ 15,499	$ 21,061		
Marketable securities	16,148	5,555		
Inventories	14,324	12,125		
Goodwill	1,278	1,265		
Total liabilities and equity	$144,603	$138,898		

16–17. Find the following ratios for Motorola Credit Corporation's annual report: **(a)** total debt to total assets, **(b)** return on

eXcel equity, **(c)** asset turnover (to nearest cent), and **(d)** profit margin on net sales. Round to the nearest hundredth percent. *LU 16-3(2)*

	(dollars in millions)
Net revenue (sales)	$ 265
Net earnings	147
Total assets	2,015
Total liabilities	1,768
Total stockholders' equity	427

16–18. Assume figures were presented for the past 5 years on merchandise sold at Chicago department and discount stores ($ million). Sales in 2016 were $3,154; in 2015, $3,414; in 2014, $3,208; in 2013, $3,152; and in 2012, $3,216. Using 2012 as the base year, complete a trend analysis. Round each percent to the nearest whole percent. *LU 16-3(1)*

16–19. Don Williams received a memo requesting that he complete a trend analysis of the following numbers using 2013 as the base year and rounding each percent to the nearest whole percent. Could you help Don with the request? *LU 16-3(1)*

	2016	2015	2014	2013
Sales	$340,000	$400,000	$420,000	$500,000
Gross profit	180,000	240,000	340,000	400,000
Net income	70,000	90,000	40,000	50,000

16–20. The French bank Société Générale reported that its profit fell 89% in the last quarter of 2011 due to the sovereign debt crisis

eXcel and economic turmoil. If its 2011 net income was 2.385 billion euros and its operating expenses totaled 17.0 billion euros, what was its gross profit? *LU 16-2(1)*

16–21. On January 1, Pete Rowe bought a ski chalet for $51,000. Pete is renting the chalet for $55 per night. He estimates he can rent the chalet for 190 nights. Pete's mortgage for principal and interest is $448 per month. Real estate tax on the chalet is $500 per year.

Pete estimates that his heating bill will run $60 per month. He expects his monthly electrical bill to be $20 per month. He pays $12 per month for cable television.

What is Pete's return on the initial investment for this year? Assume rentals drop by 30% and monthly bills for heat and electricity drop by 10% each month. What would be Pete's return on initial investment? Round to the nearest tenth percent as needed.   *LU 16-3(2)*

16–22. As the accountant for Tootsie Roll, you are asked to calculate the current ratio and the quick ratio for the following partial *eXcel* financial statement. Round to the nearest tenth.   *LU 16-3(2)*

Assets		Liabilities	
Current assets:		Current liabilities:	
Cash and cash equivalents	$ 4,224,190	Notes payable to banks	$ 672,221
Investments	32,533,769	Accounts payable	7,004,075
Accounts receivable, less allowances of		Dividends payable	576,607
$748,000 and $744,000	16,206,648	Accrued liabilities	9,826,534
Inventories:		Income taxes payable	4,471,429
Finished goods and work in progress	12,650,955		
Raw materials and supplies	10,275,858		
Prepaid expenses	2,037,710		

SUMMARY PRACTICE TEST You Tube™

Do you need help? The DVD has step-by-step worked-out solutions.

1. Given: Gross sales, $170,000; sales returns and allowances, $9,000; beginning inventory, $8,000; net purchases, $18,000; ending inventory, $5,000; and operating expenses, $56,000. Calculate **(a)** net sales, **(b)** cost of merchandise (goods) sold, **(c)** gross profit from sales, and **(d)** net income. *(pp. 402, 403) LU 16-2(1)*

2. Complete the following partial comparative balance sheet by filling in the total current assets and percent column; assume no plant and equipment (round to the nearest hundredth percent as needed). *(p. 396) LU 16-1(2)*

	Amount	Percent	Amount	Percent
Assets				
Current assets:				
Cash	$ 9,000		$ 8,000	
Accounts receivable	5,000		7,500	
Merchandise inventory	12,000		6,900	
Prepaid expenses	7,000		8,000	
Total current assets				

*Due to rounding.

3. Calculate the amount of increase or decrease and the percent change of each item, rounding to the nearest hundredth percent as needed. *(p. 396) LU 16-1(2)*

	2015	2014	Amount	Percent
Cash	$19,000	$ 8,000		
Land	70,000	30,000		
Accounts payable	21,000	10,000		

4. Complete a trend analysis for sales, rounding to the nearest whole percent and using 2013 as the base year. *(p. 405) LU 16-3(1)*

	2016	2015	2014	2013
Sales	$140,000	$350,000	$210,000	$190,000

5. From the following, prepare a balance sheet for True Corporation as of December 31, 2014. *(p. 394) LU 16-1(1)*

Building	$40,000	Mortgage note payable	$70,000
Merchandise inventory	12,000	Common stock	10,000
Cash	15,000	Retained earnings	37,000
Land	90,000	Accounts receivable	9,000
Accounts payable	50,000	Salaries payable	8,000
Prepaid rent	9,000		

6. Solve from the following facts, rounding to the nearest hundredth. *(p. 407) LU 16-3(2)*

Current assets	$14,000	Net sales	$40,000
Accounts receivable	$ 5,000	Total assets	$38,000
Current liabilities	$20,000	Net income	$10,100
Inventory	$ 4,000		

a. Current ratio

b. Acid test

c. Average day's collection

d. Asset turnover

e. Profit margin on sales

www.mhhe.com/
slater11e_vc

As a child, Jalem Getz, the CEO of BuyCostumes.com put little thought into his Halloween costumes. Now he thinks about costumes all year long.

Jalem Getz founded online business BuyCostumes in a warehouse in the Milwaukee suburbs in 1999 taking advantage of Wisconsin's central U.S. location and cheap rent. Getz used to dislike the lack of seasons in his native California. Now, he uses the extreme seasonality of the Halloween business to turn a big profit.

The company got its start as a brick-and-mortar retail business owned by Getz and partner Jon Majdoch. While still in their early 20s, the two began operating a chain of seasonal Halloween Express franchise stores, and then branched out into a couple of lamp and home accessory shops.

In 2001, the company changed its name to BuySeasons, Inc., to reflect its new broader focus. "Rather than just focus on one season, we target consumers in different seasons," said Jalem Getz. The BuyCostumes name is still in broad use.

Being an e-tailer means not having to open a retail space for just two months of the year, or stock other items. Money saved on storefronts goes to maintaining a stock of 10,000 Halloween items—100 times what most retailers carry for the season.

"Our selection sets us apart," Getz said. "A lot of customers are looking for something unique, by having that large selection we immediately build that additional goodwill."

The key to BuySeasons' success is limiting the choice of merchandise to items that can't readily be found in neighborhood stores. That means less price competition and higher margins for BuySeasons, which has been maintaining a 47.5 percent gross margin rate on the BuyCostumes.com site.

In July 2006, Liberty Media announced plans to acquire BuySeasons Inc. for an undisclosed sum. Getz will stay on as CEO.

BuyCostumes.com is the biggest online seller of costumes. It was ranked in October 2005 in Inc. magazine as the 75th–fastest growing U.S. private firm, with revenue of $17.6 million last year and three-year growth of 1,046 percent. Sales this year are expected to hit $25 million to $28 million, according to Getz.

Other online Halloween firms also predicted double-digit growth in 2005—according to a forecast by the National Retail Federation the entire industry would have a 5% gain, leading to a record $3.3 billion in sales for the entire industry.

BuySeasons' sales reached nearly $30 million in 2005, Getz said, up from $17.6 million in 2004. The company's sales are expected to post 50% annual growth over the next three years. The company bills itself as the world's largest Internet retailer of Halloween costumes and accessories.

Note: The following problems contain some data that has been created by the author.

PROBLEM 1

BuyCostumes.com is owned by BuySeasons, Inc., which also owns the Celebrate Express websites—BirthdayExpress.com, 1stWishes.com, and CostumeExpress.com. BuySeasons, Inc., is a wholly owned subsidiary of Liberty Media Corporation (LMC) and operates within the Liberty Interactive Group. Suppose LMC has the following balance sheet information (in millions):

	Current year	Prior year
Current assets	$3,914	$ 3,542
Non–current assets		
Total assets	$7,723	$10,792
Total liabilities	$2,472	$ 5,766
Total equity		
Total liabilities and equity	$7,723	$10,792

Fill in the blanks. Round to the nearest dollar and express in millions.

PROBLEM 2

Using the data from Problem 1, create a comparative balance sheet for these two years. Round to the nearest hundredth percent.

	Current year	Prior year
Current assets	$3,914	$ 3,542
Non–current assets	$3,809	$ 7,250
Total assets	$7,723	$10,792
Total liabilities	$2,472	$ 5,766
Total equity	$5,251	$ 5,026
Total liabilities and equity	$7,723	$10,792

PROBLEM 3

Imagine that the Interactive Group at Liberty Media Corporation had the following data (all figures are in millions):

Current assets	$3,379	Net income	$ 258
Current liabilities	$7,768	Net sales	$8,305
Stockholders' equity	$5,424	Cost of goods sold	$5,332

Calculate the gross profit from sales. Express your answer in millions.

PROBLEM 4

Using the data from Problem 3, calculate the current ratio. Round to the nearest hundredth.

PROBLEM 5

Again using the data from Problem 3, calculate the return on equity. Round to the nearest hundredth.

PROBLEM 6

Again using the data from Problem 3, calculate the profit margin on net sales. Round to the nearest hundredth.

PROBLEM 7

Suppose BuyCostumes.com sales were $93 million in 2012 and were projected to increase to $97 million in 2013. What percent increase would this represent? Round to the nearest hundredth percent.

PROBLEM 8

If BuyCostumes.com had 42% of the online Halloween market and its sales were $93 million, what would be the total size of this market? Round to the nearest million.

PROBLEM 9

BuyCostumes.com currently offers a 110% guarantee. Should you find the same costume for less, BuyCostumes.com will refund 110% of the difference in purchase price. Assuming you purchased the Avengers Captain America Classic Muscle Chest child costume for $39.98 from BuyCostumes.com and then found the same costume for $32.95 with tax and shipping included at another retailer, what refund would you receive using the price guarantee? Round to the nearest dollar.

Class Discussion With the rise in Internet shopping sites, it is becoming increasingly important for online retailers to find ways to differentiate themselves in the market. Check out BuyCostumes.com and one or two competitor sites and look for ways in which the company is setting itself apart from the competition. What ideas would you add for further differentiation in the market?

PROBLEM 1
Brew up some analysis!

Go to http://www.hoovers.com. Search for Starbucks Corporation. Click on the Financials link. Prepare a vertical analysis for the 3 years of balance sheets provided.

Discussion Questions

1. What might be included as part of Starbucks' assets?

2. How does this analysis assist you in evaluating the financials of Starbucks?

PROBLEM 2
Analysis with some pop!

Go to http://www.hoovers.com. Search for Coca-Cola Corporation. Click on the Financials link. The report includes information from the 3 most recent years. Perform a horizontal analysis using the income statement data of the current year compared to the previous year.

Discussion Questions

1. What does this analysis tell you about Coca-Cola's financial status?

2. How could you use this information in determining whether to invest in Coca-Cola?

PROBLEM 3
Building better ratios

Go to www.hoovers.com. Search for The Home Depot. Click on the Financials link. Calculate the current ratio and the total debt to total assets ratio for the 3 years of data provided. Are the ratios improving or deteriorating?

Discussion Questions

1. What can we learn about an organization by evaluating its current ratio?

2. What may be some of the specific debts for The Home Depot?

PROBLEM 4
What is trending?

Go to www.hoovers.com. Choose a company and view its annual financials. Print out the report and do a trend analysis of the balance sheet for the 3 years provided. Use the earliest year as the base for your calculations.

Discussion Questions

1. What does this trend analysis tell you about the company?

2. Should you perform such an analysis before investing in this company? Why or why not?

MY STORY Ken Proskie, Evanston, Illinois

Life After a Layoff

This environmental and occupational health and safety consultant was laid off at age 52. Instead of looking for another corporate job, he struck out on his own. AS TOLD TO LAUREN MUTHLER

HOW DID YOU LOSE YOUR JOB?
In April 2004, the company I worked for cut 1,400 jobs. I never thought that would happen to me because I was pretty successful.

WHAT DID YOU DO? I thought I would find another job right away, but that didn't happen, so I went to outplacement services. I took a seminar on how to start a business. Two weeks after that, my plan had completely changed. I had always considered being an independent consultant and decided I owed it to myself to try.

WAS IT A BIG FINANCIAL RISK?
My previous company had a generous severance package and my wife had a good insurance plan, so the risk was not immediate.

WHAT DID YOU NEED TO START OVER? I already had the qualifications, but I had to learn how to set up and run a business. I took a self-study course with modules on marketing, buying insurance and setting up accounting services. I read books on the subject. Then I called people on my contact list to see if they would hire me as a consultant. I went from doing nothing to being insanely busy in two to three years.

DO YOU PLAN TO EXPAND?
I won't hire employees because I am nearing retirement.

ARE YOU BETTER OFF NOW?
I pay myself roughly the same as I made before, but I'm able to put a lot more into my 401(k). At my old company, I could contribute up to $22,000 a year. Now, as both employer and employee, I can contribute up to $55,500 a year. I also set my own hours.

WHAT WAS YOUR TOUGHEST PROBLEM? Because of $10,000 in start-up costs and lack of initial business, I had no salary for a year and a half.

WHAT ADVICE WOULD YOU GIVE OTHERS? Keep a network. Talk to people who know how to run a business; they will help if you ask. Don't assume people know that you need help. If you think you know what you are doing and you have the passion for it, do it. I wish I had gone out on my own sooner so that I could have made my company into a bigger and more successful enterprise. I would never go back to a corporation. ■

■ KEN PROSKIE'S NEW CAREER ALLOWS HIM TO SAVE MORE FOR HIS RETIREMENT, WORK FROM HOME, SET HIS OWN HOURS AND WALK HIS DOG AT LUNCH. HERE, HE CHECKS AIR QUALITY.

BUSINESS MATH ISSUE

Technology today makes starting a business a much more financially safe option than a few years ago.

1. List the key points of the article and information to support your position.
2. Write a group defense of your position using math calculations to support your view.

CHAPTER 17

Depreciation

What You Need To Know About **Depreciation...**

Depreciation is the amount something decreases in value over time. Although it's a very real cost, depreciation is tricky because you don't get a monthly bill for it. Cars are a unique consumer good because ending value is an important consideration - most people intend to sell their cars eventually and not simply dispose of them. Let's assume you purchase a car for $20,000. If you sell it five years later for $8,000, you will have incurred $12,000 in depreciation costs over the ownership period. Depreciation is in fact the largest ownership cost over time.

Average Depreciation as % of MSRP

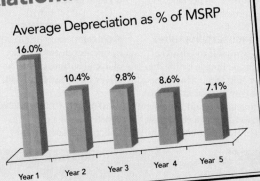

16.0%	10.4%	9.8%	8.6%	7.1%
Year 1	Year 2	Year 3	Year 4	Year 5

IntelliChoice.com

LU 17–1: Concept of Depreciation and the Straight-Line Method

1. Explain the concept and causes of depreciation (pp. 425–426).

2. Prepare a depreciation schedule and calculate partial-year depreciation (pp. 426–427).

LU 17–2: Units-of-Production Method

1. Explain how use affects the units-of-production method (p. 428).

2. Prepare a depreciation schedule (p. 428).

LU 17–3: Declining-Balance Method

1. Explain the importance of residual value in the depreciation schedule (p. 429).

2. Prepare a depreciation schedule (pp. 429–430).

LU 17–4: Modified Accelerated Cost Recovery System (MACRS) with Introduction to ACRS (1986, 1989, 2010)

1. Explain the goals of ACRS and MACRS and their limitations (p. 431).

2. Calculate depreciation using the MACRS guidelines (p. 432).

Here are key terms in this chapter. After completing the chapter, if you know the term, place a checkmark in the parentheses. If you don't know the term, look it up and put the page number where it can be found.

Accelerated Cost Recovery System (ACRS) ( ) **Accelerated depreciation** ( ) **Accumulated depreciation** ( )
Asset cost ( ) **Book value** ( ) **Declining-balance method** ( ) **Depreciation** ( ) **Depreciation expense** ( )
Depreciation schedule ( ) **Estimated useful life** ( ) **General Depreciation System (GDS)** ( ) **Modified**
Accelerated Cost Recovery System (MACRS) ( ) **Residual value** ( ) **Salvage value** ( ) **Straight-line**
method ( ) **Straight-line rate** ( ) **Trade-in value** ( ) **Units-of-production method** ( )

This chapter concentrates on depreciation—a business operating expense. You can see from the chapter opener that the average depreciation of a car in year 3 is 9.8% of the manufacturer's suggested retail price. In Learning Units 17–1 to 17–3, we discuss methods of calculating depreciation for financial reporting. In Learning Unit 17–4, we look at how tax laws force companies to report depreciation for tax purposes. Financial reporting methods and the tax-reporting methods are both legal.

Learning Unit 17–1: Concept of Depreciation and the Straight-Line Method

LO 1

Companies frequently buy assets such as equipment or buildings that will last longer than 1 year. As time passes, these assets depreciate, or lose some of their market value. The total cost of these assets cannot be shown in *1 year* as an expense of running the business. In a systematic and logical way, companies must estimate the asset cost they show as an expense of a particular period. This process is called **depreciation.** The next time you fly in a plane think how the airline will depreciate the cost of that plane over a number of years.

Remember that depreciation *does not* measure the amount of deterioration or decline in the market value of the asset. Depreciation is simply a means of recognizing that these assets are depreciating.

The depreciation process results in **depreciation expense** that involves three key factors: (1) **asset cost**—amount the company paid for the asset including freight and charges

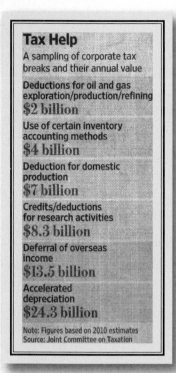

relating to the asset; (2) **estimated useful life**—number of years or time periods for which the company can use the asset; and (3) **residual value (salvage** or **trade-in value)**—expected cash value at the end of the asset's useful life.

Depreciation expense is listed on the income statement. The **accumulated depreciation** title on the balance sheet gives the amount of the asset's depreciation taken to date. Asset cost less accumulated depreciation is the asset's book value. The **book value** shows the unused amount of the asset cost that the company may depreciate in future accounting periods. At the end of the asset's life, the asset's book value is the same as its residual value—book value cannot be less than residual value.

Depending on the amount and timetable of an asset's depreciation, a company can increase or decrease its profit. If a company shows greater depreciation in earlier years, the company will have a lower reported profit and pay less in taxes. Thus, depreciation can be an indirect tax savings for the company. The *Wall Street Journal* clip "Tax Help" shows a savings of over $24.3 billion in tax breaks related to depreciation.

Later in the chapter we will discuss the different methods of computing depreciation that spread the cost of an asset over specified periods of time. However, first let's look at some of the major causes of depreciation.

Causes of Depreciation

As assets, all machines have an estimated amount of usefulness simply because as companies use the assets, the assets gradually wear out. The cause of this depreciation is *physical deterioration.*

The growth of a company can also cause depreciation. Many companies begin on a small scale. As the companies grow, they often find their equipment and buildings inadequate. The use of depreciation enables these businesses to "write off" their old, inadequate equipment and buildings. Companies cannot depreciate land. For example, a garbage dump can be depreciated but not the land.

Another cause of depreciation is the result of advances in technology. The computers that companies bought a few years ago may be in perfect working condition but outdated. Companies may find it necessary to replace these old computers with more sophisticated, faster, and possibly more economical machines. Thus, *product obsolescence* is a key factor contributing to depreciation.

Now we are ready to begin our study of depreciation methods. The first method we will study is straight-line depreciation. It is also the most common of the three depreciation methods (straight line, units of production, and declining balance). In a survey of 600 corporations, 81% responded that they used straight-line depreciation.

Straight-Line Method

The **straight-line method** of depreciation is used more than any other method. It tries to distribute the same amount of expense to each period of time. Most large companies, such as Gillette Corporation, Southwest Airlines, Campbell's Soup, and General Mills use the straight-line method. *Today, more than 90% of U.S. companies depreciate by straight line.* For example, let's assume Ajax Company bought equipment for $2,500. The company estimates that the equipment's period of "usefulness"—or *useful life*—will be 5 years. After 5 years the equipment will have a residual value (salvage value) of $500. The company decides to calculate its depreciation with the straight-line method and uses the following formula:

$$\frac{\text{Depreciation expense}}{\text{each year}} = \frac{\text{Cost} - \text{Residual value}}{\text{Estimated useful life in years}}$$

$$\frac{\$2,500 - \$500}{5 \text{ years}} = \$400 \text{ depreciation expense taken each year}$$

LO 2

Table 17.1 (p. 427) gives a summary of the equipment depreciation that Ajax Company will take over the next 5 years. Companies call this summary a **depreciation schedule.** A corporation like Southwest Airlines depreciates its flight equipment 20 to 25 years.

TABLE 17.1

Depreciation schedule for straight-line method

$$\frac{100\%}{\text{Number of years}} = \frac{100\%}{5} = 20\%$$

Thus, the company is depreciating the equipment at a 20% rate each year.

End of year	Depreciation cost of equipment	Depreciation expense for year	Accumulated depreciation at end of year	Book value at end of year (Cost − Depreciation at end of year)
1	$2,500	$400	$ 400	$2,100 ($2,500 − $400)
2	2,500	400	800	1,700
3	2,500	400	1,200	1,300
4	2,500	400	1,600	900
5	2,500	400	2,000	500
	↑ Cost stays the same.	↑ Depreciation expense is same each year.	↑ Accumulated depreciation increases by $400 each year.	↑ Book value is lowered by $400 until residual value of $500 is reached.

MONEY tips

Do not open several credit card accounts in a short period of time. Doing so negatively affects your credit rating if you are trying to buy or refinance a home.

Depreciation for Partial Years

If a company buys an asset before the 15th of the month, the company calculates the asset's depreciation for a full month. Companies do not take the full month's depreciation for assets bought after the 15th of the month. For example, assume Ajax Company (Table 17.1) bought the equipment on May 6. The company would calculate the depreciation for the first year as follows:

$$\frac{\$2,500 - \$500}{5 \text{ years}} = \$400 \times \frac{8}{12} = \$266.67$$

Now let's check your progress with the Practice Quiz before we look at the next depreciation method.

LU 17–1	PRACTICE QUIZ

Complete this **Practice Quiz** to see how you are doing.

*For **extra help** from your authors—Sharon and Jeff–see the student DVD*

You Tube™

1. Prepare a depreciation schedule using straight-line depreciation for the following:

   Cost of truck $16,000
   Residual value $ 1,000
   Life   5 years

2. If the truck were bought on February 3, what would the depreciation expense be in the first year?

✓ Solutions

1.

End of year	Cost of truck	Depreciation expense for year	Accumulated depreciation at end of year	Book value at end of year (Cost − Accumulated depreciation)
1	$16,000	$3,000	$ 3,000	$13,000 ($16,000 − $3,000)
2	16,000	3,000	6,000	10,000
3	16,000	3,000	9,000	7,000
4	16,000	3,000	12,000	4,000
5	16,000	3,000	15,000	1,000 ← Note that we are down to residual value

2. $$\frac{\$16,000 - \$1,000}{5} = \$3,000 \times \frac{11}{12} = \boxed{\$2,750}$$

Need more practice? Try this **Extra Practice Quiz** (check figures in the Interactive Chapter Organizer, p. 434). Worked-out Solutions can be found in Appendix B at end of text.

1. Prepare a depreciation schedule using straight-line depreciation for the following:

   Cost of truck $20,000
   Residual value $ 2,000
   Life   3 years

2. If the truck were bought on February 3, what would the depreciation expense be in the first year?

Learning Unit 17–2: Units-of-Production Method

LO 1

Unlike in the straight-line depreciation method, in the **units-of-production method** the passage of time is not used to determine an asset's depreciation amount. Instead, the company determines the asset's depreciation according to how much the company uses the asset. This use could be miles driven, tons hauled, or units that a machine produces. For example, when a company such as Ajax Company (in Learning Unit 17–1) buys equipment, the company estimates how many units the equipment can produce. Let's assume the equipment has a useful life of 4,000 units. The following formulas are used to calculate the equipment's depreciation for the units-of-production method.

MONEY tips

Unplug electronics when they are not in use. It will save their lifespan and your energy consumption.

$$\frac{\text{Depreciation}}{\text{per unit}} = \frac{\text{Cost} - \text{Residual value}}{\text{Total estimated units produced}} = \frac{\$2,500 - \$500}{4,000 \text{ units}} = \$.50 \text{ per unit}$$

$$\frac{\text{Depreciation}}{\text{amount}} = \frac{\text{Unit}}{\text{depreciation}} \times \frac{\text{Units}}{\text{produced}} = \$.50 \text{ times actual number of units}$$

Now we can complete Table 17.2. Note that the table gives the units produced each year.

TABLE 17.2 Depreciation schedule for units-of-production method

End of year	Cost of equipment	Units produced	Depreciation expense for year	Accumulated depreciation at end of year	Book value at end of year (Cost − Accumulated depreciation)
1	$2,500	300	$ 150 (300 × $.50)	$ 150	$2,350 ($2,500 − $150)
2	2,500	400	200	350	2,150
3	2,500	600	300	650	1,850
4	2,500	2,000	1,000	1,650	850
5	2,500	700	350	2,000	500

At the end of 5 years, the equipment produced 4,000 units. If in year 5 the equipment produced 1,500 units, only 700 could be used in the calculation, or it will go below the equipment's residual value.

Units produced per year times $.50 equals depreciation expense.

Residual value of $500 is reached. (Be sure depreciation is not taken below the residual value.)

LO 2

Let's check your understanding of this unit with the Practice Quiz.

LU 17-2 | **PRACTICE QUIZ**

Complete this **Practice Quiz** to see how you are doing.

$$\frac{\$20,000 - \$4,000}{16,000} = \$1$$

For **extra help** from your authors–Sharon and Jeff–see the student DVD

You **Tube**

From the following facts prepare a depreciation schedule:

Machine cost $20,000
Residual value $ 4,000

Expected to produce 16,000 units over its expected life

	2012	**2013**	**2014**	**2015**	**2016**
Units produced:	2,000	8,000	3,000	1,800	1,600

✓ **Solutions**

End of year	Cost of machine	Units produced	Depreciation expense for year	Accumulated depreciation at end of year	Book value at end of year (Cost − Accumulated depreciation)
1	$20,000	2,000	$2,000 (2,000 × $1)	$ 2,000	$18,000
2	20,000	8,000	8,000	10,000	10,000
3	20,000	3,000	3,000	13,000	7,000
4	20,000	1,800	1,800	14,800	5,200
5	20,000	1,600	1,200*	16,000	4,000

*Note that we can depreciate only 1,200 units since we cannot go below the residual value of $4,000.

LU 17-2a | **EXTRA PRACTICE QUIZ WITH WORKED-OUT SOLUTIONS**

Need more practice? Try this **Extra Practice Quiz** (check figures in the Interactive Chapter Organizer, p. 434). Worked-out Solutions can be found in Appendix B at end of text.

From the following facts prepare a depreciation expense:

Machine cost $30,000
Residual value $ 2,000

Expected to produce 56,000 units over its expected life

	2012	**2013**	**2014**	**2015**	**2016**
Units produced	1,000	6,000	4,000	2,000	2,500

Learning Unit 17–3: Declining-Balance Method

In the declining-balance method, we cannot depreciate below the residual value.

LO 1

LO 2

MONEY tips

Do you have enough money? Before purchasing or adopting a pet, estimate the annual cost of caring for it to determine whether you can afford it.

The **declining-balance method** is another type of **accelerated depreciation** that takes larger amounts of depreciation expense in the earlier years of the asset. The straight-line method, you recall, estimates the life of the asset and distributes the same amount of depreciation expense to each period. To take larger amounts of depreciation expense in the asset's earlier years, the declining-balance method uses up to *twice* the **straight-line rate** in the first year of depreciation. A key point to remember is that the declining-balance method does not deduct the residual value in calculating the depreciation expense. Today, the declining-balance method is the basis of current tax depreciation.

For all problems, we will use double the straight-line rate unless we indicate otherwise. Today, the rate is often 1.5 or 1.25 times the straight-line rate. Again we use our $2,500 equipment with its estimated useful life of 5 years. As we build the depreciation schedule in Table 17.3 (p. 430), note the following steps:

Step 1. Rate is equal to $\frac{100\%}{5 \text{ years}} \times 2 = 40\%$.

Or another way to look at it is that the straight-line rate is $\frac{1}{5} \times 2 = \frac{2}{5} = 40\%$.

Step 2.

Depreciation expense each year	=	Book value of equipment at beginning of year	×	Depreciation rate

| TABLE | 17.3 | Depreciation schedule for declining-balance method |

End of year	Cost of equipment	Accumulated depreciation at beginning of year	Book value at beginning of year (Cost − Accumulated depreciation)	Depreciation (Book value at beginning of year × Rate)	Accumulated depreciation at end of year	Book value at end of year (Cost − Accumulated depreciation)
1	$2,500	—	$2,500	$1,000 ($2,500 × .40)	$1,000	$1,500 ($2,500 − $1,000)
2	2,500	$1,000	1,500	600 ($1,500 × .40)	1,600	900
3	2,500	1,600	900	360 ($900 × .40)	1,960	540
4	2,500	1,960	540	40	2,000	500
5	2,500	2,000	500	—	2,000	500
	↑ Original cost of $2,500 does not change. Residual value was not subtracted.	↑ Ending accumulated depreciation of 1 year becomes next year's beginning.	↑ Cost less accumulated depreciation	↑ Note: In year 4, only $40 is taken since we cannot depreciate below residual value of $500. In year 5, no depreciation is taken.	↑ Accumulated depreciation balance plus depreciation expense this year.	↑ Book value now equals residual value.

Step 3. We cannot depreciate the equipment below its residual value ($500). The straight-line method automatically reduced the asset's book value to the residual value. This is not true with the declining-balance method. So you must be careful when you prepare the depreciation schedule.

Now let's check your progress again with another Practice Quiz.

| LU 17–3 | PRACTICE QUIZ |

Complete this **Practice Quiz** to see how you are doing.

*For **extra help** from your authors—Sharon and Jeff—see the student DVD*

You Tube™

Prepare a depreciation schedule from the following:

Cost of machine: $16,000
Rate: 40% (this is twice the straight-line rate)

Estimated life: 5 years
Residual value: $1,000

✓ **Solutions**

End of year	Cost of machine	Accumulated depreciation at beginning of year	Book value at beginning of year (Cost − Accumulated depreciation)	Depreciation (Book value at beginning of year × Rate)	Accumulated depreciation at end of year	Book value at end of year (Cost − Accumulated depreciation)
1	$16,000	$ –0–	$16,000.00	$6,400.00	$ 6,400.00	$9,600.00
2	16,000	6,400.00	9,600.00	3,840.00	10,240.00	5,760.00
3	16,000	10,240.00	5,760.00	2,304.00	12,544.00	3,456.00
4	16,000	12,544.00	3,456.00	1,382.40	13,926.40	2,073.60
5	16,000	13,926.40	2,073.60	829.44*	14,755.84	1,244.16

*Since we do not reach the residual value of $1,000, another $244.16 could have been taken as depreciation expense to bring it to the estimated residual value of $1,000.

LU 17–3a EXTRA PRACTICE QUIZ WITH WORKED-OUT SOLUTIONS

Need more practice? Try this **Extra Practice Quiz** (check figures in the Interactive Chapter Organizer, p. 434). Worked-out Solutions can be found in Appendix B at end of text.

Prepare a depreciation schedule for three years for the following:

Cost of machine: $31,000   Estimated life: 5 years
Rate: 40% (this is twice the straight-line rate)   Residual value: $1,000

Learning Unit 17–4: Modified Accelerated Cost Recovery System (MACRS) with Introduction to ACRS (1986, 1989, 2010)

© Royalty-Free/Corbis

LO 1

In Learning Units 17–1 to 17–3, we discussed the depreciation methods used for financial reporting. Since 1981, federal tax laws have been passed that state how depreciation must be taken for income tax purposes. Assets put in service from 1981 through 1986 fell under the federal **Accelerated Cost Recovery System (ACRS)** tax law enacted in 1981. The Tax Reform Act of 1986 established the **Modified Accelerated Cost Recovery System (MACRS)** for all property placed into service after December 31, 1986. This system, used by businesses to calculate depreciation for tax purposes based on the tax laws of 1986, 1989, and 2010, is also known as the **General Depreciation System (GDS)**. For the latest updates, go to www.irs.gov/form4562.

Depreciation for Tax Purposes Based on the Tax Reform Act of 1986 (MACRS)

Tables 17.4 and 17.5 (p. 432) give the classes of recovery and annual depreciation percentages that MACRS established in 1986. The key points of MACRS are:

1. It calculates depreciation for tax purposes.

2. It ignores residual value.

3. Depreciation in the first year (for personal property) is based on the assumption that the asset was purchased halfway through the year. (A new law adds a midquarter convention for all personal property if more than 40% is placed in service during the last 3 months of the taxable year.)

4. Classes 3, 5, 7, and 10 use a 200% declining-balance method for a period of years before switching to straight-line depreciation. You do not have to determine the year in which to switch since Table 17.5 builds this into the calculation.

5. Classes 15 and 20 use a 150% declining-balance method before switching to straight-line depreciation.

6. Classes 27.5 and 31.5 use straight-line depreciation.

TABLE 17.4

Modified Accelerated Cost Recovery System (MACRS) for assets placed in service after December 31, 1986

Class recovery period (life)	Asset types
3-year*	Racehorses more than 2 years old or any horse other than a racehorse that is more than 12 years old at the time placed into service; special tools of certain industries.
5-year*	Automobiles (not luxury); taxis; light general-purpose trucks; semiconductor manufacturing equipment; computer-based telephone central-office switching equipment; qualified technological equipment; property used in connection with research and experimentation.
7-year*	Railroad track; single-purpose agricultural (pigpens) or horticultural structures; fixtures; equipment; furniture.
10-year*	New law doesn't add any specific property under this class.
15-year†	Municipal wastewater treatment plants; telephone distribution plants and comparable equipment used for two-way exchange of voice and data communications.
20-year†	Municipal sewers.
27.5-year‡	Only residential rental property.
31.5-year‡	Only nonresidential real property.

*These classes use a 200% declining-balance method switching to the straight-line method.
†These classes use a 150% declining-balance method switching to the straight-line method.
‡These classes use a straight-line method.

TABLE	17.5	Annual recovery for MACRS

Recovery year	3-year class (200% D.B.)	5-year class (200% D.B.)	7-year class (200% D.B.)	10-year class (200% D.B.)	15-year class (150% D.B.)	20-year class (150% D.B.)
1	33.00	20.00	14.28	10.00	5.00	3.75
2	45.00	32.00	24.49	18.00	9.50	7.22
3	15.00*	19.20	17.49	14.40	8.55	6.68
4	7.00	11.52*	12.49	11.52	7.69	6.18
5		11.52	8.93*	9.22	6.93	5.71
6		5.76	8.93	7.37	6.23	5.28
7			8.93	6.55*	5.90*	4.89
8			4.46	6.55	5.90	4.52
9				6.55	5.90	4.46*
10				6.55	5.90	4.46
11				3.29	5.90	4.46
12					5.90	4.46
13					5.90	4.46
14					5.90	4.46
15					5.90	4.46
16					3.00	4.46

*Identifies when switch is made to straight line.

LO 2

EXAMPLE Using the same equipment cost of $2,500 for Ajax, prepare a depreciation schedule under MACRS assuming the equipment is a 5-year class and not part of the tax bill of 1989. Use Table 17.5. Note that percent figures from Table 17.5 have been converted to decimals.

MONEY tips

Consider refinancing your home to obtain a lower fixed interest rate. Determine whether your savings offset the refinance costs. A rate reduction of 1.5% is generally worth the cost.

End of year	Cost	Depreciation expense	Accumulated depreciation	Book value at end of year
1	$2,500	$500 (.20 × $2,500)	$ 500	$2,000
2	2,500	800 (.32 × $2,500)	1,300	1,200
3	2,500	480 (.1920 × $2,500)	1,780	720
4	2,500	288 (.1152 × $2,500)	2,068	432
5	2,500	288 (.1152 × $2,500)	2,356	144
6	2,500	144 (.0576 × $2,500)	2,500	–0–

LU 17–4 PRACTICE QUIZ

Complete this **Practice Quiz** to see how you are doing.

1. In 1991, Rancho Corporation bought semiconductor equipment for $80,000. Using MACRS, what is the depreciation expense in year 3?
2. What would depreciation be the first year for a wastewater treatment plant that cost $800,000?

✓ **Solutions**

1. $80,000 × .1920 = $15,360   2. $800,000 × .05 = $40,000

For **extra help** from your authors–Sharon and Jeff–see the student DVD

Need more practice? Try this **Extra Practice Quiz** (check figures in the Interactive Chapter Organizer, p. 434). Worked-out Solutions can be found in Appendix B at end of text.

1. In 1991, Rancho Corporation bought semiconductor equipment for $90,000. Using MACRS, what is the depreciation expense in year 3?

2. What would depreciation be the first year for a wastewater treatment plant that cost $900,000?

INTERACTIVE CHAPTER ORGANIZER

Topic/procedure/formula	Examples	You try it*
Straight-line method, pp. 426–427 $$\text{Depreciation expense each year} = \frac{\text{Cost} - \text{Residual value}}{\text{Estimated useful life in years}}$$ For partial years if purchased before 15th of month depreciation is taken.	Truck, $25,000; $5,000 residual value, 4-year life. $$\text{Depreciation expense} = \frac{\$25,000 - \$5,000}{4}$$ $$= \boxed{\$5,000} \text{ per year}$$	**Calculate depreciation expense** Truck, $50,000; $10,000 residual value; 4-year life.
Units-of-production method, p. 428 $$\text{Depreciation per unit} = \frac{\text{Cost} - \text{Residual value}}{\text{Total estimated units produced}}$$ Do not depreciate below residual value even if actual units are greater than estimate.	Machine, $5,000; estimated life in units, 900; residual value, $500. Assume first year produced 175 units. $$\text{Depreciation expense} = \frac{\$5,000 - \$500}{900}$$ $$= \frac{\$4,500}{900}$$ $$= \$5 \text{ depreciation per unit}$$ 175 units $\times$ $5 = $\boxed{\$875}$ depreciation expense	**Calculate depreciation expense** Machine, $4,000; estimated life in units, 700; residual value, $500. Assume first year produced 150 units.
Declining-balance method, pp. 429–430 An accelerated method. Residual value not subtracted from cost in depreciation schedule. Do not depreciate below residual value. $$\begin{array}{c}\text{Depreciation} \\ \text{expense} \\ \text{each year}\end{array} = \begin{array}{c}\text{Book} \\ \text{value of} \\ \text{equipment} \\ \text{at beginning} \\ \text{of year}\end{array} \times \begin{array}{c}\text{Depreciation} \\ \text{rate}\end{array}$$	Truck, $50,000; estimated life, 5 years; residual value, $10,000. $\frac{1}{5} = 20\% \times 2 = 40\%$ (assume double the straight-line rate) 	Year	Cost	Depreciation expense	Book value at end of year	 |---|---|---|---| 	1	$50,000	$20,000 ($50,000 × .40)	$30,000 ($50,000 − $20,000)	 	2	$50,000	$12,000 ($30,000 × .40)	$18,000 ($50,000 − $32,000)		**Calculate depreciation expense and book value for 2 years** Truck, $40,000; estimated life, 4 years; residual value, $5,000.

(continues)

INTERACTIVE CHAPTER ORGANIZER

Topic/procedure/formula	Examples	You try it*
MACRS/Tax Bill of 1989, 2010, p. 432 After December 31, 1986, depreciation calculation is modified. Tax Act of 1989, 2010, modifies way to depreciate equipment.	Auto: $8,000, 5 years. First year, .20 × $8,000 = $1,600 depreciation expense	Auto: $7,000, 5 years. Second year = ? depreciation expense

KEY TERMS	Accelerated Cost Recovery System (ACRS), p. 431 Accelerated depreciation, p. 429 Accumulated depreciation, p. 426 Asset cost, p. 425 Book value, p. 426 Declining-balance method, p. 429 Depreciation, p. 425	Depreciation expense, p. 425 Depreciation schedule, p. 426 Estimated useful life, p. 426 General Depreciation System (GDS), p. 431 Modified Accelerated Cost Recovery System (MACRS), p. 431	Residual value, p. 426 Salvage value, p. 426 Straight-line method, p. 426 Straight-line rate, p. 429 Trade-in value, p. 426 Units-of-production method, p. 428

Check Figures for Extra Practice Quizzes with Page References. (Worked-out Solutions in Appendix B.)	LU 17–1a (p. 428) 1. Book value EOY 3 $2,000 2. $5,500	LU 17–2a (p. 429) $.50; Book value EOY 5 $22,250	LU 17–3a (p. 431) *Depreciation expense year* 1. $12,400 2. $7,440 3. 4,464	LU 17–4a (p. 433) 1. $17,280 2. $45,000

*Worked-out solutions are in Appendix B.

Critical Thinking Discussion Questions with Chapter Concept Check

1. What is the difference between depreciation expense and accumulated depreciation? Why does the book value of an asset never go below the residual value?

2. Compare the straight-line method to the units-of-production method. Should both methods be based on the passage of time?

3. Why is it possible in the declining-balance method for a person to depreciate below the residual value by mistake?

4. Explain the Modified Accelerated Cost Recovery System. Do you think this system will be eliminated in the future?

5. **Chapter Concept Check.** Considering the chapter opener, search the web for a car of your choice and use concepts from this chapter to provide a depreciation schedule for the car.

END-OF-CHAPTER PROBLEMS

Check figures for odd-numbered problems in Appendix C.   Name _____   Date _____

DRILL PROBLEMS

From the following facts, complete a depreciation schedule by using the straight-line method: *LU 17-1(2)*

Given   Cost of Toyota Hybrid Highlander $30,000
Residual value $ 6,000
Estimated life   8 years

End of year	Cost of Highlander	Depreciation expense for year	Accumulated depreciation at end of year	Book value at end of year
17–1.				
17–2.				
17–3.				
17–4.				
17–5.				
17–6.				
17–7.				
17–8.				

From the following facts, prepare a depreciation schedule using the declining-balance method (twice the straight-line rate): *LU 17-3(2)*

Given   Volvo truck $25,000
Residual value $ 5,000
Estimated life   5 years

End of year	Cost of truck	Accumulated depreciation at beginning of year	Book value at beginning of year	Depreciation expense for year	Accumulated depreciation at end of year	Book value at end of year
17–9.						
17–10.						
17–11.						
17–12.						

For the first 2 years, calculate the depreciation expense for a $7,000 car under MACRS. This is a nonluxury car. *LU 17-4(2)*

MACRS	**MACRS**
17–13. Year 1	**17–14.** Year 2

Complete the following table given this information:

Cost of machine $94,000   Estimated units machine will produce   100,000
Residual value $ 4,000   Actual production: **Year 1   Year 2**
Useful life   5 years   60,000   15,000

	Depreciation Expense	
Method	Year 1	Year 2
17–15. Straight line *LU 17-1(2)*		
17–16. Units of production *LU 17-2(2)*		
17–17. Declining balance *LU 17-3(2)*		
17–18. MACRS (5-year class) *LU 17-4(2)*		

WORD PROBLEMS

17–19. Two strong months of manufacturing growth coupled with a decline in the unemployment rate are encouraging signs for the U.S. economy in the early months of 2012. Shearer's Foods, part of the $2.6 billion snack food industry, employs 1,100 people in Brewster, Ohio. If Shearer's purchased a packaging unit for $185,000 with a life expectancy of 695,000 units and a residual value of $46,000, what is the depreciation expense for year 1 if 75,000 units were produced? *LU 17-2(2)*

17–20. Lena Horn bought a Toyota Tundra on January 1 for $30,000 with an estimated life of 5 years. The residual value of the truck **eXcel** is $5,000. Assume a straight-line method of depreciation. **(a)** What will be the book value of the truck at the end of year 4? **(b)** If the Tundra was bought the first year on April 12, how much depreciation would be taken the first year? *LU 17-1(2)*

17–21. Jim Company bought a machine for $36,000 with an estimated life of 5 years. The residual value of the machine is $6,000. **eXcel** Calculate **(a)** the annual depreciation and **(b)** the book value at the end of year 3. Assume straight-line depreciation. *LU 17-1(2)*

17–22. Using Problem 17–21, calculate the first 2 years' depreciation, assuming the units-of-production method. This machine **eXcel** is expected to produce 120,000 units. In year 1, it produced 19,000 units, and in year 2, 38,000 units. *LU 17-2(2)*

17–23. Jim Clinnin purchased a used RV with 19,000 miles for $46,900. Originally the RV sold for $70,000 with a residual value of $20,000. After subtracting the residual value, depreciation allowance per mile was $.86. How much was Jim's purchase price over or below the book value? *LU 17-2(1)*

17–24. Whole Foods, the world's leader in natural and organic foods, has more than 310 stores and 62,000 employees in North America and the United Kingdom. A new store is being built in San Antonio, Texas, at the Vineyard shopping center. A commercial oven for $7,985 with a 5-year life and residual value of $1,100 was purchased for the store. What is the depreciation expense in year 2 for the oven? Use the straight-line method. *LU 17-1(2)*

17–25. Perry Wiseman of Truckers Accounting Service in Omaha, Nebraska, likes to use the straight-line method. The cost of his truck was $108,000, with a useful life of 3 years and a residual value of $35,000. What would be the book value of the truck after the first year? Round your answers to the nearest dollar. *LU 17-1(2)*

17–26. Starwood Hotels & Resorts recently announced new benefits for guests staying more than 100 nights with them per year. To stay state-of-the-art, they are expanding some of their fitness centers. If they purchased an elliptical cross-trainer for $27,750 in March 2013, what is year 5's depreciation expense if the piece of equipment qualifies for a 7-year property classification under MACRS? *LU 17-4(2)*

CHALLENGE PROBLEMS

17–27. A delivered price (including attachments) of a crawler dozer tractor is $135,000 with a residual value of 35%. The useful life of the tractor is 7,700 hours. *LU 17-2(2)*
  a. What is the total amount of depreciation allowed?
  b. What is the amount of depreciation per hour?
  c. If the tractor is operated five days a week for an average of $7\frac{1}{4}$ hours a day, what would be the depreciation for the first year?
  d. If the hours of operation were the same each year, what would be the total number of years of useful life for the tractor? Round years to the nearest whole number.

17–28. Assume a piece of equipment was purchased July 26, 2014, at a cost of $72,000. The estimated residual value is $5,400 with a useful life of 5 years. Assume a production life of 60,000 units. Compute the depreciation for years 2014 and 2015 using **(a)** straight-line and **(b)** units-of-production (in 2014, 5,000 units were produced and in 2015, 18,000 units were produced). *LU 17-1(2), LU 17-2(2)*

 SUMMARY PRACTICE TEST You Tube™

Do you need help? The DVD has step-by-step worked-out solutions.

1. Leo Lucky, owner of a Pizza Hut franchise, bought a delivery truck for $30,000. The truck has an estimated life of 5 years with a residual value of $10,000. Leo wants to know which depreciation method will be the best for his truck. He asks you to prepare a depreciation schedule using the declining-balance method at twice the straight-line rate. *(pp. 429–430) LU 17-3(2)*

2. Using MACRS, what is the depreciation for the first year on furniture costing $12,000? *(p. 432)   LU 17-4(2)*

3. Abby Matthew bought a new Jeep Commander for $30,000. The Jeep Commander has a life expectancy of 5 years with a *eXcel* residual value of $10,000. Prepare a depreciation schedule for the straight-line-method. *(pp. 426–427)   LU 17-1(2)*

4. Car.com bought a Toyota for $28,000. The Toyota has a life expectancy of 10 years with a residual value of $3,000. After *eXcel* 3 years, the Toyota was sold for $19,000. What was the difference between the book value and the amount received from selling the car if Car.com used the straight-line method of depreciation? *(pp. 426–427)   LU 17-1(2)*

5. A machine cost $70,200; it had an estimated residual value of $6,000 and an expected life of 300,000 units. What would be the depreciation in year 3 if 60,000 units were produced? (Round to nearest cent.) *(p. 428)   LU 17-2(2)*

PROBLEM 1
Computing depreciation

Go to http://www.dell.com. Find the price of a computer system that you would like to buy. Assume you bought this system for business use and the system has a residual value of $400. Compute the depreciation each year under a 5-year straight-line depreciation. Also, calculate the depreciation using MACRS (Tables 17.4 and 17.5 in the text).

Discussion Questions

1. Based on the cost of this computer system, would you keep it for more than 5 years? Why or why not?

2. Do you feel a computer system would actually be worth far less than the depreciated value you calculated? Why?

PROBLEM 2
How car values decline

Go to http://www.kbb.com. Find the price of a car you would like to buy. Assume you bought this car at that price for business use and it has a residual value of 20% of the purchase price. Compute the depreciation each year under a 5-year straight-line depreciation. Then, calculate the depreciation using MACRS (Table 17.5 in the text).

Discussion Questions

1. How does this depreciation represent the value of the car as it ages?

2. Would this depreciation impact the amount of money you would spend on a car? Why or why not?

PROBLEM 3
Calculating auto depreciation

Go to http://www.edmunds.com. Search for a target purchase price on the latest year's version of a nonluxury car. Now go to http://www.money-zine.com/Calculators/Auto-Loan-Calculators/Car-Depreciation-Calculator. Assume that you will own the car for 5 years, that its depreciation will be average, and that the car will have a residual value of 10% of the purchase price. What is the amount of the first year's depreciation? What is total depreciation over the 5 years that you own the car?

Discussion Questions

1. How does the depreciation using the online calculator compare to the depreciation using the straight-line approach?

2. What do you feel may be the difference between these two methods of computing depreciation?

PROBLEM 4
Nothing depreciates like a Deere!

Go to http://www.deere.com/wps/dcom/en_US/buying_and_finance/usa/buy_online/buy_online.page? and choose a piece of equipment. Assume a life of 5 years and a $500 residual value. Compute the depreciation for each year, using 5-year straight-line depreciation.

Discussion Questions

1. How do residual values impact depreciation?

2. Do you feel that residual values truly reflect the value of the item being depreciated? Why or why not?

LESSONS FROM THE GREAT RECESSION ARE STILL RESONATING WITH CAR BUYERS.

Choose a new vehicle and depreciation slices up to 20% off the value in the first year. Choose used and someone else takes that financial hit. But all the converts to used cars have created an unintended consequence: The used-car supply is tight and prices are at all-time highs. That doesn't mean deals aren't out there. But to find

them, you'll have to do a little more research, look in new areas and bargain smarter for the car you want.

It may be two to three years before the supply—and prices—get back to normal levels. Tom Kontos, chief economist for Adesa, a vehicle-auction company, says new-car sales and leasing recovered in 2010, so three-year-old vehicles will start coming back into the market next year and put some downward pressure on prices.

•• FIND THE DEALS

With gas near $4 a gallon, fuel-efficient vehicles are in high demand—and their prices are high, too. But manufacturers began focusing on improving small-car safety and amenities in 2008, so used-car buyers have more palatable choices now—and that is keeping a ceiling on prices. (Even so, soaring prices on some models are skewing the used-car market—see the box at right.) Your best opportunity for a bargain is among used cars that were new-model bestsellers. For example, a recent search on AutoTrader.com for 2009 compacts in Atlanta turned up 139 Honda Civics and 60 Volkswagen Jettas, but only 18 Nissan Sentras and 11 Ford Focuses. The more you have to choose from, the more room you have to negotiate.

Fuel costs are driving prices higher for midsize vehicles as well, but there's a silver lining there, too. A number of redesigned models in this segment have been introduced recently or are coming to market soon—the Toyota Camry, Chevy Malibu, Ford Fusion and Nissan Altima among them. Jonathan Piol, who is pricing manager for Edmunds.com, says these new models will spur owners who have been hold-

ing on to their old midsize cars to trade them in, which should add to the number of used vehicles.

You can find deals on full-size cars and large SUVs now that they're not in vogue. In particular, look for bargains on the truck-based, body-on-frame versions of SUVs that have recently been redesigned as crossovers, such as the Ford Explorer and Dodge Durango. Used crossovers are in high demand, however, because they're more fuel-efficient than their body-on-frame brethren and have the same number of seats. And pickup truck sales have increased as the economy has picked up, so screaming bargains in trucks are also hard to find.

•• DO YOUR HOMEWORK

After Noelle and Earl Peterson of Denver had their second child last

Sometimes It Pays to Buy New

Skyrocketing prices on some small, fuel-efficient used cars means you need to tread cautiously before you pick used over new. We asked Vincentric, an automotive data company, for three-year ownership costs for new and used Toyota Corolla LE's—including depreciation, interest on your loan, insurance, fuel costs, maintenance and repairs.

The three-year costs of a 2009 Corolla you buy from a private party are $20,520; for a 2009 certified preowned Corolla, which commands a higher initial price because it comes with a one-year comprehensive warranty, they're $22,015. But the three-year costs for a brand-new Corolla are only $20,944. When you factor in higher prices for the used Corollas plus the costs of maintenance and repairs, it's clear that buying a new one is a better deal.

year, they decided it was time for a new car. Noelle's 2004 Volvo V70 wasn't big enough to fit her whole family when her parents came to visit, and bending over to secure the child seats was a pain. She knew used-car prices were high, but she was determined to find a deal. She consulted the *Consumer Reports* reliability ratings to narrow her choices, checked safety ratings and used the appraisal tool on Edmunds.com to find a good ballpark price before she hit the dealers' lots.

The result: a 2007 Toyota Sienna LE. The one she found has all-wheel drive to get the family—or as many as seven passengers—over the river and through the woods in the winter. The dealer wanted $15,500, but Noelle stuck to her guns—and the Edmunds-recommended price—and talked him down to $14,000.

Once you've decided what type of car you want, hit the Web to find out more. In addition to its appraisal tool, Edmunds.com has reviews to help narrow your choices, and *Consumer Reports* (www.consumerreports.org) has reliability ratings parsed by model year. A subscription to the Web site costs $30 annually ($20 if you already subscribe to the magazine), or $6.95 a month. You can check safety ratings on SaferCar.gov and at the Insurance Institute for Highway Safety's Web site (www.iihs.org).

Next, find your ride—preferably several, so you can persuade sellers to compete for your offer. Cars.com and Autotrader.com are two of the biggest auto-sales sites and offer the most listings. Or check out CarGurus.com. It aggregates listings from Autobytel, Vehix and other sites and analyzes prices based on listings in your area

BUSINESS MATH ISSUE

Depreciation should never be a factor in buying or selling a car.

1. List the key points of the article and information to support your position.
2. Write a group defense of your position using math calculations to support your view.

Classroom Notes

Inventory and Overhead

Wal-Mart Radio Tags To Track Clothing

BY MIGUEL BUSTILLO

Wal-Mart Stores Inc. plans to roll out sophisticated electronic ID tags to track individual pairs of jeans and underwear, the first step in a system that advocates say better controls inventory but some critics say raises privacy concerns.

Starting next month, the retailer will place removable "smart tags" on garments that can be read by a hand-held scanner. Wal-Mart workers will be able to quickly learn, for instance, which size of Wrangler jeans is missing, with the aim of ensuring shelves are optimally stocked and inventory tightly watched.

If successful, the radio-frequency ID tags will be rolled out on other products at Wal-Mart's more than 3,750 U.S. stores.

"This ability to wave the wand and have a sense of all the products that are on the floor or in the back room in seconds is something that we feel can really transform our business," said Raul Vazquez, the executive in charge of Wal-Mart stores in the western U.S.

Before now, retailers including Wal-Mart have primarily used RFID tags, which store unique numerical identification codes that can be scanned from a distance, to track pallets of merchandise traveling through their supply chains.

LU 18–1: Assigning Costs to Ending Inventory—Specific Identification; Weighted Average; FIFO; LIFO

1. List the key assumptions of each inventory method (pp. 444–449).
2. Calculate the cost of ending inventory and cost of goods sold for each inventory method (pp. 444–449).

LU 18–2: Retail Method; Gross Profit Method; Inventory Turnover; Distribution of Overhead

1. Calculate the cost ratio and ending inventory at cost for the retail method (p. 450).
2. Calculate the estimated inventory using the gross profit method (p. 451).
3. Explain and calculate inventory turnover (p. 452).
4. Explain overhead; allocate overhead according to floor space and sales (pp. 453–454).

Here are key terms in this chapter. After completing the chapter, if you know the term, place a checkmark in the parentheses. If you don't know the term, look it up and put the page number where it can be found.

Average inventory ( ) Distribution of overhead ( ) First-in, first-out (FIFO) method ( ) GAAP ( )
Gross profit method ( ) IFRS ( ) Inventory turnover ( ) Just-in-time (JIT) inventory system ( ) Last-in, first-out (LIFO) method ( ) Overhead expenses ( ) Periodic inventory system ( ) Perpetual inventory system ( ) Retail method ( ) Specific identification method ( ) Weighted-average method ( )

The chapter opener shows how Walmart is trying to better control its inventory with sophisticated electronic ID tags. In the following *Wall Street Journal* clip "Taking Stock Of the Battle In Teen Retail" we see American Eagle Outfitters loading up on popular inventory items. Will the risk increase profits? The two methods that a company can use to monitor its inventory are the *perpetual* method and the *periodic* method.

Taking Stock Of the Battle In Teen Retail

Teen fashion is like poker. The key to getting ahead is knowing when to go all in.

That appears to be the latest play by **American Eagle Outfitters**. The company plans to raise inventory dollars per square foot by a whopping 35% in its fourth quarter, having increased comparable-store sales just 5% in the third quarter.

It is a gutsy move. If American Eagle winds up with too much merchandise on its hands, it could be forced to make catastrophic discounts that would erode profits. Indeed, big mismatches between sales and inventory have led to some of fashion's worst disasters, such as **Crocs** in 2007.

But there is reason to believe American Eagle is on the right track. The company has adopted a strategy of loading up on popular items and pricing them aggressively to get customers into the store. Once inside, the hope is that shoppers will make follow-on purchases. That is critical in the highly competitive teen category, where **Abercrombie & Fitch** and **Aéropostale** vie constantly for American Eagle's customers.

© Kumar Sriskandan/Alamy

The perpetual inventory system should be familiar to most consumers. Today, it is common for cashiers to run scanners across the product code of each item sold. These scanners read pertinent information into a computer terminal, such as the item's number, department, and price. The computer then uses the **perpetual inventory system** as it subtracts outgoing merchandise from inventory and adds incoming merchandise to inventory. However, as you probably know, the computer cannot be completely relied on to maintain an accurate count of merchandise in stock. Since some products may be stolen or lost, periodically a physical count is necessary to verify the computer count.

With the increased use of computers, many companies are changing to a perpetual inventory system of maintaining inventory records. Some small stores, however, still use the **periodic inventory system.** This system usually does not keep a running account of its inventory but relies only on a physical inventory count taken at least once a year. The store then uses various accounting methods to value the cost of its merchandise. In this chapter we discuss the periodic method of inventory.

You may wonder why a company should know the status of its inventory. In Chapter 16 we introduced you to the balance sheet and the income statement. Companies cannot accurately prepare these statements unless they have placed the correct value on their inventory. To do this, a company must know (1) the cost of its ending inventory (found on the balance sheet) and (2) the cost of the goods (merchandise) sold (found on the income statement).

No longer do retailers get a few seasonal deliveries; they now receive new items often, maybe even weekly, to keep their store looking fresh. Frequently, the same type of merchandise flows into a company at different costs. The value assumptions a company makes about the merchandise it sells affect the cost assigned to its ending inventory. Remember that different costs result in different levels of profit on a firm's financial reports.

This chapter begins by using the Blue Company to discuss four common methods (specific identification, weighted average, FIFO, and LIFO) that companies use to calculate the cost of ending inventory and the cost of goods sold. In these methods, the flow of costs does not always match the flow of goods. The chapter continues with a discussion of two methods of estimating ending inventory (retail and gross profit methods), inventory turnover, and the distribution of overhead.

Learning Unit 18–1: Assigning Costs to Ending Inventory—Specific Identification; Weighted Average; FIFO; LIFO

LO 1, 2

Blue Company is a small artist supply store. Its beginning inventory is 40 tubes of art paint that cost $320 (at $8 a tube) to bring into the store. As shown in Figure 18.1, Blue made additional purchases in April, May, October, and December. Note that because of inflation and other competitive factors, the cost of the paint rose from $8 to $13 per tube. At the end of December, Blue had 48 unsold paint tubes. During the year, Blue had 120 paint tubes to sell. Blue wants to calculate (1) the cost of ending inventory (not sold) and (2) the cost of goods sold.

Specific Identification Method

Companies that sell high-cost items such as autos, jewelry, antiques, and so on, usually use the specific identification method.

Companies use the **specific identification method** when they can identify the original purchase cost of an item with the item. For example, Blue Company color codes its paint tubes as they come into the store. Blue can then attach a specific invoice price to each paint tube.

FIGURE 18.1

Blue Company—a case study

	Number of units purchased	Cost per unit	Total cost	
Beginning inventory	40	$ 8	$ 320	
First purchase (April 1)	20	9	180	
Second purchase (May 1)	20	10	200	
Third purchase (October 1)	20	12	240	
Fourth purchase (December 1)	20	13	260	
Goods (merchandise) available for sale	120		$1,200	◄— Step 1
Units sold	72			
Units in ending inventory	48			

This makes the flow of goods and flow of costs the same. Then, when Blue computes its ending inventory and cost of goods sold, it can associate the actual invoice cost with each item sold and in inventory.

To help Blue calculate its inventory with the specific identification method, use the steps that follow.

CALCULATING THE SPECIFIC IDENTIFICATION METHOD
Step 1. Calculate the cost of goods (merchandise available for sale).
Step 2. Calculate the cost of the ending inventory.
Step 3. Calculate the cost of goods sold (Step 1 – Step 2).

First, Blue must actually count the tubes of paint on hand. Since Blue coded these paint tubes, it can identify the tubes with their purchase cost and multiply them by this cost to arrive at a total cost of ending inventory. Let's do this now.

	Cost per unit	Total cost
20 units from April 1	$ 9	$180
20 units from October 1	12	240
8 units from December 1	13	104
Cost of ending inventory		$524 ← Step 2

Blue uses the following cost of goods sold formula to determine its cost of goods sold:

$$\text{Cost of goods available for sale} - \text{Cost of ending inventory} = \text{Cost of goods sold} \quad \leftarrow \textbf{Step 3}$$

$$\$1,200 \quad - \quad \$524 \quad = \quad \boxed{\$676}$$

(Figure 18.1)

Note that the $1,200 for cost of goods available for sale comes from Figure 18.1 (p. 444). Remember, we are focusing our attention on Blue's *purchase costs*. Blue's actual *selling price* does not concern us.

Now let's look at how Blue would use the weighted-average method.

Weighted-Average Method[1]

The **weighted-average method** prices the ending inventory by using an average unit cost. Let's replay Blue Company and use the weighted-average method to find the average unit cost of its ending inventory and its cost of goods sold. Blue would use the steps that follow.

CALCULATING THE WEIGHTED-AVERAGE METHOD
Step 1. Calculate the average unit cost.
Step 2. Calculate the cost of the ending inventory.
Step 3. Calculate the cost of goods sold.

[1]Virtually all countries permit the use of the weighted-average method.

In the table that follows, Blue makes the calculation.

	Number of units purchased	Cost per unit	Total cost
Beginning inventory	40	$ 8	$ 320
First purchase (April 1)	20	9	180
Second purchase (May 1)	20	10	200
Third purchase (October 1)	20	12	240
Fourth purchase (December 1)	20	13	260
Goods (merchandise) available for sale	120		$1,200
Units sold	72		
Units in ending inventory	48		

$$\text{Weighted average unit cost} = \frac{\text{Total cost of goods available for sale}}{\text{Total number of units available for sale}} = \frac{\$1,200}{120 \text{ units}} = \$10 \text{ average unit cost}$$ ← **Step 1**

Average cost of ending inventory: 48 units at $10 = $480 ← **Step 2**

$$\text{Cost of goods available for sale} - \text{Cost of ending inventory} = \text{Cost of goods sold}$$

$$\$1,200 \quad - \quad \$480 \quad = \quad \$720$$ ← **Step 3**

Remember that some of the costs we used to determine the average unit cost were higher and others were lower. The weighted-average method, then, calculates an *average unit price* for goods. Companies with similar units of goods, such as rolls of wallpaper, often use the weighted-average method. Also, companies with homogeneous products such as fuels and grains may use the weighted-average method.

Now let's see how Blue Company would value its inventory with the FIFO method.

FIFO—First-In, First-Out Method

The **first-in, first-out (FIFO)** inventory valuation method assumes that the first goods (paint tubes for Blue) brought into the store are the first goods sold. Thus, FIFO assumes that each sale is from the oldest goods in inventory. FIFO also assumes that the inventory remaining in the store at the end of the period is the most recently acquired goods. This cost flow assumption may or may not hold in the actual physical flow of the goods. An example of a corporation using the FIFO method is Gillette Corporation.

Use the following steps to calculate inventory with the FIFO method.

CALCULATING THE FIFO INVENTORY
Step 1. List the units to be included in the ending inventory and their costs.
Step 2. Calculate the cost of the ending inventory.
Step 3. Calculate the cost of goods sold.

In the table that follows, we show how to calculate FIFO for Blue using the above steps.

FIFO (bottom up)	Number of units purchased	Cost per unit	Total cost
Beginning inventory	40	$ 8	$ 320
First purchase (April 1)	20	9	180
Second purchase (May 1)	20	10	200
Third purchase (October 1)	20	12	240
Fourth purchase (December 1)	20	13	260
Goods (merchandise) available for sale	120		$1,200
Units sold	72		
Units in ending inventory	48		

20 units from December 1 purchased at $13		$260
20 units from October 1 purchased at $12	← Step 1 →	240
8 units from May 1 purchased at $10		80
48 units result in an ending inventory cost of		$580 ← Step 2

Cost of goods available for sale	−	Cost of ending inventory	=	Cost of goods sold
$1,200	−	$580	=	$620 ← Step 3

In FIFO, the cost flow of goods tends to follow the physical flow. For example, a fish market could use FIFO because it wants to sell its old inventory first. Note that during inflation, FIFO produces a higher income than other methods. So companies using FIFO during this time must pay more taxes.

We conclude this unit by using the LIFO method to value Blue Company's inventory.

LIFO—Last-In, First-Out Method

If Blue Company chooses the **last-in, first-out (LIFO)** method of inventory valuation, then the goods sold by Blue will be the last goods brought into the store. The ending inventory would consist of the old goods that Blue bought earlier.

You can calculate inventory with the LIFO method by using the steps that follow.

CALCULATING THE LIFO INVENTORY
Step 1. List the units to be included in the ending inventory and their costs.
Step 2. Calculate the cost of the ending inventory.
Step 3. Calculate the cost of goods sold.

Now we use the above steps to calculate LIFO for Blue.

LIFO (top down)	Number of units purchased	Cost per unit	Total cost
Beginning inventory	40	$ 8	$ 320
First purchase (April 1)	20	9	180
Second purchase (May 1)	20	10	200
Third purchase (October 1)	20	12	240
Fourth purchase (December 1)	20	13	260
Goods (merchandise) available for sale	120		$1,200
Units sold	72		
Units in ending inventory	48		

40 units of beginning inventory at $8 $320

8 units from April at $9   ← Step 1 →   72

48 units result in an ending inventory cost of $392 ← Step 2

Cost of goods available for sale	−	Cost of ending inventory	=	Cost of goods sold
↑		↑		↑
$1,200	−	$392	=	$808 ← Step 3

Although LIFO doesn't always match the physical flow of goods, companies do still use it to calculate the flow of costs for products such as DVDs and computers, which have declining replacement costs. Also, during inflation, LIFO produces less income than other methods. This results in lower taxes for companies using LIFO. The following *Wall Street Journal* clip, "Balancing the Books," shows that although the LIFO method may be used inside the United States per **Generally Accepted Accounting Principles (GAAP)**, the **International Financial Reporting Standards (IFRS)** do not permit companies to use this method.

Balancing the Books

Accounting rulemakers are trying to move U.S. and global accounting standards closer together, but some significant differences remain.

	GAAP U.S. generally accepted accounting principles	IFRS International Financial Reporting Standards
NATURE OF STANDARDS	'Rules-based,' under which companies must apply detailed, bright-line rules	'Principles-based,' less-detailed rules, where companies use judgment in applying a set of guidelines
INVENTORY VALUATION	Permits 'last-in, first-out' accounting, or LIFO, which gives companies lower taxable income	Doesn't permit LIFO
DEVELOPMENT COSTS	Typically expensed against earnings every quarter	Typically capitalized on the balance sheet

Sources: American Institute of Certified Public Accountants; WSJ research

Before concluding this unit, we will make a summary for the cost of ending inventory and cost of goods sold under the weighted-average, FIFO, and LIFO methods. From this summary, you can see that in times of rising prices, LIFO gives the highest cost of goods sold ($808). This results in a tax savings for Blue. The weighted-average method tends to smooth out the fluctuations between LIFO and FIFO and falls in the middle.

The key to this discussion of inventory valuation is that different costing methods produce different results. So management, investors, and potential investors should understand the different inventory costing methods and should know which method a particular company uses. For example, Fruit of the Loom, Inc., changed its inventories from LIFO to FIFO due to cost reductions.

Let's check your understanding of this unit with a Practice Quiz.

MONEY tips

Open a flexible-spending account. Eighty-five percent of employers offer them and they help you save by using pretax dollars for several expense categories.

Inventory method	Cost of goods available for sale	Cost of ending inventory	Cost of goods sold
Weighted average	$1,200	$480 **Step 1:** Total goods, $1,200 Total units, 120 $\frac{\$1,200}{120} = \$10$ **Step 2:** $10 \times 48 = \$480$	$1,200 − $480 = $720
FIFO	$1,200	Bottom up to inventory level (48) $20 \times \$13 = \$260$ $20 \times \$12 = \quad 240$ $8 \times \$10 = \quad\underline{\ 80}$ $\qquad\qquad\quad \$580$	$1,200 − $580 = $620
LIFO	$1,200	Top down to inventory level (48) $40 \times \$8 = \$320$ $8 \times \$9 = \quad\underline{\ 72}$ $\qquad\qquad \$392$	$1,200 − $392 = $808

LU 18–1 **PRACTICE QUIZ**

Complete this **Practice Quiz** to see how you are doing.

From the following, calculate **(a)** the cost of ending inventory and **(b)** the cost of goods sold under the assumption of (1) weighted-average method, (2) FIFO, and (3) LIFO (ending inventory shows 72 units):

	Number of books purchased for resale	Cost per unit	Total
January 1 inventory	30	$3	$ 90
March 1	50	2	100
April 1	20	4	80
November 1	60	6	360

For **extra help** from your authors—Sharon and Jeff—see the student DVD

✓ Solutions

1. a. 72 units of ending inventory $\times$ $3.94 = $283.68 cost of ending inventory
($630 ÷ 160)

    b.
$$\underset{\text{available for sale}}{\text{Cost of goods}} - \underset{\text{inventory}}{\text{Cost of ending}} = \underset{\text{goods sold}}{\text{Cost of}}$$

$$\$630 \quad - \quad \$283.68 \quad = \quad \boxed{\$346.32}$$

2. a.
60 units from November 1 purchased at $6	$360
12 units from April 1 purchased at $4	48
72 units Cost of ending inventory	$408

    b.
$$\underset{\text{available for sale}}{\text{Cost of goods}} - \underset{\text{inventory}}{\text{Cost of ending}} = \underset{\text{goods sold}}{\text{Cost of}}$$

$$\$630 \quad - \quad \$408 \quad = \quad \boxed{\$222}$$

(continued on p. 450)

3. a.

30 units from January 1 purchased at $3		$ 90
42 units from March 1 purchased at $2		84
72	Cost of ending inventory	$174

b.

$$\underset{\downarrow}{\begin{array}{c}\text{Cost of goods}\\\text{available for sale}\end{array}} - \underset{\downarrow}{\begin{array}{c}\text{Cost of ending}\\\text{inventory}\end{array}} = \underset{\downarrow}{\begin{array}{c}\text{Cost of}\\\text{goods sold}\end{array}}$$

$$\$630 \quad - \quad \$174 \quad = \quad \boxed{\$456}$$

LU 18–1a EXTRA PRACTICE QUIZ WITH WORKED-OUT SOLUTIONS

Need more practice? Try this **Extra Practice Quiz** (check figures in the Interactive Chapter Organizer, p. 458). Worked-out Solutions can be found in Appendix B at end of text.

From the following, calculate **(a)** the cost of ending inventory and **(b)** the cost of goods sold under the assumption of (1) weighted-average, (2) FIFO, and (3) LIFO (ending inventory shows 58 units):

	Number of books purchased for resale	Cost per unit	Total
January 1 inventory	20	$4	$ 80
March 1	60	3	180
April 1	40	5	200
November 1	50	7	350

Learning Unit 18–2: Retail Method; Gross Profit Method; Inventory Turnover; Distribution of Overhead

Customers want stores to have products available for sale as soon as possible. This has led to outsourced warehouses offshore where tens of thousands of products can be stored ready to be quickly shipped to various stores.

When retailers receive their products, they go into one of their most important assets—their inventory. When the product is sold, it must be removed from inventory so it can be replaced or discontinued. Often these transactions occur electronically at the registers that customers use to pay for products. How is inventory controlled when the register of the store cannot perform the task of adding and subtracting products from inventory?

© Alistair Berg/Digital Vision/Getty Images

Convenience stores often try to control their inventory by taking physical inventories. This can be time-consuming and expensive. Some stores draw up monthly financial reports but do not want to spend the time or money to take a monthly physical inventory.

Many stores estimate the amount of inventory on hand. Stores may also have to estimate their inventories when they have a loss of goods due to fire, theft, flood, and the like. This unit begins with two methods of estimating the value of ending inventory—the *retail method* and the *gross profit method*.

Retail Method

Many companies use the **retail method** to estimate their inventory. As shown in Figure 18.2, this method does not require that a company calculate an inventory cost for each item. To calculate the $3,500 ending inventory in Figure 18.2 (p. 451), Green Company used the steps that follow.

LO 1

CALCULATING THE RETAIL METHOD

Step 1. Calculate the cost of goods available for sale at cost and retail: $6,300; $9,000.

Step 2. Calculate a cost ratio using the following formula:

$$\frac{\text{Cost of goods available for sale at cost}}{\text{Cost of goods available for sale at retail}} = \frac{\$6,300}{\$9,000} = .70$$

Step 3. Deduct net sales from cost of goods available for sale at retail: $9,000 − $4,000.

Step 4. Multiply the cost ratio by the ending inventory at retail: .70 × $5,000.

FIGURE 18.2

Estimating inventory with the
retail method

	Cost	Retail	
Beginning inventory	$4,000	$6,000	
Net purchases during month	2,300	3,000	
Cost of goods available for sale **(Step 1)**	$6,300	$9,000	
Less net sales for month		4,000	**(Step 3)**
Ending inventory at retail		$5,000	
Cost ratio ($6,300 ÷ $9,000) **(Step 2)**		70%	
Ending inventory at cost (.70 × $5,000) **(Step 4)**		$3,500	

Now let's look at the gross profit method.

Gross Profit Method

To use the **gross profit method** to estimate inventory, the company must keep track of (1) average gross profit rate, (2) net sales at retail, (3) beginning inventory, and (4) net purchases. You can use the following steps to calculate the gross profit method:

LO 2

CALCULATING THE GROSS PROFIT METHOD
Step 1. Calculate the cost of goods available for sale (Beginning inventory + Net purchases).
Step 2. Multiply the net sales at retail by the complement of the gross profit rate. This is the estimated cost of goods sold.
Step 3. Calculate the cost of estimated ending inventory (Step 1 − Step 2).

EXAMPLE   Assume Radar Company has the following information in its records:

Gross profit on sales	30%
Beginning inventory, January 1, 2013	$20,000
Net purchases	$ 8,000
Net sales at retail for January	$12,000

If you use the gross profit method, what is the company's estimated inventory?

The gross profit method calculates Radar's estimated cost of ending inventory at the end of January as follows:

Goods available for sale			
Beginning inventory, January 1, 2013		$20,000	
Net purchases		8,000	
Cost of goods available for sale		$28,000	← Step 1
Less estimated cost of goods sold:			
Net sales at retail	$12,000		
Cost percentage (100% − 30%)	Step 2 → .70		
Estimated cost of goods sold		8,400	
Estimated ending inventory, January 31, 2013		$19,600	← Step 3

Note that the cost of goods available for sale less the estimated cost of goods sold gives the estimated cost of ending inventory.

Since this chapter has looked at inventory flow, let's discuss inventory turnover—a key business ratio.

Inventory Turnover

Apple's New Math On Textbook Pricing

McGraw-Hill Cos. normally sells high-school textbooks for $75 a pop. Now it says it will sell electronic versions of the same books, via Apple, for $15 each. How can the publisher make that work?

It's the usual answer for this kind of digital question: "Volume," says McGraw-Hill CEO Terry McGraw.

But there's an important asterisk here, too. Normally, McGraw-Hill would sell its books directly to public schools, which would keep the texts for an average of five years.

Under Apple's new textbooks plan, though, McGraw-Hill will try something different. It will

sell its books directly to each student, who will use the book for a year, then move on. They'll be able to keep the digital text, but won't be able to resell it or pass it along to another student, and McGraw-Hill anticipates that another set of students will buy new books the following year.

So Mr. McGraw figures that over five years, he'll generate the same total sales selling $15 ebooks as he would selling $75 books.

Of course, Apple will take an undisclosed cut of sales— McGraw-Hill execs wouldn't go into details, so let's assume for now that it's Apple's standard 30%—but presumably McGraw-Hill can make up some of that by forgoing the cost of print and distribution.

Inventory turnover is the number of times the company replaces inventory during a specific time. The *Wall Street Journal* clip "Apple's New Math On Textbook Pricing" reveals that McGraw-Hill will provide electronic versions of texts to high schools through Apple's products. Now McGraw-Hill will have fewer paper and inventory costs. Companies use the following two formulas to calculate inventory turnover:

$$\text{Inventory turnover at retail} = \frac{\text{Net sales}}{\text{Average inventory at retail}}$$

$$\text{Inventory turnover at cost} = \frac{\text{Cost of goods sold}}{\text{Average inventory at cost}}$$

You should note that inventory turnover at retail is usually lower than inventory turnover at cost. This is due to theft, markdowns, spoilage, and so on. Also, retail outlets and grocery stores usually have a high turnover, but jewelry and appliance stores have a low turnover.

Now let's use an example to calculate the inventory turnover at retail and at cost.

EXAMPLE The following facts are for Abby Company, a local sporting goods store (rounded to the nearest hundredth):

Net sales	$32,000	Cost of goods sold	$22,000
Beginning inventory at retail	$11,000	Beginning inventory at cost	$ 7,500
Ending inventory at retail	$ 8,900	Ending inventory at cost	$ 5,600

With these facts, we can make the following calculations to determine **average inventory:**

$$\textbf{Average inventory} = \frac{\text{Beginning inventory} + \text{Ending inventory}}{2}$$

At retail: $\dfrac{\$32,000}{\dfrac{\$11,000 + \$8,900}{2}} = \dfrac{\$32,000}{\$9,950} = \boxed{3.22}$

At cost: $\dfrac{\$22,000}{\dfrac{\$7,500 + \$5,600}{2}} = \dfrac{\$22,000}{\$6,550} = \boxed{3.36}$

What Turnover Means   Inventory is often a company's most expensive asset. The turnover of inventory can have important implications. Too much inventory results in the use of needed space, extra insurance coverage, and so on. A low inventory turnover could indicate customer dissatisfaction, too much tied-up capital, and possible product obsolescence. A high inventory turnover might mean insufficient amounts of inventory causing stockouts that may lead to future lost sales. If inventory is moving out quickly, perhaps the company's selling price is too low compared to that of its competitors.

In recent years the **just-in-time (JIT) inventory system** from Japan has been introduced in the United States. Under ideal conditions, manufacturers must have suppliers that will provide materials daily as the manufacturing company needs them, thus eliminating inventories. The companies that are using this system, however, have often not been able to completely eliminate the need to maintain some inventory.

LO 4

Distribution of Overhead

In Chapter 16 we studied the cost of goods sold and operating expenses shown on the income statement. The operating expenses included **overhead expenses**—expenses that are *not* directly associated with a specific department or product but that contribute indirectly to the running of the business. Examples of such overhead expenses are rent, taxes, and insurance. The *Wall Street Journal* clip "Productivity Gap" indicates that the Gap's sales have not kept up with the size of its stores.

Companies must allocate their overhead expenses to the various departments in the company. The two common methods of calculating the **distribution of overhead** are by (1) floor space (square feet) or (2) sales volume.

Calculations by Floor Space   To calculate the distribution of overhead by floor space, use the steps that follow.

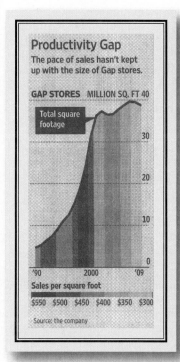

Productivity Gap
The pace of sales hasn't kept up with the size of Gap stores.

CALCULATING THE DISTRIBUTION OF OVERHEAD BY FLOOR SPACE
Step 1. Calculate the total square feet in all departments.
Step 2. Calculate the ratio for each department based on floor space.
Step 3. Multiply each department's floor space ratio by the total overhead.

EXAMPLE   Roy Company has three departments with the following floor space:

Department A	6,000 square feet
Department B	3,000 square feet
Department C	1,000 square feet

The accountant's job is to allocate $90,000 of overhead expenses to the three departments. To allocate this overhead by floor space:

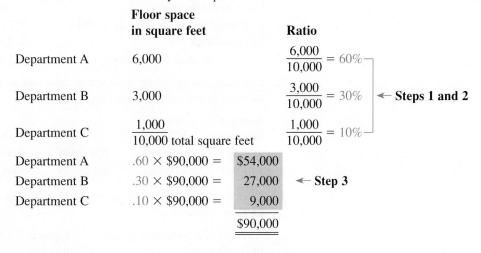

	Floor space in square feet	**Ratio**	
Department A	6,000	$\frac{6,000}{10,000} = 60\%$	
Department B	3,000	$\frac{3,000}{10,000} = 30\%$	← **Steps 1 and 2**
Department C	$\frac{1,000}{10,000}$ total square feet	$\frac{1,000}{10,000} = 10\%$	
Department A	.60 × $90,000 =	$54,000	
Department B	.30 × $90,000 =	27,000	← **Step 3**
Department C	.10 × $90,000 =	9,000	
		$90,000	

MONEY tips

Whenever possible, contribute the maximum allowed to your retirement plan(s) to defer taxes and help you prepare for a healthy financial retirement. This is especially important if your employer matches your contribution.

Calculations by Sales To calculate the distribution of overhead by sales, use the steps that follow.

CALCULATING THE DISTRIBUTION OF OVERHEAD BY SALES
Step 1. Calculate the total sales in all departments.
Step 2. Calculate the ratio for each department based on sales.
Step 3. Multiply each department's sales ratio by the total overhead.

EXAMPLE Morse Company distributes its overhead expenses based on the sales of its departments. For example, last year Morse's overhead expenses were $60,000. Sales of its two departments were as follows, along with its ratio calculation.

Since Department A makes 80% of the sales, it is allocated 80% of the overhead expenses.

	Sales	**Ratio**	
Department A	$ 80,000	$\dfrac{\$80,000}{\$100,000} = .80$	← **Steps 1 and 2**
Department B	20,000	$\dfrac{\$20,000}{\$100,000} = .20$	
Total sales	$100,000		

These ratios are then multiplied by the overhead expense to be allocated.

Department A	.80 × $60,000 =	$48,000	
Department B	.20 × $60,000 =	12,000	← **Step 3**
		$60,000	

It's time to try another Practice Quiz.

LU 18–2 | **PRACTICE QUIZ**

Complete this **Practice Quiz** to see how you are doing.

1. From the following facts, calculate the cost of ending inventory using the retail method (round the cost ratio to the nearest tenth percent):

January 1—inventory at cost	$ 18,000
January 1—inventory at retail	58,000
Net purchases at cost	220,000
Net purchases at retail	376,000
Net sales at retail	364,000

2. Given the following, calculate the estimated cost of ending inventory using the gross profit method:

Gross profit on sales	40%
Beginning inventory, January 1, 2014	$27,000
Net purchases	$ 7,500
Net sales at retail for January	$15,000

3. Calculate the inventory turnover at cost and at retail from the following (round the turnover to the nearest hundredth):

Average inventory at cost	Average inventory at retail	Net sales	Cost of goods sold
$10,590	$19,180	$109,890	$60,990

4. From the following, calculate the distribution of overhead to Departments A and B based on floor space.

Amount of overhead expense to be allocated	Square footage
$70,000	10,000 Department A
	30,000 Department B

✓ Solutions

		Cost	Retail
1.	Beginning inventory	$ 18,000	$ 58,000
	Net purchases during the month	220,000	376,000
	Cost of goods available for sale	$238,000	$434,000
	Less net sales for the month		364,000
	Ending inventory at retail		$ 70,000
	Cost ratio ($238,000 ÷ $434,000)		54.8%
	Ending inventory at cost (.548 × $70,000)		$ 38,360

2. Goods available for sale

Beginning inventory, January 1, 2014		$ 27,000
Net purchases		7,500
Cost of goods available for sale		$ 34,500
Less estimated cost of goods sold:		
Net sales at retail	$ 15,000	
Cost percentage (100% − 40%)	.60	
Estimated cost of goods sold		9,000
Estimated ending inventory, January 31, 2014		$ 25,500

3. Inventory turnover at cost $= \dfrac{\text{Cost of goods sold}}{\text{Average inventory at cost}} = \dfrac{\$60,900}{\$10,590} = \boxed{5.75}$

Inventory turnover at retail $= \dfrac{\text{Net sales}}{\text{Average inventory at retail}} = \dfrac{\$109,890}{\$19,180} = \boxed{5.73}$

4.

		Ratio		
Department A	10,000	$\dfrac{10,000}{40,000} = .25 \times \$70,000 =$	$17,500
Department B	30,000	$\dfrac{30,000}{40,000} = .75 \times \$70,000 =$	52,500
			$ 70,000

LU 18–2a EXTRA PRACTICE QUIZ WITH WORKED-OUT SOLUTIONS

Need more practice? Try this **Extra Practice Quiz** (check figures in the Interactive Chapter Organizer, p. 458). Worked-out Solutions can be found in Appendix B at end of text.

1. From the following, calculate the cost of ending inventory using the retail method (round the cost ratio to the nearest tenth percent):

January 1—inventory at cost	$ 19,000
January 1—inventory at retail	60,000
Net purchases at cost	265,000
Net purchases at retail	392,000
Net sales at retail	375,000

2. Given the following, calculate the estimated cost of ending inventory using the gross profit method:

Gross profit on sales	30%
Beginning inventory, January 1, 2014	$30,000
Net purchases	$ 8,000
Net sales at retail for January	$16,000

(continued on p. 456)

3. Calculate the inventory turnover at cost and at retail from the following (round the turnover to the nearest hundredth):

Average inventory at cost	Average inventory at retail	Net sales	Cost of goods sold
$11,200	$21,800	$129,500	$76,500

4. From the following, calculate the distribution of overhead to Departments A and B based on floor space.

Amount of overhead expense to be allocated	Square footage
$60,000	10,000 Department A
	50,000 Department B

INTERACTIVE CHAPTER ORGANIZER

Topic/procedure/formula	Examples	You try it*
Specific identification method, p. 444 Identification could be by serial number, physical description, or coding. The flow of goods and flow of costs are the same.	<table><tr><td></td><td>Cost per unit</td><td>Total cost</td></tr><tr><td>April 1, 3 units at</td><td>$7</td><td>$21</td></tr><tr><td>May 5, 4 units at</td><td>8</td><td>32</td></tr><tr><td></td><td></td><td>$53</td></tr></table>If 1 unit from each group is left, ending inventory is: 1 × $7 = $ 7 + 1 × 8 = 8 $15 <table><tr><td>Cost of goods available for sale</td><td>−</td><td>Cost of ending inventory</td><td>=</td><td>Cost of goods sold</td></tr><tr><td>$53</td><td>−</td><td>$15</td><td>=</td><td>$38</td></tr></table>	**Calculate ending inventory and cost of goods sold** <table><tr><td></td><td>Cost per unit</td><td>Total cost</td></tr><tr><td>May 1, 4 units at</td><td>$ 9</td><td></td></tr><tr><td>June 6, 3 units at</td><td>10</td><td></td></tr></table>Assume one unit from each group is left.
Weighted-average method, p. 445 $$\text{Weighted average unit cost} = \frac{\text{Total cost of goods available for sale}}{\text{Total number of units available for sale}}$$	<table><tr><td></td><td>Cost per unit</td><td>Total cost</td></tr><tr><td>1/XX, 4 units at</td><td>$4</td><td>$16</td></tr><tr><td>5/XX, 2 units at</td><td>5</td><td>10</td></tr><tr><td>8/XX, 3 units at</td><td>6</td><td>18</td></tr><tr><td></td><td></td><td>$44</td></tr></table>Unit cost = $\frac{\$44}{9}$ = $4.89 If 5 units left, cost of ending inventory is 5 units × $4.89 = $24.45	**Calculate unit cost and cost of ending inventory** <table><tr><td></td><td>Cost per unit</td><td>Total cost</td></tr><tr><td>1/XX, 6 units at</td><td>$5</td><td>$30</td></tr><tr><td>5/XX, 4 units at</td><td>6</td><td>24</td></tr><tr><td>8/XX, 5 units at</td><td>7</td><td>35</td></tr><tr><td></td><td></td><td>$89</td></tr></table>4 units left
FIFO—first-in, first-out method, p. 446 Sell old inventory first. Ending inventory is made up of last merchandise brought into store.	Using example above: 5 units left: ↓ <table><tr><td>(Last into store)</td><td>3 units at $6</td><td>$18</td></tr><tr><td></td><td>2 units at $5</td><td>10</td></tr><tr><td colspan="2">Cost of ending inventory</td><td>$28</td></tr></table>	**Calculate cost of inventory by FIFO** Use weighted-average example.

(continues)

INTERACTIVE CHAPTER ORGANIZER

Topic/procedure/formula	Examples	You try it*
LIFO—last-in, first-out method, p. 447 Sell last inventory brought into store first. Ending inventory is made up of oldest merchandise in store.	Using weighted-average example: . 5 units left: ↓ (First into store) 4 units at $4 — $16 1 unit at $5 — 5 Cost of ending inventory — $21	**Calculate cost of inventory by LIFO** Use weighted-average example.

Retail method, p. 450

Ending inventory at cost equals:

$$\frac{\text{Cost of goods available at cost}}{\text{Cost of goods available at retail}} \times \text{Ending inventory at retail}$$

(This is cost ratio.)

	Cost	Retail
Beginning inventory	$52,000	$ 83,000
Net purchases	28,000	37,000
Cost of goods available for sale	$80,000	$120,000
Less net sales for month		80,000
Ending inventory at retail		$ 40,000

Cost ratio $= \dfrac{\$80,000}{\$120,000} = .67 = 67\%$

Rounded to nearest percent.
Ending inventory at cost, $26,800
(.67 × $40,000)

Calculate cost of ending inventory at cost and at retail

	Cost	Retail
Beginning inventory	$60,000	$80,000
Net purchases	28,000	37,000

Assume net sales of $90,000.
(Round ratio to nearest percent.)

Gross profit method, p. 451

$$\text{Beg. inv.} + \text{Net purchases} - \begin{array}{c}\text{Estimated}\\\text{cost of}\\\text{goods}\\\text{sold}\end{array} = \begin{array}{c}\text{Estimated}\\\text{ending}\\\text{inventory}\end{array}$$

Goods available for sale

Beginning inventory	$30,000
Net purchases	3,000
Cost of goods available for sale	$33,000
Less: Estimated cost of goods sold:	
Net sales at retail $18,000	
Cost percentage (100% − 30%) .70	
Estimated cost of goods sold	12,600
Estimated ending inventory	$20,400

Calculate estimated ending inventory
Given: Net sales at retail of $20,000 and a 75% gross profit.

Goods available for sale

Beginning inventory	$40,000
Net purchases	2,000

Inventory turnover at retail and at cost, p. 452

$$\frac{\text{Net sales}}{\text{Average inventory at retail}} \text{ or } \frac{\text{Cost of goods sold}}{\text{Average inventory at cost}}$$

Inventory, January 1 at cost	$20,000
Inventory, December 31 at cost	48,000
Cost of goods sold	62,000

At cost:

$$\frac{\$62,000}{\dfrac{\$20,000 + \$48,000}{2}} = 1.82 \text{ (inventory turnover at cost)}$$

Calculate inventory turnover at cost
Jan 1 inventory at cost $40,000
Dec 31 inventory at cost $60,000
Cost of goods sold $90,000

(continues)

INTERACTIVE CHAPTER ORGANIZER

Topic/procedure/formula	Examples	You try it*
Distribution of overhead, p. 453 Based on floor space or sales volume, calculate: 1. Ratios of department floor space or sales to the total. 2. Multiply ratios by total amount of overhead to be distributed.	Total overhead to be distributed, $10,000 **Floor space** Department A 6,000 sq. ft. Department B 2,000 sq. ft. 8,000 sq. ft. Ratio A $= \dfrac{6,000}{8,000} = .75$ Ratio B $= \dfrac{2,000}{8,000} = .25$ Dept. A $= .75 \times \$10,000 = \$7,500$ Dept. B $= .25 \times \$10,000 = \$2,500$	**Calculate overhead cost to each department** Total overhead to be distributed, $30,000 **Floor space** Department A 4,000 sq. ft. Department B 6,000 sq. ft.
KEY TERMS	Average inventory, *p. 452* Distribution of overhead, *p. 453* First-in, first-out (FIFO) method, *p. 446* GAAP, *p. 448* Gross profit method, *p. 451* IFRS, *p. 448*	Inventory turnover, *p. 452* Just-in-time (JIT) inventory system, *p. 453* Last-in, first-out (LIFO) method, *p. 447* Overhead expenses, *p. 453* Periodic inventory system, *p. 444*	Perpetual inventory system, *p. 444* Retail method, *p. 450* Specific identification method, *p. 444* Weighted-average method, *p. 445*
Check Figures for Extra Practice Quizzes with Page References. (Worked-out Solutions in Appendix B.)	LU 18–1a (p. 450) 1. a. $276.08; b. $533.92 2. a. $390; b. $420 3. a. $194; b. $616	LU 18–2a (p. 455) 1. $48,356 2. $26,800 3. 6.83; 5.94 4. $10,200; $49,800	

*Worked-out solutions are in Appendix B.

Critical Thinking Discussion Questions with Chapter Concept Check

1. Explain how you would calculate the cost of ending inventory and cost of goods sold for specific identification, FIFO, LIFO, and weighted-average methods. Explain why during inflation, LIFO results in a tax savings for a business.

2. Explain the cost ratio in the retail method of calculating inventory. What effect will the increased use of computers have on the retail method?

3. What is inventory turnover? Explain the effect of a high inventory turnover during the Christmas shopping season.

4. How is the distribution of overhead calculated by floor space or sales? Give an example of why a store in your area cut back one department to expand another. Did it work?

5. What have you seen of levels of inventory affected by the economic crises at your local mall?

6. **Chapter Concept Check.** As we saw in the chapter opener article, Walmart is employing new techniques to track its inventory. Search the web to find the latest techniques used by other stores to control their inventory. Use all the concepts in the chapter to discuss the privacy issue as well.

END-OF-CHAPTER PROBLEMS  www.mhhe.com/slater11e

Check figures for odd-numbered problems in Appendix C.   Name _____   Date _____

DRILL PROBLEMS

18–1. Using the specific identification method, calculate **(a)** the ending inventory and **(b)** the cost of goods sold given the following: *LU 18-1(2)*

Date	Units purchased	Cost per Blackberry	Ending inventory
June 1	12 Blackberrys	$ 99	4 Blackberrys from June 1
October 1	30 Blackberrys	109	7 Blackberrys from Oct. 1
December 1	37 Blackberrys	125	10 Blackberrys from Dec. 1

From the following, **(a)** calculate the cost of ending inventory (round the average unit cost to the nearest cent) and **(b)** cost of goods sold using the weighted-average method, FIFO, and LIFO (ending inventory shows 61 units).   *LU 18-1(2)*

	Number purchased	Cost per unit	Total
January 1 inventory	40	$4	$160
April 1	60	7	420
June 1	50	8	400
November 1	55	9	495

18–2. Weighted average:

18–3. FIFO:

18–4. LIFO:

From the following, (18–5 to 18–12) calculate the cost of ending inventory and cost of goods sold for LIFO (18–13), FIFO (18–14), and the weighted-average (18–15) methods (make sure to first find total cost to complete the table); ending inventory is 49 units: *LU 18-1(2)*

Beginning inventory and purchases	Units	Unit cost	Total dollar cost
18–5. Beginning inventory, January 1	5	$2.00	
18–6. April 10	10	2.50	
18–7. May 15	12	3.00	
18–8. July 22	15	3.25	
18–9. August 19	18	4.00	
18–10. September 30	20	4.20	
18–11. November 10	32	4.40	
18–12. December 15	16	4.80	

18–13. LIFO:

Cost of ending inventory   **Cost of goods sold**

18–14. FIFO:

Cost of ending inventory   **Cost of goods sold**

18–15. Weighted average:

Cost of ending inventory   **Cost of goods sold**

18–16. From the following, calculate the cost ratio (round to the nearest hundredth percent) and the cost of ending inventory to the nearest cent under the retail method.   *LU 18-2(1)*

Net sales at retail for year	$40,000	Purchases—cost	$14,000
Beginning inventory—cost	$27,000	Purchases—retail	$19,000
Beginning inventory—retail	$49,000		

18–17. Complete the following (round answers to the nearest hundredth):   *LU 18-2(3)*

a. Average inventory at cost	b. Average inventory at retail	c. Net sales	d. Cost of goods sold	e. Inventory turnover at cost	f. Inventory turnover at retail
$14,000	$21,540	$70,000	$49,800		

Complete the following (assume $90,000 of overhead to be distributed):   *LU 18-2(4)*

	Square feet	Ratio	Amount of overhead allocated
18–18. Department A	10,000		
18–19. Department B	30,000		

18–20. Given the following, calculate the estimated cost of ending inventory using the gross profit method. *LU 18-2(2)*

Gross profit on sales	55%	Net purchases	$ 3,900
Beginning inventory	$29,000	Net sales at retail	$17,000

WORD PROBLEMS

18–21. LIFO was designed to protect cash flow in industries where prices increase rapidly. It has been used for both tax and finan-
eXcel cial statement reporting since the 1930s. The higher cost of goods sold under LIFO in these circumstances results in lower reported profit than under FIFO. In the 2012 budget, President Obama has threatened to repeal LIFO. If Exxon uses LIFO for its inventory valuation, calculate the cost of ending inventory and cost of goods sold if ending inventory is 110 barrels of crude oil. *LU 18-1(2)*

Beginning inventory and purchases	Barrels	Barrel cost	Total cost
Beginning inventory: Jan 1	125	$ 95	$11,875
March 1	50	101	5,050
June 1	65	98	6,370
September 1	75	90	6,750
December 1	50	103	5,150

18–22. Marvin Company has a beginning inventory of 12 sets of paints at a cost of $1.50 each. During the year, the store purchased 4 sets at $1.60, 6 sets at $2.20, 6 sets at $2.50, and 10 sets at $3.00. By the end of the year, 25 sets were sold. Calculate **(a)** the number of paint sets in ending inventory and **(b)** the cost of ending inventory under LIFO, FIFO, and the weighted-average methods. Round to nearest cent for the weighted average. *LU 18-1(2)*

18–23. BillFloat, based in San Francisco, California, will pay any of your qualifying bills and then automatically deduct the amount of the bill plus fees and interest from your bank account within 30 days. The company registered 190,000 users in 2011 and made 80,000 loans averaging $160 each with rates up to 36% APR, not including fees. If BillFloat wants to distribute $45,000 worth of overhead by sales, calculate the overhead expense for each department: *LU 18-2(4)*

New customer sales (NCS)	$ 5,120,000
Current customer new sales (CCNS)	4,480,000
Current customer loan extension sales (CCLES)	3,200,000

18–24. Comcast lost 135,000 customers in the last quarter of 2010 due to the economic challenges presented by the recession. Business improved in the last quarter of 2011 when it lost only 17,000 customers and things are looking up for 2012. If Comcast is upgrading its cable boxes and has 500 obsolete boxes in ending inventory, what is the cost of ending inventory using FIFO, LIFO, and the weighted-average method? *LU 18-1(2)*

Beginning inventory and purchases	Boxes	Box cost	Total cost
Beginning inventory: January 1	15,500	$15	$232,500
March 1	6,500	16	104,000
June 1	2,500	20	50,000
September 1	1,500	23	34,500
December 1	1,000	32	32,000

18–25. May's Dress Shop's inventory at cost on January 1 was $39,000. Its retail value was $59,000. During the year, May eXcel purchased additional merchandise at a cost of $195,000 with a retail value of $395,000. The net sales at retail for the year were $348,000. Calculate May's inventory at cost by the retail method. Round the cost ratio to the nearest whole percent. *LU 18-2(1)*

18–26. A sneaker outlet has made the following wholesale purchases of new running shoes: 12 pairs at $45, 18 pairs at $40, and eXcel 20 pairs at $50. An inventory taken last week indicates that 23 pairs are still in stock. Calculate the cost of this inventory by FIFO. *LU 18-1(2)*

18–27. Over the past 3 years, the gross profit rate for Jini Company was 35%. Last week a fire destroyed all Jini's inventory. Using eXcel the gross profit method, estimate the cost of inventory destroyed in the fire, given the following facts that were recorded in a fireproof safe: *LU 18-2(2)*

Beginning inventory	$ 6,000
Net purchases	64,000
Net sales at retail	49,000

18–28. Monroe Company had a beginning inventory of 350 cans of paint at $12 each on January 1 at a cost of $4,200. During the year, the following purchases were made:

February 15   280 cans at $14.00
April 30   110 cans at $14.50
July 1   100 cans at $15.00

Monroe marks up its goods at 40% on cost. At the end of the year, ending inventory showed 105 units remaining. Calculate the amount of sales assuming a FIFO flow of inventory. *LU 18-1(2)*

18–29. Logan Company uses a perpetual inventory system on a FIFO basis. Assuming inventory on January 1 was 800 units at $8 each, what is the cost of ending inventory at the end of October 5? *LU 18-1(2)*

Received			Sold	
Date	**Quantity**	**Cost per unit**	**Date**	**Quantity**
Apr. 15	220	$5	Mar. 8	500
Nov. 12	1,900	9	Oct. 5	200

SUMMARY PRACTICE TEST   You Tube

Do you need help? The DVD has step-by-step worked-out solutions.

1.   Writing.com has a beginning inventory of 16 sets of pens at a cost of $2.12 each. During the year, Writing.com purchased 8 sets at $2.15, 9 sets at $2.25, 14 sets at $3.05, and 13 sets at $3.20. By the end of the year, 29 sets were sold. Calculate **(a)** the number of pen sets in stock and **(b)** the cost of ending inventory under LIFO, FIFO, and weighted-average methods. *(pp. 445–448)   LU 18-1(2)*

2.   Lee Company allocates overhead expenses to all departments on the basis of floor space (square feet) occupied by each department. The total overhead expenses for a recent year were $200,000. Department A occupied 8,000 square feet; Department B, 20,000 square feet; and Department C, 7,000 square feet. What is the overhead allocated to Department C? In your calculations, round to the nearest whole percent. *(p. 453)   LU 18-2(4)*

3. A local college bookstore has a beginning inventory costing $80,000 and an ending inventory costing $84,000. Sales for the year were $300,000. Assume the bookstore markup rate on selling price is 70%. Based on the selling price, what is the inventory turnover at cost? Round to the nearest hundredth. *(p. 452)   LU 18-2(3)*

4. Dollar Dress Shop's inventory at cost on January 1 was $82,800. Its retail value was $87,500. During the year, Dollar purchased additional merchandise at a cost of $300,000 with a retail value of $325,000. The net sales at retail for the year were $295,000. Calculate Dollar's inventory at cost by the retail method. Round the cost ratio to the nearest whole percent. *(p. 450)   LU 18-2(1)*

5. On January 1, Randy Company had an inventory costing $95,000. During January, Randy had net purchases of $118,900. Over recent years, Randy's gross profit in January has averaged 45% on sales. The company's net sales in January were $210,800. Calculate the estimated cost of ending inventory using the gross profit method. *(p. 451)   LU 18-2(2)*

PROBLEM 1
For what it's worth

Go to http://www.hoovers.com. Using the same company for which you analyzed financial statements in Chapter 16, estimate the inventory turnover ratio. Calculate both the inventory turnover at retail and the inventory turnover at cost.

Discussion Questions

1. What does inventory turnover tell us about a company's performance?

2. Based on your analysis, would you be likely to invest in this firm? Why or why not?

PROBLEM 2
Revolving doors at Wal-Mart Stores, Inc.

Go to http://www.walmartstores.com. Follow the links to investor information and annual reports. In the most recent annual report find where Wal-Mart Stores, Inc., reports its net sales and its inventories. Use these values to estimate the inventory turnover ratio for Wal-Mart Stores.

Discussion Questions

1. How does this inventory turnover impact how Wal-Mart orders products to sell in its stores?

2. Why do you feel Walmart is able to turn over inventory so quickly?

PROBLEM 3
Inventory turnover is on the rise!

Go to http://www.investopedia.com/articles/02/060502.asp and read the article. Then calculate the inventory value for the bread company mentioned in the article, assuming the company sells 300 loaves on Monday and Tuesday (and the bread isn't stale!). Use first the FIFO, then the LIFO method.

Discussion Questions

1. Why would inventory turnover be so crucial for a bread company?

2. If this were your bread company, which inventory method would you prefer (FIFO or LIFO)? Why?

PROBLEM 4
Fair and square

Go to http://www.accountingcoach.com/online-accounting-course/36Xpg01.html and read the article. Assume you operate a small business with four departments and a total of $50,000 in overhead expenses. Allocate the overhead based on the following assumptions: department 1, 250 square feet; department 2, 300 square feet; department 3, 450 square feet; department 4, 150 square feet.

Discussion Questions

1. How does this allocation of overhead expense assist you in managing your business?

2. Why is it important to allocate overhead expense based on the square footage of departments?

✿ What You'll Find When You Shop

The Green Guide

If fuel economy is high on your list of specs for your new car, a number of technologies can satisfy that need. Which is best for you depends on your other goals. For example, do you want to be as green as possible? An electric vehicle (EV) is the answer. Want superb fuel economy without worrying about plugging in? A hybrid is a good choice. Do you crave power and the feel of gears shifting as you accelerate? If so, hybrids and EVs are likely out of contention, but diesels and turbocharged gas engines are good candidates. Check out the green options and the pros and cons of each. To compare ownership costs for traditional versus green cars, see kiplinger.com/tools/hybrid_calculator.

	Electric	Plug-In Hybrid	Hybrid	Diesel	Turbocharged Gas Engine
GREEN SCORE	🌿🌿🌿🌿	🌿🌿🌿🌿	🌿🌿	🌿🌿	🌿
EXAMPLE	Nissan Leaf SV	Chevrolet Volt	Toyota Prius II	Volkswagen Jetta TDI	Chevrolet Cruze Eco
HOW IT WORKS	A battery-powered electric motor runs all the car's systems. Charge the battery at home and you have about 100 miles to go before you need to recharge.	A battery-powered electric motor you can plug in at home operates for a limited number of miles. After the battery is depleted, a gas engine kicks in.[†]	The battery-powered electric motor assists the engine and can recapture energy from braking. The engine shuts down when you stop, saving fuel.	Small but powerful engines plus diesel fuel's high energy content make these vehicles up to 35% more efficient than comparable gas-powered vehicles.	The exhaust from the engine powers a fan, which forces more air into the engine's cylinders. This generates extra power, so smaller engines can be used.
WHY IT'S COOL	Zero tailpipe emissions, plus pickup	EV range, but without "range anxiety"	Eco-friendly without high price of a plug-in	Powerful, yet fuel-thrifty	Cheapest way to go green
TRADE-OFFS	Limited range; few public charging stations	High price premium; often underpowered	Often underpowered; battery reduces cargo area	Diesel fuel costs more than gasoline	Good but not stellar fuel economy
STICKER PRICE	$36,050*	$39,995*	$24,760	$23,545	$19,995
INVOICE PRICE	$34,557	$38,429	NA	$22,634	$19,225
ANNUAL FUEL COST#	$612 (electricity costs)	$1,000**	$968	$1,721	$1,457
OTHER POPULAR MODELS	Mitsubishi iMiev, Smart electric drive	Toyota Prius Plug-in	Ford Fusion, Honda Civic, Lexus RX	Audi A3, Mercedes E350	Kia Optima 2.0T, Nissan Juke

*Qualifies for $7,500 federal tax credit. †Note that the Volt's gas engine acts as a generator to power the electric motor. Other plug-ins revert to hybrid mode after the battery is depleted. NA Not available. #Based on 15,000 miles of city and highway driving per year. **Fuel-efficiency depends on how often you charge. To compute annual fuel costs for plug-in vehicles for our rankings, we assumed 15,000 miles of city and highway driving a year, evenly spread out over five days a week with a two-week vacation.

BUSINESS MATH ISSUE

Green cars cost more due to lack of inventory.

1. List the key points of the article and information to support your position.
2. Write a group defense of your position using math calculations to support your view.

Classroom Notes

Sales, Excise, and Property Taxes

Price Advantage | Amazon doesn't collect sales tax in Texas and most other states, which some big retailers say gives it an unfair advantage. It does collect the tax in New York and four other states. An online price comparison:

	TARGET	Walmart	amazon	
	IN HOUSTON	IN HOUSTON	IN HOUSTON	IN NEW YORK
CANON POWERSHOT SX130IS	Price: $199.99	Price: $199.00	Price: $198.99	Price: $198.99
	Sales tax: $16.50	Sales tax: $16.42	Sales tax: $0	Sales tax: $17.66
	Total price: $216.49	Total price: $215.42	Total price: $198.99	Total price: $216.65
VIZIO M470NV 47-INCH	Price: $999.99	Price: $998	Price: $948.00	Price: $948.00
	Sales tax: $86.66	Sales tax: $82.34	Sales tax: $0	Sales tax: $84.14
	Total price: $1,086.65	Total price: $1,080.34	Total price: $948.00	Total price: $1,032.14
PLAYSTATION 3	Price: $299.99	Price: $299.00	Price: $299.99	Price: $299.99
	Sales tax: $25.91	Sales tax: $25.90	Sales tax: $0	Sales tax: $26.62
	Total price: $325.90	Total price: $324.90	Total price: $299.99	Total price: $326.61

Sources: Target.com, Walmart.com, Amazon.com; Note: Prices don't include shipping. Photos from top: Canon; Vizio; Bloomberg News

LU 19–1: Sales and Excise Taxes

1. Compute sales tax on goods sold involving trade and cash discounts and shipping charges *(pp. 469–470)*.
2. Explain and calculate excise tax *(p. 470)*.

LU 19–2: Property Tax

1. Calculate the tax rate in decimal *(p. 471)*.
2. Convert tax rate in decimal to percent, per $100 of assessed value, per $1,000 of assessed value, and in mills *(p. 472)*.
3. Compute property tax due *(p. 472)*.

VOCABULARY PREVIEW

Here are key terms in this chapter. After completing the chapter, if you know the term, place a checkmark in the parentheses. If you don't know the term, look it up and put the page number where it can be found.

Assessed value ( ) Excise tax ( ) Mill ( ) Personal property ( ) Property tax ( ) Real property ( )
Sales tax ( ) Tax rate ( )

For many years, there has been a constant debate over whether sales tax should be charged for online sales. Check out the chapter opener clip to see price advantages.

As you know, in the United States sales tax rates vary from state to state. Four state capitals (Concord, New Hampshire; Dover, Delaware; Helena, Montana; and Salem, Oregon) do not impose a sales tax. However, if you live in California, Florida, Texas, or Washington, your combined state and local tax rate reaches 7% or more.

In Learning Unit 19–1 you will learn how sales taxes are calculated. This learning unit also discusses the excise tax that is collected in addition to the sales tax. Learning Unit 19–2 explains the use of property tax.

Learning Unit 19–1: Sales and Excise Taxes

Today, many states have been raising their sales tax and excise tax.

LO 1

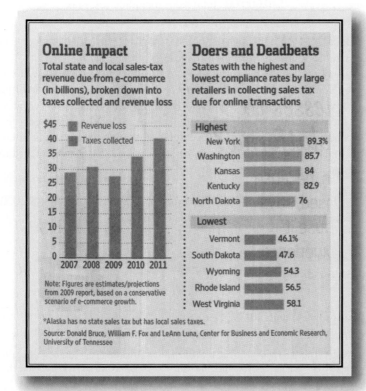

Online Impact
Total state and local sales-tax revenue due from e-commerce (in billions), broken down into taxes collected and revenue loss

- Revenue loss
- Taxes collected

$45, 40, 35, 30, 25, 20, 15, 10, 5, 0 — 2007 2008 2009 2010 2011

Note: Figures are estimates/projections from 2009 report, based on a conservative scenario of e-commerce growth.

Doers and Deadbeats
States with the highest and lowest compliance rates by large retailers in collecting sales tax due for online transactions

Highest
New York 89.3%
Washington 85.7
Kansas 84
Kentucky 82.9
North Dakota 76

Lowest
Vermont 46.1%
South Dakota 47.6
Wyoming 54.3
Rhode Island 56.5
West Virginia 58.1

*Alaska has no state sales tax but has local sales taxes.
Source: Donald Bruce, William F. Fox and LeAnn Luna, Center for Business and Economic Research, University of Tennessee

Sales Tax

In many cities, counties, and states, the sellers of certain goods and services collect **sales tax** and forward it to the appropriate government agency. Forty-five states have a sales tax. Of the 45 states, 28 states and the District of Columbia exempt food; 44 states and the District of Columbia exempt prescription drugs. The *Wall Street Journal* clip in the margin shows which states collect the most taxes from online transactions.

Sales taxes are usually computed electronically by the new cash register systems and scanners. However, it is important to know how sellers calculate sales tax manually. The example on page 470 of a car battery will show you how to manually calculate sales tax.

| Selling price of a Sears battery | $32.00 | Shipping charge | $3.50 |
| Trade discount to local garage | $10.50 | Sales tax | 5% |

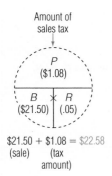

Amount of
sales tax

$21.50 + $1.08 = $22.58
(sale)   (tax
              amount)

Manual calculation

$32.00 − $10.50 = $21.50 taxable
                    ×   .05
                    ─────────
                    $ 1.08 tax
                    + 21.50 taxable
                    + 3.50 shipping
                    ─────────
                    $26.08 total price with tax and shipping

Check

100% is base + 5% is tax = 105%

1.05 × $21.50 = $22.58
                  + 3.50 shipping
                  ─────────
                  $26.08

In this example, note how the trade discount is subtracted from the selling price before any cash discounts are taken. If the buyer is entitled to a 6% cash discount, it is calculated as follows:

$$.06 \times \$21.50 = \$1.29$$

Also, remember that we do not take cash discounts on the sales tax or shipping charges.

Calculating Actual Sales   Managers often use the cash register to get a summary of their total sales for the day. The total sales figure includes the sales tax. So the sales tax must be deducted from the total sales. To illustrate this, let's assume the total sales for the day were $40,000, which included a 7% sales tax. What were the actual sales?

Hint: $40,000 is 107% of actual sales

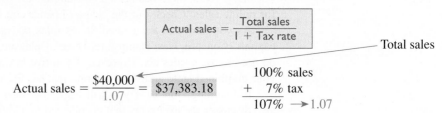

$$\text{Actual sales} = \frac{\text{Total sales}}{1 + \text{Tax rate}}$$

Total sales

$$\text{Actual sales} = \frac{\$40,000}{1.07} = \$37,383.18$$

100% sales
+   7% tax
─────────
107% → 1.07

Thus, the store's actual sales were $37,383.18. The actual sales plus the tax equals $40,000.

Check

$37,383.18 × .07 = $ 2,616.82 sales tax
                     + 37,383.18 actual sales
                     ──────────
                     $40,000.00 total sales including sales tax

LO 2

Excise Tax

Governments (local, federal, and state) levy **excise tax** on particular products and services. This can be a sizable source of revenue for these governments.

Consumers pay the excise tax in addition to the sales tax. The excise tax is based on a percent of the *retail* price of a product or service. This tax, which varies in different states, is imposed on luxury items or nonessentials. Examples of products or services subject to the excise tax include airline travel, telephone service, alcoholic beverages, jewelry, furs, fishing rods, tobacco products, and motor vehicles. Although excise tax is often calculated as a percent of the selling price, the tax can be stated as a fixed amount per item sold. The following example calculates excise tax as a percent of the selling price.[1]

MONEY tips

Launder your clothes in cold water and air-dry them to help combat the rising costs of energy.

EXAMPLE   On June 1, Angel Rowe bought a fur coat for a retail price of $5,000. Sales tax is 7% with an excise tax of 8%. Her total cost is as follows:

$5,000
+   350 sales tax (.07 × $5,000)
+   400 excise tax (.08 × $5,000)
─────────
$5,750

Let's check your progress with a Practice Quiz.

[1]If excise tax were a stated fixed amount per item, it would have to be added to the cost of goods or services before any sales tax were taken. For example, a $100 truck tire with a $4 excise tax would be $104 before the sales tax was calculated.

Complete this **Practice Quiz** to see how you are doing.

*For **extra help** from your authors–Sharon and Jeff–see the student DVD*

You Tube™

From the following shopping list, calculate the total sales tax. Food items are excluded from sales tax, which is 8%.

| Chicken | $6.10 | Orange juice | $1.29 | Shampoo | $4.10 |
| Lettuce | $ .75 | Laundry detergent | $3.65 | | |

✓ Solutions

Shampoo	$4.10
Laundry detergent	+ 3.65
	$7.75 × .08 = $.62

Need more practice? Try this **Extra Practice Quiz** (check figures in the Interactive Chapter Organizer, p. 474). Worked-out Solutions can be found in Appendix B at end of text.

From the following shopping list, calculate the total sales tax. Food items are excluded from sales tax, which is 7%.

| Chicken | $7.90 | Orange juice | $1.50 | Shampoo | $5.90 |
| Lettuce | $ .85 | Laundry detergent | $4.10 | | |

Learning Unit 19–2: Property Tax

When you own property, you must pay property tax. In this unit we listen in on a conversation between a property owner and a tax assessor.

Defining Assessed Value

Bill Adams was concerned when he read in the local paper that the property tax rate had been increased. Bill knows that the revenue the town receives from the tax helps pay for fire and police protection, schools, and other public services. However, Bill wants to know how the town set the new rate and the amount of the new property tax.

Bill went to the town assessor's office to get specific details. The assessor is a local official who estimates the fair market value of a house. Before you read the summary of Bill's discussion, note the following formula:

Property Can Have Two Meanings

Both subject to property tax

1. **Real property—** land, buildings, etc.
2. **Personal property—** possessions like jewelry, autos, furniture, etc.

> Assessed value = Assessment rate × Market value

Bill: What does *assessed value* mean?

Assessor: Assessed value is the value of the property for purposes of computing property taxes. We estimated the market value of your home at $210,000. In our town, we assess property at 30% of the market value. Thus, your home has an assessed value of $63,000 ($210,000 × .30). Usually, assessed value is rounded to the nearest dollar.

Bill: I know that the **tax rate** multiplied by my assessed value ($63,000) determines the amount of my property tax. What I would like to know is how did you set the new tax rate?

Determining the Tax Rate

LO 1

Assessor: In our town first we estimate the total amount of revenue needed to meet our budget. Then we divide the total of all assessed property into this figure to get the *tax rate*. The formula looks like this:[2]

$$\text{Tax rate} = \frac{\text{Budget needed}}{\text{Total assessed value}}$$

Our town budget is $125,000, and we have a total assessed property value of $1,930,000. Using the formula, we have the following:

$$\frac{\$125,000}{\$1,930,000} = \$.0647668 = \boxed{.0648} \text{ tax rate per dollar}$$

[2]Remember that exemptions to total assessed value include land and buildings used for educational and religious purposes and the like.

Note that the rate should be rounded up to the indicated digit, *even if the digit is less than 5.* Here we rounded to the nearest ten thousandth.

How the Tax Rate Is Expressed

Assessor: We can express the .0648 tax rate per dollar in the following forms:

LO 2

By percent	Per $100 of assessed value	Per $1,000 of assessed value	In mills
6.48%	$6.48	$64.80	64.80
(Move decimal two places to right.)	(.0648 × 100)	(.0648 × 1,000)	$\left(\frac{.0648}{.001}\right)$

A **mill** is $\frac{1}{10}$ of a cent or $\frac{1}{1,000}$ of a dollar (.001). To represent the number of mills as a tax rate per dollar, we divide the tax rate in decimal by .001. Rounding practices vary from state to state. Colorado tax bills are now rounded to the thousandth mill. An alternative to finding the rate in mills is to multiply the rate per dollar by 1,000, since a dollar has 1,000 mills. In the problems in this text, we round the mills per dollar to the nearest hundredth.

LO 3

How to Calculate Property Tax Due[3]

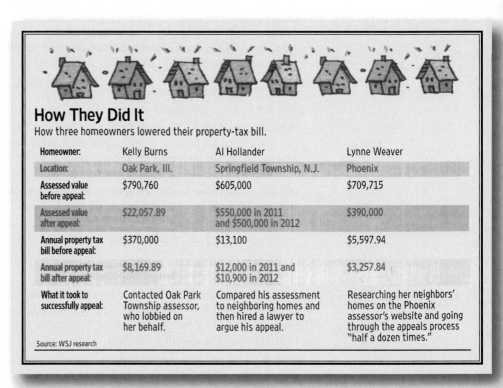

How They Did It

How three homeowners lowered their property-tax bill.

Homeowner:	Kelly Burns	Al Hollander	Lynne Weaver
Location:	Oak Park, Ill.	Springfield Township, N.J.	Phoenix
Assessed value before appeal:	$790,760	$605,000	$709,715
Assessed value after appeal:	$22,057.89	$550,000 in 2011 and $500,000 in 2012	$390,000
Annual property tax bill before appeal:	$370,000	$13,100	$5,597.94
Annual property tax bill after appeal:	$8,169.89	$12,000 in 2011 and $10,900 in 2012	$3,257.84
What it took to successfully appeal:	Contacted Oak Park Township assessor, who lobbied on her behalf.	Compared his assessment to neighboring homes and then hired a lawyer to argue his appeal.	Researching her neighbors' homes on the Phoenix assessor's website and going through the appeals process "half a dozen times."

Source: WSJ research

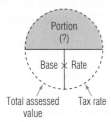

Portion
(?)

Base × Rate

Total assessed value   Tax rate

Assessor: The following formula will show you how we arrive at your **property tax:**

Total property tax due (Portion)	=	Tax rate (Rate)	×	Total assessed value (Base)
$4,082.40	=	.0648	×	$63,000

[3]Some states have credits available to reduce what the homeowner actually pays. For example, 42 out of 50 states give tax breaks to people over age 65. In Alaska, the state's homestead exemption reduces the property tax of a $168,000 house from $1,512 to $253.

We can use the other forms of the decimal tax rate to show you how the property tax will not change even when expressed in various forms:

By percent	Per $100	Per $1,000	Mills
6.48% × $63,000	$\frac{\$63,000}{\$100} = 630$	$\frac{\$63,000}{\$1,000} = 63$	Property tax due
= $4,082.40	630 × $6.48	63 × $64.80	= Mills × .001 × Assessed value
	= $4,082.40	= $4,082.40	= 64.80 × .001 × $63,000
			= $4,082.40

The *Wall Street Journal* clip on page 472 "How They Did It" shows how three home-owners lowered their property tax bill. If you own a home, this clip may save you money.
Now it's time to try the Practice Quiz.

LU 19–2   PRACTICE QUIZ

Complete this **Practice Quiz** to see how you are doing.

From the following facts: (1) calculate the assessed value of Bill's home; (2) calculate the tax rate for the community in decimal (to the nearest ten thousandth); (3) convert the decimal to **(a)** %, **(b)** per $100 of assessed value, **(c)** per $1,000 of assessed value, and **(d)** in mills (to the nearest hundredth); and (4) calculate the property tax due on Bill's home **(a)** in decimal, **(b)** per $100, **(c)** per $1,000, and **(d)** in mills.

Given

Assessed market value	40%	Total budget needed	$ 176,000
Market value of Bill's home	$210,000	Total assessed value	$1,910,000

For **extra help** from your authors–Sharon and Jeff–see the student DVD

You Tube™

✓ Solutions

1. .40 × $210,000 = $84,000

2. $\frac{\$176,000}{\$1,910,000}$ = .0922 per dollar

3. a. .0922 = 9.22%

b. .0922 × 100 = $9.22

c. .0922 × 1,000 = $92.20

d. $\frac{.0922}{.001}$ = 92.2 mills (or .0922 × 1,000)

4. a. .0922 × $84,000 = $7,744.80

b. $9.22 × 840 = $7,744.80

c. $92.20 × 84 = $7,744.80

d. 92.20 × .001 × $84,000 = $7,744.80

LU 19–2a   EXTRA PRACTICE QUIZ WITH WORKED-OUT SOLUTIONS

Need more practice? Try this **Extra Practice Quiz** (check figures in the Interactive Chapter Organizer, p. 474). Worked-out Solutions can be found in Appendix B at end of text.

From the following facts: (1) calculate the assessed value of Bill's home; (2) calculate the tax rate for the community in decimal (to the nearest ten thousandth); (3) convert the decimal to **(a)** %, **(b)** per $100 of assessed value, **(c)** per $1,000 of assessed value, and **(d)** in mills (to the nearest hundredth); and (4) calculate the property tax due on Bill's home **(a)** in decimal, **(b)** per $100, **(c)** per $1,000, and **(d)** in mills.

Given

Assessed market value	40%	Total budget needed	$ 159,000
Market value of Bill's home	$150,000	Total assessed value	$1,680,000

INTERACTIVE CHAPTER ORGANIZER

Topic/procedure/formula	Examples	You try it*
Sales tax, pp. 469–470 Sales tax is not calculated on trade discounts. Shipping charges, etc., also are not subject to sales tax. Actual sales $= \dfrac{\text{Total sales}}{1 + \text{Tax rate}}$ Cash discounts are calculated on sale price before sales tax is added on.	Calculate sales tax: Purchased 12 bags of mulch at $59.40; 10% trade discount; 5% sales tax. $59.40 − $5.94 = $53.46 $53.46 × .05 $2.67 sales tax Any cash discount would be calculated on $53.46.	**Calculate sales tax** 14 bags of mulch at $62.80; 8% trade discount; 6% sales tax
Excise tax, p. 470 Excise tax is calculated separately from sales tax and is an additional tax. It is based as a percent of the selling price. It could be stated as a fixed amount per item sold. In that case, the excise tax would be added to the cost of the item before any sales tax calculations. Rates for excise tax vary.	Jewelry $4,000 retail price Sales tax 7% Excise tax 10% $4,000 + 280 sales tax + 400 excise tax $4,680	**Calculate cost of jewelry** $6,000 retail price Sales tax 5% Excise tax 10%
Assessed value, p. 471 Assessment rate × Market value	$100,000 house; rate, 30%; $30,000 assessed value.	**Calculate assessed value** $200,000 house; rate, 40%.
Tax rate, p. 471 $\dfrac{\text{Budget needed}}{\text{Total assessed value}} = \text{Tax rate}$ (Round rate up to indicated digit even if less than 5.)	$\dfrac{\$800,000}{\$9,200,000} = .08695 = .0870$ tax rate per $1	**Calculate tax rate** Budget needed, $700,000; Total assessed value, $8,400,000. (Round up to 4 digits.)
Expressing tax rate in other forms, p. 472 1. Percent: Move decimal two places to right. Add % sign. 2. Per $100: Multiply by 100. 3. Per $1,000: Multiply by 1,000. 4. Mills: Divide by .001.	1. .0870 = 8.7% 2. .0870 × 100 = $8.70 3. .0870 × 1,000 = $87 4. $\dfrac{.0870}{.001} = 87$ mills	**Using the above tax rate, calculate tax rate in:** 1. Percent 2. Per $100 3. Per $1,000 4. Mills
Calculating property tax, pp. 472–473 $\dfrac{\text{Total property}}{\text{tax due}} = \text{Tax rate} \times \dfrac{\text{Total assessed}}{\text{value}}$ Various forms: 1. Percent × Assessed value 2. Per $100: $\dfrac{\text{Assessed value}}{\$100} \times \text{Rate}$ 3. Per $1,000: $\dfrac{\text{Assessed value}}{\$1,000} \times \text{Rate}$ 4. Mills: Mills × .001 × Assessed value	*Example:* Rate, .0870 per $1; $30,000 assessed value 1. (.087)8.7% × $30,000 = $2,610 2. $\dfrac{\$30,000}{\$100} = 300 \times \$8.70 = \$2,610$ 3. $\dfrac{\$30,000}{\$1,000} = 30 \times \$87 = \$2,610$ 4. $\dfrac{.0870}{.001} = 87$ mills 87 mills × .001 × $30,000 = $2,610	**Calculate property tax for various forms given:** $.0950 per $1; $40,000 assessed value

KEY TERMS	Assessed value, *p. 471* Excise tax, *p. 470* Mill, *p. 472*	Personal property, *p. 471* Property tax, *p. 472* Real property, *p. 471*	Sales tax, *p. 469* Tax rate, *p. 471*
Check Figures for Extra Practice Quizzes with Page References. (Worked-out Solutions in Appendix B.)	LU 19–1a (p. 471) $.70	LU 19–2a (p. 473) 1. $60,000 2. $.0946 3. a. 9.46% b. $9.46 c. 94.60 d. 94.6 mills 4. $5,676 (Due to rounding, you may use .0947 and property tax would be $5,682.)	

*Worked-out solutions are in Appendix B.

Critical Thinking Discussion Questions with Chapter Concept Check

1. Explain sales and excise taxes. Should all states have the same tax rate for sales tax?

2. Explain how to calculate actual sales when the sales tax was included in the sales figure. Is a sales tax necessary?

3. How is assessed value calculated? If you think your value is unfair, what could you do?

4. What is a mill? When we calculate property tax in mills, why do we use .001 in the calculation?

5. **Chapter Concept Check.** Keeping in mind the chapter opener, please search the web to find the latest information on taxing online sales. Do you think it is fair? Defend your position using concepts learned in this chapter.

Classroom Notes

END-OF-CHAPTER PROBLEMS connect plus+ www.mhhe.com/slater11e

Check figures for odd-numbered problems in Appendix C.   Name _____   Date _____

DRILL PROBLEMS

Calculate the following: *LU 19-1(1, 2)*

	Retail selling price	Sales tax (6%)	Excise tax (10%)	Total price including taxes
19–1.	$900			
19–2.	$1,500			

Calculate the actual sales since the sales and sales tax were rung up together. Assume a 6% sales tax and round your answer to the nearest cent. *LU 19-1(1)*

19–3. $88,000

19–4. $26,000

Calculate the assessed value of the following pieces of property: *LU 19-2(2)*

	Assessment rate	Market value	Assessed value
19–5.	30%	$130,000	
19–6.	80%	$210,000	

Calculate the tax rate in decimal form to the nearest ten thousandth: *LU 19-2(2)*

	Required budget	Total assessed value	Tax rate per dollar
19–7.	$920,000	$39,500,000	

Complete the following:

	Tax rate per dollar	In percent	Per $100	Per $1,000	Mills
19–8.	.0956				
19–9.	.0699				

Complete the amount of property tax due to the nearest cent for each situation: *LU 19-2(3)*

	Tax rate	Assessed value	Amount of property tax due
19–10.	40 mills	$ 65,000	
19–11.	$42.50 per $1,000	105,000	
19–12.	$8.75 per $100	125,000	
19–13.	$94.10 per $1,000	180,500	

WORD PROBLEMS

19–14. Be careful when signing a work-for-hire agreement if you are a songwriter. You may lose all rights to your song in the copy-right law world. If your song sells thousands on iTunes, you do not get to share in any of the publishing income. If you live in New Jersey and iTunes sold five of your songs for a total of $65,000, what is the tax owed at 7.0%? *LU 19-1(1)*
eXcel

19–15. Don Chather bought a new Dell computer for $1,995. This included a 6% sales tax. What is the amount of sales tax and the selling price before the tax? *LU 19-1(1)*
eXcel

19–16. Homeowners enjoy many benefits, including a federal tax deduction for state and local property taxes paid. Des Moines, Iowa, was voted one of the top 100 best places to live in 2011 by *Money Magazine*. With a median home price of $100,000 and property taxes at 27.23 mills, how much does the average homeowner pay in property taxes? *LU 19-2(3)*

19–17. In the town of Marblehead, the market value of a home is $280,000. The assessment rate is 40%. What is the assessed value? *LU 19-2(2)*

19–18. Bemidji, Minnesota, needs $3,850,000 for its 2013 budget. Total assessed value of property in Bemidji is $353,211,009. e**X**cel What is the tax rate expressed as a percent, per $100, per $1,000, and in mills? *LU 19-2(2)*

19–19. Lois Clark bought a ring for $6,000. She must still pay a 5% sales tax and a 10% excise tax. The jeweler is shipping the ring, so Lois must also pay a $40 shipping charge. What is the total purchase price of Lois's ring? *LU 19-1(1, 2)*

19–20. Blunt County needs $700,000 from property tax to meet its budget. The total value of assessed property in Blunt is $110,000,000. What is the tax rate of Blunt? Round to the nearest ten thousandth. Express the rate in mills. *LU 19-2(1, 2)*

19–21. Bill Shass pays a property tax of $3,200. In his community, the tax rate is 50 mills. What is Bill's assessed value? *LU 19-2(2)*

19–22. The home of Bill Burton is assessed at $80,000. The tax rate is 18.50 mills. What is the tax on Bill's home? *LU 19-2(3)*
e**X**cel

19–23. Jesse Garza has a home assessed at $285,000. The tax rate is 7.9 mills. What is the tax on Jesse's home? *LU 19-2(3)*

19–24. Bill Blake pays a property tax of $2,500. In his community, the tax rate is 55 mills. What is Bill's assessed value? Round to the nearest dollar. *LU 19-2(2)*

19–25. The property tax rate for Minneapolis is $8.73 per square foot, and the Denver rate is $2.14 a square foot. If 3,500 square feet is occupied at each location, what is the difference paid in property taxes? *LU 19-2(3)*

19–26. Ginny Fieg expanded her beauty salon by increasing her space by 20%. Ginny paid property taxes of $2,800 at 22 mills. The new rate is now 24 mills. As Ginny's accountant, estimate what she may have to pay for property taxes this year. Round the final answer to the nearest dollar. In the calculation, round assessed value to the nearest dollar. *LU 19-2(2)*

19–27. Art Neuner, an investor in real estate, bought an office condominium. The market value of the condo was $250,000 with a *eXcel* 70% assessment rate. Art feels that his return should be 12% per month on his investment after all expenses. The tax rate is $31.50 per $1,000. Art estimates it will cost $275 per month to cover general repairs, insurance, and so on. He pays a $140 condo fee per month. All utilities and heat are the responsibility of the tenant. Calculate the monthly rent for Art. Round your answer to the nearest dollar (at intermediate stages). *LU 19-2(2)*

SUMMARY PRACTICE TEST You Tube

Do you need help? The DVD has step-by-step worked-out solutions.

1. Carol Shan bought a new Apple iPod at Best Buy for $299. The price included a 5% sales tax. What are the sales tax and the selling price before the tax? *(p. 469)   LU 19-1(1)*

2. Jeff Jones bought a ring for $4,000 from Zales. He must pay a 7% sales tax and 10% excise tax. Since the jeweler is shipping the ring, Jeff must also pay a $30 shipping charge. What is the total purchase price of Jeff's ring? *(pp. 469–470) LU 19-1(1, 2)*

3. The market value of a home in Boston, Massachusetts, is $365,000. The assessment rate is 40%. What is the assessed value? *(p. 471)   LU 19-2(1)*

4. Jan County needs $910,000 from its property tax to meet the budget. The total value of assessed property in Jan is $180,000,000. What is Jan's tax rate? Round to the nearest ten-thousandth. Express the rate in mills (to the nearest tenth). *(p. 472)   LU 19-2(2)*

5. The home of Nancy Billows is assessed at $250,000. The tax rate is 4.95 mills. What is the tax on Nancy's home? *(p. 472) LU 19-2(3)*

6. V's Warehouse has a market value of $880,000. The property in V's area is assessed at 35% of the market value. The tax rate is $58.90 per $1,000 of assessed value. What is V's property tax? *(p. 472)   LU 19-2(3)*

www.mhhe.com/
slater11e_vc

A source of renewable energy, wind offers the opportunity for clean energy on a relatively small footprint. Wind turbines are used to create wind power by converting and capturing wind energy. Multiple wind turbines make up a wind farm.

The Meadow Lake Wind Farm in White County, Indiana, is one such farm. Phase I of the farm became operational in late 2009 and consisted of 121 wind turbines. Phase II went online in mid-2010 and Phases III and IV were added in late 2010 for a total of approximately 300 wind turbines. Future phases are planned to create one of the largest wind farms in the world. Meadow Lake Wind Farm is owned and operated by Horizon Wind Energy.

EDP Renewables North America, operating as Horizon Wind Energy in the U.S., is owned by EDP Renewables (EDPR). Headquartered in Madrid, Spain, EDPR is a leader in the renewable energy industry.

Five key factors go into developing a wind farm:

- Wind
- Transmission lines
- Land use
- Community
- Power plants

To achieve efficient wind development at competitive market prices, site assessment, access to transmission lines, and wind capacity are critical considerations. Site assessment includes an evaluation of the ground conditions for unevenness, existence of obstacles, and presence of mountains. Overall the goal is to match ideal wind capacity with minimal land impact. White County, Indiana, offered an ideal setting for a wind farm.

Once energy is generated by the turning of the wind turbines' blades, the energy flows to underground collections lines into a substation and then to another transmission line into an interconnected substation before flowing to power lines. For this reason, access to transmission lines is another critical factor in locating a wind farm.

In the case of the Meadow Lake Wind Farm, partnerships with area farmers are critical and allow for a high yield of wind energy with minimal obstacles or impact on agricultural production. Not only do local farmers benefit financially from their work with Horizon Wind Energy, but so too does the community, where significant dollars were added to the tax rolls. An unlimited resource, wind energy offers a win-win for White County and the communities served by this source of renewable and green energy.

Note: The following problems contain some data that has been created by the author.

PROBLEM 1

As indicated in the textbook, 45 states maintain a sales tax. What is the sales tax for Indiana where the Meadow Lake Wind Farm is located?

PROBLEM 2

As indicated in the video, nearly $1 billion was invested in the development of the Meadow Lake Wind Farm. Assuming 25% of those dollars were spent locally and subject to Indiana's sales tax, calculate the actual sales made locally. Round to the nearest cent.

PROBLEM 3

According to its state website (www.in.gov), Indiana maintains a 4% auto rental excise tax on vehicles weighing less than 11,000 pounds, when rented for less than 30 days. Suppose an EDP Renewables executive from its Great Lakes Regional Office in Bloomington, Illinois, rented a car to travel to the Meadow Lake Wind Farm to monitor operations. If the auto rental price for a 4-day rental was $140 before sales and excise tax, what was his total cost? (*Hint:* Assume that he returned the car with a full tank of gas and was not subject to other taxes or fees other than those noted in the question.) Round your answer to the nearest cent.

PROBLEM 4

Assume the salaries and benefits of White County government personnel amounted to $18,000,000 last year. If this represents 60% of the total county budget, what is the total budget for White County? Round to the nearest dollar.

PROBLEM 5

If the total assessed value of property in White County was $292,000,000 before the addition of the Meadow Lake Wind Farm to the tax rolls, what would the tax rate need to be to cover its budget as calculated in Problem 4? Round to the nearest hundredth.

PROBLEM 6

Now assuming that the Meadow Lake Wind Farm added $340,000,000 to the tax rolls for White County, what would the tax rate need to be to cover its budget as calculated in Problem 4? Round to the nearest hundredth.

PROBLEM 7

Based on your answers to Problems 5 and 6, by what percent did the tax rate change? Round to the nearest percent.

PROBLEM 8

Express the tax rate calculated in Problem 6 by percent, per $100, per $1,000, and in mills. Round to the nearest hundredth and nearest dollar as appropriate.

PROBLEM 9

According to www.city-data.com, the mean price (market value) of a detached house in White County in 2009 was $159,996. Assuming the county assesses property at 32% of the market value, and using the tax rate calculated in Problem 6, what would be the total property tax due for a house at this mean price? Round the assessed value to the nearest dollar and the tax due to the nearest cent.

Class Discussion EDP first determined the ideal location for each wind turbine in White County. It then had to negotiate with each land owner to place a turbine on his property. Many of these land owners were farmers. Discuss the pros and cons these land owners likely considered when determining whether to let EDP place a turbine on their property. What decision would you have made?

SURF TO SAVE

PROBLEM 1
Taxing choices

Go to https://treas-secure.state.mi.us/ptestimator/ptestimator.asp. Suppose you buy a home in Woodhaven, Michigan, for $150,000 and its taxable value is 50% of that. The home is in Wayne County and the Woodhaven school district. How much will you pay in property taxes if you live in the home (homestead rate)? What would your taxes be if you purchased the same home in Brownstown, which is in the same county and school district?

Discussion Questions

1. What activities are supported from this property tax revenue?

2. What may cause property taxes to increase or decrease?

PROBLEM 2
Taxing sales

Go to http://thestc.com/STrates.stm. Suppose you spend $25,350 annually on items with a sales tax and you live in Mississippi. How much money will you save in sales taxes if you move to North Carolina?

Discussion Questions

1. What accounts for these differences in sales tax among states?

2. What may cause a state to increase its sales tax rate?

PROBLEM 3
Paying the tax man

Go to http://www.comptroller.tn.gov/pa/paavt.asp. Suppose you live and own a business in a Tennessee city that taxes at a rate of $3.3900 per $100 of assessed value. Suppose your home is worth $150,000 and your commercial real estate property is worth $200,000. How much would you pay in property taxes annually?

Discussion Questions

1. Why would assessed values be below actual values?

2. How would the amount of property tax impact your house purchase?

PROBLEM 4
Filling up can really cost you!

Go to http://www.scribd.com/doc/82726304/Facts-and-Figures-2012-State-Gas-Tax-Rates. Find the amount of excise tax on gasoline in the state where you live. Suppose you purchase 1,500 gallons of diesel fuel in a year. How much would you pay in excise taxes in the first quarter of the year? How much would you pay in excise tax for the entire year?

Discussion Questions

1. Why do excise taxes vary among states?

2. What may cause an increase in excise tax rates?

MOBILE APPS   ✕

Tax Me: Sales Tax Calculator (Gary Asman)
Calculates sales tax on purchases.

Simple Sales Tax Calc (Black Bolt Soft) Calculates sales tax on purchases.

INTERNET PROJECTS   ✕

See text website
www.mhhe.com/slater11e_sse_ch19

WHAT TO DO WITH A TAX REFUND

Got the basics covered? We have plenty of other ideas. BY KIMBERLY LANKFORD

IT'S RARE TO GET A WINDFALL these days. That may be one reason so many people have so much more money than necessary withheld from their paycheck for taxes. The average refund has been around $3,000 for the past two years (most people receive their refund within three weeks of filing their returns). We usually counsel against giving Uncle Sam an interest-free loan (see below), but if you have a refund check coming your way, consider using it to bolster your personal balance sheet.

You could use the extra cash to make a dent in debt—for example, to reduce high-interest credit card debt or pay down the principal on your mortgage. Or you could beef up your long-term savings—say, by adding to your retirement savings in an IRA, or by helping your kids or grandkids save for college in a 529 account. You could rebuild your emergency fund or start saving for a down payment on your next home.

Already have those basics

■ ONE IDEA: SET UP A VACATION, NEW-CAR OR HOLIDAY-GIFT FUND.

covered? We have some other ideas:

Prepay your vacation. Set aside some money for vacation ahead of time. That will ensure you pay off your credit card balance after you return and don't accrue interest charges. Stash your refund in a separate account, then add money automatically every week (it's easy to set up an online account for one of the money market deposit accounts listed on page 62; you'll earn a bit of interest, too). You could also set up the account for other

expenses—such as a new car or holiday gifts.

Invest in your home. Your refund won't be enough to redo your kitchen or bathroom, but it can pay for some smaller home improvements. Use the extra cash to add a backsplash, paint a room or cabinets, replace your bathroom sink, swap out your faucets, organize a closet, buy some shrubs or install a programmable thermostat (see "50 Top Money Tips," April).

Load up on stocks. Use the extra cash to buy shares in a mutual fund or stock you've been considering, but may feel is too risky for your IRA or not available in your 401(k) plan. For example, if you want to invest in small-company stocks vetted by a pro, check out a new addition to the Kiplinger 25, Homestead Small-Company Stock fund (see page 23), which has a $500 minimum investment. For individual stocks, consult our "Stock Watch" columns on Kiplinger.com, including "16 Stock Picks for Risk-Averse Investors" and "6 Tech Stocks for Dividends."

If your refund this year was substantial, consider giving yourself an immediate raise by adjusting your tax withholding to increase your take-home pay. Use our tax-withholding calculator at Kiplinger.com to figure out how many allowances you should claim. (You'll need to refer to your 2011 tax return.) Then ask your employer to give you a new Form W-4 to fill out. ■

Windfalls

BROKERS PAY FOR YOUR CASH

Discount brokers are competing hard for your money; they're even willing to pay you a bounty if you give it to them. Cash incentives offered by major brokers range from a couple hundred dollars to $2,500, depending on how much money you invest.

At E*Trade, for example, open a new IRA with $250,000 or more—with a rollover from an employer retirement account or a transfer from another firm's IRA—and the broker will deposit $600 in your account. TD Ameritrade offers the same incentive for opening any kind of account. TD Ameritrade's deal ends June 30, but E*Trade's offer lasts until December 31.

Schwab is paying $200 for new IRA accounts worth $50,000, and $2,500 for a cool $1 million. Merrill Edge offers up to $500 for IRAs of $200,000 or more. Both of those offers expire on April 17, but incentives come and go.

The firms make it easy to switch. Send a recent statement from your current broker and specify whether you want to move all or just a portion of your securities and cash. Expect to pay a transfer fee of up to $75.

Before you bite, investigate fees, investment choices and commissions. An errant switch might add unwanted charges or wall you off from your favorite funds or ETFs. **JOHN MILEY**

BUSINESS MATH ISSUE

A tax refund should always be put into savings.

1. List the key points of the article and information to support your position.
2. Write a group defense of your position using math calculations to support your view.

Life, Fire, and Auto Insurance

Coming to Terms

Insurers are pitching online sales of term life insurance that don't require blood tests and other medical exams. Here's what to keep in mind before buying:

■ You might not be getting the best price in return for the convenience. In general, the healthier you are, the better the price you will get by buying a term policy the conventional way.

■ Before speeding through a deal, check out websites such as **Term4Sale.com** and **FindmyInsurance.com**. They provide quick quotes based on your birth date and other personal data. Final rates are subject to underwriting approval.

■ Price a policy through a direct seller, such as **TIAA-CREF** (www.tiaa-cref.org) or **USAA** (www.usaa.com), which are among the nation's financially strongest insurers and don't use commissioned agents, which can mean better prices.

Insuring Against Mistakes

Some things to consider when buying life insurance

■ **BUY** convertible term insurance if you don't have time to understand the risks of a proposed cash-value policy.

■ **ASK** the agent if you can get a better deal by combining one or more riders with base coverage.

■ **PAY** the minimum premium to get the policy in force, and then review the contract to decide on the best premium schedule.

■ **ASK** the agent for a commission estimate.

■ **GET** a second opinion fro[m] someone who doesn't have [a] financial stake in your purc[hase]

■ **DON'T** assume that you [have] to pay a premium just bec[ause] you get a premium notice.

■ **READ** your contract to [get] a better understanding o[f] options that you have.

■ **DON'T** drop a policy w[ithout] checking to see if it mak[es sense] to do a tax-free exchang[e for an] annuity.

Source: Glenn S. Daily

LU 20–1: Life Insurance

1. Explain the types of life insurance; calculate life insurance premiums *(pp. 486–488)*.

2. Explain and calculate cash value and other nonforfeiture options *(pp. 488–489)*.

LU 20–2: Fire Insurance

1. Explain and calculate premiums for fire insurance of buildings and their contents *(pp. 490–491)*.

2. Calculate refunds when the insured and the insurance company cancel fire insurance *(pp. 491–492)*.

3. Explain and calculate insurance loss when coinsurance is not met *(p. 492)*.

LU 20–3: Auto Insurance

1. Explain and calculate the cost of auto insurance *(pp. 494–497)*.

Here are key terms in this chapter. After completing the chapter, if you know the term, place a checkmark in the parentheses. If you don't know the term, look it up and put the page number where it can be found.

Beneficiary ( ) Bodily injury ( ) Cash value ( ) Coinsurance ( ) Collision ( ) Comprehensive insurance ( ) Compulsory insurance ( ) Deductibles ( ) Extended term insurance ( ) Face amount ( ) Fire insurance ( ) Indemnity ( ) Insured ( ) Insurer ( ) Level premium term ( ) Liability insurance ( ) No-fault insurance ( ) Nonforfeiture values ( ) Paid-up insurance ( ) Policyholder ( ) Premium ( ) Property damage ( ) Reduced paid-up insurance ( ) Short-rate table ( ) Statisticians ( ) Straight life insurance ( ) Term insurance ( ) 20-payment life ( ) 20-year endowment ( ) Universal life ( ) Whole life ( )

Are you thinking about buying life insurance? The chapter opening *Wall Street Journal* clips "Insuring Against Mistakes" and "Coming to Terms" reveal some things to consider before you make that purchase. Buyer beware!

Regardless of the type of insurance you buy—life, auto, nursing home, property, or fire—be sure to read and understand the policy before you buy the insurance. It has been reported that half of the people in the United States who have property insurance have not read their policy and 60% do not understand their policy. If you do not understand your life, fire, or auto insurance policies, this chapter should answer many of your questions. We begin by studying life insurance.

Learning Unit 20–1: Life Insurance

More Go Without Life Insurance

BY LESLIE SCISM

Nearly a third of U.S. households have no life-insurance coverage, the highest percentage in more than four decades, according to research firm Limra.

The *Wall Street Journal* clip "More Go Without Life Insurance" reveals that more than a third of all households have no life insurance. Let's look at Bob Brady and what type of life insurance he plans to buy.

Bob Brady owns Bob's Deli. He is 40 years of age, married, and has three children. Bob wants to know what type of life insurance protection will best meet his needs. Following is a discussion between an insurance agent, Rick Jones, and Bob.

Bob: I would like to buy a life insurance policy that will pay my wife $200,000 in the event of my death. My problem is that I do not have much cash. You know, bills, bills, bills. Can you explain some types of life insurance and their costs?

Rick: Let's begin by explaining some life insurance terminology. The **insured** is you—the **policyholder** receiving coverage. The **insurer** is the company selling the insurance policy. Your wife is the **beneficiary.** As the beneficiary, she is the person named in the policy to receive the insurance proceeds at the death of the insured (that's you, Bob). The amount stated in the policy, say, $200,000, is the **face amount** of the policy. The **premium** (determined by **statisticians** called *actuaries*) is the periodic payments you agree to make for the cost of the insurance policy. You can pay premiums annually, semiannually, quarterly, or monthly. The more frequent the payment, the higher the total cost due to increased paperwork, billing, and so on. Now we look at the different types of insurance.

Types of Insurance

In this section Rick explains term insurance, straight life (ordinary life), 20-payment life, 20-year endowment, and universal life insurance.

LO 1

Term Insurance[1]

Rick: The cheapest type of life insurance is **term insurance,** but it only provides *temporary* protection. Term insurance pays the face amount to your wife (beneficiary) only if you die within the period of the insurance (1, 5, 10 years, and so on).

For example, let's say you take out a 5-year term policy. The insurance company automatically allows you to renew the policy at increased rates until age 70. A new policy called **level premium term** may be less expensive than an annual term policy since each year for, say, 50 years, the premium will be fixed.

The policy of my company lets you convert to other insurance types without a medical examination. To determine your rates under 5-year term insurance, check this table (Table 20.1, p. 487). The annual premium at 40 years per $1,000 of insurance is $3.52. We use the following steps to calculate the total yearly premium.

CALCULATING ANNUAL LIFE INSURANCE PREMIUMS

Step 1. Look up the age of the insured (for females, subtract 3 years) and the type of insurance in Table 20.1. This gives the premium cost per $1,000.

Step 2. Divide the amount of coverage by $1,000 and multiply the answer by the premium cost per $1,000.

$$\frac{\$200,000 \text{ (coverage)}}{\$1,000} = 200 \times \$3.52 = \boxed{\$704}$$

| Number of thousands | Cost per $1,000 for age 40 | Annual premium |

Airport flight insurance is a type of term insurance.

From this formula you can see that for $704 per year for the next 5 years, we, your insurance company, offer to pay your wife $200,000 in the event of your death. At the end of the 5th year, you are not entitled to any cash from your paid premiums. If you do not renew your policy (at a higher rate) and die in the 6th year, we will not pay your wife anything. Term insurance provides protection for only a specific period of time.

Bob: Are you telling me that my premium does not build up any cash savings that you call **cash value**?

Rick: The term insurance policy does not build up cash savings. Let me show you a policy that does build up cash value. This policy is straight life.

Straight Life (Ordinary Life)

Rick: Straight life insurance provides *permanent* protection rather than the temporary protection provided by term insurance. The insured pays the same premium each year or

---

[1]A new term policy is available that covers policyholders until their expected retirement age.

TABLE	20.1

Life insurance rates for males (for females, subtract 3 years from the age)[2]

Age	Five-year term	Age	Straight life	Age	Twenty-payment life	Age	Twenty-year endowment
20	1.85	20	5.90	20	8.28	20	13.85
21	1.85	21	6.13	21	8.61	21	14.35
22	1.85	22	6.35	22	8.91	22	14.92
23	1.85	23	6.60	23	9.23	23	15.54
24	1.85	24	6.85	24	9.56	24	16.05
25	1.85	25	7.13	25	9.91	25	17.55
26	1.85	26	7.43	26	10.29	26	17.66
27	1.86	27	7.75	27	10.70	27	18.33
28	1.86	28	8.08	28	11.12	28	19.12
29	1.87	29	8.46	29	11.58	29	20.00
30	1.87	30	8.85	30	12.05	30	20.90
31	1.87	31	9.27	31	12.57	31	21.88
32	1.88	32	9.71	32	13.10	32	22.89
33	1.95	33	10.20	33	13.67	33	23.98
34	2.08	34	10.71	34	14.28	34	25.13
35	2.23	35	11.26	35	14.92	35	26.35
36	2.44	36	11.84	36	15.60	36	27.64
37	2.67	37	12.46	37	16.30	37	28.97
38	2.95	38	13.12	38	17.04	38	30.38
39	3.24	39	13.81	39	17.81	39	31.84
40	3.52	40	14.54	40	18.61	40	33.36
41	3.79	41	15.30	41	19.44	41	34.94
42	4.04	42	16.11	42	20.31	42	36.59
43	4.26	43	16.96	43	21.21	43	38.29
44	4.50	44	17.86	44	22.15	44	40.09

until death.[3] The premium for straight life is higher than that for term insurance because straight life provides both protection and a built-in cash savings feature. According to our table (Table 20.1), your annual premium, Bob, would be:

Face value is usually the amount paid to the beneficiary at the time of the insured's death.

$$\frac{\$200,000}{\$1,000} = 200 \times \$14.54 = \boxed{\$2,908} \text{ annual premium}$$

Bob: Compared to term, straight life is quite expensive.

Rick: Remember that term insurance has no cash value accumulating, as straight life does. Let me show you another type of insurance—20-payment life—that builds up cash value.

Twenty-Payment Life

Rick: A **20-payment life** policy is similar to straight life in that 20-payment life provides permanent protection and cash value, but you (the insured) pay premiums for only the first 20 years. After 20 years you own **paid-up insurance.** According to my table (Table 20.1), your annual premium would be:

$$\frac{\$200,000}{\$1,000} = 200 \times \$18.61 = \boxed{\$3,722} \text{ annual premium}$$

[2]The life insurance tables in this chapter show premiums for a sampling of age groups, options, and coverage available to those under 45 years of age.

[3]In the following section on nonforfeiture values, we show how a policyholder in later years can stop making payments and still be covered by using the accumulated cash value built up.

Bob: The 20-payment life policy is more expensive than straight life.

Rick: This is because you are only paying for 20 years. The shorter period of time does result in increased yearly costs. Remember that in straight life you pay premiums over your entire life. Let me show you another alternative that we call 20-year endowment.

Twenty-Year Endowment

Rick: The **20-year endowment** insurance policy is the most expensive. It is a combination of term insurance and cash value. For example, from age 40 to 60, you receive term insurance protection in that your wife would receive $200,000 should you die. At age 60, your protection *ends* and you receive the face value of the policy that equals the $200,000 cash value. Let's use my table again (Table 20.1) to see how expensive the 20-year endowment is:

$$\frac{\$200,000}{\$1,000} = 200 \times \$33.36 = \boxed{\$6,672} \text{ annual premium}$$

In summary, Bob, following is a review of the costs for the various types of insurance we have talked about:

	5-year term	Straight life	20-payment life	20-year endowment
Premium cost per year	$704	$2,908	$3,722	$6,672

Before we proceed, I have another policy that may interest you—universal life.

LO **2**

Universal Life Insurance

Rick: **Universal life** is basically a **whole-life** insurance plan with flexible premium schedules and death benefits. Under whole life, the premiums and death benefits are fixed. Universal has limited guarantees with greater risk on the holder of the policy. For example, if interest rates fall, the policyholder must pay higher premiums, increase the number of payments, or switch to smaller death benefits in the future.

Bob: That policy is not for me—too much risk. I'd prefer fixed premiums and death benefits.

Rick: OK, let's look at how straight life, 20-payment life, and 20-year endowment can build up cash value and provide an opportunity for insurance coverage without requiring additional premiums. We call these options **nonforfeiture values.**

Nonforfeiture Values

Rick: Except for term insurance, the other types of life insurance build up cash value as you pay premiums. These policies provide three options should you, the policyholder, ever want to cancel your policy, stop paying premiums, or collect the cash value. As shown in Figure 20.1, these options are: cash value; **reduced paid-up insurance;** and **extended term insurance.**

FIGURE **20.1**

Nonforfeiture options

Option 1: Cash value (cash surrender value)

a. Receive cash value of policy.

b. Policy is terminated.

The longer the policy has been in effect, the higher the cash value because more premiums have been paid in.

Option 2: Reduced paid-up insurance

a. Cash value buys protection without paying new premiums.

b. Face amount of policy is related to cash value buildup and age of insured. The **face amount is less than original policy.**

c. Policy continues for life (at a reduced face amount).

Option 3: Extended term insurance

a. Original face amount of policy continues for a certain period of time.

b. Length of policy depends on cash value built up and on insured's age.

c. This option results automatically if policyholder doesn't pay premiums and fails to elect another option.

TABLE	20.2	Nonforfeiture options based on $1,000 face value

	STRAIGHT LIFE				20-PAYMENT LIFE				20-YEAR ENDOWMENT			
Years insurance policy in force	Cash value	Amount of paid-up insurance	EXTENDED TERM Years	Day	Cash value	Amount of paid-up insurance	EXTENDED TERM Years	Day	Cash value	Amount of paid-up insurance	EXTENDED TERM Years	Day
5	29	86	9	91	71	220	19	190	92	229	23	140
10	96	259	18	76	186	521	28	195	319	520	30	160
15	148	371	20	165	317	781	32	176	610	790	35	300
20	265	550	21	300	475	1,000		Life	1,000	1,000		Life

Option 1: Cash value
$$\frac{\$200,000}{\$1,000} = 200 \times \$148 = \$29,600$$

Option 2: Reduced paid-up insurance
$$\frac{\$200,000}{\$1,000} = 200 \times \$371 = \$74,200$$

Option 3: Extended term insurance
Bob could continue this $200,000 policy for 20 years and 165 days.

MONEY tips

Review your insurance policies, coverages, and deductibles annually. Consider disability, renter's, life, auto, burial, and home. Use the same insurance company for all your insurance needs to take advantage of discounts.

For example, Bob, let's assume that at age 40 we sell you a $200,000 straight-life policy. Assume that at age 55, after the policy has been in force for 15 years, you want to stop paying premiums. From this table (Table 20.2), I can show you the options that are available.

Insight into Health and Business Insurance Often people who interview for a new job are more concerned with the salary offered than the whole health care package such as eye care, dental care, hospital and doctor care, and so on. Be sure you know exactly what the new job offers in health insurance. For employees, company health insurance and life insurance benefits can be an important job consideration.

Some of the key types of business insurance that you may need as a business owner include fire insurance, business interruption insurance (business loss until physical damages are fixed), casualty insurance (insurance against a customer's suing your business due to an accident on company property), workers' compensation (insurance against injuries or sickness from being on the job), and group insurance (life, health, and accident).

Although group health insurance costs have soared recently, many companies still pay the major portion of the cost. Some companies also provide health insurance benefits for retirees. As health costs continue to rise, we can expect to see some changes in this employee benefit.

Companies vary in the type of life insurance benefits they provide to their employees. This insurance can be a percent of the employee's salary with the employee naming the beneficiary; or in the case of key employees, the company can be the beneficiary.

If as an employer you need any of the types of insurance mentioned in this section, be sure to shop around for the best price. If you are in the job market, consider the benefits offered by a company as part of your salary and make your decisions accordingly.

In the next unit, we look specifically at fire insurance. Now let's check your understanding of this unit with a Practice Quiz.

LU 20–1   PRACTICE QUIZ

Complete this **Practice Quiz** to see how you are doing.

1. Bill Boot, age 39, purchased a $60,000, 5-year term life insurance policy. Calculate his annual premium from Table 20.1. After 4 years, what is his cash value?

2. Ginny Katz, age 32, purchased a $78,000, straight life policy. Calculate her annual premium. If after 10 years she wants to surrender her policy, what options and what amounts are available to her?

✓ **Solutions**

1. $\dfrac{\$60,000}{\$1,000} = 60 \times \$3.24 = \boxed{\$194.40}$ No cash value in term insurance.

2. $\dfrac{\$78,000}{\$1,000} = 78 \times \$8.46^* = \boxed{\$659.88}$

   Option 1: Cash value $78 \times \$96 = \boxed{\$7,488}$

   Option 2: Paid up $78 \times \$259 = \boxed{\$20,202}$

   Option 3: Extended term $\boxed{18 \text{ years and } 76 \text{ days}}$

   *For females we subtract 3 years.

LU 20–1a EXTRA PRACTICE QUIZ WITH WORKED-OUT SOLUTIONS

Need more practice? Try this **Extra Practice Quiz** (check figures in the Interactive Chapter Organizer, p. 499). Worked-out Solutions can be found in Appendix B at end of text.

1. Bill Boot, age 37, purchased a $70,000, 5-year term life insurance policy. Calculate his annual premium from Table 20.1. After 3 years, what is his cash value?

2. Ginny Katz, age 30, purchased a $95,000, straight-life policy. Calculate her annual premium. If after 5 years she wants to surrender her policy, what options and what amounts are available to her?

Learning Unit 20–2: Fire Insurance

LO 1

Periodically, some areas of the United States, especially California, have experienced drought followed by devastating fires. These fires spread quickly and destroy wooded areas and homes. When the fires occur, the first thought of the owners is the adequacy of their **fire insurance.** Homeowners are made more aware of the importance of fire insurance that provides for the replacement value of their home. Out-of-date fire insurance policies can result in great financial loss.

In this unit, Alice Swan meets with her insurance agent, Bob Jones, to discuss fire insurance needs for her new dress shop at 4 Park Plaza. (Alice owns the building.)

Alice: What is *extended coverage?*

Bob: Your basic fire insurance policy provides financial protection if fire or lightning damages your property. However, the extended coverage protects you from smoke, chemicals, water, or other damages that firefighters may cause to control the fire. We have many options available.

© Aaron Roeth Photography

Alice: What is the cost of a fire insurance policy?

Bob: Years ago, if you bought a policy for 2, 3, 5, or more years, reduced rates were available. Today, with rising costs of reimbursing losses from fires, most insurance companies write policies for 1 to 3 years. The cost of a 3-year policy premium is 3 times the annual premium. Because of rising insurance premiums, your total costs are cheaper if you buy one 3-year policy than three 1-year policies.

Alice: For my purpose, I will need coverage for 1 year. Before you give me the premium rates, what factors affect the cost of my premium?

Bob: In your case, you have several factors in your favor that will result in a lower premium. For example, (1) your building is brick, (2) the roof is fire-resistant, (3) the building is located next to a fire hydrant, (4) the building is in a good location (not next to a gas station) with easy access for the fire department, and (5) the goods within your store are not as flammable as, say, those of a paint store. I have a table here (Table 20.3, p. 491) that gives an example of typical fire insurance rates for buildings and contents (furniture, fixtures, etc.).

TABLE 20.3

Fire insurance rates per $100 of coverage for buildings and contents

| | CLASSIFICATION OF BUILDING | | | |
| | CLASS A | | CLASS B | |
Rating of area	Building	Contents	Building	Contents
1	.28	.35	.41	.54
2	.33	.47	.50	.60
3	.41	.50	.61	.65

Fire insurance premium equals premium for building and premium for contents.

Let's assume your building has an insured value of $190,000 and is rated Class B, Area No. 2, and we insure your contents for $80,000. Then we calculate your total annual premium for building and contents as follows:

$$\text{Premium} = \frac{\text{Insured value}}{\$100} \times \text{Rate}$$

Building

$$\frac{\$190,000}{\$100} = 1,900 \times \$.50 = \$950$$

Contents

$$\frac{\$80,000}{\$100} = 800 \times \$.60 = \$480$$

Total premium = $950 + $480 = $1,430

For our purpose, we round all premiums to the nearest cent. In practice, the premium is rounded to the nearest dollar.

LO 2

Canceling Fire Insurance

Alice: What if my business fails in 7 months? Do I get back any portion of my premium when I cancel?

Bob: If the insured—that's you, Alice—cancels or wants a policy for less than 1 year, we use this **short-rate table** (Table 20.4). These rates are higher because it is more expensive to process a policy for a short time. For example, if you cancel at the end of 7 months, the premium cost is 67% of the annual premium. We would calculate your refund as follows:

Short-rate premium = Annual premium × Short rate

$958.10   = $1,430   ×   .67

Refund = Annual premium − Short-rate premium

$471.90 = $1,430   − $958.10

Alice: Let's say that I don't pay my premium or follow the fire codes. What happens if your insurance company cancels me?

Bob: If the insurance company cancels you, the company is *not* allowed to use the short-rate table. To calculate what part of the premium the company may keep,[4] you can prorate

TABLE 20.4

Fire insurance short-rate and cancellation table

Time policy is in force	Percent of annual rate to be charged	Time policy is in force	Percent of annual rate to be charged
Days: 5	8%	Months: 5	52%
10	10	6	61
20	15	7	67
25	17	8	74
Months: 1	19	9	81
2	27	10	87
3	35	11	96
4	44	12	100

[4]Many companies use $\frac{\text{Days}}{365}$.

the premium based on the actual days that have elapsed. We can illustrate the amount of your refund by assuming you are canceled after 7 months:

Note that when the insurance company cancels the policy, the refund ($595.83) is greater than if the insured cancels ($471.90).

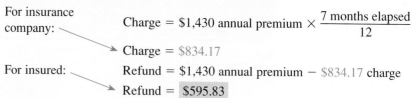

For insurance company:
$$\text{Charge} = \$1,430 \text{ annual premium} \times \frac{7 \text{ months elapsed}}{12}$$

Charge = $834.17

For insured:
Refund = $1,430 annual premium − $834.17 charge

Refund = $595.83

LO 3

Coinsurance

Alice: My friend tells me that I should meet the coinsurance clause. What is coinsurance?

Bob: Usually, fire does not destroy the entire property. **Coinsurance** means that you and the insurance company *share* the risk. The reason for this coinsurance clause[5] is to encourage property owners to purchase adequate coverage.

Alice: What is adequate coverage?

Bob: In the fire insurance industry, the usual rate for coinsurance is 80% of the current replacement cost. This cost equals the value to replace what was destroyed. If your insurance coverage is 80% of the current value, the insurance company will pay all damages up to the face value of the policy.

Alice: Hold it, Bob! Will you please show me how this coinsurance is figured?

Bob: Yes, Alice, I'll be happy to show you how we figure coinsurance. Let's begin by looking at the following steps so you can see what amount of the insurance the company will pay.

MONEY tips

Request quotes from your insurance provider using different deductibles for each policy. Choose the one that meets your financial needs. Keep the amount of each deductible in an interest-earning account for easy access if and when it is needed.

Although there are many types of property and homeowner's insurance policies, they usually include fire protection.

CALCULATING WHAT INSURANCE COMPANY PAYS WITH COINSURANCE CLAUSE

Step 1. Set up a fraction. The numerator is the actual amount of the insurance carried on the property. The denominator is the amount of insurance you should be carrying on the property to meet coinsurance (80% times the replacement value).

Step 2. Multiply the fraction by the amount of loss (up to the face value of the policy).

Let's assume for this example that you carry $60,000 fire insurance on property that will cost $100,000 to replace. If the coinsurance clause in your policy is 80% and you suffer a loss of $20,000, your insurance company will pay the following:

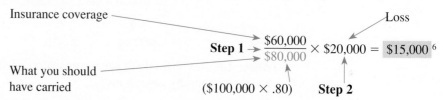

Insurance coverage

Loss

Step 1 → $\frac{\$60,000}{\$80,000} \times \$20,000 = \boxed{\$15,000}$ [6]

What you should have carried

($100,000 × .80) **Step 2**

If you had had actual insurance coverage of $80,000, then the insurance company would have paid $20,000. Remember that if the coinsurance clause is met, the most an insurance company will pay is the face value of the policy.

You are now ready for the following Practice Quiz.

LU 20–2 PRACTICE QUIZ

Complete this **Practice Quiz** to see how you are doing.

1. Calculate the total annual premium of a warehouse that has an area rating of 2 with a building classification of B. The value of the warehouse is $90,000 with contents valued at $30,000.

2. If the insured in problem 1 cancels at the end of month 9, what are the costs of the premium and the refund?

---

[5]In some states (including Wisconsin), the clause is not in effect for losses under $1,000.

[6]This kind of limited insurance payment for a loss is often called an **indemnity**.

3. Jones insures a building for $120,000 with an 80% coinsurance clause. The replacement value is $200,000. Assume a loss of $60,000 from fire. What will the insurance company pay? If the loss was $160,000 and coinsurance *was* met, what will the insurance company pay?

*For **extra help** from your authors–Sharon and Jeff–see the student DVD*

✓ Solutions

1. $\dfrac{\$90,000}{\$100} = 900 \times \$.50 = \$450$

    $\dfrac{\$30,000}{\$100} = 300 \times \$.60 = \underline{180}$

    $\phantom{\dfrac{\$30,000}{\$100} = 300 \times \$.60 = } \underline{\$630} \leftarrow$ total premium

2. $\$630 \times .81 = \boxed{\$510.30}$ $\quad \$630 - \$510.30 = \boxed{\$119.70}$

3. $\dfrac{\$120,000}{\$160,000} = \dfrac{3}{4} \times \$60,000 = \boxed{\$45,000}$

    $\qquad \uparrow$

    $(.80 \times \$200,000) \qquad \boxed{\$160,000}$ never more than face value

---

LU 20–2a EXTRA PRACTICE QUIZ WITH WORKED-OUT SOLUTIONS

Need more practice? Try this **Extra Practice Quiz** (check figures in the Interactive Chapter Organizer, p. 499). Worked-out Solutions can be found in Appendix B at end of text.

1. Calculate the total annual fire insurance premium of a warehouse that has an area rating of 3 with a building classification of A. The value of the warehouse is $80,000 with contents valued at $20,000.

2. If the insured from problem 1 cancels at the end of month 8, what are the costs of the premium and the refund?

3. Jones insures a building for $140,000 with an 80% coinsurance clause. The replacement value is $250,000. Assume a loss of $50,000 from fire. What will the insurance company pay? If the loss was $170,000 and coinsurance was met, what will the insurance company pay?

Learning Unit 20–3: Auto Insurance

If you own an auto, you have had some experience purchasing auto insurance. Often first-time auto owners do not realize that auto insurance can be a substantial expense. Insurance rates often increase when a driver is involved in an accident. Some insurance companies give reduced rates to accident-free drivers—a practice that has encouraged drivers to be more safety conscious. For example, State Farm Insurance offers a discount to drivers who maintain a safety record. An important factor in safe driving is the use of a seat belt. Make it a habit to always put on your seat belt.

In this unit we follow Shirley as she learns about auto insurance. Shirley, who just bought a new auto, has never purchased auto insurance. So she called her insurance agent, Bob Long, who agreed to meet her for lunch. We will listen in on their conversation.

Shirley: Bob, where do I start?

Liability insurance includes
1. **Bodily injury**—injury or death to people in passenger car or other cars, etc.
2. **Property damage**—injury to other people's autos, trees, buildings, hydrants, etc.

Bob: Our state has two kinds of **liability insurance,** or **compulsory insurance,** that by law you must buy (regulations and requirements vary among states). Liability insurance covers any physical damages that you inflict on others or their property. You must buy liability insurance for the following:

1. **Bodily injury** to others: 10/20. This means that the insurance company will pay damages to people injured or killed by your auto up to $10,000 for injury to one person per accident or a total of $20,000 for injuries to two or more people per accident.

2. **Property damage** to someone else's property: 5. The insurance company will pay up to $5,000 for damages that you have caused to the property of others.

Now we leave Shirley and Bob for a few moments as we calculate Shirley's premium for compulsory insurance.

TABLE 20.5

Compulsory insurance (based on class of driver)

BODILY INJURY TO OTHERS		DAMAGE TO SOMEONE ELSE'S PROPERTY	
Class	10/20	Class	5M*
10	$ 55	10	$129
17	98	17	160
18	80	18	160
20	116	20	186

Explanation of 10/20 and 5

10	20	5
Maximum paid to one person per accident for bodily injury	Maximum paid for total bodily injury per accident	Maximum paid for property damage per accident

*M means thousands.

The tables we use in this unit are for Territory 5. Other tables are available for different territories.

Calculating Premium for Compulsory Insurance[7]

Insurance companies base auto insurance rates on the territory you live in, the class of driver (class 10 is experienced driver with driver training), whether the auto is for business use, how much you drive the car, the age of the car, and the make of the car (symbol). Shirley lives in Territory 5 (suburbia). She is classified as 17 because she is an inexperienced operator licensed for less than 6 years. Her car is age 3 and symbol 4 (make of car). We use Table 20.5 to calculate Shirley's compulsory insurance. Note that the table rates in this unit are not representative of all areas of the country. In case of lawsuits, the minimum coverage may not be adequate. Some states add surcharges to the premium if the person has a poor driving record. The tables are designed to show how rates are calculated. From Table 20.5, we have the following:

$$
\begin{array}{rr}
\text{Bodily} & \$\ 98 \\
+\ \text{Property} & \underline{160} \\
& \$258 \\
\end{array}
$$

Remember that the $258 premium represents minimum coverage. Assume Shirley hits two people and the courts award them $13,000 and $5,000, respectively. Shirley would be responsible for $3,000 because the insurance company would pay only up to $10,000 per person and a total of $20,000 per accident.

Although total damages of $18,000 are less than $20,000, the insurance company pays only $15,000.

	(1)	**(2)**	
	$13,000	+ $5,000 =	$18,000
Paid by insurance company ⟶	− 10,000	− 5,000 =	− 15,000
Paid by Shirley ⟶	$ 3,000	+ $ 0 =	$ 3,000

We return to Shirley and Bob. Bob now shows Shirley how to calculate her optional insurance coverage. Remember that optional insurance coverages (Tables 20.6 to 20.10) are added to the costs in Table 20.5.

Calculating Optional Insurance Coverage

Bob: In our state, you can add optional bodily injury to the compulsory amount. If you finance your car, the lender may require specific amounts of optional insurance to protect its investment. I have two tables (Tables 20.6 and 20.7, p. 495) here that we use to calculate the option of 250/500/50. This means that in an accident the insurance company will pay $250,000 per person, up to $500,000 per accident, and up to $50,000 for property damage.

---

[7]Some states may offer medical payment insurance (a supplement to policyholders' health and accident insurance) as well as personal injury protection against uninsured or underinsured motorists.

TABLE   20.6

Bodily injury

Class	15/30	20/40	20/50	25/50	25/60	50/100	100/300	250/500	500/1,000
10	27	37	40	44	47	69	94	144	187
17	37	52	58	63	69	104	146	228	298
18	33	46	50	55	60	89	124	193	251
20	41	59	65	72	78	119	168	263	344

TABLE   20.7

Damage to someone else's property

Class	10M	25M	50M	100M
10	132	134	135	136
17	164	166	168	169
18	164	166	168	169
20	191	193	195	197

Bob then explains the tables to Shirley. By studying the tables, you can see how insurance companies figure bodily injury and damage to someone else's property. Shirley is Class 17:

Bodily

250/500 = $228

Property

50M   =   + 168

$396 premium for optional bodily injury and property damage

Note: These are additional amounts to compulsory.

Shirley: Is that all I need?

Bob: No, I would recommend two more types of optional coverage: **collision** and **comprehensive.** Collision provides protection against damages to your car caused by a moving vehicle. It covers the cost of repairs less **deductibles** (amount of repair you cover first before the insurance company pays the rest) and depreciation.[8] In collision, insurance companies pay the resale or book value. So as the car gets older, after 5 or more years, it might make sense to drop the collision. The decision depends on how much risk you are willing to assume. Comprehensive covers damages resulting from theft, fire, falling objects, and so on. Now let's calculate the cost of these two types of coverage—assuming a $100 deductible for collision and a $200 deductible for comprehensive—with some more of my tables (Tables 20.8 and 20.9, p. 496).

Collision and comprehensive are optional insurance types that pay only the insured. Note that Tables 20.8 and 20.9 are based on territory, age, and car symbol. The higher the symbol, the more expensive the car.

	Class	Age	Symbol	Premium
Collision	17	3	4	$191 ($148 + $43) Cost to reduce deductibles
Comprehensive	17	3	4	+ 56 ($52 + $4)
				$247

Total premium
for collision and
comprehensive

Shirley: Anything else?

Bob: I would also recommend that you buy towing and substitute transportation coverage. The insurance company will pay up to $25 for each tow. Under substitute transportation, the insurance company will pay you $12 a day for renting a car, up to $300 total. Again,

[8]In some states, repair to glass has no deductible and many insurance companies now use a $500 deductible instead of $300.

TABLE | **20.8** | Collision

Classes	Age group	Symbols 1–3 $300 ded.	Symbol 4 $300 ded.	Symbol 5 $300 ded.	Symbol 6 $300 ded.	Symbol 7 $300 ded.	Symbol 8 $300 ded.	Symbol 10 $300 ded.
10–20	1	180	180	187	194	214	264	279
	2	160	160	166	172	190	233	246
	3	148	148	154	166	183	221	233
	4	136	136	142	160	176	208	221
	5	124	124	130	154	169	196	208

These classes would use all this information.

To find the premium, use the age and symbol only.

Additional cost to reduce deductible

Class	From $300 to $200	From $300 to $100
10	13	27
17	20	43
18	16	33
20	26	55

TABLE | **20.9** | Comprehensive

Classes	Age group	Symbols 1–3 $300 ded.	Symbol 4 $300 ded.	Symbol 5 $300 ded.	Symbol 6 $300 ded.	Symbol 7 $300 ded.	Symbol 8 $300 ded.	Symbol 10 $300 ded.
10–25	1	61	61	65	85	123	157	211
	2	55	55	58	75	108	138	185
	3	52	52	55	73	104	131	178
	4	49	49	52	70	99	124	170
	5	47	47	49	67	94	116	163

Additional cost to reduce deductible: From $300 to $200 add $4

TABLE | **20.10**

Transportation and towing

Substitute transportation	$16
Towing and labor	4

Premiums for collision, property damage, and comprehensive are not reduced by no fault.

from another table (Table 20.10), we find the additional premium for towing and substitute transportation is $20 ($16 + $4).

We leave Shirley and Bob now as we make a summary of Shirley's total auto premium in Table 20.11 (p. 497).

No-Fault Insurance Some states have **no-fault insurance,** a type of auto insurance that was intended to reduce premium costs on bodily injury. With no fault, one forfeits the right to sue for *small* claims involving medical expense, loss of wages, and so on. Each person collects the bodily injury from his or her insurance company no matter who is at fault. In reality, no-fault insurance has not reduced premium costs, due to large lawsuits, fraud, and operating costs of insurance companies. Many states that were once considering no fault are no longer pursuing its adoption. Note that states with no-fault insurance require the purchase of *personal-injury protection (PIP)*. The most successful no-fault law seems to be in Michigan, since it has tough restrictions on the right to sue along with unlimited medical and rehabilitation benefits.

TABLE 20.11

Worksheet for calculating Shirley's auto premium

Compulsory insurance	Limits	Deductible	Premium
Bodily injury to others	$10,000 per person $20,000 per accident	None	$ 98 (Table 20.5)
Damage to someone else's property	$5,000 per accident	None	$160 (Table 20.5)
Options			
Optional bodily injury to others	$250,000 per person $500,000 per accident	None	$228 (Table 20.6)
Optional property damage	$50,000 per accident	None	$168 (Table 20.7)
Collision	Actual cash value	$100	$191 (Table 20.8) ($148 + $43)
Comprehensive	Actual cash value	$200	$ 56 (Table 20.9) ($52 + $4)
Substitute transportation	Up to $12 per day or $300 total	None	$ 16 (Table 20.10)
Towing and labor	$25 per tow	None	$ 4 (Table 20.10)
			$ 921 Total premium

It's time to take your final Practice Quiz in this chapter.

LU 20–3 PRACTICE QUIZ

Complete this **Practice Quiz** to see how you are doing.

Calculate the annual auto premium for Mel Jones who lives in Territory 5, is a driver classified 18, and has a car with age 4 and symbol 7. His state has compulsory insurance, and Mel wants to add the following options:

1. Bodily injury, 100/300.
2. Damage to someone else's property, 10M.
3. Collision, $200 deductible.
4. Comprehensive, $200 deductible.
5. Towing.

*For **extra help** from your authors–Sharon and Jeff–see the student DVD*

✓ Solutions

Compulsory

Bodily	$ 80	(Table 20.5)
Property	160	(Table 20.5)
Options		
Bodily	124	(Table 20.6)
Property	164	(Table 20.7)
Collision	192	($176 + $16)	(Table 20.8)
Comprehensive	103	($99 + $4)	(Table 20.9)
Towing	4		(Table 20.10)
Total annual premium	$827	

LU 20–3a EXTRA PRACTICE QUIZ WITH WORKED-OUT SOLUTIONS

Need more practice? Try this **Extra Practice Quiz** (check figures in the Interactive Chapter Organizer, p. 499). Worked-out Solutions can be found in Appendix B at end of text.

Calculate the annual auto premium for Mel Jones who lives in Territory 5, is a driver classified 17, and has a car with age 5 and symbol 6. His state has compulsory insurance, and Mel wants to add the following options:

1. Bodily injury, 100/300.
2. Damage to someone else's property, 10M.
3. Collision, $200 deductible.
4. Comprehensive, $200 deductible.
5. Towing.

INTERACTIVE CHAPTER ORGANIZER

Topic/procedure/formula	Examples	You try it*
Life insurance, pp. 486–488 Using Table 20.1, per $1,000: $\dfrac{\text{Coverage desired}}{\$1,000} \times \text{Rate}$ For females, subtract 3 years.	**Given** $80,000 of insurance desired; age 34; male. **1.** 5-year term: $\dfrac{\$80,000}{\$1,000} = 80 \times \$2.08 = \boxed{\$166.40}$ **2.** Straight life: $\dfrac{\$80,000}{\$1,000} = 80 \times \$10.71 = \boxed{\$856.80}$ **3.** 20-payment life: $\dfrac{\$80,000}{\$1,000} = 80 \times \$14.28 = \boxed{\$1,142.40}$ **4.** 20-year endowment: $\dfrac{\$80,000}{\$1,000} = 80 \times \$25.13 = \boxed{\$2,010.40}$	**Given** $90,000 of insurance desired; age 36; male. **Calculate these premiums:** 1. 5-year term 2. Straight life 3. 20-payment life 4. 20-year endowment
Nonforfeiture values, pp. 488–489 **By Table 20.2** Option 1: Cash surrender value. Option 2: Reduced paid-up insurance policy continues for life at reduced face amount. Option 3: Extended term—original face policy continued for a certain period of time.	A $50,000 straight-life policy was issued to Jim Rose at age 28. At age 48 Jim wants to stop paying premiums. What are his nonforfeiture options? Option 1: $\dfrac{\$50,000}{\$1,000} = 50 \times \$265$ $= \boxed{\$13,250}$ Option 2: $50 \times \$550 = \boxed{\$27,500}$ Option 3: $\boxed{21 \text{ years } 300 \text{ days}}$	**Given** $60,000 straight-life policy issued to Ron Lee at age 30. At age 50, Ron wants to stop paying premium. **Calculate his nonforfeiture options**
Fire insurance, pp. 490–491 Per $100 $\text{Premium} = \dfrac{\text{Insurance value}}{\$100} \times \text{Rate}$ Rate can be for buildings or contents.	**Given** Area 3; Class B; building insured for $90,000; contents, $30,000. Building: $\dfrac{\$90,000}{\$100} = 900 \times \$.61$ $= \boxed{\$549}$ Contents: $\dfrac{\$30,000}{\$100} = 300 \times \$.65$ $= \boxed{\$195}$ Total: $549 + $195 = $\boxed{\$744}$	**Calculate fire insurance premium** Area 3; Class B; insurance for $80,000; contents, $20,000.
Canceling fire insurance—short-rate Table 20.4 (canceling by policyholder), pp. 491–492 $\dfrac{\text{Short-rate}}{\text{premium}} = \dfrac{\text{Annual}}{\text{premium}} \times \dfrac{\text{Short}}{\text{rate}}$ $\text{Refund} = \dfrac{\text{Annual}}{\text{premium}} - \dfrac{\text{Short-rate}}{\text{premium}}$ If insurance company cancels, do not use Table 20.4.	Annual premium is $400. Short rate is .35 (cancel end of 3 months). $400 \times .35 = $140 Refund = $400 − $140 = $\boxed{\$260}$	**Calculate refund** Annual premium is $600; insurance cancels after 4 months.
Canceling by insurance company, pp. 491–492 $\text{Annual premium} \times \dfrac{\text{Months elapsed}}{12}$ (Refund is higher since company cancels.)	Using example above but if insurance company cancels at end of 3 months. $400 \times \frac{1}{4} = $100 Refund = $400 − $100 = $\boxed{\$300}$	**Calculate refund from example above if insurance company cancels**

(continues)

INTERACTIVE CHAPTER ORGANIZER

Topic/procedure/formula	Examples	You try it*
Coinsurance, p. 492 Amount insurance company pays: $\dfrac{\text{Actual} \rightarrow \text{Insurance carried (Face value)}}{\text{What coverage} \rightarrow \text{to meet coinsurance should have been (Rate} \times \text{Replacement value)}} \times \text{Loss}$ Insurance company never pays more than the face value.	**Given** Face value, $30,000; replacement value, $50,000; coinsurance rate, 80%; loss, $10,000; insurance to meet required coinsurance, $40,000. $\dfrac{\$30,000}{\$40,000} \times \$10,000 = \boxed{\$7,500}$ paid by insurance company ($50,000 × .80)	**Calculate coinsurance** **Given** Face value, $40,000; replacement, $60,000; rate, 80%; loss, $9,000.
Auto insurance, pp. 493–497 **Compulsory** Required insurance. **Optional** Added to cost of compulsory. Bodily injury—pays for injury to person caused by insured. Property damage—pays for property damage (not for insured auto). Collision—pays for damages to insured auto. Comprehensive—pays for damage to insured auto for fire, theft, etc. Towing. Substitute transportation.	Calculate the annual premium. Driver class 10; compulsory 10/20/5. **Optional** Bodily—100/300 Property—10M Collision—age 3, symbol 10, $100 deductible Comprehensive—$300 deductible ($55 + $129) 10/20/5 $184 Table 20.5 Bodily 94 Table 20.6 Property 132 Table 20.7 ($233 + $27) Collision 260 Table 20.8 Comprehensive 178 Table 20.9 Total premium $848	**Calculate annual premium** Driver class 10; compulsory 10/20/5. **Optional** Bodily—100/300 Property—10M Collision—age 5, symbol 8, $100 deductible Comprehensive—$300 deductible

KEY TERMS			
	Beneficiary, p. 485 Bodily injury, p. 493 Cash value, p. 486 Coinsurance, p. 492 Collision, p. 495 Comprehensive insurance, p. 495 Compulsory insurance, p. 493 Deductibles, p. 495 Extended term insurance, p. 488 Face amount, p. 486 Fire insurance, p. 490	Indemnity, p. 492 Insured, p. 485 Insurer, p. 485 Level premium term, p. 486 Liability insurance, p. 493 No-fault insurance, p. 496 Nonforfeiture values, p. 488 Paid-up insurance, p. 487 Policyholder, p. 485 Premium, p. 486 Property damage, p. 493	Reduced paid-up insurance, p. 488 Short-rate table, p. 491 Statisticians, p. 486 Straight life insurance, p. 486 Term insurance, p. 486 20-payment life, p. 487 20-year endowment, p. 488 Universal life, p. 488 Whole life, p. 488

| **Check Figures for Extra Practice Quizzes with Page References. (Worked-out Solutions in Appendix B.)** | LU 20–1a (p. 490)
1. $186.90; no cash value
2. $736.25
Opt. 1. $2,755
     2. $8,170
     3. 9 years and 91 days | LU 20–2a (p. 493)
1. $428
2. $111.28; $316.72
3. $35,000
Never more than $170,000 | LU 20–3a (p. 497)
$817 |

*Worked-out solutions are in Appendix B.

Critical Thinking Discussion Questions with Chapter Concept Check

1. Compare and contrast term insurance versus whole-life insurance. At what age do you think people should take out life insurance?

2. What is meant by *nonforfeiture values?* If you take the cash value option, should it be paid in a lump sum or over a number of years?

3. How do you use a short-rate table? Explain why an insurance company gets less in premiums if it cancels a policy than if the insured cancels.

4. What is coinsurance? Do you feel that an insurance company should pay more than the face value of a policy in the event of a catastrophe?

5. Explain compulsory auto insurance, collision, and comprehensive. If your car is stolen, explain the steps you might take with your insurance company.

6. "Health insurance is not that important. It would not be worth the premiums." Please take a stand.

7. **Chapter Concept Check.** Using the information in the chapter opener, visit the web and find tips for buying life insurance. Based on concepts in the chapter, what would it cost you to set up a life insurance policy that would fit your needs?

END-OF-CHAPTER PROBLEMS  www.mhhe.com/slater11e

Check figures for odd-numbered problems in Appendix C.

Name _____   Date _____

DRILL PROBLEMS

Calculate the annual premium for the following policies using Table 20.1 (for females subtract 3 years from the table). *LU 20-1(1)*

Amount of coverage (face value of policy)	Age and sex of insured	Type of insurance policy	Annual premium
20–1. $140,000	39 F	Straight life	
20–2. $120,000	42 M	20-payment life	
20–3. $150,000	29 F	5-year term	
20–4. $50,000	27 F	20-year endowment	

Calculate the following nonforfeiture options for Lee Chin, age 42, who purchased a $200,000 straight-life policy. At the end of year 20, Lee stopped paying premiums. *LU 20-1(2)*

20–5. Option 1: Cash surrender value

20–6. Option 2: Reduced paid-up insurance

20–7. Option 3: Extended term insurance

Calculate the total cost of a fire insurance premium (rounded to nearest cent) for a building and its contents given the following: *LU 20-2(1)*

Rating of area	Class	Building	Contents	Total premium cost
20–8. 3	B	$90,000	$40,000	

eXcel

Calculate the short-rate premium and refund of the following: *LU 20-2(2)*

Annual premium	Canceled after	Short-rate premium	Refund
20–9. $700	8 months by insured		
20–10. $360	4 months by insurance company		

eXcel

Complete the following: *LU 20-2(3)*

Replacement value of property	Amount of insurance	Kind of policy	Actual fire loss	Amount insurance company will pay
20–11. $100,000	$60,000	80% coinsurance	$22,000	
20–12. $60,000	$40,000	80% coinsurance	$42,000	

eXcel

Calculate the annual auto insurance premium for the following: *LU 20-3(1)*

20–13. Britney Sper, Territory 5
Class 17 operator
Compulsory, 10/20/5   _____

Optional

   a. Bodily injury, 500/1,000   _____

   b. Property damage, 25M   _____

   c. Collision, $100 deductible   _____

   Age of car is 2; symbol of car is 7

   d. Comprehensive, $200 deductible   _____

   Total annual premium   _____

WORD PROBLEMS

20–14. Life expectancy has risen to 78.3 years according to the Centers of Disease Control and Prevention. The average Roman's lifespan 2,000 years ago was 22 years. In 1900, a person was expected to live 47.3 years. In 2013, if you are a 47-year-old female, what annual premium would you pay for a $200,000, 5-year term life insurance policy? What is the cash value after 3 years?   *LU 20-1(1, 2)*

20–15. Mike Reno, age 44, saw an Insurance Solutions Direct advertisement stating that its $500,000 term policy costs $395 per year. Compare this to Table 20.1 in the text. How much would he save by going with Insurance Solutions Direct?   *LU 20-1(1)*

20–16. Margie Rale, age 38, a well-known actress, decided to take out a limited-payment life policy. She chose this since she
eXcel expects her income to decline in future years. Margie decided to take out a 20-year payment life policy with a coverage amount of $90,000. Could you advise Margie about what her annual premium will be? If she decides to stop paying premiums after 15 years, what will be her cash value?   *LU 20-1(1)*

20–17. Janette Raffa has two young children and wants to take out an additional $300,000 of 5-year term insurance. Janette is 40 years old. What will be her additional annual premium? In 3 years, what cash value will have been built up?   *LU 20-1(1)*

20–18. Roger's office building has a $320,000 value, a 2 rating, and a B building classification. The contents in the building are valued at $105,000. Could you help Roger calculate his total annual premium?   *LU 20-2(1)*

20–19. Abby Ellen's toy store is worth $400,000 and is insured for $200,000. Assume an 80% coinsurance clause and that a fire
eXcel caused $190,000 damage. What is the liability of the insurance company?   *LU 20-2(3)*

20–20. To an insurer, you are a statistic. Your premiums are based on your risk factors, including your credit rating. Bad credit increases the amount you pay for your premiums. Make certain to check your credit report annually for accuracy. Calculate the premium for someone in class 20 for 10/20/5. Then determine how much the premium will be for 50/100/50. What is the difference between the two? *LU 20-3(1)*

20–21. As given via the Internet, auto insurance quotes gathered online could vary from $947 to $1,558. A class 18 operator carries compulsory 10/20/5 insurance. He has the following optional coverage: bodily injury, 500/1,000; property damage, 50M; and collision, $200 deductible. His car is 1 year old, and the symbol of the car is 8. He has comprehensive insurance with a $200 deductible. Using your text, what is the total annual premium? *LU 20-3(1)*

20–22. Dan Miller insured his pizza shop for $100,000 for fire insurance at an annual rate per $100 of $.66. At the end of **eXcel** 11 months, Earl canceled the policy since his pizza shop went out of business. What was the cost of Earl's premium and his refund? *LU 20-2(2)*

20–23. Warren Ford insured his real estate office with a fire insurance policy for $95,000 at a cost of $.59 per $100. Eight months **eXcel** later the insurance company canceled his policy because of a failure to correct a fire hazard. What did Warren have to pay for the 8 months of coverage? Round to the nearest cent. *LU 20-2(2)*

20–24. If you had 10/20/5 coverage and were in a car accident causing injury to three people with injuries totaling $15,000, $9,000, and $5,000, how much would you have to pay out of pocket? If you had 50/100/50 coverage for the same scenario, how much would you have to pay out of pocket? What is the difference? *LU 20-3(1)*

20–25. Tina Grey bought a new Honda Civic and insured it with only 10/20/5 compulsory insurance. Driving up to her ski chalet one snowy evening, Tina hit a parked van and injured the couple inside. Tina's car had damage of $4,200, and the van she struck had damage of $5,500. After a lengthy court suit, the injured persons were awarded personal injury judgments of $16,000 and $7,900, respectively. What will the insurance company pay for this accident, and what is Tina's responsibility? *LU 20-3(1)*

20–26. Rusty Reft, who lives in Territory 5, carries 10/20/5 compulsory liability insurance along with optional collision that has a $300 deductible. Rusty was at fault in an accident that caused $3,600 damage to the other auto and $900 damage to his own. Also, the courts awarded $15,000 and $7,000, respectively, to the two passengers in the other car for personal injuries. How much will the insurance company pay, and what is Rusty's share of the responsibility? *LU 20-3(1)*

20–27. Marika Katz bought a new Blazer and insured it with only compulsory insurance 10/20/5. Driving up to her summer home one evening, Marika hit a parked car and injured the couple inside. Marika's car had damage of $7,500, and the car she struck had damage of $5,800. After a lengthy court suit, the couple struck were awarded personal injury judgments of $18,000 and $9,000, respectively. What will the insurance company pay for this accident, and what is Marika's responsibility? *LU 20-3(1)*

CHALLENGE PROBLEMS

20–28. Money.cnn.com states, "The single most important reason to own life insurance is to provide support for your dependents." Insurance4usa.com states, "Professionals suggest you have 8 to 12 times your income in life insurance." Pat and Bonnie Marsh are calculating how much life insurance they need. They have two young children with no college fund set up. Bonnie is a 35-year-old stay-at-home mom. Pat, 39, earns $68,000 per year. How much life insurance do you recommend each person have? (Note that a spouse who stays at home to raise the family generates the equivalent of a salary that needs to be taken into account. Assume Bonnie's salary is $25,000.) What will be the cost of straight-life insurance for both policies if the lowest recommended amount is used? What is the monthly premium owed? *LU 20-1(1)*

20–29. Lou Ralls insured a building and contents (area 2, class B) for $150,000. After 1 month, he canceled the policy. The next day he received a cancellation notice by the company. It stated that he was being canceled due to his previous record. How does Lou save by this insurance cancellation versus his planned cancellation? *LU 20-2(1, 2)*

Do you need help? The DVD has step-by-step worked-out solutions.

1. Howard Slater, age 44, an actor, expects his income to decline in future years. He decided to take out a 20-year payment life policy with a $90,000 coverage. What will be Howard's annual premium? If he decides to stop paying premiums after 15 years, what will be his cash value? *(pp. 486–489) LU 20-1(1, 2)*

2. J.C. Monahan, age 40, bought a straight-life insurance policy for $210,000. Calculate her annual premium. If after 20 years J.C. no longer pays her premiums, what nonforfeiture options will be available to her? *(pp. 486–489) LU 20-1(1, 2)*

3. The property of Pote's Garage is worth $900,000. Pote has a $375,000 fire insurance policy that contains an 80% coinsurance clause. What will the insurance company pay on a fire that causes $450,000 damage? If Pote meets the coinsurance, how much will the insurance company pay? *(p. 492) LU 20-2(3)*

4. Lee Collins insured her pizza shop with a $90,000 fire insurance policy at a $1.10 annual rate per $100. At the end of 7 months, Lee's pizza shop went out of business so she canceled the policy. What is the cost of Lee's premium and her refund? *(p. 491) LU 20-2(2)*

5. Charles Prose insured his real estate office with a $300,000 fire insurance policy at $.78 annual rate per $100. Nine months later the insurance company canceled his policy because Charles failed to correct a fire hazard. What was Charles's cost for the 9-month coverage? Round to the nearest cent. *(pp. 491–492) LU 20-2(2)*

6. Roger Laut, who lives in Territory 5, carries 10/20/5 compulsory liability insurance along with optional collision that has a $1,000 deductible. Roger was at fault in an accident that caused $4,800 damage to the other car and $8,800 damage to his own car. Also, the courts awarded $19,000 and $9,000, respectively, to the two passengers in the other car for personal injuries. How much does the insurance company pay, and what is Roger's share of the responsibility? *(pp. 494–497) LU 20-3(1)*

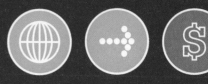

PROBLEM 1
The cost of life insurance

Go to http://www.prudential.com. Follow the link to Products and Services—Insurance. Enter the information the site asks for and get life insurance quotes for $250,000, $500,000, $750,000, and $1,000,000 of coverage. (Use a 10-year Term Essential policy.) Does the $500,000 policy cost twice as much as the $250,000 policy? Does the $1,000,000 policy cost four times as much as the $250,000 policy? Explain your result.

Discussion Questions

1. As a college student, should you take out a life insurance policy? Why or why not?

2. How can you determine the level of life insurance coverage you should purchase?

PROBLEM 2
Life insurance comparisons

Get a quote for $250,000 of life insurance from either State Farm or Prudential for 10-year level term insurance. Then, using the same profile, get a list of quotes from http://www.insure.com. How much could you save each year by buying from the least expensive company?

Discussion Questions

1. Is price the determining factor for you in choosing which life insurance policy you would purchase? Why or why not?

2. What may be the reason for the differences in pricing among these life insurance policies?

PROBLEM 3
Protecting your car

Go to http://www.allstate.com. Get a quick quote for auto insurance in your zip code. (Use 48150 if you are taking the course outside the United States.) Find out how much it would cost to insure your car. How much would you save each year if you changed your collision and comprehensive deductibles from $250 to $1,000? What extra risks would you incur? If you had an accident and paid a $1,000 deductible, how many years would it take to make up the extra $750 you paid through lower premiums? (Assume the difference in premiums does not change.)

Discussion Questions

1. What are the pros and cons of carrying a lower deductible on your car?

2. What is the rationale behind the decision to require drivers to carry automobile insurance before they are allowed to get a driver's license?

PROBLEM 4
Clear the smoke

Go to https://termlife.allstate.com/StartQuote.aspx?ZipKey=s068IS5rp7ylBnjrwrntCQ%3d%3d and get a life insurance quote using your own personal information for a $1,000,000.00 policy for a 10-year level period. How much does the premium quote change if you change your smoking status?

Discussion Questions

1. Why would insurance providers charge more for a policyholder who smokes versus one who doesn't smoke? Is this a fair business practice?

2. Other than smoking, what characteristics should increase or decrease your life insurance policy costs?

MOBILE APPS ✕

LIFE Foundation Needs Calculator (LIFE Foundation) Helps determine the level of life insurance protection needed based upon the unique characteristics of the user.

Insurance Saver (Mobile Web Solutions) Organizes all insurance policy information in one location.

INTERNET PROJECTS ✕

See text website
www.mhhe.com/slater11e_sse_ch20

4 REASONS TO RESHOP YOUR AUTO INSURANCE

Chances are you'll be able to save money on premiums. BY KIMBERLY LANKFORD

IF YOU HAVEN'T COMPARED rates for auto insurance lately, give it a try—there's a good chance you could lower your premiums. Sometimes an insurer will raise rates across the board, even for drivers with spotless records, and sometimes a change in your situation will prompt a rate spike. You may be able to save by jumping to another insurer.

1 You've been ignoring the GEICO gecko. When you reshop your rates, try an independent agent at www.iiaba.net, get price quotes at www.insweb.com or www.insurance.com, or contact insurers directly, such as at www.allstate.com, www.geico.com, www.progressive.com or www.statefarm.com. Before you switch, see how much you can save by raising your deductibles (boosting the collision deductible from $250 to $1,000 can save you 20% or more).

2 You got a speeding ticket or had an accident. In most states, tickets and at-fault accidents remain on your driving record for three or five years. Longtime customers with good driving records may not get a rate hike at all. But many insurers check motor-vehicle records every 12 or 18 months, so a speeding ticket could bump up your rates long after you were pulled over.

If your rate does rise—and especially if your policy is canceled—shop around immediately. Prospective insurers will pull your record, but some insurers care less than others about the incident. And when the accident or ticket drops off your motor-vehicle record, ask your insurer to remove the surcharge and then reshop your policy, too.

3 You have a teenage driver. A new teenage driver increases a two-car family's auto-insurance bill by an average of 58%, according to Insurance.com. Some insurers charge a lot more for teenagers, so when your teen starts to drive it's time to shop around. "One insurer's rates for young drivers can be as much as four times as high as another's," says Michael McCartin, an independent agent in College Park, Md.

You'll usually get the best deal by keeping your teen on your auto-insurance policy—even if your child is the principal driver of the vehicle he is assigned to. You will benefit from multicar and multipolicy discounts if you have homeowners coverage with the same insurer. Your child may also inherit other discounts—for example, at Travelers, kids get a safe-driver discount if their parents have had a clean driving record for five years—and most insurers offer a break of up to 15% for a grade-point average of 3.0 or higher. And if your kid goes to college more than 100 or 150 miles away without a car, you can qualify for a hefty discount.

4 You're buying a new car. Insurance costs can vary a lot depending on the car's safety and theft record and the cost to repair it. Compare premiums from a few contenders before you make your final decision. An InsWeb study found that the Kia Sedona, Mazda5, Ford Escape and Hyundai Santa Fe are the least expensive to insure, while the Acura ZDX, Audi TTS, Audi A5 and Cadillac Escalade were the most expensive.

Brad Cooper, of InsWeb, points out that vehicles that cost the least to insure may have other factors that keep premiums low. For example, a four-cylinder car with moderate horsepower is usually less expensive to insure than a six- or eight-cylinder car. InsWeb's QuickQuote (www.insweb.com/quickquote/quickquote.html) lets you look up general insurance costs for cars, but it's best to give your agent the VINs for cars you're considering. ∎

BUSINESS MATH ISSUE

The most important factor to consider when picking an insurance provider is good service.

1. List the key points of the article and information to support your position.
2. Write a group defense of your position using math calculations to support your view.

Stocks, Bonds, and Mutual Funds

LU 21–1: Stocks

1. Read, calculate, and explain stock quotations *(pp. 510–511)*.
2. Calculate dividends of preferred and common stocks; calculate return on investment *(pp. 511–513)*.

LU 21–2: Bonds

1. Read, calculate, and explain bond quotations *(p. 514)*.
2. Compare bond yields to bond premiums and discounts *(pp. 514–515)*.

LU 21–3: Mutual Funds

1. Explain and calculate net asset value and mutual fund commissions *(pp. 516–517)*.
2. Read and explain mutual fund quotations *(p. 517)*.

VOCABULARY PREVIEW

Here are key terms in this chapter. After completing the chapter, if you know the term, place a checkmark in the parentheses. If you don't know the term, look it up and put the page number where it can be found.

Bonds ( ) Bond yield ( ) Cash dividend ( ) Common stocks ( ) Cumulative preferred stock ( ) Discount ( ) Dividends ( ) Dividends in arrears ( ) Earnings per share (EPS) ( ) Mutual fund ( ) Net asset value (NAV) ( ) PE ratio ( ) Preferred stock ( ) Premium ( ) Price-earnings ratio ( ) Stockbrokers ( ) Stock certificate ( ) Stockholders ( ) Stocks ( ) Stock yield ( )

When you make financial investments there is always some degree of risk. Should you invest in stocks or bonds, or just keep your money in cash? The *Wall Street Journal* clip, "Getting the Right Mix," in the chapter opener offers some investment strategies.

Before we explain the concept of stock, consider the following general investor principles: (1) know your risk tolerance and the risk of the investments you are considering—determine whether you are a low-risk conservative investor or a high-risk speculative investor; (2) know your time frame—how soon you need your money; (3) know the liquidity of the investments you are considering—how easy it is to get your money; (4) know the return you can expect on your money—how much your money should earn; and (5) do not put "all your eggs in one basket"—diversify with a mixture of stocks, bonds, and cash equivalents. It is most important that before you seek financial advice from others, you go to the library and/or the Internet for information. When you do your own research first, you can judge the advice you receive from others.

This chapter introduces you to the major types of investments—stocks, bonds, and mutual funds. These investments indicate the performance of the companies they represent and the economy of the country at home and abroad.

Learning Unit 21–1: Stocks

We begin this unit with an introduction to the basic stock terms. Then we explain the reason why people buy stocks, newspaper stock quotations, dividends on preferred and common stocks, and return on investment.

ADAM AT HOME © 2011 Brian Basset and Rob Harrell. Reprinted with permission of UNIVERSAL UCLICK. All rights reserved.

Introduction to Basic Stock Terms

Companies sell shares of ownership in their company to raise money to finance operations, plan expansion, and so on. These ownership shares are called **stocks.** The buyers of the stock (**stockholders**) receive **stock certificates** verifying the number of shares of stock they own.

If you own 50 shares of common stock, you are entitled to 50 votes in company elections. Preferred stockholders do not have this right.

The two basic types of stock are **common stock** and **preferred stock.** Common stockholders have voting rights. Preferred stockholders do not have voting rights, but they receive preference over common stockholders in **dividends** (payments from profit) and in the company's assets if the company goes bankrupt. **Cumulative preferred stock** entitles its owners to a specific amount of dividends in 1 year. Should the company fail to pay these dividends, the **dividends in arrears** accumulate. The company pays no dividends to common stockholders until the company brings the preferred dividend payments up to date.

Why Buy Stocks?

Some investors own stock because they think the stock will become more valuable, for example, if the company makes more profit, new discoveries, and the like. Other investors own stock to share in the profit distributed by the company in dividends (cash or stock).

For various reasons, investors at different times want to sell their stock or buy more stock. Strikes, inflation, or technological changes may cause some investors to think their stock will decline in value. These investors may decide to sell. Then the law of supply and demand takes over. As more people want to sell, the stock price goes down. Should more people want to buy, the stock price would go up.

How Are Stocks Traded? Stock exchanges provide an orderly trading place for stock. You can think of these exchanges as an auction place. Only **stockbrokers** and their representatives are allowed to trade on the floor of the exchange. Stockbrokers charge commissions for stock trading—buying and selling stock for investors. As you might expect, in this age of the Internet, stock trades can also be made on the Internet. Electronic trading is growing each day.

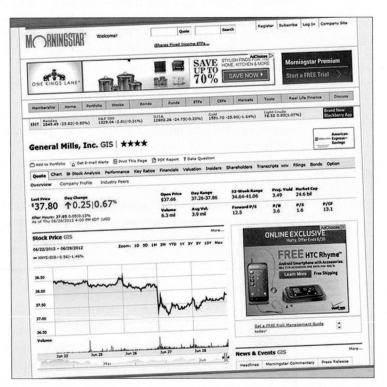

© Roberts Publishing Services

How to Read Stock Quotations in the Newspaper's Financial Section[1]

We will use General Mills stock to learn how to read the stock quotations found in your newspaper. Note the following newspaper listing of General Mills stock:

52 WEEKS				YLD		VOL		NET
HI	LO	STOCK (SYM)	DIV	%	PE	100's	CLOSE	CHG
41.06	34.64	Gen Mills (GIS)	1.21	3.1	17	239,750	39.09	−.76

The highest price at which General Mills stock traded during the past 52 weeks was $41.06 per share. This means that during the year someone was willing to pay $41.06 for a share of stock.

The lowest price at which General Mills stock traded during the year was $34.64 per share.

The newspaper lists the company name. The symbol that General Mills uses for trading is GIS. General Mills paid a dividend of $1.21 per share to stock owners last year. So if you owned 100 shares, you would have received a **cash dividend** of $121 (100 shares × $1.21).

The **stock yield** percent tells stockholders that the dividend per share is returning a rate of 3.1% to investors. This 3.1% is based on the closing price. The calculation is:

$$\text{Stock yield} = \frac{\text{Annual dividend per share}}{\text{Today's closing price per share}} = \frac{\$1.21}{\$39.09} = 3.1\% \text{ (rounded to nearest tenth percent)}$$

The 3.1% return may seem low to people who could earn a better return on their money elsewhere. Remember that if the stock price rises and you sell, your investment may result in a high rate of return.

The General Mills stock is selling at $39.09; it is selling at 17 times its **earnings per share (EPS).** Earnings per share are not listed on the stock quote.

$$\text{Earnings per share} = \text{Closing price} \div \text{Price-earnings ratio}$$
$$(\$2.30) = (\$39.09) \div (17)$$

The **price-earnings ratio,** or **PE ratio,** measures the relationship between the closing price per share of stock and the annual earnings per share. For General Mills we calculate the following price-earnings ratio. (This is not listed in the newspaper.)

$$\text{PE ratio} = \frac{\text{Closing price per share of stock}}{\text{Annual earnings per share}} = \frac{\$39.09}{\$2.30} = 17$$

If the PE ratio column shows ". . . ," this means the company has no earnings. The PE ratio will often vary depending on quality of stock, future expectations, economic conditions, and so on.

In the newspaper stock quotations for General Mills, the number in the volume column is in the 100s. Thus, to 239,750, you add two zeros to get 23,975,000. This indicates that 23,975,000 shares were traded on this day. Remember that shares of stock need a buyer and a seller to trade.

The last trade of the day, called the closing price, was at $39.09 per share.

On the *previous day,* the closing price was $39.85 (not given). The *new* close is $39.09. The result is that the closing price is down $.76 from the *previous day.*

Dividends on Preferred and Common Stocks

If you own stock in a company, the company may pay out dividends. (Not all companies pay dividends.) The amount of the dividend is determined by the net earnings of the company listed in its financial report. The clip on page 512 from *Barron's* shows some companies that have boosted their dividend.

[1]For centuries, stocks were traded and reported in fraction form. In 2001 the New York Stock Exchange and NASDAQ began the conversion to decimals, which is how it is reported today.

FIGURE 21.1

New York Stock Exchange

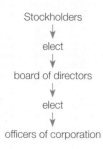

Stockholders
↓
elect
↓
board of directors
↓
elect
↓
officers of corporation

Round PE to the nearest whole number.

LO 2

DIVIDEND PAYMENT BOOSTS

Company Name-Ticker Symbol (Exchange)	Period	To	From	% Increase	Record Date	Ex-Div Date	Payment Date
Apartment Investment Mgt-AIV (NYSE)	Q	.18	.12	50.0%	2-21	2-16	2-29
Assured Guaranty Ltd-AGO (NYSE)	Q	.09	.045	100.0%	2-23	2-21	3-08
Avista Corp-AVA (NYSE)	Q	.29	.275	5.5%	2-24	2-22	3-15
BRE Properties-BRE (NYSE)	Q	.385	.375	2.7%	3-15	3-13	3-30
Barry (RG) Corp-DFZ (Nasdaq)	Q	.08	.07	14.3%	2-20	2-15	3-05
Chesapeake Lodging Tr-CHSP (NYSE)	Q	.22	.20	10.0%	3-31	3-28	4-13
Church & Dwight-CHD (NYSE)	Q	.24	.17	41.2%	2-21	2-16	3-01
Coca-Cola Enterprises-CCE (NYSE)	Q	.16	.13	23.1%	3-09	3-07	3-22
Corp Executive Board-EXBD (NYSE)	Q	.175	.15	16.7%	3-15	3-13	3-30
Diebold Inc-DBD (NYSE)	Q	.285	.28	1.8%	2-20	2-15	3-05
Dr Pepper Snapple Grp-DPS (NYSE)	Q	.34	.32	6.3%	3-19	3-15	4-06
Dun & Bradstreet-DNB (NYSE)	Q	.38	.36	5.6%	2-28	2-24	3-14
Eastern Co-EML (Nasdaq)	Q	.10	.09	11.1%	2-22	2-17	3-15
Equifax Inc-EFX (NYSE)	Q	.18	.16	12.5%	2-23	2-21	3-15
Fidelity National Finl-FNF (NYSE)	Q	.14	.12	16.7%	3-16	3-14	3-30
Harley-Davidson-HOG (NYSE)	Q	.155	.125	24.0%	2-21	2-16	3-02
Home Properties-HME (NYSE)	Q	.66	.62	6.5%	2-16	2-14	2-28
Hubbell Inc B-HUBB (NYSE)	Q	.41	.38	7.9%	3-05	3-01	4-11
Jack Henry & Associates-JKHY (Nasdaq)	Q	.115	.105	9.5%	2-21	2-16	3-08
L-3 Communications-LLL (NYSE)	Q	.50	.45	11.1%	3-01	2-28	3-15
Lorillard Inc.-LO (NYSE)	Q	1.55	1.30	19.2%	3-01	2-28	3-09
MasterCard Inc A-MA (NYSE)	Q	.30	.15	100.0%	4-09	4-05	5-09
Occidental Petroleum-OXY (NYSE)	Q	.54	.46	17.4%	3-09	3-07	4-15
Omnicom Group-OMC (NYSE)	Q	.30	.25	20.0%	3-05	3-01	4-02
Owens & Minor Inc-OMI (NYSE)	Q	.22	.20	10.0%	3-15	3-13	3-30
PartnerRe Ltd-PRE (NYSE)	Q	.62	.60	3.3%	2-17	2-15	3-01
Simon Property Inc-SPG (NYSE)	Q	.95	.90	5.6%	2-15	2-13	2-29
3M Co-MMM (NYSE)	Q	.59	.55	7.3%	2-17	2-15	3-12
Time Warner Inc-TWX (NYSE)	Q	.26	.235	10.6%	2-29	2-27	3-15
Timken Co-TKR (NYSE)	Q	.23	.20	15.0%	2-21	2-16	3-02
Tortoise Engy Infrastr-TYG (NYSE)	Q	.5575	.555	0.5%	2-22	2-17	3-01
United Parcel Svc B-UPS (NYSE)	Q	.57	.52	9.6%	2-21	2-16	3-07
Western Union Co-WU (NYSE)	Q	.10	.08	25.0%	3-16	3-14	3-30

Barron's © 2012

Earlier we stated that cumulative preferred stockholders must be paid all past and present dividends before common stockholders can receive any dividends. Following is an example to illustrate the calculation of dividends on preferred and common stocks for 2014 and 2015.

EXAMPLE   The stock records of Jason Corporation show the following:

Preferred stock issued: 20,000 shares.

Preferred stock cumulative at $.80 per share.

Common stock issued: 400,000 shares.

In 2014, Jason paid no dividends.

In 2015, Jason paid $512,000 in dividends.

Remember that common stockholders do not have the cumulative feature of preferred stockholders.

Since Jason declared no dividends in 2014, the company has $16,000 (20,000 shares × $.80 = $16,000) dividends in arrears to preferred stockholders. The dividend of $512,000 in 2015 is divided between preferred and common stockholders as follows:

	2014		2015	
Dividends paid	0		$512,000	
Preferred stockholders*	Paid: 0		Paid for 2014 (20,000 shares × $.80)	$ 16,000
	Owe: Preferred, $16,000 (20,000 shares × $.80)		Paid for 2015	16,000
				$ 32,000
Common stockholders	0		Total dividend	$512,000
			Paid preferred for 2014 and 2015	− 32,000
			To common	$480,000
			$\dfrac{\$480,000}{400,000 \text{ shares}} = \$1.20$ per share	

*For a discussion of par value (arbitrary value placed on stock for accounting purposes) and cash and stock dividend distribution, check your accounting text.

Calculating Return on Investment

Now let's learn how to calculate a return on your investment of General Mills stock, assuming the following:

Bought 200 shares at $39.09.

Sold at end of 1 year 200 shares at $41.10.

1% commission rate on buying and selling stock.

Current $1.21 dividend per share in effect.

Bought		**Sold**	
200 shares at $39.09	$7,818.00	200 shares at $41.10	$8,220.00
+ Broker's commission		− Broker's commission	
(.01 × $7,818)	+ 78.18	(.01 × $8,220.00)	− 82.20
Total cost	$7,896.18	Total receipt	$8,137.80

Note: A commission is charged on both the buying and selling of stock.

Total receipt	$8,137.80
Total cost	− 7,896.18
Net gain	$ 241.62
Dividends	+ 242.00 (200 shares × $1.21)
Total gain	$ 483.62

Portion $\dfrac{\$483.62}{\$7,896.18} = \boxed{6.12\%}$ rate of return (to nearest hundredth percent)

Base

It's time for another Practice Quiz.

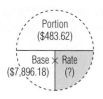

Portion ($483.62)

Base × Rate ($7,896.18) (?)

LU 21–1 PRACTICE QUIZ

Complete this **Practice Quiz** to see how you are doing.

1. From the following Texaco stock quotation **(a)** explain the letters, **(b)** estimate the company's earnings per share, and **(c)** show how "YLD %" was calculated.

52 WEEKS				**YLD**		**VOL**		**NET**
HI	**LO**	**STOCK (SYM)**	**DIV**	**%**	**PE**	**100's**	**CLOSE**	**CHG**
73.90	48.25	Texaco TX	1.80	2.5	14	13020	72.25	+0.46
(A)	(B)	(C)	(D)	(E)	(F)	(G)	(H)	(I)

2. **Given:** 30,000 shares of preferred cumulative stock at $.70 per share; 200,000 shares of common; 2014, no dividend; 2015, $109,000. How much is paid to each class of stock in 2015?

*For **extra help** from your authors—Sharon and Jeff—see the student DVD*

You Tube

✓ **Solutions**

1. **a.** (A) Highest price traded in last 52 weeks.
     (B) Lowest price traded in past 52 weeks.
     (C) Name of corporation is Texaco (symbol TX).
     (D) Dividend per share per year is $1.80.
     (E) Yield for year is 2.5%.
     (F) Texaco stock sells at 14 times its earnings.
     (G) Sales volume for the day is 1,302,000 shares.
     (H) The last price (closing price for the day) is $72.25.
     (I) Stock is up $.46 from closing price yesterday.

    b. EPS = $\dfrac{\$72.25}{14} = \$5.16$ per share

    c. $\dfrac{\$1.80}{\$72.25} = 2.5\%$

2. **Preferred:** 30,000 × $.70 = $21,000   Arrears 2014
                                   + 21,000   2015
                                   —————
                                     $42,000

    Common: $67,000 ($109,000 − $42,000)

LU 21–1a ‖ EXTRA PRACTICE QUIZ WITH WORKED-OUT SOLUTIONS

Need more practice? Try this **Extra Practice Quiz** (check figures in the Interactive Chapter Organizer, p. 519). Worked-out Solutions can be found in Appendix B at end of text.

1. From the following Goodyear stock quotation (**a**) explain the letters, (**b**) estimate the company's earnings per share, and (**c**) show how YLD % was calculated.

| 52 WEEKS | | | | YLD | | VOL | | NET |
HI	LO	STOCK (SYM)	DIV	%	PE	100'S	CLOSE	CHG
23.14	3.17	Goodyear GT	.07	.54	16	30800	13.08	+.11
(A)	(B)	(C)	(D)	(E)	(F)	(G)	(H)	(I)

2. **Given:** 40,000 shares of preferred cumulative stock at $.60 per share; 300,000 shares of common; 2014, no dividend; 2015, $210,000. How much is paid to each class of stock in 2015?

Learning Unit 21–2: Bonds

LO 1

Have you heard of the Rule of 115? This rule is used as a rough measure to show how quickly an investment will triple in value. To use the rule, divide 115 by the rate of return your money earns. For example, if a bond earns 5% interest, divide 115 by 5. This measure estimates that your money in the bond will triple in 23 years.

This unit begins by explaining the difference between bonds and stocks. Then you will learn how to read bond quotations and calculate bond yields.

Reading Bond Quotations

Sometimes companies raise money by selling bonds instead of stock. When you buy stock, you become a part owner in the company. To raise money, companies may not want to sell more stock and thus dilute the ownership of their current stock owners, so they sell bonds. **Bonds** represent a promise from the company to pay the face amount to the bond owner at a future date, along with interest payments at a stated rate.

Once a company issues bonds, they are traded as stock is. If a company goes bankrupt, bondholders have the first claim to the assets of the corporation—before stockholders. As with stock, changes in bond prices vary according to supply and demand. Brokers also charge commissions on bond trading. These commissions vary.

Bond quotes are stated in percents of the face value of the bond and not in dollars as stock is. Interest is paid semiannually.

LO 2

How to Read the Bond Section of the Newspaper

The bond section of the newspaper shows the bonds that are traded that day. The information given on bonds differs from the information given on stocks. The newspaper states bond prices in *percents of face amount, not in dollar amounts* as stock prices are stated. Also, bonds are usually in denominations of $1,000 (the face amount).

When a bond sells at a price below its face value, the bond is sold at a discount. Why? The interest that the bond pays may not be as high as the current market rate. When this happens, the bond is not as attractive to investors, and it sells for a **discount.** The opposite could, of course, also occur. The bond may sell at a **premium,** which means that the bond sells for more than its face value or the bond interest is higher than the current market rate.

Let's look at this newspaper information given for Aflac bonds:

Bonds	Current yield	Vol.	Close	Net change
Aflac 422	4.02%	214,587	99.50	−1

Note: Bond prices are stated as a percent of face amount.

The name of the company is Aflac. It produces a wide range of insurance coverage. The interest on the bond is 4%. The company pays the interest semiannually. The bond matures (comes due) in 2022. The total interest for the year is $40 (.04 × $1,000). Remember that the face value of the bond is $1,000. Now let's show this with the following formula:

> Yearly interest = Face value of bond × Stated yearly interest rate
>
> $40.00   = $1,000   ×   .04

We calculate the 4.02% yield by dividing the total annual interest of the bond by the total cost of the bond. (For our purposes, we will omit the commission cost.) We will calculate more bond yields in a moment.

Note this bond is selling for more than $1,000 since its interest is very attractive compared to other new offerings.

$$\frac{\text{Yearly interest}}{\text{Cost of bond at closing}} = \frac{\$40 \ (.04 \times \$1,000)}{\$995 \ (.9950 \times \$1,000)}$$

$$= \boxed{4.02\%} \qquad \text{This is the same as 99.50\%.}$$

On this day, $214,587 bonds were traded. Note that we do *not* add two zeros as we did to the sales volume of stock.

The last bond traded on this day was 99.50% of face value, or in dollars, $.9950.

The last trade of the day was down 1% of the face value from the last trade of yesterday. In dollars this is 1% = $10.

$$1\% = .01 \times \$1,000 = \$10$$

Thus, the closing price on this day, 99.50% + 1%, equals yesterday's close of 100.50% ($1,005). Note that *yesterday's close is not listed in today's quotations.*

Calculating Bond Yields

The Aflac bond (selling at a discount) pays 4% interest when it is yielding investors 4.02%.

$$\text{Bond yield} = \frac{\text{Total annual interest of bond}}{\text{Total current cost of bond at closing*}}$$

*We assume this to be the buyer's purchase price.

The following example will show us how to calculate **bond yields.**

EXAMPLE   Jim Smith bought 5 bonds of Aflac at the closing price of 99.50 (remember that in dollars 99.50% is $995). Jim's total cost excluding commission is:

$$5 \times \$995 = \$4,975$$

What is Jim's interest?

No matter what Jim pays for the bonds, he will still receive interest of $40 per bond (.04 × $1,000). Jim bought the bonds at $995 each, resulting in a bond yield of 4.02%. Let's calculate Jim's yield to the nearest tenth percent:

(5 bonds × $40 interest per bond per year)

$$\frac{\$200.00}{\$4,975} = 4.02\%$$

Now let's try another Practice Quiz.

MONEY tips

Spend your money wisely. Cut back on frivolous spending to provide more discretionary income for an emergency fund and retirement savings.

LU 21–2 PRACTICE QUIZ

Complete this **Practice Quiz** to see how you are doing.

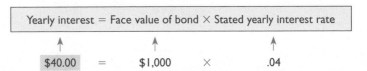

Bonds	Yield		Sales	Close	Net change
Aetna 6.375% 13	6.4		20	100.375	.875

From the above bond quotation, **(1)** calculate the cost of 5 bonds at closing (disregard commissions) and **(2)** check the current yield of 6.4%.

You Tube™

✔ Solutions

1. $100.375\% = 1.00375 \times \$1,000 = \$1,003.75 \times 5 = $ $\boxed{\$5,018.75}$
2. $6.375\% = .06375 \times \$1,000 = \$63.75$ annual interest

$$\frac{\$63.75}{\$1,003.75} = 6.35\% = \boxed{6.4\%}$$

LU 21–2a	EXTRA PRACTICE QUIZ WITH WORKED-OUT SOLUTIONS

Need more practice? Try this **Extra Practice Quiz** (check figures in the Interactive Chapter Organizer, p. 519). Worked-out Solutions can be found in Appendix B at end of text.

Bonds	Yield	Sales	Close	Net change
Aetna 7.5 14	7.5%	20	100.25	+.75

From the above bond quotation, **(1)** calculate the cost of 5 bonds at closing (disregard commissions) and **(2)** check the current yield of 7.5%.

Learning Unit 21–3: Mutual Funds

Steve Senne/AP Photo

In recent years, mutual funds have increased dramatically and people in the United States have invested billions in mutual funds. Investors can choose from several fund types—stock funds, bond funds, international funds, balanced (stocks and bonds) funds, and so on. This learning unit tells you why investors choose mutual funds and discusses the net asset value of mutual funds, mutual fund commissions, and how to read a mutual fund quotation.

DILBERT © Scott Adams/Dist. by United Feature Syndicate, Inc.

Why Investors Choose Mutual Funds

The main reasons investors choose mutual funds are the following:

LO 1

1. **Diversification.** When you invest in a mutual fund, you own a small portion of many different companies. This protects you against the poor performance of a single company but not against a sell-off in the market (stock and bond exchanges) or fluctuations in the interest rate.

2. **Professional management.** You are hiring a professional manager to look after your money when you own shares in mutual funds. The success of a particular fund is often due to the person(s) managing the fund.

3. **Liquidity.** Most funds will buy back your fund shares whenever you decide to sell.

4. **Low fund expenses.** Competition forces funds to keep their expenses low to maximize their performance. Because stocks and bonds in a mutual fund represent thousands of shareholders, funds can trade in large blocks, reducing transaction costs.

5. **Access to foreign markets.** Through mutual funds, investors can conveniently and inexpensively invest in foreign markets.

Net Asset Value

Investing in a **mutual fund** means that you buy shares in the fund's portfolio (group of stocks and/or bonds). The value of your mutual fund share is expressed in the share's **net asset value (NAV)**, which is the dollar value of one mutual fund share. You calculate the

NAV by subtracting the fund's current liabilities from the current market value of the fund's investments and dividing this by the number of shares outstanding.

$$NAV = \frac{\text{Current market value of fund's investments} - \text{Current liabilities}}{\text{Number of shares outstanding}}$$

The NAV helps investors track the value of their fund investment. After the market closes on each business day, the fund uses the closing prices of the investments it owns to find the dollar value of one fund share, or NAV. This is the price investors receive if they sell fund shares on that day or pay if they buy fund shares on that day.

Commissions When Buying Mutual Funds

The following table is a quick reference for the cost of buying mutual fund shares. Commissions vary from 0% to $8\frac{1}{2}$% depending on how the mutual fund is classified.

Classification	Commission charge*	Offer price to buy
No-load (NL) fund	No sales charge	NAV (buy directly from investment company)
Low-load (LL) fund	3% or less	NAV + commission % (buy directly from investment company or from a broker)
Load fund	$8\frac{1}{2}$% or less	NAV + commission % (buy from a broker)

*On a front-end load, you pay a commission when you purchase the fund shares, while on a back-end load, you pay when you redeem or sell. In general, if you hold the shares for more than 5 years, you pay no commission charge.

The offer price to buy a share for a low-load or load fund is the NAV plus the commission. Now let's look at how to read a mutual fund quotation.

LO 2

How to Read a Mutual Fund Quotation

We will be studying the Putnam Mutual Funds. Cindy Joelson has invested in the Growth and Income Fund with the hope that over the years this will provide her with financial security when she retires. On May 27, Cindy turns to *Barron's* and looks up the Putnam Growth Income Fund quotation.

Putnam Funds Class A:				
AmGv p	9.18	-0.01	-0.4	32.3
CATx p	8.16	0.00	3.1	31.5
ConvSec	19.82	-0.05	8.1	79.1
Dvrln p	7.53	0.02	3.5	71.7
DynAABalA	11.32	-0.01	6.1	67.9
DynAAGthA	12.68	-0.03	8.0	71.2
Eqln p	16.14	-0.10	7.5	67.8
GeorgePutBal	12.57	-0.03	4.3	54.2
GlbHlthCare p	41.41	-0.48	6.5	32.6
GlblEqty p	8.97	NA	NA	NA
Grln p	13.82	-0.06	8.9	71.6
HYAd p	5.91	0.01	3.9	68.3
HiYd p	7.61	NA	NA	NA
Incm p	6.86	0.03	1.6	62.1
IntCaO p	30.94	-0.18	13.7	80.2
IntlEq p	17.89	NA	NA	NA

	NAV	Net Chg.	YTD % Ret.	3-Yr. % Ret.
Inv p	13.60	-0.01	7.9	73.4
MultiCpGr p	53.85	-0.13	12.0	70.7
NYTx p	8.83	0.00	2.4	25.7
TFHY	12.16	0.00	3.5	50.5
TxEx p	8.87	0.00	2.6	30.7
USGv p	13.69	NA	NA	NA
Voy p	22.55	0.00	15.6	92.4

Barron's © 2012

The name of the fund is Growth and Income, which has the investment objective of growth and income securities as set forth in the fund's prospectus (document giving information about the fund). Note that this is only one fund in the Putnam family of funds.

- The $13.82 figure is the NAV plus the sales commission.
- The fund has decreased $.06 from the NAV quotation of the previous day.
- The fund has a 8.9% return this year (January through May 27). This assumes reinvestments of all distributions. Sales charges are not reflected.

Now let's check your understanding of this unit with a Practice Quiz.

MONEY tips

A will provides peace of mind to those surviving. Reread your will annually to ensure it is up-to-date. If you do not have a will, write one. There are many free resources online. Put your will in a safety deposit or fireproof box and ensure survivors can locate it.

LU 21–3 PRACTICE QUIZ

Complete this **Practice Quiz** to see how you are doing.

From the mutual fund quotation of the Schwab Health Care Growth Fund shown below, complete the following:

1. NAV

   _____

2. NAV change

   _____

3. Total return, YTD

   _____

*For **extra help** from your authors–Sharon and Jeff–see the student DVD*

You Tube

✓ **Solutions**

1. 18.33

2. −.11

3. 4.4

Schwab Funds:				
1000 Inv nr	37.99	-0.06	7.4	74.3
CoreEq n	17.99	0.00	7.1	55.3
DivEqSel n	13.99	-0.06	4.6	58.8
FunUSLgInst nr	10.07	-0.04	6.7	103.1
FunUSSmMdInst nr	10.24	-0.17	10.9	132.8
GNMA Sel n	10.55	0.00	0.2	20.0
HlthCare n	18.33	-0.11	4.4	55.0
Intl Sel nr	15.80	-0.18	8.1	49.4
IntlMstrl n	18.05	-0.18	9.6	84.5
IntlMstr S nr	18.04	-0.17	9.7	85.3
MT AllEq n	12.28	-0.12	8.0	71.2
MT Bal n	15.75	-0.08	4.9	50.5
MT Gro n	17.39	-0.12	6.4	61.1
PremIncInst nr	10.49	0.00	0.7	31.3
S&P Sel n	20.93	-0.03	6.9	72.6
SmCp Sel nr	20.88	-0.46	9.8	107.2
TotBd n	9.61	0.00	0.5	20.8
TSM Sel nr	24.34	-0.08	7.6	77.5
TxFrBd n	11.94	0.00	1.8	23.3

Barron's © 2012

LU 21–3a EXTRA PRACTICE QUIZ WITH WORKED-OUT SOLUTIONS

Need more practice? Try this **Extra Practice Quiz** (check figures in the Interactive Chapter Organizer, p. 519). Worked-out Solutions can be found in Appendix B at end of text.

From the mutual fund quotation of the Principal Investor High Yield A Fund shown below, complete the following:

1. NAV

   _____

2. NAV change

   _____

3. Total return, YTD

   _____

Principal Investors:				
BdMtgIn	10.79	0.02	1.6	45.2
DivIntlInst	9.55	-0.12	8.0	54.9
EqInclA p	18.71	-0.15	5.0	70.5
FlIncA p	11.59	-0.01	3.4	43.5
GvtHiQltyA	11.32	0.00	0.7	20.2
HighYldA p	7.61	0.00	3.8	66.3
HighYldC t	7.67	0.01	3.8	62.9
HiYld IN	10.50	0.03	3.9	74.7
InfPro IN	8.84	0.03	1.7	32.1
IntlI Inst	10.49	-0.16	9.0	45.1
LgGrIN	8.56	0.03	9.6	65.8
LgIndxI	9.40	-0.01	6.9	72.0
LgValIN	9.92	-0.06	6.6	60.8
LT2010In	11.54	-0.02	4.8	58.9
LT2020 In	11.99	-0.04	6.5	63.9
LT2020J t	11.95	-0.05	6.4	62.0
LT2030In	11.84	-0.06	7.1	67.0
LT2030J t	11.83	-0.06	7.1	64.9
LT2040I	11.99	-0.07	7.7	67.8
LT2050I	11.48	-0.07	8.1	68.6
LTStratI	10.99	0.00	3.2	44.9
MdGrIII Inst	11.30	-0.03	11.2	104.7
MdVall In	13.50	-0.04	8.4	88.4
MidCpBldA	14.28	-0.05	6.6	93.0
PLgGr2I	8.22	-0.01	8.2	70.4
PreSecI	9.81	0.04	5.1	96.1
PtrLB In	10.07	-0.02	7.1	68.0
PtrLGI In	9.78	0.00	10.1	99.9
PtrLgVal IN	11.06	-0.03	7.9	63.0
PtrLV In	10.40	-0.03	7.0	58.4
SGI In	11.37	-0.17	10.9	121.8
SmCVII IN	9.92	-0.19	9.5	98.5
RealEstSecI	18.52	-0.47	6.1	132.9
SAMBalA p	13.20	-0.05	5.3	56.0
SAMBalC t	13.06	-0.05	5.2	52.6
SAMGrA p	14.09	-0.08	6.3	61.9
SAMGrC t	13.41	-0.09	6.2	58.1
StrGrw A p	15.49	-0.12	7.5	66.0
A p	40.20	-0.33	6.6	70.9

Barron's © 2012

INTERACTIVE CHAPTER ORGANIZER

Topic/procedure/formula	Examples	You try it*
Stock yield, p. 511 <u>Annual dividend per share</u> Today's closing price per share (Round yield to nearest hundredth percent.)	Annual dividend, $.72 Today's closing price, $42.375 $\dfrac{\$.72}{\$42.375} = $ 1.70%	**Calculate stock yield to nearest hundredth percent** Annual dividend, $.88 Today's closing price, $53.88
Price-earnings ratio, p. 511 $PE = \dfrac{\text{Closing price per share of stock}}{\text{Annual earnings per share}}$ (Round answer to nearest whole number.)	From previous example: Closing price, $42.375 Annual earnings per share, $4.24 $\dfrac{\$42.375}{\$4.24} = 9.99 = $ 10	**Calculate PE ratio** From previous example: Closing price, $53.88 Annual earnings per share, $3.70

Dividends with cumulative preferred stock, p. 512
Cumulative preferred stock is entitled to all dividends in arrears before common stock receives dividend.
	2013 dividend omitted; in 2014, $400,000 in dividends paid out. Preferred is cumulative at $.90 per share; 20,000 shares of preferred issued and 100,000 shares of common issued.
	To preferred:
	  20,000 shares × $.90 = $18,000
	In arrears 2013:
	  20,000 shares × .90 = <u>18,000</u>
	  Dividend to preferred $36,000
	To common:
	  $364,000 ($400,000 − $36,000)
	  $\dfrac{\$364,000}{100,000 \text{ shares}} = \$3.64$ dividend to common per share
		Calculate dividends to preferred and common stock
		2013, no dividend
		2014, $300,000
		Preferred—$.80 cumulative, 30,000 shares issued
		Common—60,000 shares issued

Cost of a bond, p. 515 Bond prices are stated as a percent of the face value. Bonds selling for less than face value result in bond discounts. Bonds selling for more than face value result in bond premiums.	Bill purchases 5 $1,000, 12% bonds at closing price of $103\frac{1}{4}$. What is his cost (omitting commissions)? $103\frac{1}{4}\% = 103.25\% = 1.0325$ in decimal $1.0325 \times \$1,000$ bond = $1,032.50 per bond 5 bonds × $1,032.50 = $5,162.50	**Calculate cost of bonds** 6 $1,000, 3% bonds at 102.25
Bond yield, p. 515 <u>Total annual interest of bond</u> Total current cost of bond at closing (Round to nearest tenth percent.)	Calculate bond yield from last example on one bond. $\dfrac{\overset{(\$1,000 \times .12)}{\$120}}{\$1,032.50} = $ 11.6%	**Calculate bond yield** 4% bond selling for $1,011.20
Mutual fund, pp. 516–517 $NAV = \dfrac{\begin{array}{c}\text{Current market value} \\ \text{of fund's investment}\end{array} - \begin{array}{c}\text{Current} \\ \text{liabilities}\end{array}}{\text{Number of shares outstanding}}$	The NAV of the Scudder Income Bond Fund was $12.84. The NAV change was 0.01. What was the NAV yesterday? $12.83	**Calculate yesterday's NAV** Today—$12.44 Change—.05

KEY TERMS	Bonds, *p. 514* Bond yield, *p. 515* Cash dividend, *p. 511* Common stocks, *p. 510* Cumulative preferred stock, *p. 510* Discount, *p. 514* Dividends, *p. 510*	Dividends in arrears, *p. 510* Earnings per share (EPS), *p. 511* Mutual fund, *p. 516* Net asset value (NAV), *p. 516* PE ratio, *p. 511* Preferred stock, *p. 510* Premium, *p. 514*	Price-earnings ratio, *p. 511* Stockbrokers, *p. 510* Stock certificate, *p. 510* Stockholders, *p. 510* Stocks, *p. 510* Stock yield, *p. 511*

Check Figures for Extra Practice Quizzes with Page References. (Worked-out Solutions in Appendix B.)	LU 21–1a (p. 514)
	1. b. $.82 per share
	  c. $.07/$13.08 = .54%
	2. Pref. $48,000
	  Com. $162,000
		LU 21–2a (p. 516)
		1. $5,012.50
		2. $\dfrac{\$75}{\$1,002.50} = 7.48\%$
			LU 21–3a (p. 518)
			1. $7.61
			2. no change
			3. 3.8%

*Worked-out solutions are in Appendix B.

Critical Thinking Discussion Questions with Chapter Concept Check

1. Explain how to read a stock quotation. What are some of the red flags of buying stock?

2. What is the difference between odd and round lots? Explain why the commission on odd lots could be quite expensive.

3. Explain how to read a bond quote. What could be a drawback of investing in bonds?

4. Compare and contrast stock yields and bond yields. As a conservative investor, which option might be better? Defend your answer.

5. Explain what NAV means. What is the difference between a load and a no-load fund? How safe are mutual funds?

6. **Chapter Concept Check.** Review the chapter opener and then go to the web to determine what you would invest in today if you were building a portfolio. Keep in mind your age, marital status, and the financial goals you want to achieve. Use the concepts in this chapter to develop your investment strategy.

END-OF-CHAPTER PROBLEMS   McGraw Hill connect plus+   www.mhhe.com/slater11e

Check figures for odd-numbered problems in Appendix C.   Name _____   Date _____

DRILL PROBLEMS

Calculate the cost (omit commission) of buying the following shares of stock: *LU 21-1(1)*

21–1. 400 shares of General Mills at $379.88

21–2. 1,200 shares of Apple at $77.90

Calculate the yield of each of the following stocks (rounded to the nearest tenth percent):   *LU 21-1(1)*

Company	Yearly dividend	Closing price per share	Yield
21–3. Boeing	$.68	$64.63	____
21–4. Best Buy	$.07	$9.56	____

Calculate the earnings per share, price-earnings ratio (to nearest whole number), or stock price as needed: *LU 21-1(1)*

Company	Earnings per share	Closing price per share	Price-earnings ratio
21–5. BellSouth	$3.15	$40.13	____
21–6. American Express	$3.85	_____	26

21–7. Calculate the total cost of buying 400 shares of CVS at $59.38. Assume a 2% commission.   *LU 21-1(1)*

21–8. If in Problem 21–1 the 400 shares of General Mills stock were sold at $350, what would be the loss? Commission is omitted.   *LU 21-1(1)*

21–9. Given: 20,000 shares cumulative preferred stock ($2.25 dividend per share): 40,000 shares common stock. Dividends paid: 2013, $8,000; 2014, 0; and 2015, $160,000. How much will preferred and common stockholders receive each year?   *LU 21-1(2)*

For each of these bonds, calculate the total dollar amount you would pay at the quoted price (disregard commission or any interest that may have accrued):   *LU 21-2(1)*

Company	Bond price	Number of bonds purchased	Dollar amount of purchase price
21–10. Petro	87.75	3	_____
21–11. Wang	114	2	_____

For the following bonds, calculate the total annual interest, total cost, and current yield (to the nearest tenth percent): *LU 21-2(2)*

Bond	Number of bonds purchased	Selling price	Total annual interest	Total cost	Current yield
21–12. Sharn $11\frac{3}{4}$ 12	2	115	_____	_____	_____
21–13. Wang $6\frac{1}{2}$ 14	4	68.125	_____	_____	_____

21–14. From the following calculate the net asset values. Round to the nearest cent. *LU 21-3(1)*

	Current market value of fund investment	Current liabilities	Number of shares outstanding	NAV
a.	$5,550,000	$770,000	600,000	_____
b.	$13,560,000	$780,000	840,000	_____

21–15. From the following mutual fund quotation, complete the blanks: *LU 21-3(2)*

				TOTAL RETURN		
	Inv. obj.	NAV	NAV chg.	YTD	4 wks.	1 yr.
EuGr	ITL	12.04	−0.06	+8.2	+0.9	+9.6

NAV _____   NAV change _____

Total return, 1 year _____

WORD PROBLEMS

21–16. Ryan Neal bought 1,200 shares of Ford at $1.98 per share. Assume a commission of 2% of the purchase price. What is the
e**X**cel total cost to Ryan? *LU 21-1(1)*

21–17. Assume in Problem 21–16 that Ryan sells the stock for $2.25 with the same 2% commission rate. What is the bottom line
e**X**cel for Ryan? *LU 21-1(1)*

21–18. Jim Corporation pays its cumulative preferred stockholders $1.60 per share. Jim has 30,000 shares of preferred and 75,000
e**X**cel shares of common. In 2013, 2014, and 2015, due to slowdowns in the economy, Jim paid no dividends. Now in 2016, the
board of directors decided to pay out $500,000 in dividends. How much of the $500,000 does each class of stock receive
as dividends? *LU 21-1(2)*

21–19. Maytag Company earns $4.80 per share. Today the stock is trading at $59.25. The company pays an annual dividend of $1.40. Calculate **(a)** the price-earnings ratio (rounded to the nearest whole number) and **(b)** the yield on the stock (to the nearest tenth percent). *LU 21-1(1)*

21–20. Jimmy Comfort was interested in pursuing a second career after retiring from the military. He signed up with Twitter to help network with individuals in his field. Within 1 week, he received an offer from a colleague to join her start-up business in Atlanta, Georgia. Along with his salary, he receives 100 shares of stock each month. If the stock is worth $4.50 a share, what is the value of the 100 shares he receives each month? *LU 21-1(1, 2)*

21–21. The following bond was quoted in *The Wall Street Journal:*   *LU 21-2(1)*

Bonds	Curr. yld.	Vol.	Close	Net chg.
NY Tel $7\frac{1}{4}$ 11	7.2	10	100.875	$+1\frac{1}{8}$

Five bonds were purchased yesterday, and 5 bonds were purchased today. How much more did the 5 bonds cost today (in dollars)?

20–22. Seattle-based Amazon.com's stock (AMZN) was trading at $246.71 in October 2011. In early 2012, the stock was trading at $177.54. Net income fell 58% from $416 million to $177 million. If AMZN's price-earnings ratio is 130.46 with a closing price of $177.54, what are the annual earnings per share? *LU 21-1(1)*

21–23. Ron bought a bond of Bee Company for 79.25. The original bond was $5\frac{3}{4}$ 12. Ron wants to know the current yield (to the nearest tenth percent). Please help Ron with the calculation. *LU 21-2(1)*

21–24. Abby Sane decided to buy corporate bonds instead of stock. She desired to have the fixed-interest payments. She purchased 5 bonds of Meg Corporation $11\frac{3}{4}$ 09 at 88.25. As the stockbroker for Abby (assume you charge her a $5 commission per bond), please provide her with the following: **(a)** the total cost of the purchase, **(b)** total annual interest to be received, and **(c)** current yield (to nearest tenth percent). *LU 21-2(1)*

21–25. Mary Blake is considering whether to buy stocks or bonds. She has a good understanding of the pros and cons of both. The stock she is looking at is trading at $59.25, with an annual dividend of $3.99. Meanwhile, the bond is trading at 96.25, with an annual interest rate of $11\frac{1}{2}\%$. Calculate for Mary her yield (to the nearest tenth percent) for the stock and the bond. *LU 21-1(1), LU 21-2(1)*

21–26. Wall Street performs a sort of "financial alchemy" enabling the individual to benefit from institutions lending money to them, according to Adam Davidson, cofounder of NPR's "Planet Money." Individuals can invest small amounts of their money in a 401(k), pooling their capital and spreading the risk. If you invested in Fidelity New Millennium, FMILX, one of the "10 Best Rated Funds for 2012" by *The Street*, how much would you pay for 80 shares if the 52-week high is $32.26, the 52-week low is $26.38, and the NAV is $31.88? *LU 21-3(1)*

21–27. Louis Hall read in the paper that Fidelity Growth Fund has an NAV of $16.02. He called Fidelity and asked how the NAV was calculated. Fidelity gave him the following information:

Current market value of fund investment	$8,550,000
Current liabilities	$ 860,000
Number of shares outstanding	480,000

Did Fidelity provide Louis with the correct information? *LU 21-3(1)*

21–28. Lee Ray bought 130 shares of a mutual fund with an NAV of $13.10. This fund also has a load charge of $8\frac{1}{2}\%$. **(a)** What is the offer price and **(b)** what did Lee pay for his investment? *LU 21-3(1)*

21–29. Ron and Madeleine Couple received their 2010 Form 1099-DIV (dividends received) in the amount of $1,585. Ron and Madeleine are in the 28% bracket. What would be their tax liability on the dividends received? *LU 21-1(2)*

CHALLENGE PROBLEMS

21–30. Here's an example of how breakpoint discounts on sales commissions for mutual fund investors work:
Sales charge

> Less than $25,000, 5.75%
> $25,000 to $49,999, 5.50%
> $50,000 to 99,999, 4.75%
> $100,000 to $249,999, 3.75%

Nancy Dolan is interested in the T Rowe Price Mid Cap Fund. Assume the NAV is 19.43. **(a)** What minimum amount of shares must Nancy purchase to have a sales charge of 5.50%? **(b)** What are the minimum shares Nancy must purchase to have a sales charge of 4.75%? **(c)** What are the minimum shares Nancy must purchase to have a sales charge of 3.75%? **(d)** What would be the total purchase price for **(a)**, **(b)**, or **(c)**? Round up to the nearest share even if it is less than 5. *LU 21-3(1)*

21–31. On September 6, Irene Westing purchased one bond of Mick Corporation at 98.50. The bond pays $8\frac{3}{4}$ interest on June 1 and December 1. The stockbroker told Irene that she would have to pay the accrued interest and the market price of the bond and a $6 brokerage fee. What was the total purchase price for Irene? Assume a 360-day year (each month is 30 days) in calculating the accrued interest. (*Hint:* Final cost = Cost of bond + Accrued interest + Brokerage fee. Calculate time for accrued interest.) *LU 21-2(2)*

 SUMMARY PRACTICE TEST You Tube

Do you need help? The DVD has step-by-step worked-out solutions.

1. Russell Slater bought 700 shares of Disney stock at $24.90 per share. Assume a commission of 4% of the purchase price. What is the total cost to Russell? *(p. 511) LU 21-1(1)*

2. Avis Company earns $2.50 per share. Today, the stock is trading at $18.99. The company pays an annual dividend of $.25. Calculate **(a)** the price-earnings ratio (to the nearest whole number) and **(b)** the yield on the stock (to the nearest tenth percent). *(p. 511) LU 21-1(1)*

3. The stock of Aware is trading at $4.90. The price-earnings ratio is 4 times earnings. Calculate the earnings per share (to the nearest cent) for Aware. *(p. 511) LU 21-1(1)*

4. Tom Fox bought 8 bonds of UXY Company $3\frac{1}{2}$ 09 at 84 and 4 bonds of Foot Company $4\frac{1}{8}$ 10 at 93. Assume the commission on the bonds is $3 per bond. What was the total cost of all the purchases? *(p. 514) LU 21-2(1)*

5. Leah Long bought one bond of Vick Company for 147. The original bond was 8.25 10. Leah wants to know the current yield to the nearest tenth percent. Help Leah with the calculation. *(p. 515) LU 21-2(2)*

6. Cumulative preferred stockholders of Rale Company receive $.80 per share. The company has 70,000 shares outstanding. For the last 9 years, Rale paid no dividends. This year, Rale paid $400,000 in dividends. What is the amount of dividends in arrears that is still owed to preferred stockholders? *(pp. 511–512) LU 21-1(2)*

7. Bill Roundy bought 800 shares of a mutual fund with an NAV of $14.10. This fund has a load charge of 3%. **(a)** What is the offer price and **(b)** what did Bill pay for the investment? *(p. 516) LU 21-3(1)*

PROBLEM 1
Take note!

Go to http://www.treasurydirect.gov/indiv/research/indepth/tnotes/res_tnote_rates.htm. Look up the price and stated interest (coupon) on a 10-year Treasury note. What is the amount of annual interest on a $1,000 face value bond and what is the bond yield? Explain why the bond is selling at a premium or a discount.

Discussion Questions

1. Are these bonds a good investment? Why or why not?
2. What is the advantage to the U.S. government in issuing these Treasury notes?

PROBLEM 2
Peaks and valleys

Go to http://finance.yahoo.com. Choose a stock and look up its current price. Then look up its price 1 year ago using the graph to select "1y." (If either day falls on a weekend, use the preceding Friday.) What percent change in value has the stock had? How does that compare to the change in the Dow Jones Industrial Average (symbol DJIA) over the same year?

Discussion Questions

1. What do you feel contributed to this change in price for the stock you selected?
2. What does the change in the stock price versus the change in the Dow Jones Industrial Average tell you about the performance of this company versus other businesses?

PROBLEM 3
DJIA changes over time

Go to http://money.cnn.com/ and investigate the Dow Jones averages for the past 5 years. What was the lowest point value of the Dow? When did that occur? What was the highest point value? When did that occur?

Discussion Questions

1. What do you feel has caused this change to the Dow Jones?
2. Based upon the past 5 years and the performance of the Dow Jones, what do you predict to happen over the next 10 years? Why?

PROBLEM 4
NASDAQ versus NYSE

Go to http://www.nasdaq.com, pick five stocks on the NASDAQ, and then go to http://www.nyse.com and pick five stocks on the NYSE. Which set of stocks would return a better investment if it continued on the same trend as the present?

Discussion Questions

1. Why would a stock be listed on the NASDAQ versus the NYSE?
2. What characteristics would you look for in a stock before purchasing?

MOBILE APPS ☒

Stocks (The Bear Flag Republic) Tracks stocks during or after market hours from both NASDAQ and NYSE.

iFinance (OpenStack Inc.) Analyzes financial investments and answers financial questions.

INTERNET PROJECTS ☒

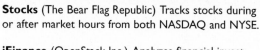

See text website
www.mhhe.com/slater11e_sse_ch21

MACY'S: BACK IN FASHION

One of the great names in retailing is showing that you can serve the middle class and still prosper. BY JENNIFER SCHONBERGER

■ MACY'S IS GOING AFTER TEENS WITH A LINE OF CLOTHING DESIGNED BY MADONNA.

IN 2007, MICHAEL DERVOS, then regional director of Macy's New York–area stores, walked past a clearance sale in the shoe department of the store in Flushing, Queens. He noticed that all the shoes were size 9 and above—even though many of the store's customers were Asian Americans, who tend to have smaller feet. Meanwhile, on the clearance rack at a Brooklyn Macy's, whose customers tended to have average-size feet, the sizes were 7 and below. Dervos swapped the stores' inventories, and the shoes sold quickly.

That incident led Macy's (symbol M) in 2009 to adopt a new strategy, called My Macy's, to boost sales by tailoring the merchandise in each store to its clientele. Customizing merchandise to local markets also helps Macy's better control inventory—and therefore helps to reduce markdowns, which translates to fatter profits.

The strategy has enabled the chain to double earnings over the past three years, a period during which most retailers serving the middle class have struggled. Over the period, Macy's stock climbed sixfold, to $41 (prices and related data are as of April 5).

The company, which owns Bloomingdale's as well, has also made a bigger push into exclusive private-label brands. In 2010, Macy's started selling the Material Girl clothing line, designed by singer Madonna, exclusively in Macy's teen departments. Last fall, Macy's rolled out "Impulse Beauty," a section in cosmetic departments that sells boutique brands. And the company recently announced plans to target shoppers born in the 1980s and '90s—the so-called Millennials—a group it thinks is key to future growth.

Another bright spot for Macy's: growing Internet sales. Online sales from Macys.com and Bloomingdales.com jumped 40% last year, to $962 million, estimates Morningstar, and are expected to grow to $2 billion this year.

All these strategies have helped Macy's perform well in a so-so economy. It has had to be resourceful because, as a retailer that primarily serves the middle class, it can't raise prices as easily as Saks Fifth Avenue and Nordstrom (which have a wealthier clientele).

The numbers tell Macy's success story best. In the year that ended last January, sales increased 5.6%, to $26.4 billion, while earnings per share jumped 36%, to $2.88. Analysts on average see sales rising 4.6%, to $27.6 billion, in the year that ends next January and earnings jumping 16%, to $3.33 per share.

Macy's is sharing the wealth. In January, its board approved a doubling of its quarterly dividend, to 20 cents per share (the stock yields 2.0%). The board also increased the company's stock-buyback cache by $1 billion.

Despite all the good news, Macy's stock is cheap. It trades at 12 times estimated earnings, compared with 21 for the average department-store stock. If gasoline prices continue to move higher, sales could drop. But Brian Sozzi, chief stock analyst for NBG Productions, an independent research firm, says that Macy's low price-earnings ratio cushions the stock price from a big hit. He thinks the stock could climb 10% over the next 12 months. And it could do far better if the economy picks up steam, as it appears to be doing. ■

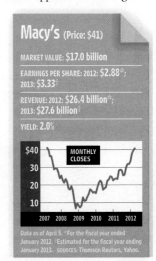

Macy's (Price: $41)

MARKET VALUE: $17.0 billion

EARNINGS PER SHARE: 2012: $2.88*; 2013: $3.33†

REVENUE: 2012: $26.4 billion*; 2013: $27.6 billion†

YIELD: 2.0%

Data as of April 5. *For the fiscal year ended January 2012. †Estimated for the fiscal year ending January 2013. SOURCES: Thomson Reuters, Yahoo.

BUSINESS MATH ISSUE

Macy's stock is not a good buy.

1. List the key points of the article and information to support your position.
2. Write a group defense of your position using math calculations to support your view.

Business Statistics

iPad Stats | A look at the people who own Apple's tablet

7.8
Number of people in the U.S., in millions, who own iPads

INCOME

$75,000 to $99,999 — 16.4%
$50,000 to $74,999 — 15.9%
11.9%
More than $100,000 — 49.4%
$25,000 to $49,999
Less than $25,000 — 6.4%

56.1
Percentage of iPad owners in the U.S. who are males

AGE

13-17	7.6%
18-24	15.2
25-34	27.0
35-44	20.3
45-54	16.4
55-64	7.3
65+	6.2

41.4
Percent of iPad owners in U.S. who have not yet received a college degree

PHONE USE

BlackBerry — 28.9%
Other — 29.6%
Android — 14.2%
iPhone — 27.3%

Figures are from a survey by research firm comScore Inc. of more than 30,000 people with mobile devices, conducted over three months ending in February. Survey participants were older than 13.

Buoy 2: Expires 15:34 EDT
Right Whale Detected: Voluntary Speed Reduction to 10 Knots or Less

10 knot SPEED REGULATION

LU 22–1: Mean, Median, and Mode

1. Define and calculate the mean *(p. 530)*.

2. Explain and calculate a weighted mean *(pp. 530–531)*.

3. Define and calculate the median *(pp. 531–532)*.

4. Define and identify the mode *(p. 532)*.

LU 22–2: Frequency Distributions and Graphs

1. Prepare a frequency distribution *(pp. 533–534)*.

2. Prepare bar, line, and circle graphs *(pp. 534–536)*.

3. Calculate price relatives and cost comparisons *(p. 536)*.

LU 22–3: Measures of Dispersion (Optional)

1. Explain and calculate the range *(p. 538)*.

2. Define and calculate the standard deviation *(pp. 538–539)*.

3. Estimate percentage of data by using standard deviations *(pp. 539–540)*.

Here are key terms in this chapter. After completing the chapter, if you know the term, place a checkmark in the parentheses. If you don't know the term, look it up and put the page number where it can be found.

Bar graph ( ) Circle graph ( ) Frequency distribution ( ) Index numbers ( ) Line graph ( ) Mean ( )
Measure of dispersion ( ) Median ( ) Mode ( ) Normal distribution ( ) Price relative ( ) Range ( )
Standard deviation ( ) Weighted mean ( )

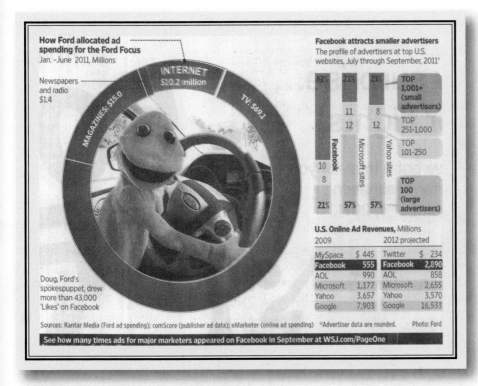

How Ford allocated ad spending for the Ford Focus
Jan.–June 2011, Millions

Newspapers and radio $1.4
INTERNET $10.2 million
MAGAZINES: $15.0
TV: $69.1

Doug, Ford's spokespuppet, drew more than 43,000 'Likes' on Facebook

Facebook attracts smaller advertisers
The profile of advertisers at top U.S. websites, July through September, 2011*

	62%	21%	23%	TOP 1,001+ (small advertisers)
		11	8	TOP 251–1,000
		12	12	TOP 101–250
	10			
	8			TOP 100 (large advertisers)
	21%	57%	57%	

Facebook   Microsoft sites   Yahoo sites

U.S. Online Ad Revenues, Millions

2009		2012 projected	
MySpace	$ 445	Twitter	$ 234
Facebook	555	Facebook	2,890
AOL	990	AOL	858
Microsoft	1,177	Microsoft	2,655
Yahoo	3,657	Yahoo	3,570
Google	7,903	Google	16,533

Sources: Kantar Media (Ford ad spending); comScore (publisher ad data); eMarketer (online ad spending) *Advertiser data are rounded. Photo: Ford

See how many times ads for major marketers appeared on Facebook in September at WSJ.com/PageOne

In this chapter we look at various techniques that analyze and graphically represent business statistics. For example, in the chapter opener we see what kind of people own an Apple tablet. The *Wall Street Journal* clip on the left shows how statistics is used to profile what kind of advertisers use Facebook, Microsoft, or Yahoo! sites. Learning Unit 22–1 discusses the mean, median, and mode. Learning Unit 22–2 explains how to gather data by using frequency distributions and express these data visually in graphs. Emphasis is placed on whether graphs are indeed giving accurate information. The chapter concludes with an introduction to index numbers—an application of statistics—and an optional learning unit on measures of dispersion.

Learning Unit 22–1: Mean, Median, and Mode

Companies frequently use averages and measurements to guide their business decisions. The mean and median are the two most common averages used to indicate a single value that represents an entire group of numbers. The mode can also be used to describe a set of data.

Mean

The accountant of Bill's Sport Shop told Bill, the owner, that the average daily sales for the week were $150.14. The accountant stressed that $150.14 was an average and did not represent specific daily sales. Bill wanted to know how the accountant arrived at $150.14.

LO 1

The accountant went on to explain that he used an arithmetic average, or **mean** (a measurement), to arrive at $150.14 (rounded to the nearest hundredth). He showed Bill the following formula:

$$\text{Mean} = \frac{\text{Sum of all values}}{\text{Number of values}}$$

The accountant used the following data:

	Sun.	Mon.	Tues.	Wed.	Thur.	Fri.	Sat.
Sport Shop sales	$400	$100	$68	$115	$120	$68	$180

To compute the mean, the accountant used these data:

$$\text{Mean} = \frac{\$400 + \$100 + \$68 + \$115 + \$120 + \$68 + \$180}{7} = \$150.14$$

LO 2

When values appear more than once, businesses often look for a **weighted mean.** The format for the weighted mean is slightly different from that for the mean. The concept, however, is the same except that you weight each value by how often it occurs (its frequency). Thus, considering the frequency of the occurrence of each value allows a weighting of each day's sales in proper importance. To calculate the weighted mean, use the following formula:

$$\text{Weighted mean} = \frac{\text{Sum of products}}{\text{Sum of frequencies}}$$

Let's change the sales data for Bill's Sport Shop and see how to calculate a weighted mean:

	Sun.	Mon.	Tues.	Wed.	Thur.	Fri.	Sat.
Sport Shop sales	$400	$100	$100	$80	$80	$100	$400

Value	Frequency	Product
$400	2	$ 800
100	3	300
80	2	160
		$1,260

The weighted mean is $\dfrac{\$1,260}{7} = \$180$

Note how we multiply each value by its frequency of occurrence to arrive at the product. Then we divide the sum of the products by the sum of the frequencies.

When you calculate your grade point average (GPA), you are using a weighted average. The following formula is used to calculate GPA:

$$\text{GPA} = \frac{\text{Total points}}{\text{Total credits}}$$

Now let's show how Jill Rivers calculated her GPA to the nearest tenth.

Given A = 4; B = 3; C = 2; D = 1; F = 0

Courses	Credits attempted	Grade received	Points (Credits × Grade)
Introduction to Computers	4	A	16 (4 × 4)
Psychology	3	B	9 (3 × 3)
English Composition	3	B	9 (3 × 3)
Business Law	3	C	6 (2 × 3)
Business Math	3	B	9 (3 × 3)
	16		49 $\frac{49}{16} = 3.1$

When high or low numbers do not significantly affect a list of numbers, the mean is a good indicator of the center of the data. If high or low numbers do have an effect, the median may be a better indicator to use.

LO 3

Median

The **median** is another measurement that indicates the center of the data. An average that has one or more extreme values is not distorted by the median. For example, let's look at the following yearly salaries of the employees of Rusty's Clothing Shop.

Alice Knight	$95,000	Jane Wang	$67,000
Jane Hess	27,000	Bill Joy	40,000
Joel Floyd	32,000		

Note how Alice's salary of $95,000 will distort an average calculated by the mean.

$$\frac{\$95,000 + \$27,000 + \$32,000 + \$67,000 + \$40,000}{5} = \boxed{\$52,200}$$

The $52,200 average salary is considerably more than the salary of three of the employees. So it is not a good representation of the store's average salary. The following *Wall Street Journal* clip "Flattening Out" shows that the median income for men plateaus when they are in their late 40s. How was that conclusion reached? We use the following steps to find the median of a group of numbers.

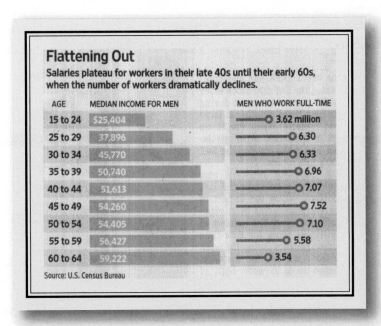

Flattening Out
Salaries plateau for workers in their late 40s until their early 60s, when the number of workers dramatically declines.

AGE	MEDIAN INCOME FOR MEN	MEN WHO WORK FULL-TIME
15 to 24	$25,404	3.62 million
25 to 29	37,896	6.30
30 to 34	45,770	6.33
35 to 39	50,740	6.96
40 to 44	51,613	7.07
45 to 49	54,260	7.52
50 to 54	54,405	7.10
55 to 59	56,427	5.58
60 to 64	59,222	3.54

Source: U.S. Census Bureau

FINDING THE MEDIAN OF A GROUP OF VALUES

Step 1. Orderly arrange values from the smallest to the largest.

Step 2. Find the middle value.

    a. *Odd number of values:* Median is the middle value. You find this by first dividing the total number of numbers by 2. The next-higher number is the median.

    b. *Even number of values:* Median is the average of the two middle values.

For Rusty's Clothing Shop, we find the median as follows:

1. Arrange values from smallest to largest:

    $27,000; $32,000; $40,000 ; $67,000; $95,000

2. Since we have a total number of five values and 5 is an odd number, we divide 5 by 2 to get $2\frac{1}{2}$. The next-higher number is 3, so our median is the third-listed number, $40,000 .

If Jane Hess ($27,000) were not on the payroll, we would find the median as follows:

1. Arrange values from smallest to largest:

    $32,000; $40,000; $67,000; $95,000

2. Average the two middle values:

$$\frac{\$40,000 + \$67,000}{2} = \$53,500$$

Note that the median results in two salaries below and two salaries above the average. Now we'll look at another measurement tool—the mode.

Mode

The **mode** is a measurement that also records values. In a series of numbers, the value that occurs most often is the mode. If all the values are different, there is no mode. If two or more numbers appear most often, you may have two or more modes. Note that we do not have to arrange the numbers in the lowest-to-highest order, although this could make it easier to find the mode.

EXAMPLE 3, 4, 5, 6, 3, 8, 9, 3, 5, 3

3 is the mode since it is listed 4 times.

Now let's check your progress with a Practice Quiz.

MONEY tips

Create a list of all your accounts and passwords and ensure a survivor knows where to locate it in the event of death. Keep the list up-to-date.

LO 4

LU 22–1 PRACTICE QUIZ

Complete this **Practice Quiz** to see how you are doing.

Barton Company's sales reps sold the following last month:

Sales rep	Sales volume	Sales rep	Sales volume
A	$16,500	C	$12,000
B	15,000	D	48,900

Calculate the mean and the median. Which is the better indicator of the center of the data? Is there a mode?

✓ **Solutions**

$$\text{Mean} = \frac{\$16,500 + \$15,000 + \$12,000 + \$48,900}{4} = \$23,100$$

$$\text{Median} = \frac{\$15,000 + \$16,500}{2} = \$15,750$$

$12,000, $15,000, $16,500, $48,900. Note how we arrange numbers from smallest to highest to calculate median.

Median is the better indicator since in calculating the mean, the $48,900 puts the average of $23,100 much too high. There is no mode.

*For **extra help** from your authors—Sharon and Jeff—see the student DVD*

Need more practice? Try this **Extra Practice Quiz** (check figures in the Interactive Chapter Organizer, p. 542). Worked-out Solutions can be found in Appendix B at end of text.

Barton's Company sales reps sold the following last month:

Sales rep	Sales volume	Sales rep	Sales volume
A	$17,000	C	$11,000
B	14,000	D	51,000

Calculate the mean and median. Which is the better indicator of the center of the data? Is there a mode?

Learning Unit 22–2: Frequency Distributions and Graphs

In this unit you will learn how to gather data and illustrate these data. Today, computer software programs can make beautiful color graphics. But how accurate are these graphics? This *Wall Street Journal* clipping gives an example of graphics that did not agree with the numbers beneath them. The clipping reminds all readers to check the numbers illustrated by the graphics. This is an old clip that is still relevant today.

What's Wrong With this Picture? Utility's Glasses Are Never Empty

By KATHLEEN DEVENY
Staff Reporter of THE WALL STREET JOURNAL

When Les Waas, an investor in Philadelphia Suburban Corp., paged through the company's 1994 annual report, he was impressed by what he saw.

The water utility had used a series of charts to represent its revenues, net income and book value per share, among other results. Each figure was represented by the level of water in a glass. Each chart showed strong growth.

Then Mr. Waas looked a little more carefully. The bars in the chart seemed to indicate far more impressive growth than the numbers beneath them. A chart showing the growth in the number of Philadelphia Suburban's water customers, for ex-

Number of Metered Water Customers (thousands)

ample, seemed to indicate the company's customer base had more than tripled since 1990. But the numbers actually increased only 6.4%.

The reason for the disparity: The charts don't begin at zero. Even an empty glass in the accompanying chart would represent a customer base of 230,000.

LO 1

Collecting raw data and organizing the data is a prerequisite to presenting statistics graphically. Let's illustrate this by looking at the following example.

A computer industry consultant wants to know how much college freshmen are willing to spend to set up a computer in their dormitory rooms. After visiting a local college dorm, the consultant gathered the following data on the amount of money 20 students spent on computers:

Price of computer	Tally	Frequency
$ 1,000	IIIII	5
2,000	I	1
3,000	IIIII	5
4,000	I	1
5,000	II	2
6,000	II	2
7,000	I	1
8,000	I	1
9,000	I	1
10,000	I	1

$1,000	$7,000	$4,000	$1,000	$ 5,000	$1,000	$3,000
5,000	2,000	3,000	3,000	3,000	8,000	9,000
3,000	6,000	6,000	1,000	10,000	1,000	

Note that these raw data are not arranged in any order. To make the data more meaningful, the consultant made the **frequency distribution** table. Think of this distribution table as a way to organize a list of numbers to show the patterns that may exist.

As you can see, 25% ($\frac{5}{20} = \frac{1}{4} = 25\%$) of the students spent $1,000 and another 25% spent $3,000. Only four students spent $7,000 or more.

Now let's see how we can use bar graphs.

LO 2

Bar Graphs

Bar graphs help readers see the changes that have occurred over a period of time. This is especially true when the same type of data is repeatedly studied. Note the following example of the use of bar graphs.

The following *Wall Street Journal* clipping, "Power Up," uses bar graphs to show the projected U.S. sales of charging gear for electric-vehicles.

GE's WattStation, above in San Fransicsco, will trail products from start-ups already sold to governments.

Let's return to our computer consultant example and make a bar graph of the computer purchases data collected by the consultant. Note that the height of the bar represents the frequency of each purchase. Bar graphs can be vertical or horizontal.

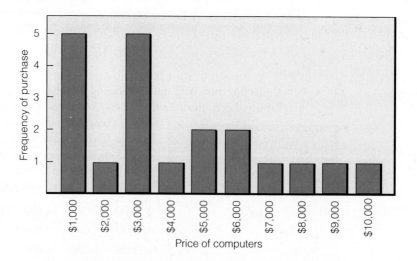

We can simplify this bar graph by grouping the prices of the computers. The grouping, or *intervals,* should be of equal sizes.

A bar graph for the grouped data follows.

Class	Frequency
$1,000–$3,000.99	11
3,001– 5,000.99	3
5,001– 7,000.99	3
7,001– 9,000.99	2
9,001–11,000.99	1

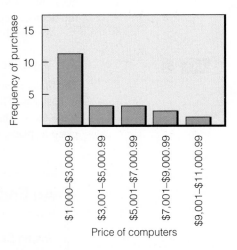

Next, let's see how we can use line graphs.

Line Graphs

A **line graph** shows trends over a period of time. Often separate lines are drawn to show the comparison between two or more trends.

Note the trend in higher emissions of carbon dioxide, which is contributing to global warming.

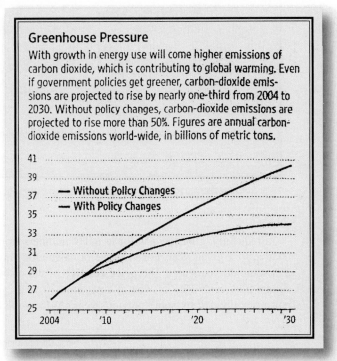

Greenhouse Pressure

With growth in energy use will come higher emissions of carbon dioxide, which is contributing to global warming. Even if government policies get greener, carbon-dioxide emissions are projected to rise by nearly one-third from 2004 to 2030. Without policy changes, carbon-dioxide emissions are projected to rise more than 50%. Figures are annual carbon-dioxide emissions world-wide, in billions of metric tons.

— Without Policy Changes
— With Policy Changes

National E. © 2005 *Higher Education Advocate.*

We conclude our discussion of graphics with the use of the circle graph.

Circle Graphs

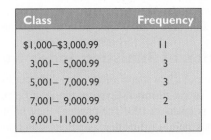

$.15 \times 360° = 54.0$
$.11 \times 360° = 39.6$
$.36 \times 360° = 129.6$
$.38 \times 360° = 136.8$
$\underline{}$
360.0

Circle graphs, often called *pie charts,* are especially helpful for showing the relationship of parts to a whole. The entire circle represents 100%, or 360°; the pie-shaped pieces represent the subcategories. Note at the middle of the following page (p. 536) how the circle graph in the *Wall Street Journal* clipping "An Enduring Challenge," uses pie charts to show the world energy outlook by 2030.

To draw a circle graph (or pie chart), begin by drawing a circle. Then take the percentages and convert each percentage to a decimal. Next multiply each decimal by 360° to get the degrees represented by the percentage. Circle graphs must total 360°.

We conclude this unit with a brief discussion of index numbers.

An Application of Statistics: Index Numbers

The financial section of a newspaper often gives different index numbers describing the changes in business. These **index numbers** express the relative changes in a variable compared with some base, which is taken as 100. The changes may be measured from time to time or from place to place. Index numbers function as percents and are calculated like percents.

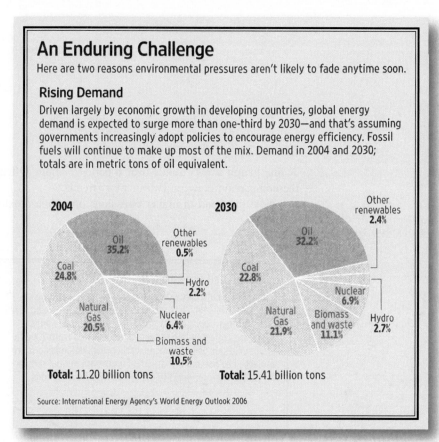

An Enduring Challenge
Here are two reasons environmental pressures aren't likely to fade anytime soon.

Rising Demand
Driven largely by economic growth in developing countries, global energy demand is expected to surge more than one-third by 2030—and that's assuming governments increasingly adopt policies to encourage energy efficiency. Fossil fuels will continue to make up most of the mix. Demand in 2004 and 2030; totals are in metric tons of oil equivalent.

2004
Oil 35.2%
Coal 24.8%
Natural Gas 20.5%
Other renewables 0.5%
Hydro 2.2%
Nuclear 6.4%
Biomass and waste 10.5%
Total: 11.20 billion tons

2030
Oil 32.2%
Coal 22.8%
Natural Gas 21.9%
Other renewables 2.4%
Nuclear 6.9%
Biomass and waste 11.1%
Hydro 2.7%
Total: 15.41 billion tons

Source: International Energy Agency's World Energy Outlook 2006

Frequently, a business will use index numbers to make comparisons of a current price relative to a given year. For example, a calculator may cost $9 today relative to a cost of $75 some 30 years ago. The **price relative** of the calculator is $\frac{\$9}{\$75} \times 100 = 12\%$. The calculator now costs 12% of what it cost some 30 years ago. A price relative, then, is the current price divided by some previous year's price—the base year—multiplied by 100.

$$\text{Price relative} = \frac{\text{Current price}}{\text{Base year's price}} \times 100$$

MONEY tips

Review your accounts annually to ensure the correct beneficiary is listed. All too often, the incorrect beneficiary is listed on life insurance policies, retirement accounts, and bank accounts.

Index numbers can also be used to estimate current prices at various geographic locations. The frequently quoted Consumer Price Index (CPI), calculated and published monthly by the U.S. Bureau of Labor Statistics, records the price relative percentage cost of many goods and services nationwide compared to a base period. Table 22.1 (p. 537) gives a portion of the CPI that uses 1982–84 as its base period. Note that the table shows, for example, that the price relative for housing in Los Angeles is 139.3% of what it cost in 1982–84. Thus, Los Angeles housing costs amounting to $100.00 in 1982–84 now cost $139.30. So if you built a $90,000 house in 1982–84, it is worth $125,370 today. (Convert 139.3% to the decimal 1.393; multiply $90,000 by 1.393 = $125,370.)

Once again, we complete the unit with a Practice Quiz.

TABLE 22.1

Consumer Price Index (in percent)

Expense	Atlanta	Chicago	New York	Los Angeles
Food	131.9	130.3	139.6	130.9
Housing	128.8	131.4	139.3	139.3
Clothing	133.8	124.3	121.8	126.4
Medical care	177.6	163.0	172.4	163.3

LU 22–2 PRACTICE QUIZ

Complete this **Practice Quiz** to see how you are doing.

1. The following is the number of sales made by 20 salespeople on a given day. Prepare a frequency distribution and a bar graph. Do not use intervals for this example.

5	8	9	1	4	4	0	3	2	8
8	9	5	1	9	6	7	5	9	10

2. Assuming the following market shares for diapers 5 years ago, prepare a circle graph:

Pampers	32%	Huggies	24%
Luvs	20%	Others	24%

3. Today a new Explorer costs $30,000. In 1991 the Explorer cost $19,000. What is the price relative? Round to the nearest tenth percent.

*For **extra help** from your authors–Sharon and Jeff–see the student DVD*

✓ Solutions

1.

Number of sales	Tally	Frequency
0	I	1
1	II	2
2	I	1
3	I	1
4	II	2
5	III	3
6	I	1
7	I	1
8	III	3
9	IIII	4
10	I	1

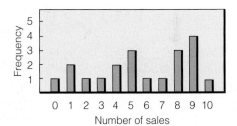

2.

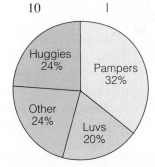

Huggies 24%
Pampers 32%
Other 24%
Luvs 20%

.32 × 360° = 115.20°
.20 × 360° = 72.00°
.24 × 360° = 86.40°
.24 × 360° = 86.40°

3. $\dfrac{\$30,000}{\$19,000} \times 100 = 157.9$

LU 22–2a EXTRA PRACTICE QUIZ WITH WORKED-OUT SOLUTIONS

Need more practice? Try this **Extra Practice Quiz** (check figures in the Interactive Chapter Organizer, p. 542). Worked-out Solutions can be found in Appendix B at end of text.

1. The following is the number of sales made by 20 salespeople on a given day. Prepare a frequency distribution and a bar graph. Do not use intervals for this example.

0	8	9	1	4	4	0	3	2	8
8	9	0	1	9	6	7	0	9	10

2. Assuming the following market shares for diapers 5 years ago, prepare a circle graph.

Pampers	40%	Huggies	25%
Luvs	20%	Others	15%

3. Today a new Explorer costs $35,000. In 1991, the Explorer cost $19,000. What is the price relative? Round to the nearest tenth percent.

Learning Unit 22–3: Measures of Dispersion (Optional)

In Learning Unit 22–1 you learned how companies use the mean, median, and mode to indicate a single value, or number, that represents an entire group of numbers, or data. Often it is valuable to know how the information is scattered (spread or dispersed) within a data set. A **measure of dispersion** is a number that describes how the numbers of a set of data are spread out or dispersed.

This learning unit discusses three measures of dispersion—range, standard deviation, and normal distribution. We begin with the range—the simplest measure of dispersion.

Range

LO 1

The **range** is the difference between the two extreme values (highest and lowest) in a group of values or a set of data. For example, often the actual extreme values of hourly temperature readings during the past 24 hours are given but not the range or difference between the high and low readings. To find the range in a group of data, subtract the lowest value from the highest value.

> Range = Highest value − Lowest value

Thus, if the high temperature reading during the past 24 hours was 90° and the low temperature reading was 60° the range is 90° − 60°, or 30°. The range is limited in its application because it gives only a general idea of the spread of values in a data set.

EXAMPLE   Find the range of the following values: 83.6, 77.3, 69.2, 93.1, 85.4, 71.6.

Range = 93.1 − 69.2 = 23.9

Standard Deviation

LO 2

Since the **standard deviation** is intended to measure the spread of data around the mean, you must first determine the mean of a set of data. The following diagram shows two sets of data—A and B. In the diagram, the means of A and B are equal. Now look at how the data in these two sets are spread or dispersed.

Data set A	Data set B
x x x x x	x x x x x
0 1 2 3 4 5 6 7 8 9 10 11 12 13	0 1 2 3 4 5 6 7 8 9 10 11 12 13
Mean = (1 + 2 + 5 + 10 + 12) ÷ 5 = 6	Mean = (4 + 4 + 5 + 8 + 9) ÷ 5 = 6

Note that although the means of data sets A and B are equal, A is more widely dispersed, which means B will have a smaller standard deviation than A.

To find the standard deviation of an ungrouped set of data, use the following steps:

FINDING THE STANDARD DEVIATION

Step 1. Find the mean of the set of data.

Step 2. Subtract the mean from each piece of data to find each deviation.

Step 3. Square each deviation (multiply the deviation by itself).

Step 4. Sum all squared deviations.

Step 5. Divide the sum of the squared deviations by $n - 1$, where n equals the number of pieces of data.

Step 6. Find the square root ($\sqrt{}$) of the number obtained in Step 5 (use a calculator). This is the standard deviation. (The square root is a number that when multiplied by itself equals the amount shown inside the square root symbol.)

Two additional points should be made. First, Step 2 sometimes results in negative numbers. Since the sum of the deviations obtained in Step 2 should always be zero, we would not be able to find the average deviation. This is why we square each deviation—to generate positive quantities only. Second, the standard deviation we refer to is used with *sample* sets of data, that is, a collection of data from a population. The population is the *entire* collection of data. When the standard deviation for a population is calculated, the sum of the squared deviations is divided by n instead of by $n - 1$. In all problems that follow, sample sets of data are being examined.

EXAMPLE   Calculate the standard deviations for the sample data sets A and B given in the diagram on p. 538. Round the final answer to the nearest tenth. Note that Step 1—find the mean—is given in the diagram.

Standard deviation of data sets A and B: The table on the left uses Steps 2 through 6 to find the standard deviation of data set A, and the table on the right uses Steps 2 through 6 to find the standard deviation of data set B.

Data	Step 2 Data − Mean	Step 3 (Data − Mean)^2
1	$1 - 6 = -5$	25
2	$2 - 6 = -4$	16
5	$5 - 6 = -1$	1
10	$10 - 6 = \ \ 4$	16
12	$12 - 6 = \ \ 6$	36
	Total 0	94 **(Step 4)**

Step 5: Divide by $n - 1$: $\dfrac{94}{5-1} = \dfrac{94}{4} = 23.5$

Step 6: The square root of   is 4.8 (rounded).

The standard deviation of data set A is 4.8.

Data	Step 2 Data − Mean	Step 3 (Data − Mean)^2
4	$4 - 6 = -2$	4
4	$4 - 6 = -2$	4
5	$5 - 6 = -1$	1
8	$8 - 6 = \ \ 2$	4
9	$9 - 6 = \ \ 3$	9
	Total 0	22 **(Step 4)**

Step 5: Divide by $n - 1$: $\dfrac{22}{5-1} = \dfrac{22}{4} = 5.5$

Step 6: The square root of   is 2.3.

The standard deviation of data set B is 2.3.

As suspected, the standard deviation of data set B is less than that of set A. The standard deviation value reinforces what we see in the diagram.

Normal Distribution

One of the most important distributions of data is the **normal distribution.** In a normal distribution, data are spread *symmetrically* about the mean. A graph of such a distribution looks like the bell-shaped curve in Figure 22.1. Many data sets are normally distributed. Examples are the life span of automobile engines, women's heights, and intelligence quotients.

FIGURE 22.1

Standard deviation and the normal distribution

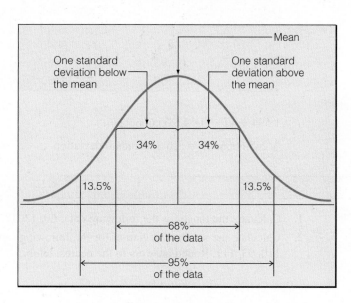

In a normal distribution, the data are spread out symmetrically—50% of the data lie above the mean, and 50% of the data lie below the mean. Additionally, if the data are normally distributed, 68% of the data should be found within one standard deviation above and below the mean. About 95% of the data should be found within two standard deviations above and below the mean. Figure 22.1 illustrates these facts.

EXAMPLE Assume that the mean useful life of a particular lightbulb is 2,000 hours and is normally distributed with a standard deviation of 300 hours. Calculate the useful life of the lightbulb with **(a)** one standard deviation of the mean and **(b)** two standard deviations of the mean; also **(c)** calculate the percent of lightbulbs that will last 2,300 hours or longer.

MONEY tips

Start achieving financial security today! Reduce spending, pay off debt, and start saving. Set small milestones, increasing them as you reach each goal. It's worth the effort and will make tomorrow financially brighter.

a. The useful life of the lightbulb one standard deviation from the mean is one standard deviation above *and* below the mean.

$$2,000 \pm 300 = 1,700 \text{ and } 2,300 \text{ hours}$$

The useful life is somewhere between 1,700 and 2,300 hours.

b. The useful life of the lightbulb within two standard deviations of the mean is within two standard deviations above *and* below the mean.

$$2,000 \pm 2(300) = 1,400 \text{ and } 2,600 \text{ hours}$$

c. Since 50% of the data in a normal distribution lie below the mean and 34% represent the amount of data one standard deviation above the mean, we must calculate the percent of data that lies beyond one standard deviation above the mean.

$$100\% - (50\% + 34\%) = \boxed{16\%}$$

So 16% of the bulbs should last 2,300 hours or longer.

It's time for another Practice Quiz.

LU 22–3 PRACTICE QUIZ

Complete this **Practice Quiz** to see how you are doing.

*For **extra help** from your authors—Sharon and Jeff—see the student DVD*

You Tube™

1. Calculate the range for the following data: 58, 13, 17, 26, 5, 41.
2. Calculate the standard deviation for the following sample set of data: 113, 92, 77, 125, 110, 93, 111. Round answers to the nearest tenth.

✓ **Solutions**

1. $58 - 5 = \boxed{53} \text{ range}$

2.

Data	Data − Mean	(Data − Mean)²
113	113 − 103 = 10	100
92	92 − 103 = −11	121
77	77 − 103 = −26	676
125	125 − 103 = 22	484
110	110 − 103 = 7	49
93	93 − 103 = −10	100
111	111 − 103 = 8	64
	Total	1,594

$$1,594 \div (7 - 1) = 265.6666667$$

$$\sqrt{265.6666667} = \boxed{16.3} \text{ standard deviation}$$

LU 22–3a EXTRA PRACTICE QUIZ WITH WORKED-OUT SOLUTIONS

Need more practice? Try this **Extra Practice Quiz** (check figures in the Interactive Chapter Organizer, p. 542). Worked-out Solutions can be found in Appendix B at end of text.

1. Calculate the range for the following data: 60, 13, 17, 26, 5, 41.
2. Calculate the standard deviation for the following sample set of data: 120, 88, 77, 125, 110, 93, 111. Round answers to the nearest tenth.

INTERACTIVE CHAPTER ORGANIZER

Topic/procedure/formula	Examples	You try it*
Mean, p. 530 $\dfrac{\text{Sum of all values}}{\text{Number of values}}$	Age of team players: 22, 28, 31, 19, 15 $\text{Mean} = \dfrac{22 + 28 + 31 + 19 + 15}{5}$ $= \boxed{23}$	**Calculate mean** 41, 29, 16, 15, 18
Weighted mean, p. 530 $\dfrac{\text{Sum of products}}{\text{Sum of frequencies}}$	<table><tr><td></td><td>S.</td><td>M.</td><td>T.</td><td>W.</td><td>Th.</td><td>F.</td><td>S.</td></tr><tr><td>Sales</td><td>$90</td><td>$75</td><td>$80</td><td>$75</td><td>$80</td><td>$90</td><td>$90</td></tr></table> Value Frequency Product $90 3 $270 75 2 150 80 2 160 7 $580 $\text{Mean} = \dfrac{\$580}{7} = \boxed{\$82.86}$	**Calculate weighted mean** <table><tr><td></td><td>S.</td><td>M.</td><td>T.</td><td>W.</td><td>Th.</td><td>Fr.</td><td>S.</td></tr><tr><td>Sales</td><td>80</td><td>90</td><td>100</td><td>80</td><td>80</td><td>90</td><td>90</td></tr></table>

Median, p. 532
1. Arrange values from smallest to largest.
2. Find the middle value.
  a. Odd number of values: median is middle value.
  $\left(\dfrac{\text{Total number of numbers}}{2}\right)$
  Next-higher number is median.
  b. Even number of values: average of two middle values.
	12, 15, 8, 6, 3
	1. 3 6 8 12 15
	2. $\dfrac{5}{2} = 2.5$
	Median is third number, $\boxed{8}$.
		Calculate median
		14, 16, 9, 7, 4

Mode, p. 532 Value that occurs most often in a set of numbers	6, 6, 8, 5, 6 Mode is 6	**Find mode** 7, 7, 4, 3, 2, 7
Frequency distribution, p. 533 Method of listing numbers or amounts not arranged in any particular way by columns for numbers (amounts), tally, and frequency	Number of sodas consumed in one day: 1, 5, 4, 3, 4, 2, 2, 3, 2, 0 <table><tr><th>Number of sodas</th><th>Tally</th><th>Frequency</th></tr><tr><td>0</td><td>I</td><td>1</td></tr><tr><td>1</td><td>I</td><td>1</td></tr><tr><td>2</td><td>III</td><td>3</td></tr><tr><td>3</td><td>II</td><td>2</td></tr><tr><td>4</td><td>II</td><td>2</td></tr><tr><td>5</td><td>I</td><td>1</td></tr></table>	**Prepare frequency distribution** Number of coffees consumed in one day: 1, 4, 5, 8, 2, 2, 3, 0
Bar graphs, p. 534 Height of bar represents frequency. Bar graph used for grouped data. Bar graphs can be vertical or horizontal.	From soda example above: 	**From coffee example above, prepare bar graph**
Line graphs, p. 535 Shows trend. Helps to put numbers in order.	**Sales** 2012 $1,000 2013 2,000 2014 3,000 	**Prepare line graph** **Sales** 2012 $5,000 2013 3,000 2014 2,000

(continues)

INTERACTIVE CHAPTER ORGANIZER

Topic/procedure/formula	Examples	You try it*
Circle graphs, p. 535–536 Circle = 360° % × 360° = Degrees of pie to represent percent Total should = 360°	60% favor diet soda 40% favor sugared soda Sugared 40% / Diet 60% .60 × 360° = 216° .40 × 360° = 144° 360°	**Create circle graph** 70% coffee drinkers 30% non-coffee-drinkers
Price relative, p. 536 Price relative = $\dfrac{\text{Current price}}{\text{Base year's price}} \times 100$	A station wagon's sticker price was $8,799 in 1982. Today it is $14,900. Price relative = $\dfrac{\$14,900}{\$8,799} \times 100 = 169.3$ (rounded to nearest tenth percent)	**Calculate price relative** Old price, $ 9,000 Today's price, 12,000
Range (optional), p. 538 Range = Highest value − Lowest value	Calculate range of the data set consisting of 5, 9, 13, 2, 8 Range = 13 − 2 = 11	**Calculate range** 6, 8, 14, 2, 9

Standard deviation (optional), p. 538
1. Calculate mean.
2. Subtract mean from each piece of data.
3. Square each deviation.
4. Sum squares.
5. Divide sum of squares by $n - 1$, where n = number of pieces of data.
6. Take square root of number obtained in Step 5, to find the standard deviation.
	Calculate the standard deviation of this set of data: 7, 2, 5, 3, 3.
	1. Mean = $\dfrac{20}{5} = 4$
	2. 7 − 4 = 3
	   2 − 4 = −2
	   5 − 4 = 1
	   3 − 4 = −1
	   3 − 4 = −1
	3. $(3)^2 = 9$
	   $(-2)^2 = 4$
	   $(1)^2 = 1$
	   $(-1)^2 = 1$
	   $(-1)^2 = 1$
	4. 16
	5. 16 ÷ 4 = 4
	6. Standard deviation = 2
		Calculate standard deviation
		8, 1, 6, 2, 2

KEY TERMS	Bar graph, *p. 534* Circle graph, *p. 536* Frequency distribution, *p. 533* Index numbers, *p. 536* Line graph, *p. 535*	Mean, *p. 530* Measure of dispersion, *p. 538* Median, *p. 531* Mode, *p. 532* Normal distribution, *p. 539*	Price relative, *p. 536* Range, *p. 538* Standard deviation, *p. 538* Weighted mean, *p. 530*
Check Figures for Extra Practice Quizzes with Page References. (Worked-out Solutions in Appendix B.)	LU 22–1a (p. 533) Mean $23,250 Median $15,500 There is no mode.	LU 22–2a (p. 537) 1. 9 IIII 4 2. Pampers 40% 144° 3. 184.2%	LU 22–3a (p. 540) 1. Range is 55. 2. Standard deviation is 17.7.

*Worked-out solutions are in Appendix B.

Critical Thinking Discussion Questions with Chapter Concept Check

1. Explain the mean, median, and mode. Give an example that shows you must be careful when you read statistics in an article.

2. Explain frequency distributions and the types of graphs. Locate a company annual report and explain how the company shows graphs to highlight its performance. Does the company need more or fewer of these visuals? Could price relatives be used?

3. Explain the statement that standard deviations are not accurate.

4. **Chapter Concept Check.** Referring to the chapter opener, visit the Apple website. Gather new statistics on the iPad and/or iPhone. Use concepts in this chapter for your presentation.

Classroom Notes

END-OF-CHAPTER PROBLEMS  www.mhhe.com/slater11e

Check figures for odd-numbered problems in Appendix C.   Name _____ Date _____

DRILL PROBLEMS (*Note:* Problems for optional Learning Unit 22–3 follow the Challenge Problem 22–24, page 549.)

Calculate the mean (to the nearest hundredth):   *LU 22-1(1)*

22–1.   14, 8, 6, 2

22–2.   8, 11, 19, 17, 15

22–3. $55.83, $66.92, $108.93

22–4. $1,001, $68.50, $33.82, $581.95

22–5.   Calculate the grade-point average: A = 4, B = 3, C = 2, D = 1, F = 0 (to nearest tenth).   *LU 22-1(2)*
eXcel

Courses	Credits	Grade
Computer Principles	3	B
Business Law	3	C
Logic	3	D
Biology	4	A
Marketing	3	B

22–6.   Find the weighted mean (to the nearest tenth):   *LU 22-1(2)*

Value	Frequency	Product
4	7	
8	3	
2	9	
4	2	

Find the median: *LU 22-1(3)*

22–7.   55, 10, 19, 38, 100, 25

22–8.   95, 103, 98, 62, 31, 15, 82

Find the mode: *LU 22-1(4)*

22–9.   8, 9, 3, 4, 12, 8, 8, 9

22–10.   22, 19, 15, 16, 18, 18, 5, 18

22–11. Given: Truck cost   2012 $30,000
          Truck cost   2008 $21,000

Calculate the price relative (rounded to the nearest tenth percent).   *LU 22-2(3)*

22–12.   Given the following sales of Lowe Corporation, prepare a line graph (run sales from $5,000 to $20,000).   *LU 22-2(2)*
eXcel

2012	$ 8,000
2013	11,000
2014	13,000
2015	18,000

22–13. Prepare a frequency distribution from the following weekly salaries of teachers at Moore Community College. Use the following intervals: *LU 22-2(1)*

$200–$299.99
$300–$399.99
$400–$499.99
$500–$599.99

$210	$505	$310	$380	$275
290	480	550	490	200
286	410	305	444	368

22–14. Prepare a bar graph from the frequency distribution in Problem 22–13. *LU 22-2(2)*

22–15. How many degrees on a circle graph would each be given from the following? *LU 22-2(2)*

Wear digital watch	42%
Wear traditional watch	51
Wear no watch	7

WORD PROBLEMS

22–16. The first Super Bowl on January 15, 1967, charged $42,000 for a 30-second commercial. For Super Bowl XLVI, NBC *eXcel* charged an average of $3.5 million for each 30 seconds and sold 70 commercial slots. Create a line graph for the following Super Bowl 30-second commercial costs: 2007, $2,385,365; 2008, $2,699,963; 2009, $2,999,960; 2010, $2,954,010; 2011, $3,100,000; and 2012, $3,500,000. *LU 22-2(2)*

22–17. The American Kennel Club announced the "Most Popular Dogs in the U.S. for 2011." Labrador retrievers remained *eXcel* number one for the 21st consecutive year. German shepherds came in second followed by beagles, golden retrievers, and Yorkshire terriers. Create a circle graph for Dogs for Life Kennel Club with the following members: 52 labrador retrievers, 33 German shepherds, 22 beagles, 15 golden retrievers, and 10 Yorkshire terriers. *LU 22-2(2)*

22–18. College graduates continue to earn significantly more than high school graduates. In fact, the wage college graduates earn has been increasing to almost twice as much as that of high school graduates. If graduates in 2013 earn $40,632, $35,554, $42,192, $33,432, $69,479 and $43,589, what is the standard deviation for this sample? Round to a whole number for each calculation. *LU 22-3(2)*

22–19. Bill Small, a travel agent, provided Alice Hall with the following information regarding the cost of her upcoming vacation. Construct a circle graph for Alice. *LU 22-2(2)*

Transportation	35%
Hotel	28
Food and entertainment	20
Miscellaneous	17

22–20. Jim Smith, a marketing student, observed how much each customer spent in a local convenience store. Based on the following results, prepare **(a)** a frequency distribution and **(b)** a bar graph. Use intervals of $0–$5.99, $6.00–$11.99, $12.00–$17.99, and $18.00–$23.99. *LU 22-2(2)*

$18.50	$18.24	$ 6.88	$9.95
16.10	3.55	14.10	6.80
12.11	3.82	2.10	
15.88	3.95	5.50	

22–21. Angie's Bakery bakes bagels. Find the weighted mean (to the nearest whole bagel) given the following daily production for June: *LU 22-1(2)*

200	150	200	150	200
150	190	360	360	150
190	190	190	200	150
360	400	400	150	200
400	360	150	400	360
400	400	200	150	150

22–22. Melvin Company reported sales in 2014 of $300,000. This compared to sales of $150,000 in 2013 and $100,000 in 2012. Construct a line graph for Melvin Company.   *LU 22-2(2)*

CHALLENGE PROBLEMS

22–23. Listed below are annual revenues for a few travel agencies:

AAA Travel Agency	$86,700,000
Riser Group	63,200,000
Casto Travel	62,900,000
Balboa Travel	36,200,000
Hunter Travel Managers	36,000,000

(a) What would be the mean and the median? **(b)** What is the total revenue percent of each agency? **(c)** Prepare a circle graph depicting the percents.   *LU 22-1(1, 2), LU 22-2(2)*

22–24. The following circle graph is a suggested budget for Ron Rye and his family for a month. Ron would like you to calculate the percent (to the hundredth) for each part of the circle graph along with the appropriate number of degrees.   *LU 22-2(2)*

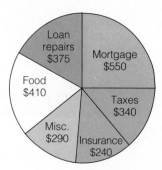

Name _____   Date _____

DRILL PROBLEMS

1. Calculate the range for the following set of data: 117, 98, 133, 52, 114, 35.   *LU 22-3(1)*

Calculate the standard deviation for the following sample sets of data. Round the final answers to the nearest tenth.   *LU 22-3(2)*

2. 83.6, 92.3, 56.5, 43.8, 77.1, 66.7

3. 7, 3, 12, 17, 5, 8, 9, 9, 13, 15, 6, 6, 4, 5

4. 41, 41, 38, 27, 53, 56, 28, 45, 47, 49, 55, 60

WORD PROBLEMS

5. The mean useful life of car batteries is 48 months. They have a standard deviation of 3. If the useful life of batteries is **eXcel** normally distributed, calculate **(a)** the percent of batteries with a useful life of less than 45 months and **(b)** the percent of batteries that will last longer than 54 months.   *LU 22-3(2)*

6. The average weight of a particular box of crackers is 24.5 ounces with a standard deviation of 0.8 ounce. The weights of the boxes are normally distributed. What percent of the boxes **(a)** weigh more than 22.9 ounces and **(b)** weigh less than 23.7 ounces?   *LU 22-3(2)*

7. An examination is normally distributed with a mean score of 77 and a standard deviation of 6. Find the percent of individuals scoring as indicated below.   *LU 22-3(2)*

   a. Between 71 and 83

   b. Between 83 and 65

   c. Above 89

   d. Less than 65

   e. Between 77 and 65

8. Listed below are the sales figures in thousands of dollars for a group of insurance salespeople. Calculate the mean sales figure and the standard deviation. *LU 22-3(1, 2)*

$117	$350	$400	$245	$420
223	275	516	265	135
486	320	285	374	190

9. The time in seconds it takes for 20 individual sewing machines to stitch a border onto a particular garment is listed below. Calculate the mean stitching time and the standard deviation to the nearest hundredth. *LU 22-3(1, 2)*

67	69	64	71	73
58	71	64	62	67
62	57	67	60	65
60	63	72	56	64

 SUMMARY PRACTICE TEST You Tube

Do you need help? The DVD has step-by-step worked-out solutions.

1. In July, Lee Realty sold 10 homes at the following prices: $140,000; $166,000; $80,000; $98,000; $185,000; $150,000; **eXcel** $108,000; $114,000; $142,000; and $250,000. Calculate the mean and median. *(pp. 530–532)   LU 22-1(1, 3)*

2. Lowes counted the number of customers entering the store for a week. The results were 1,100; 950; 1,100; 1,700; 880; 920; and 1,100. What is the mode? *(p. 532)   LU 22-1(4)*

3. This semester Hung Lee took four 3-credit courses at Riverside Community College. She received an A in accounting and C's in history, psychology, and algebra. What is her cumulative grade point average (assume A = 4 and C = 2) to the nearest hundredth? *(pp. 530–531)   LU 22-1(2)*

4. Pete's Variety Shop reported the following sales for the first 20 days of May. Prepare a frequency distribution for Pete's. *(pp. 533–534)   LU 22-2(1)*

$100	$400	$600	$400	$600
100	600	300	500	700
200	600	700	500	200
100	600	100	700	700

5. Leeds Company produced the following number of maps during the first 5 weeks of last year. Prepare a bar graph. e**X**cel *(p. 534)* *LU 22-2(2)*

Week	Maps
1	800
2	600
3	400
4	700
5	300

6. Laser Corporation reported record profits of 30%. It stated in the report that the cost of sales was 40% with expenses of 30%. Prepare a circle graph for Laser. *(pp. 535–536)* *LU 22-2(2)*

7. Today a new Explorer costs $39,900. In 1990, Explorers cost $24,000. What is the price relative to the nearest tenth percent? *(p. 536)* *LU 22-2(3)*

*8. Calculate the standard deviation for the following set of data: 7, 2, 5, 3, 3, 10. Round the final answer to the nearest tenth. *(pp. 538–539)* *LU 22-3(2)*

*Optional problem.

PROBLEM 1
Average performance?

Visit your school's website to access your grades in classes you have completed up to this point. If you have not completed more than five courses, then use grades from your high school courses. Convert your letter grades to their numerical equivalent. Compute the mean and median for your grades.

Discussion Questions

1. What do these numbers tell you about your academic performance thus far?
2. What could you do to improve your grade average?

PROBLEM 2
One mean GDP

Go to https://www.cia.gov/library/publications/the-world-factbook and choose a country in The World Factbook. Show how to use the GDP (Gross Domestic Product) purchasing power parity and the population to calculate the mean GDP for this country. If this differs from the per capita GDP listed in The World Factbook, explain why.

Discussion Questions

1. How does the GDP for the country you selected compare to the U.S.'s?
2. What do you feel may be the reason for this difference?

PROBLEM 3
Driving up the money!

Go to http://www.nascar.com. Go to the driver standings for the Nationwide Series. Calculate the range, mean, median, and mode of the top 15 drivers' earnings after the most recent race. If the season is not currently in progress, use the final earnings results of the previous season.

Discussion Questions

1. How does the median relate to the highest-paid driver?
2. How does the median relate to the lowest-paid driver?

PROBLEM 4
Far and wide?

Track the time you spend commuting (driving, walking, bicycling, etc.) to work and/or school for 1 week. Record each trip as a separate time. Once you have recorded all of your commute times, calculate the mean and median for your commutes. Compare your answers with other students and discuss the differences.

Discussion Questions

1. What options are available for you to commute to school and work?
2. Based on your commute time analysis, would these other options increase or decrease your average commute time?

MOBILE APPS ✕

Calculator: Statistics (SaleCalc Software) Calculates basic statistics.

Mean, Median, Mode & Range Calculator (Kristin Whitehead) Quickly calculates the mean, median, mode, and range of a set of numbers.

INTERNET PROJECTS ✕

See text website
www.mhhe.com/slater11e_sse_ch22

PERSONAL FINANCE

A KIPLINGER APPROACH

▶ WILLS ◀

Q: HIRE A LAWYER TO WRITE A WILL, OR DO IT YOURSELF?

DO THIS | **Hire a lawyer** in most situations—it could save your family confusion and squabbles later. A lawyer's assistance is essential if your circumstances are complex, unusual or involve significant assets. You can search for a lawyer who specializes in estate planning at www.actec.org or www.naepc.org. Costs depend on your situation and your region, but you'll probably pay at least $300. If money is tight, check with your state's bar association to find low-cost legal help, says lawyer Danielle Mayoras, coauthor of *Trial & Heirs*.

DO THIS | **Write a do-it-yourself will** if you need a short-term fix until you can hire a lawyer or if your situation is very straightforward—say, you're leaving everything to one person. But even small mistakes could cause problems down the road. Sites such as LegalZoom.com ($69 for a basic will) and Nolo.com ($59 for a basic will) provide forms and guidance on drafting your own will. If you go this route, make sure you meet your state's requirements, such as having independent witnesses sign the document. You may be able to ask a lawyer to review the will for a small fee.

▶ INSURANCE ◀

Q: BUY LONG-TERM-CARE INSURANCE, OR SELF-INSURE?

DO THIS | **Choose long-term-care insurance** if the cost of a nursing-home stay would devastate your savings. The median cost of one year in a private room in a nursing home topped $77,000 in 2011, and round-the-clock home care costs even more. The long-term-care insurance industry has been in turmoil recently, with insurers exiting the business or raising rates. But a healthy 55-year-old could still find a policy for about $2,000 to $3,000 per year that provides $150 in daily benefits, with inflation protection, for up to three years. You can save on premiums with a policy that boosts annual benefits based on increases in the consumer price index, rather than rising by 5% compounded each year. A three-year benefit period covers average long-term-care needs, but you can hedge your bets by buying a shared-benefit policy with a spouse, which provides a pool of benefits you both can use. You may also get a discount of up to 15% by buying a policy through your employer.

OR THAT | **Self-insure** if you have very deep pockets. But incurring hundreds of thousands of dollars in potential long-term-care expenses is a huge hit for even the wealthiest seniors. You can compromise by buying a policy that combines life insurance and long-term-care coverage, or combines annuities and long-term care. A $100,000 combo annuity, for example, may provide up to $300,000 in long-term-care benefits; unused portions of the annuity—minus any long-term-care payouts—may be left to heirs. These policies are also a way to get long-term-care insurance if you can't qualify for a stand-alone policy, and they help you avoid long-term-care rate increases.

> **"You could buy a policy that combines life insurance with long-term-care coverage, or combines annuities and long-term care."**

BUSINESS MATH ISSUE

When you look at all of the statistics it is evident that long-term care is not worth the premiums.

1. List the key points of the article and information to support your position.
2. Write a group defense of your position using math calculations to support your view.

Learning Unit 1–1 : Reading, Writing, and Rounding Whole Numbers

DRILL PROBLEMS

1. Express the following numbers in verbal form:
   a. 7,821 _____

   b. 160,501 _____

   c. 2,098,767 _____

   d. 58,003 _____

   e. 50,025,212,015 _____

2. Write in numeric form:
   a. Eighty thousand, two hundred eighty-one _____
   b. Fifty-eight thousand, three _____
   c. Two hundred eighty thousand, five _____
   d. Three million, ten _____
   e. Sixty-seven thousand, seven hundred sixty _____

3. Round the following numbers:
   a. To the nearest ten:
      76 _____   379 _____   855 _____   5,981 _____   206 _____
   b. To the nearest hundred:
      9,664 _____   2,074 _____   888 _____   271 _____   75 _____
   c. To the nearest thousand:
      21,486 _____   621 _____   3,504 _____   9,735 _____

4. Round off each number to the nearest ten, nearest hundred, nearest thousand, and round all the way. (Remember that you are rounding the original number each time.)

	Nearest ten	Nearest hundred	Nearest thousand	Round all the way
a. 4,752	_____	_____	_____	_____
b. 70,351	_____	_____	_____	_____
c. 9,386	_____	_____	_____	_____
d. 4,983	_____	_____	_____	_____
e. 408,119	_____	_____	_____	_____
f. 30,051	_____	_____	_____	_____

5. Name the place position (place value) of the underlined digit.
   a. 8,<u>3</u>48 _____
   b. <u>9</u>,734 _____
   c. 3<u>4</u>7,107 _____
   d. 7<u>2</u>3 _____
   e. <u>2</u>8,200,000,121 _____
   f. <u>7</u>06,359,005 _____
   g. 27,<u>5</u>63,530 _____

WORD PROBLEMS

6. Gim Smith was shopping for an Apple computer. He went to three different websites and found the computer he wanted at three different prices. At website A the price was $2,018, at website B the price was $1,985, and at website C the price was $2,030. What is the approximate price Gim will have to pay for the computer? Round to the nearest thousand. (Just one price.)

7. Amy Parker had to write a check at the bookstore when she purchased her books for the new semester. The total cost of the books was $564. How will she write this amount in verbal form on her check?

8. Matt Schaeffer was listening to the news and heard that steel production last week was one million, five hundred eighty-seven thousand tons. Express this amount in numeric form.

9. Jackie Martin is the city clerk and must go to the aldermen's meetings and take notes on what is discussed. At last night's meeting, they were discussing repairs for the public library, which will cost three hundred seventy-five thousand, nine hundred eighty-five dollars. Write this in numeric form as Jackie would.

10. A government survey revealed that 25,963,400 people are employed as office workers. To show the approximate number of office workers, round the number all the way.

11. Bob Donaldson wished to present his top student with a certificate of achievement at the end of the school year in 2004. To make it appear more official, he wanted to write the year in verbal form. How did he write the year?

12. Nancy Morrissey has a problem reading large numbers and determining place value. She asked her brother to name the place value of the 4 in the number 13,542,966. Can you tell Nancy the place value of the 4? What is the place value of the 3?

The 4 is in the _____ place.

The 3 is in the _____ place.

Learning Unit 1–2 :   Adding and Subtracting Whole Numbers

DRILL PROBLEMS

1. Add by totaling each separate column:

a.	668	b.	43	c.	493	d.	36	e.	716	f.	535	g.	751	h.	75,730
	338		58		826		76		458		107		378		48,531
			96				43		397		778		135		15,797
							24		139		215		747		
									478		391		368		

2. Estimate by rounding all the way, and then add the actual numbers:

a.	580	b.	1,470	c.	475
	971		7,631		837
	548		4,383		213
	430				775
	506				432

d.	442	e.	2,571	f.	10,928
	609		3,625		9,321
	766		4,091		12,654
	410		928		15,492
	128				

3. Estimate by rounding all the way, and then subtract the actual numbers:

a. 90
   − 38

b. 91
   − 33

c. 68
   − 59

d. 981
   − 283

e. 622
   − 328

f. 1,125
   − 913

4. Subtract and check:

a. 4,947
   − 4,362

b. 3,724
   − 2,138

c. 474,820
   − 85,847

d. 50,000
   − 21,762

e. 65,003
   − 24,987

f. 15,715
   − 3,503

5. In the following sales report, total the rows and the columns, and then check that the grand total is the same both horizontally and vertically.

Salesperson	Region 1	Region 2	Region 3	Total
a. Becker	$ 5,692	$ 7,403	$ 3,591	
b. Edwards	7,652	7,590	3,021	
c. Graff	6,545	6,738	4,545	
d. Jackson	6,937	6,950	4,913	
e. Total				

WORD PROBLEMS

6. June Long owes $8,600 on her car loan for a new chevy volt, plus interest of $620. How much will it cost her to pay off this loan?

7. Sales at Rich's Convenience Store were $3,587 on Monday, $3,944 on Tuesday, $4,007 on Wednesday, $3,890 on Thursday, and $4,545 on Friday. What were the total sales for the week?

8. Poor's Variety Store sold $5,000 worth of lottery tickets in the first week of August; it sold $289 less in the second week. How much were the lottery ticket sales in the second week of August?

9. A truck weighed 9,550 pounds when it was empty. After being filled with rubbish, it was driven to the dump where it weighed in at 22,347 pounds. How much did the rubbish weigh?

10. Joanne Hoster had $610 in her checking account when she went to the bookstore. Joanne purchased an accounting book for $140, the working papers for $30, and a study guide for $35. After Joanne writes a check for the entire purchase, how much money will remain in her checking account?

11. A used Ford truck is advertised with a base price of $6,986 delivered. However, the window sticker on the truck reads as follows: tinted glass, $210; automatic transmission, $650; power steering, $210; power brakes, $215; safety locks, $95; air conditioning, $1,056. Estimate the total price, including the accessories, by rounding all the way and *then* calculating the exact price.

12. Four different stores are offering the same make and model of a Panasonic LCD television:

Store A	Store B	Store C	Store D
$1,285	$1,380	$1,440	$1,355

Find the difference between the highest price and the lowest price. Check your answer.

13. A Xerox XC830 copy machine has a suggested retail price of $1,395. The net price is $649. How much is the discount on the copy machine?

Learning Unit 1–3 : Multiplying and Dividing Whole Numbers

DRILL PROBLEMS

1. In the following problems, first estimate by rounding all the way, and then work the actual problems and check:

Actual	Estimate	Check
a. 160		
$\times 15$		

b. 4,216		
$\times 45$		

c. 52,376		
$\times 309$		

d. 3,106		
$\times 28$		

2. Multiply; use the shortcut when applicable:

   a.   4,072
          $\times$ 100

   b.   5,100
          $\times$ 40

   c.   76,000
          $\times$ 1,200

   d. 93 $\times$ 100,000

3. Divide by rounding all the way; then do the actual calculation and check showing the remainder as a whole number.

Actual	Estimate	Check

   a. 8)7,709

   b. 26)5,910

   c. 151)3,783

   d. 46)19,550

4. Divide by the shortcut method:

   a. 200)5,400

   b. 50)5,650

   c. 1,200)43,200

   d. 17,000)510,000

WORD PROBLEMS

5. Mia Kaminsky sells state lottery tickets in her variety store. If Mia's Variety Store sells 720 lottery tickets per day, how many tickets will be sold in a 7-day period?

6. Arlex Oil Company employs 100 people who are eligible for profit sharing. The financial manager has announced that the profits to be shared amount to $64,000. How much will each employee receive?

7. John Duncan's employer withheld $4,056 in federal taxes from his pay for the year. If equal deductions are made each week, what is John's weekly deduction?

8. Anne Domingoes drives a Volvo that gets 32 miles per gallon of gasoline. How many miles can she travel on 25 gallons of gas?

9. How many 8-inch pieces of yellow ribbon can be cut from a spool of ribbon that contains 6 yards (1 yard = 36 inches)?

10. The number of commercials aired per day on a local television station is 672. How many commercials are aired in 1 year?

11. The computer department at City College purchased 18 computers at a cost of $2,400 each. What was the total price for the computer purchase?

12. Net income for Goodwin's Partnership was $64,500. The five partners share profits and losses equally. What was each partner's share?

13. Ben Krenshaw's supervisor at the construction site told Ben to divide a load of 1,423 bricks into stacks containing 35 bricks each. How many stacks will there be when Ben has finished the job? How many "extra" bricks will there be?

Learning Unit 2–1 : Types of Fractions and Conversion Procedures

DRILL PROBLEMS

1. Identify the type of fraction—proper, improper, or mixed number:

   a. $\dfrac{7}{8}$
   b. $\dfrac{31}{29}$
   c. $\dfrac{29}{27}$

   d. $9\dfrac{3}{11}$
   e. $\dfrac{18}{5}$
   f. $9\dfrac{1}{8}$

2. Convert to a mixed number:

   a. $\dfrac{29}{4}$
   b. $\dfrac{137}{8}$
   c. $\dfrac{27}{5}$

   d. $\dfrac{29}{9}$
   e. $\dfrac{71}{8}$
   f. $\dfrac{43}{6}$

3. Convert the mixed number to an improper fraction:

   a. $9\dfrac{1}{5}$
   b. $12\dfrac{3}{11}$
   c. $4\dfrac{3}{7}$

   d. $20\dfrac{4}{9}$
   e. $10\dfrac{11}{12}$
   f. $17\dfrac{2}{3}$

4. Tell whether the fractions in each pair are equivalent or not:

   a. $\dfrac{3}{4}\quad\dfrac{9}{12}$ _____
   b. $\dfrac{2}{3}\quad\dfrac{12}{18}$ _____
   c. $\dfrac{7}{8}\quad\dfrac{15}{16}$ _____

   d. $\dfrac{4}{5}\quad\dfrac{12}{15}$ _____
   e. $\dfrac{3}{2}\quad\dfrac{9}{4}$ _____
   f. $\dfrac{5}{8}\quad\dfrac{7}{11}$ _____

   g. $\dfrac{7}{12}\quad\dfrac{7}{24}$ _____
   h. $\dfrac{5}{4}\quad\dfrac{30}{24}$ _____
   i. $\dfrac{10}{26}\quad\dfrac{12}{26}$ _____

5. Find the greatest common divisor by the step approach and reduce to lowest terms:

a. $\dfrac{36}{42}$

b. $\dfrac{30}{75}$

c. $\dfrac{74}{148}$

d. $\dfrac{15}{600}$

e. $\dfrac{96}{132}$

f. $\dfrac{84}{154}$

6. Convert to higher terms:

a. $\dfrac{9}{10} = \dfrac{}{70}$

b. $\dfrac{2}{15} = \dfrac{}{30}$

c. $\dfrac{6}{11} = \dfrac{}{132}$

d. $\dfrac{4}{9} = \dfrac{}{36}$

e. $\dfrac{7}{20} = \dfrac{}{100}$

f. $\dfrac{7}{8} = \dfrac{}{560}$

WORD PROBLEMS

7. Ken drove to college in $3\frac{1}{4}$ hours. How many quarter-hours is that? Show your answer as an improper fraction.

8. Mary looked in the refrigerator for a dozen eggs. When she found the box, only 5 eggs were left. What fractional part of the box of eggs was left?

9. At a recent meeting of a local Boosters Club, 17 of the 25 members attending were men. What fraction of those in attendance were men?

10. By weight, water is two parts out of three parts of the human body. What fraction of the body is water?

11. Three out of 5 students who begin college will continue until they receive their degree. Show in fractional form how many out of 100 beginning students will graduate.

12. Tina and her friends came in late to a party and found only $\frac{3}{4}$ of a pizza remaining. In order for everyone to get some pizza, she wanted to divide it into smaller pieces. If she divides the pizza into twelfths, how many pieces will she have? Show your answer in fractional form.

13. Sharon and Spunky noted that it took them 35 minutes to do their exercise routine. What fractional part of an hour is that? Show your answer in lowest terms.

14. Norman and his friend ordered several pizzas, which were all cut into eighths. The group ate 43 pieces of pizza. How many pizzas did they eat? Show your answer as a mixed number.

Learning Unit 2–2 :   Adding and Subtracting Fractions

DRILL PROBLEMS

1. Find the least common denominator (LCD) for each of the following groups of denominators using the prime numbers:

a. 8, 16, 32

b. 9, 15, 20

c. 12, 15, 32

d. 7, 9, 14, 28

2. Add and reduce to lowest terms or change to a mixed number if needed:

a. $\frac{1}{9} + \frac{4}{9}$

b. $\frac{5}{12} + \frac{8}{15}$

c. $\frac{7}{8} + \frac{5}{12}$

d. $7\frac{2}{3} + 5\frac{1}{4}$

e. $\frac{2}{3} + \frac{4}{9} + \frac{1}{4}$

3. Subtract and reduce to lowest terms:

a. $\dfrac{5}{9} - \dfrac{2}{9}$ **b.** $\dfrac{14}{15} - \dfrac{4}{15}$ **c.** $\dfrac{8}{9} - \dfrac{5}{6}$ **d.** $\dfrac{7}{12} - \dfrac{9}{16}$

e. $33\dfrac{5}{8} - 27\dfrac{1}{2}$ **f.** $9 - 2\dfrac{3}{7}$ **g.** $15\dfrac{1}{3} - 9\dfrac{7}{12}$

h. $92\dfrac{3}{10} - 35\dfrac{7}{15}$ **i.** $93 - 57\dfrac{5}{12}$ **j.** $22\dfrac{5}{8} - 17\dfrac{1}{4}$

WORD PROBLEMS

4. Dan Lund took a cross-country trip. He drove $5\dfrac{3}{8}$ hours on Monday, $6\dfrac{1}{2}$ hours on Tuesday, $9\dfrac{3}{4}$ hours on Wednesday, $6\dfrac{3}{8}$ hours on Thursday, and $10\dfrac{1}{4}$ hours on Friday. Find the total number of hours Dan drove in the first 5 days of his trip.

5. Sharon Parker bought 20 yards of material to make curtains. She used $4\dfrac{1}{2}$ yards for one bedroom window, $8\dfrac{3}{5}$ yards for another bedroom window, and $3\dfrac{7}{8}$ yards for a hall window. How much material did she have left?

6. Molly Ring visited a local gym and lost $2\dfrac{1}{4}$ pounds the first weekend and $6\dfrac{1}{8}$ pounds in week 2. What is Molly's total weight loss?

7. Bill Williams had to drive $46\frac{1}{4}$ miles to work. After driving $28\frac{5}{6}$ miles he noticed he was low on gas and had to decide whether he should stop to fill the gas tank. How many more miles does Bill have to drive to get to work?

8. Albert's Lumber Yard purchased $52\frac{1}{2}$ cords of lumber on Monday and $48\frac{3}{4}$ cords on Tuesday. It sold $21\frac{3}{8}$ cords on Friday. How many cords of lumber remain at Albert's Lumber Yard?

9. At Arlen Oil Company, where Dave Bursett is the service manager, it took $42\frac{1}{3}$ hours to clean five boilers. After a new cleaning tool was purchased, the time for cleaning five boilers was reduced to $37\frac{4}{9}$ hours. How much time was saved?

Learning Unit 2–3 : Multiplying and Dividing Fractions

DRILL PROBLEMS

1. Multiply; use the cancellation technique:

a. $\dfrac{6}{13} \times \dfrac{26}{12}$

b. $\dfrac{3}{8} \times \dfrac{2}{3}$

c. $\dfrac{5}{7} \times \dfrac{9}{10}$

d. $\dfrac{3}{4} \times \dfrac{9}{13} \times \dfrac{26}{27}$

e. $6\dfrac{2}{5} \times 3\dfrac{1}{8}$

f. $2\dfrac{2}{3} \times 2\dfrac{7}{10}$

g. $45 \times \dfrac{7}{9}$

h. $3\dfrac{1}{9} \times 1\dfrac{2}{7} \times \dfrac{3}{4}$

i. $\dfrac{3}{4} \times \dfrac{7}{9} \times 3\dfrac{1}{3}$

j. $\dfrac{1}{8} \times 6\dfrac{2}{3} \times \dfrac{1}{10}$

2. Multiply; do not use canceling but reduce by finding the greatest common divisor:

   a. $\dfrac{3}{4} \times \dfrac{8}{9}$

   b. $\dfrac{7}{16} \times \dfrac{8}{13}$

3. Multiply or divide as indicated:

   a. $\dfrac{25}{36} \div \dfrac{5}{9}$

   b. $\dfrac{18}{8} \div \dfrac{12}{16}$

   c. $2\dfrac{6}{7} \div 2\dfrac{2}{5}$

   d. $3\dfrac{1}{4} \div 16$

   e. $24 \div 1\dfrac{1}{3}$

   f. $6 \times \dfrac{3}{2}$

   g. $3\dfrac{1}{5} \times 7\dfrac{1}{2}$

   h. $\dfrac{3}{8} \div \dfrac{7}{4}$

   i. $9 \div 3\dfrac{3}{4}$

   j. $\dfrac{11}{24} \times \dfrac{24}{33}$

   k. $\dfrac{12}{14} \div 27$

   l. $\dfrac{3}{5} \times \dfrac{2}{7} \div \dfrac{3}{10}$

WORD PROBLEMS

4. Mary Smith plans to make 12 meatloafs to store in her freezer. Each meatloaf requires $2\frac{1}{4}$ pounds of ground beef. How much ground beef does Mary need?

5. Judy Carter purchased a real estate lot for \$24,000. She sold it 2 years later for $1\frac{5}{8}$ times as much as she had paid for it. What was the selling price?

6. Lynn Clarkson saw an ad for a camcorder that cost $980. She knew of a discount store that would sell it to her for a markdown of $\frac{3}{20}$ off the advertised price. How much is the discount she can get?

7. To raise money for their club, the members of the Marketing Club purchased 68 bushels of popcorn to resell. They plan to repackage the popcorn in bags that hold $\frac{2}{21}$ of a bushel each. How many bags of popcorn will they be able to fill?

8. Richard Tracy paid a total of $375 for lumber costing $9\frac{3}{8}$ per foot. How many feet did he purchase?

9. While training for a marathon, Kristin Woods jogged $7\frac{3}{4}$ miles per hour for $2\frac{2}{3}$ hours. How many miles did Kristin jog?

10. On a map, 1 inch represents 240 miles. How many miles are represented by $\frac{3}{8}$ of an inch?

11. In Massachusetts, the governor wants to allot $\frac{1}{6}$ of the total sales tax collections to public education. The total sales tax collected is $2,472,000; how much will go to education?

Learning Unit 3–1: Rounding Decimals; Fraction and Decimal Conversions

DRILL PROBLEMS

1. Write in decimal:
    a. Sixty-two hundredths _____
    b. Six tenths _____
    c. Nine hundred fifty-three thousandths _____
    d. Four hundred one thousandths _____
    e. Six hundredths _____

2. Round each decimal to the place indicated:
    a. .8624 to the nearest thousandth _____
    b. .051 to the nearest tenth _____
    c. 8.207 to the nearest hundredth _____
    d. 2.094 to the nearest hundredth _____
    e. .511172 to the nearest ten thousandth _____

3. Name the place position of the underlined digit:
    a. .8$\underline{2}$6 _____
    b. .91$\underline{4}$ _____
    c. 3.$\underline{1}$169 _____
    d. 53.17$\underline{5}$ _____
    e. 1.017$\underline{4}$ _____

4. Convert to fractions (do not reduce):

a. .91 _____

b. .426 _____

c. 2.516 _____

d. .62$\frac{1}{2}$ _____

e. 13.007 _____

f. 5.03$\frac{1}{4}$ _____

5. Convert to fractions and reduce to lowest terms:

a. .4

b. .44

c. .53

d. .336

e. .096

f. .125

g. .3125

h. .008

i. 2.625

j. 5.75

k. 3.375

l. 9.04

6. Convert the following fractions to decimals and round your answer to the nearest hundredth:

a. $\frac{1}{8}$

b. $\frac{7}{16}$

c. $\frac{2}{3}$

d. $\frac{3}{4}$

e. $\frac{9}{16}$

f. $\frac{5}{6}$

g. $\frac{7}{9}$

h. $\frac{38}{79}$

i. $2\frac{3}{8}$

j. $9\frac{1}{3}$

k. $11\frac{19}{50}$

l. $6\frac{21}{32}$

m. $4\frac{83}{97}$

n. $1\frac{2}{5}$

o. $2\frac{2}{11}$

p. $13\frac{30}{42}$

WORD PROBLEMS

7. Alan Angel got 2 hits in his first 7 times at bat. What is his average to the nearest thousandths place?

8. Bill Breen earned $1,555, and his employer calculated that Bill's total FICA deduction should be $118.9575. Round this deduction to the nearest cent.

9. At the local college, .566 of the students are men. Convert to a fraction. Do not reduce.

10. The average television set is watched 2,400 hours a year. If there are 8,760 hours in a year, what fractional part of the year is spent watching television? Reduce to lowest terms.

11. On Saturday, the employees at the Empire Fish Company work only $\frac{1}{3}$ of a day. How could this be expressed as a decimal to the nearest thousandth?

12. The North Shore Cinema has 610 seats. At a recent film screening there were 55 vacant seats. Show as a fraction the number of filled seats. Reduce as needed.

13. Michael Sullivan was planning his marketing strategy for a new product his company had produced. He was fascinated to discover that Rhode Island, the smallest state in the United States, was only twenty thousand, five hundred seven ten millionths the size of the largest state, Alaska. Write this number in decimal.

14. Bull Moose Company purchased a new manufacturing plant, located on an acre of land, for a total price of $2,250,000. The accountant determined that $\frac{3}{7}$ of the total price should be allocated as the price of the building. What decimal portion is the price of the building? Round to the nearest thousandth.

Learning Unit 3–2 : Adding, Subtracting, Multiplying, and Dividing Decimals

DRILL PROBLEMS

1. Rearrange vertically and add:
   a. 7.57 + 6.2 + 13.008 + 4.83

   b. 1.0625 + 4.0881 + .0775

   c. .903 + .078 + .17 + .1 + .96

   d. 3.38 + .175 + .0186 + .2

2. Rearrange and subtract:
   a. .96 − .43

   b. .885 − .069

   c. 11.67 − .935

   d. 261.2 − 8.08

3. Multiply and round to the nearest tenth:
   a. 13.6 × .02

   b. 1.73 × .069

c. 400×3.7 **d.** 0.025×5.6

4. Divide and round to the nearest hundredth:
   a. $13.869 \div .6$ **b.** $1.0088 \div .14$ **c.** $18.7 \div 2.16$ **d.** $15.64 \div .34$

5. Complete by the shortcut method:
   a. $6.87 \times 1,000$ **b.** $927,530 \div 100$ **c.** $27.2 \div 1,000$
   d. $.21 \times 1,000$ **e.** 347×100 **f.** $347 \div 100$
   g. $.0021 \div 10$ **h.** $85.44 \times 10,000$ **i.** 83.298×100
   j. $23.0109 \div 100$

WORD PROBLEMS (Use *Business Math Handbook* Tables as Needed.)

6. Andy Hay noted his Ford Explorer odometer reading of 18,969.4 at the beginning of his vacation. At the end of his vacation the reading was 21,510.4. How many miles did he drive during his vacation?

7. Jeanne Allyn purchased 12.25 yards of ribbon for a craft project. The ribbon cost 37¢ per yard. What was the total cost of the ribbon?

8. Leo Green wanted to find out the gas mileage for his company truck. When he filled the gas tank, he wrote down the odometer reading of 9,650.7. The next time he filled the gas tank the odometer reading was 10,112.2. He looked at the gas pump and saw that he had taken 18.5 gallons of gas. Find the gas mileage per gallon for Leo's truck. Round to the nearest tenth.

9. At Halley's Rent-a-Car, the cost per day to rent a medium-size car is $35.25 plus 37¢ a mile. What would be the charge to rent this car for 1 day if you drove 205.4 miles?

10. A trip to Mexico costs 6,000 pesos. What is this in U.S. dollars? Check your answer.

11. If a commemorative gold coin weighs 7.842 grams, find the number of coins that can be produced from 116 grams of gold. Round to the nearest whole number.

Learning Unit 4–1 : The Checking Account

DRILL PROBLEMS

1. The following is a deposit slip made out by Fred Young of the F. W. Young Company.

   a. How much cash did Young deposit? _____

   b. How many checks did Young deposit? _____

   c. What was the total amount deposited? _____

					ADDITIONAL CHECKS		
		DESCRIPTION	DOLLARS	CENTS	DESCRIPTION	DOLLARS	CENTS
Fleet Bank	This deposit is subject to: proof and verification, the Uniform Commercial Code, the collection and availability policy of this bank.	BILLS	415	XX	7.		
Checking Deposit		COIN	15	64	8.		
TO THE ACCOUNT OF DATE 3/27/14		LIST CHECKS 1 53-1297	188	44	9.		
NAME		2 51-1509	98	37	10.		
(PLEASE PRINT) PLEASE ENTER CLEARLY		3 53-1290	150	06	11.		
PLEASE ENDORSE ALL CHECKS YOUR ACCOUNT NUMBER		4.			12.		
		5.			13.		
		6.			14.		
		SUB TOTAL ITEMS 1-6			SUB TOTAL ITEMS 7-14		
					TOTAL		

⑈5 2⑈ 2000 ⑈7⑈

2. Blackstone Company had a balance of $2,173.18 in its checking account. Henry James, Blackstone's accountant, made a deposit that consisted of 2 fifty-dollar bills, 120 ten-dollar bills, 6 five-dollar bills, 14 one-dollar bills, $9.54 in change, plus two checks they had accepted, one for $16.38 and the other for $102.50. Find the amount of the deposit and the new balance in Blackstone's checking account.

3. Answer the following questions using the illustration:

No. 113	$ 750 00/100		Jones Company			No. 113

October 4 20 *XX*
To *Neuner Realty*
For *real estate*

	DOLLARS	CENTS
BALANCE	1,020	93
AMT. DEPOSITED	2,756	80
TOTAL	3,777	73
AMT. THIS CHECK	750	00
BALANCE FORWARD	3,027	73

Jones Company
22 Aster Road
Salem, MA 01970

PAY TO THE ORDER OF _____ *Neuner Realty Company* _____ $ 750 00/100

October 4 20 *XX*   5-13/110

Seven Hundred Fifty and 00/100 _____ DOLLARS

FLEET BANK OF MASSACHUSETTS,
NATIONAL ASSOCIATION
Fleet Bank BOSTON, MASSACHUSETTS

Kevin Jones

MEMO _____ *real estate*

⑆011000138⑆   14 0380 113

a. Who is the payee? _____

b. Who is the drawer? _____

c. Who is the drawee? _____

d. What is the bank's identification number _____

e. What is Jones Company's account number? _____

f. What was the balance in the account on September 30? _____

g. For how much did Jones write Check No. 113? _____

h. How much was deposited on October 1? _____

i. How much was left after Check No. 113 was written? _____

4. Write each of the following amounts in verbal form as you would on a check:

a. $40 _____

b. $245.75 _____

c. $3.98 _____

d. $1,205.05 _____

e. $3,013 _____

f. $510.10 _____

Learning Unit 4–2 : Bank Statement and Reconciliation Process; Trends in Online Banking

WORD PROBLEMS

1. Find the bank balance on January 31.

Date	Checks and payments			Deposits	Balance
January 1					401.17
January 2	108.64				_____
January 5	116.50			432.16	_____
January 6	14.92	150.00	10.00		_____
January 11	12.29			633.89	_____
January 18	108.64	18.60			_____
January 25	43.91	23.77		657.22	_____
January 26	75.00				_____
January 31	6.75 sc				_____

2. Joe Madruga, of Madruga's Taxi Service, received a bank statement for the month of May showing a balance of $932.36. His records show that the bank had not yet recorded two of his deposits, one for $521.50 and the other for $98.46. There are outstanding checks in the amounts of $41.67, $135.18, and $25.30. The statement also shows a service charge of $3.38. The balance in the check register is $1,353.55. Prepare a bank reconciliation for Madruga's as of May 31.

3. In reconciling the checking account for Nasser Enterprises, Beth Accomando found that the bank had collected a $3,000 promissory note on the company's behalf and had charged a $15 collection fee. There was also a service charge of $7.25. What amount should be added/subtracted from the checkbook balance to bring it up to date?

   Add: _____   Deduct: _____

4. In reconciling the checking account for Colonial Cleaners, Steve Papa found that a check for $34.50 had been recorded in the check register as $43.50. The bank returned an NSF check in the amount of $62.55. Interest income of $8.25 was earned and a service charge of $10.32 was assessed. What amount should be added/subtracted from the checkbook balance to bring it up to date?

   Add: _____   Deduct: _____

5. Matthew Stokes was completing the bank reconciliation for Parker's Tool and Die Company. The check register balance was $1,503.67. Matthew found that a $76.00 check had been recorded in the check register as $67.00; that a note for $1,500 had been collected by the bank for Parker's and the collection fee was $12.00; that $15.60 interest was earned on the account; and that an $8.35 service charge had been assessed. What should the check register balance be after Matthew updates it with the bank reconciliation information?

6. Consumers, community activists, and politicians are decrying the new line of accounts because several include a $3 service charge for some customers who use bank tellers for transactions that can be done through an automated teller machine. Bill Wade banks at a local bank that charges this fee. He was having difficulty balancing his checkbook because he did not notice this fee on his bank statement. His bank statement showed a balance of $822.18. Bill's checkbook had a balance of $206.48. Check No. 406 for $116.08 and Check No. 407 for $12.50 were outstanding. A $521 deposit was not on the statement. Bill has his payroll check electronically deposited to his checking account—the payroll check was for $1,015.12. (Bill's payroll checks vary each month.) There are also a $1 service fee and a teller fee of $6. Complete Bill's bank reconciliation.

7. At First National Bank in San Diego, some customers have to pay $25 each year as an ATM card fee. John Levi banks at First National Bank and just received his bank statement showing a balance of $829.25; his checkbook balance is $467.40. The bank statement shows an ATM card fee of $25.00, teller fee of $9.00, interest of $1.80, and John's $880 IRS refund check, which was processed by the IRS and deposited to his account. John has two checks that have not cleared—No. 112 for $620.10 and No. 113 for $206.05. There is also a deposit in transit for $1,312.10. Prepare John's bank reconciliation.

Learning Unit 5–1 : Solving Equations for the Unknown

DRILL PROBLEMS

1. Write equations for the following situations. Use N for the unknown number. Do not solve the equations.

   a. Three times a number is 180.

   b. A number increased by 13 equals 25.

   c. Seven less than a number is 5.

   d. Fifty-seven decreased by 3 times a number is 21.

   e. Fourteen added to one-third of a number is 18.

   f. Twice the sum of a number and 4 is 32.

   g. Three-fourths of a number is 9.

   h. Two times a number plus 3 times the same number plus 8 is 68.

2. Solve for the unknown number:

   a. $C + 40 = 90$

   b. $29 + M = 44$

   c. $D - 77 = 98$

   d. $7N = 63$

   e. $\dfrac{X}{12} = 11$

   f. $3Q + 4Q + 2Q = 108$

   g. $H + 5H + 3 = 57$

   h. $2(N - 3) = 62$

   i. $\dfrac{3R}{4} = 27$

   j. $E - 32 = 41$

   k. $5(2T - 2) = 120$

   l. $12W - 5W = 98$

m. $49 - X = \quad 37$

n. $12(V + 2) = \quad 84$

o. $7D + 4 = \quad 5D + 14$

p. $7(T - 2) = \quad 2T - 9$

Learning Unit 5-2 : Solving Word Problems for the Unknown

WORD PROBLEMS

1. A sweater at the Gap was marked down $30. The sale price was $50. What was the original price?

Unknown(s)	Variables(s)	Relationship

2. Goodwin's Corporation found that $\frac{2}{3}$ of its employees were vested in their retirement plan. If 124 employees are vested, what is the total number of employees at Goodwin's?

Unknown(s)	Variables(s)	Relationship

3. Eileen Haskin's utility and telephone bills for the month totaled $180. The utility bill was 3 times as much as the telephone bill. How much was each bill?

Unknown(s)	Variables(s)	Relationship

4. Ryan and his friends went to the golf course to hunt for golf balls. Ryan found 15 more than $\frac{1}{3}$ of the total number of golf balls that were found. How many golf balls were found if Ryan found 75 golf balls?

Unknown(s)	Variables(s)	Relationship

5. Linda Mills and Sherry Somers sold 459 tickets for the Advertising Club's raffle. If Linda sold 8 times as many tickets as Sherry, how many tickets did each one sell?

Unknown(s)	Variables(s)	Relationship

6. Jason Mazzola wanted to buy a suit at Giblee's. Jason did not have enough money with him, so Mr. Giblee told him he would hold the suit if Jason gave him a deposit of $\frac{1}{5}$ of the cost of the suit. Jason agreed and gave Mr. Giblee $79. What was the price of the suit?

Unknown(s)	Variables(s)	Relationship

7. Peter sold watches ($7) and necklaces ($4) at a flea market. Total sales were $300. People bought 3 times as many watches as necklaces. How many of each did Peter sell? What were the total dollar sales of each?

Unknown(s)	Variables(s)	Price	Relationship

8. Peter sold watches ($7) and necklaces ($4) at a flea market. Total sales for 48 watches and necklaces were $300. How many of each did Peter sell? What were the total dollar sales of each?

Unknown(s)	Variables(s)	Price	Relationship

9. A 3,000 piece of direct mailing cost $1,435. Printing cost is $550, about $3\frac{1}{2}$ times the cost of typesetting. How much did the typesetting cost? Round to the nearest cent.

Unknown(s)	Variables(s)	Relationship

10. In 2014, Tony Rigato, owner of MRM, saw an increase in sales to $13.5 million. Rigato states that since 2011, sales have more than tripled. What were his sales in 2011?

Unknown(s)	Variables(s)	Relationship

Learning Unit 6–1 : Conversions

DRILL PROBLEMS

1. Convert the following to percents; round to the nearest tenth of a percent if needed:

   a. .04 _____ %   **b.** .729 _____ %   **c.** .009 _____ %

   d. 8.3 _____ %   **e.** 5.26 _____ %   **f.** 6 _____ %

   g. .0105 _____ %   **h.** .1180 _____ %   **i.** 5.0375 _____ %

   j. .862 _____ %   **k.** .2615 _____ %   **l.** .8 _____ %

   m. .025 _____ %   **n.** .06 _____ %

2. Convert the following to decimals; do not round:

   a. 68% _____   **b.** .09% _____   **c.** 4.7% _____

   d. 9.67% _____   **e.** .2% _____   **f.** $\frac{1}{4}$% _____

   g. .76% _____   **h.** 110% _____   **i.** $12\frac{1}{2}$% _____

   j. 5% _____   **k.** .004% _____   **l.** $7\frac{5}{10}$% _____

   m. $\frac{3}{4}$% _____   **n.** 1% _____

3. Convert the following to percents; round to the nearest tenth of a percent if needed:

   a. $\frac{7}{10}$ _____ %   **b.** $\frac{1}{5}$ _____ %   **c.** $1\frac{5}{8}$ _____ %

   d. $\frac{2}{7}$ _____ %   **e.** 2 _____ %   **f.** $\frac{14}{100}$ _____ %

   g. $\frac{1}{6}$ _____ %   **h.** $\frac{1}{2}$ _____ %   **i.** $\frac{3}{5}$ _____ %

   j. $\frac{3}{25}$ _____ %   **k.** $\frac{5}{16}$ _____ %   **l.** $\frac{11}{50}$ _____ %

   m. $4\frac{3}{4}$ _____ %   **n.** $\frac{3}{200}$ _____ %

4. Convert the following to fractions in simplest form:

   a. 40% _____   **b.** 15% _____   **c.** 50% _____

   d. 75% _____   **e.** 35% _____   **f.** 85% _____

   g. $12\frac{1}{2}$% _____   **h.** $37\frac{1}{2}$% _____   **i.** $33\frac{1}{3}$% _____

   l. $5\frac{3}{4}$% _____

   j. 3% _____   **k.** 8.5% _____

   m. 100% _____   **n.** 10% _____

5. Complete the following table by finding the missing fraction, decimal, or percent equivalent:

	Fraction	Decimal	Percent		Fraction	Decimal	Percent
a.		.25	25%	h.	$\frac{1}{6}$	$.16\overline{6}$	
b.	$\frac{3}{8}$		$37\frac{1}{2}\%$	i.		$.083\overline{3}$	$8\frac{1}{3}\%$
c.	$\frac{1}{2}$	.5		j.	$\frac{1}{9}$		$11\frac{1}{9}\%$
d.	$\frac{2}{3}$		$66\frac{2}{3}\%$	k.		.3125	$31\frac{1}{4}\%$
e.		.4	40%	l.	$\frac{3}{40}$	.075	
f.	$\frac{3}{5}$	.6		m.	$\frac{1}{5}$		20%
g.	$\frac{7}{10}$		70%	n.		1.125	$112\frac{1}{2}\%$

WORD PROBLEMS

6. If in 2013, Mutual of New York reported that 80% of its new sales came from existing clients. What fractional part of its new sales came from existing clients? Reduce to simplest form.

7. Six hundred ninety corporations and design firms competed for the Industrial Design Excellence Award (IDEA). Twenty were selected as the year's best and received gold awards. Show the gold award winners as a fraction; then show what percent of the entrants received gold awards. Round to the nearest tenth of a percent.

8. If in the first half of 2013, stock prices in the Standard & Poor's 500-stock index rose 4.1%. Show the increase as a decimal.

9. In the recent banking crisis, many banks were unable to cover their bad loans. Citicorp, the nation's largest real estate lender, was reported as having only enough reserves to cover 39% of its bad loans. What fractional part of its loan losses was covered?

10. Dave Mattera spent his vacation in Las Vegas. He ordered breakfast in his room, and when he went downstairs to the coffee shop, he discovered that the same breakfast was much less expensive. He had paid 1.884 times as much for the breakfast in his room. What was the percent of increase for the breakfast in his room?

11. Putnam Management Company of Boston recently increased its management fee by .09%. What is the increase as a decimal? What is the same increase as a fraction?

12. Joel Black and Karen Whyte formed a partnership and drew up a partnership agreement, with profits and losses to be divided equally after each partner receives a $7\frac{1}{2}\%$ return on his or her capital contribution. Show their return on investment as a decimal and as a fraction. Reduce.

Learning Unit 6–2 :   Application of Percents—Portion Formula

DRILL PROBLEMS

1. Fill in the amount of the base, rate, and portion in each of the following statements:

   a. The Logans spend $4,000 a month on food, which is 30% of their monthly income of $20,000.

     Base   _____   Rate   _____   Portion   _____

   b. Rocky Norman got a $15 discount when he purchased a new camera. This was 20% off the sticker price of $75.

     Base   _____   Rate   _____   Portion   _____

   c. Mary Burns got a 12% senior citizens discount when she bought a $7.00 movie ticket. She saved $0.84.

     Base   _____   Rate   _____   Portion   _____

   d. Arthur Bogey received a commission of $13,500 when he sold the Brown's house for $225,000. His commission rate is 6%.

     Base   _____   Rate   _____   Portion   _____

   e. Leo Davis deposited $5,000 in a certificate of deposit (CD). A year later he received an interest payment of $450, which was a yield of 9%.

     Base   _____   Rate   _____   Portion   _____

   f. Grace Tremblay is on a diet that allows her to eat 1,600 calories per day. For breakfast she had 600 calories, which is $37\frac{1}{2}\%$ of her allowance.

     Base   _____   Rate   _____   Portion   _____

2. Find the portion; round to the nearest hundredth if necessary:

   a. 7% of 74 _____   **b.** 12% of 205 _____   **c.** 16% of 630 _____

   d. 7.5% of 920 _____   **e.** 25% of 1,004 _____   **f.** 10% of 79 _____

   g. 103% of 44 _____   **h.** 30% of 78 _____   **i.** .2% of 50 _____

   j. 1% of 5,622 _____   **k.** $6\frac{1}{4}\%$ of 480 _____   **l.** 150% of 10 _____

   m. 100% of 34 _____   **n.** $\frac{1}{2}\%$ of 27 _____

3. Find the rate; round to the nearest tenth of a percent as needed:

   a. 30 is what percent of 90? _____   **b.** 6 is what percent of 200? _____

   c. 275 is what percent of 1,000? _____   **d.** .8 is what percent of 44? _____

   e. 67 is what percent of 2,010? _____   **f.** 550 is what percent of 250? _____

   g. 13 is what percent of 650? _____   **h.** $15 is what percent of $455? _____

   i. .05 is what percent of 100? _____   **j.** $6.25 is what percent of $10? _____

4. Find the base; round to the nearest tenth as needed:

   a. 63 is 30% of _____   **b.** 60 is 33% of _____   **c.** 150 is 25% of _____

   d. 47 is 1% of _____   **e.** $21 is 120% of _____   **f.** 2.26 is 40% of _____

   g. 75 is $12\frac{1}{2}\%$ of _____   **h.** 18 is 22.2% of _____   **i.** $37.50 is 50% of _____

   j. 250 is 100% of _____

5. Find the percent of increase or decrease; round to the nearest tenth percent as needed:

	Last year	This year	Amount of change	Percent of change
a.	5,962	4,378	_____	_____
b.	$10,995	$12,250	_____	_____
c.	120,000	140,000	_____	_____
d.	120,000	100,000	_____	_____

WORD PROBLEMS

6. A machine that originally cost $8,000 was sold for $800 at the end of 5 years. What percent of the original cost is the selling price?

7. Joanne Byrne invested $75,000 in a candy shop and is making 12% per year on her investment. How much money per year is she making on her investment?

8. There was a fire in Bill Porper's store that caused 2,780 inventory items to be destroyed. Before the fire, 9,565 inventory items were in the store. What percent of inventory was destroyed? Round to nearest tenth percent.

9. Elyse's Dress Shoppe makes 25% of its sales for cash. If the cash receipts on January 21 were $799, what were the total sales for the day?

10. The YMCA is holding a fund-raiser to collect money for a new gym floor. So far it has collected $7,875, which is 63% of the goal. What is the amount of the goal? How much more money must the YMCA collect?

11. Leslie Tracey purchased her home for $51,500. She sold it last year for $221,200. What percent profit did she make on the sale? Round to nearest tenth percent.

12. Maplewood Park Tool & Die had an annual production of 375,165 units this year. This is 140% of the annual production last year. What was last year's annual production?

Learning Unit 7–1 : Trade Discounts—Single and Chain*

DRILL PROBLEMS

1. Calculate the trade discount amount for each of the following items:

Item	List price	Trade discount	Trade discount amount
a. iPhone	$ 200	20%	_____
b. Flat-screen TV	$1,200	30%	_____
c. Suit	$ 500	10%	_____
d. Bicycle	$ 800	$12\frac{1}{2}$	_____
e. David Yurman bracelet	$ 950	40%	_____

2. Calculate the net price for each of the following items:

Item	List price	Trade discount amount	Net price
a. Home Depot table	$600	$250	_____
b. Bookcase	$525	$129	_____
c. Rocking chair	$480	$ 95	_____

3. Fill in the missing amount for each of the following items:

Item	List price	Trade discount amount	Net price
a. Sears electric saw	_____	$19	$56.00
b. Electric drill	$90	_____	$68.50
c. Ladder	$56	$15.25	_____

4. For each of the following, find the percent paid (complement of trade discount) and the net price:

List price	Trade discount	Percent paid	Net price
a. $45	15%	_____	_____
b. $195	12.2%	_____	_____
c. $325	50%	_____	_____
d. $120	18%	_____	_____

5. In each of the following examples, find the net price equivalent rate and the single equivalent discount rate:

Chain discount	Net price equivalent rate	Single equivalent discount rate
a. 25/5	_____	_____
b. 15/15	_____	_____
c. 15/10/5	_____	_____
d. 12/12/6	_____	_____

*Freight problems to be shown in LU 7–2 material.

6. In each of the following examples, find the net price and the trade discount:

List price	Chain discount	Net price	Trade discount
a. $5,000	10/10/5	_____	_____
b. $7,500	9/6/3	_____	_____
c. $898	20/7/2	_____	_____
d. $1,500	25/10	_____	_____

7. The list price of a handheld calculator is $19.50, and the trade discount is 18%. Find the trade discount amount.

8. The list price of a silver picture frame is $29.95, and the trade discount is 15%. Find the trade discount amount and the net price.

9. The net price of a set of pots and pans is $65, and the trade discount is 20%. What is the list price?

10. Jennie's Variety Store has the opportunity to purchase candy from three different wholesalers; each of the wholesalers offers a different chain discount. Company A offers 25/5/5, Company B offers 20/10/5, and Company C offers 15/20. Which company should Jennie deal with? *Hint:* Choose the company with the highest single equivalent discount rate.

11. The list price of a television set is $625. Find the net price after a series discount of 30/20/10.

12. Mandy's Accessories Shop purchased 12 purses with a total list price of $726. What was the net price of each purse if the wholesaler offered a chain discount of 25/20?

13. Kransberg Furniture Store purchased a bedroom set for $1,097.25 from Furniture Wholesalers. The list price of the set was $1,995. What trade discount rate did Kransberg receive?

14. Susan Monk teaches second grade and receives a discount at the local art supply store. Recently she paid $47.25 for art supplies after receiving a chain discount of 30/10. What was the regular price of the art supplies?

Learning Unit 7-2 : Cash Discounts, Credit Terms, and Partial Payments

DRILL PROBLEMS

1. Complete the following table:

	Date of invoice	Date goods received	Terms	Last day of discount period	End of credit period
a.	February 8		2/10, n/30	_____	_____
b.	August 26		2/10, n/30	_____	_____
c.	October 17		3/10, n/60	_____	_____
d.	March 11	May 10	3/10, n/30, ROG	_____	_____
e.	September 14		2/10, EOM	_____	_____
f.	May 31		2/10, EOM	_____	_____

2. Calculate the cash discount and the net amount paid.

	Invoice amount	Cash discount rate	Discount amount	Net amount paid
a.	$75	3%	_____	_____
b.	$1,559	2%	_____	_____
c.	$546.25	2%	_____	_____
d.	$9,788.75	1%	_____	_____

3. Use the complement of the cash discount to calculate the net amount paid. Assume all invoices are paid within the discount period.

	Terms of invoice	Amount of invoice	Complement	Net amount paid
a.	3/10, n/30	$1,400	_____	_____
b.	3/10, n/30 ROG	$4,500	_____	_____
c.	2/10, EOM	$375.50	_____	_____
d.	1/15, n/45	$3,998	_____	_____

4. Calculate the amount of cash discount and the net amount paid.

	Date of invoice	Terms of invoice	Amount of invoice	Date paid	Cash discount	Amount paid
a.	January 12	2/10, n/30	$5,320	January 22	_____	_____
b.	May 28	2/10, n/30	$975	June 7	_____	_____
c.	August 15	2/10, n/30	$7,700	August 26	_____	_____
d.	March 8	2/10, EOM	$480	April 10	_____	_____
e.	January 24	3/10, n/60	$1,225	February 3	_____	_____

5. Complete the following table:

	Total invoice	Freight charges included in invoice total	Date of invoice	Terms of invoice	Date of payment	Cash discount	Amount paid
a.	$852	$12.50	3/19	2/10, n/30	3/29	_____	_____
b.	$669.57	$15.63	7/28	3/10, EOM	9/10	_____	_____
c.	$500	$11.50	4/25	2/10, n/60	6/5	_____	_____
d.	$188	$9.70	1/12	2/10, EOM	2/10	_____	_____

6. In the following table, assume that all the partial payments were made within the discount period.

	Amount of invoice	Terms of invoice	Partial payment	Amount to be credited	Balance outstanding
a.	$481.90	2/10, n/30	$90.00	_____	_____
b.	$1,000	2/10, EOM	$500.00	_____	_____
c.	$782.88	3/10, n/30, ROG	$275.00	_____	_____
d.	$318.80	2/15, n/60	$200.00	_____	_____

WORD PROBLEMS

7. Ray Chemical Company received an invoice for $16,500, dated March 14, with terms of 2/10, n/30. If the invoice was paid March 22, what was the amount due?

8. On May 27, Trotter Hardware Store received an invoice for trash barrels purchased for $13,650 with terms of 3/10, EOM; the freight charge, which is included in the price, is $412. What are **(a)** the last day of the discount period and **(b)** the amount of the payment due on this date?

9. The Glass Sailboat received an invoice for $930.50 with terms 2/10, n/30 on April 19. On April 29, it sent a payment of $430.50. **(a)** How much credit will be given on the total due? **(b)** What is the new balance due?

10. Dallas Ductworks offers cash discounts of 2/10, 1/15, n/30 on all purchases. If an invoice for $544 dated July 18 is paid on August 2, what is the amount due?

11. The list price of a Luminox watch is $299.90 with trade discounts of 10/20 and terms of 3/10, n/30. If a retailer pays the invoice within the discount period, what amount must the retailer pay?

12. The invoice of a sneakers supplier totaled $2,488.50, was dated February 7, and offered terms 2/10, ROG. The shipment of sneakers was received on March 7. What are **(a)** the last date of the discount period and **(b)** the amount of the discount that will be lost if the invoice is paid after that date?

13. Starburst Toy Company receives an invoice amounting to $1,152.30 with terms of 2/10, EOM and dated November 6. If a partial payment of $750 is made on December 8, what are **(a)** the credit given for the partial payment and **(b)** the balance due on the invoice?

14. Todd's Sporting Goods received an invoice for soccer equipment dated July 26 with terms 3/10, 1/15, n/30 in the amount of $3,225.83, which included shipping charges of $375.50. If this bill is paid on August 5, what amount must be paid?

Learning Unit 8–1 :   Markups Based on Cost (100%)

DRILL PROBLEMS

1. Fill in the missing numbers:

	Cost	Dollar markup	Selling price
a.	$14.80	$4.10	_____
b.	$8.32	_____	$11.04
c.	$25.27	_____	$29.62
d.	_____	$75.00	$165.00
e.	$86.54	$29.77	_____

2. Calculate the markup based on cost; round to the nearest cent.

	Cost	Markup (percent of cost)	Dollar markup
a.	$425.00	30%	_____
b.	$1.52	20%	_____
c.	$9.90	$12\frac{1}{2}$	_____
d.	$298.10	50%	_____
e.	$74.25	38%	_____
f.	$552.25	100%	_____

3. Calculate the dollar markup and rate of the markup as a percent of cost, rounding percents to nearest tenth percent. Verify your result, which may be slightly off due to rounding.

	Cost	Selling price	Dollar markup	Markup (percent of cost)	Verify
a.	$2.50	$4.50	_____	_____	_____
b.	$12.50	$19.00	_____	_____	_____
c.	$0.97	$1.25	_____	_____	_____
d.	$132.25	$175.00	_____	_____	_____
e.	$65.00	$89.99	_____	_____	_____

4. Calculate the dollar markup and the selling price.

	Cost	Markup (percent of cost)	Dollar markup	Selling price
a.	$2.20	40%	_____	_____
b.	$2.80	16%	_____	_____
c.	$840.00	$12\frac{1}{2}$%	_____	_____
d.	$24.36	30%	_____	_____

5. Calculate the cost, rounding to the nearest cent.

Selling price	Rate of markup based on cost	Cost
a. $1.98	30%	_____
b. $360.00	60%	_____
c. $447.50	20%	_____
d. $1,250.00	100%	_____

6. Find the missing numbers. Round money to the nearest cent and percents to the nearest tenth percent.

Cost	Dollar markup	Percent markup on cost	Selling price
a. $72.00	_____	40%	_____
b. _____	$7.00	_____	$35.00
c. $8.80	$1.10	_____	_____
d. _____	_____	28%	$19.84
e. $175.00	_____	_____	$236.25

WORD PROBLEMS

7. If the cost of a Pottery Barn chair is $499 and the markup rate is 40% of the cost, what are **(a)** the dollar markup and **(b)** the selling price?

8. If Barry's Furniture Store purchased a floor lamp for $120 and plans to add a markup of $90, **(a)** what will the selling price be and **(b)** what is the markup as a percent of cost?

9. If Lesjardin's Jewelry Store is selling a gold bracelet for $349, which includes a markup of 35% on cost, what are **(a)** Lesjardin's cost and **(b)** the amount of the dollar markup?

10. Toll's Variety Store sells an alarm clock for $14.75. The alarm clock cost Toll's $9.90. What is the markup amount as a percent of cost? Round to the nearest whole percent.

11. Swanson's Audio Supply marks up its merchandise by 40% on cost. If the markup on a cassette player is $85, what are **(a)** the cost of the cassette player and **(b)** the selling price?

12. Brown's Department Store is selling a shirt for $55. If the markup is 70% on cost, what is Brown's cost (to the nearest cent)?

13. Ward's Greenhouse purchased tomato flats for $5.75 each. Ward's has decided to use a markup of 42% on cost. Find the selling price.

Learning Unit 8–2 : Markups Based on Selling Price (100%)

DRILL PROBLEMS

1. Calculate the markup based on the selling price.

Selling price	Markup (percent of selling price)	Dollar markup
a. $25.00	40%	_____
b. $230.00	25%	_____
c. $81.00	42.5%	_____
d. $72.88	$37\frac{1}{2}\%$	_____
e. $1.98	$7\frac{1}{2}\%$	_____

2. Calculate the dollar markup and the markup as a percent of selling price (to the nearest tenth percent). Verify your answer, which may be slightly off due to rounding.

Cost	Selling price	Dollar markup	Markup (percent of selling price)	Verify
a. $2.50	$4.25	_____	_____	_____
b. $16.00	$24.00	_____	_____	_____
c. $45.25	$85.00	_____	_____	_____
d. $0.19	$0.25	_____	_____	____
e. $5.50	$8.98	_____	_____	_____

3. Given the *cost* and the markup as a percent of *selling price,* calculate the selling price.

Cost	Markup (percent of selling price)	Selling price
a. $5.90	15%	_____
b. $600	32%	_____
c. $15	50%	_____
d. $120	30%	_____
e. $0.29	20%	_____

4. Given the selling price and the percent markup on selling price, calculate the cost.

Cost	Markup (percent of selling price)	Selling price
a. _____	40%	$6.25
b. _____	20%	$16.25
c. _____	19%	$63.89
d. _____	$62\frac{1}{2}\%$	$44.00

5. Calculate the equivalent rate of markup, rounding to the nearest hundredth percent.

Markup on cost	Markup on selling price		Markup on cost	Markup on selling price
a. 40%	_____	**b.** 50%		_____
c. _____	50%	**d.** _____		35%
e. _____	40%			

WORD PROBLEMS

6. Fisher Equipment is selling a Wet/Dry Shop Vac for $49.97. If Fisher's markup is 40% of the selling price, what is the cost of the Shop Vac?

7. Gove Lumber Company purchased a 10-inch table saw for $225 and will mark up the price 35% on the selling price. What will the selling price be?

8. To realize a sufficient gross margin, City Paint and Supply Company marks up its paint 27% on the selling price. If a gallon of Latex Semi-Gloss Enamel has a markup of $4.02, find **(a)** the selling price and **(b)** the cost.

9. A Magnavox 20-inch color TV cost $180 and sells for $297. What is the markup based on the selling price? Round to the nearest hundredth percent.

10. Bargain Furniture sells a five-piece country maple bedroom set for $1,299. The cost of this set is $700. What are **(a)** the markup on the bedroom set, **(b)** the markup percent on cost, and **(c)** the markup percent on the selling price? Round to the nearest hundredth percent.

11. Robert's Department Store marks up its sundries by 28% on the selling price. If a 6.4-ounce tube of toothpaste costs $1.65, what will the selling price be?

12. To be competitive, Tinker Toys must sell the DS software for $89.99. To meet expenses and make a sufficient profit, Tinker Toys must add a markup on the selling price of 23%. What is the maximum amount that Tinker Toys can afford to pay a wholesaler for the DS software?

13. Nicole's Restaurant charges $7.50 for a linguini dinner that costs $2.75 for the ingredients. What rate of markup is earned on the selling price? Round to the nearest hundredth percent.

Learning Unit 8–3 :   Markdowns and Perishables

DRILL PROBLEMS

1. Find the dollar markdown and the sale price.

Original selling price	Markdown percent	Dollar markdown	Sale price
a. $200	40%	_____	_____
b. $2,099.98	25%	_____	_____
c. $729	30%	_____	_____

2. Find the dollar markdown and the markdown percent on original selling price.

Original selling price	Sale price	Dollar markdown	Markdown percent
a. $19.50	$9.75	_____	_____
b. $250	$175	_____	_____
c. $39.95	$29.96	_____	_____

3. Find the original selling price.

Sale price	Markdown percent	Original selling price
a. $328	20%	_____
b. $15.85	15%	_____

4. Calculate the final selling price.

Original selling price	First markdown	Second markdown	Final markup	Final selling price
a. $4.96	25%	8%	5%	_____
b. $130	30%	10%	20%	_____

5. Find the missing amounts.

Number of units	Unit cost	Total cost	Estimated* spoilage	Desired markup (percent of cost)	Total selling price	Selling price per unit
a. 72	$3	_____	12%	50%	_____	_____
b. 50	$0.90	_____	16%	42%	_____	_____

*Round to the nearest whole unit as needed.

WORD PROBLEMS

6. Speedy King is having a 30%-off sale on their box springs and mattresses. A queen-size, back-supporter mattress is priced at $325. What is the sale price of the mattress?

7. Murray and Sons sells a Dell computer for $602.27. It is having a sale, and the computer is marked down to $499.88. What is the percent of the markdown?

8. Coleman's is having a clearance sale. A lamp with an original selling price of $249 is now selling for $198. Find the percent of the markdown. Round to the nearest hundredth percent.

9. Johnny's Sports Shop has advertised markdowns on certain items of 22%. A soccer ball is marked with a sale price of $16.50. What was the original price of the soccer ball?

10. Sam Grillo sells seasonal furnishings. Near the end of the summer a five-piece patio set that was priced $349.99 had not been sold, so he marked it down by 12%. As Labor Day approached, he still had not sold the patio set, so he marked it down an additional 18%. What was the final selling price of the patio set?

11. Calsey's Department Store sells their down comforters for a regular price of $325. During its white sale the comforters were marked down 22%. Then, at the end of the sale, Calsey's held a special promotion and gave a second markdown of 10%. When the sale was over, the remaining comforters were marked up 20%. What was the final selling price of the remaining comforters?

12. The New Howard Bakery wants to make a 60% profit on the cost of its pies. To calculate the price of the pies, it estimated that the usual amount of spoilage is five pies. Calculate the selling price for each pie if the number of pies baked each day is 24 and the cost of the ingredients for each pie is $1.80.

13. Sunshine Bakery bakes 660 loaves of bread each day and estimates that 10% of the bread will go stale before it is sold and thus will have to be discarded. The owner of the bakery wishes to realize a 55% markup on cost on the bread. If the cost to make a loaf of bread is $0.46, what should the owner sell each loaf for?

Learning Unit 8-4 : Breakeven Analysis

DRILL PROBLEMS

1. Calculate the contribution margin.

	Selling Price per unit	Variable cost per unit	Contribution margin
a.	$14.00	$8.00	
b.	$15.99	$4.88	
c.	$18.99	$4.99	
d.	$251.86	$110.00	
e.	$510.99	$310.00	
f.	$1,000.10	$410.00	

2. Calculate the selling price per unit.

	Selling price per unit	Variable cost per unit	Contribution margin
a.		$12.18	$ 4.10
b.		$19.19	$ 5.18
c.		$21.00	$13.00
d.		$41.00	$14.88
e.		$128.10	$79.50
f.		$99.99	$60.00

3. Calculate the breakeven point, rounding to the nearest whole unit.

	Break even point	Fixed cost	Selling price per unit	Variable cost per unit
a.		$50,000	$4.00	$1.00
b.		$30,000	$6.00	$2.00
c.		$20,000	$9.00	$3.00
d.		$100,000	$12.00	$4.00
e.		$120,000	$14.00	$5.00
f.		$90,000	$26.00	$8.00

WORD PROBLEMS

4. Jones Co. produces bars of candy. Each bar sells for $3.99. The variable cost per unit is $2.85. What is the contribution margin for Jones Co.?

5. Logan Co. produces stuffed animals. They have $40,000 in fixed costs. Logan sells each animal for $19.99 with a $12.10 cost per unit. What is the breakeven point for Logan? Round to the nearest whole number.

6. Ranyo Company produces lawn mowers. It has a breakeven point of 6,000 lawn mowers. If its contribution margin is $150, what is Ranyo's fixed cost?

7. Moore company has $100,000 in fixed costs. Its contribution margin is $4.50. Calculate the breakeven point for Moore to the nearest whole number.

Learning Unit 9–1 : Calculating Various Types of Employees' Gross Pay

DRILL PROBLEMS

1. Fill in the missing amounts for each of the following employees. Do not round the overtime rate in your calculations and round your final answers to the nearest cent.

Employee	Total hours	Rate per hour	Regular pay	Overtime pay	Gross pay
a. Mel Jones	38	$11.25	_____	_____	_____
b. Casey Guitare	43	$9.00	_____	_____	_____
c. Norma Harris	37	$7.50	_____	_____	_____
d. Ed Jackson	45	$12.25	_____	_____	_____

2. Calculate each employee's gross from the following data. Do not round the overtime rate in your calculation but round your final answers to the nearest cent.

Employee	S	M	Tu	W	Th	F	S	Total hours	Rate per hour	Regular pay	Overtime pay	Gross pay
a. L. Adams	0	8	8	8	8	8	0	_____	$8.10	_____	_____	_____
b. M. Card	0	9	8	9	8	8	4	_____	$11.35	_____	_____	_____
c. P. Kline	2	$7\frac{1}{2}$	$8\frac{1}{4}$	8	$10\frac{3}{4}$	9	2	_____	$10.60	_____	_____	_____
d. J. Mack	0	$9\frac{1}{2}$	$9\frac{3}{4}$	$9\frac{1}{2}$	10	10	4	_____	$9.95	_____	_____	_____

3. Calculate the gross wages of the following production workers.

Employee	Rate per unit	No. of units produced	Gross pay
a. A. Bossie	$0.67	655	_____
b. J. Carson	$0.87\frac{1}{2}$	703	_____

4. Using the given differential scale, calculate the gross wages of the following production workers.

Units produced	Amount per unit
From 1–50	$.55
From 51–100	.65
From 101–200	.72
More than 200	.95

Employee	Units produced	Gross pay
a. F. Burns	190	_____
b. B. English	210	_____
c. E. Jackson	200	_____

5. Calculate the following salespersons' gross wages.
   a. Straight commission:

Employee	Net sales	Commission	Gross pay
M. Salley	$40,000	13%	_____

b. Straight commission with draw:

Employee	Net sales	Commission	Draw	Commission minus draw
G. Gorsbeck	$38,000	12%	$600	_____

c. Variable commission scale:

Up to $25,000	8%
Excess of $25,000 to $40,000	10%
More than $40,000	12%

Employee	Net sales	Gross pay
H. Lloyd	$42,000	_____

d. Salary plus commission:

Employee	Salary	Commission	Quota	Net sales	Gross pay
P. Floyd	$2,500	3%	$400,000	$475,000	_____

WORD PROBLEMS

For all problems with overtime, be sure to round only the final answer.

6. In the first week of December, Dana Robinson worked 52 hours. His regular rate of pay is $11.25 per hour. What was Dana's gross pay for the week?

7. Davis Fisheries pays its workers for each box of fish they pack. Sunny Melanson receives $.30 per box. During the third week of July, Sunny packed 2,410 boxes of fish. What was Sunny's gross pay?

8. Maye George is a real estate broker who receives a straight commission of 6%. What would her commission be for a house that sold for $197,500?

9. Devon Company pays Eileen Haskins a straight commission of $12\frac{1}{2}\%$ on net sales. In January, Devon gave Eileen a draw of $600. She had net sales that month of $35,570. What was Eileen's commission minus draw?

10. Parker and Company pays Selma Stokes on a variable commission scale. In a month when Selma had net sales of $155,000, what was her gross pay based on the following schedule?

Net sales	Commission rate
Up to $40,000	5%
Excess of $40,000 to $75,000	5.5%
Excess of $75,000 to $100,000	6%
More than $100,000	7%

11. Marsh Furniture Company pays Joshua Charles a monthly salary of $1,900 plus a commission of $2\frac{1}{2}\%$ on sales over $12,500. Last month, Joshua had net sales of $17,799. What was Joshua's gross pay for the month?

12. Amy McWha works at Lamplighter Bookstore where she earns $7.75 per hour plus a commission of 2% on her weekly sales in excess of $1,500. Last week, Amy worked 39 hours and had total sales of $2,250. What was Amy's gross pay for the week?

Learning Unit 9-2 : Computing Payroll Deductions for Employees' Pay; Employers' Responsibilities

DRILL PROBLEMS

Use tables in the *Business Math Handbook* (assume FICA rates in text).

Employee	Allowances and marital status	Cumulative earnings	Salary per week	Taxable earnings S.S.		Medicare
1. Pete Small	M—3	$109,600	$2,300	a. _____		b. _____
2. Alice Hall	M—1	$110,100	$1,100	c. _____		d. _____
3. Jean Rose	M—2	$120,200	$2,000	e. _____		f. _____

4. What is the tax for Social Security and Medicare for Pete in Problem 1?

5. Calculate Pete's FIT by the percentage method.

6. What would employer's contribute for this week's payroll for SUTA and FUTA?

WORD PROBLEMS

7. Cynthia Pratt has earned $108,600 thus far this year. This week she earned $3,500. Find her total FICA tax deduction (Social Security and Medicare).

8. If Cynthia (Problem 7) earns $1,050 the following week, what will be her new total FICA tax deduction?

9. Roger Alley, a service dispatcher, has weekly earnings of $750. He claimed four allowances on his W-4 form and is married. Besides his FIT and FICA deductions, he has deductions of $35.16 for medical insurance and $17.25 for union dues. Calculate his net earnings for the third week in February. Use the percentage method.

10. Nicole Mariotte is unmarried and claimed one withholding allowance on her W-4 form. In the second week of February, she earned $707.35. Deductions from her pay included federal withholding, Social Security, Medicare, health insurance for $47.75, and $30.00 for the company meal plan. What is Nicole's net pay for the week? Use the percentage method.

11. Gerald Knowlton had total gross earnings of $109,800 in the last week of November. His earnings for the first week in December were $804.70. His employer uses the percentage method to calculate federal withholding. If Gerald is married, claims two allowances, and has medical insurance of $52.25 deducted each week from his pay, what is his net pay for the week?

Learning Unit 10–1 : Calculation of Simple Interest and Maturity Value

DRILL PROBLEMS

1. Find the simple interest for each of the following loans:

	Principal	Rate	Time	Interest
a.	$12,000	2%	1 year	_____
b.	$3,000	12%	3 years	_____
c.	$18,000	$8\frac{1}{2}$%	10 months	_____

2. Find the simple interest for each of the following loans; use the exact interest method. Use the days-in-a-year calendar in the text when needed.

	Principal	Rate	Time	Interest
a.	$900	4%	30 days	_____
b.	$4,290	8%	250 days	_____
c.	$1,500	8%	Made March 11 Due July 11	_____

3. Find the simple interest for each of the following loans using the ordinary interest method (Banker's Rule).

	Principal	Rate	Time	Interest
a.	$5,250	$7\frac{1}{2}$%	120 days	_____
b.	$700	3%	70 days	_____
c.	$2,600	11%	Made on June 15 Due October 17	_____

WORD PROBLEMS

4. On October 17, Gill Iowa borrowed $6,000 at a rate of 4%. She promised to repay the loan in 7 months. What are **(a)** the amount of the simple interest and **(b)** the total amount owed upon maturity?

5. Marjorie Folsom borrowed $5,500 to purchase a computer. The loan was for 9 months at an annual interest rate of $12\frac{1}{2}$%. What are **(a)** the amount of interest Marjorie must pay and **(b)** the maturity value of the loan?

6. Eric has a loan for $1,200 at an ordinary interest rate of 9.5% for 80 days. Julie has a loan for $1,200 at an exact interest rate of 9.5% for 80 days. Calculate **(a)** the total amount due on Eric's loan and **(b)** the total amount due on Julie's loan.

7. Roger Lee borrowed $5,280 at $13\frac{1}{2}$% on May 24 and agreed to repay the loan on August 24. The lender calculates interest using the exact interest method. How much will Roger be required to pay on August 24?

8. On March 8, Jack Faltin borrowed $10,225 at $9\frac{3}{4}$%. He signed a note agreeing to repay the loan and interest on November 8. If the lender calculates interest using the ordinary interest method, what will Jack's repayment be?

9. Dianne Smith's real estate taxes of $641.49 were due on November 1, 2013. Due to financial difficulties, Dianne was unable to pay her tax bill until January 15, 2014. The penalty for late payment is $13\frac{3}{8}$% ordinary interest. What is the penalty Dianne will have to pay, and what is Dianne's total payment on January 15?

10. On August 8, Rex Eason had a credit card balance of $550, but he was unable to pay his bill. The credit card company charges interest of $18\frac{1}{2}$% annually on late payments. What amount will Rex have to pay if he pays his bill 1 month late?

11. An issue of *Your Money* discussed average consumers who carry a balance of $2,000 on one credit card. If the yearly rate of interest is 18%, how much are consumers paying in interest per year?

12. AFBA Industrial Bank of Colorado Springs, Colorado, charges a credit card interest rate of 11% per year. If you had a credit card debt of $1,500, what would your interest amount be after 3 months?

Learning Unit 10–2 : Finding Unknown in Simple Interest Formula

DRILL PROBLEMS

1. Find the principal in each of the following. Round to the nearest cent. Assume 360 days. *Calculator hint:* Do denominator calculation first, do not round; when answer is displayed, save it in memory by pressing [M+]. Now key in the numerator (interest amount), [÷], [MR], [=] for the answer. Be sure to clear memory after each problem by pressing [MR] again so that the M is no longer in the display.

	Rate	Time	Interest	Principal
a.	8%	70 days	$68	_____
b.	11%	90 days	$125	_____
c.	9%	120 days	$103	_____
d.	$8\frac{1}{2}$%	60 days	$150	_____

2. Find the rate in each of the following. Round to the nearest tenth of a percent. Assume 360 days.

Principal	Time	Interest	Rate
a. $7,500	120 days	$350	_____
b. $975	60 days	$25	_____
c. $20,800	220 days	$910	_____
d. $150	30 days	$2.10	_____

3. Find the time (to the nearest day) in each of the following. Assuming ordinary interest, use 360 days.

Principal	Rate	Interest	Time (days)	Time (years) (Round to nearest hundredth)
a. $400	11%	$7.33	_____	_____
b. $7,000	12.5%	$292	_____	_____
c. $1,550	9.2%	$106.95	_____	_____
d. $157,000	10.75%	$6,797.88	_____	_____

4. Complete the following. Assume 360 days for all examples.

Principal	Rate (nearest tenth percent)	Time (nearest day)	Simple interest
a. $345	_____	150 days	$14.38
b. _____	12.5%	90 days	$46.88
c. $750	12.2%	_____	$19.06
d. $20,260	16.7%	110 days	_____

WORD PROBLEMS

Use 360 days.

5. In June, Becky opened a $20,000 bank CD paying 1% interest, but she had to withdraw the money in a few days to cover one child's college tuition. The bank charged her $1,000 in penalties for the withdrawal. What percent of the $20,000 was she charged?

6. Dr. Vaccarro invested his money at $12\frac{1}{2}\%$ for 175 days and earned interest of $760. How much money did Dr. Vaccarro invest?

7. If you invested $10,000 at 5% interest in a 6-month CD compounding interest daily, you would earn $252.43 in interest. How much would the same $10,000 invested in a bank paying simple interest earn?

8. Thomas Kyrouz opened a savings account and deposited $750 in a bank that was paying 2.5% simple interest. How much were his savings worth in 200 days?

9. Mary Millitello paid the bank $53.90 in interest on a 66-day loan at 9.8%. How much money did Mary borrow? Round to the nearest dollar.

10. If Anthony Lucido deposits $2,400 for 66 days and makes $60.72 in interest, what interest rate is he receiving?

11. Find how long in days David Wong must invest $23,500 of his company's cash at 8.4% in order to earn $652.50 in interest.

Learning Unit 10–3 : U.S. Rule—Making Partial Note Payments before Due Date

DRILL PROBLEMS

1. A merchant borrowed $3,000 for 320 days at 11% (assume a 360-day year). Use the U.S. Rule to complete the following table:

Payment number	Payment day	Amount paid	Interest to date	Principal payment	Adjusted balance
					$3,000
1	75	$500	_____	_____	_____
2	160	$750	_____	_____	_____
3	220	$1,000	_____	_____	_____
4	320	_____	_____	_____	_____

2. Use the U.S. Rule to solve for total interest costs, balances, and final payments; use ordinary interest.

   Given
   Principal, $6,000, 5%, 100 days
   Partial payments on 30th day, $2,000
                       on 70th day, $1,000

WORD PROBLEMS

3. John Joseph borrowed $10,800 for 1 year at 14%. After 60 days, he paid $2,500 on the note. On the 200th day, he paid an additional $5,000. Use the U.S. Rule and ordinary interest to find the final balance due.

4. Doris Davis borrowed $8,200 on March 5 for 90 days at $8\frac{3}{4}$%. After 32 days, Doris made a payment on the loan of $2,700. On the 65th day, she made another payment of $2,500. What is her final payment if you use the U.S. Rule with ordinary interest?

5. David Ring borrowed $6,000 on a 13%, 60-day note. After 10 days, David paid $500 on the note. On day 40, David paid $900 on the note. What are the total interest and ending balance due by the U.S. Rule? Use ordinary interest.

Learning Unit 11–1 : Structure of Promissory Notes; the Simple Discount Note

DRILL PROBLEMS

1. Identify each of the following characteristics of promissory notes with an **I** for simple interest note, a **D** for simple discount note, or a **B** if it is true for both.

___ Interest is computed on face value, or what is actually borrowed.

___ A promissory note for a loan usually less than 1 year.

___ Borrower receives proceeds = Face value − Bank discount.

___ Maturity value = Face value + Interest.

___ Maturity value = Face value.

___ Borrower receives the face value.

___ Paid back by one payment at maturity.

___ Interest computed on maturity value, or what will be repaid, and not on actual amount borrowed.

2. Find the bank discount and the proceeds for the following; assume 360 days:

	Maturity value	Discount rate	Time (days)	Bank discount	Proceeds
a.	$8,000	3%	120	_____	_____
b.	$4,550	8.1%	110	_____	_____
c.	$19,350	12.7%	55	_____	_____
d.	$63,400	10%	90	_____	_____
e.	$13,490	7.9%	200	_____	_____
f.	$780	$12\frac{1}{2}$%	65	_____	_____

3. Find the effective rate of interest for each of the loans in Problem 2. Use the answers you calculated in Problem 2 to solve these problems; round to the nearest tenth percent.

	Maturity value	Discount rate	Time (days)	Effective rate
a.	$7,000	2%	90	_____
b.	$4,550	8.1%	110	_____
c.	$19,350	12.7%	55	_____
d.	$63,400	10%	90	_____
e.	$13,490	7.9%	200	_____
f.	$780	$12\frac{1}{2}\%$	65	_____

WORD PROBLEMS

Assume 360 days.

4. Kaylee Putty signed a $8,000 note for 140 days at a discount rate of 5%. Find the discount and the proceeds Kaylee received.

5. The Salem Cooperative Bank charges an $8\frac{3}{4}\%$ discount rate. What are the discount and the proceeds for a $16,200 note for 60 days?

6. Bill Jackson is planning to buy a used car. He went to City Credit Union to take out a loan for $6,400 for 300 days. If the credit union charges a discount rate of $11\frac{1}{2}\%$, what will the proceeds of this loan be?

7. Mike Drislane goes to the bank and signs a note for $9,700. The bank charges a 15% discount rate. Find the discount and the proceeds if the loan is for 210 days.

8. Flora Foley plans to have a deck built on the back of her house. She decides to take out a loan at the bank for $14,300. She signs a note promising to pay back the loan in 280 days. If the note was discounted at 9.2%, how much money will Flora receive from the bank?

9. At the end of 280 days, Flora (Problem 8) must pay back the loan. What is the maturity value of the loan?

10. Dave Cassidy signed a $7,855 note at a bank that charges a 14.2% discount rate. If the loan is for 190 days, find **(a)** the proceeds and **(b)** the effective rate charged by the bank (to the nearest tenth percent).

11. How much money must Dave (Problem 10) pay back to the bank?

Learning Unit 11–2 : Discounting an Interest-Bearing Note before Maturity

DRILL PROBLEMS

1. Calculate the maturity value for each of the following promissory notes; use 360 days:

Date of note	Principal of note	Length of note (days)	Interest rate	Maturity value
a. June 9	$5,000	180	3%	_____
b. August 23	$15,990	85	13%	_____
c. December 10	$985	30	11.5%	_____

2. Find the maturity date and the discount period for the following; assume no leap years. *Hint:* See Exact Days-in-a-Year Calendar, Chapter 7.

Date of note	Length of note (days)	Date of discount	Maturity date	Discount period
a. March 11	200	June 28	_____	_____
b. January 22	60	March 2	_____	_____
c. April 19	85	June 6	_____	_____
d. November 17	120	February 15	_____	_____

3. Find the bank discount for each of the following; use 360 days:

Date of note	Principal of note	Length of note	Interest rate	Bank discount rate	Date of discount	Bank discount
a. October 5	$2,475	88 days	11%	9.5%	December 10	_____
b. June 13	$9,055	112 days	15%	16%	August 11	_____
c. March 20	$1,065	75 days	12%	11.5%	May 24	_____

4. Find the proceeds for each of the discounted notes in Problem 3.

    a. _____

    b. _____

    c. _____

WORD PROBLEMS

5. Connors Company received a $4,000, 90-day, 10% note dated April 6 from one of its customers. Connors Company held the note until May 16, when the company discounted it at a bank at a discount rate of 12%. What were the proceeds that Connors Company received?

6. Souza & Sons accepted a 9%, $22,000, 120-day note from one of its customers on July 22. On October 2, the company discounted the note at Cooperative Bank. The discount rate was 12%. What were **(a)** the bank discount and **(b)** the proceeds?

7. The Fargate Store accepted an $8,250, 75-day, 9% note from one of its customers on March 18. Fargate discounted the note at Parkside National Bank at $9\frac{1}{2}$% on March 29. What proceeds did Fargate receive?

8. On November 1, Marjorie's Clothing Store accepted a $5,200, $8\frac{1}{2}$%, 90-day note from Mary Rose in granting her a time extension on her bill. On January 13, Marjorie discounted the note at Seawater Bank, which charged a 10% discount rate. What were the proceeds that Majorie received?

9. On December 3, Duncan's Company accepted a $5,000, 90-day, 12% note from Al Finney in exchange for a $5,000 bill that was past due. On January 29, Duncan discounted the note at The Sidwell Bank at 13.1%. What were the proceeds from the note?

10. On February 26, Sullivan Company accepted a 60-day, 10% note in exchange for a $1,500 past-due bill from Tabot Company. On March 28, Sullivan Company discounted at National Bank the note received from Tabot Company. The bank discount rate was 12%. What are **(a)** the bank discount and **(b)** the proceeds?

11. On June 4, Johnson Company received from Marty Russo a 30-day, 11% note for $720 to settle Russo's debt. On June 17, Johnson discounted the note at Eastern Bank at 15%. What proceeds did Johnson receive?

12. On December 15, Lawlers Company went to the bank and discounted a 10%, 90-day, $14,000 note dated October 21. The bank charged a discount rate of 12%. What were the proceeds of the note?

Learning Unit 12–1 : Compound Interest (Future Value)—The Big Picture

DRILL PROBLEMS

1. In the following examples, calculate manually the amount at year-end for each of the deposits, assuming that interest is compounded annually. Round to the nearest cent each year.

	Principal	Rate	Number of years	Year 1	Year 2	Year 3	Year 4
a.	$530	4%	2	_____	_____		
b.	$1,980	12%	4	_____	_____	_____	_____

2. In the following examples, calculate the simple interest, the compound interest, and the difference between the two. Round to the nearest cent; do not use tables.

	Principal	Rate	Number of years	Simple interest	Compound interest	Difference
a.	$4,600	10%	2	_____	_____	_____
b.	$18,400	9%	4	_____	_____	_____
c.	$855	$7\frac{1}{5}\%$	3	_____	_____	_____

3. Find the future value and the compound interest using the Future Value of $1 at Compound Interest table or the Compound Daily table. Round to the nearest cent.

	Principal	Investment terms	Future value	Compound interest
a.	$20,000	6 years at 4% compounded annually	_____	_____
b.	$10,000	6 years at 8% compounded quarterly	_____	_____
c.	$8,400	7 years at 12% compounded semiannually	_____	_____
d.	$2,500	15 years at 10% compounded daily	_____	_____
e.	$9,600	5 years at 6% compounded quarterly	_____	_____
f.	$20,000	2 years at 6% compounded monthly	_____	_____

4. Calculate the effective rate (APY) of interest using the Future Value of $1 at Compound Interest table.

Investment terms	Effective rate (annual percentage yield)
a. 12% compounded quarterly	_____
b. 12% compounded semiannually	_____
c. 6% compounded quarterly	_____

WORD PROBLEMS

5. John Mackey deposited $7,000 in his savings account at Salem Savings Bank. If the bank pays 2% interest compounded semi annually, what will be the balance of his account at the end of 3 years?

6. Pine Valley Savings Bank offers a certificate of deposit at 12% interest compounded quarterly. What is the effective rate (APY) of interest?

7. Jack Billings loaned $6,000 to his brother-in-law Dan, who was opening a new business. Dan promised to repay the loan at the end of 5 years, with interest of 8% compounded semiannually. How much will Dan pay Jack at the end of 5 years?

8. Eileen Hogarty deposits $5,630 in City Bank, which pays 12% interest compounded quarterly. How much money will Eileen have in her account at the end of 7 years?

9. If Kevin Bassage deposits $3,500 in Scarsdale Savings Bank, which pays 8% interest compounded quarterly, what will be in his account at the end of 6 years? How much interest will he have earned at that time?

10. Arlington Trust pays 6% compounded semiannually. How much interest would be earned on $7,200 for 1 year?

11. Paladium Savings Bank pays 9% compounded quarterly. Find the amount and the interest on $3,000 after three quarters. Do not use a table.

12. David Siderski bought a $8,000 bank certificate paying 4% compounded semiannually. How much money did he obtain upon cashing in the certificate 3 years later?

13. An issue of *Your Money* showed that the more frequently the bank compounds your money, the better. Consider a $10,000 investment earning 6% interest in a 5-year certificate of deposit at the following three banks. What would be the interest earned at each bank?
   a. Bank A (simple interest, no compounding)
   b. Bank B (quarterly compounding)
   c. Bank C (daily compounding)

Learning Unit 12–2 :   Present Value—The Big Picture

1. Use the *Business Math Handbook* to find the table factor for each of the following:

	Future value	Rate	Number of years	Compounded	Table value
a.	$1.00	2%	5	Annually	_____
b.	$1.00	12%	8	Semiannually	_____
c.	$1.00	6%	10	Quarterly	_____
d.	$1.00	12%	2	Monthly	_____
e.	$1.00	8%	15	Semiannually	_____

2. Use the *Business Math Handbook* to find the table factor and the present value for each of the following:

	Future value	Rate	Number of years	Compounded	Table value	Present value
a.	$1,000	2%	6	Semiannually	_____	_____
b.	$1,000	16%	7	Quarterly	_____	_____
c.	$1,000	8%	7	Quarterly	_____	_____
d.	$1,000	8%	7	Semiannually	_____	_____
e.	$1,000	8%	7	Annually	_____	_____

3. Find the present value and the interest earned for the following:

	Future value	Number of years	Rate	Compounded	Present value	Interest earned
a.	$2,500	6	8%	Annually	_____	_____
b.	$4,600	10	6%	Semiannually	_____	_____
c.	$12,800	8	10%	Semiannually	_____	_____
d.	$28,400	7	8%	Quarterly	_____	_____
e.	$53,050	1	12%	Monthly	_____	_____

4. Find the missing amount (present value or future value) for each of the following:

	Present value	Investment terms	Future value
a.	$3,500	5 years at 8% compounded annually	_____
b.	_____	6 years at 12% compounded semiannually	$9,000
c.	$4,700	9 years at 14% compounded semiannually	_____

WORD PROBLEMS

Solve for future value or present value.

5. Paul Palumbo assumes that he will need to have a new roof put on his house in 4 years. He estimates that the roof will cost him $17,000 at that time. What amount of money should Paul invest today at 2%, compounded semiannually, to be able to pay for the roof?

6. Tilton, a pharmacist, rents his store and has signed a lease that will expire in 3 years. When the lease expires, Tilton wants to buy his own store. He wants to have a down payment of $35,000 at that time. How much money should Tilton invest today at 6%, compounded quarterly, to yield $35,000?

7. Brad Morrissey loans $8,200 to his brother-in-law. He will be repaid at the end of 5 years, with interest at 10% compounded semiannually. Find out how much he will be repaid.

8. The owner of Waverly Sheet Metal Company plans to buy some new machinery in 6 years. He estimates that the machines he wishes to purchase will cost $39,700 at that time. What must he invest today at 8%, compounded semiannually, to have sufficient money to purchase the new machines?

9. Paul Stevens's grandparents want to buy him a car when he graduates from college in 4 years. They feel that they should have $27,000 in the bank at that time. How much should they invest at 12%, compounded quarterly, to reach their goal?

10. Gilda Nardi deposits $5,325 in a bank that pays 12% interest compounded quarterly. Find the amount she will have at the end of 7 years.

11. Mary Wilson wants to buy a new set of golf clubs in 2 years. They will cost $775. How much money should she invest today at 9%, compounded annually, so that she will have enough money to buy the new clubs?

12. Jack Beggs plans to invest $30,000 at 10%, compounded semiannually, for 5 years. What is the future value of the investment?

13. Ron Thrift expects his Honda Pilot will last 3 more years. Ron does not like to finance his purchases. He went to First National Bank to find out how much money he should put in the bank to purchase a $20,300 car in 3 years. The bank's 3-year CD is compounded quarterly with a 4% rate. How much should Ron invest in the CD?

14. The Downers Grove YMCA had a fund-raising campaign to build a swimming pool in 6 years. Members raised $825,000; the pool is estimated to cost $1,230,000. The money will be placed in Downers Grove Bank, which pays daily interest at 6%. Will the YMCA have enough money to pay for the pool in 6 years?

Learning Unit 13–1 : Annuities: Ordinary Annuity and Annuity Due (Find Future Value)

DRILL PROBLEMS

1. Find the value of the following ordinary annuities; calculate manually:

Amount of each annual deposit	Interest rate	Value at end of year 1	Value at end of year 2	Value at end of year 3
a. $1,000	8%	_____	_____	_____
b. $2,500	12%	_____	_____	_____
c. $7,200	10%	_____	_____	_____

2. Use the Ordinary Annuity Table: Compound Sum of an Annuity of $1 to find the value of the following ordinary annuities:

Annuity payment	Payment period	Term of annuity	Interest rate	Value of annuity
a. $650	Semiannually	5 years	6%	_____
b. $3,790	Annually	13 years	12%	_____
c. $500	Quarterly	1 year	8%	_____

3. Find the annuity due (deposits are made at beginning of period) for each of the following using the Ordinary Annuity Table:

Amount of payment	Payment period	Interest rate	Time (years)	Amount of annuity
a. $900	Annually	7%	6	_____
b. $1,200	Annually	11%	4	_____
c. $550	Semiannually	10%	9	_____

4. Find the amount of each annuity:

Amount of payment	Payment period	Interest rate	Time (years)	Type of annuity	Amount of annuity
a. $600	Semiannually	12%	8	Ordinary	_____
b. $600	Semiannually	12%	8	Due	_____
c. $1,100	Annually	9%	7	Ordinary	_____

WORD PROBLEMS

5. At the end of each year for the next 9 years, D'Aldo Company will deposit $25,000 in an ordinary annuity account paying 9% interest compounded annually. Find the value of the annuity at the end of the 9 years.

6. David McCarthy is a professional baseball player who expects to play in the major leagues for 10 years. To save for the future, he will deposit $50,000 at the beginning of each year into an account that pays 11% interest compounded annually. How much will he have in this account at the end of 10 years?

7. Tom and Sue plan to get married. Because they hope to have a large wedding, they are going to deposit $1,000 at the end of each month into an account that pays 24% compounded monthly. How much will they have in this account at the end of 1 year?

8. Chris Dennen deposits $15,000 at the end of each year for 13 years into an account paying 7% interest compounded annually. What is the value of her annuity at the end of 13 years? How much interest will she have earned?

9. Amanda Blinn is 52 years old today and has just opened an IRA. She plans to deposit $500 at the end of each quarter into her account. If Amanda retires on her 62nd birthday, what amount will she have in her account if the account pays 8% interest compounded quarterly?

10. Jerry Davis won the citywide sweepstakes and will receive a check for $2,000 at the beginning of each 6 months for the next 5 years. If Jerry deposits each check in an account that pays 8% compounded semiannually, how much will he have at the end of 5 years?

11. Mary Hynes purchased an ordinary annuity from an investment broker at 8% interest compounded semiannually. If her semiannual deposit is $600, what will be the value of the annuity at the end of 15 years?

Learning Unit 13–2 : Present Value of an Ordinary Annuity (Find Present Value)

DRILL PROBLEMS

1. Use the Present Value of an Annuity of $1 table to find the amount to be invested today to receive a stream of payments for a given number of years in the future. Show the manual check of your answer. (Check may be a few pennies off due to rounding.)

Amount of expected payments	Payment period	Interest rate	Term of annuity	Present value of annuity
a. $1,500	Yearly	9%	2 years	_____
b. $2,700	Yearly	13%	3 years	_____
c. $2,700	Yearly	6%	3 years	_____

2. Find the present value of the following annuities. Use the Present Value of an Annuity of $1 table.

Amount of each payment	Payment period	Interest rate	Time (years)	Compounded	Present value of annuity
a. $2,000	Year	7%	25	Annually	_____
b. $7,000	Year	11%	12	Annually	_____
c. $850	6 months	12%	5	Semiannually	_____
d. $1,950	6 months	14%	9	Semiannually	_____
e. $500	Quarter	12%	10	Quarterly	_____

WORD PROBLEMS

3. Tom Hanson would like to receive $200 each quarter for the 4 years he is in college. If his bank account pays 8% compounded quarterly, how much must he have in his account when he begins college?

4. Jean Reith has just retired and will receive a $12,500 retirement check every 6 months for the next 20 years. If her employer can invest money at 12% compounded semiannually, what amount must be invested today to make the semiannual payments to Jean?

5. Tom Herrick will pay $4,500 at the end of each year for the next 7 years to pay the balance of his college loans. If Tom can invest his money at 7% compounded annually, how much must he invest today to make the annual payments?

6. Helen Grahan is planning an extended sabbatical for the next 3 years. She would like to invest a lump sum of money at 10% interest so that she can withdraw $6,000 every 6 months while on sabbatical. What is the amount of the lump sum that Helen must invest?

7. Linda Rudd has signed a rental contract for office equipment, agreeing to pay $3,200 at the end of each quarter for the next 5 years. If Linda can invest money at 12% compounded quarterly, find the lump sum she can deposit today to make the payments for the length of the contract.

8. Sam Adams is considering lending his brother John $6,000. John said that he would repay Sam $775 every 6 months for 4 years. If money can be invested at 8%, calculate the equivalent cash value of the offer today. Should Sam go ahead with the loan?

9. The State Lotto Game offers a grand prize of $1,000,000 paid in 20 yearly payments of $50,000. If the state treasurer can invest money at 9% compounded annually, how much must she invest today to make the payments to the grand prize winner?

10. Thomas Martin's uncle has promised him upon graduation a gift of $20,000 in cash or $2,000 every quarter for the next 3 years. If money can be invested at 8%, which offer will Thomas accept? (Thomas is a business major.)

11. Paul Sasso is selling a piece of land. He has received two solid offers. Jason Smith has offered a $60,000 down payment and $50,000 a year for the next 5 years. Kevin Bassage offered $35,000 down and $55,000 a year for the next 5 years. If money can be invested at 7% compounded annually, which offer should Paul accept? (To make the comparison, find the equivalent cash price of each offer.)

12. Abe Hoster decided to retire to Spain in 10 years. What amount should Abe invest today so that he will be able to withdraw $30,000 at the end of each year for 20 years after he retires? Assume he can invest money at 8% interest compounded annually.

Learning Unit 13–3 : Sinking Funds (Find Periodic Payments)

DRILL PROBLEMS

1. Given the number of years and the interest rate, use the Sinking Fund Table based on $1 to calculate the amount of the periodic payment.

Frequency of payment	Length of time	Interest rate	Future amount	Sinking fund payment
a. Annually	19 years	5%	$125,000	_____
b. Annually	7 years	10%	$205,000	_____
c. Semiannually	10 years	6%	$37,500	_____
d. Quarterly	9 years	12%	$12,750	_____
e. Quarterly	6 years	8%	$25,600	_____

2. Find the amount of each payment into the sinking fund and the amount of interest earned.

	Maturity value	Interest rate	Term (years)	Frequency of payment	Sinking fund payment	Interest earned
a.	$45,500	5%	13	Annually	_____	_____
b.	$8,500	10%	20	Semiannually	_____	_____
c.	$11,000	8%	5	Quarterly	_____	_____
d.	$66,600	12%	$7\frac{1}{2}$	Semiannually	_____	_____

WORD PROBLEMS

3. To finance a new police station, the town of Pine Valley issued bonds totaling $600,000. The town treasurer set up a sinking fund at 8% compounded quarterly in order to redeem the bonds in 7 years. What is the quarterly payment that must be deposited into the fund?

4. Arlex Oil Corporation plans to build a new garage in 6 years. To finance the project, the financial manager established a $250,000 sinking fund at 6% compounded semianually. Find the semiannual payment required for the fund.

5. The City Fisheries Corporation sold $300,000 worth of bonds that must be redeemed in 9 years. The corporation agreed to set up a sinking fund to accumulate the $300,000. Find the amount of the periodic payments made into the fund if payments are made annually and the fund earns 8% compounded annually.

6. Gregory Mines Corporation wishes to purchase a new piece of equipment in 4 years. The estimated price of the equipment is $100,000. If the corporation makes periodic payments into a sinking fund with 12% interest compounded quarterly, find the amount of the periodic payments.

7. The Best Corporation must buy a new piece of machinery in $4\frac{1}{2}$ years that will cost $350,000. If the firm sets up a sinking fund to finance this new machine, what will the quarterly deposits be assuming the fund earns 8% interest compounded quarterly?

8. The Lowest-Price-in-Town Company needs $75,500 in 6 years to pay off a debt. The company makes a decision to set up a sinking fund and make semiannual deposits. What will their payments be if the fund pays 10% interest compounded semiannually?

9. The WIR Company plans to renovate their offices in 5 years. They estimate that the cost will be $235,000. If they set up a sinking fund that pays 12% quarterly, what will their quarterly payments be?

Learning Unit 14–1 : Cost of Installment Buying

DRILL PROBLEMS

1. For the following installment problems, find the amount financed and the finance charge.

	Sale price	Down payment	Number of monthly payments	Monthly payment	Amount financed	Finance charge
a.	$1,500	$300	24	$58	_____	_____
b.	$12,000	$3,000	30	$340	_____	_____
c.	$62,500	$4,700	48	$1,500	_____	_____
d.	$4,975	$620	18	$272	_____	_____
e.	$825	$82.50	12	$67.45	_____	_____

2. For each of the above purchases, find the deferred payment price.

	Sale price	Down payment	Number of monthly payments	Monthly payment	Deferred payment price
a.	$1,500	$300	24	$58	_____
b.	$12,000	$3,000	30	$340	_____
c.	$62,500	$4,700	48	$1,500	_____
d.	$4,975	$620	18	$272	_____
e.	$825	$82.50	12	$67.45	_____

3. Use the Annual Percentage Rate Table per $100 to calculate the estimated APR for each of the previous purchases.

	Sale price	Down payment	Number of monthly payments	Monthly payment	Annual percentage rate
a.	$1,500	$300	24	$58	_____
b.	$12,000	$3,000	30	$340	_____
c.	$62,500	$4,700	48	$1,500	_____
d.	$4,975	$620	18	$272	_____
e.	$825	$82.50	12	$67.45	_____

4. Given the following information, calculate the monthly payment by the loan amortization table.

	Amount financed	Interest rate	Number of months of loan	Monthly payment
a.	$12,000	10%	18	_____
b.	$18,000	11%	36	_____
c.	$25,500	13.50%	54	_____

WORD PROBLEMS

5. Jill Walsh purchases a bedroom set for a cash price of $3,920. The down payment is $392, and the monthly installment payment is $176 for 24 months. Find **(a)** the amount financed, **(b)** the finance charge, and **(c)** the deferred payment price.

6. An automaker promotion loan on a $20,000 automobile and a down payment of 20% are being financed for 48 months. The monthly payments will be $367.74. What will be the APR for this auto loan? Use the table in the *Business Math Handbook*.

7. David Nason purchased a recreational vehicle for $25,000. David went to City Bank to finance the purchase. The bank required that David make a 10% down payment and monthly payments of $571.50 for 4 years. Find **(a)** the amount financed, **(b)** the finance charge, and **(c)** the deferred payment that David paid.

8. Calculate the estimated APR that David (Problem 7) was charged per $100 using the Annual Percentage Rate Table.

9. Young's Motors advertised a new car for $16,720. They offered an installment plan of 5% down and 42 monthly payments of $470. What are **(a)** the deferred payment price and **(b)** the estimated APR for this car? Use the table.

10. Angie French bought a used car for $9,000. Angie put down $2,000 and financed the balance at 11.50% for 36 months. What is her monthly payment? Use the loan amortization table.

Learning Unit 14–2 : Revolving Charge Credit Cards

DRILL PROBLEMS

1. Use the U.S. Rule to calculate the outstanding balance due for each of the following independent situations:

	Monthly payment number	Outstanding balance due	$1\frac{1}{2}$% interest payment	Amount of monthly payment	Reduction in balance due	Outstanding balance due
a.	1	$9,000.00	_____	$600	_____	_____
b.	5	$5,625.00	_____	$1,000	_____	_____
c.	4	$926.50	_____	$250	_____	_____
d.	12	$62,391.28	_____	$1,200	_____	_____
e.	8	$3,255.19	_____	$325	_____	_____

2. Complete the missing data for a $6,500 purchase made on credit. The annual interest charge on this revolving charge account is 18%, or $1\frac{1}{2}$% interest on previous month's balance. Use the U.S. Rule.

Monthly payment number	Outstanding balance due	$1\frac{1}{2}$% interest payment	Amount of monthly payment	Reduction in balance due	Outstanding balance due
1	$6,500	_____	$700	_____	_____
2	_____	_____	$700	_____	_____
3	_____	_____	$700	_____	_____

3. Calculate the average billing daily balance for each of the monthly statements for the following revolving credit accounts; assume a 30-day billing cycle:

Billing date	Previous balance	Payment date	Payment amount	Charge date(s)	Charge amount(s)	Average daily balance
a. 4/10	$329	4/25	$35	4/29	$56	_____
b. 6/15	$573	6/25	$60	6/26	$25	
				6/30	$72	_____
c. 9/15	$335.50	9/20	$33.55	9/25	$12.50	
				9/26	$108	_____

4. Find the finance charge for each monthly statement (Problem 3) if the annual percentage rate is 15%.

   a. _____   b. _____   c. _____

WORD PROBLEMS

5. Niki Marshall is going to buy a new bedroom set at Scottie's Furniture Store, where she has a revolving charge account. The cost of the bedroom set is $5,500. Niki does not plan to charge anything else to her account until she has completely paid for the bedroom set. Scottie's Furniture Store charges an annual percentage rate of 18%, or $1\frac{1}{2}$% per month. Niki plans to pay $1,000 per month until she has paid for the bedroom set. Set up a schedule for Niki to show her outstanding balance at the end of each month after her $1,000 payment and also the amount of her final payment. Use the U.S. Rule.

6. Frances Dollof received her monthly statement from Brown's Department Store. The following is part of the information contained on that statement. Finance charge is calculated on the average daily balance.

Date	Reference	Department	Description	Amount
Dec. 15	5921	359	Petite sportswear	84.98
Dec. 15	9612	432	Footwear	55.99
Dec. 15	2600	126	Women's fragrance	35.18
Dec. 23	6247	61	Ralph Lauren towels	20.99
Dec. 24	0129	998	Payment received—thank you	100.00CR

Previous balance		Annual percentage rate	Billing date
719.04	12/13	18%	JAN 13

Brown's Charge Account Terms
Payment is required in monthly installments upon receipt of monthly statement in accordance with Brown's payment terms.

When my new balance is:	My minimum required payment is:	When my new balance is:	My minimum required payment is:
Up to $20.00	New Balance	$350.01 to $400.00	$40.00
$ 20.01 to $200.00	$20.00	$400.01 to $450.00	$45.00
$200.01 to $250.00	$25.00	$450.01 to $500.00	$50.00
$250.01 to $300.00	$30.00	More than $500.00	$50.00 plus
$300.01 to $350.00	$35.00		$10.00 for each $50.00 (or fraction thereof) of New Balance over $500.00

   a. Calculate the average daily balance for the month.

   b. What is Ms. Dollof's finance charge?

   c. What is the new balance for Ms. Dollof's account?

   d. What is the minimum payment Frances is required to pay according to Brown's payment terms?

7. What is the finance charge for a Brown's customer who has an average daily balance of $3,422.67?
8. What is the minimum payment for a Brown's customer with a new balance of $522.00?
9. What is the minimum payment for a Brown's customer with a new balance of $325.01?
10. What is the new balance for a Brown's customer with a previous balance of $309.35 whose purchases totaled $213.00, given that the customer made a payment of $75.00 and the finance charge was $4.65?

RECAP OF WORD PROBLEMS IN LU 14–1

11. A home equity loan on a $20,000 automobile with a down payment of 20% is being financed for 48 months. The interest is tax deductible. The monthly payments will be $401.97. What is the APR on this loan? Use the table in the *Business Math Handbook*. If the person is in the 28% income tax bracket, what will be the tax savings with this type of a loan?

12. An automobile with a total transaction price of $20,000 with a down payment of 20% is being financed for 48 months. Banks and credit unions require a monthly payment of $400.36. What is the APR for this auto loan? Use the table in the *Business Math Handbook*.

13. Assume you received a $2,000 rebate that brought the price of a car down to $20,000; the financing rate was for 48 months, and your total interest was $3,279. Using the table in the *Business Math Handbook*, what was your APR?

Learning Unit 15–1 : Types of Mortgages and the Monthly Mortgage Payment

DRILL PROBLEMS

1. Use the table in the *Business Math Handbook* to calculate the monthly payment for principal and interest for the following mortgages:

Price of home	Down payment	Interest rate	Term in years	Monthly payment
a. $200,000	15%	6%	25	_____
b. $200,000	15%	$5\frac{1}{2}\%$	30	_____
c. $450,000	10%	$11\frac{3}{4}\%$	30	_____
d. $450,000	10%	11%	30	_____

2. For each of the mortgages, calculate the amount of interest that will be paid over the life of the loan.

Price of home	Down payment	Interest rate	Term in years	Total interest paid
a. $200,000	15%	$6\frac{1}{2}\%$	25	_____
b. $200,000	15%	$10\frac{1}{2}\%$	30	_____
c. $450,000	10%	$11\frac{3}{4}\%$	30	_____
d. $450,000	10%	11%	30	_____

3. Calculate the increase in the monthly mortgage payments for each of the rate increases in the following mortgages. Then calculate what percent of change the increase represents, rounded to the nearest tenth percent.

Mortgage amount	Term in years	Interest rate	Increase in interest rate	Increase in monthly payment	Percent change
a. $175,000	22	9%	1%	_____	_____
b. $300,000	30	$11\frac{3}{4}\%$	$\frac{3}{4}\%$	_____	_____

4. Calculate the increase in total interest paid for the increase in interest rates in Problem 3.

Mortgage amount	Term in years	Interest rate	Increase in interest rate	Increase in total interest paid
a. $175,000	22	9%	1%	_____
b. $300,000	30	$11\frac{3}{4}\%$	$\frac{3}{4}\%$	_____

WORD PROBLEMS

5. The Counties are planning to purchase a new home that costs $150,000. The bank is charging them 6% interest and requires a 20% down payment. The Counties are planning to take a 25-year mortgage. How much will their monthly payment be for principal and interest?

6. The MacEacherns wish to buy a new house that costs $299,000. The bank requires a 15% down payment and charges $11\frac{1}{2}\%$ interest. If the MacEacherns take out a 15-year mortgage, what will their monthly payment for principal and interest be?

7. Because the monthly payments are so high, the MacEacherns (Problem 6) want to know what the monthly payments would be for **(a)** a 25-year mortgage and **(b)** a 30-year mortgage. Calculate these two payments.

8. If the MacEacherns choose a 30-year mortgage instead of a 15-year mortgage, **(a)** how much money will they "save" monthly and **(b)** how much more interest will they pay over the life of the loan?

9. If the MacEacherns choose the 25-year mortgage instead of the 30-year mortgage, **(a)** how much more will they pay monthly and **(b)** how much less interest will they pay over the life of the loan?

10. Larry and Doris Davis plan to purchase a new home that costs $415,000. The bank that they are dealing with requires a 20% down payment and charges $12\frac{3}{4}\%$. The Davises are planning to take a 25-year mortgage. What will the monthly payment be?

11. How much interest will the Davises (Problem 10) pay over the life of the loan?

Learning Unit 15–2 : Amortization Schedule—Breaking Down the Monthly Payment

DRILL PROBLEMS

1. In the following, calculate the monthly payment for each mortgage, the portion of the first monthly payment that goes to interest, and the portion of the payment that goes toward the principal.

Amount of mortgage	Interest rate	Term in years	Monthly payment	Portion to interest	Portion to principal
a. $170,000	8%	22	_____	_____	_____
b. $222,000	$11\frac{3}{4}\%$	30	_____	_____	_____
c. $167,000	$10\frac{1}{2}\%$	25	_____	_____	_____
d. $307,000	13%	15	_____	_____	_____
e. $409,500	$12\frac{1}{2}\%$	20	_____	_____	_____

2. Prepare an amortization schedule for the first 3 months of a 25-year, 12% mortgage on $265,000.

Payment number	Monthly payment	Portion to interest	Portion to principal	Balance of loan outstanding
1	_____	_____	_____	_____
2	_____	_____	_____	_____
3	_____	_____	_____	_____

3. Prepare an amortization schedule for the first 4 months of a 30-year, $10\frac{1}{2}$% mortgage on $195,500.

Payment number	Monthly payment	Portion to interest	Portion to principal	Balance of loan outstanding
1	_____	_____	_____	_____
2	_____	_____	_____	_____
3	_____	_____	_____	_____
4	_____	_____	_____	_____

WORD PROBLEMS

4. Jim and Janice Hurst are buying a new home for $235,000. The bank that is financing the home requires a 20% down payment and charges a $13\frac{1}{2}$% interest rate. Janice wants to know **(a)** what the monthly payment for the principal and interest will be if they take out a 30-year mortgage and **(b)** how much of the first payment will be for interest on the loan.

5. The Hursts (Problem 4) thought that a lot of their money was going to interest. They asked the banker just how much they would be paying for interest over the life of the loan. Calculate the total amount of interest that the Hursts will pay.

6. The banker told the Hursts (Problem 4) that they could, of course, save on the interest payments if they took out a loan for a shorter period of time. Jim and Janice decided to see if they could afford a 15-year mortgage. Calculate how much more the Hursts would have to pay each month for principal and interest if they took a 15-year mortgage for their loan.

7. The Hursts (Problem 4) thought that they might be able to afford this, but first wanted to see **(a)** how much of the first payment would go to the principal and **(b)** how much total interest they would be paying with a 15-year mortgage.

8.

	1980	2014
Cost of median-priced new home	$44,200	$136,600
10% down payment	$4,420	
Fixed-rate, 30-year mortgage		
Interest rate	8.9%	$7\frac{1}{2}$%
Total monthly principal and interest	$316	

Complete the 2014 year.

9. You can't count on your home mortgage lender to keep you from getting in debt over your head. The old standards of allowing 28% of your income for mortgage debt (including taxes and insurance) usually still apply. If your total monthly payment is $1,033, what should be your annual income to buy a home?

10. Assume that a 30-year fixed-rate mortgage for $100,000 was 9% at one date as opposed to 7% the previous year. What is the difference in monthly payments for these 2 years?

11. If you had a $100,000 mortgage with $7\frac{1}{2}$% interest for 25 years and wanted a $7\frac{1}{2}$% loan for 35 years, what would be the change in monthly payments? How much more would you pay in interest?

Learning Unit 16–1 :   Balance Sheet—Report as of a Particular Date

DRILL PROBLEMS

1. Complete the balance sheet for David Harrison, Attorney, and show that

   Assets = Liabilities + Owner's equity

Account totals are as follows: accounts receivable, $4,800; office supplies, $375; building (net), $130,000; accounts payable, $1,200; notes payable, $137,200; cash, $2,250; prepaid insurance, $1,050; office equipment (net), $11,250; land, $75,000; capital, $85,900; and salaries payable, $425.

DAVID HARRISON, ATTORNEY		
Balance Sheet		
December 31, 2014		
Assets		
Current assets:		
Cash	_____	
Accounts receivable	_____	
Prepaid insurance	_____	
Office supplies	_____	
Total current assets		_____
Plant and equipment:		
Office equipment (net)	_____	
Building (net)	_____	
Land	_____	
Total plant and equipment		_____
Total assets		======
Liabilities		
Current liabilities:		
Accounts payable	_____	
Salaries payable	_____	
Total current liabilities		_____
Long-term liabilities:		
Notes payable	_____	
Total liabilities		_____
Owner's Equity		
David Harrison, capital, December 31, 2014		_____
Total liabilities and owner's equity		======

2. Given the amounts in each of the accounts of Fisher-George Electric Corporation, fill in these amounts on the balance sheet to show that

   Assets = Liabilities + Stockholders' equity

Account totals are as follows: cash, $2,500; merchandise inventory, $1,325; automobiles (net), $9,250; common stock, $10,000; accounts payable, $275; office equipment (net), $5,065; accounts receivable, $300; retained earnings, $6,895; prepaid insurance, $1,075; salaries payable, $175; and mortgage payable, $2,170.

FISHER-GEORGE ELECTRIC CORPORATION
Balance Sheet
December 31, 2014

Assets

Current assets:
  Cash   _____

  Accounts receivable   _____

  Merchandise inventory   _____

  Prepaid insurance   _____

    Total current assets   _____

Plant and equipment:

  Office equipment (net)   _____

  Automobiles (net)   _____

    Total plant and equipment   _____

Total assets   ══════

Liabilities

Current liabilities:

  Accounts payable   _____

  Salaries payable   _____

    Total current liabilities   _____

Long-term liabilities:

  Mortgage payable   _____

    Total liabilities   _____

Stockholders' Equity

Common stock   _____

Retained earnings   _____

    Total stockholders' equity   _____

Total liabilities and stockholders' equity   ══════

3. Complete a vertical analysis of the following partial balance sheet; round all percents to the nearest hundredth percent.

THREEMAX, INC.
Comparative Balance Sheet Vertical Analysis
At December 31, 2013 and 2014

	2013		2014	
	Amount	Percent	Amount	Percent
Assets				
Cash	$ 8,500	_____	$ 10,200	_____
Accounts receivable (net)	11,750	_____	15,300	_____
Merchandise inventory	55,430	_____	54,370	_____
Store supplies	700	_____	532	_____
Office supplies	650	_____	640	_____
Prepaid insurance	2,450	_____	2,675	_____
Office equipment (net)	12,000	_____	14,300	_____
Store equipment (net)	32,000	_____	31,000	_____
Building (net)	75,400	_____	80,500	_____
Land	200,000	_____	150,000	_____
Total assets	$398,880	_____	$359,517	_____

4. Complete a horizontal analysis of the following partial balance sheet; round all percents to the nearest hundredth percent.

THREEMAX, INC. Comparative Balance Sheet Horizontal Analysis At December 31, 2013 and 2014				
	2014	2013	Change	Percent
Assets				
Cash	$ 8,500	$ 10,200	_____	_____
Accounts receivable (net)	11,750	15,300	_____	_____
Merchandise inventory	55,430	54,370	_____	_____
Store supplies	700	532	_____	_____
Office supplies	650	640	_____	_____
Prepaid insurance	2,450	2,675	_____	_____
Office equipment (net)	12,000	14,300	_____	_____
Store equipment (net)	32,000	31,000	_____	_____
Building (net)	75,400	80,500	_____	_____
Land	200,000	150,000	_____	_____
Total assets	$398,880	$359,517		

Learning Unit 16–2 : Income Statement—Report for a Specific Period of Time

DRILL PROBLEMS

1. Complete the income statement for the year ended December 31, 2014, for Foley Realty, doing all the necessary addition. Account totals are as follows: office salaries expense, $15,255; advertising expense, $2,400; rent expense, $18,000; telephone expense, $650; insurance expense, $1,550; office supplies, $980; depreciation expense, office equipment, $990; depreciation expense, automobile, $2,100; sales commissions earned, $98,400; and management fees earned, $1,260.

FOLEY REALTY Income Statement For the Year Ended December 31, 2014	
Revenues:	
Sales commissions earned	_____
Management fees earned	_____
Total revenues	
Operating expenses:	
Office salaries expense	_____
Advertising expense	_____
Rent expense	_____
Telephone expense	_____
Insurance expense	_____
Office supplies expense	_____
Depreciation expense, office equipment	_____
Depreciation expense, automobile	_____
Total operating expenses	_____
Net income	_____

2. Complete the income statement for Toll's, Inc., a merchandising concern, doing all the necessary addition and subtraction. Sales were $250,000; sales returns and allowances were $1,400; sales discounts were $2,100; merchandise inventory, December 31, 2013, was $42,000; purchases were $156,000; purchases returns and allowances were $1,100; purchases discounts were $3,000; merchandise inventory, December 31, 2014, was $47,000; selling expenses were $37,000; and general and administrative expenses were $29,000.

TOLL'S, INC. Income Statement For the Year Ended December 31, 2014			
Revenues:			
Sales			_____
Less: Sales return and allowances		_____	
Sales discounts		_____	_____
Net sales			_____
Cost of goods sold:			
Merchandise inventory, December 31, 2013		_____	
Purchases	_____		
Less: Purchases returns and allowances	_____		
Purchase discounts	_____	_____	
Cost of net purchases		_____	
Goods available for sale		_____	
Merchandise inventory, December 31, 2014		_____	
Total cost of goods sold			_____
Gross profit from sales			_____
Operating expenses:			
Selling expenses		_____	
General and administrative expenses		_____	
Total operating expenses			_____
Net income			======

3. Complete a vertical analysis of the following partial income statement; round all percents to the nearest hundredth percent. Note net sales are 100%.

THREEMAX, INC. Comparative Income Statement Vertical Analysis For Years Ended December 31, 2013 and 2014				
	2014		2013	
	Amount	Percent	Amount	Percent
Sales	$795,450		$665,532	
Sales returns and allowances	−6,250		−5,340	
Sales discounts	−6,470	....	−5,125	....
Net sales	$782,730	....	$655,067	....
Cost of goods sold:				
Beginning inventory	$ 75,394		$ 81,083	
Purchases	575,980		467,920	
Purchase discounts	−4,976	....	−2,290	....
Goods available for sale	$646,398		$546,713	
Less ending inventory	−66,254	....	−65,712	....
Total costs of goods sold	$580,144	....	$481,001	....
Gross profit	$202,586		$174,066	

4. Complete a horizontal analysis of the following partial income statement. Rround all percents to the nearest hundredth percent.

THREEMAX, INC. Comparative Income Statement Horizontal Analysis For Years Ended December 31, 2014 and 2013				
	2014	2013	Change	Percent
Sales	$795,450	$665,532	_____	_____
Sales returns and allowances	−6,250	−5,340	_____	_____
Sales discounts	−6,470	−5,125	_____	_____
Net sales	$782,730	$655,067	_____	_____
Cost of goods sold:				
Beginning inventory	$ 75,394	$ 81,083	_____	_____
Purchases	575,980	467,920	_____	_____
Purchase discounts	−4,976	−2,290	_____	_____
Goods available for sale	$646,398	$546,713	_____	_____
Less ending inventory	−66,254	−65,712	_____	_____
Total cost of goods sold	$580,144	$481,001	_____	_____
Gross profit	$202,586	$174,066	_____	_____

Learning Unit 16–3 : Trend and Ratio Analysis

DRILL PROBLEMS

1. Express each amount as a percent of the base-year (2012) amount. Round to the nearest tenth percent.

	2015	2014	2013	2012
Sales	$562,791	$560,776	$588,096	$601,982
Percent				
Gross profit	$168,837	$196,271	$235,238	$270,891
Percent				
Net income	$67,934	$65,927	$56,737	$62,762
Percent				

2. If current assets = $42,500 and current liabilities = $56,400, what is the current ratio (to the nearest hundredth)?

3. In Problem 2, if inventory = $20,500 and prepaid expenses = $9,750, what is the quick ratio, or acid test (to the nearest hundredth)?

4. If accounts receivable = $36,720 and net sales = $249,700, what is the average day's collection (to the nearest whole day)?

5. If total liabilities = $243,000 and total assets = $409,870, what is the ratio of total debt to total assets (to the nearest hundredth percent)?

6. If net income = $55,970 and total stockholders' equity = $440,780, what is the return on equity (to the nearest hundredth percent)?

7. If net sales = $900,000 and total assets = $1,090,000, what is the asset turnover (to the nearest hundredth)?

8. In Problem 7, if the net income is $36,600, what is the profit margin on net sales (to the nearest hundredth percent)?

WORD PROBLEMS

9. Calculate trend percentages for the following items using 2012 as the base year. Round to the nearest hundredth percent.

	2015	**2014**	**2013**	**2012**
Sales	$298,000	$280,000	$264,000	$249,250
Cost of goods sold	187,085	175,227	164,687	156,785
Accounts receivable	29,820	28,850	27,300	26,250

10. According to the balance sheet for Ralph's Market, current assets = $165,500 and current liabilities = $70,500. Find the current ratio (to the nearest hundredth).

11. On the balance sheet for Ralph's Market (Problem 10), merchandise inventory = $102,000. Find the quick ratio (acid test).

12. The balance sheet of Moses Contractors shows cash of $5,500, accounts receivable of $64,500, an inventory of $42,500, and current liabilities of $57,500. Find Moses' current ratio and acid test ratio (both to the nearest hundredth).

13. Moses' income statement shows gross sales of $413,000, sales returns of $8,600, and net income of $22,300. Find the profit margin on net sales (to the nearest hundredth percent).

14. Given:

Cash	$ 39,000	Retained earnings	$194,000
Accounts receivable	109,000	Net sales	825,000
Inventory	150,000	Cost of goods sold	528,000
Prepaid expenses	48,000	Operating expenses	209,300
Plant and equipment (net)	487,000	Interest expense	13,500
Accounts payable	46,000	Income taxes	32,400
Other current liabilities	43,000	Net income	41,800
Long-term liabilities	225,000		
Common stock	325,000		

Calculate (to nearest hundredth or hundredth percent as needed):

a. Current ratio.   **b.** Quick ratio.   **c.** Average day's collection.

d. Total debt to total assets.   **e.** Return on equity.   **f.** Asset turnover.

g. Profit margin on net sales.

15. The Vale Group lost $18.4 million in profits for the year 2013 as sales dropped to $401 million. Sales in 2012 were $450.6 million. What percent is the decrease in Vale's sales? Round to the nearest hundredth percent.

Learning Unit 17-1 : Concept of Depreciation and the Straight-Line Method

DRILL PROBLEMS

1. Find the annual straight-line rate of depreciation, given the following estimated lives.

Life	Annual rate	Life	Annual rate
a. 25 years	_____	**b.** 4 years	_____
c. 10 years	_____	**d.** 5 years	_____
e. 8 years	_____	**f.** 30 years	_____

2. Find the annual depreciation using the straight-line depreciation method. Round to the nearest whole dollar.

	Cost of asset	Residual value	Useful life	Annual depreciation
a.	$2,460	$400	4 years	_____
b.	$24,300	$2,000	6 years	_____
c.	$350,000	$42,500	12 years	_____
d.	$17,325	$5,000	5 years	_____
e.	$2,550,000	$75,000	30 years	_____

3. Find the annual depreciation and ending book value for the first year using the straight-line depreciation method. Round to the nearest dollar.

	Cost	Residual value	Useful life	Annual depreciation	Ending book value
a.	$6,700	$600	3 years	_____	_____
b.	$11,600	$500	6 years	_____	_____
c.	$9,980	–0–	5 years	_____	_____
d.	$36,950	$2,500	12 years	_____	_____
e.	$101,690	$3,600	27 years	_____	_____

4. Find the first-year depreciation to the nearest dollar for the following assets, which were only owned for part of a year. Round to the nearest whole dollar the annual depreciation for in-between calculations.

	Date of purchase	Cost of asset	Residual value	Useful life	First year depreciation
a.	April 8	$10,500	$1,200	4 years	_____
b.	July 12	$23,900	$3,200	6 years	_____
c.	June 19	$8,880	$800	3 years	_____
d.	November 2	$125,675	$6,000	17 years	_____
e.	May 25	$44,050	–0–	9 years	_____

WORD PROBLEMS

5. North Shore Grinding purchased a lathe for $37,500. This machine has a residual value of $3,000 and an expected useful life of 4 years. Prepare a depreciation schedule for the lathe using the straight-line depreciation method.

6. Colby Wayne paid $7,750 for a photocopy machine with an estimated life of 6 years and a residual value of $900. Prepare a depreciation schedule using the straight-line depreciation method. Round to the nearest whole dollar. (Last year's depreciation may have to be adjusted due to rounding.)

7. The Leo Brothers purchased a machine for $8,400 that has an estimated life of 3 years. At the end of 3 years the machine will have no value. Prepare a depreciation schedule using the straight-line depreciation method for this machine.

8. Fox Realty bought a computer table for $1,700. The estimated useful life of the table is 7 years. The residual value at the end of 7 years is $370. Find (a) the annual rate of depreciation to the nearest hundredth percent, (b) the annual amount of depreciation, and (c) the book value of the table at the end of the *third* year using the straight-line depreciation method.

9. Cashman, Inc., purchased an overhead projector for $560. It has an estimated useful life of 6 years, at which time it will have no remaining value. Find the book value at the end of 5 years using the straight-line depreciation method. Round the annual depreciation to the nearest whole dollar.

10. Shelley Corporation purchased a new machine for $15,000. The estimated life of the machine is 12 years with a residual value of $2,400. Find (a) the annual rate of depreciation by the straight-line method to the nearest hundredth percent, (b) the annual amount of depreciation, (c) the accumulated depreciation at the end of 7 years, and (d) the book value at the end of 9 years.

11. Wolfe Ltd. purchased a supercomputer for $75,000 on July 7, 2013. The computer has an estimated life of 5 years and will have a residual value of $15,000. Find (a) the annual depreciation amount by the straight-line method, (b) the depreciation amount for 2013, (c) the accumulated depreciation at the end of 2014, and (d) the book value at the end of 2015.

Learning Unit 17-2 : Units-of-Production Method

DRILL PROBLEMS

1. Find the depreciation per unit for each of the following assets. Round to three decimal places.

Cost of asset	Residual value	Estimated production	Depreciation per unit
a. $3,500	$800	9,000 units	_____
b. $309,560	$22,000	1,500,000 units	_____
c. $54,890	$6,500	275,000 units	_____

2. Find the annual depreciation expense for each of the assets in Problem 1.

Cost of asset	Residual value	Estimated production	Depreciation per unit	Units produced	Amount of depreciation
a. $3,500	$800	9,000 units	_____	3,000	_____
b. $309,560	$22,000	1,500,000 units	_____	45,500	_____
c. $54,890	$6,500	275,000 units	_____	4,788	_____

3. Find the book value at the end of the first year for each of the assets in Problems 1 and 2.

Cost of asset	Residual value	Estimated production	Depreciation per unit	Units produced	Book value
a. $3,500	$800	9,000 units	_____	3,000	_____
b. $309,560	$22,000	1,500,000 units	_____	45,500	_____
c. $54,890	$6,500	275,000 units	_____	4,788	_____

4. Calculate the accumulated depreciation at the end of year 2 for each of the following machines. Carry out the unit depreciation to three decimal places.

Cost of machine	Residual value	Estimated life	Hours used during year 1	Hours used during year 2	Accumulated depreciation
a. $67,900	$4,300	19,000 hours	5,430	4,856	_____
b. $3,810	$600	33,000 hours	10,500	9,330	_____
c. $25,000	$4,900	80,000 hours	7,000	12,600	_____

WORD PROBLEMS

5. Prepare a depreciation schedule for the following machine: The machine cost $63,400; it has an estimated residual value of $5,300 and expected life of 290,500 units. The units produced were:

Year 1	95,000 units
Year 2	80,000 units
Year 3	50,000 units
Year 4	35,500 units
Year 5	30,000 units

6. Forsmann & Smythe purchased a new machine that cost $46,030. The machine has a residual value of $2,200 and estimated output of 430,000 hours. Prepare a units-of-production depreciation schedule for this machine, rounding the unit depreciation to three decimal places. The hours of use were:

Year 1	90,000 hours
Year 2	150,000 hours
Year 3	105,000 hours
Year 4	90,000 hours

7. Young Electrical Company depreciates its vans using the units-of-production method. The cost of its new van was $24,600, the useful life is 125,000 miles, and the trade-in value is $5,250. What are (a) the depreciation expense per mile (to three decimal places) and (b) the book value at the end of the first year if it is driven 29,667 miles?

8. Tremblay Manufacturing Company purchased a new machine for $52,000. The machine has an estimated useful life of 185,000 hours and a residual value of $10,000. The machine was used for 51,200 hours the first year. Find (a) the depreciation rate per hour, rounded to three decimal places, (b) the depreciation expense for the first year, and (c) the book value of the machine at the end of the first year.

Learning Unit 17–3 : Declining-Balance Method

DRILL PROBLEMS

1. Find the declining-balance rate of depreciation, given the following estimated lives.

Life	Declining rate
a. 25 years	_____
b. 10 years	_____
c. 8 years	_____

2. Find the first year depreciation amount for the following assets using the declining-balance depreciation method. Round to the nearest whole dollar.

	Cost of asset	Residual value	Useful life	First year depreciation
a.	$2,460	$400	4 years	_____
b.	$24,300	$2,000	6 years	_____
c.	$350,000	$42,500	12 years	_____
d.	$17,325	$5,000	5 years	_____
e.	$2,550,000	$75,000	30 years	_____

3. Find the depreciation expense and ending book value for the first year, using the declining-balance depreciation method. Round to the nearest dollar.

	Cost	Residual value	Useful life	First year depreciation	Ending book value
a.	$6,700	$600	3 years	_____	_____
b.	$11,600	$500	6 years	_____	_____
c.	$9,980	–0–	5 years	_____	_____
d.	$36,950	$2,500	12 years	_____	_____
e.	$101,690	$3,600	27 years	_____	_____

WORD PROBLEMS

4. North Shore Grinding purchased a lathe for $37,500. This machine has a residual value of $3,000 and an expected useful life of 4 years. Prepare a depreciation schedule for the lathe using the declining-balance depreciation method. Round to the nearest whole dollar.

5. Colby Wayne paid $7,750 for a photocopy machine with an estimated life of 6 years and a residual value of $900. Prepare a depreciation schedule using the declining-balance depreciation method. Round to the nearest whole dollar.

6. The Leo Brothers purchased a machine for $8,400 that has an estimated life of 3 years. At the end of 3 years, the machine will have no value. Prepare a depreciation schedule for this machine. Round to the nearest whole dollar.

7. Fox Realty bought a computer table for $1,700. The estimated useful life of the table is 7 years. The residual value at the end of 7 years is $370. Find (a) the declining depreciation rate to the nearest hundredth percent, (b) the amount of depreciation at the end of the *third* year, and (c) the book value of the table at the end of the *third* year using the declining-balance depreciation method. Round to the nearest whole dollar.

8. Cashman, Inc., purchased an overhead projector for $560. It has an estimated useful life of 6 years, at which time it will have no remaining value. Find the book value at the end of 5 years using the declining-balance depreciation method. Round to the nearest whole dollar.

9. Shelley Corporation purchased a new machine for $15,000. The estimated life of the machine is 12 years with a residual value of $2,400. Find **(a)** the declining-balance depreciation rate as a fraction and as a percent (hundredth percent), **(b)** the amount of depreciation at the end of the first year, **(c)** the accumulated depreciation at the end of 7 years, and **(d)** the book value at the end of 9 years. Round to the nearest dollar.

Learning Unit 17–4 : Modified Accelerated Cost Recovery System (MACRS) with Introduction to ACRS

DRILL PROBLEMS

1. Using the MACRS method of depreciation, find the recovery rate, first-year depreciation expense, and book value of the asset at the end of the first year. Round to the nearest whole dollar.

Cost of asset	Recovery period	Recovery rate	Depreciation expense	End-of-year book value
a. $2,500	3 years	_____	_____	_____
b. $52,980	3 years	_____	_____	_____
c. $4,250	5 years	_____	_____	_____
d. $128,950	10 years	_____	_____	_____
e. $13,775	5 years	_____	_____	_____

2. Find the accumulated depreciation at the end of the second year for each of the following assets. Round to the nearest whole dollar.

Cost of asset	Recovery period	Accumulated depreciation at end of 2nd year using MACRS	Book value at end of 2nd year using MACRS
a. $2,500	3 years	_____	_____
b. $52,980	3 years	_____	_____
c. $4,250	5 years	_____	_____
d. $128,950	10 years	_____	_____
e. $13,775	5 years	_____	_____

WORD PROBLEMS

3. Colby Wayne paid $7,750 for a photocopy machine that is classified as equipment and has a residual value of $900. Prepare a depreciation schedule using the MACRS depreciation method. Round all calculations to the nearest whole dollar.

4. Fox Realty bought a computer table for $1,700. The table is classified as furniture. The residual value at the end of the table's useful life is $370. Using the MACRS depreciation method, find **(a)** the amount of depreciation at the end of the *third* year, **(b)** the total accumulated depreciation at the end of year 3, and **(c)** the book value of the table at the end of the *third* year. Round all calculations to the nearest dollar.

5. Cashman, Inc., purchased an overhead projector for $560. It is classified as office equipment and will have no residual value. Find the book value at the end of 5 years using the MACRS depreciation method. Round to the nearest whole dollar.

6. Shelley Corporation purchased a new machine for $15,000. The machine is comparable to equipment used for two-way exchange of voice and data with a residual value of $2,400. Find **(a)** the amount of depreciation at the end of the first year, **(b)** the accumulated depreciation at the end of 7 years, and **(c)** the book value at the end of 9 years. Round to the nearest dollar.

7.* Wolfe Ltd. purchased a supercomputer for $75,000 at the beginning of 1996. The computer is classified as a 5-year asset and will have a residual value of $15,000. Using MACRS, find **(a)** the depreciation amount for 1996, **(b)** the accumulated depreciation at the end of 1997, **(c)** the book value at the end of 1998, and **(d)** the last year that the asset will be depreciated.

*These problems are placed here for a quick review.

8.[*] Cummins Engine Company uses a straight-line depreciation method to calculate the cost of an asset of $1,200,000 with a $200,000 residual value and a life expectancy of 15 years. How much would Cummins have for depreciation expense for each of the first 2 years? Round to the nearest dollar for each year.

9. An article in an issue of *Management Accounting* stated that Cummins Engine Company changed its depreciation. The cost of its asset was $1,200,000 with a $200,000 residual value (with a life expectancy of 15 years) and an estimated productive capacity of 864,000 products. Cummins produced 59,000 products this year. What would it write off for depreciation using the units-of-production method?

*These problems are placed here for a quick review.

Learning Unit 18–1 : Assigning Costs to Ending Inventory—Specific Identification; Weighted Average; FIFO; LIFO

DRILL PROBLEMS

1. Given the value of the beginning inventory, purchases for the year, and ending inventory, find the cost of goods available for sale and the cost of goods sold.

	Beginning inventory	Purchases	Ending inventory	Cost of goods available for sale	Cost of goods sold
a.	$1,000	$4,120	$2,100	_____	_____
b.	$52,400	$270,846	$49,700	_____	_____
c.	$205	$48,445	$376	_____	_____
d.	$78,470	$2,788,560	$100,600	_____	_____
e.	$965	$53,799	$2,876	_____	_____

2. Find the missing amounts; then calculate the number of units available for sale and the cost of the goods available for sale.

Date	Category	Quantity	Unit cost	Total cost
January 1	Beginning inventory	1,207	$45	_____
February 7	Purchase	850	$46	_____
April 19	Purchase	700	$47	_____
July 5	Purchase	1,050	$49	_____
November 2	Purchase	450	$52	_____
Goods available for sale		_____		_____

3. Using the *specific identification* method, find the ending inventory and cost of goods sold for the merchandising concern in Problem 2.

Remaining inventory	Unit cost	Total cost
20 units from beginning inventory	_____	_____
35 units from February 7	_____	_____
257 units from July 5	_____	_____
400 units from November 2	_____	_____
Cost of ending inventory		_____
Cost of goods sold		_____

4. Using the *weighted-average* method, find the average cost per unit (to the nearest cent) and the cost of ending inventory.

Units available for sale	Cost of goods available for sale	Units in ending inventory	Weighted-average unit cost	Cost of ending inventory
a. 2,350	$120,320	1,265	_____	_____
b. 7,090	$151,017	1,876	_____	_____
c. 855	$12,790	989	_____	_____
d. 12,964	$125,970	9,542	_____	_____
e. 235,780	$507,398	239,013	_____	_____

5. Use the *FIFO* method of inventory valuation to determine the value of ending inventory, which consists of 40 units, and the cost of goods sold.

Date	Category	Quantity	Unit cost	Total cost
January 1	Beginning inventory	37	$219.00	_____
March 5	Purchases	18	230.60	_____
June 17	Purchases	22	255.70	_____
October 18	Purchases	34	264.00	_____
Goods available for sale		___		_____

Ending inventory = _____   Cost of goods sold = _____

6. Use the *LIFO* method of inventory valuation to determine the value of the ending inventory, which consists of 40 units, and the cost of goods sold.

Date	Category	Quantity	Unit cost	Total cost
January 1	Beginning inventory	37	$219.00	_____
March 5	Purchases	18	230.60	_____
June 17	Purchases	22	255.70	_____
October 18	Purchases	34	264.00	_____
Goods available for sale		___		_____

Ending inventory = _____   Cost of goods sold = _____

WORD PROBLEMS

7. At the beginning of September, Green's of Gloucester had 13 yellow raincoats in stock. These raincoats cost $36.80 each. During the month, Green's purchased 14 raincoats for $37.50 each and 16 raincoats for $38.40 each, and they sold 26 raincoats. Calculate **(a)** the average unit cost rounded to the nearest cent and **(b)** the ending inventory value using the weighted-average method.

8. If Green's of Gloucester (Problem 7) used the FIFO method, what would the value of the ending inventory be?

9. If Green's of Gloucester (Problem 7) used the LIFO method, what would the value of the ending inventory be?

10. Hobby Caterers purchased recycled-paper sketch pads during the year as follows:

January	350 pads for $.27 each
March	400 pads for $.31 each
July	200 pads for $.36 each
October	850 pads for $.26 each
November	400 pads for $.31 each

At the end of the year, the company had 775 of these sketch pads in stock. Find the ending inventory value using **(a)** the weighted-average method (round to the nearest cent), **(b)** the FIFO method, and **(c)** the LIFO method.

11. On March 1, Sandler's Shoe Store had the following sports shoes in stock:

13 pairs running shoes for $33 a pair
22 pairs walking shoes for $29 a pair
35 pairs aerobic shoes for $26 a pair
21 pairs cross-trainers for $52 a pair

During the month Sandler's sold 10 pairs of running shoes, 15 pairs of walking shoes, 28 pairs of aerobic shoes, and 12 pairs of cross-trainers. Use the specific identification method to find **(a)** the cost of the goods available for sale, **(b)** the value of the ending inventory, and **(c)** the cost of goods sold.

Learning Unit 18–2 : Retail Method; Gross Profit Method; Inventory Turnover; Distribution of Overhead

DRILL PROBLEMS

1. Given the following information, calculate **(a)** the goods available for sale at cost and retail, **(b)** the cost ratio (to the nearest thousandth), **(c)** the ending inventory at retail, and **(d)** the cost of the March 31 inventory (to the nearest dollar) by the retail inventory method.

	Cost	Retail
Beginning inventory, March 1	$57,300	$95,500
Purchases during March	$28,400	$48,000
Sales during March		$79,000

2. Given the following information, use the gross profit method to calculate **(a)** the cost of goods available for sale, **(b)** the cost percentage, **(c)** the estimated cost of goods sold, and **(d)** the estimated cost of the inventory as of April 30.

Beginning inventory, April 1	$30,000
Net purchases during April	81,800
Sales during April	98,000
Average gross profit on sales	40%

3. Given the following information, find the average inventory.

Merchandise inventory, January 1, 200A	$82,000
Merchandise inventory, December 31, 200A	$88,000

4. Given the following information, find the inventory turnover for the company in Problem 3 to the nearest hundredth.

Cost of goods sold (12/31/0A)	$625,000

5. Given the following information, calculate the **(a)** average inventory at retail, **(b)** average inventory at cost, **(c)** inventory turnover at retail, and **(d)** inventory turnover at cost. Round to the nearest hundredth.

	Cost	Retail
Merchandise inventory, January 1	$ 250,000	$ 355,000
Merchandise inventory, December 31	$ 235,000	$ 329,000
Cost of goods sold	$1,525,000	
Sales		$2,001,000

6. Given the floor space for the following departments, find the entire floor space and the percent each department represents.

		Percent of floor space
Department A	15,000 square feet	_____
Department B	25,000 square feet	_____
Department C	10,000 square feet	_____
Total floor space	50,000 square feet	_____

7. If the total overhead for all the departments (Problem 6) is $200,000, how much of the overhead expense should be allocated to each department?

Overhead/department

Department A _____

Department B _____

Department C _____

WORD PROBLEMS

8. During the accounting period, Ward's Greenery sold $290,000 of merchandise at marked retail prices. At the end of the period, the following information was available from Ward's records:

	Cost	Retail
Beginning inventory	$ 53,000	$ 79,000
Net purchases	$204,000	$280,000

Use the retail method to estimate Ward's ending inventory at cost. Round the cost ratio to the nearest thousandth.

9. On January 1, Benny's Retail Mart had a $49,000 inventory at cost. During the first quarter of the year, Benny's made net purchases of $199,900. Benny's records show that during the past several years, the store's gross profit on sales has averaged 35%. If Benny's records show $275,000 in sales for the quarter, estimate the ending inventory for the first quarter, using the gross profit method.

10. On April 4, there was a big fire and the entire inventory of R. W. Wilson Company was destroyed. The company records were salvaged. They showed the following information:

Sales (January 1 through April 4)	$127,000
Merchandise inventory, January 1	16,000
Net purchases	71,250

On January 1, the inventory was priced to sell for $38,000 and additional items bought during the period were priced to sell for $102,000. Using the retail method, calculate the cost of the inventory that was destroyed by the fire. Round the cost ratio to the nearest thousandth.

11. During the past 4 years, the average gross margin on sales for R. W. Wilson Company was 36% of net sales. Using the data in Problem 10 and the gross profit method, calculate the cost of the ending inventory destroyed by fire.

12. Chase Bank has to make a decision on whether to grant a loan to Sally's Furniture store. The lending officer is interested in how often Sally's inventory turns over. Using selected information from Sally's income statement, calculate the inventory turnover for Sally's Furniture Store (to the nearest hundredth).

Merchandise inventory, January 1	$ 43,000
Merchandise inventory, December 31	55,000
Cost of goods sold	128,000

13. Wanting to know more about a business he was considering buying, Jake Paige studied the business's books. He found that beginning inventory for the previous year was $51,000 at cost and $91,800 at retail, ending inventory was $44,000 at cost and $72,600 at retail, sales were $251,000, and cost of goods sold was $154,000. Using this information, calculate for Jake the inventory turnover at cost and the inventory turnover at retail.

14. Ralph's Retail Outlet has calculated its expenses for the year. Total overhead expenses are $147,000. Ralph's accountant must allocate this overhead to four different departments. Given the following information regarding the floor space occupied by each department, calculate how much overhead expense should be allocated to each department.

Department W	12,000 square feet	Department Y	14,000 square feet
Department X	9,000 square feet	Department Z	7,000 square feet

15. How much overhead would be allocated to each department of Ralph's Retail Outlet (Problem 14) if the basis of allocation were the sales of each department? Sales for each of the departments were:

Department W	$110,000	Department Y	$170,000
Department X	$120,000	Department Z	$100,000

Learning Unit 19–1 : Sales and Excise Taxes

DRILL PROBLEMS

1. Calculate the sales tax and the total amount due for each of the following:

	Total sales	Sales tax rate	Sales tax	Total amount due
a.	$536	5%	_____	_____
b.	$11,980	6%	_____	_____
c.	$3,090	$8\frac{1}{4}\%$	_____	_____
d.	$17.65	$5\frac{1}{2}\%$	_____	_____
e.	$294	7.42%	_____	_____

2. Find the amount of actual sales and amount of sales tax on the following total receipts:

	Total receipts	Sales tax rate	Actual sales	Sales tax
a.	$27,932.15	5.5%	_____	_____
b.	$35,911.53	7%	_____	_____
c.	$115,677.06	$6\frac{1}{2}\%$	_____	_____
d.	$142.96	$5\frac{1}{4}\%$	_____	_____
e.	$5,799.24	4.75%	_____	_____

3. Find the sales tax, excise tax, and total cost for each of the following items:

	Retail price	Sales tax, 5.2%	Excise tax, 11%	Total cost
a.	$399	_____	_____	_____
b.	$22,684	_____	_____	_____
c.	$7,703	_____	_____	_____

4. Calculate the amount, subtotal, sales tax, and total amount due of the following:

Quantity	Description	Unit price	Amount
3	Taxable item	$4.30	_____
2	Taxable item	$5.23	_____
4	Taxable item	$1.20	_____
		Subtotal	_____
		5% sales tax	_____
		Total	_____

5. Given the sales tax rate and the amount of the sales tax, calculate the price of the following purchases (before tax was added):

	Tax rate	Tax amount	Price of purchase
a.	7%	$71.61	_____
b.	$5\frac{1}{2}\%$	$3.22	_____

6. Given the sales tax rate and the total price (including tax), calculate the price of the following purchases (before the tax was added):

	Tax rate	Total price	Price of purchase
a.	5%	$340.20	_____
b.	6%	$1,224.30	_____

WORD PROBLEMS

7. In a state with a 4.75% sales tax, what will be the sales tax and the total price of a video game marked $110?

8. Browning's invoice included a sales tax of $38.15. If the sales tax rate is 6%, what was the total cost of the taxable goods on the invoice?

9. David Bowan paid a total of $2,763 for a new computer. If this includes a sales tax of 5.3%, what was the marked price of the computer?

10. After a 5% sales tax and a 12% excise tax, the total cost of a leather jacket was $972. What was the selling price of the jacket?

11. A customer at the RDM Discount Store purchased four tubes of toothpaste priced at $1.88 each, six toothbrushes for $1.69 each, and three bottles of shampoo for $2.39 each. What did the customer have to pay if the sales tax is $5\frac{1}{2}$%?

12. Bill Harrington purchased a mountain bike for $875. Bill had to pay a sales tax of 6% and an excise tax of 11%. What was the total amount Bill had to pay for his mountain bike?

13. Donna DeCoff received a bill for $754 for a new chair she had purchased. The bill included a 6.2% sales tax and a delivery charge of $26. What was the selling price of the chair?

Learning Unit 19–2 : Property Tax

DRILL PROBLEMS

1. Find the assessed value of the following properties, rounding to the nearest whole dollar:

Market value	Assessment rate	Assessed value	Market value	Assessment rate	Assessed value
a. $195,000	35%	_____	d. $2,585,400	65%	_____
b. $1,550,900	50%	_____	e. $349,500	85%	_____
c. $75,000	75%	_____			

2. Find the tax rate for each of the following municipalities, rounding to the nearest tenth of a percent:

Budget needed	Total assessed value	Tax rate	Budget needed	Total assessed value	Tax rate
a. $2,594,000	$44,392,000	_____	d. $13,540,000	$143,555,500	_____
b. $17,989,000	$221,900,000	_____	e. $1,099,000	$12,687,000	_____
c. $6,750,000	$47,635,000	_____			

3. Express each of the following tax rates in all the indicated forms:

By percent	Per $100 of assessed value	Per $1,000 of assessed value	In mills
a. 7.45%	_____	_____	_____
b. _____	$14.24	_____	_____
c. _____	_____	_____	90.8
d. _____	_____	$62.00	_____

4. Calculate the property tax due for each of the following:

Total assessed value	Tax rate	Total property tax due	Total assessed value	Tax rate	Total property tax due
a. $12,900	$6.60 per $100	_____	e. $78,900	59 mills	_____
b. $175,400	43 mills	_____	f. $225,550	$11.39 per $1,000	_____
c. $320,500	2.7%	_____	g. $198,750	$2.63 per $100	_____
d. $2,480,000	$17.85 per $1,000	_____			

WORD PROBLEMS

5. The county of Chelsea approved a budget of $3,450,000, which had to be raised through property taxation. If the total assessed value of properties in the county of Chelsea was $37,923,854, what will the tax rate be? The tax rate is stated per $100 of assessed valuation.

6. Linda Tawse lives in Camden and her home has a market value of $235,000. Property in Camden is assessed at 55% of its market value, and the tax rate for the current year is $64.75 per $1,000. What is the assessed valuation of Linda's home?

7. Using the information in Problem 6, find the amount of property tax that Linda will have to pay.

8. Mary Faye Souza has property with a fair market value of $219,500. Property in Mary Faye's city is assessed at 65% of its market value and the tax rate is $3.64 per $100. How much is Mary Faye's property tax due?

9. Cagney's Greenhouse has a fair market value of $1,880,000. Property is assessed at 35% by the city. The tax rate is 6.4%. What is the property tax due for Cagney's Greenhouse?

10. In Chester County, property is assessed at 40% of its market value, the residential tax rate is $12.30 per $1,000, and the commercial tax rate is $13.85 per $1,000. What is the property tax due on a home that has a market value of $205,000?

11. Using the information in Problem 10, find the property tax due on a grocery store with a market value of $5,875,000.

12. Bob Rose's home is assessed at $195,900. Last year the tax rate was 11.8 mills, and this year the rate was raised to 13.2 mills. How much more will Bob have to pay in taxes this year?

Learning Unit 20–1 : Life Insurance

DRILL PROBLEMS

1. Use the table in the *Business Math Handbook* to find the annual premium per $1,000 of life insurance and calculate the annual premiums for each policy listed. Assume the insureds are males.

	Face value of policy	Type of insurance	Age at issue	Annual premium per $1,000	Number of $1,000s in face value	Annual premium
a.	$25,000	Straight life	31			
b.	$40,500	20-year endowment	40			
c.	$200,000	Straight life	44			
d.	$62,500	20-payment life	25			
e.	$12,250	5-year term	35			
f.	$42,500	20-year endowment	42			

2. Use Table 20.1 to find the annual premium for each of the following life insurance policies. Assume the insured is a 30-year-old male.

	Face value of policy	Five-year term policy	Straight life policy	Twenty-payment life policy	Twenty-year endowment
a.	$50,000				
b.	$1,000,000				
c.	$250,000				
d.	$72,500				

3. Use the table in the *Business Math Handbook* to find the annual premium for each of the following life insurance policies. Assume the insured is a 30-year-old female.

	Face value of policy	Five-year term policy	Straight life policy	Twenty-payment life policy	Twenty-year endowment
a.	$50,000				
b.	$1,000,000				
c.	$250,000				
d.	$72,500				

4. Use the table in the *Business Math Handbook* to find the nonforfeiture options for the following policies:

	Years policy in force	Type of policy	Face value	Cash value	Amount of paid-up insurance	Extended term
a.	10	Straight life	$25,000	_____	_____	_____
b.	20	20-year endowment	$500,000	_____	_____	_____
c.	5	20-payment life	$2,000,000	_____	_____	_____
d.	15	Straight life	$750,000	_____	_____	_____
e.	5	20-year endowment	$93,500	_____	_____	_____

WORD PROBLEMS

5. If Mr. Davis, aged 39, buys a $90,000 straight life policy, what is the amount of his annual premium?

6. If Miss Jennie McDonald, age 27, takes out a $65,000 20-year endowment policy, what premium amount will she pay each year?

7. If Gary Thomas decides to cash in his $45,000 20-payment life insurance policy after 15 years, what cash surrender value will he receive?

8. Mary Allyn purchased a $70,000 20-year endowment policy when she was 26 years old. Ten years later, she decided that she could no longer afford the premiums. If Mary decides to convert her policy to paid-up insurance, what amount of paid-up insurance coverage will she have?

9. Peter and Jane Rizzo are both 28 years old and are both planning to take out $50,000 straight life insurance policies. What is the difference in the annual premiums they will have to pay?

10. Paul Nasser purchased a $125,000 straight life policy when he was 30 years old. He is now 50 years old. Two months ago, he slipped in the bathtub and injured his back; he will not be able to return to his regular job for several months. Due to a lack of income, he feels that he can no longer continue to pay the premiums on his life insurance policy. If Paul decides to surrender his policy for cash, how much cash will he receive?

11. If Paul Nasser (Problem 10) chooses to convert his policy to paid-up insurance, what will the face value of his new policy be?

Learning Unit 20–2 :   Fire Insurance

DRILL PROBLEMS

1. Use the tables in the *Business Math Handbook* to find the premium for each of the following:

	Rating of area	Building class	Building value	Value of contents	Total annual premium
a.	3	A	$80,000	$32,000	_____
b.	2	B	$340,000	$202,000	_____
c.	2	A	$221,700	$190,000	_____
d.	1	B	$96,400	$23,400	_____
e.	3	B	$65,780	$62,000	_____

2. Use the tables in the *Business Math Handbook* to find the short-term premium and the amount of refund due if the insured cancels.

	Annual premium	Months of coverage	Short-term premium	Refund due
a.	$1,860	3	_____	_____
b.	$650	7	_____	_____
c.	$1,200	10	_____	_____
d.	$341	12	_____	_____
e.	$1,051	4	_____	_____

3. Find the amount to be paid for each of the following losses:

	Property value	Coinsurance clause	Insurance required	Insurance carried	Amount of loss	Insurance company pays (indemnity)
a.	$85,000	80%	_____	$70,000	$60,000	_____
b.	$52,000	80%	_____	$45,000	$50,000	_____
c.	$44,000	80%	_____	$33,000	$33,000	_____
d.	$182,000	80%	_____	$127,400	$61,000	_____

WORD PROBLEMS

4. Mary Rose wants to purchase fire insurance for her building, which is rated as Class B; the rating of the area is 2. If her building is worth $225,000 and the contents are worth $70,000, what will her annual premium be?

5. Janet Ambrose owns a Class A building valued at $180,000. The contents of the building are valued at $145,000. The territory rating is 3. What is her annual fire insurance premium?

6. Jack Altshuler owns a building worth $355,500. The contents are worth $120,000. The classification of the building is B, and the rating of the area is 1. What annual premium must Jack pay for his fire insurance?

7. Jay Viola owns a store valued at $460,000. His fire insurance policy (which has an 80% coinsurance clause) has a face value of $345,000. A recent fire resulted in a loss of $125,000. How much will the insurance company pay?

8. The building that is owned by Tally's Garage is valued at $275,000 and is insured for $225,000. The policy has an 80% coinsurance clause. If there is a fire in the building and the damages amount to $220,000, how much of the loss will be paid for by the insurance company?

9. Michael Dannon owns a building worth $420,000. He has a fire insurance policy with a face value of $336,000 (there is an 80% coinsurance clause). There was recently a fire that resulted in a $400,000 loss. How much money will he receive from the insurance company?

10. Rice's Rent-A-Center business is worth $375,000. He has purchased a $250,000 fire insurance policy. The policy has an 80% coinsurance clause. What will Rice's reimbursement be **(a)** after a $150,000 fire and **(b)** after a $330,000 fire?

11. If Maria's Pizza Shop is valued at $210,000 and is insured for $147,000 with a policy that contains an 80% coinsurance clause, what settlement is due after a fire that causes **(a)** $150,000 in damages and **(b)** $175,000 in damages?

Learning Unit 20-3 :   Auto Insurance

DRILL PROBLEMS

1. Calculate the annual premium for compulsory coverage for each of the following.

	Driver classification	Bodily	Property	Total premium
a.	17	_____	_____	_____
b.	20	_____	_____	_____
c.	10	_____	_____	_____

2. Calculate the amount of money the insurance company and the driver should pay for each of the following accidents, assuming the driver carries compulsory insurance only.

Accident and court award	Insurance company pays	Driver pays
a. Driver hit one person and court awarded $15,000.	_____	_____
b. Driver hit one person and court awarded $12,000 for personal injury.	_____	_____
c. Driver hit two people; court awarded first person $9,000 and the second person $12,000.	_____	_____

3. Calculate the additional premium payment for each of the following options.

Optional insurance coverage	Addition to premium
a. Bodily injury 50/100/25, driver class 20	_____
b. Bodily injury 25/60/10, driver class 17	_____
c. Collision insurance, driver class 10, age group 3, symbol 5, deductible $100	_____
d. Comprehensive insurance, driver class 10, age group 3, symbol 5, deductible $200	_____
e. Substitute transportation, towing, and labor; driver class 10, age group 3, symbol 5	_____

4. Compute the annual premium for compulsory insurance with optional liability coverage for bodily injury and damage to someone else's property.

Driver classification	Bodily coverage	Premium
a. 17	50/100/25	_____
b. 20	100/300/10	_____
c. 10	25/60/25	_____
d. 18	250/500/50	_____
e. 20	25/50/10	_____

5. Calculate the annual premium for each of the following drivers with the indicated options. All drivers must carry compulsory insurance.

Driver classification	Car age	Car symbol	Bodily injury	Collision	Comprehensive	Transportation and towing	Annual premium
a. 10	2	4	50/100/10	$100 deductible	$300 deductible	Yes	_____
b. 18	3	2	25/60/25	$200 deductible	$200 deductible	Yes	_____

WORD PROBLEMS

6. Ann Centerino's driver classification is 10. She carries only compulsory insurance coverage. What annual insurance premium must she pay?

7. Gary Hines is a class 18 driver. He wants to add optional bodily injury and property damage of 250/500/50 to his compulsory insurance coverage. What will be Gary's total annual premium?

8. Sara Goldberg wants optional bodily injury coverage of 50/100/25 and collision coverage with a deductible of $300 in addition to the compulsory coverage her state requires. Sara is a class 17 driver and has a symbol 4 car that is 2 years old. What annual premium must Sara pay?

9. Karen Babson has just purchased a new car with a symbol of 8. She wants bodily injury and property liability of 500/1,000/100, comprehensive and collision insurance with a $200 deductible, and transportation and towing coverage. If Karen is a class 10 driver, what will be her annual insurance premium? There is no compulsory insurance requirement in her state. Assume age group 1.

10. Craig Haberland is a class 18 driver. He has a 5-year-old car with a symbol of 4. His state requires compulsory insurance coverage. In addition, he wishes to purchase collision and comprehensive coverage with the maximum deductible. He also wants towing insurance. What will Craig's annual insurance premium be?

11. Nancy Poland has an insurance policy with limits of 10/20. If Nancy injures a pedestrian and the judge awards damages of $18,000, **(a)** how much will the insurance company pay and **(b)** how much will Nancy pay?

12. Peter Bell carries insurance with bodily injury limits of 25/60. Peter is in an accident and is charged with injuring four people. The judge awards damages of $10,000 to each of the injured parties. How much will the insurance company pay? How much will Peter pay?

13. Jerry Greeley carries an insurance policy with bodily injury limits of 25/60. Jerry is in an accident and is charged with injuring four people. If the judge awards damages of $20,000 to each of the injured parties, **(a)** how much will the insurance company pay and **(b)** how much will Jerry pay?

14. An issue of *Your Money* reported that the Illinois Department of Insurance gave a typical premium for a brick house in Chicago built in 1950, assuming no policy discounts and a replacement cost estimated at $100,000. With a $100 deductible, the annual premium will be $653. Using the rate in your textbook, with a rating area 3 and class B, what would be the annual premium? (This problem reviews fire insurance.)

15. An issue of *Money* ran a story on cutting car insurance premiums. Raising the car insurance deductible to $500 will cut the collision premium 15%. Theresa Mendex insures her car; her age group is 5 and symbol is 5. What would be her reduction if she changed her policy to a $500 deductible? What would the collision insurance now cost?

16. Robert Stuono lost his life insurance when he was downsized from an investment banking company early this year. So Stuono, age 44, enlisted the help of an independent agent who works with several insurance companies. His goal is $350,000 in term coverage with a level premium for 5 years. What will Robert's annual premium be for term insurance? (This problem reviews life insurance.)

Learning Unit 21–1 : Stocks

DRILL PROBLEMS

52 weeks		Stocks	SYM	Div	Yld %	PE	Vol 100s	High	Low	Close	Net chg
Hi	Lo										
43.88	25.51	Disney	DIS	.21	.8	49	49633	27.69	26.50	27.69	+0.63

1. From the listed information for Disney, complete the following:
   a. _____ was the highest price at which Disney stock traded during the year.
   b. _____ was the lowest price at which Disney stock traded during the year.
   c. _____ was the amount of the dividend Disney paid to shareholders last year.
   d. _____ is the dividend amount a shareholder with 100 shares would receive.
   e. _____ is the rate of return the stock yielded to its stockholders.
   f. _____ is how many times the earnings per share the stock is selling for.
   g. _____ is the number of shares traded on the day of this stock quote.
   h. _____ is the highest price paid for Disney stock on this day.
   i. _____ is the lowest price paid for Disney stock on this day.
   j. _____ is the change in price from yesterday's closing price.

2. Use the Disney information to show how the yield percent was calculated.

3. What was the price of the last trade of Disney stock yesterday?

WORD PROBLEMS

4. Assume a stockbroker's commission of 2%. What will it cost to purchase 200 shares of Saplent Corporation at $10.75?

5. In Problem 4, the stockbroker's commission for selling stock is the same as that for buying stock. If the customer who purchased 200 shares at $10.75 sells the 200 shares of stock at the end of the year at $18.12, what will be the gain on investment?

6. Holtz Corporation's records show 80,000 shares of preferred stock issued. The preferred dividend is $2 per share, which is cumulative. The records show 750,000 shares of common stock issued. In 2012, no dividends were paid. In 2013, the board of directors declared a dividend of $582,500. What are (a) the total amount of dividends paid to preferred stockholders, (b) the total amount of dividends paid to common stockholders, and (c) the amount of the common dividend per share?

7. Melissa Tucker bought 300 shares of Delta Air Lines stock listed at $61.22 per share. What is the total amount she paid if the stockbroker's commission is 2.5%?

8. A year later, Melissa (Problem 7) sold the stock she had purchased. The market price of the stock at this time was $72.43. Delta Air Lines had paid its shareholders a dividend of $1.20 per share. If the stockbroker's commission to sell stock is 2.5%, what gain did Melissa realize?

9. The board of directors of Parker Electronics, Inc., declared a $539,000 dividend. If the corporation has 70,000 shares of common stock outstanding, what is the dividend per share?

Learning Unit 21–2 : Bonds

DRILL PROBLEMS

Bond	Current yield	Sales	Close	Net change
IBM $10\frac{1}{4}$ 18	10.0	11	102.5	+.125

1. From the bond listing above complete the following:
   a. _____ is the name of the company.
   b. _____ is the percent of interest paid on the bond.
   c. _____ is the year in which the bond matures.
   d. _____ is the total interest for the year.
   e. _____ was the previous day's closing price on the IBM bond.

2. Show how to calculate the current yield of 10.0% for IBM. (Trade commissions have been omitted.)

3. Use the information for the IBM bonds to calculate (a) the amount the last bond traded for on this day and (b) the amount the last bond traded for yesterday.

4. What will be the annual interest payment (a) to the bondholder assuming he paid $101\frac{3}{4}$ and (b) to the bondholder who purchased the bond for $102\frac{1}{2}$?

5. If Terry Gambol purchased three IBM bonds at this day's closing price, (a) what will be her total cost excluding commission and (b) how much interest will she receive for the year?

6. Calculate the bond yield (to the nearest tenth percent) for each of the following:

	Bond interest rate	Purchase price	Bond yield
a.	7%	97	_____
b.	$9\frac{1}{2}$%	101.625	_____
c.	$13\frac{1}{4}$%	104.25	_____

7. For each of the following, state whether the bond sold at a premium or a discount and give the amount of the premium or discount.

Bond interest rate	Purchase price	Premium or discount
a. 7%	97	_____
b. $9\frac{1}{2}$%	101.625	_____
c. $13\frac{1}{4}$%	104.25	_____

WORD PROBLEMS

8. Rob Morrisey purchased a $1,000 bond that was quoted at 102.25 and paying $8\frac{7}{8}$% interest. **(a)** How much did Rob pay for the bond? **(b)** What was the premium or discount? **(c)** How much annual interest will he receive?

9. Jackie Anderson purchased a bond that was quoted at 62.50 and paying interest of $10\frac{1}{2}$%. **(a)** How much did Jackie pay for the bond? **(b)** What was the premium or discount? **(c)** What interest will Jackie receive annually? **(d)** What is the bond's current annual yield (to the nearest tenth percent)?

10. Swartz Company issued bonds totaling $2,000,000 in order to purchase updated equipment. If the bonds pay interest of 11%, what is the total amount of interest the Swartz Company must pay semiannually?

11. The RJR and ACyan companies have both issued bonds that are paying $7\frac{3}{8}$% interest. The quoted price of the RJR bond is 94.125, and the quoted price of the ACyan bond is $102\frac{7}{8}$. Find the current annual yield on each (to the nearest tenth percent).

12. Mary Rowe purchased 25 of Chrysler Corporation $8\frac{3}{8}$% bonds of 2009. The bonds closed at 93.25. Find **(a)** the total purchase price and **(b)** the amount of the first semiannual interest payment Mary will receive.

13. What is the annual yield (to the nearest hundredth percent) of the bonds Mary Rowe purchased?

14. Mary Rowe purchased a $1,000 bond listed as ARch $10\frac{7}{8}$ 19 for 122.75. What is the annual yield of this bond (to the nearest tenth percent)?

Learning Unit 21–3 : Mutual Funds

DRILL PROBLEMS

From the following, calculate the NAV. Round to the nearest cent.

Current market value of fund investments	Current liabilities	Number of shares outstanding	NAV
1. $6,800,000	$850,000	500,000	_____
2. $11,425,000	$690,000	810,000	_____
3. $22,580,000	$1,300,000	1,400,000	_____

Complete the following using this information:

NAV	Net change	Fund name	Inv. obj.	YTD %Ret	Total return 1 Yr R
$23.48	+.14	EuroA	Eu	+37.3	+7.6 E

4. NAV _____

5. NAV change _____

6. Total return year to date _____

7. Return for the last 12 months _____

8. What does an E rating mean? _____

Calculate the commission (load) charge and the offer to buy.

NAV	% commission (load) charge	Dollar amount of commission (load) charge	Offer price
9. $17.00	$8\frac{1}{2}\%$	_____	_____
10. $21.55	6%	_____	_____
11. $14.10	4%	_____	_____

WORD PROBLEMS

12. Paul wanted to know how his Fidelity mutual fund $14.33 NAV in the newspaper was calculated. He called Fidelity, and he received the following information:

Current market value of fund investment	$7,500,000
Current liabilities	$910,000
Number of shares outstanding	460,000

Please calculate the NAV for Paul. Was the NAV in the newspaper correct?

13. Jeff Jones bought 150 shares of Putnam Vista Fund. The NAV of the fund was $9.88. The offer price was $10.49. What did Jeff pay for these 150 shares?

14. Pam Long purchased 300 shares of the no-load Scudder's European Growth Company Fund. The NAV is $12.61. What did Pam pay for the 300 shares?

15. Assume in Problem 14 that 8 years later Pam sells her 300 shares. The NAV at the time of sale was $12.20. What is the amount of her profit or loss on the sale?

16. Financial planner J. Michael Martin recommended that Jim Kelly choose a long-term bond because it gives high income while Kelly waits for better stock market opportunities down the road. The bond Martin recommended matures in 2012 and was originally issued at $8\frac{1}{2}\%$ interest and the current yield is 7.9%. What would be the current selling price for this bond and how would that price appear in the bond quotations?

17.

Bonds		Vol.	Close	Net chg.
Comp USA $9\frac{1}{2}$	14	70	102.375	−.125
GMA 7	22	5	101.625	−1.25

From the above information, compare the two bonds for:

a. When the bonds expire.
b. The yield of each bond.
c. The current selling price.
d. Whether the bond is selling at a discount or premium.
e. Yesterday's bond close.

Learning Unit 22–1 : Mean, Median, and Mode

Note: Optional problems for LU 22–3 are found on page 549.

DRILL PROBLEMS

1. Find the mean for the following lists of numbers. Round to the nearest hundredth.
   a. 12, 16, 20, 25, 29   Mean _____
   b. 80, 91, 98, 82, 68, 82, 79, 90   Mean _____
   c. 9.5, 12.3, 10.5, 7.5, 10.1, 18.4, 9.8, 6.2, 11.1, 4.8, 10.6   Mean _____

2. Find the weighted mean for the following. Round to the nearest hundredth.
   a. 4, 4, 6, 8, 8, 13, 4, 6, 8   Weighted mean _____
   b. 82, 85, 87, 82, 82, 90, 87, 63, 100, 85, 87   Weighted mean _____

3. Find the median for the following:
   a. 56, 89, 47, 36, 90, 63, 55, 82, 46, 81   Median _____
   b. 59, 22, 39, 47, 33, 98, 50, 73, 54, 46, 99   Median _____

4. Find the mode for the following:
   24, 35, 49, 35, 52, 35, 52   Mode _____

5. Find the mean, median, and mode for each of the following:
   a. 72, 48, 62, 54, 73, 62, 75, 57, 62, 58, 78
      Mean _____   Median _____   Mode _____
   b. $0.50, $1.19, $0.58, $1.19, $2.83, $1.71, $2.21, $0.58, $1.29, $0.58
      Mean _____   Median _____   Mode _____
   c. $92, $113, $99, $117, $99, $105, $119, $112, $95, $116, $102, $120
      Mean _____   Median _____   Mode _____
   d. 88, 105, 120, 119, 105, 128, 160, 151, 90, 153, 107, 119, 105
      Mean _____   Median _____   Mode _____

WORD PROBLEMS

6. The sales for the year at the 8 Bed and Linen Stores were $1,442,897, $1,556,793, $1,703,767, $1,093,320, $1,443,984, $1,665,308, $1,197,692, and $1,880,443. Find the mean earnings for a Bed and Linen Store for the year.

7. To avoid having an extreme number affect the average, the manager of Bed and Linen Stores (Problem 6) would like you to find the median earnings for the 8 stores.

8. The Bed and Linen Store in Salem sells many different towels. Following are the prices of all the towels that were sold on Wednesday: $7.98, $9.98, $9.98, $11.49, $11.98, $7.98, $12.49, $12.49, $11.49, $9.98, $9.98, $16.00, and $7.98. Find the mean price of a towel.

9. Looking at the towel prices, the Salem manager (Problem 8) decided that he should have calculated a weighted mean. Find the weighted mean price of a towel.

10. The manager of the Salem Bed and Linen Store above would like to find another measure of the central tendency called the *median*. Find the median price for the towels sold.

11. The manager at the Salem Bed and Linen Store would like to know the most popular towel among the group of towels sold on Wednesday. Find the mode for the towel prices for Wednesday.

Learning Unit 22–2 : Frequency Distributions and Graphs

DRILL PROBLEMS

1. A local dairy distributor wants to know how many containers of yogurt health club members consume in a month. The distributor gathered the following data:

17	17	22	14	26	23	23	15	18	16
18	15	23	18	29	20	24	17	12	15
18	19	18	20	28	21	25	21	26	14
16	18	15	19	27	15	22	19	19	13
20	17	13	24	28	18	28	20	17	16

Construct a frequency distribution table to organize these data.

2. Construct a bar graph for the Problem 1 data. The height of each bar should represent the frequency of each amount consumed.

3. To simplify the amount of data concerning yogurt consumption, construct a relative frequency distribution table. The range will be from 1 to 30 with five class intervals: 1–6, 7–12, 13–18, 19–24, and 25–30.

4. Construct a bar graph for the grouped data.

5. Prepare a pie chart to represent the above data.

WORD PROBLEMS

6. The women's department of a local department store lists its total sales for the year: January, $39,800; February, $22,400; March, $32,500; April, $33,000; May, $30,000; June, $29,200; July, $26,400; August, $24,800; September, $34,000; October, $34,200; November, $38,400; December, $41,100. Draw a line graph to represent the monthly sales of the women's department for the year. The vertical axis should represent the dollar amount of the sales.

7. The following list shows the number of television sets sold in a year by the sales associates at Souza's TV and Appliance Store.

115	125	139	127	142	153	169	126	141
130	137	150	169	157	146	173	168	156
140	146	134	123	142	129	141	122	141

Construct a relative frequency distribution table to represent the data. The range will be from 115 to 174 with intervals of 10.

8. Use the data in the distribution table for Problem 7 to construct a bar graph for the grouped data.

9. Expenses for Flora Foley Real Estate Agency for the month of June were as follows: salaries expense, $2,790; utilities expense, $280; rent expense, $2,000; commissions expense, $4,800; and other expenses, $340. Present these data in a circle graph. (First calculate the percent relationship between each item and the total, then determine the number of degrees that represents each item.)

10. Today a new Jeep costs $25,000. In 1970, the Jeep cost $4,500. What is the price relative? (Round to the nearest tenth percent.)

Worked-Out Solutions to Extra Practice Quizzes and You Try It Problems

Chapter 1

LU 1-1a

1. **a.** Eight thousand, six hundred eighty-two
   b. Fifty-six thousand, two hundred ninety-five
   c. Seven hundred thirty-two billion, three hundred ten million, four hundred forty-four thousand, eight hundred eighty-eight

2. **a.** $43 = 40$ **b.** $654 = 700$ **c.** $7,328 = 7,000$ **d.** $5,980 = 6,000$

3. Kellogg's sales and profit:

	The facts	Solving for?	Steps to take	Key points
BLUEPRINT	*Sales:* Three million, two hundred ninety-one thousand dollars. *Profit:* Four hundred five thousand dollars.	Sales and profit rounded all the way.	Express each verbal form in numeric form. Identify leftmost digit in each number.	Rounding all the way means only the leftmost digit will remain. All other digits become zeros.

Steps to solving problem

1. Convert verbal to numeric.
   Three million, two hundred ninety-one thousand ⟶ $3,291,000
   Four hundred five thousand ⟶ $ 405,000

2. Identify leftmost digit of each number.
      $3,291,000 $405,000
         ↓   ↓
     $3,000,000 $400,000

LU 1-2a

1.
```
    10
    18
    19
    24
 26,090
```

2.
Estimate	Actual
3,000	3,482
7,000	6,981
+ 5,000	5,490
15,000	15,953

3.

```
  8 17717
  9,787          Check
 −5,968          3,819
  3,819        + 5,968
                 9,787
```

4. Jackson Manufacturing Company over- or underestimated sales:

	The facts	Solving for?	Steps to take	Key points
BLUEPRINT	*Projected 2013 sales:* $878,000 *Major clients:* $492,900 *Other clients:* $342,000	How much were sales over- or underestimated?	Total projected sales − Total actual sales = Over- or underestimated sales.	Projected sales (minuend) − Actual sales (subtrahend) = Difference.

Steps to solving problem

1. Calculate total actual sales.
     $492,900
     + 342,000
     $834,900

2. Calculate over- or underestimated sales.
     $878,000
     − 834,900
     $ 43,100 (overestimated)

LU 1-3a

1.

Estimate	Actual	Check
5,000	4,938	$9 \times 4,938 = 44,442$
$\times\ 20$	$\times\ 19$	$10 \times 4,938 = +49,380$
100,000	44442	93,822
	4938	
	93,822	

2. $86 \times 19 = 1,634 + 5$ zeros $= 163,400,000$

3. $86 + 4$ zeros $= 860,000$

4.

Rounding	Actual		Check
200	245	R24	$26 \times 245 = 6,370$
30)6,000	26)6,394		$+ 24$
6 0	52		6,394
	119		
	104		
	154		
	130		
	24		

5. Drop 3 zeros $= 3)\overline{99}$ (quotient 33)

6. General Motors' total cost per year:

	The facts	Solving for?	Steps to take	Key points
BLUEPRINT	*Cars produced each workday: 850* *Workweek: 5 days* *Cost per car: $7,000*	Total cost per year.	Cars produced per week × 52 = Total cars produced per year. Total cars produced per year × Total cost per car = Total cost per year.	Whenever possible, use multiplication and division shortcuts with zeros. Multiplication can be checked by division.

Steps to solving problem

1. Calculate total cars produced per week. $5 \times 850 = 4,250$ cars produced per week

2. Calculate total cars produced per year.   4,250 cars × 52 weeks = 221,000 total cars produced per year

3. Calculate total cost per year.   221,000 cars × $7,000 = $1,547,000,000 (multiply 221 × 7 and add zeros)

       Check $1,547,000,000 ÷ 221,000 = $7,000 (drop 3 zeros before dividing)

You Try It

1. 571 → Five hundred seventy-one

    7,943 → Seven thousand, nine hundred forty-three

2. 691 = 691 = 690

     Identify   Less
     digit   than 5

3. 429,685 → 429,685 → 400,000

     Identify   Less
     digit   than 5

4.
76
$+ 38$
114

5.
5 1 2
6̷2̷9̷
$- 134$
495

6.
491
$\times\ 28$
3928
982
13,748

   13 × 10 = 130 (attach 1 zero)

   13 × 1,000 = 13,000 (attach 3 zeros)

7.
5 R15
16)95
80
15

   4,000 ÷ 100 = 40 (drop 2 zeros)

   4,000 ÷ 1,000 = 4 (drop 3 zeros)

Chapter 2

LU 2-1a

1.
  a. Proper
  b. Improper
  c. Mixed
  d. Improper

2.
$$\begin{array}{r} 22\ \ 1/7 \\ 7\overline{)155} \\ \underline{14} \\ 15 \\ \underline{14} \\ 1 \end{array}$$

3. $\dfrac{(9 \times 8) + 7}{9} = \dfrac{79}{9}$

4.
  a.
$$\begin{array}{r} 1 \\ 42\overline{)70} \\ \underline{42} \\ 28 \end{array} \qquad \begin{array}{r} 1 \\ 28\overline{)42} \\ \underline{28} \\ 14 \end{array} \qquad \begin{array}{r} 2 \\ 14\overline{)28} \\ \underline{28} \\ 0 \end{array}$$

14 is greatest common divisor

$$\frac{42 \div 14}{70 \div 14} = \frac{3}{5}$$

  b.
$$\begin{array}{r} 1 \\ 96\overline{)182} \\ \underline{96} \\ 86 \end{array} \qquad \begin{array}{r} 1 \\ 86\overline{)96} \\ \underline{86} \\ 10 \end{array} \qquad \begin{array}{r} 8 \\ 10\overline{)86} \\ \underline{80} \\ 6 \end{array}$$

$$\begin{array}{r} 1 \\ 6\overline{)10} \\ \underline{6} \\ 4 \end{array} \qquad \begin{array}{r} 1 \\ 4\overline{)6} \\ \underline{4} \\ 2 \end{array} \qquad \begin{array}{r} 2 \\ 2\overline{)4} \\ \underline{4} \\ 0 \end{array}$$

$$\frac{96 \div 2}{182 \div 2} = \frac{48}{91}$$

5.
  a. $\dfrac{300}{30} = 10 \times 16 = 160$
    b. $\dfrac{60}{20} = 3 \times 9 = 27$

LU 2-2a

1.

2/10	15	9	4
3/ 5	15	9	2
5/ 5	5	3	2
1	1	3	2

$\text{LCD} = 2 \times 3 \times 5 \times 1 \times 1 \times 3 \times 2 = 180$

2.
  a. $\dfrac{2}{25} + \dfrac{3}{5} = \dfrac{2}{25} + \dfrac{15}{25} = \dfrac{17}{25}$

$$\left(\begin{array}{l} \dfrac{3}{5} = \dfrac{?}{25} \\ 25 \div 5 = 5 \times 3 = 15 \end{array} \right)$$

  b.
$$\begin{array}{r} 3\dfrac{3}{8} \\ +6\dfrac{1}{32} \\ \hline \end{array} \qquad \begin{array}{r} 3\dfrac{12}{32} \\ +6\dfrac{1}{32} \\ \hline 9\dfrac{13}{32} \end{array}$$

$\dfrac{3}{8} = \dfrac{?}{32}$

$32 \div 8 = 4 \times 3 = 12$

3.
  a.
$$\begin{array}{r} \dfrac{5}{6} = \dfrac{5}{6} \\ -\dfrac{1}{3} = \dfrac{2}{6} \\ \hline \dfrac{3}{6} = \dfrac{1}{2} \end{array}$$

  b.
$$\begin{array}{r} 9\dfrac{1}{8} = \quad 9\dfrac{4}{32} = \quad 8\dfrac{36}{32} \\ -3\dfrac{7}{32} = -3\dfrac{7}{32} = -3\dfrac{7}{32} \\ \hline 5\dfrac{29}{32} \end{array}$$

$\left(\dfrac{32}{32} + \dfrac{4}{32} \right)$

c. Note how we showed the 6 as $5\frac{5}{5}$

$$5\frac{5}{5}$$
$$-1\frac{2}{5}$$
$$\overline{\quad 4\frac{3}{5}\quad}$$

4. $209\frac{1}{8}$ $209\frac{1}{8}$ $985\frac{1}{4}$ $985\frac{2}{8}$ $984\frac{10}{8}$

$\underline{+382\frac{1}{4}}$ $\underline{+382\frac{2}{8}}$ $591\frac{3}{8}$ $\underline{-591\frac{3}{8}}$ $\underline{-591\frac{3}{8}}$

        $591\frac{3}{8}$ sq. feet $393\frac{7}{8}$ sq. feet

LU 2-3a

1. a. $\dfrac{\overset{1}{\cancel{6}}}{8} \times \dfrac{3}{\underset{1}{\cancel{6}}} = \dfrac{3}{8}$ b. $\dfrac{\overset{6}{\cancel{42}}}{1} \times \dfrac{1}{\underset{1}{7}} = \dfrac{6}{1} = 6$

2. $\dfrac{13}{117} \times \dfrac{9}{5} = \dfrac{117}{585}$

$$\begin{array}{r} 5 \\ 117\overline{)585} \\ \underline{585} \\ 0 \end{array}$$

117 is great common divisor

$$\frac{117 \div 117}{585 \div 117} = \frac{1}{5}$$

3. a. $\dfrac{1}{8} \times \dfrac{5}{4} = \dfrac{5}{32}$ b. $\dfrac{61}{6} \times \dfrac{7}{6} = \dfrac{427}{36} = 11\dfrac{31}{36}$

4. Total cost of Jill's new home:

	The facts	Solving for?	Steps to take	Key points
BLUEPRINT	*Jill's mobile home:* $10\frac{1}{8}$ as expensive as her brother's. *Brother paid:* $10,000	Total cost of Jill's new home.	$10\frac{1}{8}$ × Total cost of Jill's brother's mobile home = Total cost of Jill's new home.	Canceling is an alternative to reducing.

Steps to solving problem

1. Convert $10\frac{1}{8}$ to a mixed number. $\dfrac{81}{8}$

2. Calculate the total cost of Jill's home. $\dfrac{81}{\underset{1}{8}} \times \$\overset{1,250}{\cancel{10,000}} = \$101,250$

You Try It

1. $\frac{3}{10}$ proper, $\frac{9}{8}$ improper, $1\frac{4}{5}$ mixed

2. $\frac{18}{7} = 2\frac{4}{7}$ $5\frac{1}{7} = \frac{35 + 1}{7} = \frac{36}{7}$

3. $\frac{16 \div 8}{24 \div 8} = \frac{2}{3}$ 4. $\frac{20}{50} = 20\overline{)50}$
$$\begin{array}{r} 2 \\ 20\overline{)50} \\ \underline{40} \\ 10 \end{array}$$
$$\begin{array}{r} 2 \\ 10\overline{)20} \\ \underline{20} \\ 0 \end{array}$$

10 is greatest common denominator

5. $\frac{16}{31} = \frac{}{310}$
$310 \div 31 = 10 \qquad 10 \times 16 = 160$

6. $\frac{3}{7} + \frac{2}{7} = \frac{5}{7} \qquad \frac{5}{7} - \frac{2}{7} = \frac{3}{7}$
$$\begin{array}{r} \frac{5}{8} = \frac{25}{40} \\ + \frac{3}{40} = \frac{3}{40} \\ \hline \frac{28}{40} = \frac{7}{10} \end{array}$$

7. Prime numbers 2, 3, 5, 7, 11, 13, 17

8. $\frac{1}{2} + \frac{1}{4} + \frac{1}{5} = 2\overline{)\begin{array}{ccc} 2 & 4 & 5 \\ 1 & 2 & 5 \end{array}}$
$2 \times 1 \times 2 \times 5 = 20$ LCD

9. $2\frac{1}{4}$
$+ 3\frac{3}{4}$
$\overline{5\frac{4}{4} = 6}$

10. $11\frac{1}{3}$ $10\frac{4}{3}$
$-2\frac{2}{3}$ $-2\frac{2}{3}$
$\overline{\qquad\qquad 8\frac{2}{3}}$

11. $\frac{4}{5} \times \frac{25}{26} = \frac{\overset{2}{\cancel{4}}}{\underset{1}{\cancel{5}}} \times \frac{\overset{5}{\cancel{25}}}{\underset{13}{\cancel{26}}} = \frac{10}{13}$

12. $2\frac{1}{4} \times 3\frac{1}{4} = \frac{9}{4} \times \frac{13}{4} = \frac{117}{16} = 7\frac{5}{16}$

13. $\frac{1}{8} \div \frac{1}{4} = \frac{1}{\underset{2}{\cancel{8}}} \times \frac{\overset{1}{\cancel{4}}}{1} = \frac{1}{2}$

14. $3\frac{1}{4} \div 1\frac{4}{5} = \frac{13}{4} \div \frac{9}{5} = \frac{13}{4} \times \frac{5}{9} = \frac{65}{36}$

Chapter 3

LU 3-1a

1. .309 (3 places to right of decimal)

2. Hundredths

3. Ten thousandths

4. **a.** .8 (identified digit 8 – digit to right less than 5)   **b.** .844 (identified digit 3 – digit to right greater than 5)

5. **a.** .9 (identified digit 6 – digit to right greater than 5)   **b.** .879 (identified digit 9 – digit to right less than 5)

6. .0008 (4 places)

7. .00016 (5 places)

8. $\frac{938}{1,000} \left(\frac{938}{1 + 3 \text{ zeros}} \right)$

9. $17\frac{95}{100}$

10. $\frac{325}{10,000} \left(\frac{325}{1 + 4 \text{ zeros}} \quad \frac{1}{4} \times .01 = .0025 + .03 = .0325 \right)$

11. .125 = .13

12. .571 = .57

13. 13.111 = 13.11

LU 3-2a

1.
$$\begin{array}{r} 16.0000 \\ .8310 \\ 9.8500 \\ 17.8321 \\ \hline 44.5131 \end{array}$$

2.
$$\begin{array}{r} {}^{14\ 17} \\ {}^{8\ \ \cancel{4}\cancel{7}13} \\ 29.\cancel{5}\cancel{8}\cancel{3}2 \\ -.9980 \\ \hline 28.5852 \end{array}$$

3.
$$\begin{array}{r} 29.64 \\ \times 18.2 \\ \hline 5928 \\ 23712 \\ 2964 \\ \hline 539.448 = 539.4 \end{array}$$

4.
$$774.08 = 774.09$$
$$\begin{array}{r} 494\overline{)382400.00} \\ \underline{3458} \\ 3660 \\ \underline{3458} \\ 2020 \\ \underline{1976} \\ 4400 \\ \underline{3952} \\ 448 \end{array}$$

5. 17.48 = 1,748

6. 8.432 = 8.432

7. .9643 = .9643

8. A: $8.88 ÷ 64 = $.14   B: $7.25 ÷ 50 = $.15   Buy A

9. Avis Rent-A-Car total rental charge:

	The facts	Solving for?	Steps to take	Key points
BLUEPRINT	*Cost per day:* $29.99 22 cents per mile. Drove 709.8 miles. 2-day rental.	Total rental charge.	Total cost for 2 days' rental + Total cost of driving = Total rental charge.	In multiplication, count the number of decimal places. Starting from right to left in the product, insert decimal in appropriate place. Round to nearest cent.

Steps to solving problem

1. Calculate total costs for 2 days' rental. $29.99 × 2 = $59.98

2. Calculate the total cost of driving. $.22 × 709.8 = $156.156 = $156.16

3. Calculate the total rental charge.

$$\begin{array}{r} \$\ 59.98 \\ +\ 156.16 \\ \hline \$216.14 \end{array}$$

10. 7,000 × $.0717 = $501.90

Check $501.90 × 13.9461 = 6,999.5 pesos due to rounding

You Try It

1. .8256 → Ten thousandths place

2. .841 = .8

↑↑

Less than 5

3. $\frac{9}{1,000}$ = .009

$\frac{3}{10,000}$ = .0003

4. $\frac{1}{7}$ = .142 = .1

5. $5\frac{4}{5} = \frac{4}{5}$ = .80 + 5 = 5.80

6. .865 $\frac{865}{}$ $\frac{865}{1}$ $\frac{865}{1,000}$ (attach 3 zeros)

7.
$$\begin{array}{r} 1.7 \\ 3.0 \\ .8 \\ \hline 5.5 \end{array} \qquad \begin{array}{r} \overset{5\ 10}{6.\cancel{0}0} \\ -4.10 \\ \hline 1.90 \end{array}$$

8. 3.49 (2 places)

$$\begin{array}{r} .015 \text{ (3 places)} \\ \hline 1745 \\ 349 \\ \hline .05235 \end{array}$$

9.
$$\begin{array}{r} 1.5 \\ 33)\overline{49.5} \\ 33 \\ \hline 165 \\ 165 \\ \hline 0 \end{array}$$

10.
$$.46 = .5$$
$$\begin{array}{r} 3.2)\overline{1.480} \\ 128 \\ \hline 200 \\ 192 \end{array}$$

11. 6.92 × 100 = 692 (move 2 places to right)

6.92 ÷ 100 = .0692 (move 2 places to left)

Chapter 4

LU 4-1a

1.

LU 4-2a

EARL MILLER			
Bank Reconciliation as of March 8, 2013			
Checkbook balance		**Bank balance**	
Earl's checkbook balance	$1,200.10	Bank balance	$ 300.10
Add:		Add:	
Interest	24.06	Deposit in transit	1,200.50
	$1,224.16		$1,500.60
Deduct:		Deduct:	
Deposited check returned fee	$30.00	Outstanding checks:	
		No. 300	$22.88
ATM	15.00	45.00	No. 302	15.90
		No. 303	282.66	321.44
Reconciled balance	$1,179.16	Reconciled balance	$1,179.16

You Try It

Sample

			Checkbook		
1. Pete Co. 24-111-9	Pay to the order of Reel Bank Pete Co. 24-111-9	Pay to the order of Reel Bank for deposit only Pete Co. 24-111-9	**Beg. balance**		$300
			2. *Less:* NSF	$50	
			ATM service charge	20	70
			Ending balance		$230

Chapter 5

LU 5-1a

1.
   a. $\frac{1}{2}Q - 8 = 16$
   b. $12(Q + 41) = 1,200$
   c. $7 - 2Q = 1$

   d. $4Q - 2 = 24$
   e. $3Q + 3 = 19$
   f. $2Q - 6 = 5$

2.
   a. $B + 14 = 70$
   $\dfrac{-14}{B} = \dfrac{-14}{56}$

   b. $\dfrac{\cancel{5}D}{\cancel{5}} = \dfrac{250}{5}$
   $D = 50$

   c. $\dfrac{\cancel{11}B}{\cancel{11}} = \dfrac{121}{11}$
   $B = 11$

   d. $8\left(\dfrac{B}{8}\right) = 90(8)$
   $B = 720$

   e. $\dfrac{B}{2} + 2 = 250$
   $\dfrac{-2}{\dfrac{B}{2}} = \dfrac{-2}{248}$
   $2\left(\dfrac{B}{2}\right) = 248(2)$
   $B = 496$

   f. $3(B - 6) = 18$
   $3B - 18 = 18$
   $\dfrac{+18}{\dfrac{3B}{3}} = \dfrac{+18}{\dfrac{36}{3}}$
   $B = 12$

LU 5-2a

1.

	Unknown(s)	Variable(s)	Relationship
BLUEPRINT	Original price	P*	P − $50 = Sale price Sale price = $140

*P = Original price.

1. Mechanical steps
$P - \$50 = \$140$
$\dfrac{+\ 50}{P} = \dfrac{+\ 50}{\$190}$

2.

	Unknown(s)	Variable(s)	Relationship
BLUEPRINT	Yearly salary	S*	$\frac{1}{7}S$ Entertainment = $7,000

*S = Salary.

2. Mechanical steps

$$\frac{1}{7}S = \$7,000$$

$$7\left(\frac{S}{7}\right) = \$7,000(7)$$

$$S = \$49,000$$

3.

	Unknown(s)	Variable(s)	Relationship
BLUEPRINT	Micro Morse	8C* C	5C $-\,C$ 49 computers

*C = Computers.

3. Mechanical steps

$$8C - C = 49$$

$$\frac{-7C}{7} = \frac{49}{7}$$

$$C = 7 \ (\textit{Morse})$$
$$8C = 56 \ (\textit{Micro})$$

4.

	Unknown(s)	Variable(s)	Relationship
BLUEPRINT	*Stoves sold:* Susie Cara	2S* S	2S +S 360 stoves

*S = Stoves.

4. Mechanical steps

$$2S + S = 360$$

$$\frac{-3S}{3} = \frac{360}{3}$$

$$S = 120 \ (\textit{Cara})$$
$$2S = 240 \ (\textit{Susie})$$

5.

	Unknown(s)	Variable(s)	Price	Relationship
BLUEPRINT	Meatball Cheese	M 3M	$7 6	7M + 18M $1,800 total sales

5. Mechanical steps

$$7M + 18M = 1,800$$

$$\frac{25M}{25} = \frac{1,800}{25}$$

$$M = 72 \quad (\text{meatball})$$
$$3M = 216 \ (\text{cheese})$$

Check

$$(72 \times \$7) + (216 \times \$6) = \$1,800$$

$$\$504 + \$1,296 = \$1,800$$

$$\$1,800 = \$1,800$$

6.

	Unknown(s)	Variable(s)	Price	Relationship
BLUEPRINT	*Unit sales:* Meatball Cheese	M* 288 − M	$7 6	6M + 6(288 − M) $1,800 total sales

*We assign the variable to the most expensive item to make the mechanical steps easier to complete.

6. Mechanical steps

$$7M + 6(288 - M) = \$1,800$$
$$7M + 1,728 - 6M = \$1,800$$
$$M + 1,728 = \$1,800$$
$$-1,728 = -1,728$$
$$M = 72$$
$$Meatball = 72$$
$$Cheese = 288 - 72 = 216$$

Check

$$72(\$7) + 216\,(\$6) = \$504 + \$1,296$$
$$= \$1,800$$

You Try It

1.
$$E + 15 = 14$$
$$\underline{-15 \quad -15}$$
$$E = -1$$

2.
$$B - 40 = 80$$
$$\underline{+40 \quad +40}$$
$$B = 120$$

3.
$$\frac{5C}{5} = 75$$
$$C = 15$$

4.
$$\frac{A}{6} = 60 \quad (6)\frac{A}{6} = 6(60)$$
$$A = 360$$

5.
$$\frac{C}{4} + 10 = 17$$
$$\underline{-10 \quad -10}$$
$$\frac{C}{4} = 7$$
$$(4)\frac{C}{4} = 7(4)$$
$$C = 28$$

6.
$$7(B - 10) = 35$$
$$7B - 70 = 35$$
$$\underline{+70 \quad +70}$$
$$\frac{7B}{7} = \frac{105}{7}$$
$$B = 15$$

7. $5B + 3B = 16$

$$\frac{8B}{8} = \frac{16}{8}$$

$$B = 2$$

Sit. 1. $P - \$53 = \$110$

$$\frac{+53 \quad +53}{P \quad = \$163}$$

Sit. 2. $\frac{1}{7}B = \$6,000$

$$7\left(\frac{B}{7}\right) = 6,000\,(7)$$

$$B = \$42,000$$

Sit. 3. $95 - S = 640$

$$\frac{8S}{8} = \frac{640}{8}$$

$$S = 80 \qquad 9S = 720$$

Sit. 4. $9S + S = 640$

$$\frac{10S}{10} = \frac{640}{10}$$

$$S = 64 \qquad 9S = 576$$

Sit. 5. $1,200\,N + 300\,N = 15,000$

$$\frac{1,500\,N}{1,500} = \frac{15,000}{1,500}$$

$$N = 10$$

$$3\,N = 30$$

Sit. 6. $400\,S + 300\,(40 - S) = 15,000$

$$400\,S + 12,000 - 300\,S = 15,000$$

$$100\,S + 12,000 = 15,000$$

$$\frac{-12,000 \quad -12,000}{}$$

$$\frac{100\,S}{100} = \frac{3,000}{100}$$

$$S = 30$$

$$40 - S = 10$$

Chapter 6

LU 6-1a

1. $.44.44 = 44.4\%$

2. $.78.2 = 78.2\%$

3. $.00.6 = .6\%$

4. $7.93.333 = 793.3\%$

5. $\frac{1}{5}\% = .20\% = .0020$

6. $7\frac{4}{5}\% = 7.80\% = .0780$

7. $92\% = .92 = .92$

8. $765.8\% = 7.65.8 = 7.658$

9. $\frac{1}{3} = .33.333 = 33.33\%$

10. $\frac{3}{7} = .42.857 = 42.86\%$

11. $17\% = 17 \times \frac{1}{100} = \frac{17}{100}$

12. $82\frac{1}{4}\% = \frac{329}{4} \times \frac{1}{100} = \frac{329}{400}$

13. $150\% = 150 \times \frac{1}{100} = \frac{150}{100} = 1\frac{50}{100} = 1\frac{1}{2}$

14. $\frac{1}{4}\% = \frac{1}{4} \times \frac{1}{100} = \frac{1}{400}$

15. $17\frac{8}{10}\% = \frac{178}{10} \times \frac{1}{100} = \frac{178}{1,000} = \frac{89}{500}$

LU 6-2a

1. $504 = 1,200 \times .42$

$(P) = (B) \times (R)$

2. $\$560 = \$8,000 \times .07$

$(P) = (B) \times (R)$

3. $\frac{(P)510}{(B)6,000} = .085 = 8.5\%$

4. $\frac{(P)400}{(B)900} = .444 = 44.4\%$

5. $\frac{(P)30}{(R).60} = 50(B)$

6. $\frac{(P)1,200}{(R).035} = 34,285.7(B)$

7. Percent of Professor Ford's class that did not receive the A grade:

	The facts	Solving for?	Steps to take	Key points
BLUEPRINT	10 As. 25 in class.	Percent that did not receive A.	Identify key elements. Base: 25 Rate: ? Portion: 15(25 − 10). Rate = $\dfrac{\text{Portion}}{\text{Base}}$	Portion (15) Base × Rate (25) (?) The whole Portion and rate must relate to same piece of base.

Steps to solving problem

1. Set up the formula.

$$\text{Rate} = \frac{\text{Portion}}{\text{Base}}$$

2. Calculate the rate.

$$R = \frac{15}{25}$$

$$R = 60\%$$

8. Abby Biernet's original order:

	The facts	Solving for?	Steps to take	Key points
BLUEPRINT	70% of the order not in. 90 lobsters received.	Total order of lobsters.	Identify key elements. *Base:* ? *Rate:* 30 (100% − 70%) *Portion:* 90. $$\text{Base} = \frac{\text{Portion}}{\text{Rate}}$$	Portion (90) Base × Rate (?) (.30) 90 lobsters represent 30% of the order Portion and rate must relate to same piece of base.

Steps to solving problem

1. Set up the formula.

$$\text{Base} = \frac{\text{Portion}}{\text{Rate}}$$

2. Calculate the base.

$$B = \frac{90}{.30} \longleftarrow \text{90 lobsters are 30\% of base}$$

$$B = 300 \text{ lobsters}$$

9. Dunkin' Donuts Company sales for 2014:

	The facts	Solving for?	Steps to take	Key points
BLUEPRINT	*2013:* $400,000 sales. *2014:* Sales up 35% from 2013.	Sales for 2014.	Identify key elements. *Base:* $300,000 *Rate:* 1.35. Old year 100% New year + 35 ——— 135% *Portion:* ? Portion = Base × Rate	2014 sales Portion (?) Base × Rate ($400,000) (1.35) 2013 sales When rate is greater than 100%, portion will be larger than base.

Steps to solving problem

1. Set up the formula.

Portion = Base × Rate

2. Calculate the portion.

$$P = \$400,000 \times 1.35$$

$$P = \$540,000$$

10. Percent decrease in Apple Computer price:

	The facts	Solving for?	Steps to take	Key points
BLUEPRINT	Apple Computer was $1,800; now $1,000.	Percent decrease in price.	Identify key elements. *Base*: $1,800 *Rate*: ? *Portion*: $800 ($1,800 − $1,000) $\text{Rate} = \dfrac{\text{Portion}}{\text{Base}}$	Difference in price Portion ($800) Base × Rate ($1,800) (?) Original price

Steps to solving problem

1. Set up the formula. $\text{Rate} = \dfrac{\text{Portion}}{\text{Base}}$

2. Calculate the rate. $R = \dfrac{\$800}{\$1,800}$
$R = 44.44\%$

11. Percent increase in Boston Celtics ticket:

	The facts	Solving for?	Steps to take	Key points
BLUEPRINT	$14 ticket (old). $75 ticket (new).	Percent increase in price.	Identify key elements. *Base*: $14 *Rate*: ? *Portion*: $61 ($75 − $14) $\text{Rate} = \dfrac{\text{Portion}}{\text{Base}}$	Difference in price Portion $61 Base × Rate ($14) (?) Original price When portion is greater than base, rate will be greater than 100%.

Steps to solving problem

1. Set up the formula. $\text{Rate} = \dfrac{\text{Portion}}{\text{Base}}$

2. Calculate the rate. $R = \dfrac{\$61}{\$14}$
$R = 435,714 = 435.71\%$

You Try It

1. $.92 = 92\%$
$.009 = .9\%$
$5.46 = 546\%$

2. $\dfrac{2}{9} = 22.222\% = 22.22\%$

3. $78\% = .0078$ (2 places to left)
$96\% = .96$ (2 places to left)
$246\% = 2.46$ (2 places to left)

$7\dfrac{3}{4}\% = 7.75\% = .0775$

$\dfrac{3}{4}\% = .75\% = .0075$

$\dfrac{1}{2}\% = .50\% = .0050$

4. $\dfrac{3}{5} = .60 = 60\%$

5. $74\% \rightarrow 74 \times \dfrac{1}{100} = \dfrac{74}{100} = \dfrac{37}{50}$

$\dfrac{1}{5}\% \rightarrow \dfrac{1}{5} \times \dfrac{1}{100} = \dfrac{1}{500}$

$121\% \rightarrow 121 \times \dfrac{1}{100} = \dfrac{121}{100} = 1\dfrac{21}{100}$

$17\dfrac{1}{5}\% \rightarrow \dfrac{86}{5} \times \dfrac{1}{100} = \dfrac{86}{500} = \dfrac{43}{250}$

$17.75\% \rightarrow 17\dfrac{3}{4}\% = \dfrac{71}{4} \times \dfrac{1}{100} = \dfrac{71}{400}$

6. Portion ($1,600) = Base ($2,000) × Rate (.80)

7. Rate (25%) = $\dfrac{\text{Portion (\$500)}}{\text{Base (\$2,000)}}$

8. Base ($1,000) = $\dfrac{\text{Portion (\$200)}}{\text{Rate (.20)}}$

9. $\dfrac{\text{Difference in price (\$100)}}{\text{Base (orig. \$500)}} = 20\%$

Chapter 7

LU 7-1a

1. Dining room set trade discount amount and net price:

	The facts	Solving for?	Steps to take	Key points
BLUEPRINT	List price: $16,000. Trade discount rate: 30%.	Trade discount amount. Net price.	Trade discount amount = List price × Trade discount rate. Net price = List price × Complement of trade discount rate.	Trade discount amount. Portion (?). Base ($16,000) × Rate (.30). List price. Trade discount rate.

Steps to solving problem

1. Calculate the trade discount. $16,000 × .30 = $4,800 Trade discount amount
2. Calculate the net price. $16,000 × .70 = $11,200 (100% − 30% = 70%)

2. Video system list price:

	The facts	Solving for?	Steps to take	Key points
BLUEPRINT	Net price: $400. Trade discount rate: 20%.	List price.	List price = $\dfrac{\text{Net price}}{\text{Complement of trade discount}}$	Net price. Portion $400. Base (?) × Rate (.80). List price. 100% −20%

Steps to solving problem

1. Calculate the complement of trade discount

$$\begin{array}{r} 100\% \\ -\ 20\% \\ \hline 80\% = .80 \end{array}$$

2. Calculate the list price. $\dfrac{\$400}{.80} = \$500$

3. Lamps Outlet's net price and trade discount amount:

	The facts	Solving for?	Steps to take	Key points
BLUEPRINT	List price: $14,000. Chain discount: 4/8/20.	Net price. Trade discount amount.	Net price = List price × Net price equivalent rate. Trade discount amount = List price × Single equivalent discount rate.	Do not round off net price equivalent rate or single equivalent discount rate.

Steps to solving problem

1. Calculate the complement of each chain discount.

$$\begin{array}{ccc} 100\% & 100\% & 100\% \\ -\ 4 & -\ 8 & -\ 20 \\ \hline 96\% & 92\% & 80\% \end{array}$$

2. Calculate the net price equivalent rate.   .96 × .92 × .80 = .70656
3. Calculate the net price. $14,000 × .70656 = $9,891.84
4. Calculate the single equivalent discount rate.

$$\begin{array}{r} 1.00000 \\ -\ .70656 \\ \hline .29344 \end{array}$$

5. Calculate the trade discount amount. $14,000 × .29344 = $4,108.16

LU 7-2a

1. End of discount period: July 8 + 10 days = July 18
   End of credit period: By Table 7.1, July 8 =

   $$\begin{array}{r} 189 \text{ days} \\ +30 \text{ days} \\ \hline 219 \rightarrow \text{search} \longrightarrow \text{Aug. 7} \end{array}$$

2. End of discount period: June 12 + 10 days = June 22
   End of credit period: By Table 7.1, June 12 =

   $$\begin{array}{r} 163 \text{ days} \\ +30 \text{ days} \\ \hline 193 \rightarrow \text{search} \longrightarrow \text{July 12} \end{array}$$

3. End of discount period: By Table 7.1, May 12 =

   $$\begin{array}{r} 132 \text{ days} \\ +30 \text{ days} \\ \hline 162 \rightarrow \text{search} \longrightarrow \text{June 11} \end{array}$$

   End of credit period: By Table 7.1, May 12 =

   $$\begin{array}{r} 132 \text{ days} \\ +60 \text{ days} \\ \hline 192 \rightarrow \text{search} \longrightarrow \text{July 11} \end{array}$$

4. End of discount period: May 10
   End of credit period: May 10 + 20 = May 30

5. End of discount period: June 10
   End of credit period: June 10 + 20 = June 30

6. Vasko Corporation's cost of equipment:

	The facts	Solving for?	Steps to take	Key points
BLUEPRINT	List price: $9,000. Trade discount rate: 30%. Terms: 2/10 EOM. Invoice date: 6/29 Date paid: 8/9	Cost of equipment.	Net price = List price × Complement of trade discount rate. EOM before 25th: Discount period is 1st 10 days of month that follow sale.	Trade discounts are deducted before cash discounts are taken. Cash discounts are not taken on freight or returns.

Steps to solving problem

1. Calculate the net price. $9,000 × .70 = $6,300   100%
   − 30%
2. Calculate the discount period.   Until Aug. 10
3. Calculate the cost of office equipment. $6,300 × .98 = $6,174   100%
   − 2%

7. $\dfrac{\$600}{.98} = \$612.24$ Credited

   $700 − $612.24 = $87.76 Balance outstanding

You Try It

1. $700 × .20 = $140

2. $\begin{array}{r} 1.00 \\ -\ .20 \\ \hline .80 \end{array}$ $700 × .80 = $560

3. Seller will pay the freight

4. $\dfrac{\$240}{.40} = \$600$

   (100% − 60%)

5. $\begin{array}{l} \$200 \\ \times\ .06 \\ \hline \$12.00 \end{array}$ $\begin{array}{l} \$188 \\ \times\ .08 \\ \hline \$15.04 \end{array}$

   $\begin{array}{r} \$188.00 \\ -\ 15.04 \\ \hline \$172.96 \end{array}$ .94 × .92 = $\begin{array}{r} .8648 \text{ NPER} \\ \times\ \$200 \\ \hline \$172.96 \end{array}$

6. .94 × .92 × $2,000 = $1,729.60

7. $\begin{array}{r} 1.0000 \\ -\ .8648 \quad (.94 \times .92) \\ \hline .1352 \times \$2,000 = \$270.40 \end{array}$

8. $\begin{array}{r} \$2,000 \\ -\ 80 \quad (\text{Freight and returns}) \\ \hline \$1,920 \times .02 = \$38.40 \end{array}$

9. April 12, May 2

10. $\begin{array}{r} \$700 \\ -\ 100 \\ \hline \$600 \times .98 = \$588 \\ +\ 100 \\ \hline \$688 \end{array}$

11. No discount; pay full $700

12. November 10; November 13

13. $300/.98 = $306.12

Chapter 8

LU 8-1a

1. Irene's dollar markup and percent markup on cost:

	The facts	Solving for?	Steps to take	Key points
BLUEPRINT	Desk cost: $800. Desk selling price: $1,200.	$\quad\quad$ % $\quad$ \$ $C\quad$ 100% $\quad$ \$ 800 $+ M\quad$ 50$^2\quad$ 400^1 $= S\quad$ 150% $\quad$ \$1,200 ^{1}Dollar markup. ^{2}Percent markup on cost.	$\dfrac{\text{Dollar}}{\text{markup}} = \dfrac{\text{Selling}}{\text{price}} - \text{Cost.}$ $\dfrac{\text{Percent}}{\text{markup}} = \dfrac{\text{Dollar markup}}{\text{Cost}}$ on cost	Dollar markup Portion $400 Base $\times$ Rate $800 $\quad$ (?) Cost

Steps to solving problem

1. Calculate the dollar markup.

$$\text{Dollar markup} = \text{Selling price} - \text{Cost}$$
$$\$400 \quad\quad = \quad \$1,200 \quad - \$800$$

2. Calculate the percent markup on cost.

$$\text{Percent markup on cost} = \dfrac{\text{Dollar markup}}{\text{Cost}}$$
$$= \dfrac{\$400}{\$800} = 50\%$$

Check

$$\text{Selling price} = \text{Cost} + \text{Markup} \quad \text{or} \quad \text{Cost}\ (B) = \dfrac{\text{Dollar markup}\ (P)}{\text{Percent markup on cost}\ (R)}$$

$$\$1,200 = \$800 + .50(\$800) \quad\quad\quad = \dfrac{\$400}{.50} = \$800$$

$$\$1,200 = \$800 + \$400$$
$$\$1,200 = \$1,200$$

2. Dollar markup and selling price of doll:

	The facts	Solving for?	Steps to take	Key points
BLUEPRINT	Doll cost: $14 each. Markup on cost: 38%.	$\quad\quad$ % $\quad$ \$ $C\quad$ 100% $\quad$ \$14.00 $+M\quad$ 38 $\quad$ 5.32^1 $= S\quad$ 138% $\quad$ \$19.32^2 ^{1}Dollar markup. ^{2}Selling price.	Dollar markup: $S = C + M$ $S = \text{Cost} \times \left(\begin{array}{c}\text{Percent} \\ 1 + \text{markup} \\ \text{on cost}\end{array}\right)$	Selling price Portion (?) Base $\times$ Rate ($14) $\quad$ (1.38) Cost $\quad\quad$ 100% $\quad\quad\quad$ +38%

Steps to solving problem

1. Calculate the dollar markup.

$$S = C + M$$
$$S = \$14.00 + .38(\$14.00)$$
$$S = \$14.00 + \$5.32 \quad \longleftarrow \text{ Dollar markup}$$

2. Calculate the selling price.

$$S = \$19.32$$

Check

$$\text{Selling price} = \text{Cost} \times (1 + \text{Percent markup on cost}) = \$14.00 \times 1.38 = \$19.32$$
$$\quad\ (P) \quad\quad\quad\quad (B) \quad\quad\quad\quad\quad\quad (R)$$

3. Cost and dollar markup

The facts	Solving for?	Steps to take	Key points
Selling price: $16. Markup on cost: 42%.	$\begin{array}{ccc} & \% & \$ \\ C & 100\% & \$11.27 \\ +\ M & 42 & 4.73^1 \\ \hline =\ S & 142\% & \$16.00^2 \end{array}$ ^{1}Cost. ^{2}Dollar markup.	$S = C + M$ or $\text{Cost} = \dfrac{\text{Selling price}}{1 + \dfrac{\text{Percent}}{\text{markup on cost}}}$ $M = S - C$	Selling price Portion $16 Base × Rate (?) (1.42) Cost 100% +42%

Steps to solving problem

1. Calculate the cost.

$$S = C + M$$
$$\$16 = C + .42C$$
$$\frac{\$16}{1.42} = \frac{\cancel{1.42}C}{\cancel{1.42}}$$
$$\$11.27 = C$$

2. Calculate the dollar markup.

$$M = S - C$$
$$M = \$16 - \$11.27$$
$$M = \$4.73$$

Check

$$\text{Cost } (B) = \frac{\text{Selling price } (P)}{1 + \text{Percent markup on cost } (R)} \qquad \frac{\$16}{1.42} = \$11.27$$

LU 8-2a

1. Irene's dollar markup and percent markup on selling price:

The facts	Solving for?	Steps to take	Key points
Desk cost: $800. Desk selling price: $1,200.	$\begin{array}{ccc} & \% & \$ \\ C & 66.7\% & \$800 \\ +\ M & 33.3^2 & 400^1 \\ \hline =\ S & 100\% & \$1,200 \end{array}$ ^{1}Dollar markup. ^{2}Percent markup on selling price.	$\dfrac{\text{Dollar}}{\text{markup}} = \dfrac{\text{Selling}}{\text{price}} - \text{Cost}$ $\dfrac{\text{Percent}}{\text{markup on}} = \dfrac{\text{Dollar}}{\text{markup}}$ $\text{selling price} \quad \dfrac{}{\text{Selling}}$ $\qquad\qquad\qquad \text{price}$	Markup Portion $400 Base × Rate $1,200 (?) Selling price

Steps to solving problem

1. Calculate the dollar markup.

$$\begin{array}{rcl} \text{Dollar markup} &=& \text{Selling price} - \text{Cost} \\ \$400 &=& \$1,200 \quad - \$800 \end{array}$$

2. Calculate the percent markup on selling price.

$$\begin{array}{rcl} \dfrac{\text{Percent markup}}{\text{on selling price}} &=& \dfrac{\text{Dollar markup}}{\text{Selling price}} \\[2mm] &=& \dfrac{\$400}{\$1,200} = 33.3\% \end{array}$$

Check

$$\text{Selling price} = \text{Cost} + \text{Markup} \qquad \text{or} \qquad \text{Selling price } (B) = \frac{\text{Dollar markup } (P)}{\text{Percent markup on selling price } (R)}$$

$$\$1,200 = \$800 + .333(\$1,200)$$

$$\$1,200 = \$800 + \$399.60$$

$$\$1,200 = \$1,199.60 \text{ (off due to rounding)} \qquad\qquad = \frac{\$400}{.333} = \$1,201.20 \text{ (off due to rounding)}$$

2. Selling price of doll and dollar markup:

	The facts	Solving for?	Steps to take	Key points
BLUEPRINT	Doll cost: $14 each. Markup on selling price: 38%.	$\begin{array}{lll} & \% & \$ \\ C & 62\% & \$14.00 \\ +M & 38 & 8.58^2 \\ =S & 100\% & \$22.58^1 \end{array}$ ^{1}Selling price. ^{2}Dollar markup.	$S = C + M$ or $S = \dfrac{\text{Cost}}{1 - \begin{array}{c}\text{Percent markup}\\\text{on selling price}\end{array}}$	Cost Portion $14 Base × Rate (?) (.62) Selling price 100% −38%

Steps to solving problem

1. Calculate the selling price.

$$S = C + M$$
$$S = \$14.00 + .38S$$
$$\underline{-.38S} \qquad \underline{-.38S}$$
$$\frac{.62S}{.62} = \frac{\$14.00}{.62}$$
$$S = \$22.58$$

2. Calculate the dollar markup.

$$M = S - C$$
$$\$8.58 = \$22.58 - \$14.00$$

Check

$$\text{Selling price } (B) = \frac{\text{Cost } (P)}{1 - \text{Percent markup on selling price } (R)} = \frac{\$14.00}{.62} = \$22.58$$

3. Dollar markup and cost:

	The facts	Solving for?	Steps to take	Key points
BLUEPRINT	Selling price: $16. Markup on selling price: 42%.	$\begin{array}{lll} & \% & \$ \\ C & 58\% & \$\ 9.28^2 \\ +M & 42 & 6.72^1 \\ =S & 100\% & \$16.00 \end{array}$ ^{1}Dollar markup. ^{2}Cost.	$S = C + M$ or $\text{Cost} = \text{Selling price} \times$ $\left(1 - \begin{array}{c}\text{Percent markup}\\\text{on selling price}\end{array}\right)$	Cost Portion (?) Base × Rate ($16) (.58) Selling price 100% −42%

Steps to solving problem

1. Calculate the dollar markup.

$$S = C + M$$
$$\$16.00 = C + .42(\$16.00)$$

2. Calculate the cost.

$$\$16.00 = C + \$6.72 \leftarrow \text{Dollar markup}$$
$$\underline{-6.72} \qquad \underline{-6.72}$$
$$\$9.28 = C$$

Check

$$\underset{(P)}{\text{Cost}} = \underset{(B)}{\text{Selling price}} \times \underset{(R)}{(1 - \text{Percent markup on selling price})} = \$16.00 \times .58 = \$9.28$$

$$(1.00 - .42)$$

4. $\text{Cost} = \dfrac{\$5}{\$7} = 71.4\%$ $\qquad\qquad \dfrac{.417}{1 - .417} = \dfrac{.417}{.583} = 71.5\%$

   $\text{Selling price} = \dfrac{\$5}{\$12} = 41.7\%$ $\qquad \dfrac{.714}{1 + .714} = \dfrac{.714}{1.714} = 41.7\%$ (due to rounding)

LU 8-3a

1.

$$S = C + M$$

$$S = \$800 + .30S$$

$$\underline{-.30S \qquad\quad -.30S}$$

$$\frac{.70S}{.70} = \frac{\$800}{.70}$$

$$S = \$1,142.86$$

Check

$$S = \frac{\text{Cost}}{1 - \text{Percent markup on selling price}}$$

$$S = \frac{\$800}{1 - .30} = \frac{\$800}{.70} = \$1,142.86$$

First markdown: $.90 \times \$1,142.86 = \$1,028.57$ selling price
Second markdown: $.95 \times \$1,028.57 = \$977.14$
Markup: $1.02 \times \$977.14 = \$996.68$ final selling price

$$\$1,142.86 - \$996.68 = \frac{\$146.18}{\$1,142.86} = 12.79\%$$

2.

The facts	Solving for?	Steps to take	Key points
500 lb. tomatoes at $.16 per pound. *Spoilage:* 10% *Markup cost:* 55%.	Price of tomatoes per pound.	Total cost. Total dollar markup. Total selling price. Spoilage amount *TS = TC + TM*	Markup is based on cost.

(BLUEPRINT)

Steps in solving problem

1. Calculate the total cost.

$$TC = 500 \text{ lb.} \times \$.16 = \$80.00$$

2. Calculate the total dollar markup.

$$TS = TC + TM$$

$$TS = \$80.00 + .55(\$80.00)$$

$$TS = \$80.00 + \$44.00 \;\longleftarrow\; \text{Total dollar markup}$$

3. Calculate the total selling price.

$$TS = \$124.00 \;\longleftarrow\; \text{Total selling price}$$

4. Calculate the tomato loss.

$$500 \text{ lb.} \times .10 = 50 \text{ lb. spoilage}$$

5. Calculate the selling price per pound of tomatoes.

$$\frac{\$124.00}{450} = \$.28 \text{ per pound (rounded to nearest hundredth)}$$

$$(500 - 50)$$

LU 8-4a

$$\$240 - \$80 = \$160 \qquad \frac{\$96,000}{\$160} = 600 \text{ units}$$

You Try It

1. $S = C + M$
$S = \$400 + \$200$
$S = \$600$

2. $\dfrac{\$50}{\$200} = 25\%$

$\dfrac{\$50}{.25} = \$200$

3. $S = C + M$
$S = \$8 + .10(\$8)$
$S = \$8 + \$.80$
$S = \$8.80$

4. $S = C + M$
$\$200 = C + .60\,C$
$\dfrac{\$200}{1.60} = \dfrac{1.60C}{1.60}$
$\$125 = C$

5. $M = S - C$
$(\$2,500) = (\$4,500) - (\$2,000)$

6. $\dfrac{\$700}{\$2,800} = 25\%$

$\dfrac{\$700}{.50} = \$1,400$

7.
$$S = C + M$$
$$S = \$800 + .40(S)$$
$$\frac{-.40 \qquad -.40}{\frac{.60\,S}{.60} = \frac{\$800}{.60}}$$
$$S = \$1333.33$$

8.
$$S = C + M$$
$$\$2,000 = C + .70(\$2,000)$$
$$2,000 = C + \$1,400$$
$$\frac{-1,400 \qquad -1,400}{\$600 = C}$$

9. $\dfrac{.47}{1 + .47} = \dfrac{.47}{1.47} = 32\%$ rounded

10.
$$\begin{array}{r} \$50 \\ \times\ .20 \\ \hline \$10 \end{array} \qquad \frac{\$10}{\$50} = 20\%$$

11.
$$TS = TC + TM$$
$$TS = \$9 + .30(\$9)$$
$$TS = \$9 + \$2.7$$
$$TS = \$11.70$$
$$\frac{\$11.70}{45} = \$.26$$

12. $\dfrac{\$70,000}{\$20} = 3{,}500$ units

Chapter 9

LU 9-1a

1. 40 hours × \$12.00 = \$480.00
14 hours × \$18.00 = $\underline{\$252.00}$ (\$12.00 × 1.5 = \$18.00)
 \$732.00

2. \$210,000 × .08 =
$$\begin{array}{r} \$16,800 \\ -\ 4,000 \\ \hline \$12,800 \end{array}$$

3. Gross pay = \$1,200 + (\$3,000 × .01) + (\$8,000 × .03) + (\$20,000 × .05) + (\$20,000 × .08)
= \$1,200 + \$30 + \$240 + \$1,000 + \$1,600
= \$4,070

LU 9-2a

1.
Social Security

$$\begin{array}{r} \$110,100 \\ -\ 109,600 \\ \hline \$\quad 500 \end{array} \times .062 = \$31$$

Medicare

\$10,000 × .0145 = \$145.00

FIT
Percentage method:
$316.67 × 1 =
$$\begin{array}{r} \$10,000.00 \\ -\ \$316.67 \\ \hline \$\ 9,683.33 \end{array}$$ (Table 9.1)

\$7,317 to \$15,067 → \$1,453.65 plus 28% of excess over \$7,317 (Table 9.2)

$$\begin{array}{r} \$9,683.33 \\ -\ 7,317.00 \\ \hline \$2,366.33 \end{array} \qquad \begin{array}{r} \$1,453.65 \\ +\ 662.57\ (\$2,366.33 \times .28) \\ \hline \$2,116.22 \end{array}$$

2. 13 weeks × \$200 = \$ 2,600
13 weeks × \$800 = 10,400 (\$10,400 − \$7,000) → \$3,400
13 weeks × \$950 = $\underline{12,350}$ (\$12,350 − \$7,000) → $\underline{5,350}$ } exempt wages (not taxed
 \$25,350 \$8,750 } for FUTA or SUTA)

\$25,350 − \$8,750 = \$16,600 taxable wages
SUTA = .051 × \$16,600 = \$846.60
FUTA = .008 × \$16,600 = \$132.80

Note: FUTA remains at .008 whether SUTA rate is higher or lower than standard.

You Try It

1. 38 hrs × $9.25 = $351.50

2.   **Reg $ Overtime $**
    (40 × $7) + (3 × $10.50)
       $280   + $31.50 = $311.50 gross pay

3. 2,250 × $.79 = $1,777.50

4. 600 × $.79 = $474
   300 × $.88 = + 264
              $738

5. $175,000 × .07 = $12,286.96

6. $6,000 × .05 = $300
   $2,000 × .09 = 180
   $4,000 × .12 = 480
               $960

7. $600 + ($6,000 × .04)
   $600 + 240 = $840

8. Gross $490.00
   Less: FIT   41.69 $490.00
         SS   30.38   − 73.08
         Med.   7.11 $416.92 × .10 = $41.69
            $410.82

9. Social Security = $110,100 × .062 = $682,62
   Medicare = $150,000 × .0145 = $2,175

10. $1,400.00   ($73.08 × 3)
       219.24 $33.40 + .15($690.76)
     1,180.76 $33.40 + $103.61
    − 490.00 $137.01 FIT
     $ 690.76

11. FUTA $200 × .008 = $1.60
    SUTA $200 × .054 = $10.80

Chapter 10

LU 10-1a

1. $16,000 \times .03 \times \dfrac{8}{12} = \$320$

2. $15,000 \times .06 \times 6 = \$5,400$

3. $50,000 \times .07 \times \dfrac{18}{12} = \$5,250$

4. August 14 → 226 $\$20,000 \times .07 \times \dfrac{100}{365} = \$383.56$
    May 6 → − 126
              100      $MV = \$20,000 + \$383.56 = \$20,383.56$

5. $\$20,000 \times .07 \times \dfrac{100}{360} = \$388.89$ $MV = \$20,000 + \$388.89 = \$20,388.89$

LU 10-2a

1. $\dfrac{\$9,000}{.04 \times \dfrac{90}{360}} = \dfrac{\$9,000}{.01} = \$900,000$ $P = \dfrac{I}{R \times T}$

2. $\dfrac{\$280}{\$6,000 \times \dfrac{180}{360}} = \dfrac{\$280}{\$3,000} = 9.33\%$ $R = \dfrac{I}{P \times T}$

3. $\dfrac{\$190}{\$900 \times .06} = \dfrac{\$190}{\$54} = 3.52 \times 360 = 1,267 \text{ days}$ $T = \dfrac{I}{P \times R}$

LU 10-3a

$\$4,000 \times .04 \times \dfrac{15}{360} = \$6.67$ $\begin{array}{r} \$2,000.00 \\ -\quad 9.19 \\ \hline \$1,990.81 \end{array}$ $\begin{array}{r} \$3,306.67 \\ -1,990.81 \\ \hline \$1,315.86 \end{array}$

$\begin{array}{r} \$ 700.00 \\ -\quad 6.67 \\ \hline \$ 693.33 \end{array}$ $\begin{array}{r} \$ 4,000.00 \\ -\quad 693.33 \\ \hline \$ 3,306.67 \end{array}$ $\$1,315.86 \times .04 \times \dfrac{20}{360} = \$2.92$

$\$3,306.67 \times .04 \times \dfrac{25}{360} = \$9.19$ $\begin{array}{r} \$\quad 2.92 \\ +\ 1,315.86 \\ \hline \$1,318.78 \end{array}$

You Try It

1. $\$4,000 \times .03 \times \dfrac{18}{12} = \$180$

2. $\$3,000 \times .04 \times \dfrac{45}{365} = \$14.79$ $\begin{array}{ll} \text{Feb 22} & 53 \\ \text{Jan 8} & \underline{-\ 8} \\ & 45 \end{array}$

3. $\$3,000 \times .04 \times \dfrac{45}{360} = \$15.00$

4. $\$2,000 \times .04 \times \dfrac{90}{360} = \$20$

5. $\dfrac{\$20}{.04 \times \dfrac{90}{360}} = \$2,000$

6. $\dfrac{\$20}{\$2,000 \times \dfrac{90}{360}} = 4\%$

7. $\dfrac{20}{\$2,000 \times .04} = .25 \times 360 = 90$ days

8. $\$4,000 \times .04 \times \dfrac{30}{360} = \$13.33$

$\begin{array}{r} \$400.00 \\ -\ \ 13.33 \\ \hline \$386.67 \end{array}$

$\$4,000 - 386.67 = \$3,613.33$

$\$3,613.33 \times .04 \times \dfrac{40}{360} = \$16.06$

$\$300 - \$16.06 = \$283.94$

$\$3,613.33 - \$283.94 = \$3,329.39$

$\$3,329.39 \times .04 \times \dfrac{20}{360} = \$7.40$

$\$3,329.39 + \$7.40 = \$3,336.79$

Total interest $= \$13.33 + \$16.06 + \$7.40 = \$36.79$

Chapter 11

LU 11-1a

1. **a.** Maturity value = Face value = $\$14,000$

   b. Bank discount = $MV \times$ Bank discount rate $\times$ Time

$$= \$14,000 \times .045 \times \frac{60}{360}$$

$$= \$105$$

   c. Proceeds = $MV -$ Bank discount

$$= \$14,000 - \$105$$

$$= \$13,895$$

   d. Effective rate $= \dfrac{\text{Interest}}{\text{Proceeds} \times \text{Time}}$

$$= \frac{\$105}{\$13,895 \times \dfrac{60}{360}}$$

$$= 4.53\%$$

2. $\$10,000 \times .04 \times \dfrac{13}{52} = \$100$ interest $\dfrac{\$100}{\$9,900 \times \dfrac{13}{52}} = 4.04\%$

LU 11-2a

1. **a.** $I = \$40,000 \times .05 \times \dfrac{170}{360} = \$944.44$

   $MV = \$40,000 + \$944.44 = \$40,944.44$

   b. Discount period = $170 - 61 = 109$ days.

   $\begin{array}{lr} \text{April} & 30 \\ & \underline{-\ 10} \\ & 20 \\ \text{May} & \underline{+\ 31} \\ & 51 \\ \text{June} & \underline{+\ 10} \\ & 61 \end{array}$ **or by table:**
   $\begin{array}{lr} \text{June 8} & 161 \\ \text{April 8} & \underline{-\ 100} \\ & 61 \end{array}$

   c. Bank discount $= \$40,944.44 \times .02 \times \dfrac{109}{360} = \$247.94$

   d. Proceeds $= \$40,944.44 - \$247.94 = \$40,696.50$

You Try It

1. $4,000 \times .02 \times \frac{30}{360} = \$6.67$

$ 4000.00
−   6.67
$3,993.33 Proceeds

2. $15,000 \times .04 \times \frac{40}{360} = \$66.67$

$15,000.00
−   66.67

$\dfrac{\$66.67}{\$14,933.33 \times \frac{40}{360}} = 4.02\%$

3. Dec 15   349
Nov 5   −309
         40 days

$2,000 \times .03 \times \frac{60}{360} = \$10$

MV = $2,010   (Left to go)

$2,010 \times .05 \times \frac{20}{360} = \$5.58$

$2,010 − $5.58 = $2,004.42 Proceeds

Chapter 12

LU 12-1a

1. **a.** $4(4 \times 1)$ **b.** $541.21   **c.** $41.27 ($541.27 − $500)

$500 \times 1.02 = \$510 \times 1.02 = \$520.20 \times 1.02 = \$530.60 \times 1.02 = \$541.21$

2. 500×1.0824 (4 periods at 2%) = $541.20

3. 16 periods, 2%, $7,000 \times 1.3728 = \$9,609.60$

4. 4 periods, $1\frac{1}{2}\%$

$8,000 \times 1.0614 = \$8,491.20$
       − 8,000.00
       $ 491.20

$\dfrac{\$491.20}{\$8,000} = 6.14\%$

5. $1,800 \times 1.3498 = \$2,429.64$

LU 12-2a

1. 14 periods (7 years × 2) $2\frac{1}{2}\%$ (5% ÷ 2)   .7077 $6,369.30 ($9,000 × .7077)

2. 20 periods (20 years × 1)   4% (4% ÷ 1)   .4564 $9,128 ($20,000 × .4564)

3. 6 years × 4 = 24 periods $\dfrac{8\%}{4} = 2\%$ .6217 × $40,000 = $24,868

4. 4 × 4 years = 16 periods $\dfrac{4\%}{4} = 1\%$ .8528 × $28,000 = $23,878.40

You Try It

1. $200 $ 208
× 1.04   × 1.04
$208 $216.32

2. $4,000 × 1.4258 (3% 12 periods)
= $5,703.20

3. Table 1.0609 (3% 2 periods)
↓
6.09%
$4,000 × 1.0609 = $4,243.60
        − 4,000.00
        $ 243.60

$\dfrac{\$243.60}{\$4,000.00} = 6.09\%$

4. Table $.7880 (1.5% 16 periods)
    × $6,000
    $4,728

Chapter 13

LU 13-1a

1. **a.** **Step 1.** Periods = 4 years × 2 = 8
        4% ÷ 2 = 2%

Step 2. Factor = 8.5829
Step 3. $5,000 × 8.5829 = $42,914.50

b. Periods = 4 years × 2   **Step 1**
      = 8 + 1 = 9
4% ÷ 2 = 2%

Factor = 9.7546   **Step 2**
$5,000 × 9.7546 = $48,773   **Step 3**
−1 payment   − $ 5,000   **Step 4**
           $43,773

2. **Step 1.** 6 years × 2 = 12 + 1 = 13 Periods $\quad \dfrac{6\%}{2} = 3\%$

   Step 2. Table factor, 15.6178
   Step 3. $2,500 × 15.6178 = $39,044.50
   Step 4. $\dfrac{-\ \ 2,500.00}{\$36,544.50}$

LU 13-2a

1. **Step 1.** Periods = 5 years × 2 = 10; Rate = 5% ÷ 2 = $2\frac{1}{2}\%$
   Step 2. Factor, 8.7521
   Step 3. $20,000 × 8.7521 = $175,042

2. **Step 1.** Periods = 10; Rate = 4%
   Step 2. Factor, 8.1109
   Step 3. $15,000 × 8.1109 = $121,663.50

3. **Step 1.** Calculate present value of annuity; 30 periods, 3%

   $80,000 × 19.6004 = $1,568,032

   Step 2. Find the present value of $1,568,032 × .8626 = $1,352,584.40

LU 13-3a

20 years × 2 = 40 Per. $\quad \dfrac{6\%}{2} = 3\%\quad$ $120,000 × .0133 = $1,596

Check

$1,596 × 75.4012 = $120,340

You Try It

1. 4.4399 (7% 4 periods)
   $\underline{\times 6,000}$
   $26,639.40

2. $6,000 × 5.7507 = $ $$$34,504.20 (7% 5 periods)
   $\underline{- 6000.00}$
   $$$28,504.20

3. 5.2421 (4% 6 periods)
   $\underline{\times \$\ 20,000}$
   $104,842

4. .0302 (5% 20 periods)
   $\underline{\times \$400,000}$
   $ 12,080

Chapter 14

LU 14-1a

1. **a.** $13,999 − $1,480 = $12,519
   b. $17,700 ($295 × 60) − $12,519 = $5,181
   c. $17,700 ($295 × 60) + $1,480 = $19,180
   d. $\dfrac{\$5,181}{\$12,519} × \$100 = \$41.39$; between 14.50% and 14.75%
   e. $\dfrac{\$5,181 + \$12,519}{60} = \$295$

2. $\dfrac{\$8,000}{\$1,000} = 8 × \$20.28 = \$162.24$ (8%, 60 months)

LU 14-2a

1.

Month	Balance due	Interest	Monthly payment	Reduction in balance	Balance outstanding
1	$300	$3.75 (.0125 × $300)	$20	$16.25 ($20 − $3.75)	$283.75
2	$283.75	$3.55 (.0125 × $283.75)	$20	$16.45	$267.30

2. Average daily balance calculated as follows:

No. of days of current balance	Current balance	Extension
3	$400	$1,200
7	300 ($400 − $100)	2,100
5	360 ($300 + $60)	1,800
5	340 ($360 − $20)	1,700
11	540 ($340 + $200)	5,940

$31 - 20 (3 + 7 + 5 + 5)$

Average daily balance $= \dfrac{\$12,740}{31} = \$410.97$

Finance charge $= \$410.97 \times 2\% = \$8.22$

You Try It

1. $5,400$ amount financed
$\underline{-\quad 100}$
$\$5,300$

2. $\qquad\qquad \$7,799.40$
$\$129.99 \times 60 = \underline{-\ 5300.00}$
$\qquad\qquad\quad \$2,499.40$ FC

3. $7,799.40 + \$100 = \$7,899.40$

4. $\dfrac{\$2,499.40}{\$5,300.00} \times \$100 = 47.16$ (between 16.25% and 16.50%)

5. $\dfrac{\$2,499.40 + \$5,300}{60} = \$129.99$

$\dfrac{\$5,300}{1,000} = 5.3 \times 24.32 = \$128.9$
(off due to using 16% instead of using between 16.25% and 16.50%)

6. $\$5,000 \times .035 = \quad \$175$
$\$275 - \$175 = \quad \$100$
$\$5,000 - \$100 = \$4,900$

7. 12 days × $200 = $2,400
4 days × $120 [$200 − $80] = $480
14 days × $180 [$120 + $60] = $2,520
Total = $5,400
$5,400/30 = $180 daily balance
Finance charge = $180 × 2.5% = $4.50

Chapter 15

LU 15-1a

1. $180,000 − $54,000 = $126,000

$\dfrac{\$126,000}{\$1,000} = 126 \times 6.66 = \$839.16$

$176,097.60 = $302,097.60 − $126,000
($839.16 × 360)   30 years × 12 payments per year

2. 5% = $676.62 monthly payment
(126 × $5.37)

Total interest cost $117,583.20 = ($676.62 × 360) − $126,000
Savings $58,514.40 = $176,097.60 − $117,583.20

LU 15-2a

$70,000 mortgage; monthly payment of $466.20 (70 × $6.66)

Payment number	Principal (current)	PORTION TO— Interest	PORTION TO— Principal reduction	Balance of principal
1	$70,000	$408.33 $70,000 × .07 × $\frac{1}{12}$	$57.87 ($466.20 − $408.33)	$69,942.13 ($70,000 − $57.87)
2	$69,942.13	$69,942.13 × .07 × $\frac{1}{12}$ $408	($466.20 − $408.00) $58.20	($69,942.13 − $58.20) $69,883.93

You Try It

1. $\dfrac{\$70,000}{\$1,000} = 70 \times \$4.50 = \$315$

2. 30 years $= \begin{array}{r} 360 \text{ payments} \\ \times \$ \quad\;\; 315 \\ \hline \$113,400 \end{array}$ $- \$70,000 = \$43,400$ interest

3.

Payment	Interest	Principal reduction	Balance
1	$204.17	$110.83	$69,889.17
	$\left(\$70,000 \times .035 \times \dfrac{1}{12} = \$204.17\right)$	($315 − $204.17)	($70,000 − $110.83)
2	203.84	$111.16	$69,778.01
	$\left(\$69,889.17 \times .035 \times \dfrac{1}{12}\right)$	($315 − $203.84)	($69,889.17 − $111.16)

Chapter 16

LU 16-1a

		2014	2013
1.	a. Cash	$\dfrac{\$38,000}{\$180,000} = 21.11\%$	$\dfrac{\$35,000}{\$140,000} = 25.00\%$
	b. Accounts receivable	$\dfrac{\$19,000}{\$180,000} = 10.56\%$	$\dfrac{\$18,000}{\$140,000} = 12.86\%$
	c. Merchandise inventory	$\dfrac{\$16,000}{\$180,000} = 8.89\%$	$\dfrac{\$11,000}{\$140,000} = 7.86\%$
	d. Prepaid expenses	$\dfrac{\$20,000}{\$180,000} = 11.11\%$	$\dfrac{\$16,000}{\$140,000} = 11.43\%$

2. $\begin{array}{r} \$16,000 \\ -\;11,000 \\ \hline \$\;5,000 \end{array}$ Percent $= \dfrac{\$5,000}{\$11,000} = 45.45\%$

LU 16-2a

1. a. $36,000 − $2,800 = $33,200
   (Gross sales − Sales returns and allowances)

   b. $5,900 + $6,800 − $5,200 = $7,500
   (Beginning inventory + Net purchases − Ending inventory)

   c. $33,200 − $7,500 = $25,700
   (Net sales − Cost of merchandise sold)

   d. $25,700 − $8,100 = $17,600
   (Gross profit from sales − Operating expenses)

LU 16-3a

		2015	2014	2013	2012
1.	Sales	36%	86%	71%	100%
		$\left(\dfrac{\$25,000}{\$70,000}\right)$	$\left(\dfrac{\$60,000}{\$70,000}\right)$	$\left(\dfrac{\$50,000}{\$70,000}\right)$	

2. a. $\dfrac{\text{CA}}{\text{CL}} = \dfrac{\$14,000}{\$9,000} = 1.6$

   b. $\dfrac{\text{CA} - \text{Inv.}}{\text{CL}} = \dfrac{\$14,000 - \$3,900}{\$9,000} = 1.12$

   c. $\dfrac{\text{AR}}{\frac{\text{Net sales}}{360}} = \dfrac{\$5,500}{\frac{\$36,500}{360}} = 54.2$ days

   d. $\dfrac{\text{NI}}{\text{Net sales}} = \dfrac{\$8,000}{\$36,500} = 21.92\%$

You Try It

1.
$$\begin{array}{rr} \$\ 400 & 40\% \\ +\ 600 & 60\% \\ \hline \$1,000 & 100\% \end{array}$$

2.

	2014	**2013**	**Change**	**%**	
Cash	$8,000	2,000	$6,000	300%	$\dfrac{\$6,000}{\$2,000}$

3. $400 − $20 − $5 = $375 net sales

4. $50 + $200 − $20 = $230

5. $400 − $250 = $150 gross profit

6. $210 − $180 = $30 net income

7.

2016	**2015**	**2014**
1,200	800	1,000
120%	80%	100%
$\left(\dfrac{1,200}{1,000}\right)$	$\dfrac{200}{1,000}$	

8. $\dfrac{\$40,000}{\$160,000} = .25$

9. $\dfrac{\$40,000 - \$2,000 - \$3,000}{\$160,000} = \dfrac{\$35,000}{\$160,000} = .22$

10. $\dfrac{\$4,000}{\dfrac{\$60,000}{360}} = 24$ days

11. $\dfrac{\$180,000}{\$70,000} = 257.14$

12. $\dfrac{\$16,000}{-\$90,000} = -17.78\%$

13. $\dfrac{\$60,000}{70,000} = .86$

14. $\dfrac{\$16,000}{\$60,000} = .27$

Chapter 17

LU 17-1a

1.

End of year	Cost of truck	Depreciation expense for year	Accumulated depreciation at end of year	Book value at end of year (Cost − Accumulated depreciation)
1	$20,000	$6,000	$ 6,000	$14,000 ($20,000 − $6,000)
2	20,000	6,000	12,000	8,000
3	20,000	6,000	18,000	2,000

2. $\dfrac{\$20,000 - \$2,000}{3} = \$6,000 \times \dfrac{11}{12} = \$5,500$

LU 17-2a

1. $\dfrac{\$30,000 - \$2,000}{56,000} = \$.50$

End of year	Cost of machine	Units produced	Depreciation expense for year	Accumulated depreciation at end of year	Book value at end of year (Cost − Accumulated depreciation)
2012	$30,000	1,000	$500 ($1,000 × $.50)	$ 500	$ 29,500
2013	30,000	6,000	3,000	3,500	26,500
2014	30,000	4,000	2,000	5,500	24,500
2015	30,000	2,000	1,000	6,500	23,500
2016	30,000	2,500	1,250	7,750	22,250

LU 17-3a

End of year	Cost of machine	Accumulated depreciation at beginning of year	Book value at beginning of year (Cost − Accumulated depreciation)	Depreciation (Book value at beginning of year × Rate)	Accumulated depreciation at end of year	Book value at end of year (Cost − Accumulated depreciation)
1	$31,000	$ -0-	$31,000	$12,400	$12,400	$18,600
2	31,000	12,400	18,600	7,440	19,840	11,160
3	31,000	19,840	11,160	4,464	24,304	*6,696

*An additional $5,696 could have been taken to reach residual value.

LU 17-4a

1. $90,000 \times .1920 = \$17,280$

2. $900,000 \times .05 = \$45,000$

You Try It

1. $\dfrac{\$50,000 - \$10,000}{4} = \dfrac{\$40,000}{4} = \$10,000$ per year

2. $\dfrac{\$4,000 - \$500}{700} = \dfrac{\$3,500}{700} = \$5$ depreciation per unit

   $150 \times \$5 = \$750$

3.

Year	Cost	Depreciation expense	Book value at end of year
1	$40,000	$20,000 ($40,000 × .50)	$20,000
2	$20,000	10,000 ($20,000 × .50) =	$10,000

4. $.20 \times \$7,000 = \$1,400$ depreciation expense

Chapter 18

LU 18-1a

1.   **a.** 58 units of ending inventory $\times \$4.76 = \$276.08$ Cost of ending inventory

   b. $\underset{\text{available for sale}}{\text{Cost of goods}} - \underset{\text{inventory}}{\text{Cost of ending}} = \underset{\text{goods sold}}{\text{Cost of}}$

   $\$810 \quad - \quad \$276.08 \quad = \quad \$533.92$

2.   **a.** 50 units from November 1 purchased at $7 $350
   $\underline{\ 8}$ units from April 1 purchased at $5 $\underline{+ \ 40}$
   58 units $390 Cost of ending inventory

   b. $\underset{\text{available for sale}}{\text{Cost of goods}} - \underset{\text{inventory}}{\text{Cost of ending}} = \underset{\text{goods sold}}{\text{Cost of}}$

   $\$810 \quad - \quad \$390 \quad = \quad \$420$

3.   **a.** 20 units from January 1 purchased at $4 $ 80
   $\underline{38}$ units from March 1 purchased at $3 $\underline{+ \ 114}$
   58 units $194 Cost of ending inventory

   b. $\underset{\text{available for sale}}{\text{Cost of goods}} - \underset{\text{inventory}}{\text{Cost of ending}} = \underset{\text{goods sold}}{\text{Cost of}}$

   $\$810 \quad - \quad \$194 \quad = \quad \$616$

LU 18-2a

	Cost	Retail
1. Beginning inventory	$ 19,000	$ 60,000
Net purchases during the month	265,000	392,000
Cost of goods available for sale	$284,000	$452,000
Less net sales for the month		375,000
Ending inventory at retail		$ 77,000
Cost ratio ($284,000 ÷ $452,000)		62.8%
Ending inventory at cost (.628 × $77,000)		$ 48,356

2. Goods available for sale

Beginning inventory, January 1, 2014		$ 30,000
Net purchases		8,000
Cost of goods available for sale		$ 38,000
Less estimated cost of goods sold:		
Net sales at retail	$ 16,000	
Cost percentage (100% − 30%)	.70	
Estimated cost of goods sold		$ 11,200
Estimated ending inventory, January 31, 2014		$ 26,800

3. $\text{Inventory turnover at cost} = \dfrac{\text{Cost of goods sold}}{\text{Average inventory at cost}} = \dfrac{\$76,500}{\$11,200} = 6.83$

$\text{Inventory turnover at retail} = \dfrac{\text{Net sales}}{\text{Average inventory at retail}} = \dfrac{\$129,500}{\$21,800} = 5.94$

Ratio

4. Department A 10,000 $\dfrac{10,000}{60,000} = .17 \times \$60,000 = \$10,200$

Department B $\dfrac{50,000}{60,000}$ $\dfrac{50,000}{60,000} = .83 \times \$60,000 = \dfrac{49,800}{\$60,000}$

You Try It

1. 4 × 9 = 36
    3 × 10 = 30
    66 total cost
    1 × $9 = $9
    1 × $10 = $10
    $19
    $66 − 19 = $47 Cost of goods sold

2. $\dfrac{89}{15}$ = $5.93 unit cost

    4 × $5.93 = $23.72

3. FIFO   4 × $7 = $28

4. LIFO   4 × $.5 = $20

5.

	Cost	Retail
Cost of goods available for sale	$88,000	$117,000
		− 90,000
Net sales		$ 27,000

Cost ratio: $\dfrac{\$88,000}{\$117,000}$ = 75%

.75 × $27,000 = $20,250

6. Cost of goods available for sale $42,000

Net sales at retail	$20,000	
	× .25	
COGS at retail		5,000
Ending inventory		$37,000

7. $\dfrac{\$90,000}{\dfrac{\$40,000 + \$60,000}{2}} = \dfrac{\$90,000}{\$50,000} = 1.8$

8. Total sq. ft. for dept. 10,000
    .40 to Dept A $30,000 × .40 = $12,000
    .60 to Dept B   30,000 × .60 = 18,000

Chapter 19

LU 19-1a

Shampoo	$ 5.90
Laundry detergent	4.10
	$10.00 × .07 = $.70

LU 19-2a

1. $.40 \times \$150,000 = \$60,000$

2. $\dfrac{\$159,000}{\$1,680,000} = .0946$ per dollar

3. a. $.09.46 = 9.46\%$

   b. $.09.46 \times 100 = \$9.46$

   c. $.094.6 \times 1,000 = \$94.60$

   d. $\dfrac{.0946}{.001} = 94.6$ mills (or $.0946 \times 1,000$)

4. $.0946 \times \$60,000 \qquad\qquad = \$5,676$
   $\$9.46 \times 600 \qquad\qquad\quad = \$5,676$
   $\$94.60 \times 60 \qquad\qquad\quad = \$5,676$
   $94.60 \times .001 \times \$60,000 = \$5,676$

You Try It

1. $\$62.80 - \$5.02 = \$57.78$
   $\underline{\times \quad .06}$
   $\$3.47$ sales tax

2. $\$6,000 + \$30 + \$60 = \$6,090$

3. $\$200,000 \times .40 = \$80,000$ assessed value

4. $\dfrac{\$700,000}{\$8,400,000} = .0833$

5. 1. 8.3% 2. $\$8.33$
   3. $\$83$ 4. $\dfrac{.0833}{.001} = 83.3 = 83$ mills

6. 1. $9.5\% \times \$40,000 = \$3,800$
   2. $\dfrac{\$40,000}{\$100} = 400 \times \$9.50 = \$3,800$
   3. $\dfrac{\$40,000}{\$1,000} = 40 \times \$95 = \$3,800$
   4. $\dfrac{\$.0950}{.001} = 95 \times .001 \times \$40,000 = \$3,800$

Chapter 20

LU 20-1a

1. $\dfrac{\$70,000}{\$1,000} = 70 \times \$2.67 = \$186.90$ No cash value in term insurance

2. $\dfrac{\$95,000}{\$1,000} = 95 \times \$7.75^* = \$736.25$

   Option 1: Cash value $\qquad 95 \times \$29 = \$2,755$
   Option 2: Paid up $\qquad\quad 95 \times \$86 = \$8,170$
   Option 3: Extended term $\quad 9$ years 91 days
   *For females we subtract 3 years.

LU 20-2a

1. $\dfrac{\$80,000}{100} = 800 \times \$.41 = \$328 \qquad \dfrac{\$20,000}{100} = 200 \times \$.50 = \dfrac{\$100}{\$428} \longleftarrow$ total premium

2. $\$428 \times .74 = \$316.72 \qquad\qquad \$428 - \$316.72 = \$111.28$

3. $\dfrac{\$140,000}{\$200,000} = \dfrac{7}{10} \times \$50,000 = \$35,000$

   $\quad\quad\uparrow$
   $(.80 \times \$250,000) \quad \$170,000$ never more than face value

LU 20-3a

Compulsory		
Bodily	$ 98	(Table 20.5)
Property	160	(Table 20.5)
Options		
Bodily	146	(Table 20.6)
Property	164	(Table 20.7)
Collision	174 ($154 + $20)	(Table 20.8)
Comprehensive	71 ($67 + $4)	(Table 20.9)
Towing	4	(Table 20.10)
Towing annual premium	$817	

You Try It

1. 1. $\dfrac{\$90,000}{\$1,000} = 90 \times \$2.44 = \$219.60$

2. $\dfrac{\$90,000}{\$1,000} = 90 \times \$11.84 = \$1,065.60$

3. $\dfrac{\$90,000}{\$1,000} = 90 \times \$15.60 = \$1,404.00$

4. $\dfrac{\$90,000}{\$1,000} = 90 \times \$27.64 = \$2,487.60$

2. Option 1: $\dfrac{\$60,000}{\$1,000} = 60 \times \$265 = \$15,900$

Option 2: $60 \times \$550 = \$33,000$

Option 3: 21 yr 300 days

3. $\dfrac{\$80,000}{\$100} = 800 \times \$.61 = \$488$

$\dfrac{\$20,000}{\$100} = 200 \times \$.65 = \$130$

 Total $\underline{\$618}$

4. $600 \times \$.44 = \$264$

Refund $\$600 - \$264 = \$336$

5. $\$600 \times \dfrac{1}{3} = \$200$

$\$600 - \$200 = \$400$

6. $\dfrac{\$40,000}{\$60,000} \times \$9,000 = \$6,000$

7.
10/20/5	$184 ($55 + $129)
Bodily	94
Property	132
Collision	196
Comprehensive	178
Comprehensive	$\underline{\underline{\$784}}$

Chapter 21

LU 21-1a

1. **a.** (A) Highest price traded in last 52 weeks.

(B) Lowest price traded in past 52 weeks.

(C) Name of corporation is Good Year (symbol GT).

(D) Dividend per share per year is .07.

(E) Yield for year is .54%.

(F) Good Year stock sells at 16 times its earnings.

(G) Sales volume for the day is 3,080,000.

(H) The last price (closing price for the day) is $13.08.

(I) Stock is up $.11 from closing price yesterday.

b. EPS $= \dfrac{\$13.08}{16} = \$.82$ per share $\qquad$ **c.** $\dfrac{\$.07}{\$13.08} = .54\%$

2. Preferred: $40,000 \times \$.60 = \$24,000 \qquad$ Arrears 2014

$\dfrac{+\ 24,000}{\$48,000}$ 2015

Common: $162,000 ($210,000 − $48,000)

LU 21-2a

1. $100.25\% \times \$1,000 = \$1,002.50 \times 5 = \$5,012.50$

2. $7\frac{1}{2}\% = .075 \times \$1,000 = \$75$ annual interest $\qquad \dfrac{\$75.00}{\$1,002.50} = 7.48\%$

LU 21-3a

1. 7.61 $\qquad$ **2.** 0.00 $\qquad$ **3.** 3.8%

You Try It

1. $\dfrac{\$.88}{\$53.88} = 1.63\%$

2. $\dfrac{\$53.88}{\$3.70} = 14.56 = 15$

3. $30,000 \times \$.80 = 24,000$

$30,000 \times \$.80 = \underline{24,000}$

$48,000$ to preferred

$\begin{array}{r}\$300,000\\ -\ \ 48,000\\ \hline \$252,000\end{array} \div 60,000 = \$4.20$ to common

4. $\$1,022.25 \times 6 = \$6,133.50$

5. $\dfrac{\$40}{1,011.20} = 3.96\%$

6. $\$12.44 + \$.05 = \$12.49$

Chapter 22

LU 22-1a

$$\text{Mean} = \frac{\$17,000 + \$14,000 + \$11,000 + \$51,000}{4} = \$23,250$$

$$\text{Median} = \frac{\$14,000 + \$17,000}{2} = \$15,500 \qquad \$11,000, \boxed{\$14,000, \$17,000,} \; \$51,000.$$

Note how we arrange numbers from smallest to highest to calculate median.

Median is the better indicator since in calculating the mean, the $51,000 puts the average of $23,250 much too high. There is no mode.

LU 22-2a

1.

Number of sales	Tally	Frequency
0	IIII	4
1	II	2
2	I	1
3	I	1
4	II	2
5		0
6	I	1
7	I	1
8	III	3
9	IIII	4
10	I	1

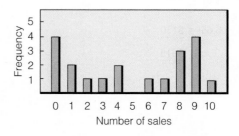

2.

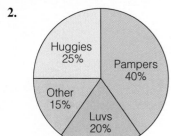

.40 × 360° = 144°
.20 × 360° = 72°
.25 × 360° = 90°
.15 × 360° = 54°

3. $\dfrac{\$35,000}{\$19,000} \times 100 = 184.21$

LU 22-3a

1. 60 − 5 = 55 range

2.

Data	Data − Mean	(Data − Mean)²
120	120 − 103 = 17	289
88	88 − 103 = −15	225
77	77 − 103 = −26	676
125	125 − 103 = 22	484
110	110 − 103 = 7	49
93	93 − 103 = −10	100
111	111 − 103 = 8	64
	Total	1,887

1,887 ÷ (7 − 1) = 314.5
$\sqrt{314.5} = 17.7$ standard deviation

You Try It

1. $\dfrac{41 + 29 + 16 + 15 + 18}{5} = 23.8$

2.
Value	Frequency	Product
80	2	160
90	3	270
100	$\dfrac{1}{6}$	$\dfrac{100}{690}$

Mean $= \dfrac{690}{6} = 115$

3. 4 7 ⑨ 14 16

4.
Coffees consumed	Tally	Frequency
0	I	1
1	I	1
2	II	2
3	I	1
4	I	1
5	I	1
6		0
7		0
8	I	1

5.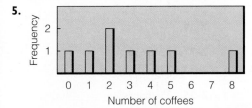

6.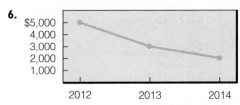

7.

.70 × 360° = 252°

.30 × 360° = 108°

8. 7

9. $\dfrac{\$12{,}000}{\$9{,}000} \times 100 = 133.3$

10. Range = 14 − 2 = 12

11. 1. Mean $= \dfrac{19}{5} = 3.8$

    2. 8 − 3.8 = 4.2

      1 − 3.8 = −2.8

      6 − 3.8 = 2.2

      2 − 3.8 = −1.8

      2 − 3.8 = −1.8

    3. $(4.2)^2 = 17.64$

      $(-2.8)^2 = 7.84$

      $(2.2)^2 = 4.84$

      $(-1.8)^2 = 3.24$

      $\underline{(-1.8)^2 = 3.24}$

    4.   36.8

    5. 36.8 ÷ 4 = 9.2

    6. Standard deviation = 3.03

Check Figures

Odd-Numbered Drill and Word Problems for End-of-Chapter Problems.

Challenge Problems (all).

Summary Practice Tests (all).

Cumulative Reviews (all).

Odd-Numbered Additional Assignments by Learning Unit from Appendix A.

Check Figures to Drill and Word Problems (Odds), Challenge Problems, Summary Practice Tests, and Cumulative Reviews

Chapter 1

End-of-Chapter Problems

1–1. 94
1–3. 176
1–5. 13,580
1–7. 113,690
1–9. 38
1–11. 3,600
1–13. 1,074
1–15. 31,110
1–17. 340,531
1–19. 126,000
1–21. 90
1–23. 86 R4
1–25. 405
1–27. 1,616
1–29. 24,876
1–31. 17,989; 18,000
1–33. 80
1–35. 133
1–37. 216
1–39. 19 R21
1–41. 7,690; 6,990
1–43. 70,470; 72,000
1–45. 700
1–47. $27,738
1–49. $240; $200; $1,200; $1,080
1–51. $2,436; $3,056; $620 more
1–53. 905,600
1–55. 1,080
1–57. a. $4,569
    b. $4,600
    c. $31
1–59. $25
1–61. $1,872,000
1–63. $4,815; $250,380
1–65. $64,180
1–67. 200,000; 10,400,000
1–69. $1,486
1–71. Average $33; no concern
1–73. $40 per sq yard

1–75. $7,680 difference between drugstore and bakery
1–76. $12,000 difference

Summary Practice Test

1. 7,017,243
2. Nine million, six hundred twenty-two thousand, three hundred sixty-four
3. a. 70
    b. 900
    c. 8,000
    d. 10,000
4. 17,000; 17,692
5. 8,100,000; 8,011,758
6. 829,412,000
7. 379 R19
8. 100
9. $95
10. $500; no
11. $1,000

Chapter 2

End-of-Chapter Problems

2–1. Proper
2–3. Improper
2–5. $61\frac{2}{5}$
2–7. $\frac{59}{3}$
2–9. $\frac{11}{13}$
2–11. 60 ($2 \times 2 \times 3 \times 5$)
2–13. 96 ($2 \times 2 \times 2 \times 2 \times 2 \times 3$)
2–15. $\frac{13}{21}$
2–17. $15\frac{5}{12}$
2–19. $\frac{5}{6}$
2–21. $7\frac{4}{9}$

2–23. $\frac{5}{16}$
2–25. $\frac{3}{25}$
2–27. $\frac{1}{3}$
2–29. $\frac{7}{18}$
2–31. $215,658
2–33. 234,701
2–35. $35\frac{1}{4}$ hours
2–37. $10\frac{3}{4}$ hours
2–39. $6\frac{1}{2}$ gallons
2–41. $875
2–43. $\frac{23}{36}$
2–45. 156,467,484
2–47. $3\frac{3}{4}$ lbs apple; $8\frac{1}{8}$ cups flour; $\frac{5}{8}$ cup marg.; $5\frac{15}{16}$ cups sugar; 5 teaspoons cin.
2–49. 400 people
2–51. 275 gloves
2–53. $450
2–55. $45\frac{3}{16}$
2–57. $62,500,000; $37,500,000
2–59. $\frac{3}{8}$
2–61. $2\frac{3}{5}$ hours
2–63. $8\frac{31}{48}$ feet; Yes
2–64. a. 400 homes b. $320,000
    c. 3,000 people; 2,500 people
    d. $112.50 e. $8,800,000

Summary Practice Test

1. Mixed number
2. Proper
3. Improper
4. $18\frac{1}{9}$
5. $\frac{65}{8}$
6. $9;\frac{7}{10}$
7. 64
8. 24 ($2 \times 2 \times 3 \times 2 \times 1 \times 1 \times 1$)
9. $6\frac{17}{20}$
10. $\frac{1}{4}$
11. $6\frac{2}{21}$
12. $\frac{1}{14}$
13. $3\frac{5}{6}$ hours
14. 7,840 rolls
15. a. 60,000 veggie
    b. 30,000 regular
16. $39\frac{1}{2}$ hours
17. $26

Chapter 3

End-of-Chapter Problems

3–1. Hundredths
3–3. .7; .74; .739
3–5. 5.8; 5.83; 5.831
3–7. 6.6; 6.56; 6.556
3–9. $4,822.78
3–11. .08
3–13. .06
3–15. .91
3–17. 16.61
3–19. $\frac{71}{100}$
3–21. $\frac{125}{10,000}$
3–23. $\frac{825}{1,000}$
3–25. $\frac{7,065}{10,000}$
3–27. $28\frac{48}{100}$
3–29. .005
3–31. .0085
3–33. 818.1279
3–35. 3.4
3–37. 2.32
3–39. 1.2; 1.26791
3–41. 4; 4.0425
3–43. 24,526.67
3–45. 161.29

3–47. 6,824.15
3–49. .04
3–51. .63
3–53. 2.585
3–55. .0086
3–57. 486
3–59. 3.950
3–61. 7,913.2
3–63. .583
3–65. $19.57
3–67. $1.40
3–69. $119.47
3–71. $29.00
3–73. $785.4 million
3–75. $423.16
3–77. $105.08
3–79. $325.03
3–81. $1.7 billion
3–83. $1.58; $3,713
3–85. $6,465.60
3–86. Yes, $16,200
3–87. $560.45

Summary Practice Test

1. 767.849
2. .7
3. .07
4. .007
5. $\frac{9}{10}$
6. $6\frac{97}{100}$
7. $\frac{685}{1,000}$
8. .29
9. .13
10. 4.57
11. .08
12. 390.2702
13. 9.2
14. 118.67
15. 34,684.01
16. 62,940
17. 832,224,982.1
18. $24.56
19. $936.30
20. $385.40
21. A $.12
22. $453.60
23. $28.10

Cumulative Review 1, 2, 3

1. $405
2. $200,000
3. $50,560,000
4. $10.00
5. $225,000
6. $750
7. $369.56
8. $130,000,000
9. $63.64

Chapter 4

End-of-Chapter Problems

4–1. $4,720.33
4–3. $4,705.33
4–5. $753
4–7. $540.82
4–9. $577.95
4–11. $998.86
4–13. $6,489
4–14. $1,862.13
4–15. $3,061.67

Summary Practice Test

1. End Bal. $15,649.12
2. $8,730
3. $1,282.70
4. $10,968.50

Chapter 5

End-of-Chapter Problems

5–1. $C = 355$
5–3. $Q = 300$
5–5. $Y = 15$
5–7. $Y = 12$
5–9. $P = 25$
5–11. Fred 25; Lee 35
5–13. Hugh 50; Joe 250
5–15. 50 shorts; 200 T-shirts
5–17. $B = 70$
5–19. $N = 63$
5–21. $Y = 7$
5–23. $P = 610.99
5–25. Pete = 90; Bill = 450
5–27. 48 boxes pens; 240 batteries
5–29. $A = 135$
5–31. $M = 60$
5–33. 211 Boston; 253 Colorado Springs
5–35. $W = 129$
5–37. Shift 1: 3,360; shift 2: 2,240
5–39. 22 boxes of hammers
      18 boxes of wrenches
5–41. 135,797 lenders
5–42. a. 2.5
      b. 15 miles
      c. 6 hours
5–43. $B = 4$

Summary Practice Test

1. $541.90
2. $84,000
3. Sears 70; Buy 560
4. Abby 200; Jill 1,000
5. 13 dishes; 78 pots
6. Pasta 300; 1,300 pizzas

Chapter 6

End-of-Chapter Problems

6–1. 78%
6–3. 70%

6–5. 356.1%
6–7. .08
6–9. .643
6–11. 1.19
6–13. 8.3%
6–15. 87.5%
6–17. $\dfrac{1}{25}$
6–19. $\dfrac{19}{60}$
6–21. $\dfrac{27}{400}$
6–23. 10.5
6–25. 102.5
6–27. 156.6
6–29. 114.88
6–31. 16.2
6–33. 141.67
6–35. 10,000
6–37. 17,777.78
6–39. 108.2%
6–41. 110%
6–43. 400%
6–45. 59.40
6–47. 1,100
6–49. 40%
6–51. +20%
6–53. 80%
6–55. $10,000
6–57. $640 per month
6–59. 677.78%
6–61. 6%
6–63. 16%
6–65. Yes, $15,480
6–67. 900
6–69. $742,500
6–71. $220,000
6–73. 33.3%
6–75. 1.4%
6–77. $39,063.83
6–79. $138.89
6–81. $1,900
6–83. $102.50
6–85. 3.7%
6–87. $2,571
6–89. $41,176
6–91. 40%
6–93. 585,000
6–94. **a.** 68%
   b. 125%
   c. $749,028
   d. $20
   e. 7 people
6–95. $55,429

Summary Practice Test
   1. 92.1%
   2. 40%
   3. 1,588%
   4. 800%
   5. .42

6. .0798
7. 4.0
8. .0025
9. 16.7%
10. 33.3%
11. $\dfrac{31}{160}$
12. $\dfrac{31}{500}$
13. $540,000
14. $2,330,000
15. 75%
16. 2.67%
17. $382.61
18. $639
19. $150,000

Chapter 7

End-of-Chapter Problems
7–1. .9603; .0397; $23.78; $575.22
7–3. .893079; .106921; $28.76; $240.24
7–5. $369.70; $80.30
7–7. $1,392.59; $457.41
7–9. June 28; July 18
7–11. June 15; July 5
7–13. July 10; July 30
7–15. $138; $6,862
7–17. $2; $198
7–19. $408.16; $291.84
7–21. $59.80; $239.20
7–23. .648; .352; $54.56; $100.44
7–25. $576.06; $48.94
7–27. $5,100; $5,250
7–29. $5,850
7–31. $1,357.03
7–33. $8,173.20
7–35. $8,333.33; $11,666.67
7–37. $99.99
7–39. $489.90; $711.10
7–41. $4,658.97
7–43. $1,083.46; $116.54
7–45. $5,008.45
7–47. $2,925.30
7–48. **a.** $1,500
   b. 8.34%
   c. $164.95
   d. $16,330.05
   e. $1,664.95
7–49. $4,794.99

Summary Practice Test
   1. $332.50
   2. $211.11
   3. $819.89; $79.11
   4. **a.** Nov. 14; Dec. 4
      b. March 20; April 9
      c. June 10; June 30
      d. Jan. 10; Jan. 30
   5. $15; $285

6. $7,120
7. B: 20.95%
8. $1,938.78; $6,061.22
9. $7,076.35

Chapter 8

End-of-Chapter Problems
8–1. $100; $600
8–3. $4,285.71
8–5. $6.90; 45.70%
8–7. $450; $550
8–9. $110.83
8–11. $34.20; 69.8%
8–13. 11%
8–15. $3,830.40; $1,169.60; 23.39%
8–17. 16,250; $4.00
8–19. $166.67
8–21. $14.29
8–23. $600; $262.50
8–25. $84
8–27. 42.86%
8–29. $3.56
8–31. 20,000
8–33. $558.60
8–35. $195
8–37. $129.99
8–39. $2.31
8–41. 12,000
8–42. $266
8–43. $94.98; $20.36; loss

Summary Practice Test
   1. $126
   2. 30.26%
   3. $482.76; $217.24
   4. $79; 37.97%
   5. $133.33
   6. $292.50
   7. 27.27%
   8. $160
   9. 25.9%
   10. $1.15
   11. 11,500

Cumulative Review 6, 7, 8
   1. 650,000
   2. $296.35
   3. $133
   4. $2,562.14
   5. $48.75
   6. $259.26
   7. $1.96; $1.89

Chapter 9

End-of-Chapter Problems
9–1. 39; $310.05
9–3. $12.00; $452
9–5. $1,680
9–7. $60
9–9. $13,000
9–11. $4,500

9–13. $11,900; $6,900; $138; $388
9–15. $378.20; $101.50
9–17. $177.98; $99.20; $23.20; $1,299.62
9–19. $752.60; $113.60
9–21. $1,290.80
9–23. $202.99
9–25. $825
9–27. $1,086.17
9–29. $357; $56
9–31. $1,077.86
9–32. a. $233.38
    b. $196.19
    c. $37.19
9–33. $1,653.60, $193.13 understated; $52

Summary Practice Test
1. 49; $428
2. $794
3. $24,700
4. $465; $290
5. $271.86
6. $798 SUTA; $112 FUTA; no tax in quarter 2

Chapter 10

End-of-Chapter Problems
10–1. $637.50; $17,637.50
10–3. $1,012.50; $21,012.50
10–5. $28.23; $613.23
10–7. $20.38; $1,020.38
10–9. $73.78; $1,273.78
10–11. $1,904.76
10–13. $4,390.61 balance due
10–15. $618.75; $15,618.75
10–17. $2,377.70; Save $1.08
10–19. 4.7 years
10–21. $21,596.11
10–23. $714.87; $44.87
10–25. 266 days
10–27. $2,608.65
10–29. $18,666.85
10–31. 12.37%
10–33. 72 days
10–35. 5.6%
10–36. a. $1,000
    b. 8%
    c. $280; $1,400
10–37. $7.82; $275.33

Summary Practice Test
1. $27.23; $2,038.11
2. $86,400
3. $14,901.25
4. $14,888.90
5. $32,516
6. $191.09; $10,191.09

Chapter 11

End-of-Chapter Problems
11–1. $211.11; $15,788.89
11–3. 25 days

11–5. $51,451.39; 57; $733.18; $50,718.21
11–7. 4.04%
11–9. $7,566.67; 6.9%
11–11. $8,937
11–13. ¥20,188
11–15. $5,133.33; 56; $71.87; $5,061.46
11–17. $4,836.44
11–18. a. $90.13
    b. $177.50
    c. 3.64%
    d. 3.61%
11–19. $2,127.66; 9.57%

Summary Practice Test
1. $160,000
2. $302.22; $16,697.98; $17,000; 4.1%
3. $61,132.87
4. $71,264.84
5. $57,462.50; 7.6%
6. 5.58%

Chapter 12

End-of-Chapter Problems
12–1. 4; 3%; $1,800.81; $200.81
12–3. $15,450; $450
12–5. 12.55%
12–7. 16; $1\frac{1}{2}$%; .7880; $4,728
12–9. 28; 3%; .4371; $7,692.96
12–11. 2.2879 × $7,692.96
12–13. $64,188
12–15. Mystic $4,775
12–17. $25,734.40
12–19. $3,807
12–21. 5.06%
12–23. $37,644
12–25. Yes, $17,908 (compounding) or $8,376 (p.v.)
12–27. $3,739.20
12–29. $13,883.30
12–31. $105,878.50
12–32. $689,125; $34,125 Bank B

Summary Practice Test
1. $48,760
2. $31,160
3. $133,123.12
4. No, $26,898 (compounding) or $22,308 (p.v.)
5. 6.14%
6. $46,137
7. $187,470
8. $28,916.10

Chapter 13

End-of-Chapter Problems
13–1. $203,182
13–3. $209,278
13–5. $3,118.59

13–7. End of first year $2,405.71
13–9. $1,410
13–11. $3,397.20
13–13. $124,937.70; $168,254.70
13–15. $1,245
13–17. $900,655
13–19. $33,444
13–21. $13,838.25
13–23. Annuity $12,219.11 or $12,219.93
13–25. $3,625.60
13–27. $111,013.29
13–29. $404,313.97
13–30. $199.29
13–31. $120,747.09

Summary Practice Test
1. $100,952.82
2. $33,914.88 or $33,913.57
3. $108,722.40
4. $2,120
5. $2,054
6. $264,915.20
7. $83,304.59
8. $237,501.36
9. $473,811.99
10. $713,776.37

Cumulative Review 10, 11, 12, 13
1. Annuity $2,058.62 or $2,058.59
2. $5,118.70
3. $116,963.02
4. $3,113.92
5. $5,797.92
6. $18,465.20
7. $29,632.35
8. $55,251

Chapter 14

End-of-Chapter Problems
14–1. Finance charge $3,600
14–3. Finance charge $1,279.76; 12.75%–13%
14–5. $119.39; $119.37
14–7. $2,741; $41.12
14–9. $1,191.67
14–11. a. $4,050 b. $1,656 c. $5,756
    d. $40.89, falls between 14.25% and 14.50%
    e. $95.10
14–13. $415.12; $340.66; $74.46
14–15. $940.36
14–17. Peg is correct
14–18. 15.48%

Summary Practice Test
1. $26,500; $4,100
2. $52.66
3. 4.25% to 4.5%
4. $6,005.30
5. $400; $8

Chapter 15

End-of-Chapter Problems

15–1. $651.30
15–3. $894.60
15–5. $118,796
15–7. $1,679.04; $1,656.25; $22.79; $158,977.21
15–9. $145,395
15–11. $636.16; $117,017.60
15–13. Payment 3, $119,857.38
15–15. $84,240
15–17. $942.50
15–18. $793.50
15–19. a. $92,495.50
    b. $1,690.15
    c. $415,954

Summary Practice Test

1. $1,020; $850; $169,830
2. $499.84; $91,942.40
3. a. $434.97; $75,589.20
   b. $460.08; $84,628.80
   c. $486; $93,960
   d. $512.73; $103,582.80
4. $5.71; $1,027.80
5. $251,676

Chapter 16

End-of-Chapter Problems

16–1. Total assets $74,000
16–3. Inventory −16.67%; mortgage note +13.79%
16–5. Net sales 13.62%; Net earnings 2013 47.92%
16–7. Depreciation $100; + 16.67%
16–9. 1.43; 1.79
16–11. .20; .23
16–13. .06; .08
16–15. 13.57%
16–17. 87.74%; 34.43%; .13; 55.47%
16–19. 2016 68% sales
16–21. $3,470; $431
16–22. 3.5; 2.3

Summary Practice Test

1. a. $161,000
   b. $21,000
   c. $140,000
   d. $84,000
2. Acc. rec. 15.15%; 24.67%
3. Cash $11,000; 137.50%
4. 2013; 74%
5. Total assets $175,000
6. a. .70   b. .50   c. 45 days
   d. 1.05   e. .25

Chapter 17

End-of-Chapter Problems

17–1. Book value (end of year) $27,000
17–3. Book value (end of year) $21,000
17–5. Book value (end of year) $15,000
17–7. Book value (end of year) $9,000
17–9. Book value (end of year) $15,000
17–11. Book value (end of year) $5,400
17–13. $1,400
17–15. $18,000
17–17. $22,560
17–19. $15,000
17–21. $6,000; $18,000
17–23. $6,760 below
17–25. $83,667
17–27. a. $87,750   b. $11.40
    c. $21,489   d. 4 years
17–28. $13,320; $1.11

Summary Practice Test

1. Book value end of year 2: $10,800
2. $1,713.60
3. Acc. dep., $4,000; $8,000; $12,000; $16,000; $20,000
4. $1,500
5. $12,600

Chapter 18

End-of-Chapter Problems

18–1. $2,409; $6,674
18–3. $543; $932
18–5. $10
18–7. $36
18–9. $72
18–11. $140.80
18–13. $147.75; $345.60
18–15. $188.65; $304.70
18–17. 3.56; 3.25
18–19. .75; $67,500
18–21. $10,550; $24,645
18–23. $45,000
18–25. $55,120
18–27. $38,150
18–28. $13,499.50
18–29. $1,900

Summary Practice Test

1. a. 31   b. $66.87; $93.30; $80.29
2. $40,000
3. 1.10
4. $109,275
5. $97,960

Chapter 19

End-of-Chapter Problems

19–1. $1,044
19–3. $83,018.87
19–5. $39,000
19–7. $.0233
19–9. 6.99%; $6.99; $69.90; 69.90
19–11. $4,462.50
19–13. $16,985.05
19–15. $112.92
19–17. $112,000
19–19. $6,940
19–21. $64,000
19–23. $2,251.50
19–25. $23,065 more in Minn.
19–26. $3,665
19–27. $979

Summary Practice Test

1. $284.76; $14.24
2. $4,710
3. $146,000
4. 5.1 mills
5. $1,237.50
6. $18,141.20

Chapter 20

End-of-Chapter Problems

20–1. $1,657.60
20–3. $277.50
20–5. $53,000
20–7. 21 years, 300 days
20–9. $518; $182
20–11. $16,500
20–13. $1,067
20–15. $1,855 cheaper
20–17. $801
20–19. $118,750
20–21. $1,100
20–23. $373.67
20–25. $22,900; $10,700
20–27. $24,000; $16,300
20–28. $7,512.64; $1,942.00; $787.89
20–29. $176.00

Summary Practice Test

1. $1,993.50; $28,530
2. $2,616.60; $55,650; $115,500; 21 years 300 days
3. $234,375; $450,000
4. $990; $326.70
5. $1,755
6. Insurance company pays $31,600; Roger pays $10,000

Chapter 21

End-of-Chapter Problems

21–1. $151,952
21–3. 1.1%
21–5. 13
21–7. $24,227.04
21–9. 2013   preferred $8,000
    2014   0
    2015   preferred $127,000
    common $33,000
21–11. $2,280
21–13. $260; $2,725; 9.5%
21–15. $12.04; −$.06; 9.6%
21–17. Gain $222.48

21–19. 12; 2.4%

21–21. $5,043.75; $56.25

21–23. 7.3%

21–25. Stock 6.7%; bond 11.9%

21–27. Yes, $16.02

21–29. $443.80

21–30. **a.** 1,287 shares

b. 2,574 shares

c. 5,147 shares

d. $26,381.76 for (a);
$52,388.43 for (b);
$103,756.44 for (c)

21–31. $1,014.33

Summary Practice Test

1. $18,127.26

2. 8; 1.3%

3. $1.23

4. $10,476

5. 5.6%

6. $160,000

7. $14.52; $11,616

Chapter 22

End-of-Chapter Problems

22–1. 7.50

22–3. $77.23

22–5. 2.7

22–7. 31.5

22–9. 8

22–11. 142.9

22–13. $200–$299.99 卌

22–15. Traditional watch 183.6°

22–17.

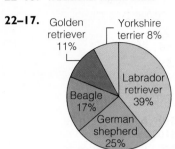

22–19. Transportation   126°

Hotel   100.8°

Food   72°

Miscellaneous   61.2°

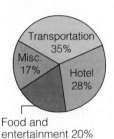

22–21. 250

22–23. **a.** 57,000,000 mean
62,900,000 median

b. AAA = 30.42%
Riser = 22.18%
Casto = 22.07%
Balbon = 12.70%
Hunter = 12.63%

22–24. 24.94%; 15.42%; 10.88%; 13.15%;
18.59%; 17.01%

Optional Assignment

1. 98

3. 4.3

5. 16%; 2.5%

7. 68%; 81.5%; 2.5%; 2.5%; 47.5%

9. 5.02

Summary Practice Test

1. $143,300; $141,000

2. 1,100

3. 2.50

4. 100; 卌; 4

5. Bar 1 on horizontal axis goes up to 800 on vertical axis

6. Profits   108°
Cost of sales   144°
Expense   108°

7. 166.3%

8. 3.0 standard deviation

Check Figures (Odds) to Additional Assignments by Learning Unit from Appendix A

LU 1–1

1. **a.** Seven thousand, eight hundred twenty-one
   d. Fifty-eight thousand, three

3. **a.** 80; 380; 860; 5,980; 210
   c. 21,000; 1,000; 4,000; 10,000

5. **a.** Hundreds place
   c. Ten thousands place
   e. Billions place

7. Five hundred sixty-five

9. $375,985

11. Two thousand, four

LU 1–2

1. **a.** 1,006
   c. 1,319
   d. 179

3. **a.** Estimated 50; 52
   c. Estimated 10; 9

5. $71,577

7. $19,973

9. 12,797 lbs

11. Estimated $9,400; $9,422

13. $746 discount

LU 1–3

1. **a.** Estimated 4,000; actual 2,400
   c. Estimated 15,000,000;
   actual 16,184,184

3. **a.** Estimated 1,000; actual 963 R5
   c. Estimated 20; actual 25 R8

5. 5,040

7. $78

9. 27

11. $43,200

13. 40 stacks and 23 "extra" bricks

LU 2–1

1. **a.** Proper
   b. Improper
   c. Improper
   d. Mixed number
   e. Improper
   f. Mixed number

3. **a.** $\frac{46}{5}$ **c.** $\frac{31}{7}$ **f.** $\frac{53}{3}$

5. **a.** 6; $\frac{6}{7}$ **b.** 15; $\frac{2}{5}$ **e.** 12; $\frac{8}{11}$

7. $\frac{13}{4}$

9. $\frac{17}{25}$

11. $\frac{60}{100}$

13. $\frac{7}{12}$

LU 2–2

1. **a.** 32   **b.** 180   **c.** 480   **d.** 252

3. **a.** $\frac{1}{3}$ **b.** $\frac{2}{3}$ **e.** $6\frac{1}{8}$ **h.** $56\frac{5}{6}$

5. $3\frac{1}{40}$ yards

7. $17\frac{5}{12}$ miles

9. $4\frac{8}{9}$ hours

LU 2–3

1. **a.** $\overset{1}{\underset{1}{\cancel{6}}}_{13} \times \overset{\overset{2}{\cancel{26}}}{\underset{2}{\cancel{12}}} = 1$

3. **a.** $1\frac{1}{4}$ **b.** 3   **g.** 24   **l.** $\frac{4}{7}$

5. $39,000

7. 714

9. $20\frac{2}{3}$ miles

11. $412,000

LU 3–1

1. **a.** .62   **b.** .6   **c.** .953
   d. .401   **e.** .06

3. a. Hundredths place
  d. Thousandths place

5. a. $\frac{2}{5}$ **b.** $\frac{11}{25}$

  g. $\frac{5}{16}$ **l.** $9\frac{1}{25}$

7. .286

9. $\frac{566}{1,000}$

11. .333

13. .0020507

LU 3–2

1. a. 31.608 **b.** 5.2281 **d.** 3.7736
3. a. .3 **b.** .1 **c.** 1,480.0 **d.** .1
5. a. 6,870 **c.** .0272
  e. 34,700 **i.** 8,329.8
7. $4.53
9. $111.25
11. 15

LU 4–1

1. a. $430.64 **b.** 3 **c.** $867.51
3. a. Neuner Realty Co.
  b. Kevin Jones
  h. $2,756.80

LU 4–2

1. $1,435.42
3. Add $3,000; deduct $22.25
5. $2,989.92
7. $1,315.20

LU 5–1

1. a. $3N = 180$ **e.** $14 + \frac{N}{3} = 18$
  h. $2N + 3N + 8 = 68$

LU 5–2

1. $80
3. $45 telephone; $135 utility
5. 51 tickets—Sherry;
  408 tickets—Linda
7. 12 necklaces ($48);
  36 watches ($252)
9. $157.14

LU 6–1

1. a. 4% **b.** 72.9% **i.** 503.8% **l.** 80%
3. a. 70% **c.** 162.5%
  h. 50% **n.** 1.5%
5. a. $\frac{1}{4}$ **b.** .375 **c.** 50%
  d. $.\overline{666}$ **n.** $1\frac{1}{8}$
7. 2.9%
9. $\frac{39}{100}$
11. $\frac{9}{10,000}$

LU 6–2

1. a. $20,000; 30%; $4,000
  c. $7.00; 12%; $.84
3. a. 33.3% **b.** 3% **c.** 27.5%
5. a. −1,584; −26.6%
  d. −20,000; −16.7%
7. $9,000
9. $3,196
11. 329.5%

LU 7–1

1. a. $40 **b.** $360 **c.** $50
  d. $100 **e.** $380
3. a. $75 **b.** $21.50; $40.75
5. a. .7125; .2875 **b.** .7225; .2775
7. $3.51
9. $81.25
11. $315
13. 45%

LU 7–2

1. a. February 18; March 10
  d. May 20; June 9
  e. October 10; October 30
3. a. .97; $1,358
  c. .98; $367.99
5. a. $16.79; $835.21
7. $16,170
9. a. $439.29 **b.** $491.21
11. $209.45
13. a. $765.31 **b.** $386.99

LU 8–1

1. a. $18.90 **b.** $2.72
  c. $4.35 **d.** $90 **e.** $116.31
3. a. $2; 80% **b.** $6.50; 52%
  c. $.28; 28.9%
5. a. $1.52 **b.** $225
  c. $372.92 **d.** $625
7. a. $199.60 **b.** $698.60
9. a. $258.52 **b.** $90.48
11. a. $212.50 **b.** $297.50
13. $8.17

LU 8–2

1. a. $5.40 **b.** $57.50
  c. $34.43 **d.** $27.33 **e.** $.15
3. a. $6.94 **b.** $882.35 **c.** $30
  d. $171.43
5. a. 28.57% **b.** 33.33% **d.** 53.85%
7. $346.15
9. 39.39%
11. $2.29
13. 63.33%

LU 8–3

1. a. $80; $120
  b. $525; $1,574.98
3. a. $410 **b.** $18.65

5. a. $216; $324; $5.14
  b. $45; $63.90; $1.52
7. 17%
9. $21.15
11. $273.78
13. $.79

LU 8–4

1. a. $6.00 **b.** $11.11
3. a. 16,667 **b.** 7,500
5. 5,070
7. 22,222

LU 9–1

1. a. $427.50; 0; $427.50
  b. $360; $40.50; $400.50
3. a. $438.85 **b.** $615.13
5. a. $5,200 **b.** $3,960
  c. $3,740 **d.** $4,750
7. $723.00
9. $3,846.25
11. $2,032.48

LU 9–2

1. a. $500; $2,300
3. $0; $2,000
5. $328.59
7. $143.75
9. $594.44
11. $663.50

LU 10–1

1. a. $240 **b.** $1,080 **c.** $1,275
3. a. $131.25 **b.** $4.08 **c.** $98.51
5. a. $515.63 **b.** $6,015.63
7. a. $5,459.66
9. $659.36
11. $360

LU 10–2

1. a. $4,371.44 **b.** $4,545.45
  c. $3,433.33
3. a. 60; .17 **b.** 120; .33
  c. 270; .75 **d.** 145; .40
5. 5%
7. $250
9. $3,000
11. 119 days

LU 10–3

1. a. $2,568.75; $1,885.47; $920.04
3. $4,267.59
5. $4,715.30; $115.30

LU 11–1

1. I; B; D; I; D; I; B; D
3. a. 2%
  c. 13%
5. $15,963.75

7. $848.75; $8,851.25
9. $14,300
11. $7,855

LU 11–2

1. a. $5,075.00
   b. $16,480.80
   c. $994.44
3. a. $14.76
   b. $223.25
   c. $3.49
5. $4,031.67
7. $8,262.74
9. $5,088.16
11. $721.45

LU 12–1

1. a. $573.25 year 2
   b. $3,115.57 year 4
3. a. $25,306; $5,306
   b. $16,084; $6,084
5. $7,430.50
7. $8,881.20
9. $2,129.40
11. $3,207.09; $207.09
13. $3,000; $3,469; $3,498

LU 12–2

1. a. .9804 **b.** .3936 **c.** .5513
3. a. $1,575.50; $924.50
   b. $2,547.02; $2,052.98
5. $14,509.50
7. $13,356.98
9. $16,826.40
11. $652.32
13. $18,014.22

LU 13–1

1. a. $1,000; $2,080; $3,246.40
3. a. $6,888.60 **b.** $6,273.36
5. $325,525
7. $13,412
9. $30,200.85
11. $33,650.94

LU 13–2

1. a. $2,638.65 **b.** $6,375.24; $7,217.10
3. $2,715.54
5. $24,251.85
7. $47,608
9. $456,425
11. Accept Jason $265,010

LU 13–3

1. a. $4,087.50 **b.** $21,607
   c. $1,395 **d.** $201.45
   e. $842.24
3. $16,200
5. $24,030

7. $16,345
9. $8,742

LU 14–1

1. a. $1,200; $192
   b. $9,000; $1,200
3. a. 14.75% **b.** 10%
   c. 11.25%
5. a. $3,528 **b.** $696
   c. $4,616
7. a. $22,500 **b.** $4,932
   c. $29,932
9. a. $20,576 **b.** 12.75%

LU 14–2

1. a. $465; $8,535
   b. $915.62; $4,709.38
3. a. $332.03 **b.** $584.83
   c. $384.28
5. Final payment $784.39
7. $51.34
9. $35
11. $922.48
13. 7.50% to 7.75%

LU 15–1

1. a. $1,096.50 **b.** $965.60;
   $4,090.50; $3,859.65
3. a. $117.25, 7.7%
   b. $174, 5.7%
5. $774
7. $2,584.71; $2,518.63
9. a. $66.08 **b.** $131,293.80
11. $773,560

LU 15–2

1. a. $1,371.90; $1,133.33; $238.57
3. #4 balance outstanding $195,183.05
5. $587,612.80
7. $327.12; $251,581.60
9. $44,271.43
11. $61,800

LU 16–1

1. Total assets $224,725
3. Merch. inventory 13.90%; 15.12%

LU 16–2

1. Net income $57,765
3. Purchases 73.59%; 71.43%

LU 16–3

1. Sales 2015, 93.5%; 2014, 93.2%
3. .22
5. 59.29%
7. .83
9. COGS 119.33%; 111.76%;
   105.04%

11. .90
13. 5.51%
15. 11.01%

LU 17–1

1. a. 4% **b.** 25% **c.** 10%
   d. 20%
3. a. $2,033; $4,667
   b. $1,850; $9,750
5. $8,625 depreciation per year
7. $2,800 depreciation per year
9. $95
11. a. $12,000 **b.** $6,000
   c. $18,000 **d.** $45,000

LU 17–2

1. a. $.300 **b.** $.192 **c.** $.176
3. a. $.300, $2,600
   b. $.192, $300,824
5. $5,300 book value end of year 5
7. a. $.155 **b.** $20,001.61

LU 17–3

1. a. 8% **b.** 20% **c.** 25%
3. a. $4,467; $2,233
   b. $3,867; $7,733
5. $121, year 6
7. a. 28.57% **b.** $248 **c.** $619
9. a. 16.67% **b.** $2,500
   c. $10,814 **d.** $2,907

LU 17–4

1. a. 33%; $825; $1,675
3. Depreciation year 8, $346
5. $125
7. a. $15,000 **b.** $39,000
   c. $21,600 **d.** 2001
9. $68,440

LU 18–1

1. a. $5,120; $3,020
   b. $323,246; $273,546
3. $35,903; $165,262
5. $10,510.20; $16,345
7. $37.62; $639.54
9. $628.40
11. $3,069; $952; $2,117

LU 18–2

1. a. $85,700; $143,500; .597; $64,500;
   $38,507
3. $85,000
5. $342,000; $242,500; 5.85; 6.29
7. $60,000; $100,000; $40,000
9. $70,150
11. $5,970
13. 3.24; 3.05
15. $32,340; $35,280; $49,980;
   $29,400

LU 19–1

1. **a.** $26.80; $562.80
   b. $718.80; $12,698.80
3. **a.** $20.75; $43.89; $463.64
5. Total is **(a)** $1,023; **(b)** $58.55
7. $5.23; $115.23
9. $2,623.93
11. $26.20
13. $685.50

LU 19–2

1. **a.** $68,250 **b.** $775,450
3. **a.** $7.45; $74.50; 74.50
5. $9.10
7. $8,368.94
9. $42,112
11. $32,547.50

LU 20–1

1. **a.** $9.27; 25; $231.75
3. **a.** $93.00; $387.50; $535.00; $916.50
5. $1,242.90
7. $14,265
9. $47.50 more
11. $68,750

LU 20–2

1. **a.** $488 **b.** $2,912
3. **a.** $68,000; $60,000
   b. $41,600; $45,000
5. $1,463
7. $117,187.50

9. $336,000
11. **a.** $131,250 **b.** $147,000

LU 20–3

1. **a.** $98; $160; $258
3. **a.** $312 **b.** $233 **c.** $181
   d. $59; $20
5. **a.** $647 **b.** $706
7. $601
9. $781
11. $10,000; $8,000
13. $60,000; $20,000
15. $19.50; $110.50

LU 21–1

1. **a.** $43.88 **f.** 49
3. $27.06
5. $1,358.52 gain
7. $18,825.15
9. $7.70

LU 21–2

1. **a.** IBM **b.** $10\frac{1}{4}$ **c.** 2018
   d. $102.50 **e.** 102.375
3. **a.** $1,025
   b. $1,023.75
5. **a.** $3,075
   b. $307.50
7. **a.** $30 discount
   b. $16.25 premium
   c. $42.50 premium
9. **a.** $625 **b.** $375 discount
   c. $105 **d.** 16.8%

11. 7.8%; 7.2%
13. 8.98%

LU 21–3

1. $11.90
3. $15.20
5. +$.14
7. 7.6%
9. $1.45; $18.45
11. $.56; $14.66
13. $1,573.50
15. $123.00 loss
17. **a.** 2014; 2022
    b. 9.3% Comp USA; 6.9% GMA
    c. $1,023.75 Comp USA
    $1,016.25 GMA
    d. Both at premium
    e. $1,025 Comp USA; $1,028.75 GMA

LU 22–1

1. **a.** 20.4 **b.** 83.75 **c.** 10.07
3. **a.** 59.5 **b.** 50
5. **a.** 63.7; 62; 62
7. $1,500,388.50
9. $10.75
11. $9.98

LU 22–2

1. 18: ||||| || 7
3. 25–30: ||||| ||| 8
5. 7.2°
7. 145–154: |||| 4
9. 98.4°; 9.9°; 70.5°; 169.2°; 11.9°

Classroom Notes

Classroom Notes

Classroom Notes

Classroom Notes

Metric System

The Boston Globe

John Sullivan: Angie, I drove into the gas station last night to fill the tank up. Did I get upset! The pumps were not in gallons but in liters. This country (U.S.) going to metric is sure making it confusing.

Angie Smith: Don't get upset. Let me first explain the key units of measure in metric, and then I'll show you a convenient table I keep in my purse to convert metric to U.S. (also called customary system), and U.S. to metric. Let's go on.

The metric system is really a decimal system in which each unit of measure is exactly 10 times as large as the previous unit. In a moment, we will see how this aids in conversions. First, look at the middle column (Units) of this to see the basic units of measure:

U.S.	Thousands	Hundreds	Tens	Units	Tenths	Hundredths	Thousandths
Metric	Kilo-	Hecto-	Deka-	Gram	Deci-	Centi-	Milli-
	1,000	100	10	Meter	.1	.01	.001
				Liter			
				1			

- Weight: Gram (think of it as $\frac{1}{30}$ of an ounce).
- Length: Meter (think of it for now as a little more than a yard).
- Volume: Liter (a little more than a quart).

To aid you in looking at this, think of a decimeter, a centimeter, or a millimeter as being "shorter" (smaller) than a meter, whereas a dekameter, hectometer, and kilometer are "larger" than a meter. For example:

1 centimeter $= \frac{1}{100}$ of a meter; or 100 centimeters equals 1 meter.

1 millimeter $= \frac{1}{1,000}$ meter; or 1,000 millimeters equals 1 meter.

1 hectometer $= 100$ meters.

1 kilometer $= 1,000$ meters.

Remember we could have used the same setup for grams or liters. Note the summary here.

Length	Volume	Mass
1 meter:	1 liter:	1 gram:
= 10 decimeters	= 10 deciliters	= 10 decigrams
= 100 centimeters	= 100 centiliters	= 100 centigrams
= 1,000 millimeters	= 1,000 milliliters	= 1,000 milligrams
= .1 dekameter	= .1 dekaliter	= .1 dekagram
= .01 hectometer	= .01 hectoliter	= .01 hectogram
= .001 kilometer	= .001 kiloliter	= .001 kilogram

Practice these conversions and check solutions.

1	PRACTICE QUIZ

Convert the following:

1. 7.2 meters to centimeters
2. .89 meter to millimeters
3. 64 centimeters to meters
4. 350 grams to kilograms
5. 7.4 liters to centiliters
6. 2,500 milligrams to grams

✓ **Solutions**

1. 7.2 meters = 7.2 × 100 = 720 centimeters (remember, 1 meter = 100 centimeters)
2. .89 meter = .89 × 1,000 = 890 millimeters (remember, 1 meter = 1,000 millimeters)
3. 64 centimeters = 64/100 = .64 meters (remember, 1 meter = 100 centimeters)
4. 350 grams = $\frac{350}{1,000}$ = .35 kilograms (remember 1 kilogram = 1,000 grams)
5. 7.4 liters = 7.4 × 100 = 740 centiliters (remember, 1 liter = 100 centiliters)
6. 2,500 milligrams = $\frac{2,500}{1,000}$ = 2.5 grams (remember, 1 gram = 1,000 milligrams

Angie: Look at the table of conversions and I'll show you how easy it is. Note how we can convert liters to gallons. Using the conversion from meters to U.S. (liters to gallons), we see that you multiply numbers of liters by .26, so for 37.95 liters we get 37.95 × .26 = 9.84 gallons.

Common conversion factors for U.S./metric					
A. To convert from U.S. to	**Metric**	**Multiply by**	**B. To convert from metric to**	**U.S.**	**Multiply by**
Length:			*Length:*		
Inches (in)	Meters (m)	.025	Meters (m)	Inches (in)	39.37
Feet (ft)	Meters (m)	.31	Meters (m)	Feet (ft)	3.28
Yards (yd)	Meters (m)	.91	Meters (m)	Yards (yd)	1.1
Miles	Kilometers (km)	1.6	Kilometers (km)	Miles	.62
Weight:			*Weight:*		
Ounces (oz)	Grams (g)	28	Grams (g)	Ounces (oz)	.035
Pounds (lb)	Grams (g)	454	Grams (g)	Pounds (lb)	.0022
Pounds (lb)	Kilograms (kg)	.45	Kilograms (kg)	Pounds (lb)	2.2
Volume or capacity:			*Volume or capacity:*		
Pints	Liters (L)	.47	Liters (L)	Pints	2.1
Quarts	Liters (L)	.95	Liters (L)	Quarts	1.06
Gallons (gal)	Liters (L)	3.8	Liters (L)	Gallons	.26

John: How would I convert 6 miles to kilometers?

Angie: Take the number of miles times 1.6, thus 6 miles × 1.6 = 9.6 kilometers.

John: If I weigh 120 pounds, what is my weight in kilograms?

Angie: 120 times .45 (use the conversion table) equals 54 kilograms.

John: OK. Last night, when I bought 16.6 liters of gas, I really bought 4.3 gallons (16.6 liters times .26).

2   PRACTICE QUIZ

Convert the following:

1. 10 meters to yards
2. 110 quarts to liters
3. 78 kilometers to miles
4. 52 yards to meters
5. 82 meters to inches
6. 292 miles to kilometers

✓ Solutions

1. 10 meters × 1.1 = 11 yards
2. 110 quarts × .95 = 104.5 liters
3. 78 kilometers × .62 = 48.36 miles
4. 52 yards × .91 = 47.32 meters
5. 82 meters × 39.37 = 3,228.34 inches
6. 292 miles × 1.6 = 467.20 kilometers

Appendix D: Problems

DRILL PROBLEMS

Convert:

1. 65 centimeters to meters

2. 7.85 meters to centimeters

3. 44 centiliters to liters

4. 1,500 grams to kilograms

5. 842 millimeters to meters

6. 9.4 kilograms to grams

7. .854 kilograms to grams

8. 5.9 meters to millimeters

9. 8.91 kilograms to grams

10. 2.3 meters to millimeters

Convert, rounding to the nearest tenth:

11. 50.9 kilograms to pounds

12. 8.9 pounds to grams

13. 395 kilometers to miles

14. 33 yards to meters

15. 13.9 pounds to grams

16. 594 miles to kilometers

17. 4.9 feet to meters

18. 9.9 feet to meters

19. 100 yards to meters

20. 40.9 kilograms to pounds

21. 895 miles to kilometers

22. 1,000 grams to pounds

23. 79.1 meters to yards

24. 12 liters to quarts

25. 2.92 meters to feet

26. 5 liters to gallons

27. 8.7 meters to feet

28. 8 gallons to liters

29. 1,600 grams to pounds

30. 310 meters to yards

WORD PROBLEM

31. A metric ton is 39.4 bushels of corn. The Russians bought 450,000 metric tons of U.S. corn, valued at $58 million, for delivery after September 30. Convert the number of bushels purchased from metric tons to bushels of corn.

Glossary/Index

Note: Page numbers followed by n indicate material found in footnotes.

Accelerated Cost Recovery System (ACRS) *Tax law enacted in 1981 for assets put in service from 1981 through 1986*, 431

Accelerated depreciation *Computes more depreciation expense in the early years of the asset's life than in the later years*, 429

Accounts payable *Amounts owed to creditors for services or items purchased*, 394

Accounts receivable *Amount owed by customers to a business from previous sales*, 394

Accumulated depreciation *Amount of depreciation that has accumulated on plant and equipment assets*, 426

Acid test *Current assets less inventory less prepaid expenses divided by current liabilities*, 407

ACRS; *see* **Accelerated Cost Recovery System**

Adams, Scott, 142

Addends *Numbers that are combined in the addition process*, 10. *Example:* 8 + 9 = 17, in which 8 and 9 are the addends

Addition
  of decimals, 71–72
  estimating, 11
  of fractions, 41–43
  of mixed numbers, 43–44
  of whole numbers, 10–11

Adesa, 440

Adjustable rate mortgage (ARM) *Rate of mortgage is lower than a fixed rate mortgage. Rates adjusted without refinancing. Caps available to limit how high rate can go for each adjustment period over term of loan*, 374

Adjusted balance *The balance after partial payment less interest is subtracted from the principal*, 270–271

Adjusted bank balance *Current balance of checkbook after reconciliation process*, 98

Aflac, 514–515

Albertsons, 45

Alliant Credit Union, 115

Amazon, 88, 180, 243, 468

American Eagle Outfitters, 443

American Express, 240, 356, 370

Amortization *Process of paying back a loan (principal plus interest) by equal periodic payments (see amortization schedule)*, 350
  on installment loans, 350, 354
  on mortgages, 375–376, 378–379

Amortization schedule *Shows monthly payment to pay back loan at maturity. Payment also includes interest. Note payment is fixed at same amount each month*, 379

Amortization table *A table that shows each periodic payment on a loan or mortgage*, 375–376

Amount financed *Cash price less down payment*, 350

Analysis; *see* **Horizontal analysis**; **Ratio analysis**; **Trend analysis**; **Vertical analysis**

Andriotis, AnnaMaria, 380

Annual percentage rate (APR) *True or effective annual interest rate charged by sellers. Required to be stated by Truth in Lending Act*, 351–353

Annual percentage rate (APR) table *Effective annual rate of interest on a loan or installment purchase as shown by table lookup*, 351–353

Annual percentage yield (APY) *Truth in savings law forced banks to report actual interest in form of APY. Interest yield must be calculated on actual number of days bank has the money*, 306–307

Annuities certain *Annuities that have stated beginning and ending dates*, 325

Annuity *Stream of equal payments made at periodic times*, 324
  contingent, 325
  future value, 324–325
  lump sum versus, 332
  payment periods, 324, 329
  term, 324

Annuity due *Annuity that is paid (or received) at the beginning of the time period*, 325
  future value, 327–329

Apple, 74, 88, 207, 240, 243, 452, 529

Apps, banking, 101

APR; *see* **Annual percentage rate**

APY; *see* **Annual percentage yield**

ARM; *see* **Adjustable rate mortgage**

Assessed value *Value of a property that an assessor sets (usually a percent of property's market value) that is used in calculating property taxes*, 471

Asset cost *Amount company paid for the asset*, 425–426

Asset turnover *Net sales divided by total assets*, 407

Assets *Things of value owned by a business*, 394; *see also* **Depreciation**
  acid test, 407
  on balance sheet, 392, 394
  book value, 426
  current, 394
  land, 394, 426
  liquid, 516
  plant and equipment, 394
  quick, 407

ATM *Automatic teller machine that allows customer of a bank to transfer funds and make deposits or withdrawals*, 91

Audi, 466, 507

Automatic teller machines; *see* **ATM**

Automobile insurance
  compulsory, 493–494
  deductibles, 495
  no-fault, 496
  optional, 494–496
  premiums, 494, 497, 507
  shopping for, 507

Average daily balance *Sum of daily balances divided by number of days in billing cycle*, 357–358

Average inventory *Total of all inventories divided by number of times inventory taken*, 452

Averages; *see* **Mean**; **Median**

Balance sheet *Financial report that lists assets, liabilities, and equity. Report reflects the financial position of the company as of a particular date*, 392
  assets, 392, 394
  elements, 393–395

horizontal analysis, 395–397
  liabilities, 392, 394–395
  owner's equity, 393, 395
  vertical analysis, 395, 396

Baldwin, Mike, 14

Bank discount *The amount of interest charged by a bank on a note. (Maturity value × Bank discount rate × Number of days bank holds note ÷ 360)*, 286, 289

Bank discount rate *Percent of interest*, 286

Bank of America, 370, 372

Bank reconciliation *Process of comparing the bank balance to the checkbook balance so adjustments can be made regarding checks outstanding, deposits in transit, and the like*, 98–101

Bank statement *Report sent by the bank to the owner of the checking account indicating checks processed, deposits made, and so on, along with beginning and ending balances*, 96–97

Banker's Rule *Time is exact days/360 in calculating simple interest*, 267

Banking apps *Special client application programs like checking account balances, paying bills, and transferring funds for those doing online banking*, 101

Banks
  debit cards, 91–92, 370
  fees, 92, 94
  industry trends, 96
  interest rates, 306–307
  technology, 91, 96, 101

Bar graph *Visual representation using horizontal or vertical bars to make comparison or to show relationship on items of similar makeup*, 534–535

Base *Number that represents the whole 100%. It is the whole to which something is being compared. Usually follows word "of"*, 149
  solving for, 152–153

Bater, Jeff, 288

Baumbach, Paul, 283

BE; *see* **Breakeven point**

Bell, Peter, 375

Beneficiary *Person(s) designated to receive the face value of the life insurance when insured dies*, 485–486

Benefit corporation *A new type of corporation with less responsibility to stockholders. These are environmentally friendly corporations*, 393

Benefits, employment, 489

Bernier, Suzanne, 63

Bertolucci, Jeff, 88, 240

Best Buy, 88, 180, 207

Biweekly *Every 2 weeks (26 times in a year)*, 244

Biweekly mortgage *Mortgage payments made every 2 weeks rather than monthly. This payment method takes years off the life of the mortgage and substantially reduces the cost of interest*, 374

Blank endorsement *Current owner of check signs name on back. Whoever presents checks for payment receives the money*, 94

Bodily injury *Auto insurance that pays damages to people injured or killed by your auto,* 493–495, 496

Bond discount *Bond selling for less than the face value,* 514

Bond premium *Bond selling for more than the face value,* 514

Bond yield *Total annual interest divided by total cost,* 515

Bonds *Written promise by a company that borrows money usually with fixed-interest payment until maturity (repayment time),* 514
  quotations, 514–515
  returns, 514, 515

Book value *Cost less accumulated depreciation,* 426

Borrowing; *see* **Loans**

Breakeven analysis, 224–225

Breakeven point (BE) *Point at which seller has covered all expenses and costs and has made no profit or suffered a loss,* 225

Brobeck, Stephen, 115

Brokers; *see* **Stockbrokers**

Building *An asset listed on a balance sheet,* 394; *see also* **Fire insurance**

Business insurance, 489

Bustello, Miguel, 442

Campbell Soup, 398, 399, 426

Cancellation *Reducing process that is used to simplify the multiplication and division of fractions,* 48. *Example:*

$$\frac{1}{\overset{}{\underset{3}{\cancel{6}}}} \times \frac{\overset{2}{\cancel{4}}}{7}$$

Cancellation of fire insurance, 491–492

Capital *Owners' investment in the business,* 393

Carvin, Michael, 392

Cash, 394

Cash advance *Money borrowed by holder of credit card. It is recorded as another purchase and is used in the calculation of the average daily balance,* 357

Cash discount *Savings that result from early payment by taking advantage of discounts offered by the seller; discount is not taken on freight or taxes,* 177, 185–186
  credit periods, 186–188
  credit terms, 188–191
  word problem, 191–192

Cash dividend *Cash distribution of company's profit to owners of stock,* 511; *see also* **Dividends**

Cash value *Except for term insurance, this indicates the value of the policy when terminated. Options fall under the heading of nonforfeiture values,* 486, 487, 488, 489

Cecala, Guy, 388

Centi- (Appendix D) *Prefix indicating .01 of a basic metric unit,* D-1

Chain discount *Two or more trade discounts that are applied to the balance remaining after the previous discount is taken. Often called a series discount,* 182

Check cards, 91–92

Check register *Record-keeping device that records checks paid and deposits made by companies using a checking account,* 93

Check stub *Provides a record of checks written. It is attached to the check,* 93

Checking accounts
  adjusted balances, 98
  fees, 94

  opening, 92
  reconciling, 96–97, 98–101
  statements, 96–97
  using, 93–94

Checks *Written documents signed by appropriate person that direct the bank to pay a specific amount of money to a particular person or company,* 92
  depositing, 94
  endorsements, 94
  outstanding, 98
  writing, 92–93

Circle graph *A visual representation of the parts to the whole,* 535–536

Citibank, 240, 357

Clark, Jane Bennett, 33

Closing costs *Costs incurred when property passes from seller to buyer such as for credit reports, recording costs, points, and so on,* 377

CM; *see* **Contribution margin**

CM *Abbreviation for* **credit memorandum.** *The bank is adding to your account. The CM is found on the bank statement,* 99. *Example:* Bank collects a note for you.

Cohn, Laura, 345

Coinsurance *Type of fire insurance in which the insurer and insured share the risk. Usually there is an 80% coinsurance clause,* 492

Collision *Optional auto insurance that pays for the repairs to your auto from an accident after deductible is met. Insurance company will only pay for repairs up to the value of the auto (less deductible),* 495, 496

Commissions *Payments based on established performance criteria,* 246
  overrides, 247
  salary plus, 247
  straight, 246
  variable, 246

Commissions, broker, 513, 517

Common denominator *To add two or more fractions, denominators must be the same,* 41–43

Common stocks *Units of ownership called shares,* 395, 510; *see also* **Stocks**

Comparative statement *Statement showing data from two or more periods side by side,* 395
  balance sheets, 395–397
  income statements, 403–404

Complement *100% less the stated percent,* 181. *Example:* 18% → 82% is the complement (100% – 18%).

Compound amount *The future value of a loan or investment,* 302

Compound interest *The interest that is calculated periodically and then added to the principal. The next period the interest is calculated on the adjusted principal (old principal plus interest),* 301–302; *see also* **Annuity**
  calculating, 303, 304–305
  compared to simple interest, 303–306
  effective rate, 307
  periods, 302
  rates, 302
  sinking funds, 333–334

Compounded annually *Interest on balance calculated once a year,* 302

Compounded daily *Interest calculated on balance each day,* 302, 307–308

Compounded monthly *Interest on balance calculated twelve times a year,* 302

Compounded quarterly *Interest on balance calculated four times a year,* 302

Compounded semiannually *Interest on balance calculated two times a year,* 302

Compounding *Calculating the interest periodically over the life of the loan and adding it to the principal,* 301–302
  continuous, 307–308
  relationship to present value, 309–312

Comprehensive insurance *Optional auto insurance that pays for damages to the auto caused by factors other than from collision (fire, vandalism, theft, and the like),* 495, 496

Compulsory insurance *Insurance required by law—standard coverage,* 493–494

Connexus Credit Union, 115

Constants *Numbers that have a fixed value such as 3 or –7. Placed on right side of equation; also called knowns,* 119

Consumer Federation of America, 115, 240

Consumer Price Index (CPI), 536, 537

Contingent annuities *Beginning and ending dates of the annuity are uncertain (not fixed),* 325

Contingent liability *Potential liability that may or may not result from discounting a note,* 289

Contribution margin (CM) *Difference between selling price and variable cost,* 225

Conversion periods *How often (a period of time) the interest is calculated in the compounding process. Example:* Daily—each day; monthly—12 times a year; quarterly—every 3 months; semiannually—every 6 months

Conversions
  to decimal fractions, 69–70
  to decimals, 68–69, 145–146
  foreign currency, 74
  of mixed numbers, 38, 69
  to percents, 144–146, 147

Cooper, Brad, 507

Corporation *Company with many owners or stockholders. Equity of these owners is called stockholders' equity,* 393

Cost *Price retailers pay to manufacturer or supplier to bring merchandise into store,* 209; *see also* **Closing costs; Inventory costs**
  asset, 425–426
  fixed, 224
  markups based on, 210–213, 218–219
  variable, 224

Cost of merchandise (goods) sold *Beginning inventory + Net purchases – Ending inventory,* 400, 401, 402, 444

Costco, 88, 207, 240

CPI; *see* **Consumer Price Index**

Credit; *see also* **Loans**
  closed-end, 350
  FICO scores, 349
  open-end, 350, 356
  regulations, 351, 356
  revolving, 355–357

Credit card, 91–92
  average daily balances, 357–358
  balances, 355–358
  interest calculations, 357–358

Credit card *A piece of plastic that allows you to buy on credit,* 370

Credit Card Act *A federal statute passed in 2009 to provide fair and transparent practices to the extension of credit,* 356, 370

Credit due dates, calculating, 186–188

Credit memo (CM) *Bank transactions that increase customer's account,* 99

Credit period *Credit days are counted from date of invoice. Has no relationship to the discount period*, 186
  due dates, 186–188
  end of, 186
Credit reports, 349
Credit scores, 349, 373
Credit terms, 188–191
Credit unions, 115, 370
CreditSesame.com, 299
Cumulative preferred stock *Holders of preferred stock must receive current year and any dividends in arrears before any dividends are paid out to the holders of common stock*, 510, 512
Current assets *Assets that are used up or converted into cash within 1 year or operating cycle*, 394
Current liabilities *Obligations of a company due within 1 year*, 394
Current ratio *Current assets divided by current liabilities*, 407

Daily balance *Calculated to determine customer's finance charge: Previous balance + Any cash advances + Purchases – Payments*, 358; *see also* **Average daily balance**
Days, 186
Debit card *Transactions result in money being immediately deducted from customer's checking account*, 91–92, 370
Debit memo (DM) *A debit transaction bank does for customers*, 99
Deca- (Appendix D) *Prefix indicating 10 times basic metric unit*, D-1
Deci- (Appendix D) *Prefix indicating .1 of basic metric unit*, D-1
Decimal equivalent *Decimal represents the same value as the fraction*, 68. *Example:*

$$.05 = \frac{5}{100}$$

Decimal fraction *Decimal representing a fraction; the denominator has a power of 10*, 68
  converting to, 69–70
  converting to decimals, 68
Decimal point *Center of the decimal system—located between units and tenths. Numbers to left are whole numbers; to the right are decimal numbers*, 4, 66
Decimal system *The U.S. base 10 numbering system that uses the 10 single-digit numbers shown on a calculator*, 4
Decimals *Numbers written to the right of a decimal point*, 66. *Example: 5.3, 18.22*
  adding, 71–72
  applications, 74
  converting fractions to, 68–69
  converting percents to, 145–146
  converting to percents, 144–145
  dividing, 73, 74–75
  mixed, 69–70
  multiplying, 73, 74–75
  pure, 69–70
  reading, 67
  repeating, 67
  rounding, 67–68
  subtracting, 71–72
Declining-balance method *Accelerated method of depreciation. The depreciation each year is calculated by book value beginning each year times the rate*, 429–430

Deductibles *Amount insured pays before insurance company pays. Usually the higher the deductible, the lower the premium will be*, 495
Deductions *Amounts deducted from gross earnings to arrive at net pay*, 245, 248–251
Deferred payment price *Total of all monthly payments plus down payment*, 351
Dell, 240
Denominator *The number of a common fraction below the division line (bar)*, 36. *Example:*

$$\frac{8}{9}, \text{ in which 9 is the denominator}$$

  least common, 41–43
Deposit slip *Document that shows date, name, account number, and items making up a deposit*, 92, 93
Deposits in transit *Deposits not received or processed by bank at the time the bank statement is prepared*, 99
Depreciation *Process of allocating the cost of an asset (less residual value) over the asset's estimated life*, 425
  accelerated, 429
  accumulated, 426
  declining-balance method, 429–430
  for partial years, 427
  straight-line method, 426–427, 429
  for tax purposes, 431–432
  units-of-production method, 428
Depreciation causes *Normal use, product obsolescence, aging, and so on*, 426
Depreciation expense *Process involving asset cost, estimated useful life, and residual value (salvage or trade-in value)*, 425–426
Depreciation schedule *Table showing amount of depreciation expense, accumulated depreciation, and book value for each period of time for a plant asset*, 426–427
Dervos, Michael, 527
Deveny, Kathleen, 533
DHL Global Delivery, 342
Difference *The resulting answer from a subtraction problem*, 11. *Example:* Minuend less subtrahend equals difference: 215 – 15 = 200
Differential pay schedule *Pay rate is based on a schedule of units completed*, 246
Digit *Our decimal number system of 10 characters from 0 to 9*, 4
Discount, 514
Discount *Amount bond sells below $1,000*, 514
Discount period *Amount of time to take advantage of a cash discount*, 186, 290
Discounting a note *Receiving cash from selling a note to a bank before the due date of a note. Steps to discount include: (1) calculate maturity value, (2) calculate number of days bank waits for money, (3) calculate bank discount, and (4) calculate proceeds*, 289–290
Discounting Treasury bills, 288
Discounts; *see* **Cash discount; Trade discount**
Distribution of overhead *Companies distribute overhead by floor space or sales volume*, 453–454
Dividend *Number in the division process that is being divided by another*, 16. *Example:*

  15 ÷ 5, in which 15 is the dividend.

  estimating, 17
  shortcuts, 17

Dividends *Distribution of company's profit in cash or stock to owners of stock*, 510
  amounts, 511–512
  cash, 511
Dividends in arrears *Dividends that accumulate when a company fails to pay cumulative dividends to preferred stockholders*, 510
Division
  of decimals, 73, 74–75
  of fractions, 49
  of mixed numbers, 49
  of whole numbers, 16
Divisor *Number in the division process that is dividing into another*, 16. *Example:*

  15 ÷ 5, in which 5 is the divisor.

DM *Abbreviation for debit memorandum. The bank is charging your account. The DM is found on the bank statement*, 99. *Example: NSF*
Dollar markdown *Original selling price less the reduction to price. Markdown may be stated as a percent of the original selling price*, 222. *Example:*

$$\frac{\text{Dollar markdown}}{\text{Original selling price}}$$

Dollar markup *Selling price less cost. Difference is the amount of the markup. Markup is also expressed in percent*, 210, 211–212, 216
Down payment *Amount of initial cash payment made when item is purchased*, 350
Drafts *Written orders like checks instructing a bank, credit union, or savings and loan institution to pay your money to a person or organization*, 92
Draw *The receiving of advance wages to cover business or personal expenses. Once wages are earned, drawing amount reduces actual amount received*, 246
Drawee *One ordered to pay the check*, 93
Drawer *One who writes the check*, 93
Due date *Maturity date, or when the note will be repaid*, 186–188
Dunkin' Donuts, 17, 324

E*Trade, 483
Earnings, retained, 395; *see also* **Profit; Wages**
Earnings per share (EPS) *Annual earnings ÷ Total number of shares outstanding*, 511
eBay, 88, 265, 285
Eckblad, Marshall, 390
Edmunds.com, 349
EDP Renewables, 480
Effective rate *True rate of interest. The more frequent the compounding, the higher the effective rate*, 288
  annual percentage yield, 306–307
  for compound interest, 307
  of simple discount note, 287–288
  of simple interest note, 287
Efrati, Amir, 117, 142
EFT; *see* **Electronic funds transfer**
Electronic deposits *Credit card run through terminal which approves (or disapproves) the amount and adds it to company's bank balance*, 98
Electronic funds transfer (EFT) *A computerized operation that electronically transfers funds among parties without the use of paper checks*, 98

Employees; *see* **Commissions; Payroll; Wages**
Employee's Withholding Allowance Certificate (W-4) *Completed by employee to indicate allowance claimed to determine amount of FIT that is deducted,* 248, 249
Employers
  insurance, 489
  responsibilities, 251–252
  workers' compensation, 489
Employment benefits, 489
End of credit period *Last day from date of invoice when customer can take cash discount,* 186
End of month (EOM) *(also proximo) Cash discount period begins at the end of the month invoice is dated. After the 25th discount period, one additional month results,* 190–191
Endorse *Signing the back of the check; thus ownership is transferred to another party,* 94
Endowment life *Form of insurance that pays at maturity a fixed amount of money to insured or to the beneficiary. Insurance coverage would terminate when paid—similar to term life,* 488
Enron, 392
EOM; *see* **End of month**
EPS; *see* **Earnings per share**
Equation *Math statement that shows equality for expressions or numbers, or both,* 118
Equation equality rule, 120
Equation solving
  equation equality rule, 120
  like unknowns rule, 122
  multiple processes rule, 121
  opposite process rule, 119
  parentheses rule, 121
  solving for the unknown rule, 119
  for unknown, 118–122
Equivalent (fractional) *Two or more fractions equivalent in value,* 39
Escrow account *Lending institution requires that each month $\frac{1}{12}$ of the insurance cost and real estate taxes be kept in a special account,* 377
Estate planning, 553
Estimated useful life *How long asset will be in use,* 426
Estimating
  addition, 11
  division, 17
  multiplication, 15
Exact days, 187, 188
Exact interest *Calculating simple interest using 365 days per year in time,* 266–267
Excise tax *Tax that government levies on particular products and services. Tax on specific luxury items or nonessentials,* 470
Expenses *Cost of doing business; listed on the income statement,* 401
  depreciation, 426
  operating, 210, 399, 401
  overhead, 453–454
  prepaid, 394
Expression *A meaningful combination of numbers and letters called terms,* 118, 119
Extended term insurance *Resulting from nonforfeiture, it keeps the policy for the full face value going without further premium payments for a specific period of time,* 488

Face amount *Dollar amount stated in policy,* 486
Face value *Amount of insurance that is stated on*

the policy. It is usually the maximum amount for which the insurance company is liable, 487
  of fire insurance, 492
  of life insurance, 488
  of promissory notes, 286
Facebook, 14, 142, 176, 209, 243, 400, 529
Fair Credit and Charge Card Disclosure Act of 1988 *Act that tightens controls on credit card companies soliciting new business,* 356
Fair Isaac Corporation, 349
Fair Labor Standards Act *Federal law has minimum wage standards and the requirement of overtime pay. There are many exemptions for administrative personnel and for others,* 244
Family Dollar, 143
FC; *see* **Fixed cost**
Federal Express, 342
Federal income tax (FIT) withholding *Federal tax withheld from paycheck,* 249–251
Federal Insurance Contribution Act (FICA) *Percent of base amount of each employee's salary. FICA taxes used to fund retirement, disabled workers, Medicare, and so on. FICA is now broken down into Social Security and Medicare,* 249
Federal Reserve, 266
Federal Unemployment Tax Act (FUTA) *Tax paid by employer. Current rate is .8% on first $7,000 of earnings,* 251, 252
Federal withholding tax; *see* **Federal Income tax**
FICA; *see* **Federal Insurance Contribution Act**
FICO scores, 349
Fiegerman, Seth, 388
FIFO; *see* **First-in, first-out method**
Finance charge *Total payments – Actual loan cost,* 350, 356–358
Financial statements; *see* **Balance sheet; Income statement; Ratio analysis; Trend analysis**
Fire insurance *Stipulated percent (normally 80%) of value that is required for insurance company to pay to reimburse one's losses,* 490
  for businesses, 489, 490–491
  canceling, 491–492
  coinsurance, 492
  premiums, 490–491
  short-rate table, 491
First-in, first-out (FIFO) method *This method assumes the first inventory brought into the store will be the first sold. Ending inventory is made up of goods most recently purchased,* 446–447
FIT; *see* **Federal Income tax withholding**
Fixed cost (FC) *Costs that do not change with increase or decrease in sales,* 224
Fixed rate mortgage *Monthly payment fixed over number of years, usually 30 years,* 374
FOB destination *Seller pays cost of freight in getting goods to buyer's location,* 180
FOB shipping point *Buyer pays cost of freight in getting goods to his location,* 179
Ford Motor Company, 153, 440, 466, 507
Foreclosure *A legal process used by lender to recover balance of the loan from the borrower who has stopped making payments on the loan,* 373
Foreign currency conversions, 74
Formula *Equation that expresses in symbols a general fact, rule, or principle,* 118

Fraction *Expresses a part of a whole number,* 36. *Example:*

$$\frac{5}{6} \text{ expresses 5 parts out of 6}$$

  adding, 41–43
  converting to decimals, 68–69
  converting to percents, 147
  converting to whole or mixed numbers, 37–38
  denominators, 36
  dividing, 49
  higher terms, 39
  improper, 37–38
  lowest terms, 38–39
  multiplying, 47–48
  numerators, 36
  proper, 36–37
  subtracting, 44
  types, 36–37
Freight terms *Determine how freight will be paid. Most common freight terms are FOB shipping point and FOB destination,* 179–180
Frequency distribution *Shows by table the number of times event(s) occurs,* 533–534, 539–540
Fruit of the Loom, Inc., 449
Fry's Electronics, 207
Full endorsement *This endorsement identifies the next person or company to whom the check is to be transferred,* 94
FUTA; *see* **Federal Unemployment Tax Act**
Future value (FV) *Final amount of the loan or investment at the end of the last period. Also called compound amount,* 301–302
  relationship to present value, 309–312
Future value of annuity *Future dollar amount of a series of payments plus interest,* 324–325
  annuity due, 327–329
  ordinary annuity, 325–327, 329
Future value table, 304, 305
FV; *see* **Future value**

GAAP *Accounting rules or standards set by a U.S. policy board to establish commonly accepted reporting of accounting information,* 448
Gabriel, Stuart, 380
Gamer Grub, 290, 291
Gap, 209, 210–212, 215–216, 453
Gazelle, 88
GDS; *see* **General Depreciation System**
General Depreciation System (GDS) *Most common (MACRS) system to calculate depreciation,* 431
General Mills, 402, 426, 511, 513
Generally Accepted Accounting Principles; *see* **GAAP**
Gerstner, Lisa, 299
Gillette Corporation, 426, 446
Gillis, Jack, 240
Goldwasser, Joan, 115, 370
Google Inc., 41, 71, 117, 142, 207, 243
Graduated-payment mortgage (GPM) *Borrower pays less at beginning of mortgage. As years go on, the payments increase,* 374
Gram (Appendix D) *Basic unit of weight in metric system. An ounce equals about 28 grams,* D-1, D-2
Graphs
  bar, 534–535
  circle, 535–536

line, 535
misleading, 533
Greatest common divisor *The largest possible number that will divide evenly into both the numerator and denominator*, 38–39
Gross pay *Wages before deductions*, 245
Gross profit *Difference between cost of bringing goods into the store and selling price of the goods*, 209
Gross profit from sales *Net sales – Cost of goods sold*, 401, 403
Gross profit method *Used to estimate value of inventory*, 451
Gross sales *Total earned sales before sales returns and allowances or sales discounts*, 400
Groupon, 176
Gumbinger, Keith, 388

Health insurance, 489
Hecto- (Appendix D) *Prefix indicating 100 times basic metric unit*, D-1
Hershey's, 12
Higher terms *Expressing a fraction with a new numerator and denominator that is equivalent to the original*, 39. *Example:*

$$\frac{2}{9} \rightarrow \frac{6}{27}$$

Hobson, Katherine, 116
Home equity loan *Cheap and readily accessible lines of credit backed by equity in your home; tax-deductible; rates can be locked in*, 374
Honda, 65, 349, 440, 466
Horizontal analysis *Method of analyzing financial reports where each total this period is compared by amount of percent to the same total last period*, 395
of balance sheet, 395–397
of income statement, 404
Housing costs, 377; *see also* **Mortgage**
Hyundai, 507

IBM, 179, 180
IFRS *Accounting rules or standards used internationally to establish commonly accepted reporting of accounting information*, 448
Improper fraction *Fraction that has a value equal to or greater than 1; numerator is equal to or greater than the denominator*, 37–38. *Example:*

$$\frac{6}{6}, \frac{14}{9}$$

Income statement *Financial report that lists the revenues and expenses for a specific period of time. It reflects how well the company is performing*, 399
depreciation expense, 426
elements, 400–401
formulas, 402–403
horizontal analysis, 404
net income, 399
operating expenses, 399, 401
revenues, 399, 400
vertical analysis, 403
Income tax or FIT *Tax that depends on allowances claimed, marital status, and wages earned*, 249–251
Indemnity *Insurance company's payment to insured for loss*, 492n
Index numbers *Express the relative changes in a variable compared with some base, which is taken as 100*, 536

Individual retirement account (IRA) *An account established for retirement planning*, 141, 345, 483
Installment cost *Down payment + (Number of payments × Monthly payment). Also called deferred payment*, 350, 351
Installment loan *Loan paid off with a series of equal periodic payments*, 350
Installment purchases *Purchase of an item(s) that requires periodic payments for a specific period of time, usually with a high rate of interest*, 350
amortization, 350
amount financed, 350
deferred payment price, 351
down payments, 350
finance charge, 350
monthly payments, 353–354
Insurance; *see also* **Life insurance**
auto, 493–496
business, 489
fire, 490–492
health, 489
long-term care, 553
workers' compensation, 489
Insured *Customer or policyholder*, 485
Insurer *The insurance company that issues the policy*, 485
Interest *Principal × Rate × Time*, 265
annual percentage rate, 351–353
annual percentage yield, 306–307
compound, 301–302, 303–306
on installment loans, 350
on mortgages, 376–377, 388
nominal rates, 306–307
rate, 269
on revolving charge accounts, 356–358
simple, 265–267, 268–269
Interest rates
on loans, 265, 266
on mortgages, 374, 376–377
on promissory notes, 286
Interest-bearing note *Maturity value of note is greater than amount borrowed since interest is added on*, 286
Interest-only mortgage *Type of mortgage where in early years only interest payment is required*, 374
International Financial Reporting Standards; *see* **IFRS**
Inventory
average, 452
on balance sheet, 444
merchandise, 394, 400
Inventory control
comparison of methods, 448–449
periodic method, 444
perpetual method, 444
physical counts, 444, 450
Inventory costs
FIFO method, 446–447
gross profit method, 451
LIFO method, 447–448
retail method, 450–451
specific identification method, 444–445
weighted-average method, 445–446
Inventory turnover *Ratio that indicates how quickly inventory turns:*

$$\frac{\text{Cost of goods sold}}{\text{Average inventory at cost}}, 452–453$$

Investments; *see also* **Stocks**
bonds, 514–515
mutual funds, 516–517
principles, 509
returns, 513, 514
Invoice *Document recording purchase and sales transactions*, 178
credit periods, 186–188
credit terms, 188–191
partial payments, 192
IRA; *see* **Individual retirement account**

J. M. Smucker, 143
Jargon, Julie, 399
JIT, *see* **Just–in-time inventory system**
JPMorgan Chase & Co., 101, 372
Just-in-time (JIT) inventory system *System that eliminates inventories. Suppliers provide materials daily as manufacturing company needs them*, 453

Kahler, Rick, 388
Kardashians, 370
Karp, Hannah, 178
Kellogg Co., 390
Kia, 466, 507
Killam, Caitlin, 283
Kilo- (Appendix D) *Prefix indicating 1,000 times basic metric unit*, D-1
Kiplinger, Knight, 63
Kmart, 222
Known *A number or fact that is specified*, 119
Koch, Jim, 291
Kohl's Corp., 180
Kontos, Tom, 440
Korn, Melissa, 143

Lake Michigan Credit Union, 115
Land *Asset on balance sheet that does not depreciate*, 394, 426
Lankford, Kimberly, 141, 262, 483, 507
Last-in, first-out (LIFO) method *This method assumes the last inventory brought into the store will be the first sold. Ending inventory is made up of the oldest goods purchased*, 447–448
Least common denominator (LCD) *Smallest nonzero whole number into which all denominators will divide evenly*, 41–43. *Example:*

$$\frac{2}{3} \text{ and } \frac{1}{4} \quad \text{LCD} = 12$$

Leestma, David, 33
Leitz, Linda, 63
Lending Club Corp., 265, 285
Level premium term *Insurance premium that is fixed, say, for 50 years*, 486
Liabilities *Amount business owes to creditors*, 394
on balance sheet, 392, 394–395
contingent, 289
current, 394
long-term, 395
Liability insurance *Insurance for bodily injury to others and damage to someone else's property*, 493
Life insurance
for employees, 489
nonforfeiture values, 488–489
premiums, 486, 487
terminology, 485–486
types, 486–488
LIFO; *see* **Last-in, first-out method**
Light, Joe, 243
Like fractions *Proper fractions with the same denominators*, 41, 44

Like terms *Terms that are made up with the same variable: A + 2A + 3A = 6A*

Like unknowns rule, 122

Limited payment life (20-payment life) *Premiums are for 20 years (a fixed period) and provide paid-up insurance for the full face value of the policy,* 487–488

Line graphs *Graphical presentation that involves a time element. Shows trends, failures, backlogs, and the like,* 535

Line of credit *Provides immediate financing up to an approved limit*

Liquid assets *Cash or other assets that can be converted quickly into cash,* 516

List price *Suggested retail price paid by customers,* 178, 181–182

Liter (Appendix D) *Basic unit of measure in metric, for volume,* D-1, D-2

Loan amortization table *Table used to calculate monthly payments,* 354–355

Loans; *see also* **Credit; Installment purchases; Interest; Mortgage; Promissory note**
  compound amounts, 302
  home equity, 374
  interest rates, 265, 266
  maturity value, 265
  partial payments, 270–271
  principal, 265, 268–269

Long-term care insurance, 553

Long-term liabilities *Debts or obligations that company does not have to pay within 1 year,* 395

Loten, Angus, 265, 285

Lowest terms *Expressing a fraction when no number divides evenly into the numerator and denominator except the number 1,* 38–39. *Example:*

$$\frac{5}{10} \rightarrow \frac{1}{2}$$

MACRS; *see* **Modified Accelerated Cost Recovery System**

Macy's, 208, 209, 527

Madonna, 527

Maker *One who writes the note,* 286

Mallard Advisors, 283

Maltby, Emily, 284

Margin *Difference between cost of bringing goods into store and selling price of goods,* 209

Markdowns *Reductions from original selling price caused by seasonal changes, special promotions, and so on,* 222

Markup *Amount retailers add to cost of goods to cover operating expenses and make a profit,* 209
  based on cost, 210–213, 218–219
  based on selling price, 215–219
  dollar amount, 210, 211–212, 216

Markup percent calculation *Markup percent on cost × Cost = Dollar markup; or Markup percent on selling price × Selling price = Dollar markup,* 210–212, 215–216

MasterCard, 370

Mattioli, Dana, 180

Maturity date *Date the principal and interest are due,* 286

Maturity value (MV) *Principal plus interest (if interest is charged). Represents amount due on the due date,* 265

Maturity value of note *Amount of cash paid on the due date. If interest-bearing*

maturity, value is greater than amount borrowed, 286

Mazda, 507

McCartin, Michael, 507

McDonald's, 2, 3, 35, 242, 251, 405

McGraw-Hill Co.s, 178, 180, 182, 452

McQueen, M. P., 372

Mean *Statistical term that is found by:*

$$\frac{\text{Sum of all figures}}{\text{Number of figures}}, 530–531$$

Measure of dispersion *Number that describes how the numbers of a set of data are spread out or dispersed,* 538–539

Median *Statistical term that represents the central point or midpoint of a series of numbers,* 531–532

Medicare *Part of FICA tax that has no minimum base,* 249

Mercedes, 466

Merchandise inventory *Cost of goods for resale,* 394, 400; *see also* **Inventory**

Meter (Appendix D) *Basic unit of length in metric system. A meter is a little longer than a yard,* D-1, D-2

Metric system (Appendix D) *A decimal system of weights and measures. The basic units are meters, grams, and liters,* D-1–D-2

Microsoft, 529

Miley, John, 63, 483

Mill, 472

$\frac{1}{10}$ *of a cent or* $\frac{1}{1,000}$ *of a dollar.*

In decimal, it is .001. In application:

$$\frac{\text{Property}}{\text{tax due}} = \text{Mills} \times .001 \times \text{Assessed valuation}$$

Milli- (Appendix D) *Prefix indicating .001 of basic metric unit,* D-1

Minuend *In a subtraction problem, the larger number from which another is subtracted,* 11. *Example:* 50 – 40 = 10

Mitsubishi, 466

Mixed decimal *Combination of a whole number and decimal, such as 59.8, 810.85,* 69–70

Mixed number *Sum of a whole number greater than zero and a proper fraction,* 37. *Example:*

$$2\frac{1}{4}, 3\frac{3}{9}$$

  adding, 43–44
  converting fractions to, 38
  converting to decimals, 69
  dividing, 49
  multiplying, 48
  subtracting, 44–45

Mobile banking *Doing banking transactions on a mobile device such as a smartphone or tablet,* 96, 101

Mode *Value that occurs most often in a series of numbers,* 532

Modified Accelerated Cost Recovery System (MACRS) *Part of Tax Reform Act of 1986 that revised depreciation schedules of ACRS. Tax Bill of 1989, 2010 updates MACRS,* 431–432

Monthly *Some employers pay employees monthly,* 244

Monthly payment *Amount paid each period to pay off part of a mortgage,* 375–377, 378–379

Morningstar, 527

Morrison, Denise, 399

Morrison, Scott, 176

Mortgage *Cost of home less down payment,* 374
  amortization, 375–376, 378–379
  biweekly, 374
  closing costs, 377
  escrow account, 377
  fixed rate, 374
  foreclosures, 373
  interest cost, 376–377, 388
  interest-only, 374
  monthly payments, 375–377, 378–379
  points, 377
  refinancing, 380, 388
  reverse, 374–375
  types, 374

Mortgage note payable *Debt owed on a building that is a long-term liability; often the building is the collateral,* 395

Motor vehicle insurance; *see* **Automobile insurance**

Mullin, Keith, 291

Multiple processes rule, 121

Multiplicand *The first or top number being multiplied in a multiplication problem,* 14. *Example:*

Product = Multiplicand × Multiplier
12 = 20 × 2

Multiplication
  checking, 15
  of decimals, 73, 74–75
  estimating, 15
  of fractions, 47–48
  of mixed numbers, 48
  shortcuts, 15–16
  of whole numbers, 14–15

Multiplier *The second or bottom number doing the multiplication in a problem,* 14. *Example:*

Product = Multiplicand × Multiplier
12 = 20 × 2

Muthler, Lauren, 423

Mutual fund *Investors buy shares in the fund's portfolio (group of stocks and/or bonds),* 516
  commissions, 517
  net asset values, 516–517
  quotations, 517

MV; *see* **Maturity value**

National Credit Union Administration, 115

NAV; *see* **Net asset value**

Nazari, Adrian, 299

Net asset value (NAV) *The dollar value of one mutual fund share; calculated by subtracting current liabilities from current market value of fund's investments and dividing this by number of shares outstanding,* 516–517

Net income *Gross profit less operating expenses,* 210, 401, 403

Net pay; *see* **Net wages**

Net price *List price less amount of trade discount. The net price is before any cash discount,* 178, 181, 182–183; *see also* **Trade discount**

Net price equivalent rate *When multiplied times the list price, this rate or factor produces the actual cost to the buyer. Rate is found by taking the complement of each term in the discount and multiplying them together (do not round off),* 182–183

Net proceeds *Maturity value less bank discount,* 287

Net profit (net income) *Gross profit – Operating expenses,* 210

Net purchases *Purchases – Purchase discounts – Purchase returns and allowances,* 401

Net sales *Gross sales – Sales discounts – Sales returns and allowances,* 400, 402, 407

Net wages *Gross pay less deductions,* 251

Net worth *Assets less liabilities*

Newegg.com, 180

Nissan, 440, 466

No-fault insurance *Involves bodily injury. Damage (before a certain level) that is paid by an insurance company no matter who is to blame,* 496

Nominal rate *Stated rate,* 306–307

Nonforfeiture values *When a life insurance policy is terminated (except term), it represents (1) the available cash value, (2) additional extended term, or (3) additional paid-up insurance,* 488–489

Non-interest-bearing note *Note where the maturity value will be equal to the amount of money borrowed since no additional interest is charged,* 286, 290

Nonsufficient funds (NSF) *Drawer's account lacked sufficient funds to pay written amount of check,* 99

Noodles & Company, 237

Normal distribution *Data are spread symmetrically about the mean,* 539–540

Notes; *see also* **Loans**
discounting, 289–290
interest-bearing, 286
simple discount, 286–288
simple interest, 287

NSF; *see* **Nonsufficient funds**

Number of periods *Number of years times number of times interest is compounded per year,* 302

Numerator *Number of a common fraction above the division line (bar),* 36. *Example:*

$\frac{8}{9}$ in which 8 is the numerator

Office Depot, 207

Olson, Mark W., 392

Open-end credit *Set payment period. Also, additional credit amounts can be added up to a set limit. It is a revolving charge account,* 350, 356

Operating expenses (overhead) *Regular expenses of doing business. These are not costs,* 210
on income statement, 399, 401
overhead, 453–454

Opposite process rule, 119

Ordinary annuity *Annuity that is paid (or received) at end of the time period,* 325; *see also* **Annuity**
future value, 325–327, 329
present value, 330–331

Ordinary dating *Cash discount is available within the discount period. Full amount due by end of credit period if discount is missed,* 188–189

Ordinary interest *Calculating simple interest using 360 days per year in time,* 267

Ordinary life insurance; *see* **Straight life insurance**

Outstanding balance *Amount left to be paid on a loan,* 356

Outstanding checks *Checks written but not yet processed by the bank before bank statement preparation,* 98

Overdraft *Occurs when company or person wrote a check without enough money in the bank to pay for it (NSF check),* 97n

Overhead expenses *Operating expenses not directly associated with a specific department or product,* 453–454; *see also* **Operating expenses**

Override *Commission that managers receive due to sales by people that they supervise,* 247

Overtime *Time-and-a-half pay for more than 40 hours of work,* 244–245

Owner's equity; *see* **Capital**; **Stockholders' equity**

P&G; *see* **Procter & Gamble**

Paid-up insurance *A certain level of insurance can continue, although the premiums are terminated. This results from the nonforfeiture value (except term). Result is a reduced paid-up policy until death,* 487

Panaccione, Carlo, 345

Panasonic, 207

Parentheses rule, 121

Partial payments, 192

Partial products *Numbers between multiplier and product,* 14

Partial quotient *Occurs when divisor doesn't divide evenly into the dividend,* 16

Partnership *Business with two or more owners,* 393

Pay periods, 244

Payee *One who is named to receive the amount of the check,* 93
of promissory notes, 286

Payment periods *Length of payments used to calculate maturity value,* 324, 329

Payroll; *see also* **Commissions**; **Wages**
calculations, 244–247
deductions, 245, 248–251
pay periods, 244
unemployment taxes, 251–252

Payroll register *Multicolumn form to record payroll data,* 248

PE ratio; *see* **Price-earnings (PE) ratio**

Pentagon Federal Credit Union, 299

Percent *Stands for hundredths,* 143–144. *Example:*

4% is 4 parts of one hundred, or $\frac{4}{100}$

converting decimals to, 144–145
converting fractions to, 147
converting to decimals, 145–146
fractional, 146
portion formula, 149–153
rounding, 145

Percent decrease *Calculated by decrease in price over original amount,* 154, 155–156

Percent increase *Calculated by increase in price over original amount,* 153, 154–155

Percent markup on cost *Dollar markup divided by the cost; thus, markup is a percent of the cost,* 210–213, 218–219

Percent markup on selling price *Dollar markup divided by the selling price; thus, markup is a percent of the selling price,* 216, 218–219

Percentage method *A method to calculate withholdings. Opposite of wage bracket method,* 249–251

Periodic inventory system *Physical count of inventory taken at end of a time period. Inventory records are not continually updated,* 444

Periods *Number of years times the number of times compounded per year (see* **Conversion period***),* 302

Perishables *Goods or services with a limited life,* 222–223

Perpetual inventory system *Inventory records are continually updated; opposite of periodic inventory system,* 444

Personal property *Items of possession, like cars, home, furnishings, jewelry, and so on. These are taxed by the property tax (don't forget real property is also taxed),* 471

Peterson, Earl, 440

Peterson, Noelle, 440

Pew Research, 63

Phair, Stephanie, 177

Piecework *Compensation based on the number of items produced or completed,* 245

Piol, Jonathan, 440

Place value *The digit value that results from its position in a number,* 4, 5, 66–67

Plant and equipment *Assets that will last longer than 1 year,* 394

PMI; *see* **Private Mortgage Insurance**

Point of sale *Terminal that accepts cards (like those used at ATMs) to purchase items at retail outlets. No cash is physically exchanged*

Points *Percentage(s) of mortgage that represents an additional cost of borrowing. It is a one-time payment made at closing,* 377

Policy *Written insurance contract,* 485–486

Policyholder *The insured,* 485

Portion *Amount or part that results from multiplying the base times the rate. Not expressed as a percent; it is expressed as a number,* 149
formula, 149–153
solving for, 150–151

Powell, Ken, 402

Preferred stock *Type of stock that has a preference regarding a corporation's profits and assets,* 510, 512

Premium *Periodic payments that one makes for various kinds of insurance protection,* 486
for auto insurance, 494, 497, 507
for fire insurance, 490–491

Premium on bonds *Bond purchase price above $1,000,* 514

Prepaid expenses *Items a company buys that have not been used are shown as assets,* 394

Prepaid rent *Rent paid in advance,* 396, 397

Present value (PV) *How much money will have to be deposited today (or at some date) to reach a specific amount of maturity (in the future),* 302
relationship to future value, 309–312

Present value of an ordinary annuity *Amount of money needed today to receive a specified stream (annuity) of money in the future,* 330–331

Present value table, 310, 311

Price relative *The quotient of the current price divided by some previous year's price—the base year—multiplied by 100,* 536

Price-earnings (PE) ratio *Closing price per share of stock divided by earnings per share,* 511

Prices; *see also* **Markup**; **Trade discount**
deferred payment, 351
list, 178, 181–182
net, 178, 181, 182–183
selling, 209, 212, 222–223, 225
Prime number *Whole number greater than 1 that is only divisible by itself and 1, 42–43. Examples: 2, 3, 5*
Principal *Amount of money that is originally borrowed, loaned, or deposited,* 265, 268–269
Private Mortgage Insurance (PMI), 377
Proceeds *Maturity value less the bank charge,* 286–287, 289
Procter & Gamble (P&G), 178
Product *Answer of a multiplication process, such as:*

$$\begin{array}{ccccc} \text{Product} & = & \text{Multiplicand} & \times & \text{Multiplier} \\ 50 & = & 5 & \times & 10 \end{array}, 14$$

Profit
gross, 209, 401, 403, 451
net, 210
on net sales, 407
Promissory note *Written unconditional promise to pay a certain sum (with or without interest) at a fixed time in the future,* 286
discounting, 289–290
interest-bearing, 286
non-interest-bearing, 286, 290
simple discount notes, 286–288
structure, 286
Proper fractions *Fractions with a value less than 1; numerator is smaller than denominator, such as $\frac{5}{9}$,* 36–37
converting to decimals, 69
dividing, 49
reciprocals, 49
Property damage *Auto insurance covering damages that are caused to the property of others,* 493–495
Property tax *Tax that raises revenue for school districts, cities, counties, and the like,* 471
assessed value, 471
calculating, 472–473
rates, 471–472
Property tax due *Tax rate × Assessed valuation,* 472
Proskie, Ken, 423
Prosper Marketplace Inc., 265, 285
Proximo (prox) *Same as end of month,* 190n
Purchase discounts *Savings received by buyer for paying for merchandise before a certain date,* 401
Purchase returns and allowances *Cost of merchandise returned to store due to damage, defects, and so on. An allowance is a cost reduction that results when buyer keeps or buys damaged goods,* 400
Purchases *Merchandise for resale; listed on the income statement,* 400
Pure decimal *Has no whole number(s) to the left of the decimal point, such as .45,* 69–70
Putnam Mutual Funds, 517
PV; *see* **Present value**

Quick assets *Current assets – Inventory – Prepaid expenses,* 407
Quick ratio *(Current assets – Inventory – Prepaid expenses) ÷ Current liabilities,* 407
Quotient *The answer of a division problem,* 16

Radio Shack, 88
Ramirez, Elva, 177
Randall, Maya Jackson, 375
Range *Difference between the highest and lowest values in a group of values or set of data,* 538
Rapoport, Michael, 392
Rate *Percent that is multiplied times the base that indicates what part of the base we are trying to compare to. Rate is not a whole number,* 149
solving for, 151–152
Rate for each period *Annual rate divided by number of times interest is compounded in one year,* 302
Rate of interest *Percent of interest that is used to compute the interest charge on a loan for a specific time,* 265, 266; *see also* **Interest rates**
Ratio analysis *Relationship of one number to another,* 405–406
Real estate; *see also* **Mortgage**
buildings, 394
housing, 377
land, 394, 426
short sales, 373
Real property *Land, buildings, and so on, which are taxed by the property tax,* 471
Receipt of goods (ROG) *Used in calculating the cash discount period; begins the day that the goods are received,* 189–190
Reciprocal of a fraction *The interchanging of the numerator and the denominator. Inverted number is the reciprocal,* 49. *Example:*

$$\frac{6}{7} \to \frac{7}{6}$$

Reduced paid-up insurance *Insurance that uses cash value to buy protection, face amount is less than original policy, and policy continues for life,* 488
Rehmann Financial, 283
Remainder *Leftover amount in division,* 16
Repeating decimals *Decimal numbers that repeat themselves continuously and thus do not end,* 67
Residual value *Estimated value of a plant asset after depreciation is taken (or end of useful life),* 426
Restrictive endorsement *Check must be deposited to the payee's account. This restricts one from cashing it,* 94
Retail method *Method to estimate cost of ending inventory. The cost ratio times ending inventory at retail equals the ending cost of inventory,* 450
Retailers; *see also* **Markup**; **Trade discount**
breakeven analysis, 224–225
costs, 209
free shipping, 180
inventories, 444, 450
markdowns, 222
online, 177, 180, 469
perishables, 222
Retained earnings *Amount of earnings that is kept in the business,* 395
Retirement savings, 141, 321, 345
Return on equity *Net income divided by stockholders' equity,* 407
Returns and allowances, 400
Returns on investment, 513
Revenues *Total earned sales (cash or credit) less any sales discounts, returns, or allowances,* 399, 400

Reverse mortgage *Federal Housing Administration makes it possible for older homeowners to live in their homes and get cash or monthly income,* 374–375
Revolving charge account *Charges for a customer are allowed up to a specified maximum, a minimum monthly payment is required, and interest is charged on balance outstanding,* 356–358
Risk, in investing, 509; *see also* **Insurance**
ROG *Receipt of goods; cash discount period begins when goods are received, not ordered,* 189–190
Rosenthal, Larry, 345
Roth IRAs, 141, 345
Rounding
percents, 145
whole numbers, 6–7
Rounding all the way *Process to estimate actual answer. When rounding all the way, only one nonzero digit is left. Rounding all the way gives the least degree of accuracy,* 6–7, 11. *Example:* 1,251 to 1,000; 2,995 to 3,000
Rounding decimals *Reducing the number of decimals to an indicated position, such as 59.59 → 59.6 to the nearest tenth,* 67–68
Rule of 115, 514

Salaries; *see* **Payroll**; **Wages**
Salaries payable *Obligations that a company must pay within 1 year for salaries earned but unpaid,* 395
Sales
actual, 470
distribution of overhead, 454
gross, 400
gross profit, 401, 403
net, 400, 402, 407
Sales (not trade) discounts *Reductions in selling price of goods due to early customer payment,* 400
Sales returns and allowances *Reductions in price or reductions in revenue due to goods returned because of product defects, errors, and so on. When the buyer keeps the damaged goods, an allowance results,* 400
Sales tax *Tax levied on consumers for certain sales of merchandise or services by states, counties, or various local governments,* 469
calculating, 469–470
on online sales, 469
rates, 469
Salvage value *Cost less accumulated depreciation,* 426
Sam Adams, 291
Sam's Club, 33
Samsung Group, 178, 240
Sara Lee Corp., 390
Sarbanes-Oxley Act, 391, 392
Scannell, Kara, 392
Scarsella, Anthony, 88
Schonberger, Jennifer, 527
Schwab, 483
Scism, Leslie, 485
Secure First Credit Union, 370
Segur, Bill, 345
Segur, Susan, 345
Selling price *Cost plus markup equals selling price,* 209; *see also* **Markup**
breakeven analysis, 225
formula, 212
of perishables, 222–223

Semiannually *Twice a year,* 302
Semimonthly *Twice a month,* 244
Series discounts; *see* **Chain discount**
Short sale *A real estate sale when amount received is less than balance of the debt,* 373
Short-rate table *Fire insurance rate table used when insured cancels the policy,* 491
Short-term policy *Fire insurance policy for less than 1 year*
Sidel, Robin, 92
Signature card *Information card signed by person opening a checking account,* 92
Simple discount note *A note in which bank deducts interest in advance,* 286–288
Simple interest *Interest is only calculated on the principal. In I = P × R × T, the interest plus original principal equals the maturity value of an interest-bearing note,* 265
  Banker's Rule, 267
  compared to compound interest, 303–306
  exact interest method, 266–267
  ordinary interest method, 267
  U.S. Rule, 270–271
Simple interest formula, 266

$$\text{Interest} = \text{Principal} \times \text{Rate} \times \text{Time}$$

$$\text{Principal} = \frac{\text{Interest}}{\text{Rate} \times \text{Time}}$$

$$\text{Rate} = \frac{\text{Interest}}{\text{Principal} \times \text{Time}}$$

$$\text{Time} = \frac{\text{Interest}}{\text{Principal} \times \text{Rate}}$$

  finding unknown, 268–269
Simple interest notes, 287
Single equivalent discount rate *Rate or factor as a single discount that calculates the amount of the trade discount by multiplying the rate times the list price. This single equivalent discount replaces a series of chain discounts. The single equivalent rate is (1 – Net price equivalent rate),* 183–184
Single trade discount *Company gives only one trade discount,* 180–181
Sinking fund *An annuity in which the stream of deposits with appropriate interest will equal a specified amount in the future,* 333–334
SIT; *see* **State Income tax**
Six Flags, 173
Sliding scale commissions *Different commission. Rates depend on different levels of sales*
Slobin, Sarah, 2
Smith, Anne Kates, 175
Smith, Ethan, 144
Smits, Marcel, 390
Social Security *Part of FICA tax that has a minimum base,* 249, 321
Sole proprietorship *A business owned by one person,* 393
Solving for the unknown rule, 119
Sony, 207
Southwest Airlines, 426
Sozzi, Brian, 527
Specific identification method *This method calculates the cost of ending inventory by identifying each item remaining to invoice price,* 444–445
Sprint, 240

Standard deviation *Measures the spread of data around the mean,* 538–539
Staples, 207, 240
Starbucks, 3
State Farm Insurance, 493
State income tax (SIT) *Taxation rate imposed by individual states. State rates vary. Some states do not have a state income tax,* 251
State Unemployment Tax Act (SUTA) *Tax paid by employer. Rate varies depending on amount of unemployment the company experiences,* 252
Statements; *see* **Bank statement**
Statistician *A person who is skilled at compiling statistics,* 486
Statistics
  dispersion measures, 538–539
  frequency distributions, 533–534, 539–540
  graphs, 533, 534–536
  index numbers, 536
  mean, median, and mode, 530–532
  normal distribution, 539–540
Step approach to finding largest common divisor, 38–39
Stewart, William, 283
Stock certificate *Evidence of ownership in a corporation,* 510
Stock yield *Dividend per share divided by the closing price per share,* 511
Stockbrokers *People who with their representatives do the trading on the floor of the stock exchange,* 510
Stockholder *One who owns stock in a company,* 393, 510
Stockholders' equity *Assets less liabilities,* 393, 395
  return on, 407
Stocks *Ownership shares in the company sold to buyers, who receive stock certificates,* 510
  dividends, 510, 511–512
  preferred, 510, 512
  quotations, 511
  returns on investment, 513
  terminology, 509–510
  trading, 510
Straight commission *Wages calculated as a percent of the value of goods sold,* 246
Straight life insurance *Protection (full value of policy) results from continual payment of premiums by insured. Until death or retirement, nonforfeiture values exist for straight life,* 486–487, 488
Straight-line method *Method of depreciation that spreads an equal amount of depreciation each year over the life of the assets,* 426–427, 429
Straight-line rate (rate of depreciation) *One divided by number of years of expected life,* 429
Stratford, Michael, 283
Subprime loan *A loan with a rate higher than prime due to uncertainty of payment,* 374
Subtraction
  of decimals, 71–72
  of fractions, 44
  of mixed numbers, 44–45
  of whole numbers, 11–12
Subtrahend *In a subtraction problem, smaller number that is being subtracted from another,* 11. *Example:* 30 in

$$150 - 30 = 120$$

Subway, 2, 3
Sum *Total in the adding process,* 10
SUTA; *see* **State Unemployment Tax Act**

Target, 468
Tax rate, 471–472

$$\frac{\text{Budget needed}}{\text{Total assessed value}}$$

Tax Reform Act of 1986, 431
Taxes
  depreciation, 431
  excise, 470
  FICA, 249–251
  income, 249–251
  property, 471–473
  sales, 469–470
  unemployment, 251–252
TD Ameritrade, 483
Technology
  inventory control, 443
  product obsolescence, 426
Term
  of annuity, 324
  of promissory notes, 286
Term insurance *Inexpensive life insurance that provides protection for a specific period of time. No nonforfeiture values exist for term,* 486
Term of the annuity *Time period from the first to last payment of a stream of payments,* 324
Term policy *Period of time that the policy is in effect,* 486
Terms of the sale *Criteria on invoice showing when cash discounts are available, such as rate and time period,* 186
Thompson, Fred, 375
TIAA-CREF, 484
Tilp, Andy, 283
Time *Expressed as years or fractional years, used to calculate simple interest,* 266–267, 269
Toshiba, 207
Toyota, 75, 153–154, 440, 466
Toys "R" Us, 180, 405
Trade discount *Reduction off original selling price (list price) not related to early payment,* 177
  chain, 182
  complement method, 181
  discount sheets, 179
  formula, 178
  net price equivalent rate, 182–183
  single, 180–181
  single equivalent discount rate, 183–184
  word problem, 191–192
Trade discount amount *List price less net price,* 178
Trade discount rate *Trade discount amount given in percent,* 178
  complements, 181
Trade-in value *Estimated value of a plant asset after depreciation is taken (or end of useful life),* 426
Travelers, 507
Travelex, 370
Treasury bill *Loan to the federal government for 91 days (13 weeks), 182 days (26 weeks), or 1 year,* 288
Trend analysis *Analyzing each number as a percentage of a base year,* 405
Trillium Valley Financial Planning, 283

Truth in Lending Act *Federal law that requires sellers to inform buyers, in writing, of (1) the finance charge and (2) the annual percentage rate. The law doesn't dictate what can be charged,* 351

Truth in Savings law, 306

Turnover, *see* **Asset turnover; Inventory turnover**

20-payment life *Provides permanent protection and cash value, but insured pays premiums for first 20 years,* 487–488

20-year endowment *Most expensive life insurance policy. It is a combination of term insurance and cash value,* 488

Twitter, 4, 5

Unemployment tax *Tax paid by the employer that is used to aid unemployed persons,* 251–252

U.S. Rule *Method that allows the borrower to receive proper interest credits when paying off a loan in more than one payment before the maturity date,* 270–271

U.S. Treasury bill *A note issued by federal government to investors,* 288

Units-of-production method *Depreciation method that estimates amount of depreciation based on usage,* 428

Universal life *Whole life insurance plan with flexible premium and death benefits. This life plan has limited guarantees,* 488

Unknown *The variable we are solving for,* 119

solving for, 118–122

solving word problems, 123–126

Unlike fractions *Proper fractions with different denominators,* 41–42, 44

UPS, 342

USAA, 484

Useful life *Estimated number of years the plant asset is used,* 426

Value, assessed; *see* **Assessed value**

Value of an annuity *Sum of series of payments and interest (think of this as the maturity value of compounding),* 324–325

Variable commission scale *Company pays different commission rates for different levels of net sales,* 246

Variable cost (VC) *Costs that do change in response to change in volume of sales,* 224

Variable rate *Home mortgage rate that is not fixed over its lifetime*

Variables *Letters or symbols that represent unknowns,* 118–119

Vazquez, Raul, 442

VC; *see* **Variable cost**

Vertical analysis *Method of analyzing financial reports where each total is compared to one total,* 395. *Example:* Cash is a percent of total assets.

of balance sheet, 395, 396

of income statement, 403

Vincentric, 440

Visa, 370

Volkswagen, 440

Volvo, 440

W-4; *see* **Employee's Withholding Allowance Certificate**

Wages; *see also* **Payroll**

differential schedules, 246

gross pay, 245

minimum, 244

net, 251

overtime, 244–245

piecework, 245

Walmart, 12, 88, 180, 207, 240, 291, 442, 443, 468

Walt Disney Co., 144, 243

Walton, Sam, 291

Weekly *Once a week; some employers pay employees weekly,* 244

Weighted mean *Used to find an average when values appear more than once,* 530–531

Weighted-average method *Calculates the cost of ending inventory by applying an average unit cost to items remaining in inventory for that period of time,* 445–446

Whelan, Robbie, 291

White, Greg, 144

Whole Foods Market, 4, 5

Whole life; *see* **Straight life insurance**

Whole number *Number that is 0 or larger and doesn't contain a decimal or fraction, such as 10, 55, 92,* 4

converting fractions to, 38

converting parts, 5–6

dividing, 16

reading and writing, 4–5

rounding, 6–7

Wholesalers, *see* **Trade discount**

Wills, 553

Withholding *Amount of deduction from one's paycheck,* 248–251

Word problems

solving, 7–8

solving for unknowns, 123–126

Workers' compensation *Business insurance covering sickness or accidental injuries to employees that result from on-the-job activities,* 489

WorldCom, 392

Yahoo! 405, 529

Yields

bond, 515

stock, 511

Zimmerman, Ann, 180

Ziobro, Paul, 390

Zynga, 400